THE THIRD STATISTICAL ACCOUNT OF SCOTLAND

GLASGOW

THE CITY OF
GLASGOW
SITUATION
PROJECTION DEVISED BY R MILLER
DISTANCES OF CIRCLES FROM GLASGOW ARE MARKED IN MILES
IAGK 57
1000
2000
3000
4000
NORTH POLE
WINNIPEG
OTTAWA
NEW YORK
REYKJAVIK
GLASGOW
DUBLIN
LONDON
THE HAGUE
BRUSSELS
PARIS
BERNE
OSLO
STOCKHOLM
HELSINKI
COPENHAGEN
BERLIN
VIENNA
MOSCOW
ROME
MADRID
LISBON
ATHENS
ISTANBUL
CAIRO
JERUSALEM
TEHRAN
BASRA
40°N
50°N
60°N
70°N
80°N
110°W
100°W
90°W
80°W
70°W
60°W
50°W
40°W
30°W
20°W
10°W
0°
10°E
20°E
30°E
40°E
50°E
60°E
70°E
80°E
90°E
100°E

THE THIRD STATISTICAL ACCOUNT OF SCOTLAND

GLASGOW

EDITORS:

J. Cunnison and J. B. S. Gilfillan

COLLINS
144 CATHEDRAL STREET, GLASGOW, C.4
1958

FIRST PUBLISHED 1958

". . . . by Statistical is meant . . . . an inquiry into the state of a country for the purpose of ascertaining the quantum of happiness enjoyed by its inhabitants and the means of its future improvement."

SIR JOHN SINCLAIR, BART.
1798

PRINTED IN SCOTLAND BY
COLLINS CLEAR-TYPE PRESS

FOREWORD

By The Rt. Hon. Andrew Hood, F.E.I.S., J.P.
Lord Provost of Glasgow, 1955-8

THE publication of a *Third Statistical Account of Scotland* is an event of historical and literary importance to the country. First and Second *Accounts* (the " Old " and the " New "), issued between 1791 and 1798 and between 1834 and 1845, were published in twenty-one and fifteen volumes respectively. It is expected that thirty volumes or more will be required to give an adequate word-picture of developments in Scotland over the intervening years. In the *New Statistical Account* Glasgow was included in the volume devoted to Lanarkshire. Since then there has been a vast increase in Glasgow's population and in the city's economic importance to the country as a whole. In the present *Account*, to do justice to the changed situation, this large volume has been allocated to Glasgow alone. That is as it should be at a period when a fifth of the population of Scotland is housed within the city's boundaries.

While the Scottish Council of Social Service is sponsoring this important project, the responsibility for the preparation of the material for the *Third Statistical Account* has been entrusted to the four Universities. The editing of the volume on Glasgow is only part of the heavy burden accepted by Dr. James Cunnison and Mr. J. B. S. Gilfillan, who are to be congratulated on the success of their outstanding achievement. It is only necessary to scan the Contents and the List of Contributors to appreciate the complete adequacy of this extensive survey of every aspect of the social and industrial life of the city. Five years ago the Corporation of Glasgow voted a grant from the Common Good to the University to finance the preparation of this volume. In commending it to Glaswegians at home and abroad, I desire to express the city's appreciation and gratitude to the editors, the various contributors and all associated with them in producing a record of developments over the past century which will prove invaluable to present and future members of the Corporation and to all students of sociology.

SPECIAL ACKNOWLEDGMENTS

The editors make grateful acknowledgment to Mr. Ian' A. G. Kinniburgh, of the Geography Department, University of Glasgow, who prepared most of the line drawings for this volume ; and to Mr. H. A. Moisley, also of the Geography Department, for certain line drawings and the special information on the map at the end of the book

CONTENTS

CONTENTS

ILLUSTRATIONS

TEXT FIGURES

PLATES

PREFACE

THIS account of Glasgow is part of the *Third Statistical Account of Scotland,* of which four pilot volumes—on Ayrshire, East Lothian, Fife and the City of Aberdeen—have already been published. The whole project, which will involve the production of some 30 volumes, is sponsored by the Scottish Council of Social Service, and the preparation of the volumes has been undertaken by the four Universities. For the present volume Glasgow University accepted responsibility and the work has been supervised by two editors closely associated with the Department of Social and Economic Research. A grant by Glasgow Corporation from the Common Good of the Burgh made the undertaking possible.

The scheme of the work necessarily differs from that of the County volumes, in each of which more than half the space is devoted to accounts of the separate parishes. In Glasgow the old parochial boundaries have now lost their former significance, and the treatment is entirely by subject and not by parishes or other geographical divisions. There are thus no separate accounts by parish writers; but to retain the variety lent by such individual contributors, and at the same time to ensure adequate treatment in the many specialised fields covered, the account has been planned as a team project. Like its predecessor of 1793, it may claim to have been compiled from "the communications of several respectable inhabitants" of the district.

The account consists of 23 chapters, prepared in part by members of the staffs of the University and of the Royal College of Science & Technology, and in part by contributors outside the academic field, in such spheres as the Church, Local Government service and Journalism. Each contributor has drawn upon a vast store of willing co-operation offered by men and women in all walks of life, so that the work is to some extent an account of Glasgow by the citizens themselves.

In connection with the project, two large-scale surveys have been specially organised. To provide reliable data for the industrial sections of the account an elaborate questionnaire was circulated, with advance press publicity, to some 1,300 manufacturing firms in the Glasgow area, asking for details of their origin, development and present activities. This met with a gratifying response, and the returns have been utilised in the chapters describing the manufacturing industries of the city. For the purposes of his chapter on "The Churches" the Senior Lecturer in Sociology in the University carried out three censuses of church attendance in Glasgow, in 1954, 1955 and 1956, with the co-operation of many religious denominations. No comprehensive church census of this kind had been undertaken in Glasgow since 1851.

In view of the wealth of statistical information concerning Glasgow, in existence but not readily available to-day in compact published form, a comprehensive Statistical Appendix has been added containing tables of contemporary and past statistics relating to the various subjects dealt with in the text.

The material used in the preparation of the volume was collected mainly over a period of three years—from 1953 to 1956. The account was brought up to date as far as possible at the end of 1956. Since then, while the book has been in the press, it has been possible to make only such additions and modifications as could be contained in footnotes.

J.C.
J.B.S.G.

Part One
THE BACKGROUND

Chapter 1

THE SITE AND ITS DEVELOPMENT

J. B. S. GILFILLAN

SITUATION

GLASGOW, a city of more than a million inhabitants and the home of over a fifth of all the people living in Scotland, is one of the most northerly of the great cities of the world. It is situated in latitude 55° 51′ North, and longitude 4° 17′ West. Such figures may seem of little interest to the average Glaswegian, but it would probably surprise him to be told their implication: that George Square and the City Chambers lie closer to the Arctic Circle than Red Square and the Kremlin, and that Glasgow is situated as far westward as the Eddystone Lighthouse, off the Cornish coast of England.

Straddling the River Clyde some fourteen miles upstream from its estuary at Dumbarton, Strathclyde's ancient capital, the city is mainly concentrated on the northern bank, but has large and densely populated extensions to the south of the river, all of comparatively modern growth. The site in early times possessed an important natural advantage, to which it is probable that Glasgow's origin may ultimately be traced: the presence of shallows at this point in the Clyde, by which the river could be readily forded. Such a feature would be a primary attraction to the original settlers in the Clyde Valley, and lends some plausibility to Glasgow's claim to be not only the largest but also perhaps the oldest town in Scotland.

Geographically Glasgow forms part of Lanarkshire, the most populous of the Scottish counties. When the previous *Statistical Accounts* were drawn up it was therefore treated as a portion of that county. It has since, however, in common with Edinburgh, Aberdeen and Dundee, attained independent status as a "county of a city". Before the closing decade of the nineteenth century Glasgow actually formed part of two counties, for while the city was situated chiefly in the Nether or Lower Ward of Lanarkshire it also lay to a small extent within Renfrewshire. In 1892 it was placed wholly within Lanarkshire by an Order of the Boundary Commissioners for Scotland, and in 1893 the entire area then contained by the municipal boundary was constituted a county of a city, with administrative independence. Since that time many further adjustments of boundaries have had to be made, in order to preserve the unity of the ever expanding municipality, and these have entailed additional territorial sacrifices by the adjacent counties. Lanarkshire, Renfrewshire and Dunbartonshire have all lost substantial tracts of land to Glasgow, particularly within the last fifty years.

Geology of the Site

The physical configuration and underlying nature of the land on which the city is built have materially affected the pattern of its growth. It has frequently been said that this part of the Clyde Valley seems designed by Nature as the site of a great city, and there is some truth as well as exaggeration in the dictum. Yet it denies the credit due to generations of human skill and enterprise, for besides natural advantages to profit by there have been natural obstacles to overcome. Foremost among these, curiously enough, was the shallowness of the Clyde: for the very feature which in ancient times probably gave the initial impetus to Glasgow's growth proved later to be a serious impediment to her development as a great commercial centre and seaport. The old saying that " the Clyde made Glasgow, and Glasgow made the Clyde " is a paradox that sums up well the combination of natural and human influences that has gone to the making of the modern city.

It is to the glacial activity of the Ice Age that the most noticeable features of Glasgow's site are attributable. The pre-glacial surface features of the district are hidden by a mantle of superficial deposits, mostly of glacial origin. Fortunately, however, fairly complete evidence of the nature of the underlying rock surface has been afforded by the many drilling operations carried out in connection with coal-prospecting, the construction of docks and other works. These reveal the contours of a landscape older than the Ice Age, a landscape very different from that familiar to us to-day. Three great buried valleys, which have later been filled up by sand, gravel and other glacial deposits, are seen to have converged about Clydebank, the most notable of them—some twelve miles long—lying beneath the Bearsden district. Another of these valleys lies under the present site of Glasgow.

What is now the lower part of the Clyde Valley was once a marine estuary, as has been proved by the numerous sea-shells found in the valley's deposits. The mouth of the Clyde would then be in the vicinity of Uddingston or Rutherglen. Since 1780 many primitive dug-out canoes have been discovered underneath Glasgow in the alluvium of this former estuary. The first was found under St. Enoch Square, another near Glasgow Cross, and others beneath Stockwell Street, the Drygate, and the lands of Springfield and Clydehaugh. As the depth of silt under which these interesting relics[1] were found was twenty feet or more, a considerable fall in sea-level is indicated even within the human period, which in the case of the Glasgow district means the post-glacial period; for as yet no evidence has been forthcoming to suggest that men lived here either before or during the Ice Age.

[1] Examples are preserved in the Kelvingrove Museum. As many as seventeen canoes were unearthed from the silt in the eighty years prior to 1855, and several more have been discovered since.

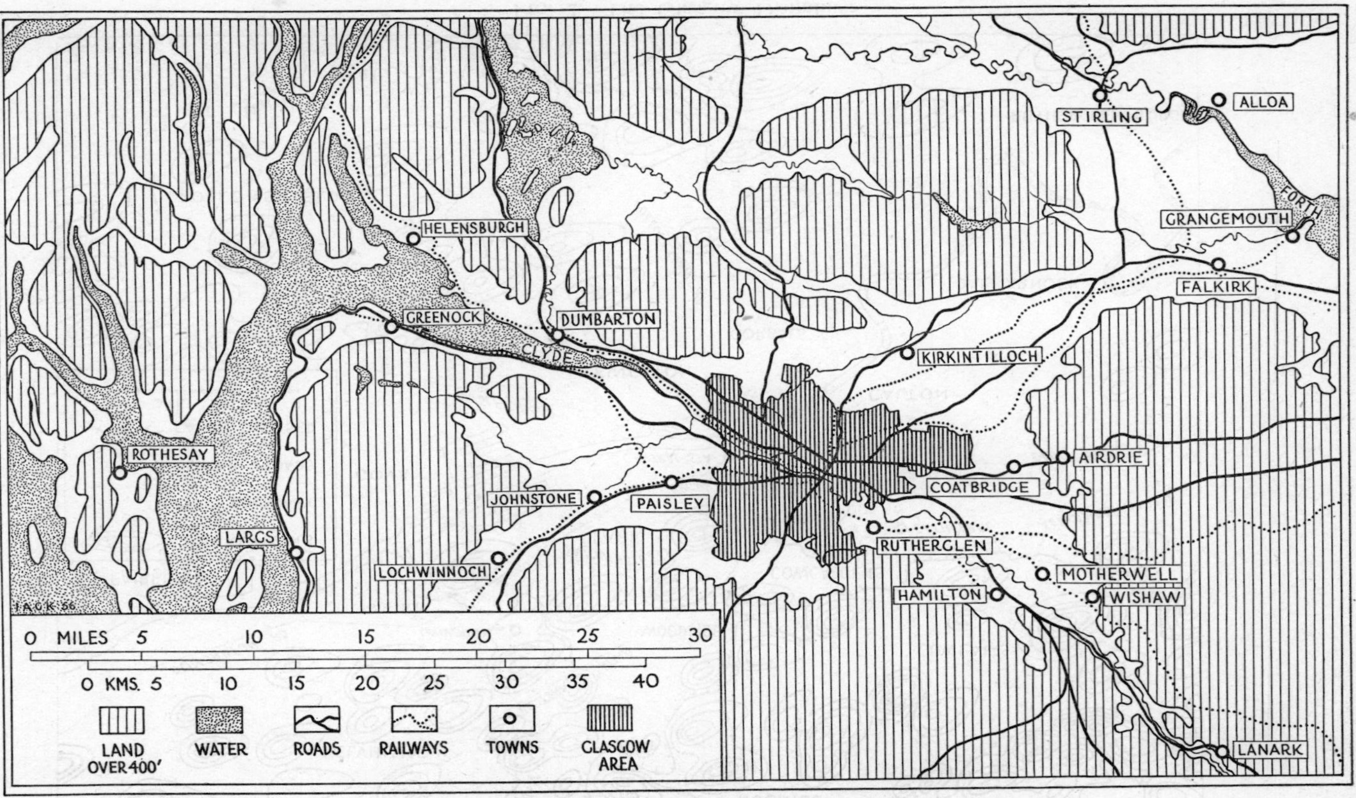

FIG. 1. Glasgow in its Regional Setting.

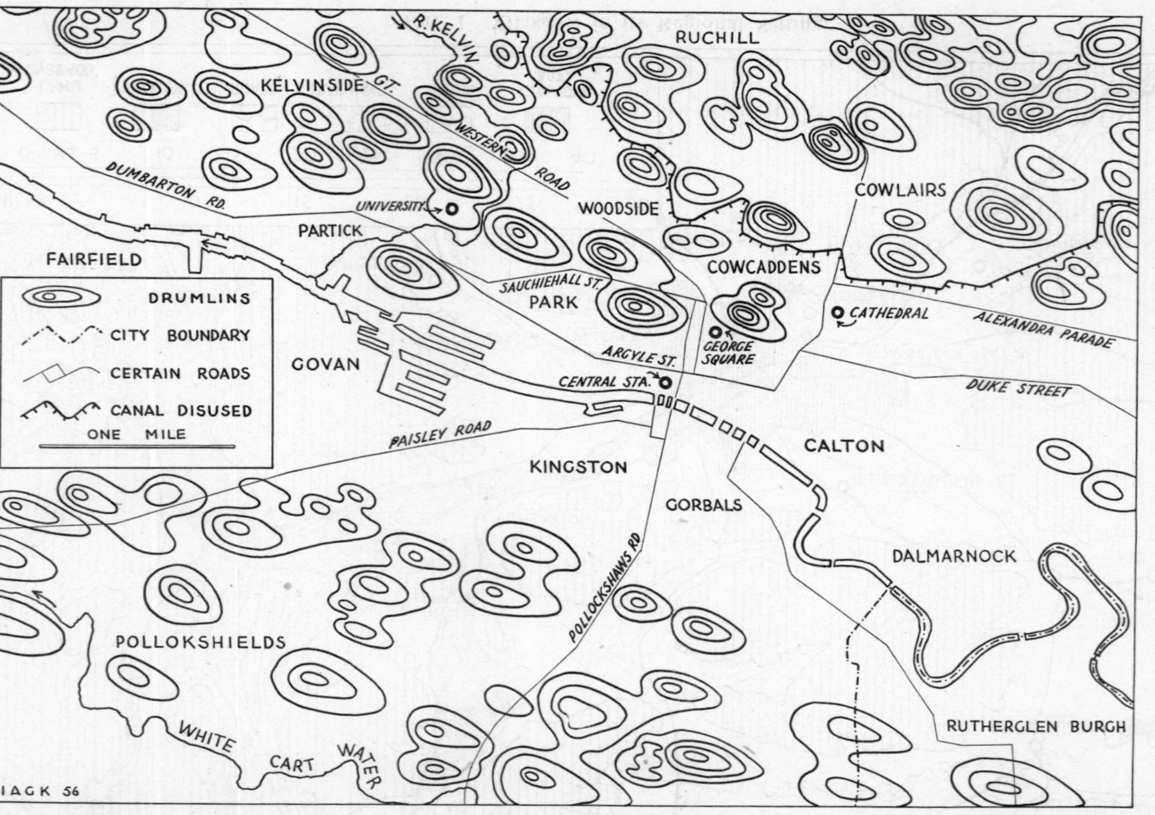

FIG. 2. The Glasgow Drumlins.

The existence of this ancient estuary, and its subsequent filling up by silt and other deposits, account for much of the present appearance of the Glasgow landscape. Thus the site of the lower part of the city, particularly towards the east and south, is very flat, and the alluvial plain extends also along the riverside on the north. Beyond this level strip of ground to the north of the Clyde, and to the west and south, the land surface becomes irregular and is broken up by a multitude of small pear-shaped hills. On their slopes the city is largely built, and to them modern Glasgow owes much of its character. A visitor to Glasgow cannot walk far without realising that, if it is not the Athens of the North, it at least resembles Rome in being "a city built upon hills". They rise fairly sharply to heights of from 100 to 250 feet, the most prominent being Garngad Hill (252′), the Necropolis (225′), Partick Hill (179′), Garnet Hill (176′), Hillhead (157′), Woodlands Hill (153′), and Blythswood Hill (135′). With the possible exception of the Necropolis, all these hills on which Glasgow stands are "drumlins", each of them a product and memorial of the Great Ice Age. They are composed of boulder clay, which is thought to have been compacted and moulded by the weight and movement of the glacial mass passing over it. It will be seen from the sketch map (Fig. 2) that the Glasgow drumlins are all oriented in the same direction, their shape indicating that the glacial movement was from the west and north-west. This is confirmed by the presence within them of an abundance of boulders of porphyritic granite, which the ice must have carried from Glen Fyne.

In addition to the boulder clay of the drumlins, there were other glacial deposits left behind by the ice when it melted which are of some significance. The most important of these, from the point of view of utility, are the stratified sands and gravels, of which extensive deposits are found and worked in the Kelvin valley, not far beyond the municipal limits. Superficial glacial deposits of the type that occur throughout the city are sometimes of advantage to an urban community, facilitating the installation of water mains, sewers, and other underground pipework for example, but in Glasgow they have often proved a serious obstacle to schemes of development. In the construction of some of the docks and shipyards much trouble was encountered because of the presence of underlying beds of sand and gravel near the riverside. Moraines, irregular dumps consisting mainly of pebbles and boulders in a sandy matrix without clay, have been deposited by the ice in various places in the Glasgow district, a notable example running north and south across the Clyde between Shettleston and Uddingston.

It is of interest to note that until about the time of the *New Statistical Account,* around 1840, all these deposits which are now recognised as glacial were believed to be the results of the biblical Flood or some great earthquake wave from the Atlantic. Glasgow itself, indeed, has a close link with the establishment of the glacial theory, which can be dated from the meeting of the British Association held in the city in that year. Moreover, a well-known citizen of Glasgow, James Smith of

Jordanhill, was a pioneer researcher in this field, his discoveries of certain shells confirming that an Arctic climate once prevailed in the Firth of Clyde.

Besides the glacial deposits there are other features of Glasgow's topography attributable to the Great Ice Age and the period following it. Raised beaches, although more generally associated with coastal districts, can be detected within the city boundary as readily as farther down the Clyde, and here as elsewhere have been taken advantage of as a basis for roads. Towards the end of the glacial period sea-level was about a hundred feet higher than at present, and the beaches formed by this Arctic sea are still visible in many places. During their formation deeper water deposits of finely laminated clays, containing Arctic shells and boulders (dropped by floating ice), were accumulating at lower levels around Glasgow. This has some economic significance, as such clays were at one time extensively worked for brick-making. After the Ice Age sea-level is believed to have been as much as a hundred feet below its present height, but a later resubmergence of the land created another raised beach—the so-called 25-foot beach which is so evident in the Clyde district. The latter, which in parts of the area is actually forty or fifty feet above present sea-level, carries most of our coast roads. Within Glasgow itself Dumbarton Road is an example of the utilisation of the level shelf of an old raised beach as a modern highway.

While the surface character of the site of Glasgow is largely due to the Ice Age, the underlying rock strata which are the deeper foundation not only of the city, but of its economic prosperity as well, are the product of earlier geological eras. The first settlers who were attracted to the place chose better than they knew: to them the site was in a strategic position geographically, but they little realised that it was also in the midst of a vast storehouse of undiscovered mineral wealth. The great Midland Valley of Scotland in which Glasgow is situated (Fig. 3) is composed principally of Old Red Sandstone and Carboniferous rocks, the latter containing the rich deposits of coal and iron to which the city owes its industrial prosperity.

Although there is little in the present appearance of the landscape to suggest it, the country around Glasgow was once a region of great volcanic activity. With the passage of time the external features of the volcanoes have been so much modified that they are no longer immediately recognisable, but their filled-up vents are actually still visible from many points in the city. Typical examples of former Carboniferous volcanoes on the outskirts of Glasgow are the hills of Dumfoyne and Dumgoyne, which are just part of a whole line of extinct volcanoes extending from Dumbarton Rock over the Kilpatrick Hills and along the northern face of the Campsies. The hard Clyde Plateau lavas which emanated from these volcanoes outcrop extensively around Glasgow in a great horse-shoe formation, being closely identifiable with the high ground to the north, west and south of the city. The gap in this circle of hills at Bowling, now occupied by the Clyde, is the

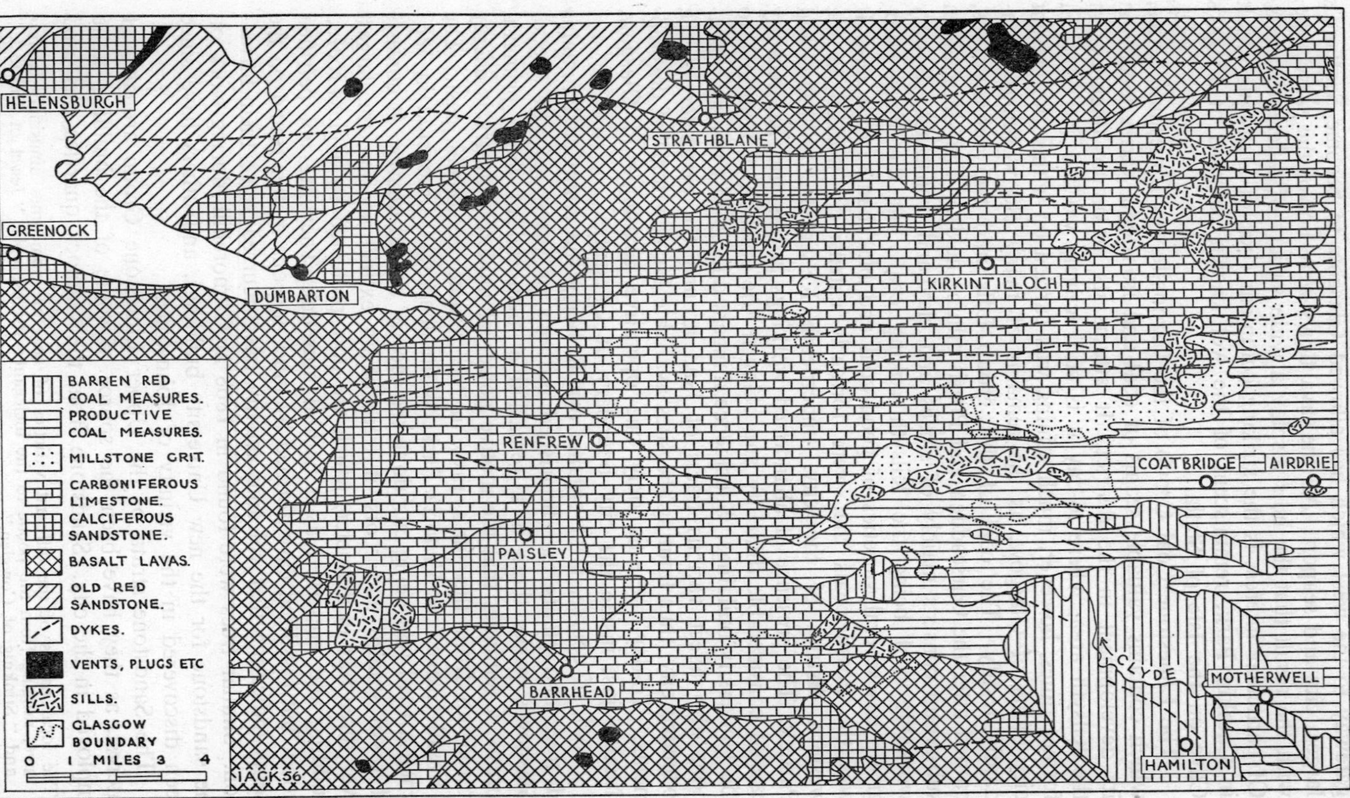
HELENSBURGH
GREENOCK
DUMBARTON
STRATHBLANE
KIRKINTILLOCH
RENFREW
PAISLEY
BARRHEAD
COATBRIDGE
AIRDRIE
MOTHERWELL
HAMILTON
CLYDE
BARREN RED COAL MEASURES.
PRODUCTIVE COAL MEASURES.
MILLSTONE GRIT.
CARBONIFEROUS LIMESTONE.
CALCIFEROUS SANDSTONE.
BASALT LAVAS.
OLD RED SANDSTONE.
DYKES.
VENTS, PLUGS ETC
SILLS.
GLASGOW BOUNDARY
0 1 MILES 3 4
IACK56

FIG. 3 Geology of the Glasgow Area.

gateway to the west which has allowed Glasgow to become Scotland's largest city and seaport. All the lava flows were not of the same type, with the result that the hills display a wide variety of different basalts. Of particular interest is the striking columnar rock of Dunsapie basalt in Cathkin Park, reminiscent of the well-known columns at Fingal's Cave on the Isle of Staffa.

The Limestone Coal Group of the Carboniferous Limestone Series, which contains valuable seams of coal and ironstone, varies locally in its development in the district. It attains its maximum thickness in the Kilsyth area, where to-day it is still actively worked for coal. In former times, however, much mining was carried on within the present city limits of Glasgow, as the remains of many old workings abundantly testify. The coal of this group falls into two sub-divisions, named after the Garscadden and Possil mining-fields.[1] The Garscadden sub-group consists mainly of shales and clayband ironstones, its only workable coal being the Kilsyth coking coal; but the Possil sub-group has several varieties of good coal and blackband ironstones. It was the Possil coals that were formerly extensively worked in the western district of the city, underneath Kelvinside, Hillhead and Partick. The presence of abandoned workings in this area has recently caused considerable difficulty and delay in the erection of additions to the University buildings. Subsidence dangers due to past mining operations also affect various tracts of land around the perimeter of the extended city, thus limiting the sites available for new housing developments. To-day there is only one operative coal-mine in Glasgow, situated just inside the city boundary at Garscube.

Coal, of course, is of organic origin, being the compacted remains of trees and plants that flourished millions of years ago. In one of Glasgow's parks there is a remarkable memorial of those primeval forests, a reminder that the motive power of modern industry is energy stored up from the sun's rays in the remote geological past. The "Fossil Grove" in Victoria Park, Whiteinch,[2] was discovered in 1887 when a road was being cut along the face of an old quarry. It consists of fossil stumps and roots of trees of an extinct species, the largest over three feet in diameter, which are now protected by a glass-roofed building and preserved as a natural museum. They are not petrified wood, but fossilised casts formed by mud, igneous matter found on the stems indicating that volcanic activity has occurred since their formation. Similar trees were found in 1868 at Gilmorehill, during work on the sandstone for the new University buildings, and others have since been discovered in the vicinity of Johnstone.

The Sandstone strata of the Upper Limestone Group are also of interest, as they have been the source of some of the building stone employed in the city. Sandstone from the Giffnock quarries was used

[1] The local names of the different varieties of coal are sometimes amusingly expressive, ranging from the poetic to the inelegant: for example, "Jewel of Giffnock" and "Stinking of Cowglen."

[2] Whiteinch was once, as its name suggests, an island. It appears thus in Blaeu's map of 1654.

in building part of the present University, the eastern side of the General Post Office, and the Glasgow Savings Bank in Ingram Street. Bishopbriggs Sandstone, rather similar in appearance to the Giffnock variety, was often used in conjunction with it, as at the University. Glasgow, however, cannot boast of any local building stone of outstanding character to compare, say, with the native granite of Aberdeen.

Another division of the Carboniferous with some economic value is the Millstone Grit, formed when the marine and shallow water conditions prevailing during the deposition of the Upper Limestone Group were terminated by the development of great river deltas. This Millstone Grit, upon which, incidentally, Glasgow Cathedral is built, consists essentially of gritty sandstones, coarse and pebbly in nature. Its industrial importance lies in the fact that it also contains fairly substantial beds of fireclay, the source of the valuable refractory clays used in the manufacture of fire bricks, an industry in which several Glasgow firms are engaged. The Lower Fireclay is worked at Glenboig and Castlecary to the north-east of the city, and the Upper Fireclay beyond Castlecary at Bonnybridge. A thin coal-seam is associated with it, but coal-seams are uncommon in the Millstone Grit and of little importance. In contrast, the lower part of the true Coal Measures, consisting of fine-grained muddy sediments, contains valuable coal-seams. These too are usually associated with fireclays. In the district to the east of the city, in more than 1200 feet of Coal Measure strata, about seventeen main coals occur, but only two of the seams exceed four feet in thickness. The great coal-fields of Lanarkshire and Ayrshire, however, are virtually on Glasgow's doorstep, and it is upon the development and utilisation of their mineral wealth that the city's past and present prosperity largely rests.

Climate

Climatic conditions have also had some influence on Glasgow's development as a city. Neither residents nor industries are likely to be attracted in large numbers to an area with an uncongenial climate, unless the natural resources of the district are so rich as to outweigh its climatic disadvantages. It must be admitted that Glasgow's reputation, where weather is concerned, is scarcely an enviable one. At the same time, however, it should be pointed out that the local climate is much less severe than is popularly supposed.

For a place situated so far north—some fifteen hundred miles nearer to the North Pole than to the Equator—the climate is really exceptionally mild. This becomes evident on comparing Glasgow's weather with that of other places in the same latitude, such as Labrador. There the land is snow-clad and the shores are frost-bound for more than half the year, and only between June and September does the temperature exceed that of Glasgow in January. It is, of course, because of the marine influence exerted by the prevailing westerly winds and the warm currents of the Atlantic Ocean that Glasgow's temperature is so unusually high for its latitude.

While the city's comparative proximity to the sea to the west and south-west tends to prevent extremes of heat or cold, the high ground enclosing it to the north and east affords some protection from the chill overland winds of winter. It is during the winter months that the ameliorating influence of the Atlantic on the mean temperature of the district is most noticeable. Snow is relatively infrequent and seldom lies long, and although keen frosts are sometimes experienced they are less severe than in more inland situations. No doubt the additional "city warmth" resulting from the growth of Glasgow's urban area over the years has served to enhance the tempering effect of these natural climatic influences.

Mild winters, however, are no new phenomenon in Glasgow. Indeed in the *New Statistical Account*, written more than a century ago, there is a rather curious remark in this connection. "In 1834 and 1835," it informs us, "the winters were so mild that ice was imported from Iceland to Glasgow."[1] Modern Glaswegians might be inclined to describe this as bringing coal to Newcastle, but a dispassionate consideration of the local meteorological records does confirm that the city enjoys a remarkably equable climate.

Glasgow is fortunate in being one of the few cities in the world whose climate has been studied in a learned memoir. This is *The Climatology of Glasgow* by L. Becker, sometime Professor of Astronomy in the University. It deals with the data collected between 1845 and 1917 at the old University Observatory on Horselethill, situated in the west end of the city about half a mile north-west of the present University buildings. Weather observations were continued there until 1936, and by courtesy of the present Professor, Dr. W. M. Smart, the records of the final nineteen years have been made available to us.

The climate of the city in the period before 1845 has been briefly described in the previous Statistical Accounts and in such works as Cleland's *Annals of Glasgow*, but the few meteorological statistics they contain do not appear to be very reliable. So little is known of the methods followed by early observers, and of the siting of their instruments, that valid comparisons between their figures and the later observations are impossible. From a study that has been made of rainfall in England from 1727 onwards, it would seem, on comparative grounds, that a rainfall at Glasgow of less than 24 inches in any year is most unlikely—yet in 1788 the rainfall of Glasgow is said to have been only 19.4 inches,[2] whereas the general rainfall for England in the same year was 22.5 inches. In 1805, if Cleland's figures are to be believed, the citizens of Glasgow had something to celebrate besides Nelson's victory at Trafalgar: the "Quantity of Rain" which fell upon them that year is reported to have been as low as 15.4 inches![3] The

[1] *New Statistical Account,* Vol. VI, p. 104.

[2] *The Statistical Account,* Vol. V (1793), p. 532.

[3] Cleland: *Annals of Glasgow* (1816), Vol. I, p. 42.

present average is about 40 inches, a yearly total of less than 30 inches being most exceptional.[1]

Such anomalies in the statistics, and the frequent changes of instruments and sites, make any study of the earlier records prior to 1868 of very doubtful value. From that date the University Observatory became an official station under the Meteorological Office, and its weather observations were recorded on a more consistent basis. In 1877 the Corporation of Glasgow apparently began to supplement the Observatory's work by instituting rainfall measurements in Queen's Park, similar observations having been begun at Crookston in 1871 or earlier. In 1901 many rain gauges were installed in local parks, and in Queen's Park by 1906 temperature also was being observed. Other parks, as they were established, gradually took part in observations. The Meteorological Office finally transferred its interest from the University Observatory to Springburn Park in 1914, when temperature observations began there. After the commencement of observations at Renfrew Airport in 1921, however, no wholehearted attempt was made to ensure that reliable "official" statistics would continue to be available from within the city. The Renfrew station is situated about three-quarters of a mile west of the city boundary, and now provides the only official figures. With the help of Glasgow Parks Department, which still maintains observations in the city,[2] and the Meteorological Office, Edinburgh, extracts have been made from all the available records, to enable a more complete account of the Glasgow climate to be presented here than would otherwise be possible.

Glasgow extends nearly 12 miles from east to west and almost 10 miles from north to south, between the extreme limits of its boundaries. With an actual area of just over 62 square miles, it probably includes as varied a surface as could be found in any city. From the river flats at Braehead, at about 20 feet, to Cathkin Braes, at almost 650 feet, there is a considerable range in altitude, although much of the older part of the town lies below 200 feet. As the average height of the city is not great, climatic figures for Renfrew (29 feet) will be more representative of Glasgow as a whole than those for Springburn (351 feet). From a scientific point of view it is unfortunate that temperature observations have been discontinued at the Belvidere Hospital station, since it is likely that a comparison between such a low-lying eastward site and other available stations would allow a complete study of climate within the city. As it is, only suggestions can be made, both as to the effect of shelter and exposure on the various slopes of the many hills, often 200 feet high, on which Glasgow stands, and also as to the effect of the city itself upon its own climate. The former is illustrated by annual rainfalls over 5% lower than Glasgow's average, in the valley of the Kelvin beside the University; the latter by the smoke haze or even cloud which, from neighbouring hills, is seen fre-

1 The writer is indebted to Mr. C. A. Halstead, of the Geography Department, University of Glasgow, for the meteorological data in the following section.

2 See Appendix Table 4.

quently to lie over the city, and to trail down-wind for a considerable distance—sometimes, it is said, even as far as Fife or Arran!

While Glasgow is the farthest north of the world's cities of over a million in population, its mean annual temperature is the same as that of Berlin some 250 miles to the south, and nearly 10° F. above that of Moscow, which it also exceeds in latitude. Both these places are 7° warmer than Glasgow in summer, but on the west coast of the continent of Europe such a summer temperature is not reached till as far south as Nantes. In winter, moreover, Berlin is colder than Glasgow by 8° F. and Moscow is colder by as much as 25° F. Glasgow is thus characterised by a cool summer and a mild winter, so that its inhabitants are seldom afflicted by uncomfortable extremes of temperature. This equability of climate—eminently desirable in an industrial and commercial centre—the city owes, as we have seen, to the prevailing moist westerly winds. These, unfortunately, also bring that "typical Glasgow weather" so loudly deplored by visitors to the city. Wind and moisture, it must be conceded, are often the first and most obvious features of Glasgow to strike them.

The mean wind velocity at Glasgow is about 10 miles an hour, which is less than that at other Scottish cities and such places as Liverpool, but half as much again as at London or Birmingham. In the Glasgow area the strongest gusts recorded are as high as at any inland place, and similarly half as high again as at these latter towns; but only seven days per annum are classed as "days with gale," whereas Liverpool has ten. The inland cities, however, have less than two such days in the year. In striking contrast to this, "calms" represent at least 15% of all observations at the Renfrew meteorological station, whereas in the London area they rarely exceed 3%. This is a clear indication of the shelter afforded by Glasgow's surrounding wall of hills. Such shelter also accounts for the rarity of northerly winds: only 2% compared with at least 7% in most other places. Their frequency is 4% at the more exposed site of the old observatory on Horselethill. The whole area shows shelter effects from these hills and the more distant Highlands when general northerly air currents prevail, and the finest crystal-clear days are often experienced then. Although Glasgow hardly ever suffers from the unpleasant "haar" of the Scottish east coast, it does feel the effects of sea breezes in the summer, and also some slight effects of cold air seeping from the surrounding upland surfaces at night. Most of the hollows which would normally trap such air, however, have been built up and are unlikely to do so now.

Moisture is an even more intangible factor to demonstrate statistically than wind. The bald statements that Glasgow has about 40 inches of rain per annum, or that it has about 230 days with rain, mask considerable local variations, but even so contrast with only three-quarters of that number of rain-days in London, which has less than two-thirds of Glasgow's total rainfall. A more interesting comparison might be made of the number of days or hours when the ground is wet in these two places, but such figures are so far not available. It is worth pointing out that whereas a total of 30 inches of rain in England represents an excess of rain over evaporation of at most 10 inches, the figure in Glasgow represents an excess of more than twice as much, since the drying power of the air is also reduced. Glasgow's average annual values of relative humidity are less than those of Liverpool and Edinburgh, but 6% greater than those of inland English cities—the difference is slight in winter but reaches 17% in July. Other quantities suggest that for the same wind velocity the air at mid-day dries the ground perhaps 60% more rapidly in central England in July than it does in Glasgow.

While midsummer days in Glasgow are an hour longer than in southern England, winter ones are an hour and a half shorter. Since the sun is more appreciated in the latter season, the fact that Glasgow in winter has less than two-thirds of the daily duration of sunshine enjoyed by the south is obviously a disadvantage of some importance. Yet fog is much less common in Glasgow, its frequency of occurrence being only about two-thirds of that in London and other large cities. The English Midlands, for instance, are much more seriously affected than Glasgow, where really dense fogs are now comparatively rare. When they do occur, fogs are both less dense and of shorter duration than formerly. This improvement is due in no small measure to the work of the smoke abatement organisations, thanks to whose efforts such memorable Glasgow fogs as those of 1909 and 1929 are unlikely to be repeated to-day. Reduction of air pollution, however, is still a pressing problem in Glasgow as in other highly industrialised areas, and much thought is being given at present to the establishment of smoke-free zones. The extent of atmospheric pollution in the city as compared with that in the open country some forty miles to the north-west is strikingly illustrated by Table I, showing the annual deposition at Glasgow and at Brenachoil (Loch Katrine).

While Glasgow is fortunate in having a frequency of fog only two-thirds of that experienced by London and some other large cities, it is less favourably placed in regard to low-lying cloud. Cloud below 1,000 feet is no more frequent than in other cities, but there are much fewer days with no low cloud than, for instance, in London: only twenty as against fifty. There is, too, a considerable difference between the amount of available daylight in the centre of Glasgow and that on the immediate outskirts. The proportions show some interesting changes over recent years. Taking Glasgow Cross and Mearnskirk Hospital as points of comparison, we have the results shown in Table II.

There has thus been a reduction in the average loss of daylight in the centre of the city since pre-war days, and the improvement is particularly striking in comparison with the wartime gloom, when virtually twilight conditions prevailed in Glasgow. A relaxation of smoke control was inevitable during the war years, but the ground then lost has since been more than regained and further progress is now being made.

On an over-all view, perhaps the most significant differences between

TABLE I

DEPOSITION IN TONS PER SQUARE MILE PER ANNUM AT GLASGOW AND LOCH KATRINE

Year	Rainfall in Millimetres	Tar	Carbonaceous less Tar	Ash	Total Insoluble	Total Soluble	Total Solids
GLASGOW							
1919	876	2.12	41.98	85.93	130.03	184.01	314.03
1929	736	2.97	54.04	115.01	172.02	123.55	295.57
1939	893	3.19	42.35	93.98	139.42	92.64	232.06
1949	966	2.86	37.47	96.16	136.49	109.23	246.72
1950	957	3.05	55.77	104.50	161.32	82.92	244.24
1951	903	3.35	44.05	113.80	161.20	82.09	243.29
1952	760	4.05	47.42	122.33	173.80	74.67	248.47
1953	739	3.76	32.71	101.16	137.63	66.85	204.48
1954	1,139	3.63	41.00	99.23	143.86	92.82	236.68
1955	714	4.01	45.85	84.43	134.29	84.27	218.56
LOCH KATRINE							
1939	1,570	1.05	6.94	3.58	11.57	114.09	125.66
1949	1,649	1.31	4.49	3.82	9.62	71.58	81.20
1950	1,429	1.41	9.59	3.26	14.26	68.69	82.95
1951	1,549	1.18	3.99	4.19	9.36	72.60	81.96
1952	1,088	1.28	2.62	3.00	6.90	48.93	55.83
1953	1,618	1.14	5.48	6.04	12.66	87.06	99.72
1954	1,749	0.98	4.64	4.45	10.07	96.13	106.20
1955	1,246	1.30	5.25	3.24	9.79	45.26	55.05

SOURCE: Health and Welfare Department, Glasgow Corporation.

TABLE II

PERCENTAGE OF AVAILABLE DAYLIGHT RECORDED AT GLASGOW CROSS

(100%-Daylight at Mearnskirk Hospital)

Year	Available Daylight (per cent)		Daylight Lost
1935-1936	69		
1936-1937	65	Pre-war Average 67	33 Per Cent
1938-1939	67		
1940-1941	59		
1941-1942	56	War-time Average 54	46 Per Cent
1942-1943	54		
1943-1944	46		
1946-1947	74		
1947-1948	84	Post-war Average 74	26 Per Cent
1948-1949	68		
1949-1950	71		
1950-1951	68		
1951-1952	62		
1952-1953	67	Immediate Five-year Average 70	30 Per Cent
1953-1954	87		
1954-1955	66		

SOURCE: Chemist and City Analyst's Department, Glasgow Corporation.

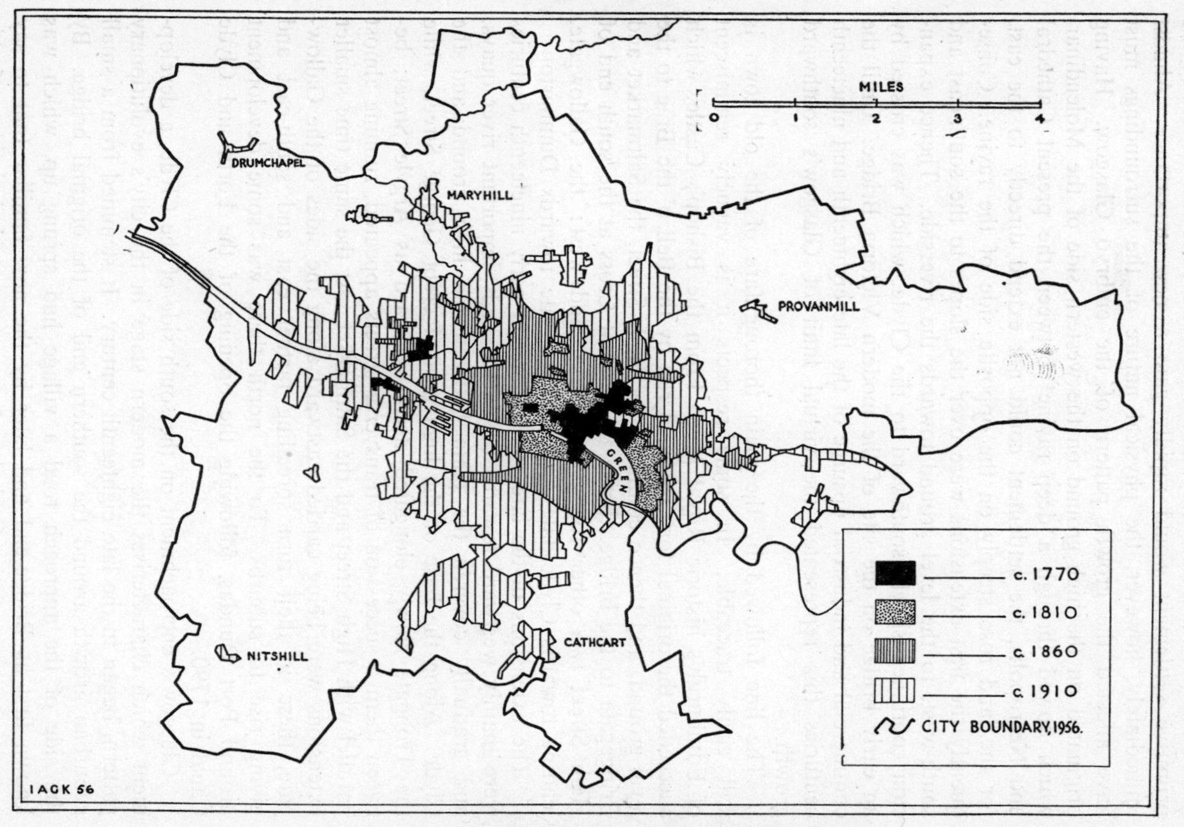

FIG. 5. The Growth of Glasgow's Built-up Areas.

The first great stimulus to its growth after Roman times came in the sixth century, with the arrival of St. Kentigern or Mungo, who is traditionally said to have established his church on the banks of the Molendinar Burn about the year 540. As an ecclesiastical centre the primitive settlement would rapidly gain a new importance. Almost immediately, however, the physical nature of the surroundings must have affected the growth pattern of the embryo Glasgow. Having originated on the high ground on the western side of the Molendinar, which flowed through a deep ravine[1] between the present Cathedral and Necropolis, the settlement could not extend directly to the east, for the land rose steeply on the opposite side of the ravine. Consequently the first extensions were over the slopes to the south-east and south-west, to the level ground towards the riverside. Thence expansion continued slowly southward to the Clyde, which was crossed by an early bridge on the site of the modern Victoria Bridge. Until the commercial and industrial upsurge of the late eighteenth and nineteenth centuries this represented the virtual limit of Glasgow's southward growth.

The line followed by the main thoroughfare of the old town is still easily traceable. In some respects it is vaguely reminiscent of Edinburgh's historic Royal Mile. From the Bishop's Castle, which succeeded the original fort, the road ran by the Bell o' the Brae to the level ground, and thence continued by High Street, the Saltmarket and Bridgegate to the bridge. From the present Cross at the south end of High Street two other roads struck east and west: the Gallowgate, leading towards Clydesdale, and the Trongate towards Dumbarton.

The extensions of the late eighteenth and early nineteenth centuries were mainly westward towards the increasingly important river quays, and gradually covered the plain between the high ground and the Clyde. Along the base of the high ground crept George Street, while the Trongate slowly elongated itself westward as Argyle Street; between them a succession of transverse streets appeared, running almost parallel with High Street and the Saltmarket. At the same time smaller extensions were being carried eastward along the sides of the Gallowgate, these in their turn spreading farther east and south-east and giving rise to suburbs. To the north there was some development around Port Dundas, following the opening of the Forth and Clyde Canal in 1790.

Glasgow's encroachment on the south side of the Clyde, a development which characterises the modern stage in the city's evolutionary pattern, began in the late eighteenth century. It stemmed from a small suburban growth around the southern end of the original bridge. By the side of the approach road a village had sprung up, which was known first as Bridge-end and later by the now familiar (not to say notorious) name of the Gorbals. As one supposed derivation of this

[1] The ravine is still partly visible, but the Molendinar—in which the ascetic Mungo, it is said was wont to immerse himself in all weathers and recite the Psalms of David!—is now degraded to an underground sewer.

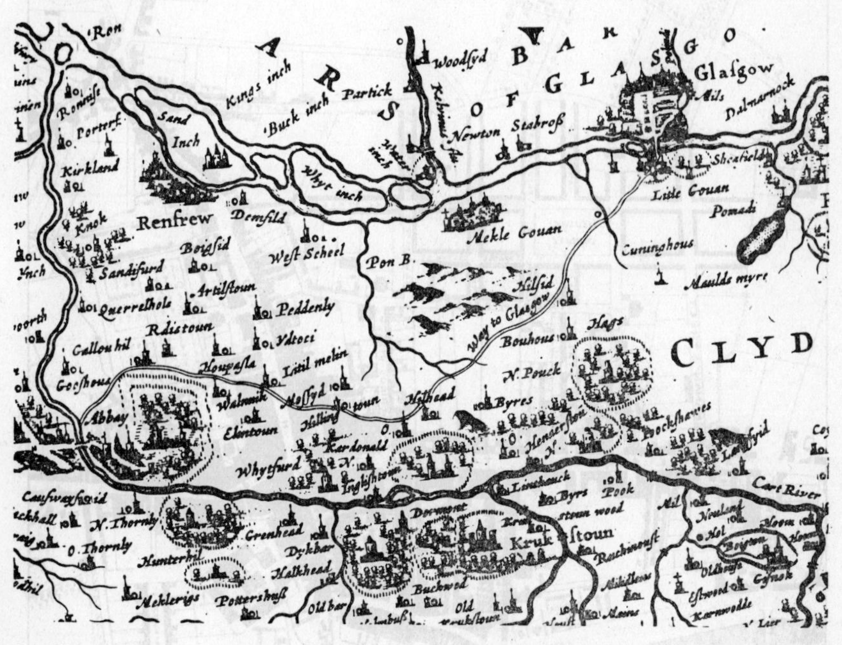

FIG. 6 The Glasgow District at the end of the Sixteenth Century.

This early map is from the Dutch cartographer Blaeu's *Atlas of Scotland,* published in 1654. It is based on a survey made about 1596 by Timothy Pont, at one time minister of Dunnet. Although it is on too small a scale to show much of the detail of the ancient city, the map reveals clearly the meandering course of the River Clyde in the days before its "improvement." Of particular interest are the islands in the river, Whyt inch and Kings inch, the former being still commemorated in the district name Whiteinch. The old forms of many other present-day place-names can also be distinguished on this map.

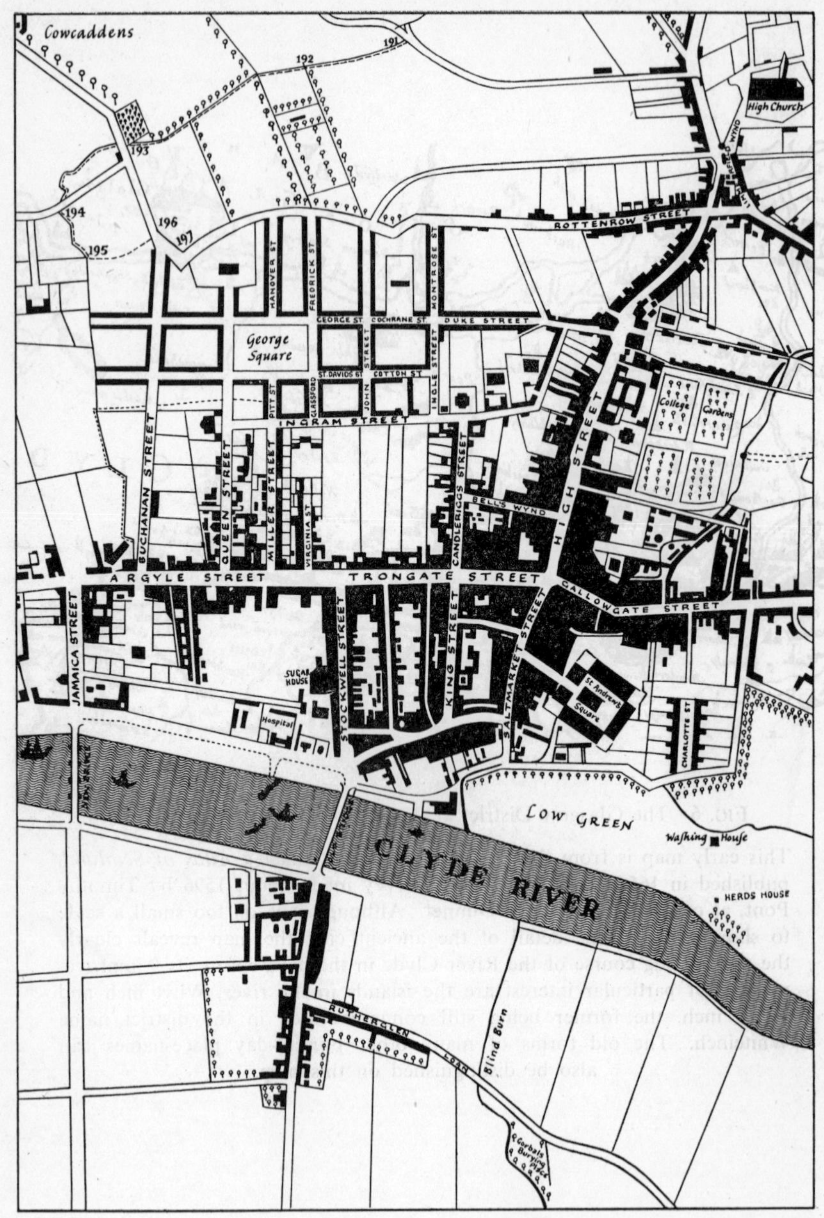

Cowcaddens
191
192
193
194
195
196
197
High Church
ROTTENROW STREET
HANOVER ST
FREDRICK ST
MONTROSE ST
GEORGE ST
COCHRANE ST
DUKE STREET
George Square
ST. DAVIDS ST
COTTON ST
PITT ST
GLASSFORD
JOHN STREET
INGRAM STREET
BUCHANAN STREET
QUEEN STREET
MILLER STREET
VIRGINIA ST
CANDLERIGGS STREET
BELL'S WYND
HIGH STREET
College
Gardens
ARGYLE STREET
TRONGATE STREET
GALLOWGATE STREET
JAMAICA STREET
STOCKWELL STREET
SUGAR HOUSE
Hospital
KING STREET
SALTMARKET STREET
St Andrews Square
CHARLOTTE ST
LOW GREEN
Washing House
HERDS HOUSE
CLYDE RIVER
RUTHERGLEN ROAD
Blind Burn
Gorbals Burying Place

FIG. 7. Barry's Plan of Glasgow, 1782.

name—“ far ” or “ distant ”—might suggest, it was for long regarded as a remote and rather isolated outpost. At the beginning of the eighteenth century it consisted merely of a few thatched houses, belonging mostly to maltmen, on either side of the highway leading south from the old bridge. Its expansion started about 1730, when a number of weavers settled in the village, and in the second half of the century its growth was rapid. In 1792, when the first *Statistical Account* was compiled, the population of the Gorbals had risen to 5,000, which led the parish minister of the time to predict that “ in 20 years a new Glasgow will probably be raised on the south side of the Clyde.” His prophecy was soon fulfilled, for after the turn of the century the humble village once occupied only by brewers and weavers became transformed into a residential suburb of the city, the home of many a prosperous Glasgow merchant. Before long this township at the southern end of the bridge was spreading to the east, west and south. Then, as the new residential areas in their turn became congested, so the frontiers of fashionable suburbia advanced still farther from the city centre.

Although in Glasgow there was no organised retreat by the wealthier classes from the old city to a planned “ New Town,” comparable with that taking place in Edinburgh at this period, there was a piece-meal movement in progress which was no less effectively altering the established pattern of the city's layout. This movement continued throughout the nineteenth century and is still apparent to-day. The central and older areas of the city were being increasingly abandoned to industry and commerce, and deserted by their former residents in favour of more salubrious quarters on the outskirts. The beginnings of the movement, which in Glasgow has been mainly directed to the south and west, are seen in the changing character of such districts as the Saltmarket, once the home of some of the wealthiest citizens. By 1800 it had degenerated into a squalid slum quarter—“ the rag fair of the city ”—and although it has since undergone much improvement there is little in its present appearance to suggest luxurious living. Its past glories, however, are enshrined in a proverbial phrase still heard occasionally on the lips of the old people: “ a' the comforts o' the Sautmarket.” While successful Glasgow business men of the seventeenth and early eighteenth centuries could find in the Saltmarket all the home comforts they desired, those of a later generation had to seek them in new districts like the Gorbals, while their successors to-day have to travel still farther from the city centre in their quest for a suitable domestic retreat.

Glasgow's extension to the south of the Clyde was accompanied by an equally spectacular westward expansion on the north side of the river. This resulted in the creation during the nineteenth century of a fashionable West End, which at the height of its development was regarded—at least by Glaswegians—as comparable in elegance and grandeur with that of London. Its glories, alas, have since in large measure departed, but the conversion of many of its original mansions into office premises and hotels, forming an extension of the city's

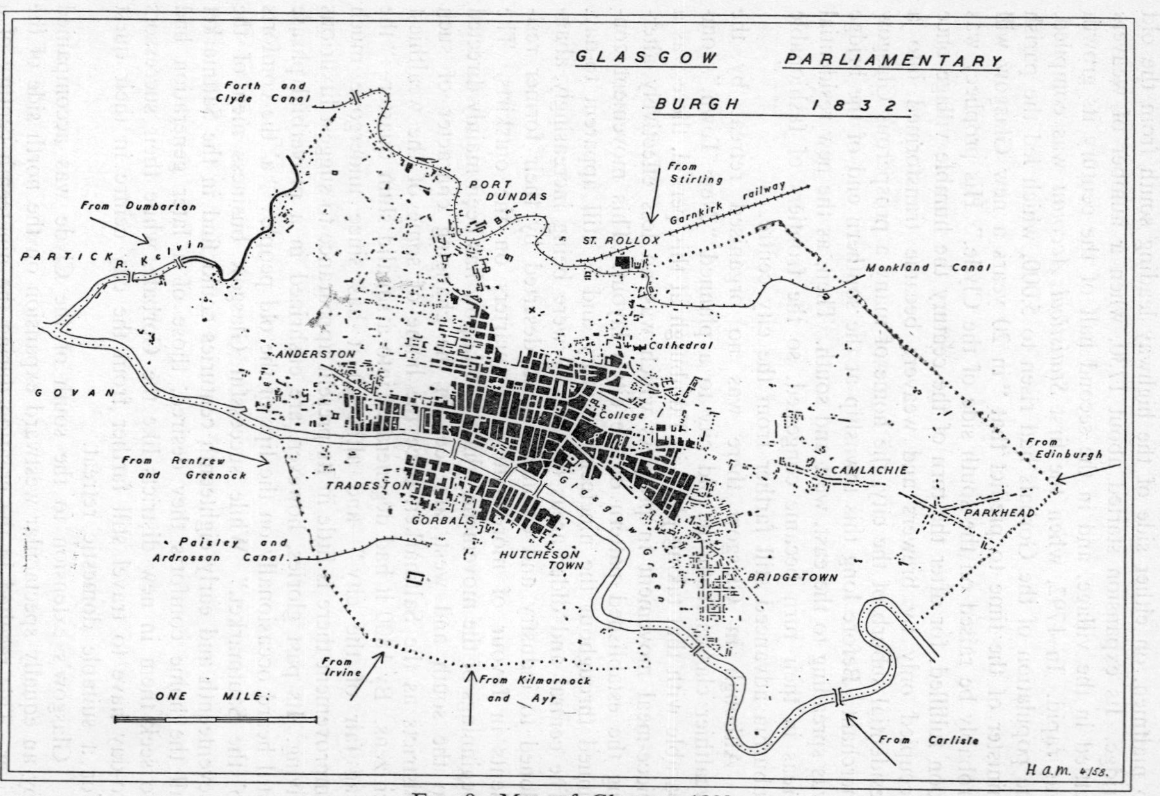

FIG. 8. Map of Glasgow 1832.

business quarter, has saved it from deteriorating in character so much as the first extensions to the south. The absence of industrial concentrations and the more varied nature of the land surface in the west, with its prominent drumlins such as Blythswood, Garnet and Gilmore Hills, and the intervening valley of the Kelvin, have also contributed to the preservation of amenity in this part of the city.

By the close of the nineteenth century the built-up area of Glasgow had extended westward from about the line of Hope Street, over Blythswood and the many other hills, to a distance of almost two miles west of the River Kelvin. One of the first of the new western streets was St. Vincent Street, which, as an early map reveals, outstripped its neighbours by passing right over Blythswood Hill to Anderston and the Dumbarton highway. Joseph Swan's view of it about 1828 shows that it was then essentially residential, but many of the houses in his engraving are now familiar to us as offices.

Sauchiehall Street, which forms the central artery of the city's western extension, is to modern Glasgow what Princes Street is to the "New Town" of Edinburgh. The æsthetic possibilities of its situation, however, have been less happily exploited. Prior to 1830 this great line of imposing shops and residential terraces was nothing more than a quiet and narrow suburban thoroughfare, known as Saughie-haugh[1] Road. An early photograph shows that even by 1890 its north side towards Charing Cross was still comparatively undeveloped.

To the north of Sauchiehall Street there gradually developed another fine highway, Great Western Road, which was eventually to displace the old route by Trongate and Argyle Street as the main outlet for fast traffic to Dumbarton and beyond. It began as a westward extension from Cowcaddens. Nothing but the name of this once pastoral district remains to remind us that it was formerly the common grazing ground for the citizens' cattle. The area to the north of Great Western Road was quite open country before 1830, but by the end of the nineteenth century it had been largely built up. Some of the finest mansions of Glasgow's merchant princes of that century were built along the farther reaches of this straight and well-planned highway. By New City Road, Cowcaddens Street, and Buchanan Street, Great Western Road is linked with the central thoroughfare of George Street, which is continued eastwards as Duke Street. By Parliamentary Road and Castle Street it is also linked with the modern Alexandra Parade, which is the outlet for the fast main routes to Stirling and Edinburgh.

Even Buchanan Street and George Street had not lost their sequestered atmosphere by the late 1820's, when Joseph Swan depicted them in his *Views of Glasgow*. Buchanan Street had been opened about 1778, its situation being described in an advertisement as "rural and agreeable"; it was not intended originally to connect it with Argyle Street. Until the second decade of the nineteenth century it was the secluded western street of the city. Those who occupied its villas were undisturbed by the noise of traffic, for it was so little frequented that grass

[1] The "willow meadow."

sprouted abundantly on the carriage-way. By 1828 Buchanan Street was becoming a busier thoroughfare but its northern end was still uncompleted at that date.

George's Square, as it was then called, had been laid out in the 1780's, and originally consisted of a spacious garden surrounded by handsome private residences. Since the early nineteenth century three sides of the square have been rebuilt, but the northern side has changed little in appearance. Paths began to be formed across the gardens in 1865, when it had become the confluence of many busy streets, and with the erection of the new City Chambers in the 'eighties George Square was transformed into the municipal centre of modern Glasgow. Its much-discussed statues accumulated steadily throughout the nineteenth century—some of them being transported from other sites in the city—but there are many people to-day who would fain see the former simplicity of the gardens restored.

While the city's extension to the south of the Clyde is inferior in its general layout to that of the west, it does possess a line of thoroughfare almost comparable with Great Western Road in boldness of design. This is Eglinton Street with its continuation, Victoria Road, sweeping south from Glasgow Bridge in an undeviating line right to the gates of Queen's Park, a mile and a half away. Its continuity, however, has been broken in recent years by the erection of a traffic barrier at its intersection with Pollokshaws Road, in an attempt to minimise congestion at Eglinton Toll. This arises from the fact that Eglinton Street and Pollokshaws Road together form the southern outlet from the city for the routes to the Ayrshire coast. Initially, of course, these thoroughfares are flanked by rather dismal rows of shops and tenements which cannot vie with the substantial terraces and mansions of the West End. But Glasgow's South Side also has its " west end " in areas like Pollokshields, and here again the physical features of the site have lent themselves to the creation of many attractive roads and avenues. Indeed, among the most striking aspects of Glasgow's layout are the numerous pleasant street vistas afforded by the newer parts of the city, even where the dwellings themselves are architecturally inferior. Confronted by these uninterrupted views of long, straight streets and roads, visitors to the city have sometimes found themselves reminded of the boulevards of Paris. There is no doubt that the undulating nature of the land on which Glasgow is built, and the proximity of the surrounding hills, combine to provide a variety of urban and rural panoramic views seldom equalled in a great industrial city.

In the picture Glasgow presents to-day the extensions of recent centuries just described contrast markedly with the portion of the city representing Old Glasgow, which is still easily recognisable by its irregular layout. Despite countless improvements down the years—involving unfortunately the demolition of almost every historic building—traces of the old closes and narrow winding streets of the early city survive in its present outlines. The area concerned is that lying on either side of High Street, between the Cathedral and the Clyde. It is still traversed from north to south by the city's ancient, if not royal, mile—now known by the successive names of Castle Street, Kirk Street, High Street, and Saltmarket. Until well on in the eighteenth century Old Glasgow consisted of little more than ten principal streets and about seventeen wynds or lanes, the shape and direction of which were largely determined by the crofting system on which the adjacent lands were held. Even the later streets laid down in the initial stages of the city's expansion had their contours fixed by the old occupation pattern of the burgh lands. Argyle Street, for example, was hemmed in on either side by the croft lands of burgesses, with the result that the extension of the city in this direction was at first limited to a form of ribbon development. Eventually streets began to be opened up north and south of the Trongate on the old agricultural holdings, but such developments were necessarily haphazard as they were dependent upon the whims of individual proprietors. Much of the ancient history of land tenure in the burgh is thus woven into the present pattern of the city's streets.

All the areas of later development are characterised by a more regular and planned layout, with straighter streets intersecting generally at right angles. The gridiron street pattern so evident in the modern commercial centre is attributable to its position relative to the Clyde, and to the many bridges constructed over the river in recent times. Thus the principal thoroughfares running parallel with the river, from east to west, are broken by a succession of cross-streets running north and south, leading to the bridges and riverside wharves. Some of the main cross-streets, such as Hope Street, Renfield Street, and West Nile Street, descend from Sauchiehall Street towards the river fairly steeply, but Buchanan Street and its neighbours farther east are more level in their lower reaches.

The erection of additional bridges over the Clyde has been a necessary concomitant of the city's expansion. Since the fourteenth century, when Bishop Rae and Lady Lochow, according to tradition, jointly financed the building of Glasgow's original stone bridge at Stockwell Street, the city's bridges have grown in number to eleven. The most easterly bridge wholly within the municipal boundary is Rutherglen Bridge, built in 1893 to replace an older structure dating from 1776. Next in order downstream are two modern erections, the Richmond Park footbridge and the Ballater Street Bridge, both terminating on Glasgow Green. A little farther downriver is the St. Andrew's Suspension Bridge for foot-passengers, built in 1856 to meet the needs of factory workers in the city's east end. Prior to its construction a ferry plied at this point, which in times of spate was a perilous crossing. Next, at the foot of the Saltmarket, is the Albert Bridge, opened in 1871 in place of one known as the Hutchesontown Bridge, which had been built only forty-two years before. Its foundations had proved unsafe, like those of its predecessor, the first Hutchesontown Bridge, which was swept away by a flood on the river in 1795 within a few months of its completion. Below this is the railway bridge opened in

1870 but rebuilt in 1900, which carried the Glasgow and South-Western Railway to its new terminus at St. Enoch Station on the north side of the Clyde. The next is Victoria Bridge, at the foot of Stockwell Street, opened in 1854 and occupying the historic site of Glasgow's first bridge. A very early bridge, probably of wood, seems to have existed here in the time of William Wallace, to be succeeded in the fourteenth or early fifteenth century by "Bishop Rae's" famous structure. It must have been a remarkable work for its period, as it survived, with only minor reconstruction, for over four hundred years. No other bridge crossed the Clyde below Bothwell until 1768 when the Broomielaw Bridge was erected.

Below Victoria Bridge is the Portland Street Suspension Bridge, a foot-bridge erected by the heritors of Gorbals in 1853. A little lower down is Glasgow Bridge, the important modern link connecting Jamaica Street with Bridge Street and Eglinton Street. Opened in 1899, it is the successor of the old Broomielaw Bridge of 1768 and Telford's Bridge of 1836, of which it is virtually a replica. It is not without significance that it has inherited the name of its ancient counterpart farther upriver, for it now bears the main weight of Glasgow's cross-river traffic. Immediately below it is the massive and rather unsightly railway bridge completed in 1879 to carry the Caledonian line to its city terminus at Central Station. The last, and most recent, of the great Glasgow bridges is the King George V Bridge at Oswald Street, which was brought into service in 1928 to ease the serious congestion—to-day unfortunately again evident—at Glasgow Bridge.

The number of bridges spanning the Clyde would be even greater, were it not for the necessity of maintaining the navigability of the river below the Broomielaw. West of that point cross-river transport is provided by a succession of ferries, and the Corporation's Underground Railway, which affords an invaluable link between Partick and Govan. Towards the close of the nineteenth century an interesting attempt was made to improve cross-river communications beyond the bridges by the boring of tunnels. Three tunnels, each sixteen feet in diameter, were constructed under the Clyde by the Harbour Tunnel Company, at a cost of over a quarter of a million pounds, and were opened to traffic in 1895. They run from Finnieston to Plantation, Govan, two being intended for vehicular traffic and the third for pedestrians, but the former are no longer in use.[1] These tunnels were purchased by the Corporation in 1926, and although the scheme was not a success renewed interest is now being taken in this method of cross-river transport, plans having been approved for a projected tunnel at Whiteinch, considerably farther downriver, which is to cost about five million pounds.

[1] The vehicular tunnels were used until 1943, but they are unsuitable for modern heavy traffic.

Municipal Boundaries

The growth of the built-up area around Glasgow referred to in the preceding account of the city's layout was partly the cause, and partly the result, of successive extensions of the municipal boundary. Once building had crept beyond the existing limits of the city to any substantial degree, it was obviously in the interests of the municipality to extend its boundaries and absorb the new growths, so as to secure rating and other powers over them. At the same time such an extension of boundaries, by bringing the benefits of municipal rights and services, was itself a stimulus to further building development in the areas concerned. The more recent boundary extensions in Glasgow have added large areas of undeveloped land to the city, which are now being utilised for the erection of new housing schemes. In the folding map at the end of this volume and in Table I in the Appendix the successive alterations of the city's boundaries since 1800 are shown.

During the nineteenth century the area of the city grew from 1,768 acres to 12,688 acres, the greater part of the increase taking place in the later decades of the century. Since 1900 the area included within the boundaries has been more than trebled, the city now embracing 39,725 acres, or slightly over 62 square miles. Although, as we have seen, Glasgow had begun to expand noticeably before the end of the eighteenth century, it was not until 1800 that any extension of boundaries occurred. Until that date the area of the city was that of the ancient royalty, which had remained unchanged for centuries. The old burgh, as defined in its charters, could not be extended, but lands could be added to the city and administered by the same government. This is what happened after 1800, and the distinction between the burgh area and the additions to the city was not only theoretical: within the old burgh the land was held by burgage tenure, whereas land within the extensions was held by feudal tenure.

The first extension in 1800 was a small one of only 96 acres, taking in part of Glasgow Green and part of the present centre of the city between Ramshorn Church and St. Enoch's Burn. In 1830 the Necropolis and the lands of Blythswood, with some adjacent lands, were added, and in 1843 the portion of the city between Castle Street and Garscube Road, south of the Canal. The first major addition took place in 1846, when the Burghs of Calton and Anderston and the greater portion of the Barony of Gorbals, with parts of the adjoining counties, were annexed to the city. This marks the beginning of Glasgow's municipal expansion to the south of the River Clyde. There were minor extensions in 1872 and 1878, when various small areas, including the remainder of the Barony of Gorbals, were incorporated. The second large addition occurred in 1891, with the absorption of no less than six burghs on the city's outskirts: Govanhill, Crosshill, Pollokshields East, Pollokshields, Hillhead and Maryhill. At the same time several suburban areas, such as Mount Florida, Langside, Shawlands, Kelvinside, Possilpark and Springburn, were brought within the city. Further minor additions were made in 1896 (Bellahouston Park, Craigton, etc.), in 1899 (the Blackhill and Shawfield areas), in 1905 (the Burgh of Kinning Park), and in 1909 (Moss Park).

The great extension of 1891, involving an addition of 5,750 acres with a population of well over ninety thousand, is the outstanding feature of Glasgow's physical expansion in the nineteenth century. It differed from the earlier boundary extensions in that the districts absorbed were mainly well-developed burghs themselves, and not mere suburban off-shoots. Hitherto the only burghs incorporated by Glasgow had been Anderston, Calton and Gorbals, in 1846. Since that date, however, many of the new urban growths on the city's outskirts had taken advantage of the powers contained in the General Police Acts of 1850 and 1862, and formed themselves into independent Police Burghs. The result was that by 1887 Glasgow was hemmed in on the north, west and south by a whole cluster of such burghs, all very conscious and jealous of their recently acquired burghal status. This presented a serious obstacle to any further expansion of the City of Glasgow. A solution of the difficulty had to be found, and in 1888 a Commission appointed by the Secretary for Scotland recommended that the city should be extended to include "the whole continuous urban area of which the present city is the centre." It was proposed that the new boundaries should embrace all the police burghs formed round the city since the passing of the General Police Act of 1850, together with the adjoining built-up portions of Lanarkshire and Renfrewshire.

Following on this recommendation the Corporation of Glasgow promoted a Bill in 1890 for the inclusion within the city of the adjacent police burghs and suburban areas, but the Bill encountered strong opposition and was rejected by the House of Lords. Its aims, nevertheless, were partly achieved, for as the result of agreements with certain of the adjoining burghs and counties the six small burghs named above were incorporated by the City of Glasgow Act, 1891, along with some county areas. The larger burghs of Govan and Partick, immediately adjoining the city, succeeded in retaining their independence until 1912, when they too were at last absorbed. In that year Pollokshaws Burgh was also taken into the city, with parts of Lanarkshire (Shettleston and Tollcross, and a portion west of Govan), Renfrewshire (Cathcart and Newlands, and a portion west of Partick), and Dunbartonshire (Dawsholm, Temple, and Knightswood North). The extension of 1912 added to Glasgow an area of 6,208 acres, with a population of 226,335. Like that of 1891, it was accomplished only in the face of strenuous opposition from the burghs and counties concerned. As originally lodged, the Bill of 1912 had proposed to incorporate also the Royal Burgh of Rutherglen, but this proud and ancient burgh has so far successfully resisted all attempts by Glasgow to absorb her. The reluctance of Glasgow's neighbours to lose their identity and their municipal independence is understandable, but in most cases what has been surrendered in status and tradition has been counterbalanced by a gain in administrative efficiency. By the end of the nineteenth century the various burghs involved had become so closely linked with Glasgow in their interests, needs and aspirations, that the affairs of the community as a whole were likely to be better directed by a unified authority, than by six or seven different councils whose individual interests and policies might conflict or overlap.

Since 1912 three further extensions of the city's boundaries have taken place, entailing the addition of over twenty thousand acres. The area of the city was in fact more than doubled within the short space of thirteen years, between 1926 and 1938. No new burghs, however, have been absorbed since 1912. Over ten thousand acres were brought into the city in 1926, again from Lanarkshire (Lambhill, Robroyston, Millerston, Carntyne and Aikenhead); Renfrewshire (Mansewood, Kennishead, Nitshill, Hurlet, Crookston, Cardonald, Scotstoun and Yoker); and Dunbartonshire (Knightswood). In 1931 there was a small addition of about five hundred acres, comprising Hogganfield and Carntyne East. The next and latest boundary extension occurred in 1938, when another great area totalling almost ten thousand acres was acquired from the adjoining counties. This consisted of largely undeveloped areas of Lanarkshire (Balmuildy, Auchinairn, Cardowan, Gartloch, Easterhouse and Queenslie); Renfrewshire (Linn Park, Jenny Lind, Darnley and Penilee); and Dunbartonshire (Drumry, Drumchapel and Summerston). These are the districts that are now being transformed by vast housing developments. Since 1938, however, the area of the City of Glasgow has remained unchanged at 39,725 acres.[1]

For administrative purposes the city is divided into 37 municipal wards, as will be seen from the map of the Glasgow Wards in Chapter 2 (Fig. 11). Their size ranges from a mere 170 acres in the densely populated Woodside Ward to as much as 4,846 acres in the sparsely inhabited Provan Ward. The wards of the city were reorganised in 1948, immediately prior to which date they were 38 in number. The portion of the city lying to the north of the Clyde is divided into 24 wards, and that to the south of the river into 13. Their combined acreage is 24,077 on the north, and 15,648 on the south. Glasgow's North Side thus comprises approximately three-fifths of the city's total area, while the South Side, which two centuries ago was practically unbuilt upon, now makes up almost two-fifths of the city.

Land Use

The way in which the land within the boundaries has been utilised has necessarily affected greatly the city's physical appearance, character and amenity. To facilitate post-war planning a comprehensive survey

[1] This is the official figure as used by the Corporation, and is the one employed throughout this volume. It differs from the acreage given in the 1951 Census Report (38,647 acres), which excludes inland water, tidal water and foreshore.

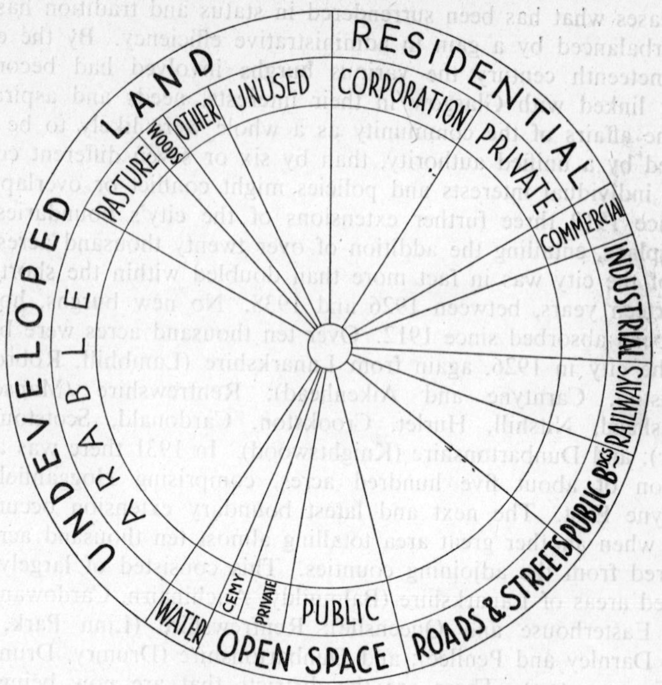

FIG. 9 Proportionate Land Use in Glasgow 1944/5

of existing land use in Glasgow was carried out by the Corporation in 1944/5, the details of which are given in the Appendix. While there have been considerable changes since that date, particularly in the acreage occupied by housing, the survey provides the only official data available regarding the relative proportions of the city's area devoted to industrial, residential and other uses. Its results are summarised in Table IV and Fig. 9.

It will be seen that at the date of the survey over 40 per cent of Glasgow's total area could be classified as undeveloped land. Less than a sixth of this, however, was actually unused land, the remainder being chiefly agricultural, with some woodlands, allotments and nurseries, and private policies. If the category described in the Table as Open Space (consisting of public and private open space, and cemeteries) is added to the foregoing, it becomes apparent that more than half of the city's area could be regarded as unbuilt upon—which means much in terms of amenity. Inevitably, of course, the distribution of this "green area" is uneven, the bulk of it lying around the perimeter in the regions of recent boundary extensions. Freely available public open space amounted to less than 3,000 acres, or under 7 per cent of the total municipal area.

The survey of land use also revealed that the area occupied by

TABLE IV

LAND USE WITHIN THE CITY OF GLASGOW, 1944/5

Description of Use	*Acreage*	*Percentage of City's Area*
Residential	6,706	16.9
Commercial	959	2.4
Industrial	2,522	6.3
Railways	1,774	4.5
Public Buildings	2,072	5.2
Open Space	4,343	10.9
Undeveloped Land	16,016	40.3
Roads and Streets	4,206	10.6
Rivers and Water	1,127	2.9
	39,725	100.0

SOURCE: Planning Department, Glasgow Corporation.

commercial and industrial premises was equivalent to more than half the area devoted to housing. Almost 16 per cent of the city's total acreage was covered by purely residential buildings, or almost 17 per cent if houses combined with shops are included. This is exclusive, of course, of all roads and streets. Roads and streets alone account for more than a tenth of Glasgow's acreage.

We have seen that while the site on which Glasgow has developed is not, as first impressions might suggest, one ideally endowed by Nature for the growth of such a great city, it is certainly blessed with sufficient natural advantages to explain the city's origin and initial expansion. Yet Glasgow's ultimate emergence as the industrial and commercial capital of Scotland cannot be attributed mainly to geographical or geological factors, however much these may have influenced its pattern of development. The chief credit must be given to the inhabitants themselves, whose personal energy and ingenuity down the centuries have overcome many natural obstacles to the city's progress. So it is with the people of Glasgow and their history that we shall concern ourselves in the chapters which follow. True to the civic motto, their faith and enterprise have let Glasgow flourish—despite a situation and climate not over congenial for spectacular growth.

Chapter 2

POPULATION, PAST AND PRESENT

D. J. ROBERTSON

THE PRESENT POPULATION

The population of Glasgow was enumerated at the Census taken on 8 April 1951 as 1,089,767. This figure is for the City of Glasgow as defined by local authority boundaries, and includes some 1,500 people on board ships in the harbour at the time of the Census. Such a total places Glasgow about thirty-seventh among the cities of the world in terms of population, and third among the cities of the United Kingdom; of the latter only London, and Birmingham (by a very narrow margin), had larger populations in 1951.

Glasgow is by a long way the largest of the four cities of Scotland. It was in 1951 over twice as big as its nearest rival, Edinburgh (487 thousands); and several times larger than either Aberdeen (183 thousands) or Dundee (177 thousands). Indeed, there were, including the four cities, only seven towns in Scotland with populations exceeding 50,000 in 1951, and Glasgow's population almost exactly equalled that of the other six put together. Further, in 1951 the population of the City of Glasgow amounted to over one fifth of the population of Scotland, which totalled 5,095,969 at the date of the Census.

In relation to the rest of Scotland, Glasgow appears as a massive urban concentration serving as a nucleus for a very large proportion of the industrialised part of the country. There are, of course, other industrial areas in Scotland besides this, such as those centred on Falkirk and Kirkcaldy, and each of the cities also has its share of industry; but the West of Scotland industrial area centred on Glasgow is, for Scotland, unique in its size and importance.

If broad divisions of the country are taken, the West Central Division of Scotland (defined by the Registrar-General as comprising the four counties of Ayr, Dunbarton, Lanark and Renfrew) included almost half of the population of Scotland in 1951. It contained within its boundaries, in addition to Glasgow, the three Scottish burghs (other than cities) with more than fifty thousand inhabitants, and twelve of the twenty Scottish burghs (other than cities) with populations of more than twenty thousand. This, however, may well be regarded as far too wide a definition of the area of industrialisation surrounding Glasgow and feeding into it. It is probably better to think in terms of the "conurbation" of which Glasgow is the centre and the largest constituent.

Conurbations have been defined in the Census Reports as "con-

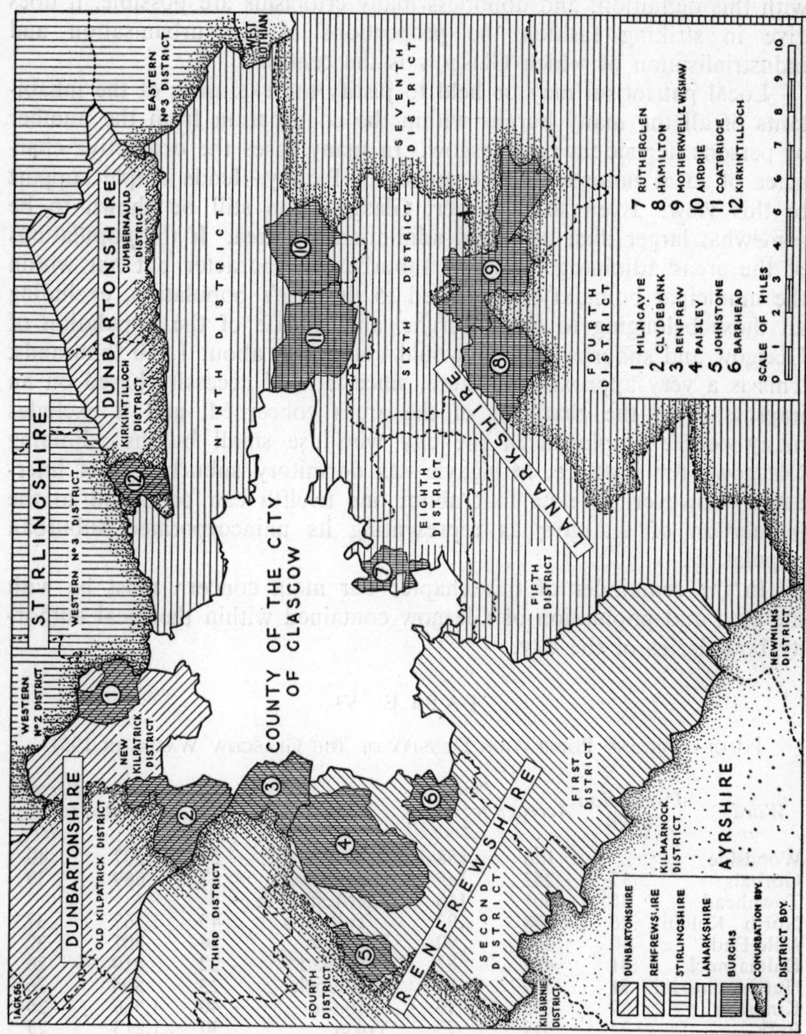

FIG. 10 The Central Clydeside Conurbation.

tinuously urbanised areas surrounding large population centres, which are, to a greater or lesser extent, focal points of economic and social activity." The Central Clydeside conurbation (Figure 10) around Glasgow, defined in this way, was found in 1951 to contain 1,758 thousands, or over one third of the population of Scotland. It included such large burghs, closely adjoining Glasgow, as Paisley, Motherwell and Wishaw, Coatbridge, Clydebank, Hamilton, Airdrie, and Rutherglen; all of which were held to form part of the continuous stretch of urban development about Glasgow. Whatever faults may be found with this definition, and doubtless many criticisms are possible, it does give in striking fashion the proportions of the urbanisation and industrialisation of which Glasgow is the centre.

Local patriotism may be held to justify the exclusion of the inhabitants of all the many burghs within the conurbation from the number of persons dependent on Glasgow. In many cases the distinctive character of local industry—for example in Paisley—lends ample support to this view. Even so, however, Glasgow can still be shown to be somewhat larger than its actual administrative area. If the populations of the areas adjoining Glasgow, suburban in character but not within the municipal boundary, are added to the city's population, excluding all those belonging to other burghs, an estimate of the population of Glasgow and suburbs in 1951 would amount to about 1,180 thousands. This is a very approximate figure, since it is of necessity based on an impression of the character of the areas concerned, and it excludes many people employed in the city who use small burghs adjoining Glasgow—for instance, Milngavie—as dormitory suburbs. It is interesting, however, to note that about one twelfth can be added to the population of Glasgow as representing its unincorporated suburban population.

In the remainder of this chapter our main concern must be with the area and population of Glasgow contained within the local authority boundaries of the city.

TABLE V[1]

POPULATION AND POPULATION DENSITY OF THE GLASGOW WARDS IN 1951

Ward	*Population* (000)	*Acreage*	*Persons to the Acre*	*Ward*	*Population* (000)	*Acreage*	*Persons to the Acre*
Woodside	27	170	158	Exchange	20	507	40
Gorbals	37	252	145	Dennistoun	27	689	39
Townhead	35	301	116	Shettleston &			
North Kelvin	26	278	93	Tollcross	43	1,167	37
Mile-End	40	443	90	Langside	26	801	32
Dalmarnock	41	487	83	Parkhead	22	819	26
Hutchesontown	31	387	80	Whiteinch	23	894	26
Kingston	27	355	76	Craigton	40	1,566	26
Park	24	317	75	Yoker	30	1,213	25
Govanhill	26	365	72	Ruchill	46	1,962	23
Govan	35	489	72	Fairfield	25	1,351	19
Kinning Park	28	402	70	Kelvinside	21	1,160	18
Partick East	23	351	67	Springburn	36	2,118	17
Calton	26	404	65	Pollokshields	40	3,239	12
Anderston	32	530	60	Pollokshaws	40	3,223	12
Partick West	27	464	58	Maryhill	26	2,210	12
Cowcaddens	27	488	56	Knightswood	18	1,614	11
Camphill	23	481	47	Cathcart	22	2,737	8
Cowlairs	28	645	43	Provan	24	4,846	5
				City of Glasgow	1,090	39,725	27

[1] Throughout this Chapter, except where otherwise indicated, the population figures are taken from the various Census reports, and the acreages are those adopted by Glasgow Corporation.

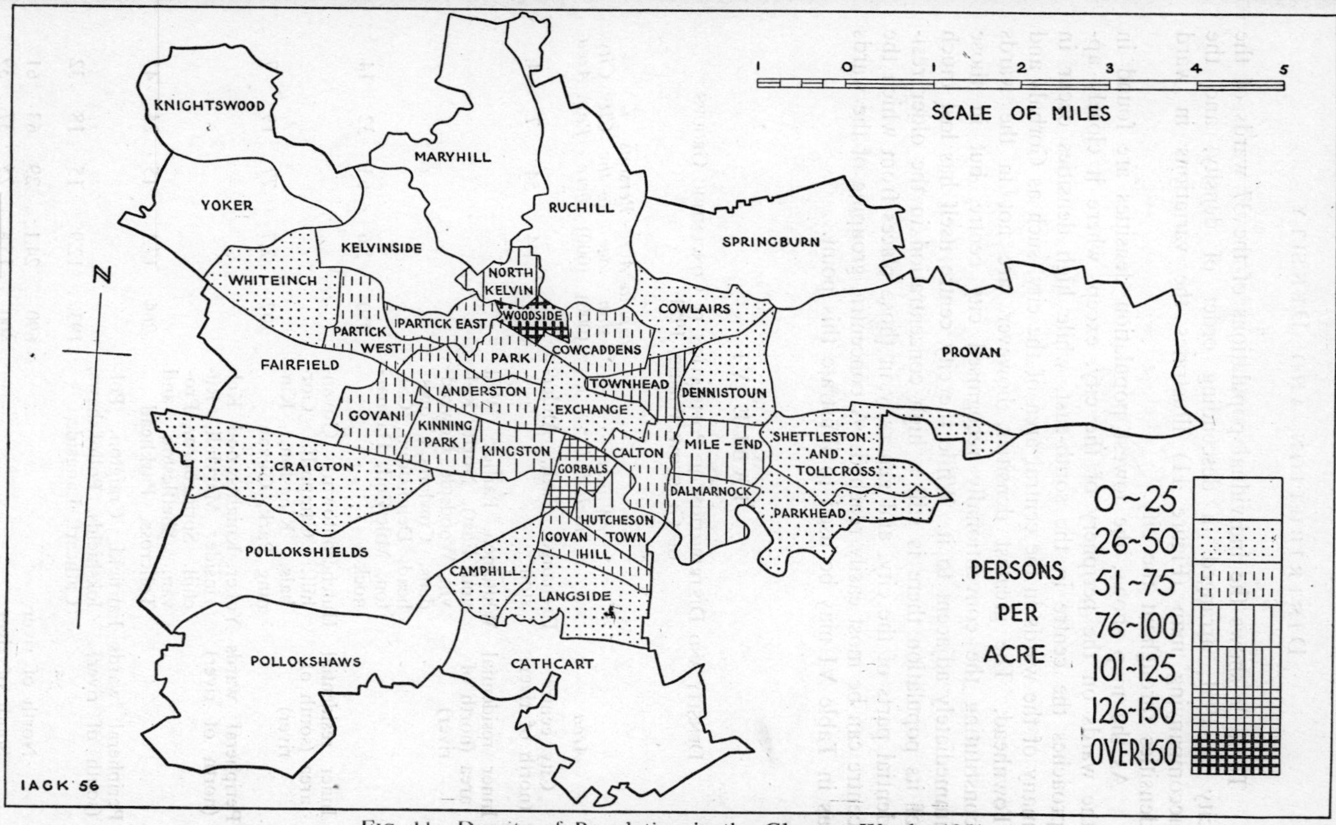

FIG. 11 Density of Population in the Glasgow Wards, 1951.

Distribution and Density

Table V shows the individual populations of the 37 wards of the city in 1951, arranged in descending order of density, and the accompanying map (Figure 11) illustrates the variations in ward densities throughout the city.

As the map shows, the lowest population densities are found in the wards on the periphery of the city, except where it closely approaches the centre in the south-east, while high densities occur in many of the wards in the central area of the city, such as Gorbals and Townhead. The greatest densities, however, are not in the wards constituting the conventionally recognised city centre, but in those immediately adjacent to it. While the city centre itself has lost much of its population there is still a high concentration in the older residential parts of the city, and generally in those places from which the centre can be most easily reached. A concentric grouping of the wards as in Table VI may be used to illustrate this point.

TABLE VI

Density and Distribution of Population in Concentric Groups of Glasgow Wards, 1951

Area	*Wards included*	*Population* (000)	*Acreage* (000)	*Persons to the acre*	*% City Pop.*	*% City Area*
City centre (north of river)	Exchange, Park, Anderston	76	1.4	54	7	4
Inner residential area (north of river)	Whiteinch, Partick (West and East), North Kelvin, Woodside, Cowcaddens, Cowlairs, Townhead, Dennistoun, Calton, Mile-End, Dalmarnock	350	5.6	63	32	14
Inner residential area (south of river)	Hutchesontown, Govanhill, Camphill, Gorbals, Kingston, Kinning Park, Govan	207	2.7	77	19	7
Peripheral wards (north of river)	Yoker, Knightswood, Kelvinside, Maryhill, Ruchill, Springburn, Provan, Shettleston and Tollcross, Parkhead	264	17.1	15	24	43
Peripheral wards (south of river)	Fairfield, Craigton, Pollokshields, Pollokshaws, Cathcart, Langside	193	12.9	15	18	32
North of river		690	24.1	29	63	61
South of river		400	15.6	25	37	39
City of Glasgow		1,090	39.7	27	100	100

The actual city centre is seen to be less densely populated than the inner residential areas of the city, which, both north and south of the river, have very high densities. The more outlying regions on both sides of the river have comparatively low densities. Taken in conjunction, Tables V and VI enable the distribution of the population to be briefly summarised. Only a small proportion of Glasgow's inhabitants—about seven per cent—actually live in the City Centre; and the Exchange ward, which is roughly coterminous with the commercial and shopping centre, is the home of less than a fiftieth of the city's population. More than half the people of Glasgow—fifty-one per cent—live in the residential districts lying round the centre. In many of these districts the inhabitants live close together in tenements (which are often in an indifferent state of repair). The remaining forty-two per cent of the population live on the outer fringe of the city. Not all parts of the wards in the latter area can be described as suburban, but a high proportion of them can; consequently a good part of this forty-two per cent may be regarded as living in the nearer suburbs of Glasgow. Of the city's total population slightly less than two thirds live north of the Clyde, while rather more than one third live on the south side of the river.

The figures of density given above gain in meaning when they are set against those of other cities, as in Table VII. Glasgow is seen to be much more densely populated than any of the other cities of Scotland, its population density being closely comparable with that of the major industrial cities of England, though such comparisons, and indeed all density statistics, are much influenced by the generosity with which boundaries may or may not be drawn to include open spaces, and with which land is or is not devoted to housing purposes.

TABLE VII

Density of Population of Various Cities of the United Kingdom in 1951

City	*Population* (000)	*Acreage* (000)	*Persons to the acre*
Edinburgh	467	33.2	14
Aberdeen	183	11.0	17
Dundee	177	12.3	14
Birmingham	1,112	51.1	22
Liverpool	790	27.3	29
Manchester	703	27.3	26
Glasgow	1,090	39.7	27

The trends of figures of the density of population of Glasgow may also be examined over a period of time, though this is difficult to do because of boundary changes, which may involve additions to the city of large undeveloped areas with very small populations. Where such extensions have recently occurred, the population density of the city as a whole will be deceptively low. Up to the closing decade of the nineteenth century there is good ground for the contention that Glasgow's population density was increasing, but there is evidence of a distinct downward trend over the past fifty years.

The overall density of any area may be expressed as the relation between its total population and its acreage. In the case of Glasgow such density figures for the early nineteenth century, when the area enumerated at each census was not exactly defined, cannot be stated with precision, but enough is known to provide a fairly clear picture. The available data are laid out in Table VIII.

TABLE VIII

Density of Population

Year	*Area*	*Population*	*Acres*	*Density Persons to the Acre*
1801	An area approximately equal to that of the Parliamentary Burgh created in 1832	77,058	c.5,063	15
1811	— Do. —	103,224	c.5,063	20
1821	— Do. —	140,432	c.5,063	28
1831	— Do. —	193,030	c.5,063	38
1841	Parliamentary Burgh	255,650	5,063	50
1851	Parliamentary Burgh (=municipal area)	329,097	5,063	65
1861	— Do. —	395,503	5,063	78
1871	— Do. —	477,732	5,063	94
1881	Municipal Burgh	511,415	6,111	84
1891	— Do. —	565,839	6,111	93
1901	— Do. —	761,709	12,688	60
1911	— Do. —	784,496	12,975	60
1921	— Do. —	1,034,174	19,183	54
1931	— Do. —	1,088,461	29,509	36
1951	— Do. —	1,089,767	39,725	27

The area enumerated at the first four census dates, 1801 to 1831, as " City and Suburbs " was not very different from that of the Parliamentary Burgh set up under the Reform Act of 1832. This was enumerated for the first time in 1841, but the Census Report of 1851 in reviewing the progress of the previous half-century gives the population of " nearly the same " area for the period 1801-1831. On this basis —which makes possible a comparison of density in a roughly constant area from 1801 right up to 1871—the overall density of Glasgow's population in 1801 was 15 persons to the acre. By 1851 the figure had risen to 65 and by 1871 to 94 persons to the acre. In the census years 1851 to 1871 the parliamentary and municipal boundaries coincided, but by the end of the century the municipal burgh reached far beyond the original parliamentary limits. The density of population within the municipal area as extended by boundary alterations declined to 84 persons to the acre in 1881 but rose again to 93 persons to the acre in the census of 1891. Thereafter it fell to 60 at the turn of the century and has continued to decline almost without interruption to 27 persons to the acre in 1951.

All the foregoing figures and comparisons refer to overall densities of population. The impression they give is therefore much influenced by the extent to which in any given area housing has a major or minor claim on land use. Before a true impression of the present position can be obtained a detailed survey of land use is essential, to reveal what proportion of the city's area is devoted to housing and freely available recreational space as opposed to that used for commercial, industrial and other purposes. Such a survey was that undertaken by the Planning Department of Glasgow Corporation in 1944/5, the results of which have been summarised in Chapter 1 and are printed in full in the Appendix.[1] As a guide to present conditions it unfortunately has two defects: first, it is now some years out of date, much new housing having been completed since; and second, it is based on the ward divisions of the city as they existed prior to the reorganisation of wards in 1948. For these reasons the results, if related to the 1951 population figures, must be regarded as approximate, and can only be utilised for certain groups of wards and for the areas of those wards which were left unchanged by the 1948 reorganisation. Subject to these limitations, the land use data may be employed to give estimates of net residential density[2] as in Table IX.

TABLE IX

NET RESIDENTIAL DENSITY OF POPULATION IN CERTAIN AREAS OF GLASGOW AT 1951 POPULATION AND 1945 LAND USE[3]

Area	*Population in 1951 (000)*	*Residential Land in 1945*		*Net Residential Density*	*Public Open Spaces in 1945*		
		Acres	*% Total Area*		*Acres*	*% Total Area*	*Acres per 1,000 persons*
Hutchesontown	31.0	55	14	564	41	10.6	1.3
Gorbals	36.6	69	27	530	2	0.8	0.05
Woodside	26.9	58	34	464	3	1.8	0.1
Park & Anderston	55.7	159	19	350	85	10.1	1.5
Cowcaddens	27.2	53	10	514	5	1.0	0.2
Govanhill	26.4	93	25	284	6	1.6	0.2
Ruchill & North Kelvin	71.7	321	14	223	128	5.7	1.8
Maryhill	25.5	133	6	192	24	1.1	0.9
Camphill & Pollokshaws	62.2	479	13	130	179	4.8	2.9
Langside & Cathcart	47.4	669	19	71	472	13.5	10.0
Craigton & Pollokshields	80.4	1,264	26	64	487	10.1	6.1
Glasgow	1,089.8	6,706	17	163	2,749	6.9	2.5

Table IX emphasises the distinction between the total area of land in the wards and the area occupied by housing. In the selection of

1 Tables 2 and 3.

2 "Net Residential Density" = persons per acre occupied by houses, their curtilages, and roads serving them.

3 Land use may be generally classified as residential, open space, commercial, industrial, railways, public buildings, roads and streets, rivers and water. "Open space" includes public open space, private open space, cemeteries, agricultural land, woodlands, allotments, policies, and unused land; but only the first of these is considered here, as it alone is expressly designed for the free recreational use of the citizens.

areas shown, none has more than 34 per cent of its land so utilised: the remainder is made up of open space, roads and streets, ground used for commercial, industrial or public purposes, or land which is not available for use, being under water. The effect of the net residential density calculation is to bring out more vividly the differences between various parts of the city. Among the areas shown in the table the older areas with a large proportion of tenements have very high residential densities. The introduction of housing estates reduces the residential density (as, for example, in Ruchill and Maryhill), and the densities are noticeably lower in wards on the periphery which are composed largely of middle-class dwellings or Corporation housing estates (such as the last three areas shown). It is noteworthy, too, that some of the areas with high densities have little public open space; indeed the largest concentrations of it are in the areas with least residential density, namely Craigton and Pollokshields, and Langside and Cathcart. One or two of the areas have large amounts of open space other than that devoted to public recreation: such land affords breathing space, if not the full benefits of free parkland. Again, however, areas with this type of open space tend to be those which already have lower residential densities, although Ruchill and Maryhill, which have above average densities, also have quite a lot of farm land within their boundaries at the outer limits of the developing city.

Mr. Robert Grieve, basing his statements on a study of population densities in Glasgow made by the City Engineer at the time of the land use survey, brings out vividly and concisely the implications of such high residential densities. He notes[1] that "the Glasgow densities were staggering. It was found for example that 700,000 people lived on 1,800 acres in and around Central Glasgow at an average gross density of 400 persons to the acre; one-seventh of Scotland's population was thus compressed into three square miles of Central Glasgow. In some parts of that area net densities rose to as high as 700 persons to the acre." House building since the end of the war has altered these figures but has unfortunately not destroyed their general import. Moreover, such high densities in areas which are mainly due or overdue for redevelopment set town planners difficult problems of finding alternative sites for housing. Even if redevelopment were to take place at what are currently regarded as high densities (net residential densities of 120 persons per acre), it would not be possible to get anything like the same number of people back into the areas they come from. Given that most building land in Glasgow is now built on, a considerable overspill of population out of Glasgow is necessary if redevelopment is to be completed. Estimates indicate very large figures for such overspill amounting to a quarter or more of the present population of the city.

Residential density figures put a different light on the comparison of Glasgow's density and that of other cities. Mr. Grieve[2] has made a

[1] Robert Grieve, *The Clyde Valley—A Review*. Paper delivered to the Town and Country Planning Summer School held at St. Andrews in 1954 and reprinted for the Town and Country Planning Association (Scottish Section).
[2] *Op. cit.*

comparison of this kind between Glasgow and Birmingham and Manchester at the end of the war. Some of his figures appear in Table X.

TABLE X

COMPARISONS OF LAND USE AND RESIDENTIAL DENSITY OF POPULATIONS OF GLASGOW, BIRMINGHAM AND MANCHESTER

Land use as % of Total Area:	*Glasgow*	*Birmingham*	*Manchester*
Open Space	11.3%	13.7%	11.5%
Undeveloped (including agriculture)	41.5%	29.7%	20.8%
Industry	8.8%	6.7%	8.2%
Commerce, Public Buildings and Transport	15.1%	7.1%	17.3%
Housing	23.3%	42.8%	42.2%
Total Areas of Cities (Acres)	38,598[1]	51,150	21,481
Total Populations (Thousands)	1,089	1,112	702
Density of Housing Areas in persons per acre	121.0	48.1	77.4

Housing densities are much greater in Glasgow than in either of these two cities. Birmingham has more land at its disposal relative to population while both Manchester and Birmingham have used more of their land area for housing. The high figure for undeveloped land in Glasgow has undoubtedly now been reduced by the extremely large house-building programme of the Corporation which again will have lowered the housing density somewhat. A substantial part of the undeveloped land is however unusable and reflects the extent to which land within the narrow boundaries of the city is undermined and liable to subsidence.

THE GROWTH OF THE POPULATION

Like other great industrial cities, Glasgow has experienced a spectacular growth in population since the beginning of last century. Much of this growth can be attributed to migration movements, and the rest to the relationship between births and deaths and to changes in this relation. These factors will be discussed in due course, but first of all a brief sketch of the growth of Glasgow's population must be given.

In 1801 the first official Census gave the population of Glasgow as some 77 thousands. Earlier estimates—of varying reliability—are avail-

[1] The figure of the area of Glasgow given here differs from that given in Table IV Chapter 1, and the percentage distribution of land use given here for Glasgow conveys a somewhat different impression from that in the earlier Table. The causes of the differences are that Mr. Grieve has deducted " rivers and water " from the total area figure, and has distributed the acreage devoted to " roads and streets " among " industry ", " commerce etc.", and " housing ". The figures given here are appropriate to the comparison Mr. Grieve makes with Birmingham and Manchester. The reader who wishes to cite data on land use in Glasgow would be better to use the more detailed figures in Table IV of Chapter 1.

able as far back as 1300, and these are shown in Table XI with the results of each Census since 1801.

TABLE XI

POPULATION OF GLASGOW AT VARIOUS DATES[1]

Year	*Population Estimates* (000)	*Year*	*Census Population* (000)
1300	1.5	1801	77
1450	2	1811	101
1490	2.9	1821	147
1556	4.5	1831	202
1600	7	1841	256
1610	7.6	1851	329
1660	14	1861	396
1690	15	1871	478
1708	12	1881	511
1712	13.8	1891	566
1740	17	1901	762
1755	23.5	1911	784
1763	28.3	1921	1,034
1780	42	1931	1,088
1791	66	1951	1,090

The Table shows the extremely rapid growth of Glasgow's population during the nineteenth century, from 77 thousands in 1801 to almost ten times that number in 1901. Between 1901 and 1951 the population has increased from 762 thousands to 1090 thousands, but by far the greater part of this latter growth is seen to have occurred in the second decade of the century. In many cases, of course, striking increases are attributable to extensions of the city's boundaries. The major incorporations of surrounding built-up areas occurred in 1846, in 1891, and in 1912; and in 1926 and 1938 various suburban and largely undeveloped areas were incorporated. The Registrar-General[2] lends his authority to the view that the boundary changes have been so complex as to make impossible any accurate estimate of the population of the present area of the city in past years. Population figures for an unchanging area of the city, which would eliminate the effects of boundary alterations, cannot be supplied. Estimates of the earlier population of the present area of the city can be given only for a few dates. These are shown in Table XII; it should be emphasised that the estimates for 1871 and 1901 are rather conjectural, though the figures given for later years should be accurate enough.

Two points emerge from this table. Firstly, as might be expected, the rate of growth of the population of the area that is now Glasgow has been less rapid than that of the city itself, which owes its growth

[1] The area of enumeration has varied considerably throughout the period. In the above Table the returns from 1801 to 1831 relate to the area described in the Census Reports as "Glasgow City (including Suburbs)," the suburbs including the Parishes of Barony and Gorbals; from 1841 to 1871 the returns are for the Parliamentary Burgh which equalled the municipal area in the census years 1851 to 1871; and from 1881 to 1951 for the Municipal Burgh. The population on board ships in the harbour is normally included.

[2] Census of Scotland, 1951: Vol. I, Part 2, p. 5.

TABLE XII

ESTIMATES OF THE POPULATION OF THE PRESENT AREA OF GLASGOW AT VARIOUS DATES

Year	*Estimated Population* (000)	*Year*	*Estimated Population* (000)
1871	600	1921	1,056
1901	950	1931	1,093
		1951	1,090

in numbers partly to the incorporation of surrounding districts. Secondly, any gain in the city's population recorded between 1931 and 1951 is seen to have been more apparent than real, being due to the extension of boundaries. The population of the area now known as Glasgow actually declined during these years. Indeed, if the Census returns of 1931 and 1951 are corrected to allow for persons who were temporary visitors and temporary absentees on the Census night, a decrease of 4,340 is revealed in the resident population of the City of Glasgow itself during the period. It should be pointed out, however, that the population would have increased but for the casualties suffered in the late war. In the *Book of Remembrance* compiled by the Corporation of Glasgow 9,202 deaths due to the war are recorded. Moreover, the under-statement of population in the 1951 Census resulting from the absence in the armed forces of people who normally live in the city is known to have been considerably greater than in 1931. For these reasons the decline in the resident population between 1931 and 1951 is of less significance than might at first sight appear, though similar circumstances must certainly have affected other cities also.

The rapidity of the growth of Glasgow's population since 1801 is perhaps best appreciated by comparing it with that of other areas. Between 1801 and 1871, while Scotland's population doubled, that of Glasgow increased over six times. By 1951 the population of Scotland was over three times as large as at the beginning of the nineteenth century, but Glasgow's had grown to more than fourteen times its 1801 level. Thus the city far outpaced the country as a whole in rate of growth, and even if due allowance is made for the effect of boundary changes the difference is still apparent. Comparing the population of Glasgow to-day with that of the same area in 1871, we find that it has increased by 82% while that of Scotland in the same period has increased by only 52%. Whereas Glasgow at the beginning of the nineteenth century contained less than 5% of the population of Scotland, to-day it comprises over 21% of the country's total population.

The West Central Division of the country, of which Glasgow is a part, has also outdistanced the rest of Scotland during the period. By 1871 the population of this Division (comprising the counties of Ayr, Dunbarton, Lanark and Renfrew) was almost four times, and by 1951 over seven times as large as in 1801. In the period up to 1871 Glasgow was pulling the surrounding area with it (since Glasgow's population increased by over six times as against an increase of almost four times in the Division), but in the subsequent period Glasgow's rate of population growth has been somewhat less rapid in comparison with that of the region as a whole (the Division's population increased by 95% and Glasgow's population by 82%). Perhaps the most noteworthy feature of the graph of Glasgow's population is that, although it followed a steeply rising curve from 1801, the curve flattened out around

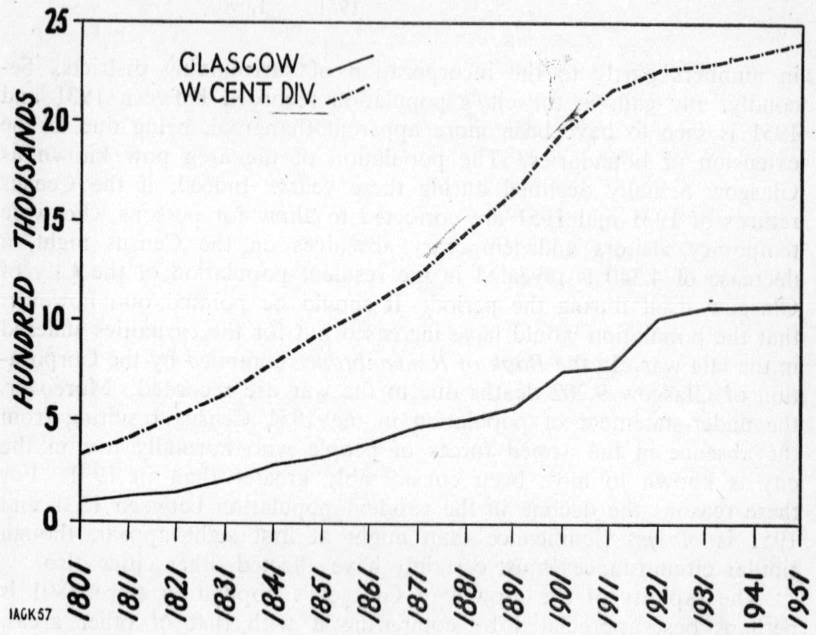

FIG. 12 Population of Glasgow and of West Central Division of Scotland, 1801-1951.

the second decade of the present century, since when the population of the city has hardly grown at all; and between 1931 and 1951, while both the country as a whole and the West Central Division were increasing in population, there was no corresponding rise in Glasgow.

Several circumstances may contribute to this slowing up—and indeed virtual cessation—of the growth of the population of Glasgow. For one thing there is the quite perceptible tendency of the population of Scotland to move eastwards, a movement in which it is to be presumed Glasgow shares. There is secondly the drift out of Scotland to England and overseas, which, it is at least possible, has been affecting Glasgow more severely than other places. There is evidence, too, of an increasing movement of population from within the boundaries of the city to nearby suburbs or adjacent burghs. All of these movements affect the rate of growth of Glasgow's population relatively to that of other parts of Scotland. In absolute terms, too, the curve of population growth is greatly affected by the tendency, common to other parts of Scotland and even more to England, for the birth rate to fall towards a level which is barely sufficient to maintain population increase. All this, in its total effect, gives reason to doubt the popular easy assumption that Glasgow is, and will remain, a city of the same importance as hitherto. The slowing of its growth may be parallelled to some extent by a decline in the rate of growth of the country as a whole, but it is also possible that Glasgow will fail to keep its place relatively to other parts. Yet the assumption that it will maintain its position is widespread and deep-rooted: it was surprising how much popular reaction was evident in Glasgow following the announcement that Birmingham had supplanted Glasgow as the second city of the United Kingdom.

The growth of the population of the city has naturally affected the distribution of the inhabitants within it. Perhaps the pattern is most easily seen by picturing the way in which the advancing boundaries encroached on the surrounding areas. Glasgow originated on the north side of the Clyde and first developed there. The earliest adjustments of the boundary occurred on that side. By the 1840's the city was developing westwards and southwards across the river. The boundary then advanced in all directions, except where hindered by neighbouring burghs that successfully resisted incorporation (such as Rutherglen), until the city reached its present dimensions. In its distribution the population within the city has followed a similar pattern of movement outward from the centre, until in many places it has spilled over into suburbs in the surrounding counties. A glance at the changing populations of wards and groups of wards, where these can be directly compared in 1931 and 1951, shows in all cases an increase in the outlying wards and a decrease in the central wards. This picture is laid out (for the same ward groups as in Table IX) in Table XIII and for the city as a whole, as far as practicable, in Figure 13.

TABLE XIII

CHANGES IN POPULATION OF CERTAIN COMPARABLE AREAS OF GLASGOW BETWEEN 1931 AND 1951

Area (1951)	*Population change per cent since* 1931 (*same area*)	*Area* (1951)	*Population change per cent since* 1931 (*same area*)
Cowcaddens	−23.8	Maryhill	−0.6
Gorbals	−21.7	Langside and Cathcart	+7.1
Hutchesontown	−20.3	Ruchill and North Kelvin	+15.2
Govanhill	−18.9	Camphill and Pollokshaws	+52.7
Woodside	−18.5	Craigton and Pollokshields	+178.8
Park and Anderston	−18.0	Glasgow City	−0.3

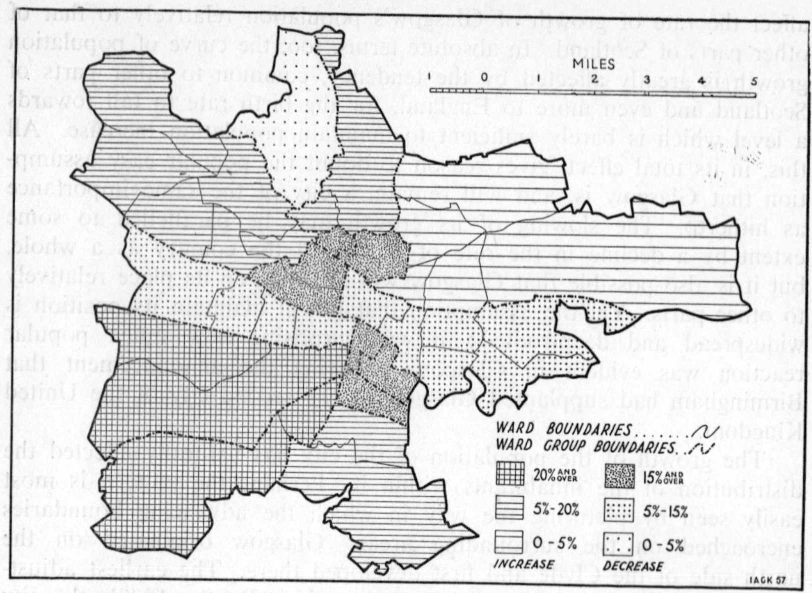

FIG. 13. Population Changes in Certain Wards and Ward Groups, 1931-1951 (1951 Area).

The heaviest losses have occurred in the "old" areas such as Cowcaddens, Gorbals and Hutchesontown, while the areas of growing population have tended to be those on the outskirts of the city, such as Craigton and Pollokshaws.

Glasgow's development south of the Clyde has, as we have seen in the preceding chapter, been going on for quite a long time. It became fashionable at one period in the early nineteenth century to live in the suburbs immediately south of the river, in the area known as the Gorbals; and it is to this period that we owe the substantial and solidly-built houses of that district. Each of the major extensions of boundaries in 1846, 1891, and 1912 (and some of the lesser extensions in other years) meant a further encroachment of Glasgow on the south side of the river. In 1846 most of the Barony of Gorbals, by then quite a large suburb, was brought within the city boundaries. In 1891 the burghs of Pollokshields, Pollokshields East, Govanhill and Crosshill—with a total population of about 28,000—were incorporated, along with a number of suburban areas on the south side. The 1905 alteration of boundaries added the Burgh of Kinning Park, with about 14,000 people; and in 1912 the incorporation of the ancient Burgh of Govan, with its 90,000 inhabitants, and Pollokshaws Burgh, with 13,000, still further increased the area and population of Glasgow on the south side of the Clyde. The population of the city north of the river was also, of course, growing during the whole of this period, both through the normal factors creating growth and through boundary extension—which has resulted, for instance, in the incorporation since 1891 of the burghs of Maryhill, Hillhead and Partick, the last having 67,000 people when it was added in 1912. Since at the beginning of the nineteenth century all of Glasgow lay to the north of the river, and the extensions to the south are of later date, it can be said that there has been a shift in population southwards. Whatever the fluctuations in this movement in some of the earlier periods, such a shift certainly appears to be going on at present. While in 1901 a quarter of Glasgow's population lived south of the river, by 1931 a third lived there, and by 1951 thirty-seven per cent. Indeed, the population north of the river declined between 1931 and 1951, whereas the population south of the river grew between these years, and that without the aid of any major increases of population resulting from boundary extensions.

The extent of the redistribution of population that has taken place in Glasgow since 1931 may be further illustrated by the census returns for the civil parishes. While there is no parish completely within the city, portions of twelve are included within its boundaries, and two of them—Glasgow and Govan—contain the bulk of its population. Table XIV shows the population of the various portions of parishes lying within the city boundary in 1951, and that of the same areas in 1931, with the percentage increase or decrease during the period.

TABLE XIV

CHANGES IN POPULATION OF CIVIL PARISHES WITHIN GLASGOW (1951 BOUNDARY) BETWEEN 1931 AND 1951

Civil Parishes (Glasgow portions)	*Population* 1931	1951	*Percentage Increase or Decrease*
New Kilpatrick	18,347	28,657	+ 56.2
Cathcart	58,684	58,666	0.0
Eastwood	20,198	40,551	+ 100.8
Paisley	11,588	65,614	+ 466.2
Renfrew	25,548	34,405	+ 34.7
Glasgow	590,893	539,942	− 8.6
Govan	364,786	311,984	− 14.5
Cadder	2,116	7,855	+ 271.2
Rutherglen	73	1,385	+ 1,797.3
Carmunnock	120	271	+ 125.8
Old Monkland	949	395	− 58.4
Neilston	35	42	+ 20.0
	1,093,337	1,089,767	− 0.3

SOURCE: *Census of Scotland*, 1951, Vol. I, Part 2, *p.* 8.

Since the numbers of people recorded in these parishes differ so greatly, it is difficult to be dogmatic about the import of the percentage changes. It is however worthy of note that the two main (and relatively central) parishes of Glasgow and Govan have shown declines in population, while the sections of the civil parishes which are rather more outlying have shown increases.

Natural Increase and Migration

There are always two possible constituents of population change in any area: the extent to which the number of births differs from the number of deaths (the "natural increase" of the population); and the extent to which the number of immigrants exceeds, or falls short of, the number of emigrants (the balance of migration). These quantities can be determined most easily with the aid of the decennial census returns and the Registrar-General's annual estimates (available from the 1850's) of births and deaths; and they provide the best impression obtainable of the effects of migration movements to and from the city. A recent book[1] has detailed the information relating to Glasgow for the period from 1861 to 1911, and this is set out in Table XV.

TABLE XV

Natural Increase and Migration at Glasgow, 1861-1911

Period	*Net Increase in Population*	*Natural Increase*	*Balance of Migration*
	(000)	(000)	(000)
1861-1871	+88	+47	+41
1871-1881	+20	+58	−38
1881-1891	+54	+65	−11
1891-1901	+104	+75	+29
1901-1911	+23	+105	−82

Over this whole period the number of births invariably exceeded the number of deaths, and this resulted, in each decade, in a natural increase of the population. Migration, however, was much less steady in direction; in three of the decades, more people moved out of the city than into it, resulting in a loss by migration; and in only two of the decades was there an excess of immigrants over emigrants and a consequent gain by migration. This result, however, in so far as it relates to the effects of migration, is largely illusory. The recurring difficulty of boundary changes again complicates the issue. The work referred to makes a similar calculation for an area which it calls Glasgow and suburbs, which includes much of the area eventually absorbed by Glasgow, especially the older suburban districts. In that wider area the losses by migration in 1871-81 and in 1881-91 disappear, showing that much of the emigration from the city was only to the immediate suburbs. Thus if the inner suburbs are included in Glasgow then the conclusion is that from 1861 to 1901 the city grew both by natural increase and by migration. In the decade 1901-11 however there was a net movement of population out of the city. The position since 1911 is shown in Table XVI.

[1] A. K. Cairncross: *Home and Foreign Investment,* 1870-1913 (1953), p. 23.

John Watson

Plate 1. VIEW OF GLASGOW FROM STOBCROSS, LOOKING NORTH

T. & R. Annan

Plate 2. GREAT WESTERN ROAD

TABLE XVI

NATURAL INCREASE AND MIGRATION AT GLASGOW, 1911-1951

Period	*Net Increase in Population* (000)	*Natural Increase* (000)	*Balance of Migration* (000)
1911-1921 (1921 area)	+26	+93	−67
1921-1931 (1931 area)	+37	+88	−51
1931-1951 (1951 area)	−4	+135	−139

The table shows that the natural increase in population due to the excess of births over deaths has continued without interruption since 1911, but throughout the whole of this period, and indeed since 1901, there has been a constant drift away from the city as a result of migration. This time the loss cannot be accounted for as simply a move to the suburbs. In an earlier section of this chapter the extent of the suburbs lying around Glasgow and not incorporated in the city (or in other burghs) was commented upon; but the population of these suburban regions grew by a total of only 67 thousands in the period from 1901 to 1951, an increase insufficient to account for the losses suffered by Glasgow. The conclusion from this analysis must be that after a period of gains from migration for which estimates have been given from 1861 (but which in fact covered most of the nineteenth century), the City of Glasgow has been losing population by migration since 1901.

It is not certain where these people went. Undoubtedly some moved to other towns in the district and to other parts of Scotland. But Scotland as a whole during the period lost fairly large numbers through migration to England and overseas, especially in the 1920's, and many of the emigrants must have been from Glasgow. Since the war of 1939-45, too, Glasgow has contributed to all these movements. Between 1 July 1946, and 30 June 1950, Glasgow lost a number equivalent to 5% of its 1946 population through migration.[1] Of this number the equivalent of 1.9% of the 1946 population were lost as a result of the balance of movement to and from other parts of Scotland; 1.6% were lost to overseas; and 1.5% went in the drift southwards to England. Glasgow was losing population to the rest of Scotland, and at the same time was contributing more than proportionately to the Scottish loss to England and overseas. Scotland lost a total of only 2.3% of her 1946 population as against the 5% lost by Glasgow. Statistics of this kind seem to provide fairly adequate evidence for the contention that there is at present a move by migration away from Glasgow.

A more detailed analysis showing the extent and age-structure of migration affecting the population of Glasgow in the period 1931-1951 has been undertaken for this chapter by Dr. C. E. V. Leser. His results are tabulated in summary form below. Table XVII shows the loss by migration according to sex and age in 1951, expressed as the difference

[1] Discussed at greater length in two articles by D. J. Robertson in *The Glasgow Herald* of 18/9/50 and 19/9/50.

between the actual population revealed by the 1951 census and the population expected in 1951 from Glasgow Life Tables and actual births.

TABLE XVII

THE AGE-STRUCTURE OF MIGRATION AT GLASGOW
CENSUS 1931—CENSUS 1951

Sex & Age	*Population 1951* *Actual* (000)	*Expected* (000)	*Loss by Migration* (000)	*Percentage Loss in each Age-Group*
Males				
0—14	137	146	−9	6
15—19	37	46	−9	20
20—24	38	47	−9	18
25—29	41	50	−9	18
30—34	36	45	−10	21
35—39	38	45	−7	15
40—44	38	44	−5	12
45—49	36	39	−3	7
50—59	55	59	−4	6
60—69	37	39	−2	5
70 and over	24	24	0	2
	519	584	−66	11
Females				
70 and ever	32	33	−1	3
0—14	133	142	−8	6
15—19	43	45	−2	4
20—24	43	46	−3	6
25—29	43	49	−6	12
30—34	39	45	−5	12
35—39	42	49	−7	14
40—44	41	48	−7	15
45—49	39	44	−5	12
50—59	67	72	−5	7
60—69	48	52	−5	9
	571	626	−55	9

The loss by migration calculated on the basis of expected deaths in the period 1931-51 is thus about 120 thousands, as compared with the figure of 139 thousands shown in Table XVI, which was based on actual deaths during the period. This difference is insufficient to affect the general truth of the age-structure analysis given above, which reveals that those lost by migration are predominantly young male adults of working age.

BIRTHPLACES

As to the source of those immigrants to Glasgow who contributed to the growth of the city in the nineteenth century, it is well known that Glasgow was then the centre of attraction for many Irish and Highland people (as well as for people from the surrounding countryside); in the twentieth century, however, there has probably been more of an

English than of an Irish element in the inward movement. The birthplaces of the population resident in Glasgow in 1881 and 1911 are shown in Table XVIII.

TABLE XVIII

BIRTHPLACES OF THE POPULATION OF GLASGOW IN 1881 AND 1911

	1881		1911	
Birthplace	*Number* (000)	*Percentage of Total Population*	*Number* (000)	*Percentage of Total Population*
Scotland	406	83	688	87
of which				
Glasgow	(252)	(52)	(483)	(62)
Crofting Counties[1]	(19)	(4)	(25)	(3)
England	15	3	29	4
Ireland	63	13	53	7
Elsewhere	4	1	14	2
	488	100	784	100

This table has several interesting features. In 1881, by which time the biggest movements out of Ireland were over, no less than 13%—that is, more than one in eight—of the population of Glasgow were Irish-born. Although the Crofting Counties represent considerably less than the whole area of the Highlands, these counties—relatively small in population—had contributed enough people to produce the result that 4% of Glasgow's population in 1881 had been born within their boundaries. English-born were many fewer than those born in Ireland and amounted to only 3%. While 83% of Glasgow's population were Scottish-born, less than two thirds of them had been born in Glasgow itself. All this indicates a considerable immigration to the city in the preceding decades.

By 1911 the population of Glasgow, as already noted, was no longer gaining from migration, and there is further evidence of this in the birthplace data. The proportion of people who had been born within the city had risen considerably, which suggests a more static population with less assistance to its growth from outside. There had been quite a striking reduction in the proportion of Irish-born, which again strongly suggests that the Irish immigration was over, and that these were likely to be older people rather than new immigrants. Certainly the Irish element in the population was not being replaced by fresh blood. There had been a similar, although less striking, decline in the proportion born in the Crofting Counties. In contrast, there had been a slight rise in the number born in England and in other countries. The general effect of these changes was to make the proportion of Scottish-born living in Glasgow higher than it had been. These results are in conformity with the thesis that Glasgow was no longer a major centre of attraction for people from other parts.

Table XIX brings the story of the birthplaces of the Glasgow

[1] Orkney, Shetland, Argyll, Inverness, Ross & Cromarty, Sutherland, Caithness.

population up to date, giving in slightly more detail the position at 1951, while Table 22 in the Appendix shows the changes during the preceding hundred years.

TABLE XIX

BIRTHPLACES OF THE POPULATION OF GLASGOW IN 1951

Birthplace	*Number* (000)	*Percentage of Total Population*	*Birthplace*	*Number* (000)	*Percentage of Total Population*
Scotland	1,001	92	England	37	3
of which			Wales	2	—
Glasgow	810	74	Ireland	34	3
West Central (excl. Glasgow)	95	9	British Dominions, Colonies, etc.	5	—
East Central	41	4	Foreign Countries (British Subjects)	5	—
Northern	43	4	Foreign Countries (Aliens)	5	—
Southern	9	1			
Not stated	3	—			

The 1951 birthplace structure of the Glasgow population shows that the trends becoming evident by 1911 have continued. While the population born in Scotland has risen, there has been an even greater increase in the proportion born in Glasgow. Now nearly three-quarters of Glasgow's inhabitants are actual natives of the city, whereas only about half of the population seventy years ago could claim Glasgow as their birthplace. Of the other Scottish-born inhabitants of Glasgow, half have come from the counties surrounding the city. The proportion of Irish-born has fallen considerably, and is now exceeded by the proportion born in England. All told, however, relatively few of the present population of Glasgow come from outside Scotland; and while England and Ireland are the main source of such incomers, neither has contributed very high proportions. This confirms once more the impression of a city more likely to have been losing than gaining population from migration.

ALIENS

TABLE XX

BIRTHPLACES OF PRINCIPAL GROUPS OF ALIEN NATIONALS IN GLASGOW AT CENSUS DATES 1951 AND 1931

Birthplaces	*Number* 1951	1931
Poland	1,164	483
Italy	1,067	1,688
Russia	1,002	1,606
U.S.A.	437	373
Germany	364	162
Norway	135	51
France	106	167

While the aliens in Glasgow are comparatively few in number they are nevertheless an interesting group and merit further study. The birthplaces of the principal groups as recorded in the 1951 Census are given in Table XX, together with the corresponding figures for 1931.

These census statistics are likely to include a number of casual visitors and tourists and to exclude a number of aliens who, though normally resident in Glasgow, were absent from the city on the night of the Census. Fuller details of the alien population of Glasgow are contained in the records kept by the police, with whom all resident aliens are required to register. Abstracts from these records of the numbers, nationalities and occupations of the registered aliens have been made available through the courtesy of the Chief Constable. There follows here (Tables XXI and XXII) a summary of some of the information contained therein. A fuller analysis of the nationalities of registered aliens is given in Appendix Table 31.

TABLE XXI

REGISTERED ALIENS IN GLASGOW BY PRINCIPAL NATIONALITIES,[1] AT VARIOUS DATES, 1931 TO 1954

	Years						
Nationality	1931	1935	1939	1943	1947	1951	1954
American (U.S.A.)	468	405	331	440	184	196	211
Austrian	114	84	92	103	113	56	—
Belgian	57	—	—	136	—	—	—
Chinese	—	—	—	378	—	—	—
Danish	70	—	—	—	—	—	—
Dutch	—	—	—	117	51	71	71
Egyptian	—	—	71	—	—	—	—
French	118	82	—	—	82	115	100
German	215	135	401	536	195	262	273
Italian	1,929	1,532	1,419	1,448	1,224	1,084	1,025
Lithuanian	203	208	192	190	147	146	112
Norwegian	62	—	—	1,367	69	93	138
Polish	113	94	121	646	1,005	1,083	975
Portuguese	—	—	—	—	66	—	—
Russian	3,181	2,526	2,117	1,885	1,421	991	797
Swedish	57	—	—	141	—	—	—
Swiss	98	65	68	—	64	76	70
Miscellaneous and Uncertain	381	441	468	792	421	368	466
Total	7,066	5,572	5,280	8,179	5,042	4,541	4,238

[1] Those nationalities with 50 or more representatives in the years in question.

In Table XXI the numbers of the principal nationalities of resident aliens in Glasgow are shown for various years. This list of nationalities is extensive but if those nationalities with smaller numbers are counted in, then, in 1954, there were representatives of no fewer than forty-nine different nationalities resident in Glasgow.

The table confirms the general impression that the total alien population of the city is tending to decline: apart from the war years there is a steady fall in the total numbers shown here. The numbers of different nationalities however have been moving in different ways. The decline in the total number of aliens is quite largely due to the decline in the White Russian population ("Russian" and "Lithuanian" in the table), presumably because of death. The number of Italians, the next most numerous group over the years, has also been falling though much more slowly. In this case it seems likely that quite a number have become naturalised, a process in the case of those who stayed on for which the war with Italy was presumably an incentive. The number of Poles is now much greater than before the war. The Polish Army formed part of the garrison of Scotland in war years with its headquarters at Kincardine—this, together with political changes in Poland since the war, seems a sufficient explanation. Glasgow would appear to have a regular small number of resident Americans, Germans, French and Swiss, but some other nationals have been in Glasgow at one time and not at another. The Chinese who were in Glasgow in 1943 were largely part of a Chinese seamen's pool which is no longer in Glasgow. The Egyptians who were in Glasgow before the war were possibly students. During the war years Glasgow was the home of quite a large number of Norwegians (and also some Belgians), most of whom have now left.

It is interesting to consider what work these aliens do in Glasgow. Unfortunately the list of occupations they follow—from gardeners to air line managers—is so enormous as to rule out its detailed presentation here. Table XXII attempts to summarise some of the story by giving for January 1955 those occupational descriptions to which more than a hundred aliens can be allocated, and by showing the numbers in these occupations for those nationalities of whom there were more than a hundred registered in the city at January 1955.

The occupations of almost three-quarters of the total alien population are separated out here. The high proportion of housewives is not unexpected. It is also to be expected that there should be a good proportion of students and a number of retired persons. The occupational analysis of the registered aliens, however, shows how marked is their concentration in shops and cafés, whether as owners or employees, and in domestic service. About one in three of the aliens who are at work are in these occupations. The numbers in the clothing trade and the numbers of unskilled labourers are also relatively high.

If the occupations of aliens of the different principal nationalities shown in Table XXII are analysed, interesting differences emerge. Of the Italians, as no resident of Glasgow can fail to suspect, over a quarter are proprietors of cafés and restaurants, and almost as many again are salesmen and shop assistants—presumably in the same type of shop. In fact, considerably over three-quarters of occupied Italians are engaged on this type of work, domestic service and hotel work. In contrast the Polish population is much more spread out, as is suggested by the fact that almost half of the occupied Poles are in occupations

TABLE XXII

PRINCIPAL OCCUPATIONS OF REGISTERED ALIENS IN GLASGOW BY PRINCIPAL NATIONALITIES AT JANUARY 1955[1]

Occupation	*Nationality*[2] I	P	R	G	A	S[3]	B[4]	O	T
Indoor domestic servants and others engaged in personal service	178	100	14	42	10	11	6	60	421
Proprietors of cafés, restaurants, etc.	274	5	2	—	—	—	2	8	291
Salesmen and shop assistants	219	19	15	3	15	2	1	11	285
Unskilled labourers	16	111	27	14	11	7	26	34	246
Cutters, pressers, and other garment and cap makers	3	52	56	6	1	1	7	13	139
Road, rail and water transport workers	4	57	4	13	12	11	3	27	131
Fitters and machine erectors	25	40	4	12	16	5	2	22	126
Building trade workers	24	51	5	—	4	—	2	32	118
Housewives	184	81	376	75	30	9	45	87	887
Students	10	7	—	19	15	90	—	130	271
Retired	—	8	105	2	17	7	8	5	152
Others	82	415	181	87	77	47	35	212	1136
Totals	1019	946	789	273	208	190	137	641	4203

[1] Occupations with more than one hundred representatives, and nationalities with a total of more than one hundred registered aliens.
[2] I—Italian, P—Polish, R—Russian, G—German, A—U.S.A., S—Scandinavian B—Baltic, O—Others, T—Totals.
[3] Mainly Norwegians.
[4] Mainly Lithuanians.

other than those enumerated here. There is however some concentration in domestic service, unskilled labour, transport (especially road transport) and garment making. A suggested origin of many of these Poles in the wartime Polish Army is reflected in the low proportion of housewives. Among the (White) Russian aliens there are noticeably high proportions of housewives and of retired persons, suggesting a long-settled group. Apart from a concentration in garment making, there is no great evidence that this nationality is specially confined to one type of occupation (though forty-two are registered as managers of wholesale or retail businesses). There is a good number of German domestics and German housewives in the city but otherwise German occupations are diverse (though twenty-two German nurses are registered). The aliens from the U.S.A. are not concentrated in any one occupational group, nor are those from the former Baltic countries or from Scandinavia, except that in the last-named case a very large number are students, and eighteen appear as professional engineers.

SEX, AGE AND CONJUGAL CONDITION

That women are more plentiful than men is a fairly well known circumstance, and Table XXIII demonstrates that it is of long standing. There is not, however, any material difference between Glasgow and Scotland in this feature at present, and there does not seem to have been very much difference in earlier years.

TABLE XXIII

PERCENTAGE OF FEMALES IN GLASGOW AND SCOTLAND IN CERTAIN YEARS

Year	*Percentage of Females* *Glasgow*	*Scotland*
1801	54	53
1851	53	52
1901	51	51
1951	52	52

Table XXIV details the age structure of the population of Glasgow and compares it with that of Scotland in 1901 and 1951.

TABLE XXIV

PERCENTAGE AGE DISTRIBUTION BY SEX OF THE GLASGOW AND SCOTTISH POPULATIONS IN 1901 AND 1951

	Male Under 15	15-34	35-64	65 & *over*	*Female* Under 15	15-34	35-64	65 & *over*
1901								
Glasgow	33	39	26	2	32	38	26	4
Scotland	35	36	25	4	32	35	27	6
1951								
Glasgow	26	29	37	8	23	30	38	9
Scotland	26	28	37	9	23	28	38	11

The drop in the proportion of young people and the increase in that of the old are evident in both Glasgow and Scotland between 1901 and 1951. Another general tendency also appears: the higher proportion of women over 65 as compared with men. If Glasgow is compared with Scotland there are no very striking differences for either sex and at either date. The proportion of old people, however, is lower in Glasgow than in Scotland, and the population of working age is higher.

The age distribution varies greatly from one area to another within the city. Some districts have a preponderance of young people while others attract the old. Table XXV shows those wards that appear to be particular examples of each type.

If a large part of Pollokshaws Ward (which includes new housing estates) is excepted, it is possible to generalise broadly about those

TABLE XXV

YOUNG AND OLD IN CERTAIN GLASGOW WARDS IN 1951

Young Wards with over 28% under 15 years	Percentages Under 15 years	65 years & over	*Old* Wards with over 12% aged 65 years and over	Percentages 65 years & over	Under 15 years
Dalmarnock	28.2	7.1	Park	12.2	16.8
Mile-End	29.1	6.9	Kelvinside	15.6	15.3
Cowcaddens	30.1	7.3	Partick East	13.2	17.9
Hutchesontown	28.7	6.9	Camphill	15.0	16.3
Gorbals	29.4	6.8	Langside	13.1	17.4
Kingston	29.3	7.0	Cathcart	12.9	19.1
Govan	29.3	6.9	Average for Glasgow	8.6	24.8
Pollokshaws	31.5	4.9			

wards with above normal proportions of young people: they are older residential areas mainly of tenements, in the inner residential parts of the city. The tenements still have a high proportion of children in their populations, and have a lower than average proportion of old people. The contrasting wards with a high percentage of old people are not quite so easily defined. With the exception of parts of Kelvinside and Cathcart, they are not the most recently built districts of the city. To a large extent, for example in Camphill and Langside, they consist of flatted properties or tenements, which are, however, generally in better repair and more likely to be "middle-class" than those in the areas with a high proportion of young people. In other places, for example the Park Ward, they consist of old but substantial terrace houses. These areas with a high proportion of old have low proportions of young people. If an overall generalisation may be risked, it would be that the older tenements house many children while the tenements and terrace houses in the inner suburbs and residential parts of the city have a high concentration of old people.

TABLE XXVI

CONJUGAL CONDITION OF THE GLASGOW AND SCOTTISH POPULATIONS IN 1901 AND 1951

	Males over 15 (Percent of all Males over 15) 1901 *Glas.*	1901 *Scot.*	1951 *Glas.*	1951 *Scot.*	*Females over 15 (Percent of all Females over 15)* 1901 *Glas.*	1901 *Scot.*	1951 *Glas.*	1951 *Scot.*
Single	47	47	33	32	43	44	32	32
Married	48	48	61	62	46	45	55	55
Widowed or Divorced	5	5	6	6	11	11	13	13

In Table XXVI the conjugal condition of the population over 15 years of age is shown in broad percentages, for Glasgow and for Scotland, in 1901 and 1951. It can be seen that the proportion of married people has risen markedly since 1901. The longer expectation of life of women, combined no doubt with a tendency for men to be older than their wives, accounts for the much higher proportion of widows than widowers, a feature common to Glasgow and Scotland alike. Similarly there do not appear to be any noteworthy distinctions in Glasgow's experience in respect of the proportion of the population entering into matrimony.

BIRTHS AND DEATHS

Table XXVII gives the rates of births and deaths in Glasgow and Scotland for a number of years since 1861, expressed in terms of births and deaths per thousand persons living.

TABLE XXVII

BIRTH RATES AND DEATH RATES FOR GLASGOW AND SCOTLAND, 1861-1955

Year	*Birth Rate per 1,000*		*Death Rate per 1,000*	
	Glasgow[1]	*Scotland*	*Glasgow*[1]	*Scotland*
1861	41.6	34.9	27.5	21.3
1871	38.4	34.5	32.1	22.2
1881	37.3	33.7	25.2	19.3
1891	35.0	31.2	25.3	20.7
1901	31.8	29.5	21.2	17.9
1911	27.7	25.6	17.7	15.1
1921	31.5	25.2	15.7	13.6
1931	21.1	19.0	14.2	13.3
1941	18.6	17.5	14.9	14.7
1946	21.6	20.3	13.3	13.1
1947	23.7	22.0	14.0	12.9
1948	20.4	19.4	12.5	11.8
1949	19.2	18.5	13.0	12.3
1950	18.4	17.9	12.9	12.4
1951	18.4	17.7	13.1	12.9
1952	18.7	17.7	12.7	12.0
1953	18.6	17.8	11.8	11.5
1954	19.3	18.0	11.7	12.0
1955	19.4	18.0	12.3	12.0

It will be seen that the birth and death rates for both Glasgow and Scotland have been falling fairly steadily since 1860. The birth rate, however, has always exceeded the death rate, so that the population has increased (migration having been insufficient to affect the situation); but the fall in the death rate has meant, of course, an increase in older people.

This table shows that, although the birth and death rates for Glasgow since 1861 have followed in their movements those for Scotland as a whole, they differ from the Scottish figures in one important respect: while the trends are similar, both the birth rate and the death rate have been consistently higher in the city than in the country as a whole. In the early years of the period the gaps between the Scottish and Glasgow rates were fairly large. These were the years

1 Births and deaths from 1921 are corrected for transfers.

of rapid growth in the city, when conditions were likely to lead both to a high number of births and to a high proportion of deaths. The gaps have certainly closed since then, but there is still a difference.

An aspect of the birth rate worthy of comment is the incidence of illegitimate births. The percentages of such births to all births in Glasgow and Scotland are set out in Table XXVIII.

TABLE XXVIII

ILLEGITIMATE BIRTHS IN GLASGOW AND SCOTLAND, 1871-1955

Year	*Illegitimate Births (Percent of all Births)*		*Year*	*Illegitimate Births (Percent of all Births)*	
	Glasgow	*Scotland*		*Glasgow*	*Scotland*
1871	9.3	9.5	1931	6.2	7.2
1881	7.9	8.3	1951	5.3	5.1
1891	7.8	7.7	1952	4.7	4.8
1901	6.1	6.3	1953	5.0	4.7
1911	6.8	7.6	1954	4.9	4.5
1921	6.5	7.1	1955	4.7	4.3

Here again the data for Glasgow follow the same trend as those for Scotland. The percentage of illegitimate births has fallen considerably since 1871, although not consistently, since there was a rise in the first decades of this century. At each year shown the level for Glasgow has been either lower than that for Scotland, or only very slightly above it. The present rate of illegitimate births means that about 1 in 20 births is at present illegitimate, as against about 1 in 11 in 1871 and about 1 in 16 in 1901.

The late Medical Officer of Health for Glasgow worked out the illegitimate birth rate per 1,000 unmarried women and widows between the ages of 16 and 44. Some of his figures are shown in Table XXIX.

TABLE XXIX

ILLEGITIMATE BIRTHS IN RELATION TO UNMARRIED WOMEN IN GLASGOW, 1871-1952

Year	*Rate per* 1,000 *Unmarried Women and Widows,* 16-44 *years*	*Year*	*Rate per* 1,000 *Unmarried Women and Widows,* 16-44 *years*
1871	27	1921	13
1881	22	1931	10
1891	21	1951	10
1901	14	1952	9
1911	14		

There has thus been a marked decline in the rate of illegitimate births, and this decline has been considerably greater than that of the general birth rate over these years.

Infant mortality—the death rate for babies under one year old—has, like the general death rate, been consistently higher in Glasgow than in Scotland as a whole. Again the gap is closing, but it still exists.

TABLE XXX

INFANT MORTALITY (DEATHS UNDER 1 YEAR) FOR GLASGOW AND SCOTLAND 1861-1955

Year	*Death Rate per 1,000 Births*		*Year*	*Death Rate per 1,000 Births*	
	Glasgow	*Scotland*		*Glasgow*	*Scotland*
1861	154	111	1947	77	56
1871	191	130	1948	56	45
1881	144	113	1949	49	41
1891	148	128	1950	44	39
1901	149	129	1951	46	37
1911	139	113	1952	41	35
1921	106	90	1953	36	31
1931	105	82	1954	35	31
1941	111	83	1955	36	30
1946	67	54			

The trends of the infant mortality rate shown in Table XXX are both interesting and important. From 1861 to 1900 there was no marked fall in the figures despite a fall in general death rates. In the first four decades of this century infant mortality rates were lower, but until after 1941 they did not fall below 80 per thousand live births in Scotland as a whole, nor below 100 in Glasgow. New medical and pharmaceutical discoveries have achieved one of their most striking successes in the reduction of infant mortality in recent years: by 1955 the rates were down to 30 for Scotland and 36 for Glasgow. This means that in Glasgow, throughout the second half of the nineteenth century, it was usual for one out of every six or seven babies to die within their first year of life, whereas the proportion is now reduced to about one in twenty-eight. That is certainly a very considerable achievement.

Dr. C. E. V. Leser has carried the discussion of the balance of births and deaths in Glasgow very much further in the following section which concludes this chapter.

THE BALANCE OF BIRTHS AND DEATHS

C. E. V. LESER

A BROAD picture of fertility and mortality in Glasgow has already been obtained by a study of its crude birth and death rates, relating the total number of births and deaths in a given year to the total size of population over the last decade, and by a comparison with the birth and death rates for Scotland as a whole. Such a comparison would suggest that fertility and mortality in Glasgow have been subject to the same process of decline as in Scotland as a whole but have been consistently higher in the city than in the rest of the country.

But these rates do not offer a reliable measure of the true changes and differences in fertility and mortality, since they are influenced by the age-distribution of the population. A city may have a high birth rate not only on account of a high level of fertility but also in consequence of an influx of women in the reproductive age-groups; unless this influx is constantly maintained, its influence on the number of births will wear off. Alternatively, the death rate of a town may be high because a large proportion of its population are new-born children and old people who are subject to heavy rates of mortality.

A better measure of fertility than the crude birth rate is the female—or maternal—gross reproduction rate. This indicates the number of girls born, on the average, to a woman in the course of her life at the current fertility levels of each age-group, provided she survives until the end of her reproductive period. If the gross reproduction rate falls consistently below 1, the population does not replace itself and must ultimately fall in size, no matter how low mortality may be.

To work out the exact value of the gross reproduction rate, it is necessary to know, apart from the age-distribution of the population, the age at death of all persons who died in a particular year. This information is not available for Glasgow, and for Scotland it is available only from 1938 onwards; but for the years 1911 and 1931, estimates of the gross reproduction rate of Scotland as well as Glasgow and other burghs have been made by Dr. Enid Charles.[1] Further estimates of the gross reproduction rate of Glasgow have now been made for the years 1939 and 1951, for which the age-distribution of the population is known from the National Registration Enquiry and the Census of Population respectively (though in the case of 1939 not completely, on account of evacuation). These estimates can be compared with the corresponding figures for Scotland which have been published in the Registrar-General's Annual Reports.

TABLE XXXI

ESTIMATED GROSS REPRODUCTION RATES FOR GLASGOW AND SCOTLAND

Year	*Glasgow*	*Scotland*
1911	1.59	1.61
1931	1.24	1.18
1939	1.11	1.06
1951	1.16	1.17

From the results set out in Table XXXI, it can be seen that there has not been a large difference between the gross reproduction rates of the city and the country as a whole. Moreover, the difference has not been consistently in one direction; fertility in Glasgow appears to have been slightly below the Scottish average in 1911 and 1951 but somewhat above it in 1931 and 1939. In Glasgow as in Scotland, fertility declined between 1911 and 1939 but recovered to some extent after the war and was above the 1939 level in 1951; but both the

1 "Differential Fertility in Scotland 1911-31": *Transactions of the Royal Society of Edinburgh,* Vol. 59, 1936-39.

decline and the recovery have been less marked in the city than in the country as a whole.

It follows that the consistently high birth rate in Glasgow cannot be interpreted as reflecting a genuinely high level of fertility in comparison with the rest of Scotland—certainly not for recent years. On the contrary, it has been brought about by the age-structure of the population. According to the Registrar-General's estimates for 1951, 14.3% of all women in Scotland were between the ages of 20 and 30 —in the age-groups responsible for nearly 60% of all births—but in Glasgow at the 1951 Population Census the corresponding proportion was 15.1%. It is this preponderance of young women in Glasgow which is shown up in the high birth rate, and the true level of fertility is now no higher or rather lower than in the remainder of Scotland.

A "favourable" age-distribution from the point of view of births —one that helps to raise the crude birth-rate of a population—is generally also favourable from the point of view of deaths in that it tends to lower the crude death-rate. We cannot, therefore, expect to find an explanation for the relatively high death rate of Glasgow in the age-structure of the city's population but, on the contrary, must be prepared to find mortality to be really higher in the city than outside, and the difference may, in fact, be partly concealed in the death rate figures.

It is not only among new-born infants that the mortality of Glasgow is high relatively to the country as a whole. Calculations made by the Government Actuary and presented by the Registrar-General show that the number of deaths in Glasgow is relatively high at each age level, though the difference between city and country tends to diminish at the upper age groups.

TABLE XXXII

PERCENTAGE EXCESS OF DEATHS IN GLASGOW OVER NUMBER EXPECTED ON BASIS OF SCOTTISH MORTALITY EXPERIENCE, 1950-52

Age Group	*Males*	*Females*
0-14	19	25
15-24	14	42
25-34	14	30
35-44	21	20
45-54	24	15
55-64	23	19
65-74	17	13
75-84	13	9
85 & over	7	3
All ages	18	14

On the average, Glasgow has an 18% higher male mortality and a 14% higher female mortality than Scotland as a whole, or an excess of about one-sixth. This difference is much larger than that shown up in the crude death rates for any of the years 1950-2 in Table XXVII.

Another way of looking at the problem is by the study of life-tables, which have been officially constructed for Glasgow as well as Scotland with regard to the averages for the years 1930-32 and 1950-52. An abstract of some of the salient features of these life tables is provided by Table XXXIII.

TABLE XXXIII

SURVIVORS TO THE AGE OF 65 OUT OF 10,000 BIRTHS, AND EXPECTATION OF LIFE AT BIRTH, GLASGOW AND SCOTLAND, 1930-32 AND 1950-52

	Males		*Females*	
	Glasgow	*Scotland*	*Glasgow*	*Scotland*
Survivors to age 65:				
1930-32	4,390	5,132	5,082	5,755
1950-52	5,458	6,088	6,749	7,212
Life expectation at birth				
1930-32	51.3	56.0	55.2	59.5
1950-52	62.0	64.4	66.3	68.7

The table shows clearly the great progress that has been made in reducing Glasgow's mortality during the 1930's and 1940's, but at the same time the gap that still exists between the city and the rest of the country. For example, whilst the mortality rates prevailing around 1931 would have permitted only nine out of twenty new-born males to reach the age of 65, almost eleven out of twenty will do so at the 1951 mortality experience; but in the country as a whole, the corresponding proportion is more than six out of ten. Similarly, the expectation of life at birth has increased by about eleven years for both sexes during the two decades in Glasgow but is still about two years below the national level.

In 1931, the difference between the life expectation for Scotland and Glasgow amounted to 4-5 years. But it is not permissible to infer that the mortality differential has narrowed down. It has, however, been shown, for males at any rate, that the gap has in fact diminished, though not to the extent suggested by the table.[1]

Incidentally, the reciprocal of the expectation of life, the "life-table death rate," gives an indication of the level which the crude death rate would approach if the mortality experience remained unchanged. For both sexes combined, the expectation of life in 1950-2 works out at 64.1 years for Glasgow and 66.0 years for Scotland, and the life-table death rate thus at 15.6 per thousand in the city and 15.0 per thousand in the country as a whole. Unless a very substantial further improvement takes place, Glasgow's death rate cannot be long maintained at its current low level in the neighbourhood of 13 per thousand.

By using the current life-table for Glasgow in conjunction with the analysis of fertility made for the city, the net reproduction rate can be worked out for Glasgow in 1951 and compared with the official figure for Scotland, published in the Registrar-General's Annual Reports.

[1] C. E. V. Leser, *Variations in Mortality and Life Expectation. Population Statistics,* Vol. IX, No. 1, July 1955, pp. 67-71, especially p. 71.

This indicates the number of girls born, on the average, to a woman at current fertility and mortality levels during her life-time.

As a result, the net reproduction rate of Glasgow in 1951 is estimated at 1.07, as compared with 1.10 for Scotland. Whilst thus the balance of births and deaths is less favourable in Glasgow than in the remainder of Scotland, the number of births in the city is more than sufficient for replacing the existing population.

Chapter 3

THE HISTORICAL SETTING

J. B. S. GILFILLAN

Glasgow Before 1700

The City's Origins

In contrast to many of the great industrial cities of to-day, Glasgow has a proud and ancient history extending far back over the centuries before the dawn of the industrial age. This was not one of those hitherto unknown townships which had greatness thrust upon them by the exigencies of the Industrial Revolution. Nor was Glasgow born great; but she can claim to have achieved greatness—largely by the efforts of her own citizens—at a very early period in her history, long before some of her modern rivals even existed.

This *Third Statistical Account* must be primarily concerned with describing the developments of recent times. But Glasgow's growth in size and importance during the past century or two, remarkable as this has been, is seen when viewed in historical perspective as no more than the setting of the seal upon an already long-established position in the West. It is the purpose of this chapter to bring into perspective the picture given in the rest of the *Account* and to illustrate—necessarily only in outline—something of the background from which modern Glasgow has emerged.

The picture revealed by history is in sharp contrast to the contemporary scene. Even the most patriotic Glaswegian would have some hesitation in recognising his native city in the description given by its old name Glasghu—" the dear green place." His difficulty, however, would be solely with reference to the prevailing colour: Glasgow may have assumed a more sombre hue but, as a popular music-hall song reminds us, it is still a place dear to those who belong to it. The origins of the name are as obscure as those of the city itself, and various derivations have been suggested by historians in the past. Some have held that it comes from Gaelic words meaning " a grey hound " or " a grey smith," while others have found a more appropriate interpretation, " dark glen," alluding to the gloomy ravine through which the Molendinar flowed near the Cathedral, close by the supposed site of original settlement. To-day it is generally believed that the name is the Celtic " Gleschu," or " Glasghu,"[1] at one time written

[1] *Glas*, green; *ghu*, dear.

"Glesco"—remarkably similar to its modern pronunciation in the local vernacular!

Such is thought to have been the name of the primitive settlement found here by Kentigern or Mungo ("dear one") when he arrived about 543 to preach Christianity to the inhabitants of Strathclyde. It is perhaps fitting that Glasgow, whose origins are so obscure, should have as Patron one of the most shadowy figures in the calendar of saints. Of the numerous legends that have gathered around him some of the more miraculous are commemorated in the arms of the city,[1] but in comparison with St. Columba of Iona or even St. Ninian of Whithorn the true life and achievements of Mungo are quite unknown to us. Several centuries before his coming the Romans had probably given the first impulse to Glasgow's growth, but what may have been the fate of the tiny community by the ford on the Clyde when the Antonine Wall to the north was finally abandoned and the legions withdrew is equally conjectural. There can be little doubt, however, that the church established by Kentigern in the sixth century became the focal point around which Glasgow began to flourish.

Virtually nothing further is known of the city's history until the beginning of the twelfth century, when the see of Glasgow was restored after an investigation ordered by David, then Prince of Cumbria (Strathclyde), in 1115. It is apparent from the deed then drawn up that by that date a cathedral had already been endowed. On his becoming king in 1124 one of the first acts of this "sair sanct to the croun" was to give to the see the lands of Partick,[2] besides returning to it many former possessions of which it had been deprived. On 7 July 1136, Bishop John Achaius, in the presence of David I, consecrated a church on the site of the present Cathedral, but some years afterwards it seems to have been destroyed by fire. Bishop Jocelin (1175-99), one of the most notable and energetic incumbents of the see, began the rebuilding of the Cathedral and to him may be attributed part of the existing structure. The choir and crypt, as we know them to-day, were completed in the episcopate of William de Bondington (1233-58).

Bishop's Burgh and University Town

It was through the efforts of Bishop Jocelin that Glasgow first attained the status of a burgh. He might be said to have been the founder not only of the city's present Cathedral but also of its commerce. At this time Glasgow was a mere village, its houses clustered round the Cathedral being occupied mainly by the clergy and their dependants, its trade and industry insignificant. In order to encourage the latter and promote the temporal welfare of his see, Jocelin between 1175 and 1178 obtained a charter from William the Lion making

1 The name of Mungo's mother (St. Thenew) still survives as a local place-name, in the corrupt form "St. Enoch."

2 Partick, once known as Pertmet, has been described as "the Balmoral of Strathclydian royalty"—it was a favourite retreat of the Kings of Strathclyde, whose capital was Dumbarton.

Glasgow a burgh, held of the bishop, with the right to have a weekly market. A further charter, granted about 1189, conferred the privilege of an annual fair in summer—the origin of our " Glasgow Fair." It was not until the seventeenth century that the city became a royal burgh, held directly of the king, but it enjoyed the freedoms and customs of a king's burgh from the beginning. Thus Glasgow's early commercial aspirations were watched by unfriendly eyes in Rutherglen and Dumbarton, both of which were king's burghs jealous of any encroachment on their exclusive rights of trade. Despite Dumbarton's opposition, Glasgow's bishop in the thirteenth century secured for his burgesses the privilege of free trading in Argyll and Lennox; and successfully resisted the claims of Rutherglen, obtaining protection from the levying of toll or custom by that burgh within Glasgow, or nearer than the cross of Shettleston. From its infancy, therefore, the city had to fight to achieve progress. Commercial rivalry with Dumbarton in particular was to become increasingly bitter as the centuries advanced.

Apart from some incidents connected with the Scottish War of Independence,[1] Glasgow does not figure prominently again in the national history until the fifteenth century. Then two major events occurred: in 1451 the cathedral city became also the seat of a university; and in 1492 was raised to the status of an archbishopric. Glasgow now indeed began to flourish—but rather through ecclesiastical rivalry, perhaps, than " through the preaching of the Word." There had long been a traditional competition between the sees of Glasgow and St. Andrews, and the foundation of the first Scottish university at St. Andrews in 1412 conferred on the eastern see a distinction that was probably not altogether palatable to the Bishop of Glasgow. Considering that Scots students had previously—and indeed still—travelled abroad in search of higher education, it seems unlikely that a second university in the west was thought essential merely to avoid the dangers and difficulties of the overland journey to St. Andrews. Nor does there appear to have been any overwhelming demand for university education in the west, to judge from the paucity of students enrolled at Glasgow in the first hundred years or so of the new foundation's existence. When it is remembered, however, that the training of an educated clergy for service in the local see was the primary object of these early Scottish universities, and that inter-see rivalry was strong, the appearance in a small and poor country like Scotland of no less than three[2] in the fifteenth century is more readily understood. This was a period when Lollardy and other heretical opinions were rife—Oxford University, to which many Scots students had formerly gone, had become suspect because of Wycliffe's teachings—and the church authorities in Scotland doubtless felt that their best defence against the " new thought " lay in control of the education of their own clergy.

[1] " Blind Harry " describes how in the battle of the Bell o' the Brae, on the site of High Street, Wallace routed the English under Percy in 1300; five years later he was betrayed to the English at Robroyston.

[2] The third, Aberdeen, was founded in 1495, Edinburgh University did not come into being until 1583, in post-Reformation times.

Such considerations would carry due weight with Pope Nicholas V, who on 7 January 1451 granted a Bull authorising the establishment in Glasgow of "a *studium generale* wherein might flourish theology, canon and civil law, as well as the arts and any other lawful faculty." Its constitution was modelled on that of the University of Bologna, then one of the most famous seats of learning in Europe, but supreme authority was vested in Bishop William Turnbull and his successors as Chancellors.[1] Existing church buildings, such as the Cathedral or the Black Friars' monastery (founded in the High Street in the thirteenth century), served initially as lecture-rooms, but it was not long before the new University acquired humble premises of its own. The Faculty of Arts soon became dominant and the distinction between the College of Arts and the University arose very early in the foundation's history.[2] A house on the south side of the Rottenrow was the first *paedagogium* or College of Arts, but about 1460 a successor to this "Auld Pedagogy" was established on the east side of the High Street, which was to be the site of the University for over four hundred years.

Sir James Hamilton of Cadzow, first Lord Hamilton, made a gift of the ground, on condition that, before the meals of the members of the Faculty, prayer was to be offered for his own soul and those of various relatives. This observance—needless to say—has long since lapsed, but in another respect the terms of Lord Hamilton's grant have had an influence on the University's life down to our own day. In setting up his "college" he conveyed the land not to the University, nor to the Faculty of Arts as a body, but to Duncan Bunch, its principal regent,[3] and his successors in office. The emergence of the "principal" as the true active head of Glasgow's University may be traced to this period. Some adjacent lands were given by Sir Thomas Arthurlie, but the development of the University—although promising at first—was slow. Indeed by the early sixteenth century it was in danger of becoming moribund, and it seems to have suffered from the general laxity and corruption then prevalent in the Church. But it could already boast some famous names—John Major, Robert Henryson, and David Beaton, for example. By the time of the Reformation, however, its condition was such that it appeared to Queen Mary "rather to be the decay of ane universitie nor ony wyse to be recknit ane establisst foundatioun."

Prior to the creation of the University, higher educational provision in the city was limited to that of the Grammar School, which had existed since at least the early fourteenth century and was under the supervision of the chancellor of the Cathedral. He was the Education

1 In Bologna the corresponding privileges were held by the Rector. The latter office gradually became an honorary one in Glasgow.

2 The complex story of the relations and disputes between them cannot be given here. For a fuller account of the University's history, the reader is referred to J. D. Mackie's *The University of Glasgow. 1451 to 1951* (1954).

3 The teaching masters were known as regents, and took their students through the whole course. This system was not finally abandoned in favour of a specialist professoriate until 1727. A similar system existed in the High School of Glasgow until the latter half of the nineteenth century.

Authority of the period, without whose licence no one could keep a grammar school or even give private instruction in grammar and the rudiments to the youth of the city. A priest who dared to do so in 1494 was prosecuted for infringing the burgh school's monopoly. Endowments for the support of the master of Glasgow's Grammar School, in the form of a tenement of land and a chaplaincy, are recorded in 1461 and in 1494. In the fifteenth century the school occupied a site on the west side of the High Street, where it remained until the 1780's, when it was moved to new premises on the lands of Ramshorn.

The foundation of the University in the fifteenth century did much both to enhance the prestige and to encourage the growth of the city. Up to this time Glasgow, although a cathedral city of long standing, was still really no more than a village. The natural advantages of the place and the possibilities of its situation were, however, already recognised; indeed the Papal Bull founding the University referred to Glasgow as a place well suited and adapted to that purpose, on account of "the mildness of the climate, the plenty of victuals, and of other things necessary for the use of man." By the latter part of the fifteenth century the population was about 2,000. In the High Street area new building lots were taken up following the opening of the University, and in a charter of 1491 there is some evidence of the development of commerce. This charter conferred on the Bishop the right to have a free tron in the city, where all merchandise might be weighed and the due customs exacted. A considerable revenue was derived from these customs, and of this revenue the University had a share through various grants by the Bishops. The weighing device was situated near the market cross, in the street that was then known as St. Thenew's Gait but which thus gradually came to be known as the Trongate. It was about this period too that the somewhat sinister name of the Gallowgate had its origin, with the building up of the road leading to the Gallow Muir or town's common, where executions were at one time carried out.

Glasgow was beginning to expand in a modest way, but as yet its life was centred mainly on the clergy and the students, the remainder of the population consisting almost entirely of servants and tradesmen dependent on Cathedral and University for their livelihood. Apart from some fishing and cloth making there was little local industry, the bulk of the articles used in the city being imported from England or Flanders. The beginnings of Glasgow's overseas trade may be traced to this period, however, for it was in the fifteenth century that William Elphinstone settled in the city as a merchant. Curing salmon (with which the limpid Clyde then abounded) and herring, he exported them to France and brought back return cargoes of brandy and salt. The curing and export of salmon and herring continued to be the chief foreign trade of Glasgow until the Union of 1707. Life was simple, but leisurely and pleasant, in this attractive country town, with its numerous gardens and orchards interspersed among the straggling thatched houses, over which towered the Cathedral and Palace of the Bishop.

In his hands were firmly held the reins of local government. Towards the close of the fifteenth century new lustre was added to his dignity and influence with the erection of the see into an Archbishopric in 1492,[1] having jurisdiction over the bishops of Dunkeld, Dunblane, Galloway and Argyll.

With the gradual development of commerce and industry in the city, merchants and craftsmen began to wield an increasing influence in the burgh's affairs. The merchants of Glasgow are found associated and acting through a president in 1569, but the exact nature of their constitution and the length of time it had existed are uncertain. Seals of cause, certificates which conferred on a craft the status of an incorporation, were possibly granted to crafts in Glasgow in the fifteenth century, but the earliest that has survived is one to the skinners and furriers dated 1516.[2] Granted by the Archbishop and the magistrates and council jointly, the seal of cause stipulates the qualifications and entry fees required of craftsmen, lays down regulations to ensure a satisfactory standard of workmanship, and prescribes the contribution they must make "for upholding the altar of St. Mungo." Each craft had its own special altar in the Cathedral, to which money and wax had to be contributed, but after such "altarages" were abolished at the Reformation these contributions were devoted to the poor. Thus originated the charitable activities of the incorporations of trades, an aspect which remains prominent to this day. It was not until the seventeenth century that organised Guildry developed in Glasgow.

The Reformation Period

In the turbulent events of the Reformation period Glasgow was closely concerned, and indeed the city can possibly claim an intimate link with the early life of John Knox. A "Joannes Knox" who matriculated at the University of Glasgow in 1522 may have been the future Reformer, for it is known that the latter was a pupil of John Major, the theologian and historian, who taught at Glasgow until 1523 and thereafter at St. Andrews. As there is some uncertainty as to the exact date of Knox's birth, however, it is doubtful if Glasgow's university can claim him as its alumnus.[3] His antagonism towards Mary Queen of Scots seems to have been shared by the majority of Glasgow's citizens, many of whom played an active part in her final defeat at Langside[4] in 1568. During her minority, in 1544, the city had been the scene of a memorable encounter between the Regent Arran and the Earl of Glencairn, which became known as the Battle of the Butts. The

[1] St. Andrews had attained this status twenty years earlier, in 1472.

[2] By the early seventeenth century there were 14 crafts in the city, 7 of which were incorporated prior to the Reformation.

[3] If he was born in 1513 or 1515, and not 1505 as was once generally accepted, his college days are more likely to have been spent entirely at St. Andrews.

[4] The site of this battle is commemorated by a monument, and by the place-name "Battlefield."

Bishop's Palace had been garrisoned by the Earl of Lennox and was besieged by Arran. Having held out for ten days, it surrendered under promise of quarter, but the promise was not kept. All but two of the defenders, it is said, were massacred. To avenge this treachery Glencairn mustered about 800 men and met the Regent's army at "The Butts," where the wappenschaws were held, in the Gallowgate. Assisted by Robert Boyd of Kilmarnock with a party of horse, however, the Regent defeated Glencairn after a bloody skirmish in which some 300 are said to have been killed on both sides. He then gave the city up to plunder, because of the sympathy shown by the Provost and the inhabitants to his opponents. According to one account, "the very doors and windows of many dwelling-houses were carried away." Such treatment Glasgow did not quickly forget.

In 1558, when the spiritual zeal of the Reformers was beginning to overflow into physical violence, the Archbishop of Glasgow found it advisable to obtain from his regality bailie, the Duke of Chatelherault,[1] a guarantee of protection. The Duke refers in the document to "this perillous and dangerous tyme, quhair detestabil heresies ryses and increasis in the diocy of Glasgow" and promises to defend the Archbishop and chapter and to assist in the crushing of heretics. Despite this undertaking, however, Chatelherault later joined the Protestant Lords of the Congregation. In July, 1560, a month before the Scottish Parliament recognised the reformed faith as the established religion of the land, Archbishop Beaton of Glasgow fled to France, taking with him the records and treasures of the see. The archives, which included the Red Book of Glasgow dating from the reign of Robert III, were deposited in the Scots College in Paris, where they remained until the outbreak of the Revolution. They were then sent for safety to St. Omer, but many were never recovered. The loss of these invaluable documents is the main reason for our scanty knowledge of Glasgow's pre-Reformation history. There is a tradition that the Cathedral was saved from the destructive violence of the Reformers only by the opposition of local craftsmen, although the authenticity of this story is doubtful. Exact details are not known, but damage to the external fabric of religious buildings in Glasgow appears to have been slight, while interior features such as images and altars were effectively removed by the combined action of departing priests and invading iconoclasts.

The freeing of church endowments brought little financial benefit to the University, but it profited in a less material sense from the events of the Reformation. A vigorous new broom—the scholarly Presbyterian, Andrew Melville, appointed Principal in 1574—and a new constitution (the *nova erectio* of 1577) served to arrest the decay which had been threatening to overwhelm it. Almost all its members had been scattered, and its records, charters and mace[2] had accompanied the

1 Titular ancestor of the Dukes of Hamilton.

2 Restored to the University in 1590, the mace (dating from 1465) is still used on ceremonial occasions.

Chancellor, Archbishop Beaton, in his precipitate flight to France. The object of the *nova erectio* was " to collect the remains " of the University, and so effectively was this accomplished under the enthusiastic hand of Melville that at the end of his six years' principalship " there was no place in Europe comparable to Glasgow . . . for a plentiful and good cheap market of all kinds of languages, arts, and sciences." So claimed his nephew and biographer, James Melville, himself a regent in the University, and there was probably some justice as well as exaggeration in his boast.

Of course much of the outward splendour, both of academic and of town life, departed from Glasgow with the passing of the old faith. The pomp and circumstance surrounding the Archbishop and his palace in Roman Catholic times, to say nothing of the wealth which his lordly revenue and retinue brought to the city,[1] were no doubt missed by the populace, and in both Church and University the loss of stately and colourful ceremonial must have cast an unaccustomed gloom over the day-to-day life of the city. Apart from the Cathedral, Glasgow had contained two monasteries of Dominicans and Franciscans—Blackfriars and Greyfriars—founded in the thirteenth and fifteenth centuries respectively. Both were deserted, if not destroyed, in 1560, but the church of the Blackfriars continued to be used as a place of worship after the Reformation.[2] So too did the new collegiate church of St. Mary and St. Ann, a recent foundation of the sixteenth century which reappeared in Protestant guise as the Tron Kirk, after a period of thirty years' abandonment. Following the Reformation this church, situated on the south side of the Trongate, was disposed of by the Town Council (who had previously endowed it with sixteen acres of the common moor), but they reacquired the property about 1592 when the growing population of the city made an additional place of worship necessary. The population of Glasgow at the time of the Reformation has been estimated at about 4,500, but by 1600, according to a census taken by the kirk session, it had increased to 7,000. There is a reflection of this growth in the subdivision of the city into parishes, which is an important development of the post-Reformation period. Until 1588 there was only one minister, with a " reader " or assistant, in Glasgow but in that year a second minister was translated to the city from Edinburgh. Services were held in the Cathedral and in the old church of the Blackfriars, which was now known as the " College Kirk." After the renovation of the collegiate church of St. Mary as the Tron Kirk in 1592 a third city minister was appointed to it. A fourth was appointed in 1595, and given charge of the landward district of

[1] A deed of gift at this period refers to the losses incurred by the city through the removal of the commissary courts, which before the Reformation had brought great numbers of people into Glasgow from the surrounding country.

[2] The site of the Greyfriars monastery and its cemetery later passed into the possession of the University. Both monasteries were situated in the vicinity of High Street, almost opposite each other. In 1563 Queen Mary, while visiting Glasgow, gave 13 acres of the lands of the Blackfriars to the University, which she observed to be in a sorry state, its buildings unfinished.

Glasgow, thereafter known as the Barony Parish. At first the Barony parishioners were temporarily accommodated in the Blackfriars church, but eventually they were allotted the crypt of the Cathedral, which remained their place of worship until the end of the eighteenth century when a separate church was built for the Barony. Following the disjunction of the urban and landward congregations, the town itself was divided into two parishes in 1599—a change which a cautious magistracy and council agreed to only on condition "that the towne be nocht burdenit for beitting and bigging of kirkis nor furnising of ma ministeris nor thai have alreddy."

The City at the close of the Sixteenth Century

The records of the Town Council, which exist—although not in completeness—from 1573 onwards, throw some light on the state of municipal affairs in Glasgow at the end of the sixteenth century. The Council was elected annually at the Michaelmas court, held in late September or early October. As feudal superior the Archbishop, or, when episcopacy was in abeyance, the lord of the regality, exercised the right to nominate the Provost.[1] The bailies, by now three in number, were also chosen by him from a leet drawn up by the Provost, bailies and retiring Council. These new bailies, together with those holding office in the previous year, then nominated the new Council. In 1574 the members chosen numbered fourteen, including the town treasurer and master of work. The officials appointed included five "liners" (their work corresponding to that now performed by the Dean of Guild Court), a water bailie to maintain order among the fishermen and seamen on the Clyde (Glasgow still has its "river bailie"), and a common procurator. Statutes were passed annually regulating the town's markets, the prices of provisions, and such matters as the cleansing of streets.

There was a regular "riding of the marches" to preserve the boundaries and prevent encroachment on the town's common lands. One such perambulation was made at the Whitsunday court held in late May or early June, and at this court the common good revenues, such as market and bridge dues, and the rents of the town mills, were set to tacksmen. The treasurer, master of work, and town clerk were also elected at the Whitsunday court. There was another perambulation of the marches at the end of June, when the entire community gathered on the "Symmerhill," which is thought to have been in the area of the present Cowcaddens. Among the business transacted at this court was the appointment of the town's "menstrales" or bagpipers, colourful characters of Old Glasgow who unfortunately find no place in the modern scene. These worthies, who regarded themselves as local dignitaries of hardly less consequence than the bailies, passed through the

1 It was only towards the end of the eighteenth century that the title "Lord Provost" began to be regularly used in Glasgow.

town each morning and evening playing their pipes,[1] and it was also part of their duty to beat the town's drum on such occasions as the making of proclamations. Their official uniform included a coat of blue cloth, on which the town's arms were emblazoned in crimson. At another court, held in the open air near the site of the Greyfriars Monastery, the town's July fair was proclaimed with due ceremony each year. Disturbances at the Glasgow Fair in those days, as now, were not unknown, and to assist in quelling the high spirits of undesirables each stall-holder was instructed to have "ane halbert, jak, and steilbonet" ready to his hand. High-days and holidays aside, however, the citizens of Glasgow three or four centuries ago were not altogether peaceable in their daily dealings with one another, if we are to judge by the frequent "trublance," "stryking," "schutyng," "scarting," "dinging" and "flyting" for which men, and only too often women, were hauled before the bailies.

A more pleasant picture of Glasgow at the close of the sixteenth century is given by Bishop Lesley in his *History of Scotland* published in 1578. His description of this "noble toune" lying "beyond the water of Clyd" reveals the city's growing importance as a commercial centre of the West of Scotland. "Surelie," he says, "Glasgow is the most renouned market in all the west, honorable and celebrat." He enumerates its exports to the east: "verie fatt kye," herring and salmon, ox hides, wool and skins, butter "that nane better," and cheese. To the Highlands and Islands, and to Ireland, Glasgow at this time was sending all kinds of grain, wines, ales and other drinks, including "aqua vitae." Lesley was but one of many writers who were to record the favourable impression that the city's appearance then made upon its visitors: "It is a verie fair situatione and plesand, abundant in gairdine herbs, aple trees, and orchardis. Farther, it hes a verie commodious seyporte, quhairin litle schipis ten myles frome the sey restis besyde the brig, quhilke brig haveing 8 bowis is ane gret delectatione to the lukeris upon it."[2]

The harbour on which the Bishop bestowed such a flattering description was as yet in its infancy. Already however the importance of securing adequate access to the sea had been recognised by the citizens as vital to Glasgow's future prosperity. In the early sixteenth century the channel of the Clyde, for some thirteen miles below the city, was so obstructed by fords, shoals and sandbanks that it was hardly navigable even by small boats. The first serious attempt to improve matters seems to have been made in 1556, when the inhabitants of Glasgow, Renfrew and Dumbarton entered into an agreement

[1] This they apparently found thirsty work, for the authorities felt it necessary to enjoin them "to leiff thair extraordiner drinking sua that thai may pass honestlie throu the towne in thair service."

[2] The eight-arched "brig" referred to is, of course, Glasgow's first stone bridge, built in the fourteenth or early fifteenth century. It remained the only bridge across the Clyde at Glasgow until Jamaica Street Bridge was built in 1768. See Chapter 1.

to work on the river, for six weeks at a time, with the object of removing the ford at Dumbuck. It was not until the eighteenth century, however, that any real success was achieved in the deepening of the Clyde's upper reaches.[1]

The Royal Burgh, 1611-1700

While Glasgow in the sixteenth century seems to have outrivalled all other Scottish towns in beauty of aspect,[2] it could claim only eleventh place in 1535, and fifth place in 1591, as regards taxable value. The subsequent improvement in the latter respect was unfortunately only to be gained with some sacrifice in the former. It is with the erection of the city into a royal burgh in 1611 that Glasgow's modern history as a commercial and industrial centre may be said to begin, but it must be emphasised that the change in status that occurred at this date was in many ways more nominal than real. As far as trading privileges were concerned, Glasgow since the twelfth century—although only a bishop's burgh—had enjoyed freedoms and customs similar to those of royal burghs held directly of the king. Its burgesses could engage in foreign and domestic trade as freely as those of the neighbouring royal burghs of Rutherglen, Renfrew and Dumbarton. The only important respect in which the inhabitants of Glasgow had inferior rights was in the election of their provost and magistrates, who as we have seen were nominated by the bishop, not by the burgesses themselves.

Several notable developments in the city's municipal government took place in the early years of the seventeenth century, including an abortive attempt to secure for the burgesses the right of electing their own magistrates. As in other Scottish burghs there was considerable animosity and jealousy between the merchants and craftsmen. The latter outnumbered the former, and claimed an equal share not only in municipal government but also in the city's seafaring trade. In 1604 the burgesses of merchant rank in Glasgow numbered 213, while those of trades rank numbered 363.[3] The claims of the craftsmen were stoutly resisted by the merchants, and according to McUre, the city's first historian, the " terrible heats, strifes, and animosities " which resulted nearly ended in bloodshed. After intervention by magistrates and ministers, however, a happy solution was reached with the grant of a Letter of Guildry in 1605. This provided for the election of a Dean of Guild and of a Deacon Convener, each with a seat on the Town Council; and made equitable regulations regarding the admission of merchants and craftsmen to guildry membership.

1 See Chapter 10 (Transport).

2 As Hume Brown has pointed out, it was the only place in Scotland of which strangers spoke with unqualified enthusiasm.

3 These were divided among the trade incorporations as follows: hammermen, 29; baxters, 27;; tailors, 65; cordiners, 50; websters, 30; " marinellis " and fishers, 17; bonnetmakers, 7; walkers and litsters, 5; skinners, 21; mediciners, 2; coopers, 23; masons, 11; wrights, 21; maltmen and mealmen, 55. Marwick, *Early Glasgow* (1911), pp. 185-6.

In the same year steps were taken towards securing municipal freedom in the election of magistrates, but internal dissensions arose which defeated the movement.[1] Riotous disturbances ensued in the summer of 1606 and the old method of election was retained. By an Act of Parliament passed in July, 1606, episcopacy had been re-established in the kingdom, but John Spottiswoode, Beaton's successor as Archbishop of Glasgow, appears to have exercised his powers with discretion and promoted an amicable settlement of the dispute. It was not until 1641 that a decisive development towards electoral reform took place. In that year the Town Council was authorised by Parliament to elect the bailies, while the Provost was to be chosen by the Duke of Lennox (in place of the Archbishop, episcopacy again being in abeyance) from a leet of three persons named by the Council. From the restoration of episcopacy in 1661 until its final abolition in 1690 the Provost was chosen by the Archbishop, but his rights of election which then devolved on the Crown were conferred upon the Town Council in the latter year.

Thus it was only in 1690 that Glasgow attained full independence as a royal burgh, although it had nominally acquired such status earlier in the century by a charter granted by James VI in 1611. This charter, confirmed by a later grant of 1636, gave the city specific rights on the River Clyde from the Broomielaw to the Cloch, clarifying the position in relation to neighbouring royal burghs and removing one of the greatest obstacles to Glasgow's commercial expansion. At first Irvine on the Ayrshire coast, 25 miles away, had been used by Glasgow merchants as a seaport for their foreign trade, but by the end of the sixteenth century the harbour there was becoming badly silted up. A reference in the council records in 1609 to " a pier and port " at the Broomielaw, and to efforts to improve the river channel, indicates that merchandise was brought upriver in small boats from vessels lying in the vicinity of Dumbarton or Greenock. In 1662 a quay was constructed at the Broomielaw to improve the facilities for loading and unloading the small boats there, and five years later 13 acres of land were acquired at Newark, near Greenock, where the harbour of " Port Glasgow " was established. This met the city's needs until the second half of the eighteenth century, when the growth of the tobacco trade and subsequent industrial development stimulated further efforts to deepen the river so that large vessels might bring their cargoes right up to the Broomielaw.[2]

Cromwell's commissioner, Tucker, in his report of 1656, reveals Glasgow's growing importance as a centre of trade. Apart from those connected with the University, the city's inhabitants were all traders and dealers. Its merchants traded with the West Highlands, Ireland, France and Norway, and some had in the past ventured as far as

[1] The subsequent evolution of Glasgow's Merchants House and Trades House is referred to in Chapter 18.

[2] See Chapter 10 (Transport).

Barbados. At this period Glasgow's shipping comprised 12 vessels, and was exceeded only by that of Leith. The population of the city is believed to have doubled between 1610 and 1660 to 14,678, making it the second largest city in Scotland.[1] Much of its new-found prosperity must be attributed to the freedom of trade enjoyed under the Commonwealth, but following the Restoration in 1660 the English Navigation Acts closed the colonies to Scottish merchants. Between the Restoration and the Revolution Glasgow experienced a severe set-back in its fortunes, and its population by 1688 appears to have fallen below 12,000. This was an unhappy period in the city's history, when political unrest and religious persecution contributed to the depression of the times. As the Provost was then still the nominee of the Archbishop, the Town Council tended to favour the episcopal party, but many of the burgesses made common cause with the Covenanters. Among the clergy who refused to conform to prelacy and had to give up their livings were Patrick Gillespie, Principal of the University, and Donald Cargill, minister of the Barony. Since that memorable time in 1638 when the General Assembly had met in Glasgow and abolished episcopacy in defiance of Charles I, the inhabitants of the city had suffered much for the cause of the Covenant. Montrose had fined them heavily after the Battle of Kilsyth in 1645, and three years later the Provost and bailies had been deposed for contumacy. To add to the town's miseries, plague and famine had devastated the burgh in 1645-8 (a divine judgment in the eyes of some, no doubt, for setting at nought the divine authority of the king) and in 1652 a great fire had destroyed a third of the city's houses. On the latter occasion it was Cromwell who detected "the hand of an angry God."

Following the Restoration came the religious persecution of the "Killing Times." The suppression of conventicles within burghs was the responsibility of the magistrates, and in the summer of 1674 a fine of £100 sterling was imposed on the city by the Privy Council because a conventicle had been held in Glasgow by Donald Cargill and others. The dreaded "Highland Host" of Lauderdale entered the city in January, 1678, before proceeding on its oppressive mission through the disaffected districts of the south-west. After his defeat at Drumclog in the following year Claverhouse retired to Glasgow, and with the garrison in the city prepared to meet an expected onslaught from the victorious covenanting forces. In a skirmish on the Gallowmuir which followed it was obvious that the sympathies of many citizens were with the Covenanters, but the town authorities contributed financial support to the king's army. Many of Glasgow's inhabitants suffered imprisonment for their faith at this period, and the city also had its quota of martyrs. A tablet in the Cathedral burial ground was raised to commemorate nine men "who all suffered at the cross of Glasgow for their testimony to the covenants and work of Reforma-

[1] Exceeded only by Edinburgh. Robert Baillie, at the same date, records that the city "in its proportions, thryves above all the land." *Letters and Journals*, i., 319.

tion" between 1666 and 1688.[1] Three others were commemorated by a Martyrs' Fountain at the Howgate, in the east wall of Castle Street.

The closing decade of the seventeenth century saw Glasgow in rather a decayed state, but nevertheless in trade and revenue it now held second place among the towns of Scotland, as compared with eleventh place in 1535. A report from the city to the Convention of Royal Burghs in 1692 shows that its foreign trade then amounted to over £17,000 sterling annually. It possessed 15 ships totalling 1,182 tons, and 8 lighters, as well as a share of 4 ships belonging to unfree burghs. But the report also states that "by the decay of trade a great number and many of the best of their houses are waste, yea that there is near 500 houses standing waste, and that those inhabited are fallen near a third pairt of the rent they payed formerly." Such was the cost[2] to the city of the religious and political strife through which the country had passed, but in the comparative tranquillity that followed the Revolution Settlement men's minds turned again towards trade and industry. The seeds of Glasgow's industrial future had already been sown, and merely awaited the congenial climate of post-Union times to bring them to fruition in the following century. In 1667 sugar refining was begun in the first of several "sugar-houses" erected in the city, and as early as 1674 there is evidence of an interest in Virginian tobacco on the part of Glasgow merchants. Such trade as they had with the English colonies in America at this period, however, was necessarily small and surreptitious.

William Paterson's proposal to establish a Scottish colony on the Isthmus of Darien met with enthusiastic support in Glasgow, whose merchants saw in this project a last hope of restoring their city's decaying fortunes. It was an enthusiasm founded on despair, not on considered commercial judgment, that led many normally cautious Scots to risk their all on this ill-conceived venture. Patriotic fervour, enflamed by jealousy of England and a desire to beat her at her own colonising game, added zest to the speculation. The Town Council of Glasgow, on behalf of the burgh, invested £3,000 sterling in the enterprise; many citizens took up stock to the limit of their means, and some joined the expedition in person. The last to sail left the Clyde in the late summer of 1699, unaware of the disaster that had already overtaken the first colonists. News of the collapse of the Darien scheme did not reach Glasgow until the following year, and it was hardly believed until the full horror of the story (too well-known to require repetition here) was told by the few emaciated survivors who returned. Many fortunes were gone, the financial loss in Glasgow being so great that it was 18 years before the city again possessed ships of its own.

[1] It was inscribed with one of those doggerel epitaphs typical of the period:

"These nine, with others in this yard,
Whose heads and bodies were not spared,
Their testimonies, foes, to bury,
Caus'd beat the drums then in great fury,
They'll know at Resurrection Day
To murder saints was no sweet play."

[2] Although possibly exaggerated.

Thus the seventeenth century ended in an atmosphere of gloom, despair and recrimination, the blame for the people's misfortunes being laid mainly on England and King William. It is scarcely surprising that Glasgow was to prove one of the staunchest opponents of the impending Union of Parliaments, unaware that therein lay the key to her future greatness.

Glasgow After 1700

The Foundation of the Modern City

The eighteenth century saw the transformation of Glasgow from a small attractive town of 12,000 inhabitants into a rising industrial city with a population exceeding that of Edinburgh. It gained the latter distinction at the cost of an earlier claim to superiority over the Capital in point of beauty: in the preceding century one of Cromwell's soldiers described Glasgow as "not so big or rich yet . . . a much sweeter and more delightful place than Edinburgh." It was in 1723 that John Macky penned his famous but rather inelegant tribute to Glasgow, "the beautifullest little city I have seen in Britain."[1] Fifty years later Pennant, with a more moderate enthusiasm, described it as "the best built of any modern second rate city I ever saw." By that time Glasgow was beginning to lose its sequestered rural appearance and was judged by the character of its streets and buildings rather than by its surroundings.

It is indicative of the city's growing importance that in 1702, when proposals for a Treaty of Union were being discussed, the Provost of Glasgow was one of the Commissioners appointed to travel to London for the purpose. The ordinary people of Glasgow, like the mass of the country's inhabitants, were violently opposed to the Union, particularly as the city was thereby to lose its independent representation in Parliament. Since 1546, if not earlier, Glasgow had sent a member to the Scottish Parliament, but in the United Kingdom Parliament the city was to have only joint representation with Dumbarton, Renfrew and Rutherglen, her ancient rivals. This, with the anti-English feeling engendered by recent events such as the Darien disaster, and the recurrent fear of episcopacy, led to outbreaks of mob violence in the winter of 1706 when the Treaty was under consideration by the Scottish Parliament. The spark which set off the conflagration was a sermon preached by the minister of the Tron Kirk, at the Sacramental Fast Day in November. He concluded his discourse with an exhortation to his congregation to "be up and be valiant for the city of God," which was regarded as a direct injunction to revolt. Within two hours drums were beating in

[1] Shortly afterwards it was described as "one of the cleanliest, most beautiful, and best-built cities in Great Britain" by Daniel Defoe (1726).

the streets and the city was at the mercy of the mob, and when on the following day the Provost refused a request by the deacons of crafts to address a remonstrance to Parliament anent the Union, the council-house and the Provost's house were attacked. He himself had to flee for safety to Edinburgh. For four weeks the city was in an uproar, which subsided only after a detachment of dragoons was sent from the Capital to quell the rioters. After the passing of the Treaty of Union the arrested ring-leaders—no doubt to placate popular feeling—were liberated without further punishment.

Unpopular as it was at first, the Union of 1707 before very long brought new prosperity to Glasgow and enabled her to profit from her situation on the western seaboard. Previously the city's merchants had traded principally with France and Holland, where they were at a disadvantage compared with their rivals on the east coast. Now the American colonies were open to Scottish traders, and Glasgow was soon exporting goods to Maryland, Virginia and the Carolinas, bringing back tobacco leaf as return cargo. The refining of sugar and the making of soap[1] were the only industries of importance carried on in the city at the beginning of the eighteenth century, but other manufactures were quickly developed to meet the demands of the colonial markets. Linen and cotton checks and plaidings, which had been made in the city on a modest scale since the time of the Commonwealth and were already acquiring some celebrity in the home market (even in fashionable and aristocratic Edinburgh), formed the basis of a new export industry in textiles. Under the stimulus of the American trade and the encouragement of the linen industry by the State, Glasgow soon began to attain prominence as a manufacturing centre. Defoe, writing within twenty years of the Union, mentions the importance of linen in the city's economy: " they make a very great quantity of it and send it to the plantations as their principal merchandise." He also refers to the manufacture of muslins, " which they make so good and fine that great quantities of them are sent into England and to the British plantations, where they sell at a good price." Glasgow weavers thus early established a reputation for skilful workmanship in fine textiles—an accomplishment which was to stand the city in good stead when its tobacco trade collapsed later in the century.

The rise and the fall of Glasgow's tobacco trade were almost equally spectacular. At first the merchants engaged in it had no ships of their own, the vessels employed being chartered from English ports, chiefly Whitehaven. It was not until 1718 that a Glasgow-owned tobacco ship crossed the Atlantic, and this was a small vessel of only 60 tons, built at Greenock. The early success of the Glasgow merchants may have been due to the simplicity and frugality of their trading methods. It was strictly a barter trade initially. A supercargo (who might even be the captain of the ship himself) went out with

[1] A company to engage in whaling and soap-making had been founded in the city by 1674. It had a blubber factory at Greenock, where its five ships were based, and a " soaperie " in the Candleriggs.

'Scotland' Magazine

Plate 3. SAUCHIEHALL STREET

Aero-Pictorial

Plate 4. THE CITY BRIDGES

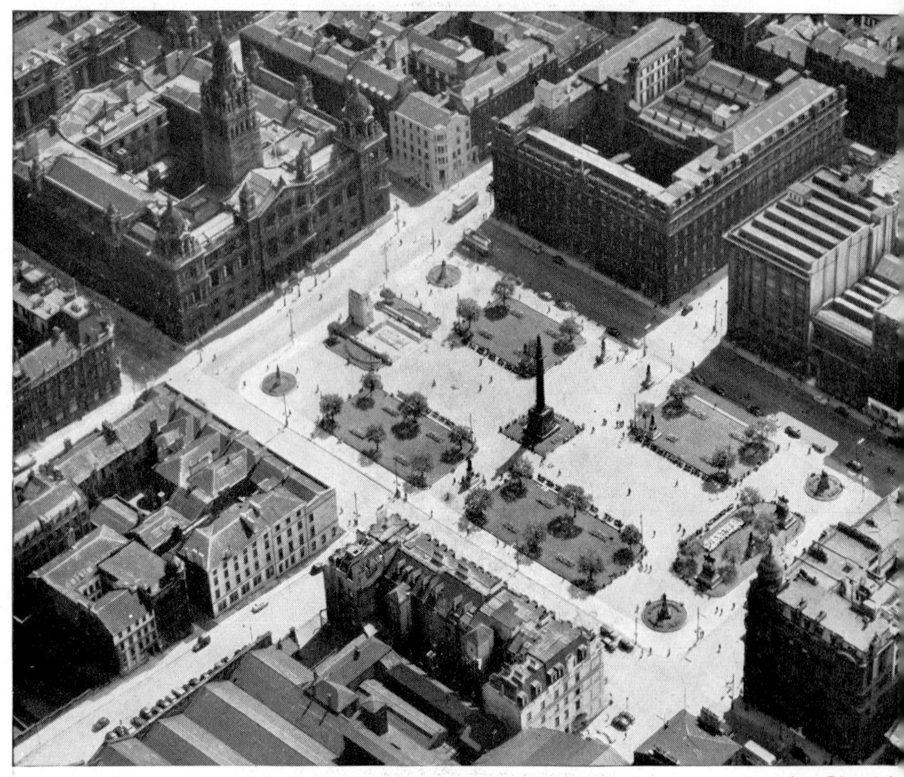

Aero-Pictorial

Plate 5. GEORGE SQUARE

each vessel, and on arrival he bartered his goods for tobacco leaf. His instructions were to remain until he had either sold all his goods, or obtained sufficient tobacco with which to load his ship, when he was to return to the Clyde with his cargo and any goods that were left. The profit on each venture was thus known and realised at once. So successful were these early Glasgow traders that English tobacco merchants, suffering from their competition, accused them of fraudulent dealing. Not only were the Glasgow tobacco houses acquiring the bulk of the foreign export trade; they were even underselling English dealers in their own home markets. To do so, they must have been content with more modest profits than their English rivals. The merchants of London, Bristol, Liverpool and Whitehaven combined together to crush the Scottish trade, complaining to the Government that it was based on a system of customs evasion. An official enquiry was held in 1721, and it says much for the impartiality of the united British Parliament that the result was entirely favourable to the Scots. The Lords of the Treasury declared that the complaints were groundless, and that they arose "from a spirit of envy, and not from a regard to the interests of trade or of the King's revenue."

By 1723 there were twenty or thirty ships engaged in the trade from the Clyde, and four years later, according to Defoe, the Glasgow merchants were sending "near fifty sail of ships every year to Virginia, New England, and other English colonies in America." For the first—and not the last—time in her history Glasgow was profiting from the fact that she was situated considerably nearer to America than were her English rivals. This geographical advantage meant more in the days of sailing ships than it does to-day. Defoe records that Glasgow vessels were often "at the Capes of Virginia before the London ships got clear of the Channel," thus saving a month or six weeks on the whole voyage. It was not until about 1735 that Glasgow finally triumphed over southern competition and interference, but thereafter the development of the city's tobacco trade was phenomenal. Resident agents were appointed in the colonies and methods of trading became more complex: in forward dealings whole crops of tobacco were often purchased before they were even planted, and princely fortunes were amassed rapidly by successful speculators. The number of ships engaged in the trade rose steadily, and by the time of the American War of Independence the city's shipping amounted to between three and four hundred vessels.

More than half the tobacco trade of Britain had become concentrated in the hands of Glasgow merchants: of the 90,000 hogsheads imported into Great Britain in 1772, 49,000 came to Glasgow. There were then some 38 firms in the business, many of them dealing in vast sums annually. Smollett tells us in *Humphry Clinker* that one merchant, John Glassford, alone owned 25 ships and traded for above half a million sterling a year. He and the other "tobacco lords" of the period have become legendary figures in Glasgow's history, which is hardly surprising when it is remembered that they formed the first commercial aristocracy the city had ever known. Their flamboyant scarlet cloaks, their gold-headed canes, their pompous parade on the Plainstanes, betray them as *nouveaux riches*—unaccustomed to their sudden prosperity, and perhaps even a little unsure of its permanence.

By its nature the tobacco trade brought great wealth to a comparatively small number of individuals, its value to the city as a whole lying not so much in its immediate effects as in the accumulation of capital that was to make possible the financing of industrial development in later years. It was largely an *entrepôt* trade, the tobacco arriving in the Clyde being almost all re-exported to France, Holland, Germany, Italy and Norway.[1] The "farmers general" of the French Customs were the principal purchasers. In 1771 46 million lb. of tobacco came to the Clyde, and of this quantity nearly 44 million lb. were re-shipped abroad. The trade hinged entirely on the mercantile theories of the time, as exemplified in the Navigation Acts, and its basis was highly artificial. It was made possible only by the restrictions which prevented the colonies from trading directly with the Continent themselves. The revolt of the colonies in 1775 brought a sudden end to Glasgow's prosperity, but although many traders were ruined some great fortunes had already been made and safely secured. American property was lost through confiscation, but the estates acquired in the West Indies by Glasgow merchants remained. Moreover much capital amassed in the tobacco trade had already been invested in new industries producing goods for the home and the colonial market, and further funds were now freed for the development of such industries.

The need to supply outward cargoes for the tobacco ships had stimulated the growth of a wide variety of local industries in the West of Scotland during the eighteenth century. By 1771, indeed, there was a favourable trade balance of home-produced exports amounting to about half a million pounds sterling.[2] Linen goods formed the chief item, the value of textiles exported from the Clyde in that year amounting to £450,000. The city's products included checkered handkerchiefs, diaper, damask, cambric, lawn, muslin handkerchiefs, "Glasgows" or lawn mixed with cotton, carolines, and inkle wares.[3]. Spencer's *English Traveller* (1771) enumerates, besides the herring trade and the tobacco trade, the manufacture of woollen cloth, stockings, shalloons, cottons and muslins; it also mentions the sugar trade, distilling, the manufacture of boots, shoes and other leather goods, including saddles, and the making of house furniture. Pottery had become established as a Glasgow industry in 1748 and the city had also glassworks, tanworks and ropeworks.

This period too saw the beginnings of the iron trade, with the

[1] Much of the sugar and rum which Glasgow imported from America and the West Indies was similarly re-exported.

[2] The figures (in £000's) were: Imports, £1,386; re-exports (chiefly tobacco), £1,354; home produced exports (chiefly linen), £503.

[3] Inkles (tapes) were a Dutch monopoly until 1732, when a Glasgow man, Alexander Harvie, at the risk of his life, brought two inkle looms and a Dutch workman to the city from Haarlem. This workman afterwards went to Manchester, thus introducing the secret of the process to England.

establishment of the Smithfield Company's works at Broomielaw Croft on the Clyde about 1732. A rolling, slitting and forging mill was built by this company on the Kelvin, near Partick, in 1738. The bar iron used was imported mainly from Russia and Sweden. Like the tobacco lords, the early Scottish iron masters were severely hit by the American War of Independence, for the wrought iron goods they manufactured were mainly for export to the colonies. Their market was artificially protected by an Act of 1750 which prohibited the erection of any new ironworks by the colonists, who were thus rendered dependent on British manufacturers for their supplies of agricultural tools and similar goods. With the loss of its free market on the outbreak of the American Revolution in 1775, and the subsequent commercial depression of the Napoleonic Wars, Glasgow's iron trade was partially eclipsed until its emergence in a new form, using locally produced ores, in the nineteenth century.[1]

Echoes of an Auld Sang

The development of commerce and industry after the Union of 1707 was soon reflected in a renewed growth in the city's population. Between 1708 and 1763 it more than doubled, from 12,766 to 28,300, and by 1780 it had increased to 42,000. The eighteenth century, however, was not altogether a period of peaceful and uninterrupted progress in Glasgow. Political and religious strife, it is true, were no longer such dominant factors in the life of the community as formerly, but the echoes of the "auld sang" that ended in 1707 were slow to die away. Distrust and discontent lingered on, even after the material benefits brought to the city by the Union began to become apparent. The Jacobite cause had its sympathisers among the inhabitants of Glasgow, although the city officially showed its loyalty to King George during the Rebellion of 1715.[2] The Town Council offered a regiment of 500 men to the Government, and this force was despatched to the Duke of Argyll's camp at Stirling, while the city was fortified against the Highlanders by numerous entrenchments and barricades. In the winter of 1715 over 350 rebel prisoners were lodged in the castle prison in Glasgow. They apparently did not suffer their incarceration meekly, for a constant guard of about a hundred men had to be maintained to prevent their escape.

Smouldering discontent and anti-English feeling flared up in 1725, when the Government attempted to impose a malt tax which was regarded as a contravention of the terms of the Treaty of Union. On the day when the tax came into effect a mob obstructed the excisemen in Glasgow, which led to intervention by the military. This merely served as an incentive to further violence, and the

1 See Chapter 5 (Iron and Steel).

2 It was amid the troubles of the 'Fifteen that the city's first newspaper, *The Glasgow Courant*, made its brief appearance. See Chapter 19.

crowd not only attacked the soldiers but vented their wrath on the house of Campbell of Shawfield, M.P. for the Glasgow district of burghs, who had supported the tax in Parliament. He had also made himself unpopular with his constituents because of his views on the tobacco trade. His fine "Shawfield Mansion," which stood in the Trongate and was regarded as the most handsome house in the city, was completely ransacked; but he and his family, apparently forewarned, had retired to his country residence a few days before the riots broke out. In subsequent collisions between the mob and the military 9 persons were killed and 17 wounded.

The army authorities were displeased with the attitude of the Provost and Magistrates, who were reluctant to order military intervention and consequently were suspected of sympathy with the rioters. General Wade took possession of the city with a large force, and Duncan Forbes of Culloden, the Lord Advocate, who accompanied him, started an investigation into the affair. The result was that 19 citizens were handed over to the military and taken to Edinburgh Castle. Worse was to follow. All the magistrates, from the Provost to the Deacon-Convener, were arrested at the instance of the Lord Advocate and thrown ignominiously into their own Tolbooth. Later they too were lodged in Edinburgh Castle but were liberated on bail after a day's detention and allowed to return home. They were met by about 200 of their fellow-citizens six miles outside Glasgow, and this reception committee, we are told, "escorted them home with every demonstration of respect, amid the joyous ringing of bells."

This episode provides a curious picture of the relations between local and central government in the early eighteenth century. Incidentally it is perhaps the only occasion in history when the Glasgow Town Council have been hailed as the popular heroes of the hour. It seems unlikely, however, that there was much substance in the charge that the magistrates had sympathised with the rioters and turned a blind eye on the sacking of Campbell's house. It was their misfortune that on the night of the attack on the Shawfield Mansion they had retired to spend a convivial evening in a tavern. There, at a late hour, the Provost was confronted with the news and an offer from the army of military aid, which he declined. In the circumstances it may be doubted if the city fathers reached this fateful decision after sober reflection. No further punishment was inflicted on them beyond the indignities they had already suffered, but their humbler fellow-citizens were less fortunate. Of the nineteen rioters arrested, two were banished, nine were whipped through the streets of Glasgow, and eight endured lengthy imprisonment. Local feeling was further embittered when Campbell of Shawfield, on application to Parliament, was granted indemnity for his losses, which together with other expenses, amounting in all to about £9,000, the city had to pay. For half a century the "Shawfield affair" was remembered with a deep sense of grievance and injustice by the inhabitants of Glasgow.

As the city's commercial prosperity increased, however, anti-Union feelings gradually subsided. The Jacobite Rebellion of 1745 found little sympathy or support in Glasgow, where the romantic appeal of Charles Edward Stuart seems to have captivated only the fair sex: the Presbyterian and mercantile interests of their menfolk were proof against his charms. The city demonstrated its loyalty to the House of Hanover by raising two battalions of 600 men, but at the time when they were most needed in Glasgow these volunteers were withdrawn for the protection of Edinburgh. On its victorious southward march the Pretender's army made a threatening move towards Glasgow. Charles had demanded from the magistrates £15,000 sterling, all the arms they possessed, and the arrears of taxes due to the Government. After temporising, in the hope of relief from Sir John Cope's forces, the magistrates succeeded in satisfying the Prince with only £5,000 in cash and £500 in goods. Three months later, on Christmas Day, 1745, the advance guard of the Pretender's army entered Glasgow in its retreat from Derby. The main body of ragged and starving Highlanders, a sorry contrast to the glittering host that had marched south from Scotland on its glorious adventure, arrived the following day. Glasgow, unprotected, was at their mercy. As a centre of Whiggism it might well have been sacked and burned, and there is a tradition that only the intervention of Cameron of Lochiel saved it from this fate.

Certainly the inhabitants of Glasgow—with the exception of a few ladies, one of whom, Clementina Walkinshaw, was to follow him into exile as his mistress—had given Charles little cause to love them. He contented himself, however, with re-equipping his tattered army at the city's expense. All told, Glasgow's enforced contributions to the Jacobite cause amounted to over £14,000, but the city later received £10,000 from Parliament in 1749 as part compensation for its losses. The Prince remained in the city until 3 January 1746, holding court in the Shawfield Mansion, which despite its rough treatment twenty years earlier was still considered the most elegant in town.[1] He held a grand review of his refurbished troops on the Green, but this failed to arouse any enthusiasm among the inhabitants—no doubt it reminded them too forcibly of the 6,000 blue bonnets and other clothing they were paying for! Charles himself complained that nowhere had he made so few friends as in Glasgow, and it seems that the sixty adherents he did procure during his stay were merely the lowest of the rabble. Provost Cochrane, who showed commendable courage and diplomacy in his dealings with the Pretender, claimed that he made but one recruit—and that "ane drunken shoemaker, who must soon have fled his country for debt, if not for treason." The news of the final Jacobite defeat at Culloden was hailed with rejoicing in Glasgow, the more so as the city's volunteers had suffered heavy casualties at the hands of the Highlanders in the Battle of Falkirk.

1 It now belonged to Glassford of Dugaldston, the merchant prince.

The Tobacco Lords and the American Revolution

The next occasion when the city raised volunteers for the service of the Crown was during the American War of Independence, when the very basis of Glasgow's new-found prosperity, the tobacco trade, was threatened. At first it was the policy of the Government to rely on foreign mercenaries, and English M.P.s scorned the idea of raising even a militia in Scotland, except as a feeder to the English regiments of the line. As the war progressed, however, they were forced to modify their views and in 1778 regiments were raised in both Edinburgh and Glasgow. The Glasgow regiment was the 83rd Foot or Royal Glasgow Volunteers. That nationalist feeling in Scotland seventy years after the Union was still strong is shown by the fact that both regiments declined to enrol Englishmen. The officers of the Royal Glasgow Volunteers protested against being compelled to admit English recruits to their ranks.[1] With one notable exception the tobacco lords threw their accustomed dignity to the winds and formed themselves into a recruiting corps. Thus Glasgow was treated to the curious spectacle of James Finlay (father of Kirkman Finlay[2] of Castle Toward) playing the bagpipes, while John Wardrop, a Virginia merchant, beat a drum, with other notabilities acting as fifers and standard-bearers. In addition to generous bounty money, young men joining the regiment were offered a burgess ticket free of expense, and this the newly-enrolled recruits proudly displayed behind their cockades when parading the streets. Prominent merchants such as Speirs of Elderslie and Cunningham of Lainshaw, motivated by a judicious mixture of patriotism and self-interest,[3] hired their tobacco ships as transports; but Glassford of Dugaldston, the prince of them all, is said to have disapproved of coercive measures against the colonists and to have laid up most of his 25 ships in Port Glasgow harbour. After serving in America and in the Channel Islands the Glasgow regiment was disbanded on the Green at the conclusion of the war in 1783.

The return of peace was not accompanied by an immediate return of prosperity to Glasgow, and the outlook for its swelling population —now approaching the 50,000 mark—seemed gloomy. A disastrous harvest in 1782 had added the threat of famine to the miseries of unemployment, at the same time accelerating the flow of immigrants to the city from the surrounding countryside where poverty and distress were acute. That year was also long remembered for one of the worst floods ever experienced in Glasgow, when the Clyde rose twenty feet

1 Sir Herbert Maxwell (Ed.), *The Lowland Scots Regiments* (1918), p. 328.

2 See p. 320.

3 Cunningham made a great fortune out of the war by buying up existing stocks of tobacco at the outbreak of hostilities and re-selling them during the subsequent scarcity. The house of this leading tobacco lord can still be seen in Glasgow— with the addition of a portico it became the Royal Exchange, now the Stirling Library.

above its ordinary level and inundated the Gorbals, Bridgegate, Saltmarket, Stockwell Street and Jamaica Street. While only one person was drowned, serious losses were sustained through the destruction of the contents of riverside warehouses and the drowning of horses and cattle.

There were, however, some happier portents. Three events in 1783 provide clear signs of a reviving interest in commerce and industry: the founding of Glasgow's Chamber of Commerce and Manufactures, the first in the British Isles, for the protection of the interests of the city's traders; the establishment of a branch of the Royal Bank of Scotland in Glasgow;[1] and the publication of the first Glasgow Directory. The latter gives us an intimate glimpse of the city's social structure at that period, and reveals that the business community was concentrated in High Street, Saltmarket, Trongate, Gallowgate, Candleriggs, Bridgegate and the Wynds. A sheriff-substitute could still reside with dignity and comfort in the Saltmarket, and a Town Clerk was not above living in the Gallowgate, while quite a covey of lawyers inhabited the Laigh Kirk Close. The great merchants who had amassed and secured their fortunes before the war, however, had built new and more palatial mansions to the west. And it was upon them and their capital that Glasgow's industrial future depended.

The Birth of the Cotton Industry

Some of that capital had already been invested in the linen industry, and now that the tobacco trade had vanished further outlets were being sought in textiles. It was Glasgow's good fortune that just when a new industry—cotton—was born, she had both the capital and the skilled labour resources necessary to develop it. Even her much-maligned climate for once proved an asset: the humid atmospheric conditions of the west suited the manufacturing processes. A cotton-spinning mill was established at Rothesay in 1778, and two years later James Monteith erected a large mill at Anderston. The number of cotton mills in Scotland increased from 19 in 1787 to 134 in 1834, by which date almost all of them lay within 25 miles of Glasgow.[2] As they were initially dependent on water-power their location was determined by the availability of suitable rivers, and the countryside round Glasgow (although not the city itself) abounded in swift-flowing streams.

One of the greatest of the new factories was built near the Falls of Clyde at Lanark. Opened in 1786, this historic "New Lanark" mill is still in active operation.[3] Its founder, David Dale, was an outstanding figure of the times—in more senses than one. This rotund gentleman (his dimensions were the subject of many witticisms, which no one seems to have enjoyed more than himself) was one of the first great

1 For the earlier local banks in the city see Chapter 12 (Finance).

2 The history of the cotton industry is given in greater detail in Chapter 8 (Textiles and Clothing).

3 It is now run by the Gourock Ropework Company.

"self-made" men of Glasgow's industrial age. Some of his contemporaries suggested that Sir Walter Scott used him as the model for his Bailie Nicol Jarvie in *Rob Roy,* but with the addition of some romantic Jacobite connections. Dale himself was the son of an Ayrshire shopkeeper, and graduated from herd boy and hawker to cotton manufacturer, Turkey-red dyer, and banker. His life-story was in many respects typical of that of the textile magnates of his day. He entered the trade as a linen weaver, when the industry was still in the "domestic" stage. Then he started to deal in linen yarn, travelling round the countryside visiting farm-houses and cottages, and later established a small business in Glasgow as an importer of Dutch and French yarns. From this he turned to manufacturing, purchasing Dutch looms on which he wove inkles[1] and other linen cloths. By 1783 he had attained such prominence in the commercial life of the city that, despite his humble origins, he was appointed Vice-President of the newly established Chamber of Commerce. Its President and founder, Provost Patrick Colquhoun, was in contrast a member of the merchant aristocracy of the tobacco period, who had been brought up in affluent circumstances.[2]

David Dale's acceptance into what had been virtually a hereditary hierarchy was more than a personal triumph: it marked the birth of a new line of "merchant princes" in Glasgow and the passing of an era. Some thirty years later even the office of Provost was to be attained by a weaver's son—Henry Monteith, another great name in the city's early cotton industry. His father, James Monteith of Anderston, and David Dale were among those Glasgow manufacturers who invited Arkwright, the inventor of the spinning frame, to visit Glasgow in 1783. Arkwright was associated with Dale in the founding of the New Lanark cotton mills, which by 1793 were the largest of their kind in Britain. Their 1,300 workers included paupers from various parishes in Scotland, and orphan children whose diet, clothing, accommodation and secular and religious training were carefully supervised by Dale. He was the first of many Glasgow industrialists to combine evangelism and practical philanthropy with successful business activity—examples of such men can still be found in the city. After the famous social reformer, Robert Owen, became his son-in-law and took over the mill, New Lanark was internationally known as a model of industrial welfare. Many of the schemes usually credited to Owen, however, were originated by Dale.

The poor of Glasgow also had good cause to be grateful to this kindly man, who would charter ships to bring in grain for their relief in years of famine and depression during the French Wars at the close of the century. Among his numerous other activities, he played a part in the founding of the "Old Scotch Independents"—a sect which

1 See p. 98, footnote 3.

2 Unlike many of the younger members of the tobacco aristocracy, Patrick Colquhoun (1745-1820) attained prominence in his own right. He left Glasgow in 1789 for London, where, among other achievements, he published a treatise on the *Wealth, Power and Resources of the British Empire* (1814), which earned him fame as "the first British statistician."

seceded from the Church of Scotland in 1768—and preached every Sunday in his own chapel, popularly dubbed the "Candle Kirk," in Greyfriars Wynd. When prosperity came to him as a cotton manufacturer, he built a fine house, designed by Robert Adam, in Charlotte Street beside Glasgow Green. This house, which survived until recently, was well worthy of preservation both as an architectural specimen of the "new town" of the eighteenth century, and as a memorial of Dale himself. Instead it has shared the fate of so many other historic buildings in Glasgow. Despite a public outcry, the city's Education Committee, into whose possession it had fallen, demolished it to make way for a school playground in 1953.

The Sky Darkens

As yet, thanks to the dependence on water-power, the factory system had not altered the face of Glasgow to any marked extent. But with the increase of population and the building of new houses the city was rapidly growing, and was no longer the salubrious country town of Daniel Defoe's day. In the early nineteenth century, however, life was still pleasant and colourful. It was not until the 'twenties and 'thirties that factory chimneys really began to darken the sky, and a gloomy pall began to settle over the city. Mechanisation had so far been virtually confined to the spinning branch of the cotton industry, although some early experiments in power-loom weaving had been made in Glasgow even before the close of the eighteenth century—in one of which the motive power took the curious form of a large Newfoundland dog operating a treadmill. The first real threat to the supremacy of the hand-loom weaver came in 1801, when John Monteith set up 200 power-looms in his factory at Pollokshaws. At this time the earnings of hand-loom weavers were so good that they formed a minor aristocracy, and indeed gold-headed canes and red cloaks, once the insignia of the tobacco lords, were now sported, if tradition is to be believed, by the Glasgow weaver and his wife when attending church on Sundays. But with improvements to the power-loom and the development of steam-power the advance of mechanisation was rapid, and the wages of the best weavers dropped from £2 a week at the beginning of the century (a huge sum in those days, equal to the earnings of many professional men) to a few shillings in the 1840's.

It was in 1765 that James Watt of Greenock, working as a mathematical-instrument maker in the University,[1] devised the idea of the separate condenser after repairing a model of Newcomen's primitive steam engine. Some have attributed his inspiration to his mother's kettle, but Glasgow prefers to believe the story that the idea came to him when walking on Glasgow Green. For many years steam engines were used mainly for pumping water from coal mines. The first to

[1] Not being a member of an incorporated trade, he was precluded from working outside the College precincts.

be used in Glasgow for cotton spinning was installed at Springfield in 1792, and their adoption thereafter seems to have been fairly rapid, for in 1814 an Act of Parliament was obtained "for the regulation of steam engines, chimneys, etc., in the city and suburbs." Four years later there were reported to be within the city "eighteen steam weaving factories, containing 2,800 looms, and producing 8,400 pieces of cloth weekly." By that date Glasgow had altogether 52 cotton mills, with a production valued at upwards of five million pounds annually. There were also 18 calico printing works and 17 calendering houses. By 1854 the number of cotton factories had risen to 92, employing over 24,000 workers. In the financial crisis of 1857, however, the industry was severely weakened and, as recorded in a subsequent chapter, only remnants of it survived in Glasgow after the interruption of raw cotton supplies by the American Civil War.

Twice within a span of a hundred years Glasgow's economy had been profoundly shaken by events on the other side of the Atlantic, but fortunately by this time the city had already found a new basis of prosperity in engineering and shipbuilding. Instead of depending on exotic importations such as tobacco and cotton, Glasgow had begun to exploit the rich store of indigenous wealth that lay buried beneath her own doorstep.

The Rise of Heavy Industry

As early as the sixteenth century the mineral resources of the area had been tentatively explored. In 1578 it is recorded that the Archbishop let the "coilheuchtis and colis within the baronie of glasgw" for three years, at an annual rent of forty pounds Scots and the delivery of "thirteen scoir and ten laidis of colis." A century later, in 1655, we find the Town Council agreeing to advance, for the good of the city's inhabitants, the sum of two thousand merks to "Patrick Bryce weiver and James Andersone in Gorballis" for the working of the coal-pits in the Gorbals for thirteen years. They were forbidden to charge the citizens more than four shillings (that is, 4d. sterling) for each hutch of coal, and were not to employ more than eight "hewars." By 1778 there were ten collieries in the vicinity of the city, but the annual production was only about 82,000 tons—including some coal exported from the Broomielaw and sold at Port Glasgow and Greenock. The coal-fields of Old and New Monkland, however, were now being developed some twelve miles to the east of the city, and it was to facilitate a plentiful supply from this area that the Monkland Canal, completed in 1790, was projected.[1] By 1836 the number of pits in the neighbourhood of Glasgow had increased to 37, from which about 561,000 tons were brought to the city, and about 124,000 tons of this were exported. Shortly after the middle of the nineteenth century over a million tons of coal were coming into Glasgow annually, a reflection of the rapid

[1] See Chapter 10 (Transport).

adoption of steam-power in industry as well as of the growth in the number of domestic consumers.

Of the local pits in the Glasgow area, the Govan collieries were probably the most profitable. In 1823 nearly 300 vessels were loaded at the harbour with Govan coal, and the Town Council, believing that rich seams lay beneath Glasgow Green, became convinced that the city could share in this prosperous activity. Professional advice encouraged them to think that five seams of workable coal would be found in the Green, but although boring operations were carried on for a year or two the project came to nothing. In the course of the nineteenth century the local seams in the immediate vicinity of Glasgow were gradually worked out, and to-day there is only one active colliery within the city boundary, at Garscube.

The discovery of the value of "blackband ironstone" in 1801 by David Mushet marked the beginning of the modern Scottish iron industry, which Glasgow, by virtue of its strategic position, was destined to dominate. It was not until after the development of the hot blast by J. B. Neilson in 1828, however, that the industry really began to expand.[1] Meanwhile, stemming initially from the mechanisation of the textile industry, and stimulated by the development of the steamship from 1812 onwards,[2] mechanical engineering was rising into prominence in Glasgow. It is easier to account for the success of the city's cotton weavers than to explain the rapid pre-eminence attained by the Glasgow engineer. Here there was no tradition of acquired skill, and indeed the city's inhabitants had been more remarkable for their ingenuity in filching the inventions of others in the eighteenth century than for the display of any mechanical aptitude of their own. We have seen how the secret of the manufacture of "inkles" or tapes was stolen from Holland, and it is rather ironic that, as a result of the successful exploitation of the process thus acquired, such products in their modern adhesive form are known as "Scotch tapes" in America to this day. Most of the machinery for the weaving shops and the early textile mills was brought to Glasgow from England or the Continent, and at first it was mainly of wooden construction. It was in maintaining and repairing such imported machinery that the city's first mechanics learned their craft.[3]

They proved industrious apprentices and soon displayed an aptitude for modifying and improving the inventions of others. Thus, while Glasgow can claim no credit for the initial mechanical developments in the cotton industry—which were largely the work of Englishmen like Hargreaves, Arkwright and Crompton—the city may boast of humbler pioneers: William Kelly, for example, who in 1792 obtained

[1] See Chapter 5 (Iron and Steel).

[2] The early history of shipbuilding on the Clyde has been incorporated in Chapter 6.

[3] By the early nineteenth century there were several firms in Glasgow making textile machinery, the proprietors of these works in many cases being themselves cotton manufacturers. William Dunn, for example, who later owned several cotton mills in Dunbartonshire, started life as an apprentice wright in Glasgow and then established his own machine shop in the city. His customers included some of the largest spinning firms in the country.

a patent for operating Crompton's mule by water-power; Neil Snodgrass, who invented in 1797 a scutching or blowing machine for cleaning cotton fibres, which was adopted in Manchester some ten years later and improved by Arkwright and others; and Henry Houldsworth, who was responsible for important improvements in the roving process. The father of mechanical engineering in Glasgow, and indeed of the Industrial Revolution itself, was of course James Watt, but even his notable invention was the result of an attempt to improve an English machine, the primitive "fire" engine of Newcomen, a Dartmouth blacksmith. Watt's development of the steam engine in 1765 brought no immediate benefit to Glasgow, but rather to its modern rival, Birmingham, as it was there that he established his works with his colleague Boulton, after a brief and ill-starred partnership with Dr. Roebuck of Carron Iron Works. Until 1800 Boulton and Watt enjoyed an "exclusive privilege" of making steam engines, but thereafter this new branch of engineering made rapid strides in Glasgow and by 1835 there were about 14 firms engaged in it. Its growth was due initially to the power requirements of the collieries and the textile factories, but with the advent of the steamship the city's engineers were able to turn their experience to good account and develop a new specialty in marine engineering.[1]

The adoption of iron in the construction of ships, which in Glasgow began with the launching of Neilson's *Fairy Queen* in 1831 and became general in the 1840's, brought shipbuilding itself within the city's orbit. As long as the industry was based on wood Glasgow was unfavourably placed compared with towns on the lower reaches of the Clyde, but now she had the advantage of ready access to a raw material which abounded in her own hinterland. Simultaneously with the application of iron to shipbuilding came the enormous demand for the metal created by railway development, which reached its maniacal peak in the mid-'forties,[2] and the railways not only stimulated the iron industry but brought a new branch of mechanical engineering to Glasgow, that of locomotive construction. The locomotives for the Glasgow-Garnkirk line, which was opened in 1831, were built by a Glasgow engineering firm. At first several general engineering concerns made both marine and railway engines, but by mid-century, when the modern system of passenger lines had been inaugurated, locomotive construction was emerging as a specialised branch of the city's industry.[3] As both customers and carriers of the products of the mines, ironworks and engineering shops, the railways greatly fostered the growth of heavy industry in the area. So too did the ships, now being launched in steadily increasing numbers from the Clyde yards—not, as is too often the case to-day, merely to forsake their native river and carry on their trade at some other port. Glasgow, by the second half of the nineteenth

[1] Of the 310 steam engines that were at work in the Glasgow area by 1825, 176 were in the textile industry, 68 in steamships, 58 in collieries, 7 in quarries, and 1 in an ironworks.

[2] See Chapter 10 (Transport).

[3] See Chapter 7 (Other Engineering).

century, had developed her harbour and extensive overseas shipping connections, without which the city could have had little share in the prosperity Britain was then enjoying as " the workshop of the world." At mid-century, as a unique aerial drawing made in 1853 confirms, smoking factory chimneys and crowded wharves were already dominant features in the Glasgow landscape.

The Struggle for Reform

The social problems created by such rapid industrial and commercial expansion were inevitably great, and many of them remain unsolved to this day. Between 1780 and 1811 the population rose from 42,000 to almost 101,000, and it more than doubled itself again in the next twenty years. This achievement was signalised by severe outbreaks of typhus and cholera in 1831 and 1832, when so many citizens died that special ground had to be acquired for their burial; Glasgow could hardly find houseroom for its living, let alone its dead. Disease was also rampant in the body politic, where the ancient system of government was wholly unrepresentative of the new industrial community and patently incapable of meeting its needs. Social and political unrest emphasised the urgency of reform, at both the national and municipal levels. Those who lacked the franchise were prompt to blame the Government for the dislocation of trade and the attendant distress that followed the Napoleonic Wars, and it was early in the nineteenth century that Glasgow first acquired its notoriety in southern eyes as a hotbed of radicalism. Many of its citizens, not by any means confined to the humbler ranks of society, had shown sympathy with the liberal ideals of the French Revolution. The Government of Pitt was not popular, and reform societies such as the Friends of the People found many adherents in Glasgow. However in the later stages of the Napoleonic conflict the city adequately affirmed its patriotism, not only raising money and numerous volunteers for the defence of Britain,[1] but providing a national hero of the war, Sir John Moore of Corunna. He was the first of the city's sons to be honoured with a statue in George Square.

Although it was not until after the close of the war in 1815 that serious political disturbances occurred in Glasgow, earlier incidents, such as a bread riot in 1800 and a number of strikes at the cotton mills, had led to the establishment of the city's first effective police force in that year.[2] Even at this early period in Glasgow's industrial history every twelfth house in the city had become a dram-shop, and drunkenness and lawlessness were rife. The Editor of a radical Edinburgh

1 It was at this period, when detachments of the regular army had to be continuously quartered in Glasgow, that infantry barracks were built on the north side of Gallowgate. They continued to be occupied from 1795 until 1877, when the present Maryhill Barracks were completed.

2 For the subsequent development of the Glasgow Police Force, see Chapters 17 and 20.

newspaper had remarked some years earlier that " notwithstanding the severe manner in which delinquents are treated by the magistrates of Glasgow, and the close and rigorous confinement they undergo in Bridewells, yet in no place are crimes more frequent than in that city." Lest it be thought that inter-city rivalry swayed his judgment, it should be added that this Edinburgh journalist was unusually impartial: for after referring to the " dreadful accounts of rapes, robberies and murders committed in and about the city of Glasgow " he goes on to record the " melancholy fact " that " no place in Europe contains so great a number of licensed low drinking houses, in proportion to its size, as the metropolis of Scotland."[1]

After Waterloo, Glasgow's ex-servicemen returned to find trade depressed and unemployment severe, the plight of the handloom weavers being particularly ominous in view of advancing mechanisation in the cotton industry. The weaver, from the nature of his craft a reader and a thinker, and traditionally a revolutionary in both politics and religion, was a prominent figure in the radical movement of the times. It was more than just the fear of starvation that led him to campaign for the repeal of the Corn Laws and cheaper bread, and his programme went considerably further: the acknowledgment of the Rights of Man—though to the less literate this meant simply the right to combine and to strike, perhaps—the grant of universal suffrage and reform of parliament and local government. In 1816 a crowd of 40,000 malcontents (nearly equivalent to the city's entire population in the year 1780) gathered in a field near Glasgow and passed resolutions for presentation to the Prince Regent demanding repeal of the Corn Laws. The magistrates, scenting rebellion in the air, alerted the 42nd Highlanders and the Dragoons. News of the seditious attitude of the populace soon reached London. It no doubt gained colour on its journey—" Red Clydeside " has always appeared in most vivid hues to southern eyes—and the Government was seriously perturbed.

According to Peter Mackenzie,[2] Lord Sidmouth asked Glasgow's M.P., Kirkman Finlay, to devise means of obtaining information for the Government about treasonable activities in the city. An *agent provocateur*, in the person of Alexander Richmond, an unprincipled Pollokshaws weaver, was Finlay's unhappy choice. As a result of Richmond's machinations a Calton weaver named M'Kinlay was brought to trial for high treason, but the case against him collapsed. So too did that against the Rev. Neil Douglas, a seventy-years-old dissenting minister in Glasgow, who enlivened his sermons and his congregations by equating King George with Nebuchadnezzar, the Prince Regent with the prodigal son, the Lord Provost with Beelzebub, and the House of Commons with " a den of the most infernal corruption." Such uninhibited pulpit invective was in full accord with the wholesome Glasgow tradition begun by Zachary Boyd of the Barony

1 James Tytler's *Historical Register or Edinburgh Monthly Intelligencer*, October, 1791.
2 *Reminiscences of Glasgow* (1865), i, 113.

when preaching before Cromwell in 1650,[1] and continued by the Rev. James Clark of the Tron Kirk during the Union negotiations in 1706.

Towards the close of 1819, when unemployment was particularly severe, there was a recrudescence of political unrest in the city and the surrounding countryside. Richmond, the Government's spy, is credited with artificially fomenting much of the trouble, but there is no doubt that Glasgow was the headquarters of the reformers. The extent to which any treasonable organisation really existed is open to question, and it would seem that many of those who rose in armed revolt were deceived and instigated to rebellion by unscrupulous government agents. Not inappropriately, it was on All Fools' Day, 1 April 1820, that a manifesto calling on the people to rise and assert their rights was surreptitiously posted up on the streets of the city.[2] It was impressively signed "By order of the Committee of Organisation for forming a Provisional Government." After a tense week, during which the city was placed under curfew and all available military forces were deployed in readiness to quell the anticipated rising, a royal proclamation was read at the Cross offering a reward of £500 for the discovery of the authors and printers of this treasonable document. Meanwhile *agents provocateurs* were active, and the most fantastic rumours were spread: England was in arms for reform, an army was on its way from France to give support to the insurgents, and French troops were to camp on Cathkin Braes.

Led to believe that a force of English reformers was advancing on Falkirk to capture the Carron Iron Works (important suppliers of Government ordnance), some seventy ardent revolutionaries, armed with pikes, swords and muskets, marched from Glasgow to lend their support. At the village of Condorrat they were joined by a weaver named John Baird and several others, but on approaching Falkirk they found no English revolutionaries in sight. Instead a troop of the 7th Hussars descended upon them while resting at Bonnymuir. Taken by surprise, they gamely but misguidedly resisted the overwhelming force, only to be captured and securely lodged in Stirling Castle. This rather pathetic skirmish has its place in history as "the Radical War" of 1820, for it was not lightly regarded by the Government of the day. The King appointed a Special Commission for the trial of the rebels under the English treason law, which had been imposed on Scotland after the Union, and 18 of the men captured at Bonnymuir were brought before a court of Oyer and Terminer at Stirling, charged with high treason. Apart from Baird and three others, all the accused belonged to

[1] According to the well-known story, Boyd's denunciations so infuriated Cromwell's secretary that he asked permission to "pistol the scoundrel." Oliver, however, invited Zachary to supper, kept the worthy minister out of bed until the small hours of the morning by engaging in a three hours' prayer—leaving Boyd not in the least discomfited, and indeed rather more favourably disposed to his malicious host than before! The Tron Kirk incident in 1706 has already been mentioned (p. 95).

[2] It appeared also in various other places in the counties of Lanark, Renfrew, Dunbarton, Ayr and Stirling.

Glasgow.[1] Despite an eloquent defence by the famous Francis Jeffrey, all were convicted; John Baird, the Condorrat weaver, and Andrew Hardie,[2] a weaver from Glasgow, were executed as ringleaders, while the others were transported. A sixty-years-old Strathaven weaver, James Wilson, who had been arrested prior to the Bonnymuir incident, was hanged and beheaded in Glasgow before a crowd of about 20,000 people. These three men were hailed as martyrs to the cause of Reform, and the Government gained nothing by the severity of its measures.[3]

In succeeding years the demand for Reform became more insistent. In 1831 a procession of the trades, accompanied by a crowd of about 150,000, marched to Glasgow Green and demanded the franchise. There was a further mass demonstration the following year, and in June 1832 the Reform Bill, enfranchising £10 householders, became law. The concession was still far short of universal suffrage, for while the population of the Parliamentary Burgh set up under the Reform Act exceeded 200,000, the number on the electoral roll was only 7,024. Now, however, Glasgow had two M.P.s of its own, directly elected, a notable advance on the former system whereby delegates from the self-electing Town Council had a quarter-share in the election of one member to represent four burghs. The reformed parliament at once embarked on the task of municipal reform, the Burgh Reform Act of 1833 ending the "close system" of council election in the royal burghs which had existed in Glasgow since 1690.[4] While the qualifications for the parliamentary and municipal vote were now identical, the municipal burgh at this time was smaller than the parliamentary, and at first there were only some 4,000 municipal electors on the roll. By 1841 the parliamentary electorate numbered 8,783 (about 3.4 per cent of the population) and the municipal electorate 5,506.[5] The subsequent history of Glasgow's municipal and parliamentary representation is dealt with in Chapter 13.

The Community tackles its Problems

The disintegration of the ancient framework of municipal government was accelerated, and indeed rendered inevitable, by the mass of new social problems created by the city's rapid industrial expansion. As the population increased so too did lawlessness, disease, poverty

1 A great-granduncle of the writer was among those indicted, but the official report of the trial records that he was "not in custody." He had in fact escaped to America, where his descendants remain to this day.

2 Forebear of Keir Hardie, the founder of the Scottish Labour Party and the first Socialist M.P.

3 More violent riots, in which six persons were killed when troops fired on a mob attacking a factory, occurred in Glasgow during the depression of 1848, but this "Chartist" uprising was not followed by any executions.

4 Traces of the old system survive in the *ex officio* membership of the Corporation still enjoyed—despite recent attempts to abolish the right—by the Dean of Guild (head of the Merchants House) and the Deacon Convener of the Trades.

5 Exact figures of the population of the municipal burgh in 1841 are not available.

and illiteracy. The old parish and burgh authorities had neither the power nor the financial means to provide adequate services to combat these problems. Thus in the nineteenth century a succession of new local government bodies, deriving the necessary revenue from rates levied on the populace, were brought into being to administer such services as police, sanitation, poor relief and education.

The public were naturally unwilling to pay rates to an authority like the old Town Council, over which they had no electoral control—"no taxation without representation" was a maxim as popular at home as it had been in the American colonies, and no less stubbornly upheld. Early attempts by the Town Council to provide police services failed because it had no authority to impose an assessment for such purposes, and when in 1800 the old method of "watch and ward" by the burgesses was finally replaced by a regular system of police, financed by rating, a separate body of "commissioners" elected by the rate-payers was set up to administer it. The city was divided into 24 "wards," each of which elected a commissioner, and these 24 commissioners together with the magistrates, Dean of Guild and Deacon Convener, constituted the police board. Thus the first step was taken towards placing the administration of local government on a democratic basis, many years before the Town Council itself ceased to be a self-electing oligarchy.

One of the less happy results of the creation of an effective police system in the city in the early nineteenth century was the migration of many criminally-disposed inhabitants to the suburbs, where tumult and disorder became rampant. Gradually, however, the suburban districts acquired similar police powers under separate Acts of Parliament, Gorbals in 1808, Calton in 1819, and Anderston in 1824. In 1846, when Glasgow's municipal boundary was altered to correspond with that of the Parliamentary Burgh set up under the Reform Act of 1832, their police systems were integrated with that of the city.[1] As the Town Council was now a more representative body, in consequence of the Municipal Reform Act, the need for a separately elected board of police commissioners had disappeared and from 1846 its place was taken by a "police and statute labour committee" elected by the Council. This new police board functioned until 1877, when the management of police affairs was vested in the magistrates and Council who, under the Police Amendment Act of 1890, were described as "police commissioners." Finally, by the Glasgow Corporation and Police Act, 1895, the municipal and police government of the city was consolidated in the Corporation, which was to become the sole authority responsible for the management of municipal affairs.

Attempts to combat poverty, disease and illiteracy among Glasgow's overcrowded masses in the nineteenth century led to the creation of similar governmental machinery—Parochial Boards, Boards of

[1] An account of the successive extensions of the municipal area has already been given in Chapter 1. The political aspects of these amalgamations with adjacent burghs are considered in Chapter 13.

Health, School Boards—whose independent functions and responsibilities were eventually also merged in the Corporation, which thus became an ever more complex organisation of departments and committees. The Corporation, too, gradually assumed responsibility for the provision of such services as water (1855), gas (1869), electricity (1890), public transport (1891) and even telephones,[1] acquiring or developing undertakings originally established in the city by private enterprise.[2] Intervention by the municipal authority in these fields was justified on the grounds that the services were essential to the community, involved the use of the corporate property, and were either actual or potential monopolies. Within the last decade, in the period following the Second World War, the Corporation has been relieved of some of its responsibilities through the nationalisation of gas and electricity undertakings, and the introduction of the National Health Service. The history of the various public services, including the development of housing, health and social welfare, will be outlined in later chapters, but a brief account must be given here of the growth of educational facilities in the city.

The Growth of the City's Schools

Until 1872, when popularly elected School Boards were established throughout Scotland, the control of education lay largely in the hands of the Church. Even Glasgow's ancient burgh school, which had passed from the Church to the Town Council at the Reformation, remained under the more or less active supervision of the Presbytery for three hundred years thereafter. The Church's legal right of superintendence over parish schools was unquestionable, but her authority over burgh schools in post-Reformation times was less clearly established. Under various Acts of the old Scottish Parliament and the General Assembly, however, no school-master could be appointed without examination and approval by the Presbytery of the bounds.[3] That the Glasgow Town Council accepted ecclesiastical supervision of their school management after the Reformation is apparent from the burgh records. When they chose a new master in 1582, for example, it was "by advice of the masters of the university, and others having power by Act of Parliament," and in 1615 we find the magistrates requesting the aid of the Presbytery in choosing his successor. The Church's advice was sought not only in regard to the teaching staff but also in the arrangement of the curriculum: the masters of the college and the ministers of the

1 Glasgow's venture into municipal telephony lasted only from 1900 until 1907, when the Corporation's system was sold to the Post Office. The experiment entailed a loss of £17,000 to the Common Good.

2 The tramways belonged to the city from the inauguration of the system in 1872, but until 1894 they were operated under lease by a private company.

3 The General Assembly was constant in its exhortations to Presbyteries to visit the schools and ascertain the sufficiency and qualifications of masters, but not all Presbyteries showed equal enthusiasm for the task. The Presbytery of Glasgow, on the evidence of its own records, was fairly active in this duty.

city prepared a course of study for Glasgow's grammar school in 1685, at the same time providing that the pupils should be regularly examined twice a year by men of eminence and learning, appointed by the Town Council and the University. During the three centuries of its management the Council appears to have served the school well, and maintained a close and beneficial link with Church and University. In 1835 some professors and ministers were still associated with the Town Council in the management, but in 1861 the long connection between school and church was formally severed by Act of Parliament, which provided that masters should no longer be subject to the government and discipline of the Established Church, or to trial of their qualifications by Presbyteries.

Until 1815 a four or five years' course in Latin was the mainstay of the school curriculum, but in that year provision was made for a one year's course in Greek.[1] It was not until 1834, after much opposition from the rector, that English, modern languages, geography and mathematics were introduced into Glasgow's grammar school, which then acquired its present name of "the High School." It acquired its present site in Elmbank Street (originally that of Glasgow Academy) in 1878, the new School Board taking full advantage of the Education Act of 1872, and its successive amendments, to improve both the amenities and the curriculum. Through a reduction of fees the higher education available at the High School was thrown open to a wider section of the community, but despite several attempts at abolition it remains a fee-paying school to this day.

In the seventeenth and eighteenth centuries a multitude of small private schools existed in Glasgow, and it was in these more humble seminaries that the bulk of the city's population received its elementary education. In the 1780's the Presbytery carried out a survey which revealed more than 60 schools in which the masters were supported only by their pupils' fees, ranging from 1s. 6d. to 5s. a quarter. Most of these schools taught only reading, the Catechism, and possibly a little writing. There were many other private schools of a superior type, charging higher fees, with a more exclusive clientele and more advanced curricula. Some were erected and managed by voluntary subscribers, and assumed the fashionable title of "academies," but neither of Glasgow's two well-known academies of the present day is of eighteenth century origin. Glasgow Academy was founded in 1846 and Kelvinside Academy in 1877, the former moving to its present site near Kelvin Bridge in 1878. The original building of Glasgow Academy (designed by Charles Wilson, who was also responsible for the striking Italian hall of the Faculty of Procurators in St. George's Place) now forms the central block of the High School.

[1] In a curriculum drawn up for Glasgow's burgh school not long after the Reformation it was recommended that towards the end of their fifth year the scholars should study the elements of Greek grammar. Greek, however, remained very much the province of the universities, which came to regard its teaching in schools as an encroachment on their preserves. An unseemly dispute arose in this connection between Edinburgh's High School and University in 1772.

Despite the large number of private schools—ranging from the humble " dame-school " to the high-class " seminaries " for young ladies and gentlemen—and the various charity and church schools which Glasgow possessed at the end of the eighteenth century, the proportion of children receiving education was tending to decline. The greatest threat to educational progress was the growth of the cotton industry, which offered employment to children between seven and eight years of age, who could earn as much in a week as would pay a quarter's school fees. Poor families, not surprisingly, found the temptation of such an additional income overwhelming, and preferred to forget about education and keep their children at the mills. The writer of the first *Statistical Account of Glasgow* felt it essential to encourage parents to send their offspring to school at the age of six, so that they might have the benefit of at least one year's education before their working life began! It was to meet this problem, and prevent the loss of what little education such children might already have received, that the Sunday School movement (originally aiming primarily at secular instruction) was developed. In 1806 *The Glasgow Herald*, referring to " a number of Gratis Sabbath Evening Schools, which are taught in this City and Neighbourhood," remarked: " Most poor children are put to some kind of employment as soon as they can walk abroad. Sabbath is the only day they have to themselves, and the evening of that day can be devoted to their instruction without interfering with other duties." The redoubtable Dr. Thomas Chalmers, whose noted experiments in voluntary poor relief in Glasgow are referred to in a subsequent chapter,[1] established between forty and fifty Sabbath Schools, with the support of the Town Council but not of his brother clergy, who —like Dr. Moodie of Edinburgh[2]—seem to have regarded them as hotbeds of disaffection and sedition.

Among those in Glasgow who supported Chalmers in his efforts to provide for the instruction of poor children was David Stow, a young merchant whose name was to become famous in the annals of education. Before meeting Dr. Chalmers he had already founded a Sabbath school of his own in the Saltmarket and together they conceived the idea of extending their activities to week-days. In 1826, with the assistance of friends, Stow succeeded in forming the Glasgow Infant School Society, and in the following year established a day school in the Drygate for a hundred pupils, where he developed educational methods far in advance of his time. Laying aside the traditional well-worn tools of the dominie's craft—the Shorter Catechism and the tawse —he evolved a system based on " natural " methods of instruction, with such successful results that his principles were adopted in many other schools throughout the country. Impressed by the need for

1 See Chapter 21.

2 Immortalised in one of Kay's " Portraits," which depicts his forcible dispersion of a Sabbath Evening School in 1799. The clergy's opposition arose from the fact that the movement's originators were sectarians, and from the suspicion that the teachers were political propagandists " notoriously disaffected to the civil constitution of the country."

efficient teacher-training, he was instrumental in founding in 1836 the Normal School for the Training of Teachers, which was the first college of its kind in Britain.[1] After the Disruption in 1843 Stow began raising funds for the establishment of a new college in connection with the Free Church, and this was erected in Cowcaddens Street, not far from the original college in Dundas Vale, in 1845, and eventually named Stow College. A third training college for teachers was opened in Glasgow in 1895, at Dowanhill, in connection with the Roman Catholic Church. The present Jordanhill Training College was opened in 1922, superseding Dundas Vale and Stow.

The churches in the early nineteenth century made valiant efforts to provide additional schools for the city's continually swelling population, and, as new parishes were created to meet the religious needs of overcrowded areas, the erection of church buildings was usually quickly followed by the opening of a school. In some cases assistance was received from government grants, but many of the new schools were entirely financed by individual congregations. The so-called Sessional schools of the Established Church, which were under the superintendence of the Kirk Sessions, were ably conducted on principles similar to those of Stow's Normal School. In addition several large charity schools, endowed by the bequests of individuals, were under church management or the joint administration of church and town council.

About 1835 it was estimated that children attending school in Glasgow represented only a fourteenth of the population, while in Scotland as a whole the proportion was an eleventh. A sixth was considered at that time to be the desirable figure.[2] Thirty years later, in 1865, it was found that less than half the children of school age in Glasgow were on school rolls, and more than a fifth of these were in schools regarded as "indifferent" or "bad." One school, no doubt of the last category, consisted of two rooms, one of which served as the teacher's kitchen, parlour and bedroom, and also as the junior classroom. "Both rooms were packed full of dirty, ragged children," reported the inspectors, "and some of them were accommodated in the kitchen bed." Although the city's schools had increased in number—particularly after the Disruption in 1843, when many Free Church congregations built new schools of their own—many were still hopelessly inadequate as regards both accommodation and staff. But by the 'sixties it appears that Glasgow, with its multiplicity of church, endowed, and private schools, was well provided compared with most industrial towns; the trouble, in the opinion of some educationists, was not so much lack of accommodation, as lack of co-operation from parents in sending their children to school. The proportion of children receiving secondary education, however, was steadily increasing. It is worth recalling that in Scotland at this period 1 out of 205 pupils was

1 Among the candidates for its Rectorship was Thomas Carlyle, but he was passed over in favour of John M'Crie, son of the biographer of Knox and Melville.

2 The proportion in Glasgow in 1954 was slightly over a sixth.

enjoying the benefit of secondary education, as compared with 1 out of 1,300 in England, while the ratio of university students to the population was six times that of England. Those were the days when Scottish higher education was the envy not only of the rest of Britain, but of Europe.

The Education (Scotland) Act of 1872 transferred both parish and burgh schools to the control of local *ad hoc* authorities known as School Boards, and created a central supervisory authority, the "Scotch" Education Department. The first School Board of Glasgow was elected in March of the following year. The Govan and other district School Boards in the neighbourhood of the city were elected about the same time. There were 39 candidates for the 15 seats on the Glasgow Board, but not much more than half the qualified electorate (which numbered 101,871) went to the poll, despite active and prolonged canvassing by both religious and secular interests. Reactionary feeling against church control was evident at the Board's first meeting, which began with a noisy argument as to whether the proceedings should be opened with prayer. Under the new Act attendance at school was compulsory between the ages of 5 and 13, the leaving age being raised to 14 in 1901.[1] Elementary education did not become free until 1889, but the fees charged were small and in cases of poverty were payable by the Parochial Boards. On taking office the Board found that the children of school age within their area numbered 87,294, whereas the city's 228 schools had accommodation for no more than 57,290. The number of pupils on the rolls, however, was only 52,644. Nearly 35,000 children of school age were therefore unaccounted for. Moreover it was decided that 41 schools with accommodation for 7,300 pupils would have to be abandoned as unsuitable. To meet the deficiency the Board acquired nine permanent day schools in various parts of the city, and opened a number of temporary premises until 30 new schools with accommodation for 22,000 could be built. Many other schools were subsequently abandoned, and by 1895 accommodation for over 66,000 children was available, concentrated in 67 board schools. At the same date other schools within the Board's district brought the total to 114, accommodating over 94,000. Thus between 1873 and 1895 the number of schools was halved and their accommodation increased by 65 per cent. The number on the roll had meanwhile risen from 52,644 to 90,269, an increase of 71 per cent.[2]

Secondary education was greatly developed after 1872. School Boards were empowered to extend the curricula of ordinary schools far beyond elementary subjects, and many "grant-aided primary schools with higher departments" or "Higher Grade Board Schools" thus made their appearance. The former burgh schools, in which classics, mathematics, modern languages and science were now taught, became

1 It remained thus until 1947, when it became 15.

2 The salaries of Glasgow's teachers at the close of the nineteenth century are of interest: in 1892 head masters received from £200 to £600 a year, second masters from £110 to £185, assistant masters from £65 to £150, and assistant mistresses from £35 to £120.

known as Secondary or " High " Schools under School Board management. Apart from these, and not under the School Boards, there were the independent " Proprietary " Secondary Schools (a notable addition to the two Academies was the Park School for girls, founded in 1880), and the " Endowed " Secondary Schools. The latter group included four schools under the management of the Roman Catholic Church—two for boys (St. Aloysius' College and St. Mungo's Academy) and two for girls (Our Lady and St. Francis, and the Convent School, Garnethill). The other endowed schools were the two Hutchesons' Grammar Schools, and Allan Glen's Institution.

In the early seventeenth century two brothers, George and Thomas Hutcheson, who were notaries and writers in the city, had bequeathed a site and funds for the founding of a hospital for the aged and for the education of poor children. Their original bequests amounted to just over £3,817, but through judicious management and additional benefactions the assets of the Trust by the end of the nineteenth century were worth nearly half a million. The original hospital, founded in 1640, was on the north side of the Trongate (at the foot of the present Hutcheson Street), and accommodated a small number of old men and boys, the latter being educated in a school on the premises. The buildings were demolished in 1802 and replaced by the structure now known as Hutchesons' Hospital in Ingram Street, two quaint seventeenth century statues of the founders being preserved on its façade. It now houses the offices of the Trust, which as well as supporting the two well-known grammar schools administers various other charities. The scope of the Trust was greatly widened in 1872, and powers were obtained to enable it to promote secondary education in the city. A boys' school was opened in Hutchesontown and a girls' school in Gorbals. The latter, together with the High School for Girls (founded in 1894 and managed by the School Board) met the demand for the higher education of girls which was becoming apparent in the late nineteenth century.

Allan Glen was a Glasgow wright, under whose will the institution bearing his name, at the corner of Cathedral Street and North Hanover Street, was established in 1853. There, in accordance with the original bequest, " a good practical education " was given gratuitously to about 50 boys, sons of tradesmen or artisans. In 1876, however, the powers of this Trust also were extended by an Act of Parliament, and the institution ceased to give free elementary education (the Education Act of 1872 having rendered the charity's original purpose less valuable). The school was transformed into a secondary and technical one, specialising in the training of boys for industrial and mercantile careers. Under the scheme of the Education Endowments Commission of 1886 Allan Glen's School became an integral, but educationally distinct, part of the Glasgow and West of Scotland Technical College, the Governors of which became its managers.[1] It quickly established a reputation as one of the leading " Science Schools " in Britain. With its modest fees,

[1] It was transferred to the Glasgow School Board, however, in 1912.

and many free scholarships and bursaries, the school was an invaluable adjunct to the city's facilities for higher and technical education. By the end of the nineteenth century the total number of pupils taking advantage of secondary education within the municipality of Glasgow was 4,738, representing rather more than 6 per 1,000 of the population.[1]

As a result of the successive extensions of the city's boundaries Glasgow's schools by 1900 were under the jurisdiction of five different School Boards. This diversity of administration was ended by the Education (Scotland) Act, 1918, which for Scotland's 947 School Boards (with over 5,000 members) substituted 38 "Education Authorities" (with less than 1,000 members). These were still to be separately elected *ad hoc* authorities, the proposal of the original Bill to place education under the direct control of the County Councils as in England having met strong opposition. An Education Authority was set up for each County and for each of several "scheduled burghs," of which Glasgow was one. Among other clauses, the 1918 Act provided for the transference to the Education Authority of Roman Catholic, Episcopal, and other voluntary schools, the institution of minimum scales of salaries for teachers, the regulation of the employment of young people in industrial and commercial undertakings, and the introduction of more extensive arrangements for the medical inspection and treatment of school children (first instituted by an Act of 1908). The Act of 1918 also provided for the raising of the school-leaving age to 15, but this was not accomplished until 1947. By the Local Government (Scotland) Act, 1929, the functions of the Glasgow Education Authority were transferred to the Corporation, which now manages the city's schools through its Education Committee.[2]

Developments in the University

The University, which had suffered a serious setback and loss of revenue with the restoration of Episcopacy in 1660, resumed its progress after the Revolution Settlement. It was in the closing decade of the seventeenth century that the finishing touches were added to the "Old College" buildings, the main portion of which had been completed soon after 1632. The eighteenth century—though marred by an initial period of stagnation and indiscipline—was the University's Golden Age, when its influence and repute derived lustre from such names as William Cullen, in medicine; Joseph Black, in chemistry; Francis Hutcheson and Adam Smith, in philosophy and logic. Lapsed chairs were restored, new professorships were established, and the roll of matriculated students greatly increased. Whereas the teaching staff at the Restoration numbered only 7, by the end of the eighteenth century it had risen to 16, while the students had grown in number

1 Between 1919 and 1939 the proportion of secondary school pupils rose from 6 per cent to 10 per cent of all school pupils in Glasgow.

2 The more recent aspects of educational development in Glasgow are treated in Chapter 16.

from about 100 to 700.[1] Within thirty years there was an addition of seven chairs, some of them revivals, others new foundations: mathematics (1691), humanity (1706), oriental languages (1709), civil law (1712), medicine (1712), church history (1716), and anatomy (1718).

The appointment of Francis Hutcheson to the Chair of Moral Philosophy in 1728 was an important landmark in the University's progress, not least because he was the first to abandon the ancient tradition of lecturing in the Latin tongue. By his adoption of English and his introduction of modern text-books he breathed new life into the dry bones of medieval scholasticism, and his example was gradually, if at first reluctantly, followed by his colleagues. A less happy development of this period was the discontinuance of college residence (by 1704 only 40 students were "living in"). The Common Table had been given up in 1694. These changes stemmed partly from the increase in the number of students and partly from the unpopularity of the petty rules and repressive discipline to which they were subjected. As students still entered the university at a very early age (13 to 15, sometimes even 11 or 12) there was of course some reason for strict supervision.

Soon after the middle of the eighteenth century systematic medical teaching was established in Glasgow, and the opening of the Royal Infirmary in 1794 led to a marked increase in the number of medical students. Between 1790 and 1814 the number rose from 54 to 352. During the first sixty years of the nineteenth century twelve new chairs were founded, most of these in the Medical Faculty. The development of both Medicine and Law, however, was hampered by the existence of the old privileged incorporations in the city, the Faculty of Physicians and Surgeons (founded 1599) and the Faculty of Procurators (incorporated 1796). The University's medical school did not become firmly established until after 1858. In that year sweeping changes were made in the University's constitution and government by the Scottish Universities Act, which terminated the separate existence and jurisdiction of the old College of Arts, so long the cause of much unseemly dispute. Hitherto the main business of the University had been conducted by two distinct bodies: the Senate, consisting of the Rector,[2] the Dean of Faculties, the Principal,[3] and all the professors; and the Faculty, or College Meeting, which comprised the Principal and the 13 professors whose chairs were founded before 1800. This dual control was ended by the Act of 1858, which transferred the whole powers of both courts to the Senate. Two new bodies were created, the University Court and

1 As early as 1702 there were over 400 students, 323 of these in Arts, but this was an exceptional period when there was a great demand for clergymen to replace those expelled from their charges at the Revolution. In 1696 the students numbered about 250.

2 Originally the active head of the University, the Rector exercised jurisdiction over all its members and was elected by the votes of both masters and students. The office, however, tended to fall into the hands of the professors, who between 1717 and 1726 succeeded in depriving the students of their vote altogether. Professors continued to take part in the elections, often with more enthusiasm than dignity, until 1858. The Rector is now elected by the matriculated students.

3 Until 1858 the Principal had to be an ordained minister of the Church.

the General Council, the powers of these being greatly enlarged by the Universities (Scotland) Act, 1889. The Court, containing many members outside the professoriate, was given the administration of the whole revenue and property of the University, the functions of the Senate being restricted to the regulation of the teaching and discipline. The General Council, including all the graduates of the University, was empowered to consider "all questions affecting the well-being and prosperity" of the University and to make representations on such matters to the Court, to which it elected four members.

Despite the high development of scientific activity in Glasgow in the nineteenth century—stimulated by the remarkable genius of William Thomson, Lord Kelvin—it was only in 1893 that a separate Faculty of Science was created, and not until thirty years later did a Faculty of Engineering, as such, make its appearance. By 1900, in the five faculties of Arts, Science, Medicine, Law, and Theology, there was a total of 31 chairs, 18 of these having been founded during the nineteenth century. The students now numbered 2,033, of whom 341 were women—female students having been admitted to the University for the first time in 1892. The extraordinary expansion that has taken place since 1900, involving the creation of 47 new chairs and an increase in the student population to over 7,500 in 1948-9, will be outlined in a subsequent chapter.[1]

TABLE XXXIV

UNIVERSITY CHAIRS ESTABLISHED PRIOR TO 1900
ARRANGED ACCORDING TO THE THEN EXISTING FACULTIES

Chairs	*Dates of foundation*	*Chairs*	*Dates of foundation*
Faculty of Medicine		*Faculty of Arts*	
Practice of Medicine	1637	Humanity	1682
Anatomy	1718	Mathematics	1691
Zoology[2]	1807	Greek	1704
Midwifery	1815	Logic & Rhetoric	1727
Surgery	1815	Moral Philosophy	1727
Chemistry	1817	Natural Philosophy	1727
Botany (as a separate chair from Anatomy)	1818	English Language & Literature	1861
Materia Medica	1831	History	1893
Forensic Medicine	1839	Political Economy	1896
Physiology[3]	1839	*Faculty of Law*	
Clinical Medicine	1874	Law	1712
Clinical Surgery	1874	Conveyancing	1861
Pathology	1893	*Faculty of Theology*	
Faculty of Science		Divinity	1640
Astronomy	1760	Hebrew & Semitic Languages[4]	1709
Civil Engineering & Mechanics	1840	Ecclesiastical History	1716
Naval Architecture	1883	Divinity & Biblical Criticism	1861

[1] See Chapter 16 (Education).
[2] "Natural History" until 1903.
[3] "Theory of Physic or Institutes of Medicine" until 1893.
[4] "Oriental Languages" until 1893.

Glasgow's Cultural Reawakening

Amid the stress and toil of industrial expansion, and the highly competitive conditions of early nineteenth century life, Glasgow's inhabitants had less time for relaxation and the cultivation of leisure interests than their forefathers. The happy and rather boisterous bonhomie of former days, when the city was a compact unit and social life revolved around its taverns, clubs and dancing assemblies, was replaced by a more serious and self-centred outlook, with business interests ever paramount. By the beginning of Victoria's reign, however, Glasgow's business men were feeling more assured of their new-found prosperity, and with returning confidence came a broadening of interests and a revival of social and cultural activity. Few of them probably were aware that in the eighteenth century their city had already achieved some momentary glory in the arts.

Robert Foulis, who, with his brother Andrew, brought Glasgow international fame as a centre of elegant book-printing,[1] was the first to encourage appreciation of the fine arts among the inhabitants. In 1753 he embarked on a remarkable plan to establish an Academy of Arts, in which instruction could be given in drawing, painting and modelling, and what would now be called industrial design. He formed a collection of several hundred paintings (not all of them, alas, genuine) and brought artists from the Continent to act as instructors. The venture was largely financed out of his own pocket, but he was assisted by some private patrons—the first of the city's long line of merchant connoisseurs—and also by the University, which gave him the use of part of its new library. Here, early in 1754, the Foulis Academy was opened —fourteen years before the founding of London's Royal Academy of Arts, the plan of which may well have owed something to Glasgow's example. The establishment functioned for over twenty years, its annual shows doing much to stimulate local interest in art, but financially it was a failure. In 1775, when Andrew Foulis died, it was closed, and after a disastrous auction of its pictures Robert also died, overwhelmed by debt and heart-broken at the collapse of his cherished scheme.

Almost a hundred years were to pass before Glasgow regained any prominence in the world of art. In the early nineteenth century, however, a number of artists were to be found in the city—mainly portrait painters, who in the days before photography could always obtain commissions in a prospering community where social prestige was being increasingly sought after. From the 1820's onwards a succession of institutes and private individuals took up the work begun by the Foulis brothers, organising exhibitions and forming collections of masterpieces by judicious purchases at home and abroad. Almost every year after 1821, when the city's first Institute of Fine Arts was established, exhibitions were held for the encouragement of local artists by such

[1] See Chapter 9 (Other Manufacturing Industries).

bodies as the Dilettanti Society (1825), the West of Scotland Academy (1840)—progenitor of the present Glasgow School of Art—and the later Institute of Fine Arts (1861), which subsequently became the Royal Glasgow Institute of Fine Arts.

It became fashionable among Glasgow's prosperous merchants and industrialists to collect paintings, and in pursuing this hobby they did not lay aside their accustomed business acumen, with the result that many shrewd acquisitions were made. More surprising is the taste and foresight that is revealed by the contents of most of their collections. The pictures which graced the walls of the great new West End mansions were not infrequently bequeathed to the city at their owners' deaths. One noted collector, John Bell, a rather crusty bachelor, went so far as to build a noble structure by the banks of the Kelvin in 1846 expressly to house his extensive art collection. This was North Park House, which some forty years later became Queen Margaret College for women students (an ironic fate for a misogynist's mansion!). In modern times it has perhaps come nearer to fulfilling its founder's original object, as a palace of the arts and disseminator of " culture " among the populace, having since 1938 been the B.B.C.'s Glasgow broadcasting centre.[1] It was Bell's intention to bequeath both the house and the collection to the community, but unfortunately he died before his plans were finalised.

The city was more fortunate in the case of Bailie Archibald McLellan's collection. In 1854 this remarkable Glasgow coachbuilder, whose enthusiasm for art outran his means, opened his " McLellan Galleries " in Sauchiehall Street where the public could view his pictures for a modest admission charge. For thirty years he had devoted his spare time to gathering a collection of works of art illustrative of the characteristics and progress of the various schools of painting in Italy, Germany, Spain, the Low Countries and France since the Renaissance. He died, insolvent, in 1854, leaving his gallery, his collection—and his debts—to the city. Many people, perhaps recalling the Foulis episode a century earlier, were sceptical of the genuineness of the collection. Some members of the Town Council, who did not have to look this gift-horse in the mouth to see that it was saddled with debt, actually described the paintings as " a heap of rubbish."

McLellan's trustees had to find £44,500 to settle with his creditors, and in face of much opposition the Council agreed to pay £15,000 for the pictures and the remainder for the building in which they were housed. Subsequently many of the pictures were disposed of very cheaply, on the advice of eminent " authorities " in the art world whose wisdom may now be doubted, but the remaining 280 items became the nucleus of Glasgow's renowned permanent collection. Now housed in the municipal Art Gallery at Kelvingrove, opened in 1902, it is acknowl-

[1] It was in Glasgow that the first official broadcasting station in Scotland was established, in March 1923. Subsequently stations were opened in Edinburgh, Aberdeen and Dundee. With the recent advent of television John Bell's old house has again become a home of the visual arts, and a new extension for permanent television studios is about to be built there.

edged to be the finest and most comprehensive municipal collection in Britain. Several of Bailie McLellan's once despised acquisitions are *each* worth to-day three or four times the sum paid for his entire collection by the Town Council a century ago. The city has had many later benefactors, notably Sir William Burrell, a former Glasgow ship-owner, who in 1944 continued a noble tradition by presenting an outstanding collection of pictures, tapestries, ceramics and other items, valued at £1½ million. More recently he has donated funds of almost half a million further, to house the collection in suitable smoke-free surroundings outwith the city, and to purchase additional works of art.

By the late nineteenth century Glasgow's art connoisseurs had become noted for their perception and the unfettered independence of their judgment and taste. Except in a few strongholds of academic tradition, such as the Glasgow Art Club, slavish obedience to the dictates and prevailing fashions of the Royal Academies was almost unknown. A reluctance to accept other people's opinions unquestioningly is in many ways a local characteristic—dissent and unorthodoxy in religion and in politics, one recalls, were never more violent than in the south-west. Perhaps, too, the very lack of a lengthy artistic tradition in Glasgow contributed to the preservation of a freshness of outlook, and a willingness to view experiment with an unprejudiced eye. It was in this congenial artistic climate of the late nineteenth century that a native school of painters flourished for the first time in Glasgow's history. Not since the days of the Foulis brothers in printing had the city exercised a comparable influence on European culture. Local patriotism, of course, has sometimes tended to exaggerate the importance of this "Glasgow school" of impressionist painters. No member of the group achieved the status of Manet, Monet or Renoir, its French inspirers, but its contribution was sufficiently distinctive to wield an influence on artistic development in not a few other countries of Europe.

Most, but not by any means all, of the Glasgow School were Scotsmen. W. Y. Macgregor, who first stimulated the movement by bringing together artists who shared his dislike of photographic realism and superfluous detail, was a Scottish landscape painter; so too was James Paterson, one of the first of the group to achieve international recognition. E. A. Hornel, however, was an Australian, and John Lavery—who was later to enjoy world fame as a portrait painter—was an Irishman. Other noted names were James Guthrie, Joseph Crawhall, George Henry, Stuart Park, Macaulay Stevenson and E. A. Walton. The group flourished for some twenty years, several of its younger members being products of Glasgow's School of Art, which in the closing decade of the century took up occupation of the striking building on Garnethill designed for it by Charles Rennie Mackintosh, the city's famous pioneer of modern functional architecture.[1]

1 Other local examples of his work are Queen's Cross Church (St. Cuthbert's), and Scotland Street School.

The late nineteenth century revival in art was accompanied by a lesser, but hardly less significant, development in literature. From the time of Tobias Smollett (1721-71), a Dunbartonshire man with whom Glasgow can claim a connection only because he studied there, no novelist of any note arose in the city until the appearance of "Hugh Foulis," Neil Munro (1864-1930). In the earlier nineteenth century the best portrayals of Glasgow life were written by outsiders, notably Scott's *Rob Roy* and Galt's *The Entail,* although the stirring events of the Radical War in 1820 inspired at least one novel by a humbler author, which enjoyed an ephemeral success. At this period Glasgow's only outstanding claimant to literary fame was Thomas Campbell (1777-1844), the "Poet of Liberty." It was in Edinburgh, however, that he wrote *The Pleasures of Hope,* which put him in the first rank of poets when scarcely twenty-two. In 1826 the students of his native city honoured him by electing him Lord Rector of the University, despite "severe opposition on the part of the professors." The honour, moreover, was twice repeated. His poetic fame has since dwindled, but it is perhaps some compensation to Glasgow to know that through him the city can claim some credit for the founding of London University, in which Campbell took an active part. Many minor poets and writers, several of them encouraged by Dr. Hedderwick's *Glasgow Citizen,* flourished in the nineteenth century, but it was the *Evening Times* that took Glasgow by storm with the publication in 1902 of J. J. Bell's humorous sketches of a Glasgow laddie, *Wee Macgreegor.* Neil Munro, of the *Evening News,* scored an equally resounding success with his tales of that immortal "puffer,"[1] the *Vital Spark,* and its skipper, Para Handy. Having produced both poets and novelists of repute, it remained to Glasgow to produce a playwright. Dr. O. H. Mavor ("James Bridie") was to fill this gap more than adequately, although his genius was perhaps less appreciated in his own country than in England.[2]

Historic Survivals

A city with its roots buried so deep in history, and with so many notable men and events associated with it, might be expected to be conscious of its debt to the past and anxious to acknowledge it by preserving some tangible memorials of its heritage. The community as a whole cannot be condemned as lacking historical consciousness, for Glasgow in recent centuries has nurtured a vigorous brood of local chroniclers and antiquarians, and to-day the activities of numerous clubs and societies testify to a lively interest in the city's past. Books, essays and other written records exist in profusion for those with the time and inclination to read them, but unhappily it is largely only on

[1] See p. 324.

[2] Recent developments in the arts in Glasgow are discussed more fully in Chapter 19 (Leisure Interests).

paper that Old Glasgow has been preserved. Apart from a few scattered, mutilated fragments, a priceless heritage of stone and lime has been squandered in the process of the city's "improvement" over the past hundred years.

The disintegration of Old Glasgow began in the 1860's, when the city fathers launched a long-overdue attack on the slums which had been created by unrestricted housing development during the preceding decades of industrial expansion.[1] In an excess of reforming zeal, however, they not only tore down the "backlands" and other notorious rabbit-warrens but also demolished many old houses of historic interest, in High Street, Gallowgate, Saltmarket and the Gorbals. The destruction begun by the Town Council was continued by the railway companies, whose lines leading to new termini in the city centre cut relentlessly through the heart of Glasgow's former merchant quarter, the Bridgegate. Here had stood the mansions of many eminent families, the city's early banks, the Merchants' Hall, and the Assembly Rooms which in the eighteenth century had echoed with the gaiety of civic balls, led off by the elegant Duchess of Douglas.

The greatest loss of all, however, was that of the Old College in High Street, deserted by the University in 1870 for more salubrious and commodious (but architecturally less worthy) premises on Gilmorehill. When even the city's supposed custodian of tradition and culture turned its back on Old Glasgow and joined the march westward, who can blame others for abandoning their heritage? Even at the time of their destruction the college buildings were recognised by informed architectural opinion as the finest group of seventeenth century buildings in Scotland, comparable with the best in Oxford and Cambridge. Nevertheless the University, with the backing of the Town Council, allowed its hallowed precincts to become a goods station and its gardens a marshalling yard.[2] The decision was not taken hurriedly, nor without protest. As early as 1845 efforts were being made to sell the buildings to a railway company—to the disgust of Lord Cockburn, a former Rector, who confided in his *Journal* the belief that the Professors were mainly influenced by the selfish desire of getting better houses. In his view the head of the smiling lion which adorned the stairway of the Old College was "more worth preserving than the heads of all the professors." It would have pleased old Henry Cockburn to know that the lion and unicorn staircase was saved from the wreckage and transferred to Gilmorehill. So too was a portion of the seventeenth century College façade, which, distorted into a new shape, became Pearce Lodge.[3]

A catalogue of Glasgow's many serious architectural losses would

1 See Chapter 14 (Housing).

2 The two quadrangles, one as a railway station and the other as a brewer's yard, survived until almost the beginning of the present century, but even in this more enlightened period nothing was done to preserve them. It is rather ironic that, in the new development plan for the city, College Goods Yard is now itself condemned.

3 The name commemorates Sir William Pearce, of the Fairfield Shipbuilding Company.

make sad reading and will not be attempted here. It is enough to mention Kelvingrove House, a much-admired Adam mansion, which the Town Council saw fit to destroy at the time of the 1911 Exhibition—to make room for a bogus representation of Falkland Palace; the fine classical church in St. Enoch Square designed by David Hamilton, which until its removal some twenty years ago effectively terminated the vista of Buchanan Street—now ruined by the anti-climax of a mock-baronial Underground station; David Dale's house in Charlotte Street, one of the few eighteenth century houses left in Glasgow, which the city's Education Committee insisted on demolishing in 1953 in order to extend the playground of an adjoining school; and the ancient Peel of Drumry, destroyed by the Corporation's Housing Committee in 1956, in the face of the strongest representations from responsible bodies and individuals throughout Scotland, and despite generous offers of funds for its preservation.

Even the few historic buildings that survive have not all escaped unblemished. Glasgow Cathedral, for example, the noblest Gothic church in Scotland, was shorn of its western tower and fifteenth century consistory house by the " improving " hands of the Council and Church authorities a century ago. It was further humbled by being overshadowed by the gigantic mass of the new Royal Infirmary buildings, begun in 1907 to replace the by then inadequate infirmary of 1792,[1] which had been beautifully designed by Robert Adam. The old buildings had been erected on the site of the former Bishop's Palace. In this connection a further notorious example of Glasgow's capacity for vandalism occurred. Despite protests and appeals from all over the world, the Lister Ward—scene of Joseph Lister's revolutionary demonstration of antiseptic surgery in the 1860's—was ruthlessly demolished in 1924. The veneration with which it was regarded elsewhere may be gathered from the fact that a single brick from the ward was given a hallowed resting place in the University of Rochester, New York, while the Wellcome Medical Museum retrieved all that it could find in the demolishers' scrap-heap in Glasgow in order to re-erect the ward as a permanent memorial to Lord Lister in London.

The oldest house that has survived in Glasgow is Provand's Lordship, dating from the late fifteenth century. Its name recalls that part of the building served as the manse of the prebendary of Barlanark, whose canonry lands were Provan. The oldest portion of the structure was built to accommodate the clergy of St. Nicholas's Hospital, an almshouse founded about 1460.[2] Provand's Lordship is now preserved as a museum. Provan Hall, on the city's eastern outskirts, was the country seat of the prebendaries of Barlanark and its older part is an interesting example of the type of house occupied by the more prosperous of the smaller sixteenth century lairds. It was extended considerably

[1] The development of Glasgow's hospitals and other health services is described in Chapter 15 (Health).

[2] Its more correct name, therefore, is the Preceptor's House of the Hospital of St. Nicholas. The office of Preceptor still exists—since 1884 it has been held *ex officio* by the Lord Provost.

in the seventeenth and eighteenth centuries, the buildings now being under the care of the National Trust for Scotland. A more historic monument is Crookston Castle, set on a hill on the city's south-western fringe, where the development of new housing estates has brought ancient and modern styles of domestic architecture into strong juxtaposition. This fourteenth century stronghold was the principal home of the Stewarts of Darnley, Earls of Lennox, and once Provosts of Glasgow.

Among the more fragmentary survivals of Old Glasgow is the Tolbooth Steeple at the Cross, dating from 1626. The city's ancient market cross was taken down in 1659 and thereafter vanished. According to " Senex," a local historian, it was buried in St. Andrew Square, but attempts to recover it met with no success. The Steeple, which is all that remains of the once greatly admired Tolbooth, contains a carillon of 16 bells erected in 1881 (replacing an older set of 1736, which delighted the citizens with a different tune every day of the week) but they are rarely played to-day. Nearby is the Tron spire, which belonged to the pre-Reformation church of St. Mary and St. Ann, and survived a spectacular fire in 1792. This conflagration—started, it is said, by the pranks of a band of youths not inappropriately known as the " Hell-Fire Club "—was responsible for the loss of valuable early records of the Glasgow Presbytery, which used the Tron Kirk Session House as its meeting-place. The Adam building which replaced the burnt church is now used as a Corporation workshop. A third disembodied steeple which commemorates the city's past is to be found adorning the fish-market. Its Dutch characteristics and its weather-vane in the form of a ship, the emblem of the Merchants, reveal it as a relic of the seventeenth century Merchants' Hall which was formerly one of the glories of the Bridgegate.

Some buildings which form interesting links with past ages and personalities are so obscured by modern growths that they are unknown to the bulk of the city's inhabitants, who daily pass them by unnoticing. An example is the old home of Sheriff Glassford Bell, who a century ago was a prominent figure in Glasgow's literary and artistic circles. Its Georgian pillared portico lies hidden behind a tall hoarding at the corner of Grant Street and St. George's Road. The house is now occupied as business premises, but its former associations are not altogether forgotten: one of its rooms is the meeting-place of Glasgow's oldest literary club, known as " Ours," which dates from 1871 and has a small and exclusive all-male membership.

For the irreparable loss of so many historic buildings Glasgow has only itself to blame. The city, unlike many other great industrial centres, suffered comparatively little damage from enemy action in the two World Wars. Indeed in the War of 1914-18 neither Zeppelins nor aeroplanes raided Glasgow, although bombs were dropped on Edinburgh. During the Second World War of 1939-45, despite an extensive balloon barrage and other anti-aircraft protection, enemy aircraft bombed the city on several occasions, but relatively few casualties occurred within the municipal limits.[1] George Square narrowly escaped destruction in a night attack in September 1940, and it was during the last air raid on Glasgow, in March 1943, that the only really serious architectural loss was suffered—the destruction of one of Alexander Thomson's churches. " Greek " Thomson, as he was popularly dubbed because of his fondness for colonnades and porticos, was the best-known of the city's Victorian architects. He is remembered for his St. Vincent Street and Caledonia Road churches, his " Egyptian Halls " which occasionally attract the eyes of the curious passer-by in Union Street, and his graceful domestic buildings such as Great Western Terrace. If our nineteenth century forefathers were blind to the historical worth of much of Old Glasgow, they at least showed—on the whole—a redeeming wisdom in their choice of architects for their New Town.[2]

1 The heavy and prolonged night raids in the spring of 1941 were mainly concentrated on Clydebank and Greenock.

2 Of the many famous architects of the period, David Hamilton, Alexander Thomson, Charles Rennie Mackintosh, and Sir J. J. Burnet were all natives of the city.

Part Two

THE CITY'S ECONOMY

Chapter 4

INDUSTRIES—PRELIMINARY SURVEY

THE INDUSTRIAL PATTERN

C. E. V. LESER

Industrial Distribution of Insured Employees

To men the world over. Glasgow means shipbuilding. What other industries occupy the energies of the city's workers is less widely known; and even among those who know the facts there has been in recent times a lack of agreement as to their significance. In particular two conflicting impressions have been held as to Glasgow's industrial pattern. According to one of them the city is remarkable for the diversity of its products and the variety of the industries within its boundaries. It has even been claimed that they are more varied than those of any other district within the Empire. On the other hand, the economy of Glasgow has been thought to be unduly dependent on shipbuilding and heavy engineering products. The city's industrial pattern is believed by many to be responsible both for the undoubtedly great severity of the depression in the 1930's, compared with other British industrial towns, and for the relative failure of its economy to expand during the inter-war period. In view of this, Glasgow was included in the Scottish Development Area set up under the Distribution of Industry Act of 1945.

Which of the impressions is the correct one? And if there be a kernel of truth in both of them, which of them contains the greater truth? In order to give an answer to these questions, we shall have to find a measure which will enable the industrial pattern of Glasgow to be compared with the industrial patterns of Scotland as a whole, of Britain as a whole and of other areas within Britain.

In theory, there are two ways of measuring the industrial pattern: by using figures for the value of net output, or the number of persons working, in various industry groups, and by expressing these figures as percentages of the total value or total number. But in practice only the second of these alternatives is available, since output data of the kind that exist for Britain or for Scotland are lacking for smaller areas such as the city of Glasgow. Statistics of the number of persons working in various industries in the city are, however, obtainable, and it is these figures, supplied through the courtesy of the Ministry of Labour, which form the basis of our analysis.

Ideally, we should like to know the distribution over the various industry groups of all persons normally working in the city of Glasgow. The actual data available fall short of the ideal data in several respects. In the first place, they refer to all insured employees, whether employed or unemployed, but exclude all self-employed persons;[1] this of course applies equally to other areas which are compared with the city and is not a serious limitation. Secondly, the figures are estimates based on the number of insurance cards exchanged in Glasgow, and in firms with different trades this exchange does not always take place at the Employment Exchange nearest to the place of work; in particular there have been some changes in the practice of railway, electricity and other government establishments during the last few years, and a reliable indication of the year-to-year changes in the industrial pattern is not obtainable. Lastly, the data now include the Hillington Employment Exchange and therefore include workers at the Hillington Industrial Estate which is just outside the city boundary; this has the effect of raising the proportion of workers in the vehicle industries, in which the manufacture of aircraft engines is included, to a higher level than a strict delimitation to the city boundaries would show, but does not make any other appreciable difference.

The Ministry of Labour return referred to is given in the Appendix, Table 33. The table shows as at mid-1955 the estimated number of insured employees in the Glasgow Area (10 City Exchanges and Hillington Exchange), distinguishing males and females; and how the total of 542,867[2] was then distributed throughout the various industries and industry groups included in the Standard Industrial Classification.

For the present discussion an abbreviated table (Table XXXV) has

TABLE XXXV

ESTIMATED NUMBER (IN THOUSANDS) OF INSURED EMPLOYEES IN THE GLASGOW AREA AT MID-1955 AND PERCENTAGE DISTRIBUTION OF TOTAL BY INDUSTRIES

	Insured Employees					
	M. (000)	F. (000)	T. (000)		T. %	
Iron and Steel	12.9	1.4	14.3	130.4	2.6	24.0
Shipbuilding & Marine Engineering	26.6	1.9	28.5		5.3	
Other Engineering	72.1	15.5	87.6		16.1	
Textiles and Clothing	8.8	28.4	37.2		6.9	
Other Manufacturing Industries	47.0	33.8	80.8		14.9	
Transport and Communication	41.6	9.4	51.0		9.4	
Commerce and Finance	58.3	78.6	136.9		25.2	
	267.3	169.0	436.3		80.4	
Remaining Industries & Services	68.8	37.8	106.6		19.6	
All Industries and Services	336.1	206.8	542.9		100.0	

1 An approximate estimate of the number of self-employed persons in Glasgow (including Hillington and Rutherglen) in 1953 was over 20,000.

2 This number plus the 314 ex-service personnel not yet allocated to any industry, makes the grand total 543,181, as shown in Appendix Table 33.

been compiled by selecting from the full returns (with some re-grouping) the numbers of insured employees in the industries dealt with in the chapters immediately following. These industries account for 436,300 out of the total of 542,900 insured employees, or 80.4%.

Comparative Industrial Patterns of Glasgow, Scotland and Gt. Britain

We may now turn to a study of the comparative industrial character of the Glasgow area, of Scotland as a whole, and of Great Britain. To begin with, a very broad indication can be given by dividing the working population into three categories: those engaged in primary production, namely agriculture, forestry, fishing, mining and quarrying; those in factory or manufacturing trades; and those in other trades providing mainly local services, like building, transport and distribution. This is done in Table XXXVI.

TABLE XXXVI

PERCENTAGE DISTRIBUTION OF INSURED EMPLOYEES BY INDUSTRIAL CATEGORIES[1] IN 1953

	Glasgow %	*Scotland* %	*Great Britain* %
Primary Production	0.7	10.2	7.8
Manufacturing	46.2	38.5	41.4
Other Trades	53.1	51.3	50.8
	100.0	100.0	100.0

It is not surprising to find primary production playing a much smaller part in the economy of Glasgow than in that of either Scotland or Britain as a whole, since agriculture and mining are not generally activities associated with a city. Indeed, it may be more of a surprise to find that the boundaries of the city are so drawn as to include a certain amount of agricultural land and a coal mine, which accounts for these trades playing any part at all in Glasgow's economic life. Again, the fact that manufacturing is relatively more important in Glasgow than in Scotland or Britain as a whole is in accordance with one's conception of the town; but the fact that less than half of Glasgow's insured population is engaged in a manufacturing trade may be less in conformity with one's preconceived ideas. As in Scotland and Britain as a whole, the trades providing chiefly local services absorb more than half of the employed population, for Glasgow is not only an industrial but also an important commercial centre.

A more detailed picture is given by Table XXXVII showing the relative importance of each of the 24 industrial groups which form the basis of the Standard Industrial Classification. The adoption of value of net output, instead of man-power, as a yardstick for the relative

[1] For this comparative study the year 1953 is chosen rather than 1955. The resulting percentages differ in no important respect from those of 1955.

contribution of each industrial sector would tend to modify the results obtained. Industries with a relatively high output per head—e.g. the chemical group, the food, drink and tobacco group, and the gas, electricity and water group of trades—would then appear more important, and industries like the clothing and building trades in which output per head is low would appear less important than they do in Table XXXVII. The comparison with Scotland or Britain would not, however, be substantially affected.

TABLE XXXVII

PROPORTION OF INSURED EMPLOYEES IN EACH INDUSTRY GROUP IN GLASGOW, SCOTLAND AND GREAT BRITAIN IN 1953

	% of all Insured Employees[1]		
Industry Groups	*Glasgow*	*Scotland*	*Great Britain*
Agriculture, forestry, fishing	.28	5.29	3.57
Mining and quarrying	.42	4.86	4.22
Treatment of non-metalliferous mining products other than coal	.76	1.17	1.61
Chemicals and allied trades	1.59	1.90	2.36
Metal manufacture	3.13	3.01	2.66
Engineering, shipbuilding and electrical goods	12.86	9.65	9.24
Vehicles	5.57	3.42	5.26
Metal goods not elsewhere specified	1.58	1.37	2.35
Precision instruments, jewellery, etc.	.72	.38	.65
Textiles	2.74	5.72	4.66
Leather, leather goods and fur	.46	.25	.35
Clothing	4.39	1.84	3.13
Food, drink and tobacco	6.60	5.08	4.07
Manufactures of wood and cork	1.79	1.43	1.42
Paper and printing	3.37	2.44	2.44
Other manufacturing industries	.61	.87	1.23
Building and contracting	6.48	7.60	6.41
Gas, electricity and water supply	1.26	1.31	1.80
Transport and communication	9.13	8.76	8.17
Distributive trades	15.60	11.52	10.62
Insurance, banking and finance	2.16	1.43	2.13
Public administration and defence	3.86	5.75	6.42
Professional services	8.57	7.96	7.35
Miscellaneous services	6.07	6.98	7.87
Total	100.00	100.00	100.00

SOURCE: Calculated from unpublished Ministry of Labour Statistics, *Digest of Scottish Statistics* and *Ministry of Labour Gazette.*

Of the manufacturing industries, the metal and engineering trades —the five groups beginning with "Metal manufacture" and ending with "Precision instruments, jewellery etc."—are of particular importance; in Glasgow, as in Scotland or Britain as a whole, they account for about one-half of the total factory employment. It is seen that each of these five groups has a greater share in the economy of Glasgow than in that of Scotland, and each group except "Metal goods not elsewhere specified"—including bolts and nuts, wire, hollow-ware, etc. —a greater share in Glasgow than in Britain as a whole. But there

[1] Excluding ex-service personnel not classified by industry.

are many other industry groups to which the same applies, and in particular Glasgow is seen to be an important centre of the clothing trade and of food, drink and tobacco production as well as of the metal and engineering trades. The only manufacturing groups in which Glasgow is relatively deficient—taking either Scotland or Britain as standard—are " Treatment of non-metalliferous mining products other than coal "—a group including the production of china, glass, bricks and other building materials—" Chemicals and allied trades," " Textiles " and " Other manufacturing industries " which include the production of rubber goods, linoleum etc. The deficiency is particularly marked in the textile field, where Glasgow's most important contribution is carpet manufacture, though there is also a small woollen industry, some hosiery manufacture etc., in the city.

Apart from " agriculture, forestry, fishing " and " mining and quarrying " the only non-manufacturing industrial group which is much under-represented in Glasgow is " Public administration and defence," partly owing to the location elsewhere of the headquarters of central government and defence, and partly owing to economies of scale with regard to local government which are possible in a large city. A somewhat surprising feature is also the comparatively low proportion of workers in the building and contracting trades which hardly exceeds the British and falls well below the Scottish average.

On the other hand, the distributive trades are very strongly represented in Glasgow. A more detailed analysis shows that this feature is specially marked in the field of wholesale distribution. For in 1953, 4.94% of all insured employees in Glasgow were working in purely wholesale trades, compared with 2.07% in Scotland and 2.12% in Britain. For the retail trade, the corresponding proportions are 9.18% in Glasgow, 8.39% in Scotland and 7.33% in Britain; in mixed categories 1.48% in Glasgow as against 1.06% in Scotland and 1.17% in Britain. Although the wholesale trades do not, of course, absorb as much labour as the retail trades, the difference is remarkably small in Glasgow, and it is the centralisation of wholesale distribution in the city which is primarily responsible for the high proportion of its labour force engaged in distribution.

But the differences which Glasgow's industrial pattern shows from the Scottish or British pattern are perhaps less remarkable than the general similarity which it bears to these national patterns which, incidentally, are also very much alike. This becomes clear when Glasgow is contrasted with other British cities, say with Birmingham, which has practically the same size of population but a very different industrial set-up, being very largely dependent upon the motor car industry and allied metal and engineering trades and being far less a commercial than an industrial centre.

From figures published in the City of Birmingham's *Abstract of Statistics*, Number 2, it can be calculated that the metal and engineering trades there accounted for 48.3% of all employment in 1951, but the textile, leather and clothing trades together for only 2.3%. The proportions applicable to Glasgow in the same year were 23.3% for metal and engineering, and 7.9% for textile, leather and clothing; these are far nearer to the British averages than are the Birmingham figures. In order to obtain more conclusive evidence, the extent to which the industrial pattern of a city or other area differs from that of the country as a whole—or, more strictly speaking, from that of the rest of the country—may be summarised in a single figure by means of the coefficient of specialisation, which has been described in more detail elsewhere.[1] On the basis of 24 industry groups, the coefficient of specialisation within Great Britain in 1951 works out as 17.1% for Glasgow but as 31.3% for Birmingham. In this sense it certainly seems appropriate to speak of Glasgow's industrial pattern as being remarkably diversified.

The industrial groups shown in Table XXXVII do not tell the whole story, as there may well be important differences in the extent to which individual industries are represented, differences which are concealed in the group averages. For example, shipbuilding and marine engineering employed in 1953 5.50% of Glasgow's insured employee population, compared with 1.41% in Britain as a whole; for the electrical engineering trades on the other hand, the proportion in the city was only 0.81% as against 2.86% in Britain. The concentration of "shipbuilding, engineering and electrical goods" in Glasgow therefore does not extend to all the trades in this group. Similarly with regard to the vehicle group. The locomotive industry, including railway workshops, employed in 1953 2.06% of the labour force in Glasgow against 0.40% in Great Britain; the manufacture of motor vehicles 0.72% in Glasgow and 1.42% in Britain.

There is thus some justification for the view that Glasgow, in the same way as the whole of Scotland, specialises in the older, heavier metal industries at the expense of the newer, lighter engineering trades. At the same time, this argument should not be carried too far. Glasgow is rich in a variety of engineering industries other than shipbuilding and marine engineering, as well as in consumer goods industries and service trades of many kinds.

Perhaps we come nearer to the truth in considering Glasgow not in isolation but in connection with its economic "hinterland," as it were, viz. the remainder of the Clyde Valley. This area, consisting of Lanarkshire (excluding Glasgow), Renfrewshire, Dunbartonshire and Northern Ayrshire, is in fact far more dependent on basic heavy industries than is Glasgow City. This can best be shown by working out sets of location factors, as defined by Professor P. Sargent Florence,[2] which has been done by dividing the percentages of insured employees in each industry group for Glasgow as well as for the rest of the Clyde Valley by the corresponding percentages for Britain as a whole. The resulting figures are presented in Table XXXVIII.

[1] Cf. C. E. V. Leser, *Some Aspects of the Industrial Structure of Scotland* (1951), pp. 9-11.

[2] *The Statistical Method in Economics and Political Science* (1929), pp. 327-8.

TABLE XXXVIII

LOCATION FACTOR OF EACH INDUSTRY GROUP IN GLASGOW AND IN THE REST OF THE CLYDE VALLEY, 1951

Industry Group	*Location Factor* *Glasgow*	*Rest of Clyde Valley*
Agriculture, forestry, fishing	.06	.56
Mining and quarrying	.16	1.16
Treatment of non-metalliferous mining products other than coal	.51	1.19
Chemical and allied trades	.78	1.56
Metal manufacture	1.14	2.54
Engineering, shipbuilding and electrical goods	1.38	2.21
Vehicles	1.10	.46
Metal goods not elsewhere specified	.70	.98
Precision instruments, jewellery, etc.	1.04	.70
Textiles	.61	1.94
Leather, leather goods and fur	1.26	.74
Clothing	1.35	.48
Food, drink and tobacco	1.56	.80
Manufacture of wood and cork	1.30	.66
Paper and printing	1.22	.42
Other manufacturing industries	.43	.54
Building and contracting	1.04	1.07
Gas, electricity and water supply	1.01	.61
Transport and communications	1.23	.77
Distributive trades	1.51	.79
Insurance, banking and finance	.91	.29
Public administration and defence	.56	.74
Professional services	1.13	.82
Miscellaneous services	.72	.63

SOURCE: Calculated from unpublished Ministry of Labour statistics and *Ministry of Labour Gazette.*

In Table XXXVIII a location factor of over 1 indicates that the industry group is well represented in the area, a factor of less than 1 that the industry group is under-represented. The tabulation shows that 9 out of 14 manufacturing groups and 5 out of 10 non-manufacturing groups are well represented in Glasgow; whilst in the rest of the Clyde Valley only 5 manufacturing and 2 other groups are well represented, but 2 of them very strongly, i.e. they have a location factor of over 2. Moreover, 5 out of the 7 industry groups which have a location factor of over 1 in the Clyde Valley outside Glasgow contain, in the main, producers' goods industries which are more sensitive to the trade cycle than consumer goods industries. The only other industry groups that are well represented there are building and textiles; and most of the textile industries, though producing consumer goods, are sensitive to a slump, owing to severe competition from abroad in home and export markets and to other factors.

While Glasgow by itself does not, therefore, appear to be particularly vulnerable, economically speaking, most of the surrounding area with which it forms an economic unit is indeed very vulnerable. A more detailed analysis carried out for 1947 showed that West Dunbarton, Renfrewshire and Lanarkshire (excluding Glasgow) are each far more vulnerable than Glasgow, and only Northern Ayrshire is in a similar position to the city, which is little above the British average for vulnerability.[1]

But the city's industries have strong links with the industries in the surrounding area; in particular, the fate of its consumer goods industries and service trades is bound up with the level of employment in the basic industries in the Clyde Valley outside the city. In the 1930's, these industries were severely affected by the depression and this was aggravated by a long-term decline in some of the older industries which took place at the same time as an expansion of other trades. This state of affairs had its repercussions on the city which became the centre of a depressed area, in spite of its great variety of industries. Such then appears to be the explanation of the paradox stated at the beginning of this chapter.

Recent Changes in the Industrial Pattern

The industrial depression of the 1930's with its severe unemployment was replaced dramatically, here as elsewhere, by conditions of full employment—the result of deliberate policy. The change had its effects on the industrial pattern of the city and it is worth while to look back to see what changes did indeed take place in that pattern. The statistics available are not strictly comparable owing to changes in industrial classification and the extension of the insurance scheme in 1948. But an attempt has been made to adjust the 1938 figures so as to bring them on to a comparable basis, and by using these estimates Table XXXIX has been constructed, which shows the changes that have taken place for some broad industrial groups.

TABLE XXXIX

THE INDUSTRIAL PATTERN OF GLASGOW, 1938 AND 1953

	% of Insured Employees 1938	1953
Metal and engineering trades	18.6	23.9
Textile, leather and clothing trades	7.8	7.6
Other manufacturing trades	13.9	14.7
All manufacturing	40.3	46.2
Other industrial production	8.7	8.2
All industrial production	49.0	54.4
Transport and distribution	31.9	24.7
Other industries and services	19.1	20.9
Total	100.0	100.0

SOURCE: Calculated from unpublished Ministry of Labour statistics; 1938 partly estimated.

1 Cf. *Some Aspects of the Industrial Structure of Scotland*, p. 43.

The outstanding change has been the increasing importance of the metal industries and of manufacturing in general at the expense of some of the commercial trades. This development is not peculiar to Glasgow but is part of the nation-wide changes in industrial pattern that have taken place during and after the Second World War. Recent developments have brought about the establishment of newer metal and metal-using industries in the city, but it is the revived demand from the traditional industries that has been responsible for the major part of this shift in emphasis.

FORMATIVE INFLUENCES

JOHN LOUDON, PAUL HANIKA AND G. D. COSTAIN

Location Factors

It is now necessary to trace some of the important factors which have contributed to the emergence of the industrial pattern which has just been examined. In the later chapters of this volume the special influences affecting the growth of each main industry contributing to the general pattern will be considered. The purpose of the present section is two-fold: to remind the reader of the broad features in Glasgow's industrial and commercial history on the basis of which the main industries have grown, and to bring out the types of influence which have in fact led firms in different industries to establish themselves in Glasgow.

Before the Union of 1707 Glasgow's trade was very limited. At the beginning of the eighteenth century America became the goal of the city's merchants, and the Act of Union, with the removal of the vexatious Navigation Laws, led the way for commercial trading in Glasgow's favour. The geographical position of the city was now an advantage: for example, it was reckoned that Glasgow was fourteen to twenty days nearer Virginia than was London. Thus for a time Glasgow flourished on maritime adventure and became the main emporium for tobacco. In addition to bringing great wealth, this trading created a commercial structure of banking and warehousing experience, emphasised the importance of deepening the River Clyde and thus greatly assisted the later establishing of Glasgow as a manufacturing centre. Trade with Virginia, Carolina and Maryland created a demand for linen in exchange for tobacco and the textile industry in Glasgow showed signs of great promise. The American War of Independence in 1776 however led to the collapse of the tobacco trade, and Glasgow business men had to look for some other outlet for investment.

This they found in cotton manufacture. Invention in textile machinery had been proceeding rapidly in England. The damp, temperate climate of Glasgow made it most suitable for the production of cotton goods, and Watt's invention of the steam engine provided a new source of power. By the beginning of the nineteenth century, there were 107 cotton mills in Glasgow using steam-driven machinery. Glasgow's industry however suffered severely from the outbreak in 1861 of the American Civil War, as a result of which the main source of raw cotton was cut off, and it was, no doubt, with the previous example in mind of how successful businesses could be destroyed when raw material supplies were outwith local control, that Glasgow business men looked for new outlets in the development of basic materials within their own area.

The industrial development of these basic materials, such as coal, fireclay, limestone and ironstone which were found in the Central Lowlands of Scotland, had begun towards the end of the eighteenth century. Ironworks were started in Glasgow and Lanarkshire, and coal pits were opened up all over Central Scotland to meet the new demands for coal. The well-known Glasgow iron works—"Dixon's Blazes," Clyde, Parkhead and Blochairn—were all in production by the mid-nineteenth century. Thus Glasgow's industry was changing from textiles to metal-working on the basis of wrought iron and cast iron.

Technical developments in the process of steel-making took place and by the year 1880 methods of producing steel from phosphoric ores had been discovered and thus local ore supplies could be used in steel-making. Consequently, Parkhead and Blochairn Works converted their plant to the making of steel, David Colville established his works at Motherwell and the Steel Company of Scotland started at Hallside.

The application of iron to ship-construction had begun about 1840. Steel succeeded iron: by 1879 hull construction of steel accounted for 10% of the Clyde's output, and by 1890, well over 90% of ships' hulls on the Clyde were constructed with steel. By the late nineteenth century, therefore, the use of iron and steel had given Glasgow an advantage as a shipbuilding area, for the hinterland of the river was an enormous industrial district, producing large quantities of metal and coal.

In order to get first-hand and specific information as to the considerations which weighed with firms in deciding to establish themselves in Glasgow, a special enquiry was made of some 1,300 manufacturing firms in the city. The replies (received from about 400 of the firms) disclosed the operation of a variety of factors, the most widely operative of which are discussed in the following pages.

The factor most frequently mentioned as decisive was the local residence of principals. Among the older firms this factor was predominant; and among the smaller of the younger firms it has remained significant. On the whole, however, this factor weighs less heavily to-day than it did in the past. For this change, improvements in transport and communications are no doubt to some extent responsible; but other developments count. A growing number of Glasgow's industrial establishments to-day are branches of concerns whose headquarters lie outside Scotland—in England, or in America, Canada, Italy and elsewhere overseas. Nevertheless, of the 400 firms about 300 were in 1955 still completely independent concerns under local control. Of the remainder 50% belonged to purely Scottish-controlled groups, 65% were under British control other than Scottish, and the remainder under foreign control, mainly American.[1]

Proximity to the source of supply of their raw materials was for many firms in different industries an important contributing factor in their choice of location. It has already been seen how important in the growth of Glasgow's main industries was the availability of coal, ironstone and other basic materials in the Central Lowlands of Scotland. But the blackband iron deposits in Lanarkshire became exhausted and new sources had to be found. Now the supply is imported from North and West Africa, Sweden, Newfoundland and Spain. Steelmakers are finding that scrap steel is neither too plentiful nor cheap enough to buy from foreign countries with the result that there is an increased demand for pig-iron in the area.

Coal as a basic material still plays an important part in Glasgow's industrial success. It is required for the coke-ovens at the various iron-works and is still extracted from Lanarkshire, but supplies have also to be brought from Ayrshire, Fife and Northern England. Steelmaking also requires large tonnages of coal. But the local industry was seriously weakened by the upheaval of the First World War (1914-18), the prolonged economic depression of the 'twenties and 'thirties, and the difficulties of the Second World War (1939-45). Advanced planning and adequate replacement of the industry's working assets were neglected. After 1940 the demand for coal increased whilst at the same time the ability to produce it decreased. On 1 January 1947 the National Coal Board took over all the collieries previously managed and operated by private concerns and plans have now been put into operation which will involve an expenditure of £100 million for new sinkings and for the reconstruction and development of existing collieries. The aim is not only to prevent further shrinkage in total output but to increase Scottish output to 30 million tons per annum by 1965. Research is proceeding in many directions together with explorations and borings, in the hope of ensuring that Glasgow will remain favourably situated with regard to coal production.

A number of the firms gave the availability of suitable labour as a main factor which determined their choice of Glasgow for the location of their business. What constitutes " suitable " labour—male or female, skilled or unskilled—differs in different industries and has in fact undergone considerable change in the course of the last century and a half of industrial development. At the beginning of the nineteenth century it was considered that with the increasing use of the power-

[1] Among the combine firms covered by this sample investigation, a considerable degree of independence exists, 52% claiming to have complete local autonomy in matters of sales and production policy, and a further 17% claiming partial autonomy.

driven machine human labour and in particular skilled labour would become less important. On the contrary, mechanisation made more and more demands on skilled labour and technicians. Glasgow thus came to possess a large skilled labour force; a force which, because of the nature of the city's main industries, is predominantly male. The position in 1955 is illustrated by the returns, which showed that 89,000 operatives were distributed as in Table XL.

TABLE XL

ANALYSIS OF OPERATIVES IN 400 MANUFACTURING FIRMS[1] IN GLASGOW, 1955

	Males	*Females*	*Total*
Skilled (time-served)	24,726	4.411	29,137
Skilled (others)	5,033	3,730	8,763
Semi-skilled	13,913	5,350	19,263
Unskilled	15,043	7,168	22,211
Apprentices	6,790	103	6,893
Learners	937	1,919	2,856
Total	66,442	22,681	89,123

As a result of the preponderance of heavy industry in the past, there has been an out-of-balance demand on the labour pool, leaving a high percentage of female labour not industrially employed. The present tendency in the manufacturing industries to employ more and more unskilled and semi-skilled female labour, so releasing the skilled male labour demanded by the new technological advances, will thus suit Glasgow. Already in many areas throughout the country the introduction of modern automatic processes is being hampered by the shortage of skilled craftsmen, technicians and technologists.

As regards education and training for industry Glasgow is well catered for by secondary schools, technical schools, commercial and technical colleges and the University. Many thousands attend these centres for either full-time study, day-release courses or part-time evening courses. Many extensions are already under way at these educational centres and still more are in the planning stages.

At the same time the number of University graduates employed in manufacturing industries in Glasgow is not large. The 395 firms which gave information on this point, employing over 89,000 operatives, had a total of 469 graduates on their staffs. Of these 85 were graduates in Arts, 125 in Science, 251 in Engineering, 7 in Law and 1 in Medicine. Their distribution by industrial groups is shown in Table XLI.

The presence of a source of power supply has been mentioned as a factor determining their location in Glasgow by firms in certain types of industry. Glasgow's easy access to plentiful coal supplies, and its good water supply, have always favoured industries in which steam-raising plant is used. Since the introduction of steam power in industry, many prominent engineering concerns have been engaged in the manu-

[1] Excluding Aircraft Manufacturers, omitted for Security reasons.

TABLE XLI

ANALYSIS OF GRADUATES EMPLOYED BY 395 MANUFACTURING FIRMS IN GLASGOW, 1955

Industrial Group	Firms	Operatives	Graduates					
			Total	*Arts*	*Science*	*Engineering*	*Law*	*Medicine*
Shipb'd'g & Marine Eng'ing	13	21,073	18	1	8	8	1	—
Vehicles[1]	7	6,089	27	5	4	18	—	—
Other Engineering and Metals	135	25,244	238	34	54	146	4	—
Food, Drink, Tobacco	48	10,654	33	11	16	5	1	—
Paper and Printing	28	5,548	29	19	5	4	—	1
Chemicals and allied trades	17	730	23	2	20	1	—	—
Textiles and Clothing	82	13,797	22	5	7	9	1	—
Others	65	5,963	29	6	10	13	—	—
Total in sample	395	89,098	419	83	124	204	7	1

facture of boilers, condensers and all forms of heat exchangers; and now Glasgow not only satisfies local needs for this equipment but exports considerable quantities. Oil-firing equipment is both manufactured and used. Supplies of oil are available from the huge storage tanks on the Clyde estuary, and Glasgow consumers have the benefit of reduced rates as a result of the price-zoning arrangement of the oil companies, whereby charges vary according to distance from the distributing depots.

Although electric power was used in 1879 to illuminate Queen Street and St. Enoch stations, it was not until the year 1890 that the first electric street lamps were in use and a public supply became available. The Corporation of Glasgow and the Clyde Valley Electrical Power Company tackled the generation and supply of electric power with great vigour right from the early days. Even prior to the establishment of the Grid System in 1926 as the result of the Electricity (Supply) Act, electric power was reliable and economic in Glasgow. Since 1947, Glasgow has obtained its power from the South of Scotland Electricity Board. Generating supply is ahead of an ever-increasing demand; a new station was opened at Braehead in 1951 and the Loch Sloy Hydro-Electric Scheme now supplements the supply at peak loadings.[2]

Many firms mention proximity to their markets as a location factor. The Glasgow area itself affords a large market for the city's basic services and for many of its manufactures. Certain engineering firms and furnishing traders found a ready-made local market in the ship-

1 Excluding Aircraft Manufacturers, omitted for Security reasons.

2 The new power station at Braehead is operating at a thermal efficiency of 28.5% as a result of extensive engineering research. As an indication of the size of these stations it may be recorded that a station with 360,000 kilowatt capacity may burn 3,500 tons of coal a day.

building industry. The main industries, however, have their markets spread throughout the United Kingdom, the Commonwealth, the Colonies, and the continents of Europe, America and Asia; they are thus, and have been over the past hundred years, dependent on good transport facilities.[1] The development of these for the main industries' bulk consignments has enabled Glasgow's other interests to avail themselves of already established trade-routes and in the last ten years has greatly assisted these smaller industries to explore export markets.

Movement of large quantities of goods and the need for speed encouraged enterprise by city traders from the sixteenth century onwards. Later local merchants and the Town Council spent large sums of money on the deepening of the River Clyde as far as the Broomielaw. The " making of the Clyde " became so important that the management of river affairs passed in 1840 from the Town Council to a separate board, known as the Clyde Navigation Trust. The Trustees first directed their activities to deepening the river to keep ahead of the advances of steamships and then provided tidal dock accommodation, from the small Kingston Dock of 1867 to the King George V Dock opened in 1929/31. In addition to providing tidal basins, they proceeded with " quay fronting " the river.

Ship-repairing has always been of major importance, and the Trustees kept in step with these developments by providing graving docks at Govan. The first graving dock was opened in 1875, the second in 1886 and by 1900 the third graving dock, 280 feet in length, was laid down. Cross-river ferries, vehicular and passenger, were also put into service. Much specialised equipment for handling materials has been installed in recent times—for example, the Meadowside Granary which in 1955 handled a total of 421,000 tons of grain.

In 1955 the Trustees embarked on large-scale alterations at the General Terminus quay to permit the simultaneous unloading of two of the largest vessels at present engaged in the ore-carrying trade. This scheme, run in conjunction with British Railways, will service the Colvilles organisation with large-scale ore imports for their iron and steel development programme.

By the mid-nineteenth century the city had seen almost a hundred years of continuous progress in transport, first in the period of " canals and metalled roads " and later in what might be regarded as the " railway and steamship " period. By 1886 there were 48 railway companies in Scotland. Facilities within the city were fully developed for freight and passenger traffic and gradually amalgamation of companies took place, so that by 1921 only two companies operated rail traffic within Glasgow, namely the London and North Eastern Railway (L.N.E.R.) and the London Midland and Scottish Railway (L.M.S.). Finally, by the Transport Act of 1947, the railways were nationalised and " British Railways " was formed.

To-day there is an excellent passenger service from Glasgow to the principal towns of Great Britain; for example there are:

[1] See Chapter 10 (Transport and Communication).

15 services from Glasgow to London daily
36 „ „ „ „ Edinburgh daily
6 „ „ „ „ Manchester daily
5 „ „ „ „ Liverpool daily.

Express freight services have been continually increased during recent years and there are now more than twice as many as were available in 1938. Freight services are operated to Aberdeen, Edinburgh, Leeds, London and Newcastle to arrive at their destination the morning after despatch; while to Birmingham, Bristol and Hull they will bring the goods to their destination on the second morning after despatch. If so requested, freight services will provide container facilities, which afford the advantages of door to door conveyance, minimum use of packing materials and avoidance of intermediate handling of commodities. Railway container service is also operated for shipment to Northern Ireland, Eire, Channel Islands and the Continent of Europe.

With the development of the petrol-driven and later the diesel-driven truck, road transport facilities have in the past thirty years continued to increase daily in the Glasgow area. Road haulage contractors built up a huge network of available routes and several local contractors specialise in transporters with multi-bogey cradles for the transport of heavy machines, structures, and other products weighing upwards of 100 tons.

Several main trunk roads have been developed, such as Glasgow to Edinburgh (put down by 1930) and later Glasgow to Kilmarnock, and Glasgow to Dumbarton. Developments are now under way on the Glasgow to Stirling route. The Glasgow Corporation have had specialist advice on new arrangements within the city itself and have this year (1956) been granted approval for a tunnel roadway under the Clyde at Whiteinch. Passenger traffic within the city in the nineteenth century proceeded from the coach to the horse-drawn tramcars of 1871. Steam-driven tramcars followed and by 1894 the electrically driven tram was in operation. Since 1929, the petrol-driven and later the diesel-driven bus has been operated within the city. Now many tramcar routes are being scrapped in favour of the trolley-bus.

The city's airport is at Renfrew. It was opened during the First World War to fly out military aircraft manufactured in Glasgow. From 1919 to 1924, many small private air transport firms failed to make economic returns but by 1933 regular airlines were established. In those days it was considered that the fixed wing type of aircraft could compete economically only on routes across water—hence the early services to islands on the west coast and to Orkney and Shetland. In 1934 Railway Air Services provided a link between Glasgow, Birmingham and London. In 1937 the Midland and Scottish Air Ferries and Northern Scottish Airways amalgamated to form Scottish Airways, and in 1946 British European Airways was formed by Act of Parliament. The following figures show the growth of freight handled at Renfrew:

Cargo handled in 1949— 356 short tons
1954— 969 short tons
1955—1564 short tons

Thus, with the development of main scheduled trunk services to principal towns in the United Kingdom plus inter-line working with Eire, Iceland, Isle of Man, Norway, France, Italy, America and Canada (via Prestwick), Renfrew airport is firmly established and expanding.

Among firms established in Glasgow within the past 20 years the availability of suitable sites for factory buildings is frequently mentioned as a powerful factor in attracting them to the area. This new attraction has come through the operations of Scottish Industrial Estates, Ltd. One element in the policy of full employment which came to have significance for Glasgow's industrial pattern was the designation, under the Special Areas (Development and Improvement) Act of 1934, of certain areas of the country as depressed areas. Although the City of Glasgow was not included in the Schedule of this Act, the neighbouring counties of Lanark, Dunbarton and Renfrew were; and as already mentioned, the omission of Glasgow was made good under the Distribution of Industry Act of 1945 when Glasgow was included in the Scottish Development Area. In the meantime, in 1936, a Scottish Economic Committee, under the Chairmanship of Lord Bilsland, was established and began a period of planned development. In 1937 one of the most important and tangible results of its activities was the establishment of the first industrial estate in Scotland, located at Hillington, Glasgow. This has had far-reaching results not only in stimulating recent industrial prosperity in Glasgow but in safeguarding the city's prosperity in the future.

The location and siting of plants are no longer as haphazard to-day as in previous years. In addition to having to consider business factors, industrial firms must now consult and adhere to the 1945 Distribution of Industry Act and the various Town and Country Planning Acts. The organisation which Scottish Industrial Estates Ltd. has built up since 1937, with intimate and up-to-date information on facts and procedures, has proved of the greatest assistance in such matters. The S.I.E. Company, subject to Board of Trade approval, is prepared to provide a standard factory for occupation on lease with low rental, of modern construction and with the possibility of expansion: thus with the minimum outlay a business can be established. To secure approval, schemes must provide employment for labour available in the district. S.I.E. accepts responsibility and provides for the architectural and structural design features. Site preparation, building construction, electricity, water, gas and heating services are all arranged by S.I.E., leaving the business man free from all the worries as well as the capital expenditure involved. On these estates the S.I.E. Catering Department also provides canteen facilities for operatives, staff and management. As a special feature, S.I.E. can provide further amenities and accept responsibility for layout of estate gardens with shrubs, trees and flowers.

An application from an existing Glasgow firm for a factory on an Industrial Estate will be considered only if it involves a definite extension of an existing enterprise which would not involve the closing of an existing production unit; or if the factory in present use has been condemned by the Local Authorities as unsuitable for industrial use; or if the applicant is occupying a factory, lease of which is about to expire and it can be proved that no fresh lease will be granted.

By October 1955, S.I.E.'s activities in Scotland had housed 357 firms, giving a total factory space of 15¾ million square feet, and other firms were on the waiting lists. Of this total, developments in Glasgow were as in Table XLII.

TABLE XLII

INDUSTRIAL ESTATES IN THE GLASGOW AREA

Estate	*Factory and Administrative Space Built (sq. feet)*	*Space available for development (sq. feet)*
Hillington	4,220,968	39,897
North Cardonald (ext. to Hillington)	336,054	163,964
Queenslie	702,508	581,224
Thornliebank	222,207	35,059
Carntyne	190,306	—
Craigton	370,367	150,000

SOURCE: Scottish Industrial Estates Ltd.

Already Glasgow has benefited from this remarkable and adventurous development. The industrial activities of the area have been greatly diversified by many small and medium-sized concerns. Among the larger concerns is Rolls-Royce, which has once again brought Glasgow back into the aircraft industry, an industry which showed such signs of progress during the First World War.

LABOUR RESOURCES

"Full employment" has led to a wider recognition of the need to make the most effective use of available labour resources. During the early 'fifties firms tended to hold on to labour—especially skilled men—in periods of decreased demand for their product, for fear of not being able to secure appropriate skills for re-engagement later. This applied especially to shipbuilding and some forms of engineering where infrequent but individually sizeable contracts provide work for large numbers for prolonged periods. More recently labour has been released, when not strictly needed, to minimise production costs so that labour resources have been used more advantageously.

The "short-week" procedure—spreading under-employment which the firm expects to be of limited duration—is not generally experienced in Glasgow except when fiscal measures seriously reduce the sale of consumer goods (Templeton's carpet factories provided an example in April 1956). When redundant employees can no longer be discarded in the certain knowledge that they will remain available for re-engagement, companies tend to base their operations more and more on "sales forecasting" and "production budgets" derived from such forecasts, in order to maintain employment at a steady level.

The need to husband labour resources has led to closer study of labour turnover and its relative cost. Differences in labour turnover rates between individual firms vary widely and even averages would only serve to disguise the extremes which vary from 5% or less for skilled men to nearly 50% for young girls and women. The high figure for females is explained by the fact that women part-time workers leave when family circumstances of one kind or another make it possible or necessary for them to do so, and that girls may terminate their employment on marriage or subsequent pregnancy. The position in Glasgow is perhaps more stable than in the English Midlands where pressure of demand encourages employers to outbid other firms, not only by the wages offered but also by inducements of various kinds such as "plenty of overtime" and "excellent canteen facilities." Generally small employers succeed in holding labour turnover to a smaller figure than larger concerns, but there are some where labour turnover is exceptionally high because physical working conditions fall below acceptable standards or wages are at the legal minimum.

Shortages of labour have caused many firms to employ foreign workers, especially Poles who remained in Scotland after the disbanding of the Polish Military Forces which had been principally stationed in Scotland during the Second World War and immediately afterwards. Others express their willingness to employ foreigners. Foreign labour is not confined to unskilled tasks—suitably qualified individuals have progressed to skilled work and technicians' posts, such as cost accounting and production planning and control.

The questionnaires circulated among local manufacturing firms brought out the existence of acute shortages in certain classes of skilled workers, especially toolmakers, draughtsmen and technologists. In 1952 the Scottish Council (Development and Industry) investigated the position of toolmaking (which was known to hold back production) and found 250 men employed in "jobbing" toolmaking firms in Scotland when 750 would have been appropriate. Such firms (some of them in Glasgow) were, as a result, assisted to expand, with encouraging success to judge from reports of the increasing ease with which manufacturing firms could get their tooling work done through subcontracting it to such firms. In respect of technologists the same body found that a demand for 1,100 annually had to find what satisfaction it could from a supply of 500, not all of whom would be available for industry in any event.

For skilled labour and draughtsmen most firms rely, necessarily under the conditions outlined, on their own efforts for replacements and expansion by instituting apprenticeship schemes, if their size warrants such a course, or on co-operation with technical colleges. A small supply flows from the Government Training Centre in Hillington which provides 148 places and offers facilities for the training of watch and clock repairers, motor repairers, machine operators, agricultural fitters and blacksmiths, hairdressers, draughtsmen and radio/television mechanics.

To sum up, labour resources in Glasgow are strained, though not by any means equally in all grades. Shortage of skilled workers is being tackled by training, a process made easier by the adoption of modern methods of "job breakdown" with the goodwill and co-operation of certain unions. This applies in particular to the "general" unions who are trying to assist in developing the skills at the command of their members as a solid claim to advancement, instead of merely demanding wage increases.

Management

The need for training in management is also more widely recognised. An analysis of a representative sample of Glasgow firms shows that of a group of small independent firms one in seven provided planned training for executive and supervisory management. Of a group of larger firms, mainly members of combines, one in three provided such training. More than half of the whole group depended entirely on their own resources for such training, while about one third made use of both internal and external resources.

The post-war years have seen a considerable development in Glasgow in the field of management studies. The Glasgow School of Management Studies is organised under the joint control of the governing bodies of the Royal College of Science and Technology and the Scottish College of Commerce. It combines the resources of the Departments of Industrial Administration and Management Studies of these Institutions and offers a wide range of full-time and evening courses in general and specialist aspects of management. A residential centre for management studies is also established at Chesters, Bearsden, presented to the Royal College of Science and Technology by Mr. Alexander Turnbull, Vice-Chairman of Governors. Management studies in the College were started in a small way in 1928 in the Department of Civil and Mechanical Engineering. In 1947 a separate Department of Industrial Administration was formed, of which this residential centre is the latest development.

A request to the University from leading industrialists in Glasgow for teaching of management to senior executives was met by the establishment, in 1952 at the University, of a three-year evening course of studies in economics, accountancy, industrial relations, and psychology. The teaching is upon principles rather than upon techniques, and is thus complementary to the teaching of the Glasgow School of Management Studies. The lectures, 40 per annum, are delivered by members of the University staff and by experienced industrialists and business men. The course is limited to 35 members each year. Those who have completed the full course become members of the University Management Club which holds meetings from time to time to hear leading speakers on the subject of management. It is significant of Glasgow's continuing position in the forefront of scientific and technical development that while in the United Kingdom as a whole in the period 1938-56 the number of university students of science and technology increased by 124%, in Glasgow the increase was 175%.

From such evidence it might seem that the city's industrial future is assured. But although the outstanding change in the industrial pattern in recent years has been the growing importance of the productive industries as opposed to the commercial trades, this change may well be reversed in the future. Glasgow may again become less of an industrial and more of a commercial centre. New industries are more likely to be established and to grow outside than inside the city, which has little space within its present limits and will do well to shed some of its industrial population in favour of new towns. But its fate will remain bound up with that of the region of which it forms the centre, and given a prosperous West of Scotland the city's consumer goods industries and services should continue to let Glasgow flourish.

Chapter 5

IRON AND STEEL

R. H. CAMPBELL

ALTHOUGH the city of Glasgow is not, and never has been, the seat of the major part of the iron and steel industries of Scotland it is nonetheless the focal point of the area in which they are situated. Indeed about 1830, before the growth of these industries on a large scale, the city was, by present day standards, still relatively small, with a population of only about 200,000. Then its prosperity was dependent mainly on extensive trading and on the manufacture of cotton. Consequently, the development of the modern economic structure of the city has been so intimately associated with that of the heavy industries of the West of Scotland that a discussion of the iron and steel industries of Glasgow must be very largely a discussion of the iron and steel industries of that wider area. This is by no means an illegitimate approach, since it can be argued that the economic character of Glasgow, unlike that of the other major ports on Britain's western seaboard, has been dominated by the development of the hinterland rather than the reverse. This domination was beginning when the *New Statistical Account* of the city was written in 1835.

NINETEENTH CENTURY DEVELOPMENTS

Iron

The iron trade of the south-west of Scotland was based on the plentiful natural resources of north Lanarkshire, and later, although to a lesser extent, of north Ayrshire and Stirlingshire. In 1801 David Mushet, at that time manager of the Calder Ironworks, discovered the rich field of blackband ironstone which lay in the coal measures near Glasgow, but the ore, though valuable, proved difficult to smelt until in 1828 J. B. Neilson, the manager of the Glasgow Gas Company, patented the process of using hot air in the blast at the furnaces. Both Mushet and Neilson carried out early experiments in their respective fields at the Clyde Ironworks at Tollcross, just outside the present boundary of the City of Glasgow and now the main plant in Scotland producing pig-iron. With the Lanarkshire hard splint coal, uncoked, the production of pig-iron became a highly profitable undertaking in

Scotland. On these technical and geological foundations the pig-iron industry of the nineteenth century was erected.

The advantages thus opened were quickly exploited by Scottish ironmasters. The number of furnaces increased from 27 in 1830, with a production of about 37,500 tons of pig-iron annually, to about 100 with a production of some 400,000 tons about 1840. The upward trend in production continued, to 1,000,000 tons in 1860 and 1,206,000 tons —the peak for the nineteenth century—in 1870.

In spite of this rapid expansion of pig-iron production in Scotland the later processes of iron manufacture did not grow commensurately. Steel-making was, of course, virtually non-existent until the second half of the nineteenth century, although before 1840 about 100 tons of steel were made annually at Calderbank, beyond the present boundary of Glasgow. The other uses for pig-iron were in the foundry, to make various castings, and, by way of the puddling furnace, in the forge for various types of malleable iron work, of which during most of the nineteenth century the manufacture of rails was of prime importance.

Because of the composition of "Scotch" pig-iron, which made it highly suitable for castings, it was to the growth of the foundries that the expansion of its manufacture gave the strongest impulse. The foundries already in Glasgow, estimated at twenty about 1830, and mostly very small, now rapidly increased in size and others were added to their number. In contrast, malleable iron production, in which lay the greatest possibilities for expansion, lagged behind. Within Glasgow attempts of any consequence to develop it were few; in the early days they were limited to the efforts of William Dixon at St. Rollox and then afterwards at Govan. Later other malleable iron works appeared, but even Blochairn, the most notable of those within the city, did not have a strikingly successful career. The same fate attended many of the major enterprises in the iron producing districts themselves. So within Scotland as a whole, and even more especially within the City of Glasgow, the importance of the foundry as against the forge in the utilisation of pig-iron was greater than in many other areas of the United Kingdom.

The finished iron trade, in spite of its growth in the nineteenth century, was still insufficient by far to consume the total Scottish output of pig-iron. Even the consumption of half was rarely reached, the usual proportion being about one third. The pig-iron trade of Scotland was never, therefore, integrated with further processes. Its progress was greatly dependent on events outwith Scotland. Consequently large quantities of pig-iron were exported to England and Wales and, especially as the nineteenth century progressed, to foreign countries so that by the early 'seventies about 40 per cent of Scottish production was being shipped overseas.

The City of Glasgow's contribution to the growth of the pig-iron trade was mainly on the distributive, or commercial, side rather than in direct production, which within the city boundary was indeed comparatively unimportant. Often, however, the direction of firms in the surrounding area became centred in Glasgow, as offices in the city were purchased, or, as was the case in later years, erected for various firms. Thus, although the works of the Bairds, the leading Scottish ironmasters, were in the Coatbridge area and in Ayrshire, their head offices were in West George Street, Glasgow. But Glasgow's most important contribution was in providing the necessary commercial link between the blast furnaces in Lanarkshire, Ayrshire and elsewhere and the consumers of their produce throughout the world. There was the obvious natural connection *via* the Clyde by ship to destinations anywhere: transport costs could therefore be kept much lower than in land-locked areas such as Staffordshire. Moreover, within Glasgow there grew up a special commercial fraternity concerned with the problems of distributing the iron. Of the firms of iron-brokers which formed its nucleus some still survive in a small way, operating chiefly within the city and the West of Scotland, but others, such as William Jacks & Co., in which Bonar Law was a partner, have attained world-wide dimensions.

A peculiar feature of the distribution of Scotch pig-iron was the system of storing the metal, mainly by the old Glasgow firm of Connal & Co., which continues to carry on business in its picturesque West George Street offices (a building modelled on the Ritter Inn at Heidelberg), although it is now engaged in other activities. Connal & Co., a firm of independent storekeepers for the trade, issued warrants against iron deposited in their stores. These warrants were simply certificates stating that a certain quantity of iron—in Glasgow usually 500 tons—had been lodged in store; but they were freely bought and sold by ironbrokers on the Glasgow Pig-Iron Market, which met daily in the Royal Exchange. The market was popularly known as the Glasgow Pig-Iron "Ring," because the meetings actually took place in a ring of chairs in the far left-hand corner of the Exchange. Dealings in warrants were equivalent to dealings in goods, since, on presentation of the document to Connal & Co. and the payment of any necessary storage charges, the iron could be withdrawn from store. Because of price fluctuations, however, these warrants became a popular medium for speculation, and were bought and sold by many who had no intention whatever of using the iron but were attracted by the possibility of large capital gains. Every conceivable factor, economic and non-economic, affected the willingness of such speculators to purchase, although the influence of Bank Rate was always particularly potent. Throughout the nineteenth century the price of pig-iron warrants fluctuated wildly, from £7 9s. a ton in March 1873 to £1 18s. 4d. in May 1886.

Until the close of the nineteenth century, when the influence of the market began to decline, the prices on the Ring were taken as standards throughout the whole world. The system functioned well only so long as a large part of the pig-iron production of Britain came from Scotland and the Scottish ironmasters were willing to put their iron into store. The appearance of the iron trade in both the north-east and then later in the north-west of England destroyed this necessary basis. At first the Glasgow market tried to retain its position by including dealings in Middlesbrough and hematite warrants, as well as in the traditional Scotch pig, but the reluctance and eventual refusal of the Middlesbrough manufacturers to deal through Glasgow, combined with the geographical spread of the iron trade, detracted from the market's commanding position. Before the First World War the Ring was almost moribund, but the war hastened its disappearance, which might otherwise have been more gradual. It was finally closed by order of the Ministry of Munitions on 31 May 1916, though the Scottish Pig-Iron Trade Association, of which the merchants dealing in the Ring were members, was dissolved only on 4 April 1934.

The pig-iron industry in Scotland continued to flourish until the early 1870's, although after the commercial crisis of 1857, when the Western Bank of Scotland closed its doors, its progress was less rapid. By 1870, however, three factors were gravely undermining the trade's prosperity. First, throughout the world there was increasing competition as the local iron industries in countries which were Scotland's chief customers (especially the United States and Germany), grew from negligible to considerable proportions, and attained moreover a high degree of technical development. At home also, and within their own special field of the production of foundry pig-iron, the Scots had to meet fierce competition from the iron producers centred in the Cleveland area around Middlesbrough. There, through the use of the local ironstone, the trade grew rapidly between 1850 and 1870, in exactly the same way as in the south-west of Scotland between 1830 and 1850. The costs of production were so low that pig-iron could be delivered in Coatbridge even below the price at which the local producers found production profitable. Thus from the 1860's onwards Cleveland pig-iron entered Scotland in increasing quantities.

Second, although Scottish ironmasters had been quick to accept and develop Neilson's hot-blast, for about forty years thereafter they showed a remarkable imperviousness to technical progress. For years the small size of the Scottish furnace, the low temperature of the blast and above all the failure to utilize the waste gases which escaped from the open tops of the furnaces attracted much adverse comment from outside observers. This lack of technical progress can be partly explained by the fact that, without radical changes in the construction of the furnaces, a harder coal than the native splint was required before much advance could be made in the matter of size of furnace and temperature of blast. No such excuse, however, could be offered for the prodigal waste of gases and their heating power. Only after 1870, when the fortunes of the trade were declining, did the ironmasters show once again some of the progressive spirit of the 1830's. It seems likely that the high profits they earned after the innovation of the hot blast made them lethargic and so hindered progress. Certainly the inability to keep the five-year-old Mining School in the Andersonian

University in existence after 1864 reflects no credit on the technological interests of the ironmasters of Scotland in the nineteenth century.

Third, the geological advantages enjoyed by the industry were diminishing. Since the best seams of blackband ironstone were exhausted, either thinner seams or the less valuable clayband and slateyband ores had to be worked. Moreover the advantages inherent in the native ores had now lost much of their former significance, for the processes in vogue in steelmaking up till about 1880, even although they were not extensively used, required pig-iron from non-phosphoric, or hematite, ores, which were not found in Scotland. Ore had therefore to be imported, in the main from Spain, and so costs of production inevitably rose. Supplies of coal, of course, remained adequate, although not those of particularly valuable grades such as the important splint coal in Lanarkshire, nor those from the collieries situated most conveniently to the ironworks. It was only in the present century that the exhaustion of the coal measures became a vital problem.

Steel

The modern steel industry dates from Bessemer's patenting of his manufacturing process in 1855, but the Scottish steel industry is of more recent origin.[1] As in malleable iron production, so in steelmaking, if less conspicuously, Scotland lagged behind other areas. This lag may be partly attributed to the failure of early experiments with the Bessemer converter in Scotland: in Glasgow the first attempt to use the new process was made by Dixon at Govan under the personal supervision of Bessemer himself, but because ordinary Scotch phosphoric pig-iron was used the results were disastrous. But even the introduction of the Siemens open-hearth furnace, the next major technical change in the industry, still left unsolved the problem of how to use phosphoric ores. Nevertheless the first major steel-making enterprise in Scotland, the Steel Company of Scotland, founded in 1871, used this process. In 1873 the company built the first open-hearth plant at Hallside, not far beyond the present city boundary, and until 1879, when a few other firms entered the field, was the sole manufacturer of open-hearth steel in Scotland. It was not until 1880, when the development of the basic process of steel-making by Gilchrist and Thomas had made the use of phosphoric pig-iron possible, that the growth of the modern Scottish steel industry really began. Unfortunately Scottish ores were still not the most suitable for the Thomas process. Consequently, with some relatively minor exceptions, Scottish steel-makers until the First World War did not change from the manufacture of acid steel, on which of necessity the earliest ventures in the field had been built. Admittedly the belief in the superiority of acid

1 Steel is of two fundamental types, basic and acid, depending on whether the pig-iron used in its manufacture has been produced from phosphoric or non-phosphoric (hematite) ore. To-day the different processes of steel-making, Bessemer converter and open-hearth furnace, manufacture both types.

steel also militated against any change. The open-hearth furnace, and not the Bessemer converter, was almost exclusively used, not only because it allowed greater control to be exercised in manufacture but also because it made possible the use of a much larger quantity of scrap than would have been the case with the Bessemer process. Since the supplies of scrap on the Clyde were plentiful, a process using much scrap relatively to pig-iron, which had to be manufactured from imported ores, was naturally attractive. While this process lessened its dependence on supplies of imported ore to make hematite pig-iron, the Scottish steel industry was nonetheless different from the early Scottish iron industry. The latter was, at least in origin, completely indigenous, all the material required for production being in Scotland. It has never been so with steel-making.

TWENTIETH CENTURY DEVELOPMENTS

1901 to 1939

At the beginning of the present century increasing competition, especially international, weakened the economic position of the Scottish iron and steel industries and was probably a factor contributing to the appearance at that time of amalgamations among firms in various branches of the Scottish trade. In 1900 fifteen Scottish firms amalgamated to form the Rivet, Bolt & Nut Company, with the object no doubt partly of increasing efficiency but mainly of eliminating competition. This company survived the years of depression in shipbuilding which followed, while a joint concern founded by the Clyde shipbuilders as a rival in the same field did not. In 1912 eight tube-making concerns, four of them in Glasgow, joined together to form the Scottish Tube Company Ltd. In the same year a series of attempts at amalgamation culminated successfully in the formation of the Scottish Iron and Steel Company, through the fusion of thirteen malleable iron and steel-making concerns. Sir John Clapham's comment on this amalgamation is significant: "an industry rather backward in organisation compared, for example, with the North-East Coast or with the Ruhr, and for the prosecution of which Scotland had lost some of the geographical and geological advantages which she had once possessed, was trying to strengthen itself by the recognised method of amalgamation."[1] But when in 1913 the iron and steel industries of Scotland produced 1,369,000 tons of pig-iron (mostly hematite) and 1,431,000 tons of steel ingots and castings their problems were still small compared with those the future was to bring. During the First World War steel-making capacity in Scotland was greatly expanded and in 1918 2,000,000 tons of steel were produced, a figure which unhappily was not touched again until the Second World War.

[1] J. H. Clapham: *An Economic History of Modern Britain* (1938), Vol. III, pp. 271-272.

After the First World War all the problems that had been accumulating for half a century and more were emphasised and driven home by the world-wide economic depression. The loss of natural advantages continued. Scottish ore production became negligible; in 1913 less than 600,000 tons were mined; in 1920 less than 280,000 tons, in 1929 a mere 25,000 tons against the 3,000,000 tons and more in the 1870's. But since after the war the blast furnaces produced mainly hematite pig-iron for the acid process in the steelworks the exhaustion of home supplies of phosphoric ores was less important than it might have been. In any case the use of foundry pig-iron, Scotland's special product, was decreasing because of the growing use of basic steel. The major geological concern of the industry between the wars, however, was over the supplies not of ore but of coals, particularly good coking coals. The supplies of these were so limited that the Balfour Committee[1] in 1928 sweepingly decided that " Scotland has no good coking coal," though this was disputed by the Scottish ironmasters and steel-makers. There were in fact adequate supplies of semi-coking varieties, which could be utilised, but only at increased cost.

The consequences of the worsened position of the industry were widespread. Production of pig-iron declined to just over 600,000 tons in 1929 and to less than 500,000 tons in 1937. Thus after the First World War the character of the Scottish pig-iron trade was completely changed. The decline in its international importance which had started before 1913 continued after 1918, and by 1930 foreign shipments of pig-iron were negligible. The closing of the Glasgow Iron Ring in 1916 is significant as the end not only of a remarkable produce market but also of a Scottish industry of international repute in which the City of Glasgow had a peculiarly important commercial interest.

Fortunately, while there was this pronounced decline in pig-iron production in Scotland after the First World War, steel production was well maintained and in some years even increased over the 1913 figure, being 1,582,000 and 1,895,000 tons respectively in the two relatively prosperous years of 1929 and 1937. Nevertheless these figures represented a lower proportion of the total United Kingdom's supplies than before the war. At these levels of steel production the supplies of pig-iron from the Scottish blast furnaces were quite inadequate to meet the needs of the steelworks, and the steel-makers had to face the need of obtaining part of their supplies elsewhere. The problem was particularly intensified for the basic steel producers since the Scottish ironworks continued to specialise in the production of hematite iron. Thus even in 1937 198,000 tons of hematite pig-iron were produced against 117,000 tons of basic iron (in addition to 182,000 tons of foundry and forge pig) while only 466,000 tons of acid open-hearth steel were made against 1,392,000 of basic open-hearth (in addition to 37,000 tons by other processes). The problems of bringing supplies of pig-iron into

1 Committee on Industry and Trade (Balfour Committee): *Survey of Metal Industries* (1928), p. 22.

Scotland were, therefore, more pronounced for those steel-makers using the basic process, who were placed at a peculiar disadvantage against their continental competitors with ample supplies of basic ores. The Scottish practice of using a large quantity of scrap in the open-hearth furnaces alleviated the problem considerably, but nevertheless it was estimated that to be self-sufficient in the inter-war years Scotland would have had to produce about 1,000,000 tons of pig-iron annually, or about double its then current level of production.

In spite of increasing difficulties there is some doubt if between the wars or earlier the Scottish iron and steel industries made full use of the technological skill and knowledge which might have lessened their disadvantages. Fortunately advances were made in scientific education. In 1887 the Chair of Metallurgy was founded at the Glasgow and West of Scotland Technical College (now the Royal College of Science & Technology), although the subject had already been taught for three years in the College of Arts and Science by Humboldt Sexton. In 1892 the West of Scotland Iron and Steel Institute was formed at Coatbridge, moving into Glasgow almost at once. Moreover between the wars Scottish steel-masters were responsible for important developments in the production of alloy steels. Yet, against these advances in the Scottish iron and steel industries have to be set certain failures and drawbacks. It is remarkable that the pig-iron production per furnace in blast in Scotland, which was only 16,000 tons annually in 1915, was still only 33,000 tons in 1937, a figure which had been reached by the whole United Kingdom in 1915; while even the United Kingdom's performance compared adversely with that of other countries. The nature and use of uncoked Scottish coal was partly responsible for the difference but this alone can hardly have accounted for such a striking lag. Scottish steelworks, largely because of their age, were badly designed to obtain many of the economies of scale. Indeed in 1921 the bad layout of the Lanarkshire steelworks formed the grounds of an appeal by their owners against a proposed increase in rateable values.

The most striking economies, particularly in fuel consumption, can, of course, be obtained only when the various processes of production are integrated. Such integration was lacking in Scotland, simply because the extensive use of scrap, and, though of much less importance, of imported pig-iron, made cold metal practice the normal method of Scottish steel-making. As the scrap ratio has declined so the need for, and advantages to be derived from, integration have increased. Consequently, integrated plants have appeared. Ravenscraig, Motherwell, will be the most outstanding example but Clydebridge has used hot metal practice since 1938.

In passing it should also be noted that in the period between the wars the City of Glasgow was thought by some to have caused delay in the installation of modern coking equipment at Gartsherrie, a desirable step towards integration, by refusing to purchase the surplus gas which would be produced, and which it was necessary to sell to make the installation an economic success. At the time it was asserted[1] that Glasgow was the only large city associated with the iron industry which did not use coke oven gas and also that there were no adverse circumstances from the municipal point of view which made its use impossible.

The integration of the industry and indeed the whole question of its technological efficiency cannot, however, be considered apart from the topic of its reorganisation and relocation—a matter of particular concern in the 1930's. As the consumption of fuel in the furnaces fell, the original advantages of their location on the coalfields were considerably diminished. Thus the industry between the wars was faced with a dilemma: to obtain the advantages of integration, of particular importance if costs were to be lowered through heat conservation, the furnaces should be near the steelworks, which were inland; but, on the other hand, to reduce the costs of transporting the ore, the furnaces should be located on the lower reaches of the Clyde (at one time a site near Erskine was suggested). In 1929 a plan proposing a new location downriver, known as the "Weir Scheme," was put forward. Had it been implemented, it was held, the cost of slabs would have been lowered from the then current average of £6 12s. a ton to £5. But, for a variety of reasons, the scheme was not adopted. The problem of location, which was still unsolved when the war began, reappeared briefly at its close to be settled in favour of an inland location.

1939 to 1955

As in the War of 1914 to 1918 so in that of 1939 to 1945 the problems of the iron and steel industries were in abeyance. Again production increased, particularly to supply the plates for the intensive activity of Clyde shipyards, as well as a vast variety of armaments. In the last war, however, there was not as great an extension of fixed capital as between 1917 and 1919. After the war the nationalisation of the iron and steel industries presented them with new sets of problems. Under the Iron and Steel Act, 1949, the securities of all the leading Scottish companies were vested in the Iron and Steel Corporation of Great Britain on 15 February 1951. The effect, except obviously on ownership, was slight. The Iron and Steel Act of 1953 provided that the industry should be returned to private hands by a gradual process. When in 1954 and in 1955 respectively Stewarts & Lloyds and Colvilles were returned, the major Glasgow companies in the iron and steel trades were no longer state owned.

Although the industries which have emerged from the Second World War are very different from those of the years after 1918, certain of the geological problems which caused concern in these earlier years are still present. No ore is now produced in Scotland. British

[1] *Report of Investigations into the Industrial Conditions in certain Depressed Areas*, Cmd. 4728 (1933-34), XIII, 313, p. 225.

ores (mainly from the Midlands) are used, but only in times of difficulty, as for instance during the war. Almost all supplies now come from abroad. In 1954 imported ores consumed in the Scottish furnaces amounted to 1,436,000 tons, and these came mainly from Sweden, French North Africa and Newfoundland: Spain, once Scotland's major foreign supplier, contributed only 85,000 tons. To facilitate the unloading of ore Colvilles in 1954, as part of their development plans, began the erection at the General Terminus Quay of a new installation which would allow two of the largest ships at present engaged on the ore carrying trade to be unloaded at the same time.

The belief which held sway in some quarters until about 1930 that Scottish coal could not be easily coked has happily now been disproved and the coal used in the coke ovens, 1,479,000 tons in 1954, is mostly local except for some brought from the south, chiefly from Durham, for blending. However the development of these local coals, not normally considered good coking varieties, requires considerable expenditure and may prove a major factor limiting future expansion of pig-iron production. Nonetheless if no longer producing ore, Scotland is still practically self-sufficient as regards the coal requirements of the furnaces.

The production of pig-iron, as might be expected, is considerably greater than before the war. In 1935 it was 863,000 tons and in 1954 947,000 tons. Moreover the transition from acid to basic processes in steel-making has been reflected in a changed proportion of hematite to basic pig-iron. Consequently whereas in 1938 Scotland produced 202,000 tons hematite, 71,000 tons basic and 131,000 tons foundry and forge iron, in 1954 the relative quantities were 41,000 tons hematite, 809,000 tons basic, 97,000 tons foundry and no forge iron at all. Although the production of pig-iron is now about double the output of the years immediately before the war, Scottish blast furnaces do not yet supply all Scotland's pig-iron requirements. Fortunately Scottish steel-makers continue to use a large quantity of scrap in the open-hearth furnaces, although the proportion is less than before the war. In 1938 scrap consumed as a proportion of steel produced was 79 per cent but in 1954 it was only 67 per cent, which was nevertheless considerably greater than the national average of 56 per cent. There will probably be difficulties in the future in maintaining this high scrap ratio. Admittedly the West of Scotland, because of the presence of shipbreaking yards, is well placed to obtain as adequate supplies as may be available anywhere, but nevertheless even at the moment home supplies are inadequate and scrap has to be imported. The retention of old vessels in service, because of the high costs of replacement, and national attempts to raise the quality of scrap used in steel-making are likely to diminish home supplies still further.

There seems, therefore, to be no doubt that the ratio of pig-iron to scrap used by the Scottish steel-makers will have to increase in the future. Certainly a severe shortage of the necessary high-grade scrap was a major factor leading to a sharp fall in Scottish steel output in

1951 and 1952 and has also, among other reasons, led Scottish producers to produce less acid and more basic steel. Consequently perhaps the most crucial question facing the industry to-day is whether or not the Scottish blast furnaces, without the special advantages they had in past days, can meet these requirements of the steelworks for more pig-iron at a reasonable cost. The answer will in turn rest largely on whether the local coals can provide adequate supplies of coke economically. Unless this is possible, Glasgow and the West of Scotland's acquired advantages of a skilled labour force, an established reputation in steel manufacture, and proximity to markets may well be insufficient to compensate for the loss of the natural geological advantages, which originally made it a centre of the ferrous metal trades. The industry hopes, however, that the problems will be overcome and that Scottish pig-iron production, which in 1954 was 947,000 tons, will be 1,200,000 by 1958. In like manner steel production is expected to increase from its present level of 2,232,000 tons of ingots and castings in 1954 (2,139,000 tons and 93,000 tons respectively) to 2,600,000 tons in 1958. It should, however, be recorded that some authorities doubt the wisdom of attempting this in an area which has lost so much of its former supremacy as the West of Scotland.

It seems fairly obvious that at the present day the further possible progress of the iron and steel industries of Glasgow and the South-West of Scotland rests on their ability to keep to the front of any technical change and advance and so to offset their diminished natural advantages. To this end an important development in the academic field was the institution in the metallurgy course at the Royal College of Science and Technology in 1946 of a course of study aimed at combining academic and practical work by arranging for students to spend, over a period of four years, six months alternately in the College and in industry, a system already followed successfully in certain University courses in other subjects. The West of Scotland Iron and Steel Institute (which is completely independent of the Iron and Steel Institute, and has over 400 members), continues its scientific work by means of monthly meetings during the winter and the publication of its *Journal*. Recently it began holding day conferences on specific topics, which have attracted visitors from the Continent. There are also signs that within the industrial field proper much of the accumulated backwardness of a century's failure to keep in the van of technical progress is being made good. A decision has at last been taken on the question of resiting the furnaces—this time against a new location downriver. At least this is the implication of the proposal, the approval of which by the Iron and Steel Board was announced in July 1954, contained in Colvilles' major development plans for Ravenscraig, Motherwell, near the existing Dalzell Works. This scheme, which is expected to cost over £20,000,000, includes the construction of two batteries of coke ovens, each of 35 ovens, and a blast furnace of 25 feet 6 inches hearth diameter to produce 1,000 tons of pig-iron daily. By these developments Colvilles hope to increase the ratio of pig-iron to scrap utilised in their steelworks. In addition their steel production is expected to reach 2,000,000 tons annually. Although it is probable that there will be yet further expansion by Colvilles at Ravenscraig, it may be that at the moment insufficient attention is being paid to the need for an increased development of plate mills to provide the large plate output required from Scottish steel-makers.[1] In any case it is fairly certain that in the West of Scotland this need will become considerable in the near future.

Perhaps the most striking technical change since before the war has been in the output per furnace in blast in Scotland, much of it owing to the three modern furnaces of the Clyde Ironworks. In 1937 it was 33,000 tons against the United Kingdom average of 69,000 tons. In 1954 it was 105,000 tons against the United Kingdom's 119,000 tons, a relatively minor difference. The arguments formerly advanced that the raw materials used in Scotland made large furnaces impracticable no longer seem to be valid. Improvements have also taken place in the manufacture of steel in Scotland. As the industry has become decreasingly dependent on imported pig-iron and on scrap, integration has taken place and hot metal practice now accounts for about 20 per cent of the output. As integration proceeds and supplies of Scottish pig-iron displace imported metal and scrap, the proportion is likely to rise still further. Moreover, although the open-hearth furnace still predominates in Scotland (in 1954 of a total of 109 steel furnaces, 64 were open-hearth and 26 electric arc), they are now mainly producing basic rather than acid steel. (In 1954 53 of the open-hearth furnaces were basic and 11 acid.) Thus in 1954 only 160,000 tons of acid open-hearth and 1,975,000 tons of basic open-hearth were produced, compared with 422,000 tons and 1,146,000 tons respectively in 1938 and 1,310,000 tons and 173,000 tons respectively in 1915.

The relative importance of the iron and steel industries in Glasgow and the West of Scotland has thus altered greatly since the nineteenth century. A hundred years ago, and even until 1900, pig-iron was the predominant ferrous metal in the city's commerce and activities. To-day steel-making and the subsequent processes of manufacture are of much greater importance. The Scottish pig-iron trade is now important only as a support to these later processes. It no longer has that considerable element of independent existence from other Scottish industries which so characterised it during the years of the world-wide predominance of Scotch pig, obtained by Connal warrants, f.o.b. Glasgow.

The Firms in Glasgow To-day

In Glasgow to-day iron and steel manufacturing predominates over iron and steel making. The head offices of some of the steel-makers are within the city (for instance those of Colvilles in West George Street), whence direction passes beyond the city boundary to their works out-

[1] Since the above was written expansion on these lines has been announced.

side. There is indeed only one concern producing pig-iron within the city, the old-established works at Govanhill. Founded by William Dixon in 1839, they were separated from the coal interests of William Dixon Ltd., when the latter were nationalised in 1947, to form Dixon's Ironworks. These were in turn nationalised in 1951, and after the de-nationalisation of the iron and steel industry in 1953 were acquired by Colvilles. For years the glare from the old open-topped furnaces in these works earned for them the local name of Dixon's Blazes. Here the three small furnaces (there are also three others which are, however, obsolete) produce about one-eighth of Scotland's output of basic iron. The Clyde Ironworks, by far the most important of the four works in Scotland producing pig-iron, lie just beyond the city boundary at Tollcross, but they are within the Glasgow Exchange Area of the Ministry of Labour. For many years the Clyde Ironworks were owned by the Dunlop family, whose fortunes were originally founded in the tobacco trade that flourished in Glasgow before the American War of Independence. In 1930, however, David Colville & Sons Ltd. and James Dunlop & Co. Ltd. merged to form Colvilles Ltd. Technically Clyde is one of the foremost works in Britain. The three furnaces, which produce basic iron, are modern and reasonably large, with hearth diameters of between 18 and 22 feet. One of them indeed was the first in Europe to be equipped for high top pressure operation. Clyde has Scotland's only sintering plant. There too the integration with further processes of manufacture has been carried out to a considerable extent. Supplies of hot metal go to Colvilles' Clydebridge steelworks on the other side of the river, as well, of course, as supplies of cold metal to other melting shops. By the bringing into operation in 1952 of new coke ovens, which make the plant self-sufficient in coke, Clyde at any rate is committed to the hope that the fundamental problem of ensuring adequate supplies of coking coal in Scotland at an economic rate can be overcome. Thus whatever difficulties may face pig-iron producing establishments in Scotland, the major group of blast furnaces is best fitted of all to withstand them.

As with the manufacture of pig-iron so with steel the major part of Scottish production comes from North Lanarkshire, outwith but close to the city. Clydebridge, for instance, is just across the river from the Clyde Ironworks. Within the city proper, however, are two establishments with steel-making plant where, of course, further manufacture is also carried out. The first, and much the more important, is the Parkhead works of William Beardmore & Co., popularly known as Parkhead Forge, with about 4,000 employees. Parkhead is one of the major Scottish steel-making plants. A forge was originally set up in 1830 which, after passing through the hands of Robert Napier, the shipbuilder and marine engineer, and then of William Rigby, came under the control of the Beardmores in the middle of the nineteenth century. Beardmore's, with five open-hearth and two electric arc furnaces, continue to follow the old Scottish practice of producing a large quantity of acid open-hearth steel which is considered necessary for the high-quality goods they produce. But indicative of the changed output of Scottish furnaces is the fact that the only work in Scotland which can now supply them with hematite pig-iron is Gartsherrie, where basic, hematite and foundry iron are still all produced, and where a proposed modernisation of the furnaces has been announced. The electric process, which Beardmore's developed especially during the war to provide uniform and good-quality steel, has, in spite of the definite advantages of its product, some drawbacks, particularly its cost. For a firm specialising in high-grade alloy and carbon steels, such as Beardmore's, however, this is not so serious. And, what is in Scotland probably an added advantage, the process can take an all-scrap charge. During and since the war Parkhead has, of course, been kept exceptionally active, not only on service requirements, guns, tanks and other armaments, but on a multifarious variety of heavy forgings.[1] The only other steel furnace within the city is at the works of the Springfield Steel Co., steel founders, which has one small open-hearth acid furnace and also one stock converter.

The further fabrication of iron and steel in Glasgow takes place in about 40 different establishments throughout the city. In these there is the diversity which is only to be expected in a city of Glasgow's size and industrial capacities. Of major importance are the works which carry out rolling and manufacture (also carried out in the steel-producing establishments themselves) but which are supplied with steel from other plants. Thus, for instance, the Steel Company of Scotland, one of the Colville group of companies, although its steel-producing works with seven open-hearth furnaces are at Hallside, also owns the Govan Shafting and Engineering Company (purchased in 1925) where bright steel bars are produced, and the old works at Blochairn, both within the city. At the latter works until recently there were also steel-making furnaces but in 1950, when the acute shortage of scrap caused a restriction of production by the temporary closing of several furnaces, those at Blochairn were dismantled and used for scrap. Blochairn is now supplied with steel from Lanarkshire.

Apart from the manufacture of heavy steel products by these firms the most important use of steel in Scotland is in tube-making. In 1954 about 12 per cent (216,600 tons out of 1,706,400 tons) of total Scottish steel deliveries were tubes and pipes. The chief name in tube manufacture in Scotland, and indeed a chief name throughout the world, is Stewarts & Lloyds. A Glasgow firm, which was started in 1860 by Andrew Stewart at the Clyde Tube Works on the site now occupied by St. Enoch Station, amalgamated with Lloyd & Lloyd of Birmingham in 1903 to become Stewarts & Lloyds. Gradually they acquired control of a major part of Scottish tube-making. Of special interest was the acquisition in 1932 of the Scottish Tube Co. Ltd., which had been formed in 1912 through the amalgamation of eight firms, four of their

[1] Since the above was written Beardmores have announced a reconstruction scheme to cover a period of five years at an estimated cost of £1,600,000. The open-hearth furnaces are to be replaced by electric arc furnaces, which will increase the capacity of the melting shop by 30 per cent.

works being within Glasgow. More important was the earlier merger with the Clydesdale Iron and Steel Co. in 1890, when the firm became a public company as A. & J. Stewart and Clydesdale Ltd. At the Mossend works of the Clydesdale Company steel-making was linked to the manufacture of tubes, and here in the last few years an extension of steel-making and tube-making facilities has been carried out. Further plans for the development of Mossend are among the main capital development schemes at present before the Scottish trade. Although the major part of Stewarts & Lloyds' activities are no longer in Glasgow, nor indeed within Scotland, Glasgow still retains the head office of the firm in Oswald Street. Beyond the city boundary, but within the Ministry of Labour's Glasgow Exchange Area, there are other tube-making firms, although not of comparable size.

The most widespread manufacture of tubes and pipes within Glasgow itself is not from steel but from cast iron in the foundries, of which there are more than a dozen, their employees varying in number from less than twenty to almost a thousand. Several of these foundries specialise in cast iron pipe production, as for instance the old firm of Shaw & McInnes, established more than a century ago. Others produce, in addition to cast iron piping, almost any type of casting required by their customers, among whom, especially with the smaller establishments, the shipyards predominate. Indeed the importance of this connection with the shipyards was illustrated recently by one of the newest additions to the city's foundries, that of Carron Company in Washington Street. This firm opened a foundry in the city in 1950 primarily because proximity to its customers in the shipyards would enable work to be carried out more easily than from the distance of Falkirk. On the other hand it is rather remarkable that few of the foundries are entirely dependent on the demand from shipbuilding for the disposal of their products. Indeed, on a rough estimate, the shipyards seem to take only about a quarter of the total output of the foundries of Glasgow. This lack of dependence on the shipyards is even greater in the case of certain foundries—particularly those attached to engineering establishments—which specialise in peculiar, non-marine lines. An example, which is also of interest in its own right, is the foundry of The Mirrlees Watson Co., where goods are produced for the manufacture of various types of machinery, especially for complete sugar cane factories, as well as evaporators for salt plants, pumping plants for water and sewage schemes, and other types of equipment, of which incidentally a very large proportion are directly exported. On the other hand foundries specialising in non-marine work are offset by those attached to some of the shipyards, as for instance that of Harland & Wolff in Govan.

Apart from the major methods of manufacturing iron and steel a number of lesser processes of a more detailed character are also carried out in the city. First, there are wire manufacturers producing all types of wire articles, in some cases, however, also with other goods. Their products have over the years undergone comparatively little change apart from an increase in the variety of metals and an increasingly finer gauge. Second, the manufacture of bolts, nuts and rivets has, not surprisingly in view of the proximity of the shipyards, four representatives, both large and small, within the city, and other firms also make some of these goods as side-lines. A branch factory which Guest, Keen & Nettlefolds opened in 1946 at Hillington, just outside the city boundary, was a notable addition to this field. Lastly, there is a group of firms within the city producing a multitude of different commodities—chains, nails, galvanised sheets, upholstery springs, expanded metal, shot, files, safes and other goods. The firms forming this miscellaneous group are, with some exceptions, mainly rather small, having generally under a hundred and more often under fifty employees.

The Present Position of the Industry

There is thus a wide variety of iron and steel manufacture in Glasgow, but it would be false to think of the industry as supplying its diverse products in anything approaching equal proportions. Firms making light metal goods are completely overshadowed in importance by the manufacturers of the heavy products, for instance by Beardmore's at Parkhead. The preponderating influence of the heavy steel products is, of course, simply a reflection of the dependence of the iron and steel industries of the city on shipbuilding and constructional engineering. In Scotland the output of plates has become of increasing importance, helped by the use of welding and pre-fabrication in shipbuilding, which appeared during the recent war. Thus, while the production of plates in the whole of the United Kingdom was in 1954 less than 16 per cent of the total finished steel output, in Scotland it was 33 per cent. Most of the plates, however, are produced at Colvilles' Lanarkshire works. Within Glasgow, Blochairn, also of course in the Colvilles group, alone makes a substantial contribution in this field, providing about 20 per cent of the total Scottish production. Blochairn now specialises entirely in the manufacture of steel plates. Moreover even some of the lighter steel products of Glasgow firms are used in shipbuilding: for example, material for the hull and engines as supplied by the rivet, bolt and nut manufacturers.

Even when considering the total demand for Scottish steel it would be wrong to think that the demand from the shipyards is the only important element in Scotland. Although in 1954 the heavy industries took over 50 per cent of Scottish steel delivered to consumers in the United Kingdom, only 21 per cent went to the shipbuilders and marine engineers (but this proportion would probably be higher if the figures of deliveries to Scottish consumers only were considered). These national figures suggest that although the shipyards may take some of the production from almost every iron and steel firm in Glasgow they do not take a major part.

Yet this degree of dependence on the heavy industries is a dangerous feature of the iron and steel trades of the city. It means that they are still susceptible to a sharp decline in demand, as happened between the wars, if the heavy industries should become less actively employed. Some believe that a considerable fall in the output of British shipyards is to be expected even although a high level of activity may persist in other sectors of the economy. In either event, but of course particularly in the face of a general recession, the iron and steel industries of Glasgow would suffer heavily. While they are prosperous to-day, it would therefore be unrealistic to refuse to recognise the possibility at some future date of a lessened demand for their output, with all its attendant evils of unemployment and stoppages.

Since 1945, in contrast to their experience in the inter-war period, and in spite of a temporary shortage of orders for certain specifications at the beginning of 1954, the iron and steel producers and manufacturers have been actively employed. Their major problems have been concerned with scarcity of raw materials. The labour force engaged in mid-1955 in the Glasgow Employment Exchange Area in the manufacture of ferrous metals was over 14,200 of whom almost 10 per cent were women. Apart from those engaged in office and administrative work, women are employed in the industry in only a few unskilled or semi-skilled tasks. Naturally the proportion of female to male labour is higher in the lighter metal undertakings than at the heavy works, at some of which (Parkhead for instance) there are no female operatives at all. The present level of activity in the iron and steel trades of the city is demonstrated simply by the fact that a proportion of the labour force in almost every iron and steel establishment is working overtime, in certain cases by quite a considerable amount. Yet, understandably, except in some of the largest firms, and of course in those, such as Parkhead, where the continuous nature of the operations requires it, shift work is almost non-existent.

Whether these conditions will last or whether there will be a relapse into the conditions of the inter-war years is difficult to determine. In Lanarkshire there are, as has been indicated, strong possibilities of still further expansion of the iron and steel industries, but this seems impossible within Glasgow itself. Indeed it is interesting to notice that few of the ferrous metal undertakings within the city are of recent origin. A majority, even among the smaller firms, where it would be least expected, were founded before 1914—many well back in the nineteenth century. Moreover a surprising number of the older firms, despite the fact that many are of considerable age, still remain in the hands of the founder's descendants. Thus Begg, Cousland & Co., George Boyd & Co., Thomas Bishop, and others, although over a century old, have not passed into other hands. As might be expected this continuity is strongest among the smaller firms, but even one of the very largest, Stewarts & Lloyds, still has a member of the Stewart family as its chairman. Indeed most of the firms are completely indigenous to the city, even if some of them have since spread out of it. They were founded by local residents who saw the profitable possibilities of a situation, favourable for access both to raw materials and to markets. One cannot but note that, with three or four interesting but small exceptions, such native enterprise no longer seems prevalent. Indeed the major iron and steel undertakings which have been established in the city since the war are branches of large parent concerns situated elsewhere, the best example being Carron Company's new foundry. The period of Glasgow's expansion in iron and steel appears to be over. While there is every reason to anticipate more favourable conditions in the future than have been known since 1913, the decreased advantages of production in the city make any large-scale expansion seem impossible. At best we can hope that Glasgow's interest in iron and steel will remain as it is to-day—prosperous but with only limited possibilities of expansion before it.

Chapter 6

SHIPBUILDING AND MARINE ENGINEERING

A. M. ROBB

ORIGINS OF THE INDUSTRY

SHIPBUILDING does not figure prominently in the early history of Scotland, still less does shipbuilding on the Clyde, yet it might be said that ships have been built on Clydeside since the very dawn of history itself. Indeed some early examples of "Clyde built" craft still survive as witnesses to the fact: those primitive canoes, referred to in a previous chapter, which were discovered in the silt beneath the streets of Glasgow within recent times and are now preserved in the museums. It would be pleasant, if fanciful, to imagine that the Clyde shipyard worker of to-day has inherited some of his traditional skill from the hands that fashioned those ancient craft, and to trace a continuity in shipbuilding on the river from the first small canoes to such modern ocean giants as the *Queen Elizabeth.* The contrast they present is strikingly symbolic of the industry's development, but it is a development largely of the past hundred and fifty years.

Apart from the building of a few ships by King Robert the Bruce near his castle of Cardross on the Clyde in the fourteenth century, and some naval construction at Dumbarton in the reign of James IV (using timber floated down the River Leven from the forests of Luss),[1] early records of shipbuilding on the west coast of Scotland are meagre. Until the American colonies were thrown open to Scottish traders by the Union of Parliaments in 1707, all the advantage lay with the east coast because of its proximity to the continent of Europe. Even in the east the only notable achievement was the building of *The Great Michael* at Newhaven, near Leith, by James IV in 1511-12.[2] There must, however, have been some merchant shipbuilding on the west coast, since there seems to have been a lively coastal trade, and some trade with the Continent. A galley appears to have been built at Glasgow in the sixteenth century, and toward the close of that century the city is said to have owned six ships with a total tonnage of

[1] Oak for the roof of Glasgow Cathedral also came from this source.

[2] "In this same year the King of Scotland bigged a great ship, called *The Great Michael,* which was the greatest ship, and of most strength, that ever sailed in *England* or *France* . . . She was Twelvescore Foot of Length, and 36 Foot within the Sides . . . She had three hundred Marines to sail her; she had sixscore of Gunners to use her Artillery; and had a thousand Men of War . . ." Pitscottie's *History of Scotland.*

279, the largest being of 92 tons.[1] But until after the development of Glasgow's colonial trade in the eighteenth century shipbuilding on the Clyde remained spasmodic and insignificant.

Strangely enough, the first major stimulus to growth came not with the rise of the American trade but with its collapse in the War of Independence. Indeed this war may be said to have secured independence not only for the American colonies, but also for Scottish shipbuilding. Initially Glasgow's trade with the Plantations had been carried on mainly in small vessels chartered from Whitehaven in England. It was not until 1718 that a locally owned ship was engaged in the trade, and although the number and size of Glasgow's tobacco ships rapidly increased thereafter, all the large vessels belonging to the Clyde were built in American yards. This dependence on overseas builders was abruptly ended by the revolt of the colonies, and, as the first *Statistical Account* informs us, " since the Americans established their independence, shipbuilding has gone on briskly in the ports of Clyde, and in other ports all over Britain." The largest merchant vessel hitherto built in Scotland was launched at Greenock about 1791.[2]

It would seem, however, that shipbuilding was still regarded as comparatively unimportant, for in the *Statistical Account* it is barely mentioned; the scarcity of references to shipbuilding may, however, be an indication of the interests of the parish ministers who provided the information rather than of the state of the industry. The merely general reference in the Account of Greenock just quoted, for example, is rather surprising in view of the fact that the Scotts had been building ships there for the better part of a century by the time it was written. Indeed there seem to have been several shipyards in Greenock and Port Glasgow at the time of the Account, although only two of the associated names, Scott of Greenock and Wood of Port Glasgow, are outstanding in shipbuilding history.[3]

As regards other parishes within the middle belt of Scotland, the only detailed references to shipbuilding in the first *Statistical Account* related to North Leith, the district in which *The Great Michael* was built, and to Newton-upon-Ayr. At North Leith it was the principal manufacture, " a number of fine vessels from 200 to 300 tons " having lately been built there. This parish could boast of two recently excavated dry docks, and five master-builders employing about 152 carpenters, whose skill was rewarded with 1s. 10d. a day. The shipyard workers on the west coast had similar wages, but the industry here was only beginning to develop. Although shipbuilding had been carried on at the harbour of Newton-upon-Ayr for many years, it had not until recently " met with any particular encouragement." But now, reports the parish minister, " the business seems to proceed with spirit and vigour. . . . Oak wood is brought from England and Wales, fir

1 Scott and Cunnison, *The Clyde Valley Industries* (1924), p. 8.
2 *Statistical Account of Scotland*, Vol. V, p. 581, Greenock (1793).
3 John Shields, *Clyde Built* (1949).

from Dantzick; the extent of the trade, at this time, will be about £5,000 per annum."

As for Glasgow itself, the "several respectable inhabitants" who compiled the Account did not mention shipbuilding at all. Nor did the minister of Port Glasgow, except perhaps indirectly. We have seen that the parish minister of Greenock regarded the American War of Independence as a stimulus to shipbuilding. His neighbour in Port Glasgow took a different view, blaming it for the stagnation of trade and the cessation of population growth in his parish. "In consequence of it," he complained, "Glasgow, upon which the people here chiefly depended hitherto, became no longer a commercial, but a manufacturing city, and consequently was no longer the immediate source of wealth to them." This, however, was rather a short-term view, for although the loss of the colonies practically stopped Glasgow's trade with North America, and proved the ruin of many of her merchants, some princely fortunes had already been secured from tobacco and were ready for investment in new ventures, such as the cotton industry. Although only indirectly, shipbuilding—and indeed later marine engineering—were to benefit considerably from the development of the textile industries. Shipbuilding's own turn was to come, but it was not until the advent of steam propulsion that it became a comparatively profitable field for investment. It is indicative of the relative position of these industries at the dawn of the steamship era that in the *General Report* drawn up by Sir John Sinclair, and published in 1814, the textile industry was given primacy, with a value assessed at upward of eight millions sterling per annum; whereas "Shipbuilding, and those branches in which timber is chiefly employed, exclusive of the fitting up of houses," were valued at about one million.[1] But two years before, in 1812, Henry Bell's *Comet*—sailing "by the power of Wind, Air, and Steam" as his advertisements proclaimed—had made its appearance on the Clyde, an event which marks the beginning of the modern epoch in shipbuilding.

The Advent of Steam Propulsion

Several attempts to adapt the steam engine to the purposes of marine propulsion had been made in Scotland during the latter part of the eighteenth century. In 1788 Patrick Miller and James Taylor, with the assistance of William Symington as engineer, had successfully demonstrated their "double pleasure boat" (so called because it was built in the form of two separate hulls with the paddle-wheels between them) on Loch Dalswinton in Dumfriesshire. Subsequent experiments were made by Symington on the Forth and Clyde Canal in 1789 and 1802, his stern-wheeler *Charlotte Dundas* towing two laden barges a distance of nineteen miles in six hours—a feat which astonished the

1 Sinclair, *General Report of the Agricultural State and Political Circumstances of Scotland* (1814).

spectators as much as it alarmed the canal proprietors. The wash she created was thought to endanger the banks of the canal, and so the project was abandoned.[1] But among the interested witnesses of these experiments was Henry Bell, a native of Torphichen, who had been successively a stone-mason, a millwright, and an engineer, before coming to settle in Glasgow about 1790 as a house-carpenter. In 1807 Bell betook himself to the village of Helensburgh, then a rising watering-place, and while his wife presided over the Baths Inn there this jack-of-all-trades, by dint of a natural mechanical ingenuity and dogged perseverance, succeeded in accomplishing what others in this country, better qualified and better financed, had just failed to achieve—a practicable steamship. Despite some support from Lord Nelson before 1805, his attempts to interest the Admiralty in his schemes for steam propulsion, a subject which had engaged his attention since 1786, were fruitless; and had it not been for lack of capital he might well have succeeded in constructing his own prototype long before he did. At last, however, in 1812, his dreams took practical shape in a Port Glasgow shipyard. Like many another inventive genius, he had to contend not only with difficulties and setbacks of a technical nature, but with poverty and ridicule. Peter Mackenzie, who had known him personally, tells us in his *Reminiscences of Glasgow* that Bell was poor and virtually despised at that time, and "was vexed and wearied almost to death by the rude jibes and jeers levelled at him while fitting up his little vessel."

Derision quickly changed to wonder when the *Comet,* with full steam up, proudly took the water in 1812. Built by the Woods of Port Glasgow, she was engined by John Robertson of Glasgow, but the boiler and main castings for her engine were made in the foundry of David Napier. While it is true that Bell was anticipated in America by Fulton, who had also been inspired by Symington's work and successfully placed a steamboat (propelled by an engine made by Boulton & Watt) on the Hudson River in 1807, there is no doubt that the *Comet* was the first really practicable steam vessel in Europe. Her appearance on the Clyde in 1812 was probably as awesome and miraculous to the country-folk who crowded to the riverside as that of the heavenly phenomenon of the previous year which gave her the name; it was certainly a portent of a new age of prosperity for Clyde shipbuilding.

As is to be expected, shipbuilding was deemed worthy of fuller mention in the reports of Clydeside parishes in the *New Statistical Account* published in the 1840's, and engineering also finds a place. That the industry was still of relatively minor significance on the upper reaches of the river is apparent on comparing the Glasgow report with those of, say, Greenock and Port Glasgow. Indeed in the original draft of the Glasgow account there is but the scanty note: "Since the deepening of the river, ship-building has been introduced here. A large

[1] But for the death of Lord Dundas, the chairman of the canal company, the outcome might have been different. His enthusiasm for the experiment (the vessel was named after his daughter) was not shared by his fellow-directors.

steam vessel for the Mediterranean trade was lately launched at Glasgow." This reveals the main reason, of course, for the delayed development of the industry in Glasgow—the ever-recurring difficulty of the shallowness of the Clyde. There was also, however, a significant reference to the provision of a quay-side crane "for shipping steam-boat boilers, and other articles of thirty tons . . ." Moreover, in an addendum to the original draft there is a reference to "a launch of a rather unusual nature" which had taken place at Broomielaw harbour in 1835. An *iron* steamer, 45 feet long, had been built by Tod & McGregor, transported by carriage to the crane, and lowered into the water, to proceed immediately on a trial trip; steam had been raised before the carriage left the yard where the ship had been built—presumably the repair yard which was the initial venture of Tod & McGregor. Such was the humble beginning in Glasgow of iron shipbuilding, which, allied with the now rapidly developing methods of steam propulsion, was soon to revolutionise the whole industry.

The Start of Iron Construction

Although this was one of the first iron ships launched in Glasgow, the use of iron as a constructional material in shipbuilding dates back to a much earlier period. Even before the time of Henry Bell's *Comet* (which was of course a wooden vessel) there had been a few iron barges in England, and in 1819 the *Vulcan*, built by Thomas Wilson at Faskine,[1] had successfully begun to ply as a passenger boat for canal service —despite the prophecies of the wiseacres who thought that iron could not float. The first iron steamship in Scotland was the little *Aglaia* of 30 tons, built by David Napier in 1827 for service on Loch Eck, and the first to run on the Clyde was Neilson's *Fairy Queen*, built four years later. But as regards sea-going vessels, the pioneers in iron shipbuilding on the Clyde were David Tod and John McGregor, two ex-foremen of Robert Napier who had established a yard of their own in Govan, from which they launched the *Royal Sovereign* in 1839, followed by the *Royal George* and the *Princess Royal*, all for service between Glasgow and Liverpool.

Early Marine Engineering

Meanwhile Glasgow's interests and reputation in marine engineering were steadily increasing. Steam engines had been made in the city since 1800, when the exclusive right to manufacture the Watt engine enjoyed by Boulton & Watt expired, so that Glasgow engineers had

[1] Incidentally, the *Vulcan* was designed by Sir John Robison, son of the John Robison who was a life-long friend of James Watt and had indeed directed his attention to the steam engine; John Robison was a midshipman on the boat carrying General Wolfe to the landing at Quebec, and he recorded the famous recitation of Gray's *Elegy* and Wolfe's noble evaluation.

acquired considerable experience in this work before the demand for marine engines arose. By the time of the *New Statistical Account* the engineering industry was firmly established in the city: "to such an extent is this business carried on here for every part of the country, that there are now fourteen firms who make steam-engines or mill machinery. Some of the works are more like national than private undertakings. Three houses alone employ upwards of 1000 persons in this important branch of trade."

Despite its later development, marine engineering no less than shipbuilding was assisted by the influence of the American War of Independence. This war, as we have seen, gave a direct stimulus to shipbuilding, and a direct stimulus to the textile industry; and but for the demand for steam engines in the great textile mills it might not have been possible to provide the engines required by the shipbuilders to follow up the success of the *Comet*. Cleland's *Annals of Glasgow*, published in 1816, gives particulars of the first twenty steamers built on the Clyde, from the *Comet* launched in 1812 to the *Rothesay Castle* launched in 1816. The twenty sets of machinery were made by seven firms, five sets by Duncan McArthur in Camlachie, at the works subsequently run by David Napier, and four sets by James Cook in Tradeston. The hulls were built by six firms, Wood at Port Glasgow building nine, and a Denny at Dumbarton building five. The name of Scott does not appear on the list. That firm did not build its first steamer until a slightly later date, and did not start making marine engines until 1825. It is rather interesting to note the expenditure on the building of a steamship in those early times. Cleland records the costs of the nineteenth ship on his list, the *Albion*, 73 feet long by 16 feet beam, built by Wood of Port Glasgow, with a 20 (nominal?) h.p. engine by Cook of Tradeston:

Carpenter, for hull etc.	£1000
Engineer, paddles etc.	1600
Joiner, Upholsterer, and miscellaneous furnishings	850
	£3450

THE CLYDE'S OUTPUT, 1800-1900

An approximate indication of the development of shipbuilding on the Clyde, year by year throughout the greater part of the nineteenth century, is provided by Fig. 14. The data from which the diagram was prepared were obtained, for the period to 1890, mainly from Statistical Reports submitted by successive City Chamberlains to the Lord Provost and Magistrates of Glasgow; for the period from 1892 to 1900 the figures were provided by Lloyd's Register of Shipping. There are discrepancies in figures from different sources, and there are some

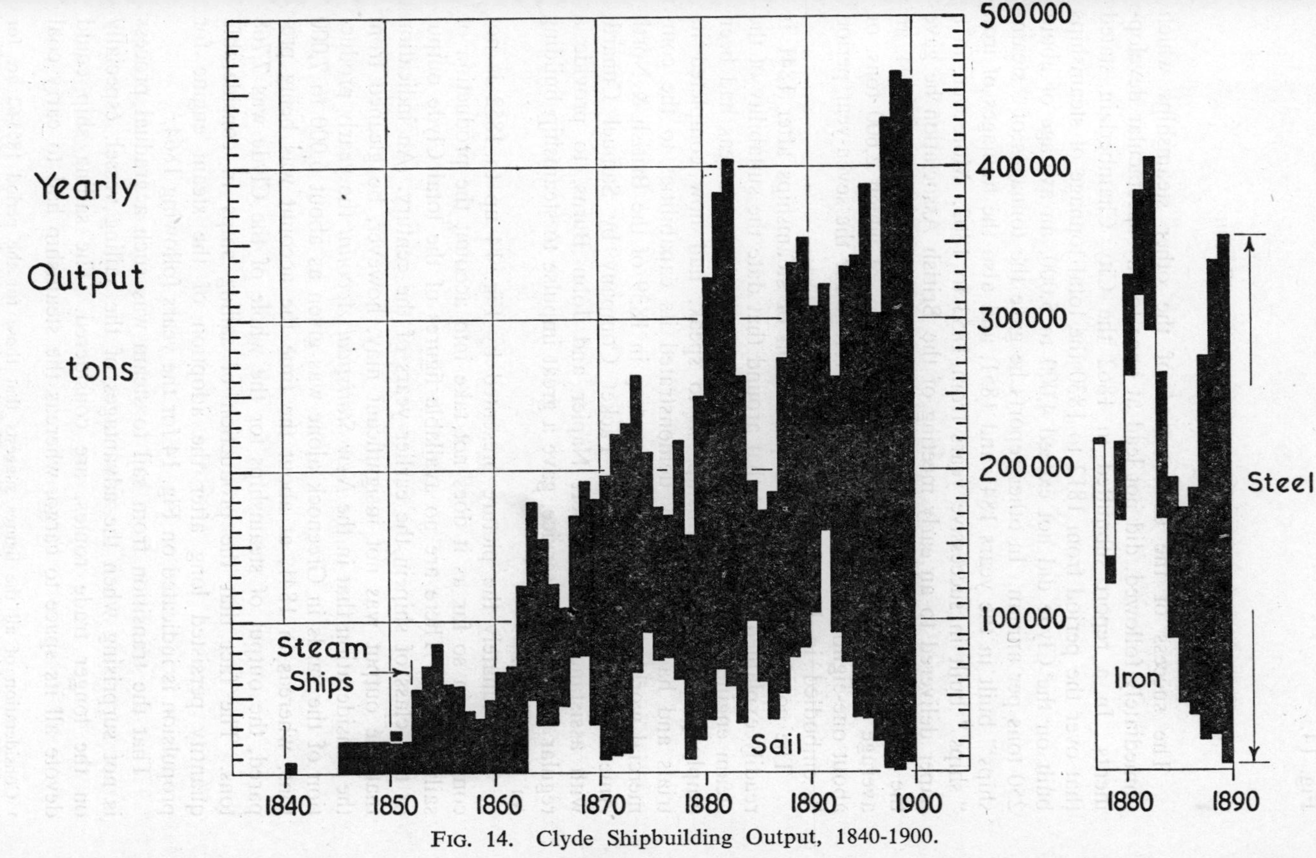

FIG. 14. Clyde Shipbuilding Output, 1840-1900.

differences in the bases of the reckoning; but it is considered that possible minor errors do not materially affect the pattern presented by Fig. 14.

The Transition from Sail to Steam

The success of the *Comet,* and of the other steamships which immediately followed, did not lead at once to any spectacular developments. In a report submitted in 1862 the City Chamberlain stated that over the period from 1812 to 1830 the total tonnage of steamships built on the Clyde did not exceed 4,000 to 5,000, an average of about 250 tons per annum. In other reports he gave the tonnages of " steamships " built in the years 1841 and 1851, and also the tonnages of iron " ships " built in successive years from 1853 to 1862. Moreover, in a paper delivered to an early meeting of the British Association he gave the total tonnage of steamships over the period 1846-52 as 147,604, an average of practically 21,100 tons per annum, of which 2,600 tons, or about one-eighth, were of wood. The average for the seven-year period is embodied in Fig. 14.

The considerably increased production of steamships after 1841 is readily explained by the fact that around that date the suitability of the steam engine for the propulsion of ships over the open seas had been amply proven. The steamship, so to speak, had now completed its trials and had convincingly demonstrated its capabilities to the commercial world. Moreover, the founding in 1839 of the British & North American Royal Mail Steam Packet Company by Samuel Cunard, with assistance from Robert Napier and John Burns, to provide a regular transatlantic service, gave a great impulse to steamship building on the Clyde.

Unfortunately the picture presented by Fig. 14 up to 1852 is not complete, in so far as it does not take into account the production of sailing ships. There are no available figures of the total Clyde output of that class of ship in the earlier years of the century. An indication that the output was not insignificant may, however, be gleaned from the consideration that in the *New Statistical Account* the yearly production of the yards in Greenock alone was given as about 6,000 to 7,000 tons, whereas in 1841, at about the time the account was being prepared, the output of steamships for the whole of the Clyde was 7,768 tons. The fact that the production of sailing ships in considerable quantity persisted long after the adoption of the steam engine for propulsion is indicated on Fig. 14 for the years following 1864.[1]

That the transition from sail to steam was such a gradual process is not surprising when the advantages of the sailing vessel, especially on the longer trade routes, are considered. The sailing ship could devote all its space to cargo, whereas the steamship had to carry coal

[1] Consideration of all the figures suggests that those for the period 1853-62 are for iron *steam*ships, although the City Chamberlain presented them as for iron *ships*.

as well. Not only were the engines inefficient in regard to fuel consumption, but coaling stations on trade routes were few and far between, so that enormous bunker capacity was required. On long voyages so little space was left for cargo that only passengers and mail could really be carried profitably by steamships, even in the 1860's. These were the years when the famous China clippers were being built, many of them in Clyde yards: most notably the *Cutty Sark*, launched at Dumbarton in 1869. The Glasgow shipbuilders, Stephen of Linthouse, produced several fine clippers, including some of the first vessels of the City Line, at the Kelvinhaugh[1] yard between 1859 and 1869. But this final burst of glory in sail was soon over. The opening of the Suez Canal in the latter year foreshadowed the doom of the sailing ship; for not only was the route to the east thereby shortened, but the distance between coaling stations was reduced, which enabled steamships to carry much more cargo than formerly. Thereafter the clippers were employed for a time in bringing wool and grain from Australia, and nitrate from the west coast of South America, but the opening of the Panama Canal in 1915 robbed sail of its supremacy there also. As Fig. 14 indicates, there was a revival in the production of sailing ships in the late 'eighties and early 'nineties, reaching a peak of about 160,000 tons in 1892, closely approximating to the tonnage of steamships launched on the Clyde in that year. In times of depression the sailing vessel could still find custom on account of its cheapness, but it could no longer compete with the steamship on equal terms when trade was good. After 1892 the number and tonnage of sailing ships built on the Clyde steadily declined until the turn of the century, when there was another, but minor, revival of sailing ship construction.

The Transition from Wood to Iron

The increasing output of the Clyde shipyards after 1841 is attributable not only to the adoption of steam propulsion, but to the growing use of iron as the main element in construction in place of wood. Reference to the first iron ships launched on the Clyde in the 1830's has already been made. From these modest beginnings the production of iron steamships jumped to an average of about 18,600 tons per annum over the period 1846-52; and there may have been some iron sailing ships of which there is no record.[2] Of the 247 steam vessels built on the Clyde during that period only 14 were of wood.

At first many eminent seafarers predicted that iron vessels would prove disastrous failures, and not only prejudice but the active hostility of vested interests had to be overcome before iron could assert its superiority over the traditional methods of timber construction. The

[1] The site is now occupied by the Queen's Dock and the Yorkhill quays, the Stephens moving downriver to Linthouse in 1870.

[2] The *Iron Duke* of 393 tons, launched in 1840, is said to have been the first seagoing sailing vessel built of iron on the Clyde. Ship-rigged, she sailed from Glasgow to India. Gillespie, *Glasgow and the Clyde* (1876), p. 73.

transition from wood to iron was further retarded by the lack of accurate scientific knowledge concerning the new material's capabilities, and much research and experimental work had still to be done. It was not until 1855 that Lloyd's underwriters mastered their distrust of iron vessels and made any regular rating arrangements for them. The factors which eventually decided the supremacy of iron, however, were first, the economy of large vessels for overseas trade, and second, the introduction of the propeller in place of the paddle-wheel. Timber was unsuitable for the stresses to which large ships are exposed, and it could not withstand the vibration caused by the propeller of a powerful steamship. Just when the rival merits of iron and wood were being argued, it so happened that the screw propeller was gaining ascendancy over the paddle in the case of larger vessels, thus strengthening the argument in favour of iron.

The last wooden Cunard liner, the *Arabia*, of 2,400 tons, was built in 1852, and by the late 'sixties wood had ceased to be a main element in construction for all but very small craft. But what was known as "composite" construction—wood planking on iron frames and beams, an arrangement designed to combine the advantages of both materials—persisted for special craft to a much later date. It was largely adopted for the China tea clippers, the last of which was built in 1869. By the 'seventies, because of the excessive cost as compared with overall iron construction, very few composite ships were being produced, and iron was at last displacing wood even in the domain of sail.

The Transition from Iron to Steel

From 1863 onward the production illustrated in Fig. 14 covers steamships and sailing ships, and all methods of construction. The supplementary diagram on the right-hand side of the main diagram illustrates a major change in construction which was introduced rapidly after 1878, the use of mild steel in place of iron. Because of the greater strength of steel, a ship constructed of this material could be made lighter than an iron one, the saving of weight amounting to about 16 per cent. Until the late 1870's, however, steel had been little used for ships and it was regarded with widespread distrust by shipbuilders, largely owing to the difficulty of obtaining really reliable steel plates and bars. Both an improvement in quality and a reduction in price were necessary before it could be generally adopted, and the inventions of Siemens in 1867 and of Thomas and Gilchrist in 1878 were decisive factors here.[1]

The possibilities of steel in the construction of large ships were first demonstrated by the French Admiralty in the *Redoutable*, a vessel built at L'Orient in 1874 from steel made both by the Bessemer and

[1] For further details of these steel-manufacturing processes see Chapter 5 (Iron and Steel).

by the Siemens process, and the British Admiralty had begun to experiment along similar lines. Steel had actually been used in the construction of some ships built on the Thames for running the Northern blockade during the American Civil War, but the intensive development in the application of the newer material started on Clydeside. In 1877 John Elder built two steel paddle-steamers at Govan for service on the English Channel; in 1878 James and George Thomson completed the steel paddle steamer *Columba*; and in 1879 William Denny & Brothers of Dumbarton, after turning out several small vessels, launched the *Rotomahana*, which was the first ocean-going steamer to be built of mild steel. It was constructed for the Union Steamship Company of New Zealand, being followed in 1880 by the *Buenos Ayrean*, of just over 4,000 tons, for the Allan Line, the first steel ship for transatlantic service. The third steel liner launched on the Clyde also came from a Dunbartonshire yard. She was the Cunarder *Servia*, built in 1881 by J. & G. Thomson. This vessel, 515 feet in length and with a gross tonnage of 7,392, was the largest ship yet constructed, with the exception of the famous *Great Eastern*.

The adoption of mild steel by other shipbuilders in the early 'eighties was due in no small measure to the intrepid example and persuasive eloquence of William Denny of Dumbarton. Of the 18,000 tons of steel shipping launched on the Clyde in 1879, 8,930 tons, or very nearly one half, were produced by his yard alone. The greater cost of steel compared with iron tended at first to retard its adoption, but the price gradually fell as improved processes of manufacture made possible increased production, until eventually it became cheaper and also more readily obtainable than iron. As steel fell in price its use rapidly spread among Clyde shipbuilders, and within a decade it practically replaced iron altogether. Between 1879 and 1889 the tonnage of steel shipping launched on the river rose from 18,000 to 326,136 tons, while the iron and wood tonnage dropped from 156,750 to 8,885 tons. The proportion of steel-built vessels had risen from 10.3 per cent to 97.2 per cent in the course of ten years, a phenomenal development unequalled in any other shipbuilding area of Britain.[1] The rapidity of the transition is partly attributable to the proximity of the great steelworks which had sprung up in Scotland since 1871, and the distance of some of the sources of supply formerly depended upon for iron plates. A notable example of the conjunction of steel production with shipbuilding and marine engineering occurred in 1899, when John Brown & Company, the great Sheffield steel firm, acquired the Clydebank Engineering and Shipbuilding Works (formerly J. & G. Thomson) as " it was desired to find some automatic outlet in the shipbuilding trade " for their heavy forgings.[2] This tendency toward integration and combination, such a marked feature of the expansion of heavy industry, was one of the most striking consequences of the

[1] Cormack, *An Economic History of Shipbuilding and Marine Engineering* (unpublished thesis).

[2] Sir Allan Grant, *Steel and Ships* (1950), pp. 37, 58-9. For similar reasons John Brown & Co. acquired an interest in Harland & Wolff in 1906.

transition from wood to iron and from iron to steel in the construction of ships.

Progress in Marine Engineering

An important subsidiary development arising from the successful substitution of mild steel for iron was the improvement of the boiler, an advance of great significance in marine engineering. Until about 1878, when improvements in the quality of steel made it suitable for marine boiler construction, steam pressure was the limiting factor in engine development. Attempts to obtain higher powers by increasing pressure with the orthodox iron boiler usually ended in failure—and sometimes in disaster. In 1844 a new steamer called the *Telegraph*, operating on the "high-pressure principle" and designed to outdistance all her rivals on the Clyde, blew up when about to leave the quay at Helensburgh. Eighteen people were killed in the explosion and many others were injured. "The mid section of the vessel," reported an eye-witness, "was blown to pieces, down to the water's edge, and its machinery was discharged as if from a cannon's mouth, far up on the beach."[1] A similar tragedy had occurred on the opposite shore of the Clyde nine years earlier, when the *Earl Grey* burst her boiler at Greenock Pier on the return trip from Dunoon to Glasgow.[2]

In 1845 the common working pressure was about 10 lb. per sq. inch above atmospheric pressure, and by the middle 'fifties it had been increased to around 20-30 lb. per sq. inch. The demand for a saving in the consumption of fuel pointed toward the adoption of higher pressures. There was, however, an objection to the complete expansion of the higher pressure steam within a single cylinder: the difference in temperature between the steam when entering the cylinder and when leaving it was so great that considerable losses were entailed by initial condensation and subsequent re-evaporation. Accordingly, in order to reduce the range of temperature, the higher pressure steam demanded expansion in two stages, first in a "high pressure" and then in a "low pressure" cylinder. Thus the "simple" engine, with the expansion of the steam all completed within one cylinder, developed into the "compound" engine, with the initial expansion of the steam carried out in one cylinder, and the final expansion carried out in one, and occasionally two, other cylinders. The simple engine held the field, until about the sixth decade, when it was superseded by the much more economical compound engine. Concurrently the boiler pressure increased to 60 lb. per sq. inch in common practice, and to 80 and even 100 lb. per sq. inch in exceptional cases.

The demand for higher steam pressures entailed a radical modification in boiler design. So long as the pressures were low the boilers

[1] Macleod: *Nonagenarian Reminiscences of Garelochside and Helensburgh* (1883), pp. 72-3.

[2] Gillespie: *Glasgow and the Clyde* (1876), p. 61.

could be built roughly in the form of boxes, proportioned to suit the spaces available in the ships. But the flat surfaces could not remain flat, and the boilers maintain steam-tightness, under the higher pressures. The capacity to resist the higher pressures demanded a cylindrical form for the boiler; and initially the water, and steam, were contained within cylinders of small diameter, and so relatively great strength, with the gases produced by combustion playing around them. The type of boiler so initiated became known in due course as the " water-tube " boiler, whereas the older type, and developments from it, have often been termed " tank " boilers; the distinction between the two types can be indicated also by the terms " externally fired " and " internally fired."

In 1857 John Scott, at Greenock, built a ship with a water-tube boiler working at a pressure of 125 lb. per sq. inch, supplying steam to a compound engine. The boiler was not successful, and after no very long service was discarded and replaced by a boiler working at a pressure of 60 lb. per sq. inch. In succeeding years a variety of designs of water-tube boiler were proposed and tried in the mercantile marine, but none was successful. In fact a simpler solution to the problem of the boiler best suited for the increased pressures had been attained. In 1862 James Howden designed a cylindrical " tank " boiler which, although not the first cylindrical boiler fitted into a ship, was the first of the so-called " Scotch " boilers which were almost universal in the mercantile marine for the next 60-70 years. Incidentally the establishment founded by James Howden plays a large part in the industrial activity of Clydeside, notably in plant associated with the combustion of fuel in boilers.

The introduction of the water-tube boiler was directly responsible for the next development of the engine. Around 1870 John Elder & Co. received an order for a ship for which the owners desired a particular type of water-tube boiler, to work at a pressure of 150 lb. per sq. inch. A. C. Kirk, responsible for the design of the engine, appreciated that the expansion of the steam must be carried out in three stages from such a pressure if the losses inherent in the simple engine were not to be found again in the compound engine. So developed the first " triple-expansion " engine, fitted in the ship *Propontis,* built in 1874. The boilers were not, however, satisfactory and were soon replaced by others working at 90 lb. per sq. inch; the engine gave satisfactory service for years.

The first satisfactory triple-expansion engine on deep-sea service was also designed by A. C. Kirk. It was fitted in the *Aberdeen,* built for service to Australia and China in 1882. In this case the boilers were of the Scotch type to which reference has been made, constructed of steel, the material which was beginning to displace iron for the hulls. The working pressure was 125 lb. per sq. inch. From that time the development of the triple-expansion engine was dictated by the desire for economy in fuel, not by the need for increased power. The most powerful compound engines fitted in the British mercantile marine were those of the single-screw Cunard liners *Umbria* and *Etruria,* built in the middle 'eighties; with steam at a pressure of 110 lb. per sq. inch expanded in one high-pressure and two low-pressure cylinders each engine developed about 14,000 horse-power. The most powerful reciprocating engines fitted in the British mercantile marine were those of the succeeding Cunard liners *Campania* and *Lucania,* built in the early 'nineties and fitted with twin screws; with steam at a pressure of 165 lb. per sq. inch, and triple expansion, each engine developed about 15,000 horse-power, not very much more than the power developed by the engine of the *Umbria.*

The ultimate stage in the search for economy with the reciprocating steam engine was quadruple expansion. This development had no relation to any demand for increased power. When the 30,000 horse-power transmitted along the two propeller shafts of the *Campania* was exceeded by the 45,000 horse-power transmitted along the two propeller shafts of the German liner *Kaiser Wilhelm II* the additional power was obtained by fitting two quadruple-expansion engines on each shaft. At the stage of highest general development of the reciprocating steam engine common practice had become stable with the association of Scotch boilers working at about 180 lb. per sq. inch for triple-expansion engines and at about 220 lb. per sq. inch for the less common quadruple-expansion engines. By the close of the nineteenth century water-tube boilers were being almost exclusively used for naval vessels, although they had not as yet been widely adopted in the mercantile marine. John Brown and Company of Clydebank and the Fairfield Shipbuilding and Engineering Co. of Govan were already manufacturing them for installation in their warships, and were soon to be followed by Denny of Dumbarton and others. Babcock & Wilcox had meanwhile established at Renfrew the largest factory in Britain for the construction of water-tube boilers, both for marine and for land purposes, in 1897.

Increase in Size of Ships

A matter of some interest is the variation in the size of the average steamship over the years. Fig. 15 traces the variation in average size up to 1900, with the total Clyde output presented as a background. It is apparent that over the years the average size of steamships has tended to increase, the tendency indicating the known economy of transportation by larger units when the volume of trade is adequate. It is apparent also that the fluctuations in average size correspond roughly to the fluctuations in total output, thus indicating the importance of the larger ship in the prosperity of the industry.

There is, however, a qualification to be made in the consideration of Fig. 15. The figures for production over the years 1892-1900 do not include ships of small tonnage, whereas those for the period 1864-1892 cover the production of all sizes of ship. Accordingly the average sizes

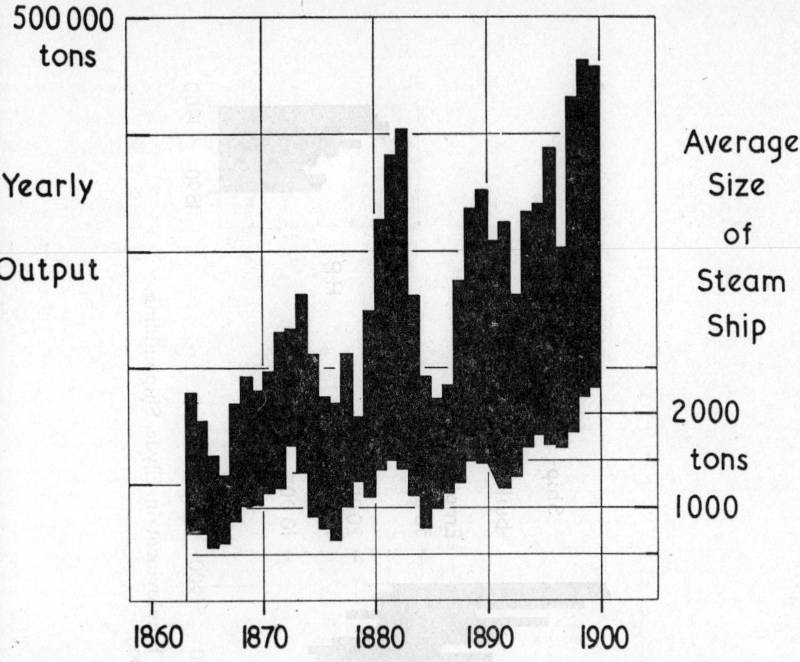

FIG. 15. Average Size of Steam Ships Built on the Clyde, 1860-1900.

for the period 1892-1900 are slightly exaggerated in relation to the average sizes for the earlier period.

The Industry at the Close of the Nineteenth Century

In a handbook of the industries of Glasgow and the West of Scotland published in connection with the meeting of the British Association in Glasgow in 1901 there are some figures relating to the period 1890-1900. These are presented graphically in the three diagrams of Fig. 16. The left-hand diagram shows the relation between total production and the production for foreign ownership. The middle diagram shows the variation in the number of men and apprentices employed in shipbuilding, excluding marine engineering, presented against total production as a background. It is apparent that the fluctuations in employment do not correspond exactly to the fluctuations in production. The right-hand diagram shows the variation in the horse-power of propelling machinery produced year by year over the period.

In the reports submitted by City Chamberlains in the nineteenth century there are some assessments of the value of shipbuilding production on the Clyde. During the seven years 1846-52 inclusive, the total value of steamships alone was £4,331,362, giving an average of

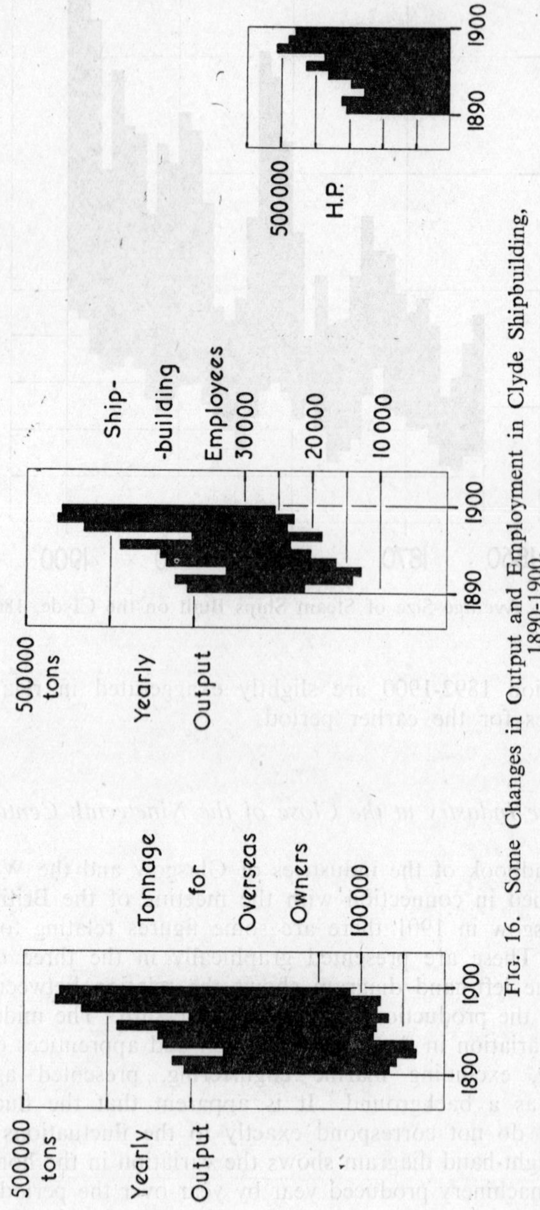

FIG. 16. Some Changes in Output and Employment in Clyde Shipbuilding, 1890-1900.

£618,766 per annum for this branch of the industry. In the year 1861 the figure was £1,759,660 (including five sailing ships of total value £50,560), and by 1864 it had risen to around five million pounds.[1] Over the seven-year period from 1863 to 1869 the value of the Clyde's production was assessed at about twenty million pounds, and in the year 1880 alone at thirteen million pounds. A return for the year 1884 shows that there were then 41 shipyards, excluding yards building only small craft, on the Clyde (including the Firth and the River Cart).

Clyde Shipbuilding Since 1900

Figure 17, showing the output of the Clyde yards since 1900, has been prepared from figures given in the Annual Trade Review published by *The Glasgow Herald*. It is a continuation into the twentieth century of Figure 14, which related to the nineteenth. Up to the end of 1950, excluding the period 1939-46, the figures of output include the tonnages of small craft such as barges and yachts, whereas the later figures do not include the tonnages of small craft; the yearly output of small craft ranges from about 1,500 tons to about 4,500 tons. The "great depression" of 1931-5 is clearly indicated on Figure 17. A minor point in this connection is that the larger output for 1934 than for 1935 is largely explained by the launching of the *Queen Mary* in the former year; a similar "peak" for 1938 is explained by the launching of the *Queen Elizabeth*.

Figure 17 indicates the production of sailing ships to the end of 1913, but a qualification is necessary. In the records of output all craft without propelling machinery are classed as sailing ships. In 1913 the output of such craft was nearly 10,000 tons. In fact, however, the last open-sea sailing ship built on the Clyde was launched in 1907. There was a minor revival of the sailing ship in 1901 and 1902; 18 were launched in 1901 and 16 in 1902. Six were launched in each of the two following years. And in 1905, 1906 and 1907, with one ship in each year, the production of open-sea sailing ships came to an end.

Figure 18 is a continuation of the left-hand diagram of Figure 16, with the minor difference that in the earlier diagram the production of tonnage for overseas owners is presented against a background of total production, whereas in Figure 18 the background is the production of merchant ship tonnage. Incidentally in Figure 18 the production for overseas owners covers, in one or two years, a small amount of tonnage for foreign navies.

[1] The American Civil War was partly responsible for this, just as in the eighteenth century the American War of Independence had stimulated shipbuilding on the Clyde. In 1862-4 Clydeside did a lucrative business in building fast steamers for running the blockade of the ports of the Southern States, and some of the swift passenger steamers already plying on the Firth were utilised in this work also.

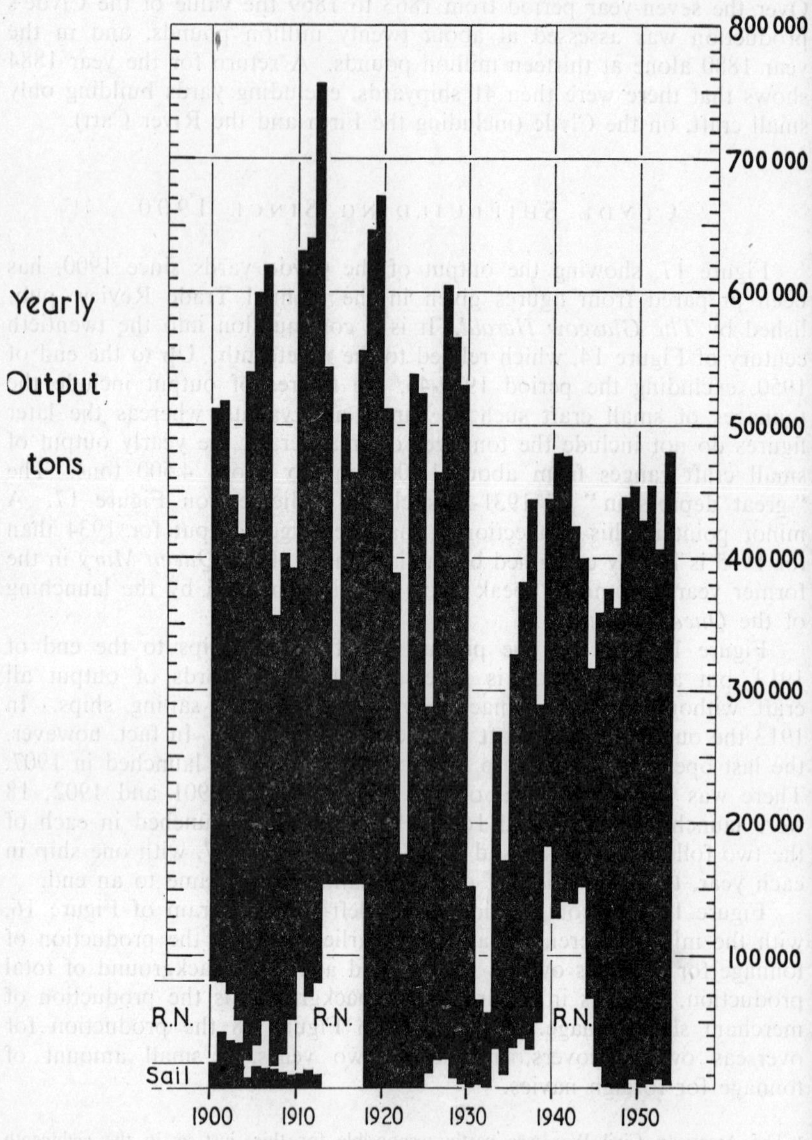

FIG. 17. Yearly Shipbuilding Output of the Clyde since 1900.

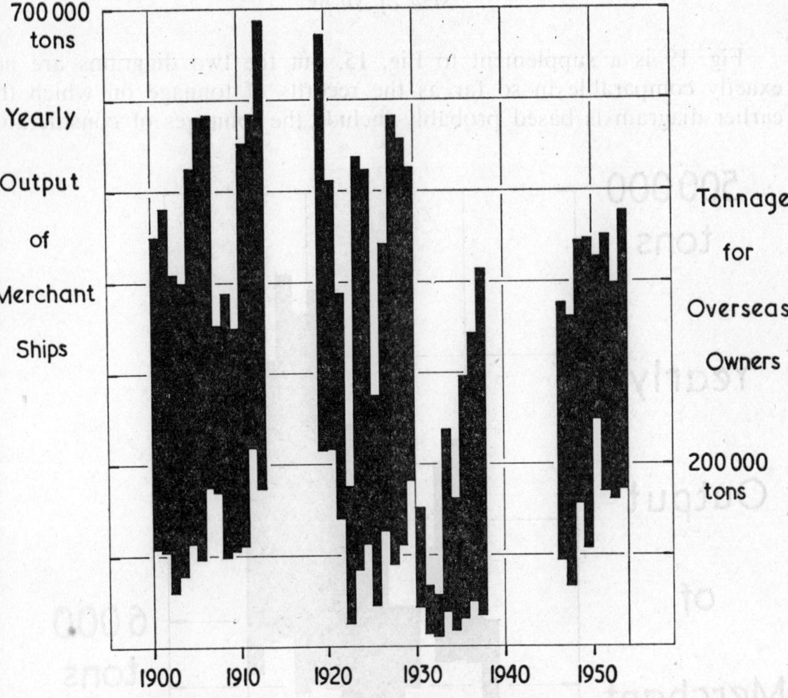

FIG. 18. Tonnage for Overseas Owners compared with Total Clyde Merchant Output, 1900-53.

Naval Vessels

Figure 17 differs from Figure 14 in so far as the tonnage of ships built to Government account, almost entirely for service with the Royal Navy, is separately indicated on the diagram. Detailed figures of output of naval tonnage for the years 1914-18 are not available; but a figure for the five-year period has been published, and an average yearly output for the period has been indicated on the diagram. For the years 1939-46 the production of ships for the Royal Navy may not be represented with complete accuracy since there is some doubt on the dates of launching of some of the minor craft; any error on this account will not, however, materially falsify the general picture. A further consideration is that a few of the ships for which the launchings have been recorded in 1946 were not completed, and the completion of some ships launched in 1945 was delayed.

Size of Ships

Fig. 19 is a supplement to Fig. 15, but the two diagrams are not exactly comparable in so far as the records of tonnage on which the earlier diagram is based probably include the tonnages of considerable

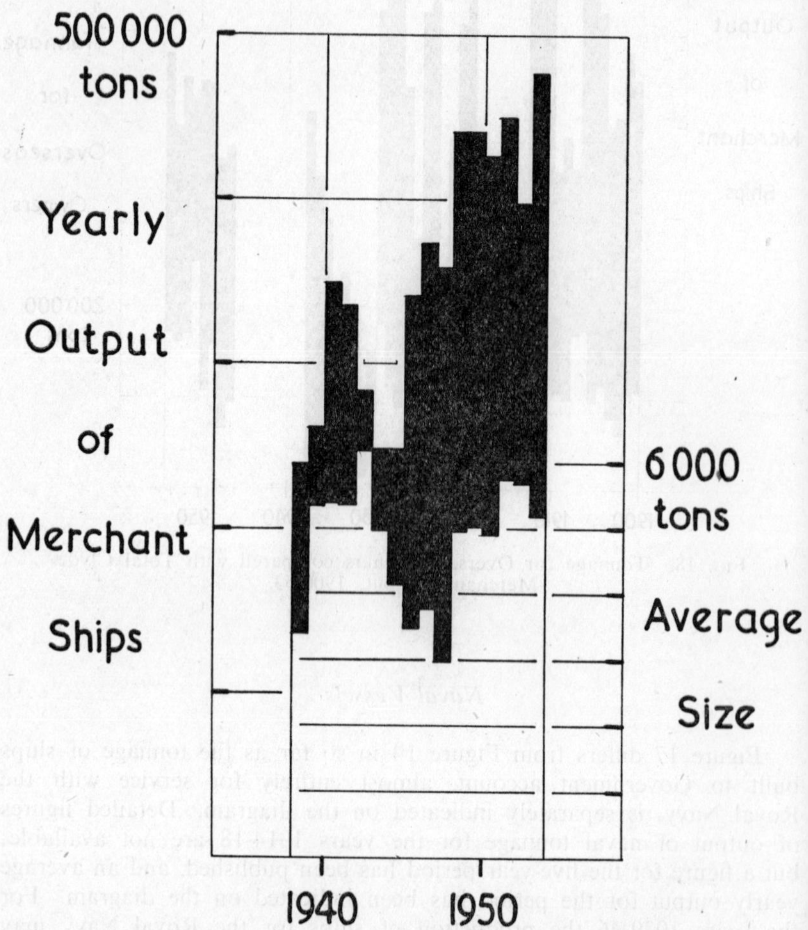

FIG. 19. Average Size of Merchant Ships built on the Clyde, 1938-53.

numbers of small craft whereas the tonnages of small craft have been excluded from the records on which Fig. 19 is based; accordingly the average tonnages shown by Fig. 15 are probably rather less than they should be for exact comparison with the figures indicated by Fig. 19. Nevertheless the absence of exact comparison does not seriously affect the indication of a marked increase in average size of ship since the beginning of the twentieth century. It is possible that the large average size of ship built during the war years was dictated by strategic considerations, and that the reduction in average size during the years immediately following the war indicates a need for the replacement of some smaller ships for trade routes not covered during the war.

Fig. 19 and Fig. 15 indicate a tendency toward bigger, and still bigger, ships; and in the early part of the present century it seemed that the tendency must continue. The tendency originated in the desire to extend the range of activity of the steamship. The longer the voyage the greater the amount of coal required, and so the larger the ship; moreover the ship had to be large enough to carry something more than merely the coal required for the propulsion. The general consideration was summed up in a very early rough, but fundamentally sound, approximation that the tonnage should be the same as the length of the voyage in miles. It was this approximation that underlay the production of the mammoth *Great Eastern* in 1859. The ship was designed for service to Australia, and the round voyage of 25,000 miles demanded the provision of bunkers for 12,000 tons of coal; wherefore the building of a ship which was not surpassed in size for nearly 50 years. Improvements in the economy of propelling machinery, and ability to obtain fuel at ports scattered over the globe, are factors which tend to restrict growth in size of ship. On the other hand the values of the cargoes transported by cargo liners demand speeds appreciably higher than in the past; and the economical attainment of the higher speeds demands increased size. Another factor in the consideration is that the discharge, and dispersal, of a widely varied assortment of cargo from a very large ship involve uneconomically long periods in port. Moreover on some trade routes there are ports which cannot be made to accommodate large ships without undue expenditure. Accordingly it would seem that there is not likely to be the steady growth in size of carriers of general cargo that was clearly evident during last century. In the oil-tanker there has, however, been spectacular growth in recent years. The larger the ship the more economically is the cargo transported. The discharge of even a very large oil cargo is a rapid process compared with the discharge of an assorted general cargo. Moreover at some ports the oil companies seem to have the capacity to handle expeditiously cargoes arriving in units up to 50,000 tons and even more. In the circumstances the limit to the size of the oil-tanker employed on main feeder services may not yet have been reached. It will be imposed by the size of dry docks available and by the size of berths available in the major shipyards.

In the case of the passenger ship the factors determining size are much the same as those operative in the case of the cargo ship, but there is, in addition, the factor of competition with air services. The building of the very large passenger ship has not always been merely a matter of prestige; the size may be determined by the speed required on service. But the speed required on service is inter-linked with the frequency of the service and the number of ships necessary to maintain it. The building of the largest ships in the British merchant navy followed from that broad consideration. It was desired to maintain a weekly service both ways across the North Atlantic throughout the season of heaviest traffic. Such a service could be maintained with two ships, only if each ship could make a crossing and "turn round" in port within the week; fortunately a full load of passengers can readily be dispersed, and by careful organisation the necessary replenishments of fuel and stores, the replacing of soiled linen and general freshening up for new passengers, can be effected in not very many hours. On this basis it was decided that two ships could maintain the service if they could be depended on to make the crossing at 28 knots. To be able to travel at such a speed without extravagant consumption of fuel the ships had to be about 1000 ft. long. That broad consideration, and not prestige, dictated the building of the two *Queens* of the North Atlantic, rather than the three, or more, ships that would have been necessary to maintain the weekly service if the speed had been less than 28 knots. It is, however, probable that these two ships will not for a long time, if ever, be surpassed in size.

It does not appear that services by air have yet materially affected services by sea across the Atlantic. The volume of passenger traffic by sea seems to be well maintained, although it is possible that the air services are taking an increasing proportion of an expanding traffic. In some services to the East there are indications of competition from the air in so far as in one fleet at least the extent of the passenger accommodation on ships of large cargo capacity has been drastically reduced. Moreover the shrinkage in the Eastern regions ruled from Europe by Europeans must have meant a considerable reduction in the numbers of officers going on, and returning from, leave. On the other hand the indications that the two major lines trading to Australia have under consideration the building of ships very much larger than the present large ships on the run suggest that there is no fear of competition from the air. Incidentally it is not yet clear whether the development represents an increase in the facilities for transport or maintenance of existing facilities by fewer ships.

Changes in Construction Methods

Not only has there been a change in the average size of ships. There have been changes in methods of construction. During recent years there has been a revolution in building methods, from riveting and piece-meal erection on open berths (where work was subject to interruption by rain and storm) to welding and pre-fabrication within building shops, resulting in substantial gains in the efficiency and cargo-carrying capacity of the ships so built. In the early days the hull was built up of innumerable small pieces, lifted separately, and all connected on the building berth. Development in design of hull structures centred mainly on the reduction in the numbers of parts to be handled. In very early days a steam riveter was available, but does not seem to have found much favour. It was not until the advent of the hydraulic riveter that mechanical power began to displace man-power in the connection of parts. There were, however, limitations on the use of the hydraulic riveter. It could not be used on all parts of a ship. It was inconvenient to use on upper portions, and, in common practice, its use was restricted to the bottoms of ships. It was, however, very convenient for use on the ground, at the end of the building berth. In this consideration there lies the beginning of the process now commonly known as pre-fabrication. By means of the hydraulic riveter several small parts could conveniently be connected to a larger part on the ground, before the whole was lifted into place; and the process was extended until it became necessary to replace the early primitive wood derricks, capable of lifting only small weights, by steel lattice-work cranes capable of dealing with considerable loads.

After the war of 1914-18 the use of compressed air in tools for riveting, caulking and drilling developed rapidly, but this particular adoption of mechanical power in substitution for man-power did not have any influence on the development of the method of pre-fabrication. The spectacular development of pre-fabrication is a consequence of the adoption of electrical power for the connection of parts—power in the form of an electric arc connecting parts by the fusion of material at the joints. With this method of connection it is convenient, and economic, to connect large pieces on the ground, within a shed, and transport them to the building berth for connection there to other large parts also transported from the pre-fabrication shed. Hence arose a demand for larger cranes; the range of capacity is now from about 20 to about 40 tons.

The substitution of electric welding for riveting was initially very gradual, and the development of the process of pre-fabrication lagged behind the extension of the process of welding. The adoption of the newer technique for connection has led to some changes in the pattern of the trades, most marked by a decline in the number of riveters and holders-on; it has led also to a decline in the number of angle-iron smiths. In April 1930 the Clyde shipyards employed 2,612 riveters and holders-on, with 207 apprentice riveters; they employed about 73 electric welders. In April 1939 the number of riveters and holders-on had fallen to 1,440, with 150 apprentices; and the number of electric welders had risen to 452, with 381 apprentices. In May 1955 the number of riveters and holders-on had declined further to 685, and 30 apprentices, 4 of them holders-on; the number of electric welders had risen to 1,806, with 480 apprentices. In April 1939 there were 67 angle-iron smiths and 8 apprentices; in May 1955 there were 5 and no apprentices.

The pattern of the trades has also been affected by the much greater elaboration of the internal arrangements and fittings of the modern ship. An indication of the trend can be gleaned from the figures of employment in two particular trades—plumbers and electricians. In 1895 there were 123 plumbers and 20 electricians employed in Clyde shipyards (the figures include apprentices). In 1905 the figures had risen to 251 and 89 respectively. For 1955 they were 1,044 and 1,292.[1]

Progress in Marine Engineering

Fig. 20 is a continuation of the right-hand diagram of Fig. 16, but shows, in addition, the production of machinery, expressed in terms of horse-power, for Government account, almost entirely for the Royal Navy. For the period 1914-18, only the total figure is available, and the diagram corresponds to the total figure although the variation over the period is probably unreliable. For the period 1939-46 the total production is known, year by year, but the production for the Royal Navy is not known. The figures of production for the Royal Navy in the later years are only approximations in the absence of exact information. The fact that in the production of machinery the demand for the Royal Navy is relatively very much larger than in the production of ships, as measured by tonnage, reflects the fact that the ships of the Royal Navy are, in relation to size, much more highly powered than ships of the mercantile marine. The most notable advance in marine engineering at the beginning of the present century was the development of the steam turbine. In the reciprocating engine the transformation of the linear motion of a piston within a cylinder into the rotary motion of a shaft entails appreciable losses from friction of moving parts; and from earliest days there have been attempts to obtain the desired rotary motion in a direct manner. Toward the end of the nineteenth century the development of the steam turbine, in which the expanding steam imparts rotary motion by impinging on "wheels" composed of series of radiating angled blades or vanes, was being pursued by Parsons in Britain, Rateau in France and Curtis in America. The Parsons turbine was the first to be adopted on an appreciable scale. Following a spectacular demonstration by an experimental craft, the *Turbinia,* at the Diamond Jubilee Naval Review at Spithead in 1897 the Parsons turbine was fitted in some torpedo-boat-destroyers for the Royal Navy; the capacity to develop high power on low weight made the turbine an attractive proposition for fast craft. The first application of the turbine for the propulsion of a merchant ship followed in 1901, when the combined enterprise of Williamson, Parsons and Denny, shipowner, engineer and shipbuilder, led to the production of the *King Edward* for service on the Clyde, a service this ship maintained for 50 years, apart from some adventures in the English Channel and North Russia between 1914 and 1919. Thereafter the progress was rapid, and the turbine offered the only possible solution to the problem of providing large powers, such as the 75,000 horse-power of

[1] A detailed table of such changes is given in the Appendix, Table 44.

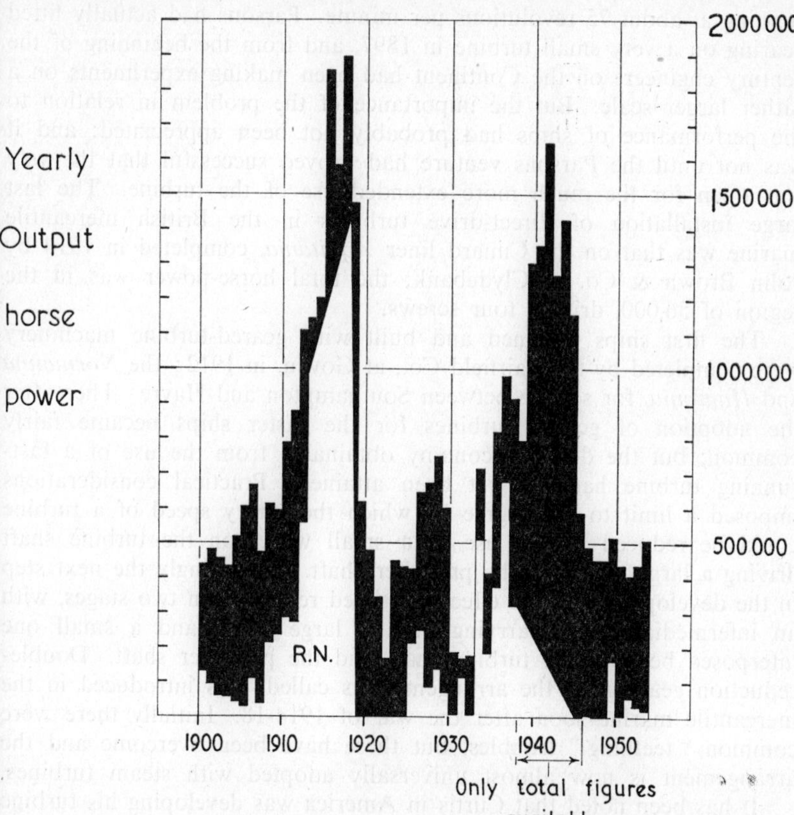

FIG. 20. Horse Power of Marine Engines built on the Clyde, 1900-53.

the *Lusitania* and *Mauretania,* and the lesser, but still large, requirements of the ships of the Royal Navy.

The early turbine machinery was open to one serious criticism—it was not very economical. Professor Sir John Biles, of Glasgow University, claimed the credit of posing the dilemma to Parsons, and suggesting the solution. In order to obtain maximum efficiency the turbine had to rotate at high speed, whereas for maximum efficiency the screw propeller which it drove had to rotate at low speed; and the practicable compromise entailed a loss of efficiency in both turbine and propeller. Hence the desirable increase in overall efficiency could be attained only by interposing speed-reduction gearing between the turbine shaft and the propeller shaft; by that means only could the turbine be rendered an attractive proposition for use in ships of the moderate and lower speeds. In 1910 Parsons removed from a cargo ship the reciprocating engine of about 1000 horse-power and replaced it by a turbine running at about 1500 revolutions per minute geared to a propeller shaft running at about 75 revolutions per minute. Parsons had actually fitted gearing on a very small turbine in 1897, and from the beginning of the century engineers on the Continent had been making experiments on a rather larger scale. But the importance of the problem in relation to the performance of ships had probably not been appreciated; and it was not until the Parsons venture had proved successful that the way was open for the much more extended use of the turbine. The last large installation of direct-drive turbines in the British mercantile marine was that on the Cunard liner *Aquitania,* completed in 1914 by John Brown & Co. at Clydebank; the total horse-power was in the region of 56,000, driving four screws.

The first ships designed and built with geared-turbine machinery were completed by the Fairfield Co., at Govan, in 1912: the *Normanna* and *Hantonia,* for service between Southampton and Havre. Thereafter the adoption of geared turbines for the faster ships became fairly common; but the desired economy obtainable from the use of a fast-running turbine had not yet been attained. Practical considerations imposed a limit to the degree by which the rotary speed of a turbine could be reduced by the use of a small wheel on the turbine shaft driving a large wheel on the propeller shaft. Accordingly the next step in the development was to effect the speed reduction in two stages, with an intermediate shaft carrying both a large wheel and a small one interposed between the turbine shaft and the propeller shaft. Double-reduction gearing, as the arrangement is called, was introduced in the mercantile marine soon after the war of 1914-18. Initially there were common "teething" troubles, but these have been overcome and the arrangement is now almost universally adopted with steam turbines.

It has been noted that Curtis in America was developing his turbine when Parsons was working in England. Not long after the Parsons turbine had been well established John Brown & Co. at Clydebank took out a licence from the Curtis Company so that they could make also the turbine of American origin. The modern turbine embodies features of both the Parsons and Curtis turbines.

The demand for higher steam pressures in the reciprocating engine led, as has been noted, to the design and construction of water-tube boilers. It has been noted also that the early water-tube boilers were not satisfactory; and there has been an indication that the adoption of the water-tube boiler in the mercantile marine was retarded in consequence of the introduction of the Scotch boiler. History repeated itself in so far as demands for increased steam pressures in turbines led to the almost universal adoption of water-tube boilers in association with turbines for the ships of higher powers. Although the water-tube boiler had only been fitfully adopted in the mercantile marine over the latter half of the nineteenth century and into the twentieth century, it had been almost universally adopted in the Royal Navy; a Yarrow boiler had been fitted in a torpedo boat in 1879. The attractiveness of the water-tube boiler lay in the fact that it was relatively very much lighter than the Scotch boiler; it was probably this consideration which dictated the first of the modern adoptions of the water-tube boilers in the mercantile marine—in the *Paris,* built by Denny in 1913 for cross-channel service. Not long after the war of 1914-18 development in the design of the turbine demanded steam pressures beyond the 220 lb. per sq. inch which marked approximately the limit for the Scotch boiler. It is true that in the 'twenties an installation of Scotch boilers working at a pressure of 300 lb. per sq. inch was fitted in a large cargo ship; but that was an isolated case with no repetition. Since about that time the adoption of water-tube boilers, of designs based on those which had been found satisfactory in the Royal Navy, has spread throughout the mercantile marine; and for steamers other than those of low power, for which the turbine is not suitable, the water-tube boiler has become universal.

During the early years of the century, while the use of the steam turbine was extending, another type of engine, now commonly known as the Diesel, was being developed on the Continent. In this engine the piston is pushed along the cylinder by the expansion of a gas, as in the steam engine; but the expanding gas is the product of the combustion of oil within the cylinder. The important feature of the new engine is that the heat necessary to initiate the combustion of the fuel is generated by the prior compression of air within the cylinder. The better name for it, therefore, is the "compression-ignition" engine. The principle of compression-ignition was actually devised in England. But the principle was developed, and first applied on a large scale, by Dr. Rudolph Diesel, in Germany; wherefore the name given to this type of engine. The first seagoing ships with Diesel engines were built in Italy and Holland in 1910. The ships were not large, and were used only on relatively short voyages. The first large ship fitted with Diesel engines for world-wide voyages was the *Selandia,* built in Denmark in 1912, followed within the same year by the *Jutlandia,* a sister ship built by Barclay, Curle & Co. at Whiteinch. Both ships were for Danish owners, and had engines built by Burmeister & Wain, of Copenhagen; incidentally, Wain was an Englishman from Stockport. For several years the Diesel engines made by Burmeister & Wain, or under licence from them, practically held the field. There are now several types available for large powers. But all large Diesel engines built on Clydeside are manufactured under licence. There is no Diesel engine of Clyde origin; the only large Diesel engine of British origin is the Doxford, developed in Sunderland by the shipbuilders and engineers of that name.

At present the steam reciprocating engine has been almost completely discarded. For the smallest powers, as in coasting ships, the Diesel engine is the most suitable. For the largest powers the combination of steam turbines and water-tube boilers is the only possibility. Over a wide range between the limits there is a choice between the turbine and the Diesel engine determined only by particular considerations.

In the record of the development of propelling machinery an important step has so far been omitted; the importance of the step has not commonly been appreciated. It has been indicated that in the *Kaiser Wilhelm II* each shaft transmitted 22,500 horse-power to the propeller. On the *Queen Elizabeth,* with four shafts, each transmits about 40,000-45,000 horse-power to a propeller. The transmission of such a large power along a shaft could not have been possible but for the use of a thrust-block invented by A. G. M. Michell, an Australian engineer and mathematician. The thrust-block is a necessary fitting on a shaft driving a screw propeller. It transmits the thrust delivered by the propeller to the structure of the ship, so that the engine merely turns the shaft, and is not affected by the thrust exerted by the rotating propeller. Prior to 1913 the thrust shaft, a relatively short shaft immediately abaft the engine, was fitted with a large number of collars. Each collar was matched with a " horse-shoe," suspended from, and rigidly secured to, a structure attached to the hull of the ship. The thrust of the propeller was transmitted from the faces of the rotating collars to the faces of the stationary horse-shoes, with films of lubricating oil between the matching faces. It was found that the thrust should be somewhere within the range from 20-50 lb. per sq. inch, with the upper end of the range open to suspicion. Provision was made for adjusting the positions of the horse-shoes as an attempt to ensure that each bore the proper share of the load. But there was never any assurance that the load could be properly distributed; and, in fact, the thrust-block was always a source of worry to every chief engineer. It is possible that about 20,000 horse-power was about the most that could be transmitted along a shaft with any approach to confidence. The Michell thrust-block has effected a transformation. With only a single collar on the thrust shaft it is possible to work with confidence to a pressure of 200-300 lb. per sq. inch, and it is now universally fitted. Incidentally the first merchant ship fitted with Michell thrust-blocks was the cross-channel steamer *Paris*, built by Denny in 1913; reference has already been made to this ship in connection with the boilers.

Fluctuations in the Industry

It has been noted, on p. 187, that 41 separate yards, excluding yards producing small craft, contributed to the output recorded for 1884. In 1901 there were 39 separate yards, and this number was maintained until 1920. In 1927 there were 31 separate yards, and in 1929 there were 29 yards. During the great depression some yards were temporarily, and others permanently, closed; the figures for output in 1931 were made up from the records of 21 yards, and in 1932 from the records of 13 yards. In 1933 there were 15 yards contributing to the output, and in 1934 there were 21 yards. Since 1947 there have been 23 yards contributing to the output (Fig. 21), although three of them are closely linked, and other two are branches of a shipbuilding organisation centred beyond the Clyde Valley.

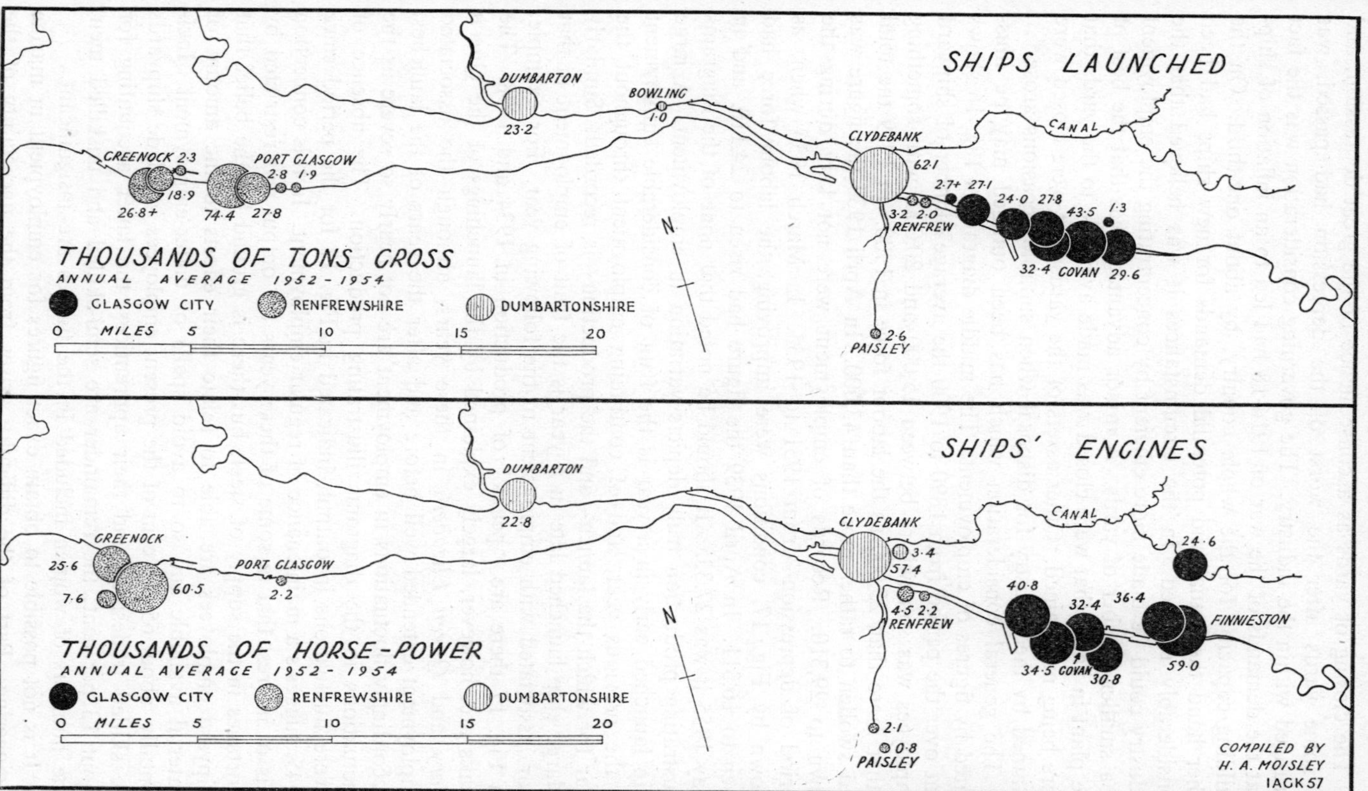

FIG. 21. Clyde Shipbuilding and Marine Engineering Establishments: Average Annual Output 1952-4.

The closing of yards as a consequence of the great depression, and of some yards after the worst of the depression had passed, was arranged within the industry. The governing consideration was the fact that the demands of the war of 1914-18 had led to an inflation of shipbuilding capacity, for the whole country, by about one-third. On the other hand the actual and potential demands for new ships had been considerably reduced. In the circumstances it was believed that the industry could be made more efficient by concentrating the employment in a smaller number of yards. A minor advantage was that the best of the plant in yards that were closed was made available to the yards that were being maintained. Other assets of the yards that were closed were retained by the industry for disposal when suitable occasions arose.

The general consideration which has been outlined may be illustrated by figures of employment. The middle diagram of Fig. 16 shows that over the period from 1890 to 1900 the average number of shipyard employees was somewhere between 15,000 and 20,000, with something rather more than 25,000 as the labour force in 1900. In 1919 the total had swollen to rather more than 43,000. In April 1930 the figure was down to 29,310. Records of employment were not kept during the period of depression—from 1931 to 1935. In March 1936 when, as shown by Fig. 17, conditions were improving, the labour force had risen to 16,311. In April 1939 the figure had risen to 24,110, and in May 1955 it was 27,335. It should be noted that none of the diagrams illustrating production truly depicts variation in employment. A large ship launched early in a year is the fruit of considerable employment in the previous year, and of continuing employment throughout the year for which the launch—and the production—is recorded. Similarly a large ship launched late in a year is the fruit of employment in that year, associated with employment in the following year. For example, on Fig. 17 there are "peaks" of production in 1934 and 1938. The peaks are, however, largely explained by the launchings of the *Queen Mary* and *Queen Elizabeth* in these years, although the associated employment extended well before and after the years of the launches. Accordingly fluctuations in employment are not nearly so severe as the fluctuations in the diagrams illustrating production. The absence of severe fluctuations in output, indicated in Fig. 17 for the period since 1945, suggests a maintenance of regular employment. In this connection it is of interest that in some of these years the output was restricted by shortages in the supply of steel; but there is ground for the belief that shipyard employees are able to relate their efforts to the amount of material available and so to avoid spells of under-employment. Incidentally, about 65 per cent of the present employees in Clyde shipyards are skilled tradesmen and their apprentices, the latter accounting for about 13 per cent; the remainder are semi-skilled and unskilled men. The numbers of women included in the figures are insignificant.

It is not possible to obtain exact figures for employment in marine engineering. Part of the difficulty arises from the uncertainty of the boundaries of marine engineering. If that branch of industry is taken to include the making of auxiliary and ancillary machinery fitted in and on ships it would be necessary to bring under consideration the employment in firms making, for instance, pumps and condensing plant. But much of the production of such firms is supplied for use on land, and it would be hard to determine the number of men at any time working only on production for service at sea. Even if it be taken that marine engineering covers only the provision of main propelling machinery there is a difficulty. Some firms making smaller types of propelling engines supply similar engines for land use; and here again it would not be easy to determine the number of men employed only on marine work. Moreover, other firms make boilers for land use as well as for marine use, and the difficulty again arises.

Value of Output

In all the diagrams illustrating the production of ships, but not the separate production of engines, the " yard-stick " of measurement is the ton. This yard-stick is very unsatisfactory, and is adopted only because it is not possible to find a better alternative. There are actually two quite different " tons " used throughout the records. For a merchant ship one ton represents, broadly, 100 cubic feet of total internal volume. For a naval ship one ton corresponds to 35 cubic feet of volume immersed in the water. It is not possible to equate the two units, and for any year in which both naval ships and merchant ships were launched the total tonnage shown on a diagram is the sum of two different quantities. Hence comparison of output year by year cannot be exact, but can be taken only as a valuable approximation. Moreover, a ton of warship is more expensive than a ton of merchant ship. Even for merchant ships a comparison of tonnages is not a comparison of values. A ton of passenger ship in 1954 corresponds to much greater elaboration in internal arrangements and in fittings than a ton of passenger ship in, say, 1904. There is a further consideration. It may be taken that with the ton as the basis for comparison the cheapest type of ship is the cargo " tramp." The oil-tanker and the cargo " liner " are much more expensive. Prior to 1914 the production of tramps predominated over the production of other types of cargo vessels. Since 1946 the production of tramps has almost ceased, whereas the production of oil-tankers and cargo liners has increased.

In the earlier years of the century there were very few oil-tankers built on the Clyde, and it was not until the 'twenties that they began to figure appreciably in the output. The development in the production of that class of ship is illustrated by Figure 22, which shows, year by year, the tonnage of oil-tankers launched, presented against a background showing total tonnage of merchant ships; figures are not available for the period 1939-46.

The total value of the output from Clydeside yards, including repair work, has been assessed at about £55 million for 1954. In this

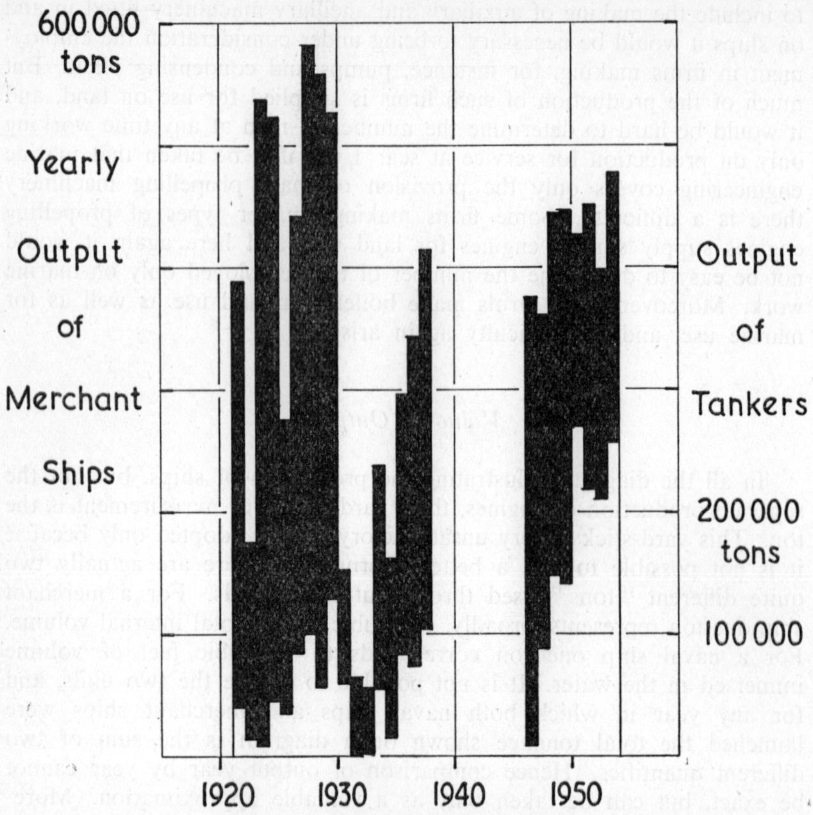

Fig. 22. Tonnage of Oil-tankers launched on the Clyde, 1921-53.

connection it must be borne in mind that shipbuilding is, in a sense, very largely an "assembly industry." For a fairly elaborate ship carrying passengers and cargo the cost of equipment, etc., merely fitted into place by the shipbuilder, including work done by sub-contractors, amounts to about 30 to 40 per cent of the total. Of the remainder, somewhere between 40 and 60 per cent represents the cost of the material on which there is considerable work done by the labour force. The equipment and fittings are not all obtainable locally, but are drawn from all over the country. Figure 23 is a reproduction, slightly modified, of a map which was prepared to show, for the Cunard liner *Queen Mary*, the districts in which contracts had been placed by the shipbuilders and their sub-contractors. The map does not, however, present a complete picture. Contracts may be placed locally for steel and for timber, but the steel-maker must obtain ore from abroad, and the timber merchant may draw his supplies from all quarters of the globe. A contract for electric cables may be placed in this country, but the fulfilment may demand the use of rubber and tin from Malaya,

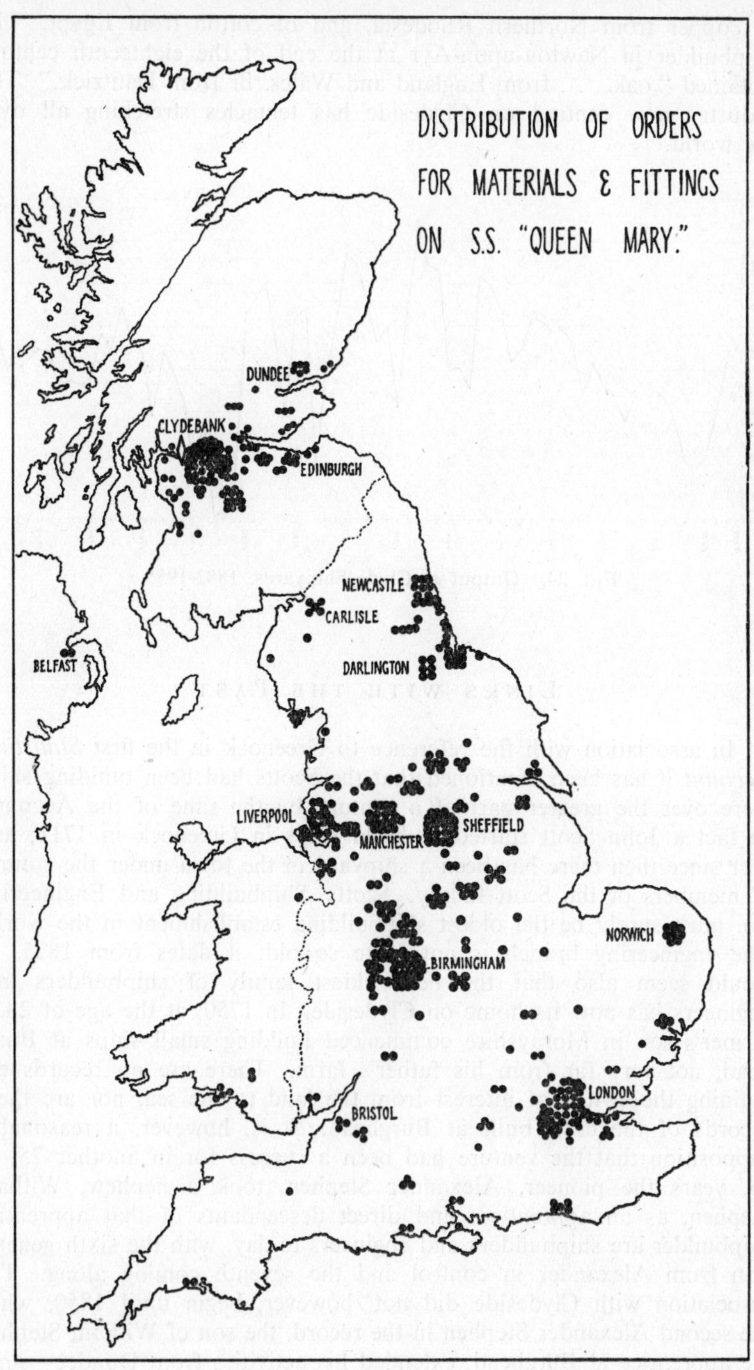
DISTRIBUTION OF ORDERS
FOR MATERIALS & FITTINGS
ON S.S. "QUEEN MARY."
DUNDEE
CLYDEBANK
EDINBURGH
NEWCASTLE
CARLISLE
BELFAST
DARLINGTON
LIVERPOOL
MANCHESTER
SHEFFIELD
NORWICH
BIRMINGHAM
LONDON
BRISTOL

FIG. 23.

of copper from Northern Rhodesia, and of cotton from Egypt. The shipbuilder in Newton-upon-Ayr at the end of the eighteenth century obtained " oak . . . from England and Wales, fir from Dantzick." The industry now centred on Clydeside has tentacles stretching all over the world.

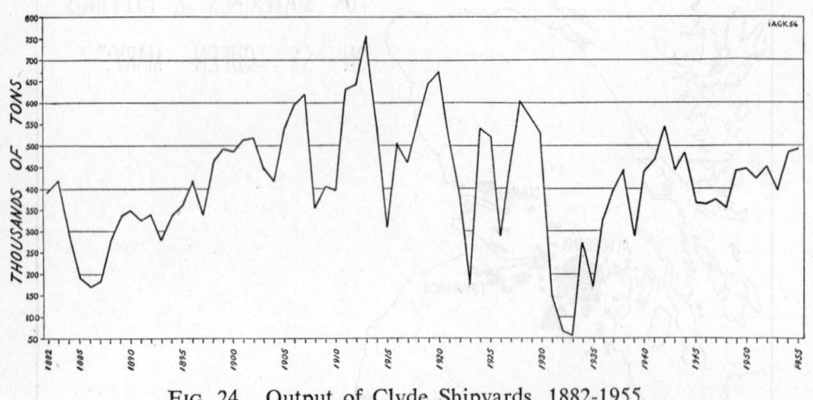

FIG. 24. Output of Clyde Shipyards, 1882-1955.

LINKS WITH THE PAST

In association with the reference to Greenock in the first *Statistical Account* it has been mentioned that the Scotts had been building ships there over the greater part of a century by the time of the Account. In fact a John Scott started to build ships in Greenock in 1711, and ever since then there has been a shipyard in the town under the control of members of the Scott family. Scotts' Shipbuilding and Engineering Co. must surely be the oldest shipbuilding establishment in the world. The engineering branch is not quite so old; it dates from 1825. It would seem also that the next oldest family of shipbuilders and engineers has now its home on Clydeside. In 1750, at the age of 28, a farmer's son in Morayshire commenced building small ships at Burghead, not very far from his father's farm. There are no records explaining the switch of interest from the land to the sea, nor are there records of the craft built at Burghead. It is, however, a reasonable supposition that the venture had been a success for in another 25, or so, years the pioneer, Alexander Stephen, took a nephew, William Stephen, as an apprentice; and direct descendants of that apprentice shipbuilder are shipbuilders and engineers to-day, with the sixth generation from Alexander in control and the seventh coming along. The association with Clydeside did not, however, begin until 1850, when the second Alexander Stephen in the record, the son of William Stephen the apprentice at Burghead, extended his activities from Dundee—since 1894 the activities have been confined to Clydeside, and the firm of

Alexander Stephen & Sons is now located at Linthouse. There is a third continuing family, the Dennys of Dumbarton. It has been noted that of the very early steam ships built on the Clyde five had hulls built by a Denny at Dumbarton. Several members of the family were concerned with the building of ships and engines in the early years of the industry, but the present firm, William Denny & Brothers, did not come into being until 1844.

There is also a continuing firm, Barclay, Curle & Co., of Whiteinch. In 1818 John Barclay commenced repairing and building ships at Stobcross, the site being chosen because of a pool in the river. The venture was successful, and activity was expanded by Robert Barclay, the son of the founder. In 1845 the manager of the shipyard was taken into partnership and the title of the firm became Robert Barclay & Curle. By 1861 the activities of the firm had been extended to cover the production of engines, and in association with that development Archibald Gilchrist was taken into the partnership. With the deaths of Robert Barclay in 1863 and of Robert Curle in 1880 the links with the earliest days were severed. There is, however, another link. The firm was constituted as a public company in 1884, and not long afterwards Archibald Gilchrist became chairman. The present chairman, James Gilchrist, follows his father, grandfather and great-grandfather in the position.

In the pattern of Clydeside history the name Napier is prominent although it disappeared from direct connection with shipbuilding after the great depression around the early 'thirties of this century. The earliest Napiers in the record were cousins, David and Robert, David the pioneer and inventor, Robert the apostle of reliability. Incidentally there was a link between the Napiers and the Dennys in so far as Robert had a Denny as a grandmother. David Napier made the boiler for the *Comet,* and so was associated with Clyde steam ships from the start. He initiated the use of steam ships in open waters by building the *Rob Roy* in 1818 for service between Greenock and Belfast; the ship was subsequently the pioneer steam ship in service across the English Channel. He is credited with the construction of the first iron steam ship on Clydeside, a small craft for service on Loch Eck. But his name does not figure so prominently in the history as that of his cousin Robert, junior to David by a couple of years. There remains, however, one link with David Napier. In 1834 two of his managers, David Tod and John McGregor, joined forces in a new venture as engineers, and soon thereafter added ship repairing and shipbuilding to their activities; the second *Statistical Account* embodies a reference to the launch of a small iron ship built by them. Their first yard was on the south side of the river, on ground near the present Mavisbank Quay, and there they built in 1839 the first iron steamer produced on the Clyde for open-water service. Subsequently they moved to a site on the west bank of the Kelvin, at the junction with the Clyde, and there they built several notable iron ships for Atlantic service. The shipyard and engine works later came under the control of the Henderson family—

the family once associated with the Anchor Line of ships—but activity is now confined to ship repairing, under the name of D. & W. Henderson: control has passed from the Henderson family.

Robert Napier was born in Dumbarton in 1791. The son of a blacksmith, he was apprenticed to his father, and in 1815 started as a smith in Glasgow. Although he had soon developed an ambition to build engines for ships he did not secure an opportunity until 1823, when he built for the *Leven* an engine which is still preserved on a pedestal near Dumbarton Castle. The quality of his work was so high that other contracts followed, and in not many more years he was acknowledged to be the leading marine engineer on Clydeside. By 1833 Napier had become deeply interested in the possibility of a transatlantic steamship service, and had prepared a fairly detailed estimate of annual income and expenditure for a ship of 800 tons and 300 horse-power; in 1839 the *British Queen,* with engines by Napier, sailed from Spithead for New York. There was interest in transatlantic steamship services also in the West, and in 1838 Samuel Cunard, a merchant in Halifax, N.S., had secured from the British Government a provisional contract for a mail service by steam ships to replace the service then carried on by small sailing ships. Early in 1839 Cunard arrived in London to make arrangements for fulfilling his contract, and, on the advice of the secretary of the East India Company, put himself in contact with Napier; Cunard was the agent of the East India Company in Halifax, and Napier had recently completed a very successful ship for the Company. The outcome of the meeting between Cunard and Napier was the founding of the fleet now known as the Cunard Line. Discussion commenced on the basis of ships of the size Napier had proposed in the estimates prepared in 1833, but subsequently Napier was satisfied that ships of 800 tons would be too small to ensure success and pressed for ships of considerably greater tonnage. Cunard demurred, on the ground that he could not provide the money for the larger ships. Napier had, however, such a reputation for wisdom and integrity that several of his friends, and their friends, subscribed the amount required and construction of four ships proceeded on the basis suggested by Napier. The original amount subscribed was £270,000, of which about one-fifth was subscribed by Cunard and the remainder by Napier and his associates. It may be that the Cunard Line is Napier's greatest memorial. Incidentally in the early days of steam ships the funnel colouring was the distinguishing mark of the builder of the engines. So it was that the first four ships of the new fleet carried the Napier funnel; and ships of the Cunard Line carry the same funnel to-day—every funnel a tribute to Robert Napier.

In 1838 Napier secured his first order from the Admiralty and provided two sets of engines, but for a period thereafter further orders were not forthcoming. It would, however, appear that Napier was not ignorant of the uses of parliamentary lobbying, for in 1844 a member of the House of Commons asked for a return of " the names of marine-engine makers with whom the Admiralty had made contracts for engines from the year 1839-1843 inclusive . . . of repairs and the cost of such repairs . . ." When the return was made it showed that the ships with engines by Napier had been in commission for 912 days and 942 days, and that the cost of repairs had amounted, respectively, to 10d. and 1s. $5\frac{1}{4}$d. per day in commission. Ships with engines by other makers had been in commission for 1173, 1095 and 912 days, with costs of repairs amounting respectively to 19s. $8\frac{3}{4}$d., 18s. $5\frac{3}{4}$d. and 17s. $6\frac{1}{2}$d., per day in commission. A succession of Admiralty contracts followed the publication of the return.

Although Napier had contracted to supply the four ships of the Cunard venture, as he had contracted for earlier ships, he had sub-let the work on the wooden hulls. He did not become a shipbuilder until 1841, when the advantages of iron hulls had become fully manifest. The firm of R. Napier & Sons remained as shipbuilders in Govan until 1900, when it was taken over by William Beardmore & Co. of Parkhead. The Parkhead Forge had been owned by Napier, and William Beardmore had become a partner when it came under the control of Rigby and Beardmore, the former a son-in-law of Napier. William Beardmore & Co. passed out of shipbuilding after the great depression, and at the same time Napier & Miller closed their shipyard at Old Kilpatrick; the senior member of the latter firm was a grandson of Robert Napier.

Although there are now no direct links with the Napiers there remain some indirect links. In 1821, before he had become a builder of marine engines, Robert Napier engaged David Elder, a millwright, as manager of his works at Camlachie, and although Elder was then past mid-life he remained with Napier for 40 years. In 1828 Napier brought James Thomson from Manchester to serve as leading smith, finisher and turner; and 10 years later he appointed him as a foreman, at the same time appointing George Thomson, brother of James, to a similar position. In 1847 the brothers Thomson established their own Clyde Bank Foundry in the Finnieston district, and five years later a shipyard on the south bank of the river at Cessnock Bank, a site which is now occupied by Prince's Dock. In 1871 they were forced by the operations of the Clyde Trust to seek a new site farther downriver, which they called Clydebank, after the name of their original engine shop at Finnieston. This was the beginning of the establishment now known as John Brown & Company, builders of the proudest ships of the Cunard fleet. The shipyard gave its name to the burgh which grew up around it.

John Elder, son of David, served his apprenticeship with Napier and was subsequently in charge of the drawing office for four years. In 1852, at the age of 28, he left Napier to become a partner in the engineering firm of Randolph, Elliot & Co.; Randolph had also been a Napier apprentice. Soon thereafter the firm became Randolph, Elder & Co. and embarked on the building of marine engines. Shipbuilding was added to their activities in 1860, and in 1868, on the retiral of Charles Randolph, the firm became John Elder & Co. On the death of John Elder in 1869 William Pearce, a shipyard manager under Napier, became head of the firm, which in 1886 became a private company under the name of the Fairfield Shipbuilding & Engineering Co. Three years later it became a public company under the same name. There is a link also with the Dennys, other than the family link which has been noted. When commencing shipbuilding Ropert Napier had, for a year or two, the services of William Denny, subsequently the founder of the Dumbarton firm, as a naval architect, and at a later date he had Walter Brock as a manager; Brock subsequently became a partner in the Dumbarton firm.

There is one more link with the remote past. The construction of the *Comet* was begun at Port Glasgow by John Wood, but before the ship was finished John Wood had died, and the work was finished by his sons, John and Charles. In due course John Wood had the highest reputation as a builder of wooden ships, and Robert Napier wanted him to build all four ships required by the Cunard venture instead of only one, the *Acadia.* John Wood retired from business in 1860, but his name is commemorated by the family of Scott, builders of coasters and small craft at Bowling and kinsmen of the Scotts of Greenock. In every generation a member of the Scott family has Wood as a secondary Christian name, to bear witness to their descent from Wood of Port Glasgow.

Chapter 7
OTHER ENGINEERING

SARAH C. AND JAMES ORR

Development in the Nineteenth Century

In spite of the variety of industries represented in Glasgow, the city is essentially the centre of an area renowned for its heavy industries and its economic fortune has long been closely linked with these industries. The characteristic heavy industrial structure of the area is the creation of what is sometimes referred to as the second phase of the industrial revolution, the phase based on coal and iron and the application of steam power. Similarly, the engineering industry itself is a product of this period of development. It is true that the earliest textile machines were mainly made of wood, but it is in the development of the iron industry and the successful application of the steam engine that modern engineering has its origin. Thus it is only natural that the two—Glasgow and the engineering industry—should be closely linked. Much of the industry, of course, is dependent, directly or indirectly, on the shipbuilding for which the Clyde is primarily noted, but this is by no means the whole story. To-day there are few branches of engineering in which Glasgow cannot claim a share.

The history of the engineering industry is inseparable from the history of industrial development in general, to which it is, of course, a basic requirement. Virtually every new industrial development has its counterpart in some further specialisation of engineering, from the main branches of which may be read a fair account of Glasgow's economic history. The accumulated engineering skill, in turn, has been extended to practically all branches of the industry and has itself been a major force in the development of new industries.

The foundations of this new craft had already been laid by the time of the second *Statistical Account* in 1845, yet there was little specific mention of it in that Account. The staple industry of Glasgow was still the cotton trade. Mention was certainly made of Watt's famous invention, of which the birthplace was Glasgow University, and of the fact that the "exclusive privilege" of manufacture had been held by Watt & Boulton of Birmingham until 1800. Thereafter the manufacture of steam engines had expanded in Glasgow and by 1845 there were 14 firms engaged in this work. Mention was also made of the railway development linking up Glasgow and the coal and iron industries of Lanarkshire, but the only indication that Glasgow was even then on the threshold of a tremendous expansion based on the heavy industries was the prophetic conclusion that there was every reason to expect a rapid growth of industry and " its extension to every article of iron manufacture." Subsequent events may be said to have fulfilled this prophecy and more. Steel has largely been substituted for iron, and it has been used in the manufacture of products not even dreamt of in 1845.

Indeed the multiplicity of activities and products of the modern engineering industry makes the task of classification and the treatment of its historical development exceedingly difficult. The position is further complicated by the fact that most firms produce a variety of products and in many cases belong to more than one of the main sections of the industry. Historically also the old-established firms have often so radically changed the nature of their activity as to move from one section of the industry to another. In what follows, therefore, an attempt has been made to pick out the main strands of development in the engineering industry, rather than to produce a complete and detailed account such as might be possible for a more uniform industry. The history of the industry inevitably includes some account, although a very summary one, of the general economic development of the area, since the engineering industry is to such a large extent a reflection of this. A more detailed account of the current position is given later in this chapter, but the problem of classification remains complex and that chosen has an admitted degree of arbitrariness.

The mechanisation of industry as we understand it to-day started with the successful harnessing of steam power and to Watt more than anyone must go the credit for putting the steam engine to work. In the early years of the nineteenth century the Glasgow engineering industry was concerned primarily with the manufacture of steam engines. By far the largest number of these were for the textile industry, where the use of steam power spread rapidly during the first half of the century. It was only natural that the new techniques should be applied to the established industry, particularly when that was the one in which the so-called industrial revolution had started. Thus the manufacture of textile machinery became a specialised branch of the Glasgow engineering industry at an early date. Some of the firms concerned started life as textile firms. In the days before the introduction of steam power it was customary for such firms to manufacture their own machines and not uncommon to find the two trades carried on together. In the new steam age some of these firms chose to concentrate entirely on machinery. One such firm was that of Houldsworths, whose Anderston foundry was attached to their cotton mills. One of the Houldsworths eventually left the cotton industry and founded the Coltness ironworks.

Another specialised branch which similarly grew out of a long-established industry was that producing sugar machinery. Sugar-boiling was established in Glasgow as early as 1667 and the eighteenth century brought extensive trading with the West Indies and latterly the start of sugar refining. In the nineteenth century mechanisation was applied to the industry and the special machinery was produced on a steadily increasing scale. By the middle of the century Glasgow was exporting machinery to all the sugar producing countries of the world. Three firms still producing sugar machinery, Blairs, Duncan Stewart & Co., and Mirrlees Watson & Co., were all founded in the period 1838 to 1840.

The first major new development, however, was the establishment of locomotive engineering, a branch destined to occupy an important place in the city's economy. The manufacture of locomotives was a by-product of the period of railway construction and the gradual replacement of the horse by the steam engine. Most of the railways in the industrial part of Scotland were constructed in the 1830's and the 1840's. The first linking up was with the collieries and the early railways were intended to be supplementary to the canals. They depended almost entirely on the transport of coal and iron, and were often worked by horses. In the 1830's, however, they became competitors of the canals and gradually established themselves as an alternative means of transport. They were still constructed primarily for goods traffic and with a view to opening up the mineral resources of Lanarkshire. In some cases both horses and steam engines were employed. Railway transport in the modern sense and the use of the steam locomotive spread slowly in Scotland at first. During the 1830's, however, there was a marked increase in the passenger traffic carried by the existing railways, and by the 1840's the steam locomotive came into its own. The modern railway system for passenger transport was inaugurated in Scotland with the opening of the Glasgow to Edinburgh line in 1842.

At first a number of general engineering firms experimented with the manufacture of the new locomotive, and some for a time combined marine and locomotive engineering. From the 1850's, however, locomotive engineering became a separate, specialised branch of the industry. The first to specialise solely in this branch of engineering was the firm of Neilson & Company of the Hyde Park Locomotive Works. The firm was founded as a general engineering concern in 1836 by a son of James Neilson, the inventor of the hot-blast, and first started the manufacture of locomotives about 1843. It is one of the three firms which amalgamated in 1903 to form the present North British Locomotive Company.

At the same time the rapidly developing coal and iron industries of Lanarkshire were making their own special demands on the engineering industry. In addition, a new and important machine tools industry was growing up in the area. Indeed, the improvement and expansion of the iron industry was providing the basis for a growing number of engineering products. The position by the middle of the century was one in which the textile industry still held its own, but side by side with it there existed a rapidly expanding group of metal industries.

Early in the second half of the century the pattern was radically altered. For some time the cotton industry had just been holding its own with difficulty against increasing foreign competition. The financial crisis of 1857 seriously weakened the industry and depleted its ranks. The final blow came with the outbreak of the American Civil War, when the industry was cut off from its main sources of supply. Many suffered heavy losses and the industry fell into a decline from which it never recovered. The young, expanding metal industries, which had been steadily gaining on the cotton industry, now reigned supreme.

In the development of the heavy industries in the Glasgow region overseas trade played an important part from the outset, although it is almost impossible to determine its relative importance in their development or disentangle its influence from that of domestic factors. No doubt many branches of engineering, if not all, started originally to supply the needs of local industries. At the same time, the presence of plentiful supplies of coal and iron in the area provided the basis for an engineering industry on a scale too vast to meet only the requirements of the domestic market and thus enabled it to satisfy a growing foreign demand for metal goods. Textile machinery provides a good illustration of the interaction of these factors. Mechanisation of the cotton industry in Glasgow was hampered at first by the lack of engineering experience and skill, but as this was gradually overcome, the manufacture of machinery became important in its own right. Some contraction naturally followed the collapse of the cotton industry and the virtual disappearance of the home market, but textile machinery has continued as an important export industry to the present time. Similarly, most of the main branches of engineering springing up in the area soon developed on a scale beyond the capacity of the home market. A tremendous expansion occurred in overseas trading during the second and third quarters of the century. The manufactured products of an industrialised Britain were exchanged for the food and raw materials of of the largely non-industrialised rest of the world. Britain became the proverbial workshop of the world and Glasgow was one of the major branches of that workshop.

During the second half of the century a considerable expansion took place in the application of steam power to ships, as a result of improvements in the engine for that purpose. The replacement of iron by steel in the 1870's completed the harnessing of the new industries to shipbuilding and the sailing ship's days were numbered. There followed a rapid growth in shipbuilding and the last quarter of the century was primarily concerned with consolidating the link-up of steel, engineering and shipbuilding. It has been said that this development gave a peculiar unity to the heavy industries of the Glasgow area and undoubtedly at this period more than any other the keynote was specialisation in marine work.

Yet even in this period the dominance of marine work was only relative, and other engineering was by no means insignificant. Many marine engineers themselves produced similar products for land use, such as boilers, while locomotive and some other branches of engineering continued to expand. From the 1870's onward, it may be said that Britain was no longer so obviously the workshop of the world. Other countries were becoming industrialised and competing in foreign markets. This was true of the continental countries, particularly Germany, and also to some extent the U.S.A. The expansion of foreign trade and the development of overseas countries helped to offset the effect of this for some of Glasgow's established industries, although to others depression became more familiar. In one industry, however, rapid expansion occurred at this time. Locomotive engineering benefited greatly from the considerable outbursts of railway construction occurring in overseas countries and its export trade spread to most parts of the world. This more than any other factor probably helps to explain the continued buoyancy of the area during the last part of the century. Indeed, the position was probably too comfortable, from the longer term point of view, and keener competition at this time might have provided the spur to continued pioneering in new lines of industrial development and prevented the excessive specialisation in heavy industries, which has remained the keynote of the area.

Export markets also figured extensively on the order books of the large structural engineering firms which began to emerge with the growing use of steel in the 1870's. They, not unnaturally, specialised in the heavy types of structures, their products being used in coal-mining, the iron and steel industry, the shipyards, and factories of all types. Bridge-building became a notable accomplishment of the area, one Glasgow firm, that of Sir William Arrol & Co., being responsible for such famous examples as the Tay and Forth Bridges, and the Tower Bridge, London.

During the latter part of the century a considerable number of engineering firms specialised in the manufacture of machine tools of various types. The products classified under this heading at this time were rather different from those to which the term machine tools would be applied to-day. This branch of engineering catered primarily for the industry of the area, and since the area specialised in the heavy industries, the tools produced were for these industries. They included punching and shearing machines, plate bending machines, planes, boring and screwing machines, and lathes. As well as supplying the needs of the local shipbuilding, heavy engineering and iron and steel industries, many of these firms had extensive business in all parts of the world. In addition to the heavy tool making, a number of firms produced scientific instruments and appliances for a wide variety of industries.

A younger branch of the industry which was also established in the area before the close of the century, was electrical engineering. The firm of Kelvin & White, now Kelvin Hughes, established before the middle of the century and specialising in mathematical and optical instruments, turned its attention to electrical instruments at an early date through its association with Lord Kelvin. Its products helped to make possible the first transatlantic cable connection. It has been said that this country was slow to adopt and develop the use of electricity on a widespread scale, although not lacking in inventors and pioneers. This is not surprising in a country where the use of steam and coal gas was already so advanced. Glasgow, however, was early in the field of electricity development, and in 1885 the city was supplied with electricity from the supply station built by Mavor & Coulson, the first in Scotland. The same firm established in 1889 the first power station for alternating current and a few years later this was purchased by the Corporation, which then became solely responsible for the city's electricity supply. By 1900 there were several firms in the city engaged in the manufacture of electrical machines and appliances of various kinds for lighting, power, ventilation and other purposes.

The closing years of the century also found engineers preoccupied with the internal combustion engine and the new horseless carriage, from which has been developed the great motor car industry of the present century. Here too Glasgow can claim important pioneers. It is recorded that a Scotsman, William Murdoch, working for Watt & Boulton, used a steam vehicle on the roads in Cornwall in 1784, complete with copper boiler, firebox and flue, but was dissuaded from patenting it by James Watt, who saw no future for it. The inventor of the modern motor car, however, was of German origin. In 1887 Daimler first put his petrol engine into a four-wheeled carriage, and for some time thereafter the Daimler engine was the most generally used in many makes of cars in different countries. The industry was handicapped in this country at first by the Red Flag Law, not repealed until 1896, according to which the maximum speed was fixed at 4 m.p.h. and vehicles had to be preceded by a man carrying a red flag. Before its repeal, however, George Johnston of Glasgow had on the road the first all-Scottish car and was fined half-a-crown for breaking this law. Technically the engine was claimed to be an improvement on the Daimler one, from which Johnston had started his experiments. The car went into commercial production in 1896 when the Mo-Car Syndicate was formed, comprising Sir William Arrol, Mr. Archibald Coats, and a Mr. Millar of Paisley. The car was of dog-cart design and the bodies were made from solid oak or mahogany by Wylie & Lochhead, cabinetmakers. Shortly after this, Alexander Govan produced his first Argyll car, although originally with a French Darracq engine. In 1899 T. Blackwood Murray and N. O. Fulton. members of George Johnston's original staff, founded the Albion Motor Car Co., now the only survivor of Scotland's motor industry.

An enterprise which might well have marked the beginning of the aircraft industry also comes into this part of Glasgow's history. In 1895 Percy Pilcher, a lecturer in naval architecture at Glasgow University, made the first glider flight in Britain at Cardross in a glider built by himself. By 1899 he had designed a glider with a wheeled undercarriage and steel springs to absorb the shock of landing, and had begun experiments on a petrol engine to be installed in the glider. These experiments were tragically terminated by his death as a result of an accident during a glider demonstration that same year, and the invention of the modern powered aeroplane was delayed until the Wright brothers' success in 1903.

In addition to the main branches of engineering mentioned, Glasgow's manufactures by the beginning of the twentieth century included a multifarious collection of metal products such as brewing, milling and bakery machinery, wheelbarrows, gas meters, safes, springs, wringers, wire, nails, bolts, nuts and screws, stoves and grates, bedsteads, lamps and candlesticks, and all types of non-ferrous metal products.

In spite of the appearance of infinite variety and diversity, however, the industrial pattern which emerged from the nineteenth century was one of extreme specialisation in the heavy industries, and this was reflected in the structure of the city's engineering industry. According to the returns of the 1901 Census Report 53,382 or some 21 per cent of the occupied male population were engaged in the category of "metals, machines, implements and conveyances." Of these, 6,306 were engaged in the iron and steel industry, 3,010 on ships and boats and 34,757 in engineering and machine making. The latter was in fact predominantly of the heavy type, and these three together accounted for nearly 83 per cent of the total in this category. In addition, tool making in the area was geared to the heavy industries. The manufacture of vehicles accounted for just over 4 per cent, and of these the largest number were employed in the manufacture of coaches and carriages, while next in importance came railway coaches and waggons. Cycle and motor manufacture together employed only 350. The diversity comes under the heading "miscellaneous," in which group are listed seventeen different trades, but together these employed only 4,819 or 9 per cent of the total in the engineering and metal trades.

Development Since 1900

During the first decade of the present century the process of industrialisation overseas continued and this country had to face increased competition in foreign trade, particularly from Germany and U.S.A. There were signs of some awareness that all was not well with the old industrial order during the years of depressed trade early in the century, but such fears were dispelled by the return of boom conditions from about 1909 onwards. The traditional heavy industries of the Glasgow area naturally benefited from the industrialisation of overseas countries, since much of the necessary capital equipment came from this country. The increasing population and wealth of the developing countries resulted in a general expansion in international trading from which Britain on balance gained, in spite of continued concentration on a few traditional industries, mainly of the heavy type. Thus the city's industrial pattern remained substantially unaltered up to 1914. Glasgow was still primarily a centre of shipbuilding and marine work, a major exporting area, and an area specialising in heavy engineering such as locomotive and structural. It is true that this was a period of consolidation rather than expansion. but conditions in the years immediately preceding 1914 appeared to justify, at least superficially, the prevailing complacency.

One of the main changes of this period was the development of the electricity industry in its many facets. The numbers employed in the manufacture of electrical apparatus of all kinds for domestic and industrial use were given for the first time as a separate group in the returns of the 1911 Census Report, when the total for Glasgow was 2,356. As electrically driven machinery replaced steam in more and more industries, electrical engineering soon passed from the general to the specialised stage of development. Mavor & Coulson, the pioneering firm in this field, turned their attention at an early date to electrical coal-cutting machinery, now their main specialty. In the shipbuilding industry much of the early application of electricity to heating and ventilation produced results capable of application in a much wider field, and for some firms this provided a healthy modification of their previous specialisation in marine work. The extensive construction of power stations and generating plant provided a new outlet for the products of the area's heavy engineering firms. Firms previously specialising in marine work turned their attention increasingly to the production of boilers and generating plant for this purpose, and for some, power station work is now more important than marine work. Structural engineers likewise found an additional market in the construction of power stations.

While statistically the traditional heavy industries remained dominant, Glasgow in this period was by no means disinterested in new developments. In the motor car industry in particular the city was well to the fore. The Mo-Car Syndicate, subsequently the Arrol Johnston Co., moved to Paisley in 1901, when its Glasgow works were destroyed by fire. Some years later, it moved to Dumfries where it continued production until the late 1920's, latterly being linked with the Aster Company. Thus the story of the Arrol Johnston cars, which gained a wide reputation throughout the country, is for the most part not Glasgow's story during this period. Mr. William Beardmore, later Lord Invernairn, joined the board of the Arrol Johnston Co., and subsequently Beardmore's acquired the Paisley works where the Beardmore taxi was manufactured. In 1906 George Johnston was associated with a new car company in Bridgeton, the A.B.C. Co., but this venture failed financially in two or three years. The firm of Bergius for a short time also entered the car market and manufactured the Kelvin car from 1904 to 1906. Finding production costly, it fitted its engine to a boat as an experiment, and so the famous Kelvin marine engine was developed. A number of other Glasgow cars of this period included the Athol and Scotia, built at Bridgeton, the St. Vincent which was assembled in Glasgow, and the Skeoch, a cycle-car. The Halley Company, which started at Finnieston in 1902 and moved to Yoker in 1906, concentrated on industrial vehicles and continued production until the late 1920's. In 1910 it produced the first motor fire-engine to be built in Scotland, which had a Drysdale pump and used bronze castings for the crankcase and gear box. But the two most important names in the history of the Glasgow motor car industry are Albion and Argyll.

The history of the Albion Company, which is now the sole surviving motor manufacturing concern in Scotland, is one of steady progress. Starting with an output of one 8 h.p. dog-cart car with tiller steering, produced with the aid of 5 works staff and 2 clerks, the firm expanded steadily until by 1913 it was producing over 500 vehicles annually and employing a total works and office staff of nearly 1,000. Commercial vehicles were added to production at an early date, and with the growing demand from industry, Albion paid more and more attention to these until they finally decided in 1913 to abandon the production of private cars entirely. By this time motor coaches had also been added to their products, and their markets extended to a number of overseas countries. The soundness of their product earned them a number of awards in Reliability Trials.

The highest achievement of the Scottish industry in car manufacture was undoubtedly the work of the Argyll Company. The designer of the Argyll car was Alex. Govan, co-founder of the Hozier Engineering Co. in Bridgeton in 1896. Although at first this firm assembled the French Darracq car, Govan's aim from the start was to produce a Scottish car of moderate price, for which he recognised the great potential demand. Govan's was a pioneering venture, before its time in its conception of large-scale production. The first Argylls used Aster engines, but later the company produced its own engines. The car gained a number of competitive awards and its popularity rapidly increased. Starting with an output of 6 cars a week, the factory had soon to be expanded. An output of 20 to 25 cars a week was reached, but even this was inadequate for the demand, and a large new factory was constructed at Alexandria. A new company, Argyll Motors, was formed with a capital of £500,000. The new factory was opened in 1906, and cost over £200,000. Govan had studied the latest factories in America and the Continent, and the Vale of Leven factory was said to surpass any in the world at that time.

Although the main scene of operations thus moved out of Glasgow in 1906, the city retained an interest in the story of the Argyll Company and the Bridgeton factory was retained. Soon after the new factory opened, Govan died of food poisoning at the early age of 39. The loss of Govan's leadership and the financial burden of the new factory soon led the company into difficulties and by 1908, when its liabilities were over £300,000, it went into partial liquidation. The company was reorganised, however, and the factory continued. The following years witnessed outstanding technical achievements. The main development was that of the single-sleeve valve engine, which the Argyll company adopted and pioneered. The inventor, Peter Burt, was a Glasgow engineer with his own firm, the Acme Engineering Company, later the Acme Wringer Company. Technically, the Burt engine was a remarkable achievement and a great improvement on the previous system. In developing it, however, the Argyll company had to face a series of legal battles, firstly with rival claimants and latterly with the inventors of the double-sleeve valve engine, then adopted by the Daimler Company.

These legal disputes, which were finally settled in Argyll's favour in 1913, were both costly and damaging to the market for the new Argyll cars. In 1913, however, an Argyll car with the Burt engine was entered for the trials at Brooklands. It was only a 15 h.p. model and in one day of 14 hours it broke 13 world records and 28 Brooklands class records. This car was the first to be fitted with the Perrot four-wheel braking system, now universally adopted. M. Perrot worked with the Argyll company from 1909 until 1914. In the matter of body design also the Argyll company was well ahead.

The cost of development in this period, however, again produced financial losses. Although these were small compared to those of 1908, the company went into voluntary liquidation in 1914. At this time their legal troubles were over, their car was gaining wide recognition and their market prospects good, and it now seems as if a little effort could have saved the firm. The industrial history of West Scotland in the interwar period might have been very different if that effort had been made.

Burt's sleeve valve engine figured in the development of another new industry in which the Glasgow engineers were showing growing interest just before the outbreak of war in 1914. In 1913 Burt designed a sleeve valve aero engine, which Argyll produced and entered for a competition at Farnborough in 1914. Although the crankshaft broke, because, it is said, of the mounting for testing, not of the design, the Argyll entry was awarded a prize. Early in the war Burt designed another aero engine for research at Farnborough, and although the sleeve valve engine was subsequently dropped, post-war researches proved its worth and some of the more recent developments by the Bristol Company were fundamentally similar in type to that of Burt.

The most advanced Glasgow firm in the field of aero-engine construction, however, was that of Beardmore's. This firm began designing and manufacturing aero engines early in the century and by 1914 was well established in this production. During the first three years of the war more flying hours by the R.F.C. were made with Beardmore engines than with any other type.

The outbreak of war in 1914 brought renewed emphasis and expansion to the heavy industries, and the city's engineering firms were mobilised in the war effort. Ships, vehicles, guns, shells and war equipment of all kinds were produced in the area, and the engineering shops were for the first time invaded by female labour. The war did not bring to Glasgow any new industrial capacity suitable for medium or light engineering in peacetime, but rather served to expand its capacity in the heavy branches. The one major development which could have become the basis of a new peacetime industry was in the field of aircraft construction. Beardmore's went in for aircraft construction on an extensive scale, with factories at Dalmuir and Inchinnan and during the war produced a total of 650 planes, ranging from small Sopwiths to four-engined Handley-Pages. In 1915 a group of the Clyde engineering and shipbuilding firms was formed for the same purpose under the leadership of G. & J. Weir of Cathcart. The group included Stephens, Denny, Barclay Curle, Napier & Miller, and Fairfield. In all, a considerable capacity for aircraft construction and the production of its many components was created, but unfortunately practically all the firms, with the exception of Beardmore, abandoned this new development and reverted to their former products when peace returned.

Glasgow at the beginning of the 1920's was still an area specialising in heavy engineering. In addition there was some motor manufacturing, and one firm engaged in aircraft construction. At first, the end of hostilities with the need for reconstruction and re-equipment brought boom conditions to the heavy industries and hopes were high that the pre-1914 situation would be restored. The boom was short-lived, however, and depression quickly followed, affecting particularly those heavy industries so prevalent in Glasgow. Prosperity of the pre-1914 variety did not return with the end of the depression and the industry of the area remained more or less in the doldrums until the advent of rearmament in the latter half of the 1930's. In the years of world depression around 1930, unemployment in this area was over 30 per cent, and for much of the rest of the period 20 per cent was typical. Although the belief that pre-1914 conditions could be restored and that all would be well was slow to die, world conditions had in fact changed in such a way and to such an extent as to make this impossible. The factors causing this had already been present well before 1914 and the war years had only served to accelerate the changes already started. Industrialisation in overseas countries had proceeded to such an extent as seriously to contract the markets for the products of the traditional heavy industries. The war and the absence of British supplies during it had accelerated this development and forced our overseas customers to seek other sources of supply. The unsettled political conditions of the interwar period and the growing economic nationalism resulted in a contraction rather than an expansion of international trading. The engineering industries of Glasgow suffered particularly from the contraction and depression of the shipbuilding industry, on which so many depended directly or indirectly, and from the contraction of export markets on which all branches depended to a considerable extent. Even the best years of the period were lean ones.

Although the years of general depression naturally had a particularly adverse effect on heavy engineering, all the main branches continued in the area, but mostly on a reduced scale. Some fared better than others, depending on their markets and the scope for variation in product. Locomotives continued to be built in the city both by the private firm and, until 1928, in the railway companies' own works. The former, depending as it did almost entirely on foreign markets, felt the lack of any extensive overseas construction comparable to the railway mania of an earlier period. Structural engineering, with its wider variety of products and bigger home market fared slightly better. In the production of heavy equipment and machine tools of a specialised type the contraction of the local heavy industries had an adverse effect on the home market, but the area retained its superiority and in this specialised line was therefore less affected by foreign competition. In electrical engineering the city was not extensively involved, the main firm now concentrating on coal-cutting and loading equipment. The other main representative, however, the Macfarlane Engineering Co., embarked on new development at this time. Previously producing mainly A.C. and D.C. motors, the firm decided in the lean years following 1918 to turn its attention to more specialised electrical work and pioneered new development, particularly in electric arc welding and in special laboratory plant. Some progress was also made in this period in the manufacture of heating and ventilating plant, frequently started primarily for ships but with increasing application in this period to factories, chiefly as a result of factory welfare legislation. A few of the established heavy industries embarked on new lines in this period, but not many. Notable among them is the shipbuilding concern of Yarrow & Co., who started in 1922 to produce land boilers, the output of which is now an important part of their activity. The firm of Howden & Co., started in the 1850's as marine engineers and adding high-speed engines and turbines for land generators early in the present century, made a special development in the interwar years of boiler auxiliaries such as fans, air pre-heaters and dust collectors, for both land and marine use, and it now specialises entirely in this work. G. & J. Weir, famous for pumps and boiler auxiliaries from the 1880's, also undertook a number of new developments in this period. To their products they added compressors, petrol pumps and refuellers, evaporators and refrigerating plant. In the process they acquired a number of concerns including that of Drysdale at Yoker, the Contraflo Engineering Co., London, Zwicky, Slough, and A. G. Mumford, Colchester. In the 1930's they carried out development work on autogyros and later produced helicopters. An old-established firm of ironfounders, Robert Maclaren & Co., founded in 1844, turned in 1922 to the manufacture of thermostats for industrial, commercial and domestic use and now specialises entirely in this work.

Several Glasgow firms continued to manufacture cars in the 1920's, but mostly on a relatively small scale. These included the Beardmore car, the Rob Roy, produced at Carntyne, the Gilchrist, assembled in Glasgow, and the Argyll, built at the old Hozier Works. The latter were acquired on the liquidation of the old company in 1914 by J. D. Brimlow and a new Argyll Motor Co. was formed with Sir John Anderson as chairman. In 1920 Brimlow produced a new Argyll car, incorporating the Burt sleeve valve engine, and manufacture of this was carried on until the late 1920's. The Halley continued for a time to manufacture commercial vehicles and in 1920 produced the first pneumatic tyred passenger coach in Britain. The latter incorporated many new features, but proved costly in development and the company suffered badly in the postwar depression. It went into liquidation in 1927, and subsequently continued on a small scale until about 1930. Beardmore's produced a commercial vehicle at Parkhead until about 1930, and Carlaw produced some vans. Other commercial vehicles produced in the city included the Caledon, the Scotia, the Sentinal and the Wallace Tractor. Albion meantime continued to expand and established a growing reputation for commercial and public service vehicles of a special type and reliability. By the beginning of the 1930's, however, only Albion remained. The great depression of that period eliminated those of the others who had survived the ups and downs of the '20's. The motor industry had become a much more large-scale and highly competitive business and was by this time concentrating in the Midlands. Most of the components were also produced in that area and the relatively small-scale Glasgow industry could not compete. Had the Argyll works at Alexandria survived the position might well have been very different. As it was, the Midlands, with its numerous small, light engineering workshops and its history of mobility, was ideally suited for the development of the industries essential to car assembly. In contrast, the Glasgow area, with its long tradition and skill in the heavy industries, lacked even the nucleus for their development. Typical of this is the case of castings. This area is accustomed to produce the heavy and specialised types required by the old industries, and the lighter castings necessary to the modern motor industry would have had to be imported.

In the field of aircraft construction Beardmore's continued to play a leading part until the late 1920's. Aero-engines were manufactured by them at Parkhead, flying boats at Dalmuir, and airships at Inchinnan. They were early pioneers in transatlantic air travel, one of their airships making the double journey in 1919. The aircraft industry at this time, however, was dependent almost entirely on scanty Government orders and was tending to concentrate in the south. Beardmore's abandoned aircraft work in the late 1920's and by the 1930's the only activity in this field in Glasgow was the development work on autogyros being carried out by G. & J. Weir, who later turned their attention to helicopters, and in 1938 produced the Weir helicopter, the first to be flown in this country.

The general picture of the interwar years, however, is one showing Glasgow at the centre of one of the main depressed or special areas created by the decline in the heavy industries and in the export trade. Unemployment was high and new industrial development almost negligible. This was the period of the so-called southward drift of industry and of the expansion of lighter industries concerned with the domestic rather than the foreign market. Many reasons have been suggested to explain Glasgow's failure to develop these new industries on any substantial scale. For one thing the nucleus of many of the new industries already existed in the Midlands and south of England, and the domestic market, now the more important, was obviously greater there. Much has also been made of the belief that heavy industry areas and their labour force are unsuited to the lighter industries. Although experiences in the Second World War have done much to modify this sweeping conclusion the traditions and customs of nearly a century undoubtedly lingered and the belief that the world of pre-1914 would eventually be restored was slow to die. As the period advanced, however, much of the labour force, far from being tied to the heavy skills, was in fact unskilled because of the lack of openings in the heavy trades.

In the particular case of engineering, there is evidence that Glasgow had its fair share of inventors and pioneers in the new medium and light branches. But inventors must have backing and the capital of the area was undoubtedly mainly in the heavy industries. Prior to 1914 many of the leaders in these industries had shown considerable interest in and given support to the newest developments in engineering. Typical of this was Sir William Arrol's interest in the young motor car industry, and Sir William Beardmore's enterprises in both the car and aircraft industries. In the interwar period, however, the depression so prevalent in the heavy industries, particularly those involved in marine work, had a damping effect on such enterprise and on the supply of capital available for new ventures. Further, in many cases, the original founder had been replaced by a less enterprising board of directors, none of whom had any personal experience of pioneering a new venture. Finally, to the lighter branches of industry, which catered primarily for the domestic market, a depressed area with heavy unemployment offered little attraction.

It was not until the late 1930's that a policy of attracting new industries to the depressed areas by the provision of industrial estates was started, and at that time the city of Glasgow was excluded from the designated Special Area. The largest estate established, however, was that at Hillington, more or less on Glasgow's door-step and now included in the Glasgow Labour Exchange area. The estate was opened in 1938 and by the end of the year some 70 firms were in production there. The most important single development on the estate was the construction of the Air Ministry's shadow factory occupied by Rolls Royce for the production of aero engines. The outbreak of war brought considerable expansion and at the peak of its production the firm employed 25,000.

From the mid 1930's onwards there was also a steady recovery in the old heavy industries of the area, as a result of the rearmament programme. The outbreak of war again called for the mobilisation of Glasgow's traditional industries. In many cases production was at first hampered by the effects of years of stagnation and by the lack of trained labour, but the shipbuilding and engineering firms were soon geared to war production. Once more ships, vehicles, guns and equipment of all types were produced, while among the most notable achievements of the area must surely rank its contribution to the Mulberry

Harbour, a major part of which was produced by the shipyards and structural engineers of Clydeside. Again the effect of the war was mainly to expand capacity in the old heavy industries, and with the notable exception of the Rolls Royce factory at Hillington, the area received little new capacity suitable for adaptation to the lighter branches of engineering. The demands on the heavy industries were made all the greater by the area's relative immunity from air attack. In spite of this, unemployment only finally disappeared in 1941 with the direction of surplus labour to the south.

Under the Distribution of Industry Act of 1945 Glasgow was included in the new Scottish Development Area of the post-war period. In addition to the original Hillington Estate, now considerably expanded, there are four new estates within the Glasgow area, at Queenslie, Carntyne, Craigton and Thornliebank. In these there are now over 200 tenants, of whom nearly a half are engaged in medium and light engineering of various kinds. In terms of numbers employed, approximately 20,000 out of a total of 26,000 or 76 per cent are engaged in these engineering firms. The largest single unit is, of course, the Rolls Royce factory at Hillington which is now concentrated entirely on the production of jet engines. A considerable addition to light engineering has been provided by the two firms manufacturing typewriters, Remington Rand and Olivetti. The rest are on a relatively small scale, at least in comparison with the traditional heavy industries of the area, which have enjoyed almost uninterrupted boom conditions since the end of the war. In addition to the expected post-war demands for replacements and reconstruction to make good the ravages of the war years, such factors as the Korean War and extensive rearmament, full employment and the attendant expansion of productive capacity, the expansion of world trade and the export drive, have all helped to maintain the level of activity in the heavy engineering firms. Glasgow still is and must surely remain the centre of an area depending basically on the heavy industries. The object of industrial estate policy can only be to introduce a greater diversity and balance.

The Present Structure

Locomotive Engineering

Locomotive engineering has justly been described as Glasgow's other great heavy industry, that is, next to shipbuilding. For nearly a century Glasgow has been the chief centre of the industry in Britain and indeed one of the greatest centres of locomotive engineering in the world. Within its boundaries are to be found the workshops of the former Caledonian and North British Railway Companies, as well as the three workshops now forming the North British Locomotive Company. The two British Railway workshops, however, are now solely concerned with repair and maintenance work and have been since the late 1920's, when, as a consequence of railway amalgamation, all new construction was concentrated in England. Thus locomotive construction in the city is now the sole prerogative of the one private firm.

As noted earlier in this chapter, this branch of engineering emerged about the 1850's and the first to specialise in it was the firm of Neilson & Company, founded as a general engineering concern in 1836. This firm's famous Hyde Park Locomotive Works, Springburn, was so called after the company's original factory which was in Hydepark Street. The second works in the present company is that of Henry Dubs, for a time manager of the Hyde Park Works, who formed his own company in 1863, the Glasgow Locomotive Works, Polmadie. The third firm in the amalgamation is that of Sharp, Stewart & Company, whose Atlas Works, Springburn, dates from 1888, when the firm moved to Glasgow from Manchester. There the firm had been founded in 1828 and engaged in locomotive building from 1833. These three firms amalgamated in 1903 to form the present North British Company, which was then the largest firm of locomotive builders in Europe, employing some 8,000 men and having over sixty acres of workshops. By 1903 the firms together had produced a total of 16,000 locomotives.

At first the private firms worked in close collaboration with the early railway companies, but the latter soon entered the field of construction themselves and finally supplied virtually all of their own requirements. The private industry was thus compelled to develop almost solely on the basis of its export trade, which it did with such success that there were said to be Glasgow locomotives in almost every country in the world. The hey-day of expanding overseas markets for this industry was the latter part of the nineteenth century and by the time of the amalgamation of the firms in 1903 the peak had already been reached. Nevertheless, the new company continued to produce about 500 locomotives annually up to 1914. In the interwar period, however, the firm suffered the general fate of the heavy industries, and the loss of export markets, on which they then depended entirely, had serious consequences. By the beginning of the 1930's one works was completely closed down and a second virtually so. Recovery began about 1936 with the start of rearmament, when the company received orders from the War Office for locomotives and light tanks. The level of activity has been maintained in the postwar period with orders from many countries engaged in industrial reconstruction. Although recently sharing in British Railways' orders, the firm still depends on overseas markets for about 95 per cent of its output. Here the position is becoming increasingly competitive. In a recent large order for the Indian railways prices quoted by manufacturers in Japan and on the Continent were about 70 per cent of the price quoted by the North British Company.

On the technical side, there have been many developments in the steam piston locomotive, from the 30-ton unit of the very early days to the condensing 230-ton giant of the present time. Output of these is

Block by courtesy of the Scottish Geographical Magazine

Plate 6. SLEZER'S VIEW OF GLASGOW FROM THE SOUTH, ABOUT 1690

Glasgow University

Plate 7. FOULIS ACADEMY OF ARTS EXHIBITION, 1761, IN THE INNER QUADRANGLE OF THE OLD COLLEGE

Plate 8.
THE SCHOOL OF ART, GARNETHILL

Designed by Charles Rennie Mackintosh

Roof of old Hengler's Circus in right foreground

T. & R. Annan

naturally hardly on mass production lines, although production of 100 of the same type is not uncommon. As well as maintaining its reputation for steam locomotives, the North British Company has experimented with other types, including the steam turbine and, more recently, a coal-burning gas turbine. The most popular and successful new development, however, has been that of the diesel engined locomotive with electric or hydraulic transmission. This was developed on the Continent in the late 1920's and its success proved there, particularly on the German State Railways. Since then most countries have been introducing diesel locomotives in place of steam, although British Railways have been slow to follow suit. In 1946 the North British Company started production of M.A.N. diesel engines under German licence and Voith hydraulic turbo transmissions for which it holds the exclusive manufacturing rights. One of its three workshops is now devoted entirely to this production. Already its output includes a diesel electric locomotive of 155 tons, the largest so far produced in this country. As part of a 15-year modernisation programme British Railways have departed from their previous custom and placed orders for 141 main-line locomotives with private firms. Of these the North British Company is contributing 31, all diesel-engined.

The company at present employs about 4,300 men, compared with 8,000 at the beginning of the century, and produces just under 200 locomotives per annum. Although this output is less than half of the peak production in the pre-1914 period, the locomotives are considerably larger and more complex. To some extent the reduction in the numbers employed is due to improved methods and increased mechanisation. By 1954 the total number of locomotives built by the three firms in the company was 28,000, and some indication of the part played by overseas markets in its development can be obtained from the fact that of these, 9,550 were for the home market, 11,300 for India, 3,300 for North and South America, and 2,550 for Europe.

All steel castings for the company are produced by an associate firm in Renfrew. A secondary line of product is that of shearing, cropping and punching machines produced in collaboration with another associate firm situated in London.

Structural Engineering

Starting as it did to supply the needs of the local heavy industries, structural engineering has retained its bias towards special and heavy structural units, with little repetition of standard lines. There are, of course, some exceptions to this, notably that of derrick cranes, of which Scotland produces 90 per cent of the United Kingdom's output. But it is in such lines as bridges, steel-framed factory buildings, dock-gates, hydro-electric pipe lines, cranes, lifts and conveyors that the industry specialises. For these it has gained a world-wide reputation and markets in many countries.

During the war the structural group in the city made a notable contribution to the Normandy invasion in the form of units for the Mulberry harbour and tank landing craft. Since the end of the war structural work has been mainly for power stations, hydro-electric pipe lines, and new factories.

There has not been much technical change in the structural field, which has very ancient traditions. The greatest changes have been the introduction of mild steel in the 1870's and the development of a stronger steel in the 1930's for lightness in long-span bridges and for the Bailey type of bridge. Some firms have experimented with aluminium alloy as a structural material, but at present the cost is greater and the material less reliable. One other change worthy of mention is the development of electric arc-welding, which is tending to replace riveting in structural work. It is also often an advantage to have units built up from rolled plates by welding instead of using castings.

At present there are some twenty firms engaged in the various types of structural engineering and together they employ over 7,000. More than half of this total are employed by the three largest firms, Arrol, Braby, and McLellan. At least four of the firms can claim to be over a hundred years old, one going back as far as 1783. Another group belongs to the period 1860 to 1880. At the other end, at least three firms were launched in the difficult interwar period, while one belongs to the present postwar era.

The largest and best-known of the city's structural firms is that of Sir William Arrol & Company. Its range of products is greater than any of the others, but its history may be taken as representative of the heavy structural group. The firm was founded in 1872 by William Arrol, who became one of the city's outstanding industrial leaders. It is famous above all, as already noted, for its bridge-building, particularly for the Forth and Tay bridges, and the Tower Bridge, London. William Arrol developed new techniques in drilling and riveting, and patented a portable hydraulic riveter which is still used. Moving bridges have become another specialty, the most important produced being those for the Manchester ship canal. The firm also produces dock gates and caisson work, and constructed the dock-gates for the Dover train ferry. It has been extensively engaged in power-station steelwork, and, more recently, in hydro-electric pipe lines. In 1910 a separate crane works was established and this has since supplied many shipyards with gantries, and docks with the largest cantilever cranes capable of lifting 250 tons. Almost from the beginning an export business was established, and to date, more products have gone south of the border than have been supplied to the Scottish market.

The firm of P. & W. MacLellan, Clutha Works, Kinning Park, produces a similar range of steel structures, but includes steel railway waggons. This firm was started as an ironmongery business in 1811, and entered the manufacturing side in 1840, when a smithy was opened in Old Wynd, Trongate. The Clutha Works were started in 1871, by which time steel was replacing iron in the structural world. A second works, also in Kinning Park, concentrates on light structural steelwork for buildings.

In terms of employment, the second largest firm in the structural group is that of F. Braby & Co. This firm, however, is not only engaged in structural work; it also rolls thin sheet steel. Its steel-rolling mill was started in 1910. It makes a variety of lighter steel products such as metal windows and partitions. This is a London firm which started in Glasgow in 1875, primarily to roll iron and steel, but Glasgow is now its main centre for sheet steel, structural and galvanising work.

Others in the same field include A. J. Main, Fleming Brothers, Lambhill Ironworks and P. & R. Fleming & Co. The latter can trace its origin back to 1783 when it was included in the Glasgow Directory as an ironmongery firm.

Although Arrol's includes cranes in its list of products the manufacture of these and other mechanical handling gear is usually a special branch of structural work. The area is particularly noted for the manufacture of cranes, in which at least four firms are engaged, with employees numbering about 1,000. The largest of these is Butter Brothers, founded in 1867 and manufacturing cranes of all types for home and export markets.

The manufacture of lifts is the special concern of two firms. A. & P. Steven, starting in 1850 as general engineers, soon turned to lifts and made its first electric lift in 1897. The other, Glasgow Engineers, Bridgeton, started in 1925, and now manufactures electric lifts of all kinds, these replacing its former hydraulic lifts.

Among the related products represented in this class of engineering work are light steel structures and architectural ironwork, conveyor structures, light metal fabrications, expanded metal work, and patent glazing bars for fixing glass. The firm engaged on this latter work, Pennycook Patent Glazing & Engineering Co., founded in 1880, can claim to be among the earliest originators of patent glazing and is the only manufacturer of this product in Scotland.

Power Plant—Boilers, Pumps and Auxiliaries

An important section of Glasgow's engineering industry is that engaged in the manufacture of boilers, pumps and other auxiliaries. In origin, of course, this section is mainly linked with the extensive shipbuilding industry of the Clyde, and insofar as it is still engaged on marine work, it rightly belongs to another chapter. Many of the firms, however, although starting with marine boilers and marine auxiliary machinery, have since added the production of similar goods for land use. In particular, the development of power stations in the last thirty years has provided an important stimulus, and in some cases the bias has shifted from marine to land work.

It is difficult to estimate exactly how many are employed in this type of work, since some firms combine it with other lines of production, the most notable example being that of Yarrow & Co., shipbuilders as well as boilermakers. An approximate estimate, however, suggests that there are about 13,000 so employed, and of these, about half are engaged in work other than marine. This work is shared by twenty firms, and the proportion of their output exported is between 20 and 30 per cent. The three largest firms are G. & J. Weir, James Howden & Co., and Yarrow & Co.

The firm of G. & J. Weir was founded by George and James Weir, who started as consultants on marine engines in 1870. They patented a boiler feed pump and other auxiliaries, and in 1886, dissatisfied with the manufacturers of their patents, they started manufacturing in Cathcart. Their factory, which was an ambitious project, included a machine shop, a brass foundry, a smithy, an iron foundry and a copper shop. The project was justified by its success, based chiefly on the inventive genius of James Weir whose numerous patents were always sound. The firm equipped two stations for the Burmah Oil Company and supplied pumps to the Anglo-Iranian Oil Company for a 150-mile pipe-line. In 1910 a centrifugal pump was developed. During the 1914-18 war the factory made shells and gun carriages, and also aero fuselages and engine cylinder blocks. In the 1920's the company expanded its former lines of production, added compressors, and acquired a controlling interest in the firm of Drysdale & Co., Yoker, manufacturers of centrifugal pumps. It also acquired a number of firms in the London area engaged on similar work. In the depressed 1930's it began development work on an autogyro, under licence, and later successfully developed a helicopter. In the recent war, in addition to its usual products, the firm made the carriage and recoil system of the famous 25-pound field gun. At present it employs a total of over 4,000 between the Cathcart works and its subsidiaries, the Argus Foundry, Thornliebank, and Weir Valves, Queenslie. Since 1946 the firm of Drysdale & Co. has also become a subsidiary. Its main products are still boiler feed pumps and auxiliaries for marine and land use, but it also makes sea-water evaporating and distilling plant, high pressure compressors and industrial refrigeration machinery.

James Howden began as a consulting engineer and designer in 1854. He was at first mainly interested in machine tools, and then in marine engines and boilers. Manufacturing was started in 1862 and the firm of Howden & Co., engineers, millwrights and boilermakers established. Howden took a special interest in the combustion process and developed a forced draught and air-preheater system for which patents were taken out in 1882. This proved successful and was adopted at sea by 1884. Thereafter the firm specialised in this line, at first mainly for marine use. By 1904 production was extended to high-speed engines and turbines for land use, chiefly in the growing field of electrical power. In the interwar period the firm developed a new mechanical method of air-preheating along with a Swedish firm, extended the production of fans for land use, particularly for power stations, and added the production of dust collectors for marine and land use. The boiler auxiliaries for land use proved so successful that the company stopped production of engines and concentrated on auxiliaries. Its power station work has become increasingly important and now only some 16 per cent of its output goes directly to the shipbuilding industry. More recently it has supplied fans to atomic energy research establishments. During the recent war it established a branch factory in the city for the production of aircraft components. Since the end of the war this factory has engaged in the production of steel furniture, latterly specialising in office furniture. In addition, the production of aircraft components has been resumed since 1952. The firm thus presents an unusual combination of heavy and light engineering. At present it employs nearly 2,300. It also has as a subsidiary the British Arc Welding (Scotland) Co.

Yarrow & Co., employing over 2,000, more strictly belongs to the shipbuilding chapter. The firm began as shipbuilders with boiler-making as a sideline, and moved from the Thames to Glasgow in 1907. Nowadays, however, production of the famous Yarrow boiler is more important than the shipbuilding activities. The company first produced a boiler for land use in 1922 and this now accounts for about one-third of its total production. Its products are used in power stations, oil refineries, and paper-mills, and the firm supplied the boilers for the Dalmarnock Power Station, Glasgow.

Drysdale & Co., Yoker, now a subsidiary of G. & J. Weir, originated as Drysdale & Pirie in 1874. The original works were in Bridgeton and were purchased on that date from Marquis Brothers, already engaged in pumping work. Although the company now concentrates solely on electrically and steam driven pumping machinery, and has always specialised in pumps, it did at one time extend its manufacture over a wide range of other products, including hand and steam cranes, hand and hydraulic presses for the tobacco industry and for shawl making, hydraulic and steam-operated lifts, riveters, tea-drying machinery and plant for a wide range of industries. The firm supplied pumps and riveters to Wm. Arrol & Co. for the building of the Forth Bridge. The business moved to its present site in 1908 and now employs over a thousand.

Alley & Maclellan (Polmadie) employs nearly 700 on the manufacture of compressors, vacuum pumps and steam engines. This firm was founded in Bridgeton in 1875 and originally produced valves, the other products being added between then and the end of the century. In 1921 the valve section was moved to Worcester, and in 1945 the firm became a subsidiary of Glenfield & Kennedy, Kilmarnock.

The Mirrlees Watson Co. is more widely associated with sugar machinery and is dealt with more fully under that heading. But its products also include pumping plant and other auxiliaries for power station and other uses, as well as evaporators and water distillers. A branch factory, that of Mirrlees (Engineers) Hillington, established in 1937, produces oil pumps. The pumps were formerly manufactured at Stockport by an associate company, established in 1907 for the manufacture of diesel engines, in which the Mirrlees Watson Co. had been engaged from 1898. The pump business was transferred to Glasgow when the Stockport company was sold to Associated British Engineering in 1945. In addition, a number of smaller firms are engaged in the production of such lines as low-pressure boilers for central heating, boilers for the paper industry, boiler auxiliaries, valves and forgings. Some of this is located in the new industrial estates.

Heating and Ventilating Apparatus

Closely allied to the power plant group, and in some cases overlapping it, are the firms specialising in the production of heating and ventilating apparatus. Indeed, notable in this field is the firm of J Howden & Co., mentioned above, important for its work in dust collectors and fans. Apart from this, the two most important firms specialising in this type of work are Thermotank and the Winsor Engineering Co. In addition, there are two smaller firms, one of which specialises in installation rather than manufacture. One other firm specialises in industrial furnaces of all types. Less than half of the output here is for shipbuilding. The total number employed by this group is about 1,800.

Thermotank was founded in 1901. The firm's products include fans, air distributors, and air conditioning, heating and ventilating equipment. Although supplying many other industries, including coal-mining, the major part of the output still goes to shipbuilding. Air conditioning of ships and the production of large industrial and mining fans, the latter up to 20 feet in diameter, are the main concerns of the Winsor Engineering Co. This firm was started in 1922, its founder breaking away from the tube-making business with which his family had been concerned since the 1850's.

Refrigerating Plant

Another closely allied branch is that engaged in the production of refrigerating plant. In this the firm of G. & J. Weir is also concerned. In addition there are three firms which specialise in this type of work. Together they employ about 1,600 and a considerable proportion of their output is exported.

The main firm here is that of L. Sterne & Co., which was founded in 1860 and now employs 1,500. The firm has a branch factory at Hillington, and produces refrigerating plant of all kinds for land and marine use. Its original products were springs, grinding wheels and grinding machines, but refrigerating machines were started in 1885. A firm now under the direction of L. Sterne & Co. and situated in Hillington, started in 1910 to manufacture valves for gas cylinders, and now produces valves for refrigerating plant and other purposes. Another

Hillington firm produces refrigerated cabinets, cold rooms, freezers and coolers.

Machinery for Special Industries

(a) *Textile Machinery.* The production of textile machinery, one of the earliest products of Glasgow's engineering industry, still provides employment for about 800, although the textile industry no longer occupies a dominant position in the area. The largest firm in this branch is that of J. & T. Boyd, Shettleston, founded in 1864 and specialising in textile machinery since 1870. Two others specialising in textile finishing machinery are Stewart & McKenzie and John Dalglish & Sons, founded in 1857 and 1872 respectively. To all of these firms export markets are of considerable importance, although some effort is now required to persuade foreign customers to come to Scotland instead of Manchester, where the main competitors in this line are to be found. A number of smaller firms manufacture pressing machines for the textile and tailoring industries and machinery for laundries, and for dry-cleaning.

(b) *Sugar Machinery.* Glasgow's connection with the sugar industry is of long standing and the city can still claim to be the greatest centre for the manufacture of sugar machinery in the world. There are over 2,000 at present employed on this work by six firms, five of whom produce machinery for the complete sugar factory, the other firm specialising only in centrifugal separators. Four of these firms are more than a hundred years old, and all of them were started before the end of last century. Most of them are primarily engaged in producing sugar machinery, but many also produce some machinery for the chemical industry, laundries, and the textile industry, and one firm combines sugar machinery and steel works plant.

The Mirrlees Watson Co. is the largest, employing 800 apart from subsidiaries. The firm was started as P. & W. McOnie in 1840, the name Mirrlees being added in 1848. By 1950 the firm had built 119 two-roller crushers and 2,202 cane mills of all sizes, along with the necessary machinery, evaporators, condensers, pumps, etc. which make up a cane sugar factory. During its lifetime it has developed a number of important inventions, including Weston centrifugal machines and Taryan evaporating apparatus, as well as establishing a diesel engine works in Stockport. It was closely associated with Watson Laidlaw & Co., formed to specialise in the production of centrifugal machinery, and in 1946 acquired a controlling interest in Blairs. It also produces some machinery for the chemical industry, some power plant equipment, and evaporators for salt plant and water distillers. About 80 per cent of its output is for export.

Three other firms which date from the same period are A. & W. Smith & Co., founded in 1837, Blairs, which started in 1838, and Duncan Stewart & Co., started about 1840. Blairs originally produced copper work for distillery and chemical plant, and copper pipes, and subsequently added sugar machinery. In 1917 it acquired the goodwill of A. & P. W. McOnie and in 1930 that of the Harvey Engineering Company, two of the oldest-established sugar machinery manufacturers. Indeed, the latter originated as early as 1788 with James Cook, who was the first to manufacture sugar machinery, and the former stems from the same root as Mirrlees Watson, now the parent company of Blairs. The firm produces plant for the chemical industry, distilling, brewing and tanning plant, food manufacture machinery, and copper and brass work of all kinds. More than half of the output is for export.

Duncan Stewart & Co. started in 1840 on the production of textile, sugar and general engineering machinery. At the beginning of the present century the company, then being controlled by Sir William Beardmore, started to develop steel-works plant, and this latterly replaced textile machinery. Since 1939 the firm has been in the Davy-United Group of steel-works plant manufacturers, but has continued its work in the design and manufacture of sugar machinery. It exports about 45 per cent of its products.

John McNeil & Co. specialises solely in cane sugar machinery. The firm was started in 1881, its founder being until then associated with one of the McOnie companies. In this case 90 per cent of output is for export markets.

The more specialised production of centrifugal machinery for sugar, chemical, laundry and textile industries is the concern of Watson Laidlaw & Co. This firm was founded in 1883 by two members of Mirrlees Watson & Co. for the manufacture of the Weston centrifugal patents. More than half of the output is exported.

(c) *Mining Machinery*. Given the importance of coal in the industrial development of the area and the proximity of the coalfields, it is natural that equipment for the mines should form an important part of the engineering industry's products. Many of the firms already mentioned contribute to this. These include Drysdale who supplies pumps; Howden, Thermotank and Winsor Engineering, fans; and the N.B. Company, locomotives. Pipes are supplied by Stewarts & Lloyds.

The area was among the earliest to introduce electrical machinery, and the firm of Mavor & Coulson has long specialised in this. This firm's early contribution to the field of electrical engineering has already been mentioned in the first section of this chapter. While still carrying on its general electrical work, the firm decided to specialise in electrical coal-cutting machinery as early as 1897 and since then has pioneered many new developments. Its success with coal-cutters brought a demand for loaders and conveyors, and here also the firm can claim several inventions, for both underground and surface use. By the 1930's it was concentrating entirely on this type of work. In addition to the main works at Bridgeton and the iron foundry at Dalmarnock, there is a large branch factory at East Kilbride, opened in 1928 and subsequently expanded, where the structural work for conveyors and loaders is concentrated. The firm has also manufactured switchgear since 1888 and expansion of this department led to the formation in 1931 of a subsidiary company, M. & C. Switchgear, with works at Kirkintilloch. A factory has been leased at Rutherglen from Scottish Industrial Estates, where rollers are manufactured for conveyors. Although specialising mainly in mining equipment, the firm also supplies conveyors and handling equipment for use by electrical and gas undertakings, quarries, etc. Its total employees in the city number over a thousand and the firm has an extensive export business.

In 1947 an American firm opened a branch factory in the Queenslie Industrial Estate where it now manufactures miners' lamps, breathing apparatus and other safety appliances.

Machine Tools

In this branch there is a bias towards heavy machine tools, which is natural in view of the area's industrial history. This is particularly true of the older firms. There are also, however, a number of firms of recent origin, a development which reflects the renewed prosperity of the engineering industry in the postwar period, and several of these are catering for the new lighter industries of the area. In all there are about 1,700 employed in the machine tools industry and many of the products are exported.

The Scottish Machine Tool Corporation was founded in 1937 and now includes in Glasgow three of the oldest firms in this branch of engineering: James Binnie, founded in 1835 and manufacturing heavy machine tools; G. & A. Harvey, founded in 1858 and manufacturing lathes, power presses and horizontal boring machines; and James Allan Senior & Son, founded in 1836 and making engineering castings; as well as two other machine tool firms outwith the city.

Heavy machine tools are manufactured by Hugh Smith & Co. (Possil), founded in 1875, as well as by firms in the locomotive, structural and sugar machinery sections of engineering. Their products include punching and shearing machines, lathes and planing machines; large shears, hydraulic presses and other steel-works plant; heavy machine tools for shipbuilding and boiler works; riveting machines and bending rolls.

A wide range of lighter machine tools are manufactured, and in some cases by firms dating from last century which have developed in this direction to meet the needs of the lighter industries and the aircraft industry of to-day. But there are several firms of more recent origin, many of them in the industrial estates, now operating in this field. In a few cases these are branch factories of English firms, of which the largest is Wickman Ltd., Coventry. Jigs, gauges, carbide tipped tools and tool holders, attachments for drilling and tapping, are among their products. The founder of one of the older firms, William Cook & Sons, dating from 1842, began as a saw doctor but soon extended his business to include manufacture. Another concern, Anderson, Whan & Co., was started as a smithy, about 1875, on the site of the present St. Enoch Hotel, by David Anderson.

Finally a number of firms in the city undertake the machining of parts under contract or sub-contract.

Motors and Cycles

Although a number of small firms in the city produce various components for the motor industry there is, as already mentioned, only one motor manufacturing firm remaining in Scotland, namely Albion Motors, Scotstoun. The firm started in 1899 and since 1913 has concentrated solely on commercial and public service vehicles. It merged with Leyland Motors in 1951. At present over 3,000 are employed and more than half of the output is for overseas markets.

Likewise the only firm of cycle manufacturers in Scotland is Argyle Cycles, Glasgow. This firm started as the Glasgow Cycle Company in 1906, a time when it was expensive to bring bicycles from the Midlands and deliveries were irregular. At first the firm produced a small range of pedal cycles, but now manufactures some 24 types, including autocycles. Output is at the rate of 100 per day, and export accounts for about 80 per cent.

Aero Engines

The most important single addition to the industry of this area in the recent period is undoubtedly the Rolls Royce aero engine works. This originated as part of the Government's rearmament programme, and the new factory for the production of Merlin engines was opened at Hillington in 1939. As already noted, during the war the numbers employed rose to a peak of 25,000. In 1947 Rolls Royce took over part of the Hillington factory and established a repair unit for piston type aero engines, and this became the repair unit for all the Rolls Royce group of factories. A Government programme of re-equipment introduced in 1951 required further expansion of manufacturing capacity and as a result a new factory has been built outwith the city, at East Kilbride, the engine repair work largely transferred to other factories in the Lanarkshire area, and the Hillington factory expanded as much as possible and devoted to the manufacture and overhaul of piston and gas turbine aero engines. The group employ a total of over 11,000 in all their Scottish factories.

King Aircraft Corporation, Hillington, have been manufacturing aircraft components since 1941.

Instruments and Electrical Equipment

These two have been grouped together because the basis of many instruments and of control equipment now tends to be electrical or electronic, and interest in this field is not confined to instrument makers in the strict sense of the word. Some of the firms already listed in other connections are concerned here, such as G. & J. Weir and Thermotank. Apart from these there are in this group firms employing over 3,000, of whom about two-thirds are employed as instrument makers proper, the remainder being concerned with electrical and electronic equipment of various kinds. This section comes into the category of light engineering, of which instrument making is one of the few branches well represented in Glasgow. In the field of electrical control equipment the city is not extensively concerned, and with a few exceptions, firms are small and of recent origin.

It is an interesting comment on University conditions in the last century that the two largest firms of instrument makers owe their prominence to University professors, who were able to combine their teaching duties with active participation in manufacturing business. Nowadays the size of both classes and curricula would surely make this impossible, even if it were permissible. The firm of Barr & Stroud was started in 1890 when Professor Barr and Professor Stroud went into partnership for the production of rangefinders. Professor Barr, who held the chair of engineering at Glasgow University until 1913, had been engaged for some time on academic research with his colleague Stroud. In response to an advertisement by the Admiralty offering a reward for the invention of a rangefinder, they successfully turned their attention to this project. At first they merely designed and assembled the rangefinders, the parts being manufactured by instrument makers in the city. In 1895 they started manufacture with one man and a boy in a small workshop in Byres Road, and by 1900 they had 100 employees. At present the firm employs 1,550 and in addition to rangefinders now produces an extended range of optical, mechanical, electrical, hydraulic and electronic precision instruments, including radar equipment. About a third of its products are exported.

Kelvin & Hughes was started in 1850 by James White who manufactured scientific instruments. Professor Thomson, later Lord Kelvin, came to be associated with the firm, which then became Kelvin & White and from 1858 concentrated on the manufacture of his patented electrical instruments. The firm later became Kelvin, Bottomley & Baird and continued to manufacture an extended range of instruments, many for marine use. In the 1920's aircraft instruments were added to its productions, but in 1935 these were transferred to a new factory in the south of England, the new site being nearer to the centre of aircraft manufacture. In 1947 the firm amalgamated with the London instrument makers, Henry Hughes & Son, and since 1953 has become a subsidiary of the English firm. The factory, now at Hillington, employs 510 and manufactures a wide range of industrial test and control equipment, including an echo sounding instrument for detecting cracks and flaws in metal. The major part of output is for export.

Dobbie McInnes started as Alex. Dobbie & Son in 1841 and in 1902 purchased the business of T. S. McInnes & Co., also started in the previous century. The production was originally that of ships' compasses, but now includes a range of engineering, industrial and scientific instruments. Engine indicators and viscometers are among the best-known of its products but a branch factory at Hillington now concentrates on electrical and electronic equipment.

A few firms specialise in electrical control equipment, with a total employment of about 500. The oldest and largest is that of Robert Maclaren & Co., started in 1841 as ironfounders, which now manufactures thermostats and float switches. A newcomer to the area is Scottish Telecommunications, which was started in 1952 as a subsidiary of the Cambridge firm, Pye Telecommunications, and manufactures radio receivers and electronic equipment. One or two other firms have recently added industrial electronic equipment to their list of products, but so far developments in this line have not been extensive.

Apart from control equipment there are four firms engaged in electrical manufacture. The largest is the Macfarlane Engineering Company. This firm started in 1911 and manufactures dynamos for special purposes, including welding generators, and laboratory plant. A considerable proportion of the business is for export. A number of firms of more recent origin are engaged on electrical equipment, making tubular heaters, water and oil heaters, electrically heated tar and bitumen equipment, motor windings, and transformers.

Other Light Engineering

There remains a rather motley collection of products whose manufacture constitutes mainly light engineering. They vary from typewriters to razor blades, and include firms established more than a century ago, as well as the newcomers of the recent postwar period. In all they provide employment for about 8,000, of whom more than half are employed by postwar firms, chiefly in the industrial estates.

Among the oldest of Glasgow's light industries is that of wire working. Wire weaving, originally by hand, is an ancient craft, and the major part of the industry in this country is in Scotland. There are over 600 employed in it in Glasgow, and its products are used by a wide variety of industries, particularly that of paper manufacture. Begg Cousland & Co. represents an amalgamation of two of the oldest firms in Glasgow engaged in this work, Alexander Cousland & Sons, started in 1843, and William Riddick & Co., founded in 1854.

The manufacture of bolts, nuts and screws provides employment for over a thousand. Here there is a mixture of old and new firms. Among the former is William Motherwell & Co., which started with the manufacture of hand-made nails, and A. P. Newall & Co., the largest in the area. In 1946 the Birmingham firm of Guest Keen & Nettlefolds opened a branch factory at Hillington for the production of mild steel wood-screws.

From the point of view of employment the largest group in this section, however, is of very recent origin in Glasgow, namely those engaged in the manufacture of typewriters. At present there are nearly 3,500 employed on this work by two branch factories in the industrial estates. The American firm, Remington Rand, started at Hillington in 1948, and as well as typewriters, also manufactures electric shavers. British Olivetti, a subsidiary of the Italian firm, started the manufacture of typewriters in the Queenslie Estate in 1947.

The manufacture of wringers has long been one of the city's light industries and at present employs some 1,300. The largest firm is that of Acme Wringers, established 1879, and now producing hand and power operated wringers at the rate of four machines per minute. The firm has an extensive export trade. The West of Scotland Wringer Co. was started in 1908 and produces wringers of various types for home and export markets.

Many firms, old and new, are engaged in the production of machinery and equipment for the food industries, including machines for packaging and labelling, as well as containers and vessels. In all there are nearly 1,000 employed in this group. Their products include hand-operated bakery machinery, equipment for mechanised bakery, vegetable cutting and food preparing machines, potato peelers, mix masters, and cooking equipment, as well as machinery for grain and flour mills, filling and packing machines, multiple bottle labelling machines, box-making machines, machines for nailing, printing, labelling and fastening; kegs, drums and tins, and stainless steel equipment for the food industries, as well as for chemical, textile and other industries.

The manufacture of chains employs about 100. Watson & McLean, the only firm of chain-makers in the city, was established in 1881. The manufacture of gas meters, an industry long established in the area, gives employment to a similar number. To this manufacture has been added the assemblage and distribution of cookers and other products.

Wheel barrows and perambulators engage the activities of one firm each and between them these employ 100 workers; a firm of bankers' engineers produces safes, deed boxes and strong rooms; the manufacture of springs of all types for light engineering, furniture and mattresses gives employment to about 200; and on the Hillington Estate an American firm, Ever-Ready Razor Products, employs over 200 on the manufacture of razor blades.

Non-ferrous Metals

Some of the larger engineering firms have their own foundries to supply their own needs and the numbers employed here are already included in the separate industries. Apart from these there are about 3,000 employed in firms specialising in the non-ferrous industry. The oldest and still the largest group are the brass-founders whose total employment is over 1,000. Of the firms supplying the textile mills in the early 1800's only one survives, John Glover & Sons, who started business before 1763. At least 50 per cent of the products of this group go to the shipyards and marine engine shops. Steven & Struthers, who started in 1866, make bronze propellers and bells. Bull's Metal & Marine, starting in 1901, also makes ships' propellers and has added more recently ships' windows. Of the dozen other mostly smaller firms having employees numbering between 20 and 125, most are general non-ferrous founders, making castings of aluminium and other alloys in addition to brass and bronze. Some have special lines in addition—Lancefield Foundry Company does coppersmith work, Wm. Ross & Sons and C. & A. Stewart make valves and boiler mountings, Kingston Brass Company makes architectural brass, and Scottish Precision Castings makes centrifugal filters.

Aluminium alloys, in spite of their increasing use for ships and superstructures, for bridges, and for a variety of trades, could be considered a neglected industry of the city except for one recent addition. The other half dozen firms are small, having each about 20 employees, making ingots and castings, ridgings and corrugated sheets. The exception is Renfrew Foundries, with an employment of something under 1000 who can claim to be the largest mechanised light alloy foundry in the United Kingdom. Starting as a part of the Rolls Royce group, this firm still directs its output largely to armaments but its aim to supply general industry throughout the country, including the motor manufacturers and the typewriter and office equipment group, has been partly achieved.

There are a few firms dealing with soft metals, the total employment being between 200 and 300. One firm has been making lead pipe and lead wire since 1844. Another makes lead traps and bends, another printing metals and solders. A firm whose main factories are in London and Kilmarnock started a branch in Hillington for repair and for the manufacture of bearings and bearing metals.

Nickel has been used as an alloy of steel for some time; it is, for example, an important element in stainless steel. It has come much to the fore recently because of the high temperature in the latest steam plants and in gas turbines, where nickel base alloys are necessary. In this area Henry Wiggin & Co., a unit of the International Nickel Company of Canada, specialises in its Thornliebank factory in making nickel alloy tubes and blading for gas turbines. There are fully 500 employed in this group.

A few firms are engaged on protective surfacing of plates, such as Electro-Platers Ltd. who have become, with their subsidiaries, the largest "jobbers plating establishment" in Great Britain. They started here in 1933. Shot blasting, metal spraying and galvanising are also undertaken.

Chapter 8

TEXTILES AND CLOTHING

COTTON AND WOOLLEN SPINNING AND WEAVING

Z. GROSICKI

COTTON

THE history of the cotton industry in Glasgow during the last hundred years makes, on the whole, sad reading: it is a tale of greatness followed by poverty, a story of expansion on a huge scale followed by an equally rapid decline. At one point in the history of cotton in Great Britain it was not quite clear whether Lancashire or Clydeside would become the cotton area; whether Manchester or Glasgow was destined to become the capital of the industry. Both had equally good qualifications—easy access from the sea, a well-developed trading community, a skilled weaving population, a suitable climate and abundant supply of water so necessary for the finishing trade. The dice became loaded against Glasgow in 1861 and this may be regarded as the crucial year during which the downward slide started. It is best, however, to consider the events in an orderly fashion.

In 1854, the city's cotton manufacturing presented the picture of a healthy boom. It fell into three main categories: (*a*) large cotton spinning and power-loom weaving firms—the two branches being often connected; (*b*) handloom weavers, and (*c*) sewed muslin makers. At that time the handloom weavers were facing fierce competition from the power-looms and were very obviously declining in numbers owing to a disastrous fall in wages. The earlier-established spinning mills were the only concerns capable of installing power-looms as the capital outlay involved was usually beyond the capacity of the handloom weaver. These spinning-cum-weaving mills frequently were of a large size, often employing 1,000 or 2,000 work people. The third section, that of the sewed muslin makers, represented a very major industry, but it completely disappeared before the end of the nineteenth century. The process consisted of the printing of a design on various fabrics, mainly book muslins, mulls or cambrics, and the subsequent embroidering of the printed portion with sewing thread usually of the excellent Sea Island quality. This embroidery was entirely a hand process. Originally the printing was a laborious hand-block operation, but in 1837 a lithographic press was first applied to this use and it brought about a remarkable increase in the volume of manufacture. This reached its zenith in 1857 by which year the four biggest Glasgow firms were said to employ between 120,000 and 150,000 women in the city, in Ayrshire and as far afield as Northern Ireland. The total number employed by all the Glasgow firms was estimated at about 200,000. But the same year brought a disaster to the trade from which it was never to recover—the collapse of the Western Bank which was financing most of the firms in the industry. The four biggest houses in the trade owed, according to current stories, more than one and a half million pounds to the bank, a huge sum in those days. As a result of the collapse, vast stocks of merchandise came under the auctioneer's hammer and were unloaded on the market at ridiculously low prices which enabled the poorer classes to start buying and wearing these embroidered muslins. This immediately caused a loss of popularity amongst the usual consumers and even when the markets became stabilised again, in 1860, the demand could not be found. In 1861 there were still 7,220 people employed in sewed muslins in Glasgow alone but the industry continued to decline and finally disappeared entirely by the end of the century. Its collapse was hastened by the development of embroidery machines in Switzerland with which the hand processing could not successfully compete even though it was considered more durable.

The cotton spinning industry had been mechanised before the weaving branch and was firmly established in the city in the 1830's. Originally the purpose of the mills was to supply cotton yarns to the handloom weavers but later many firms expanded by adding power-loom sections and also began to supply yarns to independent weaving concerns. In 1840 there were 44 cotton spinners in Glasgow alone, and this number further increased to over 50 in 1861 when this branch of the industry reached its peak. It was estimated that out of the formidable total of 1,915,000 cotton spindles employed in Scotland, Glasgow possessed about 1,200,000. There were also 11 cotton brokers supplying the needs of the industry, a breed now completely extinct. The happy state of affairs in 1860-61 was shattered the following year when supplies of cotton failed as a result of the American Civil War. As the trade was dependent almost entirely on the supply of raw material from the Southern States, the shortage that resulted between 1862 and 1866 caused a great deal of suffering in the Glasgow area, dependent as it was almost solely on this raw material for its livelihood. The experience proved how dangerous to the community a specialised unilateral expansion can be. Cotton in its era of great growth had ousted from the West of Scotland the other traditional industries of flax and silk spinning and throwing to such an extent that when the crisis came there was nothing else on which to fall back. Glasgow, except for one large flax spinning mill and one or two silk throwsters, was a cotton town.

By the end of 1866 imports of cotton began to flow freely again, this time not only from the Southern States, but also from other sources. The wheels started turning anew. But enthusiasm seems to have been lacking. Glasgow no longer boasted men of the stature and dynamic vision of Monteith and Dale who had built its textile greatness and who might have maintained its position. Competition with the more efficient Lancashire industry proved difficult. Many fortunes were lost; resources were diverted to the developing heavy industries and skilled operatives were attracted to the better paying and more stable engineering industries. The textile industries, however, still occupied a prominent position in the city as is reflected in the fact that all three Glasgow M.P.s returned in the Election of 1868 were directly connected with the spinning or finishing of textiles. But in the years between 1868 and 1890, although the number of spinning mills was maintained, there was a steady decline in the volume of trade and by 1900 most of them had disappeared. A notable exception was the Clyde Spinning Company which survived until the 1930's by specialising in the spinning of the very finest counts of yarn, mainly for export to Germany and Switzerland.

Glasgow's present-day position in the cotton industry is very humble indeed, compared with the 1860's. The number of cotton spindles may be estimated at about 100,000 compared with 1,200,000 ninety years ago. Two firms are engaged in the doubling of cotton and staple rayon yarns with additional plants for warp yarn preparation. There is one firm of spinners specialising in the manufacture of coarse yarns for mops, scouring cloths etc., and a firm of sewing thread spinners. The latter concern produces only the large type of package suitable for the making-up industry, though earlier it had also manufactured the small retail bobbin, the disappearance of which may be blamed on the proximity of the large sewing thread combines in Paisley. The above-mentioned four firms who may be considered as survivals from the past were joined in 1948 by a larger concern engaged primarily in the manufacture of cotton yarns used in the rubber tyre industry. This firm, with headquarters in Lancashire, established itself in Glasgow because of the availability of female labour, and the proximity of large rubber factories which made utilisation of the product much simpler. The cotton spinning industry in Glasgow now employs about 700 people, whereas ninety years ago it gave employment to between 2,000 and 3,000.

In connection with spinning, reference must be made to another similar industry which is represented in Glasgow. This is the ancient art of rope and twine making. The industry itself cannot be described as entirely new to the town as there are references to ropeworks within the city as far back as 1696. However, very little is heard of them afterwards until 1918, which is rather surprising in a city with such important shipping connections. It may be partly explained by the fact that large ropeworks existed for a long time in the neighbouring localities of Gourock, Greenock and Cambuslang. In 1918 the Gourock Ropework Company established a large factory in the Govan area. The factory has recently undergone extensive modernisation and enlargement, and now gives employment to about 260 workers. It produces a variety of goods, ranging from large ropes to twines and cordage. The materials used are equally diverse in character, but mainly vegetable in origin, with a large proportion represented by long staple, hard fibres of the bast or leaf family.

In comparison with spinning, the weaving branch of the cotton industry did not suffer so complete a decline, although its volume and relative importance in the city also diminished appreciably. The first to fall were the handloom weavers, which was inevitable upon the introduction of the power loom. When it is considered that about four handloom weavers are required to equal the output of one power loom, and that only one female weaver is required to operate four power looms of the non-automatic type, it becomes increasingly clear that the hand process cannot compete successfully with the mechanised operation. It may be interesting to observe at this stage the decline in handloom weavers' wages with the increase in the number of power looms in the Glasgow area:

COTTON WEAVING IN GLASGOW

	Handloom Weavers' Weekly earnings	*Number of power looms*
1806	30s. to 32s.	400
1820	10s.	2,000
1830	5s. 6d.	10,000

In spite of the disastrous fall in wages, there were still about 37,000 cotton handloom weavers in the West of Scotland in 1830 and 10,000 managed to survive until 1872. It may be suspected, however, that most of them were women and children working at home in their spare time whilst the chief bread-winner had another occupation, since it appears that the wage rate was considerably below the subsistence minimum of a single person. After 1875 they virtually disappeared from the industrial life of the region, the last survivors being the Paisley Shawl weavers, but even their highly-specialised trade was already doomed.

The first power-loom factory in the Glasgow district was established by John Monteith in Pollokshaws at the dawn of the nineteenth century. It contained 200 looms. From that date the weaving establishments multiplied until in 1861 they reached the figure of about 60. Some were quite large, employing frequently from 1,500 to 2,000 workers, and they contained in all about 20,000 looms served by up to 12,000 employees. The largest proportion was occupied in the manufacture of plain goods which gave rise to the development of the bleaching, dyeing and printing industries where another army of workers, only slightly less numerous, was employed. It is interesting to note that plain cotton goods are no longer manufactured in the city. Second in importance was the muslin trade with both plain and fancy products, while a third and much smaller section consisted of cotton lace makers.

As in cotton spinning, the American Civil War had a disastrous effect on further development. Production was almost completely halted and even the cessation of hostilities in the U.S. did not cause the resurgence of the former spirit of expansion. The war and the previous troubles caused by the collapse of the Western Bank proved such an unsettling influence that the industry was unable to resume on a normal footing. Indeed, of all the numerous firms in business in 1861, only four or five survive to-day. As stated before, no plain cotton manufacturer remained in the city after the beginning of the twentieth century and this can be explained by the fact that since it is the cheapest end of the trade, it is also the most competitive and the decline in the spinning side was directly responsible for its disappearance. It was impossible to compete with Lancashire weavers, who had their spinning mills at hand and were not forced to pay the extra transit charges on their yarn. Other fancier brands of cotton cloth could bear that charge more easily, but even so, of the 40 or 50 gingham and pullicate manufactures of the 1850's only one remains—the redoubtable firm of D. & J. Anderson, who started as far back as 1822. The firm grew in the gingham and pullicate trade (pullicates being coloured handkerchiefs or neck-cloths) and later originated a new fabric known as zephyr which achieved the peak of its popularity about 1900. Further development was towards finer qualities of poplins and fine woollen shirtings and dress materials. The firm's ginghams and other products have an unrivalled reputation in the U.S.A. and the quality of their manufacture was so excellent that the Japanese even in the period of their greatest textile expansion would not attempt to imitate it. In the home markets a major decision was reached in 1933 when the firm decided to sell directly to the retail trade; this resulted in the extension of the firm's activities to London with the opening of a sales office and a shirt factory.

In comparison with gingham makers the muslin manufacturers have suffered less. Their numbers were reduced from about twenty to four and their present-day concentration is on fancy cloths which, because of the intricacy of manufacture, cannot be easily imitated by foreign competitors. The early productions consisted mainly of various articles for the Indian market such as sarries, dhooties, mulls and muslins as well as dress and curtaining materials for home markets in the form of Madras and book muslins, lappets and similar fabrics. A development which occurred in the 1860's was the start of the manufacture of Arab yashmaghs and it is interesting to note that whilst the Indian and Burmese markets were almost entirely lost, the yashmaghs are still woven in quantity. The design of the fancy muslins and lappets improved greatly, especially in the period between 1840 and 1890. This advance was due mainly to substitution of machinery for manual operation in the clipping of unwanted extra yarn which is a feature in these fabrics. The designer of the 1840's had to bear in mind not so much the grace and balance of the pattern as the ease of access and the openings for the clippers' scissors. With the advance of machinery, the design has assumed a new charm and strength. To-day it has an attractive simplicity of pattern which to some extent was necessitated by the need for more continuous production and the comparative lack of skilled labour, both factors making the manufacture of highly complicated effects very difficult. Modern products of the remaining muslin factories include lappets, lenos, Madras and book muslins, voiles, and marquisettes in the traditional line, to which new ranges were added recently with synthetic fibres such as staple rayon, nylon, Ardil, and Terylene contributing to the variety of raw material in use. The decline of the muslin industry in particular and weaving in general has brought about the disappearance of Anderston Foundry, an engineering works which specialised in the manufacture of looms particularly suited to lappet and muslin making. It established a tradition in that type of loom, bringing forth a number of useful innovations particularly suitable for the local product, but was forced to discontinue when the demand fell with the reduction of the number of weaving firms in the city. Most weavers in the lappet trade nowadays have to arrange their own modifications in the basic loom, since there seem to be no machinery makers catering for their particular needs left in Great Britain. In spite of all these difficulties, the Glasgow group of lappet makers is in a reasonably strong position by virtue of its almost monopolistic hold on the fancier end of the trade.

The only other branch of cotton manufacture in the city with roots in the distant past is lace making. This section also has suffered a decline and now only one factory remains. It is, however, some consolation that this industry is represented in great strength in the not so distant Irvine valley district of Ayrshire, which is now considered the biggest lace manufacturing area in the whole of Great Britain.

There is, however, a brighter side to the picture. During a development period immediately prior to the Second World War or just after the end of it some new firms gained a footing in the city. Some other, older firms, having sagged badly in the 1890's and then again in the 1930's, have regained their strength and started production with a new hope. The field of cotton weaving would not be complete without a mention of a firm of towel makers who, though young compared with other establishments, have earned a high reputation for their own class of product. There is also a firm specialising in corset brocades, both rigid and elastic, using cotton, rayon, nylon and Latex yarns, as well as makers of sponge cloths, and a company producing a variety of fabrics from all-wool tartan goods through union shirtings to all-cotton fine zephyrs. The scope may be further extended to include the asbestos spinners and weavers who have a large factory in the northern part of the city, and a firm of glass fibre weavers, both concerns engaged in the manufacture of a wide range of goods for industrial purposes.

The rise of the heavy industries, so prevalent in the Glasgow of to-day, coincides with the inception of firms producing engine-cleaning cotton wastes not only for the needs of the local engineering works but also for export. Some of them also combine this with the manufacture of axle-box packing for which the large amounts of woollen waste produced by local carpet mills are utilised. To these smaller auxiliary industries, one may add a factory specialising in the making of surgical dressings which appears to progress rapidly.

The present position as compared with that obtaining ninety years ago is as follows:

Cotton Weaving in Glasgow, 1860-1954

	Looms[1]	*Operatives*[1]
1860	20,000	12,000
1954	3,300	2,200

To the concerns actively engaged in manufacture, one must add a rather unique group of firms—the so-called "manufacturers-without-looms." This may be regarded as a reminder of the city's greatness in the cotton industry in the past as the above-mentioned firms who trade under the label of manufacturers did actually produce cloth at one time, but when circumstances of declining business forced them to liquidate they discontinued their production without losing their trade connections. These firms continue in business but all the cloth they handle is woven for them on commission.

Generally, cotton manufacturing is at the moment in a reasonably healthy state, but the dwindling of the industry produces its own problems. One of them is the isolation from the sources of raw materials, which have to be procured at additional expense from Lancashire, and another is the reduction of the "pool" of trained labour. On the other hand the climate is still very favourable and the excellent shipping facilities help considerably, especially as most local firms are particularly export-minded. The varied nature of local products guards the industry against trade fluctuations and changes of fashion which in other more specialised areas often prove disastrous.

Woollen and Worsted

Glasgow is not, and never was, considered one of the traditional centres of the Scottish woollen industry. Nevertheless, a considerable number of people in the city are engaged in that branch of textile manufacture.

The industry in its home-craft form, probably one of the oldest in the district, was eclipsed first by flax spinning and weaving and later by cotton. At the time of the first *Statistical Account of Scotland* there was only one factory in Glasgow manufacturing coarse woollens and carpets. After that, several more carpet-making firms were established in the area and it appears that in 1871 there were about 4,400

[1] Including looms and operatives for allied fibres.

people employed by the various woollen manufacturers within the city boundaries. This figure undoubtedly includes knit goods operatives who may well account for over half the total, but even so, it is a substantial increase compared with the position one hundred years before that date.

It may be worth noting that this increase coincides to a marked degree with the partial decay of the cotton trade and it is also significant that during this period the transition from hand to machine operation was completed. This conversion was marked by the following stages:

1790 introduction of carding engine and spinning jenny;
1814 development of the spinning mule;
1831 adaptation of the power loom to woollen and worsted weaving.

It must be stated, however, that the wool industry did not take advantage of the vast pool of trained labour made available by the virtual disappearance of the cotton trade, and the traditional centres remained in Ayrshire, the Borders and the North, despite the suitability of Glasgow water for wool processing and the superior shipping and general trading facilities at hand.

While carpet manufacture continues, none of the woollen factories of 1870 have survived to carry on the tradition of tweed, blanket or scarf making; but the firm of William Hollins & Company, with headquarters in Nottingham, brought a new development in the 1890's in the form of cotton and wool union manufacture. Their first association with the city took the form of placing orders for commission weaving with Glasgow cotton firms but by 1900 the firm had acquired local mills and to-day all the weaving of the famous Viyella, Clydella and Dayella brands has been transferred to Glasgow. The firm, first attracted to this locality by the availability of labour with traditional weaving skill, has become one of the important features of the textile industry in the city following a period of uninterrupted growth. This has been assisted by the policy of modernisation and conversion to up-to-date automatic yarn preparation and weaving machinery. The only other manufacturer in this section of the industry is the firm of F. Friedlander, which settled in the Hillington Industrial Estate in 1937 with the assistance of the Special Areas Reconstruction Association, who were set up to aid development of distressed areas. The firm originated in Vienna in 1886 and has a great tradition in the manufacture of ladies' high-class scarves and squares. Prior to the outbreak of the 1939-45 war, all the manufacture was carried out on hand looms, but after the war a power loom section was formed to produce less expensive items for mass markets. This concern uses not only wool but also a variety of other fibres such as Angora, mohair, silk and the recent regenerated and synthetic fibres. Some of the products are screen printed within the firm, which possesses its own printing plant. About 50 per cent of the production of the above-mentioned concerns is directly exported, mainly to the United States of America. In addition to these two weaving mills, there is also a woollen spinning factory which specialises in the manufacture of carpet yarns, as well as a felt manufacturer and two curled-hair makers.

By far the biggest position in the Glasgow wool industry is occupied by carpet manufacture. This has grown from very humble beginnings to veritably gigantic proportions, dwarfing all other similar undertakings and replacing cotton as the biggest employer of the textile labour force. The establishment of Glasgow as one of the important carpet-making centres in Great Britain owes most to the firm of James Templeton & Co., who started business here in 1839. It was not an entirely new industry for the city as small establishments had been in existence as far back as the end of the eighteenth century in the district of Havannah. These became extinct at the beginning of the nineteenth century but had been replaced by the Port Eglinton Carpet Company producing the then popular three ply Scotch carpeting as well as more expensive Brussels and Wilton types and hand-tufted rugs. This company also seems to have ceased to exist, probably in the 1850's, leaving James Templeton & Co. as the only surviving firm. The inception of this concern is due to a Paisley shawl weaver, Quigley, who discovered the art of making Chenille weft with pile standing upright and placed all to one side of the fabric. Not knowing how to employ the invention, Quigley consulted James Templeton, a Paisley shawl manufacturer, who immediately saw possibilities in the new fabric. He patented the discovery in their joint names and set out from Paisley to Glasgow to establish the great firm. The reason for choosing Glasgow in preference to Paisley is shrouded in mystery, but since the Paisley shawl manufacture was essentially a homecraft industry, it may be that there were no suitable industrial premises available, whereas Glasgow, with its extensive cotton factories, may have offered this amenity. The factory, started in 1839, grew into a successful business and gave impetus to the formation of other similarly engaged firms in its vicinity.

It is of interest to note that most of them were founded by employees of James Templeton leaving to commence manufacturing on their own account. Firms originating in this way were Macfarlane Brothers in 1845, John Lyle & Sons in 1853 and Anderson & Lawson in 1860, but of these only the second still survives. At the time of James Templeton's beginnings, the known varieties of carpets included two and three ply Scotch carpeting, Brussels, Wilton, Tapestry, and Tapestry velvet, besides hand-tufted styles. The Scotch carpet had a smooth pile-less surface and James Templeton, in originating the Chenille Axminster, combined the luxurious soft pile of the Wilton with the great seamless width of the non-pile carpeting. Hitherto, pile carpets, excepting the hand-tufted products, could only be woven in comparatively narrow strips which had to be joined by seaming to make up complete carpet squares. A further advantage of Chenille was an unlimited colour scope.

In 1853 a hand loom Brussels section was started and this carpet was produced by the, then novel, jacquard method until 1856 when a separate factory was opened, equipped with power looms. Basically, the loops of the Brussels are cut to form the fibrous pile of the Wilton type but up to the advent of the twentieth century the demand for Brussels exceeded by many times that for Wilton, whilst at the present day the position has been reversed and hardly a single Brussels style is produced. Such is the change in popular taste.

The Brussels factory remained a separate subsidiary until 1906 when it was completely merged with the Chenille division. With the introduction of power to Brussels and Wilton weaving a vast field of employment was opened to female labour and in 1884 this was extended when Chenille looms became power-operated. The change-over was beneficial to the firm since male labour was becoming increasingly difficult to obtain on account of the attraction of higher wages in the heavy engineering industry which was experiencing an unprecedented boom at that time.

The reduction in cost of manufacture brought carpets within the reach of people of modest means and for the first time they were mass produced instead of being made to order. Standardisation of designs followed, bringing a further reduction in prices, so that everything seemed set for a great advance, when an American development was announced. This was a new method of carpet making by individual tuft insertion known as Spool Axminster and was introduced to the United Kingdom in 1878 at Kidderminster. This invention enabled fine cut pile carpets to be produced even more cheaply than by the Chenille method and in 1888 James Templeton & Co. secured the patent of a new version of the original invention and commenced manufacture in a new factory building in 1892. The only disadvantage of Spool Axminster was that only strips up to 36 inches in width could be produced; an invention of Templeton's own in 1914 enabled large seamless squares to be manufactured quite easily.

The 1914-18 war halted progress and the factories were mainly engaged on blanket production as a contribution to the war effort. By 1925, however, the firm were the first on the market with a full range of seamless Spool Axminster carpets, first up to 10½ feet and later to 12 feet in width. Shortly afterwards, by 1930, the newer development of Gripper Axminster was introduced by the firm, the carpet having a more limited colour range but a superior structure compared with Spool. In accordance with the policy of constant modernisation, Messrs. James Templeton have recently combined the advantage of both methods in a Spool-Gripper loom at present in the experimental stage.

Another important advance in the carpet world occurred in the early 1930's when the inventive genius of James Templeton & Co. developed the Hook Wilton loom which permitted the manufacture of this superior structure in full seamless widths instead of narrow strips. The company has become a fully vertical integration with spinning, weaving, dyeing and engineering units and with commercial representation throughout the world. Between 20 per cent and 30 per cent of the production is exported and the firm has the unique honour of having made carpets for the last three coronation ceremonies and many other Royal occasions. Its factories have been graced several times by personal Royal visits. The concern was made a public company in 1947 but even to this day there is a direct descendant of the founder serving on the Board of Directors.

Of the remaining carpet making firms, that of Anderson & Lawson was absorbed by a Kidderminster concern and the work transferred to that locality, others went into liquidation, and only John Lyle & Sons remains in the city. The founder of this last firm, John Lyle, started his career with James Templeton in the early days, but seeing no prospect of personal advancement he commenced the handloom manufacture of Chenille carpeting on his own account in 1853. From small beginnings, and in the face of fierce competition, the business continued and has grown into a medium-sized concern with happy relations between employers and operatives so that strikes, even in this present era of unrest, are unknown.

In the 1890's the mill was re-equipped with Chenille power looms and for a short period the manufacture also included Brussels and Wilton types of carpet. In pursuance of a policy of specialisation, the looms for the latter were disposed of and their place was taken in 1930 by a modern Spool Axminster plant which now produces the major proportion of the firm's output. The expansion was interrupted by the Second World War when the weaving factory and dyehouse space was requisitioned by the Ministry of Supply and converted to war uses. The production of carpets was resumed immediately after the end of hostilities and a vigorous policy of modernisation adopted. Amongst new equipment were automatic Chenille weft weaving rapier looms, installed in the early 1950's, increasing considerably the efficiency of this process. In post-war years the firm has developed a considerable export trade with Australia, New Zealand, and South Africa and at one time was exporting as much as 50 per cent of its production, though this has become stabilised around 25 per cent.

Up to 1939, all these firms were able to recruit new labour without difficulty in their locality of Bridgeton where there was a tradition of girls leaving school to enter one or other of the numerous textile mills, but the situation has deteriorated during the war and post-war years because other industries have included the district in their recruitment area and many of the people in East End tenement property have been re-housed in new estates and have sought employment near at hand.

The growth of the carpet industry has created associated industries such as carpet yarn spinning, wool "willeying" and wool broking. The city now has three wool willeying concerns, who open and partially clean the bales of wool in willeying machines prior to the spinning process. The city wool brokers have a considerable trade in raw wool imports of Indian, Pakistani, Tibetan, Moroccan and New Zealand cross bred types and they also export quantities of Scottish blackface wool.

The growth of the carpet trades in Glasgow may be shown by the following figures which include besides the carpet manufactures also companion industries:

Year	Employees
1913	2,900
1937	4,700
1954	4,500

The slight decrease in employment between 1937 and 1954 does not necessarily indicate any fall in the trade. Figures of output are not available, but the square yardage is probably greater as a result of more efficient production and more modern machinery and methods. The total labour force engaged in the whole of the woollen industry in Glasgow inclusive of cloth weavers and allied industries was as follows:

Year	Employees
1871	Approx. 1,100
1954	5,600

The growth in the industry in the last seventy years has been quite spectacular even measured in terms of the labour force, but it must be borne in mind that the increase in output must have been immeasurably greater owing to the introduction of improved and automatic machinery which would advance the production per operative very considerably. The present day portents seem to indicate that the positions will be, if not improved, at least maintained.

OTHER TEXTILES, CLOTHING, AND FINISHING

A. W. MARVIN

The Manufacture of Knitted Garments and Cloths

The manufacture of knitted garments by mechanical instead of manual control of threads is a relatively new industry in Glasgow. Unlike the cotton industry it did not participate in, or contribute to, the earlier industrial development of the city. It would appear, indeed, to have been introduced here mainly during the present century, some firms moving into the city from surrounding areas, some originating in the city during the century as complete manufacturing units. It underwent a rapid expansion in Glasgow in the period between the first and the second world wars, but since then expansion has not continued. The position is illustrated by the following figures of employment within the industry in Glasgow:

TABLE XLIII

KNITTED GARMENTS AND CLOTHS: GLASGOW, 1910-1950

Year	*Males*	*Females*	*Total*	
1910	90	580	670	(estimated)
1937	226	2,995	3,221	
1950	298	2,278	2,576	

These figures of employment, however, fail to reflect the capacity of the industry, which has been increased as a result of the introduction of new, high-production machinery combined with the application of work study in the handling of cloth in its conversion to the garment ready for the consumer. The actual production of the industry in Glasgow indeed was greater in 1950 than in any previous year, and would have been greater still but for a shortage of skilled operatives and difficulties and delays in the delivery of raw material.

The earliest methods employed by machine knitters followed the established practices of hand knitting, the loops being arranged on the machine in a straight form and the shaping of the garment achieved by increasing or decreasing the number of loops in any row during the production of the garment. The various shaped parts were then assembled to form the garment which was finished by scouring, dyeing and other similar operations. This basic method of producing full-fashioned garments is still used although the machinery and the production technique applied conform to modern design and practice. The highest quality knitwear garments are produced by this method and naturally command a high retail price which restricts sales to a small section of the consumer potential.

To cater for the larger remaining portion of that potential, the cut-up method of producing garments was introduced. In this method, rolls of fabric are produced on high-speed circular knitting machines, the fabric being dyed and possibly brushed or milled, after which the appropriate shapes are marked on the cloth, cut out and assembled to produce a complete garment. Alternatively, lengths of fabric may be produced on power flat machines. Such a method of production is faster and capable of a greater variety of design than is the former method, but the resultant quality and price are not comparable with those of a product of similar appearance produced by the first method.

The latest influence upon the industry is that introduced by the circular garment-producing machine which, as its name implies, is designed for producing garment lengths which, when taken off the machine, require the minimum of assembling and finishing.

The fashioned trade, because of its low waste rate, is able to use the high priced, high quality yarns such as cashmere, angora and lambswool, whilst that portion of the industry using bulk production methods utilises medium quality worsted yarn and also the newer synthetic fibres, these materials being less expensive than the former and being available in greater supply.

The basic activity in Glasgow in the middle of the twentieth century is the manufacture of wool outerwear garments in the form of cardigans, jumpers and twin-sets; but there is a newer and increasing demand for knitted jersey dresswear in all styles, this being dictated by the reigning fashion trend. The greater proportion of these Glasgow products is of the cut variety, whereas in the other areas of Scotland the fashioned garment is the main product. The bulk of the Glasgow production, especially for the adult consumer, is disposed of through wholesale and retail channels in the home market, but certain items are exported in considerable numbers; thus one firm of approximately 100 employees has, during the years following the Second World War, built up a fairly large export trade to the North American Continent, supplying that area with a considerable quantity of children's knitted outerwear. Certain other small firms supply the now traditional diamond pattern hose for wear with the appropriate Scottish Dress, but the production of such items is low by virtue of the semi-manual method of production, this resulting in a high cost.

A small amount of warp knitted fabric is produced, the manufacturing process employed here being a half-way stage between knitting and weaving, in so far as the yarns are wound on to beams as in the weaving industry. The main products would appear to be shawls and similar garments for infants, bed jackets, and stoles for evening wear. There is, however, the possibility of considerable expansion in this particular branch of the industry as new high-speed knitting looms, capable of greater production, are being introduced. The resulting fabric, made of fine multi- or monofilament synthetic or regenerated filaments, is being used for ladies' underwear and nightwear and is at present displacing similar garments made from finely sett, woven fabric which is produced at a much slower rate, needing possibly more basic preparation.

The knitwear manufacturer produces garments, or fabrics which are assembled into garments, in one manufacturing establishment, whilst the practice in other textile trades is to stop at the finishing of the cloth and leave the making-up of the end product, whatever it be, to either small or multiple tailors and dressmakers. Originally the manufacturer was just a knitter and imitated the products of the hand industry, but he is now a garment manufacturer who must not only copy but also create fashion to suit the development potential of his establishment.

The size of the manufacturing units is by no means equal as the largest units employ approximately 400 people, whilst the smallest employ only 10 or 20 people. During the 1939-45 period of hostilities, a small number of factories were partially destroyed or damaged by enemy action. In most cases, however, such damage has been repaired or new premises acquired, thus enabling production to be carried on. The large number of rather small units may partly explain why relatively few younger members of this branch of the industry attend any form of technological instruction, either on a day or evening basis, their number, expressed against the total employed in the area, being of the order of 1 per cent. The reduced size of the junior labour force and the increased demands made upon it by newer and possibly more vigorous light industries sited in areas around the city's perimeter may have some considerable effect. Thus, in the middle of this century, a number of knitwear mills are moving out to new premises on the more attractive industrial estates where improved canteen and other communal assets are available. The industry is at present housed in a variety of buildings of differing size and age, some being designed expressly for knitwear manufacture and having well lighted and well constructed machine flats, whilst others are in converted house, shop or manufacturing premises.

A feature of special interest in this branch of industry is that prior to 1943 there was no Trade Union in the West of Scotland catering solely for the hosiery worker, who was employed in a craft capacity. Early in that year, the Federation of Hosiery Trade Unions (a Federation operating in England and forming the workers' side of the Joint Industrial Council of the Hosiery Trade) sent organisers to form and operate a Union in Scotland. Success was immediate and within two months over 2,000 members were enrolled, these being distributed in some sixty hosiery factories in Lanarkshire, Ayrshire, West Lothian, Clackmannanshire and in the cities of Aberdeen, Edinburgh and Glasgow. Following the election of an Executive Committee drawn from Ayrshire, Alloa, Edinburgh and Glasgow, the Scottish Hosiery Union was founded. The Union was an autonomous body and in time became affiliated to the Scottish Trade Union Congress. Affiliation to the Federation of Hosiery Trade Unions was automatic and a representative of the Scottish workers sat on the Joint Industrial Council of the Hosiery Trade in England. The Scottish Union administered its own affairs with funds located at the British Linen Bank in Glasgow, the Constitution adopted being on similar lines to that adopted by other Unions affiliated to the Federation. In 1945 the National Union of Hosiery Workers was founded and the Scottish Hosiery Union then became the Scottish District of the National Union, with a full-time District Secretary chosen from a factory in Glasgow. The District is represented on the Joint Negotiating Committee of the Hosiery Trade in Scotland and has, at the time of compilation of this account, an active membership of about three thousand operatives.

Whilst the industry as a whole could expand its overall production and enter the export markets of the world to a much greater extent than at present, there would appear little hope of such an expansion taking place because the industry as an entity is not encouraging the introduction of suitably qualified senior personnel who can not only produce to requirements of present customers, but also experiment and create to suit other markets and other styles. There are available within the area educational facilities of a technological character which would fit suitable young persons for such positions, but advantage of these facilities is being taken more by students from other areas and also from abroad. The amount of finished material exported would appear to be in the region of 2 per cent of the entire production, but such a figure is difficult to verify as the exporting of such garments may not be known to the manufacturer but only to the shipper or agent acting on his behalf.

The Manufacture of Outerwear and Underwear (from woven cloth)

This is an industry which during the present century has grown from one consisting of small units supplying only the immediate locality to one whose products are advertised and known throughout the English-speaking world. Before the First World War the bulk of Glasgow's population relied for its clothing upon the products of individual tailors or upon outerwear and underwear brought in from other areas, the larger organised units of the clothing industry in Glasgow at that period employing possibly only 400 people. To-day the industry employs approximately 5,000 workers whose output, far in excess of local needs, supplies not only a large area of Scotland but also other parts of Great Britain and some overseas markets with a mixture of general and specific types of clothing in the medium to high-quality range. Thus a new industry able to utilise the local pool of female labour has become firmly established in the Glasgow area within comparatively recent years.

The growth of the labour force in the clothing industry since 1900 is shown in Table XLIV.

TABLE XLIV

Employees in the Glasgow Clothing Industry (Woven Underwear and Outerwear) 1900-1950.

Ladies' Outerwear and Underwear

Year	*Males*	*Females*	*Total*	
1900	28	190	218	(estimated)
1914	60	370	430	
1937	410	2,110	2,520	
1950	592	3,211	3,803	

Men's Outerwear and Underwear

Year	*Males*	*Females*	*Total*
1900	32	110	142
1914	91	754	845
1937	259	1,441	1,700
1950	262	1,493	1,755

A large increase in the labour force took place in the years between the wars. The growth of the industry in Glasgow in the early years of this century, and in the later years of last century, was attributable mainly to the local residence of principals and availability of capital. These were also the primary reasons for the increase in the industry between the two wars; but after the Second World War, the increase in the utilisation of labour and the construction of new factories was due more to the direction of industry to scheduled development areas where there was a possibility of a large pool of female labour, even though untrained. For a number of the firms, the choice of Glasgow as a manufacturing centre was influenced by the ease of access to the necessary raw materials (Scottish made tweeds and woollen goods). In the case of firms engaged in the conversion of medium quality cloths produced in other areas, however, the higher cost of transporting the raw material to, and the finished product away from, the mill does tend to offset the advantage of an abundant labour force, this position being possibly aggravated by the attractions of other light industries upon that labour force. As the supply of trained craft workers was somewhat limited it became necessary to resort to some form of basic training which, in one or two establishments, took the form of a training school, but in the majority of cases consisted of watching and then copying the manual dexterity of a trained worker. Such a method, whilst having an ease of application, does unfortunately allow the learner to adopt not only the good but also bad attributes of the senior operative.

The industry is located primarily in the central and central-southern sectors of the city, being accommodated in older property converted from houses and offices into larger and more suitable units. Where the new industrial estates have been located, one may find firms occupying pleasant single-floor buildings adjacent to housing estates from which suitable labour may be drawn. In view of the new town-planning projects which Glasgow Corporation now propose to apply, it would appear that a number of manufacturers whose premises are located in the city area may have to remove these premises to the industrial estates or other similar scheduled areas. Such proposals will undoubtedly have a long-term effect upon the industry and will probably result in a reduction of the number of employees and establishments in the city area as this redistribution takes place.

The type of garment manufactured varies as does the type of establishment. A number of the smaller firms specialise in small quantities of traditional garments, such as kilts and tartan skirts, in which case the cloth is cut out for each garment or piece of garment separately. In sharp contrast to the small unit catering perhaps for individual orders, there are the large manufacturing firms, whose products are often cut in layers of ten, twenty or even fifty shapes at one time. The cloth is handled in long lengths placed one upon another, the shape of each piece being then marked out on the uppermost layer and the layers of cloth cut into the appropriate shapes by electrically driven

The Glasgow Herald

Plate 9. CLYDESIDE

rotary cutters. This latter method of manufacture is applicable to coats, dresses and blouses in the average and cheaper price ranges, the price variation being decided by the quality of cloth, the general styling, the method of cutting and assembly and general finish applied to the garment. Other establishments produce shirts and sleeping garments for the male members of the community and protective clothing for industrial workers. The production of overalls from normal types of woven cloths has developed from the art of the hand seamstress and simple machining to the continuous process using a travelling conveyor on which the previously cut pieces of cloth are taken down a long line of operatives, each of whom carries out a repetitive operation designed to complete the garment in the shortest possible time.

One particular branch of the industry which has flourished over the last hundred years is that of manufacturing protective clothing from oilskin and similar material. The figures relating to turnover for the last fifty years show that its progress has been remarkable.

Turnover (in £s) in the Manufacture of Protective Clothing (Glasgow), 1905-1955 Turnover 1900 = 100

Year	*Turnover*	*Year*	*Turnover*
1905	170	1935	1,100
1910	250	1955	3,000

The labour force in Glasgow would appear to be distributed as follows:

Year	Males	Females	Total
1955	201	589	790

When compared to the more usual type of garment production it will be noted that the percentage of male labour is much higher, this being probably due to the type of material used and the form of clothing manufactured.

It is interesting to note that this industry was established a century or more ago and that one of the most important firms in existence at the time of the compilation of this Account was known for its oilskins at the time of the Battle of Waterloo. At that time and for many years after, the chief components used in the manufacture of an oilskin garment were cotton cloth (then woven locally) and linseed oil, also probably obtained from local sources. The introduction of synthetic yarns such as nylon has led to the introduction of other cloths, these proofed with poly-vinyl-chloride and derivatives of that product used as drying agents to assist in the proofing of cloths and garments. More recently the industry has extended its scope beyond the requirements of protective clothing, to include insulating cloths for cables carrying all types of electrical current used for relaying the spoken word. In this respect woven nylon tapes coated with poly-vinyl-chloride and similar composition are used in addition to the more normal type of varnished cloths and tapes by the electrical industry.

As a result of the decline of the cotton industry in the vicinity of Glasgow last century, the supply of raw materials from local sources has practically ceased, and the industry has thus to rely on Lancashire to supply the particular types of cloth required. This is a handicap and it may mean that any extension of the industry will be directed to the Manchester area rather than to Glasgow, possibly leading ultimately to a transfer to that area.

Other units engaged in the manufacture of apparel are those which produce such items as caps, ties and scarves. Of these there are a number of small units and also one or two larger mills, the latter employing over 70 per cent of the total personnel occupied in this branch of the industry. Whilst these units were originally established by virtue of residence of principals, the market has changed in location and the major portion of production is now channelled to the English market with a small proportion going for export.

Bleaching, Dyeing and Finishing

The rise and subsequent decline of the cotton industry in Scotland, and particularly in the West of Scotland, directly affected the industries formed to process the cloth after weaving and also those concerned with the preparation of yarns prior to weaving and other fabrication processes. The Parliamentary Factory Commissioners reported in 1834 " that in Scotland there are 134 cotton mills; that, with the exception of some large establishments at Aberdeen, and one at Stanley, near Perth, the cotton manufacture is almost entirely confined to Glasgow and the country immediately adjoining to a distance of about 25 miles radius; and all these mills, even including the great work at Stanley, are connected with Glasgow houses, or in the Glasgow trade." Nearly 100 of these actually belonged to Glasgow. In a parliamentary return for 1850 it was stated that at that time there were 149 cotton factories in Lanarkshire, Renfrewshire and Ayrshire employing more than 31,000 people. Such a manufacturing force, having the colossal output commensurate with that force, must have required a large finishing capacity in the immediate locality to cater adequately for its production. It is known that a number of such establishments existed: at the end of the eighteenth century no fewer than thirty print fields were in existence in the Glasgow district, these originating from the first bleach field and printworks for linen fabrics established in the middle of that century at Pollokshaws. Printing was originally carried out by wooden blocks and, as the industry progressed, by copper plates and then by copper cylinders. In addition to Pollokshaws, other areas of the city also had their mills in the late eighteenth and early nineteenth century: in Partick there was a bleachmill for cotton, employing 180 in the print field and 82 in the bleachworks; in Govan, a dye house employing 81 men and 37 women; whilst in the adjacent areas of Hutchesontown and Tradeston the cotton mills, employing about 4,000 people, operated their own bleaching and finishing equipment. It is obvious that a large number of the inhabitants of the Glasgow area must have relied upon employment in the finishing processes, even though there are no accurate data available from which such numbers may be assessed.

The demands of such a large finishing industry upon space for the natural bleaching of fabric led Charles Tennant of Glasgow, the greatest industrial chemist of his time, to experiment with lime and subsequently to produce bleaching liquid and then bleaching powder. His invention assisted in the founding of the St. Rollox Chemical Works, the largest of its type in Europe at that time, which produced the liquid and powder and, much later, sulphuric and other acids.

Glasgow's textile finishing industry was seriously affected in the 1860's by the American Civil War, this conflict causing a shortage of cotton and a consequent reduction in the production of yarn and cloth. Exports of finished goods to the American continent were also partially restricted. The fall in the production of cotton cloth reduced the need for the establishments for bleaching, dyeing and finishing which the previous prosperity had encouraged, and the failure of the Western Bank in 1857 also assisted in the decline of the industry, the subsequent recession being one from which the industry never recovered.

No description of the industry would be complete without reference to the rise and decline of Turkey red dyeing. The *New Statistical Account of Scotland* (Lanarkshire volume) records how M. Papillon, a Frenchman, together with George Macintosh, established a dye-works at Dalmarnock to carry out the new and highly secret process of Turkey red dyeing, a development which greatly increased the trade of calico printing. Its continental origin is commemorated in the name French Street, in Bridgeton, the original Dalmarnock Turkey Red Works being situated in the area between French Street and the Clyde, at that time mostly grass fields. The Dalmarnock Works were sold to Henry Monteith, a muslin manufacturer, who applied his mind to the process, introducing the discharge printing of cloth by means of the Koechlin or Thomson process, thus making his product one in great demand. He became the Rt. Hon. Henry Monteith of Carstairs, was sometime Lord Provost of Glasgow, and died in 1848 at the age of 84, renowned and famous, with a fortune built on Turkey red. The Dalmarnock Works continued under the guidance of Robert Monteith, son of Henry, until they were demolished after the retirement of Robert in the year 1873. There was increasing competition in the industry, created amongst others by the Turkey red dyers in the Vale of Leven, and this competition ultimately proved too much for the remainder of the Monteith business, which in 1904 was liquidated after a period of decay. The Turkey red process as carried out at Monteith's establishment in the latter half of the nineteenth century must have been a modification of the original process as introduced by Papillon, based upon emulsified olive oil, the coloured cloth still being dried in the open air. *The Philosophical Magazine* described the process, as carried out in the city of Glasgow, in the following terms:

"A 16 step process with emulsified gallipoli (olive) oil and soft sheep dung, plus soda ash, recommended as a 14 day steep, the longer the cloth is allowed to lie in the oil, the better."

There were at this time a number of other firms engaged in the process of Turkey red dyeing, some employing modified and shortened methods: a smaller Glasgow firm, founded in 1851, dyed hanks of cotton yarn. The Turkey red dyers, whose numbers were to some extent limited by a curtain of secrecy around new developments and techniques, enjoyed a profitable period of trading up to the First World War, 1914-18, but after that era, the introduction of Naphthol reds affected the industry, and by their general fastness had by the end of the 1930's almost eliminated the use of Turkey red in general dyeing procedure.

The general decline in the industry caused many old-established firms to close down and, in certain cases, to turn to other processes or to become a unit of an association of such firms. The purpose of such units was to develop the production of newer processes for application to the regenerated or synthetic fibres and filaments, or to process the natural fibres to induce properties not normally found in such fibres. Thus one firm of calico-printers, established in 1778, was closed down in the mid-1920's, after functioning for a while as a unit of an association; and of all the mills engaged in finishing at the height of the cotton industry in Glasgow, there are apparently not more than five or six in existence to-day.

Of the larger units still in existence, one was founded in 1795 when Glasgow was one of the chief centres of the textile trade, the choice of the present site being made on account of the proximity of large numbers of springs supplying the necessary water. This firm originally specialised in the bleaching and finishing of lawns and book muslins and was the first bleach works to bleach and finish lace curtain nets produced in the Irvine Valley. Whilst the original styles still exist, very little of the lawn or book muslin trade is now carried out in the West of Scotland, there being only one mill manufacturing such cloths in the Glasgow area. This reduction of local manufacturing capacity has resulted in this and other finishing firms developing what is known as the Manchester style of goods—voiles, marquisettes, handkerchiefs and interlinings. Others have specialised on certain finishes for poplins, dress cloths, etc. Another of the established firms has specialised on crease resistance finishes for spun rayon cloths, having gained experience in the handling of such materials by creating a successful finish on crepes when this came into prominence over forty years ago. This firm, standing probably on the site of the bleach fields of 200 years ago, by the side of the River Cart, has an up-to-date plant for bleaching, dyeing and finishing rayon fabrics, being able in addition to impregnate such fabrics with the necessary resins to create the appropriate appearance and such qualities as crease resistance. Such firms are equipped for the processing of immense quantities of cloth in roll form, and as such, draw their material not only from the few remaining Scottish mills, but also from mills in Lancashire and other areas of England. A large portion of the finished processed material (about 50 per cent) is ultimately destined for the export market. It will be noted therefore, that although the numbers employed in the industry have diminished considerably, the output is certainly greater and, spread over a diversity of cloths and markets, is felt to be more stable.

Miscellaneous Textile Industries

Under this general heading are included numerous small industries employing textile material of one type or another; but although small in size they are almost as important in the general well being and prosperity of the district as the larger, more conventional textile establishments. Some of these smaller establishments originated and developed with the growth of the shipping and shipbuilding industries along the banks of the Clyde but others are newer in both origin and product.

Among these newer industries might be mentioned the manufacture of curled hair as a filling material for the bedding and upholstery trades. It is known that the industry was located in Paisley in 1860 and that expansion of at least one firm brought this industry to Glasgow by 1880, as at that time a factory, still occupied to-day by the same firm, had been built, provided with the necessary equipment, and staffed. The manufacturing processes have not altered greatly in principle since the foundation of the industry. Nowadays, however, as in many other trades, a greater proportion of the output is of the cheaper qualities, to meet the demand for a cheaper article for the final consumer.

Curled hair is made from a mixture of horse, cattle and hog hair, the proportions used being related to the ultimate selling price. Horse tail hair is the best and most expensive, followed by cow tail hair, horse mane hair and hoghair in that order. Prior to any processing, the hair is washed to conform to standards formulated by the British Standards Institute. After the appropriate mixture of types and cost of hair has been decided, the material is put through a battery of milling and mixing machines and then spun into a rope whereby a curl is placed into each individual hair, the curl being set permanently by either boiling or steaming the ropes. This process not only fixes the curl but has also the effect of thoroughly sterilising the hair. The ropes are then dried and stored for a period of months, this allowing the hair to mature properly and also aiding the final setting of the curl.

When the hair is required to fulfil an order, whether teased or needled on hessian, ropes of the requisite quality are taken from the store, untwisted and fed into a teasing or carding machine, this being repeated with a second battery of machines. Each hair is now separated from the others and acts as a tiny spring which gives curled hair the resilience which is its purpose. With the advent of spring interior mattresses, there came a demand for hair in a form that could be easily handled, and in consequence hair is now needled on to a hessian backing which can be cut to the size necessary to cover the spring unit. This is done by laying the hair at a predetermined weight per square foot on a hessian sheet which is fed through a type of felting machine. This fixes the hair firmly to the hessian, enabling pads of any required size to be obtained.

In recent years, various other fibres have been added to the list of those originally used, the main one being coir or coconut fibre. This arrives from Ceylon in press-packed bales which are broken up to allow the fibre to be thoroughly opened and teased, any husk or short fibre having little or no stuffing value being removed by a powerful dust extraction unit. A great proportion of the fibre used is, as with hair, needled on to a hessian backing.

There would also appear to be a certain amount of wool flock used in a similar manner for a similar purpose, the flock being apparently obtained from the north of England, but the amount of such flock is small as compared with the volume of curled hair and fibre, the quantity used (not easily ascertained) being estimated to reach almost 2,000 tons per annum.

One of the older industries still in existence, but operating on a much reduced scale, is that producing all kinds of canvas goods for marine use. These include such items as hatch tarpaulins, awnings, lifeboat sails and covers. Several of these industrial concerns that were in existence in the 1850's have closed or have combined with other firms and ultimately moved into another industry. The rise of the cotton industry, and the dredging of the Clyde during last century, resulted in a large increase in the number of ships using the river. For the small trading ships the industry supplied sails and hatch covers, and for the larger vessels, which the dredging permitted to penetrate further up the river, it supplied the much larger sail requirements. The introduction of steam saw a demand for sun awnings, especially on passenger vessels. With the growth of sunbathing, there is less demand for such awnings from passenger ships but with the change from coal to oil, a demand for similar awnings has arisen from oil-tankers, which spend much of their time in the Red Sea and the Persian Gulf. For such vessels, ventilation tubes for clearing oil gases from their oil tanks are also now being supplied. It would appear, however, that the industry is faced with severe competition from English ports as a great number of shipowners have moved from Glasgow to the south or have closed down, with the result that fewer ships are coming into the river.

There would appear to be a small trade in the manufacture of jute sacks and in the reclamation of second-hand jute sacks. This industry seems to have been started about 1870 and, by virtue of the docks and especially the expansion of such industries as flour milling and cattle food manufacturing, a continuous increase in the demand for new and second-hand jute sacks has been created. Returns made by the leading firms engaged in the manufacture of such articles indicate that the increase in trade may be expected to continue for some time.

A small footwear manufacturing trade exists in Glasgow and has apparently done so for at least one hundred and seventy years, but there appears to be no continuity between the early firms and those in existence to-day. These firms are small units in comparison with those producing footwear in other areas of the United Kingdom. As such they find that the competition offered by the larger units is somewhat difficult to overcome and they have thus, especially since the cessation of hostilities in 1945, received only a small share of the general prosperity enjoyed by other local industries. These small local firms are handicapped by the heavy freight charges incurred in transporting their products to other Scottish and to English markets, and it therefore seems unlikely that any great expansion can be hoped for unless newer products for a different end use are created.

Finally, mention must be made of umbrellas, which first made their appearance in the streets of Glasgow in 1782. Four firms in the city area manufacture these articles, some having been set up around 1890 and established in Glasgow primarily because of the local residence of the principals and because of labour availability. Extension has been made into the general rainwear industry, more particularly for the wholesale trade. The industry however employs only a small number of people, the majority of these being females who are employed on covering and assembly.

Chapter 9

OTHER MANUFACTURING INDUSTRIES

J. B. S. GILFILLAN

FOOD

"FOOD fills the wame, an' keeps us livin'," as Burns forthrightly put it, and the importance of the inner man has never been underrated in the poet's "Land o' Cakes." Nor has Glasgow failed to share, and indeed enhance, Scotland's traditional reputation for wholesome nourishment. That corpulent critic, Dr. Samuel Johnson, may have found little food for thought in the conversation of the city's intelligentsia in 1773, but if disappointed in an intellectual feast[1] he "seemed to be in high glee" over the creature comforts of the Saracen's Head Inn. It was also at a Glasgow inn, in 1832, that another famous English tourist, William Cobbett, waxed fat and enthusiastic over "some *tender* beef-steaks"[2] and "exceedingly fine" mutton. Since those days the city has maintained its reputation for good food and although the production of foodstuffs has developed largely into a factory industry the traditions—and even the recipes—of the old Scots kitchens have not been forgotten.

To-day more than 27,000 people are employed in the food industry in Glasgow, distributed over the branches shown in Table XLV.

Grain Milling

Grain milling, employing about a thousand workers (predominantly men), is not now an industry of great importance in Glasgow. There are eight mills in the city, but four of these are small concerns with no more than 150 employees between them. The largest mills are those of the Riverside Milling Company in Shearer Street, Spillers's flour mills in Thurso Street, and the Regent flour mills of the Scottish Co-operative Wholesale Society in Bunhouse Road.[3]

Over a long period the number of flour mills in the city has been

1 "We had not much conversation," complains Boswell, "at Glasgow, where the professors, like their brethren at Aberdeen, did not venture to expose themselves much to the battery of cannon which they knew might play upon them." *Journal of a Tour to the Hebrides with Samuel Johnson, LL.D.*, 29 October, 1773.

2 ". . . a thing which I have not met with before in more than one out of ten beef-steak jobs in my life." Cobbett, *Tour in Scotland* (1832), pp. 143-4.

3 The name is a reminder that here Glasgow's ancient Incorporation of Bakers formerly had their premises. The bakers received a grant of their mill at Partick from the Regent Moray, for their services at the Battle of Langside in 1568.

TABLE XLV

ESTIMATED NUMBER OF INSURED EMPLOYEES IN THE FOOD INDUSTRY IN GLASGOW AT MID-1955

S.I.C. Group	*Males*	*Females*	*Total*
Grain Milling	941	180	1,121
Bread and Flour Confectionery	6,442	4,870	11,312
Biscuits	1,599	4,307	5,906
Meat and Meat Products	1,066	861	1,927
Milk Products	879	403	1,282
Sugar and Glucose	81	146	227
Cocoa, Chocolate and Sugar Confectionery	641	1,869	2,510
Preserving of Fruit and Vegetables	392	662	1,054
Miscellaneous Food Industries	897	776	1,673
	12,938	14,074	27,012

SOURCE: Ministry of Labour and National Service.

decreasing, but as there has also been a gradual fall in the quantity of flour imported into Glasgow the surviving mills find their position more favourable than formerly. Such is the experience, for example, of the old-established firm of J. & R. Snodgrass, the fourth of the large concerns, which has been engaged in the manufacture of wheat flour and wheat-meal for more than a century and a half. From 1800 or earlier until about 1858 the business was carried on in a water-driven mill at Cardonald, then in a steam-powered mill at Port Dundas until about 1865, when the firm moved to its present premises at Anderston Quay. The mill there was originally steam-powered but it is now driven by electricity. Its output has risen from 22 sacks an hour in 1913 to 30 an hour in 1937 and 35 an hour in 1954, production being entirely for the home market. In 1914 the partnership of J. & R. Snodgrass became a private limited company, which is still controlled by descendants of the original founders.

The firm of Montgomerie & Company, well known for its "Bermaline" flour, is of Glasgow origin but although it still has a factory in the city its main product is no longer manufactured there. In the 1880's John Montgomerie, a family baker and confectioner in Partick, established a wide reputation by the manufacture of a special Malt Digestive Bread, biscuits and rusks. He was a pioneer in hygienic food production and in the application of scientific principles and techniques in the baking industry. The business developed rapidly, becoming a private limited company in 1892 and a public limited company in 1897. In the latter year a flour mill and land were purchased at Haddington, East Lothian, and maltings were erected there which came into operation at the turn of the century. Malt extract is still manufactured at the Bermaline Factory in Ibrox, Glasgow, but since 1954-5 the company's main product, Bermaline flour, has been wholly manufactured at Haddington.

Bread, Cakes and Biscuits

The bakery industry has developed beyond all recognition since the early nineteenth century, when the statistically-minded Dr. Cleland calculated that "in 1822 there were 64,853 sacks of flour baked in the city and suburbs, equal to 5,317,996 quartern loaves." While home baking is happily not yet a forgotten art among Glasgow housewives, the baking of bread in the home is now almost unknown, and even scones, oatcakes and tea-cakes are being increasingly purchased in bakers' shops. The scarcities and rationing during the recent war denuded the counters and prompted a revival of domestic ingenuity in cookery, but now that the shops have again a rich variety of goods on display—including many fancy lines hitherto reserved for export—the temptation to buy the "ready-made" article is being yielded to more and more by housewives of every class.

Over 17,000 of the 27,000 insured employees in the food industry in Glasgow in 1955 were engaged in the production of bread and flour confectionery, and biscuits. Many of the biscuit manufacturers began as bakers, and in recent times some well-known bakery firms have extended their interests by entering the biscuit industry. Beatties Bakeries is the outstanding example of the growth of the bakery trade in Glasgow since the nineteenth century, and of the process of amalgamation of small units into large combines that has been taking place in this industry during the past 20 or 30 years. Since 1876, when the firm was founded by William Beattie, the business has expanded to cover areas far beyond the city, the central position of Glasgow making distribution of its products throughout Scotland more easy. Its bakeries are also well placed for securing a ready supply of flour from the mills and ports. The business developed rapidly between the wars, the numbers employed in Glasgow rising from 200 in 1913 to 2,200 in 1937; by 1954 there were 2,653 employees. Until 1913 the production consisted almost entirely of bread, but thereafter flour confectionery and cakes were added. The firm became a private limited company in 1917, and in 1928 Beatties Biscuits Ltd. was founded. Lang & Stevenson (itself an earlier combination) acquired in 1936, and W. D. Scott, acquired in 1953, are also now subsidiaries of the holding company Beatties Bakeries Ltd. About 97 per cent of production is for the home market, where the company has acquired numerous retail outlets.

Following their entry into the manufacture of biscuits and such products as "slab" cake, some bakery firms have found Glasgow a less desirable location for their business than formerly. This is because the market for biscuits is limited in Scotland,[1] and slab cake is more popular in England than in this country. Such is the experience of

[1] Nevertheless the annual consumption of biscuits in Scotland is considerably larger, in relation to the population, than in England or Wales.

Bilsland Brothers, a Glasgow firm founded in 1872, but since 1935 a subsidiary of a large parent group in England. Distribution of both slab cake and biscuits being almost entirely confined to its own group of retailing companies, the market for these products is naturally tied to the large retail groups south of the Border. Like many others this firm was originally concerned only with bread manufacture, its nineteenth-century founders considering Glasgow, as a developing industrial city, an appropriate centre for the establishment of such a business. It was not until 1924 that Bilsland Brothers added flour confectionery and cake to their production. In 1937 they began the manufacture of biscuits. The number of employees rose from 62 in 1882, ten years after the firm's establishment, to 210 just before the First World War, and to 678 in 1937. By 1954 the employees numbered 1,252; and the firm's turnover had risen from the £120,381 of 1913 to about half a million in 1937 and over two million in 1954.

Gray, Dunn & Co., founded in Glasgow in 1853, have been manufacturing biscuits for over a hundred years. Originally this firm made bread and cakes also, but it now concentrates on chocolate and sweet biscuits, in cellulose and laminated wrappings and ornamental tins—about 12 per cent of its production being directly exported. The Scot abroad and Americans, Canadians and others of Scots descent like tartan wrapping and colourful boxes depicting Highland scenes, and as many of these goods are bought in this country too for dispatch as gifts to friends and relatives overseas, the amount indirectly exported may be considerable. Macfarlane Lang & Co. is another well-known firm of biscuit manufacturers which has been established in Glasgow for more than a century, and was originally in the bakery business. It is associated with McVities Guest of Edinburgh and has a large factory in London.

The continued existence of smaller independent concerns in the biscuit trade seemed to be threatened some years ago when three of the largest and most famous Scottish manufacturers amalgamated into one big group. Moreover the modernisation of factories, to take advantage of recent large-scale developments in the mechanical handling of raw materials, demands substantial capital expenditure which the independent firm is less able to bear. Despite these adverse factors a number of independent biscuit manufacturers have survived and prospered, among the most notable being William Macdonald & Sons of Hillington. This firm, which has just recently been converted into a public company, is now engaged in an extensive scheme of factory modernisation. It has already installed plant for handling fats in bulk, and is in the process of installing automatic equipment for the bulk handling of flour, sugar and other basic raw materials. Chocolate biscuits are Macdonald's specialty, and the company's present prosperity is due in no small measure to the popularity of one particular biscuit called the "Penguin," a variety now almost as well known south of the Border as in its native Glasgow.

In the biscuit factories female workers outnumber males by more than two to one, but in the manufacture of bread and flour confectionery male labour predominates. Altogether nearly 8,000 workers are employed by the five large firms in the bakery and biscuit industry so far mentioned, and if the numbers employed in the United Co-operative Baking Society's extensive factory in McNeil Street are added the total will be well over 9,000. Among the smaller concerns are some long-established businesses whose names have become household words in Glasgow, but in many cases while the names survive the firms themselves have lost their separate identity and been absorbed in large bakery combines. The bakery and purveying business of Walter Hubbard, for example, was founded in Partick as early as 1848—about half a century before Kate Cranston made the "tea-room" a popular Glasgow institution. Hubbard's premises have served as a favourite rendezvous for inhabitants of the city's West End for several generations, and find a mention in J. J. Bell's *I Remember* among reminiscences of Hillhead in Victorian times. In 1928 the firm became a subsidiary of The City Bakeries, and of the Allied Bakeries group in London ten years later. Its name has been preserved, but the business is no longer under family control. Hubbard's great rivals, Colquhouns, were also absorbed by City Bakeries in the interwar years. Welma Bakeries, which started life in 1908 as Robert Nish Ltd., is another Glasgow firm which has been a subsidiary of Allied Bakeries since 1937.

R. A. Peacock & Son, on the other hand, is a very old concern which, although now a public company, is still directly controlled by the family of its original founder. This business moved into Glasgow in 1857 from Paisley, where it had been founded in 1827. Even before that, however, two generations of Peacocks are believed to have been bakers in Paisley. The grandfather of the present managing director was attracted to Glasgow by the tremendous increase in industrial activity in the mid-nineteenth century. The city's expansion in all directions gave the firm an opportunity, particularly after the advent of motor transport, to extend its business until it now covers practically the whole of Glasgow and the surrounding district. By the 1890's Peacock's wedding-cakes were especially celebrated and had even acquired an international fame, many being supplied "to wealthy patrons in the Colonies, India, and America, the prices ranging from one to fifty guineas."[1]

After 1900, when the original partnership became a private limited company, expansion was rapid. In 1901 a central bakery was built on the present site of Peacock's Whitefield Bakeries, and its size was trebled in 1935. In 1913 the firm controlled 18 retail shops; by 1937 there were about 45 branches, including those of an associate company, Alex. Currie & Sons, which was taken over in 1915. By 1955 the number of branches had risen to 74. The business remained a private limited company until 1928, but was forced to become a public company in that year because of the need for additional capital to

1 Stratten, *Glasgow and its Environs* (1891), p. 176.

finance its rapid growth. It now manufactures all types of bakery goods, including biscuits, oatcakes and shortbread. The variety of its products has of course increased greatly over the long period of years since the business was established.

Another well-known Glasgow firm of bakers and caterers is A. F. Reid & Sons, founded in 1858 and still entirely controlled by descendants of the original sole owner. Since 1932 it has been a private limited company. Beginning with a single shop, the business had expanded to four branches by 1904, when a new bakery was built. By 1913 another bakery had been taken over, three further branches opened, and a town restaurant established. In the period between the two world wars the firm's catering activities were greatly extended and many other branches were started. Now it has three bakeries, twenty shops and seven catering establishments, including The Burlington, The Marlborough, and the Queen's Park Rooms.

A major development of the present century which has affected all the smaller bakery concerns has been the advent of what are known in the trade as "the big bread distributors." The loaves (individually wrapped and, if desired, already sliced) produced by large manufacturers like Beatties and Bilslands, are now distributed to retailers over a very wide area of the country, with the result that the making of bread in local bakeries has undergone a substantial decline. In consequence many small firms which were originally mainly bread bakers now concentrate on roll, teabread and cake baking, and catering. This change, of course, has taken place in other cities and towns also—and competition from the large manufacturers is not limited only to bread—but it is the opinion of at least one local firm that competition and price-cutting are keener in the baking trade in Glasgow than elsewhere in Scotland.

Confectionery

There are almost a thousand manufacturers of sweets in Scotland, and the confectionery industry is prominently represented in the Glasgow area. Most of the firms are small, but one or two large manufacturers have developed in the city within the past hundred years. The most notable is Buchanan & Bros., an old family concern founded by John Buchanan of Killearn, who first began business in Glasgow in 1856. Since 1894 the firm has been a private limited company, and with two of the present directors grandsons of the founder the business is still under family control. Its growth up to the outbreak of the First World War in 1914 was immense, and was based on exports, with employees numbering over 1,200. To-day, although the numbers have fallen to about 450 and there has been a decrease in the factory's site acreage, its production capacity per square foot has increased enormously. This is because of the almost complete changeover from hand work to full mechanisation that has taken place in confectionery manufacture within recent years. In addition to sugar confectionery, chocolate and preserves, this firm makes homœopathic pills. About 9 per cent of its entire production is directly exported, ranging from exclusive Scottish sweets in tartan packs for the American market to mass-produced confectionery for the Near and Far East.

Glasgow's export trade in confectionery, however, is on the wane. The manufacturer in this area finds that to-day more and more shipping services are available to him only from the Mersey, Southampton and London, whereas formerly the world was served by the Clyde. He is thus burdened with the extra costs of freight to southern ports. Even in the home market high transport charges are a serious handicap to the Glasgow manufacturer, whose goods must be carried at least 200 miles to reach the next area with a population density equal to that of his own region. His competitors in the Midlands and in the London area, because of the higher density of population, have an overall lower average of distribution costs.

There are two outstanding examples in Glasgow of the conjunction of confectionery manufacture with the ownership of a nation-wide chain of retail shops—R. S. McColl Ltd. and Birrell Ltd. The former business was founded by a well-known Queen's Park international footballer, " Bobby " McColl, in 1901, when he and his brother Tom opened a small shop in Albert Road, Crosshill, Glasgow. The firm now has 201 shops scattered throughout the United Kingdom, many of them strategically situated at the entrance to cinemas. As with so many other great firms in the food industry, the manufacturing side of the business developed from humble beginnings. Mr. Robert McColl started making his own confectionery on a very small scale in his back shop at Albert Road. After having a small factory in Langside Road, the company took over its present premises in North Woodside Road in the early 1920's. The concern remained a private business for 24 years, but a public issue of shares was made in 1925 and in 1933 the British Cocoa and Chocolate Company acquired a controlling interest. Both Mr. R. S. and Mr. T. N. McColl are still on the Board of Directors, although neither now takes an active part in the running of the business.

One effect of increasing mechanisation in the confectionery industry has been to reduce the predominance of women in the factory labour force. This is well illustrated from the records of R. S. McColl's business. When the factory at Woodside Road began production in the 1920's, it was employing approximately 90 per cent female labour. While women are still in the majority, the proportion of female employees to-day has fallen to 70 per cent. The type of confectionery manufactured by the firm has, on the whole, changed very little over the past 55 years. At first the brothers McColl specialised in toffee and tablet making, and these two sweetmeats are still considered to be " specialties." The company, however, now also manufactures chocolate confectionery, boilings, fondants, jellies and assortments of all kinds. Production is entirely for the home market. At the " Milady " chocolate works in Anniesland Messrs Birrell produce a similarly wide variety of sweets for distribution through their own chain of retail shops. This firm is particularly well known for its chocolates. Both these concerns, having shops throughout the country, find Glasgow a very suitable central point of distribution. Indeed the company with which Birrell is associated is now concentrating all its production in Glasgow. One obvious advantage of having their own retail outlets is that they can rapidly adjust their factory production to the vagaries of consumer demand, as reflected in branch sales.

Reeves, the makers of "Ensign" chocolate and ice cream, are among the more notable of the smaller concerns in Glasgow. This company dates from 1904, when it took over the business of the Sweetmeat Automatic Company, which had been formed about 1876 to manufacture chocolates etc. for those automatic machines which have long enchanted children on railway stations and piers. Like Buchanan Bros., this firm thirty or forty years ago employed many more people than it does to-day.

While the varieties of sweets manufactured in Glasgow have undergone little alteration, there have been important changes in recent years in methods of packaging and wrapping. The aim is not only more attractive presentation, but also to ensure more hygienic handling—a long-overdue reform throughout all branches of the food industry. The days when the shopkeeper weighed out all his sweets from large bottles or open display boxes, and then transferred them into paper bags or "pokes" (which he blew open first!) are fast becoming a memory. More and more confectionery nowadays, even of the cheaper variety, comes from the factory already weighed and wrapped in cellophane bags or other packages of convenient size, ready to be handed over direct to the customer.

Proprietary Foodstuffs

There have been similar developments in "pre-packing" in many other sections of the food industry, and the range of proprietary foodstuffs marketed in cartons and tins (to say nothing of such labour-saving items as ready-made cake and soup mixes and pre-cooked oats) is now enormous. One or two Glasgow manufacturers have been prominent as pioneers in this field. James Marshall, the Semolina and Farola firm, began business in 1878 at the Ibrox Flour Mills, Glasgow. Its products were protected by trade marks in 1885, and the firm claims to be a pioneer in pre-packing refined preparations of wheat at and from that date. In 1935 it was the first in Scotland to start the manufacture of macaroni products on a commercial basis, and in recent years the pre-packing of ground rice, self-raising and plain flour, has been added to the company's activities. Since the end of the nineteenth century turnover has increased almost five-fold, excluding sales in Eire where a subsidiary company has operated since 1932. The firm has been a private limited company since 1900, and a son and two grandsons of its founder are still in control.

Creamola Food Products have been "tickling the world's palate" since 1904, when this well-known firm originated in Glasgow under the name of D. K. Porter & Co. Creamola custard was first manufactured in that year, and in 1920 the firm became a private limited company under its present name. Its founder, W. G. Hetherington, who died in 1948, was a native of Lanarkshire, and the business is still under the control of his family. Since starting in a modest building in Howard Street the company has expanded so rapidly that it has had to move its factory five times, each move being to premises at least twice the size of the previous ones. The present factory in Kinning Park, with an area of 124,000 square feet and a capacity of 1,600,000 cubic feet, is one of the largest food manufacturing establishments in Scotland. The firm has gradually added many new lines to its original custard product, including Rice Creamola and Sago Creamola, blanc-mange, desserts, milk jellies, lemonade foam crystals, steamed puddings, complete cake mixes, self-raising flour and arrowroot.

In addition to these old-established concerns there are some thriving newcomers, such as the firm of Jean MacGregor which manufactures Scotch broth and lentil broth according to traditional domestic recipes. This business was started in 1939 in the new Hillington Industrial Estate, with a capital of only £3,000. By 1952 the capital had been raised to £20,000 and the factory area has been trebled from 5,000 to 15,000 square feet. In 1948 a London firm, Stoddart & Hansford, opened a factory in Glasgow for the manufacture of cake and pudding mixtures, and the packing of desiccated coconut. Another English concern, Malga Products, makers of bakers' sundries, established a synthetic cream factory in the Cathcart district in 1953. Such firms have been attracted to Glasgow as a suitable centre for distribution of their products in Northern England, Scotland and Ireland.

A local proprietary food concern with a particularly interesting origin is Sister Laura's Infant and Invalid Food Co., of Springfield Works, Bishopbriggs.[1] The company's product was first manufactured on a small scale in Glasgow by Sister Laura M. Smith of the Royal Hospital for Sick Children. She originally devised and produced the food within the Hospital for use only by the babies under her care, but in 1912 a small company was formed to make it available to the general public. The present company was incorporated in 1920 for the purpose of developing the product and marketing it on a national scale. An associate company has been successfully established in Eire since 1938. In common with other infant-food manufacturers, however, the firm found difficulty in maintaining sales at their previous levels after the introduction of the heavily subsidised National Dried Milk by the Government in 1946. New lines, such as infants' soothing powders,

[1] This factory lies beyond the city boundary, but it is within the Ministry of Labour's Glasgow Exchange Area to which the statistical tables in this Chapter relate. The same applies, of course, to all factories in the Hillington Industrial Estate, which lies just outside the city limits.

have recently been developed, and plans are in hand to manufacture other products for babies. A subsidiary company, Wade Pharmaceuticals, formed in 1946, produces a wide variety of ethical medical preparations and galenicals.

The manufacture of coffee essence[1] is an old Glasgow industry that continues to flourish despite the fact that its principal market is in England. Indeed about half the coffee essence made in Great Britain is produced in Scotland, where there are as many as ten independent firms competing in the trade. This concentration may be partly explained by the availability of excellent supplies of soft water, which is desirable for the infusion process in manufacture. R. Paterson & Sons, the makers of "Camp" Coffee and Chicory Essence, began in 1849 by manufacturing vinegar, and later pickles and sauces. Since 1909, when the firm became a private limited company, the making of coffee and chicory essence has been the sole business. The company has been a public one since 1952, but three members of the Paterson family are still directors. Output has more than doubled since 1937, and about 5 per cent of production is for export markets, which have increased considerably in importance since the Second World War.

Drink

Drink industries of all kinds accounted for 7,839, or 1.44 per cent, of the insured employees in the Glasgow area in 1955. Of this number, 2,026 were engaged in brewing and malting, 3,738 in wholesale bottling, and the remaining 2,075 in the manufacture of "soft drinks" and other beverages. Beer and "ginger pop" may seem a strange mixture (even if as "shandy" some find it not unpalatable) but the contrast between these forms of liquid refreshment is perhaps less remarkable than that between the industries they represent: the soft drinks industry is a recent phenomenal growth, whereas brewing is of great antiquity and has its roots buried deep in Glasgow's past.

Brewing and Distilling

Few establishments in the city can boast of 400 years of continuous trading, and of having served the public under 18 successive monarchs, but that is the proud claim of Tennent's Wellpark Brewery. The name of Tennent appears to have been associated with brewing in Glasgow since pre-Reformation times, for while the present firm of J. & R. Tennent was founded in 1745 the family is believed to have operated a brewing concern at Wellpark since 1556. This business is therefore one of the oldest not only in Glasgow but in Britain, and cer-

[1] Although a beverage, coffee is not classified under Drink Industries in the Standard Industrial Classification on which Ministry of Labour statistics are based. The order of treatment in this chapter conforms with that of the S.I.C. in order to avoid discrepancies in the tables.

tainly the oldest brewing concern in Scotland. On its original site in Duke Street, where the presence of a mineral well, availability of labour, and ready access to road, rail and sea communications have favoured its continuous development, the Wellpark Brewery has expanded until it now occupies about ten acres of ground and gives employment to over a thousand workers. In addition the company owns a factory of about 1½ acres on a new site in Janefield Street, acquired in 1951. This Bridgeton establishment is devoted exclusively to wood-working and the manufacture of packing cases for the firm's extensive export trade. In recent years distribution depots for the home trade have been opened by the company at Dundee (1950), at Inverurie (1952), and at Edinburgh and Belfast (1954). Since the Second World War the business has expanded considerably, output in 1954 being more than double that of 1937, when the employees numbered only 700.

The original products of the brewery were draught beer and stout, supplied in wooden casks. Towards the middle of the nineteenth century the output was markedly increased by the introduction of bottled beer and stout. A few years later the firm began the brewing of lager beer and to-day it is one of the largest lager brewers in the United Kingdom, its product enjoying a world-wide reputation rivalling that of its famous Danish and Dutch competitors. Indeed, the company is the leading exporter of bottled beer in Britain. It is interesting to recall that at the end of the nineteenth century the firm had its own pottery and manufactured the stoneware bottles then required for its products in both home and export markets. This type of bottle is now out of date, having given way to the green or amber coloured glass bottles that are now used for all Tennent's bottled brands. A new departure of some significance is that the company has recently been very successful in producing its export lager in the American type of flat-topped cans. These cans, when packed into cartons, permit of a considerable saving in both bulk and freight compared with the bottle pack. They are beginning to achieve considerable popularity in the home market also.

A feature of the trade in recent years has been the greatly increased demand for bottled products as opposed to draught—a change partly attributable to the advent of the new domestic entertainment of television, whose devotees, it is said, have not the time to consume their leisurely pints at "the local" as in former days. The large bottling halls at the Wellpark Brewery have recently been extended and equipped with the most modern bottling plant, to increase the company's capacity and meet this rising demand; they are now considered to be the most up-to-date in Britain. Bottling of beer on a large commercial scale dates back only to about the middle of the nineteenth century, and Tennent's has been in the forefront of this development ever since.

Wellpark Brewery had acquired a world-wide trade even before the close of the eighteenth century when the first *Statistical Account of*

Scotland was compiled. At that period particularly large consignments were shipped each year from the Clyde to both North and South America. During the Victorian era the firm was classed among the chief exporters of Great Britain, and its export trade has continued to expand since those days. Since the end of the Second World War of 1939-45, however, competition in overseas markets has become extremely keen. To-day 36 per cent of the company's production is for direct export and efforts are being made to expand still further its overseas trade, as part of the national drive to increase the volume of Britain's exports.

During the four centuries of its history this old Glasgow brewery has developed into a modern integrated unit of great complexity. It has its own distribution organisation, using fleets of motorised vehicles which have superseded the familiar horse-drawn carts of the past. Beer supplies for the company's distribution depots are carried mainly by large 12-ton lorries, and in the case of the most northerly depot at Inverurie, a nightly trunk run is in operation. These depots effect delivery to their customers by locally based 5-ton lorries and light vans, while the deliveries from Glasgow are carried out by a large fleet of 8-ton and 5-ton lorries augmented by a number of articulated units with trailers—the modern "mechanical horse." The average mileage covered by the company's fleet is conservatively estimated at 100,000 miles per month, or well over a million per annum. Provision for the intake of the raw materials used in the brewing of beer—all natural products—is hardly less spectacular. In the Maltings, an enormous building situated in the heart of the brewery and one of the largest of its kind north of the Tweed, thousands of quarters of barley from the eastern counties of England and the Lothians of Scotland are annually converted into malt.

The control of this great concern has now passed out of the hands of the Tennent family. In 1901 the business was converted into a limited company to take over the private firm of J. & R. Tennent, founded in 1745. It is now a public company, part of the ordinary capital having been offered for sale to the public in 1953.

In the seventeenth century Glasgow was noted for the excellence of its ale, which was then the staple drink of the populace. Whisky was not drunk to any great extent until the 1780's—rum from the West Indies was the spirit most popular in the city—and it was only at the beginning of the nineteenth century that whisky distilling became an industry of importance. The first distillery in the city was established in the Gorbals in 1786 by William Menzies, whose licence was the fourth to be granted in Scotland. Excise duty at that time was little more than a penny a gallon, and the best malt spirits sold at about 3s. a gallon; to-day, whisky retails at 35s. or more a *bottle*.

By the close of the nineteenth century the whisky trade, as regards not only distilleries but agencies for houses situated elsewhere, had become very extensive in Glasgow, and Port Dundas could boast of a distillery which was almost the largest in the world. To-day there are only two distilleries within the city boundaries,[1] but many firms—some with distilleries in the Highlands and elsewhere—have offices in the city and premises for blending and bottling.

The Soft Drinks Industry

Having absorbed the alcoholic content of the preceding paragraphs, the reader may find it a sobering thought that the "soft drink" has displaced whisky as Scotland's national beverage. The enormous increase in the popularity of soft drinks must be numbered amongst the most notable changes in personal habits in Britain during the past thirty years: consumption rose from 45 million gallons in 1924 to 222 million gallons in 1954, and is still rising.[2] The increase seems to have been particularly marked in Scotland, where expenditure on soft drinks during 1954 was probably something over £5m. According to a Scottish aerated water manufacturer,[3] consumption of soft drinks per head of population in Scotland is now higher than in any other country in the world except America. Scots are drinking about five gallons per head per annum, compared with a United Kingdom figure of four gallons and a third (but the Americans consume about eleven gallons!) The current popularity among the youth of Glasgow and elsewhere of the variety popularly known as "coke" (Coca-Cola) is an American influence, which suggests that the Scottish thirst for soft drinks is not yet quenched and may in future years approach nearer the transatlantic level. The rise to date may be attributed in part at least to the fact that tastes acquired in youth are apt to be carried into later life. Older generations of Scots had few "aerated waters" to tempt them in their childhood, and seem never to have become particularly fond of them; but those born since the time of the First World War have been familiar with soft drinks in ever-increasing variety from their schooldays, and probably form the bulk of the present consumers.

Whatever the reason, the demand is there and Glasgow manufacturers have not been slow to meet and foster it. A feature of the soft drinks industry is the local nature of the market served by each producer, and the large number of small units engaged in the trade. Except where bulk transport and bottling at distant distribution centres is adopted, the area of distribution is necessarily limited by the high cost of transport in relation to the selling price of the product. Nevertheless during the last fifty years the firms engaged in the industry have declined in number and increased both in size and in area of distribution. In 1954 there were 15 aerated water manufacturers in Glasgow, whereas in 1900 there were as many as 50; but these were very much

[1] At Port Dundas and Hutchesontown, operated by the Distillers Company and the Scottish Grain Distilling Company respectively.

[2] This includes, however, soda water and tonic water—often the companions of whisky and gin.

[2] Mr. Robert Mitchell of Dunfermline, quoted in *The Stock Exchange Gazette*, 23 December 1955.

smaller units, operating within a very limited area with horse transport. While the number has fallen to 15 the units have greatly increased in size, producing at the rate of 400 to 500 dozen bottles an hour as compared with 40 to 70 dozen, and distributing to a radius of about 25 miles. It was not long after the First World War that the number of firms fell to around their present level: the 50 of 1900 had become 42 by 1910, 18 by 1920, and 14 by 1940. It is estimated that since 1924 the production of soft drinks in Glasgow has increased by at least five and a half if not six times, but details of actual output are not available for publication. The trade is of course a seasonal one, and is subject to considerable fluctuations from year to year according to weather—1953 was a record year in the industry's history, the output for the whole country reaching 227 million gallons, and the unusually fine summer of 1955 is pleasantly reflected in recent trading results. Production in this industry is essentially for home markets.

Of the fifteen firms manufacturing aerated waters in Glasgow in 1954, one could be classed as large, eight medium and six small. The most notable is A. G. Barr & Co., whose original "Iron Brew" has appealed to the virile tastes of more than one generation of Scottish youngsters. This firm, which like most of the others in the trade produces fruit squashes and cordials as well as aerated waters, was founded as early as 1887. Since 1904 it has been a private limited company, and its employees now number about 250 (excluding branch establishments in Irvine and Wishaw). It is a business native to Glasgow, but two other well-known companies are incomers to the city from Dundee. G. & P. Barrie extended their manufacturing activities to Glasgow in 1898, and although their head office is in Dundee where they still have a factory, they now regard Glasgow as the main centre of their manufacture. They were attracted to the city by the availability of transport and labour, and by market considerations—soft drinks are bulky and can be sold most economically in areas of dense population. Since manufacture was begun in Glasgow the company's products have remained basically unchanged, but have benefited through continual technical improvement. A development of recent years has been the growth in the production of citrus fruit drinks since 1939. The other firm of Dundee origin, Robertson Fruit Products, is a fairly new arrival, having come to Glasgow in 1938. This company, well-known for its "Stillade" fruit drinks and aerated waters, has factories in both Dundee and Aberdeen and is not mainly centred in the city. Glasgow was found a desirable location from the point of view of importation of raw materials, the firm thus saving the considerable freight charges entailed in landing goods at English ports. The large potential outlet for its products, availability of labour, and the local residence of a director were other contributory factors in the choice of Glasgow. During the war the firm's original premises at Hillington Estate were taken over under the zoning scheme and the company had to withdraw from Glasgow altogether. Since re-opening in premises in Argyle Street in 1948 the business has grown steadily. The soft drinks and squashes originally manufactured have been greatly increased in variety, and to these have been added many other products such as "Dextora" (a glucose drink), crushed fruits, fruit drinks made from fresh oranges, and also fruit drinks in cartons for sale in cinemas etc. These two Dundee firms together employ over a hundred workers in Glasgow.

Another firm, but native to Glasgow, began manufacture at Hillington Estate in 1937. This was the Citrus Products Co., makers of "Jaffajuce" fruit squash, which originated in a small factory of 4,000 square feet with 6 to 8 employees. It has now quadrupled in size, but the company has passed out of the hands of its original founders, being amalgamated with Apollinaris Ltd. in 1948 and taken over by Bovril Ltd. in 1954. Another well-known English firm, Schweppes Ltd., has factory premises in Glasgow and there are several other smaller companies manufacturing and bottling soft drinks in the city. It is an industry in which even the small family concern of two or three workers still survives.

Tobacco

As we have seen in an earlier chapter, the foundation of Glasgow's commercial prosperity after the Union of 1707 was the tobacco trade with the American colonies. The days when Glasgow handled more than half the tobacco imported into the United Kingdom and her proud Tobacco Lords strutted in scarlet-cloaked splendour on the "croon o' the causey" have long since passed, but the city whose fortunes these merchant adventurers founded still numbers tobacco among her industries. While it is one of the lesser industries, accounting for only about 2,000 of the 543,000 insured employees in the Glasgow area in 1955, it is of particular interest in view of its long survival and the continuing tradition it represents. Glasgow to-day, in fact, is still a substantial supplier of Britain's tobacco.

Both the importation and the manufacture of tobacco have had a lengthy history in Scotland, and they have not been confined exclusively to Glasgow and the West. Indeed the great Glasgow firm of Stephen Mitchell & Son, which has been engaged in the tobacco manufacturing industry in Scotland since the early eighteenth century and is thus one of the longest-established businesses of the kind in Britain, had its origins in Linlithgow. The business was founded there in 1723 by the fourth of a long line of Stephen Mitchells, one of whom was later to give Glasgow the well-known public library that bears his name. More than a century passed, however, before the firm moved to Glasgow in 1825, the change being made because of a ban by the Excise authorities on the importation of tobacco into Blackness, Linlithgow's ancient seaport. For seven years the business was carried on in the Candleriggs, but the enormous increase in the popularity of tobacco in the nineteenth century led to a transfer in 1832 to larger premises in St. Andrew Square, which continued to be the site of the firm's factory until very recently. Before the outbreak of the Second World War in 1939 the construction of a large modern factory at Alexandra Parade had been begun, but the building was requisitioned during the war and was not returned to the firm until 1946. Thereafter Stephen Mitchell & Son transferred production from St. Andrew Square to Alexandra Parade. This process was completed by September 1954, and the old premises in St. Andrew Square where the business had been situated for almost a century and a quarter were sold.

Stephen Mitchell & Son was one of the thirteen leading British tobacco firms that united in 1901 to form The Imperial Tobacco Company (of Great Britain and Ireland) Limited, in order to resist an attack launched on the British market by a powerful association of American tobacco manufacturers. Two other Glasgow firms were among the thirteen—D. & J. Macdonald (founded in 1840), who were well-known as makers of "Kilty" tobacco, and F. & J. Smith (founded in 1859), makers of "Glasgow Smoking Mixture." On joining the Imperial Tobacco Company the constituent firms ceased to be separate legal entities and became branches of the company, but they continued to trade in their own names. The Macdonald and Smith businesses, however, were subsequently incorporated into the Stephen Mitchell & Son branch. In 1904 Mitchells also acquired the home trade business of another old Glasgow firm—J. & F. Bell, makers of the famous "Three Nuns" tobacco.

Although some of the old familiar names in the Glasgow tobacco trade have disappeared new life and an even better-known name have been brought into this branch of the city's industry in recent years. W. D. & H. O. Wills, founded in Bristol in 1786, was another of the leading firms that joined the Imperial Tobacco Company on its formation in 1901. Its products have long enjoyed an extensive market in Scotland and since 1908 it has maintained its own distributing depot in Glasgow. Recently this firm decided to build a large factory in Scotland, selecting a site in Glasgow adjoining Stephen Mitchell & Son's new premises in Alexandra Parade. The choice of Glasgow was determined by its being a development area, and was made with a view to the expansion of the firm's trade in Scotland, improved distribution, and dispersal of manufacture. This new factory, giving employment to nearly a thousand workers, is of the most advanced design and first came into operation in 1953.

Thus the Imperial Tobacco Company, whose Glasgow branches at the beginning of the century comprised the three old firms of Stephen Mitchell & Son, D. & J. Macdonald, and F. & J. Smith, now has its Scottish production concentrated in two large and very modern adjacent factories in the city. The trade of these old firms was mainly in pipe tobaccos, but in the course of the present century there has been a remarkable change in smoking habits. Since 1901, in fact, the pattern of the whole United Kingdom tobacco trade has completely altered. At that time four-fifths of the tobacco consumed in this country was pipe tobacco; to-day over four-fifths is consumed in the form of cigarettes. It is said to have been the officers and men who returned from the Crimean War of 1854-6 who first made cigarette smoking fashionable in this country, but it was probably the Great War of 1914-18 that finally robbed the pipe of its ascendancy among younger men. More recently the great increase in the popularity of smoking among women of all ages has confirmed the supremacy of the cigarette. The Glasgow factory of W. D. & H. O. Wills confines itself entirely to cigarette production, while that of Stephen Mitchell & Son manufactures a wide variety of pipe tobaccos. The trade of the Imperial Tobacco Company and its branches is, it should be noted, virtually confined to the home market.

In addition to the works of the Imperial Tobacco Company there is a large factory in Glasgow owned by the Scottish Co-operative Wholesale Society. When the latter began the manufacture of tobacco in 1891 the trade was chiefly in pipe tobaccos, but they have steadily extended and modified their production to meet changing demand, developing their own brands of cigarettes to compete with those of the older makers. Although outwith the scope of this Account, brief mention must be made of the long-established firm of George Dobie & Son in nearby Paisley. Founded in 1809, it is the largest independent[1] tobacco manufacturing company in Scotland, and together with those already described completes the picture of the Tobacco Lords' descendants in Glasgow and the West to-day.

While there has been a considerable increase in the total volume of tobacco and cigarettes manufactured in the Glasgow area within the last fifty years, there is a general tendency for the numbers employed in the industry to decline. This can be attributed to various causes: increasing mechanisation; the adoption of improved production methods and layout; the replacement or modernisation of old factories; and increased and improved capital equipment. It is also, paradoxically enough, a result of the advance in the popularity of cigarettes. A much higher proportion of the tobacco manufactured in Glasgow is now in the form of cigarettes, and in the production of these a very much greater degree of mechanisation is possible than in the manufacture of pipe tobacco. It is noteworthy too that the latter branch of the industry in Glasgow employs predominantly female labour, while in the more highly mechanised manufacture of cigarettes the labour force is more evenly balanced. Taken as a whole, the tobacco industry in the Glasgow area now employs about 1½ times as many women as men.

[1] Since this was written Dobie & Son's brands have been acquired by Godfrey Phillips, in January 1956. In recent years, following the return to free trading conditions after wartime rationing of quotas, such independent concerns have suffered by competition from the larger firms. Dobie's factory at Paisley has now been taken over by Blackwood Morton, the Kilmarnock carpet manufacturers.

Paper and Printing

Paper and Board

For more than two hundred years paper-making has been an industry of some importance in Glasgow. To-day over four thousand of the city's insured employees are engaged in the making of paper and cardboard, and in the manufacture of cartons and other packages and wrappings from these materials. The development of the industry, in all its branches, has always been closely associated with that of printing; the growth of the modern "packaging" industry in particular owes much to the skill and reputation in commercial printing acquired by local firms in the past. Within recent years this branch has also been stimulated by the demands of the new light industries which have sprung up in and around Glasgow since the Second World War, for packaging material for a wide variety of goods.

Two Glasgow paper mills, those of Edward Collins & Sons at Kelvindale and the Dalsholm Paper Company, Maryhill, have an interesting history extending back to the eighteenth century. Both were established beside the River Kelvin, which seemed an attractive source of water for motive power and processing. But in 1747, only a year after his arrival in Glasgow, Edward Collins[1] found the flow of water too irregular for satisfactory working and transferred his plant several miles westward to Dalmuir, where he successfully carried on paper-making, bleaching, and the manufacture of logwood extract until his death in 1784. He was succeeded by his son Richard, and the mill at Dalmuir continued in operation until 1857. Meanwhile, however, the rapid growth of Glasgow's population, the opening of the Forth and Clyde Canal, the deepening of the Clyde and the development of cheap railway transport had made the original site at Kelvindale much more attractive. Moreover the steam engine had now largely displaced water-power for industrial purposes, so that the deficiencies of the River Kelvin were less important. Thus in 1840 paper-making was re-started at Kelvindale by Edward Collins & Sons in a new mill on the original site, which the firm occupies to this day.

The business remained a private concern until 1914, when it was formed into a limited liability company,[2] and in 1920 it became a subsidiary of The Associated Paper Mills Ltd. Seven generations of

1 He was an Englishman, from either Shropshire or Suffolk. A colourful personality suspected of Jacobitism, he is said to have told his family that before the Battle of Culloden he was conscripted against his will by the Duke of Cumberland near Edinburgh. It is possible that the Glasgow publishers whose name appears on this volume are descendants of Collins the paper-maker, but no clear evidence of the connection has yet been found. See David Keir, *The House of Collins* (1952), pp. 15-16.

2 A disastrous fire had occurred two years earlier, and it is thought that the resultant re-building and re-equipment made it necessary to seek outside capital.

the Collins family were actively concerned in it, the last member directly associated with the mill having died as recently as 1948. Few Glasgow firms can boast of such a lengthy and continuous history. Two hundred years ago, in 1756, Edward Collins was awarded a medal in Edinburgh "for the best printing paper," and the reputation for high-quality papers he then established has been upheld by his successors down the years. To-day only fine papers are manufactured at the Kelvindale works, ranging from fine and supercalendered printings, lithographic, chart, music and cartridge papers, to writing papers of various kinds, bonds, cream laids and woves, and duplicating and blotting papers. It is of interest to note that the last-named were being made by this firm as early as 1792, several years before blotting-paper came into general use.

Although also dating from the eighteenth century, the Dalsholm Paper Mills did not enjoy continuous family ownership for so long. Paper manufacture was begun on the present site about two hundred years ago under the firm name of James Macarthur & Company. This firm is still in business in Glasgow as stationers and paper makers, but it has had no connection with Dalsholm Paper Mills for about a hundred years. The present Dalsholm Paper Company Ltd. became a public company in 1934, having been a private limited company since about 1890. Like Edward Collins & Sons Ltd., it is now associated with a group of paper mills in England. In its early days the Dalsholm Mill produced only small quantities of hand-made writing and ledger papers, manufactured entirely from rags. Between 1880 and 1910 paper machines were installed and production greatly increased, but the main advance in output has taken place since 1947. The present manufacture consists almost entirely of various types of wrapping paper, which is made from waste papers and wood pulp. For high-grade writing and printing paper, such as that produced by Collins at Kelvindale, the principal raw material used is esparto grass from Spain and North Africa; but rags and chemical wood pulp are also employed. Nearly 400 workers, predominantly male, are engaged in paper-making at the Kelvindale Mill, and about 70 at Dalsholm. Much larger than either of these mills, but outside the city boundary, are the works of the Clyde Paper Company at Rutherglen and Milngavie. This company is notable as one of the two in Scotland manufacturing newsprint, and it also has the largest coating plant in the country. The bulk of its esparto paper production consists of base paper for the coating factory.

Of more recent origin are the Grove Park Paper Mills of George Stark & Sons Ltd. in North Woodside Road, founded in 1843. Formed into a private limited company in 1919, and converted to a public company in 1934, the business still maintains a link with its founder, four of the present directors being great-grandsons. Originally its products were marble and fancy coloured papers, when the sheets were coated by hand, but the output of the mills in modern times has become much more diverse to meet the needs of the printing industry, and the process is now done mechanically by brush coating machines.

The production of post-cards was formerly a very important branch of this firm's activities, but the trade has greatly diminished with the recent increases in postal charges. About 140 operatives are employed in the Grove Park Mills, but in this case the numbers of males and females are approximately equal. Chromo, enamelled and gummed papers, pasteboards, cards and coated boards constitute the present output.

Another branch of the paper industry recently represented in Glasgow was the manufacture of wallpaper, which accounted for some 250 workers in 1951 but has now virtually disappeared once again as a city industry. The production of carbon paper for use with pen, pencil or typewriter, combined with the manufacture of inked ribbons for typewriters and other office machines, and of duplicator inks, is the province of Farquharson Bros., a Glasgow business with a particularly interesting history. Its progress, indeed, is synonymous with the progress of the manufacture of carbon paper, inked ribbon and allied items in this country. When Douglas Farquharson founded his enterprise in diminutive premises in St. Vincent Street in 1900, no one in Scotland was making these products and little information was to be had regarding the processes involved. By persevering experiment in face of many baffling difficulties he and his brother, who joined him later, discovered how to make satisfactory carbons, ribbons and inks, thus giving to Scotland a new industry which was to provide employment for many people far beyond its borders. Farquharson Bros. to-day is a world-wide organisation engaged in manufacture and distribution, with a large modern factory at Anniesland, completed in 1947; there are also offices and stockrooms in London, opened in 1946. It is still the only factory in Scotland manufacturing these products. The firm has branches throughout Great Britain and Ireland, and its products are exported to 36 countries and states through agents and by direct representation.

From 10 employees in 1900 the number grew to 60 in 1913, 110 in 1937, and 200 in 1945. To-day some 225 people are employed in Glasgow and the factory span is being doubled. It is amusing to recall that when the business was founded many Glasgow offices clung tenaciously to hand-written letters, fearing that by adopting typewritten correspondence they would lose the personal touch and possibly some clients.[1] By 1913, when such prejudices were disappearing, Farquharson Bros.' sales staff had grown from two to six, a branch had been opened in Edinburgh, and representatives appointed in London and Newcastle. In that year the business was converted into a limited company, thus providing increased capital to finance its rapid extension. At the end of the First World War an Australasian subsidiary was formed, to operate the distribution of the parent company's products in

[1] In the late nineteenth century it was not unknown for lawyers to send back typewritten letters " to be properly written." Some of the products of the early machines—" typed all in shaky capitals and green ink "—were certainly unbusinesslike! See Sir John Mann, " Glimpses of Early Accountancy in Glasgow," in *The Accountants' Magazine,* June 1954.

Australia and New Zealand, and in 1922 the first London Warehouse was opened to meet the rapidly growing demand in the south. By 1936 export markets had enlarged considerably and a Norwegian subsidiary was formed in Oslo, to manufacture carbon paper and ribbons for the Scandinavian market. This factory was commandeered by Germany during the Second World War of 1939-45, but it is now functioning to capacity as before.

There have been some important developments in this industry since the war ended in 1945. In the carbon paper field the Plastic Back and other distinctive reinforced carbons have been introduced. Real silk ribbons, unobtainable during the war period, have been reintroduced on an improved basis, and nylon ribbons in addition to cotton ribbons are now manufactured. Moreover, in common with many other branches of industry, more attractive packaging—a vital factor in export markets—has been designed and adopted. In terms of value, about 64 per cent of Farquharson Bros.' output in Glasgow is for the home market, 26 per cent for direct export, and 10 per cent for indirect export. It is estimated that 52 per cent of the production is for final use by other industries.

Cardboard Boxes

The manufacture of cardboard boxes, cartons, fibre-board packing cases etc. now provides employment for over 2,000 people in Glasgow, and in view of the expansion of light industry in the area it offers considerable promise of continued development. It is only within recent times that the sales potential of attractive packaging has been fully recognised in this country, but Glasgow firms have shown commendable enterprise in meeting the needs of the manufacturers of a wide variety of consumer goods, not only in Scotland but beyond its borders. A considerable proportion of the cartons and boxes produced in Glasgow is supplied to manufacturers in England and Northern Ireland, and local firms are thus gaining valuable experience of the packaging requirements of industries not yet represented in their own area. Of the several firms in Glasgow engaged in this trade by far the largest is John Laird & Son, established in 1874. It has now passed mainly out of the hands of the family of its founder, having become a limited company in 1911 and a subsidiary of E. S. & A. Robinson Ltd. of Bristol in 1920. Beginning originally as a merchanting business, it gradually became manufacturing and steadily expanded as the requirements for protective packaging grew over the years. Since 1937 its employees have more than doubled in number and are now approaching the thousand mark. Equipped with modern apparatus for the production of cartons by the letterpress and litho processes, and for gravure and silk screen printing (an example of the adoption of new techniques for box decoration), this firm manufactures a very wide range of packaging materials for industry: cartons, rigid boxes, corrugated cases, waxed paper, cardboard drums, laminated papers, paper bags, film bags and reels, corrugated greaseproof packing, and wooden case liners. Many other smaller firms in the city manufacture folding and rigid boxes, cartons and paper bags, showcards, cut-outs etc. in similar variety, and have shared in the local expansion of this trade since the end of the War in 1945. The requirements of the food industry account for much of the demand, some firms specialising in fine corrugated papers, cellophane film products, and crimped paper cases for the bakery and confectionery trades.

Printing and Publishing

Printing, introduced into England by Caxton in 1476, took thirty years to reach Scotland; and it was not until a hundred and thirty years after Chepman and Myllar set up their press in Edinburgh in 1507 that the art began to be practised in Glasgow. In 1638 George Anderson established what is thought to have been the first printing press in the city, and in 1661 Robert Sanders, a bookseller, started a press which survived into a second generation. But up to the eighteenth century most of the booksellers and stationers in Scotland, as well as the printers, were to be found in Edinburgh. It was Glasgow, however, which was to set the standard in printing and publishing, not only for Scotland but for the whole of Europe.

The two men who conferred this glory on the city have received scant commemoration from its inhabitants. They are not among the select company of petrified notabilities who grace George Square. Only a very observant passer-by might notice in Ingram Street, engraved in the pavement fronting the old Ramshorn Kirk, the simple cross and the letters "R.F." and "A.F." which mark the burial place of the brothers Robert and Andrew Foulis—"the Elzevirs of Glasgow."[1] Robert, having with his brother visited the Continent and made a close study of the printing houses there, opened a shop in Glasgow about 1741. Two years later the title of University Printer was conferred upon him, and the Foulis Press soon acquired an illustrious reputation throughout the learned world for its elegant and accurate editions of classical authors. The brothers were fortunate to have the editorial assistance of such great Glasgow scholars of their time as Dr. Francis Hutcheson, Adam Smith, and Robert Simson the mathematician. For about thirty years the Foulis Press continued to issue its superb work,

[1] Thus Boswell complimented them; but he adds that Dr. Johnson found them tiresome conversationalists and "could not bear these men." The two Foulis brothers dined and drank tea with the eminent travellers at their Glasgow inn in 1773, and apparently proved less pleasing in person than in print: "Though good and ingenious men, they had that unsettled speculative mode of conversation which is offensive to a man regularly taught at an English school and university. I found that, instead of listening to the dictates of the sage, they had teased him with questions and doubtful disputations." Boswell's *Journal of a Tour to the Hebrides with Samuel Johnson, LL.D.*, 29 October 1773.

nothing comparable being seen again in Scotland until the advent of James MacLehose in the nineteenth century.

On such solid foundations of craftsmanship laid by these skilful and scholarly printers in the past, it would have been surprising indeed if Glasgow had failed to build the secure reputation she now enjoys in printing and publishing. From the beginning, of course, the University exerted an important influence on the development of the trade. In the seventeenth century printing was fostered directly by universities as a means of spreading knowledge, and it was no accident that George Anderson, Glasgow's first printer of 1638, was also the first Printer to the University. The list of subsequent University Printers is substantially continuous from that time, including the well-known names of Sanders, Foulis, Duncan, and MacLehose. In the Duncans we have a link with the first of the great publishing houses of the present day to which Glasgow gave birth: the firm of Blackie & Son. The original partnership was formed in 1809 under the name of W. Somerville, A. Fullerton and J. Blackie & Co. for the sale of books purchased from other publishers. Publishing of books on their own behalf began very soon afterwards, the first publication of the firm appearing in 1811. In 1829 John Blackie acquired the printing premises and plant of the Duncans, Printers to the University, and carried on there a printing establishment which was long known as W. G. Blackie & Co., Printers, Villafield. It was eventually amalgamated with the publishing house in 1892. When acquired in 1829 the floor space was approximately 3,000 square feet, but various additions were made to the premises during the nineteenth century and by 1897 the total floor space occupied had increased to 90,000 square feet. In 1931 the construction of new printing and bookbinding premises at Bishopbriggs was completed, the floor space of which is now about 225,000 square feet, and this extensive modern establishment has inherited the name of The Villafield Press. The firm's head offices in Glasgow remain, however, at Stanhope Street, the old Villafield. There are also offices in London, Bombay and Toronto. Blackie & Son's early publications were mainly of a religious character, but there were also some notable general works such as *Travels in Italy* by Dr. John Moore, father of Sir John Moore, the Glasgow-born hero of Corunna. In the second half of the nineteenth century publications of a more general nature became standard, and towards the end of that century the educational and juvenile branches of Blackie's business were developed. Since 1920 the firm has expanded considerably its publication of scientific and technical books. This old Glasgow business, which employs over 400 people and can boast a total output of some five million books, is still a private limited company controlled by the descendants of its original founder, John Blackie.

In 1819, ten years after Blackie entered business, a young man from Pollokshaws, hitherto engrossed in teaching and church work, made a humble venture into publishing and thus founded the great house of Collins. William Collins, obviously, was no ordinary young man; bred to the loom in his native village after leaving the parish school about the age of twelve, he was a clerk in John Monteith's mighty cotton mill at eighteen, where he endeavoured to improve his fellow-workers by offering them instruction in religion on Sundays, and in the three R's on week-nights. By 1814, at the age of twenty-five, he was an elder in Glasgow's Tron Kirk and (helped by Stevenson MacGill, its minister) had left the mill and opened his own private boarding school in the city. It was this youthful elder and dominie who, while visiting the Fife village of Kilmany, was attracted by the preaching of its local minister—Thomas Chalmers—and was primarily responsible for the translation of that noted divine to the Tron Parish in the following year. Out of the friendship that developed between these two like-minded social reformers the new publishing venture of "Chalmers & Collins" arose. The Chalmers of the partnership, however, was not the great Thomas himself, but his young and rather feckless brother Charles.

The interesting details of the firm's origins cannot be further dwelt on here.[1] Suffice it to say that Thomas Chalmers, having had an unhappy dispute with John Smith—the chief Glasgow bookseller of the time—Longmans of London, and Whyte of Edinburgh, over the publication of his *Tron Church Sermons* in 1819, encouraged his ambitious young elder to take up publishing and entrusted him with the MS. of his pamphlet on *The Christian and Civic Economy of Large Towns*. This, the first Collins publication, came off the press in September 1819.

The House of Collins started life as two distinct firms: Chalmers & Collins, publishers, booksellers and stationers, and William Collins & Company, printers. Charles Chalmers looked after the bookselling and stationery branches, while William Collins attended to the publishing, printing and binding. The latter received an advance of £800 from Dr. Chalmers for the printing works, which were kept separate from the retail side of the business, and were situated in the Candleriggs. Collins's partnership with Charles Chalmers, which arose through Dr. Chalmers's financial interest in the firm and was unsatisfactory from the start, lasted only until 1826, when the business got into deep water. Charles, moreover, created difficulties between his brother and William Collins, but in the end the latter was able to settle all his obligations to them both.[2] He had achieved his independence, though at the cost of saddling himself and his young firm with a heavy burden of debt. Gradually, however, the business grew and prospered under the hand of its original founder and the long line of William Collinses who succeeded him. Down the years several members of the family have made notable contributions to the civic and national life, quite apart from their activities in publishing.

At first, as in the case of Blackie & Son, the firm concentrated

1 For a full account see David Keir, *The House of Collins* (1952).

2 Charles Chalmers, after an ineffective attempt at journalism in Edinburgh, started a boarding-school with three boarders in 1827. He became a popular and accomplished schoolmaster, leased Lord Napier's house in Edinburgh and thus founded the well-known school, Merchiston Castle.

mainly on religious publications, adding thereafter the production of Bibles, school textbooks and children's books. In 1879 a paper mill at Bowling in Dunbartonshire was acquired, and at the close of that year the business was converted from a partnership into a private limited company. The year 1881 saw the introduction of the first of the well-known Collins Diaries, and by the end of the century 25 different diaries were being published in 64 different bindings. The firm's annual sales of diaries to-day run into millions. In the '90's two further paper mills were acquired at Denny in Stirlingshire, and together with the Bowling mill were converted into a separate limited company. The well-known series of Collins Pocket Classics—illustrated shilling volumes—which began to be published in 1903, would scarcely have been practicable but for such well-planned developments.[1] Since the inception of the series well over 25 million copies have been sold. This firm has been a pioneer of "the cheap edition."

William Collins Sons & Co. Ltd. was converted from a private to a public limited company in 1949, but descendants of the original founder are still closely concerned in its management. In the course of the present century the firm's employees have more than doubled in number, to nearly 2,500; this refers to Glasgow alone and excludes the branches in London and overseas. Books for abroad represent a large proportion of Collins' output, their exports reaching a record value of about £750,000 in 1949. Since the Second World War there has been a remarkable extension of the business of the firm, which is now the largest printing, binding and publishing unit in the Commonwealth, with branches in Canada, Australia, New Zealand, South Africa, and India, to say nothing of a sales organisation that is world-wide.

The name of MacLehose is synonymous with fine printing, and Robert MacLehose & Co. Ltd., the present Printers to the University, are worthy heirs of the Foulis tradition. Their best productions can stand comparison with anything that has been achieved during three centuries of printing in Glasgow. The MacLehose business has now no connection with publishing and bookselling in the city, but it was in these branches that its origin lay. James MacLehose started a bookselling business in 1838, a circulating library in 1841, and a bookbinding establishment about 1862. Two years later he was appointed Bookseller to the University, and in 1871, Publisher to the University. In the following year the MacLehose printing press—originally associated with Ayr, where James's younger brother Robert had a bookseller's business—was transferred to the building in Glassford Street, Glasgow, which George Richardson, University Printer, had occupied.

In 1881 the publishing and bookselling firm became James MacLehose & Sons, and when Robert MacLehose retired in 1894 his two nephews Robert and James purchased the printing business, becoming

[1] Illustrative of the firm's highly organised production is the fact that for many years a Pearl 24mo Bible of 850 pages was produced for *less* than a shilling. There was even a *Penny Library* series for schools, and a 3½d. *Pocket Library* of full-length novels, before the First World War rendered such bargains truly "unrepeatable."

sole partners of the University Press under the name of Robert MacLehose & Co. They had already succeeded to the publishing and bookselling business on their father's death in 1885, but the two firms were kept distinct. In 1904 the printing firm was converted into a private limited company, and the University Press was transferred from its cramped city premises to Anniesland, where it has been able to expand and develop. Following the First World War James MacLehose, then head of the firm, decided to confine his activities solely to printing. The publishing and bookselling business became successively MacLehose, Jackson & Co., Jackson, Wylie & Co., and Jackson, Son & Co. (Booksellers) Ltd., as it is now called. The MacLehose family has no longer any association with it.

In 1947 Robert MacLehose & Co. Ltd., of the University Press, was converted into a public limited company, but here the family connection remains. Its output covers a wide variety of books, university literature and commercial literature. Apart from the development of direct export business (about 14 per cent in 1955, a further 38 per cent of the firm's output being indirectly exported) the nature of the production has changed little over the years: but the character and proportions of individual products have altered, a major difference being the great increase in the use of colour. The firm is particularly noted for the printing of scientific and mathematical works, as is to be expected from its University connection. The University Presses in Scotland, however, are very different from their English counterparts: they have never been developed into printing and publishing houses on the scale of those of Oxford and Cambridge.

Commercial printing is a highly specialised branch of the trade, and in this several Glasgow firms are pre-eminent. J. & J. Murdoch, a local business whose origins go back to 1844, and McCorquodale & Co., a branch of a Lancashire firm which started operations in Glasgow ten years later, produce a wide and colourful variety of lithographed posters, showcards and labels. The former firm specialises in labels for the soft drinks industry and other bottling trades, while the latter, which was originally concerned mainly with railway posters, now handles all classes of printing including highest quality colour reproduction, and has become one of the leading British firms engaged in commercial printing. It was the proximity of main line railway termini that attracted McCorquodale & Co. to Glasgow last century, the firm at one time undertaking work for more than twelve different railways. The Glasgow business has been extensively developed by the purchase of three local printing concerns, and one in Edinburgh, which are now subsidiary companies. The company has also large works in London and elsewhere.

Another firm of local origin, Gilmour & Dean, has specialised in colour printing for a hundred years, and during that period has experienced significant changes in its clientele. Founded in 1846, this company originally produced labels and tickets for the Indian piece goods trade, but with the great reduction in the export of piece goods from Glasgow to India that branch of business has almost disappeared. Bank notes and cheques were both prominent among the firm's products in earlier days, but owing to the decrease in the number of Scottish independent banks the bank note business has now vanished; cheque printing, however, is on the increase. Meanwhile the popularisation of education since the 1870's has brought about a great increase in the printing of school books both for home and for colonial schools. About 40 per cent of the firm's present production is for export.

As is to be expected in a commercial centre such as Glasgow, the manufacture of office and legal stationery has long been carried on by a considerable number of companies. A business with a notable tradition in this field is that of Duncan Campbell & Son, which began manufacture in the city in 1826 and continued as a family concern until 1925, when it was taken over by S. Straker & Sons, a London firm of printers and stationers with an equally lengthy history. Campbell's office and pocket diaries have aided the memories of generations of Glasgow business men since Georgian times. The main changes in the firm's activities over the past hundred and thirty years have been related to the ever-widening range of printing and binding required by business houses, particularly with regard to banking and insurance.

Other developments of modern days, such as the growth of public transport and postal communications, are reflected in the work of numerous printing firms. The Glasgow Numerical Printing Company, a public limited company since 1917, has been manufacturing tramway tickets since 1878—twenty years before the horses looked askance at Glasgow's first electric tram. This firm now undertakes all kinds of numerical printing, such as counter check books etc., in addition to tram tickets and bus tickets. The manufacture of picture postcards and calendars, greetings cards for every conceivable occasion, and special stationery for parties, weddings and funerals is an industry of comparatively modern growth which is also actively represented in Glasgow. One firm, Millar & Lang, having developed from a very small beginning in the city centre in 1892, now occupies a building covering 29,000 square feet and employs nearly 200 people. About 12½ per cent of its production is for direct export, but it caters primarily for the home market where the ever-growing habit of sending greetings cards is one of the social phenomena of our times. As an easy substitute for letter-writing, whether on occasions of celebration, sorrow or illness, the printed card has become as popular with the busy (or lazy) man and woman of to-day as the telegram was with our Victorian forefathers on its first introduction. To Christmas and birthday cards, which have increased greatly in popularity since the beginning of this century, there have been added in more recent years special congratulatory cards, "get-well" cards for sending to invalids, and even (following American custom) cards for "Mother's Day" in May and "Father's Day" in September—to say nothing of the late astonishing revival of the Valentine! While there may be much to deplore in this mushroom growth of stereotyped sentiment, it forms the basis of a flourishing industry and a thriving export trade—even Africans and Indians, it seems, are adopting the greetings-card habit.

Although Edinburgh is really the centre of the manufacture of general stationery in Scotland—a reflection of the local concentration of paper mills—Glasgow has several firms engaged in this field, some of them having been established a hundred years or more. One of the larger concerns is that of John Thomlinson, which was started as a stationers' business in 1874. Several specialties have been developed through the years and this firm, now employing 160, does colour printing and makes folding boxes and cartons, in addition to envelopes and other stationery. John Watson & Co., manufacturing stationers, have been established in the city for about a hundred years. This firm was originally mainly concerned in merchanting goods, but acquired its own plant and changed to manufacturing just prior to the First World War. A larger firm, but of more recent origin, is Livingstone Brothers, dating from 1892, which manufactures stationery, envelopes, printed wrappers and paper shavings. The production of business filing systems is a thriving branch of stationery manufacture in Glasgow, represented by such firms as MacLellan & Rose who, in addition to office folders and files, make cardboard and millboard boxes, plan cases etc., at an extensive factory in the Carntyne Industrial Estate. Associated with the stationery industry in the city are a number of firms engaged in ancillary trades, such as engraving and die-cutting and copper-plate printing. Indeed the field of general stationery is a wide one and is closely interlinked with related industries. The publishing firm of William Collins, Sons & Co., already referred to, is prominent not only in the manufacture of diaries but also in the production of commercial and personal stationery of all kinds.

Wood Manufactures

More than half of the insured employees in Glasgow classified in the industrial group "Manufactures of Wood and Cork" are concerned with the making of furniture and upholstery. The other important branches, as will be seen from Table XLVI., are the timber trade and the manufacture of wooden containers.

TABLE XLVI

Estimated Number of Insured Employees in Wood Industries in Glasgow, at mid-1955

S.I.C. Group	*Males*	*Females*	*Total*
Timber	1,356	204	1,560
Furniture and Upholstery	3,398	1,407	4,805
Shop and Office Fitting	505	106	611
Wooden Containers and Baskets	1,332	349	1,681
Miscellaneous Wood and Cork Manufactures	378	275	653
	6,969	2,341	9,310

Source: Ministry of Labour and National Service.

Timber

There was a time, but it is long past, when Glasgow's timber requirements could be adequately supplied from local sources. As we have seen in an earlier chapter[1] native oak, stout enough to roof a cathedral or build a man-o'-war, was to be had at no greater distance than Luss on Loch Lomondside. The ancient Caledonian Forest which once covered Scotland is now no more, and to-day the Forestry Commission is endeavouring to replant some of the areas denuded by our improvident ancestors. Even before the end of the eighteenth century Clyde shipbuilders were importing oak from England and Wales, and fir from the Baltic. With the subsequent growth, not only of wooden shipbuilding but also of house-building and factory construction, the demand for timber in the nineteenth century increased enormously. Glasgow and its surrounding districts were large consuming areas, and as a west-coast port the city offered attractive facilities for the importing of American and Canadian woods. Moreover the large and growing exports of manufactured goods from Glasgow made possible increased return cargoes of raw materials such as timber. It is not surprising, therefore, to find that several of the timber importers in Glasgow to-day trace their origins to the first half of the nineteenth century.

The largest, although not the oldest, firm is Brownlee & Company of the City Saw Mills, Port Dundas, founded by James Brownlee in 1849. It is now the leading firm of timber merchants and saw-millers in Scotland, having acquired in recent years a number of other well-known companies as subsidiaries: Park, Dobson & Co. of Leith (1943), J. S. Dunn & Co. of Port Dundas, Glasgow (1948), J. & A. Macphee of Glasgow (1950), Robert Millar & Sons of Montrose and Aberdeen (1950), and Adam Paterson & Co. of Galashiels (1953). The parent firm has been a public company since 1896, but there are still connections with the founder's family: two of the four full-time directors are descended from a sister of James Brownlee, and one of the two part-time directors is descended from a brother. Like many other timber importing concerns, the business began as a sawmill. It was a trade sawmill, executing work mainly on a commission basis, and principally on imported softwood. Originally its site at Port Dundas was advantageous, the canal providing a cheap means of transportation from Glasgow and Greenock, but this form of transport is no longer used. Brownlee & Company now trade as timber importers and sawmillers dealing in hardwoods as well as softwoods, and as importers and merchants of plywoods, wallboards, plastics etc. A joinery factory was established in 1873 and during the two World Wars made notable contributions to the requirements of Government Departments in such lines as ammunition boxes. For over 50 years the company has

[1] See Chapter 6 (Shipbuilding).

operated a large softwood mill and storage yard at Grangemouth, which offers cheaper facilities for the importation of timber from Scandinavia and the Baltic, and indeed it now imports more there than at Glasgow. Glasgow, however, is still a more convenient centre for delivery to the bulk of the firm's customers. About 60 per cent of production is for final use by other industries, and of this proportion a quarter is for the shipbuilding industry.

On the whole, as compared with east-coast ports such as Grangemouth, Glasgow is a less desirable location than formerly for the timber merchants. Some feel that their mills would be better sited at Grangemouth, to handle the large supplies of softwoods which now arrive there from Sweden, Finland and Russia. These supplies can serve the whole industrial belt of Scotland, whereas timber arriving at Glasgow, because of carriage costs, cannot easily serve Central and East Scotland. The position was different in the early nineteenth century when cheap canal transport was available, and many of the Glasgow timber concerns founded at that time were sited to take advantage of this. One of the oldest of the surviving firms is Robinson, Dunn & Co., of the Temple Saw Mills, established in 1838 as T. & T. Dunn, and assuming its present name four years later. It was founded to meet the need for log converting machinery to deal with the logs then arriving in considerable bulk from Canada, and until about 1850 the business was that of public sawmillers only. Thereafter the partners (all Robinsons from 1860) became timber importers also. The firm became a private limited company in 1908, and a public one in 1954, but the direction is still almost entirely in the hands of the Robinson family. In addition to importing hardwoods and softwoods, the Temple Saw Mills handle plywoods and wallboards and also carry out timber preserving with creosote and "celcure" (water soluble salts) by the vacuum-pressure process. Although the total timber consumpt in the United Kingdom has fallen by 20 per cent over the past 35 years, this Glasgow firm still handles about the same quantities as in good years between the two World Wars.

Not only are greater varieties of timber now available than there were a century ago; there have been some significant changes in the requirements of the industry's customers. In both the shipbuilding and house-building trades the sections of timber used now tend to be lighter than formerly. Moreover, developments such as metal-skinned lifeboats, new welding processes, changes in agricultural implements, the growth of mechanical handling devices and the practical disappearance of horse-drawn lorries and carts have eliminated much of the sawn timber which previously figured largely in the production of the various Glasgow sawmills. The chemical treatment of wood, including fireproofing by patent processes, is now an important branch of the industry and is the specialty of the Timber Fireproofing Co., an English concern which opened a branch factory at Hillington with H.M.A. support in 1944.

Furniture and Upholstery

For design and craftsmanship Scottish furniture is justly renowned, and several manufacturers with more than a local reputation are to be found in the Glasgow district to-day. The growth of the shipbuilding industry, and particularly the advent of the luxury ocean liner with its palatial furnishings, has had much to do with the development of the furniture trade in the city during the past century. Quite apart from this, however, Glasgow manufacturers have enjoyed a reputation of long standing in the field of domestic furniture and several firms have been established for more than a hundred years. Andrew Thomson & Sons, for example, originated in 1850 when the prospect of finding more scope for his talents brought the founder to Glasgow from Argyllshire, where he had been a carpenter and cabinetmaker. This is one of the smaller firms, but small units predominate in this industry where individual craftsmanship has happily not yet been ousted by mass-production methods. Even in the larger factories employing 250 workers or more there is a tradition of personal attention to design and finish, which accounts for the distinctive character and repute of their products. Since the end of the Second World War there has been some concentration of production in the larger units, an inevitable development in view of the widening export market for Scottish-made furniture.

One of the most prominent firms is H. Morris & Co., founded in 1902, and known throughout the country and abroad as "Morris of Glasgow." During the past twenty years the business has approximately trebled in size. In addition to a wide range of domestic furniture marketed under the brand name of "Cumbrae," this firm manufactures special furniture for ships, hotels and institutions, and also blockboard, plywood, veneered plywood and architectural wood work. Its use of resin-bonded laminated timbers—a development originating in the aircraft industry during the Second World War—illustrates how modern techniques are revolutionising traditional methods of furniture construction. That this Glasgow furniture firm is a pioneer in technical developments is apparent from the fact that it has done considerable research work on low-density plastic mouldings and helicopter blades for the Research and Development Departments of the Services.

Other leading furniture manufacturers in Glasgow are Rowan & Boden of Hillington, specialists in ship furnishing, Coorsh Bros. & Co. of Bridgeton, who make bedding as well as furniture, and John McGregor & Sons, a firm which began business in Renfrew in 1904 but moved to Hillington Industrial Estate in 1950. The latter concern is well known for its "Gregart" upholstery and bedding, and "Put-u-up" bed settees. These metal-action bed settees were introduced under American licence in 1924 and now form the bulk of the firm's production, totalling some twelve to fifteen thousand per annum. This company has always specialised in domestic upholstery, the design of which has altered greatly over the past fifty years from "Victorian" to "contemporary." The development of new forms of upholstery filling and new types of springing within recent years has made possible, in conjunction with new techniques in metal and wood working, a greater freedom of design which has been exploited to the full by Glasgow manufacturers. Patent rubber upholstery such as "Dunlopillo," and latex foam cushioning on helical or serpentine springing, or even on a metal or pre-formed plywood base, are now commonly used, especially in furniture for the export market. To appreciate the revolutionary changes that have taken place in furniture design since last century we need only compare the "horse-hair sofa" of Victorian days with a modern settee made by McGregor & Sons in Glasgow—its back, seat and arms all formed from one piece of aluminium, upholstered completely with latex foam cushioning. The displacement of wood by metal in the furniture industry, it is to be hoped, may never be complete. In office and institutional furniture, however, this trend has become increasingly evident in recent times.

Wooden Containers and Baskets

As Glasgow in the nineteenth century was the principal centre of the Scotch Whisky industry, with bonded warehouses and port facilities for shipment to all parts of the world, the manufacture of casks and vats became an important subsidiary trade. The Clyde Cooperage Company, which began as MacGregor & Co. about 1840, is believed to be the oldest of its kind in Scotland. Casks for whisky, constructed from imported American oak, have always been its main product, and the firm undertakes both manufacture and reconditioning. There have been some changes in demand during the past thirty years, through the disuse of many wooden containers in favour of metal drums, tanks and other alternatives, but oak casks are still essential for the maturing of whisky at the distilleries and for the export of bulk whisky. Because of the scarcity of skilled labour in the cooperage industry, a large proportion of the work of this firm has to be farmed out.

The manufacture of wooden boxes and packing cases is carried on by many firms, some of the more prominent being the Acme Tea Chest Co. (which makes whisky cases in addition to tea chests), Brown & Co. (makers of packing cases and whisky cases), A. & G. Paterson, who are principally timber merchants and sawmillers, Hamilton, Marr & Co., and James Buchanan & Co. In this field, too, however, wood is tending to be displaced by other materials, notably fibreboard. The use of corrugated fibreboard, which usually consists of a corrugated board between two layers of kraft board, has been gaining ground particularly in America in recent years, and in the food and other industries in this country corrugated fibreboard cases are now being increasingly adopted in place of wooden ones. It has just been announced (in October 1956) that a new company is to be formed in Scotland for the manufacture of corrugated fibreboard packing cases, which will be made in the joinery department of Brownlee & Co., the Glasgow timber merchants and box makers already referred to above. The new concern is to be a joint venture between the Glasgow company and two English firms, the Alliance Box. Co. and Alders (Tamworth). Such an extension of interests by an old-established firm whose activities have hitherto been confined to wood may be significant of future trends in this branch of industry.

Packages for horticultural products are manufactured in Glasgow by the British Basket and Besto Co., which is one of the largest firms in the city engaged in the packaging industry. It originated as the British Basket Co. in 1904, and was the first firm in Britain to manufacture wood veneer packages. The production of veneer confectionery boxes was later given up in favour of fruit baskets, "chips" and "punnets." An indication of the tremendous growth of the business is given by the following estimates of the number of packages produced in certain years: 5 million in 1904, 9 million in 1913, 25 million in 1937, and 40 million in 1954. The firm has been known by its present name since 1932, when amalgamation took place with an English concern, the Besto Chip Co. In addition to the Glasgow premises, there are factories in Wisbech, Irlam, Cuxton and Evesham. Since the beginning of this century, when the business was founded to cater for the Scottish strawberry and raspberry crops, the growth of the Scottish tomato industry has assisted its expansion. Glasgow, originally attractive as a suitable port for the importation of the round logs used in manufacture, has since proved a most favourable shipping port for the firm's export trade to Eire. About a sixth of its present production is for the Irish horticultural industry.

Hickory Handles

As a curious tailpiece to this account of wood manufacture in Glasgow reference must be made to a unique industry which has existed in the city since the time of the American Civil War. The firm which gave birth to it, Robert Burley & Sons, had been founded in 1839. Its principal products originally were ships' running rigging blocks, with joinery and turnery as subsidiary activities. The manufacture of handles for joiners' and engineers' tools, however, soon became the firm's specialty. Handles were then fashioned from home-grown timber, such as ash and beech, but Robert Burley's eldest son fought on the Confederate side in the American Civil War and on returning to Glasgow brought back some samples of hickory. This wood from the Mississippi Valley was destined to be held in the skilful hands of many a Clydeside workman, for the Burleys discovered that it had ideal qualities for use with striking tools. Hickory handles have ever since been the specialty of this Glasgow firm, which is one of the best-known in the trade. Being the first to import hickory from the U.S.A., the Burleys were assured of cheap ocean transport of their raw materials. Until 1920 their factory was supplied from mills which they themselves had opened in the Southern States, and the quantities of hickory used were so great that the countryside around these mills was practically laid bare. As no replanting was done, supplies are no longer so plentiful and no satisfactory substitute has yet been found. Sufficient hickory is still forthcoming from various sources, however, to enable this peculiar Glasgow industry to continue. Robert Burley & Sons' present factory in Govan was built about 1900 and now employs some 40 workers. Ten per cent of its production, in terms of value, is exported. The firm manufactures both hickory and ash handles, and also does wood bending and turning.

Chemicals and Allied Trades

Just over 8,000, or 1.5 per cent, of the insured employees in the Glasgow area are engaged in the chemical industry and allied trades, their distribution being as shown in Table XLVII.

TABLE XLVII

Estimated Number of Insured Employees in Chemicals and Allied Trades in Glasgow at mid-1955

S.I.C. Group	*Males*	*Females*	*Total*
Coke Ovens and By-Product Works	520	2	522
Chemicals and Dyes	2,256	811	3,067
Pharmaceutical Preparations, Toilet Preparations, Perfumery	194	495	689
Explosives and Fireworks	609	287	896
Paint and Varnish	1,087	543	1,630
Soap, Candles, Glycerine, Polishes, Ink and Matches	309	288	597
Mineral Oil Refining	109	47	156
Other Oils, Greases, Glue, etc.	448	125	573
	5,532	2,598	8,130

Source: Ministry of Labour and National Service.

The growth of the chemical industry in Glasgow, as elsewhere, has been closely linked with other aspects of industrial development. It owed its birth to the requirements of the textile industries in the second half of the eighteenth century, and in the following century it became associated with the metallurgical and engineering industries: and in the later stages of the agricultural, as well as of the industrial, revolution the chemical industry has played an important part.

It is significant that the "father" of the chemical industry in Glasgow, Charles Tennant of St. Rollox, was himself connected with the textile trade as a bleacher. Following the discovery of chlorine in the late eighteenth century and James Watt's demonstration at Clober,[1] near Milngavie, of its efficiency as a bleaching agent in 1787, the time-honoured and time-consuming process of natural bleaching in the open air was soon superseded. The perfection of the method came with the introduction of "bleaching powder" (chloride of lime) by Charles Tennant, who obtained a patent for his manufacturing process. In 1798 he founded his St. Rollox works in Glasgow, an enterprise which soon became the largest chemical factory in the world. It no longer holds that distinction, and it has also lost its claim to local fame—the possession of the tallest chimney stalk in Glasgow. To-day the St. Rollox works are operated by Imperial Chemical Industries, and in place of their former wide variety of products, such as bleaching agents, acids and alkalis, they now specialise in the manufacture of sulphuric acid. When operating to capacity St. Rollox manufactures a larger quantity of acid than any other works in Scotland, its production reaching almost 40,000 tons per annum.

Sulphuric acid is also manufactured in Glasgow in the Netherfield Chemical Works of R. & J. Garroway, an old firm founded in 1817. Between that date and 1914 three generations of the Garroway family traded and manufactured in Glasgow. The business was then purchased by the late Sir Frederick L. MacLeod, and it is still controlled by his four sons and their families. For about a hundred years the same main products have been manufactured, but the production of various chemicals in small demand has been given up and the company now concentrates on larger-scale production of a few chemicals. The closing of many textile factories in Glasgow and the surrounding area (for example, calico printing works and Turkey red dyeworks) has adversely affected local chemical manufacturers, but on the other hand the expansion of steel works, with coke ovens, near the city has been a compensating development. In addition to sulphuric acid, R. & J. Garroway now manufacture aluminium sulphate, used in the purification of water and sewage and for sizing paper, and also superphosphates and compound manures for agricultural purposes.

Another Glasgow firm, that of Richard Smith, founded in 1841, has specialised in the manufacture of sulphuric, hydrochloric and nitric acids, and a variety of salts, notably Glauber's Salts, of which it is the largest maker in Scotland. This concern has now been absorbed by Scottish Tar Distillers of Falkirk, and its main products at present are hydrochloric acid and sulphites.

Chemicals for use in the leather tanning industry have also been manufactured over a long period in Glasgow. Vegetable tannins are still mainly employed, but synthetic materials known as "syntans," usually based on sulphonic acids of naphthalene and cresol, are now being adopted to reduce the length of the tanning process and to improve the grain and colour of the leather. The British Dyewood Company manufactures both types of product in its works at Parkhead,

[1] By his second marriage Watt was a son-in-law of McGregor of Clober, whose Bleachfield was established in 1763. It continued in operation until 1928.

but the majority of its consumers (as far as the home market is concerned) are now located in England. A considerable proportion of its production, however (about 24 per cent by value) is directly exported. Since 1937 the volume of the firm's business has increased at least sixfold. This concern originated in Glasgow as McArthur Scott & Co. in 1883, and was converted into a private limited company in 1898, embodying three other private companies, two of them in England and one in Scotland. The entire production was subsequently concentrated in Glasgow in 1911, when the company was reconstructed under its present name. It has now passed completely out of the ownership of the original founders, but the active management remains in the hands of their descendants. Initially this firm's customers were all textile manufacturers and tanners, whereas to-day its products go to a very wide variety of trades. While the products originally manufactured were entirely chipped and ground dyewood and tanning materials, the company now produces an extensive range of concentrated extracts and fine chemicals of vegetable origin.

Many other branches of chemical manufacture are represented in Glasgow. Alex. Hope, Jnr. & Co., for example, are the chief makers in Scotland of arsenical compounds and formaldehyde, and also manufacture Glauber's Salts. The Clydesdale Chemical Company produces activated decolourising carbon, which is used throughout the United Kingdom in making pharmaceuticals, drugs, fine chemicals, oils and special sugars. Oxygen, acetylene, and other industrial gases used so extensively in modern shipbuilding and engineering, are manufactured in Glasgow by such concerns as the British Oxygen Company, while the distillation of tar and the production of bitumen emulsions are carried on by Scottish Tar Distillers at their two works in Maryhill and Shettleston.

Sheep and cattle dips and disinfectants based on coal tar are manufactured by Robert Young & Co., a well-known Glasgow firm with a considerable export trade. One of the largest chemical firms in the city is Cooper, McDougall & Robertson, manufacturers of sheep and cattle dips, veterinary preparations, and insecticides. Cresylic acid is among this company's products. Insecticides and disinfecting fluids are also made in Glasgow by two concerns whose bleaching and washing fluids have long been familiar to the housewife—The Parazone Co., and John Paterson & Co. the makers of "Clensel." The Cromessol Co. manufactures perfumes and liquid soaps as well as disinfectants in its Glasgow factory.

With the recovery of Scottish agriculture after the severe depression which preceded the Second World War there has been a tremendous expansion in the demand for chemical fertilisers. Scottish Agricultural Industries, a subsidiary company of Imperial Chemical Industries, has factories in Aberdeen, Ayr, Carnoustie and Leith in addition to its works in Glasgow, and is the largest manufacturer of phosphatic and of compound fertilisers in Scotland. As already noted, the old Glasgow chemical firm of R. & J. Garroway also makes compound fertilisers, the use of which has increased greatly among Scottish farmers in recent years. Basic slag is one of the two principal fertilisers that are not compounded but used "straight," and its sole producers in Scotland are Colvilles' Clydebridge steelworks on the outskirts of the city.

The manufacture of fine chemicals and drugs has always been centred in Edinburgh rather than in the West of Scotland, but Glasgow has a few firms engaged in this branch of the industry. Apart from the Scottish Co-operative Wholesale Society, which produces an extensive range of pharmaceuticals, the companies are small, with a maximum of 70 to 75 employees. The most notable is Askit Ltd., makers of the well-known headache powders, who from small beginnings in 1916 can claim to have become the leading manufacturers of a proprietary medicine in Scotland. In 1924 the original concern, known as the Askit Manufacturing Co., sold the business to a group of Glasgow men who formed a private company with the present name. Its managing director, Mr. J. M. Low, has been associated with Askit since 1919, and has seen production rise from 20,000 powders in that year to 7 million in 1937 and to no less than 25 million in 1954. This progressive Glasgow firm has recently established a selling organisation in Canada to meet the demands of Scots exiles there, and in Toronto alone many thousands of Askit powers are sold every month. A sales organisation has also been established in Eire. Nearly two million powders are sold annually in Northern Ireland, and orders are received from various parts of Europe, Africa, Malaya, New Zealand and Australia. The bulk of the firm's custom, of course, is in Scotland, but lately attempts have been made to extend distribution in the Greater London area. Another, but smaller, firm in Glasgow manufacturing headache powders is Vandre Ltd., who also make travel sickness powders, disinfectants, ointments, etc. Drugs, galenicals and various medicinal preparations are made by James Taylor (Trongate) Ltd., while a branch of the Distillers Company manufactures yeast tablets, dried yeast products, and malt extract. Ephedrene, cascara and quinine are among the products of the British Dyewood Co., which has already been referred to in this chapter.

The manufacture of paint and varnish has long been an important branch of the chemical industry in Glasgow, as is to be expected in an area where such a diversity of manufacturing industries is concentrated. Its importance tends to be obscured from the public eye by the fact that its products reach the market mainly as a protective or decorative coating on the products of other industries, rather than in liquid form; although perhaps the modern injunction to "do it yourself" in such matters as home decorating has made people more familiar with paint and its manufacturers than formerly.[1] Several Glasgow firms, such as

[1] Before the War of 1939-45 it was only the exceptional and talented "handyman" who decorated his own home. The rise in tradesmen's charges since the war has forced many families in the "fixed income" group to become amateur house-painters, and they have been encouraged in this by improved paints and simplified methods of application devised by manufacturers.

Alexander, Fergusson & Co., and two smaller concerns, Thomas Macintyre & Co. and Mathews, Maclay & Manson, are well known as exporters of paints and varnishes to overseas markets. Thomas Hinshelwood & Co., another of the larger firms, has throughout its history catered particularly for the needs of the paper trade. The last quarter of the nineteenth century, when many paint factories were established and competition in the home trade became keen, saw the growth of specialisation. This firm was started in 1878 as Hannay, Gourlay & Hinshelwood, and was at first mainly a merchant business dealing in chemicals and colours for the paper industry, with only a small paint factory. Now it has seven factories, for colours, oil blending and refining, rosin size, paint, varnish, solid oil, and grease. The works, which originally covered about half an acre, now occupy three acres.

One of the largest paint firms in Glasgow, Montgomerie, Stobo & Co., specialises in decorative paints for the building trade. Since its inception in 1906 this company has expanded and widened its interests immensely, and now has branch factories in Chester and Belfast. Paints and varnishes are still its main products, but over the last few years there has been an extension of its lubricating grease and oil departments. Another prominent concern serving the building trade and the shipbuilding industry, among others, is Lewis Berger, an English firm which in 1936 absorbed the old-established Glasgow business of Alexander Miller Jnr. & Co., dating from 1850. In 1944 the firm of Blacklock & Macarthur, founded in 1878, was taken over by the Paints Division of Imperial Chemical Industries, and as a result of the installation of modern plant and other reorganisation its output has doubled during the last ten years. Whereas originally paste paints, liquid paints, anticorrosive and antifouling compositions were the chief manufactures, production is now concentrated on synthetic hard gloss paints and undercoats and is much more specialised. The manufacture of paint to detailed specifications, and to meet special conditions, both as to its use and as to methods of application, is a feature of the industry's modern development.

Few of Glasgow's paint manufacturers can trace their roots as far back as the eighteenth century, but Federated Paints Ltd. can boast a connection with a firm founded in 1780. The present company, formed in 1950, represents an amalgamation of five distinct businesses established between 1780 and 1919. It is still largely in the hands of descendants of the original founders. The persistence of a family connection, and the personal interest that accompanies it, is indeed typical of the paint industry throughout Glasgow. An interesting firm, however, which did not originate in the city is Sandeman's Varnish Ltd., which began manufacture in Glasgow in 1915. This company was an off-shoot of the Hoboken Varnish Works, near Antwerp, Belgium, the original business dating back to 1787. The Glasgow business, which is now completely separate, became a limited company in 1924 and is still controlled by descendants of its founders. In addition to varnish, it produces paints of all kinds, fused and esterified copal, and ester gum, polymerised oils, synthetic resins, driers, industrial and decorative finishes, and marine finishes.

Of the several firms manufacturing light chemicals in Glasgow the most notable is Bryant & May, whose Empire Works in Shuna Street, Maryhill, make the well-known Swan Vestas and other matches. Various polishes, in addition to bleach, insecticides and disinfectants, are manufactured by the Scottish Co-operative Wholesale Society's Glasgow factory at Shieldhall. Printing ink is the specialty of Ault & Wiborg, a recent newcomer to Scotland with a factory at Hillington. This firm purchased in 1950 the paint and cellulose business of Wilson, Blackadder & Co., dating from about 1905, and production of these lines has been continued alongside the new company's main product. The printing inks manufactured here are supplied chiefly to Scottish newspaper and periodical publishers, but about 13 per cent (by value) of the firm's total production is exported. Industrial soaps and detergents, distilled rosin oils, lubricating greases and similar products are made by Sandeman Brothers of Maryhill, a firm whose origins go back to 1883. The importation of rosin was originally facilitated by the factory's situation on the banks of the Forth and Clyde Canal, which made possible the trans-shipment of the material by barge from Bowling. To-day, however, the rosin is delivered by road instead of by canal barge, mostly from the Glasgow docks. The newer chemical products which have been developed since the demand for rosin oils diminished require the transport of raw materials from the Midlands, and in this respect the firm is less happily situated than it once was. During the inter-war period (1918 to 1939) the introduction of high-speed machinery greatly diminished the market for rosin oils and greases. By 1954, in consequence, the company's output was only 540 tons—less than in 1885, two years after the business was founded. The company had a hard struggle to replace its original products and recover to its present position, but the development of chemical mixing has to a great extent (80 per cent by weight in 1954) replaced and expanded the original output. Mineral oils, vegetable oils, castor oil and animal fats are now complementary and equal to the use of rosin. This Glasgow chemical firm provides another pleasant illustration of long-enduring family connections: one of its original founders survived till as recently as 1954, when he had reached the age of 93, and his descendants still operate the business.

Non-Metalliferous Mining Manufactures

In the rather heterogeneous group of industries classified under the heading "Treatment of Non-Metalliferous Mining Products other than Coal" the distribution of insured employees in Glasgow at mid-1955 was as shown in Table XLVIII.

TABLE XLVIII

ESTIMATED NUMBER OF INSURED EMPLOYEES ENGAGED IN THE TREATMENT OF NON-METALLIFEROUS MINING PRODUCTS OTHER THAN COAL. GLASGOW, MID-1955

S.I.C. Group	*Males*	*Females*	*Total*
Bricks and Fireclay Goods	619	70	689
China and Earthenware (inc. glazed tiles)	234	139	373
Glass (other than containers)	741	461	1,202
Glass Containers	570	59	629
Cement	26	18	44
Other Non-Metalliferous Mining Manufactures	1,474	141	1,615
	3,665	888	4,552

SOURCE: Ministry of Labour and National Service.

Pottery

The manufacture of pottery, once a thriving industry in Glasgow, has declined to insignificance; and the story of its decay, with that of the cotton trade, forms an unhappy and still controversial chapter in the city's industrial history. Like some of the early textile industries, the art of pottery manufacture reached Scotland from Holland, Glasgow's first large-scale pottery being founded by Dutch craftsmen in the mid-eighteenth century.[1] During the next hundred years many potteries were established in the city, and at the close of the Victorian era as many as 25 were in operation. The most famous was the Verreville, or Verrefield, which, as its name suggests, was built originally as a glasswork. Its products at one time included fine china and ornamental ware which commanded high prices and enjoyed an international reputation. Another concern, the Glasgow Pottery, also made excellent china at one period in its history, but in both cases it was found difficult to produce china and earthenware in the same factory and (rather in contrast to the usual Scottish attitude to this situation) the higher-quality articles were given up in favour of ordinary household and sanitary ware. In 1857 the great Britannia Pottery was established at St. Rollox, on mass production principles, this concern alone employing about a thousand workers in the late nineteenth century, but it was closed down in the Great Depression of the 1930's. Meanwhile the Verrefield works themselves had been sold in 1918 and demolished. The only survivor to-day of an industry which was still comparatively vigorous at the beginning of the twentieth century is the Govancroft Potteries, a stoneware concern founded in 1912.[2] At that time there were six stoneware potteries in the Glasgow area, besides two in the east at Portobello. Now Govancroft and A. W. Buchan of Portobello are the only manufacturers of stoneware in Scotland.

[1] It was situated near the Broomielaw and was known by the name of Delftfield. Founded in 1748, it is believed to have been the first pottery in Scotland.

[2] Its survival was recently threatened by a disastrous fire. New buildings, however, were completed in 1955 and production is to continue at Govancroft.

Survival in this branch of industry has been achieved only through constant adaptation to changing demand. Stoneware containers, such as jam jars, stone bottles and large stone jars, have fallen into disfavour with the increasing popularity of glass. When plain containers became unmarketable, the Govancroft Potteries turned to the production of coloured and decorated containers for special purposes, including even hand-decorated perfume bottles for export to America. They now make stoneware flagons in many shapes and colours for the export of Scotch whisky, miniature flagons for liqueurs, acid containers for the export of acids, and various other containers for the filling trades. Thus, through a comparative newcomer and in a rather devious way, Glasgow's former international fame as a centre of artistic pottery has in some measure been preserved.

The manufacture of industrial porous ceramics was begun at a factory on the Hillington Estate in 1938 by Aerox Filters Ltd., now known as Aerox Ltd. This firm has since opened a branch factory at Crawley, Sussex, for the manufacture of equipment ancillary to its ceramic production in Glasgow. Its main markets are in the south and on the Continent, about a quarter of its production being exported. With this solitary exception there have been no new developments in the china and earthenware industry in Glasgow within recent years.

Tobacco Clay Pipes

Perhaps the most quaint and picturesque survival from Glasgow's industrial past is the manufacture of clay pipes, which is still carried on by two firms in the city. Their survival is the more surprising in view of the small number of such pipes now to be seen, even in the mouths of old Glasgow workmen, once their staunchest devotees. The briar seems likely to oust the "cutty" completely before long, for young men have no love for clay pipes, to which indeed a certain social stigma has in course of time become attached—this being both a cause and a result, possibly, of their decline in number.[1] It is curious to recall that throughout the nineteenth century Glasgow was the chief seat of the clay pipe industry in Britain, although it had not been so long engaged in the manufacture as Derbyshire or Shropshire. The pipe clay was brought by sea to Glasgow from open mines in South Devon, and even at the beginning of the present century some 2,000 tons were used annually in the city, where the industry gave employment to about 600 people. To-day about a tenth of that number is employed by the two surviving firms, D. McDougall & Co. and William White & Son.

McDougall's factory in Charles Street, St. Rollox, is the larger and the business, dating from about 1846, has been a limited company since 1909. Half a century ago more than 400 different patterns of pipes

[1] A Glasgow newspaper, however, has recently reported that clay pipes are coming back to favour among city business men—who "are smoking them in secret"! *Evening Citizen*, 8 November 1957.

were manufactured here, although the type chiefly made in Glasgow has always been the short ("cutty") pipe, about seven inches in length. To-day only 2 per cent of the firm's output is exported, but the position was very different in 1900. "Only a small portion of these pipes," recorded a writer at that period, "is taken up in the home market. Glasgow pipes are known to, and used by, white people, as well as our dusky brothers, all over the world, our colonies and the United States being the largest and steadiest markets."[1] The drop in production since those days has been offset to some extent by adopting new lines of business, and McDougall & Co. are now engaged in packeting whiting and washing-soda, bottling bleach, and merchanting drysalteries, in addition to the manufacture of clay pipes and pipe-clay.

Despite many attempts at mechanisation in the past, the making of clay pipes has remained a hand-craft. As such, its threatened demise is the more to be regretted. In William White & Son's factory in Gibson Street, Calton, where over 100 gross of pipes are still turned out daily, one old craftsman has been moulding clay pipes with loving care and consummate artistry for more than 60 years. Some of his productions, like the ancient clay pipes of Mexico, are elaborately moulded and ornamented, their bowls depicting historical characters or national emblems—ranging from Shakespeare and Princess Ena of Spain to Burns, Sir Walter Scott, and the Scotch Thistle.[2]

Glass

The manufacture of bottles and bottle glass began in Glasgow in 1730, the first works being situated about the southern end of the present Jamaica Street. With the growth of the beer and whisky industries in the nineteenth century the making of bottles increased greatly in importance and it is now the largest branch of the glass industry in Scotland. The manufacture has become highly mechanised in recent years, and it is now concentrated in the hands of three large concerns in Glasgow, Alloa and Irvine. In the North British Bottle Works of the United Glass Bottle Manufacturers in Glasgow several hundred workers, predominantly males, are employed.

Window glass has been manufactured in Glasgow since the 1870's, at the Firhill works on the Forth and Clyde Canal. They were started, under the name of the Glasgow Plate Glass Company, by Anthony Dixon Brogan, who had learned his trade in the famous old glassworks of the Dixons in Dumbarton.[3] In 1910 the Firhill works were purchased

[1] James Fleming, "Glass, Pottery, Brick Making, Etc." in *Local Industries of Glasgow and the West of Scotland* (1901), p. 208.

[2] See the illustrations of Adam Cuthbertson's work in the *Evening News,* 21 June, 1954.

[3] One of the early partners of the Dumbarton Glasswork Company, which was formed in the second half of the eighteenth century, was a Glasgow gentleman named Dunlop. He possessed "the most fashionable house in the Candleriggs." His associates, the Dixons, a family prominent in one branch as coal and iron masters (Dixon's Blazes), also had interests in bottle works in Glasgow and Greenock.

by Chance Brothers of Smethwick, near Birmingham, a firm which had been manufacturing window glass in England for over a century. Despite the much higher cost of haulage of raw materials to Glasgow than to the firm's other works, the Firhill factory's output has been expanded by about 80 per cent in the past twenty years. In addition to meeting Scottish requirements its products are shipped from the Clyde to most parts of the world, exports amounting to some 40 per cent of the total output.

From this Glasgow factory, so closely linked with some of the earliest Scottish glassmakers, has sprung one of the most modern developments in the industry—the manufacture of glass fibres. It was to provide a new activity and works-occupation at the time of the slump of 1930-1 that Chance Brothers tentatively began to produce glass fibres at their Glasgow factory. At that period they were being manufactured nowhere else in Britain on a commercial scale. After continued development Glass Fibres Ltd. was formed in 1938 as a subsidiary of Chance Brothers at their Murano Street Factory, Firhill. The development of bulk production of glass fibres from large glass-melting tanks made it desirable in 1944-5 for a factory to be established in proximity to the glass-making industry at St. Helens in Lancashire. In 1946 the company, now known as Fibreglass Ltd., acquired the glass fibre factory of Pilkington Brothers at St. Helens, and also became their subsidiary. Head Office functions were located at offices in St. Helens, and the Glasgow factory has subsequently been developed as a manufacturing division. Both Chance Brothers and Fibreglass are now subsidiary companies of Pilkington Brothers.

While glass wool materials are made at St. Helens, the main plant for manufacturing glass yarn and tapes is in Glasgow, and is the largest engaged in this work outside the United States. The material used comes from St. Helens in the form of small glass marbles, which are re-melted and drawn into strands containing 100 or 200 filaments, each only two ten-thousandths of an inch in diameter. These strands are then twisted and doubled to form yarns which can be woven on normal textile plant. The continuous filament yarns and tapes are now widely used for electrical insulation purposes, and this new " man-made " fibre has many other ever-increasing applications. Some idea of the growth of the industry in Glasgow may be given by the following figures: at the end of 1939, eighteen months after its establishment as a separate company, Glass Fibres Ltd. had a total of 300 employed and its sales output for that year was £76,000. For the year to March 1955 the Glasgow Division output was estimated as probably worth £775,000, the employees now numbering nearly 600.

In yet another branch of the glass industry Glasgow can claim to be a pioneer. The largest factory making mirrors in Scotland—that of the City Glass Co.—is situated in Glasgow, and it was here that silvering glass was first made in Scotland on an endless belt. A new development is the manufacture of mirrors by mass production methods, and this company is also producing a flexible type of glass for interior decoration, composed of mirror glass cut into small segments. There is obviously no lack of either vitality or variety in the glass industry of modern Glasgow.

It used to be claimed that Scotland made almost everything, and that to a large extent meant Glasgow and the district around it. This is no longer true, but the variety of the city's secondary industries may be indicated by mentioning some of their many products not yet referred to in the limited space at our disposal—products ranging from abrasives, bagpipes, brushes and brooms, cork boards and stoppers, to lampshades, mousetraps, peat moss, perambulators, spectacles, sports equipment, toys, and umbrellas. Indeed, on reviewing the scene of intense industrial activity presented in this and the preceding chapters, one can only echo Bramble's comment on the city two centuries ago in *Humphry Clinker*: " It is a perfect beehive in point of industry."

Chapter 10

TRANSPORT AND COMMUNICATION

HISTORICAL DEVELOPMENT

WM. C. GALBRAITH

GLASGOW, as has been indicated in an earlier chapter, is a city whose site was determined by considerations of transport—it is a bridge town, a traffic centre and a port—but, although it was always important in its own setting, it was not till after the Union of the Scottish and English Parliaments in 1707 that the West of Scotland began to grow in importance and Glasgow began to show the possibilities inherent in its situation. Up to the seventeenth century it was little more than a country market town, less important as a centre of trade than Aberdeen or Perth, its growth being limited by the shallowness of the River Clyde which was navigable only for small boats.

It appears, however, that as early as 1546 there was some shipping belonging to the town, as its owners were instructed not to annoy the ships of Henry VIII, the Queen's Uncle. In 1556 the first recorded attempt was made to deepen the Clyde, when the burgesses of Glasgow, Renfrew and Dumbarton laboured for six weeks, without success, in an attempt to remove the sandbanks and ford at Dumbuck. In 1597 Glasgow possessed six small ships engaged in importing French wines. Irvine on the Ayrshire coast was certainly used about this time as the outport of Glasgow but by 1620 " the port and harbry being now much decayed from qwhat it was anciently," Glasgow had to look elsewhere. In January 1575 the city had joined with Dumbarton in resisting the Ayr ship *Elizabeth's* attempt to break bulk (i.e. sell retail) at Newark (the future Port Glasgow) and thus infringe the rights of royal burghs but soon Glasgow began to use Newark Bay for unloading ships' cargoes into small craft, in which they were brought upriver. Lesley in 1578 writes that Glasgow " has a verie commodious sea-porte," and by 1609 there was reported to be a " pier and port " at the Broomielaw; these could not be deemed adequate by any later age.

Dumbarton's harbour seems to have been silting up but it hung on grimly to what it considered its rights and on 13 December 1609 secured from James VI a charter by which all vessels were instructed not to break bulk till they reached Dumbarton and there make market. Glasgow regarded this as very prejudicial and immediately made strenuous opposition. Negotiations proved abortive but on 8 April 1611 James granted a charter to Glasgow, making it a royal burgh (it had been a bishop's burgh for 435 years) and conferring the right of loading and unloading ships and buying all sorts of merchandise, home and foreign. Armed with this, Glasgow went at once to the Court of Session whose decision negatived Dumbarton's claims. There was still to be friction between the two burghs for two hundred years but Glasgow had won its position and immediately resumed its attack on the great stones in the river at Dumbuck ford. This time the effort would appear to have been more successful as on 28 June 1633 Glasgow charters were confirmed by the Scots Parliament in consideration of the expense incurred by Glasgow in making the Clyde navigable. That efforts had been maintained is shown by payments made in 1631 and 1632 for "mending the water of Clyde." On 16 October 1636 Charles I granted a charter to Glasgow, describing the city as "at that time and for many ages bypast, the chief and most distinguished burgh in the Western Part of his kingdom" and alluded to the great sums of money which it had expended for many years in making the Clyde navigable for ships and vessels. He also granted to the burgh freedom of the roadstead of Newark or any other roadstead between the bridge of Glasgow and the Clochstane and the right to build ports and roadsteads, bulwarks and jetty heads to render the river more navigable as far as the spring tide flows. He also commended Glasgow for "mending, repairing and upholding the bridge over the river, which greatly conduces to the furtherance of traffic."

In 1656 Cromwell's Commissioner, Thomas Tucker, mentions Glasgow as trading with the West Highlands, Ireland, France, Norway and even "as farre as the Barbadoes." In 1662, when the shipping of the city was almost three and a half times that of 1597, the town council determined that a little quay be built at the Broomielaw; John Clark, mason, built the wall and "all the masters of families were required to send out their servants to carry sand for filling up the back of the new quay." In 1667 it was considered necessary to keep a register of ships.[1] Glasgow also decided that more adequate provision be made for them. Land at Newark was bought and on 20 January 1668 Charles II incorporated it into the "port and harbour of Glasgow." On 27 January the first steps were taken though it was not till 1676 that John Clark began operations and New Port or Port Glasgow began to function. Meanwhile farther down the river Greenock on 5 June 1635 had received its first charter as a free burgh of barony from Charles I. This was extended in 1670 by Charles II, giving Greenock power to repair and build free ports, harbours and havens. Thus commenced a rivalry which was to be much more effective than Dumbarton's. In 1696 several Glasgow burgesses even loaded their ships at Greenock and not at the town's free port of Port Glasgow; they were duly libelled and charged. At the same time "rules and lawes to be observed for the harbour and key att Portglasgow and at the key of the Broomielaw and dews to be payed" were drawn up in some detail. In

[1] By 1692 Glasgow's tonnage totalled 1,182 tons and consisted of 15 ships, besides 8 lighters.

1722 the town council of Glasgow resolved to extend its quay and two years later it was reported that the cost of "the building of the Bromilaw key, and filling with redd, and of timber for the front" would amount to £1,833 6s. 6d. sterling.[1] McUre, writing in 1736, stated, "there is not such a fresh water harbour to be seen in any place in Britain. It is strongly fenced with beams of oak, fastened with iron butts within the wall thereof that the great boards of ice in time of thaw may not offend it." There were vessels to fill it; in 1727 Defoe reported "near fifty sail of ships every year" departing to America.

By 1757 Glasgow, whose population had grown to 23,546, was very different from the city of fifty years before. The industrial age had started; and it was becoming evident that further steps to improve the navigability of the Clyde must be taken if Glasgow was to maintain her progress and position. In 1755 John Smeaton, the engineer of the Eddystone Lighthouse and the Forth and Clyde Canal, was employed to report on the best methods for deepening the Clyde and a first Act of Parliament was secured in 1759.

An English engineer, John Golborne of Chester, who was consulted in 1768, recommended the building of jetties at intervals along the course of the river to confine it to a narrower channel, which could be dredged to encourage scouring by the tide. His suggestions were embodied in an Act of Parliament obtained in 1770—which also appointed the Town Council as trustees of the river—and three years later he was employed to carry out his plan. He undertook to make the river 6 feet deep and 300 feet wide at low water, by erecting 117 jetties on either side, but he succeeded in deepening the Clyde ten inches more than his £2,300 contract stipulated—being rewarded with an additional £1,500 and a silver cup. Between 1799 and 1806, on the advice of Rennie and Telford, the jetties were linked by parallel dykes to secure a continuous uniform channel. As a result in 1806 a vessel of 120 tons drawing 8½ feet reached the Broomielaw on an ordinary spring tide direct from Lisbon. Now at last Glasgow could feel that the sea had reached her very door.[2]

In November 1808 the city was first officially recognised as a separate port of register,[3] independent of Port Glasgow and Greenock. In the following year the Town Council of Glasgow (trustees of the river since 1770) were constituted statutory trustees with separate finances. Soon the increase of trade and shipping in the river induced the Clyde Trustees to ask for more powers and bring in five other members by an Act of 1825. In 1840 the Trust was reconstituted with 23 town council representatives and 10 others, all still from the Glasgow area. In 1858 the composition became 10 elected by the town council, 6 by the trading interests and 9 by the shipowners and ratepayers. In 1905, the Trust having acquired control of Erskine Ferry and Renfrew Har-

[1] 30,000 merks Scots.
[2] This meant that the Harbour of Glasgow had to grow. For later development of quays and docks see Appendix Table 59.
[3] In 1780 Glasgow had been raised from a "creek" to a "member port," the first ship to pay dues being the *Triton*, with 60 pipes of French wine. Glasgow was declared a head port for Customs in 1815.

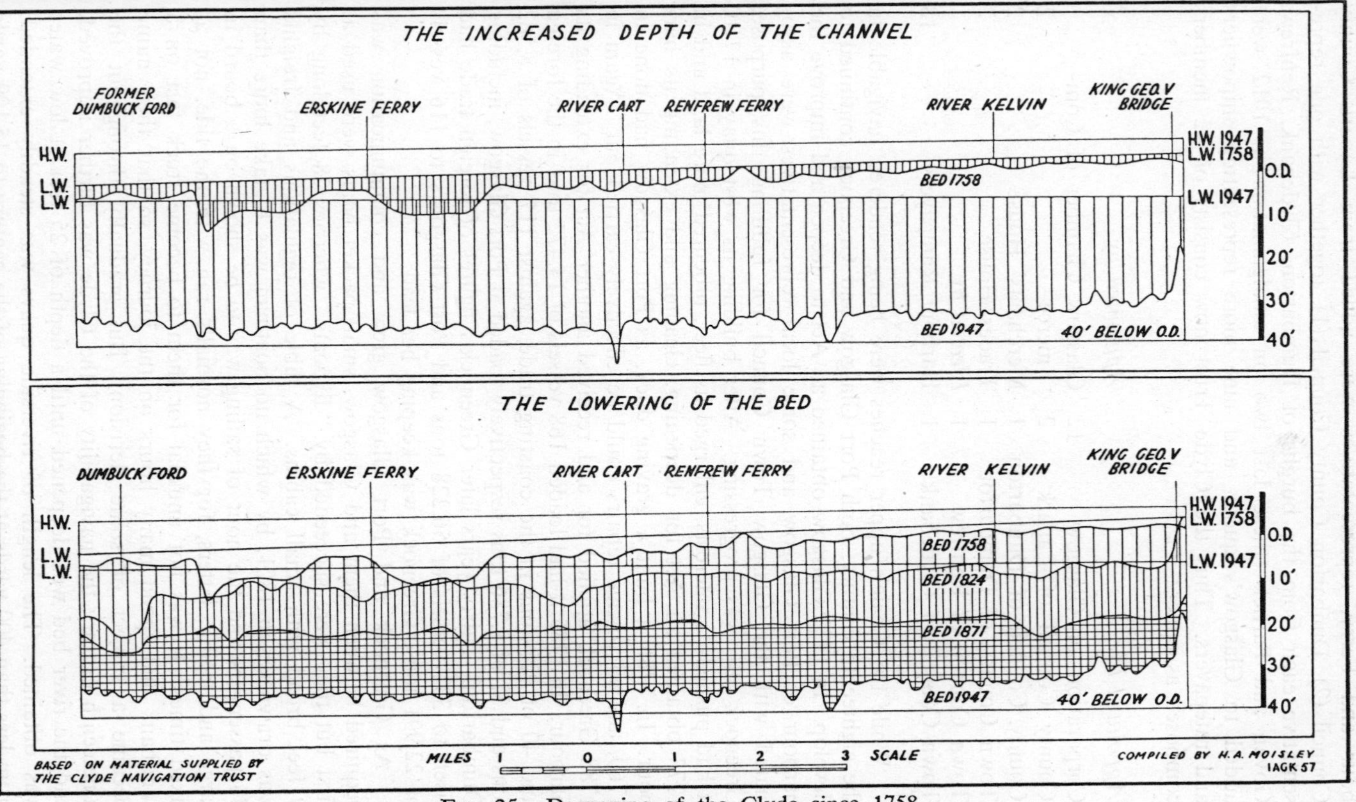

FIG. 25. Deepening of the Clyde since 1758.

bour and Ferry, representatives were added from Lanark County Council (2), Dunbarton County Council (1), together with one representative each from the burghs of Dumbarton, Clydebank, Renfrew, Govan and Partick—these last two on amalgamation in 1912 were added to Glasgow's quota—and nine more representing shipowners and ratepayers. Thus the Clyde Trust now consists of 42 members composed as under:

Appointed by		*Appointed by*	
Corporation of Glasgow	12	Glasgow Chamber of Commerce	2
County Council of Lanark	2	Merchants' House	2
County Council of Dunbarton	1	Trades House	2
Town Council of Dumbarton	1	*Elected by*	
Town Council of Renfrew	1		
Town Council of Clydebank	1	Harbour Ratepayers	18

While the Clyde's upper reaches were being rendered navigable in the eighteenth century, both Port Glasgow and Greenock continued to develop. In 1772 Glasgow obtained an Act to deepen and improve the harbour of Port Glasgow and some local representatives were associated with the Glasgow Town Council for fulfilling this purpose. Greenock also was progressing. After building its west quay in 1710, it had pushed its interests, enlarged its fleet, procured more land and in 1773 obtained an Act for deepening, cleaning and extending its harbour. In 1786 it built a graving dock, as Port Glasgow had done in 1760, and so voyage repairs could be effectively carried out. Again in 1788 Greenock applied for and received another Act for extending its harbour. In 1785 it had loaded 168 vessels of 14,472 tons in the foreign and 40 of 928 tons in the coasting trade, against 117 vessels of 8,562 tons and 37 of 1,786 tons respectively loaded at Port Glasgow, including Dumbarton. Thirty years later Greenock's figures of foreign trade had risen to 332 vessels of 56,228 tons and Port Glasgow's to 116 vessels of 22,991 tons; Greenock was keeping her lead.

As Greenock and Port Glasgow grew and communication was required between them and Glasgow, small packet boats were used at first but they were succeeded by "flyboats," wherries 28 feet long by 9 feet broad with small cabins. A table of regulations and freights was drawn up in 1801, by which no boatman was to take more than 40 passengers and the hour of sailing was to be shown on a board in large and legible letters, for they normally ran with the tide, not at fixed times. It was not unusual for them to become stuck fast on a sandbank and spend many hours on the journey, so that their name became a subject of some derision. But gradually throughout the nineteenth century the navigability of the Clyde was further improved, and the river bed was deepened until a depth of 25 feet at low water was obtained. The length of riverside quays was steadily extended, from less than 400 yards at the beginning of the century to 15,109 yards in 1900. In 1830 a Port Glasgow Harbour Act was obtained by which the Glasgow Town Council plus ten members from Port Glasgow were empowered to form in Newark Bay a wet dock of some ten acres. This, the first of its kind in Scotland, was completed in 1836 at a cost of £35,000; but in 1839 the quay collapsed and, there being no funds to repair it, the gates were removed and the harbour again became tidal. Every other dock on the Clyde, except the inner part of the James Watt Dock at Greenock built in 1872 and the small inner basin at Ardrossan, has been built tidal, in contrast with those at London, Bristol, Liverpool and Leith. Glasgow's small Kingston Dock was opened in 1867, to be followed by the Queen's Dock (1877-80), the Prince's Dock (1897), Rothesay Dock (1907) and King George V Dock (1931). The growth of the trade of the port is indicated by the fact that, whereas the tonnage of shipping arriving in 1828 was about 700,000 tons, by 1867 it was 1,800,000 tons and by 1900 it was 4,400,000 tons. The volume of goods handled in 1867 was 1,600,000 tons, but by 1900 it had risen to 7,300,000 tons, and by 1913 to 10,100,000 tons.

Inland Waterways

The development of inland water transport facilities began about the same time as that of the river and harbour, in the second half of the eighteenth century. In 1769 the Glasgow Magistrates felt the need of securing for the city a plentiful supply of coals, then most easily available in Old and New Monkland, twelve miles to the east. A canal was thought to be the best method of achieving this and James Watt was appointed to survey the ground; an Act was obtained and ten miles constructed, when the company found itself in financial difficulty and had to sell out at quarter value. The Monkland Canal was completed by the new owners in 1790 and coal began to come to the city by it. In the spring of 1813 three passage boats, horse drawn, were put on it and completed the run to Sheepford (10 miles) within one mile of Airdrie, in two hours and a half. This service continued until railways superseded it, and the transport of coal continued into the twentieth century, gradually falling off till the canal was closed in 1952.

Something more ambitious, however, had been suggested by Daniel Defoe in his *Tour of Scotland*, published in 1727. "If this city," he wrote, "could have a communication with the Firth of Forth so as to send their tobacco and sugar by water to Alloway, below Stirling, they would probably in a few years double their trade." It was not till 1763 that the tract for such a canal was surveyed by John Smeaton; a Bill for a four-feet-deep ditch canal was prepared in 1767 but this was withdrawn in favour of another, which became law in 1768, for "a navigation capable of conveying large vessels from Sea to Sea." Begun immediately from the Grangemouth end, the cut into the Old Basin at Hamilton Hill near Garscube Road was opened on 10 November 1777. Financial troubles delayed completion of the Forth and Clyde Canal to Bowling till 1790, when the Glasgow cut was also extended to Port Dundas and connected to the Monkland Canal which was completed in the same year. This was considered a great engineering achievement.[1] At first the company put on track boats carrying goods and passengers, but in 1808 replaced them with three purely passenger boats, which performed the run from Port Dundas to Lock No. 16 at Falkirk (25 miles) in five hours and a half. In 1822 the Forth and Clyde Navigation was extended by the Union Canal from Falkirk to Edinburgh, and in 1846 the other end at Bowling was completed by building an outer basin and lock. These two canals were bought by the Caledonian Railway in 1867; the Monkland is now closed and the traffic on the Forth and Clyde has dwindled to a mere trickle. Another canal, aiming at Ardrossan, was opened to Paisley and Johnstone in 1811, but, although used for a time by freight and passage boats, it was in 1885 filled in and converted into the Glasgow and South Western Railway's " Canal line." Its fate was symbolic of the ousting by the railway of the inland waterway in general.

Road Transport

Road transport also began to improve rapidly in the latter part of the eighteenth century, when agricultural improvement was transforming the countryside around Glasgow,[2] and emphasising the need for better rural communications. Up to about 1750 land transport was all by horseback, but after the first Turnpike Acts concerning the area were passed in 1752-3 road-making proceeded apace. A coach began to run to Edinburgh in 1758, taking 11 to 12 hours on the road. About 1788 this was succeeded by " diligences " which took between 7 and 8 hours, and in 1799 the Royal Telegraph coach brought this down to 6 hours. The London mail by way of Carlisle—hitherto it had come *via* Edinburgh—first reached Glasgow in 1788. By 1819 fifteen public coaches ran out from Glasgow daily and ten small coaches ran in the city itself—the first local service. All the vehicles in the city at that date totalled 103 4-wheeled and 155 2-wheeled carriages. By 1833 there was an average of 61 stage coaches departing and arriving daily.

As Glasgow began to grow in size the question of local transport loomed more important. The first horse-drawn omnibuses began to run in 1834 between the Broomielaw, Port Dundas and Port Eglinton, i.e. the Canal ports. Then under Robert Frame and Andrew Menzies from 1889 suburban buses began to go to Partick and Govan and Rutherglen and many intermediate parts. Menzies early saw the advantage of tramways, using rails in the streets; so he formed the Glasgow

[1] The canal was almost 39 miles in length, with aqueducts over the Luggie, the Kelvin and many other rivers, and with 39 locks and 33 drawbridges. Unfortunately the locks " for large vessels " only allowed for those of 68 feet keel by 19 feet beam, drawing 7ft. of water.

[2] In 1740 potatoes were first grown at Neilston and Kilsyth; turnips were first cultivated in 1760.

Tramway and Omnibus company and arranged for it to lease tramways to be laid by the Corporation. The first line, opened on 19 August 1872, extended from St. George's Cross to Eglinton Toll; other lines were soon added and when Menzies died in 1873 the company had 50 cars. Ten years later it had 233; in 1894 the Corporation took over the running of the system with 305 cars, still using horses, but on 13 October 1898 ran the first electric tramcar from Mitchell Street to Springburn. Soon the whole system was electrified and by 1902 had 536 cars; then began steady expansion by which the 73 miles of single track became 197 in 1912 and 271 in 1931. The Glasgow tramway system, based on Pinkston Power Station, became known as the cheapest and most efficient in the whole country; in 1912 it carried 179 million passengers at ½d. out of a total of 297 million. It then had 843 cars. By 1943 the number had grown to 1207. Corporation motor buses were introduced in 1924 and trolley or trackless trams in 1949[1]; a decision has now been made to give up the tramways, which is regretted by many who profess to enjoy their "smoothness and comfort." The finances in spite of cheap fares were till the last few years wonderfully buoyant; in 1917 all the outstanding capital liabilities of the undertaking were paid off and the same was again done during the Second World War. Postwar difficulties, however, have led to financial decline.

Other tramways in the area should also be noted. The Vale of Clyde Tramways, authorised 13 July 1871, ran horse cars from Govan to St. Vincent Place; they afterwards ceased to run past Paisley Road Toll. In 1878 they were replaced by steam cars, which were very fast in comparison; fares were 2d. inside and 1d. outside on top (but with a risk of sparks and smuts, so the inside accommodation was more popular). The Govan and Ibrox Tramways, running from the Toll to Whitefield Road, were opened in 1878. Both of these concerns were bought by Govan Town Council in 1893, leased to the Glasgow Tramway Company and then transferred to Glasgow Corporation in 1896. The Airdrie and Coatbridge Tramways Company, formed in 1900, connected these two towns by some fifteen double-deckers, but was taken over by Glasgow Corporation in 1922 and connected at Langloan to the city. The Paisley District Tramways Company started with horse trams and was a much bigger concern; and it served from May 1904 Paisley, Renfrew, Elderslie, Johnstone, Kilbarchan, Barrhead, Nitshill, Darnley and Thornliebank. In 1923, with 72 cars, it was taken over by the Glasgow system with which it had made contact at three places, and the two systems were integrated; it was then possible to travel from Airdrie to Ferguslie for the sum of 2d.[1] Two other systems which touched the Glasgow system were in the end

1 By November 1957 these amounted to 117 vehicles.

2 The Baillieston to Airdrie service was closed on 3 November 1956 when two other branches outwith the city, namely, Farme Cross to Cambuslang and Maryhill Park to Milngavie were also closed. The Paisley system ran for six months longer till 11 May 1957. So the service through Clydebank to Dalmuir West is now the only tramway route outwith the city.

replaced by the buses of the Central Scottish Motor Traction Company. The Dumbarton Burgh and County Tramways Company was incorporated in 1907 to work an electric system from Dalmuir through Old Kilpatrick, Bowling, Milton, Dumbarton, Alexandria, to Balloch for Loch Lomond, with branches to Bonhill and Jamestown, and to Barloan; it had a fleet of 32 cars. In 1900 the Hamilton, Motherwell and Wishaw Tramway Company was incorporated but by the time it was opened in July 1903 extensions were in prospect and the name was altered to the Lanarkshire Tramways Company. Eighty-eight cars ran on the 27 miles of track which were authorised but of this nothing now remains.

In 1897 the Glasgow District Subway Company opened a double underground circular line using cable operation, with fifteen stations from Govan and Partick to the centre of the city. There were difficulties in constructing the tunnels and the company spent a million and a half pounds and was really never out of financial difficulties. The method of haulage by a continuous rope also gave constant trouble and by 1923 the company felt that it would have to close down. So the Glasgow Corporation took it over and in 1935 electrified both lines; now officially called the Underground, but still the "Subway" by its older patrons, it has at last begun to pay and performs a very useful part in Glasgow transport. Its cramped dimensions, however, and the limited area it serves, have restricted its development. It really only came into its own with the "black-out" conditions of the recent war, which made it a very popular mode of travel.

Motor bus operation by the Corporation, having begun in 1924, expanded considerably with the development of new housing areas, though the policy was to confine the buses to the longer distance services and to areas not served by trams.[1] Motor omnibus services, run by private operators, between Glasgow and surrounding areas began on a small scale before 1914. They developed rapidly in the 1920's, and gradually the various small operators were absorbed by the larger undertakings, such as the Scottish Motor Traction Company (founded in Edinburgh in 1905), the Scottish General Transport Company (Kilmarnock, 1913), W. Alexander and Sons (Falkirk, 1924) and the Glasgow General Omnibus and Motor Company (1926). Meanwhile tramway companies serving the neighbouring industrial area, such as the Dunbartonshire and Lanarkshire companies, were converting their undertakings to motor bus operation. Eventually, in 1932, the larger undertakings were reorganised under the control of the Scottish Motor Traction Company, in which the L.M.S. and L.N.E. railways had acquired an interest in 1929. The Scottish General Company became the Western S.M.T. Company, while the Glasgow General Company became the Central S.M.T. Company, and later absorbed the Lanarkshire Traction Company, which was the old tramway company under a new name. The S.M.T. interests in this group of companies were

[1] These in November 1957 amount to 919 vehicles, housed in five garages.

bought out by the British Transport Commission in 1948, and they became the Scottish Group of the present day.

THE RAILWAYS

The earliest railway near Glasgow was the Monkland and Kirkintilloch line, which was really a feeder for the Monkland Canal, although ultimately partly incorporated in the Caledonian Railway main line and a North British branch line. It was opened in 1826, but the first railway to reach Glasgow was the Garnkirk and Glasgow, opened in 1831 from a station at St. Rollox, and later extended to Coatbridge. By this line minerals and then passengers were first brought into the city. In 1846 it was purchased by the "Caley," afterwards regraded into Buchanan Street Station, and on 15 February 1848 brought the first London train into Glasgow *via* Carlisle and Beattock. Actually from 1 July 1847 there had been a railway connection *via* York and Edinburgh with breaks at Tyne and Tweed but temporary bridges were ready by 15 October 1848 when services ran right through by the East Coast Route. Glasgow had become near London. The railway to the Scottish Capital had been opened on 18 February 1842 by the completion of the Edinburgh and Glasgow Railway from Queen Street, Glasgow to Haymarket, Edinburgh, the line being extended four and a half years later to Waverley; in 1865 it became part of the North British system, which incorporated the Helensburgh line also. The latter had begun with an amusingly isolated railway, the Bowling-Balloch, opened 16 June 1850 and leased to J. & G. Burns, as it had to be fed by a steamer service from Glasgow. Eight years later it was connected to Glasgow Queen Street at one end and to Helensburgh at the other. In 1894 the line was extended to Fort William and in 1901 to Mallaig, thus forming the West Highland Line and providing by MacBrayne's steamers the shortest route to Skye, Lewis and the Outer Hebrides.

But the first railway to put Glasgow in touch with a whole area was the Glasgow, Paisley, Kilmarnock and Ayr, which was opened in 1840 and speedily acquired the first Scottish railway, the Kilmarnock and Troon, built in 1811 as a horse tramway. In 1850 this combined with the Glasgow, Dumfries and Carlisle to form the Glasgow and South Western Railway; but it was not till 1876 when the Midland Railway reached Carlisle from London that the G. & S. W. R. could offer a through service. Meanwhile it had been developing its own area, reaching Castle Douglas in 1860, Kirkcudbright in 1864, Girvan in 1860 and Stranraer from there in 1876. It also shared in the Portpatrick and Wigtownshire Joint Railway which reached Stranraer in 1861 and connected with the Larne steamer service to Ireland. In 1869 it built the line from Kilmacolm to Greenock (Prince's Pier), which gave it connection with the Clyde Coast, as it had had with Arran *via*

Ardrossan for fifteen years. In 1873 a route to Kilmarnock *via* Barrhead was opened by the G. & S. W. R. jointly with the Caley, who in 1890 used this to reach Ardrossan and a Caley steamer route to Arran. Then in 1876 a railway bridge over the Clyde was built and the Sou'-West brought its trains into the fine new terminus of St. Enoch's. In 1885 it took over the Paisley Canal and laid an additional line westwards on the track the canal had followed.

In 1841 the Glasgow, Paisley and Greenock Railway was opened; aiming not only at mainland but also at coast steamer traffic it proved better at railway management and dropped the latter. The railway was taken over in 1851 by the Caledonian Railway, which by its Clydesdale Junction line, opened in July 1849, could run from Motherwell to Gushetfaulds, just south of Dixon's Blazes, and by the Govan and Pollok line could complete the connection. The Greenock Engine Works became the Caledonian locomotive works till St. Rollox was begun in 1856. The Greenock line with the Ayr line ran into Bridge Street Station, just south of the Clyde; but the Caley was just as keen to get across the river as the Sou'-West and on 1 August 1879 was able to open the Central Station right on Gordon Street. Major additions to it in 1890 and 1906 made it the finest station in Glasgow and allowed Bridge Street Station to be closed. The Glasgow Central Railway from Rutherglen to Maryhill was completed by 1896 and the Cathcart District Railway in 1894; both added much to the facilities provided from the Central but the dirt of many tunnels has lost them popularity and they await electrification if they are to be adequately used again.

In 1865 there had been built a railway from Port Glasgow to Wemyss Bay, from which place steamers had a short and speedy sail to Rothesay. This was taken over by the Caledonian Railway in 1890, when the trains were also run into Central Station, a move which was much appreciated by Rothesay travellers. Meantime on 1 June 1889 the Caledonian line to Greenock had been extended to Gourock through the longest tunnel in Scotland, 2,115 yards: the excavations from the tunnel were used to fill in the whole west shore of Gourock Bay and form a half-mile pier and station where trains run alongside the steamers. With the amalgamation of the railways Gourock supplanted Prince's Pier, Greenock, but its facilities were better.

Steamship Services

Closely linked with railway development, of course, are the local steamer services on the Clyde estuary. The modern Clyde passenger steamers are the successors of the packet boats and flyboats of the early nineteenth century already referred to. Although before the end of the eighteenth century the steam engine, by James Watt's inventions, had become a propulsive power which was transforming industry, it was not until 1801 that the first effective steam-driven ship—William Symington's *Charlotte Dundas*—ran on the Forth and Clyde Canal. The Clyde was now navigable and the *Comet* of 1812 and its many successors began by driving the flyboats off the river and giving a daily service (though timed to suit tides) to Port Glasgow and Greenock, which was soon extended to Dunoon and Rothesay, the Gareloch and Lochgoil, Ardrishaig and Inveraray, Arran and Campbeltown. Many who had travelled by coach and horseback found travelling by steamer much cheaper and more comfortable. In Clyde steamers there was a cabin, more or less cushioned, and a forecabin with bare boards, in which steerage passengers travelled at about half cabin rates. In the Irish and English services deck passengers were also taken at about a quarter or sometimes less. So the advent of steamers meant not only the replacement of flyboat and coach but the creation of many new travellers who had previously been content to stay at home.

As engines became more economical and vessels more commodious, fares became lower and the inducement to travel thus greater. The result was that the whole Clyde area became in summer an extension of Glasgow; there was also a closer section which became an extended suburbia. For the middle classes Cowal, Bute, Cumbrae, Arran and later Mid-Argyll and Kintyre became holiday haunts with the father often travelling daily to his business in town for part of the period; to make this possible fast services to Glasgow in the morning and back at night were required—it was on these runs that racing between rival steamers often occurred. For others who could not afford to stay away from home day sailings became popular and eventually covered almost the whole Firth of Clyde; but many took these sails from a holiday centre such as Helensburgh, Gourock, Largs, Dunoon or Rothesay. All that did not come just at once—it was the development of several decades.

To return to the vessels themselves, we must realise that to begin with they were like sailing ships of the time: bluff in the bows and not very fast. David Napier, one of the Clyde's most versatile engineers and inventors, who had provided the boiler for the first *Comet*, set himself the task of finding the best hull form to use the new prime mover. The form of hull adopted in 1818 for his *Rob Roy*, which opened all the year communication between Greenock and Belfast and then between Calais and Dover, became standard and older boats were lengthened and altered to it.[1] The mail route from Holyhead to Dublin was then supplied by two of Napier's steamers and the practicability of navigating all coastal and cross channel services by steam established. Regular services were run between Greenock and Belfast, Greenock and Liverpool, and Greenock and Dublin and these were soon routed from Glasgow as the river was deepened.

It would be impossible to name all the Glasgow citizens who con-

1 Even before this, Clyde-built steam vessels had opened up steam navigation on the Mersey, the Thames and the Rhine, while others built to similar designs were placed on every river and estuary.

tributed to the growth of Glasgow's shipping but several should be noted. Kirkman Finlay, who was much concerned with the setting up of weaving factories, was also a most enterprising merchant. He did much to destroy the monopoly of the East India Company and in 1816 sent the first vessel—the *Earl of Buckingham* of 600 tons—from Glasgow to India. He was chairman of the leading firm owning Clyde steamers, the Castle Steam Packet Company, which ran the Dunoon, Rothesay, Loch Fyne and Arran services. David Napier, as well as being an inventor, opened up the Holy Loch area with a steamboat service, putting an iron paddle steamer, the *Aglaia,* on Loch Eck, with connections by a steam road carriage from Kilmun and another steamer from Strachur to Inveraray. He was the first traffic integrator. After he went to London his engineer cousin, Robert Napier, besides being a part owner of many of the ships which he built, was with his sons owner of many Clyde and West Highland steamers, the last of which was the blockade-running *Neptune* of 1861. But it was as the builder of reliable steamers, not only for the river but for the coastal services and then for the new Atlantic service of the Cunard Company that he not only made his own name but also the name of the Clyde.[1]

Another notable contributor to Glasgow's commercial progress was Sir George Burns, who came into shipping almost by accident. A son of the minister of the Barony, he had with his brother James launched out in a produce business, though trained to the cotton trade. In 1824 the brothers Kidd, agents for six Liverpool smacks, having died, James suggested applying for the agency. George applied and was appointed. Agency led to ownership in sail and ownership in sail to ownership in steam. Soon he was in the Liverpool trade, the Ayr trade, the Belfast trade, the West Highland trade, the Londonderry trade, the Dublin trade, and then in 1839 came his participation, originally with a small share but finally with one third, in the great Cunard enterprise of the North Atlantic passenger fleet which commenced with the *Britannia, Acadia, Caledonia* and *Columbia.* Meanwhile in 1846 he bought up the Castle Company and the Clyde steamers which ran for the Greenock Railway, and for the next four years had the lion's share of the Clyde trade along with the Bowling-Balloch Railway. In February 1851, however, he decided to take up Mediterranean services and to give up the Clyde and West Highland fleets. David Hutcheson, who had been with the Kidds and become his chief clerk, took over the latter along with his own brother Alexander and David MacBrayne, the son of Burns' sister Elizabeth. This firm, first under the senior partner and then after 28 years under the junior partner alone, opened up the cargo and tourist traffic to almost every island and corner of the Scottish West Coast. The Burns' Liverpool and Irish fleet continued under family management till in 1920 it was bought over by Coast Lines of Liverpool and amalgamated in 1922 with the smaller but older Laird fleet (now known as the Burns & Laird Lines, Ltd.).

Actually the first steamer to cross the Atlantic was the Clyde-

[1] See Chapter 6 (Shipbuilding).

engined (but Leith built) *Sirius*, but it was the Cunard fleet running from Liverpool which established a regular service and defeated American competition. It was not till 1850 that Tod & McGregor's screw steamer *City of Glasgow* showed the possibility of a direct Glasgow to New York passenger service. Two other companies failed but in 1856 Handyside & Henderson, who had been in the Glasgow-Lisbon trade from 1838, took it up and the Anchor Line which they founded has kept up that connection now for 100 years. From 1859 Handyside was replaced by John Henderson, who with his brother Thomas developed the Atlantic service and the Mediterranean service, which latter, with the opening of the Suez Canal, soon extended to India; there was also an Italian emigrant service to New York. From 1865 to 1939 this company ran a weekly passenger and cargo service from Glasgow, which carried many emigrants from the Continent and Ireland, as well as from Scotland and England. Just before 1914 this was maintained by the *Columbia* (1902), *Caledonia* (1904), *California* (1907) and *Cameronia* (1911), a very fine fleet for the times. From 1911 till 1931 the Anchor Line was associated with the Cunard Line but with the depression the firms separated and the Anchor Line changed hands. The fine passenger vessels which kept up the New York sailings between the wars—the *Cameronia* (1920), *Tuscania* (1922), *California* (1923), *Transylvania* (1925) and *Caledonia* (1925)—formed the largest fleet sailing regularly from the Clyde, but the Second World War closed down this service; it is now cargo only across the Atlantic but the Anchor Line maintains passenger and cargo services to India.

In 1854 Hugh Allan commenced a service from Glasgow to Montreal and gradually developed a regular trade not only from the Clyde but also from the Mersey and the Thames. The Allan Line was ultimately absorbed by the Canadian Pacific to the considerable loss of Glasgow. Their *Victorian* (1904) and *Virginian* (1905) were the first turbine liners on the Atlantic service, as their *Buenos Ayrean* (1880) had been the first steel liner. In 1891 the Allan Line had a North Atlantic fleet of 37 steamers with weekly services from Glasgow to Canada and Glasgow to New York, fortnightly from Glasgow to Boston and Glasgow to Philadelphia, and monthly from Glasgow to the Plate: two others ran from Liverpool and one from London. They decreased gradually till amalgamation in 1917 reduced the number to 15 (it had been 20 in 1914).

In 1855 John and William Donaldson founded the firm of Donaldson Brothers who till 1870 were only concerned with sail to the Plate. In 1870, however, they inaugurated a steam service and in 1878 started a Glasgow-Canada service. Till 1905 this was mainly a cargo service but in that year the cargo vessel *Athenia* was converted into a passenger vessel, to be joined ultimately by three other new craft, thus allowing for a weekly service. So early in the century there were three large liners leaving the Clyde every Saturday for America—an Anchor with two or three black funnels, an Allan with a red, white and black one, and a Donaldson with a black, white and black stack—capable among them of carrying some 4,500 people. In 1916 the Anchor Line took over a controlling interest in the four Donaldson passenger ships, the survivors of which afterwards ran in co-operation with the Cunard Line. After 1935 the Donaldson Atlantic Line, a new firm, ran the *Athenia* (1923) and *Letitia* (1925), the former becoming on 3 September 1939 the first victim of the German submarine attacks of the Second World War. In the latter years of the war some of the greatest fleets of passenger vessels ever assembled sailed from the Tail of the Bank but in the postwar period the once great passenger trade of the Clyde has been reduced to the occasional call of a Cunard or Canadian Pacific liner on its way to or from Liverpool. But Prestwick Airport, normally fog free, handles a great passenger trade.

Of other ocean services Glasgow has not been neglectful. George Smith & Sons, already owning 29 iron sailing ships in the India trade, decided in 1870 to build steamers and so inaugurated the City Line, now part of the Ellerman fleet. The opening of the Suez Canal caused Patrick Henderson & Co. to concentrate their sailing ships on the New Zealand trade and replace their Rangoon traders in steam; this service still runs. The Clan Line of Charles Cayzer & Co., later Cayzer, Irvine & Co., running to South Africa and India, was also a Glasgow firm but is now managed in London; in January 1956 it took over a controlling interest in a merger with the Union-Castle Line, also of Scots foundation. There were also towards the end of the nineteenth century several well-known lines of sailing ships, the Castle Line of Thomas Skinner & Co., the Blair Line of Thomson & Gray, the Shire Line of Thomas Law & Co. and the Loch and Sea Lines of the Glasgow Shipping Company. These have all given up but until the Second World War there were over thirty smaller firms owning steamers not on regular services.[1] Unfortunately many of these small firms have been wound up and only some half dozen now (1957) survive. Glasgow shipowners are fewer to-day.

Up till 1840 the Clyde river steamers had run from the Bridge Wharf or Broomielaw but in the next year the Greenock Railway was opened and steamers were bought to run in connection with it; after six years they were given up and plans made for the Glasgow boats to call. By 1852 the Caledonian Railway had taken over the line and again tried steamers of its own for two years before again giving up. In 1865 the Wemyss Bay Railway on opening tried ownership twice and gave up. In 1866 the North British Railway began running its own steamers, from Helensburgh, failed and gave up, but tried again in 1870, this time successfully. In 1869 the Glasgow and South Western Railway reached Greenock and by providing trains almost alongside steamers diverted most of the traffic from the Caledonian without owning any

[1] One such is Maclay and MacIntyre, of which the then head, Sir Joseph (afterwards Lord) Maclay was in 1916 made the first Shipping Controller and contributed much to the winning of the First World War.

vessels. But when in 1889 the Caledonian tunnelled through to Gourock and put their own vessels on, the Glasgow and South Western fought back and did likewise. As the North British Railway, to secure a service of trains alongside their steamers, had substituted Craigendoran Pier in 1883 for Helensburgh, the 'nineties found three railway companies running fleets against each other with the private owners being gradually pushed out as their craft were surpassed. Yet it was a private owner, Captain James Williamson, who in conjunction with William Denny & Brothers and Sir Charles Parsons inaugurated the first commercial turbine steamer *King Edward* which in 1901 triumphantly demonstrated the feasibility and economy of a turbine-driven Clyde steamer. The same concern in 1926 demonstrated high-pressure turbines in the vessel *King George V*.

In 1900 there were 10 Caledonian craft, 10 G. & S. W., 9 N. B., and 17 privately owned, amounting to 15,175 tons with a capacity for carrying 52,249 passengers; in 1906 the number was the same, 46, but the tonnage rose to 16,560 and the capacity to 56,824 passengers. In 1909 by mutual consent competition was reduced and by 1922 war losses and the scrapping of old ships had reduced the fleet to 30, consisting of 5 Caledonian, 6 G. & S. W., 6 N. B. and 13 privately owned of 12,447 tons with a capacity of 39,617 passengers. Next year the grouping of the railways brought the first two fleets under London Midland and Scottish Railway control. This company in 1928 took over with Coast Lines the business of David MacBrayne Ltd.; the two firms of Turbine Steamers Ltd. and Williamson Buchanan Steamers Ltd. were taken over in 1935 and the Campbeltown Steamers in 1937, so that only the London and North Eastern Railway vessels, the successors of the N.B.R., were outside L.M.S.R. control. With Second War losses and subsequent scrappings the Clyde fleet was in 1947 of 10,188 tons and had a capacity of 25,199 passengers. British Railways took over in the next year and have now substituted new motor craft for older vessels, increasing the tonnage to 11,110 tons but reducing the capacity to 21,126 passengers.[1] To-day in the summer no boat is kept spare, whereas in 1906 three or four were so retained, but the wasteful competition of that time meant much surplus tonnage kept. Monopoly even under a publicly owned concern has its difficulties, as the Clyde learned in the early 1950's, when it was only after a very considerable agitation that many smaller piers, not closed by economic necessity, were retained in service. Central piers, such as Dunoon, Rothesay and Brodick with connecting motor buses, had by that time taken over the duties of many smaller piers and the four motor car ferries, which maintain the main services, do not call at any small piers at all. None of the ferry landings such as Corrie, Pirnmill or King's Cross have functioned since 1939. Of the 77 piers and ferries used for landing in the early years of the century only 30 are functioning now in 1957.

[1] With the new vessel *Glen Sannox* (1957) this became 12,217 tons and 26,055 passengers.

In Glasgow Harbour below the Jamaica Bridge and King George V Bridge there has been for many years a service of ferries. At first the craft employed were ordinary rowing boats, propelled by oars, and evidently sometimes also used for putting passengers on and off the Clyde steamers. Unfortunately these were not infrequently overloaded and some of the ferry boats were sunk by the wash of passing vessels. So in 1865 the Clyde Trust built a double-ended steam ferry with boiler and engine amidships and a propeller and steering wheel at either end, to carry about 90 passengers; other similar vessels followed and replaced the rowing boats. By 1930 nineteen of these had been built but from 1934 diesel engines have replaced steam and the number of passengers has risen to 140. At Govan and lower down the river the transport of vehicles had to be considered. It was first secured by a hand-operated chain ferry, replaced in 1867 by a power-operated chain ferry; this type is still in use at Erskine and Renfrew. But for Whiteinch, Govan and Finnieston vehicular ferries, a new type was built, in 1890 and afterwards, of double twin screw steam and later diesel vessels, which carry variable platforms, adjustable to road level as the tide falls and rises.

The Clyde never had the complicated local water services once enjoyed on the Thames but there were some such. In 1817 David Napier ran the *Marion* from Glasgow to Rutherglen and in the middle 1850's Thomas Seath, the Rutherglen shipbuilder, ran the *Artizan* on the same run, following her with the *Royal Burgh* and the *Royal Reefer*. But in 1884 the same builder produced for the Clyde Trust six small screw steamers, *Clutha* Nos. 1 to 6, carrying from 235 to 350 passengers. These ran from the Victoria Bridge, calling at floating landing stages down to Whiteinch, some four and a half miles, at a standard 1d. fare. In 1890-1 four more were added and the service grew so that in 1896 twelve were in service and were carrying some two and a half million passengers annually. The opening of the Subway (underground railway) next year affected them somewhat but the introduction of the Corporation's electric trams in 1901 provided an opposition which was too much for them and at the end of 1903 they were withdrawn. Thus ended almost twenty years of water buses.

Local trade in coal, lime and other bulk products up to a hundred years ago was carried in sloops, schooners, gabbarts and other wooden craft. But, as iron hulls for passenger steamers became general in the 1840's, they were also tried for cargo carrying, propelled by a screw. Ability to use the Forth and Clyde Canal being a desirable factor, these craft were restricted to the size of its locks, being made about 66 feet long by about 19 feet broad. The engines, placed right aft, at first exhausted into the air, from which fact the boats were called " puffers," and though the engines now fitted may be more normal, the name has stuck. For a hundred years puffers have carried loads across Scotland and to every corner of the Clyde and West Highlands. Where there is a pier they can come in at high tide and sit on the bottom as they discharge their cargoes but they can equally well lie on a suitable shore and fill up the carts which come alongside on the hard sand. A slightly bigger type, 84 feet long, fits the locks of the Crinan Canal and can take almost half as much again as the 90 to 100 tons carried by modern puffers. Altogether some four hundred puffers have been built but, except in the service to the islands, they are now suffering from the competition of the alternative motor lorry transport available. Yet J. & J. Hay have been puffer owners for a hundred years and Ross & Marshall for over eighty. Larger coasters with two or even three holds are engaged in tramp services to and from Ireland, England and Wales. But regular coastal routes are still run by the vessels of the Clyde Shipping Company as for the last hundred years, and the Bristol Channel trade is maintained by William Sloan and Co. as for over ninety years. Coast Lines took over Langlands and Lamonts, as well as many of the coastal traders. But all alike have cut out the passenger side of the business and confined themselves to cargo; and in that too they are well aware of road transport and the opposition which it offers.

It is interesting to note the reasons for this given by Mr. Alan D. Cuthbert, Joint Managing Director of the Clyde Shipping Company. (1) Full use of passenger accommodation was for three or four months only. (2) Port dues are assessed on net tonnage of whole ship including passenger space, whether occupied or not. (3) A stewardess is necessary if ladies are carried. (4) Regulations require a radio officer when there are more than 12 passengers, in spite of the efficiency of the radio telephone used. (5) Regulations for survey of passenger vessels are more stringent and more expensive than for cargo vessels. (6) Satisfying modern standards for crew makes difficult the provision of space for passengers in a composite vessel mostly dependent on cargo earnings. (7) Adherence to a passenger sailing programme incurs overtime for dock labour, which could be avoided by retaining the ship for cargo working next day. Yet in spite of being only cargo vessels nowadays, they give Glasgow and the West of Scotland the sea services needed by an island nation and use the Firth and River Clyde as made by God and developed by man.

THE PRESENT SYSTEM

J. F. SLEEMAN

The Port of Glasgow To-day

Quays and Docks

The Clyde Navigation Trust has under its care the whole of the river, from Albert Bridge, Glasgow, to Newark Castle, Port Glasgow, a distance of 18 miles. The bulk of the trade is, however, concentrated in the port of Glasgow proper, which may be said to consist of the river quays and docks occupying the six miles between Albert Bridge and Rothesay Dock, Clydebank. All the quays and docks are open to the tide without locks. The various port facilities can be conveniently grouped as under:

The upper river quays include the Upper Harbour, or Customs House Quay, between Jamaica and Albert Bridges, and the quays on both sides of the river between George V Bridge and Finnieston, together with Kingston Dock. Customs House Quay is used mainly by river barges unloading sand and gravel. The lower quays are used by coastal shipping and the berths are mostly allocated to various shipping companies. General Terminus Quay, on the south bank, was used by British Railways, and was formerly an important centre of coal export. A plan is at present under way to construct new wharfage facilities there to unload 12,000 ton iron-ore ships for rail delivery to Clyde Iron Works.

Queen's Dock is on the north bank below Finnieston and Prince's Dock is opposite it on the south bank, below Plantation. The two docks, and the adjoining Plantation and Stobcross Quays, and Yorkhill basin, are used mainly for the foreign-going general cargo trade. The Trustees' three graving docks are situated just to the west of Prince's Dock. There are also three privately owned graving docks lower down the river, at Meadowside and Elderslie.

Below the Queen's and Prince's Dock the river banks on both sides are largely occupied by shipbuilding yards. On the north side, however, above Whiteinch, are three installations belonging to the Trust, the Meadowside Granary, the Merklands Animal Lairage, and the large fruitsheds adjoining it.

King George V Dock at Shieldhall on the south bank was opened in 1931, and the west side of it was equipped only during the recent war. Its berths are allocated to regular ocean liner companies. Shieldhall Riverside Berthage, which adjoins, serves neighbouring factories and timber depots. To the west of this dock are situated the Deanside and Braehead transit depots, built during the recent war to handle the greatly increased traffic through the docks.

Rothesay Dock is outside the city boundary and lies between Yoker and Clydebank. It is used mainly for the discharge of iron ore and the shipping of coal. On the south side of the river, adjoining Renfrew Ferry, are the Trust's main workshops and slipway.

Summary details of dock and quay facilities are given in Table XLIX.

TABLE XLIX

DOCK AND QUAY FACILITIES IN GLASGOW, 1956

Docks	*Quays* *linear yards*	*Land area* *acres*	*Water area* *acres*	*Depth at* L.W.O.S.T. *ft.*
Kingston	789	4.66	4.61	13–24
Queen's	3334	25.49	33.75	18–20
Prince's	3737⅓	39.84	35.00	20–27
King George V	1734	48.61	19.95	32
Rothesay	2044⅔	54.24	20.43	24
Yorkhill Basins	1079⅔	15.46	3.79	25
Riverside quays				
North	4593	44.57	255.09 (North and South)	13–24
South	4234⅔	32.16		
Total	21,546⅓	265.03	372.62	

SOURCE: Clyde Navigation Trust.

The Trustees provide cranes and sheds, but do not carry out stevedoring and master porterage, except at Meadowside Granary. Stevedores and master porters are, however, licensed by the Trustees. Towing is carried out by two contractors, the Clyde Shipping Company and Steel & Bennie. Lighterage traffic is virtually absent from the Clyde, since the factories and warehouses to and from which traffic is consigned rarely have a water frontage. Pilotage is carried out by the Clyde Pilotage Authority, and is compulsory between Glasgow and Gourock, or, for passenger ships, between Glasgow and Cumbrae.

The Trade of the Port

Glasgow is essentially a regional industrial port serving Scotland and part of Northern England, rather than Britain as a whole. It has little passenger traffic.

In the value of its overseas trade, Glasgow ranks fifth among British ports, coming after London, Liverpool, Hull and Manchester, and accounting for about 4 per cent of the total. As an exporting port it ranks third, after London and Liverpool, because of its valuable export of machinery and other local manufactures, and it handled about

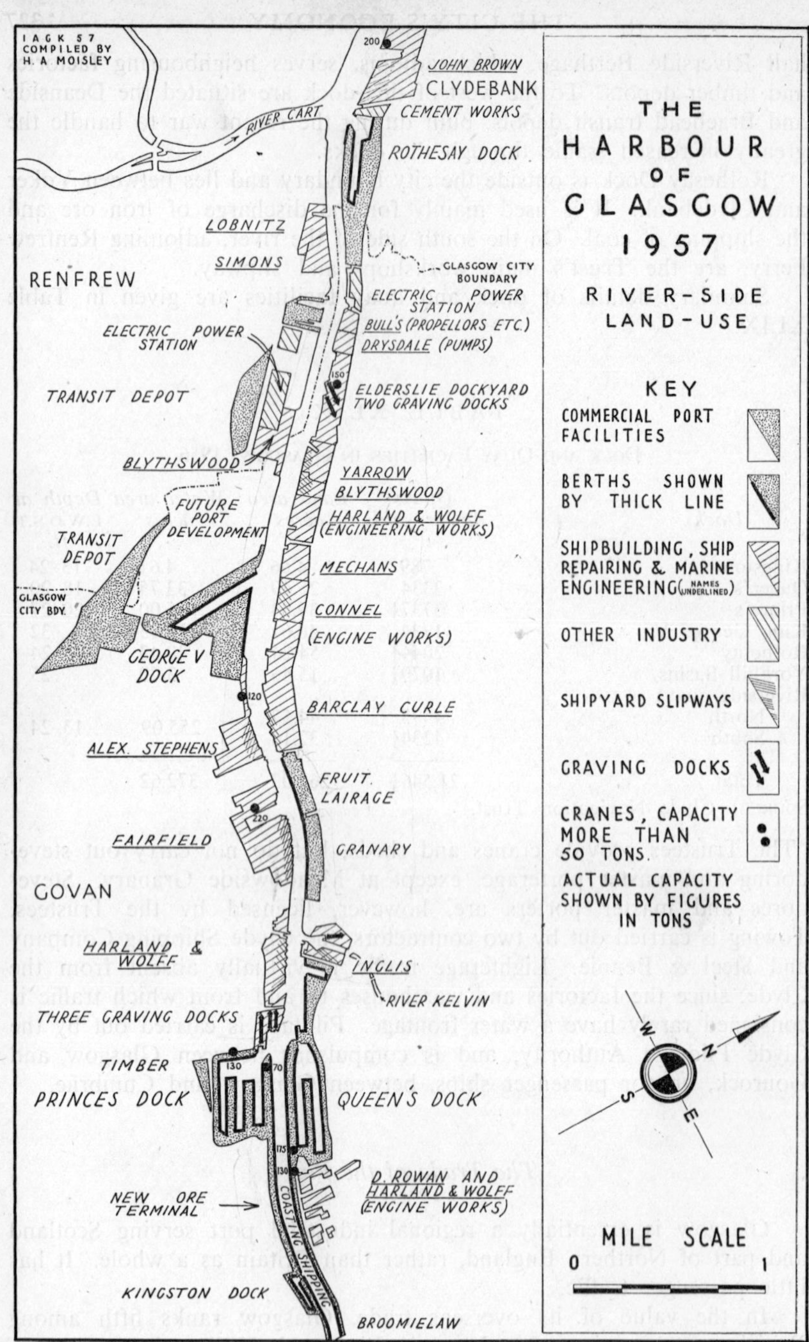
IAGK 57
COMPILED BY
H. A MOISLEY
THE
HARBOUR
OF
GLASGOW
1957
RIVER-SIDE
LAND-USE
KEY
COMMERCIAL PORT FACILITIES
BERTHS SHOWN BY THICK LINE
SHIPBUILDING, SHIP REPAIRING & MARINE ENGINEERING (NAMES UNDERLINED)
OTHER INDUSTRY
SHIPYARD SLIPWAYS
GRAVING DOCKS
CRANES, CAPACITY MORE THAN 50 TONS.
ACTUAL CAPACITY SHOWN BY FIGURES IN TONS
MILE SCALE
0
1
N
E
S
W
JOHN BROWN
CLYDEBANK
CEMENT WORKS
RIVER CART
ROTHESAY DOCK
LOBNITZ
SIMONS
RENFREW
GLASGOW CITY BOUNDARY
ELECTRIC POWER STATION
BULL'S (PROPELLORS ETC.)
DRYSDALE (PUMPS)
ELECTRIC POWER STATION
TRANSIT DEPOT
ELDERSLIE DOCKYARD TWO GRAVING DOCKS
BLYTHSWOOD
YARROW
BLYTHSWOOD
FUTURE PORT DEVELOPMENT
HARLAND & WOLFF (ENGINEERING WORKS)
TRANSIT DEPOT
MECHANS
GLASGOW CITY BDY.
CONNEL
(ENGINE WORKS)
GEORGE V DOCK
BARCLAY CURLE
ALEX. STEPHENS
FRUIT LAIRAGE
FAIRFIELD
GRANARY
GOVAN
HARLAND & WOLFF
INGLIS
RIVER KELVIN
THREE GRAVING DOCKS
TIMBER
PRINCES DOCK
QUEEN'S DOCK
D. ROWAN AND HARLAND & WOLFF (ENGINE WORKS)
NEW ORE TERMINAL
COASTING SHIPPING
KINGSTON DOCK
BROOMIELAW
200
150
120
220
130
70
115
130

FIG. 26.

six per cent by value of Britain's foreign exports in 1954. As an importing port, on the other hand, it came only seventh, behind Bristol and Southampton, and accounted for only about three per cent of the total.

Table L shows the average annual tonnage of shipping and of goods recorded by the Clyde Navigation Trust for five-year periods since 1900. The figures refer to the whole of the Trust's area, but the port of Glasgow proper accounts for the overwhelming preponderance of the traffic.

TABLE L

CLYDE NAVIGATION TRUST—TONNAGE OF VESSELS AND GOODS 1859-1955

Period	*Tonnage (000 tons)*			
	Vessels (arrivals only)	*Goods*		
		Imports	*Exports*	*Total*
Annual Totals				
1859-60	—	—		1192
1869-70	1,992	860	1062	1921
1879-80	2,994	1252	1401	2653
1889-90	3,497	2118	2678	4795
1899-1900	4,362	3106	4110	7215
Five-yearly averages	*(arrivals and departures)*			
1901-05	10,087	3479	4816	8295
1906-10	11,884	3869	5790	9660
1911-15	13,027	3810	6179	9990
1916-20	9,965	3686	4331	8018
1921-25	12,209	2855	4145	7000
1926-30	13,769	2974	4085	7059
1931-35	13,024	2481	3488	5975
1936-40	15,489	3625	3297	6922
1941-45	15,992	5258	3482	8740
1946-50	11,927	3646	2029	5675
Annual totals				
1950-51	13,569	3412	2244	5655
1951-52	13,681	3952	2058	6010
1952-53	14,225	3764	1869	5634
1953-54	14,554	4013	1906	5920
1954-55	14,634	4724	1995	6719

SOURCE: Based on the Clyde Navigation Trust's *Annual Statistics.*

Up to the late 1930's, the volume of exports regularly exceeded the volume of imports. This was due to the predominance of coal exports, which in 1906-10, for instance, averaged 3,155,000 tons annually, including both foreign and coastal trade, and also exports for ships' bunkers. Even in 1926-30, they still averaged 2,418,000 tons annually, and in 1931-5, 2,283,000 tons. The shrinkage of exports tonnage since 1946 is entirely due to the falling off of coal shipments, which in 1946-50 averaged only 517,000 tons annually.[1]

The volume of imports shrank considerably in the 1920's and 1930's

[1] In 1954-5 coal shipments amounted to only 234,993 tons, including bunkers.

and this was due mainly to the drop in iron ore imports, owing to the depressed state of the local iron and steel industry. There were marked shrinkages in 1921-2, 1926-7, and 1931-3, with recoveries in 1923-5, 1928-9 and from 1934 onwards. Iron ore imports had averaged 1,192,000 tons annually in 1906-10, but in 1926-30 the average was only 405,300 tons, and in 1931-5 it fell to 143,000 tons.

Import volumes rose steeply to record heights during the years 1941-5, when the diversion of ships from east coast ports led to the Clyde's becoming one of the chief wartime ports. Export tonnages also expanded during the war years, but less markedly, for coal shipments were already beginning to fall off from about 1942.

Of the total tonnage of goods in 1954-5, foreign trade accounted for some 4,626,000 tons, or 69 per cent, and coastwise trade for 2,093,000 tons or 31 per cent. The proportion of foreign trade was higher in earlier years—e.g. about 73 per cent in 1912-13 and the same in the early 'twenties. The reduction is due largely to the falling off in foreign coal shipments and in iron ore imports.

By volume in 1954-5 imports (foreign and coastal together) accounted for 70 per cent of the total and exports for 30 per cent. By value, however, the position is quite different, since the imports consist largely of bulky goods of low value. Iron ore, for instance, accounted for 1,235,000 tons, or 26 per cent, grain for 553,000 tons, or 12 per cent, and oil for 836,000 tons, or 17½ per cent. Thus these three items together made up 55½ per cent of total import tonnage. The exports, on the other hand, are now predominantly manufactured goods of greater value, the only bulk items of importance in 1954-5 being coal (235,000 tons or 11.8 per cent), and iron and steel (448,000 tons or 22.5 per cent).

Figures of trade by value are available, for foreign trade only, from the *Annual Statement of Trade of the United Kingdom.* Particulars for 1954 are given in Table LI.

By value in foreign trade, exports in 1954 exceeded imports considerably. Imports, as is usual in Britain, consisted mainly of foodstuffs and raw materials, and the most valuable single classes were crude petroleum, grain, and fruit and vegetables, with the bulky iron ore imports considerably further down the scale. Over 75 per cent of the exports consisted of manufactured goods, the only important exception being whisky. Among manufactures, the most valuable single classes were machinery, iron and steel goods, vehicles, ships, cotton goods (mainly sewing threads from Paisley), metal manufactures and floor coverings. Re-exports were unimportant, for Glasgow has little entrepôt trade.

Glasgow is not an important passenger port, apart from local coastal and Irish services. Long-distance passengers embarked in the year ending 31 June 1953, for instance, numbered 9,097, and those landed, only 1,195. Short-distance passengers embarked and landed totalled 487,166, of whom 214,008 were accounted for by the Clyde Coast pleasure steamers and the West Highland services, 236,007 by

TABLE LI

FOREIGN TRADE OF GLASGOW BY VALUE, 1954

IMPORTS

	£000	Per cent of Total
Class A, Food, Drink and Tobacco:		
Grain and Flour	12,976	12.3
Fruit and Vegetables	8,228	7.8
Meat	5,177	4.9
Tobacco	4,250	4.0
Live animals for food	3,497	3.3
Dairy produce	1,446	1.4
Other	7,684	7.3
Total	43,258	41.1
Class B, Basic Materials:		
Iron ore and scrap	6,408	6.1
Wood and timber	3,084	2.9
Oil seeds	3,014	2.9
Rubber	2,740	2.6
Wool	2,306	2.2
Hemp and flax	1,763	1.7
Other	6,962	6.6
Total	26,277	25.0
Class C, Mineral Fuels and Lubricants:		
Crude petroleum	17,555	16.7
Refined oils	2,061	2.0
Coal	1,061	1.0
Other	425	0.4
Total	21,100	20.1
Class D, Manufactured Goods:		
Machinery	3,313	3.1
Paper and cardboard	1,885	1.8
Non-ferrous metals	1,472	1.4
Chemicals	1,174	1.1
Other	6,197	5.9
Total	14,041	13.3
Class E, Miscellaneous:		
Total	535	0.5
Total imports	105,213	100.0

EXPORTS

	£000	Per cent of Total
Class A, Food, Drink and Tobacco:		
Whisky	26,650	17.0
Other	6,868	4.4
Total	33,518	21.4
Class B, Basic Materials:		
Total	2,463	1.6
Class C, Mineral Fuels and Lubricants:		
Total (including coal and coke—238)	738	0.5
Class D, Manufactured Goods:		
Machinery—non-electric	34,135	21.8
Iron and steel	13,854	8.8
Vehicles—road, rail and air	11,675	7.4
New ships for foreign owners	10,194	6.5
Cotton yarns, threads and fabrics	6,835	4.4
Metal manufactures	6.189	3.9
Floor coverings	5,266	3.4
Jute, linen, hemp and misc. goods	4,892	3.1
Chemicals	4,201	2.7
Electrical machinery and appliances	3,592	2.3
Paper and cardboard	3,183	2.0
Woollen yarns and fabrics	2,991	1.9
Other	11,386	7.3
Total	118,393	75.5
Class E, Miscellaneous:		
Total	1,725	1.1
Total exports	156,838	100.0
Re-exports	921	—

SOURCE: *Annual Statement of Trade of the United Kingdom.*

the Northern Ireland services and the remainder by services to and from the Irish Republic.[1]

Ships and Shipping Companies

Glasgow, as we have seen, was first recognised as a separate port of register in 1809, but before that date many ships belonging to Glasgow shipowners were registered at Port Glasgow or Greenock. As late as 1820 there were still only 84 ships, totalling 6,384 tons, registered in Glasgow, as against 114, of 18,255 tons, at Port Glasgow, 341 of 46,171 tons, at Greenock, and 121, of 10,487 tons, at Irvine. Numbers and tonnage of ships registered in Glasgow at later dates are given below:

SHIPS REGISTERED AT GLASGOW HARBOUR

Year	*Number of Ships*	*Net Tonnage*
1860	660	212,028
1900	1,605	1,582,229
1938	1,060	1,371,433
1953	710	874,485
1954	703	840,896

SOURCE: *Annual Returns Navigation and Shipping, U.K.*, and H.M. Customs, Glasgow.

Figures of registration are less significant nowadays than they once were, since the practice is for all the ships owned by a firm with the head office in a certain port to be registered in that port irrespective of whether they ever trade there. The fact that Glasgow in 1938 came third among British ports in the tonnage of shipping registered, but only fifth in value of foreign trade, thus reflects the extensive development of local shipping firms.

Glasgow has a considerable number of locally established shipping concerns. Some 30 companies are recorded as having head offices in Glasgow, with fleets varying from 30 or more down to one or two. Three are engaged on regular foreign-going passenger and cargo services, though they do not all operate passenger services from Glasgow. Four operate regular foreign-going cargo services, two operate regular coastal passenger and cargo services and three operate regular coastal cargo services. The remainder are general tramp owners apart from one specialist oil-tanker firm, and one (a subsidiary of Imperial Chemicals Ltd.) which specialises in carrying chemicals.

In addition to the local firms, many other lines naturally use the port, and regular cargo services are available, at varying intervals, to and from most of the important ports of the world.

[1] Figures supplied by the Clyde Navigation Trust.

Railways

The Railway System

The railway system of the Glasgow area owes its form largely to the competition between the three companies of pre-grouping days, the Caledonian, North British, and Glasgow and South-Western.

The main routes radiating from the city are as follows:

(1) The former Caledonian main line to Carlisle *via* Motherwell, Carstairs and Beattock, and to England *via* the West Coast Route.
(2) An offshoot from this, to Edinburgh *via* Holytown and Midcalder.
(3) The Glasgow and South-Western main line to Carlisle *via* Kilmarnock and Dumfries and to England *via* the Midland route.
(4) To Paisley, Kilwinning, Ayr and Stranraer, with an offshoot from Kilwinning to Ardrossan and Largs.
(5) To Greenock (Princes Pier) *via* Bridge of Weir.
(6) To Paisley, Port Glasgow, Greenock and the Clyde Coast.
(7) To Dumbarton and Helensburgh and to Fort William and Mallaig *via* the West Highland line.
(8) To Larbert, Stirling, Perth, Dundee, Aberdeen and Inverness, with an offshoot from Dunblane to Oban.
(9) To Edinburgh *via* Falkirk, and thence to England *via* the East Coast route, with connections to Fife *via* the Forth Bridge.
(10) A subsidiary line to Edinburgh *via* Bathgate.

There is also a number of branch lines serving places such as Milngavie, Kirkintilloch, Hamilton, East Kilbride, Uplawmoor and Balloch, as well as a fairly dense network of suburban lines developed in the days before mechanical road transport. The main features of this are the two low-level lines, through Queen Street and Central Low-Level stations respectively, and their connections to Springburn, Coatbridge, Hamilton, Rutherglen, Maryhill, Clydebank, Milngavie and Dumbarton, and, on the south side of the river, the Cathcart Circle and its extension to Kirkhill. As a result of the competition of the pre-grouping companies there is a good deal of duplication. For instance there are two lines between Glasgow and Dumbarton which cross and recross one another continually, two lines between Glasgow and Ardrossan, of which one is now abandoned, and likewise between Glasgow and Coatbridge, Hamilton and Maryhill. In recent years, with the rise of road transport, this has meant the existence of railway facilities which are often very lightly used—and many suburban stations have been closed to passenger traffic.

Goods Traffic

The three main goods stations are all situated on the north-eastern side of the city, within easy reach of the city centre. The allocation of traffic between them still follows the division of pre-grouping days. Buchanan Street handles traffic to and from the former Caledonian and Highland sections, and England *via* the West Coast route. High Street handles traffic to and from the former North British and Great North of Scotland sections, and England *via* the East Coast route. College, which occupies the site vacated by the University in 1870, handles the former Glasgow and South Western traffic, and English traffic *via* the Midland route.

These three stations handle the great bulk of the general goods traffic to and from the city. The traffic in small consignments alone, mostly to and from the shops and warehouses of the central area, amounts to some 950 tons daily, of which roughly 450 tons are handled by Buchanan Street, 280 tons by College, and 220 tons by High Street.

Table LII gives details of freight traffic forwarded by some twenty goods stations and private sidings in the inner area of Glasgow:

TABLE LII

TONNAGE OF FREIGHT TRAFFIC FORWARDED BY TWENTY GOODS STATIONS IN GLASGOW IN THE YEAR 1952

	Tonnage	*Percentage of total forwardings*		*Tonnage*	*Percentage of total forwardings*
Iron and steel	286,434	17.9	Machinery	10,475	0.7
Iron and steel scrap	185,991	11.7	Beer	9,551	0.6
Pig iron	91,833	5.8	Confectionery and preserves	9,443	0.6
Creosote and pitch	53,447	3.3	Tobacco	9,015	0.6
Slag, ashes and waste material	49,727	3.1	Butter, cheese and lard	6,246	0.4
Grain	37,079	2.3	Paper	4,527	0.3
Timber	30,902	1.9	Inflammable liquids	4,421	0.3
Wines and Spirits	30,675	1.9	Bricks and Tiles	4,020	0.3
Manure	28,115	1.8	Oils (not dangerous)	2,106	0.1
Iron Ore	26,023	1.6	Total of above	936,390	58.7
Textiles	16,931	1.1	Total all goods	1,596,000	100.0
Chemicals	14,741	0.9			
Gravel and sand	13,030	0.8			
Fruit	11,658	0.7			

SOURCE: British Railways.

The greatest tonnages of traffic forwarded consist of the materials, products and by-products of the iron and steel industry, and this is the more true because the figures for iron ore given in the table do not include the heavy traffic from Rothesay Dock, which is outside the area covered. For the rest, substantial quantities of traffic are provided by the distilling and brewing, textile, chemical, engineering, tobacco, confectionery and preserves, and paper industries, as well as in the distribution of imported goods such as grain, timber, fruit and dairy produce. The 600,000 tons not analysed include a heterogeneous collection of manufactured articles, as well as certain types of imported raw materials, and a considerable traffic in returned empties.

Passenger Traffic

There are four main passenger termini, Central, St. Enoch, Queen Street and Buchanan Street. Central and Queen Street have also low level stations which are through stations running at right angles to the main line termini above. All are situated conveniently for the city centre, and within ten minutes' walk of each other. Central and St. Enoch are large, commodious stations, with 13 and 12 platforms respectively, and more than adequate for the traffic they carry, though the working of St. Enoch is hampered by a sharply curved rail approach. Buchanan Street, though not very imposing in appearance, is big enough for the traffic it carries. Queen Street, on the other hand, is cramped and awkward in layout, and is situated at the bottom of an incline 1½ miles in length, with a gradient of 1 in 42, most of it in a tunnel which begins only a few yards from the platform ends. Though adequate as regards number of platforms, it is most difficult and costly to work. The two low level stations have all the defects which result from the use of steam engines on underground lines. Queen Street Low Level still carries a considerable local traffic, but traffic at Central Low Level has fallen off heavily in recent years.

Roughly speaking, Central is the station for England *via* the West Coast route, for Greenock and the Clyde Coast, for local services in Lanarkshire and for Edinburgh *via* Holytown. St. Enoch serves Ayrshire, Stranraer, Dumfries and England *via* the Midland route. Queen Street serves Edinburgh, England *via* the East Coast, Helensburgh and the West Highland line, while Buchanan Street is the station for Stirling, Oban, Perth, Aberdeen, Inverness and Fife. During the winter St. Enoch and Buchanan Street are closed on Sundays, and their traffic is dealt with by Central and Queen Street respectively.

Figures of the average numbers of passengers and trains at the main Glasgow stations are given in Tables LIII (a) and LIII (b).

The average daily number of passengers shows a small increase since 1949 in most cases. This is a reversal of the previous trend, for it was estimated in the *Inglis Report* that both Central and St. Enoch stations were carrying only 60 per cent or less of the traffic they had handled 50 years previously.

Three quarters of the daily passengers in 1949 were estimated to be short-distance travellers. Both Central and St. Enoch carry a heavy local traffic in addition to their long-distance traffic. Buchanan Street

TABLE LIII(a)

AVERAGE DAILY NUMBER OF PASSENGERS AT GLASGOW MAIN LINE STATIONS,[1] 1949 AND 1953

	1949	1953
Central High Level	50,484	52,934
Central Low Level	4,110	3,953
St. Enoch	23,128	24,650
Buchanan Street	5,856	6,590
Queen Street High Level	9,168	8,345
Queen Street Low Level	13,962	15,120
Total	106,708	111,592

TABLE LIII(b)

AVERAGE DAILY NUMBER OF TRAINS AT GLASGOW MAIN LINE STATIONS,[1] 1953

	Short distance	*Long distance*
Central High Level	396	38
Central Low Level	150	—
St. Enoch	208	16
Buchanan Street	19	45
Queen Street High Level	78	24
Queen Street Low Level	486	8
Total	1,337	131

is primarily a long-distance station with little local traffic. In the case of Queen Street, the long-distance traffic is concentrated on the High Level station, and the local traffic on the Low Level.

The evidence that is available suggests that long-distance traffic has not undergone much change in the last few years. On the other hand, there appears to have been a revival of short-distance traffic, which earlier had been severely affected by road competition. In the last few years, the combined influence of higher tram and bus fares, and cheap day fares by rail, seems to have tempted a certain number of local travellers back to the railway.

Interesting light was thrown on the trends of suburban traffic by some figures presented in the *Inglis Report* of the number of bookings (excluding seasons) at the Glasgow suburban stations of the former Caledonian Railway, in 1913, 1922 and 1949 and, by the courtesy of British Railways, it has been possible to bring these figures up to 1952. Between 1913 and 1949 the total annual bookings at all these stations taken together fell by 57 per cent. Between 1949 and 1952, on the other hand, they rose by 25 per cent, to a level 47 per cent below that of 1913.

The only stations at which bookings did not fall between 1913 and 1949 were a few in the neighbourhood of which extensive housing or

[1] Figures for 1949 from the Report on Passenger Traffic in Glasgow and District (Inglis Report), British Transport Commission, 1951. Figures for 1953 kindly provided by British Railways.

other development had taken place. The biggest falls were at some of the stations in the inner area, such as Eglinton Street and St. Rollox and the stations on the Central Low Level Line.

On the other hand, between 1949 and 1952, increases of bookings were registered at all except 17 of the 60 stations considered. The most marked exceptions once again were the stations on the Central Low Level line. Some of the most marked increases were once again in areas of rapid development, such as East Kilbride, Burnside, Croftfoot, King's Park, Muirend, Giffnock, Nitshill and Williamwood, but considerable increases were also shown at stations like Barrhead, Cambuslang, Carmyle, Cathcart, Langside and Newlands, Maxwell Park, Mount Florida, Pollokshields East and West, Pollokshaws East, Queen's Park, and Shawlands, which serve areas where there has not been a great deal of recent new building. This suggests that there has been a genuine increase in the use of the railway. Indeed, there are many cases nowadays where the railway cheap day return fare is lower than the double fare by Corporation Transport. Provided there is a reasonably frequent service, the railways are showing that they can compete successfully for local traffic, where rail and road fares are more or less comparable.

Nevertheless, even the recent rise in traffic does not necessarily guarantee that the traffic carried on many of these suburban services will be heavy enough to make them remunerative to operate. Distances in the Glasgow suburban area are too short to give the railways the sort of advantages which they enjoy, for instance, in Greater London.

ROAD TRANSPORT

Numbers of Vehicles Licensed

Table LIV gives the numbers of mechanically propelled vehicles licensed in Glasgow at 30 September 1955, with comparable figures for Birmingham, Liverpool and Manchester.

TABLE LIV

MECHANICALLY PROPELLED ROAD VEHICLES LICENSED IN QUARTER ENDED 30 SEPTEMBER 1955

	Glasgow	*Birmingham*	*Liverpool*	*Manchester*
Population (1951 Census)	1,089,767	1,112,340	789,532	703,175
Motor cycles	6,979	30,579	12,769	12,551
Pedestrian controlled vehicles	32	88	156	13
Hackney vehicles other than tramcars	1,562	2,244	1,437	1,919
Tramcars	1,031	—	180	—
Tractors	837	797	905	437
Goods vehicles	19,384	30,097	14,894	20,552
Private cars	29,071	86,845	29,858	34,811
Exempt vehicles	439	1,041	416	448
Total	59,335	151,691	60,615	70,731

SOURCE: Ministry of Transport.

These figures refer only to vehicles actually registered in the cities concerned; therefore they do not include many vehicles owned by residents or firms in neighbouring areas which form part of the traffic using the city streets. Nevertheless, some interesting comparisons can be made. The large numbers of private cars and motor cycles in Birmingham, as compared with the other cities, probably reflect the fact that Birmingham is a centre of the motor industry, as well as an area of higher average income. Glasgow's supremacy in the matter of tramcars is also brought out: in 1955 the city had nearly 45 per cent of all the tramcars still registered in Great Britain. In comparison with Liverpool and Manchester, however, Glasgow appears to have a smaller number of private cars and especially of motor cycles, relative to the population.

Of the total of 1,562 hackney carriages registered in Glasgow, 401 were taxis or private hire cars and 1,161 were public service vehicles. The last figure, however, does not take account of the large numbers of buses of the Scottish Group companies which use the Glasgow streets, but are registered with surrounding authorities.

Goods Transport

Details of road goods transport operations are as usual very difficult to discover. Of the total of 19,384 goods vehicles licensed in Glasgow at 30 September 1955, 15,926 were of under three tons capacity, and 3,458 of three tons and over.[1] Most of the smaller vehicles would be engaged in local delivery work, while the larger vehicles would tend to be used mainly for longer-distance operations.

Road goods services are divided between British Road Services, the independent hauliers, and the C Licence operators, that is, the traders who use vehicles to carry their own goods.

British Road Services have estimated that in 1956 they had about 450 vehicles engaged on their services in the Glasgow area. These carried about 1,200,000 tons of long-distance traffic and about 130,000 tons of local traffic.[2] Not all these vehicles were registered in Glasgow, however.

As to the independent hauliers, the Road Haulage Association had in 1956 175 members whose head offices were within the city boundaries, and a number of others in the immediately surrounding areas. The total vehicle tonnage authorised by the licences of these 175 firms amounted to 6,457 tons unladen weight. The firms varied considerably in size. The 16 which had an authorised tonnage of over 100 tons each, accounted between them for 45.5 per cent of the total tonnage, 62 medium sized firms, with from 20 to 99 tons authorised, accounted for 42.7 per cent of the tonnage, and 97 small firms, each

1 Figures supplied by courtesy of the Local Taxation Officer for the City of Glasgow.
2 Figures supplied by courtesy of British Road Services, Scottish Division.

with under 20 tons authorised, accounted for the remaining 12 per cent.[1]

This was by no means a complete picture. There are a number of hauliers who are not members of the Association. In addition, there are the vehicles operated by C Licence holders, which probably form the greatest proportion of the total, but about which no particulars are available. For the country as a whole, there has been a marked tendency for the numbers of C Licences to increase in recent years.

Motor Bus and Coach Services (other than Corporation Transport)

Motor bus and coach services into and out of Glasgow, other than those operated by Glasgow Corporation, are almost entirely in the hands of the companies of the Scottish Group, owned by the British Transport Commission. In addition, there are the West Highland services operated by David MacBrayne, which is also a subsidiary of the Commission, but the only "independents" still operating regular services from Glasgow are Northern Roadways, with express services to London, Birmingham and Scarborough; and Lowland Motorways, which operates local services in some of the new housing areas in the east of the city.

The division of the services between the companies of the Scottish Group is as follows:

W. Alexander & Sons.—Services to the North and North East, serving Milngavie, Aberfoyle, Stirling, Falkirk, Kilsyth and beyond, and intermediate points.

David Lawson.—Local services to the Kirkintilloch, Lenzie and Campsie Glen areas.

Scottish Omnibuses.—Coatbridge, Airdrie, Bathgate, Edinburgh and intermediate points.

Central S.M.T. Co.—Services into Lanarkshire—Hamilton, Motherwell, Lanark, East Kilbride, etc., also Dumbarton, Helensburgh and Balloch.

Western S.M.T. Co.—Renfrewshire and Ayrshire—e.g. Paisley, Greenock, Kilmarnock, Ayr and intermediate points.

Country bus services in Glasgow terminate at three bus stations and four street stances. The three bus stations, at Killermont Street,[2] Dundas Street and Waterloo Street, are reasonably commodious and well equipped, but at the four street stances, at Clyde Street, Carlton Place, St. Enoch Square and Renfrew Street there is no provision of shelter or waiting accommodation of any kind. Plans for a new bus station in Clyde Street or Carlton Place have so far come to nothing.

[1] Figures by courtesy of the Road Haulage Association, Scottish Area.

[2] The main entrance to this station is in Buchanan Street, but the name Killermont Street is commonly used to avoid confusion with Buchanan Street railway station.

The allocation of services between terminals is also confusing. In general, services to the north and east leave from Killermont Street, but some of them, especially in the Kirkintilloch direction. leave from Dundas Street, while the newly established services to the Drumchapel Housing Estate start from Renfrew Street. Services into Lanarkshire are mostly divided between Killermont Street and Waterloo Street except for a few services which use Carlton Place. Those to Balloch and Helensburgh use Waterloo Street. Services for Renfrewshire and Ayrshire are divided between Waterloo Street and Clyde Street, except for those to Greenock *via* Renfrew, which start from St. Enoch. MacBrayne's services start from the company's own station in Parliamentary Road.

The approximate daily numbers of buses using the main stations and stances were estimated for the *Inglis Report* in 1949, and the figures are given below:

APPROXIMATE DAILY NUMBER OF BUSES TO AND FROM GLASGOW BUS TERMINI,[1] 1949

Stations		*Stances*	
Killermont Street	2,380	Clyde Street	1,420
Dundas Street	850	Carlton Place	330
Waterloo Street	2,370	St. Enoch Square	280

In 1949 there was estimated to be a total of some 7,625 buses of the Scottish Group operating into and out of the city daily, 3,816 inwards and 3,809 outwards, and it was estimated that they carried some 239,000 passengers daily. This compared with a total of 97,000 rail passengers daily, of whom 70,000 were classified as local, but, as we saw above, there have since been signs of a slight swing in favour of the railway.

The network of bus services into and out of Glasgow is extremely dense, especially to the south-east, into Lanarkshire, to the west, to Paisley and Johnstone, and to the north-west, down the north bank of the Clyde. Buses operate every two or three minutes by various routes between Glasgow and Hamilton, Motherwell and Wishaw, and almost as frequently to places like Paisley, Dumbarton and Balloch, Milngavie, Kirkintilloch and Muirhead. Most of the larger towns of Central and Western Scotland, such as Stirling, Falkirk, Grangemouth, Airdrie, Coatbridge, Edinburgh, Lanark, Kilmarnock, Ayr and Helensburgh are linked with Glasgow by services every fifteen or twenty minutes, and many other places can be reached at half-hourly or hourly intervals.

A feature of Glasgow bus facilities is the number of comparatively distant places which can be reached directly by through stage services. Through routes operate for instance to places as far off as Campbeltown, Oban, Crieff, Dundee, St. Andrews, Kirkcaldy, Edinburgh, Peebles, Dumfries and Stranraer and they are often used by passengers

[1] The Renfrew Street terminal was not used for the local services of the Scottish Group at that date.

making the through journey, because they serve places beyond the range of the railways' cheap day return tickets.

Express services are less numerous, because of Glasgow's relative isolation from other large centres of population. Fairly frequent limited stop services are run between Glasgow and Edinburgh, and between Glasgow and Perth and Dundee. There are longer-distance express services, on which seats must be booked in advance, to London, Birmingham, Liverpool, Manchester, Newcastle and Aberdeen. Summer seasonal services are also run to Blackpool, Scarborough, Whitley Bay, Inverness and Portree.

Some light is thrown on the extent of local bus travel by the figures given in the *Inglis Report* for weekly carryings between Glasgow and 18 neighbouring places, by rail, Scottish Group bus services, and Corporation Transport services, in 1949.[1] These indicate that the Corporation services carried the biggest proportion of the traffic in the case of places immediately outside the city, such as Coatbridge, Dalmuir, Clydebank, Clarkston and Renfrew, for all of which Corporation trams and buses had over 40 per cent of the total number, and for most of which they carried more than half the total. For most of the towns which were rather farther away, such as Kirkintilloch, Airdrie, Cambuslang, Motherwell, Milngavie, Barrhead, Paisley, Johnstone, Wishaw and Larkhall, the Scottish Group companies had the largest proportion, over half in most cases, the percentages ranging from 48 at Cambuslang and 56 at Paisley, up to nearly 80 in the case of Wishaw and Larkhall, and over 90 in the case of Kirkintilloch and Johnstone. The railways carried only some ten to twenty per cent of the total traffic in all but a few cases. At Helensburgh and Greenock with their fast business services and large numbers of season ticket holders, they did have more than half the total, nearly 75 per cent in the case of Helensburgh and nearly 60 per cent in that of Greenock. Other places where the railway traffic was relatively high were Motherwell (31 per cent) and Paisley (28 per cent), both of which have fast and fairly frequent train services. On the other hand, the railway proportion fell to 5 per cent at Clarkston and Johnstone, where rail services were comparatively poor and road services very frequent.

Although there is evidence of some return of local traffic to the railways since 1949, these figures show the extent to which the highly developed railway system of the Glasgow area had come to be replaced for daily travelling by the more convenient and frequent and usually cheaper road services.

Corporation Transport Services

Glasgow Corporation Transport Department provides the local passenger services within the city and in some of the immediately adjoining areas. The Department now operates trams, motor buses, trolley-

1 *Inglis Report*, Table 5, p. 29.

buses and the Underground Railway. The numbers of vehicles in stock at 31 May 1956 were as follows:

Trams	988	of which 355 were double-bogey cars, mostly modern, and 633 were older 4-wheeled cars.
Motor buses	833	
Trolleybuses	95	
Underground cars	50	

At the end of 1953 trams were being operated on 28 routes, trolleybuses on four routes, and motor buses on 47 routes. In addition, a number of all night services were operated by motor buses.

The growth of the undertaking's traffic is shown in Table LV.

TABLE LV

GLASGOW CORPORATION TRANSPORT—ANNUAL VEHICLE-MILEAGES AND PASSENGERS IN CERTAIN YEARS (000's)

Year ended 31 May	*Tramways* Car-miles run	*Tramways* Passengers carried	*Motor-Buses* Bus-miles run	*Motor-Buses* Passengers carried	*Trolleybuses* Bus-miles run	*Trolleybuses* Passengers carried	*Underground* Train-miles run	*Underground* Passengers carried
1896[1]	6,933	86,403						
1900	9,657	127,628						
1905	17,944	195,768						
1910	20,974	222,731						
1915	24,214	336,251						
1920	26,459	509,340						
1925	30,937	439,341	227	1,340			1,227	20,008
1930	35,868	470,021	5,566	48,067			1,173	19,969
1935	35,678	449,652	13,056	78,962			1,061	14,413
1939	39,386	496,429	20,731	129,577			1,483	25,807
1945	36,042	571,653	14,939	136,263			1,486	34,210
1946	36,930	584,287	15,353	140,627			1,484	35,003
1947	38,361	587,334	17,128	142,729			1,485	36,582
1948	38,865	595,673	18,172	152,845			1,489	37,187
1949	38,489	583,748	20,396	178,133	76[2]	1,676[2]	1,486	37,344
1950	36,607	537,727	23,174	209,485	1,104	20,105	1,548	37,290
1951	35,909	504,646	25,230	214,568	1,416	25,430	1,504	36,669
1952	35,111	478,561	25,586	218,067	1,295	24,100	1,504	37,113
1953	32,581	442,270	25,108	216,470	1,589	26,313	1,476	35,971
1954	30,397	396,913	25,596	211,209	2,775	42,660	1,453	33,621
1955	29,640	383,861	25,761	211,728	2,947	45,083	1,470	34,371
1956	29,099	367,347	26,331	215,228	2,990	44,203	1,478	34,481

SOURCE: Glasgow Transport Department.

In spite of the rapid extension of bus services to serve new housing areas, Glasgow is still a tramway city, in the sense that the tramways still carry the bulk of the traffic, especially on the busiest routes. Indeed, up to 1948 tramcar mileage run and passengers carried were

[1] First full financial year of operation. The Corporation took over on 1 July, 1894.
[2] Two months only.

still expanding. There are signs, however, that the tramway ascendancy is beginning to wane. A number of outlying services have already been converted to motor buses. Since 1949, trolleybuses have been gradually introduced on four of the main routes. The most recent conversion, which took place in July 1952, brought them through the city centre *via* West Nile Street, Glassford Street and Stockwell Street. The point has now been reached where a large number of the older tramcars are due for replacement, and tracks will need renewal. The decision has been taken not to invest in new tramcars, but gradually to replace them with motor buses or trolleybuses. One fact affecting the problem is that the Transport Department has its own power station at Pinkston. If this is to be retained, that is one argument in favour of retaining trams, or replacing them with trolleybuses, rather than going over completely to motor buses.

In the postwar years the Department, in common with most other municipal transport undertakings, faced considerable financial difficulties. Costs of labour, materials and power rose steeply. Services had to be extended to make good wartime curtailments and to serve newly developing areas. The numbers of passengers carried did not expand as fast as the vehicle-mileage which had to be run to carry them and, in fact, in the last few years the number of passengers has fallen slightly from the peak figure reached in 1950. Fare increases could only be obtained slowly, because of the need to obtain the permission of the Ministry of Transport and the Area Licensing Authorities, and because of the danger of discouraging traffic by too drastic rises.

These unfortunate influences reached a peak in 1951-2, by the end of which year the undertaking had a cumulative deficit of over £2,500,000. After then the tide seemed to have turned. The rise of costs was halted, and considerable economies were achieved by cutting down services at slack periods. Fare increases enabled revenue to catch up, so that the years 1952-3 and 1953-4 ended with considerable surpluses. More recently, however, there has been a further reversal of trends. Costs have begun to rise once again, while in 1954-5 revenue began to fall off. This was partly because the Corporation gave up operating certain routes outside the city boundary, and partly it reflected an actual loss of traffic. Consequently the year ended with a deficit of £67,676. For 1955-6, in spite of an increase of revenue owing to higher fares, a further rise in costs led to a working loss of £135,415.[1]

As with all local passenger transport undertakings, the problem of the peak load is an acute one. The main traffic peaks come, of course, at the morning and evening rush hours, but there is a subsidiary peak at lunch time, and traffic in the afternoon is higher than it is in the later morning, or in the evening after the rush hour. The percentages of the fleets which are idle at off-peak periods have been estimated as follows:

1 Corporation Transport Department. Report of the General Manager for the year 1955-6.

Glasgow Corporation Transport—Percentage of Fleet which was Idle at Off-Peak Periods (1953)

Off-Peak Period	*Tramways*	*Motor Buses*	*Trolleybuses*
Late morning	57.5	63.5	64.7
Afternoon	38.9	54.5	52.9
Late evening	55.9	56.5	60.8

Source: Corporation Transport Department.

The position does not appear to have changed greatly since before the war, but, with the growing development of housing estates on the outskirts of the city, it is not likely to get any easier. Already it is estimated that the Pollok and Priesthill estates alone require some 90 buses to meet their needs, and the large-scale developments now taking place at Drumchapel and Castlemilk are necessitating several new bus services which are likely to be heavily loaded at peak periods, but only lightly used at off-peak times. The problem of how the services of the Corporation Transport Department, the Scottish Group companies and the railways can best be used to meet Glasgow's future transport needs, remains to be solved.

Fares on Glasgow Corporation Transport

The following information is taken from the General Manager's Report for 1955-6:

Glasgow Corporation Transport—Fares

Average Distance in Miles Allowed at each Fare[1]

	1d	2d	2½d	3d	4d	6d	7d	9d	1/-	*Average per mile (pence)*
Tramways										
Adults	—	—	1.17	—	2.35	5.45	—	—	—	1.275
Juveniles	1.17	2.35	—	5.45	—	—	—	—	—	0.620
Trolleybuses										
Adults	—	—	1.12	—	2.22	4.32	—	—	—	1.592
Juveniles	1.12	2.22	—	4.32	—	—	—	—	—	0.766
Motor buses										
Adults	—	—	1.16	—	2.37	3.49	6.43	—	—	1.377
Juveniles	1.16	2.37	—	3.49	6.43	—	—	—	—	0.620
Night-service	—	—	—	—	—	—	—	5.35	5.23	1.802

Underground Fares	Adults	Juveniles	Average distance (miles)
3 stations	2d	1d	1.32
4 stations	3d	2d	1.76
Over 4 stations	4d	2d	2.19 to 6.56

[1] Fares have again been revised upwards (1957). The minimum fare is now 3d. on any vehicle; the maximum fare on tram and trolley bus is 6d. and on motor bus 8d.

Glasgow can no longer boast the pre-eminence in cheapness which it enjoyed in the days of ½d. fares and the 2d. maximum on the trams, for which a journey of up to 15 miles could be taken. Nevertheless, in spite of frequent increases in recent years, the level still compares favourably with many other towns, especially over longer distances. On the trams and trolleybuses, the minimum fare is now 2½d. for two stages, and the maximum 6d., while on the buses the minimum is 2½d. with maximum of 7d.

Traffic Congestion and Accidents

Like most cities, Glasgow has a problem of traffic congestion, resulting from the growth of traffic on a road system which is no longer adequate to carry it.

The main factors involved in the Glasgow traffic problem may be summarised as follows:

(1) The main radial roads leading out of the city are inadequate for heavy modern traffic. This is particularly true, for instance, of London Road, the main artery to Carlisle and England, of Paisley Road and Paisley Road West and of Dumbarton Road, but it applies to most of the others as well. Great Western Road is an exception, providing a broad artery from the City Centre right out to Drumchapel and on by the Boulevard to Dumbarton, but it can only be reached through the congestion of the Cowcaddens or Sauchiehall Street and Cambridge Street. Similarly, Edinburgh Road forms part of the arterial road from Glasgow to Edinburgh, but to get to it from the city centre means making one's way along Cathedral Street or Parliamentary Road, and on along Alexandra Parade, before coming to the modern arterial road.

(2) There is a complete lack of adequate ring roads to take traffic round the city centre from one main road to another. This is especially true on the western side, where there are no cross-river connections for vehicles below George V Bridge, other than the often overcrowded ferries at Finnieston, Govan, Whiteinch and Renfrew. Hence the urgent need for some such project as the Whiteinch Tunnel, to save cross-river traffic from having to make the detour through the city centre.

(3) There is a serious problem of congestion in the city centre, where, in addition to heavy local traffic, through traffic from east to west must cross that from north to south. The problem is made worse by the absence of adequate parking facilities, and by the presence of tramcars in many of the central streets. The gridiron layout of the central area helps to some extent, by providing a number of parallel routes both

north and south and east and west, but on the other hand, it means that there are intersections every fifty yards or so, where traffic is held up at lights or police controlled crossings. Anyone who has seen Renfield Street at busy periods, with each block from one traffic light to the next packed solid with trams, so that sometimes they cannot move when the lights turn green, because the block ahead is full, will know what this can mean.

A measure of the changes in the volume of traffic over the years can be obtained from the Ministry of Transport figures for the fifteen census points in Glasgow. By August 1954, when the census was resumed, the average daily number of vehicles had once again passed the 1938 level. The three busiest of the fifteen points were in Alexandra Parade, Paisley Road (at Carnoustie Street), and Great Western Road (at Southpark Avenue), each with a daily average of between 13,000 and 14,000 vehicles, followed by Pollokshaws Road with just under 12,000. The other points[1] all had roughly between 6,000 and 8,500 vehicles daily. Wednesdays and Fridays are the days when traffic is usually busiest, but there is not much difference between weekdays. Sunday traffic is only about 60 per cent of the weekday average. More detailed surveys for the Pollokshaws Road census point indicate that daily traffic is naturally heavier in summer than in winter, especially on Sundays, but not necessarily on Saturdays, when there is much football traffic.

The census figures indicate that the number of motor cars on the roads was only 3 per cent greater in 1954 than in 1938, whereas the number of motor cycles had gone up by as much as 74 per cent.[2] Motor goods vehicles were up by 55 per cent and motor buses and coaches by 16 per cent, while tramcars were down by 12 per cent. Pedal cycles had fallen in number by 51 per cent, and horse-drawn vehicles by no less than 91 per cent. The total number of vehicles recorded had risen by only 7 per cent, but owing to changes in the proportions of different types of vehicles, it was estimated that this represented an increase of traffic weight of some 28 per cent. The census, it was pointed out, emphasised the need for road widening, especially in Paisley Road, Alexandra Parade, Pollokshaws Road and the inner parts of Great Western Road.

Parking facilities are a serious problem. In a survey carried out by the City Engineer's Department in 1950, it was found that in the city centre there was accommodation in official parking places for only about 760 vehicles, with a possibility of providing additional parking places to hold another 530. Private garages and car parks were being used by some 620 vehicles, and had accommodation for another 390, but these are not always in convenient situations. Whereas in March

[1] The other points were as follows: London Road (Belvedere Hospital), Dalmarnock Road, Cumbernauld Road, Maryhill Road, Great Western Road (Garscadden Road), Renfield Street, Gallowgate, Duke Street, Springburn Road, Dumbarton Road (Yoker Ferry Road), and Argyle Street (Douglas Street).

[2] This was a reversal of the previous trend, for the number of motor cycles had fallen between 1935 and 1938.

1950 some 1,720 to 1,750 vehicles were found to be parked in the streets other than in official parking places, by March 1956 this number had increased to between 4,600 and 4,800.

Unofficial parking has been to some extent cut down by the no-waiting regulations introduced in a number of central streets in 1952, and since extended. In most cases a ban was imposed on waiting, except for limited periods, by vehicles loading and unloading goods, between the hours of 12 noon and 6 p.m. on Mondays to Fridays, and between 11 a.m. and 1 p.m. on Saturdays. In several streets unilateral parking has been introduced between 10 a.m. and 6 p.m. A survey undertaken by the Scottish branch of the Road Research Laboratory showed a considerable reduction of congestion after the first introduction of the new regulations, the average speed of travel through the central streets being increased from 9.3 m.p.h. to 10.8 m.p.h., and their capacity to hold traffic having risen. At the same time, traffic speeds and flows in central Glasgow were found to be considerably lower than those in Central London. This was partly because the Glasgow streets are narrower, but also because of the presence of tramcars and the more frequent intersections in Glasgow. Advantage has also been taken of the gridiron pattern of the city centre to introduce one-way traffic regulations, notably in the area between Sauchiehall Street and the river, to the west of Renfield Street.

The number of road accidents involving death or injury has shown some decline from its wartime peak.

NUMBERS KILLED AND INJURED IN ROAD ACCIDENTS IN GLASGOW

	Killed	*Injured*
1943	193	3,041
1944	180	2,884
1945	139	2,766
1946	119	2,781
1947	125	2,934
1948	97	2,608
1949	111	2,730
1950	109	2,807
1951	97	2,645
1952	92	2,371
1953	108	2,969
1954	115	3,059
1955	109	3,198

SOURCE: Annual Reports of Chief Constable.

The number of casualties in relation to the population appears to be lower in Glasgow than in Great Britain as a whole, the figures for 1954 being 1 in 343 of the city's population, as against 1 in 207 for Great Britain. The proportion of the casualties which occurs among children is, however, unduly high. In 1952, 753 out of 2,463 casualties were of persons under 15 years of age, or 31.6 per cent, as compared with 19.7 per cent for Great Britain as a whole; 571, or 23.2 per cent, were under 10 years old. Persons over 60 accounted for 341 of the casualties or 13.8 per cent, and for no fewer than 36 of the 92 fatal accidents.

The peak period for accidents is the early evening, one third of the total number of casualties taking place between 4 p.m. and 8 p.m. Between the days of the week, there does not appear to be much difference, except that the level on Sunday is less than half that on week days, and that there is a slight tendency for casualties to be more numerous at the end of the week than the beginning, with the highest rate on Saturdays.

Accidents tend to be heavily concentrated on the main traffic routes, especially where these are heavily built up and run through densely populated districts. High figures are shown on roads like Dumbarton Road, Paisley Road, Springburn Road, Pollokshaws Road, Gallowgate, Duke Street and London Road, whereas the figures are lower, for instance, in Great Western Road which is less densely built up. In the city centre, where traffic moves more slowly, the incidence is less, except in Argyle Street and on the main bridges and their approaches.

Road Planning Proposals

Considerable thought has naturally been given to the future development of Glasgow's road system, in the hope of alleviating congestion. The *City Development Plan,*[1] published in 1951, contained long-term proposals for the reconstruction of the main roads. The aim was to provide two ring roads, a series of nine arterial roads, radiating from the inner ring to the city boundary, and a number of sub-arterial roads. The arterial roads were intended to have dual carriage-ways, and ultimately to be restricted to certain types of traffic and to have connections with service roads reduced to a minimum. The sub-arterial roads would have fifty-foot carriage-ways and access to them would ultimately be restricted also, though less stringently. The line of existing roads would be followed as far as possible, but extensive new building would be required. The Whiteinch-Linthouse Tunnel forms an essential link in the ring roads, but the idea of a bridge at Carnoustie Street, which featured in the *First Planning Report* of 1944, has been shelved, because of the interference with navigation involved. The Plan also envisages the building of those parts of the outer, or " C " Ring Road, proposed in the *Clyde Valley Regional Plan,* which lie within the city boundaries.

These are long-term proposals and there are many difficulties in the way of their achievement. Most of the roads concerned are closely built-up, with side roads at frequent intervals, and to convert them into restricted arterial roads would be exceedingly costly and would involve great interference with existing property and with the movements of existing road users. It is therefore unlikely that a plan of this sort

[1] Corporation of the City of Glasgow, *Development Plan,* 1951.

could be carried out for many years, if only because of the limitation of the national investment programme. Preliminary work has, however, been begun on the Whiteinch Tunnel, and it is hoped that it may be possible to complete it before so very long.

AIR TRANSPORT

In spite of its recent development air transport has already become an accepted part of the transport facilities available to the city. Notwithstanding higher fares, the air has definite advantages in the way of speed and comfort especially where surface transport is slow or involves sea crossings, as in the case of the service between Glasgow and the Highlands and Islands, and Glasgow and Ireland. Although the routes serving the Hebrides, the Far North, and the Orkneys and Shetlands are not economic from the point of view of the operators, because of sparse traffic and frequent landing and taking off, yet the advantage in time and comfort is so great that air travel has become firmly established among travellers on these routes.

Where surface facilities are better, air transport does not come into its own except for fairly long distances, for the saving of time is otherwise insufficient, when account is taken of the journeys to and from airports at each end. In the case of journeys to and from London, however, air travel becomes more worth while, since it makes it possible to undertake a day trip without having to spend two nights in the train. In recent winter seasons, British European Airways have offered a reduced return fare of £9 on the London service, which is about the same as the first class rail fare, and have been able to attract quite a lot of new business at a time of year when traffic is normally low.

The Glasgow airport is situated at Renfrew. It is reasonably accessible for the city centre, though not ideal, since it lies near the river and is thus liable to fog. Its future also is somewhat uncertain, for the flight approach would be interfered with if the Clyde Navigation Trust carried out its proposed developments to the west of King George V Dock. New terminal buildings have now been built to replace makeshift premises. The airport is owned and managed by the Ministry of Transport and Civil Aviation. The city terminal for the special airport buses is in St. Enoch Square. In addition, Glasgow is served by the transatlantic and other long distance services which use Prestwick Airport, some thirty miles away.

Regular services from Renfrew are operated by British European Airways, by the Irish airline Aer Lingus, Icelandic Airways and Manx Air Lines. Seasonal services are also operated by Starways Ltd., B.K.S. Air Transport and Flying Tiger Airlines. The routes and the approximate number of daily flights in 1955-6 were as follows:

SERVICES FROM RENFREW AIRPORT[1]
APPROXIMATE NUMBER OF FLIGHTS DAILY

Route	*Winter*	*Summer*
British European Airways		
Paris	—	2 (week days)
London	5	5-9
Manchester	2	2
Birmingham	2	2
Belfast	1-3	3-5
Benbecula-Stornoway	1 (week days only)	1-2 (week days only)
Tiree	Four times weekly	1-2
Barra	Twice weekly	Three times weekly
Campbeltown-Islay	1 (week days only)	2 (week days only)
Inverness-Wick-Orkney	1 (week days only)	1 (week days only) (with extra services to Inverness and Wick)
Aberdeen	1 (week days only)	1 (week days only)
Isle of Man	—	Fridays only (2 services)
Channel Islands	—	Sats. and Sundays only
Aer Lingus		
Dublin	1-3	2-6

Icelandic Airways

Weekly services between Reykjavik and Copenhagen, and Reykjavik and London, each calling at Renfrew in both directions.

Manx Airlines

Services to Isle of Man varying between twice weekly, three times weekly and daily according to the time of year.

The last few years have seen a considerable increase in the traffic at Renfrew, as shown by the following figures:

TRAFFIC AT RENFREW AIRPORT

	Passengers	*Freight* (*short tons*)	*Air Mail* (*short tons*)
1947	77,000	n.a.	n.a.
1948	107,000	n.a.	n.a.
1949	133,000	349	n.a.
1950	138,000	410	n.a.
1951	139,500	496	n.a.
1952	160,000	493	340
1953	210,000	770	354
1954	258,000	969	456
1955	306,000	1,569[2]	685[2]

SOURCE: Ministry of Transport and Civil Aviation.

The bulk of the passengers are still carried in the summer months. In 1955, for instance, 73½ per cent were carried in the months of April to October inclusive and 50½ per cent in June to September inclusive.

[1] Official timetables of British European Airways and Aer Lingus and the Ministry of Transport and Civil Aviation. The services to Newcastle and various points in Northern Europe formerly operated by Hunting-Clan Air Transport Ltd. have been withdrawn and it is uncertain whether they will be re-introduced.

[2] The freight and mail totals for 1955 were inflated by the diversion of traffic to special air services during the rail strike in June.

The relative proportion of winter travel is increasing slowly, for in 1955 26½ per cent of the total number were carried in January, February, March, November and December taken together, as against 22 per cent in 1950. Freight carryings are still very small compared with surface transport.

Post, Telegraph and Telephone Services

The earliest record of postal services in Glasgow refers to the activities of a local officer called the "post," who was appointed and paid by the town council, apparently to carry mail to and from Edinburgh and also to deliver it locally. A nation-wide postal system was first established under Charles I in 1635 and in 1662 there was a regular post instituted between Edinburgh and Portpatrick *via* Glasgow. In 1715 there were three mails a week between Glasgow and Edinburgh, still carried by footrunner, a riding post not being established until 1717. The first direct mail coach service from London *via* Carlisle was begun in 1782, and a local penny post was established in the Glasgow area in 1798.

In the early nineteenth century the postal establishment was still small. In 1832, for instance, the staff consisted of a postmaster, 8 clerks, 18 letter carriers, 2 stampers and 1 sorter. After the introduction of the country-wide Penny Post in 1840, business soon grew and, after a number of changes of premises, the present General Post Office in George Square was opened in 1857. It was considerably extended in 1880.

The first telephone exchange in Glasgow, the ancestor of the present Douglas Exchange, was opened at 140 Douglas Street in 1879. Two other independent systems were started in the following year, but in 1881 all three of them were taken over by the newly formed National Telephone Company. In 1896 the Post Office took over the trunk lines, but the local networks remained in the hands of the Company.

Glasgow Corporation had, however, taken the lead in the agitation for municipal telephones. The Corporation eventually received its licence from the Postmaster-General and established its service in competition with the National Telephone Company in 1901. The new service was not successful financially, for the initial cost of the plant was underestimated and the charges made were too low. Experience soon showed that competitive telephone systems were uneconomic, since they involved duplication of lines and exchanges, and subscribers had to be connected to both if they wanted a complete service. By 1906, when the Company had 27,856 lines in the Glasgow area, the Corporation had acquired 12,821 subscribers, of whom about half also subscribed to the Company.

The Corporation system was sold to the Post Office in 1906 for £310,000 which involved a loss of £75,000 on the original investment. From then on, by working agreement between the Post Office and the

Company, the two systems were worked more or less as one. As new exchanges were built in various districts, the subscribers of both systems were gradually transferred to them. The unification of the Glasgow telephone service was formally completed in 1911, when the National Telephone Company was taken over by the Post Office.

Below are given some details of postal and associated services in the Glasgow postal and telephone areas[1] in 1954-5:

POST OFFICE SERVICES, 1954-5

Number of post offices	254
Total postal staff	6,957
Letters delivered	275,600,000
Letters posted	263,700,000
Letters in transit	89,100,000
Parcels delivered	6,500,000
Parcels posted	6,500,000
Parcels in transit	7,600,000
Telegrams delivered	981,000
Telegrams despatched	941,000
Telephone exchanges—Automatic	48
Manual	22
Telephone subscribers	187,280
Telephone calls handled	170,300,000

SOURCE: Head Postmaster, Glasgow.

Postal traffic figures refer to the year ending 31 October, and telephone and telegraph figures to the year ending 31 March.

THE FUTURE OF GLASGOW TRANSPORT

A good deal of thought has been given in recent years to the future development of Glasgow's transport facilities, especially on the passenger side. With the growing dispersal of the population into new housing estates, both inside and outside the city boundaries, and with the parallel development of new industrial estates, the demands on road transport facilities are likely to grow steadily. The roads are already congested, especially in the central areas, and reconstruction on an adequate scale is likely to be almost prohibitively costly. Meanwhile, there exists an extensive network of railways, built in the days of railway monopoly, which has come to be comparatively little used since the development of road transport. It is not surprising, therefore, that attention has been focused on the possibility of making more effective use of the railways.

So far as passenger traffic is concerned, the situation was thoroughly examined by the Inglis Committee, whose *Report* to the British Transport Commission was published in 1951.[2] The central feature of their

[1] The main difference between the Glasgow Postal and Telephone Areas is that the latter includes Paisley and neighbouring districts in East Renfrewshire and North Ayrshire, which are excluded from the Glasgow Postal Area.

[2] British Transport Commission, *Report on Passenger Transport in Glasgow and District,* 1951.

recommendations was the provision of improved rail services by the gradual electrification of the Glasgow suburban lines and of the lines leading to neighbouring towns, as far away as Gourock, Wemyss Bay, Helensburgh, Airdrie, Hamilton, East Kilbride and (eventually) Kilmarnock and Ayr. The lines through Queen Street Low Level, to Helensburgh, Balloch, Milngavie and Airdrie, are now being electrified, and so is the Cathcart Circle. It is hoped to complete the first stage of this development by 1960. Faster, cleaner and more frequent rail services may do much to attract traffic back from the roads.

Meanwhile, public transport operators, both passenger and goods, are facing steadily growing competition from privately owned transport, by car or motor cycle, or by C licence lorry. The question may well be, therefore, one of winning passengers from using their own cars to using the railway, as much as one between train and bus. The answer will depend largely on how far the growing difficulty of driving and finding parking space in congested city streets outweighs the convenience of controlling one's own means of transport. But here Glasgow shares in a world-wide problem.

Chapter 11

COMMERCE

M. GASKIN

INTRODUCTION

COMMERCE, the name we give to the business of exchanging goods as distinct from producing them, plays an important part in the economic life of cities and towns. In some towns the commerce is simply the minimum necessary to sustain their economy, but probably most towns perform commercial functions for a wider population than their own. This is the case with Glasgow, for although it is an industrial rather than a commercial city, it is also a port and the centre of the industrial West of Scotland; as a consequence its commerce is comparatively highly developed.

There are many stages in the handling of goods, between producer and consumer. They can be divided broadly into two, the wholesale and the retail and, in the main, we shall be examining the commerce of Glasgow under these two general heads. At the outset however it must be said that, for the most part, we are concerned with the commercial function only where it is carried on by organisations that specialise in it. A considerable amount of the commercial handling of goods is carried on by the actual producers of goods, and this may cut out all or some of the independent organisations that would otherwise contribute to the exchange and distribution of them. In the case of services there is usually direct contact between producer and consumer, but this is an exception to our plan in that something will be said here about the provision of these in Glasgow. The area of the survey therefore will be first retail distribution, then wholesale distribution; a section on services will follow that on the retail trade, while after dealing with the wholesale trade, there will be a separate section on the Co-operative movement, and also a section on the foreign commerce of the city.

Table LVI gives for 1951 and 1955 the numbers employed with the corresponding percentages (together with national percentages for comparison) in those activities with which we shall be dealing in this chapter and the next. It shows that distribution, services, and finance account for just over a quarter of the Glasgow total. From the comparison with the national percentages it appears that the distributive trades are of more than average importance in Glasgow, while services are less so. The high proportion in distribution is to some extent an urban feature, but in part it reflects Glasgow's position as a distributive centre for a wide area of Western Scotland.

TABLE LVI

Employment in Distribution, Finance and Services in Glasgow[1] in 1951 and 1955

Group[2]	*Numbers employed in Glasgow* 1951	1955	*Percentage of insured employees* 1951 Glas.	1951 G.B.	1955 Glas.	1955 G.B.
	000s	000s	%	%	%	%
Distributive Trades	88.9	83.5	15.5	11.7	15.4	12.3
Insurance, Banking, Finance	10.9	11.8	1.9	2.0	2.2	2.1
Professional services[3]	10.7	10.4	1.9	...	1.9	...
Miscellaneous services	32.9	31.2	5.8	8.5	5.8	8.1

Source: Ministry of Labour and National Service.

TABLE LVII

Employment in the Distributive Trades of Glasgow in 1951 and 1955 Percentage of the Total in Various Trades

Trade	1951 %	1955 %
Dealing[4]	8.4	9.1
Wholesale Food and Drink	9.5	8.2
Wholesale Non-Food	25.2	23.1
Retail Food and Drink[5]	22.1	22.2
Retail Non-Food	32.1	35.0
Retail Confectionery, Tobacco, Newspapers	2.7	2.4
	100.0	100.0

Source: Ministry of Labour and National Service.

Table LVII gives the distribution of employment, for the same years, within the distributive trades of Glasgow. Retail distribution accounts for almost 60 per cent of the total, while wholesale distribution, including dealing, accounts for slightly more than 40 per cent. From both tables some changes can be observed between 1951 and 1955. The absolute total employed in distribution fell by 5,400, or about 6 per cent. This probably reflects the attraction of other types of occupation under conditions of full employment; as we shall see later, staffing difficulties form an important problem for the retail trader at the present time. Within the changed total the shares of the various branches of the distributive trades have altered. A striking change is the increase in the percentage of the total employed in the non-food retail trades: this was an absolute as well as a relative rise, and prob-

[1] Area of the ten city employment exchanges and Hillington exchange.

[2] With the exception of Professional Services the groups are as defined in Standard Industrial Classification.

[3] Professional Services include Law, Accountancy, and Other Professional and Business Services. Medicine, Dentistry, Education and Religion are excluded.

[4] Includes coal, builders' materials, grain, agricultural supplies (wholesale and retail), other industrial materials and machinery (Standard Industrial Classification: groups ZEL, ZEM).

[5] Excludes catering.

ably reflects the influence of increasing supplies and sales of these goods between 1951 and 1955. At the same time however there was a decline in the proportion employed in the non-food wholesale trades: this may be reconciled with the previous point on the grounds that the main increase in the sale of non-food goods was in the larger durable goods items, which normally pass directly from producer to retailer. In the textile branch of the non-food trades, where wholesaling is important, there was a decline between these two years.

Retail Trade

The Report of the official Census of Distribution and Other Services, 1950, enables us to give a reasonably precise statistical account of the distributive and service trades in Glasgow.[1]

In 1950, according to the Census, Glasgow's shops were comparatively speaking few and large. Altogether, including market stalls, kiosks, travelling vans, hawkers, pedlars, etc. as well as permanent shops, they numbered 11,213 or 103 for every 10,000 people. This ratio was lower than the corresponding British figure (108) but higher than the Scottish figure (98). It was remarkably low for a city: for the six largest cities in Great Britain (excluding London) the average number of shops per 10,000 inhabitants was 116.

TABLE LVIII

Glasgow's Retail Trade: Some Comparisons

	Glasgow	*Six Provincial Cities*[3] *Average*	*Scotland*	*Great Britain*
Establishments[2] per 10,000 popn.	103	116	98	108
Sales per Establishment	£11,600	£10,300	£10,200	£9,300
Full-Time Workers per Establishment	4.5	3.7	4.1	3.4
Sales per Full-time Worker	£2,600	£2,800	£2,500	£2,700

Source: *Census of Distribution and Other Services,* 1951, Vol. I, Tables 3, 5, and 8.

The relative fewness of shops in Glasgow is associated with comparatively high average sales; that is, measuring size by sales, Glasgow's shops are comparatively big. The average sales per Glasgow shop were £11,600 compared with a British figure of £9,300, a Scottish figure of £10,200 (£9,800 excluding Glasgow), and a six cities figure of £10,300. The size of the Glasgow figure may be due to the extremely high degree of concentration of population within the urban area; this

1 The Census was taken in 1951 but information was collected, in the main, for the calendar year 1950 (some trades were allowed to give figures for the year ending April 1951). The coverage for the country as a whole was estimated at 91 per cent of retail establishments, handling 95 per cent of the total trade.

2 For full definition of establishments included see Census, Vol. I, p. 5.

3 Birmingham, Glasgow, Leeds, Liverpool, Manchester and Sheffield.

increases the number of customers within buying range of any given shop giving scope for economies of scale, and also, together with the character of residential building in the city, places limits on the density of shop sites.

When we turn to the detailed picture, obtained by breaking down the totals into shop types, the clearness of this pattern is considerably diminished. Within the important group of food shops, for instance, Glasgow's grocery shops are relatively few and big, but dairies are numerous and small; butchers' shops are large, but in about the same ratio to population as in the country as a whole; bread and flour confectioners' are small but not especially numerous; greengrocers' are both comparatively few and small.

Glasgow's grocers present the clearest example of the relation of size and numbers: there were only 19 of them per 10,000 people, compared with a British figure of 26, a six cities figure of 27, and a Scottish figure of 22; they were also correspondingly large. But it must be noted that the dairy shops in which Glasgow abounds have, in recent years, widened their range until they are now in effect small grocery shops.

Consumption habits, so far as they are peculiar to the city, play some part in modifying the size and number of food shops. From Table LIX an idea of the comparative consumption of four types of foodstuff may be gained: this table shows the sales per head of population of four types of food retailer, calculated for Glasgow, Scotland, and Great Britain. But it should be stressed that the sales figures used are based on shop types, and the dividing lines between these are becoming increasingly blurred as traders extend the range of their goods to include those of other types of shop. Thus, for example, the total sales of greengrocers do not represent the total consumption of fruit and vegetables as quantities of these goods are also sold by grocers.

TABLE LIX

SALES OF FOOD RETAILERS PER HEAD OF POPULATION IN 1950

Food Type	*Glasgow* £	*Scotland* £	*Great Britain* £
Fruit and Vegetables[1]	3.0	2.5	3.6
Bread and Flour Confections	2.6	4.5	2.9
Fish	1.9	1.5	1.2
Meat	5.5	5.6	5.1

SOURCE: *Census of Distribution and Other Services,* 1950, Vol. I, Tables 3, 5 and 8.

From these figures it appears that Scottish consumption of some foods diverges markedly from that of the rest of Britain, a conclusion that was confirmed by a sample survey of food consumption made in

[1] Includes the sales of greengrocers also selling fish.

1953 by the National Food Survey Committee. The figures presented here show some peculiarities of consumption in Glasgow. The consumption of fruit and vegetables, for instance, diverges from the Scottish towards the British figure and this may partly account for greengrocery shops being relatively more numerous in Glasgow than in Scotland as a whole. The consumption of bread and flour confections is low in Glasgow, and this seems to affect the size of such shops, rather than their number. The consumption of fish in Glasgow is remarkably high (a fact that was also revealed in a wartime survey of consumption) and this obviously accounts for the high number of fish shops, 3.1 per 10,000 compared with 2.4 for Scotland and 1.7 for Great Britain. In the case of meat the closeness of the Scottish and the Glasgow figures suggests that consumption is an important factor in determining the number and size of shops.

Sweets, tobacco and newspaper shops are relatively numerous in Glasgow, although their average size is not markedly different from elsewhere. Within the group total the Census figures confirm the impression that one gets of rather more of the specialised non-tobacco-selling sweet shop in Glasgow than elsewhere. Apart from this the tendency for Glasgow's shops to be, on average, bigger and fewer appears in clothing and boot and shoe shops, in bookshops, in furniture and jewellery shops, and in coal dealing. One notable exception is found in Glasgow's department stores: according to the Census figures these are smaller and more numerous than in other cities. An important general feature of Glasgow's shops is that many of them—especially in the centre—serve customers from a much wider area than the city itself. Glasgow is the shopping centre for a considerable area of Scotland; people come from the east (even from Edinburgh), as well as from the industrial west, to shop in Glasgow. An indication of this can be gained from the Census figures. If we take the sales of six broad groups of establishments—clothing, hardware, books and stationery, furniture, jewellery and leather and sports goods, and the "general" group (department stores, variety stores, etc.)—we find that Glasgow with 21 per cent of the population of Scotland accounts for 31 per cent of the total sales of these groups in Scotland.

Changes in the Number of Shops

Evidence as to changes going on in the number and size of shops is generally lacking but some pointers can be mentioned. With the physical expansion of the city, and following the recent relaxation of controls, the number of shops in the city is almost certainly growing. The Corporation have built 208 shops since the end of 1945 and these probably represent the majority of the new permanent shops opened within the city in this period. The numbers of shops built by the Corporation since 1918 are as follows:

Period	No.
1918-1939	268
1940-1945	9
1946-1955	208
Total	485

Corporation policy (to be discussed later in this chapter) is likely to be an important influence in determining the rate of increase of shops. The availability of sites within the old built-up areas is limited and in any case with a static or declining population in these areas there will not be much incentive to expansion. A factor to be borne in mind is the use of mobile shops: the numbers of these are not known but they have increased in recent years, and are used particularly in serving the new estates. (They vary, of course, from vans conducting little more than a delivery service to converted buses which, in the range of stock carried, are literally shops on wheels).

One change in the number of shops that is documented is a marked contraction during the war years. An enquiry made in 1942 for the National Institute of Economic and Social Research into the wartime position of the retailer in Glasgow and Leeds, concluded that about one fifth of the shops that were open in January 1940 had closed by the end of 1941, and that the process was accelerating. The rate of casualty, revealed in the Leeds enquiry, was highest for the smallest types of shops, and non-food shops were relatively worst hit; the reason for closure given most often was "bad trade," though this included causes like shortage of supplies and cases where the shopkeeper had gone into munitions. It is understood that, in Glasgow, a type which was severely hit was the small "parlour" shop, carried on perhaps in a tenement room, where provisions and groceries could be bought in quantities smaller than the ordinary grocer would deal in. Rationing, and perhaps higher working-class incomes, caused these to disappear. (Food rationing incidentally caused problems for other shops, like dairies, which previously sold a very narrow range of provisions; their response was to widen the range of their goods).

Structure and Organisation

Over the last hundred years there have been very important changes in the structure of the retail trade and the organisations that conduct it, changes which are still going on. The general result of these changes is that a large proportion of retail trade has come to be conducted by large-scale retailing organisations. There are three types of these—co-operative societies, multiple stores, and department stores—and they each have their origins in the middle or later years of the nineteenth century. Estimates of the share of the different types of retailer in the total trade of the U.K. since 1900, are given in Table LX.

TABLE LX

ESTIMATED CHANGES IN THE SHARE OF LARGE RETAILERS IN TOTAL RETAIL TRADE OF THE U.K.

Type of Organisation	*Percentage of Total Retail Sales* 1900	1939	1950
Co-operatives	6-7	10-11½	10-12
Multiples[1]	3-4½	4½-5½	4½-6
Department Stores	1-2	18-19½	18-20½
Others (by difference)	86½-90	63½-67½	61½-67½

SOURCE: J. B. Jeffreys: *Retail Trading in Great Britain, 1850-1950* (1954), Table 18, p. 73.

TABLE LXI

DISTRIBUTION OF RETAIL TRADE BY ORGANISATION IN 1950

	Great Britain		*Scotland*		*Towns of 250,000 and over*	
Type of Organisation	*Percentage of Total Establishments*	*of Total Sales*	*Percentage of Total Establishments*	*of Total Sales*	*Percentage of Total Establishments*	*of Total Sales*
Co-operatives	5.0	12.0	9.2	20.1	4.3	11.1
Multiples[1]	10.7	23.5	10.6	18.2	11.1	24.1
Others[2]	84.3	64.4	80.2	61.8	84.6	64.9

SOURCE: *Census of Distribution and Other Services, 1950,* Volume II, Tables 9 and 10.

In Table LXI we give similar figures, but with slightly different definitions of organisation, showing the position in Great Britain, Scotland and towns of 250,000 population and over, as given for 1950 by the Census of Distribution. From this it appears that in that year multiples and co-operatives had 15 per cent of the total establishments in Great Britain and accounted for 35 per cent of total sales. In Scotland their share of total sales was greater, 38 per cent, but within the total the co-operatives had a bigger share.

It is not possible to give a comparable statistical picture for Glasgow. The share of the co-operatives, however, in total retail sales in 1950 can be calculated. In that year total sales of the eight Glasgow societies amounted to nearly £13 millions, and if we add to this an estimate equal to one half of the Clydebank Society's sales (roughly one half of this Society's members live within the city) we get a round figure of £14 millions; this represents 11 per cent of the total retail sales shown by the Census. This proportion is considerably less than the Scottish average but the same as the average of the towns in Great Britain with over a quarter million inhabitants.

Later in this chapter a section will be devoted to the co-operatives.

[1] Organisations having 10 or more branches.
[2] Organisations with under 10 branches.

Here we shall have a look at the multiples and department stores, giving what statistics we have come by, and reviewing their general position and their historical development in Glasgow.

The Multiples

There are no published figures of the proportion of Glasgow's trade conducted by the multiple concerns, but in Table LXII we give for various trades some information about the numbers of establishments owned by the multiples, which are defined here as firms owning ten or more branches.

TABLE LXII

MULTIPLE SHOPS: PERCENTAGE OF ALL ESTABLISHMENTS OWNED BY FIRMS WITH 10 OR MORE SHOPS, IN GLASGOW, GREAT BRITAIN, AND THE LARGER TOWNS

Branch of Retail Trade	*Glasgow* %	*Great Britain* %	*Towns over 250,000 population* %
Grocery	20	12	19
Meat	11	10	10
Dairying	33	13	11
Bread and Flour Confectionery	36	13	26
Sweets-Tobacco-Newspapers[1]	18	6	9

SOURCE: Kelly's *Directory of Glasgow, 1951, Census of Distribution and Other Services,* Vol. I, Table 8: Vol. II, Table 10.

These figures show that, as far as numbers of shops are concerned, there has been a comparatively strong growth of the multiples in Glasgow. In the grocery and meat trades the Glasgow percentage is practically the same as the average for the large towns. In the other three trades shown, however, and especially in dairying, the Glasgow percentage of multiples is very much higher than either the British or the large towns average. Of course, the important point is what proportion of the total sales in any particular branch falls to the multiples and this may differ from the percentage of the total shops operated by them. From Table LXI it can be seen that although the multiples in 1950 had roughly the same proportion of the total shops in Scotland as in Britain as a whole, their proportion of total sales was lower. However, on grounds partly of general impression as to the size of multiple establishments in Glasgow, partly of the comparatively lesser importance of the co-operatives, we are inclined to think that the proportion of Glasgow's retail trade conducted by the multiples is nearer to the national figures (about one quarter) than to the Scottish figure (about one fifth).

Glasgow has some interesting and notable connections with the

[1] This group includes only those retailers of tobacco and newspapers who also sell sweet confectionery.

development of multiple store trading. Thomas Lipton, the founder of one of the earliest and largest national chains of provision stores, was born in Glasgow, of Irish parents, and he began his career as a provision dealer at Stobcross where he opened his first shop in 1878. Lipton was one of the pioneers of the multiple; his career parallelled that of others who built up great systems of branch shops through the sale of cheap goods—in his case imported provisions, and later, tea—to the working classes. His business rapidly outgrew its origins and became nation-wide, so much so that in the 1890's the headquarters were transferred to London. In the interwar years he joined with three other large national multiples to form the Home and Colonial group. This group has acquired considerable interests in the multiple grocery trade of Glasgow, although not through the Lipton connection. Something will be said about it in a moment.

Another old Glasgow firm of grocers which has a wide network of branches is Cooper & Company. The founder of this firm, Thomas G. Bishop, opened his first shop in Howard Court in 1871 and soon made a name for himself in the tea business. The headquarters of this firm are still in Howard Street; until very recently a son of the founder was chairman of the company. The firm is now associated with two English regional groups of multiple grocers, and together with these controls 270 branches throughout the country.

Besides firms like those of Lipton and Bishop, which planted their branches widely over the country at large, there also grew up multiples which concentrated their attention on a single city or region and which consequently came to be far more prominent in these areas than the national concerns. In Glasgow four grocery firms (one was actually a Paisley firm), all of them dating from the 1870's and early '80's and starting as family concerns, built up considerable branch systems. In three cases the main period of growth was in the years 1900-14, while the fourth grew considerably in the interwar years. All four firms have now come under the control of the Home and Colonial group and are administered by a subsidiary company, Scottish Retail Investments Ltd. On the board of this company are members of three of the original founding families of these firms. Altogether, counting a number of branches of their national chains, this group owns 383 shops in Glasgow; this is out of a total of some 440 multiple grocery establishments in the city.

In an entirely different branch of the retail trade, the sale of women's outerwear, a Glasgow concern has had a remarkable career of expansion in recent years. This is the Morrison group which, through all its subsidiaries, owns more than 260 women's outerwear shops throughout the country. This group had its origin in a business started some fifty years ago in Glasgow by Mrs. Edith Morrison, who had come here from Esthonia. The firm became a public company in 1926 at which time it had twenty shops; since then there has been a rapid extension of branches (roughly one half of the present total has been added since the last war) and it is now one of the leading firms in the sale of women's fashion goods. Mrs. Morrison herself has retired, and the business, which is wholly administered from Glasgow, is directed by her sons.[1]

This does not exhaust the list of multiple retail concerns with Glasgow roots. In the sweet confectionery trade there are two multiples which between them own some hundreds of branches throughout the country (125 in Glasgow). In the dairy trade—which now includes a wide range of groceries, provisions and confectionery—there is one Glasgow firm with some 80 branches in the city. Besides these, however, there are about twenty Glasgow retail firms with between 10 and 40 branches: they are to be found in the sweet confectionery, meat, bread and flour confectionery, dairy, greengrocery, fish, drapery and boot and shoe trades.

So much for some of Glasgow's own multiple concerns. Like all large towns the city has its growing quota of the branches of national multiples. The frontages of the Trongate, of Argyle Street and Union Street are now largely occupied by the branches of nationally known multiple tailoring, furniture and boot and shoe concerns. Sauchiehall Street, still keeping something of its reputation as a fashion street, is attracting the shops of the multiple fashion firms. The multiple variety shops, long established in the main shopping streets, and at some points further out, are also expanding the numbers of their branches, mainly at points outside the city centre.

The Department Stores

A department store is a shop in which a variety of goods are sold under one roof, the shop being organised into departments around which the public are free to wander. As a type of shop it developed during the second half of the last century; in many cases its origins were in the retail drapery houses of the time, of which Glasgow possessed a large number. According to the Census of Distribution there were 18 department stores in 1950; they had average sales of £208,000, and they employed just under 5,000 full-time workers.

Glasgow men have played a notable part in the development of this type of shop. One of them, John Anderson, was one of the original pioneers of department store trading. In his later years he claimed: "In 1845 I introduced the idea of universal trading (the idea was original) in the drapery trade." His venture of combining different branches of trade under one roof was very successful: he moved from Clyde Terrace to the Polytechnic Rooms in Jamaica Street, and from there to Argyle Street, where, taking the name of his previous premises with him, he built Anderson's Royal Polytechnic. In 1925 this store was bought by Lewis's, who built their present shop on the site, and in the present name of which—Lewis's Royal Polytechnic—John Ander-

[1] Morrison's Associated Companies Ltd. has now (1957) been acquired by Great Universal Stores, Ltd.

son's enterprise is still remembered. Anderson demonstrated that there was an advantage in selling many things under one roof. He was an inspired buyer, ransacking the markets of Europe to provide goods for his Glasgow ventures. His methods—constant advertising, large-scale buying, low prices—were those which many successors were to follow.

Beginning his career rather later than Anderson, Walter Wilson, the founder of the Colosseum, and later of Trérons, was another notable pioneer in this field. He began as a hatter, and in 1869 took premises in the old Polytechnic recently vacated by Anderson. At first he concentrated on hats, buying in quantity from the manufacturers. In the early '80's, following a tour of America and Europe, he began to add other departments, and by 1882 there were twenty departments in the Colosseum. Wilson's career echoes that of his contemporary, David Lewis, in England. There was the same aggressive policy in buying on a large scale and selling at low prices (" store " prices); the same flamboyant advertising, with its variety of stunts, spectacles (e.g. the Christmas " Fairylands ") and competitions; there was even the same, rather surprising, foray into the mass tea trade in the 1880's (Wilson claimed to be the first to sell Ceylon tea in Glasgow; he seems to have preceded Lipton in this).

Wilson's Colosseum became a widely known store catering for a predominantly working-class clientele. In the 1890's he opened a chain of branches on this model and also, under the name of Tréron et Cie., some high-grade fashion shops. The branch scheme failed, and by 1904 all had been closed; but in that year he opened a large high-class fashion store under the Tréron name in Sauchiehall Street, taking two floors of the McLellan Galleries for the purpose. The connection of the family with the Colosseum was ended in 1936, but Mr. Arthur Wilson, son of Walter Wilson, is a director of Trérons, which is now a department store catering for all types of customers.

Another well-known name in department store trading in Glasgow is that of the Ogg family. This family has, through a number of generations, owned the well-known Sauchiehall Street store of Copland & Lye. This firm was founded in 1878, and its first store was in Argyle Street. In the 1880's the list of departments was not very different from what it is now, though probably the drapery side was relatively more important then.

It is appropriate in speaking of the development of the department store in its Glasgow habitat, to say something of a remarkable example of growth of a Glasgow concern that has occurred in recent years. The House of Fraser, under the present Mr. Hugh Fraser, has come to control a considerable proportion of the department stores not only of Glasgow, but of Scotland. The origins of this firm lie back in the middle of the nineteenth century and are linked, curiously enough, with those of Glasgow's most prominent wholesale house. In 1849 Hugh Fraser, the founder of the firm, went into partnership with James Arthur, and they opened a retail house at No. 8 Buchanan Street, the site of the present Fraser Sons' store. A wholesale business was shortly added and both sides of the firm's activities expanded. After about seven years a split occurred in the partnership as a result of which Hugh Fraser took the retail business, and James Arthur the wholesale house which was now renamed Arthur & Company.

The recent expansion of the House of Fraser began under the present Mr. Hugh Fraser, in the middle 'thirties. It has brought the firm to the position where it controls more than thirty individual department stores, drapery and clothing shops, throughout Scotland (including thirteen in Glasgow itself), as well as a chain of multiple drapers with many shops in the industrial towns of North Eastern England.

The House of Fraser is not a "multiple" in the usual sense of a firm which operates a number of more or less identical shop units. Although most of the Fraser stores are of the department store type, they are very diverse in the character of the goods sold and the markets served; in Glasgow, for instance, they range from stores with a wholly working class clientele, to two of the more "exclusive" women's fashion shops in the city. The policy of the organisation is to preserve the individuality, including the original name, of the shops taken over, and little emphasis is placed on the ownership link between them.

The department stores, along with other types of traders, are meeting big changes in the character of their markets. The main changes are caused by redistribution of income in favour of the working class, and the relatively less favourable position of the middle classes. The result in terms of store-trading—multiple and department—is a levelling tendency which can be observed in almost all Glasgow's shops. In the trade the saying is that there is a strong tendency on the part of buyers to "shop up." This means that former middle class shops are now finding themselves catering for a wider market; with higher incomes working class people are coming to them, while some groups in the middle class are not so good a market as formerly. On the other side, stores which have customarily aimed at the working class market are raising the standard of their merchandise. Other problems of the department stores include staffing difficulties, but they have these in common with the rest of the retail trade.

The Independent Retailers

In the nature of things it is not possible to say as much about the position and history of the independent retailer as such, as about the large-scale retailers. The result may be to give the impression of disproportionate attention to the latter. It must be remembered that the greater proportion of the total retail trade of Glasgow is probably still in the hands of traders who operate a single shop, or at most a few branches. But as the figures presented here show, the independent has lost ground in this century and the process is continuing. The extension of the larger concerns in the older areas of the city is probably limited by the scarcity of sites, but when independent traders retire it is usually only the bigger concerns that have the resources to make a reasonable bid for the business.

Among the independents that might be mentioned as bringing a touch of colour into the city's trade are the barrowmen (and women), and the stall-keepers in the retail markets. In the side-streets opening off Renfield Street second-hand book dealers still ply their trade from barrows, though numbers are now much reduced. On London Road, the "Barrows," a market in which second-hand goods of every kind are sold from barrows and stalls, still thrives, while in a lane off the Bridgegate there is a group of markets, known collectively as Paddy's Market (though not the original of that name, which was in Greendyke Street and has now ceased to exist) in which hawkers, who are almost all women, lease stalls for the sale mainly of second-hand clothing.

Labour in the Retail Trade

The Census of Distribution collected figures of employment in the distributive trade and a number of interesting points emerge from these. In 1950 the retail trades of Glasgow employed some 50,000 full-time workers and a further 9,000 part-time workers. Of the full-time workers 57 per cent were women; for the country as a whole the figure was 48 per cent and for the six cities, 54 per cent. The use of part-time workers in Glasgow is comparatively small: 17 of them were employed for every 100 full-time workers compared with a national figure of 25, and a six cities figure of 22. Glasgow's figure contrasted markedly with that of Birmingham where there were 29 part-timers per 100 full-timers.

In numbers of full-time workers per shop Glasgow shows a high average: for all shops it was 4.5 compared with a national figure of 3.4 and a six cities figure of 3.7 (see Table LVIII, also Appendix Table 45). Along with this high number of workers per shop there was a rather low level of sales per worker, £2,600 compared with an average of £2,800 for the six cities. In this figure there was again a marked difference between Glasgow and Birmingham, where the average sales per full-time worker was nearly £3,200. The difference is partly, but by no means wholly, due to the greater number of part-timers in Birmingham's shops; the main reason for it must be sought in a difference in the relative scarcity of labour between the two cities. It is interesting to see that in this the Glasgow and Scottish figures are very similar: the comparison between them and the national figures seems to confirm what one would expect, that the retail trades tend to be more "labour-intensive" in places where labour is relatively less scarce.

However, in spite of a comparatively larger supply of labour on which to draw, the retail trades of Glasgow have been meeting the same difficulties in staffing as the retail trader elsewhere. All types of traders in the city say that staffing is a great problem to them—a problem of getting a sufficient number of workers of the quality they like, and of keeping them. The labour market of the postwar period has been subject to the condition of labour scarcity due to high levels of aggregate demand and full employment. The retail trades however are subject to special pressures. In the first place the six-day week is a great discouragement to recruitment. Secondly, the fact is that retail trading shares, with the service trades, the difficulty of increasing the productivity of its labour. In an advancing industrial society the pace in productivity and wages is set by the manufacturing trades; the others, including distribution, have continually to adapt themselves to this, and they tend to feel it as a difficulty in obtaining an adequate supply of labour.

Part of the answer to the problem lies in changes in methods of trading and we shall say something about this in the next section. Other expedients include the employment of more married women; the department stores, for example, are employing more of these than before the war. Many of the shops and organisations approached believed that they do not get the same "type" of worker as they did before the war. To the extent that this is true, it again probably reflects the relatively weak position of the distributive trades as buyers of labour, under modern conditions. Partly a consequence of this is the problem of labour turnover which, as in other trades, is very much higher to-day than before the war (one large firm put their labour turnover at 60 per cent per annum).

Trading Methods

Over the last hundred years the retail trade has seen very great changes in organisation and methods of trading. To-day, marketing methods are not so spectacular as when Thomas Lipton paraded live pigs or three-ton cheeses through the streets of the city, but far-reaching changes are nevertheless going on. There has been, in this century, a general trend towards more impersonal methods of selling. This has culminated since the war in the appearance and spread of the self-service principle—the system where goods are displayed in open racks and the customer serves himself. This has made its appearance in Glasgow. With one exception it is so far confined to the food trades, mainly to the sale of groceries and provisions, though some of the stores concerned sell some vegetables, and a few sell meat.

In mid-1955 there were 48 self-service shops. Of these 29, or 60 per cent, were operated by co-operatives who, almost throughout the country, have been very active in embracing self-service; this percentage is practically the same as the national figure. Other types of trader—independent and multiple—were slower in adopting the principle, but there have been signs recently of much greater activity by the large multiples: between 1953 and 1955 the proportion of all self-service shops operated by them rose from 18 to 23 per cent. In Glasgow, as can be seen from Table LXIII, the multiples show a more than average development of self-service; the independents show practically none—in mid-1955 no independent grocer had opened a self-service store.

TABLE LXIII

SELF-SERVICE SHOPS[1] IN GLASGOW—AUGUST 1955

Co-operatives	*Multiples*	*Department Stores*	*Others*	*Total*
29	17	1	1	48

SOURCE: *Directory of Stores, 1955-6,* Annual Supplement to *"Self Service,"* August 1955.

There is no definite evidence yet that the self-service system is going to provide the answer to the labour problems which we discussed in the last section. In the enquiries made for this survey two co-operative societies mentioned staff shortage as a possible motive for the adoption of self-service, but neither of the two multiples approached seemed to consider this an important factor. According to one firm the labour-saving had not been so great as anticipated, but sales had gone up, and it might in the end be possible to handle a bigger turnover without a proportionate increase in staff. There are signs that self-service is popular with consumers (though not everywhere) and the stimulus to adopt it may come from the consumer's preference. However it is interesting to notice that both the multiples approached regarded their self-service ventures as experimental. A possible brake on the progress of self-service in Glasgow is the space limitation in existing shops and the scarcity of new sites.

Although there is no definite connection between difficulties of staffing and self-service trading as such, conditions in the labour market are having a long-term influence on the kind of service offered by shops. The tendency to-day in all types of shops is towards a more impersonal service. It is carried to its greatest length, short of self-service, in the multiple variety stores. But in the department stores, and even the small shops, the customer is left more and more to make his own choice, the assistant being there merely to transact the sale.

Another aspect of trading methods that has taken on an increased importance in recent years is the extension of credit trading in its various forms. At the present time all forms of credit trading are on the increase. The most striking is hire-purchase which is operated by very many shops of all types and sizes. Its progress in the most recent years has been limited by official control over the size of initial deposits and over the period of repayment. Such controls are likely to be permanent, but hire purchase is on the increase; it is also spreading, socially, to groups which previously eschewed it. Some department stores operate systems of instalment purchase (for durable goods of

1 Ordinary shops, or departments within ordinary shops, only. One co-operative society operated 7 mobile self-service shops, and these are not included in the totals.

certain kinds) which differ from hire purchase in shorter terms of credit and the absence of interest charges. Those store that allow monthly accounts have experienced a big increase in the amount of credit outstanding on this count. One store said that to-day about one third of all sales were charged to monthly accounts, compared with about one quarter before the war.

Two other forms of credit trading, used predominantly by working-class people, are the trading "check," and the facilities provided by the credit draper (or "Scotch" draper). Under the check system a customer is provided with a voucher with which he can make an immediate purchase, and for which he himself pays by instalments spread over a period of twenty weeks. The checks are handled by special companies which collect the instalments on them, and redeem them from the shopkeeper. There is a poundage charge to the customer, and the checks are redeemed from the shopkeeper at a certain discount on their face value. The principal goods on which checks are spent are drapery and footwear, but almost anything can be bought with them, and they are accepted by a very large number of shops, including the leading multiples. One distinctive feature of check trading in Glasgow is the use of the "travelling check"—a check which a customer can spend in several shops, as distinct from the "token check," used in England, which can only be spent in one shop.

Three check companies operate in Glasgow; two of them are domiciled here and the third is a large national concern. According to one of the local companies about three quarters of the city's check business is done by the two local companies. This company also reports that the check business in Glasgow is increasing.

The other system—that of the credit draper—involves the extension of credit by the shopkeeper or merchant himself. A trader sells goods and takes payment in instalments which he often collects himself. The period of credit ranges up to thirty weeks. According to information supplied by the Scottish Credit Traders Federal Board there are over one hundred credit traders in Glasgow; they operate from central premises and they deal principally in clothing and soft household goods, although many of them have been increasing their range to include carpets, china, electrical goods and furniture. The Board reports a "decided increase" in credit trading since the war.

Distribution of Retail Trading

Finally, before we leave the retail trade, something should be said about the distribution of shops in Glasgow, and changes in it. The pattern of distribution of shops in Glasgow is distinctly linear; the shops line the old arterial routes through the city (e.g. Maryhill Road, Paisley Road, Pollokshaws Road, Parliamentary Road). There are certain nuclei, usually at the junction between routes, where trade is probably greater and the shops bigger; but beyond them the shops usually continue along the routeways. The linear pattern is also stamped on the central shopping area: broadly this runs from Glasgow Cross along the Trongate and Argyle Street, up Union Street and Renfield Street, and then along Sauchiehall Street. Only in the case of lower Buchanan Street and Union Street do two major shopping thoroughfares run parallel and near to one another.

In the mid-nineteenth century the Trongate and Argyle Street formed the shopping centre. Sauchiehall Street was developed later in the century and in the early stages some shops migrated from the old to the newer shopping area. To-day Argyle Street is very much a working-class shopping street. Buchanan Street, at its lower end, still caters for more expensive tastes and in one section of its length provides the nearest approach in Glasgow to a " man's street."

Sauchiehall Street was originally developed as a fashion street, and there is still a tradition that it is hard to sell household goods there. As a fashion street it served a middle class market: to-day both the fashion element and the middle class character have been considerably diluted, though they are still detectably there. Actually, with changes in the character of the shops (e.g. the opening of multiple variety stores), and in shopping habits, Sauchiehall Street is very much a place where all the classes mingle, though perhaps more on the pavements than in the shops. It has also become the main cinema street of the city.

A question anxiously asked, and to some extent answered, is whether in view of increasing congestion in the city centre there should be some dispersal of shopping facilities. There are signs that some of the road-junctions outside the centre—e.g. St. George's Cross, Paisley Road Toll—may develop into sub-centres. One of the big multiple variety stores is now building stores at a number of these points; it may be followed by others and also by the department stores. One region that would seem to cry out for such development is the Bridge Street area, on the south side, but whether trade could be drawn here by actual planning measures is problematical.

The tendency for Glasgow's shops to line the routeways is true only of the areas of the city built before 1914. The newer parts, built since then, present an altogether different aspect. As the routes enter these districts the shops cease, and whenever they reappear it is usually in groups of six, or at the most a dozen. In the estates built by the Corporation the distribution of the shops is determined by policy in regard to shops.

The Corporation's policy in the new estates is to build shops at a density of roughly 6 to every 1,000 houses. If we take the estates completed, or under active construction, at the end of 1955, and on which shops are built, the total number of houses in the schemes is 84,000; the number of shops is 540. This is only a rough guide to policy but it confirms the ratio already mentioned. If we assume that there are four people to each Corporation house, the density of shops to population is about 12 to 15 per 10,000 people. This may be compared with an average over the whole city, in 1950, of 103 per 10,000. The two figures are not entirely comparable since the city figure includes the central shops which serve the whole city (and beyond). Also one would expect newly-built shops to be of greater than average size. However, with all allowances of this kind, the density of shops in the new estates seems to be remarkably low, and is probably an explanation of the increased use of mobile shops in them.

Corporation shops are usually built in suites of six, four doubles and two singles. The letting policy is that one third of the accommodation (one double and one single shop) is automatically offered to the co-operative societies; the rest go to the highest bidders. A typical suite contains a co-operative grocery store and a co-operative dairy or butcher's shop, one multiple grocery store (occasionally an independent grocer), one newsagent, a butcher if the second co-operative shop is a dairy, and then either a fruiterer, a baker, or occasionally a chemist. The suites are scattered through the estates and the resulting pattern is one of dispersed nuclei of shops. In three estates it is planned to build two centres which will each contain thirty shops and the nucleated pattern will be accentuated in these areas.

The Service Trades

Before turning to look at wholesale distribution something should be said about the service trades of Glasgow. The service trades are those in which the provision of a service, as distinct from a commodity, plays a big part (though not necessarily the whole part).

The 1950 Census of Distribution collected statistics of the service trades.[1] The figures for Glasgow show certain similarities with the corresponding retail trade figures. Compared with other cities, Glasgow's service establishments tend to be large and few: in 1950 there were 23 per 10,000 inhabitants, against 31 for the six largest provincial cities; sales per establishment were £8,100 for Glasgow, £6,400 for the six cities. This comparison applied to all the sub-groups of services: in the most important of these, the catering, there were about one-third fewer establishments in Glasgow, with sales per establishment about one-third higher than in the six provincial cities. The sellers and repairers of motor vehicles (including garages) and cycles are also, apparently, considerably larger on average than their counterparts elsewhere. Interestingly enough, however, sales per worker, while being lower in Glasgow's service trades than in other cities, were only slightly so (£1,430 against £1,460), and in the important catering group they were higher (£960 against £840).

It is not easy to give a statistical account of trends in the service trades, but some general comments can be made. The demand for

[1] For the service trades the Census covered 80-90 per cent of the establishments accounting for 86-90 per cent of the total trade. Certain types of establishments were included in the service trades in which the sale of goods played a big part, e.g. all establishments selling cars and cycles and their accessories.

restaurant facilities is higher now than before the war, the public having taken to "eating out" more during the war. An indication of this is the extension of restaurants in shops. In spite of this increased demand, however, some old catering establishments have closed down in recent years. The best known are, perhaps, the famous Cranston's tearooms, which have now all closed or been taken over by other firms. The Cranstons set up their tearoom in the 'nineties and in their day they were pioneers of this kind of restaurant. (They also achieved fame for the interior decorations by Charles Rennie Mackintosh.) New concerns have grown up to serve the demand. The trend is towards speedier meals—either the quick service of simplified meals, or the snack bar type of service. This is said to be because lunch times are now shorter.

Turning to one particular type of catering establishment, the public house, we have some figures provided by the Registrar of the City Police. Numbers of licensed public houses in the city at three dates were:

1913	1,411
1938	1,136
1956	1,080

Numbers have thus declined considerably since 1913. This is not necessarily an indication of smaller sales of beverages by public houses, but the consumption of these, per head, has almost certainly declined. The number of public houses in the city is being influenced by Corporation policy in planning its estates, and this is likely to be even more the case in future. In the estates built hitherto the Corporation has made no provision whatsoever for public houses. A change in this policy is impending in the case of Hutchesontown-Gorbals redevelopment plan; the proposal here is that sites for public houses will be sold or feued.

The number of hotels listed in the 1955 edition of Kelly's Directory of Glasgow was 50. In addition there were 41 private and 3 temperance hotels. One would not expect Glasgow to exercise many claims on the time of tourists and other visitors to Scotland, but the provision of accommodation is quite important. The following figures of the number of persons accommodated in hotels, boarding houses and apartment houses in the city are taken from a publication of the Scottish Tourist Board:

Year ending 30 September	1951:	621,032
,, ,, ,, ,,	1953:	683,568
,, ,, ,, ,,	1955:	684,950

No indication is given of the average duration of stay. Probably a considerable proportion of these sojourners are tourists passing through the city on the way to the north. For instance, some motor-coach tours coming from England make use of Glasgow as a stopping place.

Since the end of wartime petrol rationing, and with the increase in the supplies of new cars to the home market, all the trades connected with the selling and servicing of vehicles have expanded. The number of second-hand car dealers has risen, and garages have been re-equipped. There is an acute shortage of overnight garaging facilities in the city areas; while the general scarcity of sites probably inhibits the opening up of new service stations.

One type of service establishment that was not included in the Census but which is expanding very rapidly at present is that of the dry cleaner. A great number of these have been opened in recent years, some by individual cleaners and some by multiple concerns. In the case of some multiple concerns the branches are collecting centres, the cleaning process being performed in specialised premises. In other cases, and particularly with individual cleaners, the valeting and cleaning processes are performed in the shop. "Launderettes," that is premises (usually shops) containing batteries of washing machines in which, for a small fee, the weekly wash may be done, have not yet appeared in any numbers in Glasgow, although they are very popular in some English towns.

Wholesale Distribution

The wholesale distributive trades are a more difficult section of business to define and describe. This can be illustrated by the scope of the Census of Distribution as applied to the wholesale trades. The Census included in its returns not simply those firms which bought from producers or importers and sold to retailers: it covered a wide variety of dealers selling industrial materials and components as well as finished goods; of agents buying and selling on commission; of undertakings providing warehousing and storage services. In addition firms were included which combined wholesale trading with production, retail trading, and importing and exporting activities, although as far as possible the wholesaling activities in themselves were separated from the others for Census purposes. From this it can be seen that the wholesale trades as such are more varied than the retail trades; and as a consequence global figures, such as some of those provided by the Census, have to be used much more cautiously.

In Volume III of the Census Report, figures of the wholesale trades on a town basis are provided, and those for Glasgow are reproduced in Appendix Table 47. According to the Census, which covers somewhere in the region of 90 per cent of all organisations within its scope, there were 2,715 establishments engaged in wholesale trading (by the Census definition) in Glasgow in 1950. These establishments employed 36,000 full-time workers and had sales amounting to £420 m. The sales total greatly exceeds the total of retail sales in the city; one reason for this is that it contains a considerable volume of sales of materials and components to manufacturers; another is that some goods are bought and sold by more than one intermediary; thirdly there is the fact that Glasgow, as an important commercial centre, is a wholesale centre for a wide area of Scotland, and in some trades, parts of England as well. To make some comparisons with other cities, the total sales of the wholesale trades in Glasgow in 1950 exceeded those of Birmingham (£331 m.) but fell short of those of Manchester (£689 m.); it was also less than the Liverpool total (£553 m.), but only because this included a large figure for raw cotton (£233 m.). Within the Glasgow figure the most important groups were: Groceries, Confectionery and Drinks (£107 m.); Other Food (£53 m.); Clothing, Footwear and Textiles (£68 m.); and Industrial Raw Materials £50 m. (of which Yarns were £39 m.).

The wholesale trades expanded greatly in the second half of the last century, the increasing flow of goods from producer to consumer creating a need for intermediaries at the wholesale as well as the retail stage. In this century, with the increase in direct selling between producers and retailers, and with the growth of large-scale retailers (multiples, co-operatives) who buy very little from wholesalers, the trend has been to a relative contraction. In a recent study[1] of distribution covering all but a few minor commodities it was concluded that about 40 per cent of all goods were handled by intermediaries between the producer or importer and the retailer. But the proportion varies very much between trades. From enquiries it appears that the experience of the wholesale consumer goods trade in Glasgow, in recent decades, has been broadly typical of wholesale distribution in general. For example, in branches where large-scale retailing has made great headway there has been a reduction in numbers or, in some trades, a change of function by existing firms.

Wholesale Drapery and Textile Trade

Glasgow has long been prominent in the wholesale textile trade and here the trends already described have been experiencd. There has been a decline in numbers as well as changes in function, in this case a switch by some firms to what is, in effect, retail trading. With the development of independent wholesaling in the drapery trade, in the middle decades of the last century, Glasgow came to have many wholesale houses. Through travellers and branch warehouses these firms supplied a wide range of textiles and clothing to all parts of Britain, while through agents they supplied markets aboard. Up to 1914 the trade seems to have expanded with no undue setbacks; in the interwar years a severe blow was sustained. The general state of depression, with two periods of severe price-falls, in 1920-1 and

[1] J. H. Jeffreys, with M. McColl and G. L. Levett, *The Distribution of Consumer Goods* (1950).

1929-31, hit the wholesale drapers severely, and several Glasgow houses went out of business or were forced to amalgamate.

The difficulties of these years have been told with candour in the recently published history of Arthur & Company. This firm, which celebrates its centenary this year (1956), is one of the oldest and largest wholesale houses in Glasgow. In common with other wholesalers the firm sustained very heavy losses in both the 1920-1 and 1929-31 slumps, due to the fall in the price of goods held in stock. In 1920-1 over £400,000 had to be paid out for the cancellation of commitments. In 1929 falling prices again brought difficulties, and in the early 1930's a complete reconstruction was carried out: the number of departments was reduced and the range of goods narrowed. It is noteworthy that in 1922 two other very old Glasgow houses—J. & W. Campbell & Co., founded in 1817, and Stewart & MacDonald, founded in 1826—amalgamated. With these difficulties imposed by the general economic situation of the interwar period, there was also the long-run erosion of the wholesalers' position due to the rise of the multiple and the continued growth of the department store.

One response to these difficulties has been the development of "customer's customer" trade. Broadly this is a procedure whereby a retailer gives one of his customers a "line" to visit a warehouse to choose some article. This system has been developed by some wholesalers to the point where it is virtually a form of retail trade, carried on with the assistance of agents. The "principal customer" is not a retailer in the ordinary sense but may simply be a householder with a connection among a circle of friends: these come to the warehouse for their requirements, the goods being sold on credit. The tendency at present appears to be for this type of "customer's customer" trade to increase.

The total number of wholesale drapers in Glasgow is not known, since there are still many small drapery houses which do not belong to the principal association. This is the Wholesale Textile Association (Scottish Branch) and it has 25 members in Glasgow. As has been said, the larger firms supply customers all over the country (and meet the competition of wholesalers from others towns, in Glasgow); the smaller firms, employing up to half a dozen travellers, probably concentrate more on the local market.

A branch of the wholesale drapery trade that has shrunk considerably since the beginning of the century is the export trade. In the later decades of the last century the wholesale drapers of Glasgow, along with those in other large textile centres, built up a considerable export trade, mainly in textiles (piece-goods) and made-up garments, but with a wide range of other goods as well. The principal markets were in the Dominions, but there were also strong connections with the Far East. The principal customers in these places were merchants, traders and storekeepers, and business was done through representatives and agents. The heyday of the trade was in the period 1880-1900, a time when the new countries were developing rapidly, and growing immigrant populations had to be clothed and equipped with household textiles. It continued strongly down to the First World War and in the boom that followed it; the volume of Arthur & Company's export business reached its highest point in 1920. But with the collapse of the postwar boom the trade fell away rapidly and the interwar years saw a considerable withdrawal from it. The reasons were not simply those connected with trade depression. The position of the export merchant has been considerably undermined by the development of direct selling by manufacturers and, especially in the case of the wholesale drapers, by the growth of industry in their former markets. Many of these countries began to manufacture for themselves the kind of consumer goods which had formed the staple lines of the wholesaler-exporters. To-day the export trade of these firms is not wholly dead, but it is a mere shadow of its former self: according to one firm its exports are about one-eighth, by value, of what they were at their peak.

Wholesale Groceries and Provisions Trade

In the grocery and provisions trade it is interesting to see that the traditional distinction between grocer and provision-dealer, now almost non-existent at the retail stage, still persists in the wholesale trade. The wholesale provision merchant sells butter, cheese, eggs, bacon and lard; the wholesale grocer sells pulses, sugar, tea, biscuits, preserves; both sell canned goods. The wholesale provision dealer's trade is a more specialised one involving certain processing activities such as the maturing of cheese, and the curing, smoking and rolling of bacon. This difference is given as a reason for the difference in numbers between the two sections: there are 8 wholesale grocers, but approximately 40 wholesale provision dealers. Probably these processing activities are associated with a greater variety of demand which permits the existence of a relatively large number of firms. Also, however, the wholesale provision trade has suffered rather less than the wholesale grocery trade from the trend to direct dealing between retailer and producer, or retailer and importer.[1] A number of the wholesale provision dealers in Glasgow (the number was put at " about a dozen ") are also importers bringing in provisions which are sold to wholesalers throughout Scotland. Some provisions are imported by importing firms domiciled elsewhere, e.g. London, and sold here through agents.

Both traders have had their periods of difficulty, and numbers of firms to-day are smaller than earlier in the century. Numbers have fallen even since 1938: in the wholesale grocery trade from some 12 to 15 firms to the present 8; in the wholesale provision trade from 54 to the present 40. The decline in numbers is due partly to amalgama-

[1] It has been estimated that in 1938 50 per cent of provisions passed through wholesalers, compared with 35 per cent of groceries. See Jeffreys, McColl and Levett, *op. cit.* p. 20.

tions, partly to retirals from business. Representatives of neither trade could recall any actual failures during the interwar years. Both trades report a tendency to concentration in fewer, larger firms. Both also report some decline in outlets due to growth of multiples and co-operatives. In the case of the wholesale provision trade it was said that there has been a considerable growth in industrial catering—the supplying of industrial canteens—since the war. It was also stated—though not by a wholesaler—that the wholesalers are increasing their trade with hotels and boarding houses.

The Wholesale Markets

In some important food trades the wholesale business is carried on in and around markets owned and maintained by Glasgow Corporation. There are five of these markets—Cattle, Meat, Fruit, Fish and Cheese—and we must say something about the business and organisation of them.

The Cheese Market will not detain us long. It is the smallest of the markets and contains only two firms, both of which handle other provisions besides cheese. Furthermore, as there are numerous other firms engaged in the wholesale provisions trade it appears that the cheese market as such merely forms a fractional part of this trade.

The Cattle and Meat Markets

Glasgow has both a livestock market and a meat market; they are situated, adjacent to one another and to the abattoir, in Calton. Livestock sold in the cattle market are drawn from the main producing counties of Scotland, although between January 1940 and July 1954, under the control of fat livestock by the Ministry of Food, the market could accept beasts only from an area within a few miles of the city. This produced a considerable decline in activity in the market: the numbers of beasts sold fell and there are to-day only three firms operating in the market compared with ten pre-war. The period since the lifting of the control is too short to give any indications of the future, but there have been rises in the numbers of livestock sold, particularly cattle. One firm in the market, approached on this question, was doubtful of a restoration of the market to its former position.

The main purchasers of livestock are wholesalers buying for local slaughter and consumption, but there is some buying for this purpose by retail butchers. It is said, however, that whereas before the war about a fifth to a quarter of retailers bought some supplies on the hoof the number has declined, the necessary skill having been lost during the period of food control when butchers got all their supplies in carcass form. In the autumn many sheep and lambs are bought in the market

TABLE LXIV

CATTLE MARKET: LIVESTOCK HANDLED

Year[1]	Number of Beasts				
	Cattle	*Calves*	*Sheep*	*Pigs*	*Horses*
1937-8	26,377	6,042	324,347	13,127	4,561
1945-6	5,851	4,351	82,645	11,593	2,707
1947-8	4,496	3,829	58,889	16,577	2,179
1949-50	3,897	3,192	79,466	29,187	997
1951-2	6,499	2,986	61,338	19,290	458
1953-4	4,672	2,928	68,695	29,065	168
1955-6	11,050	3,343	89,587	12,216	58

SOURCE: General Manager, Markets Department, Corporation of Glasgow.

for consignment to Smithfield and other English markets. There is also some trade—again, sheep and lambs—in stores for fattening.

The Glasgow meat market supplies home-killed and imported meat to a wide area around the city; towns up to a distance of 60 miles draw some of their supplies from Glasgow, while a certain amount of meat is sent to Liverpool and London. The main source of supply of home-killed meat is from animals bought at markets throughout Scotland, in the North of England and in Ireland. With the exception of calves, practically all the home-killed meat sold in the market is slaughtered in the city abattoir. The tables on page 379 show the throughput in the in the market.

Broadly there are two methods by which meat is sold at wholesale. Meat may be sold by wholesalers from beasts purchased, slaughtered and dressed by them. Alternatively, livestock may be "consigned" to the market by dealers, who specialise in buying on the hoof and supplying the particular requirements of different markets, and also by farmers; such livestock is slaughtered, dressed and sold on a commission basis, by salesmen who are known as commission agents. According to information supplied most of the firms dealing in home-killed meat in the Glasgow market sell predominantly on a commission basis; about half-a-dozen firms mainly buy their own stock.

Imported meat, frozen and chilled, comes to Glasgow from London and Liverpool. Some meat was landed here prior to 1939 but since de-control there has been no resumption of these landings. Imported meat is sold in the market either by branches or subsidiaries of the big meat importing firms, or by local firms acting either as agents for an importing firm or for shippers abroad, or as sub-agents for principal agents in London. There are six imported meat firms operating directly in the market, but three of these sell home meat on consignment. Two of the importing firms are Dominion firms only recently (presumably since de-control) established in the market. During the period of control, of course, all meat was imported by the Ministry of Food, which released its stocks to the established importing firms.

[1] Year ended 31 May in each case.

TABLE LXV

ABATTOIR: THROUGHPUT

Year[1]	Cattle	Calves	Sheep	Pigs
	Number of Beasts			
1937-8	73,298	4,966	318,198	45,804
1945-6	91,054	4,326	310,935	35,619
1947-8	78,219	6,876	273,511	23,862
1949-50	76,512	6,014	326,770	59,198
1951-2	85,650	19,860	283,243	97,646
1953-4	74,044	17,809	358,593	112,313
1955-6	115,505	13,732	421,099	88,412

SOURCE: General Manager, Markets Department, Corporation of Glasgow.

TABLE LXVI

MEAT MARKET: HOME KILLED SUPPLIES

Year[2]	Cattle	Calves	Sheep	Pigs[3]
	Number of Carcasses			
1937-8	66,631	22,728	292,921	6,609
1945-6	91,163	56,391	312,333	403
1947-8	78,026	53,136	272,577	707
1949-50	78,004	54,149	327,328	5,918
1951-2	89,116	53,567	285,698	27,241
1953-4	78,369	37,055	369,688	67,332
1955-6	109,670	11,991	413,833	2,050

SOURCE: General Manager, Markets Department, Corporation of Glasgow.

TABLE LXVII

MEAT MARKET: SUPPLIES OF CHILLED AND FROZEN MEAT

Year[4]	Cattle Carcasses	Calves Carcasses	Sheep Carcasses	Pigs Carcasses	Cases[5]
1937-8	53,506	136	106,152	33,823	341,595
1945-6	8,425	340	295,133	15,788	268,300
1947-8	30,501	316	466,654	1,974	144,421
1949-50	33,054	—	381,139	5,335	72,347
1951-2	11,191	12	380,230	1,993	53,905
1953-4	18,892	—	272,495	2,718	37,892
1955-6	48,191	188	138,121	5,068	127,505

SOURCE: General Manager, Markets Department, Corporation of Glasgow.

The proportions of imported and home-killed meat handled in the market seems to be more or less in line with national averages for consumption of these types of meat. Over the three years ending 31 May 1956 about one quarter of the cattle carcasses exposed for sale

1 Year ended 31 May in each case.

2 Year ended 31 May in each case.

3 These figures do not include pigs slaughtered in the Glasgow Abattoir as these are exempt from dues.

4 Year ended 31 May in each case.

5 Cases containing cuts of meat, e.g. rumps, and, to some extent, offals, which are mainly imported.

in the market were imported, while for sheep the proportion was one third. These figures underestimate the proportion of imported meat sold since they exclude " cases " of meat which are mainly imported. In the year ending 31 May 1956 the number of carcasses of home-killed cattle sold in the market was equal to 4 per cent of the total slaughterings in the country during that period; for sheep, the corresponding figure was 5 per cent.

It is said that the number and size of firms has not changed materially since the prewar period. There has been the addition of the two importing firms already mentioned; also, two old-established firms in the market have been taken over by the Fatstock Marketing Corporation. This Corporation is a body set up in 1954 by farmers themselves, acting through the National Farmers' Union. They did so out of dissatisfaction with the prices received for fat livestock, particularly in the auction rings. The Corporation buys stock and also sells on commission.

The Fish Market

The Glasgow fish market is in the Bridgegate; the present hall was built in 1872 around the base of the old Merchants' House, which dates from 1651. Glasgow is a fish-conscious city: enquiries during the war revealed a higher average consumption of fish here than in other big towns, and the 1950 Census figures confirm this. The fish market, which contains some 46 wholesale firms, serves an area with a radius of about fifty miles around the city.

Practically all the fish comes in by road from the fishing ports Aberdeen is the main port of supply, but Granton, Lossiemouth and other east coast towns send supplies. Supplies are also drawn from the west, from Oban, Ayr and Campbeltown. At certain times of the year, particularly in the spring, seine-netters from the east coast fish in western waters, and the catches are landed at western ports. Recently one Glasgow firm has started a daily service of refrigerated vans on the run from Aberdeen.

The amount of fish and game sold in the Glasgow fish market is shown in Table LXVIII.

These figures show that supplies of fresh fish after a postwar peak in 1947-8 have tended to decline; the sale of cured fish also appears to have fallen somewhat from the early postwar years, but there is a certain doubt about these figures since there have been changes in the size of boxes used for cured fish. Herring, after a postwar rise, has resumed the downward trend that was present before the war; the 1938 figure for instance represented a considerable decline on the mid-1920 figure, when the annual total was in the region of 150,000 boxes. The decline in the amount of herring handled, formerly a staple item of the trade, has been attributed to the departure of the fish from Loch Fyne and the subsequent drop in, and erratic nature of, supplies. (At one time

TABLE LXVIII

FISH MARKET: SUPPLIES HANDLED

Year[1]	Fresh fish Boxes 6 stone	Herring Boxes 6 stone	Cured Fish Boxes 1 stone	Rabbits Hampers 1 cwt.	Fowl Boxes 1 cwt.	Game Brace 3 lb.	Venison cwt
1937-8	568,814	47,387	1,819,927[2]	14,841	14,566	3,428	64
1945-6	693,430	40,131	1,341,069	1,668	—	795	—
1947-8	933,182	63,100	982,460	1,704	1,522	—	—
1949-50	742,006	38,707	967,896	4,963	5,120	—	—
1951-2	621,341	28,688	834,352	14,953	20,621	567	142
1953-4	573,326	18,893	749,011	14,021	30,313	—	475
1955-6	586,059	18,028	896,123	668	34,970	—	285

SOURCE: General Manager, Markets Department, Corporation of Glasgow.

herring caught overnight in Loch Fyne provided breakfasts for Lanarkshire miners the following morning.) But changing demand has obviously been the major factor here. The recent fall in the amount of rabbits sold is due, of course, to myxamatosis. Game has fallen off as a result, it is said, of the attraction of supplies to the London market. Fowl, on the other hand, have increased.

Towns vary in the types and sizes of fish that they will take. Glasgow, it seems, mainly prefers haddock, whiting and sole, and in particular sizes. The popularity of whiting dates only from the 1920's. The decline of the herring has been referred to, and it might be added that the kipper trade has shrunk also; the actual business of kippering is now very small in Glasgow. A general change in the trade is the great increase in the filleting of fish at the coast. The development of block filleting has permitted the use of sizes of fish previously considered too small, and large quantities of these fillets are sold daily in the Glasgow market.

It is said that there has been a considerable change in the quality of fish supplies to the market in recent years, and that this is connected with changes in the methods of the fishing industry itself. Before the war about two thirds of the fish sold in Glasgow was trawler-caught. To-day this proportion is only a third, the rest coming from seine-net boats. These boats stay at sea only for short periods and their catches are usually in the market within forty-eight hours. The result is that supplies in the market are fresher, on average, than formerly. It may be noted that some Glasgow firms operate trawlers: between 30 and 40 of the Granton trawler fleet are so owned. The proportion of the landings of this fleet being sent to Glasgow and Edinburgh has in recent years declined from about three quarters to about one third.

1 Year ended 31 May in each case.

2 There is doubt about this figure arising from the units in which cured fish was measured in 1938. According to a trade source cured fish came in half-stone boxes before the war, and this probably accounts for the size of the total for 1938.

The Fruit Market

The fruit and vegetable trade forms a large and important market centred on the Candleriggs. The actual market building houses 29 firms, but the market in the economic sense contains about 54 firms, those not housed in the market building having premises in the surrounding streets. The market draws fruit and vegetables from all the growing regions of the country, as well as importing produce from abroad. The area served by the Glasgow market covers the whole of Scotland and extends, according to price conditions, into the North of England and Northern Ireland.

Of the firms in the market about 10 are importers; the rest are wholesale merchants. All home-grown produce is handled by merchants on a " consignment " basis, i.e. the merchant acting as agent for the grower. Some imported produce is also handled on this basis, where the importing is done by an official marketing board of the growing country. Otherwise, importing is carried out by the importing firms, and the produce is sold either by auction or by private treaty. The estimate given to us was that, in the Glasgow market, about two thirds of imported produce is sold by auction, the rest being sold by private treaty. This compares with about half-and-half in some English markets. Of the importing houses seven are auction brokers, the others selling by private treaty. The auction sales are attended by buyers from all over Scotland.

In the matter of imported supplies there is constant liaison between the various ports and markets; supplies for Glasgow may be drawn from any of these according to the distributions of landings. It is estimated that about three quarters of the imported produce consumed in Scotland is landed at Glasgow and Leith; and that about two thirds of this amount is distributed in the West of Scotland.

Changes are going on in the handling of fruit and vegetables at the retail end. There has been an increase in pre-packaging, especially (though not exclusively) for the self-service shops. There has also been a considerable growth in the sale of frozen fruit and vegetables. It would appear that this latter development, if it continues, will affect the position of the wholesaler since the processing firms operate on a large enough scale to buy directly from growers. It is said that the numbers of retailers in Glasgow buying fresh produce directly from growers is not high, though there is a certain seasonal increase in this trade in the summer months.

Second-Hand Car Market

Finally, while dealing with markets, we should mention the second-hand car market. The part of the cattle market formerly devoted to horse sales is now used as a market for the sale of second-hand cars. Three firms of auctioneers operate in this market, which is the biggest in Scotland. Dealers from all over Scotland use this market to obtain cars, while in recent years, at the time of seasonal peak demand, during the summer, English dealers have also bought here. The auctions, however, are not confined to dealers and private purchasers may also bid.

The Royal Exchange

A commercial institution embodying a number of markets that has disappeared since the last war, is the Royal Exchange. The Exchange was a place where businessmen foregathered to deal in commodities like coal and iron, and in services like shipping and insurance. The Iron Ring, to which reference is made in another chapter,[1] was an important part of the business on the floor of the Exchange. With the final disappearance of the Ring in the First World War, and also with the coming of the telephone which obviated the need for a common meeting place in many kinds of business dealings, the Royal Exchange declined considerably. The building in which the Royal Exchange was housed from the eighteen-forties onwards was a conversion made at that time of a mansion built in 1778 by William Cunningham, a tobacco merchant. Since the closing of the Exchange this has been turned into a public library, and in the basement it houses the Stirling Commercial Library.

THE CO-OPERATIVE MOVEMENT

The co-operatives play a big part in retail distribution in Glasgow. In 1950, using census figures in conjunction with co-operative statistics, they accounted for about one tenth of all retail sales in the city. On the wholesale side Glasgow houses the headquarters of the S.C.W.S., which is the body formed to handle the wholesale supply of all Scottish retail societies, and which now engages extensively in actual production.

The Retail Societies

Retail co-operative distribution in the city is carried on by a considerable number of independent societies. At the present time eight societies have their headquarters, and most of their shops, within the city. These are the Cowlairs, Glasgow Eastern, Glasgow South, London Road, St. George, St. Rollox, Shettleston and Tollcross Co-operative Societies. Two others—the Rutherglen and Clydebank Co-operative

[1] See Chapter 5 (Iron and Steel).

Societies—operate within the city, the latter very extensively, having more than one third of its shops and more than one half of its members within the city area.

Although there were some notable early societies of the "victualling" type, such as the Govan Victualling Society (1777-1909) and the Parkhead and Westmuir Economical Society (1831-1885), the modern co-operative movement in Glasgow, operating on the "Rochdale" principle of dividends according to purchases, dates effectively from the 1860's and '70's. A Glasgow Society formed in 1857, failed in 1865, but others that followed, like the St. Rollox (1860), the Glasgow Eastern (1865), Kinning Park (now Glasgow South, 1871) and the St. George (1871) survived the early difficulties and grew.

The societies were established in various districts of the city, or in what were then villages outside it. In every case the early years saw great difficulties in the gathering of sufficient capital, in the recruitment of suitable staff (especially good managers), and in hostility on the part of traders and some employers to be contended with. The movement was strengthened by the founding of the S.C.W.S. in 1868 and the United Co-operative Baking Society (U.C.B.S.) a year later, and by the 'nineties it was firmly established. Some of the early societies foundered, or amalgamated with others. At the turn of the century there were fourteen societies with their headquarters in the area now covered by the city, and further unions have reduced this to the present eight.

Let us look at the recent statistics of co-operative retail trading in Glasgow. In 1954 the eight societies had 210,239 members. Some of this number would be resident outside the city, and there would be some duplication of membership, due to people moving to new areas but retaining membership of their former society. Against this, about one half of the 36,000 members of the Clydebank Society live within the Glasgow city area. Altogether there are perhaps 220,000 co-operators in Glasgow, and if we take the number of occupied houses as an indication of the number of households, this means that about two out of every three households hold membership of the movement. However the proportion of the city's retail trade carried on by the societies is much less than this: as has been shown earlier, figures for 1950 put this proportion in the region of 11 per cent. (An average of this kind, of course, obscures the considerable importance of the co-operatives in, say, groceries, where the proportion of the total trade handled by them is very much higher than this.) This percentage is very near that for Britain as a whole, which is surprising in that Glasgow, with its long history of co-operation and its industrial character, is the kind of city where one might expect to find a movement of more than average strength.

In Table LXIX some statistics of the membership and sales of the Glasgow societies are given for four separate years; sales per member are compared with movements of total consumers' expenditure:

Glasgow Corporation Transport Department

Plate 11. HORSE-DRAWN TRAM
These were finally withdrawn in 1902

Glasgow Corporation Transport Department

Plate 12. TROLLEY-BUS

These were first introduced in 1949

TABLE LXIX

MEMBERSHIP AND SALES PER MEMBER OF GLASGOW CO-OPERATIVE SOCIETIES[1]

Year	*Total no. of members*	*Total Sales* £000's	*Sales per member* £s	*Index of sales per member at constant-prices*[2] 1938=100	*Index of U.K. consumers' expenditure at constant-prices*[3] 1938=100
1938	135,443	5,203	32	100	100
1945	154,957	8,111	52	113	96[4] (93)[4]
1950	185,294	12,968	70	119	103 (97)
1954	210,239	17,953	85	116	111 (103)

SOURCE: Glasgow and District Co-operative Association: *Annual Statistical Statements.*

Between 1938 and 1954 the combined membership of the eight Glasgow societies rose by over 50 per cent. Total sales, in money terms, increased threefold. To get a rough idea of the change in the "real" volume of sales we can adjust the sales figures by means of a retail price index, always bearing in mind the fact that any index of this kind includes the prices of many goods and services not sold by the co-operatives. Making this adjustment it appears that the real volume of co-operative sales in Glasgow rose by about one half between 1938 and 1954. This increase has come mainly through the extension of membership, but there has been some rise in the level of real sales per member. In some ways sales per member is the more significant test of the success of the co-operative idea and it is interesting to attempt a comparative measure of it. In Table LXIX above we have set an index of real sales per member alongside an index of the national total of consumers' expenditure, also in real terms. This comparison is subject to many qualifications, one of the more important being the fact that the national totals cover the whole range of goods and services consumed; the co-operatives only set out to supply a fraction of this range. Nevertheless, and bearing in mind the qualifications, there are some divergences between the two sets of figures which are sufficiently marked to be significant. The rise in real sales per member during the war years contrasts sharply with the fall in the national figure, either with or without adjustment for population change. This contrasting movement was probably linked with an improved position of the Glasgow working-class, due to full employment; but, also, it probably reflected a comparative improvement of the position of the co-operatives under wartime trading conditions.

1 All societies with head offices within the city area. Anniesland Co-operative Society is included in 1938 and 1945, but not thereafter following amalgamation with Clydebank.

2 The sales per member are deflated by the Interim Index of Retail Prices as calculated back to 1938 by the London and Cambridge Economic Service.

3 Consumers' expenditure totals are taken from the Blue Book, *National Income and Expenditure*, 1957, Table 20, p. 17. Index numbers in brackets are of consumers' expenditure adjusted for changes in the U.K. population.

4 Figure for 1946.

Under rationing there was a tendency for people to concentrate their purchases of foodstuffs and the co-operatives appear to have been favoured by this trend. In the most recent period, 1950-54, a different trend appeared: real sales per member were no longer rising and may have declined somewhat, while national consumption was expanding. To some extent this would be due to an increased consumption of goods and services (e.g. motoring) which the co-operatives do not supply. But perhaps it also indicates some failure on the part of the co-operatives to attract a proportionate share of rising real expenditure.

In line with a general trend in the co-operative movement as a whole the dividends on purchases paid by Glasgow societies are lower to-day than in the immediate prewar years. The average dividend of the eight societies—calculated by weighting the individual dividends by the total sales of each society—was 1s. 11¾d. per £ of purchases in 1938, and 1s. 6d. in 1954. To give a comparison over roughly the same period, the average level of dividend in Britain as a whole fell from 1s. 10½d. in 1942 to 1s. 0¼d. in 1954. One of the main reasons given for the decline in dividends is a proportionate fall in the retail margins on many goods, compared with prewar.

Altogether, in late 1955, there were 699 co-operative branches, belonging to ten societies, within the city limits, while there were another seven branches operated by the U.C.B.S. The number of branches has grown considerably since the war: in this period nine societies have opened 113 branches within the city. The Corporation's policy in the letting of shops in the new estates—the co-operatives are automatically offered approximately a third of the accommodation in all suites of new shops—has aided this expansion.

Changes in trading methods are important. In the country as a whole the co-operative societies have been pioneers of the self-service principle, and the Glasgow societies as a body have not lagged in this development. In 1955 61 per cent of all self-service shops in the U.K. belonged to co-operatives: for Glasgow the figure was 60 per cent and for Scotland as a whole 78 per cent. There are marked differences in this between Glasgow societies. The three smallest, covering central areas of the city, had no self-service shops in 1955. Shettleston and Glasgow South have been most active in this development, and this is to be expected in that both serve areas of new housing. The introduction of self-service is easiest where shops are being opened in new housing estates; in most of these self-service is operated from the start. There has also in recent years been an increase in the number of travelling shops operated by the co-operatives; the Glasgow societies operate a number of these mainly in the new housing areas.

A development in which the co-operatives are probably not participating on a scale commensurate with their importance is hire purchase trading, but six of the Glasgow societies now have hire purchase schemes while other forms of credit trading, such as mutuality clubs are operated. There is a certain tradition of hostility towards credit trading in the co-operative movement and this may have held back the growth of hire purchase. Also to be considered, however, is the comparative lack of success of the co-operatives in the distribution of "dry goods"—clothing and drapery, and consumers' durable goods. Most of the societies are dealing in these goods, but there is no sign that they are effectively meeting the competition of the department stores and the multiples.

One of the greatest gaps in co-operative trading in Glasgow is the failure to establish a large department store in the central shopping areas. The reasons for this are closely bound up with the structure of the co-operative movement in Glasgow. This structure is unusual in the number of independent societies operating within one city; it is not exactly parallelled in any of the other large cities. One consequence is that Glasgow societies are relatively small in terms of membership: if all the co-operators in the city were organised in one society it would be the fifth largest in the country; as it is, in 1954, the largest Glasgow society came twenty-first in point of membership.

The multiplicity of societies is the result of the movement's history in Glasgow. Some of the early failures encouraged a cautious attitude in the spreading of branches with the result that societies were started on a locality basis and tended at first to concentrate on consolidating themselves in their own district. Once the societies were established, resistances, of various kinds, to amalgamation, were generated. The sentiments of local memberships were an obstacle to union. Differences in trading policies—for example difference with regard to dividends and prices—were another. Very important, however, have been the strong vested interests within the executives and staffs of the societies. Concentration would probably tend to reduce the number of offices in the societies and this, naturally enough, is not welcomed by those whose energies and ambitions have found a fruitful outlet in the movement. Staffs, also, are not always in favour of unions, at the higher levels because of fear of redundancy, but also lower down because of differences between societies in particular benefits like bonuses and superannuation rights.

The economic disadvantages of this structure are manifold. Some kinds of services, particularly transport, are relatively expensive for the smaller societies to operate. There is overlapping of delivery rounds. Certain types of trading, e.g. in dry goods, are most efficiently operated on a scale that the smaller societies cannot achieve. The growth of the city area, and the redistribution of its population over time, have brought and continue to bring serious problems to the movement in its fragmented state. Expansion of the city limits has created districts not covered by the boundary agreement of 1902, and the expansion of societies into these areas has caused overlapping and persistent disputes over territories. More serious than this, however, is the problem created by the redevelopment of the central area of the city. Under this plan, which is already under way, the central area of the city will lose population. Altogether four societies serve areas in which the population is due to decline: they thus face the prospect of declining membership, withdrawal of capital, and excess distributive capacity. Three of the remaining societies serve areas which will gain population: they can look forward to an expanding trade in what have been termed the "semi-monopoly" conditions of the new housing areas. The redrawing of boundary lines is not the answer, since to give some declining area societies access to areas of expansion would involve the creation of "detached" areas, and hence would increase fragmentation and lead to further losses of operating efficiency.

Changes of this kind would pose problems even for a unified society, but the present structure gives them a peculiar twist. A final consequence of it, already referred to, is the lack of a central department store. This is due entirely to a failure to reach agreement with the societies whose areas would be affected. At one time there was a central store which fulfilled this function: this was the Drapery and Furnishing Society, a federation formed in 1886 by twelve societies. This society had a large store at Glasgow Cross, and enjoyed a period of success. Its eventual failure was due to a mixture of reasons—the development of dry goods stores by individual societies, an incursion by the D. & F. into groceries in competition with other societies, and the difficulties of reconciling the interests of individual and federated members. It finally closed down in 1951. Of course, all the societies have departments selling such things as drapery, clothing, furniture, radios etc., and there are also arrangements whereby a member can purchase "on a line" at the S.C.W.S. warehouse, where his own society either does not stock a particular article, or does not carry a big range of it. However it is difficult to resist the conclusion that the absence of a large co-operative store in the central shopping area is causing the loss of a lot of potential trade to department stores, as well as to the multiple tailors and furniture dealers. (It may also partly explain the comparative lowness of the proportion of the city's total retail trade enjoyed by co-operatives: a good deal of this trade is with people from outside the city and these will shop in the centre.)

The disadvantages of the fragmented structure of the movement have been overcome to some extent by joint action. The Glasgow and District Co-operative Association is one example of this: formed in 1866, it acts as a consultative body for the eighteen societies within and around Glasgow and organises the educational work which plays an important part in the activities and the aims of the movement. Another important body is the Glasgow Co-operative Managers' Committee. This was set up in 1933 to secure uniform prices of staple goods and it played an important part in meeting the severely competitive conditions of the 'thirties. Under wartime and postwar trading conditions it enabled the societies to act together in negotiations over supplies. Finally, there are some inter-society agreements for the joint provision of services, for warehousing, and for the sale of dry goods by some societies to the members of other societies.

The annual reports of the Glasgow and District Co-operative Association tell of unremitting but largely fruitless efforts at amalgamation. The latest successful union was that of the Kinning Park and Pollokshaws Societies in 1950 to form the Glasgow South; with more than 80,000 members this is the largest society in the city. There is no doubt that the solution to many co-operative problems would be the merging of existing societies into larger ones, but there is an important respect in which the consequences of amalgamation would not be advantageous. The co-operative movement embodies the principle of democratic control by members. The apathy of members, giving low attendances at meetings, causes the reality to fall far short of the ideal. But there is some life in the principle, and the merging of the smaller societies into one or two big ones would undoubtedly do it harm.

The Wholesale Society

The headquarters of the Scottish Co-operative Wholesale Society are in Glasgow, while many of the distributive and productive activities of the society are carried on in the city. The S.C.W.S. was founded in 1868 to extend the principle of co-operative trading back to the wholesale stage, and so to help in extending and consolidating the co-operative movement as a whole. In the 1880's the society entered the field of production and a wide variety of manufactures have been developed. Membership of the society is confined to registered co-operative societies and to employees of the S.C.W.S. itself.

Glasgow is an important focus of the activities of the S.C.W.S. From warehouses in Glasgow something like three quarters of the total distributive trade of the society is carried on. About two thirds of the distribution of groceries takes place from Glasgow. Many productive activities—in all twenty-five separate ones—are carried on in the city. At Shieldhall, where the first land was acquired in 1887, the society has developed what is in effect a trading estate with fourteen distinct manufacturing units.

The society also engages in certain retail trading activities which are managed from Glasgow. It operates retail branches of a general kind in parts of the country—particularly the North and West—where co-operatives have not arisen or, having arisen, have failed to thrive. The first of these stores was opened in 1908, and to-day there are 131 retail branches containing 330 shop units. Another quite separate development is the opening of a chain of retail drug stores. This began in 1937 and there are now 41 chemists shops in various towns throughout the country. With the technical supervision and specialisation necessary in the pharmaceutical trade, it was decided that it would be advantageous for it to be concentrated in the hands of the Wholesale Society.

The growth of the S.C.W.S. in the ninety-odd years of its existence may be illustrated with some figures. In 1869, its first complete year of operation, the net sales of the S.C.W.S. were £81,000; by 1900 they had risen to £5.4 m.; in 1954 they were £88.2 m. Within these totals there has been a great rise in the sales of productive departments, from £82,000 in 1900, to £10 million in 1954. This growth is shown in Table LXX.

TABLE LXX

S.C.W.S.: NET SALES OF THE DEPARTMENTS

Year	*Distributive Departments* £000's	*Productive Departments* £000's	*Buying and Service Departments*[1] £000's	*Retail Branches* £000's
1900	4,830	82	553	—
1920	25,650	384	3,525	...
1930	15,010	...	2,672	...
1940	20,540	...	8,645	...
1950	38,810	10,944	19,495	...
1954	47,414	9,883	25,098	5,848

SOURCE: S.C.W.S. Ltd.

To assess the real progress of the Society allowance must be made for changes in the value of money and this is difficult to do with any precision. It appears that in each of the periods 1900-20 and 1920-40 the real volume of the sales of the distributive departments (broadly these cover the wholesale trading function) increased by roughly one half. Since 1940, however, there seems to have been, at the most, only a comparatively small growth in real volume. In the productive and buying and service departments there has been considerable growth since the early years of the century, with a very considerable expansion in the interwar years. The sales of the productive departments show a decline in money terms—the "real" decline must have been greater—in the most recent period.

FOREIGN COMMERCE

An important part of the general commerce of the city is that connected with overseas trade. The fortunes of the city were originally built up on merchant trading from the Clyde. Glasgow is now a manufacturing rather than a trading city, but the overseas trade of the city is still very important. The trade figures of the port for the most recent year are given in a previous chapter,[2] and here we shall just say something about the commercial aspects of this trade.

Much of the trade that passes through the port of Glasgow does not involve the work of firms and institutions of a purely commercial kind within the city. To-day many manufacturers producing for export markets deal directly with those markets, or with agents in them, and

[1] These comprise such departments as creameries, farms, laundries, funeral undertaking, hotels. They also include retail drug stores.

[2] Chapter 10, Table L.

while in moving their goods through a port they frequently rely on forwarding agents or shipbrokers in that port, the commercial connection with the port is no greater than that. This is the case with a large proportion of the goods exported from Glasgow—exports like whisky, railway equipment, heavy engineering equipment. In some cases, e.g. iron and steel, exporting is still done by merchants in the city. Similarly, many imports are bulk raw materials such as crude petroleum, wheat and tobacco, which are imported directly by the large firms that will process them. In some cases however, e.g. fruit, provisions and meat (to some extent, also, wheat), the actual importing is done by import merchants or by wholesaler-importers.

The movement of goods through the port does involve the work of certain specialists within the city. Many producing firms that deal directly with foreign buyers or their agents do not themselves have the specialised staffs to deal with the work involved in shipping the goods. The handling of the dock work, the Customs formalities, and all the necessary documentation involved in the movement of goods through the port is undertaken by forwarding agents, of whom there are 41 in Glasgow. The shipbrokers may also be involved. At one time the task of a shipbroker was to link bulk cargoes with vessels available for charter. To-day, with little chartering done on the Clyde, many shipbrokers act as loading brokers for liner companies, finding cargo, bringing it to the dock and having it loaded. There are nearly sixty shipbrokers in Glasgow, and in addition thirteen of the forwarding agents also act in this capacity.

A type of foreign trade of which there are still some notable examples in the city is that of the general foreign merchant—the trader who, acting as a principal, deals in a range of goods. Some Glasgow merchant houses have long-established connections with particular markets overseas—for example Cowie Brothers in Burma, and Brown, Macfarlane & Company in Japan. Firms like these buy in many markets and their purchasing is by no means confined to this country. So far as home purchasing is concerned there appears to have been some decline in the amount of goods of purely local manufacture bought and exported by them. In some cases sources of supply, as well as points of export, have shifted south. The trading conditions of the post-war period have raised considerable difficulties for such merchanting firms. However, in this century there has been a tendency for this type of trading to decline, due to such factors as the growth of industry in many countries previously dependent on imported goods, and the growing trend to direct dealing between producers and their overseas customers.

Chapter 12

FINANCE

M. GASKIN

INTRODUCTION

THE proportion of Glasgow's insured population engaged in occupations connected with finance is about two per cent (see Table LVI above). Compared with other branches of the city's economic life this is a low figure, but the importance of finance in the economy of a region, or of a country for that matter, cannot be measured solely by the relative size of its labour force. Finance is a strategic element in the economy: an adequate supply of it is vital to the operation of business and the development of industry.

Financially Britain is highly integrated: the flow of funds of all kinds between the various regions is relatively free, and the whole tends to form a set of markets each nationally unified, in funds of various kinds. This does not mean, however, that regional finance has no interest. The financial institutions of a region are important to it on three grounds. In the first place the participation of an area in national financial markets depends on the presence in it of efficient institutions. Secondly, the movement of funds between the regional sectors is not perfectly free, so that local institutions and local supplies of finance may have a special importance. Thirdly, the presence of particular concentrations of financial institutions in a place is an aspect of specialisation which, by its influence on incomes and occupation, may have further effects on the economic and social life of the place.

Large cities tend to be foci of financial activity because of the greater concentration of business in them, but between cities there are variations in the kind of financial activities specialised in. For instance, along with other Scottish cities, Glasgow has played a considerable part in the promotion of investment trusts, while in the field of capital flotation it has one of the only three issuing houses outside London. On the other hand, compared with, say, Edinburgh or Liverpool, it is not conspicuously an " insurance city " (although it has a long and important history of marine underwriting).

The variety and complexity of national finance makes it difficult to present an ordered account of the financial life of a city like Glasgow where all the main types of institution are to be found. Here we shall deal with it under three broad headings: first, institutions of the " banking type," by which we mean those that borrow on short-term; secondly, those concerned with, or in, long-term borrowing; thirdly, insurance institutions. In a final section something will be said about a profession closely associated with financial activities of all kinds—that of accountancy.

"Banking Type" Institutions

The Banks Themselves

Of all institutions engaged in raising and distributing finance the joint-stock banks are the most important. Glasgow is served by all the Scottish banks, and as a city it has seen some interesting passages in Scottish banking history.

Banking in Scotland developed in Edinburgh at the end of the seventeenth and during the first half of the eighteenth century. When, in the middle years of the eighteenth century, private banking firms were established in Glasgow, they had to contend with the opposition of the Edinburgh banks. In the 1830's there was a strong development of joint-stock banking in Glasgow in response to the great expansion of the economy of the West of Scotland. By the middle years of the nineteenth century there was a clearly defined group of Glasgow banks which on some issues, for instance, Peel's Bank Acts, took up an opposing view to that of the Edinburgh banks. During the ensuing hundred years this group was whittled away by failures and amalgamations, until to-day only one bank has its headquarters in the city. The two failures were big ones and caused considerable hardship to shareholders: in both cases the banks concerned were unlimited companies. First came the collapse of the Western Bank, in 1857, due to bad management; far too much of its resources had been lent to four merchanting firms, while it had also been lending unwisely in America. In the trade recession of that year and the accompanying financial crisis, the four firms went bankrupt and the Western Bank itself was forced to close. The net loss to shareholders, including their capital, was nearly £3 m. Then, 21 years later, the City of Glasgow Bank fell. Here again there had been an undue concentration of resources on a few big borrowers, but in this case fraud was added to mismanagement, and a number of the directors served prison sentences. The loss to shareholders, including capital, was over £6 m. In this case the hardship caused to shareholders was very great indeed and aroused widespread (and practical) sympathy; it also played an important part in stimulating the Government to frame the Companies Act of 1879, by which established banks were enabled to adopt limitation of shareholders' liability.

Fortunately, this exhausts the list of failures; the other notable reduction in the ranks of Glasgow banks occurred recently as the result of a merger. In 1952 the Union Bank of Scotland, which had its head office in Glasgow, amalgamated with the oldest of the Scottish banks, the Bank of Scotland. This was a straight merger of two institutions more or less equal in size, but it was decided, naturally, to retain the name of the older bank with its traditional position of seniority among the Scottish banks. In 1952 by an exchange of shares the capital of the Union Bank was acquired by the Bank of Scotland, but the merging of the two banks into a single institution was not fully achieved until 1955.

With this merger an old and honoured name in Scottish banking history has gone. The Union, as its name implied, was originally the product of a number of amalgamations: between 1836 and 1849 the Glasgow Union Banking Company acquired, or amalgamated with, a number of private banks, principally in Glasgow and the West of Scotland, to form the Union Bank of Scotland, which in accordance with the trends of the time was a public joint-stock company. Most of the uniting banks had long histories: one, the Glasgow and Ship Bank, went back (with an interruption of one year) to 1750, while another, the Thistle Bank, had been founded in 1761. One important merger was with Sir William Forbes, Hunter & Co., an Edinburgh bank; following this a second head office was established in Edinburgh and the Union became the first of the Scottish banks to have two principal offices. In the middle of last century the Union was one of the biggest of the Scottish banks, but in the second half of the century it failed to grow as rapidly as some of the others. In the present century it did not follow some of the other banks in affiliating with English banks, and it remained one of the smallest of the unaffiliated banks. Following the merger the Bank of Scotland controls assets which at 29 February 1956 amounted to £226 m., making it one of the largest of the Scottish banks. Its branches in Scotland number 393, with a further 46 sub-offices.

The reason for this recent merger was presumably the desire on the part of both banks to secure the advantages of a larger organisation. A larger bank secures rationalisation at two levels—at the level of higher management where an increased volume of assets can be handled without a proportionate increase of staff, and at the level of branch organisation where the elimination of surplus capacity, particularly among smaller branches, will be possible. In connection with the latter point, the pace at which the closing of redundant branches can proceed is limited by considerations both of existing staff and customers; so far (1956) only three branches have been closed although a comparison of the branch lists of the two original banks suggests that quite a number of closures will be possible in the long run. But there is another important advantage of size in banking operations: a larger organisation possessing a greater volume of assets can undertake larger individual transactions than a smaller institution. This is very important in an age when firms grow to ever-greater sizes and when the outstanding bank debts of an important company may equal an appreciable proportion of the total advances of a single bank: it is particularly important in Scotland where, compared with England, banking is characterised by smallness of scale.

Considerations such as these must have influenced another recent merger involving a Glasgow bank. On the first day of 1950 the Clydesdale Bank and the North of Scotland Bank united to form the Clydesdale & North of Scotland Bank with its head office in Glasgow, and a chief office in Aberdeen. Both these banks were affiliated to an English bank, the Midland, so that the decision to merge them depended simply on the parent bank. The Clydesdale was founded in Glasgow in 1838 with the object of increasing the banking facilities of the West of Scotland. It grew rapidly, absorbing several smaller banks and weathering the financial storms of the third quarter of the nineteenth century. In the 1870's it opened some branches in Cumberland, which at that time was closely connected with the city's iron and steel industry, and in so doing precipitated a conflict between the English and the Scottish banks on the whole question of Scottish banks operating in England. In 1920, by an exchange of shares, the bank became affiliated to the Midland Bank. The immediately compelling reason for this move was the very favourable terms offered by the Midland, but in recommending acceptance the directors of the Clydesdale probably felt that, on a longer view, there were great advantages to be reaped by affiliating to a bank with a very wide network of connections at home and abroad.

The North of Scotland Bank was the product of the union, in 1908, of two old Aberdeen banks, the Town and County Bank, founded in 1825, and the North of Scotland, formed in 1836. This bank had its strongest connection with, and most of its branches in, the north-east. It became an affiliate of the Midland in 1924.

The advantages of merging these two banks were presumably those that we have already discussed. The scope for reducing the number of branches is probably less than in the case of the merger of the Bank of Scotland and the Union, since the Clydesdale Bank and the North Bank had differing regional concentrations of branches. However, the union will have considerably broadened the business of the resulting bank: to the Clydesdale's connections with the West of Scotland have been added the strong connections of the North Bank with the agricultural and fishing interests of the north-east. The main administration is done from Glasgow, but the strong interests of the bank in the north-east are underlined by the fact that its second office is in Aberdeen, and that there is a local board which sits in the north. The number of branches listed in the last balance sheet (31 December 1955) was 317, with 23 sub-offices and 2 mobile branches. The total assets of the bank at that date were £212 m.. making it one of the largest of the Scottish banks.

Let us turn now to consider the general business of banking, in Glasgow. The joint-stock banks have two main functions: they are financial intermediaries, borrowing from one group of people and lending to another; secondly, through the system of payments by cheque, in conjunction with current accounts, they operate " a vast system of payments and record "—the system through which the great bulk of all transactions are settled. In addition to these there are important subsidiary functions such as foreign exchange dealing, the accepting of bills, and trusteeship work. Nearly three quarters of the total resources of the banking system are lent, in one form or another, to the Government; the remainder is lent to industry and trade and forms an appreciable part of the working capital of the country. (In general the banks do not provide fixed capital.) The main features of the banks' lending activities in Glasgow are those of the city's economy. The banks provide short-term capital to all the main industries of the city—metals, engineering, shipbuilding, and the distributive trades, although the dependence of shipbuilding on bank finance is comparatively small. It is probable that the business of the bigger firms in the area around Glasgow tends to be conducted within Glasgow, in the larger city branches.

Within the activities of the banking system the service of current accounts is increasingly important. In this the branches have an important part to play. In 1956 there were some 230 branches (excluding sub-branches) of the six Scottish banks in Glasgow; this represented one branch to about every 4,700 people.

One banking activity which is very strong in Glasgow is the business connected with foreign exchange: all the banks have their chief foreign exchange departments in the city. The buying and selling of foreign currencies on behalf of clients, of remitting to and collecting from abroad, of arranging documentary credits—these are traditional functions (in some cases modern developments of them) of the banker. Since 1939 the conditions under which these have been performed have been very different from those ruling previously. The free buying and selling of foreign currencies by private individuals has been in suspension, transactions in such currencies being subject to exchange control.

Under the régime of exchange control the joint-stock banks were appointed "authorised" agents of the authority administering the control—the Bank of England. As such they possess certain powers of action, which in recent years have been widened, and certain responsibilities for seeing that transactions take place according to control regulations. To facilitate the work of the Scottish banks, an exchange control office of the Bank of England was opened in Glasgow in mid-1940. This office is still open: it is there for the reference, by the banks, of applications falling outside the authorities granted to them. As these authorities have increased in recent years there has been some reduction in the need for reference to the Bank of England.

Since 1951 there has been a considerable restoration of the mechanism of the foreign exchange market. The banks have been empowered to deal in currencies—in spot and forward markets—between themselves and with banks abroad. Arbitrage in the currencies of Western European countries, on the part of authorised dealers, has been restored; while the sterling exchange rate has been "unpegged" to the extent of allowing fluctuations within a narrow range. It should be emphasised that this has been a restoration of a market mechanism and not a return to freedom of transaction in foreign currencies: the apparatus of the exchange control remains, and its regulations have to be complied with. But it does mean that some of the work of the foreign departments of banks—particularly that concerned with currency dealings—is now much nearer to what it was pre-war than at any time since 1939.

Finally, on joint-stock banking in Glasgow there are one or two points concerning administration and note-issue in which the economic and financial importance of the city receives recognition. The Clydesdale & North is of course administered from Glasgow; in the case of the Bank of Scotland, with its strong connection with the city through the former Union Bank, a committee of directors meets in Glasgow each week; and with some of the other banks, the board of directors meets in Glasgow at intervals. Connections with the city are strengthened in most cases by the presence of Glasgow men on the boards. On the question of note-issue, under the Currency and Bank Notes Act, 1928, the number of offices at which the legal-tender cover for Scottish banknotes issued in excess of the very low fiduciary amount might be held was increased. Previously such cover had to be held at the head office of each bank, but it then became permissible to hold it at either of two authorised offices (per bank) in Scotland, or at the Bank of England. In the case of each Scottish bank one of its authorised offices is in Glasgow.

A bank of a rather different kind is the *Glasgow Savings Bank*. The savings bank movement began in the second decade of last century with the object of encouraging thrift among poorer people by providing them with a secure depository for their savings. The first savings bank to be opened in Glasgow was set up in 1815. By 1835 this bank was not thriving and in the following year a new bank was founded under an Act of Parliament of 1835 extending to Scottish savings banks the privilege of depositing funds with the National Debt Commissioners. It is this bank which to-day serves the city.

In 1845, nine years after opening, it had over 22,000 accounts, and deposits amounted to £393,000. In 1955 (at 20 November) there were £88.2 m. of deposits in nearly 700,000 accounts, with a further £8.6 m. of Government stock held on the bank's register on behalf of depositors. The total funds of the bank (including reserves and surpluses) now exceed £100 m. The Glasgow Savings Bank is (and has been for a long time) the largest savings bank in Britain.

The bank operates through 59 branch offices. The first of these was opened in 1869; others followed as the city grew, but until 1929 there were only two branches outside the city. In that year the Motherwell Savings Bank amalgamated with the Glasgow bank, and this has been followed by amalgamations with eight other independent savings banks in the West of Scotland. To-day the bank has 29 branches outside the city in towns as far apart as Oban and Girvan; it is in fact the savings bank for a wide area of Western Scotland.

Recent changes in the funds lodged with the Glasgow Savings Bank are shown in Table LXXI.

TABLE LXXI

DEPOSITS OF THE GLASGOW SAVINGS BANK

Year[1]	Deposits: Ordinary Dept.	Deposits: Special Investment Dept.	Securities in Stock Dept.[2]	Total
	£000s	£000s	£000s	£000s
1938	23,129	11,425	3,915	38,469
1949	75,237	10,763	7,532	93,533
1951	75,347	10,564	7,736	93,646
1953	71,605	12,699	8,134	92,437
1955	70,048	18,161	8,582	96,796

SOURCE: Annual Reports of the Glasgow Savings Bank.

The tremendous expansion in the monetary total of the bank's resource, since prewar, can be seen. The expansion levelled off in 1949 and for a period deposits tended to decline. In 1954 an increase again appeared and this has continued.

There have been considerable changes in the composition of deposits. During the wartime and postwar expansion deposits in the Special Investment Department were more or less stationary. The funds deposited in this type of account normally earn a higher rate of interest than those in the Ordinary Department (where it is fixed at 2½ per cent), and withdrawal of them is subject to notice. Also, they are subject to a limit of £2,000, and the depositor must hold £50 in an Ordinary account. Unlike the funds in the Ordinary Department, which are automatically lent to the National Debt Commissioners, funds in this department can be lent to local authorities on the security of local rates, and then can also be invested in redeemable government securities. During the war, and in the immediate postwar period, there were restrictions on the borrowing powers of local authorities (up to 1951 they were compelled to borrow only from the Public Works Loans Board) and this, coupled with the elimination, between 1944 and 1954, of the difference in interest rates between the two departments, and more stringent conditions of deposit, kept the funds in the Special Investment Department static. Since 1951 interest rates generally have risen; local authorities have been encouraged to seek funds from sources outside the P.W.L.B.; and with the rise in rates on mortgage loans to these authorities it has been possible to offer higher rates on funds placed in the Special Investment Department. In 1951 this rate was raised to 2¾ per cent and there have been further rises, to reach 4 per cent in May 1956. This has led to a marked increase in the deposits in this department, and in the most recent years the increase in the total funds of the bank has come wholly from these deposits.

[1] Figures refer to 20 November in each year.
[2] Securities held on behalf of depositors.

With the rise in interest rates following the new monetary policy begun at the end of 1951, the interest rate in the Ordinary Department has ceased to be competitive with other forms of holding savings. This has led to a decline in deposits, some by transfer to the Special Investment Department, but some have gone into other types of institutions and assets. It is interesting to see that the rate of decline in Ordinary deposits has slowed down during the last two years when the opportunities for earning a higher rate of interest have been greatest. This may mean that the present level of Ordinary deposits represents something like the minimum of liquid deposits desired by the users of the Savings Bank. Of course, if prices and incomes continue to rise there is bound to be an increase in the total of liquid deposits held by the public. Another factor suggests itself as helping to maintain the level of Ordinary deposits during the last four years: in 1952 the Scottish joint-stock banks for the first time imposed charges on the service of current accounts, and this may have caused an increased use of deposits in the Ordinary Department as running cash balances. However, the bank itself reports that there has been little indication that this practice has been adopted. It is noteworthy that there has been a continuing rise in cash turnover, in spite of the stability of deposits. In the year ending 20 November 1952, the total of withdrawals from, and payments (including interest) into, Ordinary accounts was £25.4 m., while in the year ending at the same date in 1955, with a lower level of deposits, this total was £62.0 m. This in itself is not an indication of an increased use of Ordinary deposits as current accounts, since the period has been one of rising prices; but it points to a lower savings element in the funds deposited in this department.

The trustee savings banks are a part of the national savings movement; they form one of the outlets for small savings. The future of these savings depends on what happens to personal savings as a whole. Of course, if the inflationary rise in prices and the money supply continues, there is bound to be some increase in the money balances of depositors in trustee and other savings banks. For savings to grow at a faster rate than this will require a disposition on the part of income earners to save an increased proportion of their real income. There has been a rise in personal savings in recent years but it remains to be seen how far this revival will go. The ability of the trustee savings banks to attract funds will depend on the competitiveness of their interest rates, and it is likely that, while the present high rates persist, it will be in the Special Investment Department that growth will occur.

Building Societies and Hire-Purchase Finance Companies

Two other important types of financial institution which lend funds borrowed at short term are building societies and hire-purchase finance companies. Both types of organisation are active in Glasgow, but for the most part this activity is carried on by the branches of national institutions with their headquarters elsewhere.

The resources and lending of the building societies have been increasing greatly in recent years, with the rise in house purchase. House purchase has increased with the resumption of private building, but also on account of the decline in the letting of houses and flats due to rent restriction. The building societies obtain their resources by accepting money on deposit, subject to varying conditions of withdrawal (some deposits, or part of some deposits, are withdrawable on demand). Interest is paid, usually free of tax, and the gross rate is normally higher (at present, considerably so) than that offered by the banks on deposit accounts.

The building society world is composed of a few giants with resources between one and three hundred million, some medium-sized societies with up to one hundred million, and a large number of small societies with resources varying from twenty thousand to half-a-million pounds. If one were to try to discern any concentrations in the location of the head offices of societies, the industrial towns of Lancashire and Yorkshire might present one such; but, on the whole, building societies are widely scattered. All the large and medium-sized societies have branches and agencies throughout the country.

Glasgow is not the home of any large society. According to the Building Societies Yearbook, 1955, which lists all members of the Building Societies Association, there are only three small societies, mustering under £700,000 of resources, which have their head offices in Glasgow. Including these there are altogether 29 societies operating in Glasgow, through 30 offices. In 15 cases these offices are agencies, usually solicitors or accountants. As far as mere numbers of offices go, the Glasgow figure is comparatively low: compared, that is, with Manchester, which has 52 societies operating through 60 offices (including 6 head offices); with Birmingham which has almost the same, 51 societies and 59 offices (with 4 head offices); and Edinburgh which has 36 societies and offices (with 10 head offices). If numbers of offices are an index of building society business then Glasgow exhibits a comparatively low level of activity in this line. Perhaps the character of the city's housing, with its large proportion of flats which, until recent years, were rented rather than bought by the occupiers, may explain an apparent lack of interest in the city on the part of the building societies.

The business of hire-purchase finance has also seen a considerable growth in recent years. For a long time after the war there were controls over capital issues by, or loans to, hire-purchase finance companies. Later these were relaxed, but in the most recent years curbs have been re-introduced in the shape of higher initial deposit requirements on hire-purchase contracts. The range of goods financed by hire-purchase is now very wide and includes producers' goods—industrial machinery and office equipment—so that it has become a factor of some significance in the finance of industry, and especially for the smaller firms. The main types of goods purchased on hire-purchase contracts are vehicles and consumers' durable goods—furniture, radios, cycles, electrical appliances. Expenditure on these goods has been rising considerably in recent years, and this, coupled with the spread of hire-purchase to social classes which previously eschewed it, has increased the demand for this type of finance.

Under the restrictions on capital issues it was possible to float new companies provided the capital was under £50,000. This led to the appearance of a large number of small companies, alongside the one or two established giants. The sources of finance for such companies, apart from their own funds, are the banks and other institutions, and deposits by the public, for which, currently, very high rates of interest are being offered. Such deposits are usually withdrawable only at notice.

Glasgow is served by branches of the large national hire-purchase finance companies. There are also at least half a dozen small companies, of local origin, all of which are recent formations.

The Corporation as a Depository of Funds

A small financial activity of the banking type, which should be noticed, is carried on by the Corporation. The Corporation accepts money on deposit at seven days' notice, or for fixed periods of three to six months and thereafter at seven days' notice The rates of interest paid are based on the rates ruling in the short-loan market in London. The main depositors are industrial and commercial undertakings, insurance companies, investment trusts and the savings banks. Over the last six years these deposits have averaged £7.5 m., but they have been increasing substantially in the last three years.

INSTITUTIONS ENGAGED IN LONG-TERM FINANCE

In the institutions engaged in the handling of long-term capital, or of assets representing it, we can make a division into three groups: the Stock Exchange, the New Issues Market, and the Investment Trusts. This division is partly dictated by the institutions themselves, but in part it is functional since some institutions, e.g. stockbroking firms, will appear under more than one heading. It must be regarded rather as a method of clarifying a complex field of financial activities, than as indicating three clearly demarcated groups of institutions.

The Stock Exchange

The Glasgow Stock Exchange is one of the largest and most important of the provincial stock exchanges. It was founded in 1844; in that year the Stock Exchange Association was formed with 28 members. This was not the beginning of stock-dealing in the city: the earliest record of a stockbroker doing business is of one, James Watson, who began business in 1830. Watson, who later became a Lord Provost of the city and a chairman of the Stock Exchange, in that year issued a list of 22 stocks in which he dealt. To-day the number of members of the Association is 147. On the official list of the Exchange there are over a thousand securities, and this is far from being the total number of stocks that may be traded in, since securities on the list of any British stock exchange may be bought and sold on the Glasgow market.

With an exception to be noted presently, dealing on the Glasgow Stock Exchange takes place without the intervention of jobbers. This system is common to the provincial exchanges and is in contrast to the London Stock Exchange. At London there is a division of function between brokers and jobbers: the brokers deal with the public, executing their orders to buy and sell; the jobbers act as middlemen between brokers. In Glasgow certain brokers are "dealers" which means that they perform the function of jobber in local securities (those of firms within 25 miles of the city): they are prepared to buy and hold these on their own account, thus "making a market" in them. There are also on the Exchange firms which are known as "shunters": these are prepared to "shunt" stocks with a national market between the Glasgow Exchange and other exchanges. They do this in response to any price differences which open up between markets. The effect of this activity is a twofold one: it keeps prices in line between all markets, and it connects the provincial markets with the London jobbers who make a market and also have a steadying effect on price. According to information supplied to us there are some ten firms in Glasgow engaged in either dealing or shunting. Of course, all brokers are free to deal with brokers in any other market, and a considerable proportion of inter-market business by-passes the shunters.

In recent decades there have been important changes affecting the business of the Glasgow Stock Exchange, along with all other stock markets. Compared with pre-war, for instance, there has been a reduction in the number of stocks due partly to nationalisation, partly to the sale of overseas assets like the Argentine railways. Also, the war led to the virtual disappearance of dollar securities, although in the most recent years there has been an increasing supply of these through the London market.

More important than change in the number of stocks is the change in the number and the nature of the market's customers. Before the First World War nine-tenths of business was on behalf of the well-to-do private investor. Since then the numbers and the investing activities of such investors have been very greatly reduced by redistributive taxation and a comparatively high rate of stamp duty. To-day, it is the institutions—insurance companies, banks, pensions funds, investment trusts—which bring the major part of the market's business. The effect has been a contraction of business, with a very considerable reduction in the type of business which the broker found most remunerative. Further, it is considered that the provincial exchanges have suffered comparatively heavily by these changes in that there is a tendency for institutional business to be done in London. This is said to be particularly the case with the large " switching " operations in gilt-edged; these are undertaken by the institutions to take advantage of fractional differences in yields between stocks; to be worthwhile they have to be undertaken on a large scale which means that they are normally done through the London Market.

One gets the impression that the Scottish exchanges—at any rate Glasgow and Edinburgh—possibly benefit from the large number of institutions domiciled in Scotland. The locally based institutions do make considerable use of the local exchange, and it is not unknown, for instance, for a Scottish institution—insurance company or bank—to insist on a Scottish broker's name appearing on all its contracts. This means that if the transaction is put through in, say, London, the Scottish broker splits the commission with the London broker. In return, of course, the institutions get from local brokers numerous services in the way of market intelligence and quotations.

However, the general movements in stock market business have had their effect on the Glasgow Exchange. Perhaps one sign of this is the fact that dealings in Mining and Rubber shares, having been brought back to the main floor of the Exchange during the last war, have remained there. Because of the volume of business the Mining market had to be put into a separate room in 1895, and it was joined by Rubber in 1910. A surer indication is the decline that has been going on since 1929 in the membership.

Year	1900	1920	1930	1938	1946	1950	1955
No. of Members	188	257	277	261	203	182	147

It appears from these figures that the rate of decline has increased in recent years. It is said that the changes in business, particularly the growth of institutional business, have favoured the large stockbroking firm compared with the smaller firm, since it is the larger firms that either concentrate on, or are favoured by (it is not altogether clear which applies), the institutions. It is difficult to test such a thesis adequately but we can examine the size distribution of stockbroking firms at two points of time.

TABLE LXXII

SIZE OF STOCKBROKING FIRMS IN GLASGOW

	1930	1954
No. of Single-Partner Firms[1]	73	39
„ „ Two-Partner Firms	44	23
„ „ Three-Partner Firms	13	10
„ „ Four-Partner Firms	10	7
„ „ Five and Six-Partner Firms	6	1
	146	80

SOURCE: Official list of members and firms.

These figures give some support to the view that the larger firms have fared better than the smaller ones, though they do not tell us why. There is a striking exception in the group of very large firms—those with 5 or 6 partners—but the numbers of the firms with 3 and 4 partners have kept up markedly better than those with 1 and 2 partners.

The position of the Glasgow Stock Exchange as a part of the wider stock market of the country as a whole has been described. In terms of local finance a provincial exchange provides a market where the shares of locally-known companies can be dealt in; hence it confers a benefit on local industry. But from the point of view of the market itself, dealings in the shares of purely local companies are a mere fraction of the total business.

We mentioned earlier that there had been a decline in the number of securities dealt in. On the other side, the postwar years have seen a considerable number of new issues, or of introductions of stock to the Glasgow exchange. Table LXXIII gives some idea of the volume and types of such issues in a number of postwar years.

This table shows that of the new securities receiving quotations on the Glasgow market the overwhelming proportion were national issues, that is, a London quotation was also received, and in the majority of cases Glasgow institutions were not specially involved in the business of issue. Only a small proportion of these new securities received their quotations only at Glasgow, and although the amount of these would be greater if we included new issues quoted at Glasgow and Edinburgh alone, the picture would not be radically altered. These issues, receiving quotations on local exchanges, are typically made by small or medium-sized local firms, but the amount of them does not indicate the total flotation of local firms: the new issues of large local firms are made on a national basis.

A word of caution is necessary about the interpretation of the figures in Table LXXIII: some of the jumps in the volume of parti-

[1] In each year the official list included some names without addresses, telegraphic or otherwise. It has been assumed that these were inactive members and they have not been included as single-partner firms. In 1930 nine (including one member with an address in England), and in 1954 two, such names have been omitted.

TABLE LXXIII

PERMISSION TO DEAL AND OFFICIAL QUOTATIONS ON THE GLASGOW STOCK EXCHANGE[1]

	1947	1949	1951	1953	1955
	£000s	£000s	£000s	£000s	£000s
National[2]					
Rights	4,000	2,356	9,600	2,618	10,671
Bonuses	750	11,914	26,548	72,599	119,709
Public Offers[3]	3,771	4,726	15,500	65,000	14,500
Introductions	1,275	4,561	2,238	1,813	2,192
Placings	25	2,048	100	890	12,692
Glasgow Only[4]					
Rights	—	—	260	251	200
Bonuses	—	2,097	—	1,071	300
Public Offers	—	236	—	—	—
Introductions	—	160	185	—	—
Placings	73	—	50	—	—

SOURCE: The Secretary, The Glasgow Stock Exchange Association.

cular types of issue, e.g. " public offers " in 1953, and " placings " in 1955, are due simply to the incidence of one or two very large issues in these particular years. We must turn now to discuss the business of new issues itself in Glasgow.

The New Issues Market

The floating of new issues of securities is an important branch of the activities of the long-term capital market. The very considerable preparation involved in the issuing of securities not previously dealt in on the Stock Exchange is undertaken partly by specialised institutions known as Issuing Houses, and partly by stockbrokers. Practically all the issuing houses are situated in London, but of the three which are not, one is in Glasgow. This is Glasgow Industrial Finance Ltd., founded in 1946 by a group of Glasgow and Edinburgh Investment Trusts to provide the full range of services required in the issue of shares. Up to January 1955 G.I.F. Ltd. handled 41 issuing operations involving securities with a total nominal value of just under £12 m.; the amount of cash involved was practically £15 m. Of these operations 17 were " placings," 12 were offers to existing shareholders, and 7 were " offers for sale "; the remainder included one " introduction," one

1 Totals are nominal values of securities issued. For definitions of the various types of new issue see p. 406 footnote.

2 These are issues in which London quotations and permissions to deal were also obtained.

3 These comprise " public issues " and " offers for sale " as defined below, p. 406 footnote.

4 Issues in which quotations and permissions to deal were obtained on the Glasgow Exchange only.

" bonus " issue, and one " public issue."[1] It is thought that approximately 40 per cent of the total business done has been to finance expansion. A large part of the remainder has resulted from the conversion of private companies to public for quotation purposes (the usual object of this is to avoid the reputedly excessive valuation of shares in private companies by the Inland Revenue, when assessing death duties). The firms served have all been local firms: they have included engineering, brewing, publishing, paper-making and footwear manufacturing firms, as well as some in the distributive trades.

The experience of G.I.F. Ltd. has shown that there is a demand for the services of a provincial issuing house. Such a firm brings two special advantages to the industry of the region it serves. First it offers a means of floating an issue to those firms—apparently they exist—which are inhibited from going to London by a fear of " the City." Secondly, through the local knowledge of its directors it can back a local issue which London might turn down. Thus, although the sources of finance tapped by the local issuing house are probably not very different from those available to London houses, from the point of view of the small local firm there is a definite benefit in having a local issuing house.

There may also be benefits to local financial institutions. The business of underwriting new issues, that is, of contracting in advance to take any part of an issue that remains unsold, is undertaken largely by the institutions, especially insurance companies, investment trusts and pensions funds. The numerous Scottish institutions play their part in the underwriting business of the country as a whole and do not depend for it on local issuing operations. But the presence of a substantial issuing house in Glasgow is some safeguard that they will continue to get a share of underwriting business. It may also benefit local stockbroking firms since their services in connection with issues earn commission; there might be a tendency on the part of a London house floating a Scottish issue to employ London brokers, where the firm is nationally known.

An important consideration in the floating of an issue is the costs involved. These can be heavy, particularly for a small issue, since some of the elements are fixed in size. G.I.F. Ltd. claim that the costs of floating an issue through them compare favourably with those of a London house.

A number of Glasgow stockbroking firms engage in new issue business. According to the *Issuing House Yearbook,* published by *The*

[1] The definition of these technical terms is briefly as follows: a " public issue " is the issue of shares by prospectus to the public, the company concerned retaining ownership of the shares until sold; an " offer for sale " is the sale to the public of a block of shares previously acquired by an issuing house; a " placing " is the sale, privately, of a block of shares, to clients of brokers and of the issuing house; an " introduction " is the sale privately of a number of shares on the conversion of a private company to a public company (to comply with a Stock Exchange rule about a minimum of shares being available to the public); a " rights " issue is an issue of shares offered in the first place to existing shareholders; a " bonus " issue is a gift of new shares to existing shareholders to increase the value of a company's issued share capital.

Times newspaper, 19 Glasgow firms were associated in some way with issuing operations between 1946 and 1954. All issuing operations require the services of stockbrokers—to assist in negotiations for obtaining a quotation on the Stock Exchange, to provide access to a range of clients who may buy the new shares, and to secure underwriting connections. But in the provinces stockbrokers frequently undertake issuing operations as principals (especially the smaller " placings," " introductions," " rights " and " bonus " issues).

According to the *Issuing House Yearbook,* which it may be noted is an incomplete source of information on these points, there were about 130 issues between 1946 and 1954 in which Glasgow stockbrokers were in some way concerned. In rather more than half of these the brokers concerned were acting as principals, usually in conjunction with brokers in London or in one of the other Scottish cities. The majority of these issues were " placings," " bonus " issues to shareholders, and " introductions." There were quite a number of combined conversions and issues on behalf of Scottish investment trusts.

It is very rarely that an entirely new enterprise is founded by an issue of shares to the public. Most public companies start life as private firms (e.g. partnerships or private companies) and only secure public status, with a quotation on the Stock Exchange, when they have grown to a certain size. But because of lack of finance they frequently find such growth difficult, and as a result of the airing given to this question by the Macmillan Report, 1931, a number of institutions both private and public have been set up to provide finance to developing companies.

In Glasgow an institution of this kind was set up in 1948: Glasgow Industrial Finance (Development) Ltd. As the name indicates, there is close connection between this company and the Glasgow issuing house, G.I.F. Ltd. The two are separate companies, but G.I.F.(D.) was formed by the same group of trusts as G.I.F. and with the object of working closely with it. G.I.F.(D.) is a development company: its object is to provide finance to private companies which have not yet reached the stage where a public issue is feasible, or which could, after a period of development, make an issue on better terms. It is also prepared to provide finance for development purposes to companies wishing to remain private.

The Company was formed by the acquisition of the issued capital of the South Western Investment Trust. The motives behind it were partly a feeling that something of this kind was needed in Scotland, partly a desire to fill a gap in the line of financing institutions formed by G.I.F. and the investment trusts. The broad object was to take on small, promising firms capable of development, and to nurse them to the point where G.I.F. could take over and arrange a public issue. The finance employed by G.I.F.(D.) was to form a revolving fund.

In the event these objects have not been fully realised. Out of some two hundred enquiries about assistance, from all kinds of firms,

11 have been accepted for development. But the growth of these firms has been disappointing and none has so far reached the point of making an issue. One contributing factor causing slowness of growth of firms like these is the present high rates of taxation. The problems of growth in developing enterprises have only come under close scrutiny in recent times. Organisations like G.I.F.(D.) are operating on ground that is imperfectly known, and of which knowledge is only obtained through operating experience. One thing is certain: there is undoubtedly a need for an institution of this kind in Scotland (perhaps more than one) if native enterprises are to be given every chance to grow.

Before leaving the question of development and new issue it should be mentioned that one large national finance company—United Dominion Trust Ltd.—has a branch office in Glasgow. This company, besides engaging on a considerable scale in hire-purchase finance, makes medium-term loans to industrialists for development purposes and also handles new issues.

Investment Trusts

Glasgow has a strong association with the founding and management of an important type of financial institution, the investment trust. An investment trust is a company formed to buy and hold stock exchange securities of all kinds. It issues shares, preference and ordinary, and it raises debenture capital. The holder of shares in an investment trust, no matter how small his holding, secures at one remove a spread of risk which would otherwise only be available to someone with considerable funds to invest. A further advantage to the holder of investment trust equities is that of "gearing"; the raising of a proportion of the capital on fixed interest obligations ensures that when the average yields on the trust's holdings is high, the dividend payable on the ordinary shares stands even higher; on the other hand the risks of low, or even no, dividend in times of low profit are increased.

Scotland has played a prominent part in the development of the investment trust. The first Scottish trust was founded in 1873 in Dundee by Robert Fleming, a pioneer of the trust movement. To-day the promotion and management of investment trusts outside London is practically confined to Dundee, Edinburgh and Glasgow.

Glasgow's entry into the trust field was relatively late. The first Glasgow trust was founded in 1907, and only two others followed before 1914. During this earlier period of the trusts' history, the energies and finance of the West of Scotland were being absorbed into other fields of enterprise and investment. In 1914 Edinburgh had 25 trusts and Dundee 8, compared with Glasgow's 3.

The main period of trust promotion in Glasgow was the later nineteen-twenties. There was a boom in trusts at that time; promotion was easy as trust shares went to a premium as soon as they were issued.

It is said, also, that there was encouragement from the insurance companies. Perhaps the depression in the native industries of the west provides one reason why the trust idea was taken up so strongly in Glasgow at that time. Between 1924 and 1929, 16 trusts were formed in Glasgow out of a Scottish total of 31. Altogether, at the present time, 22 investment trusts quoted on the Stock Exchange have their registered offices in Glasgow out of a Scottish total of 73. They have a total nominal capital (ordinary, preference and debenture) of some £36 m., which is between a fifth and a quarter of the Scottish total; the market value of their investments, as shown on balance sheets appearing between July 1954 and June 1955, was approximately £70 m.

In Glasgow the accountancy profession has played a leading part in promoting investment trusts; many of the directors are chartered accountants, and all the trusts are managed by accounting firms. In all, 7 firms are involved, but 3 firms manage 18 of the Glasgow trusts. Also it may be noted that 11 London trusts are managed by branches of, or firms associated with, 4 Glasgow firms of accountants.

The composition of investment trusts' portfolios heavily favours equities. In 1954-5, of the 21 Glasgow trusts giving information on their holdings none had less than 79 per cent (by market values) in ordinary and deferred ordinary shares; 7 had more than 90 per cent. These percentages are considerably higher than prewar: in 1937-8, out of 20 trusts giving information, 8 had less than 40 per cent of their portfolios in ordinary and deferred ordinary shares, while only 5 had more than 60 per cent. Just how much of this change is due to the appreciation of ordinary shares and how much to re-investment policy it is not possible to say, but it is probable that policy is at least as important as the rise in equity prices. According to sample figures given in a recent article in *The Economist* (18 August 1956), Scottish investment trusts as a whole show a rather higher percentage of their portfolios invested in equities, than English trusts.

There has been a good deal of variation in the geographical distribution of portfolio securities in recent years. Scottish investment trusts have traditionally held a high proportion of overseas, and especially North American, securities. Inevitably this proportion fell drastically during the recent war, but in late years there has been a remarkable restoration of the trusts' holdings of overseas, and especially American, securities. In 1954-5, out of 18 Glasgow trusts, 13 had more than 20 per cent of their portfolios in U.S. securities, while 14 had higher percentages of Dominion and Empire securities than before the war. The present pattern seems to be a proportion of American securities at least as high as pre-war, with a higher proportion of home, Dominion and Empire securities. Foreign securities, other than American, are down on pre-war.

In the 1930's the investment trusts suffered severely. There was default on foreign bonds; some British securities were converted to lower rates of interest; everywhere the profitability of enterprise was low due to economic depression. The Scottish trusts with their comparatively high prior charges[1] were very vulnerable, and especially those, like the Glasgow trusts, which had had only a short life, and consequently little time to accumulate reserves. Of the 23 Glasgow trusts quoted in the 1930's, 12 paid no ordinary dividend in some years between 1931 and 1936. In some cases preference dividends were also "passed." It is significant that, of all the Glasgow trusts, those formed before 1914 weathered the interwar depression best, although even their dividends fell. The Second World War was another phase of difficulty for some trusts due to the loss of earnings on investments in countries affected by the war. The dividends of most Glasgow trusts dipped during the war years, but four trusts paid no dividends at all between 1939 and 1945, and three others paid none in some years. After the war dividends began to recover, but only slowly up to 1950. Since that year they have risen steeply, and many of the trusts are now paying ordinary dividends of 20 per cent and over. In addition most trusts have accumulated substantial visible reserves, while at present levels of security prices all have considerable invisible reserves in the great excess of the market values of portfolios over their book valuation.

The effects of the local concentration of investment trust managements as regards number of staff employed are very slight. In the case of one trust-managing group, portfolios amounting to about £12 m. are handled by a staff of 18. If we assume that to be the average ratio the total number of people involved in running the Glasgow trusts will be rather more than one hundred. The main local effects of these institutions may well flow from their activities as underwriters of new issues. This is an important ancillary activity of investment trusts, and the existence of such institutions locally, acquainted with local firms, may ease somewhat the business of issue for these firms. Through their promotion of Glasgow Industrial Finance Ltd. and also G.I.F.(D.) Ltd., the Scottish investment trusts generally are making a positive contribution to the supplying of finance to Scottish industry.

INSURANCE

Insurance is not in the first place a matter of finance, but insurance companies are nevertheless very important financial institutions. This is because their business involves the handling of very large funds which have to be invested for varying periods of time. Even in the case of non-life assurance (fire, accident, etc.) where there is a comparatively close relationship between current claims and premiums, there are large funds to be invested for short periods, while considerable reserves are

[1] In 1954-5 the proportion of debentures within the issued capital of the Glasgow trusts was about 45 per cent (about one eleventh of debenture capital was in terminable, i.e. short-term, loans and debentures). Besides this there was a considerable proportion of preference shares within total share capital. When most of the Glasgow trusts were being promoted, the common view was that shares should be issued in the ratio of 60 preference to 40 ordinary, and to-day this distribution is observable in 16 of the trusts. The high proportion of debenture and preference capital produces a high "gearing" of the capital stock.

held in securities of longer term. In the case of life assurance the companies and societies have a growing volume of funds to invest each year, partly because life assurance is increasing and premium income exceeds claims, partly as a consequence of the growing popularity of policies with a large savings element, like endowment policies and the various policies employed in group pensions schemes.

Glasgow is not conspicuously a " centre " of insurance business. There are only four assurance societies of any size with their headquarters in the city. Two of these, the Scottish Amicable and the Scottish Mutual, are mutual life offices, and they come into the medium-sized group of such offices. The combined funds (life and annuity) of these two societies amounted to £57 m. at the end of 1955; some idea of the present rate of growth of life office assets can be obtained from the fact that in 1951 this total was £37 m. The Scottish Amicable was formed in 1826, one of the earliest of a number of Scottish formations in the 1820's and '30's. This society has an unbroken bonus record going back to its foundation. It has recently introduced a Double Bonus policy—a policy which receives bonus at double the rate of the ordinary with-profits policy. The Scottish Mutual Assurance Society was founded in 1883 and is the youngest of the Scottish mutual offices. It was originally a limited company and only became a mutual office in 1952. The word " Temperance " figured in the original title, and the society still gives special terms to total abstainers. The business of these offices is not, of course, confined to Scotland: according to information obtained from one of them, Scottish business amounted to about one third of the total.

The other two Glasgow societies of any size, the Scottish Legal Life and the City of Glasgow, are industrial assurance societies. " Industrial " assurance is simply life assurance adapted to the needs of the weekly wage-earners; it deals in policies for comparatively small sums the premiums for which are collected in frequent, often weekly, instalments by special collectors. The industrial assurance movement dates from the middle decades of last century and its main strength is in the industrial areas of the country. It has two roots: one in the local friendly societies which developed in the first half of the nineteenth century to assure sickness benefits and burial expenses to their members; the other in limited companies formed to bring life assurance to the wage-earners. This twofold root is reflected in a continuing division of the field between " companies," which have shareholders and distribute dividends, and " societies " in which all income accrues to the policy-holding members.

Both the Glasgow industrial offices are " societies," and they have a long history, being among the earliest of the larger industrial assurance societies. The Scottish Legal Life was founded in 1852, and the City of Glasgow in 1862. A third old-established Glasgow society, the Scottish United Reform, amalgamated with the Scottish Legal Life in 1953. By modern industrial office standards neither of the existing Glasgow societies is very big; their combined funds (industrial and ordinary life) at the end of 1955 were £24 m. One of the societies reports that in a recent year about one quarter of its premium income was collected in Scotland, about three fifths of this coming from Glasgow itself. The main trend reported in this business is an increasing preference for the Endowment, as compared with the Whole Life, type of policy.

Besides these societies there are numbers of smaller insurance institutions with their head offices in Glasgow. For the most part they specialise in particular types of insurance—fire, boiler, employers' liability etc. One of the larger of them—the Scottish General Insurance Company, dealing mainly in fire, accident and motor insurance—has over thirty branches throughout the country; it was founded in 1919, and in 1933 became allied to a large Perth company. Finally, all the main societies and companies of the country operate in Glasgow through branch offices: altogether more than 160 insurance institutions, big and small, are represented in the city.

Underwriting in Glasgow

A branch of insurance in which Glasgow has long played an important part is the business of underwriting. Evidence of underwriting activity in the city can be found as far back as 1744; it was fostered by, and grew alongside, the marine and mercantile interests which provided both the demand for the service and the private fortunes against which risks could be underwritten. By the three-quarter mark of that century underwriting was an established business; from a notice dated 1778, it is apparent that a clear distinction between underwriters and brokers had emerged by then. In 1818 the " Association of Underwriters and Insurance Brokers in Glasgow " was constituted and housed then, as now, in the Royal Exchange. During the nineteenth century Glasgow's importance as an underwriting centre increased very much and it became one of the two principal centres of this business in the country, outside London (the other being Liverpool).

Underwriting is the oldest application of the insurance principle. This principle consists in the fact that if one takes in a sufficiently large number of insurances where a particular hazard is present, it is possible, on the basis of experience, to predict within a reasonable degree of error the number of insurances in which the hazard will be realised. The eventual loss, due to the realisation of the hazard, can be estimated at a certain cost (the " premium ") applicable to all similar insurances.

The business of underwriting involves three separable functions which may be performed by separate individuals, although this is not always the case. First there is the function of bearing the risk—accepting liability for realised losses; secondly, there is the task of deciding whether or not any given risk shall be underwritten and of apportioning it among those willing to bear it; thirdly, there is the function of bringing people with risks to insure into contact with those willing to underwrite them. Where the three functions are performed by separate individuals these are knowns respectively as the *underwriting member,* the *underwriter*, and the *broker*.

Traditionally the underwriting member was a man of substance, very often a merchant, who had no other connection with the business of insurance. To-day there are considerably fewer of these than there were—at least there are fewer willing to underwrite—and the ultimate underwriting of risks in the Glasgow market is usually done by an insurance company. To-day many underwriters are *underwriting agents,* accepting risks on behalf of a number of companies which have appointed them as their agents. In Glasgow there is only one syndicate of private underwriting members. The underwriter, or underwriting agent, may combine his function with either of the other two. In Glasgow all the fifteen firms engaged in underwriting are brokers *and* underwriting agents; in contrast to this, at Lloyds brokering and underwriting are carried on by separate firms.

The principal underwriting business in Glasgow to-day is hull business; this accounts for about 90 per cent of the total. The underwriting of the construction risks of shipbuilders plays some part in the remainder. A considerable amount of business is done and some large sums are insured. But in this field Glasgow has suffered a decline from her earlier prominence. The removal of the head offices of some shipping lines to London, after the First World War, took away business from Glasgow underwriters. Again, as in all insurance, size of business is an advantage, giving a greater spread of risks: the narrower market in Glasgow (compared with, say, London) has reduced its attractiveness to the private underwriting member. Moreover, it has not had the advantage, enjoyed for example by Liverpool, of being the headquarters of a number of marine insurance offices. Finally, one recent development that should be mentioned is that two or three Glasgow firms have lately become associated with firms at Lloyds.

Export Credit Insurance

One type of insurance that deserves a separate mention is that performed by the Export Credits Guarantee Department, which has a branch in Glasgow. E.C.G.D. is a Government department, set up in its present form in 1930, which undertakes to insure exporters against certain risks. The chief risks insured are losses caused by the failure to receive payment for goods exported for such reasons as insolvency of the buyer, default, or governmental interference with the transfer of currencies. The E.C.G.D. does not cover the whole risk; on the ordinary credit policies the amount covered is 85 per cent of some risks, 90 per cent of others. Other policies give exporters certain kinds of cover in dollar markets, e.g. on losses incurred on stocks held abroad, and on the cost of unfavourable market surveys.

The Glasgow office of E.C.G.D. is one of 13 branches; it was opened in 1935 and serves the whole of the western and northern districts of Scotland, the eastern counties and the borders being served by the Edinburgh office. Altogether about 6 per cent of the Department's business is handled in Glasgow. The proportion of the total export trade insured by E.C.G.D. in 1955-6 was 13 per cent or £353 m., so that some £30 m. of insurance business was handled in Glasgow.

The Accountancy Profession

The profession of accountancy is the servant of all industry and commerce, but this is perhaps the most appropriate chapter in which to say something about it. Glasgow was one of the earliest homes of an organised profession of accountants. In 1855 the accountants of Glasgow formed themselves into the Institute of Accountants and Actuaries in Glasgow and obtained incorporation by Royal Charter; they thus followed by one year the Society of Accountants in Edinburgh, which was the first professional association in the world. The Glasgow Institute retained its independence until 1951, when it amalgamated with the Edinburgh and Aberdeen societies to form the Institute of Chartered Accountants of Scotland.

Glasgow accounts for a large proportion of the membership of this body—1,339 out of a total membership in Scotland of 3,255, and an overall total of 5,962. Of the chartered accountants in the city, 464 work on their own account or as partners in firms. In all there are 167 firms, with a further 38 accountants in practice on their own. In the 1956 Official Directory of the Institute, a total of 492 Glasgow members are entered as working in ordinary businesses, public corporations and institutions, a high proportion of them being secretaries or directors. The remaining 383 either work in the offices of accountancy firms, or are listed in the Directory without indication of their present posts (presumably some will be retired members).

Some Glasgow firms have branches elsewhere, in London or other English towns. In some cases these are virtually separate firms with their own partners; in others they are branch offices established to facilitate the handling of the business of clients of the head office.

The chartered accountants are not the sole representatives of their profession in the city but they greatly outnumber the members of other accountancy bodies. According to the Post Office Directory there are 60 members of the Society of Incorporated Accountants, while Kelly's Directory lists 25 members of the Association of Certified and Corporate Accountants in Glasgow.

* * *

From this description of the finance of Glasgow it is apparent that, for a provincial city, it has an unusual variety of financial institutions. Whether or not this variety has any special effects on the supply of finance it is difficult to say. One point to bear in mind here is that finance is not wholly confined to the institutions we have described. Some capital funds move through less formal channels: loans and mortgages are arranged privately through solicitors and accountants, and such arrangements are often very important for small, local enterprises. This happens in Glasgow, as elsewhere, but it is difficult to estimate the scale on which it takes place. As far as the major institutions are concerned Glasgow is undoubtedly well served: there is an adequate representation of those, like banks and building societies, which channel funds to and from national markets; while through those concerned with initiating, or supporting by underwriting, new capital issues, it avoids one potential deficiency in the regional supply of finance.

Finally, we might ask to what extent Glasgow shows a special concentration of financial occupations. The figures (see Table LVI p. 355) rather surprisingly show that the proportion of Glasgow's employed population engaged in financial occupations is the same as the average for the country as a whole. It is possible that the country average is pulled up by a high figure for London. Figures recently published by the Registrar-General show that, in 1951, 1½ per cent of the employed population of Scotland was engaged in financial occupations, and a comparison of this figure with Glasgow's 2 per cent may give a truer indication of the relative concentration of financial activities in the city. These figures are not very big, but the comparative difference in favour of Glasgow is quite large, and it probably represents an even greater concentration of the high-income receivers of the financial world. Altogether, from what we have surveyed here, it is clear that Glasgow has as many claims as any large provincial city, and probably more than most, to be regarded as a financial "centre."

The late F. V. Pessl (from the Glasgow Photographic Survey, 1955)

Plate 13. THE TOWN COUNCIL IN SESSION

The Right Hon. the Lord Provost, Mr. Andrew Hood, in the chair

Glasgow Corporation Architectural & Planning Department

Plate 14. HUTCHESONTOWN, SHOWING PROPOSED REDEVELOPMENT

Part Three

PUBLIC ADMINISTRATION AND SERVICES

Chapter 13

GOVERNMENT

THE MACHINERY OF LOCAL GOVERNMENT AND JUSTICE

ROBERT BAIRD

Growth of the Municipality

FROM 21 December, 1613—when James VI of Scotland and I of England granted to Glasgow the "Tenandry of Ratonraw"[1] in recognition of the "expenses incurred by the City in supporting the Metropolitan Church and upholding the Bridge"—until the passing of the Royalty of Glasgow Extension Act in 1800 the boundaries of Glasgow remained unchanged. Between 1800 and 1938, the area of the municipality multiplied more than twenty-two-and-a-half times. There have been five great "annexations"—in 1846,[2], 1891, 1912, 1926 and 1938—and these together brought in 35,383 acres. The remaining additions of 2,574 acres within this time required ten separate Acts of Parliament to bring them about.

Two of the major extensions deserve special comment. They were of much greater significance in the political and social history of Glasgow than mere raids upon the territories of the Counties of Lanarkshire, Renfrewshire and Dunbartonshire. The Parliamentary Constituency of Glasgow formed in 1832 after the Report of the Parliamentary Boundaries Commission of that year was more extensive in some directions than the ancient Royalty of the City but it did not include that part of the Royalty lying to the north of the Forth and Clyde Canal on the west of Castle Street and to the north of Garngad Road on the east of Castle Street. The Glasgow Municipal Extension Act of 1846 made the Local Government boundaries of the City the same as its Parliamentary boundaries; so that this northern part of the Royalty was cut off from Glasgow's municipal area as defined by the Act.[3] The

[1] Lands just outside the North Port of the City. The return for the lands was to be 36/8d. Scots which was the amount of the ancient feufarm paid by the Sub-Deans of the Cathedral plus 3/4d. Scots "in augmentation of the Royal Rental."

[2] Prior to the Act of 1846, by which the greater part of the Barony of Gorbals together with certain lands on its east and west boundaries were added to the City, the entire municipal area lay to the north of the Clyde. For details of the various extensions see Table 1 in Appendix and end-map.

[3] Until this area was restored to the City by the Glasgow Municipal Act of 1872, the ancient Royalty had to be specially referred to in empowering Acts relating to Glasgow.

1846 Act more than doubled the City area by bringing in what had been until then three separate and independent burghs lying hard up against the City's east, south and south-west boundaries. These were Calton, Gorbals and Anderston. Calton had obtained its burghal charter in 1817 and in 1840 had had its police powers extended and continued for another twenty-one years. It was active as a local authority and in 1844 had promoted a Bill in Parliament in an attempt to annex the area of Bridgeton. Bridgeton had retaliated by applying to have itself erected into a burgh. Both applications were heard and rejected in 1845 by a Parliamentary Committee.[1]

Gorbals was a very ancient Burgh of Barony and Regality but for two hundred years had been in the anomalous position of having its magistrates appointed by the magistrates and town council of Glasgow who were its feudal superiors.[2] During a large part of that time Glasgow had been struggling to free itself from the same kind of treatment at the hands of its own feudal superiors. But Gorbals, too, was an active local authority. It obtained its first set of police powers in 1808 and its fourth by the Act of 1843;[3] and by the latter Act the jurisdiction of its Board of Police Commissioners had been extended over all the land on the south of the Clyde lying within the parliamentary boundary of Glasgow fixed in 1832.

Anderston had been erected into a Burgh of Barony by Royal Charter in 1824, and an Act of Parliament in 1843[4] extending its police powers also annexed to the burgh parts of the lands of Blythswood and Newtonhill and others, with lands in Lancefield, Finnieston; Stobcross and adjacent areas. In 1844 Anderston Town Council had gone a step further in its expansion programme and promoted a Bill to annex the lands of Woodside, whereupon Glasgow felt compelled to try to do exactly the same thing. Glasgow was smarting under the virtual rejection of a Bill framed in 1842 to incorporate all the three burghs on her boundaries which were competing with her for territory—a Bill eventually passed in a very truncated form as the Extension Act of 1843. The Committee of the House of Commons which heard and rejected all these competing claims for territory stated in 1845 that unless the city and the suburban burghs could agree among themselves upon a scheme of police administration covering their joint territories, the Government would have to deal with the matter. After conferences between committees of Glasgow Town Council, Glasgow Police Board, the suburban burghs and other interested parties, the Bill, which passed as the Glasgow Municipal Extension Act of 1846, was agreed. In

1 In spite of the inter-burghal struggle the extensions to Glasgow made by the 1846 Act had, in fact, been recommended in the 1835 Report of the Royal Commission on Municipal Corporations in Scotland. This Commission was set up in 1833, the year in which the Scotch Burghs Reform Act ended the centuries-old "closed corporations" in the towns.

2 This was the result of the sale of the Superiority of Gorbals to Glasgow in 1647 by the successors of Sir George Elphinstone—Provost of the City of Glasgow in 1605—to whom the feudal superiority had been conveyed in 1601 by the Archbishop of Glasgow.

3 The year in which Glasgow's proposal to annex Gorbals was rejected by Parliament.

4 In spite of Glasgow's claims for extension.

addition to the three suburban burghs and the land which *they* had already annexed this Act brought within the municipality Bridgeton, Dalmarnock, part of Parkhead, Camlachie, Dennistoun, Garngad and lands to the west of the city which now form part of the municipal wards of Park, Woodside and North Kelvinside. The eastermost point of the city's boundaries was now brought up to the junction of the old and new Shettleston Roads and the western boundary to the line of the River Kelvin.

The 1891 " amalgamations "[1] received Parliamentary authority only after a long and bitter struggle between Glasgow and the areas about to be submerged. This struggle was resolved only after seven months of intensive enquiry by the Glasgow Boundary Commission which reported in 1888. The history of this struggle is of some interest.

The General Police (Scotland) Act of 1850 and the General Police and Improvement (Scotland) Act of 1862 had made it possible for " populous places "—at first of 1,200 and later of 700 population—to become independent Police Burghs after going through certain procedural requirements. Various parts of " the Suburbs of Glasgow "[2] availed themselves of these Acts to obtain burghal status and local government powers—Partick in 1852; Maryhill in 1856; Govan in 1864; Hillhead in 1869; Kinning Park and Crosshill both in 1871 (after active opposition by Glasgow at the hearings before the Sheriff of Renfrewshire); West Pollokshields in 1876; Govanhill in 1877 (after a long fight between Glasgow and Crosshill about an area lying between them which was described as " no man's land ") and East Pollokshields in 1879. In 1881 Kelvinside, too, took the first steps towards obtaining independent burghal status but eventually abandoned the proposal. Within a few weeks both Hillhead and Partick burghs applied to the Sheriff of Lanarkshire to annex Kelvinside. However, after lengthy enquiry, the Sheriff refused both applications. In the same year East Pollokshields tried to annex Titwood: it failed in that year but it did succeed in 1884.

Both the Town Council and the Police Board of Glasgow had become alarmed by these events and by their failure to prevent the expansion of the suburban burghs, but they looked hopefully to the Parliamentary Elections Redistribution Act of 1885 for an extension of the parliamentary boundaries of the city beyond the existing municipal limits; having in mind the fact that the extension of the parliamentary boundaries beyond the municipal boundaries in 1832 had provided a strong argument in favour of the subsequent extension of the municipal boundaries in 1846 to the then parliamentary limits. But the Act of 1885 disappointed Glasgow; the parliamentary boundaries were set on the existing limits of municipal and police jurisdiction.

The appointment of the Glasgow Boundary Commission in 1887 finally gave Glasgow its opportunity to argue that " the principles

[1] This word had come to be preferred by city officials responsible for arguing the Town's frequent expansionist proposals.

[2] As the official Glasgow case argued before the Boundary Commission of 1887 described them.

recognised by the Boundaries Commission and the Legislature in 1832" justified the inclusion within the city of the nine burghs that had sprung up on its outskirts, together with the districts of Polmadie, Mount Florida, Langside, Shawlands, Crossmyloof, Strathbungo, Bellahouston and certain lands in and around the Queen's Park (all to the south of the City) and also the districts of Kelvinside, Scotstounhill, Dawsholm, Possil, Springburn and adjoining lands (all to the north of the city).[1] Although the Report of the Commissioners conceded almost the whole of Glasgow's claims the 1891 Act which followed the Report gave Glasgow only six of the nine burghs,[2] and almost all the land asked for on the south of the Clyde,[3] but of the land claimed on the north of the river only Springburn and part of Kelvinside up to Anniesland Cross.

The Burgh of Kinning Park disappeared into the maw of the giant in 1905, and the last of the independent Police Burghs touching the city boundaries (Partick, Govan and Pollokshaws) were swallowed up by the Act of 1912. For the rest of the 1912 extensions and for all subsequent extensions to the city territory the town's arguments have been with the counties of Lanarkshire, Renfrewshire and Dunbartonshire.

The extensions of the first half of the nineteenth century were largely concerned with taking in built-up areas already encircled by city territories or so closely compacted with them as to create technical difficulties in the separate supply of police, lighting, paving and cleansing services. In the latter half of the century the development of the river work and of the water supply, drainage and sewage services provided strong reasons for expansion. In the twentieth century the positive policies towards Housing and Town Planning have been major factors in the drive for "liebensraum." Nowadays extension is away from the river outwards to the north, east and south-west in search of space for housing development. The Planning Report of the City Engineer in 1946 envisaged no necessary extension of the city area for housing purposes, but this conclusion was opposed by the Report of the Clyde Valley Regional Planning Advisory Committee. The 1952 Report of the City Architect on Glasgow's housing needs calculated that space outside the present boundaries would have to be found for 137,000 houses (out of a total of 345,000 calculated as the city's needs) if permission for the building of 8,000 houses in the "Eastern areas"[4] were not granted by the Secretary of State for Scotland. In fact permission to build 5,000 houses in this area was granted.

1 Pollokshaws, then a Burgh of Barony, was not included in the Glasgow claim and lay well to the south of the boundary argued for in the Glasgow case; and yet the Commissioners thought that the inclusion of Pollokshaws within the city boundaries should have been considered.

2 Partick, Govan and Kinning Park lived to fight another day.

3 Bringing the southernmost point of the city's boundaries up to the line of the White Cart.

4 That part of the city area lying to the north of the Edinburgh Road and eastward of the Queenslie Industrial Estate outward to the east city boundary.

The Town Council

The first election of a Town Council for Glasgow following the Burgh Reform Act was held on a thoroughly wet Tuesday, 5 November 1833; but the rain "appears to have prevented very few of the electors from coming forward to exercise their newly acquired privilege."[1] The numbers of those who turned out in the rain are not known, but at the Census of 1831 the municipal electorate had been 5,506 and the parliamentary electorate 8,783. The Burgh Reform Act of 1833 gave the municipal franchise to those qualified for the parliamentary franchise, so that the total municipal vote in 1833 could not have been more than 9,000 out of a total city population of over 202,400.

Under the Act of 1833 the city was divided into five wards. Six councillors were to be elected for each ward, and two of each six (the first two being those receiving the lowest number of votes in each ward in 1833) were to retire each subsequent year in order to provide for the system of annual election of one-third of the Council—an arrangement that has operated ever since, except in certain years of reorganisation of the wards when the whole council has come up for election. With the two *ex officio* members—the Dean of Guild and the Deacon Convener of the Trades House—the first City Council numbered thirty-two. The Dean and the Deacon are still *ex officio* members, to remind the town of the days before 1833 when the Merchants' and the Trades' Houses were the virtual masters of its government.

At the election of 1833 there was one "polling station" (opened for voting at 8 a.m.) in each of the five wards, and votes were recorded in "polling books" which were sealed at 4 p.m. when the stations closed. The seals were broken at noon the following day at the statutory meeting in the Justiciary Hall. The Act had anticipated that the counting of votes would be completed within two hours. In Glasgow it was in fact completed at 10 p.m. and that only after "the most indefatigable labour and incessant toil."[2]

On the Thursday the newly elected councillors met in the comparatively new Council Hall in Jail Square (now the Justiciary buildings). At this meeting they took the oath of allegiance and subscribed the declaration *de fideli administratione*. On Friday the 8th, the first business meeting of the elected Council was held, and by the unanimous vote of the members present, representatives of the Press were permitted to be in attendance. By some mischance this led a number of interested citizens outside the Chamber to believe that they too were to be admitted. When they tried to gain entry they were "forcibly ejected." The new Council appeared to step off with the wrong foot in the march to local democracy. This business meeting elected the Lord Provost, the five magistrates, the Water Bailie and his Depute, the Bailie of Provan and other officials. Eight of the senior "permanent"

[1] John Tweed, *The Lord Provosts of Glasgow, 1833-83* (1883), p. 1.
[2] John Tweed, *op. cit.*, p. 2.

officials were elected for one year only, but they refused to admit the Council's right to impose such terms, reserving "all claim in law to the permanency of their offices." The new Council was apparently hardly more in step with its officials than with its citizens.

At this meeting of the Council the only other item of business that was formally raised for discussion was the question whether to abolish the traditional cocked hats and gold chains of the Bailies because of the "ridiculous nature and buffoon-like appearance of the dress." This discussion was inconclusive and the day's formal business ended with the bringing in of a "glass of wine" for the Council. At this point four or five of the council members walked out in protest against the traditional practice, and at the same time indicated their objection to many other aspects of the Council's "hospitality," an earnest of the temperance issue that was to be prominent in local politics for many years to come. By now the new Council was tripping over its own feet.

In 1844, when the Council Chambers were moved to the newly built city and county buildings in Wilson Street, the Council was still one of 32 members and there had been as yet no great expansion of the city's area, yet the work of the departments was already showing signs of an expansion that was soon to become rapid.

As a result of the substantial enlargement of the city's area in 1846 the number of wards was increased to 16 and the membership of the Council to 50, still including the Dean of Guild and the Deacon Convener. The number of bailies was increased to seven, and, because of the reorganisation of wards involved, the election of that year was for all 48 representatives on the Council, each elector to have three votes in his ward. The main issue at the election of this year was the level of assessment to the Poor Rate, and "politics" played very little part in the election campaigns. There were 11,136 votes cast in all, and because of the need to establish the order of retiral of councillors in the next two years, there was voting in all 16 wards. These votes represented about 3,712 electors, a poll of just under 39 per cent. There was apparently no great enthusiasm for the opportunity to form a completely new governing body. Eleven of the sixteen wards were uncontested. Four of the five others were in the east end of the city and there the issue upon which the election was fought was the threat of encroachment upon the area of Glasgow Green.[1]

The year 1872 saw a further small addition to the area of the city and also the abolition of the "polling books" and the first municipal election by "ballot." Under the new system there were no half-hourly announcements from the polling stations throughout the day as to the state of the poll. These announcements had been a feature of election procedure in the past that had helped to sustain the interest, and at

[1] The voting was fairly heavy on this issue, the percentages being:

Ward 1—61 per cent
,, 2—68 per cent
,, 3—70 per cent
,, 4—67 per cent

In the only other contest—in Ward 16—61 per cent of the electorate turned out to the polls.

times the excitement, of election day, but in 1872 the local electorate did not appear to show any great disappointment at their loss. The ballot system in use from then on had indeed a very powerful effect in calming down what had very often been a hectic day in the municipal year.

There were contests in only seven of the sixteen wards in 1872, and only two candidates presented themselves in each. The main issue was "temperance" and *The Glasgow Herald* commented that the results in the seven contested wards represented a "decided victory for the teetotal party." "The Wine, Spirit and Beer Trade Association were, upon the whole, unfortunate in their candidates and few sensible people will regret that they have been placed at the bottom of the poll." Thus although organised party politics in municipal affairs did not come to the city until after the First World War, even fifty years before that there were the beginnings of "party" or "pressure group" organisation in the approach to and conduct of municipal affairs.

The contests in the seven wards produced 15,102 votes. The total electorate for the city was over 53,000, so that something less than 30 per cent of the electorate thought it necessary (or were given an opportunity through the nomination of candidates), to express their views on the past and present work of the Council and its plans for the future. The "apathy" about municipal affairs that we are inclined to think of as a mid-twentieth century phenomenon was in fact showing itself in the middle of the nineteenth century, though in a somewhat different form —in the form of a trend towards an increasing number of unopposed returns. The nadir of this trend was reached in 1878 and 1880 when there were 15 unopposed returns among the city's sixteen wards. Even in 1890 there were contests in only four of the sixteen wards, although the city was fighting for an expansion that would about double its area, and was launched on a large programme of positive action that had already cost a lot of money and gave every promise of costing much more in the future. In 1891—after the great expansion of the city's area, the increase in the number of wards from sixteen to twenty-five, and the number of the Council to seventy-seven—there were rival candidates in only seven of the sixteen old wards of lesser Glasgow, and even among the nine new wards (each of which was required to return three members to the Council), there were nine unopposed returns out of twenty-seven. The main issue in 1891 was again "temperance" in spite of the countless other, and more directly relevant, issues that it now appears could have been raised. There were 33,822 active voters in the fourteen contested wards—a proportion of 29.8 per cent of the total municipal electorate of 113,270. At this election there were 18,307 women voters on the roll, the municipal vote for women having been introduced in 1882-83 when 12,986 women electors were included in a total register of 79,774 voters.[1] It has been possible to calculate the

[1] By 1939-40—the year in which information as to the number of females on the register was last separately collected—their number had grown to 323,691 out of a total municipal electorate of 606,337, appreciably more than 50 per cent.

percentage polls for six of these contested wards and the figures are:—

Ward 1—54.5% (3 candidates for 1 seat)
Ward 4—73.2% (5 candidates for 1 seat)
Ward 6—88.8% (2 candidates—smallest ward)
Ward 11—46.8% (2 candidates—largest ward by far in the city)
Ward 12—55.3% (2 candidates—first contest for 16 years)
Ward 18—about 59% (4 candidates for 3 seats—new ward)

These figures suggest that in some instances where an opportunity to vote did present itself the ward electorates were not unwilling to make a fight of it—and occasionally there were enough candidates to provide the opportunity.

By 1900 there had been two further extensions of the city's area—those of 1896 and 1899. The number of wards was still the same—25—but these had been re-arranged to take in the added areas. In just over half the city wards (13 out of 25), candidates in the 1900 election were returned unopposed. In the remaining 12 wards there was a total electorate of 57,941 and of these 38,092 (65.7 per cent) voted. But again on this occasion active voting in the whole city represented something less than 30 per cent of the total power to vote.

It is interesting to see the kind of representatives that the municipality voted for (or was content to have) as its governors in 1900. Their occupations are listed in Table 65 in the Appendix, together with corresponding details for later years. The descriptions of occupations are those given by the councillors themselves and they were often extremely vague, but it is apparent that in 1900 there was a strong representation of the financially " solid " section of the industrial and commercial community—shipbuilders, shipowners, a coalmaster, ironfounders, coachbuilders etc., and some of the classes of " merchant " and " manufacturer "—together with a good number of professional men (doctors, engineers, accountants, a solicitor), and of substantial traders. The representatives of the small trader and the " working man " were few.

Before considering the changes in the composition of the council that have occurred since 1900 it is of interest to examine the record of unopposed returns in the first fourteen years of the present century.

1900	1901	1902	1903	1904	1905	1906	1907	1908
13/25	18/25	12/25	15/25	14/25	15/26	12/26	13/26	12/26

1909	1910	1911	1912	1913	1914
17/26	16/26	13/26	17/37	20/37	24/37

In 1901 three-quarters of the returns were unopposed, and in only 6 of these 15 years were as many as half the wards contested. Yet when we look at the composition of the council in 1914 it would appear that many of the changes in representation that we are inclined to think of as " postwar " and as the result of the introduction of party politics into local affairs were in fact only confirmed by the 1919 elections and merely labelled and organised by the emergence of " party " in 1920. What then was happening in the contests that did take place between 1900 and 1914?

Looking first at the polling statistics in contested elections, the figures for 1901 and 1903 were as follows:

TABLE LXXIV

PERCENTAGE POLL IN CONTESTED WARDS, 1901 AND 1903

Ward No.	*Ward Name*	1901 %	1903 %
1	Dalmarnock	49.2	
2	Calton	56.0	51.0
3	Mile-End	50.5	45.4
4	Whitevale		57.8
6	Springburn	69.0	
9	Blackfriars	56.5	
12	Broomielaw	68.0	
13	Anderston	48.5	64.8
16	Cowcaddens		58.7
17	Woodside		73.5
18	Hutchesontown		29.2
20	Kingston		66.2
22	Langside		63.5
25	Maryhill		59.5

It is not an unreasonable inference from these figures that the emergence of issues affecting single wards or neighbouring groups of wards had more to do with whether a ward was contested, and with the level of the voting, than had general municipal policies and administration. This inference is to some extent supported by the annual election statistics up to 1911. For example in 1906 and again in 1908, in both of which years 14 of the 26 seats were contested, contests took place in groups of adjoining wards and in some of these groups the polling percentages were very close (e.g. Springburn, Cowlairs, Townhead and Blackfriars in 1906 with voting figures of 66.6 per cent, 64.2 per cent, 63.7 per cent and 71.6 per cent). Again in the 1911 elections there were contests in the 7 wards nos. 2 to 8 inclusive[1] and the polling figures were: 67.6 per cent, 55.3 per cent, 58.9 per cent, 66.8 per cent, 58.8 per cent, 53.6 per cent and 58.0 per cent. Finally for a quick look at the returns for 1912 and 1914—both important electoral years, 1912 because the addition of more than 6,000 acres to the area of the city had increased the number of wards to 37, and 1914 because it was a year in which the election took place after the outbreak of war and only two years after the addition of twelve new wards to the electoral register. In 1912 there were no contests for 17 of the 37 wards, which meant that 23 of the 59 councillors were returned unopposed. The highest percentage poll was a freak one—67 per cent in Blackfriars, which

[1] Viz. Calton, Mile-End, Whitevale, Dennistoun, Springburn, Cowlairs, Townhead.

for years had returned a candidate unopposed and promptly reverted to that practice in the following year. The lowest poll (43 per cent) was returned for one of the new wards, Partick West, and four more of the new wards (Govan, Ibrox, Partick East, Cathcart) returned their first nine councillors to the city without a fight. Polling in the rest of the new wards was no heavier than in the wards of the old city and by 1914 the 11 new wards thoroughly conformed to the old city habits. In that year only 4 of them bothered to have an election and among these four the highest poll was 37 per cent and the lowest (Jordanhill) 23.9 per cent. Only one ward of the old city area (Springburn, 22 per cent) had a worse electoral return in 1914. The year was, understandably, a bad one for municipal politics and only 13 of the 37 wards were contested—the highest poll was 54.8 per cent for the businessmen's ward, Exchange.

An analysis of the occupations of the new members (or re-elected members) of the Council for the years dealt with above has revealed the fact that, although some of the " heavyweights " of the city's industry and commerce continued to seek election or re-election within the period, their numbers gradually dwindled and the vacancies were filled by independents from the professions, by middle-sized and small-sized traders and occasionally by salaried and wage-earning employees with perhaps ideals in advance of the practice of their times. Once in, the newcomers appeared to stay the course, in the main, and to be re-elected after their first three years of office. The really big change in the make-up of the Council came with the elections of 1912 for the enlarged city area. The new wards—particularly in the Govan, Partick and Pollokshaws areas—brought in more professional men, small traders and representatives of the wage-earning electors than had ever been in the Council before. And by 1914 the example had begun to spread to the wards of the old city. The seed had been sown for the postwar years.

The first postwar election in 1919 was an abnormal one and should perhaps have no implications for the general trend. But the parallels with 1914 are very close. Twenty-five of the 37 seats were uncontested; the highest poll for a contested ward was 58.7 per cent,[1] and the lowest was 26.4 per cent for Jordanhill—one of the new wards which had already demonstrated its " couldn't care less " attitude in 1914. Moreover the composition of the Council in 1919 had scarcely changed from that of 1914, and indeed, because of the circumstances, the bulk of the members were the same people. Things looked as though the " Business As Usual " notice had been put up outside the new Council Chambers[2] on the east side of George Square. But in 1920 at least three things happened to produce a substantial change in the picture—(a) a reorganisation of wards; (b) a retiral, in consequence, of all 111 elected members of the Council with an opportunity for the electorate

1 For both Govan Central and Govan Fairfield with Govan Ibrox a close third at 56.9 per cent—obviously again a local issue as no other ward except Shettleston got into the 50-60 per cent bracket.

2 Opened in 1889.

to put in a completely new Council if it so wished; and (c) last, but by no means least, the emergence of organised party politics in the municipal elections, the principal antagonists being the local Labour and Moderate parties. The resultant changes were striking.

Only 4 of the 37 wards were uncontested and 12 of the 111 Councillors returned unopposed (3 Labour and 9 Moderate). The lowest percentage poll[1] was Provan's 46.7 per cent,[2] and the highest poll was 75.8 per cent in Springburn. In 15 other wards the percentage was over 70. (See Appendix Table 66.) The new Labour Party's vote was over 321,000 and it netted them 45 seats as against the 495,900 votes and 66 seats for all other contestants. Municipal affairs had apparently been given a much-needed " shot in the arm." The " shot " has since been administered annually and it continued for a time to have its effect, but never again quite the dramatic effect of 1920.

There was a mild but noticeable reaction in 1921 when the number of uncontested seats (Moderate constituencies) went up to 7—there were only 2 wards with a poll of over 70 per cent and there were 9 between 50 per cent and 60 per cent. The spread of voting narrowed to between 53.6 per cent and 73.9 per cent and about two-thirds of the returns fell into the 60 per cent—70 per cent bracket.

In 1922 the number of unopposed returns again went up sharply to 13—and again for Moderate constituencies; but the turn-out in contested wards also went up: the top poll was Provan's at 77.9 per cent and there were 9 other wards with a percentage above 70. Only two wards dropped below 60 per cent: North Kelvin 39.2 per cent and Partick West 59.8 per cent. Labour was now fighting fewer constituencies but fighting them more intensively.

The rest of the record of unopposed returns and ward voting between 1923 and 1938 (the last election year before the outbreak of World War II) is shown in Appendix Table 66. A brief comment on these figures is all that is required here. During all these 16 years there were only five occasions on which the percentage poll for any contested ward went above 70 per cent.[3] Of the total of 493 contested results, 241 fell within the range 50-60 per cent, another 123 in the range 60-70 per cent and 103 in the range 40-50 per cent. A turn-out of between one half and two fifths of the electorate in a contested ward was the inter-war-years norm. The brightest voting year of this 16-year period was 1924, but it was no more than the tail-end of the postwar enthusiasm. The decline set in in 1925 although it was slow in the beginning. There was a slump in municipal politics in 1929 that can find its match only in 1938, 1945 and 1955. In 1930 there was a partial recovery that was sustained with some noticeable high spots up to and including 1934 and, without the high spots, into 1935. After that the signs of

1 And that by far the lowest in the city as the nearest to it was Blythswood's 54.3 per cent.

2 In 1921 the same ward returned the second highest—70.6 per cent—and in 1922 the highest—77.9 per cent—percentage poll in the city.

3 Maryhill 1924 74.4 per cent, Whitevale 1925 71.2 per cent, Ruchill 1925 70 per cent, Ruchill 1928 70.5 per cent, and Parkhead 1929 82.1 per cent.

flagging were pronounced although the continuing party interest in municipal affairs ensured that even in the bleak year 1938 only 3 seats were uncontested.

In the first postwar election in 1945, seven of the 38 wards returned candidates unopposed. In the 31 contests there were 3 polls of under 30 per cent, 11 of under 40 per cent, 14 of under 50 per cent, and only 3 between 50 per cent and 60 per cent. Another low ebb—but there had been a war, and the same thing had happened after the First World War with a subsequent dramatic recovery. This time again there was some recovery towards the standards of the interwar years. In 1947 only two returns were unopposed, four constituencies polled over 60 per cent of their electorates, 18 over 50 per cent, 11 over 40 per cent and only two dropped to the 30-40 per cent level and one below 30 per cent. The percentages were certainly on the low side of the inter-war norm, but compared with those of 1945 they seemed at least to indicate a slow reversal of what had threatened to be a progressive decline. The appearance was deceptive. By 1955 the electorate had relapsed into the uncritical satisfaction, the indifference, or whatever it was by the name of " apathy " that kept them at home and out of the polling stations on election day. The parties kept hard at it, and only two Labour strongholds returned candidates unopposed, but two wards managed to pull out less than one in five of their qualified voters (Dalmarnock and Gorbals), in another 9 between 20 per cent and 30 per cent recorded their votes, in 11 more between 30 per cent and 40 per cent, in 13 more between 40 per cent and 50 per cent, and by 0.5 per cent one single ward scraped over the 50 per cent line (Partick West). Rock bottom?—this brief review has shown that in 1878 and 1880, without the stimulus of organised party politics only one ward in the whole city was contested! The trough of a cyclical trend, to be followed by an upsurge of interest?—there has always until now been something quite specific, some large new development, to account for upswings in electoral interest and the trend of development on the executive side of modern government shows, at the moment, no sign of producing any new shot in the arm for municipal affairs.

The Courts

If the electors of Glasgow take less interest in the work of their City Council than they might, they show still less concern about the vast and intricate labours of the judicial machinery of government. The courts of justice held within the city area have now less direct connection with the executive machinery of local government than they had at one time, but there is still an important connection and the direct and indirect effects of the administration of law in these courts upon the life of the town are of fundamental importance.

The following are the courts that exercise civil or criminal jurisdiction and also sit within the area. In all cases (except those of the

Magistrate courts including that of the River Bailie, which now have no civil jurisdiction, and the Dean of Guild Court which has no criminal jurisdiction) there is some overlapping of criminal and civil jurisdictions, but except for the Sheriff Court which has extensive jurisdiction in both fields, the operation of each court is predominantly in the realm of either criminal or civil law.[1]

Criminal Courts[2]

The High Court of Justiciary on Circuit.

The Sheriff Court of Lanarkshire—sitting in Glasgow for the Glasgow Sheriff Court District of the County.

The Justices of the Peace Courts for the lower ward of the County of Lanarkshire and also for the County of the City of Glasgow.

The Burgh Magistrate or Police Courts, including the Court of the Bailie of the River and Firth of Clyde.

Civil Courts[3]

The Sheriff Courts—Ordinary Court, Appeal Court and Small Debt Court.

The Justices of the Peace Courts for the lower ward of the County of Lanark and also for the County of the City of Glasgow.

The Dean of Guild Court.

As the work of the criminal courts is referred to elsewhere in this volume,[4] little will be said about them here except in the case of the High Court of Justiciary whose sittings were until the middle of last century held in the same building as those of the Town Council, and whose sentences of death were until that time carried out publicly before the City Chambers. The criminal jurisdiction of the Sheriff Court is both summary and solemn and the town's citizens are, in the latter type of cases (as also in High Court trials), called upon to take a very direct share in the work by service upon juries. The rest of the criminal courts have restricted and closely defined summary jurisdictions.

1 The Court of Session no longer visits Glasgow on circuit as it did in the nineteenth century when trying civil causes with juries (see Act establishing Courthouse Commissioners 1836); and the potent but narrow civil powers of the High Court are seldom used.

2 *Sittings*: High Court—every three months in Jocelyn (or "Jail") Square. Sheriff Court—Summary, daily; Jury, every second Monday. J.P. Courts—Lanarkshire, Mondays; Glasgow, Thursdays and Fridays; both in the Justices' Hall, County Buildings. Burgh Magistrate Courts—daily in District Police Chambers in Central, Marine, Eastern, Southern, Northern, Maryhill and Govan Police Districts; River Bailie's Court, every lawful day, in the Court Hall, Anderston Street.

3 *Sittings*: Sheriff Courts—Ordinary, 5 weekdays; Appeal, Monday to Thursday inclusive; Small Debt, Monday to Thursday inclusive; all in County Buildings. J.P. Courts—as in preceding footnote. Dean of Guild Court—on days fixed as necessary, in Burgh Court Hall, John Street.

4 See Chapter 20 (Crime).

The jurisdictions of the civil courts in the Glasgow area are the same as those for similar courts in other parts of Scotland, the Dean of Guild Court being concerned only with matters relating to the erection of new or the alteration of existing buildings in the city area.

The *High Court of Justiciary on Circuit* has a civil jurisdiction to hear appeals from the Sheriff Small Debt Court on the grounds of corruption, incompetency, malice or oppression, but of course it functions principally as the Supreme Criminal Court of Scotland.

Until 1812 the Justiciary Court met twice a year on circuit in the Tolbooth[1] which housed also the Town Council and the only jail in the city until the opening of the new jail in Saltmarket in 1812 and of Duke Street Prison in 1826. Prisoners awaiting trial, and also convicted prisoners, male and female—for crimes or for debt—from Glasgow and from the Circuit Courts of Lanarkshire, Renfrewshire and Dunbartonshire, were all housed together in the 32 cells of the Tolbooth.

In 1812 a new building was completed at the south-west end of the Saltmarket to house the Municipal Offices, the Justiciary Courts and a new jail. This was on the site of the old slaughter house and the Skinners' Green, next to the glue works that used the offal from the slaughter house and also hard by various houses " occupied by scullions and tripe-cleaners." The new Court House was a vast improvement on the premises in the Tolbooth. The new jail had 122 cells, facilities for the segregation of prisoners of different sex and type of conviction, much improved sanitary amenities, and also provision for exercise. Although only 35 prisoners were transferred to it from the cells in the Tolbooth in 1812, by June 1819 the number of inmates had risen to 158 and the problem of overcrowding was again appearing.

The Glasgow Court House Commissioners were established by an Act of 1836 and charged, among other things, to erect a Justiciary Court House, Sheriff Court Houses and public offices for the city and the lower ward of Lanarkshire. The close link between judicial and local government functions is shown in the fact that the Commissioners were then the Lord Provost, Bailies, Dean of Guild, Deacon Convener and Treasurer of the Town Council together with five others appointed jointly by the Council and the Sheriff, and eleven more appointed by the County local government bodies, the Commissioners of Supply for Lanarkshire.[2] The Commissioners built the premises in Wilson Street (the southern half of the present County Buildings) and to them moved the Town Council, the Sheriff Court Chambers and various other public offices, leaving the building in the Saltmarket to the jail and the Justiciary Court in 1842-4. The jail had passed out of the control of the city in 1839 into the hands of the Prison Commissioners for Scotland.

In the Reports of the " Commissioners upon the Courts of Law in Scotland " (1869) it is stated that in the year 1867 the Justiciary Court

1 At the foot of High Street at Trongate. It was rebuilt in 1626.

2 Now as above but including the Sheriff and 11 members of Lanarkshire County Council instead of 11 appointees of the Commissioners of Supply.

on the West Circuit held three sessions at Glasgow, each of two courts varying in length from three to seven days. In these sessions the Court tried 140 cases involving 185 persons, of whom 35 pleaded guilty, 107 were found guilty, 30 were acquitted and 13 had the cases against them deserted or were declared to be outlaws. The Court also dealt with seven appeals from inferior courts. It was only two years before this, in 1865, that the last public execution—that of the notorious Dr. Pritchard —took place outside the South Prison on Glasgow Green.

The buildings in Jail Square are well known to a great many Glasgow people and have been the scene of many famous criminal trials centring upon inhabitants of the town whose names were for many years household words—but few Glasgow people could give directions to them if asked for " Jocelyn Square."

In 1955 the High Court of Justiciary tried 70 Glasgow cases—58 while sitting on Circuit in Jail Square, and 12 at the central court in Edinburgh. Of the 70 accused, 59 were found guilty, 5 not guilty, 2 not proven and 4 insane.

The *Sheriff Court* in Glasgow at the beginning of the nineteenth century was not popular with litigants. Its procedures were laborious and wordy, and the court was inadequately staffed and badly housed, the Sheriff Court Chambers being rooms above shops and the entrance to them being through a " pend " off Stockwell Street. At the mouth of this pend there was a public-house that was only too popular with the members of the Sheriff Clerk's staff. In addition there was no resident Sheriff Clerk until 1874,[1] the office having been farmed out for many years. Indeed there was no resident Sheriff Principal (then called Sheriff Depute) in the city in the early years of the nineteenth century, and the whole of the Court's ordinary business was dealt with by one Sheriff Substitute (nearly removed in 1816 on the grounds of incapacity).

Moreover until 1853 pleadings were entirely in writing and no oral evidence or pleadings were heard by the Sheriff. Evidence was taken on Commission by the Sheriff Clerk or his Deputes. The unpopularity of the Court can be gathered from the remarks of Mr. George Baillie,[2] himself a member of the Faculty of Procurators: " Summons as vague and general as possible . . . defences equally mystified, replies, duplies, triplies, quadruplies and sometimes as far as Nonoplies, memorials, minutes, objections, reclaiming petitions, answers etc., all well seasoned with pungent sarcasm, withering insinuations, cutting reflections, fanciful illustrations and confident expectations of justice." Perhaps it is not surprising that the Substitute sometimes gave judgment without reading the Record.

By the time of the arrival in the city of Sheriff Archibald Alison[3]

1 G. B. Young, *Reminiscences of the Glasgow Sheriff Court* (1907) pp. 10, 11.

2 George Baillie, *Reminiscences*, pp. 14, 15.

3 Later Sir Archibald, perhaps the most powerful and colourful figure in the history of the Sheriff Court in Glasgow—see, for example, the story of the arrest and conviction of the Cotton Spinners in 1837 in *Anecdotage of Glasgow* (1892) collected by Robert Alison, pp. 309-11.

in 1835 the Bench had been increased to a Sheriff Principal (now resident) and two Substitutes, though one of the latter was reputed to have so little to do that he spent a large part of his time playing his violin in Chambers.

The most popular branch of the court had always been the Small Debt Court and when its jurisdiction was extended in 1837 to £100 Scots (£8 6s. 8d. Sterling) the business of this Court expanded so rapidly that Sheriff Alison had to give it two full days a week (Thursdays and Saturdays) and even then exercise the most rigid control over the procedure in order to get through the Roll.

The Sheriff Court Act of 1853 made vast improvements in procedure in the Ordinary Court resulting in a great increase in its popularity and business. After that date evidence was no longer taken on Commission but was recorded in long hand by the judge who heard oral evidence and pleadings in open court; and while not everyone was pleased with the changes,[1] Ordinary Court business continued to increase rapidly and the number of judges had to be raised to five. Fortunately the Court House Commissioners of 1836 had provided in 1844 new and much larger accommodation for the Sheriff Court Chambers in the east wing of the new building in Wilson Street, which still forms part of the Sheriff Court premises to-day, though much has been altered and much added since that time.

The extent to which the growing commerce and industry of the city had to have recourse to the Sheriff Ordinary Courts in civil matters can be seen in figures quoted in the *Report of the Commissioners on the Courts of Law in Scotland* issued in 1869. In 1863 the Court dealt with a total of 2,027 ordinary actions of which 1,378 were defended. Where costs were awarded they were taxed on one of three scales. The average award ranged from £10 1s. 8d. to £10 6s. 8d. depending on the scale—the largest award from £44 14s. 1d. to £50 14s. 5d. and the smallest from £1 15s. 6d. to £2 14s. 8d. There were 404 appeals from the Sheriffs Substitute to the Sheriff Principal (involving 309 actions); 31 of these involved no pleadings or arguments and were dealt with in an average time of 68 days each and at an average cost ranging from 8s. 6d. to 12s. 6d. The remaining 372 appeals required written pleadings or oral argument and took on an average 103 days each at an average cost of between £1 9s. 6d. and £2 13s. 6d. In the same year, under the Debts Recovery Act, the Court gave final judgment in 256 contested cases involving a total sum claimed of £6,033—the total sum decerned for was however over £3,689 (an average of £14 8s. 3d. per case). In 210 cases costs were awarded—on the higher of two scales the average was £1 3s. 10d. and on the lower 7s. 10d. Under this Act the Court also gave judgment in 391 uncontested cases involving a total sum of over £8,340—the average per case being £21 8s. 8d. and the average cost 10s. 6d. Of the decisions of the Substitutes in the Debt

[1] e.g., Sheriff-Substitute George Skene resigned in 1855 over the introduction of oral pleading.

Recovery actions, 86 were appealed to the Sheriff Principal and 3 to the Court of Session.

In 1870 the Town Council and the Municipal Offices moved to the new City Chambers built on to the north end of the Wilson Street buildings (to face Ingram Street) and the Courts took over the whole of the Wilson Street block. This was a much needed expansion of accommodation, but the premises had always been most unsatisfactory internally—between 1844 and 1900 they had to be reconstructed five times. Again in 1895 the Town Council and Municipal Offices moved to new quarters in George Square and the County Buildings expanded to take in the whole of the block between Wilson Street and Ingram Street, where they remain to this day.

But the Sheriff Court civil business has increased so enormously that the present enlarged Bench of Sheriff Principal and nine Substitutes is hard pressed to keep up with the Rolls. In 1955 the Ordinary Court dealt with 4,443 actions, the Small Debt Court with 25,587, and in addition there passed through the Court 6,176 applications of various sorts covering such subjects as "Rates and Taxes" (536), "Lunacy and Mental Deficiency" (824), "Bankruptcy" (142), "Registration of Clubs" (114), and "Miscellaneous" (4,155). The Commissary Office of the Court recorded 6,306 Inventories of the estates of deceased persons, the total amount involved being £15,492,000. Of these Inventories 3,179 were of "Small Estates" of under £500 totalling in value £597,000. In its civil and administrative work, the Sheriff Court in Glasgow has become an indispensable instrument of the town's government.

Jurisdiction in the *Justices of the Peace* and the *Magistrate* or *Police Courts* in criminal matters is to-day limited to certain petty crimes and offences at Common Law and under statute. But although the offences are described as "petty" (the victims of wife or child assault, breaches of the peace, drunken and disorderly behaviour etc. would perhaps not so describe them) the volume of the work is immense and its importance to the social life of the city incalculable. Procedure is summary and most of the work is now done in the daily sittings of the seven Police Courts and of the Court of the River Bailie which deals with cases relating to the work of the River and Harbour Police. Separate statistics of the work of these Courts are not now published in the *Criminal Statistics of Scotland,* but in 1868 it was the Justices of the Peace Courts (then for the Lower ward of Lanarkshire, as Glasgow was not yet a County of a City[1]) that did the bulk of the work. Indeed in that year the Burgh Court appears to have exercised no jurisdiction in criminal police matters and to have confined itself to hearing 196 undefended and 3 defended actions of "removing" and one other action relating to property. In the same year the J.P. Courts dealt with 16,954 Small Debt actions involving claims totalling £28,174 14s. 9d. These courts were popular for this type of case—and no wonder,

1 In 1893 when Glasgow was made a County of a City it acquired its own Justices of the Peace Court.

as the average expenses awarded were 2s. 10d. and the average Court dues from pursuer or defender ranged between 6d. and 1s. 6d. The J.P. Small Debt Courts also occasionally heard actions for aliment of bastards, but these must have concerned questions of debt in such cases and not questions of paternity.

The J.P. Courts also once exercised a considerable criminal jurisdiction at Common Law and under statute, and in the year 1868 tried 472 cases at common law (maximum penalty £5 or 60 days' imprisonment) and 283 cases under various statutes (maximum penalty £100 or two months' imprisonment). The administrative work of the Justices in these courts was concerned mainly with licensing. In 1868 they granted 186 licences to publicans and 17 to dealers in game. In 1955 the Licensing Courts in Glasgow (now the Lord Provost and nominated Bailies—the Licensing Appeal Court being the J.P. Court for the County of the City) dealt with 1,343 applications for renewal of licences for hotels and inns, public houses and grocers and 21 other applications for licences to cover new premises and extensions.

Armed Forces

While the armed forces of the Crown are raised and maintained on a national basis, Glasgow has particularly close links with certain branches of the fighting services. The city is proud to claim as its very own regiment the Highland Light Infantry, formed in 1881 by the amalgamation of the old 71st and 74th. It was in that year that the city became the regiment's territorial area and its acknowledged home, but the association with Glasgow goes much further back. The Regiment was raised originally as the 73rd (Macleod's Highlanders) round Elgin and Glasgow in 1777. A second battalion was raised at Dumbarton in 1804, and because of the source of many of its recruits this unit became known unofficially as the "Glasgow Highlanders." Royal approval was obtained in 1808 for the addition of the city's name to its title. During the First World War of 1914-18 many volunteer battalions of the Highland Light Infantry were raised in Glasgow, and in 1922 the city's contribution was suitably recognised by the King, who authorised the H.L.I. to assume the additional title of "City of Glasgow" Regiment. Following the Second World War the city in turn honoured its regiment: in 1948 the freedom of Glasgow was granted to the H.L.I. and received on its behalf by Princess Margaret, as Colonel-in-Chief.[1]

Glasgow has also close links with the Royal Navy and the Royal Air Force. The No. 602 (City of Glasgow) Squadron of the Royal Auxiliary Air Force, and the Scottish Air Division of the Royal Naval Volunteer Reserve, both based at Abbotsinch, Paisley, had proud

[1] Since the above was written plans for the reorganisation of the British Army have been announced, including a proposal to amalgamate the Highland Light Infantry with the Royal Scots Fusiliers. If this merger, which has aroused much controversy, is carried out the H.L.I. will lose its separate identity as the City of Glasgow Regiment.

records during the Second World War. These units, however, are to disappear as a result of the Government's decision to cut defence costs, announced early in 1957. The City of Glasgow Squadron was one of the first four auxiliary air force squadrons to be formed, recruiting having started in 1925. Among its founder members were the Duke of Hamilton and D. F. MacIntyre, of Mount Everest fame. In 1940 the squadron played a prominent rôle in the Battle of Britain, and in 1944 became part of the Second Tactical Air Force. The Scottish Air Division, R.N.V.R., was founded in 1941, and later became two units: the Nos. 1830 and 1843 Squadrons. Neither of these squadrons, however, was specifically associated with the city, although many Glasgow men served in them.

PARLIAMENTARY REPRESENTATION 1832-1955

DONALD G. SOUTHGATE

The parliamentary electorate under the franchise of 1832, when separate representation in the British Parliament was first accorded to Glasgow, was less than 5 per cent of the population; under the franchise of 1868, which endured fifty years, about 15 per cent; with full adult male suffrage and a restricted woman suffrage, 1919-28, it was just over 50 per cent. To-day, when only minors, lunatics and peers are excluded, it is between 65 and 70 per cent. Table LXXV records the broadening of the franchise, the change in 1885 from a single burgh constituency to electoral divisions and, by the implication of the figures in columns 1 and 2, the boundary extension of 1918. The area included in " Glasgow " for parliamentary purposes has varied, and has at times differed considerably from the municipal area. The boundary commissioners in 1832 excluded nearly half the old royal burgh and took in 5,000 acres in all, two thirds outside the municipal area, which did not catch up until 1846. Perhaps because the parliamentary pattern had provided a target for municipal expansion, the residents of Partick and Govan in 1868 resisted inclusion in the parliamentary burgh. They were not included until 1918, for the first general election after their absorption by the municipality in 1912, at which time more than a third of the municipal population was outside the parliamentary burgh. In 1948 and 1955 the Boundary Commissioners pursued the decentralising population into the outskirts.

That was not all they did. Until 1885 the burgh was a single constituency, returning two members before 1868, and thereafter three; a constituency, in the last election under this régime, of 60,000. Seven divisions were appointed in 1885. By 1915 the growth and movement of population had given them an average electorate of over 15,000 each, varying from only 10,600 at Blackfriars-Hutchesontown to 24,000 at

Bridgeton. Redistribution was overdue, even apart from the inclusion of the newly-municipalised populations. When it came, it gave the enlarged Glasgow fifteen divisions. In 1935 they had an average constituency of nearly 43,000, varying only between the 37,000 of Hillhead and Partick and the 54,000 of Maryhill, with eleven of them lying within the range 39,986-46,696. Rather surprisingly, the bombing during the Second World War did not increase the inequalities; all the constituencies were estimated in the very defective register of 1945 as between 38,666 (Tradeston) and 47,880 (Maryhill). But post-war housing schemes and patterns necessitated redistribution in 1948, and provided a strong case for fairly frequent future redistributions. The electorate of Pollok rose from less than 55,000 to nearly 63,000 between the elections of 1950 and 1951. But the Glasgow redistribution of 1955 (Fig. 27) will always remain a classic example of over-elaborate exercise of delegated authority and wide discretion. Eleven of the fifteen divisions were altered, seven municipal wards were divided for parliamentary purposes (instead of four). Two traditional names disappeared, and two new ones emerged. Old names retained were given a radically new substance; " Govan " was now to mean mostly what " Tradeston " had formerly meant, and the new name, " Craigton," stood for most of what had been " Govan." And with what result? To leave five divisions, one of them a reception area, with over 50,000 and to increase from two to three the number with less than 41,000, none of these three being likely to expand in population! This abstruse operation was not popular locally, and it does not seem calculated to associate members of Parliament intimately with the constituencies they represent or promote local electoral enthusiasms. It did provide (much needed) stimulus by the creation of three of the most marginal seats in the United Kingdom, but two or more seats had already emerged from the redistribution of 1948 as supreme tests for party organisation and propaganda. Mr. J. N. Browne's three successive victories for the Conservative Party in 1950-51-55, years of general Conservative advance, have been won by margins of 373, 241, and 210. Conservative majorities in Scotstoun, including the by-election of October 1950, have been 239, 1319, 625 and 428. The commissioners in 1955 added Provan to the spree; Labour won by 180.

If, among party politicians, Glasgow is known for its marginal seats, this is a recent phenomenon. In the inter-war years there were only two seats out of fifteen commonly regarded as really marginal.[1] This

[1] Maryhill, generally Left but U. 1918, 1924, 1931: Partick, generally Right but Lab. 1923 and 1929. Other seats went Right or Left consistently 1922-45 inclusive, except in 1931 (when Unionists won Camlachie, Springburn, Tradeston), with the fortuitous exception of Cathcart 1922 (Right-wing vote divided, and seat won by Labour) and Kelvingrove 1945 (Scottish Nationalist and Liberal intervention probably responsible for Unionist loss).
The generally Left seats were:
Bridgeton, Camlachie, Gorbals, Govan, Shettleston, St. Rollox, Springburn, Tradeston, and, less certainly, Maryhill.
The generally Right seats were:
Pollok, Hillhead, Central, Cathcart, Kelvingrove and, when no Liberal intervened, Partick.

TABLE LXXV

Glasgow Parliamentary Elections, 1831-1955
Population of Parliamentary Burgh, Number of Electors and Votes Cast

	Population of Parliamentary Burgh		*Electors*	*Votes Cast*
e1831	193,030	1832	8,000	
e1841	255,650	to	rising to	
1851	329,097	1865	18,000	
1861	395,503	inclusive		
1871	477,156	1868	a	
		1874	53,111	
1881	488,588	1880	61,069	93,727x
m1881	510,812a	1885	75,293a	61,276
1891	565,839	1886	75,293	58,061
		1892	81,438	60,251
		1895	85,581	53,275
1901	622,372	1900	91,331	55,049y
		1906	92,471	76,744
		1910	86,507	75,001
1911	599,614	1910	87,036	73,758
e1914	1,052,000	1918	524,008ab	279,051aby
1921	1,034,174a	1922	518,897	387,458
		1923	510,013	349,926
		1924	525,982	406,311
		1929	651,339a	486,464
1931	1,027,419	1931	638,339	485,534
		1935	642,707	464,738
e1939	1,010,143	1945	733,125b	416,280b
		1950	718,626	574,702
1951	1,089,767	1951	725,538	584,388
		1955	714,084	509,865

m Population of municipal burgh with which the parliamentary was assimilated in 1885.
e Estimates, made for 1831 and 1841 by the census authorities in 1851, for 1914 by the Registrar General in 1917; that for 1939 is given by the Secretary of the British Records Association in a Chambers's Encyclopædia article.
a Additions to population by boundary extension, and to electorate by this in 1885 and 1918 and by extension of franchise in 1868, 1917 and 1928.
b Registers very defective.
x Voters might in this election cast two votes each and most did.
y One seat uncontested in 1900 and 1918.

Members of Parliament—2 until 1868, 3 for the elections of 1868, 1874 and 1880, in the undivided burgh; 7 in single-member divisions, 1885-1910 inclusive; 15 since 1918, single-member.

Electoral Qualification—1832-68, middle class property and residential qualification based on annual value.
1868-1917, " Household suffrage " for adults with certain exceptions for poorer lodgers; twelve-month residence necessary; receipt of poor relief disqualified.
1917-28, Adult male suffrage (six-months' residence) and women over 30 being local government electors or their wives.
1928 ff. Adult suffrage.
1948. Abolition of plural vote for business " occupation." No figures published for Scotland. Plural votes often decisive in the Conservative interest in the Central Division, a Labour seat since 1950.

change may give an exaggerated importance to the decision of small parties to abstain or intervene. Communist intervention saved the Central division for the Tories in 1945,[1] and gave them Govan and Scotstoun in 1950; the Communists were unable, if they wished, to give them to Labour in 1951 by abstaining, since the Liberals also abstained.

The deposition of the Liberals by the Left occurred in Glasgow after the War of 1914-18. George Barnes, General Secretary of the Amalgamated Engineers, had won a three-cornered contest in Blackfriars-Hutchesontown in 1906 (so that the Liberals agreed to support him in

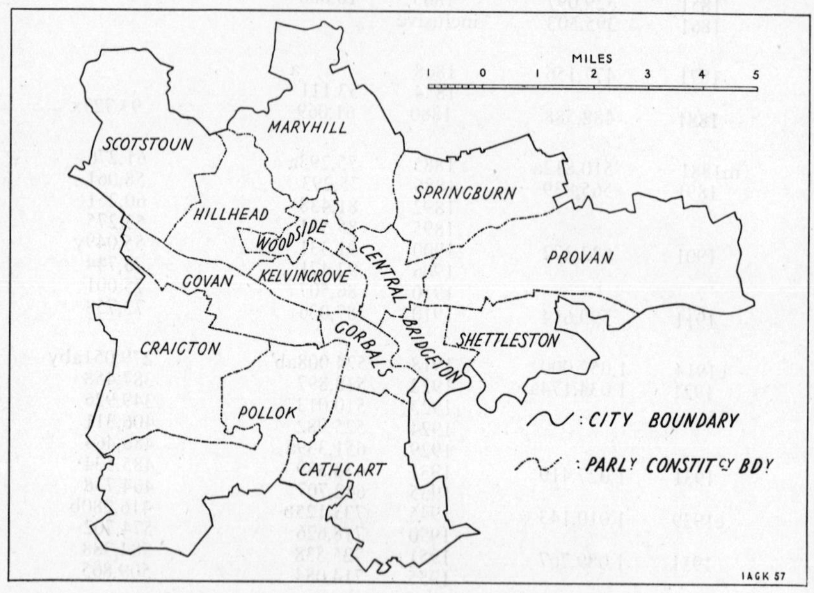

FIG. 27. The Present Parliamentary Constituencies.

1910). Labour intervention gave the Unionists Camlachie in 1892 and 1906 and twice in 1910. Between 1918 and 1945 it seems unlikely that Liberal intervention affected any result except once in 1929 and once in 1945.[2] The formerly dominant party had hardly even nuisance value in Glasgow. The figures given in Table LXXVI showing the votes actually cast, and in the main part of Table LXXVII, which reduces them to percentages, convey a misleading impression of Liberal revival in 1922-3 when the National Liberals, to their indignation, were deserted at Westminster by the Unionists, and Labour contemptuously allowed a Liberal a free run in three Unionist seats. The Unionists left

[1] The Central division had a substantial number of plural voters with a business qualification, which probably determined the retention by a Unionist of the seat on four occasions (Butler, *The Electoral System in Britain* 1918-51, p. 147). Upon the abolition of this qualification, the seat became Labour (1950 ff).

[2] 1929 Partick—Lab. maj. 399, Liberal vote 2,975. 1945 Kelvingrove—Lab. maj. 88, Liberal 919 and Scot. Nat. 1314.

the Liberals a free run in three safe Left-wing seats in 1923 and in one in 1924.

TABLE LXXVI

Glasgow Parliamentary Elections, 1880-1955
Votes Recorded for the Parties

(Where the number of candidates of the party differed from the number of seats being contested [3 in 1880, 7 in 1885-1910 inclusive except 1900 when six, 15 since 1918 except 1918 when 14] the number of candidates to whom the vote refers is given in brackets.)

	Total	*Conservative and Allies*	*Liberal*	*Labour*	*Various*
1880	93,727	22,693c	71,034		
1885	61,276	26,480	32,576(8)	978(1)	1,242(2)
1886	58,061	28,883	29,178		
1892	60,251	28,971	30,147(8)	1,133(2)	
1895	53,275	27,204	23,545	2,526(5)	
1900	55,049a	30,767	24,282		
1906	76,744	32,783	38,109	5,852(2)	
1910	75,001	31,692	33,404x(6)	6,939(2)	2,996(1)
1910	73,758	33,510	34,512x(6)	5,701(2)	35(1)

The 2,996 in 1910 were for Corbett, M.P., Unionist 1906, Liberal 1910 (2nd election).

	Total	*Conservative and Allies*	*Liberal*	*Labour*	*Other Left*	*Various*
1918	b279,051a	175,005	14,042(7)	89,013		991(1)
1922	387,458	117,783x(10)	98,541y(16)	166,637x(12)	4,497(2)	
1923	349,926	119,119x(12)	51,784y(10)	168,922x(14)	10,,021y(1)	
1924	406,311	197,667x(14)	11,238y(1)	197,406		
1929	486,464	211,554	15,941(4)	256,710	613(1)	646(1)
1931	485,534	273,866		200,237	6,479(3)	4,952(3)
1935	464,738	213,422	1,004(1)	166,150	84,162(6)	
1945	b416,280	177,063	3,994(3)	184,935x(13)	48,788(7)	1,500(2)
1950	574,702	255,223	17,919(9)	286,150	12,851(9)	2,559(2)
1951	584,398	272,165		305,922	5,955(4)	356(1)
1955	509,865	245,449		257,774	6,642(3)	

Underlined—Party forming Government after General Election.
a Unionist unopposed in one seat.
b Number of voters reduced by post-war derangement and defective registers.
c In this election there were two Conservative and three Liberal candidates for three seats, each voter being entitled to two votes.
x Party support undervalued by not contesting some seats.
y Party support overvalued by abstention of major party in some seats.

Conservatives and Allies:
Includes: Liberal Unionists from 1886. Party generally known in Scotland as "Unionist."
3 National Liberals and 1 National Labour in 1918.

Liberals:
Includes in 1918 Asquithians only.
Includes in 1922 7 Asquithians in three-cornered fight (including one against National Liberal), three Asquithians in straight fights with Unionist, and six National Liberals not now allied with the Unionists.
Includes in 1923 3 unopposed by Unionists, and in 1924, one such.

Various:
1885 Crofter 1,156 and Ind. 86.
1910 (second election) Woman Suffrage.
1918 Independent.
1929 Scottish Nationalist.
1931 Independent 4,021 (St. Rollox) and 2 New Party, 931.
1945 Scottish Nationalist 1,314; Independent 186.
1950 Scottish Nationalist, 639;; Irish anti-Partition, 1,920.
1951 "Independent Millionaire."

The national reasons for the decline of the Liberals operated in Glasgow—the mortal strife of Lloyd George and Asquith, the association of the former and the majority of the Liberal M.P.s with the Unionists, and working-class distrust of Liberal policy and leadership. This last factor had been unusually potent on Clydeside even before the Great War. It was fanned during the international conflict by the activities of the "wild Clydesiders" in propaganda, strikes, demonstrations and in gaol, with the Union of Democratic Control intervening. Later, Allied intervention against the Bolsheviks in Russia and then the depression of 1920-1 fed the sturdy plant of Socialism. Glasgow was to be the stage on which was played, and, it seems, played out, the tangled drama of Labour-I.L.P. relations. Before the First World War, a majority of Labour M.P.s in the Parliaments of 1906 and 1910 were I.L.P. men, but the parliamentary party was not committed to Socialism. The I.L.P. remained a party with local branches, while "the Labour Party" was a party in the House but not in the country. Most of the Labour M.P.s supported the war, but the I.L.P. on the whole did not. A small Labour remnant under Macdonald formed the opposition at Westminster, the I.L.P. formed the opposition in the country, and certainly on Clydeside. In 1918 "Labour" (and that meant locally the I.L.P.) fought every contested Glasgow seat. The Asquithian Liberals polled very poorly; one of their ex-cabinet ministers, McKinnon Wood, defending his seat at St. Rollox, incurred the novel penalty of the forfeited deposit.

The foundation on a national basis of the Labour Party in 1918, with a Socialist programme, made the position of the I.L.P. anomalous, because branches of the new party (from 1918 the official Opposition in Parliament) were now to be formed everywhere. But forms cannot alter facts, as Labour discovered in 1935. To the Parliament of 1931 only 52 Labour members were returned, and five of them came from Glasgow. They were Neil Maclean (Govan 1922-50), James Maxton (Bridgeton 1922-46), John McGovern (Shettleston 1930 ff) and George Buchanan (Gorbals 1922-49) with Mr. Leonard (St. Rollox, May 1931-50). Disgusted by the "gradualism" of the Labour Party, Maxton led such of the I.L.P. as he could muster out of the fold. The Independent Labour Party, so named to indicate in the 'nineties its independence of the *old* parties, resumed a separate existence independent of *Labour*. It cut no ice in England, and only a little at Merthyr Tydfil. It fought in 1935 on a narrow front in Scotland, where outside the Glasgow vicinity four candidates obtained only 11,500 as against 55,000 for the official Labour men. Even in Govan (Neil Maclean had not left the

Labour Party) and Tradeston (which was recaptured by a former Labour junior minister, Tom Henderson) the I.L.P. attackers secured only 8,382 against Labour's 28,044. But in North Lanarkshire the I.L.P. man obtained 17,267 against less than 7,000 for Labour and the Unionist triumphed through the split vote. And when Labour assaulted the four I.L.P. strongholds in Glasgow, namely Bridgeton, Shettleston, Gorbals and Camlachie (represented 1922-31 and 1935-47 by Rev. Campbell Stephen), its candidates polled a mere 7,722 against 73,993 for the four who, until Buchanan's secession in 1939 on the issue of the war, constituted the I.L.P. at Westminster. In 1945 Labour left well alone, except at Shettleston, but contested the election of Maxton's successor at Bridgeton in August 1946. That successor, like Stephen and McGovern, soon rejoined the Labour Party. The I.L.P. diehards, championed by Miss Annie Maxton, took action at Camlachie on Stephen's death in 1947; the plethora of Left-wing candidates let the Unionist in (January 1948). The vendetta was pursued in Bridgeton and Shettleston in 1950 and 1951, and at Bridgeton again in 1955, but the (ex-I.L.P.) Labour members, McGovern and Carmichael, were unshaken.

Though the Left in Glasgow has been spirited and often extreme, loyalty to personalities was marked during the internecine strife, and the Glasgow electorate has sternly eschewed the furthest extremes of both Left and Right—if it is proper to put on the Right the New Party formed in 1931 by one who had so recently been Labour's rising hope, Sir Oswald Mosley. This Fascist effort attracted less than 1,000 votes in two constituencies. The high-water marks of Communist achievement (at the polls) have been registered, not surprisingly, in 1922 at Gorbals and in 1945, when Russia was " the great, progressive ally," at Shettleston; the votes were 4,027 and 4,122, the percentages 13 and 12½. Glaswegians have also refused to deviate from the contest between the Right and the Left (as variously represented)—even to so seductive a candidate as the septuagenarian Mr. Pickard, provider of circuses (cinemas), who solicited support in Maryhill in 1951 as an " independent millionaire." The largest vote secured by a Scottish Nationalist was 1,314 in Kelvingrove in 1945, when Mr. Walter Elliot lost to Labour by 88. A dissident treasurer of the Gorbals Labour Party in 1950 united the potent appeals of " Ireland United and Scotland Free " and secured 1,919 supporters.

Taking a retrospect of Glasgow's electoral history in terms of the major parties, we see 1832-85 as a period of complete, and often unchallenged, Liberal predominance, when a middle-class electorate, and then a mass electorate dutifully following its lead, regularly sent to Westminster Radical, Protestant free-traders who were almost uniformly local merchants or manufacturers. No Conservative was returned until 1874, when Mr. Whitelaw, an ironmaster, slipped in, not merely because of the " minority representation " device introduced in 1868 (whereby, with three members to be returned, no elector might cast more than two votes), nor because this was the first election by secret ballot, but because six Liberal candidates contended together, and the single Conservative found 14,000 votes out of 75,000 enough. Not until 1880, when two Conservatives were adopted, can we measure at all accurately the party strengths;[1] in that year of Liberal revival produced by Gladstone's speeches in Midlothian the Liberal predominance was as 3:1. Glasgow was therefore often cited in 1885 as a place where the minority would not secure representation unless proportional representation was introduced into the electoral system. The case for "P.R." must stand or fall on other, and national, grounds, but so far as Glasgow was concerned the evidence for the innovators was to be stronger than they then suspected. Conservative hopes of due representation in the great cities depended upon division according to economic and social distinctions in the population; by a unique agreement, reached privately, between their leaders and the Liberal ministers, the boundary commissioners were instructed to follow this rule. In the next election, the first in the seven divisions, a great surprise occurred. The Conservatives took over 43 per cent of the votes in Glasgow, but they gained not one seat. The population of Glasgow was far from homogeneous—the presence, with a Conservative candidate, in Blackfriars-Hutchesontown, of a Liverpool businessman who had sat as an Irish member, and of a Crofter, symbolised the city's function as a magnet attracting immigrants from distressed rural areas. Yet the Conservative vote varied only between 39 per cent in this constituency and 49.4 per cent in the Central division, and only one candidate, of either side, ever secured 60 per cent of the poll before the Great War. This was A. Cameron Corbett, afterwards first Lord Rowallan, to whom Tradeston was faithful from 1885 to 1911 although his own consistency of view twice separated him from his political associates: in 1886 when the Liberal Party adopted Home Rule for Ireland, and after 1903 when the Unionists began to backslide on Free Trade. In 1885 he got 56.4 per cent as a Liberal against a Conservative, and in 1910 60.5 per cent. In 1886 he got 55 per cent as a Unionist against a Liberal and in 1900 61.2 per cent; in a straight fight with Labour in 1892, he got 81.2 per cent, and in 1895 against Liberal and Labour, 53.5 per cent. The Tariff Reformers sent against him in 1906, when a Liberal fought him, a candidate who failed to get 3 per cent. Corbett then left the Unionists without joining the Liberals, and was opposed by both in the first general election of 1910. This was the occasion of the highest turn-out ever known at a British general election—85.6 per cent. In Glasgow it was 86.7 per cent, not counting those who spoiled papers; this was very high indeed for a city where part of the population tended to be transitory and the registers over-

[1] A single Conservative polled 10,812 in 1868.
A single Conservative polled 14,134 in 1874.
In 1868 three Liberals polled 54,152.
In 1874 six Liberals polled 60,966.

But the exact Liberal strength remains obscure because some Liberals may have cast only one vote and some Conservatives may have voted for one of the Liberals to keep the others out.

optimistic.[1] In Tradeston Corbett (Ind. Lib.) took 34.1 per cent of the votes, the Unionist 33 per cent and the official Liberal 32.9 per cent.

Movement of population and redistribution altered the picture for the main contestants, now Unionists and Labour; such a balance appeared that, save in the quite exceptional circumstances of 1918 and 1931, the result at none of the eight general elections before the redistribution of 1948 diverged by more than one seat from 9 Socialist, 6 Unionist.[2] And this distribution of constituencies meant that six of the eight times the Unionists were under-represented, as compared with the Left, even taking all Left-wing votes together although they were sometimes cast in mutual antagonism. We have seen by what freakish margins a due proportion of members (8 Labour, 7 Unionist) to seats has been maintained since the 1948 redistribution.

Glasgow has contributed notably to the more eminent personnel of the House of Commons. In 1910 George Barnes became Labour's parliamentary chairman. In 1911 Andrew Bonar Law, the Glasgow industrialist and banker, became leader of the Unionists. Law had won Blackfriars in 1900 and Barnes had defeated him there in 1906. The two men sat together in wartime coalition governments, and after the 1918 election, when Barnes (Coalition Labour) held Gorbals against a Left-wing candidate and Bonar Law was elected in the Central division, were members of Lloyd George's cabinet of five. Sir Robert Horne (U. Hillhead, 1918-37) had a meteoric ministerial career in 1919-22 at the Ministry of Labour, Board of Trade and Treasury. Bonar Law was Prime Minister in 1922-3. Of Secretaries for Scotland, Glasgow has

1 Comparison of Glasgow polling level with contested seats in Great Britain in general (adjusted as per Butler, *op. cit.* Table 21).

	1906	1910	1910	1918	1922	1923	1924
Gt. Britain	83.3	85.6	81.0	57.6	71.3	70.8	76.6
Glasgow	83.0	86.7	84.7	58.3	74.7	68.6	77.2
		+1%	+3½%		+3½%	−2%	

	1929	1935	1935	1945	1950	1951	1955
Gt. Britain	76.1	76.3	71.2	72.7	84.0	82.5	76.8
Glasgow	74.7	76.0	72.3	56.7	80.5	80.6	71.5
	−1½%		+1%	−16%	−3½%	−2%	−5%

Examination of the decline of electoral participation since the late war shows that it has been confined to the safe Labour seats and Kelvingrove, with the Central division as the worst offender. Attendance is very high in the Unionist stronghold of Cathcart and above average in Hillhead, and high in the marginal seats. The figures for 1955 were:

Glasgow Poll 71.5% Labour Seats (safe): Central −8½%; Gorbals −6½%; Bridgeton −5½%; Shettleston −2½%; Springburn −2½%; Maryhill −1½%; Govan average.

Labour Seats (marginal): Provan +3½%.

Unionist seats (marginal): Scotstoun +8½%; Craigton +5½%; Woodside +1½%; Kelvingrove −3½%.

Unionist seats (safe): Hillhead +1½%; Pollok +4½%; Cathcart + 4½%.

This implies more effective organisation, and greater doggedness and solidarity among the Unionists.

2 See note (1) page 438.

TABLE LXXVII

GLASGOW PARLIAMENTARY ELECTIONS, 1880-1955
PERCENTAGE SHARE OF TOTAL VOTES, BY PARTIES
AND NUMBERS OF MEMBERS RETURNED

Turnout	*Year*	*C.&L.U.*	*M.P.s*	*Lib.*	*M.P.s*	*Lab.*	*M.P.s*	*Other*	*M.P.s*
76% app.	1880	24.2%	0	76.8%	3				
81.4	1885	43.2	0	53.2	7	1.6%(1)		1.9%(2)	
77.1	1886	49.8	3	50.2	4				
74.0	1892	47.7	3	50.4	4	1.9(2)			
61.1	1895	51.1	5	44.1	2	4.8(5)			
72.2	1900	55.9	7	44.1	0				
83.0	1906	42.7	2	49.7	4	7.6(2)	1		
86.7	1910	42.3	2	44.5(6)	3	y9.3(2)	1	3.9(1)	1
84.7	1910	45.6	2	46.7(6)	4	y7.7(2)	1		
		Right	*M.P.s*	*Lib.*		*Left*	*M.P.s*		
58.3	1918	59.2	14	5.0(7)		35.5	1		
74.7	1922	45.5	5	y10.1(10)		44.4(12)	10		
68.6	1923	34.1(12)	5	y14.8(10)		51.1	10		
77.2	1924	48.6(14)	7	y2.8(1)		48.6	8		
74.7	1929	43.5	5	3.3(4)		52.9	10		
76.0	1931	56.4	10			42.6	5		
72.3	1935	45.9	6	0.2(1)		53.9	9	(4 I.L.P.)	
56.7	1945	42.4	5	1.0(3)		56.1	10	(3 I.L.P.)	
80.5	1950	44.4	7	3.1(9)		52.0	8		
80.6	1951	46.6	7			53.4	8		
71.5	1955	48.1	7			51.9	8		

y Party support overvalued in constituencies fought, by absence of candidates from one of the main parties (counting Liberals as such before 1918 and Labour afterwards).

The Right here included National Liberals with Unionists in 1922 as well as 1918. But, dissociated from the Unionists, the Nat. Libs. slumped less heavily than they did in the 1922 election. A more accurate picture of the trends as they affected the Unionists and Labour is given by the following:

Party shares in five constituencies where Unionists and Labour fought each election, 1918-23 inclusive

1918	Unionist	63%	Labour	30.8%	Liberal	6.2% (4)
1922	,,	41.3	,,	51.6	,,	7.1 (4)
1923	,,	41.2	,,	54.1	,,	4.7 (2)
1924	,,	(47.8)	,,	50.6	,,	(1.2) (1)
1929	,,	41.3	,,	56.2 (inc. 1 Com.)	,,	1.8 (1)
1931	,,	53.1	,,	45.5 (inc. 1 Com.)		

In 1924 the Unionists had 41.6% with only four candidates, as they did not oppose the Liberal in St. Rollox; on the reasonable assumption that the Conservative would have got four fifths of the votes that went to the Liberal (had there been a three-cornered contest) the above estimate has been made.

returned Sir George Trevelyan (L. Bridgeton 1887-97);[1] T. McKinnon Wood (L. St. Rollox 1906-18); Sir John Gilmour (U. Pollock 1918-40), who was appointed in 1926 first Secretary of State; and Mr. Walter Elliot (Kelvingrove, U. 1924-45 and 1955 ff). J. Wheatley, the hero of the rent strike of 1920 (Shettleston 1922-30) was Minister of Health in the first Labour government of 1924. But in the last generation it was for its stormy House of Commons " characters," the " wild Clydesidors," that Glasgow was famous. Their local fame was at first extra-

[1] He came as a refugee after his brief Unionist aberration which had cost him the representation of the Border burghs.

parliamentary, their tone anti-parliamentary. It is perhaps fitting to recall that "Geordie" Buchanan became Under-Secretary for Scotland (1945), and few tributes to that constitutional system, a small part of which we have been describing, have been more moving than the considered judgment of the veteran "Jimmy" Maxton.[1]

1 The basic figures for the Section "Parliamentary Representation, 1832-1955," were taken from three sources—Dod's *Parliamentary Companion* and the Constitutional Year-Books until 1945, and after then *The Times, House of Commons*. But the writer is responsible for all calculations and categories.

Chapter 14

HOUSING

ROBERT BAIRD

INTRODUCTION

ONE hundred and ten years ago—in 1846—municipal Glasgow more than doubled its size by a single Act of Parliament, and for the first time crossed the Clyde to take in most of the ancient Barony of Gorbals on the south bank of the river and the green fields on the Barony's boundaries. The extensions of that year brought the city's area up to 5,063 acres within which, according to the 1851 Census, there were 64,611 houses[1] at a density of 12.8 houses to the acre. By 1951 the city's area had increased to 39,725 acres and the number of houses to 294,467, and the density of building over the whole area was down to 7.4 houses[2] to the acre.

This is, on the face of it, a substantial improvement in housing density, particularly in view of the intensive industrial and commercial development of the nineteenth century and of the fact that many parts of the city now regarded as " central " were green fields and garden grounds in 1851. But the Second Planning Report of the City Engineer showed that in 1946 there were about 172,000 houses (58.4 per cent of the 1951 total for the city) occupying only 1,810 acres (4.5 per cent of the city's area) at a density of 95 houses to the acre. This Report also estimated that 83 per cent of these houses were of one or two apartments only, that 91 per cent were without proper sanitary facilities, and that 56 per cent did not even have separate water-closet accommodation. According to this estimate the number of one-roomed and two-roomed houses in this central area of the city in 1946 was greater than the number of similar houses in the whole city five years later.

In spite then of more than thirty years of positive State housing policies, and ten years' intensive postwar investment in the building of new houses, there would still appear to be a " city within a city," a nineteenth century housing " hangover " in the midst of a twentieth century housing spree. Glasgow has for long had a bad reputation for housing conditions. The novelist, the playwright and the propagandist

[1] This is in fact the Census figure for " families " which the Report itself recommended for use as the number of " houses " in view of the unsuitability to Scottish conditions of the definition of a " house " for Census purposes. The use of the figure for " families " in this connection does not of course take into account the amount of sharing of houses by more than one household. (See notes in Appendix p. 862.)

[2] Using the 1951 figure for " families," the strictly comparable density would be 7.7 to the acre.

for social reform have found rich material in the slums of the nineteenth century and the remains of them that have survived into the middle of the twentieth, but they give no indication of the size of the problems facing the city's housing authorities and no picture of the improvements that have been wrought or of the developments that are envisaged.

HOUSE-BUILDING SINCE 1850

By the middle of the nineteenth century the central area of Glasgow, and particularly the area of the "ancient city," was a congested mass of tenement houses. Tenements had been built in Glasgow even before the period of industrialisation began, and many reasons have been given to explain the tenement as a characteristic of Scottish urban life: e.g., the climate and the weather; the local supply of good stone and a preference for it as a building material; the close commercial and industrial organisation of a community around a communications bottleneck, or around a natural defensive[1] vantage point, or within the protection and enrichment of an established centre of religion; the rising values of building ground and the economies in building costs to be gained by building upwards rather than outwards. Whatever the order of importance of the reasons offered, they combined to make the nineteenth the century of the tenement in Glasgow.

By the middle of the century the one-roomed and room-and-kitchen stone cottages, and the two-storeyed cottage-type houses (with or without attics) containing single families or two families, with an outside stair giving access to the top flat—all of which had been typical of the housing in or near the centre of the city only a hundred years before—were to be found only on the city's outskirts and in its suburbs. The many terrace houses that had been the homes of the well-to-do in former years and were now being engulfed by the city's commercial and industrial expansion, were in the process of being abandoned by their former owners and divided up to house many more families than they had been built for. The earlier tenements of four storeys or more in height with stone walls of two feet or more in thickness,[2] built in the centre of the town in large rectangular blocks around open spaces or "back-greens," now found the light and air shut off from their rear windows by the "back-lands" tenements that grew up in their midst under pressure of industrial and commercial development and the scarcity of building ground. It was the mid-century "back lands" that were principally responsible for what the Royal Commission in 1917 described as "groups of lightless and unventilated houses" and "clotted masses of slums" which were to keep the sanitary and public health officials busy for the next hundred years. But not all Glasgow's

1 It has even been suggested by some writers that the tenement with the typical single entry through a "close" was designed to make defence of its inhabitants easier—the comparison with the "broch" is perhaps rather strained.

2 More often than not without a damp course and therefore, because of their great thickness, acting as monumental sponges for the city's rainfall.

tenements stand condemned. With the great improvements in hygiene and sanitation made possible by the Loch Katrine water supply (1859), and under pressure of the developing social and civic consciousness illustrated by the passing of the City Improvements Acts of 1866 and 1897, the City and Burgh Police Acts and the Public Health (Scotland) Act of 1897, the standards of tenement properties built in the last half of the century showed substantial improvement. The best of these properties had two flats on each landing (with perhaps six entering from the common stair, and the two ground-floor flats forming main-door houses) and each flat had three, four or more rooms and kitchen with bathroom, water-closet, hot-water system and a scullery built off from the kitchen. These were homes for the comparatively well-to-do.

Lower in quality—the homes of what the Royal Commission described as " the superior artisan class " and the " good artisan class " —were the tenements that had three or four houses on each landing of a three or four-storeyed block, each house being of two rooms and kitchen with a bathroom, or of a room and kitchen either with a bathroom which included a water-closet, or with a water-closet alone. All the nineteenth century tenements had one or more " box beds " built into the walls (almost certainly one in the kitchen) and only in the better and later-built examples did the sanitary equipment reach the standard now considered the minimum for public health. Some information on this subject will be given later, but it is worth noting here that the worst of the congested back-land tenements had, in addition to their other potentialities for unsavouriness, immorality and ill-health, nothing more than a communal " privy " in their constricted back yards; and water-closets provided for the more fortunate slum tenants after the introduction of the city's water supply were often shared by the occupants of more than one landing or even in many cases by all the inhabitants of the " close."

Tenement building went out of favour in Glasgow after the 1914-18 war, as it did throughout Scotland, although the Royal Commission's Report had pointed out that the best of the Victorian tenements had been responsible for the marked improvement in density of occupation and sanitary conditions in the Scottish towns. However, the attack on the tenement—and particularly the congested back-lands tenements—had started in Glasgow in 1866 with the passing of the first City Improvements Act. Under this Private Act of Parliament the City Corporation was empowered as " Improvement Trustees " to acquire land by agreement and clear out insanitary areas, to widen existing streets and to make new streets, to establish a public park in the north-east of the city,[1] and also for the first time to " erect and maintain houses for mechanics, labourers and other persons of the poorer and working classes and either let or sell these." This power to build houses, according to the Report of the Glasgow Municipal Commission on the Housing of the Poor " seems indeed to have been almost re-

[1] The park named in the Trustees' powers—Alexandra Park—was opened in 1870.

garded by the Corporation as a permission that had found its way into the Act by mistake."

The Police Board had, under Acts of 1873 and 1877, widened and diverted some streets, made new streets and improved some others. The lands left in their hands were passed by statute to the Improvement Trustees in 1894 to be used for the general purposes of the 1866 Act. Under that Act the Trustees were empowered to impose an assessment not exceeding 6d. per £ of rateable value for the first five years and thereafter 3d. per £ for the next ten years. The Lord Provost of the day lost his seat on the Council at the next municipal election because the maximum of 6d. per £ was imposed in the first year.

Under their original empowering Act the Trustees lost no time in buying up land, clearing buildings, widening streets and making new streets, mainly around the areas of Saltmarket, Trongate and High Street, but they made little of the power to build new houses, except for the construction of two tenements in the Drygate and the building of seven model lodging houses (six for males, one for females) in and around the centre of the city. Perhaps there was a good enough reason for this in that the property market collapsed in the depression of 1878 and the Trustees could not sell, or even feu, the land they had cleared. Some of these old properties that had been scheduled for demolition had in fact to be repaired and let, in order to bring in some income to the Trust. Indeed by 1888 certain of the properties still in the hands of the Council and still occupied were "among the worst and most insanitary in the city." The activities of city improvement had come to a stop for a time. However, as an extension of the lodging house developments, the building of a Family Home was started by the Trust in St. Andrew's Street and in 1896 it was opened for wage-earning widowers with families of young children.

In the meantime the depression in the property market had lightened and in 1888 demolition work and the erection of new buildings on cleared sites had been resumed. The first building done was of two blocks of tenement houses (with shops on the ground floor) on the east side of Saltmarket, and by 1894 almost the whole of the area scheduled for demolition in the 1866 Act had been cleared and re-built. In the process of widening 26 existing streets and making 30 new streets under the powers given by this Act, 100,000 square yards of ground were cleared of houses that had contained about 51,000 persons.

The property and powers of the Improvement Trustees were transferred to the Corporation of the City by the Glasgow Corporation and Police Act of 1895 and in 1897 a further private Improvements Act was put through Parliament by the Corporation in order to enable the city to clear and re-build on six "congested and insanitary" areas and also to build houses for the "poorest classes" on 25 acres of land to be bought. The Corporation was empowered to borrow £560,000 (including £100,000 for the building of working-class houses) and also to impose a rate of 1d. per £ for these purposes. The remarkable difference between the two enabling Acts is that the Act of 1866 provided for no Sinking Fund for the redemption of debt (and even in

1955 the work undertaken under this Act was still in deficit), whereas the Act of 1897 imposed an obligation to provide a Sinking Fund by which the whole debt of the Corporation under this head should be repaid within 60 years. The 1897 Act together with an Act of 1902 empowered the Corporation to borrow in all £710,000 and to use £250,000 of this to buy land for houses for the "poorest classes." Before 1900 all the properties within the scheduled areas had been bought (either on an agreed price basis or as a result of arbitration) for about £300,000 and by 1906 the old buildings had been demolished and new buildings erected at a cost of about £263,000. The Corporation also bought the 25 acres of land that it was empowered to buy for the building of working-class dwellings, but it handed over about eight acres to the Parks Department as they proved to be unsuitable for house-building.

By 1913 the Corporation had built (under the 1866 and 1897 Acts, but chiefly under the latter) the following houses:[1]

One apartment houses	592
Two " "	1,334
Three " "	257
Houses of larger size	16
	2,199

At that time the Improvements Committee was anxious to extend its activities in providing houses for the poorer classes and in clearing congested areas of the town, but prices for property were too high for the Corporation and the War of 1914-18 put a stop to all ambition in this direction. Since 1920 the City Improvement Acts have been very largely overshadowed by the various Housing Acts and Planning Acts, but in 1955 the following items still appeared in the city accounts under the name of the Improvement Trustees:

(a) Under the Act of 1866

Dwelling houses	1,646
Shops and business premises	394
Total Capital Value	£713,555
Annual rental	£69,520
Lodging houses (Men)	5
Lodging houses (Women)	1

[1] The rents of these houses (per annum) varied from £4 10s. to £5 10s. for a single apartment, from £5 10s. to £6 for a single apartment with a scullery and a small bedroom, and from £7 to £8 10s. for two apartments.

and (b) Under the Act of 1897

Dwelling houses	866
Shops and business premises	189
Total Capital Value	£381,565
Annual rental	£35,789

All the houses built under the Improvement Acts were in tenements, mostly of four storeys with shops on the ground floor. They were substantial and comparatively well equipped tenements and the cubic capacity of the rooms was considerably above the legal minimum then required. Nevertheless few of these houses had separate sculleries, and still fewer had separate water-closets, the standard practice being to provide one water-closet to every four tenants. It was after the First World War that the City Corporation really began to build houses. From 1919 to 1951 the Corporation built 71,287 houses and another 10,419 houses were put up by private builders receiving grants from the Corporation under the 1919, 1923 and 1924 Housing Acts. Some of these houses—particularly in the re-housing schemes[1]—were two-storey and three-storey stone-built tenements, but by far the majority were built as two-storey flats, terrace cottages and semi-detached cottages with outer walls of cavity brick construction. In some of the tenements, there were a few houses of one and two apartments, and some of the two-storey flats were of two rooms, but the bulk of the building was of houses of three and four apartments.

Although most of the house-building in Glasgow since 1919 has been the work of the Corporation and of private builders receiving financial assistance from the Corporation, private enterprise erected 10,404 houses without Corporation assistance between 1919 and 1955.[2] As in other cities, the building industry in Glasgow is represented by considerable numbers of small and moderate-sized firms and a few large or very large. Some of the latter firms located in Glasgow have names well known throughout Scotland and beyond. The smaller firms are joiners, or slaters, or plasterers, or carry on some other trade ancillary to the production or repair and renewal of houses and other buildings. Most of the very large firms—with employees running perhaps to 1,000—have many-sided businesses and contract to erect complete buildings or groups of buildings like a new housing estate. Some are speculative and build for subsequent sale. Of the largest, some are civil engineers as well as builders, and prepare roads and sewage systems in addition to erecting buildings.

A few of the large firms specialise in house-building; so far, indeed, as houses have been erected by private enterprise in Glasgow in recent years, this has been the work mainly of three or four such firms whose names are household words. Others build no houses, but are known for their public buildings, some in high-class stone work, such as banks

1 By 1951 there had been 15,412 houses demolished under the various Slum Clearance Schemes.

2 See Appendix, Table 79.

and hotels. There are some very large firms of slaters, only a few of whom, however, do new work: the majority are engaged in repair, the vigorous tenement building of 1870-1910 having bequeathed a fantastic legacy of roof-repairing to the present period. In recent years there has been much specialising in shop-fitting by Glasgow building firms.

In the Building and Contracting group of Industries (Standard Industrial Classification) the numbers of employees in the Glasgow Area of the Ministry of Labour were as follows:

	1951	1955
Building	31,090	28,148
Electric Wiring and Contracting	2,419	2,152
Civil Engineering and Contracting	4,579	4,384
Building and Contracting Total	38,088	34,684

Besides those employed by private enterprise the above numbers include those employed by the Works Department of Glasgow Corporation. In December 1954, the latter numbered 6,135: these may be classified as under:

Direct Labour	New Works (Building) Section	3,302
	New Works (Roads and Sewers) Section	877
	Mechanical Plant and Transport	368
	Maintenance Section	1,588
	Total	6,135

Number and Size of Houses

In the 90 years from 1861 to 1951 the number of houses in the city increased more than three and one half times—largely, of course, through the extension of the city boundaries but also as a result of new building. For example, in the 21 years from 1891 to 1911 inclusive, linings were granted for the erection of 57,406 houses—8,566 of one room, 22,814 of 2 rooms, 12,461 of 3 rooms, 3,154 of 4 rooms and 10,411 of 5 rooms or more. The boom building years were 1897 and 1898. There was a slight revival of building in 1902 and 1903 but from 1904 the rate of building fell away rapidly until, at the outbreak of war in 1914, practically no new building of houses was being done.

In the Glasgow of 1861 nearly three quarters of all the families lived in houses of one or two rooms.[1] By 1871 this figure was just short of 80 per cent, but by 1881 it had gone back to 76.6 per cent. The proportion of one-roomed houses in the city's ever-increasing total of houses declined steadily after 1871 until in 1951 it was only 11 per

[1] See Appendix, Table 69.

TABLE LXXVIII

PROPORTION OF HOUSES OF DIFFERENT SIZES IN EACH WARD, 1911

Ward	Houses with no. of rooms as under				
	1	2	3	4	5 & over
	%	%	%	%	%
Dalmarnock	37.3	54.3	7.3	0.7	0.4
Calton	30.1	45.8	16.8	3.3	3.1
Mile-End	34.6	56.8	7.4	0.8	0.4
Whitevale	24.3	52.0	19.3	3.2	1.1
Dennistoun	8.7	44.1	31.9	9.5	5.8
Springburn	27.7	58.5	10.0	1.9	1.8
Cowlairs	21.5	58.6	17.6	1.3	0.9
Townhead	20.5	53.8	17.7	5.3	2.7
Blackfriars	26.2	47.1	18.6	4.7	3.4
Exchange	15.4	27.4	25.2	17.9	14.2
Blythswood	4.3	14.2	14.6	26.6	40.4
Broomielaw	15.9	47.3	23.3	10.1	3.4
Anderston	19.9	53.2	20.1	4.3	2.5
Sandyford	15.1	38.1	24.9	8.2	13.8
Park	2.2	13.4	19.0	30.7	34.7
Cowcaddens	24.8	47.4	18.9	5.4	3.4
Woodside	18.5	52.9	18.0	5.4	5.1
Hutchesontown	33.3	58.7	7.2	0.5	0.2
Gorbals	15.7	40.4	30.7	7.9	5.3
Kingston	16.1	42.2	31.2	7.9	2.5
Govanhill	13.7	56.7	22.0	5.3	2.2
Langside	0.7	21.7	38.9	18.9	19.7
Pollokshields	1.2	7.3	5.9	20.9	64.6
Kelvinside	0.3	3.9	21.7	15.3	58.7
Maryhill	14.5	54.7	16.9	5.5	8.5
Kinning Park	30.7	54.5	12.3	0.9	1.5

SOURCE: *Census of Scotland 1911.*

cent compared with the 41.3 per cent of 80 years before; and from 1871 to 1921 the proportion of two-apartment houses steadily increased from 37.2 per cent to 48.4 per cent. From 1921 onwards, however, the proportion of two-roomed houses declined until in 1951 it was less than it had been 80 years before. In spite of these trends there were still almost 70 per cent of the city's families living in one- and two-roomed houses at the beginning of this century, and even in 1951 the proportion was as high as 50.6 per cent. From 1871 to 1951 the proportion of three-apartment houses rose steadily, the most rapid rate of increase occurring from 1921 onwards, and by 1951 28.2 per cent of the city's houses were of three apartments, housing 27 per cent of the total number of families. The proportion of four-apartment houses received a boost from the more generous standards of the interwar building and a still greater boost by the building done after the end of the Second World War in 1945. One fifth[1] of the city's population and 15.2 per cent of its families now live in homes of this size—the latter figures showing quite clearly that the majority of these houses were built with a particular size of family in view. Interwar and post-1945

[1] Appendix Tables 69 and 70.

building also increased the number of five-apartment houses but they still make up less than 5 per cent of the total.

However, the figures for the city as a whole conceal the substantial differences in the distribution of houses by size in the various wards. The last Census in what might be described as the "private enterprise era" of housebuilding in Glasgow was that of 1911, and details for that year are shown in the accompanying Table LXXVIII.

In 1911 there were thus three out of the 26 city wards in which over 90 per cent of the housing was of one or two apartments (Dalmarnock 91.6 per cent, Mile-End 91.4 per cent and Hutchesontown 92 per cent), three in which the proportion was over 80 per cent (Kinning Park 85.2 per cent, Springburn 86.2 per cent and Cowlairs 80.1 per cent), and seven in which it was over 70 per cent. In seven wards housing was predominantly of two and three apartments, and only in four wards—notably in Pollokshields—was housing definitely of the four- and five-apartment and larger kinds. In Langside the emphasis was on three-apartment houses (38.9 per cent) and about 60 per cent of the houses were made up of about equal numbers of two-, four- and five-apartment buildings. In Maryhill more than half the total number of houses were of the room and kitchen type. That was the state of things in 1911.

By 1951, as shown in Table LXXIX, the position had considerably improved, but in 19 wards out of the 37 in the city more than half the houses were still "single ends" or "room and kitchen." In five of these wards the proportion of such houses was 75 per cent or more and in the two worst 88.8 per cent (Hutchesontown) and 82.7 per cent (Dalmarnock). In nine more wards the proportion was over 60 per cent. In spite of these somewhat depressing figures the decline in the numbers and proportions of one-roomed houses and the increased numbers of three-apartment houses are shown in the fact that in 1951 in seventeen wards more than 70 per cent of the total number of houses were of two and three apartments. This kind of improvement is further underlined by the fact that in the rest of the city there were four wards in which more than 80 per cent of the housing was of three and four apartments.

Density of Occupation

It is, however, in the statistics of density of occupation that the changes in standards of accommodation brought about by changes in the size distribution of houses can best be seen. The main measure of density of occupation is the average number of persons to a room (or hundred rooms) throughout the city. By this overall measure there has been a steady and regular improvement in standards of accommodation over the greater part of the last ninety years.[1] In 1861 the average number of persons to a room in the city was 2.04 and in 1951 it had fallen to 1.27. The largest improvements in this measure of

[1] See Statistical Appendix Table 71.

TABLE LXXIX

PROPORTION OF HOUSES[1] OF DIFFERENT SIZES IN EACH WARD, 1951

Ward	*Houses with rooms as under* 1 %	2 %	3-5 %	6 & over %	*Total number of houses*
Shettleston & Tollcross	10.5	35.3	53.5	0.7	10,940
Parkhead	9.6	38.3	51.0	1.1	5,755
Dalmarnock	29.8	52.9	17.2	0.1	11,893
Calton	19.6	48.6	30.6	1.2	6,971
Mile-End	22.9	55.0	22.1	0.0	11,199
Dennistoun	6.1	32.3	59.2	2.4	8,070
Provan	2.5	7.1	88.9	1.5	5,618
Cowlairs	17.7	57.3	24.8	0.2	7,964
Springburn	7.7	28.1	63.1	1.1	7,819
Townhead	14.9	53.0	31.6	0.5	9,561
Exchange	13.1	38.0	46.4	2.5	4,600
Anderston	12.2	49.6	36.7	1.5	8,285
Park	4.5	14.7	66.4	14.4	6,128
Cowcaddens	19.0	59.0	21.8	0.2	7,483
Woodside	19.2	55.6	22.7	2.5	7,736
Ruchill	5.0	25.2	69.5	0.3	10,684
North Kelvin	14.6	49.8	31.0	4.6	8,069
Maryhill	8.6	48.3	41.6	1.5	6,846
Kelvinside	7.6	12.3	62.5	17.6	6,525
Partick East	6.6	16.6	61.9	14.9	6,875
Partick West	14.0	53.7	28.4	3.9	8,392
Whiteinch	5.2	38.6	50.1	6.1	6,765
Yoker	0.1	11.9	86.9	1.1	7,772
Knightswood	6.2	3.5	95.2	1.1	4,331
Hutchesontown	31.1	57.7	11.2	0.0	9,407
Gorbals	17.1	45.7	36.2	1.0	9,291
Kingston	16.0	45.4	38.1	0.5	7,262
Kinning Park	11.9	53.1	32.7	2.3	8,007
Govan	13.6	51.7	34.0	0.7	9,044
Fairfield	9.4	45.7	44.7	0.2	6,613
Craigton	0.3	1.7	93.7	4.3	10,499
Pollokshields	0.6	3.0	83.0	13.4	8,667
Camphill	3.0	20.2	69.5	7.3	7,668
Pollokshaws	5.3	15.4	76.0	3.3	8,691
Govanhill	2.8	50.4	46.5	0.3	8.272
Langside	0.9	8.9	82.2	8.0	7,830
Cathcart	1.1	18.8	65.4	14.7	6,935

SOURCE: *Census of Glasgow, 1951.*

density occurred between 1921 and 1931 (a fall of 0.23) and between 1931 and 1951 (a fall of 0.27). The city average for 1931 was 1.54, but there were seven wards where it was more than 2, and in the worst (Dalmarnock) it was just short of 2.5. In 1951 there was no area of the city where the figure was as high as 2, but in 22 wards out of 37 it was above the city average and it was only the very low densities of wards like Kelvinside, Cathcart, Langside, Camphill, Partick East and Park that kept the average for the whole city so low.

It is more revealing, however, to consider not just the averages for

[1] Private houses only. See also Appendix, Table 74.

the city as a whole but the proportion of the population living at different densities of occupation. In 1861, 63.2 per cent of the total population of the city lived at a density of more than two persons to a room; almost 20 per cent lived more than four to a room and more than 25 per cent at a density of two to three to a room. The improvement in housing standards is clearly shown by the steady rise in the proportion of population living not more than two to a room from 36.8 per cent in 1861 to 75.6 per cent in 1951. Nevertheless in 1951 there were still over 3,000 persons living more than four to a room and another 5,000 or so at a density of three to four to a room. It is worth noting that, although throughout the period 1861-1951 there was a general trend towards improvement in densities, yet the proportion of population living two to three to a room increased slightly between 1861 and 1911, as did the proportion for the 3-4 category between 1911 and 1921.

Again, the overall averages conceal some important facts that can only be seen in the details for the city wards.[1] Although the proportion of the total city population living more than four to a room was only 3 per cent in 1951, there were six wards where the proportion was more than double this (Dalmarnock 7.7 per cent, Hutchesontown 7.7 per cent, Gorbals 6.8 per cent, Woodside 6.6 per cent, Cowcaddens 6.3 per cent and Mile-End 6.3 per cent). In Dalmarnock and Hutchesontown the proportions of population living three to four to a room were more than double the city average, and in five wards more than a quarter of the population lived at a density of two to three to a room although the city average was only 16.3 per cent. On the brighter side of the picture there were eight wards in 1951 where more than 90 per cent of the population lived not more than two to a room, and eight more where this proportion was more than 80 per cent.

The social significance of these figures of occupation densities can perhaps only be fully appreciated when they are related to sizes of house. Unfortunately the Census does not give this information directly and it is a laborious business to work out the details from the figures given. Table 73 in the Appendix shows the details for houses of up to five rooms for the four Census years 1861, 1911, 1931 and 1951. The first year in which the Census gave the necessary information for the calculations was 1861. The next year chosen—1911—has been taken because it occurred towards the end of a long period of stagnation in the building industry in Glasgow (a stagnation that continued until after the end of the 1914-18 War) and also because it was the last Census year in what might be called the *laissez faire* era of occupation densities in dwelling houses.[2] The year 1931, though a depression year, was in the middle of the interwar house-building activity of local authorities. Also by that time both the central and local authorities had begun to take a more positive attitude towards density of occupa-

[1] See Appendix Table 72.

[2] Not quite completely a *laissez faire* era because of the nineteenth century legislation dealing with cubic air space in sleeping quarters, though this affected only the comparatively small number of "ticketed" houses in the city.

tion and some attempt was being made to enforce improved standards.[1]

Table 73 in the Appendix shows that by 1951 high occupational densities had ceased to be of any real concern to the city only in the larger houses. In houses of one or two rooms, the position was still acute. Of the 30,947 persons living in the city in that year at a density of " more than four " persons to a room, more than two thirds were occupants of " single ends." Moreover, about one third of the city's total population lived in houses of two rooms, and over one third of these lived more than two to a room. This is nevertheless a vast improvement on the position that existed ninety years before, when the one-roomed and two-roomed houses between them contained substantially more than two thirds of the city's population, and almost half the inhabitants of one-roomed houses lived more than four to a room, while more than 70 per cent of those living in two rooms lived at a density in excess of two to a room. In the period 1861-1911 the total number of " single enders " in the city scarcely decreased, but there was a substantial reduction (15,610) in the numbers of them living more than four to a room. The numbers in all the other density categories increased. This is to some extent the measure of the effectiveness of the primitive legislation of the nineteenth century dealing with the occupancy of houses, but it is also an illustration of the effects of the demolition of properties by the City Improvements Trust and the clearances of slum and other areas for railway development. It is also, of course, a reflection of the increasing popularity of the room and kitchen house, and to a lesser extent of the two rooms and kitchen house. In these fifty years the numbers of occupants of two-roomed houses increased by 206,978 (by far the largest rise recorded in the table referred to), and the number of occupants of three rooms went up by 107,711. This was apparently the half century of the " but and ben " and demand for the single end seemed to be on the decline.

However, in the next twenty years (1911 to 1931) there was a substantial increase (11,685) in the number of occupants of one-roomed houses in the city, and even more surprisingly about half of that increase lived " more than four " to a room. Reasons for this are probably to be found in the slum clearance activities of the City Corporation, the decline in tenement building and indeed the decline in the total of all building by private enterprise of houses to let as a result of the operation of the Rent Restrictions Acts in Scotland. Yet this was undoubtedly the period of the three-roomed and two-roomed houses and almost the whole of the substantial increases in occupancies of these houses was at densities of not more than two to a room.

The twenty-year period from 1931 to 1951 was one of decline in the numbers and proportions of all occupancies at densities of more than two to a room in houses of one to three rooms, and of substantial increases in occupancies at a density of not more than two to a room

[1] The difficulties encountered are illustrated by the provisions as to the " appointed day " for enforcement of the overcrowding provisions of the 1935 Housing Act —see *posted*.

among four-roomed and three-roomed houses. This was the result partly of the building boom of the 1930's which produced the "schemes" of two- and three-storeyed flatted houses and of detached and semi-detached bungalows and small villas in and around the city. But it was more the result of the emergence of a strongly positive government attitude towards housing and housing standards and the intensive post-1945 house-building by the city with the encouragement of government subsidy.

Domestic and Sanitary Equipment

There is no statistical information about domestic and sanitary equipment in Glasgow households in the middle of the nineteenth century, but enough is known about water supply and the sources of domestic heating to make it possible to generalise about conditions in the average home.

Few households in the city had a piped water supply before the introduction of Loch Katrine water in 1859, although two private water companies had been drawing water from the Clyde from early in the century and were supplying certain areas of the city.[1] Private and public wells, springs and pumps, the various streams that flowed through the city and the River Clyde itself were the sources of supply for most homes, and almost all household water had to be carried to the home, sometimes over long distances, although at least one enterprising citizen with an abundant spring within his own grounds operated a profitable business as a seller of water from carts in the streets. The municipal records of the early part of the century abound with complaints and requests from the citizens about sources of water for household purposes.

The water-closet was therefore almost unknown and the privy (often common to many households), the midden and the system of private contracting for the removal of household waste were as much responsible for nineteenth century plagues and epidemics as were overcrowded homes and congested buildings. Long before the last two could be dealt with, the introduction of piped water made a vast difference to the mortality statistics of the town. Before its introduction the household bath, if there was one, was a lightweight metal tub filled from pails of water that had been heated directly over the kitchen fire; the washing of clothes at home was a nightmare, and the dirt and soot which the "washing" gathered while drying in the "back green" of the tenement a heartbreak. Glasgow Green—the only public park and the largest drying green in the city—was the east-end housewife's paradise.

Again, by the middle and late nineteenth century the principal source of heating for all domestic purposes in most homes was the open coal-burning "range" let in to the chimney breast in the kitchen wall.

[1] See Chapter 17 (Other Public Services).

This had a fire-box of about one cubic foot in capacity lined on three sides with fire-brick, fronted by vertical cast iron bars, at the top of which there was a horizontal steel cross-bar that pivoted outwards and downwards to accommodate the larger pots. At the lower front of the fire-box there was a small steel platform or "hob," and beneath the box a capacious ash-pan. The cooking oven was at one side of the fire-box and was heated by an arrangement of the draught flues. This type of kitchen range, with its burnished and gleaming steels, and its black-leaded cast-iron surfaces, is still the "pride" of many Glasgow house-wives no matter how well equipped their kitchens may otherwise be with modern gas or electric cookers.

Coal gas had been introduced to the city early in the century (1818) for lighting streets and shops, and by mid-century was also being used to light "closes" and stairheads and many of the middle-class and some working-class houses in the town. The light was provided by simple flame burner (later by incandescent mantle). In kitchens the gas bracket would be fixed to the mantelpiece (which would also support the "wally dugs" or other Clydeside *lares et penates*) but "ben the house" there would be a chandelier hung centrally from the ceiling and carrying two, three or more shaded lights. Meters were first introduced in 1827 and gas cooking appliances were first let out on hire by the Corporation Gas Department in 1885. Gas fires were issued on the hire-purchase system until 1912 after which they were hired out. By 1912 too gas water-heating apparatus could be had from the Department on hire-purchase terms but at that time few houses used it. In 1913 there were 286,883 meters in use, but only 144,584 gas stoves and grills, 12,589 gas fires on hire and 6,391 gas fires on hire-purchase. In the smaller homes the gas cooking equipment consisted of a shallow square-shaped cast iron frame carrying two "rings" or two rings and a grill that stood on top of the kitchen range at that side of the fire-box on which the oven was situated. This was more or less standard equipment in most tenement houses by the turn of the century, though the heavyweight cast iron free-standing gas cooker with gas oven was becoming more widely used in the larger houses. The small gas cooker is still the only auxiliary to the kitchen range in many tenement homes to-day. Glasgow was a prime example of the "gas and water socialism" of the era but in the earlier part of the nineteenth century gas was not cheap. In 1860 it cost the consumer 5s. per thousand cubic feet. By 1900 the price had fallen to 2s. 2d., and when war broke out in 1914 the price was between 1s. and 1s. 11d. according to use and rate of consumption.

Electricity for private lighting was switched on in a small area in the centre of the city in April 1893, and by 1913 there were 27,848 consumers using over 60 million B.T. Units per annum. The price to domestic consumers was 3d. a unit, though there were lower prices for large-scale industrial and business consumption. In 1893 the price had been 7d. a unit without distinction as to user or rate of consumption.

To-day only a few of the older houses in the town do not have electricity for lighting and for low-powered domestic appliances.

Vast improvements there have been in a hundred years, but there are still many homes in the city where equipment for sanitation and personal hygiene are well below the standard that we would regard as the minimum essential. The results of a Survey carried out in 1915[1] covering 212,223 houses of from one to four apartments are as follows:

[1] Referred to in the *Report of The Royal Commission on Housing in Scotland*, 1917.

TABLE LXXX

PIPED WATER SUPPLY, 1915

Size of house	*No. of houses surveyed*	*No. with separate sinks and piped cold water supply*	*Percentage of total*	*No. with shared sink*
1 apartment	41,354	40,127	97.0%	1,227
2 "	111,451	110,804	99.4%	647
3 "	44,791	44,771	99.9%	20
4 "	14,627	14,621	99.9%	6

A piped water supply leading at least to the kitchen sink was an accepted minimum of domestic equipment forty years ago even for the smallest houses. And yet in 1951[2] there were 24,243 homes in the city that shared a piped water supply and 178 that had none at all. These numbers together fell not far short of a tenth of the number that had the exclusive use of a piped water supply, and perhaps the explanation is to be found in the increasing practice of subdividing larger houses.[3]

In relation to water-closets the 1915 Survey gave the information shown in Table LXXXI.

TABLE LXXXI

SANITARY CONVENIENCES, 1915

Size of house	*No. of houses surveyed*	*No. with separate W.C.*	*Percentage of total*	*No. sharing W.C.*
1 apartment	41,354	2,947	7.1%	38,407
2 "	111,451	42,513	38.2%	68,938
3 "	44,791	39,694	88.6%	5,097
4 "	14,627	14,274	97.6%	353

The Survey added that in the case of houses of one and two apartments sharing a water-closet, one was reckoned sufficient for four households! The long life of the Glasgow tenements and the difficulty of correcting the faults built into them are amply illustrated by the figures relating to this matter in the 1951 Census—114,960 households shared a water-closet in that year of grace, and a further 359 had not the use of any. Only 191,506 out of the 306,825 households had the

[2] See Appendix, Table 78.

[3] And also perhaps in the Census definition of a " house."

exclusive use of one. But the figures for fixed baths are even more illuminating. Although working-class tenement flats at reasonably low rentals were being built in the late nineteenth century incorporating fixed baths and hot-water systems, in 1951 there were more city households that had no fixed bath and no opportunity to share in the use of one (153,762) than there were households with the exclusive (135,277) or shared (17,786) use of a bath. That this cannot also be put down to the sub-division of large houses is shown by the fact that although 17,541 of the households who shared a bath also shared a water-closet (and this may be a result of sub-division) 97,203 of the houses which had no bath at all had also to share a water-closet. The worst conditions are concentrated in certain areas of the city and Table LXXXII (extracted from the 1951 Census) illustrates how intractable the problems are in these districts. In 11 of the 37 municipal wards there are more households that have to share a water-closet than have

TABLE LXXXII

HOUSEHOLD AMENITIES

Ward		*Exclusive use*	*Shared use*	*None*
Shettleston & Tollcross	W.C.	7,150	3,967	11
	Bath	6,174	279	4,675
Dalmarnock	W.C.	3,061	9,063	7
	Bath	1,787	229	10,115
Calton	W.C.	2,622	4,756	6
	Bath	944	310	6,130
Mile-End	W.C.	3,873	7,511	11
	Bath	1,135	101	10,155
Cowlairs	W.C.	3,776	4,357	5
	Bath	1,968	167	6,003
Townhead	W.C.	4,388	5,598	22
	Bath	1,233	384	8,371
Exchange	W.C.	2,455	2,480	7
	Bath	924	236	3,782
Anderston	W.C.	4,684	4,049	6
	Bath	1,254	527	6,958
Cowcaddens	W.C.	2,254	5,425	23
	Bath	537	106	7,059
Woodside	W.C.	3,240	5,029	16
	Bath	895	651	6,739
North Kelvin	W.C.	4,225	4,180	—
	Bath	2,058	425	5,922
Maryhill	W.C.	4,377	2,603	21
	Bath	2,821	202	3,978
Partick West	W.C.	5,417	3,154	10
	Bath	3,222	245	5,114
Hutchesontown	W.C.	1,708	7,783	18
	Bath	667	41	8,801
Gorbals	W.C.	4,153	5,544	13
	Bath	574	327	8,809
Kingston	W.C.	3,751	3,865	13
	Bath	540	166	6,923
Govan	W.C.	4,797	4,565	29
	Bath	2,674	352	6,365
Fairfield	W.C.	4,962	1,769	8
	Bath	2,733	114	3,892

the exclusive use of one and in Dalmarnock and Hutchesontown this proportion is about three and four to one respectively. In the same eleven wards and in eight other wards there are fewer households with a bath of their own than there are with no bath at all and in some areas the latter outnumber the former by more than ten to one. Conditions in the worst wards of the city are summarised in Table LXXXII.

In many homes the introduction of a water-closet and a fixed bath would be virtually impossible on the score of space alone. In many others where the architect and the plumber might say that it could be done, the landlord would almost certainly be unable to meet the cost.

Overcrowding

The first statutory " standard " of occupation upon which estimates of the amount of overcrowding could be based (and action to diminish it taken by the local authority) was contained in the Glasgow Police Act of 1866.[1] This Act laid down minimum cubic capacities for one-, two- and three-apartment houses irrespective of the number of occupants[2] and gave power to the Town Council to inspect and, if necessary, " ticket " houses which were of three apartments or less and of not more than 2,000 cubic feet in total content. Under this Act " ticketing " meant putting up on the door, after inspection and measurement of the house, a statement of the cubic capacity of the house and of the number of persons over eight years of age who might lawfully sleep therein, the number being calculated to allow 300 cubic feet of air space for every person over eight years of age and 150 cubic feet for each person under eight years. This meant, in a house with 10ft. ceilings, a minimum floor space of 6ft. by 5ft. for each person over eight years old, and 3ft. by 5ft. for each person under eight. Penalties were provided for occupation in excess of the " ticketed " maximum. The Glasgow Police (Amendment) Act of 1890 raised the minimum cubic space to 400 cubic feet for each person over ten years of age, and 200 cubic feet for each person under ten, and applied these minima to all houses whatever their number of rooms or total cubic air space (though " ticketing " was still restricted to houses of three apartments or less and total air space of 2,000 cubic feet). The report of the Glasgow Municipal Commission on the Housing of the Poor (1904) notes that in 1901 there were 55,292 inspections for overcrowding in the city within the standards laid down by the 1866 and 1890 Acts; 7,044 cases of

[1] The Public Health (Scotland) Act of 1897 empowered Scottish local authorities generally to make bye-laws regarding numbers of occupants permitted, the minimum sanitary appliances required, the cleaning of houses, stairs, etc. etc.

[2] 1 apartment, 700 cubic feet if occupied as a house before the Act,
900 cubic feet if first occupied as a house after the Act;
2 apartment, 1,200 cubic feet if occupied as a house before the Act,
1,500 cubic feet if occupied as a house after the Act,
3 apartment, 1,800 cubic feet if occupied as a house before the Act,
2,000 cubic feet if occupied as a house after the Act.

overcrowding were found, in 5,571 of which the parties were warned by the inspectors, in 615 admonished in the Police Courts, and in 858 fined in the Police Courts. The Report also estimates that considerably over 20,000 persons " were then occupying as sleeping apartments " places in which the Statute Law forbade sleeping. Without measurement of every house in the city in relation to the number of occupants it would have been impossible to assess the total amount of overcrowding that existed according to these standards. It is certain, however, that overcrowding was much in excess of what was officially noted in the Municipal Commission's Report.

The Royal Commission on Housing in Scotland[1] noted that the standard of overcrowding used in England for Census purposes was " more than two persons " to a room, but also observed that this standard had no statutory authority in Scotland. The Commission reluctantly decided to use the standard of " more than three persons " to a room in its calculation of Scotland's housing needs. The Report contains no detailed estimate[2] of the amount of overcrowding in Glasgow on the basis of this standard, but the information provided by the 1921 Census shows the housing position in Glasgow at that time. On the Royal Commission's standard of " more than three persons to a room " the houses overcrowded were of:

1 room	15,836	
2 rooms	22,543	
3 „	1,491	
4 „	52	
Total	39,922	
		or 17.8 per cent of all the houses enumerated

Had it been possible to achieve an optimum re-distribution of the available house-room according to sizes of households, Glasgow's housing needs (at three persons to a room) in 1921 would have been catered for by an additional 46,152 houses *of one room,* and in the redistribution the following houses would have been (in their existing sizes) " surplus to requirements ":

Houses of 2 rooms	9,852
„ „ 3 „	10,408
„ „ 4 „	8,638
„ „ 5+ „	17,254
Total	46,152

1 Report 1917—Cd. 8731.

2 It recommended that the Local Government Board for Scotland should carry out a detailed investigation to discover the incidence of overcrowding.

In theory then the " making down " of the " surplus " fit houses, together with an optimum redistribution of houseroom would have solved the overcrowding problem in Glasgow in 1921, on the standard of " more than three persons to a room," without any new building.

On the standard of " more than two to a room "—which the Royal Commission would have liked to see adopted—the picture would have been much different. Houses overcrowded would then have been:

Houses of	1 room	25,065
" "	2 rooms	53,580
" "	3 "	9,003
" "	4 "	835
" "	5 "	97
" "	6 "	19
" "	7 "	4
Total		88,603

or 39.4 per cent of all the houses enumerated

Optimum redistribution of houseroom on this standard would still have left a need for:

Houses of	1 room	4,997
" "	3 rooms	14,859
" "	4 "	13,539
" "	5 "	2,323
Total		35,718

and would have rendered " surplus to requirements " at their existing sizes:

Houses of	2 rooms	27,250
" "	6 "	1,772
" "	7 "	1,986
" "	8 "	4,710
Total		35,718

" Making down " could theoretically have provided all the " single ends " required, about half the three-roomed houses required, and about 10,000 of the 13,539 four-roomed houses required. About 25,000 houses of two rooms would have been scheduled for demolition and the city would have had a programme of new building of about 7,500 three-roomed, 2,200 four-roomed and 2,300 five-roomed houses to undertake.

The Housing (Scotland) Act, 1935, laid down detailed standards of permitted occupancy. These standards were defined in relation to (a) the number of rooms, (b) the floor area of the house, (c) the separation of the sleeping quarters of occupants of opposite sexes over ten years of age—except husband and wife, (d) the counting of each child between one and ten years old as "half an adult," and taking no account of children under one year. With these factors in mind, the permitted standards of occupancy of houses were:

1 room	2 adults
2 rooms	3 "
3 "	5 "
4 "	7½ "
5+ "	10 "

with two more adults for each room in excess of five.

An overcrowding survey was carried out in Glasgow under the terms of this Act. The survey was limited to houses not exceeding £45 rental per annum, i.e. 259,769 out of the 276,130 houses in the city in 1935 (94.1 per cent of the total). According to this survey almost one third of all families living in these houses were overcrowded.[1] More than half of all the one-roomed houses and nearly 43 per cent of the two-roomed houses in the city were overcrowded by this standard, and between them these two groups of houses constituted over 55 per cent of the city's total housing. The survey estimated that 46,633 *new* houses of from three to six apartments would be required in the city to abate overcrowding (i.e. after optimum redistribution of available houseroom according to the standards of the Act) and that in the process of "de-crowding" there would become "surplus to requirement" 14,936 houses of one apartment and 30,502 houses of two apartments. The highest proportions of overcrowding existed in the Dalmarnock and Mile-End wards of the city, where the proportions of overcrowded houses were 54.6 per cent and 52.9 per cent respectively. Next in order came Hutchesontown (48.1 per cent), Parkhead (43.7 per cent), Cowcaddens (43.3 per cent) and Whitevale (40 per cent). The 1935 Act's standards of occupancy were none too high by current ideals, but they set a problem for Glasgow (and for Scotland as a whole) so vast that the "appointed day" for imposition of the sanctions against overcrowding as defined in the Act was in fact never fixed by the Secretary of State. The war of 1939-45 enlarged the problem, and new and higher standards emerged to be applied in the postwar years.

In 1944 the Scottish Housing Advisory Committee recommended to the Secretary of State for Scotland that the following standards of occupancy should be applied to all houses covered by the Housing Acts (i.e. all local authority houses):

[1] See Appendix, Table 76.

No. of rooms	No. of Persons
1	0
2	2
3	4
5	8
	with an additional two persons in respect of each room over five

All children were to count fully as individual persons; sex separation for the sleeping of all children over ten years of age was obligatory; and each house had to possess a living room which was not to be used for sleeping purposes.

On the basis of this standard[1] and of the 1931 Census information the City Architect and Planning Officer produced in 1952 a Report on Glasgow's housing needs in which there is a table showing the numbers and sizes of households in Glasgow in relation to the sizes of houses occupied by them. Table LXXXIII gives a summary of the picture of overcrowding at 1931 according to the 1944 Standard.

The 1944 Standard condemned the one-roomed house without qualification, and such houses in 1931 formed 14.5 per cent of the total number of houses in the city. Two-roomed houses represented 43.6 per cent of the city's total, and more than three-quarters of these were overcrowded. Two-fifths of the three-roomed houses were also overcrowded and these formed 23.9 per cent of the total. In all, three-fifths of the city's total number of houses in 1931 would have been adjudged to be overcrowded on the 1944 Standard.[2]

Table 77 in the Appendix recalculates the amount of overcrowding on the 1944 Standard, using the 1951 Census data. Table LXXXIV summarises the facts of the situation.

Progress in " de-crowding " houses of one, two and three apartments between 1931 and 1951 has not been inconsiderable, in view of the intervention of the war years. In 1951 there were 11,955 more houses than in 1931 in these three categories[3] and 27,709 fewer over-

[1] But omitting the " sex separation factor."

[2] In the 1921 situation the 1944 standards would have shown 69.4 per cent of the numbers of houses in the city to be overcrowded and even after optimum redistribution would have put 40,680 " single ends " and 63,282 room-and-kitchen houses on the scrap heap. After all the " making down " that was possible had been done the city would still have been confronted with a building programme of about

37,700	3 room houses
39,000	4 " "
17,400	5 " "
5,400	6 " "
99,500	Houses

[3] 4,753 fewer of one apartment, 4,933 fewer of two apartments, and 21,641 more of three apartments

TABLE LXXXIII

Overcrowding in Glasgow, 1931

Houses of:—	*Numbers overcrowded*	*Percentage overcrowded of the total of this size*
1 room	37,230	100%
2 rooms	87,417	78.2
3 "	24,902	40.5
4 "	3,549	15.4
5 "	329	3.0
6 "	58	1.3
7 "	16	0.6
8 "	2	0.1
All	153,503	59.9%

TABLE LXXXIV

Overcrowding in Glasgow, 1951

Houses of:—	*Numbers overcrowded*	*Percentage overcrowded of the total of this size*
1 room	32,477	100%
2 rooms	68,050	63.7
3 "	21,313	25.6
4 "	7,468	15.5
5 "	1,006	7.1
6 "	78	1.7
7 "	26	1.0
8 "	17	1.3
All	130,435	44.2%

crowded. But overcrowding in these categories was still substantial, and had increased both in numbers and in proportions in all the other categories, particularly among houses of four apartments.

The 1952 Report of the City Architect and Planning Officer estimated that even if all the housing accommodation available could be re-distributed among households to make the optimum use of it by the 1944 standards, yet in order to comply with the 1944 standard of occupancy and on the basis of the 1931 Census figures the numbers of new houses required and the numbers surplus to requirements would have been as shown in Table LXXXV. The same calculations, based on the 1951 Census figures throughout, reveal that the numbers of new houses required and the numbers of houses surplus to requirements in 1951 would have been as shown in Table LXXXVI.

The number of new three-apartment houses required is still high and has in fact risen slightly, but there has been a substantial drop in the numbers of larger houses required. Again the number of surplus houses has dropped in all categories except the seven-apartment house, where there has been a slight rise. That is probably the size lying between houses big enough to " make down " and those which are obviously not big enough for this. There has been a dramatic drop

TABLE LXXXV

Estimated Number of Houses Required and Surplus on Basis of 1931 Census Figures

	New Houses Required	Houses Surplus to Requirements
1 apartment	—	37,230
2 ,,	—	51,739
3 ,,	41,839	—
4 ,,	37,190	—
5 ,,	12,959	—
6 ,,	2,973	—
7 ,,	—	1,162
8 ,,	—	1,361
9 ,, and over	—	3,469
Total	94,961	94,961

TABLE LXXXVI

Estimated Number of Houses Required and Surplus on Basis of 1951 Census Figures

	New Houses Required	Houses Surplus to Requirements
1 apartment	—	32,477
2 ,,	—	11,902
3 ,,	41,944	—
4 ,,	4,784	—
5 ,,	1,498	—
6 ,,	77	—
7 ,,	—	1,312
8 ,,	—	957
9 ,, and over	—	1,655
Total	48,303	48,303

(39,837 or 76 per cent) in the calculated number of surplus two-apartment houses while the actual number of these houses has been reduced by only 4,933. The number of households of one and two persons has at the same time increased by 34,904 (i.e. by 58 per cent of the 1931 figure), so that much overcrowding caused by families sharing houses could in theory be eliminated and the two-apartment house could be approaching its optimum use under the 1944 standards. The great problems that remain are (a) to cope with the 32,477 "single ends" which cannot now be regarded as suitable houses even for households of one person, and, of course, (b) to bring about something like the ideal redistribution of accommodation upon the basis of which these calculations of housing needs have been made. Without solutions to both of these problems it still is the case that 44.2 per cent of the city's housing in 1951 was overcrowded on the 1944 standard. Housing policy in Glasgow will therefore have to be directed not only to new building, but also to bringing about a substantial redistribution of existing accommodation more nearly in compliance with the 1944 optima.

The Cost of Houseroom

Table LXXXVII showing the numbers of houses in the city and their average rentals at various years from 1851 to 1915 is taken from the evidence given by the City Assessor before the Committee on Rentals of Small Dwelling Houses in Industrial Districts in Scotland.[1]

TABLE LXXXVII

AVERAGE RENTAL OF HOUSES IN GLASGOW
1851-1915

Year	*Total No. of houses*	*Average rental per house*
1851-52	60,542	£8 8 9
1860-61	85,203	9 13 2
1870-71	96,327	9 7 6
1880-81	115,099	10 12 1
1890-91	119,865	10 9 3
1895-96	144,041	12 19 5
1900-01	158,779	13 12 5
1905-06	175,278	14 2 9
1910-11	179,885	14 1 11
1911-12	180,379	13 19 0
1912-13	230,657[2]	14 5 3
1913-14	231,267	14 4 4
1914-15	231,351	14 6 8

These rentals are exclusive of occupier's rates and show an increase of just under 70 per cent in 64 years. A more detailed picture of the situation in 1906 is given by the evidence of the City Assessor before the Departmental Committee on House-letting in Scotland (1907):

TABLE LXXXVIII

RENTALS OF HOUSES IN GLASGOW, 1906

Houses at rents:—	*Number*	*Total Rental*
Under £5	11,535	£52,632
£5 to £10	82,642	660,588
£10 to £15	33,844	406,902
£15 to £20	20,808	355,149
£20 upwards	26,449	1,002,492
	175,278	£2,477,763

Although the average rental per house for the whole city in that year was £14 2s. 9d. almost half the total housing stock was in the £5 to £10 rental group, and if the houses in the £20 upwards group are excluded, the average rental per house was under £10. As occupier's

[1] Cmd. 8154 (1916) Appendix VII.

[2] Boundary extension.

rates were about 4s. and owner's rates about 2s. in the £ of rental, the gross cost of houseroom to the average tenant (in all but the top category of assessed rentals) would be about £12 a year and the average net return to his landlord would be about £9 a year. Houses of under £20 rental represented about 85 per cent of the total number of houses in the city.

By 1937-8 the total number of houses had risen to 275,815 and the average rent per house to £21 14s. Table LXXXIX (taken from a Detailed Rental of the City compiled for 1937-8 by the City Assessor's Department) shows the distribution of the total number of houses among the various rental groups:

TABLE LXXXIX

RENTALS OF HOUSES IN GLASGOW, 1937-8

Houses at rents:—	*Number*	*Average Rental*
Under £4	560	
£4 to £10	25,053	
£10 to £20	139,311	£16 6 0
£20 to £26 5s.	40,779	
£26 5s. to £30	17,358	
	223,061	
£30 to £45	38,475	
£45 to £60	8,096	£42 2 0
£60 to £90	4,732	
Over £90	1,451	
	52,754	
Grand Total	275,815	£21 14 0

About 80 per cent of the city's housing stock in 1937-8 was in the under £30 rental groups, and the average rent per house for these was £16 6s., more than half the houses in the city being in the £10 to £20 group. If we call houses in the under £30 group "representative" houses, this means that in about 30 years there had been an increase of about 60 per cent in the assessed rental of a "representative" house—but, as the owner's rate poundage had more than trebled, the net rental was only £1 4s. 3d. (about 13½ per cent) above the 1906 level. Nevertheless as occupier's rate poundage had about doubled the "representative" *gross* rental, i.e. the cost to the householder, was now about £23—that is about 90 per cent above the 1906 figure.

It has been estimated by the City Assessor's Department that in the year 1952-3 about 78 per cent of the houses in the city were in the under £30 rental group. The average assessed rental for these would have been about £17 5s. With occupier's rate poundage at 12s. 1½d. and owner's poundage at 7s. 9d., the "representative" gross and net rents for that year would have been about £27 14s. and £10 2s. 6d. respectively, i.e. the net rent figure was less than in 1937-8 and the gross rent figure about 20 per cent greater.

The true importance of these changes in the levels of rents can only be assessed against information not only about changes in the standards of accommodation such as we have already discussed, but also about changes in the levels of household earnings and local government services which are not in place here.

To conclude this chapter a word about the cost of "council" housing is necessary. The *Return of Rents of Houses owned by Local Authorities in Scotland,* 1953 (Cmd. 9235) gives the facts for Glasgow at 15 November 1953, as shown in Table XC.

TABLE XC

RENTALS OF COUNCIL HOUSES, 1953

	No. of houses of				
	2 apts. or less	*3 apts.*	*4 apts.*	*5 apts. or more*	*Total*
(a)	5,128	31,928	13,489	1,744	52,289
(b)	603	7,929	15,398	1,533	25,463
(c)	5,731	39,857	28,887	3,277	77,752

Average Standard Rents Exclusive of Rebates and Occupier's Rates

	2 apts. or less	*3 apts.*	*4 apts.*	*5 apts. or more*	*All sizes*
	£ *s.* *d.*	£ *s.* *d.*	£ *s.* *d.*	£ *s.* *d.*	£ *s.* *d.*
(a)	12 14 0	20 11 0	26 3 2	35 18 6	21 14 10
(b)	19 8 0	26 9 4	31 12 0	37 16 8	30 1 9
(c)	13 8 1	21 14 6	29 1 2	36 16 4	24 9 6

(a) Pre-1946 Act.
(b) 1950 and 1952 Acts.
(c) Combined totals.

These figures show that for all but the houses of two apartments or less built before the 1946 Act, average rentals of council houses were above the "representative" average for the city in that year. The average of £24 9s. 6d. for council houses of all sizes still leaves the whole council house group in the under £30 rateable value category, but the council house average is more than 40 per cent above the representative average. Moreover these levels of contractual rents of council houses mean that their gross rents are not far short of 50 per cent above those of representative non-council houses. In spite of this fact, and in spite of central subsidies ranging up to £46 15s. per annum per house and statutory local authority contributions ranging up to £15 10s. per annum per house, the deficit on Housing Revenue Account for the financial year 1952-3 was £811,292, the net deficit brought forward from previous years was £1,803,672 and the total deficit to be carried forward to the financial year 1953-4 was £2,614,964.

The 1947 *Review of Operations* issued by the Corporation Housing Department showed that from the tentative beginnings of local authority housebuilding after the First World War Glasgow had by 1947 completed 59,734 houses containing in all 195,477 apartments.[1] Four types of "schemes" were involved and the distribution of houses among them was as follows:

Ordinary	27,288
Intermediate	14,720
Re-housing	14,759
House purchase	676

The average cost of building a three-apartment house had gone up from £823 in 1920 to £1,062 in 1947 and of a four-apartment from £913 to £1,249.[2] The Corporation had by then built houses in all but seven of the 38 wards of the city, but the main building programmes had been in the following wards: Yoker and Knightswood, 8,155; Pollokshields, 7,500; Ruchill, 6,646; Provan, 5,715; Shettleston and Tollcross, 5,158; Parkhead, 3,061; Pollokshaws, 2,946; Springburn, 2,679; Whiteinch, 2,580; Fairfield, 2,056; Maryhill, 2,037.

There has not been a detailed "operations" report by the housing department since 1947, but in 1955 the department had completed 90,817 houses, had contracted for 10,656 more, had schemes in preparation for another 4,001, and proposed to build a further 7,390 on ground acquired. The completion of the 100,000th house built by the Corporation since 1919 was marked by an official ceremony in November 1956, at which it was formally opened by Earl Attlee.

[1] 1-apt., 135; 2-apt., 4,906; 3-apt., 35,606; 4-apt., 16,723; 5-apt., 2,364.
[2] Appendix, Table 82.

Chapter 15

HEALTH

WM. A. HORNE

(Material supplied by Medical Officers of the Health and Welfare Department, Glasgow Corporation.)

INTRODUCTION

IN recent years rapid progress has undoubtedly been made in public health, but the foundations of its success have been laid in the past. The public health service in Glasgow has passed through five distinct phases, starting with the provision of the water supply, drainage and cleansing services, following the report on the *Sanitary Conditions of the Labouring Population* prepared for the Poor Law Commissioners by Edwin Chadwick in 1842.

The second period (1863-1902), which might be called the sanitary period, commenced with the appointment of the first Medical Officer of Health and terminated with the end of the Boer War. During this period the chief concern of the Service was with cleanliness, removal of offensive conditions, control of the major infectious diseases, and the removal of adverse environmental conditions.

The Boer War brought to light the unsatisfactory physical state of the population. The Reports on Physical Training and Physical Deterioration made recommendations for the introduction of services and safeguards, some of which have not yet been fully implemented. To the third period (1902-29) belongs the institution of the Maternity and Child Welfare Service, the School Health Service, the National Health Insurance and Unemployment Schemes, the provision of school meals and milk, and the development of the services for the control of tuberculosis and venereal disease. The end of the 1914-18 war saw the commencement of large-scale local authority house construction and an attack on slums and overcrowding.

The fourth phase (1929-48) commenced with the Local Government (Scotland) Act, 1929, and the concentration of attention on the administration of those hospitals which had been transferred from the Parish Councils to the Corporation. There also took place the integration of the personal health services, the Maternity and Child Welfare and School Health Services, and the upgrading of the Poor Law hospitals.

The present phase was initiated by the National Health Service (Scotland) Act, 1947. The hospital services were nationalised, the specialist services for tuberculosis and venereal disease were integrated with the hospital service, and the provision of "free" medical attention now covered the whole community instead of only a section of it as under the National Health Insurance Act. The Local Authority found itself bereft of an appreciable amount of its work and left with what appeared at first glance as only a fragment of its original services.

While certain phases can thus be discerned in the course of public health in the last 100 years, the services provided have been continuous and the phases have tended to overlap. A good water supply and an efficient drainage system and cleansing service are as necessary now as they were in the 1840's. Overcrowding is still the dominant factor in the city and has coloured all our vital statistics. The presence of insanitary housing and overcrowding remains the largest single health problem at the present time.

Effects of Overcrowding and Insanitary Conditions

The period of the Industrial Revolution witnessed large numbers of people flocking to Glasgow as to other cities throughout Great Britain. Adverse effects gradually emerged, both from the overcrowding of individual houses and from the insanitary conditions due to the overcrowding of the city area as a whole. The most striking of these adverse results proved to be the epidemics of major infectious disease which marked the first half of the nineteenth century, a period during which the population of Glasgow increased fourfold. Outbreaks of typhus occurred in 1818, 1832, 1837 (with 2,180 deaths), 1847 (with 4,346 deaths), and 1851-2. Cholera epidemics appeared in 1832 (with 2,842 deaths), 1848-9 (with 3,772 deaths in the latter year), and 1853-4 (with 3,855 deaths in 1854). "Relapsing fever" also inflicted its toll of 1,398 deaths in 1843. High death-rates were recorded in the epidemic years—46 per thousand in 1832, 41 in 1837, 32 in 1843, 54 in 1847, 35 in 1849 and 42 in 1854.

A national effort to cope with such conditions began to make headway with the publication in 1842 of the results of the enquiry by the Poor Law Commissioners into the *Sanitary Conditions of the Labouring Population*. In 1844 the Commissioners published their further report on the *Health of Towns*. Many features of urban life, particularly of the housing districts of the poorest classes, were condemned in the reports—among them overcrowded homes, faulty drains, cesspools, the lack of privies, the injurious effect of the Window Tax (in force until 1851), narrow thoroughfares, overbuilt sites and polluted water-supplies. The housing conditions of the poorest sections of the community and even of a considerable proportion of the labouring classes were castigated with especial severity. The wynds inspected in Edinburgh and Glasgow were compared as regards filth and bad ventilation with the worst prisons; and Edwin Chadwick, the celebrated Secretary to the Commissioners, in presenting his report to Parliament in July 1842, recorded a sharp criticism of Glasgow both as regards structural arrangements and the condition of its population. The most important early response to the challenge in Glasgow was probably the power conferred on the Dean of Guild by the Police Act of 1843 to order the repair or demolition of ruinous buildings. This was notably succeeded in the second half of the century by the City Improvements Acts (of which the first was passed in 1866) and others for regulating the width of streets and the erection of new buildings.

National enactments during this period included the Cholera Acts, 1832; the Nuisance Removal (Scotland) Act, 1846; its Amending Act, 1856; and the Scottish Registration Act, 1854. Glasgow administrative measures included several Police Acts; the appointment of an Inspector of Cleansing in 1843; the introduction of gravitation upland water from Gorbals Water Works in 1848 and from Loch Katrine in 1859; the appointment of a Committee on Nuisances in 1857; a Parks and Galleries Act, 1859; the appointment of a Sanitary Committee in 1862; the appointment of the first Medical Officer of Health in 1863; the opening of the first Municipal Fever Hospital in 1865; and the appointment of the first Sanitary Inspector in 1870. Subsequent diverse but relevant events were the Cattle Sheds in Burghs (Scotland) Act, 1860; the Scottish Public Health Act, 1867; the Scottish Education Act, 1872; and the Housing of the Working Classes Act and the Infectious Diseases (Notification) Act, 1890. Among the later local measures, apart from Police Acts and the City Improvements Acts, were the opening of a new disinfection station and the completion of a fever hospital at Belvidere in 1871 and 1887 respectively; the opening of Reception Houses in 1872 and 1892; the beginning of co-operation with the School Board to prevent dissemination of infectious disease in schools in 1874; the condemnation of the privy system in 1889; the opening of Refuse Despatch Works; the acquisition of the site for Ruchill Hospital in 1892 and the opening of a disinfecting station there in 1894; the Building Regulations Act, 1892; and the issue of new bye-laws regarding cow-houses and byres in 1894.

Following these measures it was noted that during the years 1885-1894 18 nuisances were removed per annum per 100 houses occupied; 2,540 drain-tests per annum were applied; and the number of articles washed per case of infectious disease registered was 43. For the same ten year period as compared with the period 1865-74 the death rate had dropped from 30.5 to 23.2, the infantile mortality rate from 167 to 144 and the death rate from zymotic diseases from 7.4 to 3.8.

With the appointment of its own sanitary officials the Corporation had found an unfailing source of professional documentation and of campaigning zeal on the subjects of overcrowding and of the insanitary conditions resulting from it. Dr. (later Sir) William T. Gairdner, who was the city's first Medical Officer of Health (1863 to 1872) and his successor Dr. James B. Russell (1872 to 1892) did much to stir the public conscience. It was with the physical effects of overcrowding that Dr. Russell chiefly occupied himself. He focussed his attention on the city's one- and two-apartment houses; and pointed out that small houses are not only capable of being injurious to health when overcrowded but are also, by reason of their smallness, more difficult to maintain in a proper state of repair than larger houses. One of Dr. Russell's best-known studies was contained in a paper delivered to the Philosophical Society of Glasgow in November, 1888. In this he submitted the results of an investigation of the mortality statistics of the inhabitants of Glasgow for the year 1885 according to the sizes of the houses which they occupied. He found that 24.7 per cent of the population of Glasgow were then living in one-apartment houses and 44.7 per cent in two rooms, whereas the deaths in the two types of houses were respectively 27 per cent and 47 per cent of the total mortality. Adding the institutional and untraced deaths to the figures for the small houses, he found that together they provided 70.8 per cent of the population but 79.4 per cent of the deaths. On enquiry into the causes of death, he found that the death-rate from zymotic or infectious diseases (including diarrhœa) was twice as great in the 1-2 apartment houses as in medium sized houses (3-4 apartments); from acute diseases of the lungs (including consumption) one and a half times as great; and from diseases of nutrition special to children, twice as great.

When the houses of one and two apartments were compared with houses of five or more rooms the contrast was still more marked. The contemporary readers of the present *Statistical Account* will be interested to note that in his assault upon the small house Dr. Russell was at pains to include the made-down house. He especially attacked the made-down houses that comprised the entire number of the city's "ticketed" houses.[1] The adequacy of the structures for their original purposes could not be permitted to justify the diversion of the subdivided structures to new and more exacting uses.

Dr. A. K. Chalmers, who succeeded Dr. Russell and was Medical Officer of Health from 1892 to 1925, continued to make similar studies. One of these had regard to phthisis early in the present century. He reported that the death rate from phthisis was 0.7 per 1,000 in houses of four or more apartments, 1.8 in houses of two apartments and 2.4 in single-roomed dwellings. In subsequent years, the incidence of infectious diseases diminished and the insanitary environmental conditions that had figured so prominently in a city invaded by an excessive population came under adequate control: but the problem of overcrowded houses persisted. War retarded and then stimulated both private and municipal enterprise in the erection of new houses. But the magnitude of the original problem and the continued growth of the population both operated to postpone any virtual solution. The Annual Report for 1936 of the Department of Health continued to express the view that overcrowding in Scotland was a grave evil in the national life. The percentage of overcrowded houses was over 40 in

[1] For an account of ticketed houses see Chapter 14 (Housing), p. 464.

Coatbridge, Port Glasgow, Clydebank and Motherwell; 29 in Glasgow; 24 in Dundee; and 17 in Edinburgh.

In 1943 Sir John Boyd Orr's Committee on Infant Mortality in Scotland (a Sub-Committee of the Scientific Advisory Committee) reported to the Secretary of State for Scotland that the infant mortality rate in Scotland compared unfavourably with that in other parts of the English-speaking world and all other countries in the West of Europe except Spain and Portugal. The West Central region of Scotland showed the highest infant mortality of any region in Great Britain. The excessive deaths between one and twelve months were chiefly due to infectious disease; and the main contributory environmental conditions were held to be poverty, faulty feeding and bad housing.

By this time the made-down houses of Dr. Russell's days had been succeeded in formerly prosperous residential urban districts of Glasgow by sublet houses originally designed to accommodate a single family but by now leased to several sub-tenants from a principal tenant. A survey of 173 such houses in a central urban ward was carried out in one of the Divisions of the Public Health Department shortly after World War II. Most of the original houses were of 4-6 apartments but there was an average of 4.2 sub-tenancies per house. The population of the houses numbered 2,292; and it was computed that over 400 additional apartments would have been necessary to accommodate them without overcrowding according to modern standards. Of the 173 sub-divided houses only 55 still had a usable bath and only 20 had a water supply of or above minimum adequacy. There was an average of at least 13 persons per water-closet and of seven persons for each water tap. The conditions prevailing were not comparable with those of the sombre made-down houses of bygone days: but the reappearance of an old mode of overcrowding in a new form was of considerable interest. One nine-apartment house had a separate family in each apartment, including the kitchen, and a total of 36 inmates; and a four-apartment house contained 29 persons. The average number of persons in the 173 houses was 13.

The period that has now elapsed since World War II has permitted improvements in the general housing and sanitary situations. The building up of the sanitary staff after a phase of depletion has enabled the control of environmental hygiene to be resumed and prodigious achievements have been attained in public housing programmes. The population too, once stigmatised as tolerant of slums, has become more conscious of housing conditions and is not only able but willing to make greater efforts to improve them. Large and numerous demolition gaps are to be observed in old tenement areas while vast new housing schemes extend on the outskirts of the city to the municipal boundaries. An even more vigorous effort has been planned for the years immediately ahead. Meanwhile the incidence of the common infectious diseases with the exception of the mild bacillary dysenteries has further declined; and the Welfare State has diminished the incidence and mitigated the effects of poverty. Nevertheless it would be rash to forecast that the compilers of a Fourth Statistical Account will be able to report that the problem of overcrowding in Glasgow has been liquidated. The dimensions of the original legacy of inadequate housing not only entail a long period to make substantial inroads but also open up the danger of the burden being added to in due course by the deterioration of the houses at present regarded as new. It may well be that in such populous areas of long standing, as Alva Myrdal warned us in her *Nation and Family,* "A new society will for the most part always have to live in dwellings inherited from an old one."

Health Record

"There is some evidence that early in the nineteenth century the population of Glasgow was not unhealthy even when judged by the standards of the early twentieth century" (A. K. Chalmers). The death rate among children under 5 years of age was diminishing, while the reduced rate of admissions to the fever wards of Glasgow Royal Infirmary afforded local illustration of the relative freedom from typhus which the country generally had experienced throughout the opening decade of the nineteenth century. From 1816 onwards, however, until the early '70's of the century the city was devastated by recurring epidemics of infectious diseases of several kinds and of considerable magnitude. These epidemics when they occurred formed only the peaks of a high level of disease incidence, an incidence which was capable of maintaining an annual death rate frequently between 30 and 40 per thousand and rising in occasional years, as in 1832, to 46 and in 1840 to 56. Prior to 1855 the register of burials kept by wardens of churchyards was the only source of information as to the number of deaths and their causes. It was with the coming into operation of the Registration (Scotland) Act, 1855, that an accurate record of vital statistics of Glasgow became available. It is from this date that precise changes in the death rate can be observed, as illustrated in Table XCI.

TABLE XCI

Glasgow—Death Rate per 1,000 Population

Decennial Periods		*Quinquennial Periods*	
1855-64	30.1	1901-05	19.0
1865-74	30.5	1906-10	17.5
1875-84	26.9	1911-15	17.0
1885-94	23.2	1916-20	15.7
1881-90	24.2	1921-25	15.5
1891-1900	21.5		

The decline in the death rate noted in the 'seventies formed part of an extensive recession of disease both in the city and in the country generally. It was associated with the institution of the sanitary period and with the extensive clearance effected under the first City Improvement Act of 1866; and it heralded the emergence of the population from the waves of epidemic disease.

At the same time there occurred a change in the principal causes of death, as is shown in Table XCII.

TABLE XCII

GLASGOW—DEATH RATE PER MILLION

Period	*Zymotics*[1]	*Pulmonary Tuberculosis*	*Other Diseases of Lungs*	*Other Causes*	*All Causes*
1855-64	7,841	3,918	5,170	13,121	30,050
1865-74	7,377	3,940	6,522	12,692	30,530
1875-84	5,056	3,396	6,322	12,113	26,886
1885-94	3,822	2,458	5,329	11,566	23,175
1921-25	1,986	1,005	2,748	9,069	14,808

The most remarkable feature was the shrinkage of the zymotic diseases and the gradual change in the character of the total death rate. In the period 1855-64 three groups—the zymotics, pulmonary tuberculosis and other diseases of the lungs—contributed 56.5 per cent of the total death rate, and in 1885-94, 50 per cent; but in 1921-25 they contributed only 41 per cent.

The continuing changes in the character of the death rate are shown in Table XCIII, which gives the major causes of death for the four years 1925, 1935, 1945 and 1955:

TABLE XCIII

GLASGOW—MAJOR CAUSES OF DEATH IN EACH OF THE YEARS 1925, 1935, 1945 AND 1955

	1925		1935		1945		1955	
	No.	%	No.	%	No.	%	No.	%
Heart Disease	1,498	9.8	2,837	18.2	3,265	23.4	3,768	28.4
Malignant Neoplasms	1,384	9.0	1,564	10.1	1,924	13.8	2,321	17.4
Vascular Lesions of the Central Nervous System	707	4.6	1,104	7.1	1,318	9.4	1,903	14.3
Bronchitis	883	5.8	507	3.3	340	2.4	700	5.3
Violence (Suicide, Road Traffic Accidents, etc.)	618	4.0	539	3.5	553	4.0	631	4.7
Congenital Malformations and Diseases of Early Infancy	851	5.5	933	6.0	638	4.6	566	4.3
Pneumonia	1,665	10.9	1,516	9.8	555	4.0	545	4.1
Pulmonary Tuberculosis	1,012	6.6	972	6.2	1,085	7.8	369	2.8
	8,618	56.2	9,972	64.2	9,678	69.4	10,803	81.3
All Causes	15,336		15,537		13,941		13,275	

[1] Typhus, smallpox, enteric fever, scarlet fever, measles, whooping cough, diphtheria, diarrhœal diseases, erysipelas, puerperal fever, influenza, etc.

The following table is a summary of death rates per million from principal causes arranged according to the International Classification adopted in 1950:

TABLE XCIV

SUMMARY OF DEATH RATES PER MILLION FROM PRINCIPAL CAUSES

	1955	1954	1953
General Diseases—			
(a) Infectious	64	72	81
(b) Tuberculosis			
(1) Respiratory	340	387	434
(2) Non-Respiratory	31	32	40
(c) Malignant (Cancer, etc.)	2,139	2,063	2,053
Diseases of the Nervous System (including Mental Disorders)	1,994	1,964	1,789
Diseases of the Circulatory System	4,060	3,724	3,907
Diseases of Respiratory System (including Influenza)	1,284	1,029	1,138
Diseases of Digestive System	346	355	352
Congenital Defects and Diseases of Early Infancy	521	478	468
Violence	582	552	552
All Other Causes	873	1,098	1,008
	12,234	11,754	11,822

Mortality from infectious disease was reduced still further in 1955 with the rate of 64 per million. Of the 69 deaths in this group, 37 were due to diarrhœa in children under 2 years of age. There were four deaths from dysentery and one death from typhoid fever. There were no deaths from scarlet fever, diphtheria or whooping cough during 1955, but measles was the cause of death of two children under 1, two under 2 years, and one under 10 years. The mortality from tuberculosis continues its downward trend. With regard to diseases of the nervous system there was a further increase in the deaths in this group of causes—in 1955, 2,163 compared with 2,130 in 1954 and 1,941 in 1953. Vascular lesions, which rank third in the list of major causes of death, accounted for 89 per cent of the deaths in this group. Deaths from diseases of the circulatory system, which had shown a downward trend in the preceding three years, rose again in 1955 and now represent 33 per cent of the deaths from all causes. Arterio-sclerotic and degenerative heart disease, to which most of the deaths (77 per cent in 1955) are attributable, accounted for no less than 3,380 deaths. Some 49 per cent of these deaths were classified as due to coronary thrombosis, a condition developing in the arteries of the heart. This cause of death has become one of major importance in recent years, as will be seen from Table XCV, showing deaths at all ages from coronary thrombosis in the course of the last five years as contrasted with 1931 and 1941.

Similar changes have occurred in Scotland as a whole. The condition has increased with the rising pressure of life at the present time and affects particularly men with heavy responsibility in early middle life.

TABLE XCV

GLASGOW—DEATHS (ALL AGES) FROM CORONARY THROMBOSIS

	Male	*Female*	*Total*
1931	37	25	102
1941	296	168	464
1951	864	391	1,255
1952	947	545	1,492
1953	970	488	1,458
1954	958	555	1,513
1955	1,062	609	1,671

Deaths in the group " malignant neoplasms," including neoplasms of lymphatic and hæmatopoietic tissues, numbered 2,321. For the six years 1950-5 the average annual number of deaths has been 2,231, and the trend of the rate during that period was as follows:

TABLE XCVI

GLASGOW—DEATHS FROM CANCER
RATE PER MILLION

1950	2,006	1953	2,053
1951	2,002	1954	2,063
1952	2,055	1955	2,139

The two main systems affected are the respiratory and the digestive. Cancer of the digestive organs has remained stationary with approximately equal incidence in males and females. Cancer of the respiratory system, however, has shown a disturbing rise in recent years, principally among males. It forms the second condition along with coronary thrombosis which has shown a marked increase in the last twenty years as a cause of death. Table XCVII shows the number of deaths from lung cancer for the years 1931, 1941 and 1951 onwards:

TABLE XCVII

GLASGOW—DEATHS FROM CANCER OF RESPIRATORY SYSTEM

	1931	1941	1951	1952	1953	1954	1955
Males	52	146	353	421	486	460	498
Females	29	50	95	73	84	83	110
	81	196	448	494	570	543	608

This condition is at present more prevalent in males than in females and particularly at ages over 45. The position in Scotland is illustrated by the following table, which compares the mortality from lung cancer in later adult life in the period 1931-3 with 1951-3. A similar increase occurred in Britain as a whole where, in 1955, 17,000 persons died of lung cancer. The table has been obtained from an article by Dr. P. L. McKinlay in the October 1955 Health Bulletin.

TABLE XCVIII

SCOTLAND—MORTALITY FROM LUNG CANCER
TIMES INCREASE, 1931-3 AND 1951-3

Younger Age Group 45-54 *years*		*Older Age Group* 55-64 *years*	
Male	*Female*	*Male*	*Female*
3.9	1.2	6	1.7

A vast amount of research has taken place into the ætiology of lung cancer. It is known that the condition is more prevalent in males over the age of 45 who are heavy cigarette smokers. The recorded mortality rate in large towns, however, has been reported as about twice to four times the rate for residents in country districts, and a certain number of non-smokers, mainly city dwellers, also die of lung cancer. Although cigarette consumption is rather greater in urban than in rural areas, in the former it is believed that atmospheric pollution[1] or some other factor may be a predisposing cause. The results of research, however, are still inconclusive.

THE CONTROL OF INFECTIOUS DISEASE

The control of infection remains an important function of the health authority, although it is not the cholera, typhus and relapsing fever of the nineteenth century which we endeavour to control but tuberculosis, poliomyelitis and the zymotic infections such as smallpox, enteric fever and the others.

Smallpox remains an ever present danger in a city with a port, and the history of the past fifty years shows how wary a health authority must be, always on the look-out for this virulent infection which has been the cause of so much disfigurement, suffering and death in the past. During the present century Glasgow has had five outbreaks of smallpox, one of which reached epidemic proportions and lasted for five years. In each case the outbreak started with the arrival of a ship, with a passenger or member of the crew incubating smallpox, or the entry into the city of infected clothing. Table XCIX illustrates these incidents.

Compulsory infant vaccination was introduced in the middle of the nineteenth century, but in 1906 conscientious objection to vaccination was permitted, and by the National Health Service Act, 1947, compulsory infant vaccination was abolished. This action by the Government was based on the success which had been achieved with diphtheria immunisation on a voluntary basis, and it was felt that a similar success would follow voluntary vaccination. This hope has not been realised,

1 The reduction of atmospheric pollution has been a principal duty of local authorities for the past forty years, and in Glasgow considerable improvement has been effected. See Chapter 1, p. 29.

TABLE XCIX

GLASGOW—SMALLPOX

Year	*Cases*	*Deaths*
1899	1	1
1900	397	41
1901	1,394	193
1902	460	42
1903	292	24
1904	870	67
1905	4	1
1920	542	113
1929	17	—
1942	36	8
1950	19	6

and therefore a large proportion of the children born in the city are not protected against smallpox. On those occasions when smallpox becomes prevalent, however, there is an urgent desire on the part of citizens to be vaccinated at once. To date, except on one occasion, every smallpox outbreak in the city has been accompanied by a mass vaccination of the public.

Typhus first appeared in Glasgow in epidemic proportions at the beginning of the nineteenth century and recurred from time to time until the 1870's. Thereafter, no doubt associated with the concentrated energies of the sanitarians, the incidence of the disease declined until 1924 and 1925 when there were no cases in the city. Apart from eight cases, with one death, in 1926, and two cases in 1930 and one in 1931, the disease has not recurred.

Typhus is transmitted by infected body lice and is usually associated with overcrowding and uncleanliness. The control of this disease is the control of lice by the use of insecticides and by delousing infested persons and clothing. In recent years, particularly during World War II, insecticides have been developed which are lethal to lice and cause no skin irritation. The improved standard of cleanliness, the reduction in overcrowding, and the availability of insecticides make the recurrence of typhus in epidemic proportions unlikely.

Plague is a disease which till 1900 had not appeared in Glasgow since the Restoration period. Its recession eastwards after the Great Plague of London (1665) remained one of the mysteries of epidemiology until its dependence on rat migration was recognised after its reawakening in Hong Kong in 1894. From there it was distributed by shipping and in less than six years it had spread to both hemispheres. In 1898 it appeared in Oporto and in 1900-1 in Glasgow, where 48 cases of bubonic plague occurred with 16 deaths. The outbreak appeared first in the poorer parts of the city but in the following year five cases occurred in the staff of a high-class hotel. No evidence of infection from human sources was found there, but in the neighbourhood there was extensive rat infestation, and many of the animals were found to be carriers of the disease. Plague has not returned to the city since

1901, but even to this day rat infestation remains an important problem and a persistent campaign for rat destruction is still necessary.

Tuberculosis has always been a subject of the first magnitude in the City of Glasgow. Deaths from pulmonary tuberculosis made up fully 15 per cent of the total deaths in the city in 1888, but even this figure was a reduction on the tuberculosis death rate in the period 1860-4 when it was at its highest in Glasgow, 4,098 per million. In 1888, six years after Koch's discovery of the bacillus of tuberculosis, a Departmental Committee was appointed, for which Dr. J. B. Russell, Glasgow's Medical Officer of Health, prepared a comprehensive memorandum. At the turn of the century the National Association for the Prevention of Consumption was formed, and in 1901 the Corporation contributed towards the cost of sanatoria at Bellefield and Bridge of Weir. Prior to their erection the treatment of pulmonary tuberculosis was carried out in the general hospitals, but with the provision of special accommodation the number of cases of pulmonary tuberculosis treated in general hospitals fell quickly until by 1907 tuberculosis patients formed only a small percentage of the total medical admissions. In 1912 the tuberculosis accommodation for Glasgow patients was provided by 140 beds at Bridge of Weir, 52 at Bellefield and 18 for advanced cases at Lanfine. In addition, the Glasgow and Govan Parish Councils provided 272 and 144 beds respectively, making altogether 626 available beds.

The treatment of pulmonary tuberculosis was accelerated by certain provisions of the National Health Insurance Act, 1911, which enabled local authorities to qualify for building grants and also for payment for treatment. To meet the need for additional beds, the Corporation in 1911 resolved to set aside 150-170 beds in the hospital to be erected at Robroyston and to build a home or preventorium in the country for the residential treatment of children. Ground was secured at Southfield for what was to be Mearnskirk Sanatorium. Robroyston Hospital, although commenced in 1914, was not available for pulmonary tuberculosis cases until 1919. Further accommodation for tuberculosis was provided by an extension at Knightswood and Shieldhall and the completion of the sanatorium annexe for 270 beds at Ruchill in 1915. The provision of hospital accommodation at Robroyston was later expanded by the building of wards for 220 additional beds and the use between major prevalences of smallpox of a further 200 beds.

Meanwhile in 1906 a system of dispensaries had been started under the direction of the Glasgow branch of the National Association. Following the official notification of pulmonary tuberculosis in 1910 and the Public Health (Pulmonary Tuberculosis) Regulations of 1911 the local authority took over responsibility and recast the system. Five new dispensaries were opened, replacing all former dispensaries, this system remaining almost unaltered until the development of the new clinic at Belvidere.

In the diagnosis of pulmonary tuberculosis, sputum and X-ray examinations are essential. While the Public Health Laboratory was instituted in 1899 and sputum testing became reasonably efficient from that date, X-ray apparatus except in the hands of experts did not give satisfactory results until the later 1920's with the introduction of improved equipment.

Despite the intervention of the First World War the period between 1910 and 1940 was marked by steady progress. The treatment of pulmonary tuberculosis improved. Moreover, a series of enactments affecting dairies and milk production and the introduction of designated milks and tuberculin-tested herds gradually diminished bovine infection, and this was reflected in the steady decline in the cases of non-pulmonary disease. The death rates from pulmonary tuberculosis continued to decline, from 136 per 100,000 in 1910 to 86 in 1939, and the non-pulmonary death rate from 72 per 100,000 in 1910 to 22 in 1939.

The control of tuberculosis during the last fifteen years has been characterised by relatively violent changes beginning with the virtual disruption of the Tuberculosis Service in September, 1939. The results of war conditions were seen immediately in rising incidence and mortality rates and in lengthening waiting lists for sanatoria. In an attempt to relieve the bed situation suitable patients were treated outdoor by artificial pneumothorax in 1943. The introduction in 1947 of streptomycin marked the beginning of a radical change in the treatment of tuberculosis, and with the advent of chemotherapy, out-patient treatment was increasingly adopted to deal with the waiting list, which had grown to over 1,000 in 1948.

The National Health Service (Scotland) Act, 1947, brought about a division of the existing scheme of administration. The tuberculosis hospitals, sanatoria and clinics were placed under the jurisdiction of the Western Regional Hospital Board, the home medical care of the patient under the general practitioner, and there remained to the local health authority the means of prevention and education.

In 1950 B.C.G. (Bacillus Calmette-Guerin) vaccination became available in Britain and special clinics were opened in Glasgow for this purpose. The scheme of immunisation expanded rapidly, and the yearly total of vaccinations performed has risen from 435 in 1950 to almost 16,000 in 1954. The prescribed groups of the population to be protected were nurses in hospitals, especially institutions for tuberculosis, the new-born infants of tuberculous mothers, the contacts of patients suffering from open pulmonary tuberculosis, and medical students. By 1952 new-born infants in certain selected hospitals were included, and now all maternity hospitals and units within the city are providing this service. In 1953 vaccination was available to school children in their fourteenth year, and during 1955 the parents of 85 per cent of the children of this age group have agreed to initial testing and if need be vaccination.

A further measure for the prevention of infection was mass miniature radiography. The first mass miniature radiography unit in Glasgow started work in 1944, and most of the time available was devoted to the examination of persons of susceptible age groups, where the incidence of tuberculosis was high. This unit, like the rest of the tuberculosis services, was transferred to the Regional Hospital Board in 1948. More recently there have been developed community surveys by mass radiography, and there is a proposal for a survey in 1957 of the whole of the city population.[1]

During the past six years, as will be seen from Table C, Glasgow's death rate from pulmonary tuberculosis has fallen steadily, but other cities have made even greater progress:

TABLE C

PULMONARY TUBERCULOSIS
DEATH RATES PER 100,000 POPULATION FOR CERTAIN CITIES IN SCOTLAND AND ENGLAND, 1950-1955

	1950	1951	1952	1953	1954	1955
Glasgow	87	64	52	43	39	34
Edinburgh	48	33	26	23	19	10
Aberdeen	20	20	20	14	10	8
Dundee	58	40	22	17	19	15
Birmingham	43	34	25	24	20	19
Liverpool	60	52	34	33	29	24
Manchester	58	45	38	28	27	19
Newcastle-on-Tyne	62	38	33	28	27	17

The incidence of pulmonary tuberculosis, however, has not fallen, and while Table CI shows that the incidence has remained high in other cities the case rate for Glasgow is still in excess of that ruling elsewhere.

The incidence of pulmonary tuberculosis varies with age and sex. In the male, the incidence is high in the age group 15-24, then falls to a constant lower level in the age period 35-64, to decrease again at ages

[1] The Glasgow X-ray Campaign commenced on 11 March 1957, and by 12 April 714,915 persons had been X-rayed. Of this number, 641,000 belonged to Glasgow, equal to 76 per cent. of the population over 14 years of age. The provisional figure for the pulmonary tuberculosis cases disclosed is 8,000, of which 1,980 were Glasgow people suffering from active disease. This compares with the expected figure of 1,000. The remaining cases included 5,000 doubtfully active and requiring observation and 1,700 in which the disease was healed. Within four weeks of the completion of the Campaign, over 1,000 Glasgow patients had been admitted to hospital. The average number X-rayed weekly per unit was 4,760. The highest in one day for all units was 46,000 and the highest in one day for one unit was 2,775. Some 31,000 people were recalled for further X-ray, equal to 4.4 per cent. After the Campaign was ended immediate attention was given to contact tracing, the examination of contacts who had not been X-rayed during the Campaign and, where indicated, the inoculation of child contacts with B.C.G.

The astonishingly successful results achieved could not have been obtained without extensive and careful advanced planning jointly by the Corporation of Glasgow, the Western Regional Hospital Board and the Department of Health for Scotland. In collaboration with the Ministry of Health, the Department of Health for Scotland were able to secure the assistance of 27 additional units which, together with the Scottish units, made available during the Campaign 37 X-ray units, a greater number than had ever been brought together for one community survey. To the Corporation of Glasgow fell the duty of persuading the public to come forward for X-ray, and this was achieved by means of a complete and thorough publicity campaign and the co-operation of voluntary organisations and voluntary helpers. The propaganda for the Campaign was guided by a Publicity Committee on which were represented the press, the cinema and the B.B.C., and also by the expert advice of the Scottish Information Office.

TABLE CI

PULMONARY TUBERCULOSIS
CASE RATES PER 100,000 FOR CERTAIN CITIES IN
SCOTLAND AND ENGLAND, 1950-1955

	1950	1951	1952	1953	1954	1955
Glasgow	224	203	208	218	203	201
Edinburgh	139	135	152	169	170	137
Aberdeen	144	124	125	131	123	109
Dundee	287	186	156	164	171	161
Birmingham	102	107	111	111	111	103
Liverpool	196	195	108	175	144	139
Manchester	105	102	102	106	96	96
Newcastle-on-Tyne	181	166	148	164	150	133

over 65. In the case of the female, however, the incidence is much higher in the 15-24 age group but falls rapidly in the older age groups. This varying incidence is also shown in the accompanying diagram of the incidence rates for each age group and sex. (Fig. 28).

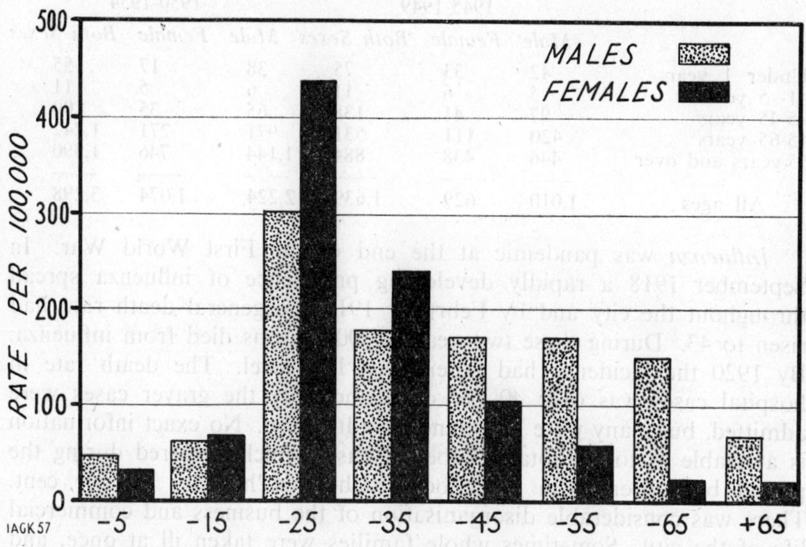

FIG. 28. Incidence of Respiratory Tuberculosis by Sex and Age-groups.

The fall in the death rates over the past years has occurred mainly at the younger age groups both in males and females, but at ages over 55 in males and over 65 in females the rate has remained stationary or in some years has even risen.

The number of beds for pulmonary tuberculosis patients has increased from 1,250 in January 1948 to 1,424 in January 1956. The newer methods of treatment have been vigorously employed, and gradually the lengthy waiting list of the 1940's has shrunk to negligible proportions. The outlook as regards tuberculosis in Scotland is more promising than it has been for many years.

Pneumonia and *bronchitis* are the principal acute diseases of the lung other than tuberculosis. Acute primary pneumonia is a notifiable disease, and during the past ten years over 40,000 patients have been notified, of whom 76 per cent were treated in hospital. Unlike bronchitis, which principally affects the later age periods, this disease affects mainly those of early and middle life. Pneumonia shows a pronounced seasonal incidence, notifications and deaths being heaviest in the first quarter of the year and lightest in the third. Low temperature, fog, and the prevalence of influenza markedly affect the incidence.

Bronchitis, on the other hand, affects principally patients over 45 years of age, as will be seen from Table CII for the quinquennia 1945-9 and 1950-4:

TABLE CII

GLASGOW—DEATHS FROM BRONCHITIS 1945-1949 AND 1950-1954

	1945-1949			1950-1954		
	Male	*Female*	*Both Sexes*	*Male*	*Female*	*Both Sexes*
Under 1 year	42	33	75	38	17	55
1- 5 years	5	6	11	6	5	11
5-45 years	97	41	138	65	35	100
45-65 years	420	111	531	971	271	1,242
65 years and over	446	438	884	1,144	746	1,890
All ages	1,010	629	1,639	2,224	1,074	3,298

Influenza was pandemic at the end of the First World War. In September 1918 a rapidly developing prevalence of influenza spread throughout the city and by February 1919 the general death rate had risen to 43. During these two years 4,000 persons died from influenza. By 1920 the incidence had fallen to a low level. The death rate in hospital cases was over 40 per cent, and only the graver cases were admitted, but many were moribund on admission. No exact information is available as to the total number of cases which occurred during the period but absenteeism in school reached as high as 30 per cent. There was considerable disorganisation of the business and commercial life of the city. Sometimes whole families were taken ill at once, and the medical and nursing professions were grossly overworked during this time.

Since 1919 influenza has returned from time to time to the city, but never in the proportions that existed in 1918-19. Periods of unusually high incidence were in 1929 when there were 878 deaths, 1937 with 496 deaths, and 1940 with 451 deaths.[1]

Cerebrospinal Fever, now more correctly called meningococcal meningitis, is one of the two principal infections of the central nervous system. It first appeared in epidemic proportions in Glasgow in 1906.

[1] In the spring and early summer of 1957 influenza due to a new variant of the virus has appeared in Asia and is rapidly reaching pandemic proportions.

The disease was virulent in attack, and during the years 1906-7, 1,197 cases were registered. Many of the cases were fulminating and ended fatally within 24-48 hours. The incidence of the disease fell sharply and remained at a low level until 1915 when it again became prevalent, particularly among servicemen. The reduction of overcrowding and improved spacing of the beds helped to reduce the spread of infection. In the period 1928-33 the disease again appeared in rather more than endemic proportions. The case fatality rate of these outbreaks was high, ranging from 75 to 50 per cent.

The next recrudescence of the disease appeared in 1940. During the war the conditions in the cities, camp life, and overcrowding, as in the First World War, led to a sharp increase in the number of cases registered during the period 1940-2. Chemotherapy, however, had improved the chances of recovery, and the case mortality rate was reduced to under 25 per cent. In recent years improved chemotherapy has again reduced the case fatality rate to the neighbourhood of 10 per cent.

Poliomyelitis, which was commonly known as infantile paralysis, is another important infectious disease of the central nervous system. It frequently leaves the patient with permanent paralysis of limbs or muscles. Epidemics of this condition have occurred notably in the United States, Scandinavia and Australia, and it is still a frequent occurrence in these countries at certain periods of the year. There have been recurrent outbreaks of poliomyelitis in Glasgow, the most important being in 1928, 1947, 1950 and 1955. It is almost always a summer disease, associated with a prolonged period of unusually warm weather. The Glasgow outbreaks have occurred in almost all cases during the months of July to October. The details of the last four outbreaks are shown in Table CIII.

TABLE CIII

GLASGOW—POLIOMYELITIS

INCIDENCE—1928, 1947, 1950 AND 1955

Year	*Total Cases*	*Paralysed*	*Percentage of Total*	*Permanently Handicapped*	*Deaths*	*All Cases Percentage Age Incidence* —5 *yrs.*	5-15	*Peak Sickening Dates*
1928	103	92	89.3%	37	8	73.0%	19.8%	6 Oct.
1947	319	262	82.1%	170	29	52.8%	32.2%	23 Aug.
		(52.8% under 5)						20 Sept.
1950	278	212	76.2%	60	11	72.6%	15.8%	1 July
		(80% under 5)						19 July
1955	246	170	69.0%	87	5	55.0%	37.0%	10 Sept.
		(60% under 5)						8 Oct.

The cause of poliomyelitis was first discovered to be a virus in 1909, but it was not until 1954 that suitable vaccines were prepared in Canada and the United States. They have now been brought into general use, after an initial set-back when, owing to manufacturing defects, one batch caused the disease in a small group, with paralysis and death. This mishap led to a review of the manufacturing processes.

In view of the success of the American virus, production was started in Britain and some vaccine was made available to Health Departments throughout the country in May and June, 1956.

Encephalitis Lethargica is a third infection of the central nervous system. The disease first appeared in epidemic form in Europe in 1915. This strange condition affected Glasgow in 1920-5 when 690 cases with 161 deaths were registered. While some patients recovered without defect, many were left with sequelæ which affected their moral, mental and physical condition. Many of the survivors became permanent invalids. One of the problems of the Glasgow outbreak was the need to deal with large numbers of patients who were incapacitated for life. Special units were set aside in Stobhill Hospital for these patients, and many others have been accommodated in mental hospitals.

Enteric Fever is the group name for typhoid and paratyphoid fevers. Statistics for this condition date from 1865 when for the first time the Registrar-General classified it apart from other fevers. It is only within the past 20 years that the annual death rate per million from this condition has been reduced to single figures.

TABLE CIV

GLASGOW—ENTERIC FEVER

DEATH RATE PER MILLION OF POPULATION

Year	Rate	Year	Rate	Year	Rate
1881–1890	230	1932	8	1944	1
1891–1900	215	1933	8	1945	3
1901–1910	127	1934	4	1946	4
1911–1915	58	1935	13	1947	3
1916–1920	23	1936	12	1948	Nil
1921–1925	11	1937	4	1949	1
1926	15	1938	4	1950	Nil
1927	9	1939	4	1951	1
1928	9	1940	5	1952	Nil
1929	6	1941	2	1953	Nil
1930	9	1942	7	1954	Nil
1931	10	1943	3	1955	1

The great decrease in the incidence and mortality of the disease can be accounted for by improvements in housing and general sanitation, by the control over the food supply, particularly milk and ice cream, and the much improved living conditions of the population. Typhoid fever outbreaks in the past have been frequently connected with water supplies. The provision of a piped water supply and a water carriage sewage system have been mainly instrumental in preventing the recurrence of the epidemics of the nineteenth century.

Outbreaks of paratyphoid fever have been mainly associated with some article of food supply: in 1927 with milk and in 1931 with ice cream; but in 1940 the origin of this widespread epidemic was not traced. The number of cases of typhoid and paratyphoid fever reported in the past thirty years is shown in Table CV.

Dysentery and Food Poisoning are two other enteric conditions that require consideration. Until the end of the Second World War dysentery in Glasgow was not an administrative problem. From the year 1943 the

TABLE CV

GLASGOW—ENTERIC FEVER

	Typhoid Fever	*Paratyphoid Fever*	*Total*
1926-30	225	301	526
1931-35	242	308	550
1936-40	92	662	754
1941-45	141	121	262
1946-50	66	57	123
1951-55	14	156	170

incidence of the disease markedly increased, and in recent years has been unusually high.

TABLE CVI

GLASGOW—BACILLARY DYSENTERY

	Case Rate per Million Population	*Death Rate per Million Population*
1943	419	8
1944	1,199	8
1945	1,404	12
1946	532	3
1947	252	3
1948	1,061	5
1949	1,262	7
1950	2,156	5
1951	1,422	4
1952	2,110	2
1953	2,509	4
1954	5,755	5
1955	5,823	4

The disease is most prevalent among children, mainly between one and five years. It is particularly troublesome if it occurs in a children's institution or home, as the carrier state is readily and frequently developed. The death rate is low and has been listed separately only from 1950 when a new international classification code was introduced.

Until the passing of the Food and Drugs (Scotland) Act, 1956, food poisoning was not notifiable in Scotland, and therefore statistics of outbreaks refer only to cases coming to the attention of the Department. Food poisoning occurs most frequently in the warmer summer months, and is of two main types, the specific group associated with the Salmonella organism and the non-specific group including those caused by a toxin. Most of these outbreaks concern individual cases of illness, but frequently there are family or larger incidents, as is shown in Table CVII.

The Food and Drugs (Scotland) Act, 1956, gives additional powers and provides for regulations on food hygiene and allied subjects, the registration of food traders and the closer supervision of food handling and restaurants. As with dysentery, however, the prevention of food poisoning is one of personal hygiene and attention to detail. Until the food worker has grasped thoroughly the need for meticulous cleanliness in food handling, food poisoning is likely to recur from time to time.

TABLE CVII

GLASGOW—FOOD POISONING

	1955		1954		1953	
	Incidents	*Cases*	*Incidents*	*Cases*	*Incidents*	*Cases*
Outbreaks	5	119	7	135	8	228
Family Outbreaks	40	133	18	46	27	78
Sporadic Cases	165	165	100	100	150	150
	210	417	125	281	185	456

Diphtheria exhibited a rising incidence extending over several years during which it gradually increased to a peak in 1940-4, to fall again to the present low level. The position in the course of the last 55 years is shown in Table CVIII.

TABLE CVIII

GLASGOW—INCIDENCE AND DEATHS FROM DIPHTHERIA IN QUINQUENNIAL PERIODS, 1900-1954 AND 1955

Period	*Registered Cases*	*Deaths*
1900-1904	3,091	539
1905-1909	6,334	736
1910-1914	9,088	886
1915-1919	7,300	802
1920-1924	9,228	712
1925-1929	11,843	633
1930-1934	11,900	633
1935-1939	12,740	580
1940-1944	17,850	614
1945-1949	4,370	96
1950-1954	368	12
1955	2	—

The highest figure recorded for any year was in 1940 with 5,190 cases and 226 deaths. In 1955 there were two cases and no deaths. This remarkable change is evidence of the progress made in the control and eradication of diphtheria in the city. The campaign for the protection of children against diphtheria by immunisation began in the latter part of 1940. Special centres were opened in maternity and child welfare and school clinics for free immunisation, and general practitioners were invited to take part in the campaign. While many children have been immunised against diphtheria, it is still necessary to emphasise the need for protection. Of the ten cases which occurred in 1954, seven were not immunised, and one, a non-immunised child of eight months, died.

Scarlet fever, in the middle of last century a severe and often fatal infection, has since assumed a much milder form, although remaining almost unaffected in incidence. Glasgow in common with the rest of the country experienced a greatly increased incidence of scarlet fever

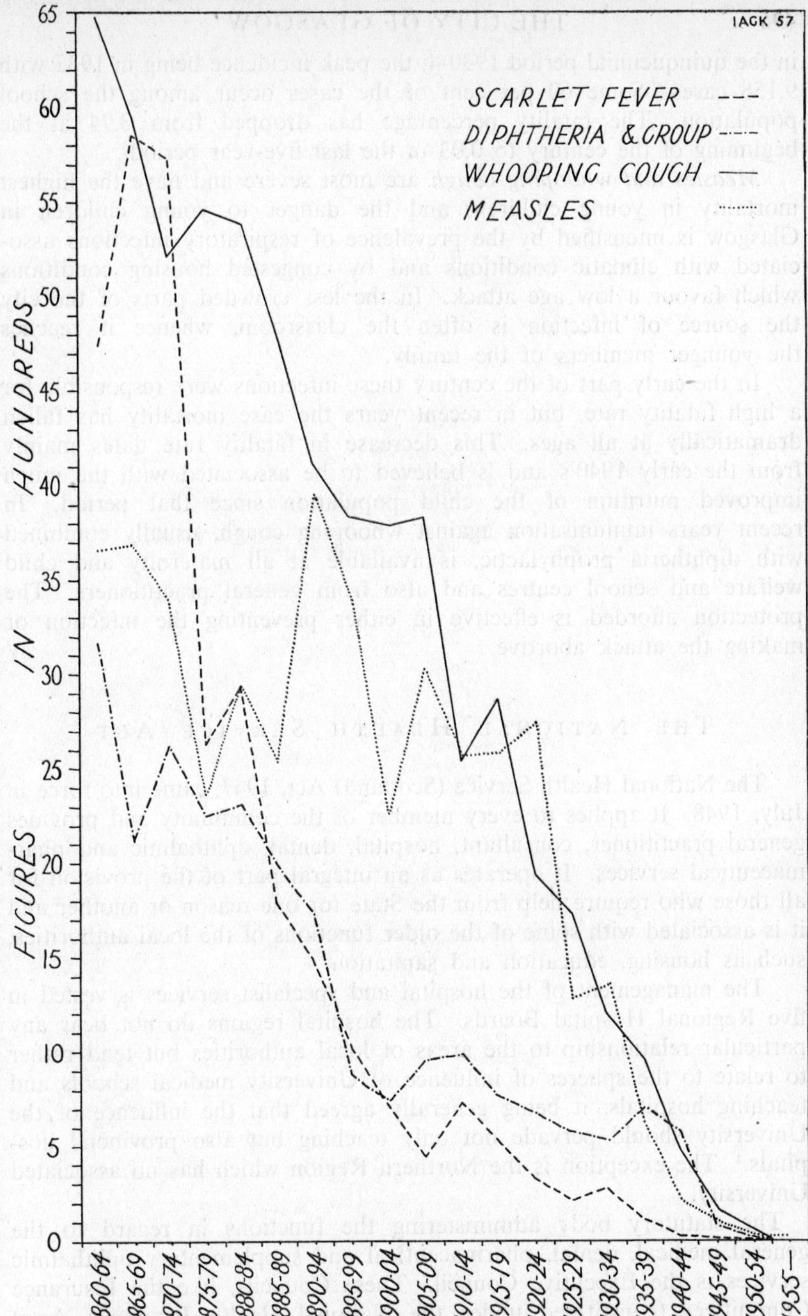

FIG. 29. Deaths per million of children under 10 from the Commoner Infectious Diseases.

in the quinquennial period 1930-4, the peak incidence being in 1932 with 9,158 cases. Some 60 per cent of the cases occur among the school population. The fatality percentage has dropped from 3.94 at the beginning of the century to 0.03 in the last five-year period.

Measles and whooping cough are most severe and have the highest mortality in young children, and the danger to young children in Glasgow is intensified by the prevalence of respiratory infections associated with climatic conditions and by congested housing conditions which favour a low age attack. In the less crowded parts of the city the source of infection is often the classroom, whence it reaches the younger members of the family.

In the early part of the century these infections were responsible for a high fatality rate, but in recent years the case mortality has fallen dramatically at all ages. This decrease in fatality rate dates mainly from the early 1940's and is believed to be associated with the much improved nutrition of the child population since that period. In recent years immunisation against whooping cough, usually combined with diphtheria prophylactic, is available at all maternity and child welfare and school centres and also from general practitioners. The protection afforded is effective in either preventing the infection or making the attack abortive.

The National Health Service Act

The National Health Service (Scotland) Act, 1947, came into force in July, 1948. It applies to every member of the community and provides general practitioner, consultant, hospital, dental, ophthalmic and pharmaceutical services. It operates as an integral part of the provision for all those who require help from the State for one reason or another and it is associated with some of the older functions of the local authorities, such as housing, education and sanitation.

The management of the hospital and specialist services is vested in five Regional Hospital Boards. The hospital regions do not bear any particular relationship to the areas of local authorities but tend rather to relate to the spheres of influence of University medical schools and teaching hospitals, it being generally agreed that the influence of the University should pervade not only teaching but also provincial hospitals.[1] The exception is the Northern Region which has no associated University.

The statutory body administering the functions in regard to the general medical, dental, pharmaceutical and supplementary ophthalmic services is the Executive Council. These Councils, like the Insurance Committees (constituted under the National Health Insurance Acts) which they replace, function within the area of one or more Local Health Authorities. Their main duty is to make arrangements with

[1] In Glasgow the three infirmaries, Royal, Western and Victoria, share along with Stobhill Hospital the bulk of the clinical teaching of medical students and the University's clinical teachers are drawn from their consultant staffs.

medical practitioners for the provision of general medical and maternity services, with dental practitioners for dental treatment, and with registered pharmacists for the supply of medicines.

Under Part III of the Act the major Local Authorities are renamed Local Health Authorities, and in addition to the existing services are given duties for the care of mothers and young children, domiciliary midwifery, health visiting, home nursing, vaccination and immunisation, prevention of illness, care and after-care, and the provision of the domestic help service. The majority of these duties were extensions of the existing services, but the powers conferred by Section 27—Prevention of Illness, Care and After-Care—giving scope for considerable developments, have not yet been fully employed.

To the Local Health Authority there still remain the environmental services dealing with the health of the family at home, the prevention of illness, the control of infectious disease, the supervision of food and its distribution, the control of atmospheric pollution, the continuance of the fight against tuberculosis, the Maternity and Child Welfare and School Health Services, and many other duties which have continued over the past years.

Hospital Service

The city's composite hospital system of to-day has been built up over the years from three principal sources—voluntary effort, the Parish authorities and the Public Health Authority. The earliest general hospital in Glasgow was that of St. Nicholas, founded about 1456. This was followed by Hutchesons' Hospital in 1639 and the Town's Hospital in 1733. These institutions no longer exist as such, although Hutchesons' Hospital still survives in the form of an educational trust. The earliest existing hospital is the Royal Infirmary, which was opened in 1794, having received its Charter in 1791. This was followed by the Western Infirmary in 1874 and the Victoria in 1890. At the same time there were growing up two parallel systems, namely, those of the Parochial Boards (Parish Councils after 1894) and the Public Health Authority. The Parish hospitals were gradually developing from the infirmaries of the poorhouses, while the Public Health Authority were establishing fever hospitals for the purpose of protecting the public by the isolation of infectious disease. The earliest of these was the Kennedy Street Hospital, opened in 1865. Indeed, this hospital was not only the earliest in Glasgow but was the first fever hospital as such in Scotland. Prior to 1865, infectious disease had been treated in the wards of the Royal Infirmary.

Following upon the passing of the Local Government (Scotland) Act, 1929, the hospitals of the Parish Council and the Public Health Authority were amalgamated under one administration, the Public Health Department. At that time the Parish Council general hospitals had accommodation for some 2,500 patients, while the infectious diseases hospitals which had had their beginnings in the Kennedy Street

TABLE

WESTERN REGIONAL

HOSPITALS UNDER THE CONTROL OF BOARDS

	Type				Other Special Branches of Surgery							
Hospital	*General, Unclassified or Misc.*	*Chronic Sick and Geriatric*	*General Medicine*	*General Surgery*	*Ear, Nose & Throat*	*Ophthalmic*	*Orthopædic*	*Neurosurgery*	*Urology*	*Burns & Plastic*	*Thoracic*	*Cancer*
1 Royal Infirmary	52	...	240	416	50	...	12	...	38	36	...	...
2 Western Infirmary	...	...	189	230	32	20	45	...	35	10	10	...
3 Victoria Infirmary	50	...	126	177	32	8	50	...	20	...	...	...
4 Stobhill	92	79	269	144	66	12	...	12	...	...	...	...
5 Southern General	191	62	281	126	28	4	...	...	...	...	...	...
6 Eastern District	...	...	109	52	...	...	...	...	...	...	...	...
7 Western District	...	...	111	57	12	...	...	...	...	...	...	...
8 R.H.S.C., Yorkhill	...	...	...	...	...	...	32	...	...	...	...	...
9 R.H.S.C., Drumchapel	...	...	...	...	...	...	...	...	...	...	...	...
10 R.H.S.C., Strathblane	...	...	...	...	...	...	...	...	...	...	...	...
11 Royal Beatson Memorial	...	...	...	...	...	...	...	...	...	...	...	70
12 Canniesburn Auxiliary	42	...	...	...	...	...	...	...	...	10	...	...
13 Glasgow Royal Maternity	...	...	...	...	...	...	...	...	...	...	...	...
14 Ross Maternity, Paisley	...	...	...	...	...	...	...	...	...	...	...	...
15 Redlands	...	...	...	...	...	...	...	...	4	...	...	...
16 Royal Samaritan	...	...	...	...	...	...	...	...	...	...	...	...
17 Philipshill Auxiliary	60	...	...	...	...	...	120	...	...	...	...	...
18 David Elder Infirmary	...	...	...	15	...	...	...	...	...	...	...	...
19 Elder Cottage	30	...	...	...	...	...	...	...	...	...	...	...
20 Shieldhall	...	120	...	...	...	...	...	...	...	...	...	...
21 Ear, Nose & Throat	...	...	...	...	113	...	...	...	...	...	...	...
22 Eye Infirmary	...	...	...	...	...	113	...	...	...	...	...	...
23 Ophthalmic Institution	...	...	...	...	...	36	...	...	...	...	...	...
24 Schaw Home, Bearsden	...	70	...	...	...	...	...	...	...	...	...	...
25 Foresthall (Hospital Portion)	...	640	...	...	...	...	...	...	...	...	...	...
26 Homœopathic	30	...	...	...	...	...	...	...	...	...	...	...
27 Homœopathic (Children)	28	...	...	...	...	...	...	...	...	...	...	...
28 Belvidere	...	...	...	...	...	...	...	...	...	...	...	...
29 Ruchill	...	...	...	...	...	...	...	...	...	...	...	...
30 Knightswood	...	...	...	...	...	...	...	...	...	...	46	...
31 Robroyston	...	...	...	...	...	...	...	...	...	...	...[1]	...
32 Mearnskirk	150	...	50 (Chest)	...	50	...	75	...	...	...	52	...
33 Bellefield Sanatorium, Lanark	...	...	...	...	...	...	...	...	...	...	...	...
34 Baird Street Auxiliary	...	...	...	...	...	...	...	...	...	...	...	...
35 Lady Hozier Home, Lanark	...	...	...	...	...	...	...	...	...	...	...	...
36 G'gow Convalescent Home, Lenzie	...	...	...	...	...	...	...	...	...	...	...	...
37 Brooksby Home, Largs	...	...	...	...	...	...	...	...	...	...	...	...
38 Killearn	60	...	60	...	...	...	172	112	...	...	...	...
39 Dental Hospital	...	...	...	...	...	...	...	...	...	...	...	...
40 Glasgow Royal Mental	...	...	...	...	...	...	...	...	...	...	...	...
41 Gartloch	...	...	130	...	...	...	...	...	...	...	...	...
42 Stoneyetts	...	...	...	...	...	...	...	...	...	...	...	...
43 Woodilee	...	...	...	...	...	...	...	...	...	...	...	...
44 Hawkhead	...	...	...	...	...	...	...	...	...	...	...	...
45 Caldwell House, Uplawmoor	...	...	...	...	...	...	...	...	...	...	...	...
46 Lennox Castle	...	...	...	...	...	...	...	...	...	...	...	...
47 Waverley Park, Kirkintilloch	...	...	...	...	...	...	...	...	...	...	...	...
Total	785	962	1565	1217	383	193	506	124	97	56	108	70

1 See Respiratory Tuberculosis.

CIX

HOSPITAL BOARD

OF MANAGEMENT IN THE GLASGOW AREA

of Bed

	Pædiatric														
	Medicine	*Surgery*	*Non-respiratory Tuberculosis*	*Respiratory Tuberculosis*	*Other Infectious Diseases*	*Gynæcology*	*Obstetric*	*Dermatology*	*Mental Observation Wards*	*Mental Hospital*	*Mental Defective*	*Convalescent and Recovery*	*Authorised Bed Complement*	*Out-patient Attendances for year ended 31 December 1955*	*Date of Opening*
1	...	...	...	...	...	50	...	24	...	...	...	...	918	399,275	1794
2	...	...	...	...	...	48	...	20	...	...	...	...	639	354,900	1874
3	...	...	...	...	...	28	...	12	...	...	...	...	503	282,443	1890
4	138	36	...	32	...	100	102	120	180	...	...	...	1,373	113,073	1904
5	28	...	...	25	...	8	63	52	80	180	...	...	1,128	143,248	1874
6	10	...	...	...	...	10	44	...	58	...	...	...	283	39,390	1904
7	9	...	...	...	...	19	46	...	...	...	...	...	254	68,150	1904
8	92	188	...	...	...	...	...	...	...	...	...	...	312	84,242	1882
9	60	40	...	...	...	...	...	...	...	...	...	...	100	—	1903
10	40	...	...	...	...	...	...	...	...	...	...	...		—	1913
11	...	...	...	...	...	...	...	...	...	...	...	...	70	1,607	1896
12	...	...	...	...	...	...	...	...	...	...	...	80	132	—	1938
13	30	...	...	...	...	15	150	...	...	...	...	...	195	65,507	1834
14	3	...	...	...	...	...	49	...	...	...	...	...	52	—	1956
15	...	...	...	...	...	43	23	...	...	...	...	...	70	9,212	1903
16	...	...	...	...	...	189	...	...	...	...	...	...	189	11,237	1886
17	...	...	...	...	...	...	...	...	...	...	...	...	180	870	1929
18	...	...	...	...	...	35	...	...	...	...	...	...	50	3,551	1925
19	...	...	...	...	...	...	...	...	...	...	...	...	30	12,568	1901
20	...	...	...	...	...	...	...	...	...	...	...	...	120	—	1895
21	...	...	...	...	...	...	...	...	...	...	...	...	113	44,546	1925
22	...	...	...	...	...	...	...	...	...	...	...	...	113	131,266	1824
23	...	...	...	...	...	...	...	...	...	...	...	...	36	33,777	1868
24	...	...	...	...	...	...	...	...	...	...	...	...	70	—	1895
25	...	...	...	...	...	...	...	...	...	...	...	...	640	—	
26	...	...	...	...	...	...	...	...	...	...	...	...	30	1,223	1914
27	...	...	...	...	...	...	...	...	...	...	...	...	28	344	1921
28	...	...	...	100	544	...	...	...	...	...	...	...	644	33,487	1870
29	...	...	...	214	450	...	...	...	...	...	...	...	710	34,956	1900
30	...	...	...	60	160	...	...	...	...	...	...	...	220	2,261	1877
31	12	...	193	424	185	...	80	...	...	...	...	...	894	7,922	1917
32	...	...	175	180	...	...	...	...	...	...	...	...	732	10,276	1930
33	...	...	...	108	...	...	...	...	...	...	...	...	108	387	1906
34	...	...	...	36	16	...	...	...	...	...	...	...	52	49,745	1906
35	...	...	...	...	...	...	...	...	...	...	...	30	30	—	1892
36	...	...	...	...	...	...	...	...	...	...	...	55	55	—	1864
37	...	...	...	...	...	...	...	...	...	...	...	30	30	—	1897
38	...	...	...	...	...	...	...	...	...	...	...	...	404	2,756	1940
39	...	...	...	...	...	...	...	...	...	...	...	...	—	65,849	1885
40	...	...	...	...	...	...	...	...	...	830	...	...	830	4,910	1814
41	...	...	...	...	...	...	...	...	...	841	...	...	971	2,043	1896
42	...	...	...	...	...	...	...	...	...	340	...	...	340	—	1913
43	...	...	...	...	...	...	...	...	...	1284	...	...	1,230	1,337	1875
44	...	...	...	...	...	...	...	...	...	1230	...	...	1,284	—	1895
45	...	...	...	...	...	...	...	...	...	...	127	...	127	—	
46	10	...	...	...	...	30	132	...	...	...	1380	...	1,552	1,385	
47	...	...	...	...	...	...	...	...	...	...	145	...	145	—	
	432	264	368	1179	1355	575	689	228	318	4705	1652	195	18,026	2,017,743	

SOURCE: Western Regional Hospital Board.

Hospital, now no longer in use, could provide accommodation for almost 2,000 patients. In addition, over 1,000 beds were available for the treatment of tuberculosis.

A steady development took place in the status of the general hospitals, and by 1948 their accommodation had been increased from 2,500 until there were in Stobhill, Southern General, Eastern and Western District Hospitals some 3,300 beds. The National Health Service (Scotland) Act, 1947, brought about a further step in the combination of the hospital facilities by the amalgamation of the Corporation and voluntary hospitals, so that the services originally provided by these separate authorities were now provided by one, the National Health Service. At the time of the actual amalgamation in 1948 the three voluntary hospitals, the Western, Royal and Victoria Infirmaries, including Canniesburn and Philipshill Auxiliary Hospitals, possessed a combined total of 2,309 beds, the four municipal general hospitals 3,406 beds, while the fever hospitals and sanatoria belonging to the municipality contributed a total of 3,660 beds, of which 1,500 were for the treatment of infectious disease and 1,540 for the treatment of tuberculosis, the remainder being scattered amongst them and used for such purposes as ear, nose and throat, maternity and gynæcology.

At this time also there were transferred from the Corporation to the Western Regional Hospital Board the various *ad hoc* clinics and dispensaries for the treatment and control of tuberculosis (5), venereal disease (4), and trachoma (1).

Table CIX gives the dates of opening, present bed accommodation, and out-patient attendances of the various hospitals in the Glasgow area now under the control of the Western Regional Hospital Board.

General Practitioner Service

As already stated, the Executive Council administers the scheme for the provision of general medical, dental, pharmaceutical and supplementary ophthalmic services. The Executive Council includes members representing the public and the medical, dental and pharmaceutical professions.

The number of doctors on the list of the Executive Council for the city and providing general medical services is 544. On these doctors' registers are 1,061,000 patients. There are in addition 131 doctors on the Glasgow list whose principal practice is outwith the city but who are responsible for 19,000 Glasgow patients. These latter doctors are also on the list of the Executive Councils of the surrounding areas. Some 12 doctors are on the Glasgow list for limited purposes such as the provision of medical services in institutions or camps or for maternity services only.

The maximum number of patients a doctor may have on his list varies according to his method of working. If he is a single-handed practitioner it is 3,500; for a practitioner with one assistant 5,500; for a member of a partnership 4,500 provided that the average list of the partnership does not exceed 3,500. Taking into account only doctors providing full medical services whose reference numbers are allocated through the Glasgow Executive Council, i.e. 532, the average number of patients on these doctors' lists is around 2,000. More than half the doctors have a list ranging from 1,000 to 3,500, although there are a few practitioners with as many as 5,000 patients.

Payment for general medical services is mainly by way of a capitation fee, to which have to be added fees for special services, for example, maternity services. The usual form of practice is the partnership of two or more doctors, in most cases two or three. There is still a considerable body of single-handed practitioners, although the general trend is against this type of practice. Applications for inclusion in the list of the Executive Council come from practitioners wishing to join an existing partnership, from successful applicants for vacancies following on the death or retiral of a practitioner, and from doctors wishing to set up new single-handed practice or a new partnership. These applications are considered by the Executive Council after obtaining the views of the Local Medical Committee, a statutory committee composed almost wholly of general medical practitioners. Any decision of the Executive Council must receive the acquiescence of the Scottish Medical Practices Committee.

The number of dentists on the list of the Executive Council as principals is 268 and as assistants 15. Unlike the medical practitioners who have a registered clientele and are remunerated by capitation fee for each patient, the dental practitioners are remunerated for services carried out. When the National Health Service (Scotland) Act, 1947, first came into operation all treatment and appliances were free. A limited charge is now made for conservative treatment and for dentures.

Supplementary ophthalmic services are provided by 28 ophthalmic medical practitioners and 220 ophthalmic opticians on the list of the Council. The number of prescriptions dispensed during the year ending 31 March 1956 involved 118,000 pairs of spectacles.

The pharmaceutical services are provided by 261 pharmacists on the list of the Council operating from 345 chemist shops. The number of prescription forms submitted during the year ending March 1956 was 3,602,640, and the cost £1,313,000. Patients are now required to pay a fee for each prescription dispensed.

Local Health Authority Services

Maternity and Child Welfare Service

Immense advances have been made in saving maternal and infant life and in improving the health of the school child, although the position revealed by our vital statistics still does not compare favourably with that of most other urban health authorities.

The present form of the Maternity and Child Welfare Service belongs to this century. Towards the close of last century the failure of sanitation to bring down the infant mortality rate to any great extent was attracting the attention of hygienists. The position in Glasgow at that time is shown in Table CX.

TABLE CX

DEATHS OF INFANTS PER 1,000 BIRTHS AT SEVERAL PERIODS

Period	0-3 *Months*	3-6 *Months*	6-12 *Months*	*Average Infant Mortality per* 1,000
1880-82	65	25	58	148
1890-92	70	25	54	149
1900-02	72	26	47	145

The increase in the diarrhœal death rate was almost entirely due to an increase in the deaths of children under 5 years of age, and in the wards of the city where this increase was occurring there was also a rise in the infant mortality rate. Consequently, this latter rate came to be regarded as an index of insanitary conditions. Causes of infant mortality other than insanitary surroundings were, however, operative, for example, illegitimacy.

TABLE CXI

GLASGOW—INFANT DEATHS PER 1,000 BIRTHS

	1880-2	1891-3[1]	1900-2
Legitimate Births	138	139	136
Illegitimate Births	266	259	265

Certain tentative administrative measures bearing on the welfare of infants and particularly infants artificially fed were taken in Glasgow in 1903 with the opening of a milk depot in Osborne Street. Milk for infants was sold both from this depot and throughout the city with the help of the retail dairies. Visitation of families supplied with this milk was undertaken voluntarily by individuals and by the Queen Margaret Settlement and various Church Committees. In October 1906 the first "infant consultation" was opened at the Settlement, to be followed in May 1907 by one in Milton Street School, Cowcaddens. Classes for mothers were also held at these centres. The first child welfare medical officer was appointed in 1906 and the first health visitor in 1907.

The Notification of Births Acts of 1907 and 1915 really created the Maternity and Child Welfare Service. The later Act enabled local authorities, with the aid of a 50 per cent grant, to make such arrange-

[1] Information for 1890 not available.

ments as they thought fit for attending to the health of the expectant and nursing mothers and of children under five years. This Act along with the Maternity and Child Welfare Act, 1918, conferred the widest possible powers on local authorities. These powers are now contained in Section 22 of the National Health Service (Scotland) Act, 1947. Additional powers are contained in Section 23 of this Act, under which it is the duty of the local health authority to provide midwives for domiciliary confinements.

In the early years of the twentieth century the care provided for the expectant mother was minimal. The great majority of mothers, unless some serious complication arose, had no ante-natal care and did not consult a doctor during pregnancy. There was no supervision of the domiciliary midwifery practice until the Midwives (Scotland) Act was passed in 1915. In 1916 the Corporation arranged that an ante-natal clinic would be held in the Royal Maternity Hospital and at Govan Maternity Home, the latter being staffed by a local authority child welfare medical officer and health visitors. The Corporation also made a grant towards the opening of a ward for ante-natal cases at the Royal Maternity Hospital. By 1923 ante-natal sessions had been established at three child welfare centres. These proved most successful, and gradually over the years a considerable development of the Corporation's ante-natal service took place. This extension became necessary when the Central Midwives Board ruled in 1931 that no midwife could accept a patient for confinement until the mother secured a medical certificate that she was a suitable case for home confinement by a midwife. Large numbers of women began to seek ante-natal advice at the clinics and a particularly rapid development took place in the early 1930's. By 1947 the number of expectant mothers seen at these clinics was 13,000 out of a total of 26,000 births which took place in the city in that year.

Under the Local Government (Scotland) Act, 1929, the general hospitals formerly administered by the Parish Councils were transferred to the Corporation and thereafter obstetric units were opened for all these hospitals. The supervision of the expectant mother was developed as a co-ordinated scheme of ante-natal clinics at the child welfare centre, and consultative clinics and maternity bed accommodation at the hospitals. With the passing of the National Health Service Act the hospital clinics and indoor accommodation were transferred to the Regional Hospital Board. Since 1948 no addition has been made to the maternity accommodation, and the proportion of births taking place in hospital still stands at approximately 50 per cent, although the total number of births has diminished to 20,000 per annum. Attendances at the local health authority clinics have declined steadily, and in 1955 fewer than 6,000 mothers received ante-natal care there.

The nursing attendance at the 8,000 births which take place at home is almost entirely provided by the domiciliary midwifery service of the Corporation. Only a small number of expectant mothers book a private maternity nurse. All midwives and maternity nurses in domiciliary practice are supervised by the Medical Officer of Health under the Midwives (Scotland) Act, 1951. The number of midwives in 1955 who notified their intention to carry on domiciliary practice, including the whole-time staff of the Corporation, was 155. They attended 8,000 births. Of this number approximately 6,500 were also attended by a medical practitioner; in such cases the midwife acts as a maternity nurse and does not carry full responsibility.

For the assistance of all expectant mothers who have their babies at home, the Corporation supply sterilised maternity outfits. During 1955, 8,596 outfits were provided. As an additional help to expectant and nursing mothers, a home help service is available to them for one or two weeks either during their pregnancy or after the confinement. Some 2,500 expectant and nursing mothers engaged the services of home helps during 1955.

Over the years there has been continuous development of the Child Welfare Service, and at the present time there are 28 centres providing 78 ante-natal and post-natal sessions and 102 child welfare sessions weekly.

The National Health Service has provided a doctor for every person, and therefore it might be expected that there would be less need for the maternity and child welfare services. It is true that a considerable reduction has taken place in the proportion of expectant mothers attending the ante-natal clinics. On the other hand, as will be seen from the following table, the infant consultations after passing through a phase during which the attendances dropped steeply have now risen again to levels above the pre-1948 figures. This rise does appear to indicate that the child welfare centres are meeting a real need, that the mothers are being given an opportunity for the careful assessment of their children's progress and are receiving satisfactory answers to their many doubts and difficulties.

TABLE CXII

ATTENDANCES AT INFANT CONSULTATIONS

	Under 1 Year		*Over 1 Year*	
	No. of Attendances		*No. of Attendances*	
Year	*Primary*	*Subsequent*	*Primary*	*Subsequent*
1947	12,104	117,904	1,123	26,795
1948	10,221	105,124	983	28,919
1949	9,120	85,536	917	24,898
1950	8,688	80,832	856	22,574
1951	8,846	80,213	762	21,180
1952	9,223	83,114	2,952	18,624
1953	9,678	86,958	3,275	19,829
1954	9,752	85,729	3,263	20,190
1955	10,155	87,735	3,863	21,374

The provision of help to mothers who are supporting their children —widows and unmarried mothers—is very necessary in a large industrial city like Glasgow. Present day conditions of full employment have brought social difficulties, particularly where a mother falls ill even for a short time or is removed to hospital and cannot arrange for the care of her children. To this end the Corporation provides 15 day nurseries open five days a week from 8 a.m. till 6 p.m., and one 24-hour nursery which closes only at weekends. Where a mother falls ill children up to five years have been provided for in two residential homes where the length of stay of any child is limited to one month. For prolonged care, help must be sought from the Children's Department.

The results of the past forty years' work are only partly illustrated by the success so far obtained in reducing maternal and child mortality. The most outstanding improvement has been the reduction in the maternal mortality rate, i.e. the number of mothers who die in proportion to every thousand births. In 1915, it was 6.37; in 1935, 7.01; and in 1955, 0.33. The infant mortality rate, i.e. the number of children under one year who die proportionate to every thousand live births, was 143 in 1915; 98 in 1935; and 36 in 1955. A further striking improvement in child health is the marked decline in deaths of children between one and five years. In 1915 the rate per thousand children in this age group was 36.2; in 1935, 8.69; and in 1955, 1.26.

We have only to look at the children of Glasgow to appreciate that the excellent work of the Maternity and Child Welfare Service is not reflected solely in a reduction in death rates. Much, however, remains to be done. The most disturbing factor shown in the vital statistics is the decreasing rate of fall in the infant and neo-natal mortality and still birth rates.

TABLE CXIII

GLASGOW INFANT MORTALITY

Year	*Still Birth Rate per* 1,000 *Live and Still Births*	*Neo-natal Mortality per* 1,000 *Births*	*Infant Mortality per* 1,000 *Births*
1947	32	35.5	77
1948	32	29.3	56
1949	30	25.3	49
1950	29	24.6	44
1951	28	25.9	46
1952	27	24.1	41
1953	27	22.2	36
1954	29	21.5	35
1955	27	22.7	36

It is generally agreed that expectant mothers require education in mothercraft and diet, but there is insufficient co-operation between the hospitals, the general practitioners and the local authority clinics in this field. Renewed efforts are being made to secure some co-ordinated scheme for this most important educational work. Without this it is unlikely that a reduction in the number of still births and premature births will take place.

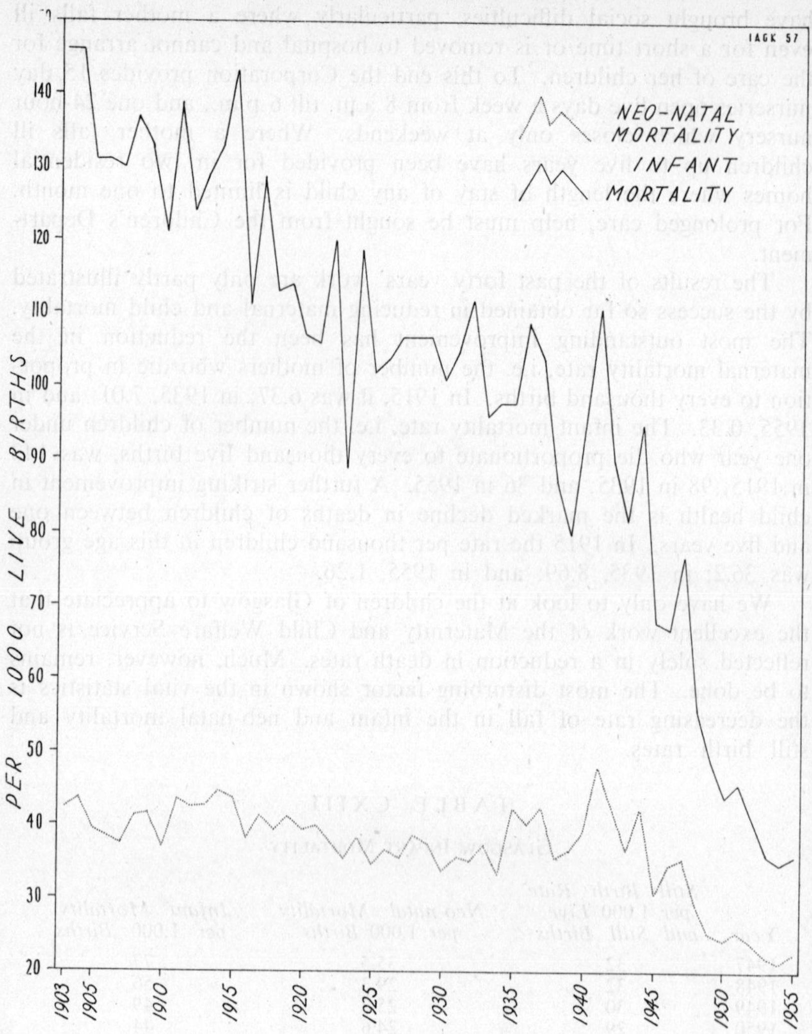

FIG. 30. Infant and Neo-natal Mortality Rates.

School Health Service

The School Health Service was conceived as the result of the general concern at the beginning of the present century regarding the unsatisfactory condition of the nation's health as indicated by the high death rate of infants under one year of age, the falling birth rate and the poor physique of Army recruits during the South African War. Reports issued by the Royal Commission on Physical Training (Scotland) in 1903 and the Inter-Departmental Committee on Physical Deterioration in 1904 stressed the need for systematic medical inspection in schools in order that the nation's health could be properly assessed and measures of a remedial or ameliorative nature applied with reasonable hope of success.

In 1904 the Medical Officer of Health for Glasgow (the late Dr. A. K. Chalmers) instituted an enquiry into the health and housing conditions of 750 children attending Glasgow schools; while in 1905 the School Board of Glasgow recorded the physical measurements of 72,857 children attending 73 schools and ascertained their housing conditions. Govan Parish School Board in 1907 anticipated the passing of the necessary legislation by initiating the systematic medical inspection of children attending schools in their area.

The Education (Scotland) Act, 1908, actually empowered the formation of a school health service although medical inspection of physically handicapped children was already permissive by the terms of the Education of Defective Children (Scotland) Act, 1906. Under the 1908 Act, a school board[1] was entitled (or compelled at the request of the " Scotch " Education Department) to provide for the medical examination and supervision of pupils attending schools in the area and to employ medical officers or nurses or arrange with voluntary agencies for the supply of nurses, and to provide appliances or other requisites. Authority was also given to take action against parents for neglect where a child was in a filthy or verminous state or was unable by reason of lack of food or clothing to take full advantage of the education provided. In the case of illness or poverty of the parents, a school board could provide for the child while under obligation to attend school or make temporary provision for any child and recover the cost from parent (or guardian) unless poverty or ill-health of parent was substantiated. The Act, however, did not envisage the provision of medical treatment, the inspecting medical officer being authorised merely to advise the parent to obtain the necessary treatment, although food and clothing could be supplied in necessitous cases.

After the Corporation of the city became the Education Authority under the Local Government (Scotland) Act, 1929, the Corporation decided to unite the School Medical Services with the Public Health Department to provide an Education Health Service, this name being altered in 1946 to the School Health Service. During the next twenty years routine medical inspection developed into the examination of children shortly after entry to school, at the age of 9-10 years, and at 13-14 years, with re-examination of special cases. Medical treatment, at first provided only for " necessitous " children, became free under the Education (Scotland) Act, 1946.

One of the most important factors in the health of the school child was the attention given to nutrition. Meals for necessitous school children had been one of the early health measures following on investigation subsequent to the Boer War. By 1922 eleven million

[1] From 1872 to 1918 education was administered by local *ad hoc* authorities called " School Boards."

meals were being supplied during the school year, of which ten million were for necessitous cases. The Education (Scotland) Act, 1942, removed the " necessitous " restriction. The provision of milk in schools was authorised in the Education (Scotland) Act, 1930, and following the passing of the Milk Act, 1934, in Glasgow a ration of one third of a pint per child was supplied at a cost of a halfpenny or free of charge to necessitous cases. School milk became a free issue in August, 1946.

Provision for handicapped children has been increasingly developed since the early 1920's with special schools for physically and mentally defective children. A hostel for blind children was opened in January 1919, and the first sight-saving class in Scotland was instituted early in 1914 at Broomloan Road School, Govan. Special classes were available for the deaf and the partially deaf. Residential school accommodation has been extended and the holiday type of school instituted. In 1945 a scheme of residential school education was inaugurated with four more schools for physically defective children and one for nursery and one for problem children. Accommodation was also available in the Biggart Memorial Children's Home, Prestwick, for physically defective children from Glasgow in need of care.

With the evacuation of children from Glasgow during the Second World War complaints were received from the reception areas, and the prevention of uncleanliness absorbed much of the time and energy of medical and nursing staff. In 1941 a scheme of " hygiene units," in charge of the senior woman assistant, was inaugurated in six selected schools, later increased to 26, to inspect children and encourage personal cleanliness.

As a result of the employment of mothers on war work, more and more nursery schools and day nurseries became necessary. By 1945 there were 25 nursery schools and 36 wartime nurseries with a total of 3,000 places. With the cessation of war the wartime nurseries were discontinued, and there now remain 36 nursery schools with places for 1,400 children and 15 day nurseries with 700 places, and a weekly nursery for 40 children whose mothers are on night-shift work.

The Education (Scotland) Acts, 1945 and 1946, gave powers to insist upon the systematic inspection of pupils, the certification of handicapped children, the classification of ineducable children as trainable and untrainable, and, as already stated, the provision of free medical and dental treatment; and gave increased powers for dealing with uncleanliness. In 1947 a cardiology service was introduced and a heart specialist attended regularly at school clinics. Occupational centres, seven in number, were opened for children classified as ineducable but trainable, and a scheme of home tuition instituted for physically handicapped children unable to attend school.

Since 1948 medical inspections and re-inspections have increased in number, and treatment facilities have also been expanded and the scope widened by the appointment of medical auxiliaries. The hygiene units already mentioned have been supplied with modern equipment and all attendants given a special course of instruction. New clinics have been developed and are planned for the new housing areas. Speech therapy has been made available to children in the schools for the handicapped and dental treatment facilities expanded. Audiometric surveys have now been instituted to detect deafness. A special clinic for asthma cases has operated since 1950, and arrangements for placing in employment physically handicapped young persons have been successfully functioning since 1951.

As the result of medical inspection in schools, continuous records of the physical condition of school children are available since the year 1910—information of a nature which is non-existent for any other group of the population.

That the physical condition of school children has consistently improved is established by the fact that the incidence of bad and very bad nutrition has fallen from 9.1 per cent in 1919-23 to 0.2 per cent in 1954; that the incidence of rickets is now negligible; that the numbers of children with major remediable defects have progressively declined and that those with no defect have increased from 6.7 per cent in 1934 to 48.1 per cent in 1954; and especially that there has been a progressive increase since 1910 in the average heights and weights of pupils. This is shown clearly for pupils in three age groups in Table CXIV.

TABLE CXIV

SCHOOL CHILDREN—AVERAGE HEIGHTS AND WEIGHTS, 1910-1954

	Heights in Inches						*Weights in lbs.*					
	At 5 yrs.		*At 9 yrs.*		*At 13 yrs.*		*At 5 yrs.*		*At 9 yrs.*		*At 13 yrs.*	
	Boys	*Girls*	*Boys*	*Girls*	*Boys*	*Girls*	*Boys*	*Girls*	*Boys*	*Girls*	*Boys*	*Girls*
1910-19	40.4	39.7	47.5	47.3	55.2	55.5	38.5	37.7	54.2	51.8	74.5	76.8
1920-29	40.7	40.2	48.7	48.3	55.5	56.1	39.1	37.9	55.5	53.7	76.8	79.5
1930-39	41.3	41.0	49.6	49.4	56.8	57.7	39.7	38.3	57.9	57.7	81.6	85.9
1940-49	42.0	41.7	50.7	50.3	58.2	58.9	41.5	39.9	60.6	58.9	86.9	91.3
1950-54	42.4	42.1	51.2	50.7	58.8	59.3	42.1	40.5	62.2	60.1	89.8	94.1

In the matter of the clothing and cleanliness of school children the improvement is no less striking. As regards the former, the following figures speak for themselves:

TABLE CXV

SCHOOL CHILDREN—AVERAGE PERCENTAGES WITH DEFECTIVE CLOTHING, 1910-1954

	1910-19	1920-29	1930-39	1940-49	1950-54
Clothing:					
Insufficient	1.3	0.4	0.1	0.1	0.0
Ragged	3.1	1.6	0.3	0.1	0.0
Dirty	2.8	2.0	0.2	0.1	0.1
Totals	7.2	4.0	0.6	0.3	0.1
Footgear:					
Unsatisfactory	2.3	1.0	0.4	0.3	0.1
None	5.2	0.8	0.0	0.0	0.0
Totals	7.5	1.8	0.4	0.3	0.1

Efforts to ensure cleanliness are unremitting. At present three main schemes are in operation:

(1) Cleanliness inspections by school nurses in more than 90 schools under the provisions of the Education (Scotland) Act, 1946 (Section 52), including advice to parents, and if necessary, compulsory cleansing at school or clinic and prosecution of parent for persistent offence. In 1954 cleanliness inspections totalled 167,218, the highest recorded, and 82 cases were referred to the Procurator Fiscal.

(2) Visits to a similar number of other schools by outdoor nurses of the Health and Welfare Department, who also visit the homes of offenders.

(3) Cleanliness supervision by senior women assistants in 26 selected schools.

The figures in Table CXVI show the progress made since 1910, interrupted by the war, but continuing again in the postwar period:

TABLE CXVI

CLEANLINESS OF GLASGOW SCHOOL CHILDREN AT ROUTINE MEDICAL INSPECTION
AVERAGE PERCENTAGES, 1910-1954

	1910-19	1920-29	1930-39	1940-49	1950-54
Head:					
Dirty	2.1	0.7	0.2	0.0	0.0
Nits	20.3	10.5	6.4	11.4	9.4
Vermin		0.8	0.3	0.3	0.2
Body:					
Dirty	1.1	1.3	0.5	0.2	0.1
Vermin	2.8	0.9	0.2	0.1	0.0
Totals	26.3	14.2	7.6	12.0	9.7

Skin diseases have diminished in number steadily. The percentage of school children found on medical inspection to have unsound teeth has fallen from 66.9 per cent in 1914 to 32.5 per cent in 1954; but dental officers still find that at least 75 per cent of the children they examine in a small number of selected schools are in need of treatment. Of external eye diseases, the prevalence of strabismus, which is the most common, shows little decline; but inflammatory conditions, such as conjunctivitis, are much reduced. Defective vision is less prevalent and "bad vision" has declined from 5.3 per cent in 1934 to 2.7 per cent in 1954. In 1954, out of 10,872 children dealt with at refraction clinics, 5,537 had spectacles prescribed. Enlarged tonsils with or without adenoid growths are mainly found among the entrants. Of such cases, 1,600 were admitted, by arrangement with three hospitals, for operation in 1954. For defective hearing, there are routine inspections by medical officers, special examinations at age seven years and an audiometric survey of nine-year-olds. Treatment services, including the services of aurists, are available. Eight speech therapists give treatment to pupils attending ordinary and special schools.

Mental and nervous cases have fallen considerably, the "dull" or "backward" from 2.0 per cent in 1914 to 0.2 in 1954. Heart conditions show little reduction. The cardiology service treats those suffering from heart disease and assesses their ability to pursue ordinary activities. Of lung cases those with acute respiratory conditions, being absent from school, do not come under inspection by school medical officers. Chronic bronchitis, formerly making up a large proportion, is now much reduced; but catarrh is still fairly prevalent, though diminishing as school age advances. For deformities, which are few, treatment is carried out at four orthopædic clinics and those in need of institutional treatment are admitted to Mearnskirk Hospital. A new school for spastics (opened January 1955) includes medical auxiliaries—two physiotherapists and a speech therapist. Treatment facilities provided through the School Health Service are thus comprehensive. The school clinic acts

(1) as a centre for specialist examination and treatment, and
(2) as a convenient place where large numbers of children suffering from minor ailments may receive treatment with the minimum loss of school time.

Without the co-operation of the teaching staffs, the objects of the school medical service would be unattainable and health progress can only be assured if parent, teacher and medical officer work in harmony. There are signs that this is being steadily accomplished, and there is no doubt that the school teachers have made and continue to make a valuable contribution by their personal interest in the children. The preservation of health is also influenced by environment and advances have been made in this connection for school children by the increasing number of schools erected on open-air principles, and by the provision of gymnasia and playing fields. Unfortunately, many of the existing schools, especially in the congested areas, are ill-adapted for this purpose and the most ideal conditions exist in the new housing schemes where modern schools and recreation facilities are provided.

Health Visiting Service

Health visitors are nurses who have undergone a special course of training for the Health Visitor Certificate. The Health Visiting Service had its origin in the Glasgow Infant Health Visitors' Association, a voluntary body consisting of ladies who visited homes where there were infants and gave advice and encouragement. This Association rendered valuable assistance to the Health Department for close on forty years.

Whole-time health visitors (Glasgow's highly popular "Green Ladies") were first appointed in the city in 1907 as one of the measures to combat the high infant and maternal mortality rates of the period.

The duty of the whole-time health visitor was mainly to teach mothers the rules regarding the maintenance of health. In 1908 Glasgow appointed three special female visitors, certified midwives with training in diseases of children. During the years which followed additional staff were appointed as the need arose. Although much voluntary work still continued, it became increasingly organised and linked with the statutory service developed after the passing of the 1915 Notification of Births (Extension) Act. Health visitors were also being appointed for the visitation and care of tuberculous patients and nurses were being attached to the School Medical Service.

Provision for full-time qualified staff began in 1925 with the institution of special training courses and examinations for nurses who wished to become health visitors. In Glasgow there has been since 1932 a training scheme conducted by the Corporation in co-operation with the University of Glasgow. Admission to the course is restricted to nurses who have had general nursing training, are State-registered, and have taken at least Part I of the midwifery training. An extension of the course was undertaken in 1941 by the appointment of a full-time tutor and by a scheme for assisting students by payment of a modified salary during the course of training.

The functions of the health visitor are primarily health education and the giving of advice on domestic problems. Her work in Glasgow at present includes the care of mothers and young children, the prevention of illness, and the after-care of tuberculous patients. Under some local authorities the health visitor has general duties on all public health problems in her area, including the health and welfare of the aged and handicapped, the care and after-care of chronic illness, and co-operation with general practitioners and hospitals. There is a considerable body who hold that the health visitor should be the principal medico-social worker in an area, dealing with all types of social problems. The Report of a recent enquiry into health visiting visualises her as a family visitor with a small district working closely with the general practitioner and the hospitals, and truly a medico-social worker playing a full part in both preventive and social medicine. On the other hand, her training and experience are of greatest use in the prevention of illness and disease by the education of parents and children.

In Glasgow some 235 health visitors are employed, 112 attached to the maternity and child welfare service, 43 to the tuberculosis service and 80 to the school health service. Owing to the shortage of trained health visitors, it has been necessary to employ on a temporary basis nurses with an initial general nursing and midwifery training.

Home Help Service

The Home Help Service provides domestic assistance where a mother has taken ill or where there are patients at home requiring domestic assistance. A Home Help Service to assist pregnant and recently confined mothers was started in a voluntary way many years ago but it was not until 1924 that the scheme of home help, restricted to maternity cases, was administered directly by the Public Health Department. At that time 30 home helps were employed and paid at the rate of 5s. a day. This early scheme continued until the early years of the war when the supply of suitable helps dwindled with the increase of women on munition work. The scheme was resuscitated in May 1941, and was restricted to families in which there was a pregnant or recently confined mother or a case of chronic disease unlikely to benefit by hospital treatment. Since the war increasing use has been made of the Home Help Service, and when the National Health Service (Scotland) Act came into force in July 1948 there were 368 home helps on the register.

During 1950 a scheme of domestic helps for tuberculous families was brought into operation to provide domiciliary care for tuberculous patients who were being nursed in their own homes while awaiting admission to hospital or after dismissal. Volunteers were invited and 45 home helps were specially enrolled. These home helps must be over 40 years of age, have no children under 15 years of age resident in their own homes, and undergo a complete medical examination and check-up every six months.

Table CXVII shows the work carried out by the Home Help Service.

TABLE CXVII

GLASGOW—HOME HELP SERVICE
CASES ASSISTED

	1953	1954	1955
Maternity	2,470	2,312	2,341
General	3,708	3,810	4.104
Tuberculosis	101	159	183
	6,279	6,281	6,628

The Home Help Service is not intended to provide permanent domestic helps but to give an opportunity for families to make their own arrangements for securing assistance. There is therefore a limit to the period for which the home help is provided. It has been necessary however to make provision for the special group of old folks living alone and included in the general section of the service are 1,291 cases receiving extended service, of whom 91 per cent are over 60 years of age.

There are at present 1,087 domestic helps employed by the local health authority, 465 on a whole-time and 622 on a part-time basis. The charge for the Home Help Service to individual patients varies according to means. The sliding scale provides for a minimum charge of 3s. per day (1s. 6d. per half-day) and a maximum of six guineas per week of 5½ days. During the year ended May 1956, the Domestic Help Service cost a total of £244,000. The revenue obtained from families was £54,000, leaving the balance to be met equally by Government grant and local rates.

Home Nursing Service

The Home Nursing Service has a long tradition in Glasgow. The work of district nursing was started by Mrs. Mary Orrell Higginbotham in Glasgow in 1875. Mrs. Higginbotham, realising the need of a skilled home nursing service for those who were unable to pay for it, anticipated the Queen Victoria Nurses by twelve years. She herself went into the homes of people who had to contend with sickness as well as

TABLE CXVIII

GLASGOW—HOME NURSING STAFF

	1955
Senior Superintendent of Home Nursing	1
Superintendents of Homes	5
Assistant Superintendents	5
	11
Queen's Nurses on General Nursing Work	80
Queen's Nurses on Maternity Work	21
State-registered Nurses in training for Queen's Roll	12
State-registered Nurses doing full-time Nursing	3
State-registered Nurses doing part-time Nursing	14
Queen's Nurses undertaking Midwifery Training in the District	—
Queen's Nurses undertaking Part I Training in Hospital	—
	141

poverty, and was thus the first district nurse in Scotland. The object of the Association she founded was "to provide thoroughly trained, experienced and reliable nurses to attend the sick poor free of charge and the working classes at a moderate fee." The district nurses visited first in the Anderston area and later in Cowcaddens and the south side of the city. In 1891 the Association was affiliated to the Queen Victoria Jubilee Institute, now the Queen's Institute of District Nursing. In 1892 there were 14 nurses on the Association's staff. The work of the staff continued to increase in all areas until the Glasgow District Nursing Association was responsible for the district nursing in all parts of the city with the exception of the Springburn and Scotstoun areas. For many years the Association has given district training to State-registered nurses and it is recognised as a training institution for pupil midwives taking the second section of their certificate course.

On the coming into operation of the National Health Service (Scotland) Act, 1947, local health authorities were obliged to provide a Home Nursing Service. In some areas the authorities absorbed the existing district nursing service, but in Glasgow it was decided that the District Nursing Association should operate as the agency of the Corporation. The local health authority is responsible for all expenditure and the provision of all new services, but the Association remains as a local training organisation.

The district nurses work in close association with the general practitioner and carry out his instructions in the care of the patients. During the year 1955 they nursed some 13,000 patients, paying 400,000 visits. The majority of the patients suffered from medical conditions, but there were also some 1,750 midwifery cases.

In addition to home nurses from the local authority Home Nursing Service, nursing help is also available from nursing agencies. These organisations are controlled by the Nurses' Agencies (Scotland) Regulations, 1945, made under powers conferred by the Nurses (Scotland) Act, 1943. In 1947 ten agencies were registered with the local authority; in 1955 the number of agencies on the roll was six.

Conclusion

The successes of the past hundred years are monuments to the men and women who devoted their lives to public health, in particular the Medical Officers of Health of the City of Glasgow, Sir William Gairdner, James B. Russell, A. K. Chalmers, Sir Alexander Macgregor and Stuart Laidlaw. Their thoughts were for the problems not only of the community but also of the individual, and they spent much of their time bringing to the recognition of the public the conditions existing in the city.

Many of the problems of the past remain with us. Sanitation, water supply and cleansing demand continued action, but housing has become a major public health concern and overcrowding recognised as a cardinal factor in the spread of disease. Tuberculosis is still a disease to be reckoned with, although the death rate is falling rapidly. Constant watch is maintained for the older infections like smallpox and plague, but now receiving attention are such diseases as poliomyelitis, coronary thrombosis and lung cancer.

Education, nutrition and the personal health services have made possible happier and healthier children than the city has ever known. Children born to-day have an expectation of life twenty years longer than those born in 1900, and the death rate among infants and children has fallen to a fraction of what it was in the past.

Now coming to the fore are ideas not on physical but on mental health—problems of behaviour and maladjustment and the development of measures to ensure a well-balanced individual, family and community life. These problems will form the work of future years and are no less important to-day than the sanitary defects and the major infections of the 1850's.

Chapter 16

EDUCATION

JOHN HIGHET

SCHOOLS

Types of Courses and of Schools

GLASGOW parents, like parents in other parts of Scotland and in England and Wales, are under statutory obligation to provide efficient education for their children between five and fifteen years of age.[1] Normally this means that the Glasgow child, willy-nilly, attends a school for a minimum of ten years of his young life. He may, however, start the process of learning, albeit very informally, any time after the age of two at a private or education authority nursery school; and at the end of the compulsory school period, full-time day or part-time day or evening instruction is available to him, if he desires or can be persuaded to take advantage of it, at schools or other educational institutes.

For the first stage—normally a period of seven years—of his compulsory school career the child attends a primary school. From here he passes, usually between the ages of 11½ and 12½, to the secondary division. A variety of secondary courses is offered, but they fall into two broad types: one of three years' duration designed mainly for those not likely to remain at school after the statutory leaving age, and the other of five or six years' duration designed for those intending to remain at school to take the Scottish Leaving Certificate, normally at the age of 17. These courses, and the schools providing them, are generally referred to, respectively, as junior and senior secondary. Some secondary schools—Glasgow has several of this type—accept all the post-primary pupils in their school area and offer as far as possible the whole range of secondary courses. Schools of this type are sometimes called "omnibus" and sometimes (as in Glasgow) "comprehensive" schools.

In order to get a reasonably clear picture of the pattern of education in Glasgow and of its national background, it is necessary to spend some time in defining terms. By "grant-aided school" is meant a school in respect of which grants are made from the Education (Scotland) Fund to the managers of the school, and it includes a public school. A public school, to the Scots, is not (as, quaintly, it is south of the border) a private school: it is a school under the management

1 Sixteen years of age in the case of a child for whom special educational provision is necessary (for example, a physically or mentally handicapped child).

of an education committee exercising powers delegated to them by a Town or County Council as Education Authority.

These are the meanings the Scottish Education Department attach to these terms in official publications. In less formal usage, however, "grant-aided" tends to signify a school under voluntary management (by a Trust or Board of Governors) which receives a grant direct from the Department (even although it may also receive a financial contribution from the Education Authority of its area): that is to say, a grant-aided school other than a public school. The Department acknowledge this usage in their own frequent practice, which is inconsistent with the pure logic of their definitions, of referring to "public and other grant-aided schools." In this chapter we shall adopt the less formal phraseology, and grant-aided schools other than public schools we shall refer to as "direct-grant schools."[1]

All public and direct-grant schools are required to conform to the regulations laid down by the Secretary of State for Scotland and set out in the Schools (Scotland) Code.[2] The remaining Scottish schools (apart from the special category of Approved Schools[3]) providing full-time education for five or more pupils of school age are designated "independent schools." These schools are not subject to the requirements of the Code, but the Secretary of State has a duty to cause inspection to be made of these as of public and direct-grant schools. An education authority may include an independent school in its scheme of educational provision if the school's accommodation and educational provision, and the qualifications of its teaching staff, are acceptable to the authority.[4] An independent school so included in an authority's scheme may receive from the authority a contribution making good its deficit on the year's working. A representative of the authority sits on the board of management of a contribution-receiving independent school, but this arrangement in practice diminishes scarcely at all the independent character of these schools.

1 The Department have recently altered their definitions to "Public School: any school under the management of an Education Authority"; "Grant-aided School: a school, other than a public school, in respect of which grants are made from the Education (Scotland) Fund to the managers of the school." As a result of this change, the Department's usage is in line with that adopted in this chapter, except that what the Department now call "grant-aided schools" we are here referring to as "direct-grant schools" (since public schools are also, strictly speaking, grant-aided).

2 The Code is a statutory instrument which is revised from time to time. The code operative when the above was written was the Schools (Scotland) Code, 1956.

3 An approved school is one providing education and training for juveniles, usually between the ages of 10 and 17, who have been sent to the school by a Court because they have committed an offence or have been found to be in need of care or protection. There are 23 such schools in Scotland, all under voluntary management except one which is managed by Glasgow Education Authority. In the year ended 31 March 1955, when the number of such schools in Scotland was 24, there were 1,381 on their rolls. At 15 January 1954, there were 311 pupils in the four Approved Schools situated in Glasgow. The Glasgow Education Authority Approved School had 87 pupils on its roll in September 1956.

4 In deciding an independent school's "acceptability" the authority will have in mind the relevant standards required by the Secretary of State. The teachers of an "included" independent school are paid according to the national scales applying to teachers of public and direct-grant schools.

Of Scotland's schools the great majority—3,209 of them—are public and direct-grant schools, and within this category direct-grant schools constitute a small minority. Of the country's public schools the overwhelming majority, in turn, are non-fee-paying, co-educational day schools. The number of independent schools is in the region of 200. At 15 January 1955, out of a total of 863,899 pupils receiving education, 839,745—97.2 per cent—attended public and direct-grant schools; 1,330 attended Approved Schools; 1,755 received education elsewhere than at school; and 21,069—2.4 per cent—attended independent schools.[1]

So much for the general picture. Let us now apply all this to Glasgow's educational structure. In addition to its public schools, Glasgow has four direct-grant schools. These four—all part of the authority's scheme, all providing primary and post-primary instruction, and all fee-paying—are: Hutchesons' Boys' Grammar School, Hutchesons' Girls' Grammar School, St. Aloysius College, and Jordanhill College School. (This last is a rather special case in that, being associated with a teachers' training college, it receives its central grant through the National Committee for the Training of Teachers.)

Next, there are in Glasgow a number of independent schools: a Scottish Education Department list of July, 1956, contains the names of 21. Six of these 21 are included in the authority's scheme and of these six, five are at present in receipt of a deficit-meeting contribution from the authority. These five, all fee-paying and providing primary and post-primary instruction, are: Craigholme, Laurel Bank, The Park, and Westbourne, all for girls; and Kelvinside Academy, for boys. Glasgow Education Authority are represented on the board of governors of each of these five schools. The sixth is Glasgow Academy which, although eligible for a contribution, has not applied for it. There is no education authority representative on its governing board.

Most of the other independent schools in the city cater in the main for primary pupils; two of them have rolls in the region of 300 but the majority are small establishments acting chiefly as preparatory schools for the city's fee-paying schools.

Two further points must be made. First, the two Hutchesons' Grammar Schools and St. Aloysius College receive, in addition to fixed grants from central funds, a contribution from the education authority to cover their annual deficits, and a contribution based on the number of their pupils; and the authority are represented on the board of governors of each of these schools. It is nevertheless in order to refer to them as direct-grant schools and to distinguish them from public schools on the one hand and independent schools on the other. Secondly, between the education authority and (at this writing) the four direct-grant schools and Kelvinside Academy there operates an administrative relationship known as the "mutual eligibility scheme," which provides for the transfer of teachers from these schools to the city's public schools, or conversely, without prejudice to promotion rights and seniority.

[1] *Education in Scotland in 1955.*

If education in Scotland is very much a preserve of the national or public system, education in Glasgow is, in turn, very much an area implementation of that system: the city's 4 direct-grant schools and its independent schools are quantitatively overshadowed by the 352 schools —177 of them primary and 79 secondary—which Glasgow Education Authority had under their jurisdiction at 1 September 1955.[1] Out of a total of 182,697 pupils receiving education in Glasgow at 15 January 1954, 177,333—97.1 per cent—were on the registers of the city's public and direct-grant schools; 311 attended the four Approved Schools situated in the city; 473 were receiving education elsewhere than at school; and 4,580—2.5 per cent—were pupils of the city's independent schools. We have already noted the percentage of Scottish pupils attending public and direct-grant schools, and the percentage attending independent schools, in January 1955; if, however, we examine the Scottish position a year earlier—on the date to which the Glasgow figures above refer[2]—we find the Glasgow proportions of 97.1 per cent and 2.5 per cent reflected exactly in the Scottish distribution.

On 14 October 1955 there were 177,709 pupils on the registers of schools under the management of Glasgow Education Authority. The number at Scottish public schools on 15 January 1955 was 824,530.[3] Thus Glasgow's public school pupils make up over one fifth of the Scottish total.[4] With responsibility for the provision of efficient education for this proportion of the country's school-children, Glasgow Corporation is the largest education authority in Scotland. The bulk of the sections that follow are concerned with the city's public educational system, including further education and finance; other sections deal, *inter alia,* with schools not under the jurisdiction of the authority, with the city's colleges and with its University.

Problems of Accommodation and Shortage of Staff

In the postwar period up to September 1955 the number of schools under the management of the Education Committee as the agent of Glasgow Corporation *qua* education authority rose by 53 to 352. Table CXIX, which gives a classification of these 352, shows that 24 of these additional schools come into the period July 1952 to September 1955—17 new primary, 2 new senior secondary, 2 special, 2 nursery and 1 residential. The two new senior secondary schools—Crookston Castle

1 A classification of these 352 schools is given in Table CXIX.

2 These are the most recent figures of the kind available. An analysis of pupils on the registers of all Glasgow schools, by age-group and type of school and class, is set out in Table 101 in the Statistical Appendix.

3 Deducting the 15,215 pupils attending all direct grant-aided schools in Scotland from the total (as at 15 January 1955) of 839,745 on the registers of all public and direct-grant schools.

4 It is interesting to note that in 1954 the number of pupils at Glasgow's independent schools also constituted more than one fifth of the total on the registers of all independent schools in Scotland.

(Protestant) and St. Augustine's (Roman Catholic) are of the type the Education Committee term "comprehensive."[1]

TABLE CXIX

NUMBER AND CLASSIFICATION OF SCHOOLS UNDER THE MANAGEMENT OF GLASGOW EDUCATION AUTHORITY AS AT 1 SEPTEMBER 1955, WITH COMPARATIVE FIGURES FOR 1952

As at July 1952	*Type of School*	*As at* 1 *September* 1955 *Prot.*	*R.C.*	*Non-Denom.*	*Total*
160	Primary	126	51	—	177
28	Junior Secondary (Group II)	15	13	—	28
20	Junior Secondary (Group I)	12	8	—	20
29	Senior Secondary (incl. Comprehensive)	24	7	—	31
237		177	79		256
	Schools for Handicapped Children:				
	(a) Physically Handicapped	1	—	—	1
	(b) Mentally Handicapped	5	3	1	9
	(c) Mentally and Physically Handicapped	5	4	—	9
	(d) Occupational Centres	—	—	10	10
	(e) Deaf	2	—	—	2
	(f) Blind, Deaf and Partially Deaf	—	1	—	1
	(g) Partially Deaf	1	—	—	1
	(h) Partially Sighted	—	—	1	1
	(i) Hospital Schools	—	—	6	6
38		14	8	18	40
38	Nursery Schools	—	—	40	40
313					336
	Residential Schools:				
	(a) Normal	2	1	—	3
	(b) Convalescent	3	1	—	4
	(c) Nursery	—	—	1	1
	(d) Physically Handicapped and Convalescent	2	2	—	4
	(e) Child Guidance (maladjusted)	—	—	1	1
12		7	4	2	13
1	Approved School	—	—	1	1
1	Agricultural School	—	—	1	1
1	Gardening School	—	—	1	1
328	Totals	198	91	63	352

SOURCES: *Progress Reports on the Work of the Education Committee, 1950-2* and *1953-5*.

At the beginning of 1947, the number of pupils in the Education Committee's schools (excluding nursery and residential but including special schools, that is, schools for handicapped children) was very nearly 163,000; a year later, by which time the raising of the school

[1] A note on Glasgow's comprehensive schools appears below, p. 526.

leaving age in 1947 from 14 to 15 had begun to take effect, it was just under 169,000. By October 1950 it was 173,332, and it went on rising until 1954, when it was 177,876.[1] This rise reflects the impact on the primary school rolls of the high birth-rate in the late 1940's: the post-primary and handicapped pupil rolls fluctuated over the period 1950-1955. Table CXX gives an analysis of the rolls of Glasgow schools under the management of the Education Authority as at October 1950, 1953 and 1955. (The omitted years show no significant difference from those given in the table.)

TABLE CXX

SCHOOLS UNDER THE MANAGEMENT OF GLASGOW EDUCATION AUTHORITY—ANALYSIS OF ROLLS, 1950, 1953 AND 1955

Pupils		1950 No.	1950 %	1953 No.	1953 %	1955 No.	1955 %
Primary	Protestant	81,372	68.7	84,880	68.6	84,604	68.2
	Roman Catholic	37,013	31.3	38,864	31.4	39,512	31.8
	Total	118,385	100.0	123,744	100.0	124,116	100.0
Secondary	Protestant	34,474	69.2	33,345	68.0	33,612	69.1
	Roman Catholic	15,317	30.8	15,657	32.0	15,016	30.9
	Total	49,791	100.0	49,002	100.0	48,628	100.0
Primary & Secondary	Protestant	115,846	68.9	118,225	68.4	118,216	68.4
	Roman Catholic	52,320	31.1	54,521	31.6	54,528	31.6
	Total	168,166	100.0	172,746	100.0	172,744	100.0
Handicapped	Protestant	3,125	60.6	3,118	60.9	3,122	62.9
	Roman Catholic	2,031	39.4	2,001	39.1	1,843	37.1
	Total	5,156	100.0	5,119	100.0	4,965	100.0
All Pupils	Protestant	118,971	68.6	121,343	68.2	121,338	68.3
	Roman Catholic	54,361	31.4	56,522	31.8	56,371	31.7
Grand Total		173,332	100.0	177,865	100.0	177,709	100.0

SOURCE: Based on data supplied by the Education Department, Glasgow Corporation.

The two most pressing problems to which the postwar period has given rise are accommodation and shortage of staff. The large new housing estates that have been established in recent years are still without adequate provision of schools, with the result that thousands of pupils are daily transported, some of them over distances of up to seven miles, to the nearest schools that have room to receive them. In September 1955, for example, 10,007 primary and 6,642 secondary pupils travelled to school daily from their homes in 11 new housing

[1] An analysis of the city's public schools' rolls (including handicapped pupils), 1954 and 1955, by denomination, stage of course, and type of handicap is given in Table 100 in the Statistical Appendix.

areas by ordinary service vehicles and by a fleet of over 100 buses specially set aside for their use. Much progress has been made with the Committee's extensive building programme, which makes provision for new schools, improvements in and extensions to some existing schools, and the replacement of obsolete and unsatisfactory school premises in the older areas of the city;[1] and—to take an example—the five new secondary schools which the Committee expect to be in operation by August 1957 will help to relieve the situation. But, as the Committee themselves are well aware, it is not only the length of time it takes to erect schools and carry out structural alterations that makes the accommodation problem one that will face them for many a day: the house-building still in progress on the outskirts of the city has further demands in store for them, and the wave of the high postwar birth-rate is due, within the next year or two, to start its sweep through the secondary classrooms.

There is, too, an element of irony in the situation, for the very achievement of putting new schools into operation aggravates the staffing deficiency. " Classes in new schools, each composed of a few pupils transferred from many schools, cannot be staffed by the withdrawal of teachers in the congested areas . . . Thus, each new school opened constitutes a new problem, staffing commitments being increased although the number of pupils in the city remains constant."[2] The increase recorded in the teaching staff in recent years—from 6,460 in 1949 to 6,841 in 1955—has accordingly done little more than keep the deficiency—officially estimated at 500—more or less constant.

Inevitably, this situation is reflected in the size of classes of Glasgow's public schools. The Schools (Scotland) Code, 1956, lays down that no class in a primary division should exceed 45, in the first three years of a secondary division 40, and in the fourth or subsequent years of a secondary division, 30. In January 1955, 429 out of 3,158 primary classes (13.6 per cent), 72 out of 1,349 1st-3rd year senior and junior secondary classes (5.8 per cent), and 21 out of 186 4th-6th year senior secondary classes (11.3 per cent) had rolls above the appropriate Code maxima.[3] The city's public and direct-grant schools had, in 1955, a ratio of 25.5 pupils per teacher.[4]

The situation would have been worse but for the continued employment of promoted members of primary staffs on full-time (instead of, as is normal, half-day) teaching duties and the return of retired

1 The programme also includes plans for 8 new schools for handicapped children, an extension of facilities for nursery schools, 3 district further education colleges, new Stow Colleges of Building and Printing, a new Stow College of Commerce and Distributive Trades, a community centre, several playing-field pavilions, a residential school and other construction projects. Details of work completed and in hand are set out in the Committee's *Progress Report*, 1953-5, pp. 43-49.

2 *Progress Report*, 1953-5, p. 10.

3 These figures are based on information supplied by Glasgow Corporation Education Department.

4 In this Glasgow compares favourably with Dunbartonshire (28.7), Lanarkshire (26.4) and Renfrewshire (25.9), but unfavourably with Aberdeen (19.0), Dundee (22.5) and Edinburgh (22.6), and with the figure for Scotland as a whole, 23.6.

teachers and the employment of uncertificated teachers.[1] In December 1955, out of a total of 6,815 teachers employed for the whole day in schools under the management of the Education Authority, 251 or 3.7 per cent were retired teachers (64 of them being over 70 years of age) and 65, or just under 1 per cent, were uncertificated.[2] Even as thus supplemented, however, the teaching force is at present, and may be for some time, insufficient to maintain full educational provision in all the city's public schools. The shortage, here as elsewhere, is particularly acute in the case of teachers of mathematics and science, and the number of such specialists in the Education Committee's employment is officially assessed as "inadequate to meet the needs of the secondary schools."[3] At certain periods in recent sessions, when staff numbers have been further reduced by illness, the Committee have been forced to put some classes in the worst affected areas on short-time (in a few cases half-time) instruction for varying spells. As recently as the beginning of session 1956-7, emergency time-tables were introduced in two junior secondary schools (Lambhill Street and Sir John Maxwell) whereby the pupils were divided into two sections, one attending from 9 a.m. to 3.20 p.m., and the other from 9.40 a.m. to 4 p.m.[4] If this experiment is deemed a success it may later be extended to other junior secondary schools.

For a time between the two world wars the Education Committee made their teachers an additional payment of about £50 above the national scales, and a recent attempt to obtain permission to revive this practice failed. Over recent years Glasgow has lost a considerable number of prospective and serving teachers to education authorities offering the inducement of a rented house, and the possibility of Glasgow's following suit is under discussion with the Housing Committee. In session 1956-7, for the first time in the city's educational history, special assistants—to the number of 131—were appointed in senior secondary schools to do advanced work in one of the main departments of the school in connection with, for example, Leaving Certificate examinations and university bursaries; and to carry out, *inter alia,* special duties associated with school organisation and extra-curricular activities. These special duties carry an additional responsibility payment of £55 a year. It is the Committee's hope that this development will help to attract teachers into service in the city and to retain those already in their employment who might be enticed elsewhere. Whether recent increases in national salary scales[5] will bring more men and women into teaching, and if so, whether Glasgow

1 "Uncertificated," it should be noted, means "not holding a Scottish certificate"—not necessarily (as many take it automatically to mean) "unqualified." Generally speaking, county education areas have a higher proportion of uncertificated teachers.

2 Cf. also the section "Teachers: *Composition of Staff,*" below.

3 *Progress Report,* 1953-5, p. 11.

4 While for pupils this will mean a shorter school day (by 40 minutes), teachers will be on duty for the full school day from 9 a.m. to 4 p.m.

5 See Section "Teachers: *Professional discontents,*" below.

schools will receive their share of recruits, remains to be seen. The glass is probably set fairer now than at any time in recent years; even so, there can be little foundation to any forecast of an early easing of Glasgow's teacher shortage.

THE WORK OF THE SCHOOLS

While it is left to education authorities to frame detailed courses, the Schools (Scotland) Code, 1956, lays down the broad lines which primary courses should follow. To indicate these will serve as a summary sketch of the work of Glasgow's primary schools. The Code requires that primary pupils shall be given instruction in reading, writing and arithmetic; in the use and understanding of written and spoken English; in music; in art and handwork; in nature study; in physical training; and, from such stage as is appropriate, in history, geography, written composition and, in the case of girls, needlework.[1]

Schemes of work for primary and for secondary schools must be approved by H.M. District Inspector of Schools. Substantial revision of schemes has been carried out recently in Glasgow, especially in junior secondary schools, to bring them into harmony with the various memoranda published by the Scottish Education Department on the teaching of secondary school subjects; but the minutiæ of these matters need not detain us. The body of the three-year course is made up of English, history, geography, arithmetic, science, art, music and physical education, with an additional subject or subjects drawn from a range of choices such as technical subjects and commercial subjects, homecraft and foreign languages.

The senior secondary course, orientated as it is to the requirements of the examination for the Scottish Leaving Certificate, varies according to the individual pupil's choice of subjects in which he will go forward for examination; but English, history or geography, arithmetic, art (in the fourth and later years, at least in the form of art appreciation), music (as a recreative subject at least), must be studied throughout the course. Languages other than English, mathematics, science and history or geography (whichever is not studied throughout) are included in the curriculum, but not necessarily studied throughout the course.[2] Pupils may select other subjects from a wide range of options, including technical subjects, commercial subjects and homecraft.[3] In

[1] *Public Education in Scotland (1952)*, p. 23.

[2] *Public Education in Scotland*, p. 25.

[3] The adequacy or inadequacy of the place occupied by Scottish studies in the curricula of Scottish public schools has been a prominent postwar debate in educational and cultural circles. While the position varies from school to school, Scottish history, literature, institutions and traditions in general appear to occupy a very minor and incidental role. (Cf. e.g., *Scotland in the Schools*: *A report on the Scottish content of our Education*, published by the Saltire Society, Edinburgh, 1953). The matter is raised here because the latest comment on the situation has come from a visiting teacher from America, Mr. Elmer Clayton. "As a teacher recently come to one of your large secondary schools," wrote Mr. Clayton in a letter to the editor of *The Scotsman* (15 October 1956), "I have been appalled by

certain Glasgow schools instruction in Gaelic and Hebrew is provided.

Control of the transfer of pupils from primary to secondary course is exercised by a Promotion Board set up by the Education Committee and consisting of 4 Head Teachers, 4 Assistant Teachers in Primary Schools, and the Director of Education as convener, while not more than four additional teachers may be co-opted for special purposes. Under the Committee's Promotion Scheme, approved by the Secretary of State, pupils who have completed the final stage of the Primary course and all others who have attained the age of 12 are given a Calibration Test comprising papers in English (including Composition) and in formal and functional arithmetic.[1] From the list of marks of all pupils presented for transfer 8 categories of pupils are determined (three categories of pupils suitable for five-year courses, three for three-year courses, one of pupils retained in primary school until the next test and one of pupils suitable for a modified Junior Secondary course.) Each school is told of the number of places in each category gained by the pupils of that school, and the actual pupils who are given the category places are determined by an order of merit which may be either:

(1) ranking by each teacher upon all-round knowledge of pupils' attainments, intelligence, and aptitudes, made before the date of the test; or

(2) ranking in order of marks obtained by pupils in the Calibration Test; or

(3) average of (1) and (2).

Head teachers are asked to be on the look-out for obvious misplacements and, after consulting with the parents, to arrange for the appropriate direction. Appeals by parents against allocations can be made, in the first instance, to the Promotion Board, and in the last resort to the Secretary of State.[2]

A word should be said here about Glasgow's comprehensive second-

the seeming ignorance of my classes of the history, topography, literature and song of their native land . . . The class informed me that they get no instruction in Scottish history . . . My colleagues inform me that it is becoming more and more impossible to take up any piece of work in prose, poetry or song dealing with Scotland, as the children are almost totally ignorant of elementary and basic knowledge about their homeland . . . Are you Scots so supine as to be uncaring about this issue?" And in his final sentence Mr. Clayton lent weight to what has always been the chief contention of the advocates of Scottish studies—that in this neglect Scotland is probably unique among nations: "In none of the other countries in which I have taught, Canada, U.S.A., Ireland and New Zealand, have I found comparably basic ignorance."

[1] On the 22nd of March, 1957, Glasgow Education Committee approved a scheme abolishing this test and providing, in its place, for a list of qualifying pupils in order of merit to be prepared by headmasters of primary schools. Headmasters will also be required to prepare estimates of the most suitable secondary courses (senior, junior, modified or retention). At this writing, the new scheme awaits the approval of the Secretary of State for Scotland.

[2] This summary leans heavily on the Education Committee's own account of the Scheme (cf. e.g., their 1950-2 Report, pp. 36-41).

ary schools. In these, senior secondary and full and modified junior secondary courses are provided in the same building or establishment. As these schools are taking the entire output from primary departments in their area, it is possible to operate a modified form of "promotion" procedure. Decisions as to type of secondary course suitable for this or that pupil need not be taken immediately, and when taken can more easily be reconsidered if experience shows this to be necessary. It is the Corporation's policy that the majority of secondary schools in the city should be of this type, and all new territorial secondary schools are being planned, and some old secondary schools reconstituted, with this end in view. This policy is not without its critics among educationists, although there is general appreciation of the advantages to be gained from the greater flexibility of these schools' "promotion" procedure and from enabling pupils, whatever the nature of their course and their mental calibre, to associate in common extra-mural activities.

The Scottish Leaving Certificate is awarded by the Scottish Education Department to pupils who have completed an approved course of five years' secondary education and who have passed the national examination in one or more subjects on the lower or higher grade.[1] This marks a change from the regulations governing the award of the certificate over a period extending back a number of years from 1950. During that time it was necessary for a pupil to pass in a group of three or four subjects, according to the grade on which the subjects were attempted.[2]

This change has not commended itself universally to educationists. Its supporters point to the fact that the hard penalty has been removed whereby a pupil failing in one subject in his group was denied his Certificate even if he passed in his other subjects and no matter how well he did so; now practically every pupil completing his course stands a good chance of rounding off his five (or six) years with a Certificate. Its detractors argue, first, that the value of the Certificate

[1] A pupil may present himself for examination at the end of his fourth year, if he intends to leave school at the end of that session, in any subjects his school authorities consider him fit to attempt, but on the lower grade only.

In this connection it should be recorded that the Secretary of State for Scotland has decided to amend the regulations governing the award of the Scottish Leaving Certificate so as to enable pupils in the fourth year of an approved secondary course to be presented in as many subjects on the lower grade (appropriately adjusted) as they are considered by the school authorities to be fit to attempt. Whereas under present conditions a pupil who takes the examination in the fourth year and remains at school for a fifth year can retain only one subject pass, under the new arrangements it is proposed that he should retain new lower grade passes obtained in the fourth year. It is further proposed that the standard of the new lower grade should be comparable with that of the ordinary level of the General Certificate of Education awarded by the English examining bodies, and that it be called the "ordinary grade.' This will be lower than the present lower grade. The Department's proposals are still under consideration by interested bodies.

[2] It is, however, still necessary to present certain prescribed subjects if the candidate intends that his certificate should qualify him for admission to a University, Training College, or Central Institution.

now depends on the number of subject-passes to which it certifies; and secondly, that so many pupils now spend the sixth year in preparation for another " go " at the examination in order to augment the subject-passes which a moderate burden of work yielded the year before, that proper sixth year work has perforce to be neglected.

In 1955, 1,331 pupils of Glasgow public schools were presented for the Certificate for the first time, and 1,237 of them were successful; 611 candidates who had gained the Certificate in a previous year were also presented.[1]

The Scottish Leaving Certificate is the only national certificate based on an external examination. The School Leaving Record, issued by education authorities to all leavers, was introduced in 1951 as an experiment and was discontinued in 1955. All Glasgow pupils who leave school without the Scottish Leaving Certificate may receive either a Secondary School Certificate or a Record of Progress and Attendance. Both are issued by the authority: the first to pupils who complete a course of at least three years' secondary education and reach a certain level of attainment, and the latter to those who do not reach this level. In session 1954-5, 5,693 pupils were presented for the (Glasgow) Secondary School Certificate, 3,928 of them being successful.

These are the schemes of work, the targets aimed at, in Glasgow's public schools. But there is more to the week-by-week programme than this summary suggests. Regular instruction in religious subjects is given in all the city's public schools by class teachers, and one period each week is devoted to instruction in what is officially described as temperance, morals and manners. In 1955, 193 Protestant schools had the services of an honorary chaplain, and all Roman Catholic public schools are regularly visited by priests.

Visual aids, no new development in Glasgow schools, make their contribution. A silent film projector and a filmstrip projector have been provided for every school, and recently sound film projectors have been provided in one third of the secondary schools. Instructional films are hired from the Scottish Central Film Library, and an annual grant of £5 per school is allowed for the purchase of filmstrips for the school filmstrip library.

All schools are fitted with equipment for receiving school broadcasts simultaneously in a number of classrooms: this is, indeed, a field in which Glasgow has pioneered. A small central stock of tape recorders is held available for issue to schools on demand. The value of school libraries is fully recognised, and in 1955 the Education Committee substantially increased the amount of school library grant and are arranging for a central library to be established in each secondary school. Through lessons and lectures the Schools Museum Service encourages pupils to make profitable use of the city's Art Galleries and Museums. Vocational guidance in co-operation with the Youth Employment Service and the Glasgow Careers Council is now one of the normal facilities provided in the secondary school. A pre-nursing

[1] *Progress Report*, 1953-5, p. 18.

course is in operation in a senior secondary school. During 1954-5, 23 schools participated in the Ship Adoption Scheme.[1]

In five city schools over a thousand pupils are taking advantage of a homework supervision scheme, whereby they return to school on several evenings each week from 5.15 to 7.15 p.m. to do, under staff supervision, the exercises and preparation set them by their class teachers. It is likely that other schools will join the scheme. Thirty-four primary schools are at present participating in a scheme of Tutorial Classes, held on the school premises on three afternoons weekly from 4.30 to 5.30. Further, evidence is not wanting that, in the words of Dr. Stewart Mackintosh, Director of Education,[2] teachers are examining the curriculum and giving thought to teaching techniques "as never before."[3] Over recent years a series of meetings was held in co-operation with the Local Association of the Educational Institute of Scotland on "The Challenge of the Primary School" and "The Challenge of the Junior Secondary School." The deliberations of the latter series anticipated many of the problems stressed and discussed by the Scottish Education Department in the memorandum published in 1955, *Junior Secondary Education.*[4]

There is much else in the record of the education service—in the work of authority, teachers, administrators and pupils—that could be mentioned, the whole testifying to a vigour and an on-looking spirit not completely sapped and crushed by the somewhat daunting conditions in which the work goes on, and bearing out the Director's claim that "in many schools pioneer work of much more than local value is being done."[5]

Yet there is another side to the story. The difficulties we have noted of accommodation and shortage of teachers, with their attendant over-

[1] Under this scheme pupils of a school exchange letters with the crew of a ship allocated to it (by the British Ship Adoption Society), visits are paid to schools by captains and crews of adopted ships, and escorted parties of pupils visit ships berthed near the city.

[2] *Progress Report,* 1953-5, p. 8.

[3] Disciplinary practice in the city's public schools is frequently criticised on the grounds that too much use is made of corporal punishment, and without suggesting that this question is necessarily involved in teachers' current deliberations, it is in place to point out here that Glasgow teachers are not as blind to ideals in this matter as their critics would imply. While some must stand guilty of a too ready and an excessive use of corporal punishment, the majority turn to it with reluctance and when all else has failed. Glasgow Education Authority, specially deprecating and condemning "any reliance on corporal punishment as the chief means of securing industry and discipline," have ruled that where it is necessary to inflict such punishment this may be done only by means of the strap supplied by the authority, and then only on the palm of the hand. In no case may a cane, pointer or other instrument be used. Punishment of this type must not be inflicted on any delicate or infirm child; on girls in and above the qualifying class except after consultation in each case with the headmaster; or in connection with home lessons unless the headmaster has satisfied himself that the case is one of obstinacy or idleness. (*Corporation of Glasgow, Education Committee Handbook,* 1954-5, p. 125.)

[4] In the Department's publication the reader will find an authoritative discussion of the problems confronting the junior secondary school—problems which, in the judgment of many educationists, combine to pose the major educational issue of our time. Not a few of the relevant questions can be summed up in the statement that the public accord the junior secondary school an inferior status, both socially and educationally, and have dashed earlier hopes that they would accept it not as a poorer but as a different type of school doing a different type of job.

[5] *Progress Report,* 1953-5, p. 8.

crowded classrooms and frequent change of staff, assuredly do not make for educational excellence. In these conditions at their worst, indeed, it may scarcely be possible for ordinarily effective educational work to be done. Certainly there is no lack, to-day, of critics of Scottish public education as a whole: many commentators whose opinion carries weight assert emphatically that mid-twentieth century Scotland has lost the leading place it once enjoyed in the educational ranking of the nations;[1] and they make no secret of the fact that Glasgow is included in this judgment and that the educational standards of most of the city's public schools are not what they were within recent memory.

THE FEE-PAYING SECONDARY SCHOOLS AND THE DEMAND FOR PLACES

Such a persuasion would at all events seem to be one of the considerations in the minds of those middle-class—and upper working-class—parents who to-day so single-mindedly strive to place their children elsewhere than at the non-fee-paying public school serving the area in which they reside. In the postwar period there has been an unprecedented demand for places in the city's fifteen fee-paying schools providing instruction up to the final stages of the senior secondary course.

A list of these schools grouped in four categories is given in Table CXXI, together with fees payable and other data. A proportion, varying from school to school, of the pupils on the registers of these schools reside outwith the city. The majority of these fifteen are long established as centres of senior secondary education in the city and are of high educational standing. A few, however, must be given particular mention. The High School—ancient pillar of the city's educational structure—the Academy, the two Hutchesons' Grammar Schools and the High School for Girls are the best-known of the city's, and among the best-known of Scottish schools. Pupils of the two Hutchesons' schools have in recent years figured prominently in the list of the first hundred places in the University Bursary competition, and they are, academically, the leading schools in the city at the time of writing. Allan Glen's is notable for its tendency to specialise in science, in training in workshop practice and in crafts. The Academy, which has a number of boarders, has an educational character of its own, and stands apart from the other 14 and indeed from all Glasgow schools in point of its being the only one entitled to the name "Public School" in the sense of the term current in England. Its claim to this exclusiveness rests on its being a member of the Headmasters' Conference. While it prepares generally for the Scottish Leaving Certificate, some of its sixth form post-Leaving Certificate boys each year sit the examination for the Oxford and Cambridge Joint Board General Certificate of Education, advanced and scholarship levels only.

[1] And—in this context the hardest pill to swallow—now lags behind even England!

TABLE CXXI

Fee-Paying Schools in Glasgow Providing Instruction up to Scottish Leaving Certificate Standard: Dates of Founding, Rolls and Fees

School	Date of Founding	Roll at a Date in June 1956	Fees per Session[1] Class or Range: Primary	Secondary
I Under Glasgow Education Authority				
Allan Glen's (boys)	1853	758	Qualifying £10 7s.	From £11 11s. to £13 16s.
High School (boys)	1824	1,006	All Classes £18 9s.	All Classes £23 2s.
High School for Girls	1894	914	All Classes £11 11s.	All Classes £16 4s.
Hillhead High (co-educational)	1885	1,785	All Classes £5 17s.	All Classes £10 7s.
Notre Dame (R.C. Girls)	1897	1,017	All Classes £5 17s.	All Classes £10 7s.
II Direct-Grant Schools				
Hutchesons' Boys' Grammar	1650	681	All Classes (from age 9) £11 17s.	From £13 19s. to £1
Hutchesons' Girls' Grammar	1876	1,008	From £10 19s. (starting at age 5) to £14 2s.	All Classes £17 5s.
Jordanhill College School (co-educational)	1920	app. 1,000	All Classes £4 15s.	All Classes £9 9s.
St. Aloysius College (R.C. boys)	1859	app. 700	All Classes £21	All Classes £22 10s.
III Independent Schools				
(a) Receiving a Contribution from the Education Authority				
Craigholme (girls)	1894	335	From £31 10s.	to £53 11s.
Kelvinside Academy (boys)	1878	580	From £37 to £65	All Classes £84.
Laurel Bank (girls)	1903	509	From £39 7s. 6d. to £48 16s. 6d.	All Classes £58 5s. 6
The Park (girls)	1880	app. 450	From £31 10s. to £59 17s.	From £63 to £66
Westbourne (girls)	1877	454	From £37 16s. to £59 17s.	All Classes £63
(b) Not receiving a Contribution				
Glasgow Academy	1845	840[2]	From £47 to £70	Transition class £80 Upper School from £ to £106

1 The fees given are those payable in session 1955-6, except in the case of Glasgow Academy, for which the figures given apply to 1956-7. Independent school fees will in most cases be increased for session 1956-7.

2 Including 40 boarders.

Where room could be found for a proportion of the growing body of annual applicants, fee-paying school rolls have increased steadily over the past 10 years; in other cases rolls have been steadily maintained at the maximum enforced by limitations of accommodation. To meet this situation of demand greatly exceeding possible intake, and at the same time to serve to some degree the end of maintaining standards, most of the schools discussed in this section subject applicants to an entrance test. Both the component items of the tests and the policy of selection vary to some degree. Some schools operate a priority scheme on a kinship basis, giving the first of the available places either to the sons and daughters of former pupils and the next set of places to brothers or sisters of present pupils, or to brothers and sisters first and the children of former pupils second. This practice again varies in that some schools apply the priority scheme without testing—the sole condition being that the applicant should be likely to profit from the school's instruction or should be in some other sense and according to the particular school's criteria a " suitable " person—while others require that all intending pupils must pass the entrance test. At least one girls' school, having satisfied itself by interview that the " daughter " and " sister " applicants are suitable, accords them their places and then gives the remaining vacancies to the first so many names on a list drawn up in chronological order of submission of application, provided only that those to whom places are offered are " suitable." It is this sort of arrangement that accounts for the growing practice of parents " putting in " a child's name for a particular school almost as soon as the ink on the birth certificate is dry.

The contemporary scramble—and it is not incorrect to use the word —for fee-paying school places has developed into a quite new and noteworthy educational and social phenomenon in the city's life. Between the wars—to go no further back—most middle-class parents had no doubt at all that their children would get a perfectly sound education at the local public school, and many of the Glasgow men and women who have reached the highest levels in a wide field of professional and public service in Scotland and beyond sat as children in the classrooms of " the local school round the corner." The academic standing of such schools as Queen's Park, Whitehill, Bellahouston, and Hyndland[1] during this period was judged to be comparable to that of,

In the case of Group I schools an additional amount—£15 per session for Primary pupils and £26 for Secondary pupils—is payable in respect of children where the parent or guardian is not a Glasgow rate-payer.

In Groups II and III schools there are additional fees—for example, a Matriculation or a sessional fee, a charge arising from a particular subject in a pupil's course, and so on—not included in the Table.

---

[1] Up to session 1928-9 these and some other senior secondary public schools were fee-paying, but the fees were very moderate indeed and few parents whose children attended these schools put on any airs because they paid, almost literally, a pound or two for their children's education. Even as they were prior to 1928 such schools can still be regarded as the local schools to which you sent your children in the justified expectation that they would fare as well there as anywhere.

A brief summary of the policy in this respect of the then Education Authority

say, the Boys' and Girls' High and the two Hutchesons' Grammar Schools, and superior to that of most of the city's independent schools. The great majority of the children of middle-class (including professional) parents attended schools of the first-mentioned type and no nonsense about it.

Now all this has changed. Those middle-class parents who choose to send their children to the public school of their area—as distinct from those for whom their children's repeated failures to gain admission elsewhere leave no alternative—are very much in a minority. The majority of middle-class, and an increasing number of upper-working-class, parents now regard fee-paying schools as the only schools suitable for their children; and the lengths to which many will go in, for example, subjecting their children to high-pressure coaching for entrance tests or, again, in adopting a domestic economy of astonishing tightness so that the money may be found for sending their children to expensive schools on which the demand for places is not so great because of the higher costs—these are only two indications of the impact this development has had on individuals and families alike.

It is no exaggeration to say that one of the most common topics of conversation among middle-class housewives—the whole matter weighs more heavily on the mothers—is the success or failure attending the attempts of their own and their circle's children to gain admission to the fee-paying schools. It is not uncommon for a discernible if temporary estrangement to affect the formerly friendly personal relationships between a woman whose children have repeatedly failed and another whose children have at last—or at the first attempt—won admission. Equally a feature in this general situation is the anxiety suffered by parents and imparted to their children—sometimes with deplorable consequences—prior to and at the entrance test set by the chosen school. The headmasters and headmistresses of the fee-paying schools might be quietly amused to hear how many details of their schools' circumstances and performance are known to these middle-class mothers and how clear these women are as to the educational ranking of the schools in question. What the ordinary observer cannot avoid noting, albeit with a twinge of wry scepticism, is that a school's position

is in place here. In August 1927 those authority schools whose designations contained the words " High School " or " Academy " were, with five exceptions, re-named simply " Secondary." Thus, for example, Bellahouston Academy became Bellahouston Senior Secondary. (It is interesting to note that the former pupils of pre-1927 Academies continue to refer to themselves as " Academicals." On the cover of the magazine of Pollokshields Senior Secondary the pre-1927 title of the school still appears—" Albert Road Academy.") A year later fees were abolished in all authority schools, again with five exceptions. The excepted schools, the same in each case, were the High School, the High School for Girls, Hillhead High, Allan Glen's, and Notre Dame High School for Girls. In the early 1940's the Corporation sought permission to put into effect their decision, taken in 1934, to abolish fees at these five schools also; but permission was refused by the Secretary of State, at the time the Rt. Hon. Thomas Johnston.

The Corporation's decision was reached mainly on the ground that it was undemocratic, and conducive to class distinction, to have a remnant of fee-paying schools in the authority's educational system. If their policy had been carried out the pressure on places at the non-authority fee-paying schools would have been even greater than it is.

in this maternal ranking varies according to whether it has still to be "tried for" or has closed its doors against her sons and daughters.

The reasons for the development we are examining are complex. Some we have in fact already noted, expressly or by implication, in the course of earlier discussion. As we have seen, there is a widespread conviction in middle-class and upper-working-class circles that the educational standards reached and maintained at the city's non-fee-paying secondary public schools are in the overwhelming majority of cases inferior to those at the fee-paying schools (including the five under the management of the Corporation), with one or two exceptions. Data in the light of which this conviction could be tested are not available to the external investigator, and a special enquiry would be beyond the scope of the present study. Nevertheless, the generalisation could be risked that few of those with inside knowledge would not in their heart of hearts subscribe to this opinion. And there are a number of considerations which lend the contention a good deal of weight: at the non-authority fee-paying schools a less crippling staff shortage leads to smaller classes and more individual attention, and the ability of heads to choose their own staff and the greater span of local autonomy are advantages of inestimable potentiality. Again, the selective process of admission in general frees the school of the burden of coping with pupils whose capabilities are well below average. Further, the effects of the process we are considering tend to work spirally, for as year after year the "top cream" is skimmed off the authority schools' bottle into the fee-paying jug so it becomes the more difficult for the former to raise standards and earn or re-establish a reputation; the gap widens and in each subsequent "cohort" of parents the greater becomes the resolve to seek admission to the fee-paying schools.

Another reason—a reason which some would hold to be the prime motivation—is this. If a child is accepted into a fee-paying school his subsequent passage to senior secondary education is likely to be reasonably smooth, whereas if he approaches that stage through the primary department of a non-fee-paying authority school he has to weather the storm of the promotion test and run the risk of being steered off his (or his parents') intended course—both figuratively and literally—from ... nior to the junior secondary type of education.

... he easier conditions and greater opportunities the fee-
... them to foster in greater measure than the
... cter, personality, and social
... numerous other activities
... classroom."[1] It is probably
... parents are referring when
... ns on the topic of fee-paying
... n instructional side to educa-
... g schools and particularly the
... " is given much attention.
... probable that the motives for

... y Academy.

shunning the local school in favour of a fee-paying school derive in the majority of cases purely from a concern for the child's educational well-being—in some cases in the narrower sense of his prospering in instruction, in other (probably the more numerous) instances, in the wider sense of " education." Yet the sociologist cannot easily ignore the possibility that an element of a concern of a rather different sort—concern this time for the social status aspects of the matter—may also be present in the minds of some parents.[1] It is certainly the case that, as a result of forces we have earlier discussed, the majority of non-fee-paying public schools now draw on pupils from a much more varied social background than formerly, while the social composition of the rolls of the fee-paying schools is in the main middle-class—in several of these schools, uniformly middle-class. Even if the five High Schools and the direct-grant schools have, generally speaking, a wider range of paternal occupational grading, with home background (though still chiefly lower-middle-class) extending in some degree to the upper-working-class, this does not necessarily weaken the above hypothesis: lower-middle and upper-working-class parents are as capable of making a social *cachet* of even moderate fee-paying as their social " superiors " are of higher fee-paying at the more exclusive schools. Again, granted that such social class colouring of motives as there may be can always and cogently be painted over by expressed concern for the educational advantage of the child, this in no sense makes the sociological hypothesis the less plausible, even if it makes it the more difficult to verify.[2]

If there is in this situation an element of what would popularly be called social snobbery, the fee-paying schools themselves are not to be held responsible for it: the deliberate inculcation of any sense of social superiority, either through an express cultivation of affectation of speech or less objectionable " social graces," is quite foreign to their formal policy. And if the predominant reason for the middle and professional classes' move away from the non-fee-paying public school is that the educational standards in these schools have fallen; and if this, however one may regret it, is in fact the case, the contribution the fee-paying schools are making to the educational provision of the city becomes an increasingly valuable one. It is in no sense to detract from this to say that the development we have been reviewing signifies the beginning of a break with an honourable tradition in the city's—and in Scottish—education.

1 This apparently total separation of " educational " and " social " or " sociological " is admittedly crude, but we cannot pause here to discuss the problem in depth.

2 One other point of sociological interest is worth noting. Some of the independent schools are finding that whereas formerly most of their pupils' fathers were in business and on the management side of industry, the majority are now professional and particularly medical men. Others have found the trend is in the opposite direction—from professional to business and industrial predominance. The recent migration to the Glasgow district of many English executives and administrators in the nationalised industries and in English concerns developing branches in Clydeside is one, though a minor, factor in the contemporary pressure on fee-paying school places.

SCHOOL LEAVING PRACTICE

Parallel with the growing appreciation of the fact that there is a shortage of trained recruits not merely for teaching but for a wide range of occupations and professions there has developed in recent years a marked interest in the leaving practices of our school children, and in particular in what has been called " premature leaving."

A measure of the extent of " wastage " early leaving may entail was provided by a Scottish Education Department enquiry which revealed that upwards of 3,500 leavers during session 1953-4 were considered by their head teachers to have been capable of taking a Scottish Leaving Certificate with at least two passes on the higher grade and three on the lower. If the more modest criterion of a Certificate with some passes in the lower grade is applied, the extent of wastage is thought to be more nearly 8,000 than 4,000 pupils annually.

Apart from this special enquiry, the Department provide a table of school leaving data for all public and grant-aided schools in Scotland in their annual report on Education in Scotland. This information was first set out in the report for 1952, and the results of an analysis which the present writer has carried out of that year's figures and those of subsequent years have appeared annually in articles published in *The Glasgow Herald*.[1] The leaving pattern that has emerged might be summed up in the following provisional generalisations[2]:

(1) Just under four fifths of all leavers leave at the first opportunity; (2) about 47 per cent of all leavers leave without completing even three years of secondary education; (3) only about one twelfth of all leavers complete the full secondary course; (4) about 94 per cent of leavers from three-year courses leave at 15; (5) three fifths or a little less of those leaving three-year courses do so without completing their course; (6) over two fifths of leavers from five-year courses leave at the minimum statutory age; (7) only a little more than a quarter complete their course before they leave; (8) somewhat more than a quarter leave before completing the equivalent, in stages, of the three-year secondary course, while 5 per cent leave before completing even S.II; (9) one tenth leave within sight of completing the full senior secondary course; and (10) the majority of those leaving after completing S.IV but not S.V are of the normal or expected age for that stage and are still young enough for staying on to make little difference.

For the purposes of the present study the Department were kind enough to supply a table giving data for Glasgow equivalent to their annual Scottish " leaving " table. This Glasgow table, relating to the year ended 7 June 1954, is reproduced in full as Table 102 in the Statistical Appendix. There follows, here, an analysis, set out in Tables

[1] The dates of the articles are: on " leaving " in 1952—30 and 31 July and 1 August 1953; on 1953 " leaving "—5 and 6 July 1954; on 1954—21 and 22 June 1955; on 1955 " Scottish leaving " and 1954 " Glasgow leaving "—14 July 1956.

[2] The 1956 leaving pattern shows a slight improvement.

CXXII and CXXIII, of the Department's Glasgow data relating to leavers from 5-year courses and of the equivalent Scottish data for the year ended 7 June 1954.[1]

TABLE CXXII

Stage Distribution of Senior Secondary School Leavers, Glasgow and Scotland, 1954

	Glasgow	Scotland
Total Leaving	6,209	22,579
	%	%
Without completing S.I	0.5	0.2
After completing—		
S.I but not S.II	8.1	4.7
S.II but not S.III	28.6	21.4
S.III but not S.IV	33.0	35.8
S.IV but not S.V	8.7	10.6
S.V but not S.VI	12.7	15.7
S.VI and beyond	8.3	11.7
	100.0[2]	100.0

TABLE CXXIII

Stage Distribution for Three Ages of Senior Secondary School Leavers, Glasgow and Scotland, 1954

	At Leaving Age		Before 16		Before 17	
	Glasgow	Scotland	Glasgow	Scotland	Glasgow	Scotland
Total Leaving	3,178	9,652	1,125	4.101	713	2,953
	%	%	%	%	%	%
Without completing S.I	0.9	0.4	0.5	0.2	—	—
After completing						
S.I but not S.II	14.7	10.1	2.7	1.8	0.3	0.3
S.II but not S.III	47.1	40.9	21.2	18.2	5.1	4.5
S.III but not S.IV	36.4	47.4	60.6	61.9	25.0	29.2
S.IV but not S.V	0.9	1.3	14.8	17.3	36.6	38.2
S.V but not S.VI	—	—	0.2	0.6	32.2	26.7
S.VI or beyond	—	—	—	—	0.8	1.2
	100.0	100.0[2]	100.0	100.0	100.0	100.0[2]

It will be seen that the Glasgow position—for example, in the proportions leaving before completing even three years of the five-year course—compares unfavourably with that for Scotland as a whole. Even if this is only to be expected—as Table CXXIV among other evidence indicates, the industrial areas in general have a low "stay-

[1] *Education in Scotland in* 1954, Table 5, p. 98.
[2] Rounded-off.

ing" index—and even if the Glasgow leaving pattern has to be seen against the Education Authority's policy of promoting qualified pupils to five-year courses regardless of their school-leaving intentions, the fact remains that if school-leaving practice in Scotland gives cause for concern, Glasgow's record, at least in the year here examined, presents an even more disquieting picture.

TABLE CXXIV

PERCENTAGE OF OCCUPIED POPULATION, GLASGOW AND CENTRAL CLYDESIDE CONURBATION, 1951, FINALLY LEAVING AN EDUCATIONAL ESTABLISHMENT AT VARIOUS AGES

Age at which full-time education ceased	*Glasgow*			*Central Clydeside Conurbation*		
	Males	*Females*	*Total*	*Males*	*Females*	*Total*
	%	%	%	%	%	%
Under 15[1]	78.6	69.6	75.6	78.1	69.0	75.2
15-18	19.4	27.4	22.1	19.7	27.5	22.2
19-21	0.6	1.8	1.0	0.7	2.1	1.2
22 and over	1.3	1.2	1.3	1.4	1.3	1.4
	100.0[2]	100.0	100.0	100.0[2]	100.0[2]	100.0
Total occupied population all stated ages	343,088	170,083	513,171	549,918	261,633	811,551

SOURCE: *Census of Scotland, 1951,* Vol. IV, Table 17, p. 652.

The Scottish Education Department through a poster displayed on school notice-boards, and headmasters and youth employment officers through interview and discussion, do what they can to impress upon the intending "early leaver" the wider employment opportunities open to holders of the Scottish Leaving Certificate;[3] and in January 1956 the Department, jointly with the Educational Institute of Scotland, issued a pamphlet entitled "Give Them Their Chance" addressed to parents and in particular to parents of pupils in the third year of the senior secondary course. It is likely that the pamphlet will be distributed at the start of each session, and educationists hope that the appeal to parents to dissuade their children from unenlightened and ill-considered decisions, and to take the larger view themselves, will in due course bear fruit.[4]

1 The vast majority in this group left at age 14. The statutory school leaving age was raised to 15 in 1947.

2 Rounded-off.

3 In their discussions with senior secondary pupils proposing to leave school before completing a full secondary course, the officers of Glasgow Youth Employment Service make this point first and with all possible emphasis. During 1954-5 the Service—which is open also to pupils of the city's independent schools—found employment for 7,827 boys and 7,576 girls. All post-primary schools now have "careers teachers" who co-operate with the service and to whom pupils may turn for information. Glasgow's Youth Employment officers also advise young workers of the further education and leisure time facilities that are open to them in the Corporation's classes and clubs and through voluntary organisations. (See next section.)

4 Evidence suggests that the initiative in "early leaving" comes in most cases from the children, with parents acquiescing without due consideration. This would therefore seem to be a matter on which Parent-Teacher Associations could be of

This subject of school-leaving practice has been treated at some length not merely because of its inherent interest and importance, but also because few things sum up more succinctly than this matter the educational questions of our day. Undoubtedly the need to earn money settled the question of when to leave school for many children long before their fifteenth birthday. But there are many others for whom the socio-psychological attraction of earning a wage and having a place, however humble, in "the great big adult world" is a far weightier factor than the actual cash in the weekly pay packet. The challenge this carries to the instructional side of schooling is obvious enough: how can we hold that we are "getting at" pupils, arousing and maintaining their interest, when they have thought for little but the blessed arrival of the next statutory leaving date? But it poses a problem for the social or sociological side of school life also. The predominant attitude of mid-'teenagers appears to be that school is no fit place for them, that it is beneath their dignity and standing as "apprentice-adults" to stay on when they are free to go.

This much seems clear: through the fierce and relentless onslaught on their minds of the mid-twentieth century media of communication our 'teen-agers are maturing earlier, in some respects at least, than we like to think and our schools seem to realise. If these respects are restricted to one small area of personality and development, and are in contrast to a continuing callowness in other respects—as typified, for example, in lack of self-reliance, of facility in self-expression, and of social graces—this merely underlines the problem. Against this background it looks as if our schools may be thwarting rather than fostering the mid-'teenager's aspirations to be accepted by society as an adolescent with developing conceptions. It may be that more use, more practical application, will have to be made in the schools of recent sociological findings in youth surveys and in the field of informal group structure and relations, and of the study of informal leadership, status, role, sense of belonging, and so on. Vague and woolly as all this may seem, to set our reflection along such lines may produce at least incidental benefits if not a solution.

Further Education

All, however, need not be lost to the "early leaver." Sooner or later he can join the band of well over 100,000 persons—in session 1951-2 the total was 104,290 and in 1955-6 it was 106,424—catered

service. Unfortunately, there are only about a dozen such Associations in Glasgow, of which (according to Mrs. J. G. Duncan, Secretary of the Council) only about half are affiliated to the Council of the Parent-Teacher Associations in Scotland. In Glasgow development seems to have been along the lines of the formation of Parents' Clubs, of which there are over 40; but these do not discharge the functions of Parent-Teacher Associations. Many Glasgow schools, however, hold a Parents' Day at least once per session on which parents are invited to attend school to see the work being done and hold informal discussions with members of the teaching staff.

for in the wide-ranging Further Education Service of the Glasgow Education Authority. As defined by the Education (Scotland) Act, 1946, "further education" comprises voluntary part-time and full-time courses of instruction, and voluntary leisure-time occupation in organised cultural training and recreative activities, for persons over school age.[1] Administratively, further education falls into two main types, formal and informal.

Taking the formal side first, 8,047 of the total of 106,424 in 1955-6 were students enrolled in day classes and courses, either full-time (1,959) or part-time (6,088), while 54,940 were enrolled in evening classes and courses—27,528 of them following courses in commercial, technical and trades subjects and 25,791 in non-vocational courses. The most popular of the non-vocational subjects coming under the head of "general provision" were Dress-making, Needlework, Arts and Crafts, Cookery, Dramatic Study, Owner-Drivers, Physical Recreation and Country Dancing. Of the 25,791 enrolment, 3,592 were in adult education courses provided partly under an agreement with the University of Glasgow Extra-Mural Education Committee and partly on the advice of the Glasgow & West of Scotland Committee on Adult Education.[2]

During the same session, 6,064 students attended day release courses—courses which young persons between the ages of 15 and 18 employed in various occupations are "released" by their employers to attend for one day or two half-days, or an arranged number of hours, per week for 44 weeks. The majority of Glasgow firms, however, like Scottish firms in general, are much less enthusiastic supporters of day-release than their counterparts south of the border. Pre-Apprenticeship and Pre-Vocational courses are provided for the building and engineering industries, for commercial work, and for nursing.

Langside College, the first "junior college" to be started in Scotland, has had a successful record as Glasgow's chief centre for day release students since it was opened in 1947. The College's total enrolment in 1955-6 was 4,564, of whom 254 followed full-time day courses and 1,133 part-time day courses. The Logan and Johnston Pre-Nursing College, opened in 1946, trains girls from the age of 15 who intend to become nurses. At the outset the College roll numbered 24; in session 1955-6 it numbered 215. The Stow College of Engineering and the David Dale College provide facilities for training in all branches of Engineering in both day and evening classes, and the other Stow Colleges (of Building, of Hairdressing and of Printing) and the Decorative Trades Institute provide day-release, pre-apprenticeship and evening courses in their respective fields.

1 The Act also provided for compulsory full-time and part-time courses of instruction in junior colleges for young persons between the ages of 15 and 18, but this provision is not yet in operation. Some employers, however, have made attendance at appropriate day "continuation classes" a compulsory part of their apprenticeship and other training schemes.

2 The work of the University in the field of adult education is described in the section, "The University," below.

Recent years have shown marked development in the Committee's formal further education service, and further extension is planned. Approval has been obtained from the Scottish Education Department for the erection of new Stow Colleges of Building, of Printing, and of Commerce and Distributive Trades, on the north and south sides of Cathedral Street. The intention is to re-group as many of the further education centres as possible in one area.

The informal branch of the Committee's further education service comprises 5 community centres, 50 parents' clubs, 42 "directly provided" youth clubs, 51 junior clubs and 8 play centres. In 1955-6 the community centres had a membership of 2,581 and the youth clubs 8,975. In addition, the 458 voluntary youth clubs for whom accommodation is provided by the Committee had an enrolment of 6,094. Training courses for youth leaders are organised, and ten district advisory panels and a Central Youth Advisory Committee—all representative of the main youth and adult organisations active in the city—were inaugurated during session 1953-4.

The total staff employed in teaching and senior administrative duties in further education in session 1955-6 was 3,866—227 employed full-time and 3,639 part-time.[1]

TEACHERS

Composition of Staff

A detailed analysis of the 6,825 teachers employed for the whole day in schools under the management of Glasgow Education Authority as at 1 October 1954—the latest date for which figures are available—is provided in Table 103 in the Statistical Appendix. The following are some of the points that emerge. Of the total number of teachers, 2,319 or 34 per cent were men and 4,506 were women; 173 (2.5 per cent) were retired and 32 (0.5 per cent) were uncertificated;[2] 3,523 "fixed" teachers[3] (51.6 per cent of the total) were employed in primary departments and 2,621 (38.4 per cent) in secondary departments. Of

[1] The work of Glasgow Education Authority does not end with the provision of the services we have reviewed in this and the preceding sections. It extends also to School Welfare—the provision of footwear and clothing, of school milk and school meals, and of holiday camps; the care and protection of children who have been ill-treated or neglected in their homes; the running of educational excursions; the provision and control of Nursery Schools (it is estimated that the 41 at present under the Committee's management will have to be increased about tenfold before the city's needs will be adequately met); and many other services. Under the Child Guidance Service, Glasgow now possesses "an almost complete School Psychological Service within reach of every child's home and school." Shortage of teachers has, however, prevented development in the provision of special facilities for the slow-learning child. In 1954-5, 4,646 children were dealt with at the city's 11 Child Guidance Clinics.

[2] As we have seen, a little more than a year later retired and uncertificated teachers numbered 251 (3.7 per cent) and 65 (just under 1 per cent).

[3] By "fixed" here is meant a teacher employed wholly or mainly in one school, in contrast to a visiting teacher serving in more than one school.

the total of 6,620 excluding retired and uncertificated teachers, 2,274 (34.4 per cent) were men and 4,345 women; 3,012 (45.5 per cent) were graduates and 3,608 were non-graduates. The graduates were almost evenly divided as between the sexes: 1,467 of them, or 48.7 per cent, were men and 1,545 women. The non-graduates, on the other hand, were overwhelmingly a female category: 2,801 or 77.6 per cent women as compared with 807 men. The majority of the latter (589) were teachers of technical subjects, and of the 202 non-graduate male holders of the General Certificate only 10 taught in secondary departments. (Normally for secondary teaching the Special Certificate is required, but holders of the General Certificate, whether graduates or not, may obtain an endorsement under Article 39 of the regulations which qualifies them to teach in secondary departments.) Primary teaching is four fifths a female preserve: 2,861 or 81 per cent of the total of 3,523 were women; in secondary departments men are in a majority, though to a much less marked extent: in this case 1,458 (55.6 per cent) of the total of 2,621 were men.

Professional Discontents

As one looks back over the educational scene of recent years what strikes one most forcibly is how vocal Scottish—and Glasgow—teachers have been in unburdening themselves of their discontents and in criticising aspects of the educational situation. At public meetings and in the correspondence columns of the press teachers have aired a catalogue of complaints and grievances with a regularity and persistence surely unequalled in their profession's history.

This was especially so in 1955, a year which will surely mark the peak in teachers' postwar protests and agitation. Few members of the public can, that year, have been left unaware of the main items on the teachers' black list: the inadequacy of salaries; the proposal in the Teachers (Superannuation) Bill that teachers' contributions should be increased from five to six per cent; the lack of an effective say in the conduct of their profession's affairs and in the administration of the educational system; the excessive demands of extra-mural and extra-curricular services; certain physical conditions such as the poor state of staff-rooms in older schools; the strain of teaching oversize classes; and—to some the most hurting of all—the deterioration of their profession's standing in the eyes of the public.

In the closing weeks of the year mounting resentment and unrest burst into spectacular demonstrations of protest. At a meeting of about 600 Glasgow members of the Scottish Schoolmasters' Association on 17 December a resolution calling for mass resignations was passed by an overwhelming majority.[1] Four days later, a meeting convened by the Glasgow Local Association of the Educational Institute of Scotland ended in some disorder after heated exchanges between the platform

[1] The proposed mass resignations, however, did not take place.

party and a section of the audience. Gradually, however, the tense atmosphere at the end of 1955 eased as events in 1956 took a material turn in the profession's favour. An increase of 7 per cent on basic salary came into effect on 1 April; at the same time, increases arising from recommendations of the Appleton Committee[1] were made in the basic salaries of graduates employed in secondary schools and of Grade I teachers in further education—the 7 per cent award, in their case, being calculated after the "Appleton" increases had been added; and revised scales, providing further increases for all teachers, came into force on 1 November 1956.

The new basic scales (which apply to Glasgow as to Scottish teach-

TABLE CXXV

BASIC SALARY SCALES FOR SCOTTISH TEACHERS, AS FROM 1 NOVEMBER 1956

Scale	Teachers	Salary
Scale I	First or second class Honours graduates in secondary schools, including corresponding teachers in technical subjects (except art)	£675–1200
Scale II	Third class Honours graduates in secondary schools	£625–1085
Scale IIIA	(with secondary school addition—£25 to £55) (a) Ordinary graduates in secondary schools (b) Non-graduate men in secondary schools who were trained under the Emergency Scheme (c) Technical graduates (d) Teachers of art (e) Teachers of commerce, music, and technology, placed in Grade III by Grading Committee	£600–1040
Scale IIIB	(a) Graduates in primary schools (b) Teachers of commerce and music (Grade IV), teachers of technology and handwork (Grade IV)	£575–985
	(c) Women teachers of domestic science (Group III Diploma)	£525–860
Scale IV	Teachers of physical education, certain teachers of technology and handwork (Grade IV)	£535–985
Scale V	(a) Teachers of agriculture and of speech and drama (b) Certain teachers of music (Grade V)	£550–925
	(c) Women primary teachers trained at training college for four years	£500–810
Scale VI	(a) Certain teachers of music (Grade VI) teachers of handwork (with no additional technological qualifications)	£515–900
	(b) Women primary teachers trained at training college for three years (c) Women teachers of domestic subjects (Group I or II Diploma)	£470–780
Scale VII	Certain teachers of commercial or trade subjects (Grade VII)	£505–795
Scale VIII	Certain uncertificated teachers	£490–740

Teachers will reach their maximum salary in their eighteenth year of service except on Scales IV, V and VI, where they will reach the maximum in the twentieth year of service.

[1] Committee on the Supply of Teachers of Mathematics and Science in Scotland (Sir Edward Appleton, Principal and Vice-Chancellor of Edinburgh University, Chairman).

ers) are shown in Table CXXV. The figures given are for men (except where otherwise stated): women's scales at 1 November 1956 were approximately 87 per cent of the men's but, under the policy of introducing equal pay in seven annual instalments, women will be paid on the same scales as men from 1961 onwards.

The award allows also for an increase in the extra payments given to teachers in posts of responsibility—head teachers, principal teachers, special assistants, and so on. The head teacher of a senior secondary school with about 1,000 or more secondary pupils may accordingly receive a total remuneration of £2,225. To give another example, a graduate infant mistress in a large primary school may earn £990. Principals of further education centres are eligible for scales ranging from £1,140 to £1,360 in a small centre dealing with elementary trade instruction, to £2,020-£2,240 in a large centre. The salaries of principals and depute principals may be further increased by £215 or £55 according to the level of work done in the centre, and the principal of a very large centre doing advanced work will have a maximum salary of £2,455.[1]

In recent history at all events no new salary scales have won universal acceptance by the different categories that comprise the profession, and the 1956 increases have proved no exception. One bone of contention is the question of just differentials: non-graduate and ordinary graduate teachers are opposed to the widening of differentials in favour of Honours graduates which the latter and the lay observer see as the main hope of attracting to the schools the specialists—in mathematics and science in particular—they so gravely and urgently need. The profession as a whole, however, may well come to regard the current award as a considerable, even if partial, achievement of their many-sided goal of professional enhancement. The salary gains of 1956 may also serve to mollify the failure to have the Superannuation Bill withdrawn or the 1 per cent rise in contributions rescinded. To the general public it will assuredly appear that the November increases have now made teaching a financially attractive occupation.

What success teachers will win on the other fronts of their struggle remains to be seen. On one item, however, in the list of teachers' grievances—the status of the profession—the following comments may be made. It is the general public that accords status, and in doing so it takes into account more than teachers' aggrieved protestations that the profession ought to have a higher standing than it has. Further, monetary rewards, while a weighty, are not the sole relevant factor in the assignment of status. However inconsistent it may seem on the part of a predominantly industrial population, the public appear to regard

[1] Teachers in the various grades of further education have also had their salaries increased. For example, the basic maximum for First and Second Class Honours graduates in further education is now £1,345. To complete the summary, it may be noted that remote school allowances have also gone up—in a " very remote school," from £70 as previously to £90, and in a " remote school " from £40 as previously to £50. A teacher in a distant island will get a further £50, as compared with £40 previously.

the washing of dirty linen in full view, the constant and vociferous airing of grouses, talk of strike action, and the frequent forthright repudiation of teaching as a career to be recommended to one's sons and one's pupils—to regard all this as behaviour somehow not quite fitting to professional people. Here a hard dilemma confronts the profession, fearful as it is of losing further face: their position in a public service being what it is, they must win over the public to their support in their efforts to improve conditions; but the more they seek to do this by giving voice to their complaints and taking unconventional action, the more they run a serious risk of further lowering of their status. Even to state the dilemma may be to point a way to resolving it. This much at all events is clear: while the salary increases of 1956 will not in themselves restore the profession's status to its former level, they provide a breathing-space teachers might profitably use for a rethinking of this issue.

Finance

However slender may be his normal concern with the educational provision his city makes for the young and not-so-young, the ratepaying—and tax-paying—citizen of Glasgow displays at least once a year a close interest in the matters we have been reviewing. This is when he is reminded by examination of his rates notice that expenditure on education is the greatest single item on his city's rating account. The reminder in the late summer of 1956 came forcibly, for he then learned that, of the increase of 2s. 10d. in the £ imposed for 1956-7—making a record all-in rate of 24s. 2d.—about 1s. in the £ reflected the rise in education costs.

Nostalgically he might look back to 1939, when the costs of the city's educational provision was £3,500,000 and the charge on the local rates £1,800,000; but that would only make less palatable the hard fact that estimated expenditure for 1956-7 is £14,435,174 and the rate-charge £4,777,894. (Since 1939 Government grants have increased from 45 per cent to 65.5 per cent—cold comfort to him when he dons the mantle of tax-payer.)

The estimate for the year to 31 May 1957 shows an increase of £1,664,717 on the actual expenditure for 1955-6 of £12,770,457—itself nearly £343,000 in excess of estimated expenditure for that year. The revenue for 1955-6 (including Government grants) was £8,751,381. To mention all this is not to engage in cheap sniping at a hard-pressed Education Committee. The biggest single item on the bill is salaries and wages—teachers' salaries in 1955-6 amounted to £5,306,408 and it is expected that in 1956-7 this figure will rise to over 6¼ million—and the next biggest, maintenance of property and equipment; and about the rising costs of either the Committee can do little. Provision of food and clothing cost, in 1955-6, £1,630,623, of which school meals

Glasgow Corporation Housing Department

Plate 15. MOSS HEIGHTS, CARDONALD
Multi-storey flats

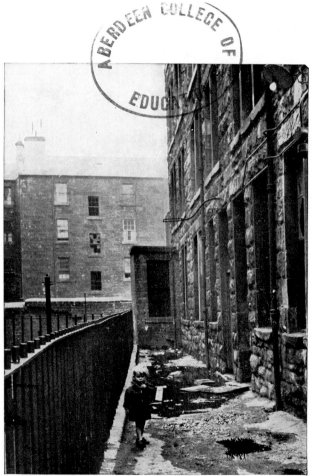

Glasgow Corporation Housing Department

Plate 16. OLD TENEMENT, BACK-COURT
RUTHERGLEN ROAD

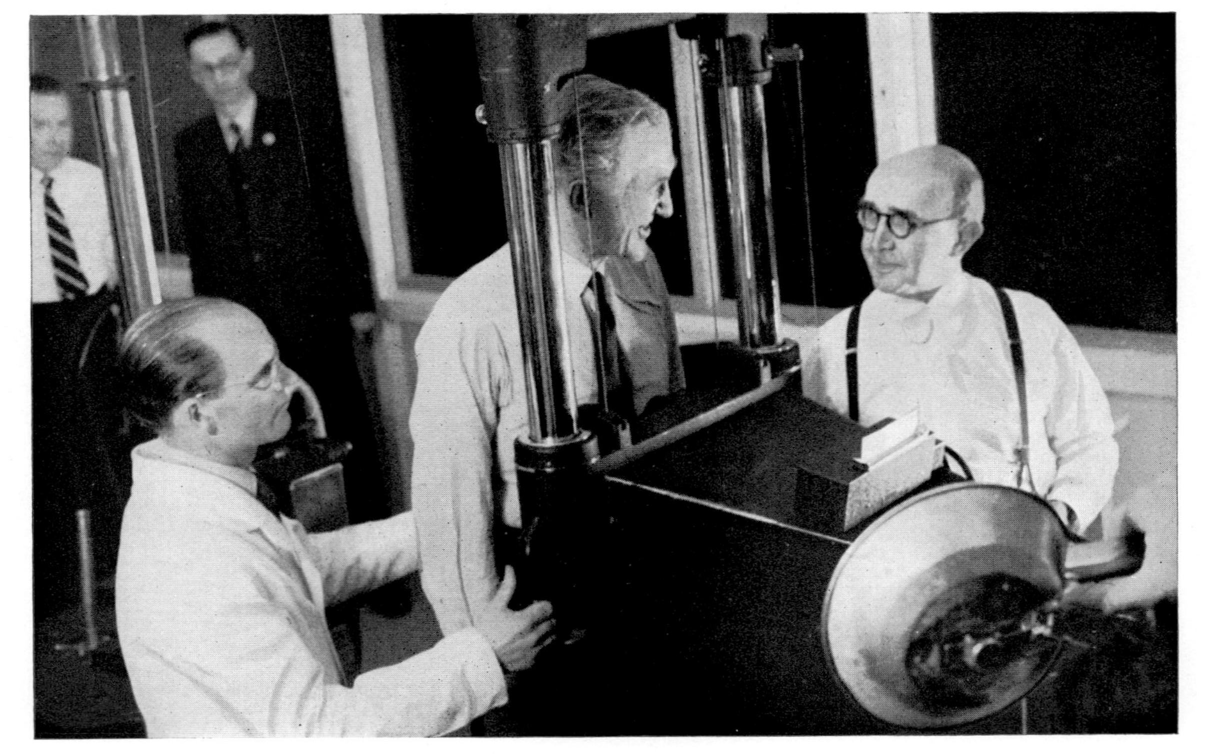

Associated Newspapers Ltd.

Plate 17. GLASGOW X-RAY CAMPAIGN, 1957

accounted for £1,267,439 and school milk £355,295.[1] The over-all cost of further education was £727,000, of which £109,802 represents the cost of the "informal" branch of the service. Another not inconsiderable item is bursaries: awards made in accordance with the provision of the Education Authority Bursaries (Scotland) Regulations, 1953 and 1955, amounted to 4,900 in number and £372,000 in cost.[2]

Allegations are made from time to time, within and outside the councils of the Corporation, of extravagance in the city's educational provision and waste in operating it.[3] Whether these are justified—they are usually hotly denied by the Education Committee—and what the possibilities might be of substantial economies that would not impair the service, it is not for this review to speculate.

THE CENTRAL INSTITUTIONS

Glasgow possesses, apart from its University, six colleges providing higher educational training, theoretical and practical, in a wide range of skills and subjects. These six, called in formal terminology Central Institutions, are under the management of independent bodies composed of influential persons interested in the activities of the Institution, of persons nominated by Education Authorities for the area served, and of local representatives of commerce, industry and the arts.[4]

Five of them are in receipt of Government grants through the Scottish Education Department, with whom they have a loose administrative relationship, and one, the West of Scotland Agricultural College,

[1] In September 1956 charges for day school meals were increased and are now fixed at 3s. 11d. per week for the first child, 3s. 6d. for a second child, and 3s. 1d. for a third and subsequent children. In nursery schools the weekly charge for midday meals is 3s. 11d. Free meals—numbering about 14,600—are supplied to necessitous children and children of large families. A "census" taken in September 1955 showed that 62,403 pupils or about one third of the total school roll received meals (61,166 of these being dinners) and 158,615 (86 per cent) received milk.

[2] These figures compare with 1,169 and £20,013 for sessions 1945-6. Of the 1955-6 totals, awards to University students (whole-time and part-time) were 937 in number and £125,701 in amount, and to students (whole-time or part-time) at Central Institutions, 918 and £87,899. (These are provisional figures: the final figures are not available at this writing.) In this matter Glasgow is one of the most generous of Scottish local authorities. For a discussion of the present Scottish system of awarding grants as it appears to an academic group see a report by the Association of University Teachers (Scotland): *Awards from Public Funds to University Students in Scotland*, 1956.

[3] One instance is the allegation by a Progressive Councillor, in August 1956, of "colossal and appalling" waste in the supply of school meals. Another example relates to further education, part of the provision of which was described about the same time by another Progressive Councillor as making available "all sorts of frills, thrills and flipperies." Less trenchantly, many Glaswegians have expressed their doubts as to whether classes on, for example, dressmaking and angling, and courses for radio amateurs, are a defensible charge on public funds. How far such critics will be placated by the news that sessional fees for non-vocational courses will be increased in session 1956-7 to 12s. 6d. for students over 21 years of age remains to be seen.

[4] There are, in addition to these, a number of colleges, not of Central Institution status, providing post-school instruction of a general or specialised kind, such as the School of Accountancy, Skerry's College, and Glasgow Tutorial College.

is grant-aided through, and in a similar relationship with, the Department of Agriculture for Scotland.[1]

Table CXXVI sets out data about the courses provided and the awards made by these six establishments, together with enrolment figures in selected years. The following notes supplement that information.

Paramount in size and educational standing is the Royal College of Science and Technology, known between 1912—when the prefix "Royal" was bestowed on its title by George V—and September 1956 as the Royal Technical College, Glasgow. In more than one respect its position is a singular one. Its relationship with the Scottish Education Department notwithstanding, it has University College status—it was accorded this status in 1919—and is in receipt of grants through the University Grants Committee. It has close links with the University, with which it has been affiliated since 1913. The form which the affiliation takes is that certain courses of study in the College are recognised by the University as leading to a degree (see Table CXXVI). Tracing its origin to the foundation of Britain's first technical college—Anderson's Institution—in 1796, the College is not only the oldest but offers the most comprehensive courses of any technical institution in the United Kingdom and is the country's leading College in the field of Applied Science. Along with the University it has made Glasgow pre-eminent as a centre of technological education; and these two in association form one of the main centres specially selected for major expansion under the Government's £97 million, five-year programme of technical education announced early in 1956. Considerable extension to, and internal replanning of, the College's already large building have taken place in recent years, and are still in progress. The formal opening of the Montrose Street Extension was planned for early 1957. A residential College for Management Studies at Chesters, Bearsden, was recently established. The College's student residence, Lochview Hall, accommodates over 40 students.

Another recent change in the title of a Glasgow college took place in 1955, when the Glasgow and West of Scotland Commercial College, dating back to 1845, became the Scottish College of Commerce in recognition of its national status and increasing prestige. The College claims that its Associateship is recognised, for such purposes as salary grading, as the equivalent of an Honours, and its Diploma as the equivalent of an Ordinary or Pass degree of a British University. Jointly with the Royal College of Science and Technology, the governing body of the College runs the Glasgow School of Management. The College also houses the Scottish Hotel School. A small extension to the College, and a hall of residence for women students taking the Hotel School course at Ross Hall, were built recently, and a new library was opened in April 1956.

The present School of Art is a development of the School of Design,

[1] The Agricultural College also receives a contribution from the Scottish Education Department.

TABLE CXXVI

CENTRAL INSTITUTIONS, GLASGOW: ENROLMENT, AWARDS AND COURSES

Central Institution	*Enrolment (numbers in brackets =full-time students)* 1947-8	1951-2	1954-5	*Awards and Courses*
Royal College of Science and Technology	5,456 (1,228)	5,658 (1,269)	5.094 (1,375)	Matriculated students who take a recognised course (which may be taken in whole or in part at the College) can present themselves for the award by the University of the degree of B.Sc. in Applied Chemistry, Architecture, Engineering (Civil, Mechanical, Electrical, Mining and Chemical) and Pharmacy. Offers also full-time courses for its own awards—the Associateship and Postgraduate Diploma.
Scottish College of Commerce	3,564 (733)	3,379 (734)	3,693 (562)	Prepares students for its own Associateships and Diplomas, and for B.Sc.(Econ.) degree of London University. Provides courses in Modern Languages for students preparing for the London B.A. degree. Full-time and part-time courses are provided in Business Administration, Management Studies, Accountancy, Secretarial Science and Modern Languages.
Glasgow School of Art	1,791 (578)	1,517 (374)	1,615[1] (472)[1]	Awards Diplomas in Drawing and Painting; Sculpture; Design and Crafts; and Commercial and Graphic Art. Provides a course in Architecture leading to a Certificate which carries exemption from the Intermediate Exam. of the R.I.B.A. (see also text). Part-time non-diploma courses are also provided.
Royal Scottish Academy of Music[2]	1,583 (93)	1,712 (127)	1,585 (134)	Provides full-time courses for (1) Diploma in Musical Education, and (2) its own Diploma (D.R.S.A.M.); and instruction for part-time students. Its associated College of Dramatic Art gives courses for Diploma in Dramatic Art or the Diploma in Speech and Drama, and for the Certificate in Dramatic Studies (issued by University). Evening classes on Voice Production, Mime and Movement and other subjects.

[1] 1955-6.

[2] Enrolment figures for the Royal Scottish Academy of Music include a number of part-time pupils aged 14 and under. In 1954-5, for example, these numbered 494.

Central Institution	*Enrolment (numbers in brackets = full-time students)* 1947-8	1951-2	1954-5	*Awards and Courses*
Glasgow and West of Scotland College of Domestic Science	2,161 (508)	1,937 (429)	1,528 (516)	Provides full-time Diploma courses for prospective Domestic Science teachers, an Institutional Management course, a Diploma course in Dietetics, and other practical courses in Cooking, Catering, Household Management, Needlework, Dressmaking and Crafts. Post-Diploma courses, non-certificate courses and evening classes are provided in a number of subjects.
West of Scotland Agricultural College	1,037 (647)	714 (438)	648 (401)	At the College in the city and at the College estate at Auchincruive, near Ayr, where practical instruction is provided, students are trained for five Scottish Diplomas—in Agriculture, Dairying (Husbandry), Dairying (Technology), Horticulture and in Poultry Husbandry. Classes are arranged in conjunction with University providing a complete course qualifying for B.Sc. Degree in Agriculture. Short courses and evening classes lead to College Certificate (e.g. in Poultry Husbandry and Bee-Keeping).

SOURCES: College Prospectuses and Annual Reports, and discussions with College officials.

founded in 1840. Its Diplomas are accepted by the Scottish Education Department as technical qualifications for the teaching of art, and its Department of Architecture forms the Glasgow School of Architecture in conjunction with the Department of Architecture at the Royal College of Science and Technology. The School of Architecture awards a Diploma, and its courses are recognised by the University as approved training for the degree of B.Sc. in Architecture.

The Royal Scottish Academy of Music, whose origins go back to the Glasgow Athenæum of 1874, was recognised as a central institution in 1939 and in 1944 was accorded the right to prefix "Royal" to its name. A programme of alterations to provide a new library, additional studies, and a students' common room is at present in hand.

Alterations recently carried out to the premises of the Glasgow and West of Scotland College of Domestic Science (founded in 1875) provided additional accommodation for the Institutional Department, including better service arrangements for the Dining Hall and facilities for instruction in various methods of large-scale service.

The first of its kind in Scotland, the West of Scotland Agricultural

College was founded in 1899. Its functions extend to advisory and research work in the College in the city, at the College estate at Auchincruive (near Ayr) and at centres in various parts of the College area.

THE UNIVERSITY[1]

If Glasgow is no longer, as it was in an earlier day, predominantly an ecclesiastical and university town, it has not turned its back entirely on its churches nor forgotten completely its principal seat of learning. Nor has the University, in its growth, forgotten or been allowed to forget the bustling commercial and industrial metropolis in which it is set. It is wholly satisfactory that the University's site on Gilmorehill overlooks the up-river docks and commands a view of the down-river shipyards; for it is not too fanciful to see in this physical relationship between crane and spire a visible symbol of a less material bond between town and gown. Quite apart from the discharge of its essential task of training and instructing, the University has since the Second World War played as central a part in the life of the community as at any time in its history.

There is much evidence of this, but we shall here instance only the following: many of its resources are now turned to the study of problems arising in the life, work and leisure of the city; a sizeable proportion of its staff serve in their own time as advisers to or officers of voluntary associations; there is regular inter-communication between University Departments and public bodies and departments of the local administration; through the University's three-year course in management studies (established in 1952) senior business and industrial executives meet members of the staff in lecture sessions and discussion groups; and there is direct contact with members of the city's adult population through the University's provisions for Extra-Mural Education. Perhaps the most striking illustration of town and gown postwar association was the week-end conference in October, 1954, on "Social Agencies and the Family in Glasgow." At this conference, which had the full support and approval of the Corporation of Glasgow and the University Court, leading representatives of the Corporation, heads and senior members of University departments, and officers of Central and Regional Government Departments examined in plenary sessions and discussion groups the impact on ordinary Glasgow families of the great social changes of the past fifty years.

Dr. R. T. Hutcheson, Secretary to the University Court and Regis-

[1] The reader is referred also to the following recent publications on the University: *The University of Glasgow, 1451-1951: A Short History* by Professor J. D. Mackie (1954); *The University of Glasgow Through Five Centuries*, a pictorial history edited by J. B. Neilson (1951); *Fortuna Domus*, a series of lectures by Heads of the older Departments (1952); and *The Book of the Fifth Centenary*, a complete record of the celebrations. The three last-mentioned works were published by the University in commemoration of the Fifth Centenary. An article by Dr. George S. Pryde, "The University of Glasgow," was published in *The Universities Review*, Vol. 20, No. 2 (January 1948).

trar, has submitted the following statement on teaching developments and material expansion:

"By 1900 there were 31 professorships in the University. Between 1900 and 1920 thirteen were added—Geology, Mining, Obstetrics, Gynæcology, Pathology (St. Mungo-Notman Chair), Scottish History and Literature, Ophthalmology, French, German, Mercantile Law, Bacteriology, Chemistry (Gardiner Chair), Physiological Chemistry, and Natural Philosophy (Cargill Chair). By 1940 twelve more had been founded—Electrical Engineering, Heat Engines (now Mechanical Engineering), Public Health, Child Health, Italian, Spanish, Accountancy, Music, Systematic Theology, Old Testament Language and Literature, New Testament Language and Literature, and Christian Ethics and Practical Theology.

The years since the war have seen the creation of a further 22 Chairs—English Language, Geography, Psychology, Civil Law, Psychological Medicine, Applied Physiology. Engineering (Mechan Chair), Education, Applied Economics, Dental Surgery, Orthodontics, Veterinary Surgery, Veterinary Pathology, Jurisprudence, Agriculture, Genetics, Mathematics (Simson Chair), Mediæval History, Economic History, Animal Husbandry, Celtic, and Engineering (Rankine Chair). Two chairs have been suppressed—Christian Ethics and New Testament.

Great as has been the increase in the number of Chairs, a much greater increase has been seen in the numbers of Lecturers and Assistants. At the beginning of the century there were 32 Lecturers and 37 Assistants; in 1920, 88 Lecturers and 63 Assistants, and to-day the totals are 420 Lecturers and 140 Assistants.

Between 1900 and the 1914-18 War, new buildings had been erected for Engineering, Botany, Natural Philosophy and some of the medical subjects, and additions to the main building included an extension to Anatomy and laboratories for Surgery.

After the First World War the Engineering Laboratories were extended, a new Zoology building was built and the West Quadrangle was completed by the University Chapel, flanked by additional rooms for the Faculty of Arts. Before the Second World War a new building for Chemistry had been begun and two thirds of this had been completed by 1939. Also just shortly before the war a small extension, the Stevenson Laboratory, was made to the Botany building, a new Observatory in University Gardens was opened and a Reading Room for students erected on the site of Hillhead House.

Since the Second World War a great deal of building has been undertaken. The remaining part of the Chemistry building has been completed as have also a large extension for Natural Philosophy (to house the 30 MeV synchrotron and to provide research rooms), a new boiler house, additions to the Zoology building and to the Anatomy building. A new Surgery Institute has been built in Church Street between the Tennent and Gardiner Institutes. Much internal reconstruction of the main building and of separate departmental buildings has been undertaken. A new Engineering building is in process of construction and it is hoped shortly to begin the erection of a new Arts building and a further extension of Natural Philosophy. All this has meant a great increase in the work of the maintenance staff and a new workshop is one of the immediate needs which it is hoped shortly to meet.

By the gift in 1921 by Lord and Lady Maclay of their house in Park Terrace in memory of two sons who fell in the 1914-18 War, a start was made with the provision of halls of residence. Strain Hall was added to Maclay Hall in 1936 by the bequest of Mr. W. W. Strain. In 1923 MacBrayne Hall was founded by the gift of Mr. Laurence MacBrayne. Queen Margaret Hall was transferred to the University in 1924. The most recent addition is Horselethill House. All these Halls have been extended over the years.

A new building for the Men's Union was opened in 1931 and the buildings vacated by the men were adapted as the Queen Margaret Union. Advanced students have been catered for by the institution of a club (Hetherington House).

Also between the wars, the new athletic ground at Westerlands was completed and a pavilion built; a further athletic ground acquired at Garscadden and a pavilion built there also.

The management of the University Gymnasium was taken over by the University Court in 1923. The present building is too small for all the activities which go on there. Plans have been prepared for a new Gymnasium with swimming bath to be erected in Oakfield Avenue.

Among the additional commitments undertaken by the University since the war is responsibility for Veterinary Education. Not only has much reconstruction of the old Veterinary College been undertaken but an Animal Hospital has been erected at Garscube. A field station has been acquired at Cochno (near Duntocher) and a number of farm buildings have been put up there. Similarly alterations have been carried out in the buildings of the Anderson College of Medicine and St. Mungo's College, which have been incorporated in the University.

The end of the building programme, however, is not yet in sight. The development plan of the University prepared by the late Sir Frank Mears envisages the complete redevelopment of the Hillhead area which has been zoned for University development in the overall plan of the city."

Table 104 in the Appendix shows the numbers of matriculated students in selected years and analyses the enrolments by sex and Faculty. Student numbers rose from 2,916 in session 1913-14 to the peak figure of 7,540 in 1948-9. Since then, with the exception of a slight rise in 1954-5, there has been an unbroken fall to 5,753 as at

November 1955. (This trend, however, will be arrested in the middle and late 1960's, when, as a consequence of the high birth-rate of 1946 and 1947 Glasgow in common with other British universities will have to meet an increased demand for places.)

In postwar sessions there have been from 3 to 4 times as many men students as women students, the male percentage rising from almost exactly 75 in 1946-7 to 80.5 in 1948-9 and then falling to 77.2 as at November 1955. This was almost exactly the male proportion in session 1913-14, but in the interwar years shown in Table 104 women formed a higher proportion—in 1918-19 and 1928-9 as high as 30 per cent—of the enrolment than they have done in any of the postwar years with the exception of 1946-7. The higher the over-all total, the higher is the proportion of male students: in three of the four sessions when enrolment passed the 7,000 mark the male proportion varied between 80 per cent and 80.5 per cent, while in the fourth it was 79 per cent.

Since 1946-7, as in 1913-14 and in general in the 1920's and 1930's, Arts has been the largest single Faculty in terms of student numbers. In 1913-14, 43.7 per cent of students were in Arts and 28.2 in Medicine and 18.8 in Science. In 1918-19, however, Medicine had 57.5 per cent compared with 25.4 in Arts and 13.5 in Science. By the late 1920's and the late 1930's Arts had re-asserted its predominance—in 1928-9 to the tune of 55.1 per cent as against Medicine's 16 per cent and Science's 10.4 per cent. In 1946-7 the distribution was: Arts, 36.5 per cent, Medicine, 18.9 per cent, Science, 18.4 per cent and Engineering 12.5 per cent; but since then there has been a more even spread over these four Faculties and at November 1955 27.3 per cent were in Arts, 26.1 per cent in Medicine, 22.3 per cent in Science and 14.4 per cent in Engineering. Enrolments in the Faculty of Law have since the war varied between 550 (1946-7) and 694 (1950-1), but they have never risen above 10 per cent of the total. By 1953-4 enrolments in Divinity had fallen from the immediate postwar figure of 114 to 65, but there was a recovery the following session to 91, and in November 1955 the figure stood at 92—1.6 per cent of the student body.

Arts is pre-eminently the favourite Faculty among women, although the postwar years can show nothing like the proportion of 84.2 per cent of all women students who were in Arts in 1928-9, compared with 5.7 per cent in Medicine and 7.9 per cent in Science. Two thirds of women students were in Arts in 1946-7, but the postwar period has shown a gradual (though not unbroken) move away from Arts into Medicine and Science. In November 1955 the number of women taking an Arts course had fallen to 53.7 per cent of all women students, while enrolments in Medicine rose from 15.9 per cent in 1946-7 to 23.1 per cent, and in Science from 14.6 per cent to 20.4 per cent over the same period. The enrolment of women in Law has varied since the war between approximately 3 and 4 per cent of women students. Normally women students in Divinity and Engineering are, literally, numbered in ones and twos, but in 1954-5 there were 3 women Divinity students and a year later 4.

The courses being followed in 1954-5, and the number of degrees awarded in various Faculties in selected years going back to 1913-14, are shown in Tables 105 and 106 of the Statistical Appendix.[1] Table 107 shows that in session 1954-5 the homes of more than three quarters—77.1 per cent—of University students (excluding students of the R.C.S.T.) were in the city or within a 30-miles radius. This compares with 71.7 per cent twenty years earlier. Somewhat contrary to general impression, there has been a decline in the proportion of students whose homes are in the United Kingdom and over 30 miles from Glasgow. But the University now has more foreign students, both absolutely and relatively, than twenty years ago, and the proportion of British Commonwealth students has doubled.

An important development in recent years has been the steady increase in the proportion of the University's revenue coming from public funds. Of a total revenue of £1,612,729 for the year ended 31 July 1955 student fees at £184,382—a large part of which sum, in any case, derives from education authority grants—accounted for 11.4 per cent, while grants to the University from local authorities (£8,700), the grant from the Education (Scotland) Fund (£21,000), and Parliamentary Grants (£1,185,937), amounting in all to £1,215,637, accounted for 75.4 per cent.

Since the war there has been notable expansion of the provisions made by the University Extra-Mural Education Committee. After a temporary decline in the early 1950's compared with the immediate postwar period up to 1949-50, both the number of classes provided and student enrolments have increased steadily in recent years to reach, in session 1955-6, the record figures of 181 and 4,014 respectively. This latter figure of student enrolment represents a level about 25 per cent higher than in the peak period of the late 1940's. The majority of classes are in Literature (36 out of 181 in 1955-6) and Science (35), followed by History (28), Social Studies (18), Art and Aesthetics (14), Philosophy and Religion (12 each) and International Affairs (11). Other subjects offered are Psychology (7 classes), Government (4) and Music (4). Alongside this development has gone an expansion in the provision of Summer Schools (including a number held at centres on the Continent) and Extension Courses.

[1] Among the interesting points brought out by my colleague, Miss Hilda R. Kahn, in an unpublished paper, "University of Glasgow: Sundry information about degrees and graduates," are these: (1) in both the Faculties of Arts and Science the number of Honours, relative to Ordinary, graduands has been on the increase; (2) the proportions obtaining First Class Honours degrees in Arts and in Science have shown a falling-off since prewar; (3) teacher training claimed the highest proportion of men graduating in Arts in 1954—29.2 per cent, compared with 16.4 per cent of Pure Science (excluding Engineering etc.) graduands. This was followed by "industrial, commercial and professional" employments (19.2 per cent of Arts and 18.8 per cent of Pure Science graduands); (4) teaching is much more popular with Ordinary than with Honours Pure Science graduates: 43.2 per cent of the former, but only 12.4 per cent of the latter proceeded to a teacher training course (men graduands, 1954). The proportion taking up "industrial, commercial and professional" posts on the other hand was hardly affected—in Arts or Pure Science—by the Ordinary/Honours classification.

The University's Extra-Mural work, both in provision and in geographical spread—from Dumfries in the South-West to Lewis in the North, and from Argyll to Lanarkshire and Stirlingshire—is unequalled in Scotland. Further, it is beginning to compare favourably with English centres in which, as a result of the less adequate provision until recently in formal education, adult education has always won greater support than in Scotland.[1]

In Glasgow itself in 1955-6 there were 87 classes and a record enrolment of 2,010. But, encouraging as this expansion is, the enrolment is still a minute proportion (less than one third of one per cent) of the 733,900 persons in Glasgow aged 20 and over—and there is nothing to prevent older 'teen-agers from joining these classes. Moreover, while the University's extra-mural provision is not in any sense expressly aimed at or designed for industrial workers, it is noteworthy that manual workers seldom constitute much more than about 10 per cent of total enrolment. It rather looks as if, from this point of view at anyrate, the traditional notion that the Scots are a nation of education-lovers is no longer, if at any time it was, borne out by the facts.

1 A factor that has restricted Scottish advance in this field is the fact that organisations providing facilities for non-residential adult education are not in receipt of direct government grants as are their counterparts in the South, with the recent exception of direct grants towards administrative costs only. The bulk of the Extra-Mural Committee's expenditure is met by a grant from the University Court, contributions from the Education Authorities of the areas served, and assistance from one or two Trusts.

Chapter 17

OTHER PUBLIC SERVICES

ROBERT BAIRD

The Growth of "Police" Functions

In March 1779 Glasgow Town Council made its first attempt to substitute an organised police force for the ancient system of watch and ward by the burgesses. A Police Inspector was appointed at a salary of £100 with a few men under his command, but the force was disbanded in 1781. In 1790 the Council set up a "night guard and patrol to watch and guard the streets." Every male citizen between the ages of 16 and 60 was liable for service on this patrol if he paid a yearly rent of £3 or more, but he could escape his tour of duty on payment of 2s. 6d. for a substitute. The city was divided into four districts and nine men to each district were required for patrol duty each night.

An Act was eventually obtained in 1800 to establish a Police Board consisting of the Lord Provost, the three magistrates, the Dean of Guild, the Deacon Convener and 24 Commissioners chosen by ballot by the ratepayers in 24 police wards of the town. This Act gave the Board power to levy an assessment for police purposes,[1] and required the town council to pay to the police board not less than £800 per annum as long as the Council continued to levy one sixth of a penny on every pint of beer or ale sold within the Royalty and Gorbals. The Act was to last for seven years and made provision also for the Board's paving, lighting and cleansing of the city streets. The Police Board's revenue for the first year amounted to about £5,000, £3,400 being obtained from the assessment, £576 from the sale of street manure, £126 from police fines, £800 from the town council and the rest from miscellaneous small sums. The Master of Police had a salary of £200, there were three sergeants at £40 each, nine officers at £30 each, 68 watchmen at a weekly wage of 10s. and a Clerk and Treasurer at a salary of £165. Under the Act there was spent in the first year £1,400 on lighting 930 lamps, £310 in street cleansing and £153 in buying "boxes" (sentry-boxes) for the watchmen. The Act was renewed in 1807 and again in 1821 with some changes, principally the appointment of two resident Commissioners for each ward whose duty it was to exercise constabulary powers and general supervision of the police functions in their areas. The resident commissioners were not members

[1] The rates of assessment were graduated according to levels of rents, e.g. 4d. in the £ on rents between £4 and £6 and 1s. in the £ on rents of £15 and upwards.

of the Police Board and had no part in the formal police administration of the town as a whole.

The first Central Police Office was built in South Albion Street in 1825. Until that time the police force had used the Old Tron Church Session House (as had the town guard before them) and later premises in Candleriggs and East Albion Street.

The extension of the city area in 1830 added nine extra wards for police purposes and the Board was increased in size by the addition of the necessary commissioners, general and resident. In 1843 the management of the functions of the Statute Labour Trustees was transferred to the Police Board, which was given power to levy an assessment of 3d. per £ of rental for Statute Labour purposes. By the same Act the town council was relieved of its obligation to pay a minimum of £800 a year to the Board as its power of taxing the beer and ale of the Royalty and Gorbals had expired in 1839. The large extensions of 1843 raised the number of police wards in the town to 36, each with its one General and two Resident Commissioners. With the reorganisation of the city for local government purposes in 1846 the Police Board was abolished and in its place there was set up a Police and Statute Labour Committee of the Town Council. This Committee consisted of the Lord Provost, Magistrates, the Dean, the Deacon and 18 other Councillors (one from each ward and two from the general council) but all its functions and workings had to be kept strictly separate from the operations of the town council and neither the Town Clerk nor the City Chamberlain was eligible to serve under the Committee. Police Courts and police offices were at the same time established in Calton, Anderston and Gorbals—the Courts to be presided over by the town magistrates with the assistance of Assessors whose appointments the Act authorised.

In 1862 a "Police Board" again made its appearance, but it was in effect the Police Committee of the 1846 Act under a new name. In 1877 this Board in turn was abolished and the Town Council became the Commissioners of Police, although again it was thought necessary to insist upon a separate system of accounts and an entirely independent organisation. Finally, in 1895 the Glasgow Corporation and Police Act united the Police Commissioners (and a number of other local governing bodies referred to later) with the Town Council under the Council's official description as "The Corporation of the City of Glasgow." By then the police force had grown to be a body of over 1,300 men costing, for pay and clothing alone, about £109,000 a year. Between 1890 and 1895 police powers had been substantially enlarged to cover such things as sanitation, sewerage, licensing (of theatres, public shows, billiard rooms, etc.) and building regulations. At the present day (1955) the authorised strength of the police force (constabulary) is 2,381 (including 44 women police), the effective strength is 2,214, the total number employed by the department is 2,548, organised in seven Divisions with 19 offices or stations throughout the city, a Police Headquarters (Administrative and C.I.D.) in St. Andrew's Street, and a Wireless

Station out of town at Cathkin Braes. Total ordinary expenditure in 1955 was £2,210,276, more than half of which went for wages and salaries. This expenditure was met to the extent of £1,011,279 by central government grants (calculated on the basis of 50 per cent of "approved" net expenditure, including police pensions), and to the extent of £1,024,338 by a rate levy on city occupiers.

In the aggregate accounts of the city the "Police Account" still covers not only the functions of the formally organised constabulary but also those various powers and duties that had accrued from time to time by Act of Parliament to the old Police Boards, Commissioners, or Committee, namely lighting, fire service, cleansing, baths and wash-houses, and public halls. It will be appropriate therefore to say something about these services here.

Lighting

In 1818 the first lamps lit by gas (1,472 of them) were put into the city streets by the Glasgow Gas-light Company. At first these lamps were little more than something of a novelty to be wondered at by the citizens but as their usefulness came to be appreciated their number steadily increased. In 1866 the Glasgow Police Act authorised the Police Board to put up lamps and lamp-posts to light the public and private streets, courts and common stairs in town. Within four years the number of street lamps had risen to 10,657 and there were in addition 17,284 stair lights in operation. The staff of the Lighting department was by then 294 and its cost to the city £29,246. Just before the First World War there were 19,437 gas lamps and 1,541 electric lamps (the latter first introduced in 1893) in the public streets, over 6,000 gas lamps, mainly incandescent, and 126 electric lamps in the private streets and courts; and over 80,000 gas and incandescent burners, and 3,449 electric lamps lighting the common stairs of tenements. The staff had risen to about 1,050 and the cost to the city to £138,866. In the 40 years that have since passed, the principal change has been, of course, to electricity although gas is still in substantial use (in 1955 the department looked after 7,723 gas lamps and 33,186 electric lamps in the city streets, together with 55,201 gas and 49,031 electric stair lights). The departmental staff had increased by only 407;[1] but the cost of lighting to the city reveals the true extent of the technical, social, and economic changes involved: at £1,076,896 it had gone up to nearly eight times the 1914 level and was equivalent to 1s. 5.24d. in the £ of the city's rental in that year.

[1] This largely, of course, as the result of the change-over to electricity.

Fire Service

Seven years after the first Police Board was founded in 1800 it was charged by statute with the duty of fire-fighting in the city and took over the existing apparatus which apparently consisted of 6 manual pumping engines with about 1,000 feet of sewn leather hose. The pumping engines were pulled to the fires by the firemen, and water for them was carried from wells or from the river. With the formation of the two private water companies in the city in 1806 and 1808 it became possible to instal a few fire-cocks in some of the town's streets and by 1816 there were 152 fire-cocks and the Board possessed about 450 yards of hose. The Board appears to have taken its fire-fighting duties very seriously and in 1834 it strictly defined the respective duties of the Superintendent and Lieutenants of Police on the one hand, and of the Superintendent of the fire department (first appointed in 1809), the firemen and the 16 carters attached to the fire department on the other. The fire department was to be formally under the command of the Superintendent of Police except at times of actual outbreak of fire when the Superintendent of the Fire department was to be responsible for the ordering out of pumping engines and water butts and was to be in charge of the operations at the site, the police force proper being commanded to turn out to all fires and give all the assistance they could under the control of the Superintendent of the fire department.

By 1862 the fire service had been speeded up by the introduction of a telegraphic linkage between the fire station and all police offices in the city, and by the stabling of the horses at the Central Fire Station so that the engines there could be on their way to a fire within two minutes of receiving a telegraphed message.

By 1864, the new Loch Katrine water supply provided a sufficient pressure at 2,700 fire cocks in the city " to send the water to the highest house " without the need for pumping-engines, and it was no longer necessary to cart water to any fire in the town.

The first steam fire engine came into use at the Central Fire Station in 1871; it could throw about 400 gallons of water per minute to a height of 180 feet. There were in addition at this station five manual engines, two hose and ladder carriages, two hand reels, and eight horses; and two drivers with sleeping quarters above the stables. The whole central force numbered 30 and a full muster was summoned by drum-beat at the station door, although the two assistant superintendents and the eight other permanent members of the central force could be summoned by bells directly connected to their homes. At this time there were also five district stations, each with seven branchmen and firemen, one manual engine, one hose, and one hand reel. Horses for drawing these district station engines were not kept by the fire department but were provided by local carters and others and it was not until 1873 that the whole fire department was equipped with its own horses. When a district fire station was in operation, its staff was in the charge of a foreman who was generally the local constable on the beat. The close link with police functions proper was still being maintained.

By the outbreak of the War of 1914-18 horse traction had disappeared, and although there were still four steam fire engines in use, there were 24 motor vehicles in the service (the majority internal-combustion pump engines). The headquarters station (opened in 1900) was in Ingram Street and there were ten district stations which could turn out in 8 to 12 seconds in daytime and in 25 to 30 seconds at night. Expenditure for fire-fighting had gone up to £31,471.

In 1955 the service used 75 motor vehicles and had 575 of a fire-fighting staff (authorised strength 582) and employed in all 631 persons at a total wage-bill of £339,491. It was organised in 13 operational fire stations throughout the city with a central Firemaster's office and administrative offices in addition. It dealt with 6,057 fire-calls and 129 other " special " calls in the previous year. Of the total cost of £459,581 in that year £103,816 was met by government grant (25 per cent of " approved " net expenditure) and £332,516 by the owner and occupier rate-payers in equal proportion, the latter sum being equivalent to a total charge on the rates of 5.71d. in the £.

Cleansing

It is difficult to imagine that the appointment of one extra man to the job of street cleaning in the city in 1777 increased the labour force by 50 per cent! When the Police Board, formed in 1800, was given the responsibility for this duty the town council scarcely seemed to realise the staggering implications for public health of the rapidly increasing accumulations of filth of all descriptions within the city boundaries. The Police Board first arranged for the job of street cleaning to be done by its own constabulary (or night-watchmen), each doing two tours of two hours' duty a week on this task. This arrangement was one of the less successful plans of the new Board, and by 1815 there were 16 scavengers permanently employed on this work at a wage of 11s. a week. Up to 1862 the Board's cleansing activities continued to cover only the sweeping of the streets; occupiers of city premises dealt with the contents of their ashpits and middens as they thought fit. From 1862 the removal of the sweepings and the collection and disposal of domestic refuse were arranged for by the Police Board through a contractor who was paid for the work. This contracting system was abolished in 1868 when the Board took over all cleansing and refuse-disposal operations. The following figures give an indication of the growth of the work of the Department between 1869 and 1914.

	1869-70	1900	1914
Staff	652	1,223	1,667
Horses	140	273	387
Net cost	£23,895	£79,225	£128,116
Material dealt with	165,000 tons	444,515 tons	387,380 tons

By 1955 the Cleansing Department employed a total staff of 2,051 (at a wage and salary bill of £1,212,439), organised in a Head Office and 20 District Depots which included stores, disposal works, garages and workshops. Two hundred and seventy-three mechanically propelled vehicles were used to deal with about 450,782 tons of refuse and the Department owned three farms and three other estates, one being a "coup" and another the site for a disposal works. Electrical current amounting to 14,339,000 units was generated at the refuse power works, and a not inappreciable amount of revenue was obtained from the sale of refuse, waste paper, etc. (£160,381). But the bulk of the total expenditure of £1,622,695 fell upon the occupiers' rates (£1,288,610) and represented 1s. 10.15d. in the £ of rental.

Baths and Wash-houses

There had been a Corporation public wash-house (for clothes) in Glasgow Green from 1742 but it was not until the Loch Katrine water supply was introduced in 1859 that the city governors became actively interested in setting up public baths and wash-houses for the whole city. The old wash-house in the Green was demolished in 1876 and on its site the Greenhead baths and wash-house were opened in 1878 with two swimming ponds (one for men and a smaller one for women), 27 private baths for men, 7 private baths for women and 40 "stalls" for clothes-washing. This establishment cost £17,190 and is still going strong. By 1914 there were 20 baths and wash-houses in the Corporation's control, some of which had no swimming ponds, some others with no private baths, but only two without stalls for clothes-washing. The era of the "steamie" had arrived.

In 1955 there were 15 establishments with baths, wash-houses and swimming pools, 11 with baths and wash-houses only, and two with clothes-washing facilities only. Attendances at the "steamies" in the year were just short of 1,800,000 and at the swimming ponds and baths just over $3\frac{1}{2}$ millions. Whether as a result of a continuing Calvinistic influence in our culture or of increased costs of supervision or simply of the principle of charging what the market will bear, it cost 50 per cent more to indulge in "mixed bathing" than it did to swim with members of one's own sex only.

Public Halls

Glasgow in 1955 was the owner of 22 public halls (excluding Kelvin Hall and People's Palace, Glasgow Green), capable of accommodating in all 25,740 people. The City Hall in Candleriggs was built in 1840 and took the place of the old town hall at Glasgow Cross and also of the Merchants' Hall in Bridgegate. The City Hall was for long a centre of the most active public social life of the town. At one time it belonged to that section of the Common Good fund of the city that owned the fruit and cheese markets and other properties in Albion Street. In 1914 its capacity was estimated by the City's Manager of Public Halls to be 3,500 persons but to-day, whether as the result of changes in structure, use, or standards of permitted accommodation, it is listed at 1,806 persons. In 1856 the Corporation bought for £29,500 the block of red sandstone buildings on the north side of Sauchiehall Street which contained the McLellan Galleries and also paid £15,000 for Bailie McLellan's collection of pictures. In 1859 the Galleries were transferred to the Parks and Galleries Trustees, and in 1909 back to the Common Good fund after the transfer of the art treasures to the Art Galleries in Kelvingrove.

In 1890 the city bought St. Andrew's Halls (which had been completed in 1877) for £37,500 and spent a further £6,000 in re-decoration and improvements. The capacity of this hall was put at 4,500 persons in 1914 and at no more than 2,434 in 1955. Three more halls came into the city's possession through the boundary extensions of 1891 (Pollokshields, Hillhead and Maryhill) and another (Dixon Hall) was bought in 1893 following upon the city's annexation of the burghs of Govanhill and Crosshill in 1891. Five more halls came within the boundaries in the annexations of 1912 (Partick, Whiteinch, Govan, Pollokshaws and the Couper Institute, Cathcart) and eventually in 1955 there were 12 halls belonging to the Common Good fund and ten more to the Police department. Since 1930 all public halls have in fact been managed by the General Finance Committee of the Corporation although deficits, if any, upon halls belonging to the Common Good Fund are still met out of that Fund's revenues whereas those on Police Department Halls are met out of occupiers' rate levies. In 1955 the deficit falling on the rates was £6,035.

Sewers and Sewage Purification

As long ago as 1602 the Convention of Burghs was urging Glasgow to do something about the increasing pollution of the Clyde by the city's sewage, and at that time there were only about 7,000 inhabitants of the city and the massive industrialisation of Clydeside was still a long way off.

The first common sewers in the town were formed in 1790, and by 1876 when the growth of the city had made the problem of sewage one of grave importance, there were only 88½ miles of common sewer to a population close on half a million; and the sewage was dumped straight into the Clyde, without any treatment whatsoever, to accumulate in the harbour and the lower reaches unless the rainfall were heavy enough to swell the river and wash some of the deposits down to the sea. And the Clyde had once been a salmon river!

The first major step to deal with the problem was not taken until 1887 although for more than 25 years before that many schemes had been proposed and all abandoned as impractical or too costly. Two examples will serve to illustrate how baffled the city appeared to have been by the problem. One scheme proposed the building of a large high-level reservoir in the upper ward of Lanarkshire from which, particularly in spells of dry weather, "artificial spates" could be released to scour the harbour and the lower reaches of the river. Another suggestion was to collect all the city's sewage at one pumping station where it could be raised to a level of 260 feet and allowed to flow by gravity in a conduit to the sandy wastes of Ayrshire. The reactions of the people of Ayrshire are not recorded.

In 1887 a Private Bill (later taken over by the Caledonian Railway Company) was promoted in Parliament asking for powers to construct a railway tunnel beneath many of the city's most important streets. The Town Council objected, particularly on the grounds that the work would interfere with the existing, and by no means adequate, sewers and sewage system. The Company then undertook to pay the whole expense of replanning and reconstructing the sewage system to the satisfaction of the local authority. The Bill was passed and a new system of drains was built to take the sewage of the east and north-east districts of the city to a works for its treatment and disposal to be specially constructed at Dalmarnock. Under an Act of 1891 this sewage works at Dalmarnock was completed and put into operation in 1894. Although, during the discussions of the middle of the nineteenth century, expert opinion had declared that there was no known process of chemical filtration and precipitation that would "effect the desired object," the Dalmarnock works was a complete success with a system of chemical precipitation and filter pressing and, later, the biological filtering of the effluent before its discharge into the river. So successful was it that in 1895 the Corporation resolved to build similar works to deal with the sewage of the rest of the area of the city on the north bank of the river.

Partick pumping station and the Dalmuir Sewage Works were opened in 1904—Kinning Park Pumping Station and the Shieldhall Sewage Works in 1910—and a fourth Works was later opened at Westthorn. The system serves not only the city of Glasgow but also the burghs of Clydebank and Rutherglen and parts of Lanarkshire, Renfrewshire and Dunbartonshire.

By 1955 there were 640.4 miles of public sewers draining into 68½ miles of main trunk sewers. In that year the four purification works treated an average of 122,468,825 gallons of sewage a day. The department employed two sludge steamers that carried an average of 1,908 tons of sludge a day out to sea for dumping. Ordinary expenditure on sewer maintenance amounted to £120,371, of which £117,971 was borne by the rates (2.03d. in the £). Capital expenditure for the year on sewers was £5,450. Ordinary expenditure for sewage purification amounted to £600,953, of which the rates carried £542,777 (9.33d. in the £). Capital expenditure on new sewers was £240,961, and for a new sludge vessel costing £134,459 a grant of £2,475 was paid by the Ministry of Labour.

Water Supply

At the beginning of the nineteenth century the principal sources of water supplies in Glasgow were 30 public wells and a number of private wells, most of which were still in use at the middle of the century. Water was of course taken from the river and streams by those who lived near them but from the centre of the city down-river the waters of the Clyde were unfit for consumption. In 1806 the Glasgow Water-works Company was formed to pump water from the Clyde at Dalmarnock into reservoirs there, thence after filtration to other reservoirs in the centre of the city, and thence again for distribution to various parts of the city and suburbs.

Another Water-works Company was formed in 1808—the Cranstonhill Company—to pump water from the Clyde at Anderston Quay into reservoirs at Cranstonhill and thence to consumers on the west side of the town. In 1819, owing to the state of the river water at Anderston, this company was forced to move its works to a site just below the works of the Glasgow Company at Dalmarnock.

These two companies had a hard struggle to exist separately and in 1838 they combined—after strong opposition by the Town Council, which was anxious to have the town's water supply in its own hands, or in the hands of a public trust.

The Gorbals Gravitation Water Company was formed in 1846 to supply the area south of the Clyde with water drawn from the Brock burn and its tributaries (about six miles south of the city) and conducted by conduits into Gorbals, Pollokshaws and Govan.

In the same year (1846) a Bill promoted by the Glasgow Company to take water from Loch Lubnaig to the city was approved by Parliament but the scheme was not proceeded with because the amount of compensation water which, the Act stipulated, must be discharged into the river Teith was more than the Company could undertake to provide. The promotion of this Loch Lubnaig scheme had been used by the Glasgow Company to persuade the town council to abandon a scheme of its own to bring water from Loch Katrine. A bitter struggle between the town council and the Glasgow water company went on for nine years until in 1855 Parliament passed the Act empowering Glasgow to bring a supply of water from Loch Katrine to the city and to take over the undertakings of the Glasgow and the Gorbals water companies. (The costs of obtaining this Bill amounted to nearly £9,000).[1] Under this Act the Glasgow Company's works were dismantled but the Gorbals Company's works were kept going as a source of extra supply to the South of the city and its suburbs there, and in 1955 the Gorbals works were still supplying areas on the south side with about 5 million gallons a day.

The Loch Katrine water supply was Glasgow's first, and perhaps still its greatest, municipal undertaking on the grand scale. Details of the construction work can be found in numerous publications,[1] and only the briefest review of the scheme can be attempted here.

The Act appointed the Town Council to be Water Commissioners and required them to appoint, from time to time, the "Water Committee" from their own members. This latter provision was repealed by Provisional Order of 1877 which re-appointed the whole council to administer the Water Acts as Commissioners. The Act also imposed certain limitations and duties upon the Water Commissioners, e.g. (1) they could raise the level of the loch no more than 4 feet above the previous summer level and draw it down no more than 3 feet below that level; (2) they could take no more than 50 million gallons a day out of the loch; (3) they were empowered to build an aqueduct from the loch and a reservoir into which to lead the waters; (4) Lochs Duchrie and Vennachar could be used to provide the necessary compensation water for the river Teith; (5) the work had to be done in such a way as to allow salmon and other fish to pass freely into and from the lochs; (6) they could lay down domestic supply pipes in the streets but owners and occupiers had to provide the essential connection pipes and water-using apparatus; (7) the domestic water rates chargeable to occupiers and the public water rates chargeable to owners of city property were authorised and defined; (8) the Commissioners could borrow up to £700,000 for the cost of the works involved and the land and properties to be bought. (In April 1859 borrowing power was increased by statute to £900,000 and in 1860 a further borrowing of £350,000 was authorised.)

Work was begun in the spring of 1856 and was completed in 1859. Queen Victoria travelled from Balmoral by train and coach and on a wet and stormy day, 15 October 1859, turned the handle that let the waters of Loch Katrine into the tunnel and works constructed to lead to the Mugdock reservoir. In March 1860 the supply was led into the city from the reservoir. The total cost of the works thus far (including alterations to the Gorbals Water-works) was £924,141. The first aque-

[1] In 1852 the number of people in Glasgow supplied with water by the water companies was about 36,000. The consumption then was just under 39 gallons per head per day inclusive of trade, industrial, municipal and domestic users.

[1] e.g. *Glasgow: The Water Supply and various Developments of the City till the close of 1900*, compiled by Sir James D. Marwick, a former town clerk of the City. (1901.)

duct from Loch Katrine to the Mugdock reservoir at Milngavie was just under 26 miles long (the distance to Glasgow itself was over 34 miles) and was 8 feet by 8 feet in size. The Mugdock reservoir had a capacity of 500 million gallons and was connected to the city by three 36-inch mains. No filtration of the water was necessary; it had only to be strained through fine copper wire.

Various minor developments in the scheme took place up to 1885 and in that year another Act of Parliament authorised the duplication of the original works. The Loch could be raised by another 5 feet, another aqueduct could be constructed, 110 million gallons a day could be taken off instead of the original 50 million gallons, and Loch Arklet could be used as a storage loch the waters of which could be led into Loch Katrine by a tunnel. These things were done and a second reservoir at Craigmaddie, Milngavie, was constructed with a capacity of 700 million gallons. By 1915 there were eight 36-inch mains from the two reservoirs to the city. To prevent pollution of the lochs, the feu rights over the whole drainage areas to the two lochs were bought for £17,700 and in 1919 the whole watershed of Loch Katrine and Loch Arklet was bought by the Corporation.

Just before the First World War a population of 1,104,000 was being supplied at a daily rate of 65.7 gallons (all kinds of consumption) a head—a total supply of 72,680,000 gallons daily; capital expenditure on the scheme had mounted to about £4½ million, of which the largest items were the cost of the 1885 duplication project (£1,917,454) and the cost of the first aqueduct, reservoir, pipes, lands, properties, compensation etc. (£1,500,538).

By 1955 capital expenditure was £9,079,533 and the average daily consumption (domestic and trade consumption together) per head of a population of 1,220,000 had risen to 74 gallons. The principal charges for this supply in 1955 were the domestic water rate of 6d. per £ payable by occupiers and the public water rate of 2.3d. per £ payable in equal proportions by owners and occupiers. Various other scales of charges were in force for supplies to areas outside the city, supplies for hydraulic power and other purposes charged by meter rates, supplies for fire appliances, and un-metered supplies for certain business and trade premises.

Gas Supply

Before 1869 two private companies supplied Glasgow and neighbourhood with gas for lighting, namely the "Glasgow Gas Light Company," formed in 1817 as a joint venture between the town council and a number of private citizens, and the "City and Suburban Gas Company of Glasgow," formed in 1843 as a purely private concern to supply gas to the City, Gorbals, Anderston, Calton, Rutherglen and neighbourhood. In 1869 the city obtained from Parliament an Act transferring these two enterprises to the Corporation. In 1891 the

Corporation also bought over the Partick, Hillhead and Maryhill Gas Company, and in the interim had acquired the works of several other small companies that had been operating near the city boundaries. By 1913 the Corporation's gas department was supplying gas from five gas-works (at Provan, Dawsholm, Tradeston, Dalmarnock and Temple) at the rate of nearly 7,733 million cubic feet a year to 286,883 consumers within an area of 98 square miles which included not only the city but also parts of Lanarkshire, Renfrewshire, Dunbartonshire and Stirlingshire. There were by then 1,048 miles of gas main pipes and the cost of gas was from 1s. 4d. to 1s. 11d. per 1,000 cubic feet. The department had at that time four show-rooms at which the most up-to-date appliances for heating, cooking and water-heating were demonstrated. Up to 1912 the department issued gas-cookers on hire and gas-fires on hire-purchase, but for some years after that date cookers were issued free of charge and fires on terms of hire. By 1913 there were 144,584 gas cookers in use by consumers free of charge, 12,589 gas fires on hire, and 6,391 gas fires on hire-purchase. There were also 286,883 gas meters in use and the department was using 741,838 tons of coal and selling 307,178 tons of coke a year. The incidental revenue from the sale of by-products was £206,072 and total revenue for the year to 31 May 1913 was £1,022,917.

In the last year of its existence before being taken over by the Scottish Gas Board under the Gas Act of 1948,[1] the department operated four principal gas works and four chemical works and owned various workshops and showrooms. There were then about 1,595 miles of gas mains serving a total population of 1,266,000. The department had issued 234,876 cookers on hire and loan and 10,862 gas fires and radiators on hire. Coal consumed was well over half a million tons and 2,863,034 gallons of oil were used in the carburetted water gas plant. Nearly a quarter of a million tons of coke were sold at an average price of 49s. 11½d. a ton. Capital expenditure had mounted to £10,423,768 and debt stood at just over £2 millions. In this last year's working the department's revenue was £3,829,205 and it made a surplus of £52,542. The charges to domestic consumers varied, according to consumption and the type of meter used, from 3s. 9d. to 4s. 8d. per 1,000 cubic feet, and to consumers on special contracts from 2s. 6½d. to 4s. 2d. per 1,000 cubic feet.

Electricity Supply

The provisional order entitled "The Glasgow Corporation Electric Lighting Order 1890" granted to the city by the Board of Trade under the Electric Lighting Acts 1882 and 1888 was confirmed by statute in October 1890. The town council were then authorised to supply electricity within the whole of the city and royal burgh for public and private purposes and given all the incidental powers neces-

[1] For statistics of gas supply in the period 1921-55 see Appendix Table 108.

sary to do this. The same Act confirmed another order of the Board of Trade in favour of the Kelvinside Electric Company Limited—Kelvinside being at that time outside the municipal boundaries—and in 1899 the Kelvinside Company was bought over by the city for £37,000. In 1892 the Corporation also bought up Mavor & Coulson's generating station in John Street for £15,000 and in the following year opened its own generating station in Waterloo Street. In 1900 the Waterloo Street station was closed as a generating station and turned into a sub-station. Two more generating stations—one at Port Dundas and another in Pollokshaws Road—were opened at the turn of the century. In 1910 when it became evident that the existing generating plant would soon become quite inadequate to deal with the mounting demand, the Corporation bought 11 acres of land upon which to build the present generating station at Dalmarnock, which was then intended to supply 100,000 Kilowatts of power. At the time of the transfer of this station to the British Electricity Authority in 1948 its capacity was 237,500 Kilowatts.

The Commissioners of Police of the burghs of Partick and Govan had obtained provisional orders in 1893 empowering them to supply their towns with electricity, and the two generating stations in these areas came within the city by the Glasgow Boundaries Act of 1912. These were closed as generating stations and converted to sub-stations taking high-tension power from the Glasgow generators and transforming it to low-tension current. One of the reasons for this decision was the very large demand for low-tension power from the ship-building and engineering firms in Govan and Partick: single firms had already made demands for power that were by themselves above the joint capacities of the existing Partick and Govan stations.

Before the outbreak of the First World War the Electricity department was selling about 66 million units a year—about 41 million for power and 25 million for lighting—at prices ranging from ¾d. a unit of industrial power supply after the first 1,000 units (1½d. a unit for the first 1,000 and ½d. a unit for consumption over 2,500 units per annum) to 3d. a unit for domestic lighting (¾d. a unit for domestic power which took even then about ½ million units a year for "heating, cooking, ironing and the working of vacuum cleaners") and varying charges between ¾d. and 3½d. a unit for lighting warehouses and business premises. Total revenue for the year (to 31 May 1913) was £345,749, gross profit £175,109 and net profit £7,520. Gross capital expenditure had reached £2,858,941, fully 50 per cent of which had been spent on underground mains. There were in all 27.848 consumers.

The department was taken over by the British Electricity Authority in 1948 under the Electricity Act of 1947.[1] The Dalmarnock station was then its only generating station but the department also operated 17 rotary sub-stations and 161 static sub-stations. There were other 501 sub-stations in the premises of consumers. The number of consumers

1 For statistics of electricity supply in the period 1949-55 see Appendix Table 109.

was 240,982 and 45 per cent of the current generated was used for power. Capital expenditure to the date of the take-over was £12,543,712 but £8,096,034 of Sinking Funds had been applied in the reduction of debt and another £1,863,876 of capital expenditure had been met out of revenue leaving debt outstanding of £2,523,893. Revenue for the final year of operation was £2,480,905 and the department made a surplus of £26,060. Prices charged for domestic supplies for lighting, heating and cooking ranged from 0.4d. to 3d. a unit, and for power supplies from 0.75d. to 1.125d. a unit. The average price charged overall was 0.81d. a unit.

LIBRARIES

The plebiscite is not a procedure now used in Glasgow's local government, except in the case of the "wet or dry" licensing polls. But three plebiscites were held in the last quarter of the nineteenth century (in 1876, 1885 and 1888) in an attempt by the City Council to adopt the Free Libraries Act and provide libraries for the town out of the rates. In each case the proposal was turned down by the ratepayers. Another attempt to adopt the Act by simple motion of the Council was made in 1897 and the motion was defeated by a majority vote. It was not until 1899, through the medium of a private Act of Parliament, that the City Corporation was empowered to set up free public libraries, to borrow £100,000 and to levy an assessment of 1d. in the £ on owners and occupiers for the purpose. The major provisions of this Act dealt with the city tramways and the library powers appear to have been slipped in as an afterthought. In April 1900 the Council decided by motion to make use of the new powers and to establish eight free libraries in the town with five reading rooms in the outlying districts.

The city had not, of course, been without libraries until the Council was empowered to supply them. In 1874 Stephen Mitchell—a name then and still associated with the tobacco trade—left a bequest of £66,998 10s. 6d. to the town council with a direction that the money should be used to set up a library to be known as the "Mitchell Library." This library is the largest in the city and was first opened in 1877 in temporary premises at 60 Ingram Street. In 1891 it was removed to Miller Street and in 1911 to its present address in North Street. On the first day of its opening in 1877 there were issued to the public 186 books out of the library's total stock of 14,000.

An older public library was that founded by Walter Stirling (1791) who bequeathed his library, his house and a sum of money to a board of directors appointed jointly by the town council, the Merchants' House, the Presbytery and the Faculty of Physicians and Surgeons, with the Lord Provost *ex officio* as president. In 1912 this library was transferred to the City Corporation.

The library service has been fortunate in the number of bequests it has received. When the decision was taken at the turn of the century to set up district libraries Dr. Andrew Carnegie (who had sailed from the Broomielaw for New York with his parents in 1849) wrote to the Lord Provost offering to honour drafts up to a total of £100,000 for this purpose. In the end he gave £20,000 more when the original fund was exhausted. There have been numerous other gifts and bequests of money and property, and there are now 35 public libraries in the city. In 1955 they issued in all 5,196,926 books and were attended by 7,380,306 people who came either to borrow books or to read them in the libraries. In that year the service cost the city £307,950, the bulk of which (£297,940) was borne by the rates, the equivalent rate poundage being 5.1d. The libraries have a total staff of 433, most of whom are female, and by far the largest item of expenditure is for salaries and wages (£147,834). Books, periodicals and binding cost a further £70,917. Capital expenditure for that year amounted to £17,000 and total capital expenditure by the Corporation to date was £424,420. The government grant to the service in the year 1954-5 was £210, being a grant of 5s. a head in respect of the average number of prisoners for whom library service was provided.

PARKS

It is impossible even to outline here the long process by which the city has acquired, in the course of the last hundred years, nearly 3,200 acres of open ground to be used as public parks and recreation grounds.[1]

The most recent Ordnance Survey map of the Glasgow area shows large patches of green distributed all over the city, with many more small patches interspersed. But until 1852 " Glasgow Green " was the only public park in the town. It had been town property since the fifteenth century—not continuously so because, like so much more of the town's property, it had been sold to meet the city's debts during the years of local misgovernment and had to be bought back during the seventeenth and eighteenth centuries. It stretches along the north bank of the Clyde eastwards for a mile and a quarter from Saltmarket. It has been used for many purposes—for recreation (at one time including the playing of golf) by the citizens, for drying nets by the Clyde salmon fishers, for grazing cattle by the burgesses and by the linen trade of the town for bleaching its wares. The Molendinar burn ran through it, but was covered over in 1817. The Green was then, and still is, used for clothes-drying by patrons of the " steamie." The addition from time to time of carriage-ways, fountains, monuments, bridges, the People's Palace and Winter Garden, various recrea-

[1] See Appendix Table 137. Further details will be found in *Municipal Glasgow* (1915) and in *Facts and Figures*, a handbook for Councillors issued annually by the City Corporation.

tional facilities including bowling greens, tennis courts, football pitches, and even at one time an open air "Gymnasium for Adults," made the Green a public park that had something to offer, not only to the "east-enders," but to all the inhabitants of the city. This fact did not go unenvied by those who lived in areas of the expanding city out of reach of the Saltmarket and particularly in the small burghs that were being swallowed up by the town's development.

Under pressure the town council in 1852 bought 66 acres of land in Kelvingrove, in the west end of the city and close by the present University site. This area has been progressively developed until Kelvingrove Park is now one of the most popular parks in the city. The river Kelvin which runs through it is not the clear and sparkling stream of the eighteenth century—indeed south of the park, after the river has run under Dumbarton Road into the Bunhouse area, it is often difficult to see the water for the thick creamy scum on the surface. But the river is one of the Park's attractions none the less and there are in addition the artificial lake, with the waterfowl which it is the children's delight to feed, the bandstand with its wide amphitheatre, handsome monuments, fountains and bridges, the Art Gallery and Museum close by, the usual recreational facilities and a roller-skating rink.

The Queen's Park—146 acres bought by the Council in 1857 as a park for residents on the south side of the city—was at one time Pathhead farm, and, at the time the town bought it, seemed to be far out of reach of most of the citizens. It did not long remain so as the city's boundaries advanced by giant strides, but so long as it did the ratepayers of Glasgow paid for the maintenance of the park and the inhabitants of the small independent burghs on the south of the River made use of it free of charge. There are the usual features—with the addition of a model yacht pond—but Queen's Park is perhaps greener and has more vegetation than parks in the more congested and industrialised parts of the city.

East, West and South had been catered for. It remained for the Council to do something for its citizens in the North. The City Improvement Trustees bought 104 acres in 1866 in the north-east of the town, laid out the ground as a public park and recreation ground and then handed it over to the Corporation as Alexandra Park. The outstanding feature of this new park was its open-air swimming pond made out of a disused quarry in the area.

The only addition to the number of parks in the town during the next quarter of a century was Cathkin Braes Park in 1886—a bequest by a Mr. James Dick. The conditions of the bequest were that these 49 acres of ground, six miles to the south of the city centre, were to be kept in their "natural" state, that the public should be allowed to roam over the whole area at will, but that there should be no provision made for sports and games.

The following is a brief list of some of the public parks that have been added since that date:

Botanic Gardens	43½ acres	1891	
Maxwell Park	21 "	1891	
Springburn Park—originally	56 "	1892	
—now	75 "		
Ruchill Park	51½ "	1892	
Maryhill Park—originally	5½ "	1892	
—now	23		
Govanhill Park	4 "	1894	(Over £3,000 per acre)
Bellahouston Park—originally	178 "	1895	
—now	175 "		
Tollcross Park—originally	82 "	1897	
—now	96½ "		
Richmond Park	44 "	1897	
Rouken Glen Park—originally	135 "	1906	(Gift of Lord Rowallan)
—now	227 "		
Elder Park	35 "	1912	(Gift to Govan Burgh, 1885)
Victoria Park	65 "	1912	(Bought by Partick Burgh, 1889)
Hogganfield Loch & Grounds	124 "	1920–1932	
Knightswood Park	141½ "	1929	
Linn Park	212 "	1919–1933	
Loch Lomond Park	200 "	1915	

Since 1930 there have been only about eight additions larger than 30 acres, and five of these have been transfers from the city's Housing Department. Pressure upon space for housing is now so intense that the era of large new parklands in the city is probably at an end. There are now (1955) 55 public parks, 82 children's playgrounds, 797 "Ornamental Open Spaces," covering in all about 3,929 acres with a further 148.72 acres still undeveloped. The parks provide 87 bowling greens, 129 tennis courts, 8 golf courses (4 of them 9 holes), 21 putting greens, 8 "pitch and putt" courses, 118 football pitches, 6 cricket pitches, 9 hockey pitches, 3 running and cycle tracks, and 2 boating lochs.

In the financial year 1954-5 ordinary expenditure of the parks department was £709,388 and ordinary revenue £103,412, the deficit of £605,976 being borne by the rates. This expenditure included £439,036 for the wages and salaries of about 1,300 of a staff. The bulk of the capital expenditure of £17,458 for the year was for the purchase of ground from the Housing Department.

Municipal Transport

The Corporation's transport undertakings belong to the Common Good Fund of the city, which means in effect that profits or losses from their operation are not accounted for in the Burgh Fund Account and are not transferred towards the reduction or increase of the city rates. The Transport Department operates electrically driven tramcars, trolleybuses and underground trains and also internal-combustion engined motor-buses. First in the field were the tramways.

Tramways

In 1870 two private companies, after strenuous opposition to their proposals by the Town Council, amalgamated and with the consent of the Council obtained Parliamentary authority to construct and work tramways in the city streets—but a condition of the Council's approval was that it should have power, if it wished to do so, to take over the Act from the company within six months of its becoming law. This the Council did, and constructed the first line, which was in operation by August 1872. The Council, however, had by then leased the tramways which it constructed under statutory authority to the Glasgow Tramway and Omnibus Company Ltd. for a period of 23 years as from July 1871, and towards the end of the lease regretted its decision when it attempted to get back from the Company what it then wanted to own and operate itself.

In the meantime Parliamentary authority was obtained for the extension of the system (and the lease of the extended tracks to the Company) in 1875, 1879, 1884, 1885 and 1893. In 1894 when the Company's lease was due to expire, the total length of track built by the city, measured as single-line track, was 63½ miles.[1] Between 1887 and 1891 the Company had been negotiating with the city for an extension of its lease beyond 1894, but the city had resolutely refused and in 1891 formally resolved to operate the tramways system itself. Then began the attempt to persuade the Company, after refusing it an extension of the lease of the tracks, to sell to the city its heritable property, horses, cars, plant and equipment—this, naturally, the Company refused to do and the Town Council had to set about the formidable task of providing all that was necessary to run the service when the private Company ceased to do so in 1894. This the Council accomplished, and during the first eleven months of operation carried 57,104,647 passengers a total distance of 5,192,031 miles at an average revenue per mile of 10.26d. and for a total revenue of £222,121 11s. The trams were, of course, horse-drawn and at 31 May 1895 (less than a year after the Corporation had started its own operation) £110,909 had been paid for horses alone. Indeed at that date total capital expenditure for the whole enterprise (less sinking fund for the track) amounted to £552,956 before deduction of depreciation.

As early as 1891 the city had obtained statutory power to operate the trams by "mechanical traction" and in 1897 it was decided to use electrical power with overhead trolley wires and to provide the first experimental section of the new system on the Springburn route (i.e. Mitchell Street to Springburn). This section was opened in October 1898 and in January 1899 the tramways committee recommended, and the Council approved, that the whole system be converted to electrical

[1] Although most of the line was laid in the streets as double track with only occasional lengths of single line.

power, and if possible the conversion be completed before the opening of the International Exhibition in May 1901. This was in fact almost completely achieved. Also in 1899 the Council decided that the tramways department should itself generate the power required for the system, and a power station at Pinkston on the Forth and Clyde Canal was in operation by 1901. The last horse-drawn cars had gone from the city streets by the end of April 1902.

In 1894 fares were reduced by the Corporation below those charged by the private Company and the department's charge was roughly ½d. for a half-mile stage. In 1913 fares ranged from ½d. for a distance of 1.15 miles to 7d. for 14.48 miles. In that year too the mileage of single track in use had gone up to 196¾, the number of cars in use to 606, the total car mileage covered in the year to 23,335,008, the average receipts per car mile to 10.36d. and the total receipts of the department to £311,480,086. In 1913 total capital expenditure (before allowing for reserves set aside for renewals and depreciation) amounted to £3,694,143—reserves set aside were £2,040,282—so that net capital expenditure was £1,653,860. Sinking fund at the same date amounted to £1,074,176 and this had all been applied in the reduction of the department's indebtedness. By 1901 it had been possible, out of revenue, to write down substantially the value of the horse-drawn equipment and also to accumulate substantial renewal and reserve funds. By 1913 the capital account was concerned only with the electric-powered system, and in that year the revenue account showed a balance of £450,827. After provision for renewal and depreciation, interest, sinking fund, taxes, etc. the department paid over to the Common Good Fund the sum of £33,003. The city's transport department (trams only) was a flourishing concern.

By 1955 the Transport Department was no longer flourishing in spite (or perhaps because) of its enormous expansion—it showed a total deficit for the year of £74,563. Tramcars had begun to go out of favour and were being replaced by the motor and trolley buses. There were still 1,027 trams in service (73 less than in the record year 1953), covering a route mileage of 256.14 (21.57 less than in 1953) and carrying in the year just short of 384 million passengers (58 million less than in 1953); but the tramways section of the Transport Department was the only one that made a loss—£210,548 after allowing for depreciation (compared with a profit of £221,292 in 1953). Tracks had disappeared from some of the city streets, which afterwards seemed to have become very much wider; and in some parts of the town there was a new and strange quietness. The great undertaking is by no means dead, but almost certainly its days are numbered.

In 1955 the staff of the department numbered 11,580, and the wage bill was £5,470,027. Between 1894 and 1955 it had paid out over £5¼ million in rates, over £2½ million in property tax, over £15½ million in capital expenditure; and had contributed almost £1½ million to the city's Common Good Fund. Its capital expenditure for 1955-6 was estimated at another £1,033,200.

Underground

The underground railway—more commonly referred to locally as the "Subway"—was taken over by the Corporation Transport Department in 1923. There were then 50 cars drawn by continuous cable, and it was not until 1935 that the system was electrified. In the financial year 1925-6 the underground carried almost 19¾ million passengers at fares of 1d. for 3 stages and 1½d. for more than three. It had spent by then £404,338 on capital equipment and in the year made an income of £100,851 for an outlay of £126,413, showing a deficit of £25,562. By 1955 there were still only 50 cars in service, the route mileage was 6.56 but the number of passengers in the year had risen to over 34 millions, and the fares to 2d. for 4 stages and 3d. for more than four. The balance of capital expenditure however then stood at £385,529, revenue had increased to £323,598 and there was a profit on the year of £31,877 after allowing for depreciation.

Motor Buses

The department started a motor bus service in 1924 with only 14 buses. In 1925-6 these 14 buses carried over 2½ million passengers but the costs of the service exceeded its earnings by £9,297 (revenue £15,467, expenditure £24,764). The fares were—2 stages 1d., 4 stages 1½d., and over four stages 2d. The charges were almost certainly too low. By 1955 they had most definitely increased—the minimum fare was 4d., (for 4 stages) and the maximum 6d. There were by then 766 buses in operation (though this was 69 less than in 1953), over more than 320 route miles carrying 211,728,936 passengers (nearly 4¾ million less than in the record 1953). Total capital expenditure to date had gone up to £3,666,661. The service however made a profit on the year's operations of £8,829 (revenue £3,210,645, expenditure £3,201,816).

Trolley Buses

The trolley bus service was started on 3 April 1949 with 20 buses. In the two months to the end of May of the same year it had carried 1,675,592 passengers and made a loss of £775. (Revenue £10,037; expenditure £10,812; capital expenditure £143,348). Fares charged were the same as for the tramcars, and they still are. The route mileage is still small—21.51—but the buses carry more than 45 million passengers a year and in 1955 made a surplus of £95,279. So far capital equipment has cost £747,040. It seems likely that this will be greatly increased in the future.

Financial Statistics

One hundred years ago—1856—the gross value of the city under the Lands Valuation (Scotland) Act (1854), which is still operative, was £1,336,475. Figures of the city's revenue and expenditure in that year are not available but in 1861, when the gross value had increased to £1,666,336, ordinary revenue was said to have been £236,677, ordinary expenditure £241,781 and outstanding debt £1,984,133. For a population of 395,503 these figures give an average rateable value per head of just over £4 and an average debt per head of £5, and show that even then the city was " in the red " over its year's working.

For the year 1880-1—the first year of the Local Taxation (Scotland) Returns—comparable figures can be obtained by adding the amounts shown separately in the Returns in the names of " Glasgow, City and Burgh," " Glasgow Corporation Water Works " and " Glasgow Police Commissioners." These figures are: revenue £1,094,195; expenditure £1,014,545; outstanding debt £4,453,940; gross valuation (as given in the Return) £3,432,112. In relation to a population in 1881 of 511,415, rateable value per head was then £6 14s. and debt per head £8 14s., but the three governing bodies, separately and combined, appear to have been in surplus on the year's operations, particularly in the " City and Burgh," to the tune of £54,219! Details of the Returns for 1880-1 are given in the Appendix[1] together with the figures for adjoining burghs which were soon to be swallowed up by Glasgow. It is interesting to note that these small local authorities—except for Maryhill—were also able to balance their accounts, although in the case of Govanhill the credit balance was only £3 and in the case of Hillhead the balance was exact. Budgeting procedure would appear to have been excellent. Glasgow's Police Commissioners spent slightly more than the Town Council and by far the largest single item in the latter's expenditure (substantially more than half of the total) was the interest on and repayment of loans. The Commissioners' largest expense was for Lighting, Cleansing and Paving—second came interest on and repayment of loans—and the cost of police functions proper came third on the list. Revenue is detailed by sources and came principally from assessments authorised under various statutes,—Police Acts, Public Health Acts, General and Special empowering statutes. Imperial subventions from Her Majesty's Treasury were received only on account of the cost of pay and clothing of Police forces. And finally, a principal reason for the apparent solvency of all these local bodies is revealed in the fact that the substantial sums borrowed during the year by each and all of them (in the case of the City and Burgh over 65 per cent of its total revenue) appear as " Revenue."

The detailed figures of revenue, expenditure and outstanding debts for the financial year 1912-13 (the first year after the large expansion of

[1] Appendix Tables 121(a) and 121(b).

the city by the annexations of 1912) are shown in Appendix Table 122. Total revenue was £4,634,109; total expenditure £4,672,669 and the total debt outstanding was £14,813,848. The valuation of the city in that year was £7,307,673 and the estimated population 1,010,805 (including the newly absorbed burghs of Govan, Partick and Pollokshaws and the added suburban areas). So that rateable value per head of population had risen by only 10s. in 32 years (1913 £7 4s.), whereas debt per head had increased in the same period by nearly £6 (£14 11s. in 1913). Figures relating to the population, rateable value, revenue and expenditure added to the city by the expansion of the previous year offer no explanation of this. The fact is simply that capital expenditure and debt accumulation were increasing much more rapidly than local taxable capacity.

Finally, a synopsis of the city accounts for the year 1954-5 is given in Appendix Table 123. The forty years since 1913 have produced some staggering changes in the statistics. The only figure that did not show a very large increase is that of the Registrar-General's estimate of population—1,084,700. Rateable value had almost doubled to £14,132,105 (gross value—£15,671,130) but rateable value per head of population (in spite of the comparatively slight increase in population) had gone up by less than £6 to £13 7s. Ordinary revenue and expenditure had multiplied nearly nine times (£40,870,170—revenue; £40,549,260—expenditure). And capital debt had increased by almost £98½ millions to £113,256,829 or by over £94¼ millions to £109,095,042 if we exclude the debt of former municipal services now nationalised. This means that debt per head of population had increased in 40 years over seven times to a level of £104 (or £100 excluding nationalised services). No detailed analysis of the outstanding loans is necessary to explain this situation. By far the bulk of the debt (£81,335,507) is for housing. The next largest item is less than a tenth of this amount—£8,015,781 for Education—and the only other items over the £ million mark are the various "Police" functions (£7,039,583), Common Good including the Transport Department (£5,253,143), Water (£4,016,387), the Municipal services now nationalised—electricity, public health and gas (£4,161,787) and the Burgh Fund (£1,320,357). Interest paid on outstanding debt during the year 1954-5 amounted to £3,633,148. Total net capital expenditure for all departments for the year amounted to £13,741,635 and the share of the housing department alone was £9,249,324—67 per cent of the total.

Among ordinary expenditures for the year the outstanding item was for Education (£11,528,787)—more than twice the figure for Housing (£5,566,857). Only the police functions proper and the Health and Welfare services topped the £2 million mark. Lighting, Cleansing, Streets, Bridges and Planning were between £1 million and £2 million. But Education, though not a revenue-producing service in the strict sense, was a good "grant producer," and the Treasury footed a bill for £7,318,292, leaving £3,695,482 to be rate-borne. Housing too was subsidised to the extent of £1,565,238, but although truly a revenue-

Glasgow Corporation School Health Service

Plate 18. AN OLD SCHOOL, OPENED 1874, STILL IN USE
ST. ANDREW'S PRIMARY R.C. SCHOOL

Glasgow Corporation School Health Service

Plate [illegible]. A NEW SCHOOL. LEITHLAND ROAD PRIMARY SCHOOL. OPENED 1951

producing service as well, a deficit on this account of £1,673,082 for the year was carried to the rates—30 per cent of the total ordinary housing expenditure for the year, and equivalent to a rate per £ of 2s. 4.75d. The total net deficit on Housing Revenue Account carried forward to 1955-6 was £4,738,129.

Total expenditure of the services in the Burgh Fund accounts (£29,765,751) was £326,478 more than total revenue (£29,439,173) but a surplus of £554,041 brought forward balanced the accounts with £227,463 to spare. The only other very large expenditure and revenue items outside the Burgh Fund Accounts were £8,322,444 (expenditure) and £8,247,882 (revenue) for the Transport undertakings of the Common Good Fund, showing a debit balance of £74,562.

Part Four

COMMUNITY LIFE

Chapter 18

WORKING CONDITIONS

OCCUPATIONS, UNEMPLOYMENT AND EARNINGS

C. E. V. LESER

OCCUPATIONS

AT the Census of population taken in 1951, 513,335 persons out of a total population of 1,089,767 in Glasgow, or 47.1 per cent, described themselves as gainfully occupied.[1] This exceeds the British average which, according to the 1 per cent sample tables of the Population Census, is put at 46.2 per cent; and it is even further above the Scottish average of 44.5 per cent. Out of the 513,335 gainfully occupied persons in Glasgow, 343,184 were males and 170,151 females; that is to say, there were about two men for every woman working. When a comparison is made with either Scotland or Britain as a whole, it is in the female section of the population that the high proportion of occupied persons in Glasgow is most remarkable. The proportion of males occupied in 1951 was 66.1 per cent in Glasgow, which is below the British average of 66.9 per cent and not very much above the Scottish average of 65.0 per cent, but among females the proportion occupied amounted to 29.8 per cent in Glasgow as compared with 27.2 per cent in Britain and 25.8 per cent in Scotland.

All these figures refer to the resident population of the city, not to its total working population, which is far larger. According to Ministry of Labour estimates at mid-1951, the number of insured persons employed in Glasgow amounted to 573,000, a figure which is reduced to about 558,000 if the Hillington Labour Exchange is excluded. But these figures take no account of self-employed persons, of whom there must be a fair number,[2] particularly in the clothing and commercial trades, and when allowance for this is made, the difference between the Ministry of Labour and the Census figures remains at 50,000 persons at the least. Whilst there is some evidence of an understatement in the number of occupied persons, particularly women, in the Population Census, there can be no doubt that the major part of this differ-

[1] This represents 62.6 per cent of the population aged 15 and over.

[2] Accurate figures are not available, but an approximate estimate of the number of self-employed persons in Glasgow (including Hillington and Rutherglen) in 1953 was over 20,000.

ence reflects the large number of people (83,135 at the date of the Census count in 1951) who come from beyond the city boundaries to spend their working day in Glasgow. There is also a considerable movement in the opposite direction, of Glasgow people travelling to work outside the city (58,927 at the same date).[1]

When enquiring about the occupations which men and women in Glasgow are following, we might concern ourselves, theoretically, with either the resident or the working population of the city. In practice the data at our disposal make it necessary to deal with the resident population covered by the Census of Population, since the Ministry of Labour statistics available distinguish between industries but not between personal occupations. There is no reason to assume that the occupational distribution of Glasgow's male and female working population differs appreciably from that shown for the resident population in the following tables.

In Table CXXVII, the number and proportion of occupied men in each of 27 occupational groups is given for 1951 and compared with the number of men in each occupational group in 1931 as well as with the occupational pattern of Scotland as a whole in 1951. This enables us to gauge both the changes that have taken place over these 20 years and the peculiarities of Glasgow's occupational pattern in relation to that of Scotland.

The outstanding feature of the occupational distribution revealed in Table CXXVII is the very large number of metal workers among the male working population, which is the result of the predominance of metal industries in Glasgow's industrial pattern combined with the fact that, in contrast to the Midlands of England, these metal industries are overwhelmingly employers of male labour. The number of metal workers has increased by nearly 6,000 between 1931 and 1951, and two out of nine men working in Glasgow, as against one out of six in Scotland as a whole, are metal workers. The number of building workers has increased even more—by over 8,000—and together with painters and wood-workers, they form one eighth of Glasgow's, compared with one ninth of Scotland's, male labour force. Most of the other skilled manual trades appear to have declined, and the number of men in them is relatively small. The number of fishermen, agricultural workers and miners forms, of course, a far smaller proportion of the total in Glasgow than in Scotland. The number of unskilled workers has also appreciably diminished but is still large—about one in eight men, which is well above the proportion in the whole of Scotland.

Other changes which have taken place during these two decades are the increase in the number of men engaged in professions and in defence, combined with a decline in the number of transport workers and commercial employees. The proportion of men engaged otherwise

[1] Over 80 per cent of the incoming workers to Glasgow come from places up to 10 miles from the city centre, 37.0 per cent from up to 5 miles and 44.9 per cent from between 5 and 10 miles, and 62.8 per cent had a journey of from 15 to 30 minutes in each direction. See Statistical Appendix Table 34.

TABLE CXXVII

OCCUPATIONS OF MEN IN GLASGOW, 1931 AND 1951, AND SCOTLAND 1951

Occupation order	*Number in Glasgow* 1931	1951	*Percentage of all occupied men* 1951 *Glasgow*	*Scotland*
Fishermen	23	22	.01	.79
Agricultural, horticultural and forestry occupations	2,196	1,802	.53	9.59
Mining and quarrying occupations	4,350	1,183	.34	5.17
Workers in the treatment of non-metalliferous mining products (other than coal)	1,294	1,052	.31	.32
Coal gas and coke makers, workers in chemical and allied trades	947	1,357	.40	.68
Workers in metal manufacture, engineering and allied trades	70,841	76,451	22.28	15.98
Textile workers	1,721	1,581	.46	1.56
Tanners, etc., leather goods makers, fur dressers	3,333	2,514	.73	.59
Makers of textile goods and articles of dress (not boots and shoes)	4,806	4,313	1.26	.69
Makers of foods, drinks and tobacco	5,739	5,222	1.52	1.57
Workers in wood, cane and cork	14,200	13,372	3.90	3.44
Makers of and workers in paper and paperboard, bookbinders, printers	5,100	4,551	1.33	1.01
Makers of products not elsewhere specified	2,424	2,383	.69	.48
Workers in building and contracting	12,214	20,805	6.06	6.09
Painters and decorators	5,850	6,941	2.02	1.81
Administrators, directors and managers	6,093	5,745	1.67	2.00
Persons employed in transport and communication	53,241	43,209	12.59	10.64
Commercial, finance and insurance occupations	41,657	30,047	8.76	8.36
Professional and technical occupations	11,426	15,665	4.56	4.62
Persons employed in defence services	5,023	9,058	2.64	3.13
Persons professionally engaged in entertainments and sport	2,464	2,181	.64	.44
Persons engaged in personal service	11,616	10,225	2.98	3.08
Clerks, typists, etc.	21,024	19,525	5.69	4.47
Warehousemen, store keepers, packers, bottlers	9,028	10,161	2.96	1.76
Stationary engine drivers, crane drivers, tractor drivers, etc., stokers, etc.	4,866	7,417	2.16	1.76
Workers in unskilled occupations	49,081	41,965	12.23	9.17
Other and undefined workers	3,200	4,437	1.29	.82
Total gainfully occupied	353,757	343,184	100.00	100.00

SOURCE: 1931 approximate figures, derived from *Census of Population for Scotland, 1931,* Vol. III.
Glasgow 1951: *Census of Scotland, 1951,* Vol. IV.
Scotland 1951: *Census 1951, Great Britain, One per cent Sample Tables,* Part I.

than in direct production—predominantly in "white collar" occupations—is generally higher in Glasgow than in the country as a whole.

The occupational distribution of women, shown in Table CXXVIII, differs in many respects from that of the men. Whilst almost one third of all the occupied men in Glasgow are either metal workers, wood workers, or building workers, little more than one out of fifty

TABLE CXXVIII

OCCUPATIONS OF WOMEN IN GLASGOW, 1931 AND 1951, AND SCOTLAND 1951

Occupation order	*Number in Glasgow* 1931	1951	*Percentage of all occupied women 1951* *Glasgow*	*Scotland*
Fishermen	—	—	—	—
Agricultural, horticultural and forestry occupations	308	157	.09	2.13
Mining and quarrying occupations	12	2	.00	.01
Workers in the treatment of non-metalliferous mining products (other than coal)	651	399	.23	.19
Coal gas and coke makers, workers in chemical and allied trades	278	168	.10	.36
Workers in metal manufacture, engineering and allied trades	1,704	2,935	1.72	1.54
Textile workers	9,128	6,220	3.66	8.22
Tanners etc., leather goods makers, fur dressers	1,112	1,147	.67	.25
Makers of textile goods and articles of dress (not boots and shoes)	16,698	17,609	10.35	5.38
Makers of foods, drinks and tobacco	5,307	4,758	2.80	2.40
Workers in wood, cane and cork	412	567	.33	.06
Makers of and workers in paper and paper-board, bookbinders, printers	5,000	4.282	2.52	1.69
Makers of products not elsewhere specified	1,327	781	.46	.47
Workers in building and contracting	2	56	.03	.07
Painters and decorators	1,476	1,034	.61	.45
Administrators, directors and managers	489	634	.37	.48
Persons employed in transport and communication	4,619	5,546	3.26	2.35
Commercial, finance and insurance occupations	28,687	25,201	14.81	14.04
Professional and technical occupations	10,775	13,029	7.66	9.32
Persons employed in defence service	28	241	.14	.17
Persons professionally engaged in entertainments and sport	435	419	.25	.16
Persons engaged in personal service	38,926	30,240	17.78	22.30
Clerks, typists, etc.	24,311	38,058	22.37	20.09
Warehousewomen, store keepers, packers, bottlers	6,379	6,524	3.83	2.72
Stationary engine drivers, crane drivers, etc., stokers, etc.	11	62	.04	.07
Workers in unskilled occupations	4,912	8,776	5.16	4.66
Other and undefined workers	902	1,306	.77	.41
Total gainfully occupied	163,889	170,151	100.00	100.00

SOURCE: As Table CXXVII.

women follows these occupations. The main women's occupations, and the proportion of all gainfully occupied women who follow them, are: clerical work (over 22 per cent), other commercial occupations like retail distribution (almost 15 per cent), personal service, including work in hotels, restaurants, etc. (almost 18 per cent), textile work and the making of textile goods and clothing (14 per cent together), professions like teaching and nursing (over 7½ per cent). More than 3 out of 4 women who go to work are found in one of these occupations.

The percentage of women who are either textile workers or textile goods workers is approximately the same as in the whole of Scotland, but owing to the range of the industries located in Glasgow, the proportion of textile workers is far lower and that of textile goods and dress makers far higher within than outside the city. Other differences from the Scottish pattern consist in the relatively high percentage of clerks and typists, shop assistants and transport workers, and the relatively low percentage in catering and other personal service among the gainfully occupied women in Glasgow. But taking a broad view, the occupational distribution of women in Glasgow does not differ fundamentally from the Scottish pattern, which is characterised by a strong tendency for women to work in specific women's occupations rather than alongside men; a tendency which appears to be rather less marked in England.

The most spectacular increase between 1931 and 1951 in the number of women working has taken place in the clerical occupations, which have absorbed 14,000 additional women, some of whom have replaced male clerks; whilst the number of women engaged in personal service has fallen by nearly 9,000, chiefly because domestic service is losing favour as a women's job. The number of women in professional occupations has also risen. In transport and commerce the number of women has increased only slightly or even fallen, but since this has been accompanied by an even larger fall in the male occupied population, some substitution of women for men can be said to have taken place. In skilled manual work the number of women has scarcely maintained itself, and as far as textile workers are concerned, it has fallen by 3,000. On the other hand, there has been an increase of nearly 4,000 in the number of unskilled women workers recorded, some of these no doubt in the newer industries.[1]

Unemployment

In the same way as the size of the total population, the size of the occupied population of Glasgow has remained practically unchanged between 1931 and 1951, a slight decrease in the number of men being almost counterbalanced by a small increase in the number of women. But this does not mean that the size of the population at work has remained constant, since these figures include all unemployed men and women looking for work. During the interwar period, the number of unemployed registered for work in the city never fell below 40,000, and in the early 1930's it was well above 100,000, while since 1947 it has generally kept well below 20,000. Of the men and women living in Glasgow there were thus almost 100,000 more at work in 1951 than there were 20 years earlier.

[1] The urgent need for labour in war-time caused many married women to take up full-time employment outside the home and this has remained a feature of the postwar era in Glasgow as elsewhere.

The course which unemployment took during the years 1923 to 1956—except the war years (1939 to 1945) for which figures were not published and would be low in any event—can be seen from Figure 31. The definition of the number of unemployed as shown here has undergone slight modifications, but the figures remain on the whole unaffected by changes in the scope of unemployment insurance and the

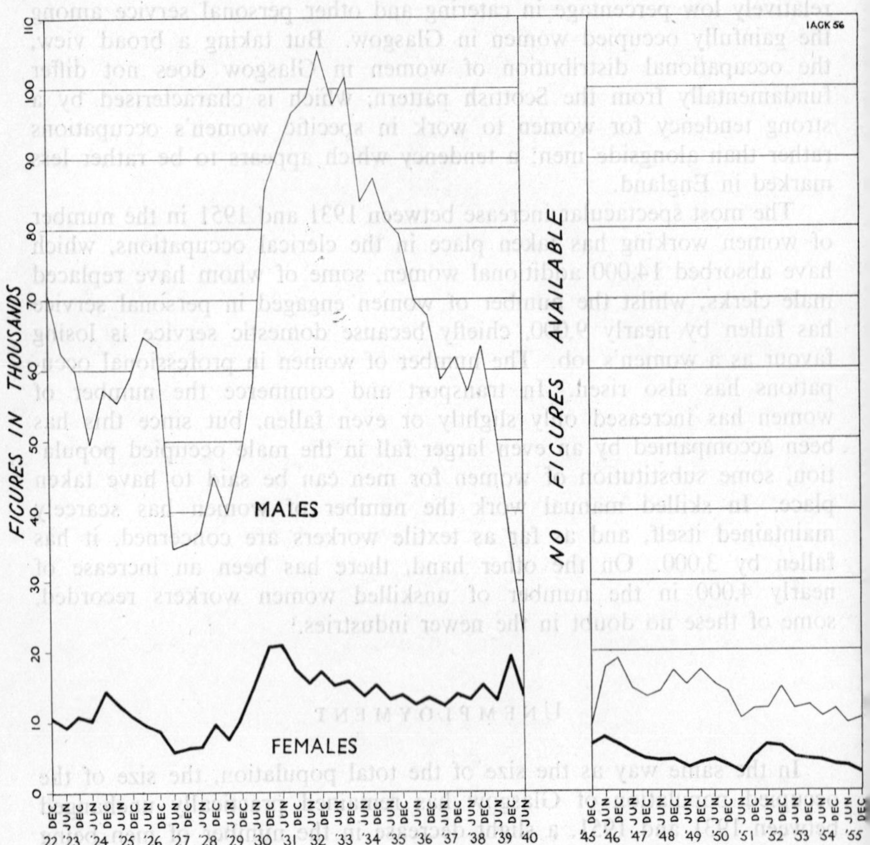

FIG. 31. Registered Unemployed in Glasgow (including Rutherglen), 1922-55.

actual number gives a better indication of the incidence of unemployment than an unemployment percentage would give. The number of unemployed has, of course, been subject to the same broad economic influences in Glasgow as elsewhere in Scotland or the United Kingdom, and the movements are the same: a fall to a relatively low level, in the prosperous years 1927 and 1928, a sharp rise in 1930 to a high level reaching its maximum in 1932, and then a gradual decline, though even by 1939 unemployment was still higher than in 1927-8. After the war there was a temporary rise in unemployment from the very low war-time level, but even the worst year—1946—was better than the best of the interwar years; and since 1947 a very low amount of unemployment has been maintained—about 3 per cent of the total working population.

Not only has unemployment as a whole been reduced but long-term unemployment in particular has diminished in importance, though it is still more prevalent in Glasgow than in Britain as a whole. This can be seen from Table CXXIX.

TABLE CXXIX

PROPORTION OF WHOLLY UNEMPLOYED IN EACH DURATION OF UNEMPLOYMENT GROUP, GLASGOW, DECEMBER 1938 AND 1953, AND GREAT BRITAIN, DECEMBER 1953

Duration of unemployment (weeks)	*Glasgow* 1938	*Glasgow* 1953	*Great Britain* 1953
Males:			
Up to 8	24.4	41.5	54.4
Over 8 and up to 26	23.1	22.0	22.9
Over 26 and up to 52	12.7	12.4	9.1
Over 52 and up to 104	12.2	10.8	7.1
Over 104	27.6	13.3	6.5
	100.0	100.0	100.0
Females:			
Up to 8	36.2	49.7	61.3
Over 8 and up to 26	31.6	28.3	26.1
Over 26 and up to 52	12.1	11.0	7.0
Over 52 and up to 104	10.3	7.7	3.9
Over 104	9.8	3.3	1.7
	100.0	100.0	100.0

SOURCE: Calculated from unpublished Ministry of Labour Statistics and *Ministry of Labour Gazette,* July 1954.

In 1938 more than a quarter of the men who were unemployed in Glasgow had been so for over 2 years; in 1953 the corresponding proportion was less than one in seven. On the other hand, more than two out of five unemployed in 1953 were men who had been out of work for 8 weeks at most, as compared with fewer than one in four before the war. This is, of course, what one would expect to find when unemployment has been reduced, since even in conditions of full employment, frictional unemployment cannot be entirely avoided. The process has gone even further elsewhere in Britain, so that for the country as a whole more than half of all out of work in 1953 were short-term unemployed (up to 8 weeks), and fewer than one in fifteen very long-term unemployed (over 2 years). In the case of women, the change has been in the same direction.

Unemployment in Glasgow is concentrated more strongly in the male sector of the labour force than it is in the rest of the country. In December 1953, out of a total of 16,368 wholly unemployed persons in Glasgow (excluding casuals and temporarily stopped), 11,734—71.7 per cent—were males and 4,634—28.3 per cent—females. The corresponding proportions were 62.6 per cent males, and 37.4 per cent females in Scotland; 65.0 per cent males and 35.0 per cent females in Great Britain.

TABLE CXXX

PERCENTAGE OF WHOLLY UNEMPLOYED IN EACH AGE GROUP, GLASGOW AND GREAT BRITAIN, DECEMBER 1953

Age Group	*Males*		*Females*	
	Glasgow	*Great Britain*	*Glasgow*	*Great Britain*
Under 20	4.9	5.1	6.7	12.7
20-39	43.1	36.7	52.0	47.3
40-54	33.7	30.8	31.9	29.4
55 and over	18.3	27.4	9.4	10.6
	100.0	100.0	100.0	100.0

SOURCE: As Table CXXIX.

A fuller analysis of the unemployed of each sex by age is supplied in Table CXXX. It shows that the proportion of unemployed men who are elderly is lower in Glasgow than in Britain on the average, while conversely Glasgow has a relatively high proportion of men in what are perhaps the best working ages—20 to 39 years—among its male unemployed population. This indicates that the somewhat greater incidence of unemployment in the city, compared with Britain as a unit, is associated with the lower age-groups rather than with the higher. Factors which may account for the difference are (a) the relatively large proportion of "secondary grade labour"[1] (suitable only for certain types of light work) among the Glasgow unemployed, and (b) the preponderance in Glasgow of heavy industries which can offer few opportunities for the employment of such men.

Among its female unemployed population, Glasgow records a comparatively large proportion of women aged 20 to 39, and a comparatively small proportion of young girls up to the age of 19. There is no obvious explanation for this phenomenon, and it does not appear to have any great social significance, unemployment among women being generally small.

EARNINGS

Information about the number of people working in Glasgow is comparatively ample; information about their earnings—wages, salaries and other income—is extremely scanty. Until a few years ago, almost the only available data on earnings related to Great Britain or the

1 Estimates of the percentage of secondary grade labour among the Glasgow male unemployed in December 1953 ranged from 24.4 per cent in the Partick Exchange area to 51.3 per cent in the Kinning Park Exchange area.

United Kingdom as a whole, and there was little evidence which would show variations between England, Wales and Scotland, or within England between different regions. For recent years, however, some information has come to light which helps us to get a picture of variations in earnings within Britain. Although the Ministry of Labour, which has the greatest amount of information at its disposal, has not so far published any regional details, this is partly compensated by data on wages and salaries published by the Board of Trade in the Census of Production and Distribution reports, and by some statistics published in the Inland Revenue reports.

As far as Scotland is concerned, all the available information suggests that wage and salary earnings, although far greater than in Northern Ireland, are at least 5 per cent lower than in Britain as a whole, both in relation to the total number of earners and, on the average, for corresponding industries and services. In the field of manufacturing, the discrepancy appears to be particularly clearly marked. Average earnings per head in Scotland seem to be not only lower than in England and Wales as a whole, but also lower than in Wales and most, or all, of the English standard regions.[1]

There is every indication that the level of wage and salary earnings in Glasgow is above the Scottish though below the British average, both for the majority of corresponding industries and occupations and for all earners taken as a whole. Indeed, in some industries and service trades the wage agreements and regulations in force provide for a set of wage rates above the Scottish average, since Scotland for this purpose is divided into two or three areas according to urban or rural character or by size of burgh, and the area including Glasgow has almost invariably the highest rates. Examples of such trades, according to the Ministry of Labour publication on "Wage Rates and Hours of Work," 1 April 1954, are: Retail bespoke tailoring, dressmaking and other clothing trades; the flour milling and other trades; printing of newspapers and general printing; retail distribution; catering trades; and hairdressing. It is likely that other trades have followed suit, if not in minimum wage rates, yet in actual earnings, and that through the payment of rates above the minimum, the working of longer hours and the effects of more bonus and incentive schemes, average earnings per head in Glasgow are lifted above the Scottish average. As regards salaries, the concentration of high-salary posts in Glasgow must raise the general average in many trades.

The overall average of earnings is influenced not only by the level of earnings in individual industries but also by the industrial pattern, according to whether high-earnings or low-earnings industries are more strongly represented. Glasgow appears to have a slight advantage in this respect over the remainder of Scotland, certainly within

1 See Phyllis Deane, "Regional variations in United Kingdom incomes from employment 1948," *Journal of the Royal Statistical Society*, Vol. 116 (1953), pp. 123-38, especially pp. 129-33; D. J. Robertson, "Wages," *The Scottish Economy* (1954), pp. 158-9; C. E. V. Leser, "Earnings in British regions in 1948," *Scottish Journal of Political Economy*, Vol. I (1954).

the field of manufacturing. For non-manufacturing trades, the position is not so clear, since one of the high-earnings industries—coal mining—is virtually absent, but this is compensated by the absence of agriculture, in which earnings are relatively low. On the whole, the influence of the industrial pattern on average earnings is likely to be a favourable one.

Some information regarding the overall earnings level can be derived from the Income Census of 1949-50 and the results published in the 94th and 95th Inland Revenue reports (Cmd. 8436 and 8726). The tables published furnish, among other things, information on the number of incomes assessed for tax as principal source of income under Schedule E and the amount of such incomes, for each county within the United Kingdom. This allows us to calculate the average income assessed for tax under Schedule E in Lanarkshire, as well as in other counties or the country as a whole. Since two thirds of the population of Lanarkshire live in Glasgow, the result has obviously some bearing on the city.

The average income so obtained for Lanarkshire in 1949-50 was £338 10s., which is well above the Scottish average of £326 2s. On the other hand, the average for the United Kingdom was £343 12s., or £344 6s. for Great Britain alone, and Lanarkshire does not reach that figure. Moreover, if the county is compared with the English counties containing large cities, we find that Middlesex (including a large part of the County of London, but not the City of London) had an average schedule E income of £371 18s., Warwickshire £367 15s., the West Riding of Yorkshire £345 10s. and Northumberland £343 4s. Lanarkshire takes a lower place in the scale than any of these counties and only manages to come on top of Lancashire—with £335 11s.—where the large proportion of women among the earners tends to pull the average down.

While money earnings thus appear to be higher in Glasgow than in the rest of Scotland but lower than in comparable English towns it is far more uncertain whether the same is true with regard to real earnings. Although the cost of living is generally lower in the countryside than in a city, this is not universally true and does not, for example, apply in the Highlands, where high transport costs make themselves felt in high prices for many commodities; and whether it is cheaper to live in the country than in town depends very largely on the pattern of one's spending habits. A comparison with English cities is equally inconclusive, for although, for example, rents are generally lower in Glasgow, standards of accommodation are lower too. Moreover, rents and prices of foods and some other items vary considerably even within the city.

LABOUR CONDITIONS AND INDUSTRIAL RELATIONS

DOUGLAS MACKENZIE

Labour Conditions

A short history of a Glasgow firm, which is still in existence, makes these observations on conditions in 1853: "They were hard times; money was scarce, competition was fierce, hours were long, the labourer was expected to be worthy of his hire." In Glasgow shipyards, for example, men worked from six o'clock in the morning to six o'clock at night, six days a week, with only two breaks for meals, while printers had a week of at least 66 hours. These conditions were by no means exceptional and are in marked contrast with those of to-day, when the average worker has an agreed 44-hour week, beyond which overtime rates must be paid. Even if overtime is taken into account, it is reckoned that the hours actually worked are, on average, around 47 a week. Moreover, while in some cases a five-and-a-half-day week is still the rule, most industries have now reduced this to five days.

Glasgow's present high level of prosperity and industrial activity is reflected in the amount of overtime which is worked in the city. A little over two thirds of 396 manufacturers who replied to a question on this point find that, to supply the needs of their customers, the working day has to be extended in this way. More than half of the firms with overtime have normally a quarter or less of their workers involved, but one eighth have more than three quarters of their workers on overtime.

The majority of wage-earners in Glasgow are not engaged in shift-working. Of the 396 firms mentioned, only 98 or 24.7 per cent have people engaged in shift-work and, even in these cases, it is exceptional to find the whole work-force involved; in fact, almost half have 10 per cent or less of their operatives on shifts. Of the companies with shift-systems, 34.7 per cent have adopted the two-shift, 6.1 per cent the three-shift, and 35.7 per cent have a small proportion of their employees on nightwork, while the remaining 23.5 per cent operate a combination of two or more of these systems.

Compared with 1853, to-day's shorter hours of labour are accompanied by rates of pay which are higher, not only in monetary terms, but in terms of purchasing power, for wages, over the period, have outstripped the rise in prices. In Glasgow in 1853, a compositor in the general printing trade received 25s. for his week's work. In 1954 he receives 169s. 6d. a week. The rates for skilled workers in shipbuilding show the same trend of higher wages and a shorter working week (see Table CXXXI). Even when allowance has been made for changes in the value of money, the skilled man has a higher standard of living than his counterpart of a hundred years ago.

These gains by craftsmen are, however, relatively insignificant when compared with the remarkable advances which have been secured by unskilled workers. Shipbuilding, a typical Glasgow industry, provides an illustration.

TABLE CXXXI

WAGES AND HOURS OF WORK IN SHIPBUILDING, 1866, 1914, 1932 AND 1954

Time-Workers 21 years of age and over	1866 *60-hour week*	1914 *54-hour week*	1932 *47-hour week* *Wage*	1932 *Increase over* 1914	1954 *44-hour week* *Wage*	1954 *Increase over* 1914	1954 *Increase over* 1932
			Gross Weekly Wages				
Fully skilled classes	25s.-30s.	About 41s. 0d.	60s. 0d.	46%	147s. 0d.	259%	145%
General labourers	12s.-16s.	23s. 6d.	41s. 0d.	74%	125s. 0d.	432%	205%

This more rapid rise in the wages of unskilled workers has greatly reduced the differentials between the two classes. Thus, in shipbuilding, whereas in 1914 the labourer's wage was only 57 per cent of the skilled man's, by 1932 it had risen to 68 per cent and by 1954 to 85 per cent. This improvement in relative position is due to several factors, one of the most important being the increase in bargaining power of the general unions on behalf of the unskilled worker. But flat-rate cost-of-living allowances, particularly during the war of 1939-1945, the increasing use of " job break-down " and the introduction of machinery capable of being handled by semi-skilled operatives, have all contributed to this change.

The twentieth century has seen holidays with pay become an accepted condition of employment for all classes of workers in both factory and office. In almost all industries, wage-earners are given two weeks' holidays with pay after a qualifying period of twelve months, and payment is also made for six public holidays in the year. The " white-collared " worker had, in general, been granted these conditions before 1939, but it was only after the war (in the case of the miners, only in 1953) that a fortnight's holiday with pay became universal.

INDUSTRIAL RELATIONS[1]

While the number of days lost through industrial disputes gives only a rough indication of the state of industrial relations, the following table shows such a striking fall that we may safely suggest that the

[1] After this Section was written, the period of comparatively peaceful industrial conditions described came to an end and was succeeded by one of numerous disputes, culminating in the strikes in the Shipbuilding and Engineering industries in early 1957.

period 1935-54 has been one of better relations and comparative peace.

TABLE CXXXII

AVERAGE YEARLY NUMBER OF DAYS LOST THROUGH STOPPAGES IN GREAT BRITAIN, 1914-54

1914-18	5,360,000
1919-21	49,140,000
1922-32[1]	7,560,000
1935-54	1,983,000

These statistics relate to Great Britain but the same trend is evident in Glasgow.

If we ignore disputes on a national scale involving industry in Glasgow, we find that, in the nine years from 1946-1954 inclusive, there were only 21 strikes of local origin and no lock-outs. Five of these disputes were concerned with wages, three being over claims for wage increases, one over piece-work rates, and the last over dissatisfaction with a recent national award. Only two industries were involved, shipbuilding and municipal services. Two other disputes, also in shipbuilding, arose, in the first place, over a claim for a five-day week and then, on a smaller scale, over the re-arrangement of working hours involved by the granting of the claim. Three stoppages occurred over the dismissal of workers on the ground of redundancy in two cases (docks and engineering) and of refusal to work late in the third (docks). Disagreement over the allocation of work led to two demarcation disputes involving some shipbuilding and engineering firms. In addition, two engineering companies lost time and production through strikes which might well have been avoided if joint consultation had been more effective.

Each of the seven remaining disputes had an origin peculiar to itself. In aircraft manufacture, the dismissal of two shop stewards, for an alleged breach of factory discipline, caused one stoppage, while a foreman's refusal to produce evidence of his qualifications to a shop steward led to another. A somewhat similar case arose in an engineering firm when shop stewards demanded that inspectors should furnish them with proof of apprenticeship at time of engagement. Workers employed on the manufacture of machinery downed tools over the employment of a non-unionist. Rejection of a demand that five men who fell into arrears with their trade union contributions should be downgraded caused a strike at a railway repair depot. Tradesmen of Glasgow Corporation came out in protest about delay in negotiations over conditions of service. The remaining stoppage was in support of a demand by a union that it should be entitled to negotiate in respect of members on the distributive side of the gas industry.

Table CXXXIII gives some indication of the duration of these 21 disputes and the numbers of workers involved.

[1] The figures for the period 1922-32 exclude 1926 when 162,000,000 days were lost mainly in the coal-mining dispute and the General Strike.

TABLE CXXXIII

INDUSTRIAL STOPPAGES, OF LOCAL ORIGIN, BY DURATION, NUMBER, AND WORKERS INVOLVED 1946-54

Duration of Stoppage	*Number of Stoppages*	*Approximate Number of Workers Involved*
1 day	2	5,430
3 days	3	4,520
7–10 days	6	52,860[1]
14–17 days	3	6,770
21 days	1	1,750
29–30 days	4	6,000
41 days	1	3,450
129 days	1	180

[1] This includes 45,000 shipbuilding workers who stopped work on 8 consecutive Saturdays.

It is noteworthy that more than half the stoppages lasted for ten days or less, and that only 180 workers took part in the most prolonged strike.

Nineteen of these disputes were settled by agreement between the parties concerned and one by joint negotiating machinery. In the remaining instance, the recommendations of a Court of Inquiry appointed by the Minister of Labour were accepted by both sides.[2]

It was during the First World War (1914-18) that the importance of welfare work in fostering good relationships in industrial establishments won recognition in Glasgow. It is a common-place reflection that when workshops were small, the good employer could take a personal interest in the well-being of his individual employees and strong ties of loyalty were often established, but that the growth of large concerns made this personal contact well-nigh impossible and other alternatives had to be found. The provision of welfare facilities was given a tremendous impetus by the Second World War (1939-45) and by the growing interest in human relations, as well as by the need, in conditions of full employment, to attract skilled workers and to cut down the cost of labour turn-over.

A growing number of firms in the area have realised the important part that personnel managers can play in promoting good relations and providing welfare arrangements. A recent survey of Glasgow producers shows that, of the 230 who gave information on this point, 41, or 17.8 per cent, have full-time personnel managers. Several of these appointments have been in existence since shortly after the First World War, but three quarters have been made since 1939. Another 12 firms state that, while there is no one on their staff devoting full time to welfare, the duties of a director or works manager embrace this function. As one would expect, most of the companies with personnel managers are

[2] This situation, in which most disputes were settled by voluntary joint negotiation, not only in Glasgow but throughout the country, held hopes for the future which have not been fulfilled in ensuing months.

large, while the reason most often given for having none is that the firm is too small to need one.

The measures adopted by Glasgow firms to ensure that their employees feel that they belong to an organisation which shows concern for them, not only as producers but as persons, are many and varied. They range from tea-breaks to playing fields, from rest-rooms to Scottish country dancing classes, from canteens to visiting chiropodists, from day outings to shower-baths. Some firms are very proud of their well equipped First-Aid rooms, which go well beyond the statutory requirements in providing, through qualified nurses, not only prompt attention for accidents, but also treatment for the prevention and cure of such ailments as colds and skin diseases. An increasing number also co-operate with the health authorities in the detection of chest complaints through mass radiography. Lost time and ill-health are reduced with gain to both employees and employers. Eighty firms, or 34.8 per cent of those who replied to a special questionnaire on the subject, stated that they provide welfare amenities of some kind. The larger firms tend to provide most of those mentioned, spending thousands of pounds per annum, but many smaller firms devote relatively large sums to the comfort and well-being of their workers. These figures do not include nationalised concerns in Glasgow, which also have excellent welfare facilities.

One hundred years ago, little or no recognition was given to the effect of pleasant surroundings and working conditions on the health and performance of the individual operative. Now the benefits of good lighting, heating, ventilation, dust extraction and agreeable colours have been widely realised. Legislation and voluntary action have produced great improvement in standards and the modern growth of industrial estates around Glasgow has provided factories which are most pleasant places in which to work.

Superannuation schemes are another form of welfare which is widespread in the city. In fact, it appears to be one of the most popular, for 51.7 per cent of the companies replying to the questionnaire make such provision. The explanation may be that, while such items as canteens are outwith the needs and the means of the small firm, pensions are a ready and acceptable indication of concern for the worker's security. Some replies gave details of the annual cost of this service, which ranged from £120 for a firm with a score of employees to £130,000 for a very large concern. Only one eighth of these schemes are exclusively for staff, the remainder including both factory and office. One company found that while staff and foremen welcomed superannuation, there was "no demand from other employees." In another case, benefit is restricted to key-men, and in a third to male employees only, probably because of the high turn-over and short working life of girls. Where no formal system exists, *ex gratia* payments and pensions are sometimes made to those with a long record of good service.

Professor Kirkaldy, Professor of Industrial Relations in the University of Cambridge, commenting on the better industrial relations of the last twenty years, recently stated[1] that the explanation of the change must be sought in an altered attitude of mind among the parties concerned, for the methods employed have remained substantially unaltered during the period. Information given by 230 Glasgow manufacturers in response to a questionnaire seems to bear this out. Of these firms, 66, or almost 30 per cent, are quite definite that their relationships with trade union representatives are now better than pre-war. Part of the credit for this may be due to the appointment of personnel managers in 14 of these firms within the last twenty years, but some other explanation must be given for the better relationships in the 37 firms which have neither personnel manager nor welfare facilities.

Symptomatic of this changed attitude is the growth, at all levels, of joint consultation, which was given a great stimulus by the urgent demands of war. It has continued to be successful between the national bodies, representing employers and workpeople, and on local bodies such as the Glasgow Productivity Committee, containing representatives of trade unions and employers. At factory and workshop level, however, opinions seem to vary about the usefulness of joint committees. At one end of the scale is to be found one Glasgow company which states that "joint consultation in this company is an obsolete term. The factory is now organised on a basis of 'Works Councils' operating through a unanimous vote principle, and having full legislative authority." On the other hand, two firms do not seem to have found such committees very valuable, for one declares that they have a committee which seldom meets and the other that the activities of its committee seemed to die out. A third company declared that "we do not believe in or use regular formal joint consultation meetings." Forty per cent of the 230 Glasgow companies have joint consultative machinery, while many small firms found that no formal meetings were required, for, as one put it, "in a small firm joint consultation is automatic." It is impossible to come to any definite conclusions about the success of joint consultation at factory level in Glasgow for mutual respect and co-operation often exist where there is no formal machinery, while all too often the energies of works committees are dissipated in the airing of petty grievances. It is of interest in this connection that several of the nationalised industries train workers and junior managers in consultative methods.

Lack of effective communications is often a major factor in preventing improvements in relations at shop floor level. An increasing number of firms use works magazines, news sheets and prominently displayed notice-boards to keep their workers abreast of the developments in the factory. Especially worthwhile is the growing practice of issuing to employees a copy of the firm's balance sheet in simplified form. Where this is done mistaken conceptions, for example, about the share of profits distributed in dividends, are frequently cleared up.

The allocation of a previously fixed share in profits to employees

[1] "Industrial Relations in Great Britain," in *International Labour Review*, December 1953.

in addition to normal wages is another method advocated to secure better relations by giving the individual worker a sense of sharing with the management in a joint undertaking. Although, in Glasgow, 42 of 230 companies declared that they operate a profit-sharing scheme, in actual fact the answers suggest that, in the majority of cases, bonus schemes rather than profit-sharing proper were meant. Earnings, profits, sales are all used as a basis for determining bonus payments. Two companies use a form of profit-sharing based on the issue of employee shares to foster a sense of having a stake in the firm.

Frustrated ambition often gives rise to disappointment and bitterness. Not only are relations soured, but ability is lost to the companies concerned. Planned training programmes and company promotion schemes are two valuable methods adopted to provide opportunities for capable employees. They also help to improve the standard of supervision which so closely affects relations in the workshop. Of 230 Glasgow manufacturers, 47, or just under 20 per cent, operate planned training schemes. Twenty-five provide training facilities for both supervisors and executives, eleven for supervisors only, and eleven for executives only. In twenty-two cases, the company provides its own training without outside help, but nine firms rely wholly on the facilities provided by such institutions as The Royal College of Science & Technology and Stow College. Sixteen supplement the training provided internally by using courses at institutions. In addition, several companies without planned programmes encourage their employees to take qualifications and courses, by paying all or part of the fees and sometimes the cost of books also.

Nine of the firms with planned training programmes also have company promotion schemes, details of which are known to all employees. In fact, there were altogether only eleven firms out of the entire sample with such promotion schemes. A considerable number, on the other hand, state that while they are too small for such formal programmes, they make a point of promoting from within.

The existence of specialist personnel departments, welfare facilities, joint consultative committees and so on is, by itself, no guarantee of healthy relations within a firm, for, in some cases, suspicion of the motives behind them make them virtually dead letters from the start. Thus while, as we have seen, much has been achieved, much still remains to be done to propagate the attitude in industrial relations which gives not only greater productivity but also greater satisfaction in work.

The Trade Union Movement

Generally, in our society, the most significant and fundamental changes occur almost imperceptibly. But the recent war provided a tremendous impetus which telescoped into a decade developments that normally might have taken a generation. Inevitably, these rapid changes, while solving many old problems, brought a train of new difficulties, and demanded from such institutions as the trade unions rapid re-adjustment of outlook and policies to meet changed conditions.

While the maintenance and improvement of wages and working conditions has always been the main purpose of Trade Unions, between the wars the prevalence of unemployment on a gigantic scale undermined their efforts at raising the standard of living, and in these years their immediate objective became the reduction of unemployment and the attainment of some degree of job security. Then came the war bringing full employment which has continued into peace and has given an unprecedented period of security and stability to employees. The trade union movement, freed from the bogey of unemployment, has turned its energies to improving the living standards of its members, and has thrown its considerable authority into the drive for greater productivity.

The power which the trade unions hold to-day is built on foundations which were laid in the latter part of the nineteenth century, and Glasgow, as one would expect, played a leading part in the establishment of the movement in Scotland. From the middle of the century the Clyde Valley had been the hub of Scottish industry, and this great concentration of workpeople provided conditions favourable to the growth of trade unionism. In 1892 the Webbs noted that nearly all of the 147,000 trade unionists in Scotland were to be found in the narrow industrial belt between the Clyde and the Forth, two thirds of the total belonging to Glasgow and neighbouring industrial centres. To-day the distribution of trade union membership would seem to be not so highly concentrated geographically, but Mr. J. D. M. Bell[1] calculates that, as recently as 1947, Glasgow still accounted for over a quarter of the estimated total of 908,982 trade unionists in Scotland. His figures yield an estimate of the growth of membership between 1924 and 1947, which is shown in Table CXXXIV.

TABLE CXXXIV

GROWTH OF TRADE UNION MEMBERSHIP BETWEEN 1924 AND 1947

	Number of Members Scotland	*Glasgow*	*Glasgow Members as % of Scottish*
1924	536,000	133,000	24.7
1947	908,982	259,000	28.4

It will be seen that Glasgow shows a higher rate of increase of membership over the period than does Scotland as a whole. By 1947 the number of trade unionists in the city had almost doubled, while Scottish membership was 170 per cent of the 1924 total.

Since the Webbs wrote, trade union membership has not only

[1] *Strength of Trade Unionism in Scotland* (1950), pp. 11 & 28. Cf. also chapter on Trade Unions by the same author in *The Scottish Economy*, ed. Cairncross (1954), pp. 280-96.

spread to other parts of the country, it has also spread to new groups of employees. In 1892 almost two thirds of the total Scottish membership were drawn from the engineering, metal, mining and building trades. This dominance of the craft unions has given way to the influence now exerted by the general workers' unions and professional organisations among such groups as teachers and civil servants. Moreover, the late nineteenth century saw the beginnings of the organisation of women workers, but, despite the efforts of such bodies as the Women's Advisory Council set up in 1926 by the General Council of the Scottish T.U.C. in the belief that the methods of organising women required special consideration, the chances of a woman worker's joining a trade union are still only approximately half those of a man.

The process of amalgamation of unions into bodies covering Scotland or the whole of Britain has generally swallowed up the purely local union,[1] but some of the national bodies can trace their beginnings to the efforts of Glasgow workers convinced that only in combination lay strength and the possibility of a better way of life. The first attempt at national organisation in the printing trade was sponsored by the Glasgow Typographical Society. The Painters' Society originated in the city in 1853, while the Scottish Horse and Motormen's Association was registered as a trade union in 1898 under the name of the Glasgow Carters' Association. The Shipconstructors' and Shipwrights' Association developed from the Shipwrights' Society, which was of Glasgow origin although it moved its headquarters in 1887 to Newcastle-on-Tyne.

Unfortunately, a fire in the Albion Hall in 1909 destroyed many of the records of Glasgow trade unionism and may well have left us in ignorance of other highlights. The period following the First World War, 1914-18, saw rapid progress in consolidation of unions into very large units, such as the British Iron, Steel and Kindred Trades Association, the Amalgamated Engineering Union, and Transport and General Workers' Union and the National Union of General and Municipal Workers. This tendency did not always meet with members' approval, and it is rather interesting to note that the Scottish Transport and General Workers' Union owes its existence to a break-away by Glasgow and Aberdeen dockers from the T.G.W.U. because of hostility to the official scheme of registration and decasualisation.

The early trade unionists were to a large extent concerned with obtaining political reforms beneficial to the working class and, to this end, joint national action was pioneered on the initiative of Glasgow when a committee for repeal of the Master and Servant Act was formed in 1864. In the same year local men also had some of the initial responsibility for the summoning of a conference of delegates from Unions and Trades Councils, which was the first British Trades Union Congress.

By 1868, the T.U.C. had taken shape as a regularly constituted annual gathering and in 1875 met in Glasgow. Local trade unionists

1 There are no unions with Glasgow titles affiliated to the S.T.U.C.

had been prominent in attempts to set up a purely Scottish body and it was in Glasgow, in 1897, that the S.T.U.C. held its first meeting, at which 55 organisations with a total membership of 41,000 were represented by 74 delegates. In 1955, the trade union membership affiliated to the S.T.U.C. was 756,903 and 435 delegates were sent by 89 unions and 46 trades councils.

Glasgow Trades Council, which was instituted in 1858 and is the oldest in Great Britain to have continued throughout its history under the title " Trades Council," brings together representatives of the unions in the area. Its main functions are recruitment, propaganda and the co-ordination of local trade union activity.

Whilst originally trades councils acted on their own initiative in both industrial and political matters, to-day their functions are very closely defined by the S.T.U.C. They are precluded from negotiations on wages and working conditions and are not policy-making bodies but must conform to and implement the policies and practices of Congress. The Glasgow Trades Council's failure to observe this latter condition caused it to be disaffiliated by the S.T.U.C. in 1951. The disaffiliated council sought an interdict to prevent the appointment of a new executive committee, but the following year a new trades council recognised by Congress was inaugurated. The dispute between the members of the old council and Congress was in the end amicably settled and some of those involved returned as delegates to the new trades council.

If this brief account suggests that the history of Trade Unionism in Glasgow has been one of effortless progress, a glance at the dramatic events on Clydeside during the First World War may help to correct the picture.[1] During that period orthodox Unionism on the Clyde (as represented by the Amalgamated Society of Engineers) met with more than one challenge to its authority, and although with the passing of wartime conditions the disruptive elements lost ground effects remained which were more than temporary and local.

The first challenge appeared in the course of a wage dispute in the engineering shops—a hang-over from prewar months. The Shop Stewards in one of the affected shops, who were at that time minor officials of the A.S.E. (although among them were some with far-reaching ideas on the control of industry), formed themselves into a Committee to oppose the moderate policy of the Union; and against the wishes of the Union the Engineers went on strike early in 1915. This success of the unofficial committee led to the multiplication of Shop Stewards, many of them not appointed by the A.S.E. but elected by the rank and file of the workers who were being increasingly irritated by wartime restrictions on labour. The introduction of Dilution of Labour under the Munitions Act of 1915 brought the growing discontent to a head; and while the majority accepted dilution as a wartime necessity, there were many who objected to the method of its operation and some who opposed it on principle. Under these condi-

[1] A set of original documents relating to the events of this period, the gift of Mr. H. E. R. Highton, is deposited in the Glasgow University Library.

tions the Committee of Shop Stewards gained popularity and grew into the Clyde Workers' Committee, whose aims, as formulated in its Constitution, went far beyond mere opposition to dilution, and included the following:— "to obtain an ever-increasing control over workshop conditions, to regulate the terms upon which the workers shall be employed and to organise the workers upon a class basis and to maintain the class struggle, until the overthrow of the wages system, the freedom of the workers and the establishment of industrial democracy have been obtained." Such a programme in wartime inevitably brought Government intervention; and in 1916 the C.W.C. was suppressed, ten of its leaders being deported

This was not, however, the end of the C.W.C. For one thing the deported members carried the idea of Workers' Committees to other districts, and organisations of labour on similar lines appeared in many parts of the country. Secondly, even in Glasgow there continued after 1916 a Provisional Committee of the C.W.C. which made itself felt in several ways. In 1917, for instance, it led a strong resistance to the new Whitley Councils and it was behind a movement in 1919 for a 40-hour week in Engineering which resulted in a strike, during which the police charged a demonstration in George Square. In this strike the C.W.C. had support from the District Committee of the A.S.E. working against the orders of its own Executive. But the Executive took a strong line, and after this incident the power of the C.W.C. declined. Yet things were never the same again. Directly, as has been shown, the Clyde movement had its effects in other districts. Indirectly it affected Trade Unionism as a whole: the Unions never regained unquestioned authority and unofficial strikes became a commonplace; and the prominence given to the ideal of control of industry by the workers strengthened industrial unionism and stimulated the progress of amalgamation among unions. And the district never quite shook off the notoriety it had acquired as "Red Clydeside."

The traditional Scottish reverence for education has been reflected in the attitude of the unions to adult education. The Glasgow branch of the Scottish Operative Masons was one of the first in the field with the formation, in the middle of last century, of a "class for mutual instruction and an association for moral, physical and intellectual improvement." This breadth of outlook still characterises trade union educational activities, which range from matters directly concerning their own affairs, to technical training and such subjects as economics and international relations. There are six workpeople's representatives on the Glasgow and West of Scotland Advisory Council for Technical Education. Several unions, such as the Transport and General Workers' Union and the Amalgamated Engineering Union, organise day or week-end schools for their members, while the National Union of General and Municipal Workers sends twice yearly an average of fourteen people from a wide variety of industries on a month's full-time course on Industrial Relations at the Royal College of Science & Technology, Glasgow.

In the Session 1947-8, Glasgow University Department of Extra-Mural Education, with the support of the Scottish Trades Union Congress, organised two tutorial classes in Trade Unionism. Each of these classes had a membership of 38, and a supplementary class started later had 30. Since then sessional classes have been held each year with varying membership, but numbers have declined in the past three years. The tutors have been University lecturers, and their subjects have covered Trade Union History, the Structure and Functions of Trade Unionism, and Problems of Wages and Collective Bargaining.

These educational schemes help to combat the apathy towards union affairs shown by the poor attendances at branch meetings, and to improve the individual member's understanding of how his efforts affect not only his own economic well-being, but that of the community as a whole. Education is just one of several methods being used by trade union officials in Glasgow, as elsewhere, in order to secure that active participation of the individual which is so vital to the success of the trade union movement.

TRADE ASSOCIATIONS

W. ALLAN GAY

Employers' Associations are of comparatively recent origin but the idea that men could benefit from mutual association dates from a much earlier period.

The Merchant Guilds of the thirteenth century for example were associations which made the merchants very powerful both in civic and national affairs. These Guilds in turn led to the formation of Craft Guilds; for the craftsmen in a burgh, although freemen, were denied entrance to the Merchant Guilds and as a result had very little say in the running of the burgh. Craft Guilds were given legal recognition through a Charter or a "Seal of Cause" but this was still not sufficient and in the royal burghs, where the Merchants were particularly powerful, the Crafts federated into a body known as the "Convenery of the Burgh."

Since Glasgow was not at first a royal burgh it did not have a Merchant Guild and consequently the fourteen Incorporated Trades, while legalised through their "Seal of Cause," had not found it necessary to federate. By the end of the sixteenth century, however, an effort was being made, on the urging of the Convention of Royal Burghs, to form a Corporate Merchant Guild in Glasgow. This move was resisted by the Crafts, who felt that even without any organisation the Merchants were able to wield more power than their numbers warranted. The dispute became so bitter that it was referred to arbitration and as a result Guildry was introduced into Glasgow. This was in 1605 and all the Incorporated Trades in the city federated to form a Convenery and a Deacon Convener was appointed.

The Trades House is the name by which this Convenery is now known and throughout the years the Trades House has played a very important part in the development of the trade of the city. At one time the Trades House had the power to make acts regulating the activities of the Crafts and it also had the right to judge on questions of dispute concerning the Crafts. These functions are now non-existent as a result of the abolition in 1846 of the exclusive privileges of trading.

There has been little change in the character or activities of either the individual Crafts or of the Trades House in the past century. To-day there is a tendency for membership of the Incorporations to be drawn from the professions rather than strictly from a craft. The Trades House had accumulated considerable funds which it administers for the benefit of the members of the various Incorporations and also for wider charities or deserving causes. It has been associated with other public bodies in the city in promoting measures which would react to the benefit of the community.

The Deacon Convener of the Trades House is *ex officio* a full member of the Corporation of Glasgow although an attempt has recently been made to break this traditional link between the Crafts and the Corporation. The Trades House takes no part whatsoever in questions affecting the relationship between employers and labour.

Another association which takes no part in industrial disputes is the Chamber of Commerce, incorporated by Royal Charter in 1783. It was established on the initiative of Patrick Colquhoun, tobacco merchant and Lord Provost of the city, with the support of a group of merchants and manufacturers, "to take cognisance of every matter and thing in the least degree connected with the interests of commerce and manufacture." At its inception the Chamber had 216 members; in January 1956 there were 3,227 members appointing 3,505 representatives.

The Chamber maintains a number of standing committees to study and advise it on questions of major importance, such as taxation, transport and legal and Parliamentary matters; and, in addition, *ad hoc* committees are appointed from time to time, to deal with specific questions.

Perhaps the most important development in its recent history has been the formation of a Junior Chamber of Commerce. Membership of the Junior Chamber is open to younger men and there are frequent meetings both of an educational and social character. The Junior Chamber will also discuss any matter of current importance and make recommendations to the senior body.

It was not until the middle of the nineteenth century that employers had any great need or inclination to join together to further their common interests. With the growth of trade unions however employers felt it necessary to protect themselves by forming associations, and several came into being during the last decade of the century, their members being drawn in the first instance from firms engaged in the same branch of trade or industry.

Glasgow, as is to be expected from the important place it has held in trade and commerce, has been particularly well served by Employers' Associations. In 1892, for example, was formed the Glasgow and District Engineers' and Boilermakers' Association. The Association was the outcome of a series of meetings to which had been invited representatives of all the principal engineering firms in the Glasgow district. The purpose of the meeting was specifically to consider the formation of an Association "to protect our interests." This particular Association has grown in size and in influence throughout the years and has frequently been called upon to act on behalf of its members in a wide range of questions relating to the employment of labour. To-day as the Scottish Engineering Employers' Association it has a membership of nearly 300 firms engaged in engineering and trades allied thereto.

There are some 60 associations with offices in Glasgow and these cater for practically every trade, including mining and quarrying, engineering and shipbuilding, building trades, civil and electrical engineering, weaving, milling, leather working, shipping and stevedoring, food manufacturing and also a wide range of retail activities. It is estimated that about 80 per cent of Glasgow firms could find an appropriate association registered within the city while the remaining 20 per cent are catered for by National Associations or by associations registered elsewhere in the country. Of the associations to be found in Glasgow one restricts its membership to city firms, six are sections of national bodies and the remainder extend their sphere of operations outwith the city limits.

There are three types of Trade Associations:

(1) those concerned with the handling of questions arising out of the employment of labour,
(2) those concerned with the regulation of prices, of outputs, of sales or of quality standards,
(3) those concerned with the supplying of advice to assist their members.

These functions are not mutually exclusive but different associations tend to concentrate on one or other of them.

The objective of a Trade Association is to further the interests of its members. As far as industrial relations are concerned this means that the association will act to prevent disputes and in the event of a dispute developing the association will on behalf of its members follow through the agreed procedure. It will also advise its members how to deal with any particular problem.

The association negotiates agreements with the trade unions either directly or through federated bodies and it will support at local or national level any measure which would be beneficial to its members.

In general the relationship between the trade association and the trade union is a formal one clearly defined within the procedures laid down to bring the two together to deal with problems of mutual interests and it would be undesirable for an association or for one of its members to ignore the agreed procedure. This does not mean of course that there are no informal contacts between officers of the association and of the union. In many cases a degree of mutual respect and goodwill exists. This has grown through informal as well as formal meetings and greatly contributes to the reaching of acceptable agreements.

To estimate the extent to which firms in Glasgow support the trade associations available a questionnaire was sent to a sample group of 400 firms in the city. The following information has been extracted from the 233 replies received:

(1) 85 per cent of the firms replying were members of some type of association and 95 per cent of these were members of an association dealing with matters relating to the employment of labour. 10 per cent (some firms are members of more than one association) had joined to get advice on technical matters while a few joined an association to obtain facilities for educational or social activities.

(2) Every firm employing more than 500 workers was a member and this means that in the sample considered over 95 per cent of wage earners are employed in firms which are members of an association.

(3) In all cases but one where there was "active" unionism the firm was a member of an association, and in several cases where there was no organised unionism there was trade association membership.

(4) Every member was satisfied with the services provided by its association.

It is probable that the proportion of non-members is higher amongst those firms which did not answer the questionnaire since being a member of an association would tend to make a management more sympathetic to the purposes of the questionnaire. Even allowing for this, however, and allowing for the fact that the sample, although representative, was relatively small, it is still apparent that there is in Glasgow a very good support for the employer associations.

Chapter 19

LEISURE INTERESTS

JACK HOUSE

CHANGES IN THE USE OF LEISURE

GLASGOW has known two kinds of leisure over the past 50 years—the customary leisure at the end of the day's work and at week-ends; and the enforced leisure which accompanies unemployment. The amount of customary leisure has increased, with shorter working hours, and the amount of enforced leisure has fortunately decreased. Enforced leisure set men to hanging about street corners (a habit which has been considerably reduced in recent years), to gambling on waste ground and by the side of the River Clyde and canals, and, strangely enough, to hiking and mountaineering. Some of the most intrepid of Glasgow climbers owe their skill to unemployment.

For example, a group of unemployed shipyard workers and engineers in Glasgow decided to try hiking, and from that proceeded to climbing. They chose the Arrochar Alps as the most convenient terrain and soon they discovered caves in the lower slopes of the mountain called The Cobbler. Every week-end (and sometimes oftener) they walked or hitch-hiked to Arrochar and then made camp in the caves of The Cobbler. From this was built the Craig-Dhu Mountaineering Club, with its own rules and songs and legends. Members of this one-time unemployed group have appeared several times on the Scottish Home Service of the B.B.C., and at least one of them has been asked to assist the Scottish Mountaineering Club in its official papers. Most of the members have now climbed the important peaks in Scotland, England and Wales, and some of them have done extensive climbing in the Swiss and French Alps.

Apart from the incidence of employment, changes in housing conditions too have made some remarkable differences in the use of leisure. There are far more suburban dwellers than ever there were in Glasgow and this has tended to a return to almost Victorian styles of amusement and entertainment for many people. In the brand-new suburb of Garthamlock not a single person turned up for an election meeting. The reason was that everybody had gone to a residents' association dance in the church hall. Yet it is not so long ago that local dances were in danger of disappearing because of the pull of the big dance halls in the centre of the city.

New districts mean that people go back to old-fashioned ways. If you take a district like Dennistoun in the days before and immediately after the war of 1914-18, you find that "going into town" (less than two miles to the centre) was considered an adventure. So Dennistoun made a great deal of its own amusement. Those were the days of the Dennistoun Amateur Minstrels, Bands of Hope lantern lectures in every church hall, concerts presented by local talent, parties in private houses, great observances of such events as Hogmanay, Hallowe'en and the King's Birthday bonfire (Guy Fawkes's Day was almost unknown then), and socials and soirees.

By the late 'twenties that style of local entertainment had almost faded away, and in the 'thirties it was virtually unknown. But it has all come back again, in modernised guise, with the new and distant suburbs such as Househillwood, Pollok, Drumchapel, Ruchazie, Barlanark, Garthamlock, and the rest. To-day the children of Househillwood will present an annual pantomime which is packed out for most of a week. Self-entertainment, which any observer in 1935 would have said had gone for ever, is now rife right round the perimeter of the city.

One change, however, is that many of the observances have become Anglified. Under commercial pressure, children insist on fireworks and bonfires on November 5th. In 1920 many Glasgow children received presents on New Year's Day, and it was even suggested that these were brought not by Father Christmas, but by a peculiarly Glasgow benefactor named Sandy Claws. To-day, throughout the entire city, tenements and villas and bungalows vie one with the other in displaying Christmas trees in the window. During the week before Christmas 1954, an observer counted 200 illuminated trees in windows from the Botanic Gardens along Great Western Road to the centre of the city. It is interesting to note that the greatest rivalry in this display is not seen in well-to-do districts, but in what are still known as working-class areas. This was also seen during the Coronation celebrations.

Domestic Entertainment

Home entertainment in the suburbs is as popular as ever it was, but there is a mechanical change in its character. The piano has been replaced by the radio set and, in many cases, by the television set. In other words, the entertainment is in the home, but it is being provided from outside. But this does keep many people within the family circle who were all too eager to leave it when they lived nearer the bright lights and did not have the "Telly." A remarkable reversion to the early days of this century is the revival of the gramophone or, as it is called now, the record player. Many young people in Glasgow have record-playing parties, to which they invite their friends. The friends are expected to bring their long-playing records along with them, and the entire evening is spent in listening to discs, not only of popular music but also of classics, ballads and esoteric forms of jazz. Even those who do not possess records or record players get a vicarious interest in this cult by going to cafés where "juke boxes" are installed.

A remarkable sight in Glasgow is to be seen any week day about noon in the gramophone department of Lewis's Store in Argyle Street. Large numbers of young people apparently forego their lunch in order to stand about in this department listening to gramophone records being played over loud-speakers. Most of the young people become animated only when dance music or jazz is played.

Glaswegians respond to radio and television much as people anywhere else do, but they have one marked peculiarity. They are inclined to be intolerant of city produced programmes and they are practically unanimous in running down the "Glasgow accent." This may seem remarkable when it is realised that the Glasgow pantomimes, which hold all the world records for long runs, depend to a large measure for their success on the use of the Glasgow accent by local comedians. But in the cinema a Glasgow audience responds with derision or embarrassed laughter to any use of the Glasgow accent from the screen. And this is not only the case as far as the exaggerated, comic version of the Glasgow accent is concerned; it obtains also when a Glasgow man or woman is speaking straightforwardly in the tongue he or she uses daily. It seems to be the mechanical reproduction of the Glasgow accent which gives offence.

A radio series about a mythical Glasgow family called "The McFlannels" was widely criticised by Glaswegians who talked in precisely the same accents. But all B.B.C. productions emanating from Glasgow are severely criticised by the Glaswegians, who nevertheless listen to local programmes in greater numbers than are found in any other B.B.C. "region." The heavy criticism dealt out to such productions by word of mouth and in the Glasgow Press may be meant to prevent authors, producers and actors from becoming swollen-headed. Or it may be the result of the Glasgow attitude described by the late James Bridie—"*Him* write a play? Ah kenn't his faither!"

Radio critics, professional and amateur, are particularly scornful of the programmes devised on radio and television for such annual events as Burns's Night, Glasgow Fair Saturday, St. Andrew's Night and Hogmanay. They are seldom happy about the appearances of the Glasgow school of comics, whose reception by listeners and viewers south of the Border is often at complete variance with the criticisms from the comedians' fellow-citizens.

Almost all this criticism is reserved for those who live and work in Glasgow or, to a lesser degree, in Scotland. Glaswegians are generally anxious to praise any fellow-citizen who has gone to London or abroad and made a success. Some of these successes may have a rather tenuous connection with Glasgow, but they are being hailed constantly as Glasgow citizens. Jack Buchanan, one of the world's leading musical comedy and film actors, was constantly styled as a Glaswegian by the Glaswegians, although he was born in Helensburgh and merely went to school at Glasgow Academy. When a celebratory booklet was issued by Glasgow Academy some years ago, the name of Jack Buchanan was not mentioned among the distinguished former pupils—which is possibly the exception that proves the rule.

Newspapers and Periodicals

Most Glasgow newspapers keep the Glasgow flag flying, even to the extent of claiming as Glaswegians famous people whose parents lived in Glasgow. But they remain critical of such stay-at-homes as the architect, Charles Rennie Macintosh, and the playwright, James Bridie —both of whom had a far higher reputation out of Glasgow than inside it.

The newspapers of Glasgow are critical of much more than the Glasgow accent and stay-at-home artists. A study of articles by feature writers and commentators and the Letters to the Editor columns indicates that there is a great deal wrong with the city and the citizens. One newspaper devotes a whole page every day to Letters to the Editor, and the vast majority of these are critical in the extreme. Outside criticism of Glasgow is, however, deeply resented, and any writer who confesses that he is English is told at once that he should go home as quickly as possible.

The main newspapers of the Glasgow Press are divided into three groups. The purely local firm is that of George Outram and it administers *The Glasgow Herald*, the *Bulletin* and the *Evening Times*. It had also a part interest in the *Evening Citizen,* but relinquished it to the Beaverbrook Press, which already held the majority of the shares. Besides the *Evening Citizen,* the Beaverbrook papers are the *Scottish Daily Express* and the *Scottish Sunday Express*. Until November 1955, the Kemsley Group was the third in Glasgow, with the *Daily Record,* the *Evening News*[1] and the *Sunday Mail*. These are now owned by the *Daily Mirror*.

There is considerable competition among these three groups, particularly in the field of evening papers. Although all these journals are produced in Glasgow, their circulation area is much wider. In the case of the morning papers, it is the whole of Scotland. The evening papers travel as far north as Oban, as far east as Kirkcaldy and Edinburgh, and as far south as Dumfries. At one time each of the evening papers included Glasgow in its title, but this was dropped when circulation went beyond the boundaries of the city.

The city's first newspaper was the *Glasgow Courant,* published on 14 November 1715, but after the fourth number the title was changed to the *West Country Intelligence*. It failed after 67 numbers and the second *Glasgow Courant* did not appear until 14 October 1745. The first permanent newspaper in Glasgow was *The Advertiser,* published in 1783. In 1801 its name was changed to *The Herald and Advertiser,*

[1] The *Evening News* ceased publication on 17 January 1957. Before then Glasgow had been the only town outside London supporting three evening newspapers.

and later that year to *The Herald*. It is now *The Glasgow Herald*. It became a daily newspaper in 1859.

The first daily newspaper in Scotland was the *North British Daily Mail*, published in Glasgow in April 1847. The first halfpenny evening newspaper was the *Evening Citizen*, published in 1864.

Two Edinburgh-produced newspapers have large offices in Glasgow. They are *The Scotsman* and the *Scottish Daily Mail*. The main issue of the *Sunday Post*, which is controlled by the Dundee firm of D. C. Thomson, is printed in Glasgow. The *Daily Herald* maintains a large staff in Glasgow, and other national newspapers are represented, as well as the Press Association.

Weekly papers in Glasgow include the *Weekly News*, the *Glasgow Observer* (a Roman Catholic periodical), and the Scottish edition of the Labour newspaper, *Forward*. *Forward* was originally produced completely in Glasgow, but now its headquarters are in London.

Several well-established weekly newspapers cater for certain large districts of Glasgow. Among them are *East Kilbride News*, the *Glasgow Eastern Standard*, the *Mercury and Advertiser* (covering Clarkston and Giffnock), the *Milngavie and Bearsden Herald*, the *Springburn and Northern News*, the *Western News*, and the *Govan Press*. One or two of these are not, strictly speaking, Glasgow newspapers, but they circulate widely in the suburbs of the city, as do the *Cambuslang Advertiser*, the *Clydebank Press*, and the *Rutherglen Reformer*.

One monthly magazine, the *Scottish Field*, is produced in Glasgow, although it is printed in Perth. There are also University, college and school magazines, of which the outstanding are "*G.U.M.*" (*Glasgow University Magazine*), *The Mask* (Royal College of Science & Technology), and *Thesus* (The Scottish Union of Students). Perhaps the most unusual publication is *The Word*, brought out monthly by Guy Aldred, and written almost entirely by the Editor. It is strongly pacifist.

Glasgow had once a large number of comic weeklies, of which *The Bailie*, *Quiz*, and *St. Mungo* were particularly renowned. *The Bailie* lasted longest, but was discontinued between World Wars I and II. Efforts to start weekly magazines since then have failed. One which set out to "tell the truth about Glasgow" was named *Well*! It lasted only two issues. A peripatetic publication entitled *The Glasgow Review* lasted somewhat longer. In the early 'thirties a monthly magazine called *The Scottish Stage* was started under independent auspices and ended in its second year as the organ of the Scottish Community Drama Association. It was restarted by the S.C.D.A. in 1935 but was abandoned at the end of the year because there was no profit. On the other hand, a monthly publication entitled *What's On and Where To Go in Glasgow* has been appearing free, and with success, for some years. Its advertisers pay for its publication.

Until the 1930's Glasgow newspapers, mainly independent or only distantly thirled to London offices, tended to a decided individuality. Now that they have been absorbed into industrial groups, the individuality has largely disappeared, though the technical production is improved immensely. Most Glasgow-produced newspapers consider Glasgow and Scottish news more important than anything which happens elsewhere in the world. Six people killed in a bus accident in Pollokshields are likely to get more space than 600 who die in an earthquake in Japan.

The one outstanding difference between Glasgow newspapers and all others is the amount of space devoted to sport, and particularly football. No newspapers anywhere in the world give such a large percentage of editorial matter to sport. In our newspaper offices the staff concentrating on sport is as large as the whole reportorial or sub-editorial department. Football news is frequently on the front page. During the football season the specially produced Sports Finals of the Glasgow evening papers on a Saturday afternoon have immeasurably the largest sales of the week. In some cases the Saturday sales are more than double the best sale of any week night. But, on the infrequent occasions when both Rangers and Celtic clubs are defeated on the same Saturday, the sales show a definite slump.

Politically, the Express group follow the vagaries of Lord Beaverbrook. While the one-time Kemsley group agreed with Lord Kemsley, there is a dichotomy in the politics of these newspapers since the *Daily Mirror* took over. Under the new ægis, the *Daily Record* follows the Left line of the *Daily Mirror*, but the *Evening News* Rightish attitude remains unchanged.[1] At one time the Outram group were remarkable because *The Glasgow Herald* was staunchly Conservative, the *Bulletin* showed a marked tendency towards Scottish Nationalism (plus photographs of weddings and other items particularly interesting to women), and the *Evening Times* leaned slightly to the Left. Changes in Editorship brought the three papers much closer politically, and in this respect the difference between *The Glasgow Herald*, the *Bulletin* and the *Evening Times* is now negligible.

The *Evening Citizen*, when still an independent newspaper, started a Church feature on Saturday mornings. This consists of articles, news stories and gossip paragraphs about the West of Scotland churches of all denominations, and columns of advertising of church services (with the exception of the Roman Catholic churches). In an American volume on the Press of the world, the *Evening Citizen* is specially mentioned as the first newspaper to publish and make a commercial success of a Church feature.

LIBRARIES

In spite of the claims of radio, television, dancing and public houses, Glaswegians are reading more than ever they did. Glasgow public libraries have been recording increases in the number of readers ever since the black-out during World War II made people dependent

[1] But see footnote, page 609.

on their own resources for entertainment. In general, Glasgow public library life differs little from life in any other public libraries. The number of books in the public libraries is slightly larger than the population, so that every citizen of Glasgow may be said to own at least one book.

Open access bookshelves are common in all Corporation libraries, and all books are issued free. Two of the 33 Corporation libraries may be specially noted. One is the Mitchell, the public library headquarters, where priceless books are kept and where there is a regular exhibition of books, periodicals, posters and programmes of various periods. The reading rooms are widely used by University and other students. The librarians have assisted in research work for a large number of films and novels and B.B.C. programmes.

The other notable library is the Stirling and Commercial, which is housed in the former Royal Exchange, in Royal Exchange Square. The Royal Exchange was, originally, the town house of one of the Tobacco Lords, William Cunninghame, and the shape of the house is still shown to Old Glasgow enthusiasts behind the Greek pillared entrance which the Royal Exchange directors added. This library is one of the show pieces of Glasgow, and even a Russian visitor who was taken there this year admitted they had no public library like it in Moscow!

Apart from the Glasgow Corporation public libraries, there are several individual libraries in the city. Baillie's Institution in Blythswood Square is especially laid out for students and has individual tables with separate lighting for each visitor. Baillie's Institution has had its ups and downs, however, and is not as widely known at the moment as it should be. It was formerly housed in an old church. (Old churches are used for many odd purposes in Glasgow.)

The Hunterian Library at Glasgow University is an exceptionally fine one, but it suffers (as does the University Fine Arts Department) from not being generally enough known among the people. There are specialised libraries in the Accountants' Hall, the Faculty of Surgeons, the Faculty of Law, the Scottish Community Drama Association, and in various schools, clubs and societies. Subscription libraries are popular too, but there has been a marked decrease in the number of small shop libraries which proliferated just before and during World War II. The main reason given by readers who stopped using the small subscription (2d. per volume) libraries is that there was not enough variety in the reading material. Glasgow readers have shown a definite tendency towards non-fiction, though fiction is still leading.

Museums and Art Galleries

Most of the museums and art galleries of Glasgow are to be found in the public parks. The biggest and by far the most popular is the Kelvingrove Art Galleries and Museum, paid for by the 1901 International Exhibition in Kelvingrove Park. The art collection is said to be the finest, by far, outside London. It may well be the finest civic collection in the world—as opposed to "national" galleries. There has long been a tradition that Glasgow merchants collect fine paintings and bequeath them to the city. When exhibitions of Old Masters are held anywhere in the world, Glasgow is usually asked to lend pictures. Apart from paintings, there is the Burrell Collection of objets d'art.

The Burrell Collection was given by Sir William Burrell, one of the world's most noted art collectors, to his native city. He made it a condition of the gift that the most valuable of the treasures should be housed in a gallery far enough from Glasgow to avoid contamination and destruction by the smoke-laden atmosphere. Glasgow Corporation thought they had solved the problem when they were given the estate of Dougalston to the north of the city. The National Coal Board have announced that they are planning to open a new mine not far from Dougalston House, and the problem of finding a suitable home for the Burrell Collection is still with us.

Regular exhibitions are held at Kelvingrove and sometimes they attract big numbers. Great crowds went to see Salvador Dali's "Le Christ" when it was first put on view. Crowds just as big go to see the annual exhibitions of paintings and drawings by Glasgow schoolchildren. Two exhibitions in recent years have drawn such numbers that queues extended all round the Art Galleries during the whole period of each show. One was an exhibition entitled "Glasgow Advancing," which demonstrated civic progress mainly through the Corporation departments. The other was the Picasso-Matisse exhibition from London. The possibly apocryphal but very indicative story of the latter exhibition was of the Glasgow man who was seen fleeing down the Kelvingrove Art Gallery steps and heard shouting, "Let me out! Let me out! I'm beginning to like it!"

Special exhibitions apart, Kelvingrove Art Galleries are always well attended on a Sunday. It is the habit of large numbers of children and young people to go there on that day, and the official attendants have an arduous job coping with them. The children race up and down the galleries, while the young people carry out the elementary and opening stages of courtship, known for several generations in Glasgow as "clicking."

Among the other park museums the two outstanding are the People's Palace in Glasgow Green and the Children's Museum in Tollcross Park. The People's Palace houses the "Old Glasgow" collection, but it must be noted that most of the people who go there are visitors to the city and not the Glaswegians who might be expected to be interested. The Children's Museum at Tollcross is said to be the only one in Britain. Its set-piece is the story of "Who Killed Cock Robin?" enacted by stuffed representatives of every bird and animal mentioned in the rhyme. There is also a small but interesting museum in Provand's Lordship, the oldest house in Glasgow (1471).

Of the semi-private museums in Glasgow, the one most visited is the Glasgow Police Museum. This is notable for a particularly fine collection of weapons used over the years by Glasgow gangsters, and for the footprint in blood of Jessie McLachlan, unjustly condemned for the murder of a maidservant in the Sandyford Place Mystery. Jessie's footprint can still be seen quite clearly in a strong light, though she made her mark in 1862.

The annual exhibition of the Fine Arts Institute is held in the McLellan Galleries, but it no longer attracts the interest which it once did in the city. Many other art shows are held in the McLellan Galleries. They range from touring exhibitions (Italian Art, for example) to a two weeks' show presented by the Glasgow Corporation Transport Department Art Club. This attracted over 1,000 visitors, but some expressed their disappointment that so few members had painted city traffic scenes. City traffic was better represented artistically in an open-air art show at Botanic Gardens, off Great Western Road, in the autumn of 1956. On the railings of the Gardens, a group of "independent" young artists were allowed to hang their paintings, in the manner of the Left Bank artists in Paris. Large crowds went to see this exhibition, and it may become an annual one.

Art exhibitions are held regularly in the British Council Rooms in West George Street, in the Glasgow Art Club, and in the art dealers' premises. There are many photographic exhibitions, and the Partick Camera Club recently sponsored a photographic survey of Glasgow as it exists to-day. The city was divided into areas and each camera club in Glasgow given its district to cover. More than 100 photographers co-operated in this effort, which culminated in an exhibition of the 300 best prints.

Scientific and Cultural Societies

In a city of over a million people, it can easily be imagined that every type of scientific, philosophical, literary, artistic and musical organisation exists. The Royal Glasgow Institute of the Fine Arts has already been mentioned. There are the Royal Philosophical Society, the Glasgow Choral Union, the Citizens' Theatre Society, the Scottish National Orchestra Society, and the Glasgow Jazz Club, an organisation which considers itself so powerful that it sent out a questionnaire on the subject of jazz to candidates at a general election. There are local branches of the Society of Authors and the P.E.N. Club, a Glasgow Civic Society, an Old Glasgow Club, and the Glasgow Tree Lovers.

Perhaps a good cross-section of the societies and organisations under review can be had by taking a winter season's letting at Saltire House. This is the clubhouse of the Saint Andrew Society (Glasgow), and has no connection with the Glasgow branch of the Saltire Society. In 1953 the lecture hall of Saltire House was let 110 times and the council room 78 times. The societies using the rooms were the Douglas Speech Training Group, the Oriana Society, Le Circle Intime, the Saltire Society, the Recorded Music Society, the Double Forte Club, the Scottish Conjurers' Association, Morrison Country Dancing Class, the Order of St. John, McKellar Ballet Class, Clyde Cruising Club, Clan Morrison, Women's Electrical Association, Clan McKinnon, and the Martyrs' Christian Band.

Music

Besides the orchestral and chamber music societies and clubs, there are groups of pipers and a Piping Society with classes for beginners, and members of brass bands in various parts of the city. Three Glasgow brass bands—Parkhead Forge, Govan Burgh and the Scottish Co-operative Wholesale Society—have won the Scottish Amateur Band Association championship at various times. Most of the big London dance bands employ Glasgow players, who have graduated through the Boys' Brigade and the brass bands to the lucrative dance band world. There are 12 jazz clubs in Glasgow, and some have resident bands with names like the Clyde Valley Stompers, Jim McHarg's Memphis Kings, McGregor's Dixielanders, and the Vintage Jazz Band. Once or twice each summer the jazz clubs hire a Clyde steamer and have what is known as a River Boat Shuffle, a cruise down the Firth of Clyde with bands playing non-stop in various parts of the steamer.

More than a dozen amateur operatic societies rehearse in Glasgow and each presents an annual performance of at least one week, usually in one of the large theatres. The standard of some of these performances is high for amateurs. The Glasgow Grand Opera Society usually present one opera a year which is little known in Glasgow. The Orpheus Club have a good reputation with their presentations of Gilbert and Sullivan. The Minerva Amateur Operatic Club have specialised in modern American musical plays like "Annie Get Your Gun" and "Brigadoon."

The Orpheus Club should not be confused with the Orpheus Choir, a body of amateur and semi-professional singers who won a world-wide reputation under the conductorship of Sir Hugh Roberton. When their conductor died, the Orpheus disbanded, but a new choir was formed called the Phœnix and its reputation is already approaching that of the Orpheus. Glasgow has a large number of amateur choirs, and most of them give at least one concert a year. In the case of the Glasgow Police Male Voice Choir, the concert is on a very large scale indeed.

Among children's choirs in Glasgow, the outstanding is the Scottish Junior Singers. Children's operettas are still performed in Glasgow church halls as they have been since Victorian days. In recent years many Glasgow boys have appeared in the Boy Scout annual "Gang Show" and the Boys' Brigade periodical "B.B. Fanfare." Each of these productions is presented in one of Glasgow's biggest theatres for a week.

Amateur Drama

Amateur drama groups are to be found everywhere. A recent count showed that 119 Glasgow amateur dramatic clubs were affiliated to the Scottish Community Drama Association, but the total number of clubs in the city, including those attached to churches and youth organisations, must be well over 200. Before World War II there were several amateur theatres in Glasgow. They included small theatres like the Tron and the Project which lasted only a season or two. But the Curtain Theatre was given a home in two mansion houses near Kelvingrove and became the Park Theatre. Those concerned in its operation later closed the Park and opened the Pitlochry Festival Theatre.

There was a strong Unity Theatre but it did not survive the success of a play entitled *The Gorbals Story*. This play toured Scotland and England under professional theatre auspices, and most of the members of Unity went into professional theatrical jobs from it.

Outstanding amateur drama groups are the Torch, the Pantheon, the Lyric Y.M.C.A., and the Jewish Institute Players. This last group has a theatre of its own in the Jewish Institute in the Gorbals, and presents a large number of plays and revues throughout the winter.

Although Glasgow Corporation have provided halls in various parts of the city, most of these are unsuitable for dramatic presentations. They were built to hold concerts and meetings. St. Andrew's Hall, the largest of these, can hold more than 2,500 people, and is the scene of political rallies and "Celebrity" concerts and performances by the Scottish National Orchestra and other musical bodies Many of the Clan and territorial associations in Glasgow hold their Annual Gatherings in St. Andrew's Hall, with a concert first and a Grand Dance to follow.

The Highlanders' Institute in Elmbank Street was founded to hold meetings and ceilidhs, but it has now proved to be too small. Its various halls and rooms are in use every night of the week. In spite of the attractions of television and radio, lectures are still popular in Glasgow, and any week night has its quota in the Christian Institute, the Central Halls, the Trades House, the Religious Institution Rooms, and church halls and community centres in all parts of the city.

THEATRES AND MUSIC-HALLS

Glasgow has been described by no less an authority than *Variety*, New York, as "the most theatre-minded city in Britain." There are five theatres and four music-halls—though plays and pantomimes are frequently produced in the music-halls as well as in the theatres. There is also the Athenæum Theatre, mainly occupied by amateur productions and those of the College of Dramatic Art attached to the Royal Scottish Academy of Music.

Three of the theatres, the King's, the Theatre Royal[1] and the Alhambra, are administered by the Howard and Wyndham group. The Citizens' Theatre (formerly the Royal Princess's) is owned by Glasgow Corporation and administered by the Citizens' Theatre company. The Citizens' was started by a private group in which the playwright James Bridie was the leader, but when the original lease of 10 years ran out, Glasgow Corporation bought it over. The fifth theatre is the Lyric, administered by the Y.M.C.A. This was originally the Royalty Theatre and the home of the first Glasgow Repertory in the years before World War I. It made a great reputation but the war killed it. The Y.M.C.A. took over the building and reorganised the stage and auditorium for concerts rather than theatrical entertainments. With the rise of the Scottish National Players and the amateur dramatic groups, the Lyric was used more and more as a theatre. It suffered considerably from a fire in 1953. Amateur operatic and drama companies contributed greatly to a rebuilding fund, and the Lyric, turned once again into something like a real theatre, is operating as usual.

The music-halls are the Empire (formerly the Palace), the Pavilion, the Metropole (formerly the Scotia, the oldest music-hall in Scotland), and the Empress. The Empress has also suffered from fire damage, but is now resuming theatrical productions. Until recently there was also the Queen's Theatre at Glasgow Cross. It was almost totally destroyed by fire and is not being rebuilt.

Touring companies have played in all the theatres, but recently there has been a strong tendency towards long-running " house " shows nurtured mainly by native talent—pantomime in the winter and revue in the summer. Some theatregoers complain that this means that Glasgow does not see good productions available to other cities in the summer time. An analysis of the summer fare of theatres in Manchester, Birmingham, Leeds and Liverpool makes one wonder what Glasgow *is* missing.

Of the regular shows in the summer, the Alhambra runs a " Five Past Eight " resident revue from May until October. The Pavilion is occupied for at least 20 weeks of the summer by the Tommy Morgan revue. There are normally resident shows in the Metropole and the Empress. Until 1954 the Theatre Royal had a regular summer season of repertory, played by the Wilson Barrett Company. This was abandoned by Mr. Barrett because it no longer paid. Since the Citizens' is closed during the summer, the King's Theatre is the only one open to touring productions.

Some years ago Glasgow was renowned as a " try-out " centre for new productions, but it has lost its place to Manchester. This, again,

[1] The Theatre Royal has now been acquired as a studio centre for commercial television.

is partly due to theatres being booked up for long-running resident shows. Glasgow is particularly famous as a pantomime centre, and normally has more pantomimes running than London can boast. (Last season there were four, compared with London's two.) Glasgow theatres also hold the world records for long pantomime runs: the Princess's for a full-length pantomime and the Metropole for a twice-nightly show. In each case the run was 26 weeks.

One of the reasons for the success of Glasgow pantomime was that it was the first to break away from the tradition that the principal boy should be the "head" (and therefore the most highly paid member of the cast) of the pantomime. Glasgow entrepreneurs realised that the comedians were the most important players and, long before it was the custom elsewhere (it is almost universal throughout Britain now), the chief comic was the "head" of the show.

The Princess's Theatre led the way in pantomime, and from it the other theatre impresarios realised that Scotch comics were essential for Scottish audiences. Most Scotch comics either belong to Glasgow or pretend that they do. Will Fyffe, who made *I Belong to Glasgow* an internationally famous song, was a Dundonian. But practically every well-known Scotch comic of the present day is a Glaswegian—Tommy Morgan, Dave Willis, Alec Finlay, Jack Anthony, Duncan Macrae, Jimmy Logan and Stanley Baxter. The greatest of all Glasgow comedians was the late Tommy Lorne. Many people remember him as the funniest man they have ever seen on the stage.

The hallmarks of the Glasgow comedian are, first, acute observation of city life at all levels, and second, a specialised use of the various forms of the Glasgow accent. Tommy Morgan presents a summer show at the Pavilion which runs for at least 20 weeks, and it is possible for English visitors to spend an evening there and not understand one word of the comic sketches. When Glasgow comedians appear outside Glasgow, however, they water down the accent. Dave Willis has appeared in Liverpool, Tommy Morgan in Middlesborough, and Jimmy Logan in London, and they have all been understood. The place where the Glasgow accent was at its most glottal was the Queen's Theatre, where non-Glaswegians required an interpreter.

One theatre with a specialised audience is the Empire. Almost every American music-hall, radio and/or television star who visits Britain makes an appearance at the Empire and is greeted with undisguised idolatry. The police are called out to control the crowds round the Empire stage door, and to assist American male stars in particular back to their hotel without injury and with their clothes. Newspaper critics complain that it is difficult to assess the performance of American male crooners because of the shrieks, shouts, moans, sighs and whistling of the young people (mainly young women) in the audience.

American film stars are also greeted ecstatically when they visit Glasgow. The time of their arrival is carefully announced, and crush barriers are erected in the Central Station. The crowd on an occasion of this sort may number up to nine or ten thousand, and it is customary for a large number of them to gather outside the Central Hotel and shout for their favourite until he makes an appearance on a balcony of the hotel. Most American stars say that the welcome they receive in Glasgow is the greatest they have ever had.

Cinemas

American films are much more popular than British films in Glasgow. British films do well in the picture houses in the centre of the city, but they seldom attract big crowds in the suburbs. Some of the suburban cinemas have great difficulty in keeping to the official quota of British films. On the other hand, a distinctively Scottish picture, like "Whisky Galore" or "The Maggie," will draw full houses. And, although Glasgow cinemagoers laugh at the Glasgow accent on the screen, they tend to dislike what they call the "English accent."

Some of the cinemas in Glasgow, notably the Coliseum and the New Savoy, were once theatres. It was possible, just after the 1914-18 war, for an act to play for 19 weeks in a different theatre every week, each reached by a Glasgow Corporation tramcar. Then films were introduced, and for some time there were variety acts and pictures on the same bill. The coming of the "talkies" in January 1929 ended that phase.

When the Cosmo Cinema opened just before World War II, with an avowed policy of presenting foreign and specialised films, cinema experts said it was inviting disaster. But the Cosmo has been a success ever since it started, and there are now three more cinemas in Glasgow which show foreign films with considerable success.

This success has affected the Glasgow Film Society, the oldest film society in the world. The Society find it almost impossible to pick foreign and unusual films which are not already available to the public through the Cosmo and the other specialised cinemas. When the Film Society was started in 1929 it was the only way to see a foreign film.

Scottish Film House in Glasgow is the headquarters of the Scottish Film Council of the British Film Institute and of various other film organisations. Part of it was, as has been stated, the Park Theatre, from which has emerged the Pitlochry Festival Theatre. That part of Scottish Film House is now a cinema. It is here that the International Film Festival is organised. Glasgow is responsible for the largest festival of amateur films in the world.

Glasgow has one of the smallest public cinemas in Europe and it has also the largest. The smallest is the Classic Cinema in Renfield Street, with just over 100 seats. The largest is Green's Playhouse, also in Renfield Street, with 4,400 seats. In this latter building there are, besides the cinema, cafés and restaurants and a big dance hall on the roof.

Dance Halls

Dancing is tremendously popular in Glasgow and there is a higher proportion of dance halls to the population than anywhere else in the British Isles. The standard of dancing was considered, up till 1940, the best in Britain. Experts now say that the standard has deteriorated because of such "foreign" influences as the arrival of American soldiers and sailors. Although the standard may have deteriorated, the number of dancers is still enormous, and many of the patrons of the big ballrooms attend four or five times a week. In a recent broadcast from Barrowland Dance Hall in the Gallowgate, a girl said that she danced seven nights a week—six nights at Barrowland and Sunday night at a special dance club.

There are more than 30 licensed dance halls in Glasgow, and a large number of small halls where dances, as distinct from "dancing," are held. No dance hall in Glasgow is licensed for the sale of alcohol, and trouble is sometimes caused by young men bringing in bottles secretly and drinking from them in the lavatory. This is sternly discouraged. The occasional fights, followed by police court appearances, on Friday and Saturday nights are most often caused because doorkeepers will not allow "drunks" to enter.

Dennistoun Palais holds 1,700 dancers and is the biggest dance hall in Glasgow. The Plaza is renowned as the place where family parties go, particularly for twenty-first birthday celebrations. "Jiving" is not encouraged in any of the big dance halls, but one, the Locarno, has experimented in having a special space apart for "jivers."

Many private and club dances are held in Glasgow, in hotels, Masonic halls, community centres and church halls. Less than 30 years ago most churches would not countenance dances, and church youth clubs held what were euphemistically called "socials." At some of these the number of dances was restricted to, say, four. But there was no restriction on "games," so the organisers would include The Grand Old Duke of York, the Eightsome Reel and items of a similar nature as games. Each of the four dances lasted for at least a quarter of an hour. Nowadays church youth clubs are, in the main, unrestricted, and no longer have to call their dances "socials."

CLUBS

Whist drives are not as popular as they once were, but bridge clubs have not yet taken their place as far as numbers are concerned. There is a good deal of gambling on cards in social clubs and in private houses. This is especially the case on the South side of the city, and taxi drivers are accustomed to being called out in the early hours of the morning to take women gamblers home.

There is practically no public " night life " in Glasgow, though a great deal goes on behind the scenes. A London firm carried out an investigation of Glasgow nocturnal habits to discover whether or not it was worth while establishing an all-night restaurant in this city. The conclusion was that it would not pay. Dance halls are sometimes open until 1 or 2 a.m., but generally close around midnight. Licensed restaurants serve alcohol with food up till 10.30 p.m., and the drink may remain on the table until 11 p.m.

There are two " night clubs " in Glasgow, the Piccadilly and the Locarno, but they observe the same licensing hours as the restaurants, although they remain open later for dancing. They are not night clubs in the London sense. The only equivalent of London night life is found at the coffee stalls in the centre of the city, where there are normally big crowds from midnight onwards. Unfortunately many undesirables are attracted, and a good deal of the vice in Glasgow has its start at the coffee stalls—although, naturally, the operators of these stalls are anxious to avoid trouble.

The social clubs of Glasgow have the power to fix their own hours. In practice they keep close to the official licensing hours which apply to restaurants and public houses. Some of the biggest and best of these clubs are finding it difficult to continue to exist, and there are frequent mentions of merging.

The oldest club in Glasgow is the Western, in Buchanan Street, founded in 1848. It is typical of Glasgow that the public house directly opposite is known, unofficially, as the Eastern Club. The Western Club and the New Club are in the tradition of heavy armchairs, dark panelling and good port.[1] The Conservative Club has made more concessions to modern taste and is one of the healthiest financially in the city. All these are exclusively male clubs, and it is perhaps significant that by far the most successful club in Glasgow is the Automobile, which opens its doors to women as well as men. There are two all-women clubs in Glasgow—the Kelvin in Royal Exchange Square, and the Ladies' Art Club in Blythswood Square.

Clubs with, to some extent, a specialised membership are the Glasgow Art Club, the Press Club, the Society of Musicians and the Literary Club, though all these have a good proportion of " lay " members. There is a large number of Service clubs, covering most Scottish regiments, the Army generally, and the Navy and R.A.F. A relic of World War I is the Old Contemptibles Association Club.

But most of the clubs in Glasgow have no premises of their own. This is true, for example, of the plethora of Burns Clubs. One of the largest Burns clubs in the world, the Scottish, is in Glasgow, but it has no home of its own. Incidentally, it is teetotal, and the Immortal Memory is drunk in lemonade.

A modern Dr. Strang who was trying to emulate his predecessor

[1] The Western and the New Clubs have amalgamated since these words were written.

and produce a volume on Glasgow clubs would need a much bigger book than the doctor did. At least one club mentioned by Dr. Strang, the Hodge Podge, still exists. Among others there are the Nomads, Ye Jovial Tramps, the Southern Medical Society (more than 100 years old), the Glasgow branch of the Wine and Food Society, and the Scottish Tramways Museum Society. Although this last club has no premises, it does possess a number of ancient tram cars, and hopes to have some day a section of tram track on which its cars can be run.

There is a large number of small and esoteric clubs, such as the 13 (which consists of precisely 13 members), the Claret Club, the Adam Smith Society, the Ours Club, the Crew One Club (a relic of World War II), and the All Saints. This last is composed of 10 Glasgow and 10 Edinburgh men and meets thrice a year to keep the old rivalry between the cities alive.

Most Glasgow schools of the academy and secondary standard have Former Pupils' clubs, though some meet merely for an annual dinner. One district of the city has a former residents' club. It is called the Old Dennistounians, and is full of men who recall the days when Dennistoun had almost as many green fields as it had houses. Old Dennistounians from all over Scotland, England and Ireland attend the annual dinner, where the atmosphere is so informal that it is not unusual for a dozen eggs and a bottle of whisky to be raffled because the committee have priced the dinner ticket too low.

Eggs and whisky also figure prominently in the annual supper of the Govan Weavers, which is held on the night of the Old Govan Fair. There are more shipbuilders than weavers in the society, but they observe the traditional menu of boiled eggs, washed down with whisky. At one time salmon was included in the supper menu but it was too difficult to get during World War II and it is no longer served.

PUBS

Glasgow public houses have been indicted for many years for their lack of social amenities, particularly as compared with the standards of Southern England. There are 1,083 pubs in Glasgow, and it is probably true that about half of them do not reach the English standard. It must be said, however, that all of them have reasonable lavatory accommodation, which is far ahead of the English standard.

"Perpendicular drinking" has been said to be the trouble with Glasgow pubs, and it has even been suggested that the Glasgow invention of square-toed shoes was to enable the Glasgow man to get closer to the bar. (Square-toed shoes were invented by Mr. Alexander Somerville, who left his money to found the St. Mungo Prize, which amounts to approximately £1,000 and is awarded every three years to the person who has done most for the city in the three preceding years.)

But many Glasgow pubs now have lounges, mostly "modern" affairs of chromium, concealed lighting and imitation leather in scarlet or bright blue. These lounges are for both sexes, and the price of drink is generally slightly higher than in the ordinary bar. There are still a fair number of pubs in Glasgow where women are not admitted, and it is only in pubs at the top and the bottom of the social scale that women are allowed to stand or sit at the bar.

Whisky, in spite of its price, and beer are still the most popular beverages in pubs, and visitors are still surprised at the Glasgow man's addiction to the "Hauf an' a hauf pint"—a half glass (or nowadays it may be a "nip") of whisky, and a half pint of beer. In some of the lower quarters of the city, whisky is thought to be too dear, and the customary combination now is a glass of cheap red wine and a half pint of beer. Pubs which sell this combination are known as "wine shops," and are not notable for their amenities.

Drinking habits have improved considerably in the slum districts of the city. During the "depressed" years of the early 1930's, there were two drinks known as "jake" and "red biddy." These were mixtures of methylated spirits and cheap red wine. It was said that a favourite practice of drinkers who wished to achieve oblivion as quickly and as cheaply as possible was to attach a tube to the gas bracket on the stair landing of a tenement and allow a "whiff" of the gas to enter a glass of milk. While it is known that this was done, it was not a general practice at all, and it gained fame because it was mentioned in newspaper reports.

Scent drinking was popular at one time, and is still known in Glasgow. Any cheap scent will satisfy the addict, but the favourite for years has been an Eau de Cologne, which costs about sixpence for a small bottle.

Before World War II experts on oblivion said it was possible to be drunk for a fortnight on 10½d. At that time the addict could buy sixpenceworth of spirits of salts (forbidden now) from any chemist. He also bought a large bottle of lemonade, which then cost fourpence ha'penny. Into the bottom of a tumbler he put a very little spirits of salts, and filled up the tumbler with lemonade. When he swallowed this mixture he rapidly became unconscious. As soon as the addict had regained consciousness (a period of time depending on the proportions of the two ingredients in the concoction), he took a glass of water. The action of the water made him drunk again. Once again, when he recovered, he took another drink of water, and kept on drinking water until it no longer had any effect. He then made a new mixture of spirits of salts and lemonade and started the process all over again. By ringing the liquid changes in this way, he could—it was said by experts in the matter—remain drunk for two weeks.

This sort of extra-mural activity has nothing to do with the Glasgow public houses. Possibly the most remarkable feature of Glasgow pub life is its geography. Glasgow Town Council do not look with favour on the provision of licences in new suburbs, and there are also some residential districts which use the Local Veto to "protect" their area.

Thus, in the Exchange Ward of the city there are 221 licensed premises for a population of 23,872 (one for every 108 persons living in the ward); in the Gorbals there are 112 licensed premises for a population of 40,525; in Maryhill there are 17 licensed premises for a population of 25,744; in Dennistoun there are four for 27,902; in Provan one for 21,010. And there are no licensed premises at all in three wards—Whiteinch, Knightswood and Cathcart.

In one street in the East End of Glasgow, the Gallowgate, there are 66 pubs. Many of the people who lived round the Gallowgate are now living in newly built Glasgow suburbs which have no pubs at all. At present the majority of men who have "flitted" to a new suburb and who like a drink travel to their former neighbourhoods and use the pubs with which they are familiar.

There are strict rules in Glasgow pubs against singing, music (apart from that provided by a radio set), and any other game but dominoes and draughts. These restrictions, plus "Temperance" propaganda, have given rise to the prevalent idea that most Glasgow pubs are mere "drinking dens" and have no social function. While this is true of a small proportion of Glasgow pubs (and particularly the "wine shops"), the amount of social activity in pubs used by working-class men is considerable. Many of these men do regard the pub as a club.

Some Glasgow pubs have an annual outing to the country or the sea. Customers pay a small subscription every week, and a committee arranges the details. An outing held by the customers of The Wee Man in the Gallowgate, for example, was to Rothesay on a Sunday. Some 50 men turned up at the Central Station. The rendezvous was the gentlemen's lavatory beside Platform 13. There each man received tickets allowing him a half glass of whisky or a bottle of beer, and had time to have a drink before the train left for Wemyss Bay. The party travelled in reserved coaches, each labelled The Wee Man. They varied widely in age, but most would be between 30 and 40. They carried with them cases of whisky and beer, two footballs, a trumpet, a wig and false moustache. As soon as they boarded the steamer at Wemyss Bay, they started a concert, in which the trumpet, the wig and the false moustache were all used.

At Rothesay they went straight to a large hotel and had luncheon. Two 'buses were waiting outside the hotel and immediately after luncheon took the party to Ettrick Bay. There they played football, paddled, and took part in various forms of athletics. A temporary bar was set up and those who had tickets left were able to have a drink. Then the 'buses took the party back to the hotel for high tea, which was followed by speeches and "harmony," when most of the songs and choruses which had been sung aboard the steamer were sung again.

On the journey back in the steamer the party held yet another concert on the deck, and a large number of day trippers from Glasgow not only joined in the singing but also provided several individual "turns." Perhaps it should be stressed here that steamer bars do not open on a Sunday, and that the high spirits were not artificially inspired.

This kind of pub outing should not be confused with the Sunday outings arranged by some groups of Glaswegians who want to take advantage of the "bona fide traveller" law and who hire 'buses to take them on a tour of country hotels for the purpose of drinking.

In recent years a number of well-known footballers have become associated with Glasgow pubs as proprietors or managers. Football is the principal subject of conversation in any Glasgow pub, so footballers' pubs are generally popular. In at least one of them there was the additional attraction that the customer could be photographed receiving his drink from the hands of his hero.

FOOTBALL

Football is the ruling passion of a great number of Glasgow males —not playing football, but watching it, gambling on it, reading about it, hearing about it, and talking about it. The filling in of football coupons has stimulated an even wider interest in the game, particularly among women. So seriously do some men support a team that its defeat makes them physically ill. The authentic remark of a young Glasgow man was, "That time Rangers got beat by the Celtic, I went to my bed for three days."

There are six senior football clubs in Glasgow—Celtic, Partick Thistle, Rangers and Queen's Park in the First Division, and Third Lanark and Clyde in the Second Division. Queen's Park, the oldest football club in Glasgow, has the distinction of being the only purely amateur club in senior football in the whole of Britain. Generally speaking, the clubs are supported by the people of the area surrounding the football grounds—Govan and Ibrox men follow Rangers, East Enders are divided between Celtic and Clyde, South Siders are for Queen's Park and Third Lanark, and north of the Clyde there is a great deal of support for Partick Thistle.

But there are other reasons. Perfervid Protestants support the Rangers, and equally perfervid Roman Catholics support Celtic. It is alleged that most of the supporters of Queen's Park wear bowler hats and speak with a "refained" accent. Clyde supporters come from the Royal Burgh of Rutherglen as well as the East End of Glasgow. The boundary line of Glasgow runs across the Clyde's playing ground at Shawfield Park, and it is possible for a player to kick the ball in Rutherglen and score a goal in Glasgow. But, generally speaking, success begets support, and Rangers and Celtic have Supporters' Clubs in almost every town of any size in Scotland.

Though the number of males playing football on any Saturday in Glasgow may not be large as compared with the population, it is nevertheless considerable. There are Junior and Juvenile teams, the Churches' League, a Roman Catholic youth league, an immense number of school and district teams, and what is believed to be the largest football league in the world—that run by the Glasgow Battalion of the Boys' Brigade. It fields some 200 teams every Saturday.

Until a few years ago Glasgow could claim to have the largest football arena in the world, Hampden Park, belonging to Queen's Park F.C. Although it is still one of the largest, it has now been beaten by grounds in South America and on the Continent. It was made to hold approximately 150,000 spectators, but the largest number ever officially accommodated there was 149,500 and, to avoid the risks of accidents, Glasgow Police now insist on the number being limited to about 135,000. Hampden is, of course, still by far the largest football ground in Britain.

The "Hampden Roar" is the name given to the amazing ululations produced from thousands of throats when the Scottish football fans are urging on the Scottish team in an international match, especially against England. It is an almost frightening sound, and English football players have been quoted as saying that the Hampden Roar is the equivalent of two goals for Scotland. Unfortunately this has not always proved true.

While most of the big football matches are held in Glasgow, the big Rugby football games are held in Edinburgh. Rugby football in Glasgow comes far behind Association football in popular support, but the number playing the game is high. Several "soccer" schools have taken up Rugby during the past few years, and sometimes suspicions are voiced that the change over is a matter of class distinction. Of the 11 principal "rugger" grounds in the Glasgow area, seven belong to Former Pupils' clubs of schools, two are owned by the University, and one by the Royal College of Science and Technology.

The chief Rugby ground is Old Anniesland, belonging to Glasgow High School F.P.s. This houses the Inter-City game between Glasgow and Edinburgh. It is used for cricket in the summer, and is usually the place selected for the Shinty Final. Shinty, said by its Highland devotees to be the oldest ball game in the world, is played by a handful of teams in Glasgow and its following, although enthusiastic, is small.

Other Outdoor Sports

The success of the television broadcasting of cricket Test matches has brought some new interest to the game of cricket in Glasgow, but it remains a minority sport. Although it is widely played in the schools, comparatively few school cricketers graduate to grown-up cricket. There are five principal Glasgow cricket clubs.

It would be difficult to name an outdoor sport which does not have its supporters in Glasgow. Archery, lacrosse, hockey, horse-riding, and the racing and field events run by athletic clubs are all to be found in the city. Two pursuits which one might not expect to find in the middle of a large town are quoiting and "the doos."

Glasgow's only quoiting club is at Townhead, on the bank of the Monkland Canal. Most of the members were trained in quoiting outside the city, and wanted to continue playing the game when they took a job in Glasgow.

The racing of "doos," or homing pigeons, is difficult in a town with as many wires and other pigeon hazards as Glasgow. Nevertheless there is a Glasgow and District Federation of Racing Pigeon Clubs. There are 16 clubs in the Federation and they entered 33,493 birds for 15 races in 1954. The members include doctors, bankers, engineers, miners and schoolboys. Most of the pigeon lofts are in the suburbs or on the outskirts of Glasgow, but one man is flying racing pigeons from a loft in the shadow of the gigantic water cooler (the second largest in Europe) at Pinkston Power Station, Port Dundas. Glasgow Corporation have laid down regulations about lofts which pigeon fanciers must obey. The loss of pigeons in the Glasgow area is high because the birds fly into wires and are killed by dogs and cats in the neighbourhood. Nevertheless there are 551 members of the Glasgow and District Federation.

At various times speedway racing, as a spectator-sport, has been popular in Glasgow. For a while three speedway tracks were operating in the city. But the craze seems to last for only a year or two, and at present it appears to have died out.

Betting

Although speedway tracks have usually operated at greyhound racing tracks, the speedway authorities have always sternly discouraged betting. This discouragement (very proper indeed where human lives are at stake) may have affected attendances, because Glasgow men and women dearly like to bet. Betting on horse and dog racing occupies a considerable amount of Glasgow time. Although betting shops are not yet legalised, it is estimated that there are well over 250 of them operating every day in Glasgow. This is in addition to the many commission agents and the even larger number of street bookmakers.

The betting shops have drab frontages and show no sign whatever of their purpose. The interiors range from the frankly functional, with a board containing details of horses and dogs running and their prices, and a counter where the bets can be placed, to the almost luxurious, with easy chairs, loud-speakers to give the latest details of the results, and a television set where the punters can while away the time between races. It is believed that the betting shops are affecting attendances at racing tracks, and particularly dog tracks, to a great extent. Many punters prefer to place their bets in comparative comfort and do not feel that it is necessary to see the dogs or the races at all.

Figures are not yet available to show what effect the betting shops have on the dog tracks, but the extent of Glasgow's interest in The

Dogs may be judged from the following figures issued by the Press Office at St. Andrew's House, Edinburgh, for the year 1954. There are four dog tracks within the Glasgow boundary—Carntyne, Albion, White City and Firhill[1] Two tracks officially outside the boundary, but actually supported mainly by Glasgow visitors, are Shawfield and Mount Vernon. These six tracks can accommodate 101,500 spectators. There is no Totalisator at Mount Vernon, but the amount of "Tote" betting at the five other tracks in 1954 was £2,227,643. Naturally there is no figure showing bets placed with bookmakers on and off the track, but the total figure of all bets placed is obviously astronomical.

The figures for these tracks are as follows:

Track	*No. of spectators*	*Amount staked on Tote*
Mount Vernon	2,500	—
Carntyne	18,000	£348,284
Albion	20,000	£466,461
White City	25,000	£490,212
Firhill[1]	20,000	£162,298
Shawfield	16,000	£760,388

There is also a track at Stepps Stadium, which is used for trotting races for ponies, etc., and which was stated in 1954 to accommodate 8,000 spectators.

The three sports in which participation is more important to the citizens than spectating are golf, tennis and bowling. Anyone who leaves or arrives at Renfrew Airport by air notices that Glasgow seems to be almost completely surrounded by cemeteries and golf courses. Golf is very much the business man's game in Glasgow, though there are eight Corporation courses in the Glasgow parks and these are so popular that, on a good day, a queue of players starts forming at 6 a.m., or even earlier. Glasgow golfers have succeeded notably in championship games and in representing Scotland in international matches.

In tennis and bowling the Glasgow Corporation facilities far outnumber those provided by private clubs. While golf is played by men and women of all ages, tennis is generally regarded as the preserve of young people, and bowling belongs to the middle-aged. Glasgow possesses 88 municipal bowling greens and 129 tennis courts, and practically all of these are in the public parks.

PARKS

Judged on a basis of population, Glasgow can claim to have more public parks than any other city or town in the United Kingdom. There

[1] Since this was written, Firhill dog track has ceased to exist.

are 50 large parks and dozens of open spaces and playgrounds, with a total area of more than 3,000 acres.[1] The parks vary in popularity, and one or two in densely populated districts are not nearly as popular as might be expected.

Despite the density of soot in the Glasgow air and the fumes from nearby works, the Glasgow parks keep up an amazingly high standard. Figures were publicised not long ago for the number of flowers planted in the five Royal Parks of Paris. It was then found that one of the 50 parks in Glasgow, Queen's Park, had more blooms than all the Royal Parks of Paris added together.

Glasgow Green is the oldest park in the city. It was bought by Glasgow Town Council in 1662, but it was a park for centuries before that. The entrance to the Green, in Jocelyn Square, was popular for many years as an open-air forum in the Hyde Park style, but flower plots have been placed there and the law-abiding Anarchists, Communists, Atheists, and others, have gone to pastures new. The stretch of the River Clyde through Glasgow Green is used by several rowing clubs, whose club and boat-houses are built on the right bank. The Green is especially popular when new exhibitions are being held in the People's Palace (where the Old Glasgow Museum is housed) and when the annual Carnival is held during the Glasgow Fair Holidays.

Probably the most popular park in the city is Kelvingrove, although many of the visitors criticise the state of the River Kelvin, which runs through the park. The effluents from paper mills and chemical and other works farther up the river form a most unpleasant scum, which often collects between the Art Galleries and the University. When an open-air exhibition of sculpture was held in Kelvingrove, one suggestion was that the advertisements should read, "Scum to see the Sculpture." In spite of this, the park is well used and in good weather crowds flock to the park bandstand, which can accommodate 4,500 people. The only roller-skating rink in Glasgow is in the open air at Kelvingrove.

Rouken Glen and Hogganfield Loch Parks provide boating, and Rouken Glen is also much visited for its waterfall. Much of Rouken Glen and of the Linn Park (through which the River Cart flows) is in a natural state, and Glasgow has also a "wild" park at Dawsholm, which is a bird sanctuary. Victoria Park is famous for its Fossil Grove, containing fossils of an extinct type of tree. Cathkin Braes Park is principally visited for the fine view over the city—when the weather is suitable.

Two Glasgow parks have artificial summits. One is Queen's Park, where the flagpole stands on an artificial mound. The other is Ruchill Park, and its summit is known locally as "Ben Whitton," after the Glasgow Corporation Director of Cleansing who built it. He took the earth excavated from the foundations of the nearby Ruchill Hospital, and added it to the top of the existing hill. The sight of the roofs of

[1] See Appendix Table 137.

the city from this vantage point would be famous in any other place but Glasgow.

The Botanic Gardens contain the largest glass building in Britain, the Kibble Palace. It is a winter garden and was presented to the city by a Mr. John Kibble. At one time it was used for concerts and meetings, and both Mr. Gladstone and the Earl of Beaconsfield gave their Rectorial addresses to the students of Glasgow University in this glass building. There are other hot-houses and the Botanic Gardens supply all the needs of the Botany Department of Glasgow University. Bananas are grown in the Kibble Palace, but are not for sale. The orchid house has 10,000 plants.

Zoo

Rouken Glen Park would have become Glasgow's first Zoo if it had not been for the outbreak of war in 1914. Efforts to start a Zoo in the city had been made since at least 1898, but had come to naught. The Rouken Glen Zoo was sponsored by Glasgow Corporation, but all plans were dropped when the Great War broke out. Between World Wars I and II other plans were put forward, but Glasgow Corporation had lost interest.

In December 1936, 35 people attended a meeting in the Department of Zoology in Glasgow University and agreed to form a Zoological Society of Glasgow. The aim of the Society was a non-commercial Zoo and by the end of 1938 more than £8,000 had been raised. An option was taken on the Calderpark Estate near the Broomhouse tram terminus, and plans were almost complete when, once again, a war stopped the building of a Glasgow Zoo.

The first turf was cut on 31 May 1946. Representatives of Lanark County Council were present, as well as representatives of Glasgow Corporation. The Zoological Society of Glasgow and West Scotland had 106 acres of ground and no water, light, heat or boundary fence. The Zoo was opened on 9 July 1947, and was a " make do and mend " affair. Some 30 acres had been made into a zoological garden whose cages, paddocks and enclosures were made from second-hand material gathered from shipbreaking yards, scrap merchants and redundant war supplies.

In spite of weather and other difficulties, the Zoo is now established, and has a good collection. It is already becoming known in Europe for its breeding of lions and tigers. When the complete plan for taking in the entire 106 acres is accomplished, the Glasgow Zoo should be one of the finest in the world.

There is some irony in the fact that, having never had a Zoo, Glasgow became possessed of two for some time. A commercial Zoo was opened at Craigend Castle, Mugdockbank, in 1950, but closed in 1954. Some of the animals are now housed in a small indoor Zoo in

Oswald Street. This has been operating for many years, and is possibly the only Zoo in the world where a magistrate of a Town Council gave an exhibition of lion taming twice a day for several years.

Indoor Sports

Glasgow has facilities for many indoor sports and recreations. There are 14 swimming ponds run by Glasgow Corporation and several private swimming clubs. Skating and curling are immensely popular at Crossmyloof Ice Rink, and many Glasgow skaters and curlers also go to Paisley Ice Rink, which is not far from the Glasgow boundary. The number of curlers in Glasgow has increased greatly with the introduction of indoor curling. A good number of business men consider curling as essential to business life as golf.

Table tennis, Badminton and basket ball are popular, and the basket ball team of the Maryhill Youth Club have met crack teams from the United States on equal terms. Squash is played, but only by a small number.

Almost all clubs have their billiards rooms, but there are also nine billiards rooms in the centre of the city. Two of these have also facilities for table tennis. As a game billiards has been almost entirely replaced by snooker in Glasgow.

Judo, wrestling and weight-lifting have their clubs and their devotees. Wrestling is also a popular sport from the spectators' point of view. All-in wrestling is banned by the Glasgow magistrates, but there is a form of wrestling known as "Under Lord Mount-Evans' rules" and this is allowed. Connoisseurs of the art find it interesting to note that the performers appear elsewhere as all-in wrestlers, but become polite when they reach Glasgow.

Amateur boxing, as a spectator sport, is more popular in Glasgow than professional boxing. Kelvin Hall is needed for the amateur championships and for international contests. This hall has also been used for professional boxing, but for various reasons (including the lack of good professional boxers), audiences have fallen off there. Glasgow professional boxers tend to the lighter weights, and followers of boxing are always hoping that the city will throw up another Benny Lynch.

Holiday Habits

Among sporting clubs which operate the whole year round (though, naturally, they have more opportunities in the summer) are cycling, rambling and mountaineering groups. Cycle clubs are keen on Sunday racing and travel considerable distances to their "meets." The racers are young men who have shown a tendency in recent years to imitate the cycle racers of the Continent in costume, equipment and habits.

Most cyclists, walkers and mountaineers are members of the Scottish Youth Hostel movement. There are also the " hikers," who clothe themselves in remarkable garments—especially the females—hang themselves about with impedimenta, travel to a tram terminus and then proceed to walk backwards as they look for car-drivers who will give them a lift.

Camping and caravanning are popular with Glaswegians, who have the advantage of so much beautiful scenery on their doorstep. Since the end of World War II, however, many Glaswegians have looked farther afield for their holidays. Campers and caravanners have been going to the far north of Scotland or to Cornwall or Wales. Many holidaymakers are air-minded and fly to the Isle of Man, Ireland, or the Continent. Aberdeen is specially favoured by Glasgow holidaymakers, who seem to regard the Firth of Clyde as too close to them to provide a real change now.

There is still a rush by Glaswegians to the Clyde resorts and the Ayrshire holiday places during the Fair Holidays, and the Lochs and the Trossachs are still popular. But over the holiday period generally, the trend is away from the places so popular with the last generation. Fortunately for the holiday places, the lack of Glaswegians is more than made up by the increased number of tourists from other parts of Scotland and, more especially, from England.

The average age of the Clyde resorts is about 100 years. At first only the wealthy people from Glasgow were able to visit them. Then, as the Industrial Revolution made itself felt in Glasgow, the middle classes and then the workers were able to take their Fair outside Glasgow too. The only remnant of the way that ordinary people celebrated the Glasgow Fair 100 years ago is the annual carnival on Glasgow Green.

The days of packing the trunk and the hamper, and going to the station in a horse-drawn cab, are over. The conception of " paw, maw and the weans " on the deck of the Clyde steamer is out-of-date. So is the idea that a town like Rothesay is turned into a miniature Glasgow during the Fair Fortnight.

Glasgow now spreads itself all over Britain and the Continent. Bus tours to France or Switzerland or Austria leave from the middle of the city. Big parties of Glasgow schoolchildren go off on conducted tours of the Continent. Boy Scout troops who once regarded a camp in Kintyre as a great adventure now make arrangements to take their tents to Brittany.

The exceptions to this trend are mainly the families with small children, and they still find the Clyde and Ayrshire convenient. There are also the die-hards who have given their heart to one place and go back to it, year by year, at every opportunity. This is especially true of the devotees of the Isle of Arran. They often claim to be miserable anywhere else. But even the number of Arranites is falling, and the island publicity committee find it necessary to run an " Arran Week " at the beginning of each summer season in order to attract attention to its amenities.

Glaswegians are popular holidaymakers. They are considered by the inhabitants of holiday resorts to be great spenders, easily pleased and bubbling over with good spirits. It is strange that they do not appear so to their fellow Glaswegians, but one would like to think that the outside opinion is the right one.

Chapter 20

CRIME

J. A. MACK

It is not surprising that Glasgow, with its history of rapid expansion and its acute deficiencies of housing and living-space, should have carried a heavy burden of crime and social disorganisation over from the early nineteenth century into the second half of the twentieth. What is remarkable is that the city's social progress, measured by the rate of decrease in the volume of recorded misbehaviour, should exceed that of the rest of Scotland in the last half-century and particularly since the war of 1939-45. It is of course unwise to read off the crime barometer at a glance. There is a bewildering variety of dials and indicators. Any major trend in the annually recorded total of crimes and offences,[1] and especially any abrupt upward or downward movement, points almost invariably to changes not only in public behaviour but also in police recording techniques and detective efficiency. Thus the Glasgow crime figures for the 1930's, and again in the last decade, reflect the major police reorganisation and the striking improvement in the efficiency of the force described later in this chapter. The main lesson of the criminal statistics, however, is that of comparative social advance. In those numerous but less serious items classed as " offences " Glasgow is well in the van of the general national improvement. In the more serious categories classed as " crimes," ranging from personal violence to petty theft and malicious mischief, Glasgow's share in the national totals has been going down steadily, and at a faster rate than the decline in Glasgow's population relative to that of Scotland, since at least the 1930's. That is the broad quantitative trend. It may not mean very much. The quality or degree of viciousness of individual crimes of violence is not noticeably changed; it is thought to have if anything increased in the years after 1945. But even so it appears that the quantum or proportion of positive and punishable offending in the population, and particularly in the adult population, is diminishing.

Offences

If the trend of offences may be regarded as throwing light on changing social standards, there has been at least one clear improve-

1 The distinction between " crimes " and " offences "—the analogous distinction in England and Wales is between " indictable offences " and " non-indictable offences " —corresponds to the common-sense distinction between crimes and nuisances.

ment in the manners of Glasgow over the past fifty years. The greatest single change in public behaviour since the days of the First World War is the almost complete disappearance of the helplessly drunk from the streets. The once horribly frequent spectacle of mass drunkenness which so impressed Beatrice Potter and Sidney Webb in the 1890's is now a thing of the past.[1] At the turn of the century the annual number of drunks appearing in the police courts was never far below 20,000. The average figure over the past ten years is 3,000, drawn from a population bigger by one third than in 1900. It is true that there has been a gradual increase in each year since 1945, when the lowest figure on record was reached at 1,836, or less than two per thousand of the city's population. But even with the increase to 3,717 in 1954 (3.4 per thousand) the volume and incidence are half that of 1938 and well below one fifth of the corresponding figures in the 1900's.[2] The general Scottish trend is broadly similar.[3]

This change can best be appreciated against the last boisterous hundred years of the city's history. Hard as it may be to credit, 1900 was probably an improvement on 1850.[4] At that time the population was rising rapidly, fed by a constant stream of Irish and Highland immigrants. It had more than doubled between 1821 and 1851: in the six years between 1851 and 1857 it increased from 329,026 to 391,400. The long-drawn out birth-pangs of the modern city were eased to some extent by a copious flow of cheap liquor. Whisky was 1s. 6d. the bottle.

The control of drunkenness, and of its consequences in violence and thieving, was to be the main task and preoccupation of the police until well into the twentieth century. They began unsupported by any but the most primitive apparatus of civic welfare, and possessing few powers. Until 1853, the year of the "Forbes Mackenzie" Act, liquor could be bought and sold at practically any time of day, week day or Sunday alike. The Act closed the public houses at 11 p.m. and earlier on Sunday. The results were at once manifest. In the last three years of the "old law," 1851 to 1853, the annual average of cases of drunkenness was just under 24,000. In the first three years of the new law, 1854 to 1856, it fell to under 18,000. In the same period Sunday drunkenness fell from an average of 1,360 to one of 490.[5]

One immediate effect of the Forbes Mackenzie Act, and of the more stringent Public House and Licensing Acts that followed it, was an increase in the illicit liquor trade conducted in shebeens and houses of ill fame. "Shadow," the roving reporter of that era, describes a typical midnight scene in 1858.[6] The author with his friends has followed an

1 Beatrice Webb, *My Apprenticeship.*

2 See Appendix Table 143.

3 J. Mack, Chapter on "Crime" in *The Scottish Economy,* Ed. Cairncross (1954), p. 229.

4 A comparative statistical statement is not possible owing to changes in classification. The figures given for the 1850's in the next paragraph refer to all items in which drunkenness is involved. Contemporary figures refer only to the single item of "drunk and incapable."

5 Duncan McLaren: *The Rise and Progress of Whisky Drinking in Scotland,* quoted by "Shadow": *Midnight Scenes and Social Photographs, Glasgow* (1858), p. 143.

6 "Shadow," *op. cit.*

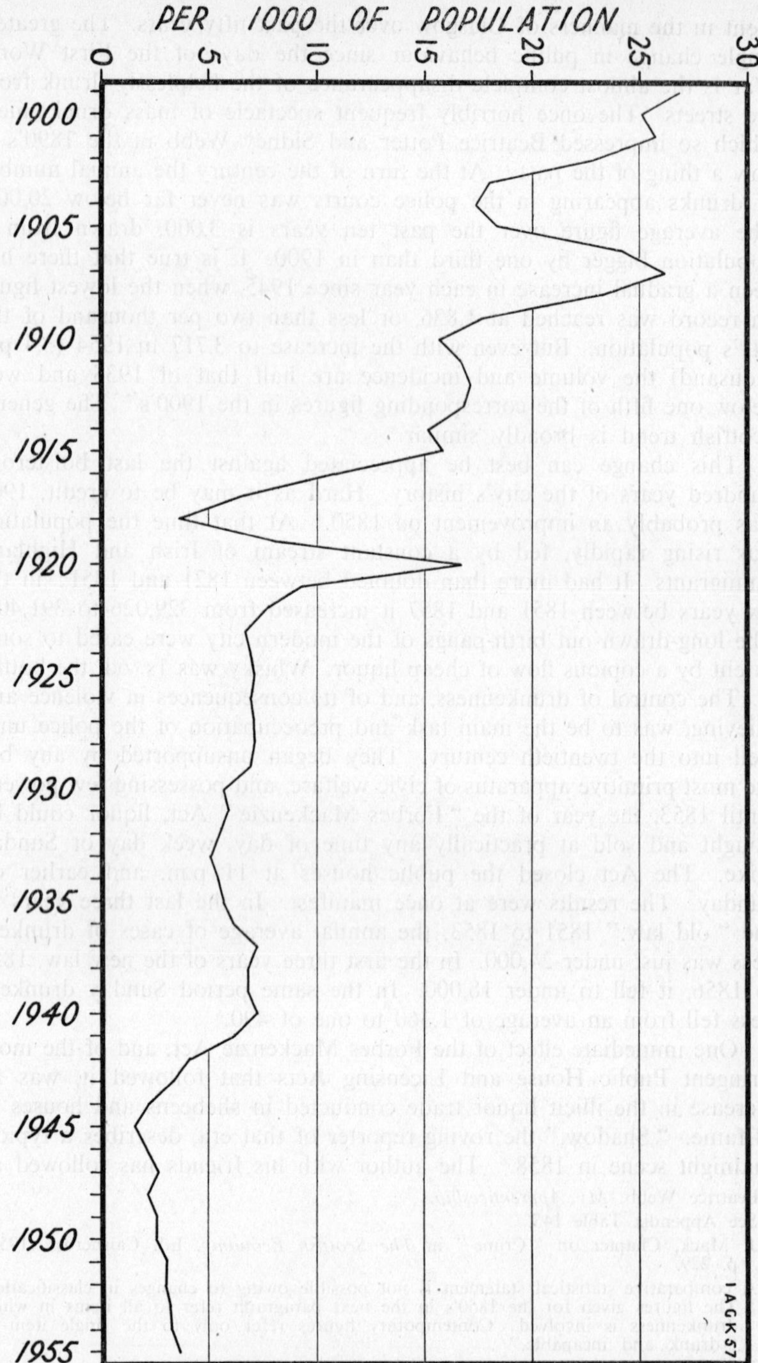

FIG. 32. Persons proceeded against for Drunkenness in Glasgow, 1899-1955.

evil-looking woman, with a half-drunk young man in tow, into a small two-room earthen-floored dwelling in a court near the Gallowgate. There are four beds with "two loathsome women" in each bed. "As we smell the whisky and pass it round, a feeling of disappointment is evidently felt. 'I doot you dinna like the whisky,' says Jenny, 'It's real gude by what we get maist times at this time o' night.' 'I daresay it is,' we remark, 'it can't be expected good at so late an hour.' A proposal is made to form a circle round the fire, and enjoy ourselves. However, giving a significant look to the young man, who by this time is again beginning to be a little elevated, we make our way towards the door, but find it locked. A trifle of money to the doorkeeper, who remonstrates against our leaving, and we forthwith take our departure, congratulating ourselves on an escape from a very dangerous den of the worst of thieves and prostitutes."

The unlicensed trade in spirits rose and fell for many years, defying all attempts at its suppression. As early as 1862 Chief Constable Smart thought that the worst of the evil was over. "The traffic in Spirits in Shebeens, or Unlicensed Premises," he reported, "was nearly put an end to by the vigorous application of Forbes Mackenzie's Act. This satisfactory result was brought about by the Magistrates, under the advice of the Town Clerk, having convicted on circumstantial evidence, instead of, as formerly, making it imperative on the prosecutor to prove a sale in each case. Little now remains to be done in the matter under either the new Public House Act or new Police Act,[1] either of which is sufficiently stringent to crush any attempt to reopen these doors."

Either the Acts were defective or their administration left much to be desired, for in 1871 occurred the celebrated exposure of the "Dark Side of Glasgow" in the *Glasgow Daily Mail*. The *Mail's* special commissioners, having investigated the city's sanitary deficiencies, turned in the closing months of 1870 to probe its "lowest phases of vice" in the Central District of Glasgow—King Street, Goosedubs, Bridgegate, Princes Street, Saltmarket, Gallowgate, High Street, and Trongate. The great Dr. Chalmers' territory, forty years after, had become a citadel of vice, with 200 houses of ill fame and 150 shebeens in an area of less than one sixteenth of a square mile.

The larger "respectable" shebeens, which made great profits, consisted of a large room holding 30 or 40, a smaller room for favoured customers, and overflow accommodation in the kitchen. There were also, in descending order of decency, the smaller shebeens in the wynds, the "wee shebeens" on the stairheads (particularly difficult to pin down) and, lowest of all, those establishments which operated at one and the same time as shebeens, brothels and thieves' kitchens. Trade went on all night, interrupted only by ineffective police visits. The police, who were required by the Public Houses Act to catch the partner in the act of selling or consuming drink, were baffled by the elusiveness of the smaller shebeens and by the elaborate system of

[1] Both of 1862.

watchers and emergency exits contrived by the larger operators. The Police Act of 1866, which authorised the magistrates to grant a warrant to enter and search any house complained against by a householder as being of habit and repute either a shebeen or a house of ill fame, was nullified by the reluctance of householders to complain.

Quite as stultifying was the failure of proprietors to keep their tenants in order, the chief culprit being the Glasgow Corporation itself. One of the most notorious localities in the Central District, the Laigh Kirk Close at 59 Trongate, containing twenty brothels and three shebeens, was a Corporation property. Its chief lessees, William John Craig and Stephen Lynch, were adept at keeping on the right side of their proprietors and of the law. But not for long. Whether stimulated or not by the *Mail,* the police in that year made a determined and effective attack on the shebeens, backed by the Magistrates and by the public opinion of the respectable classes. This was not yet the end of the story. Prosecutions for keeping shebeens continued at a high rate until the turn of the century and the item even now features occasionally in the police returns. Many people in Glasgow who are still far from decrepit can remember the lodging-houses in the high back courts of Trongate, and the aspect of their patrons[1]—a direct link with the most unsavoury chapter in Glasgow's past.

The battle to close the shebeens and their less savoury attachments was only the advanced skirmishing in the major operation of limiting and controlling the sale and consumption of drink in licensed and unlicensed houses alike. Since 1900 the main effort of the temperance movement—which has in Glasgow, understandably, been strongly and rigidly teetotal—has been to reduce the number of licences. In 1899 Glasgow had 1,742 licensed houses or one for every 424 of the population. In 1955 the number of licensed houses was 1,347, or one for every 806 of the population. It is notable that Glasgow has fewer licensed houses in relation to population than any other British city. In 1950, for example, comparative ratios were as shown in Table CXXXV.

TABLE CXXXV

LICENSED PREMISES AND DRUNKENNESS IN GLASGOW AND CERTAIN OTHER CITIES

City	*Population*	*No. Proceeded against for Drunkenness per 1,000 of population*	*Total No. of licensed Premises*	*No. of inhabitants to each licensed house*
Bristol	403,840	0.009	993	443
Birmingh'm	1,002,603	4.77	1,722	582
Glasgow	1,110,000	2.6	1,355	819
Liverpool	802,000	3.6	1,340	598
Edinburgh	439,010	2.4	807	544
Dundee	180,500	2.3	306	590

SOURCE: *Report of Chief Constable of Glasgow for 1950.*

1 As the unsympathetic "Shadow" wrote, anticipating the now discredited Lombroso: "The contour of their heads is unmistakable and the fierce animal expression of their countenances still less so." *Midnight Scenes, etc.,* p. 93.

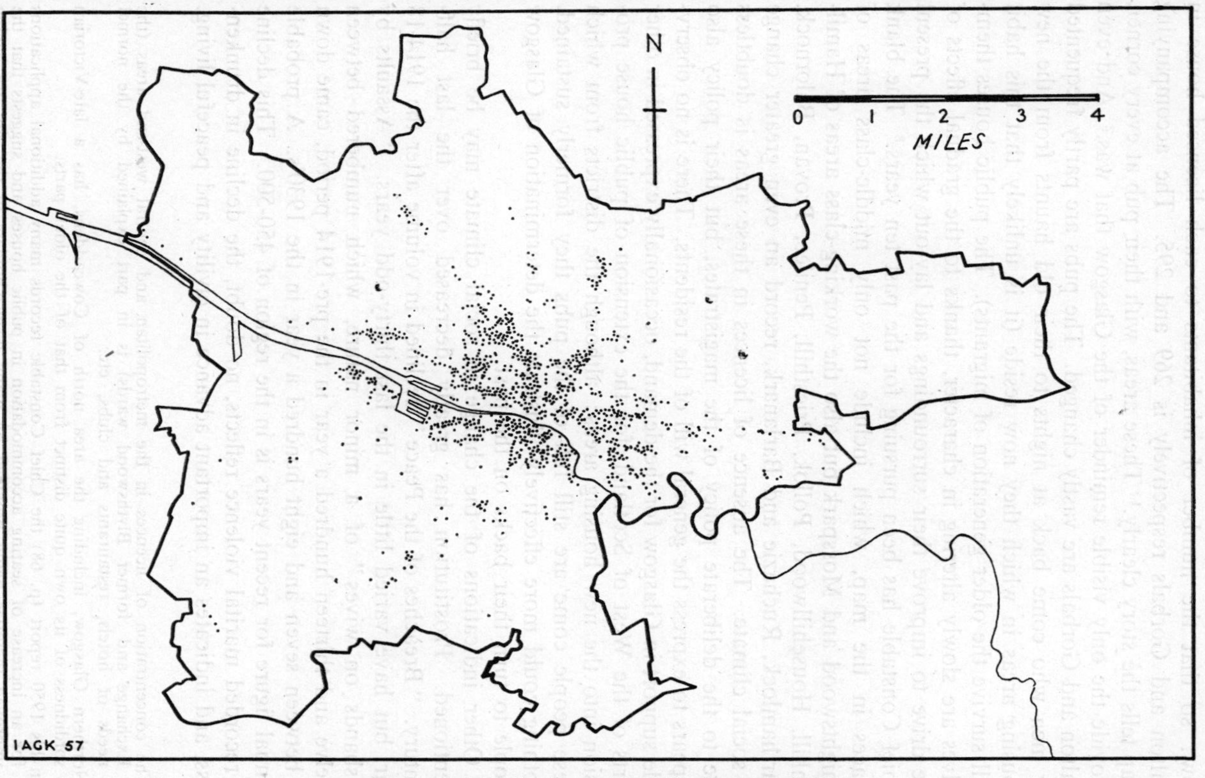

FIG. 33. Distribution of Public Houses, 1956.

But as is pointed out elsewhere in this book, the distribution of the licences is very strongly concentrated in the central districts of Glasgow: so that the number of inhabitants to each licensed house in Calton and Gorbals respectively is 269 and 295. The accompanying map tells the story clearly.[1] These areas, with their pub at every corner, provide the only visible reminder of the Glasgow that was.[2] And even Calton and Gorbals are vastly changed. The pubs are partly frequented by men who come back at nights to their old haunts from the new housing areas in which they now reside (it is unlikely that this habit will survive the older generation of migrants). The public houses themselves are slowly altering in character, thanks to the gradual effects of the drive to improve their surroundings and lay-out which the present Chief Constable has been pursuing for the past ten years.[3] The blank spaces in the map, which include not only middle-class areas of Knightswood and Mosspark but also the working-class areas of Hamiltonhill, Househillwood, Pollok, Priesthill, Penilee, Provan, Balornock, Garthamlock, Ruchazie and Barlanark, record an even greater change in social climate. The absence of licences in these areas is doubtless due to the deliberate policy of the magistrates, but their policy also appears to express the general will of the residents. There is no observable support in Glasgow for the demand, occasionally expressed in other parts of the West of Scotland, for the extension of public house provision into the new housing areas: although the districts from which these people come are still full of the pubs they formerly sustained. Nothing could more effectively illustrate the determination of Glasgow people to turn their backs on the past.

Other indications of the change in social climate may be briefly mentioned. Prostitution has greatly decreased over the last half-century. " Breaches of the Peace " declined in volume after the 1914-18 war, but have varied little in the last thirty-odd years. " Assaults by husbands on wives " of a minor nature, which numbered between twelve and thirteen hundred a year in the pre-1914 period, came down to between seven and eight hundred a year in the 1930's. A probable annual figure for recent years is in the region of 450-500.[4] This decline in recorded marital violence reflects, no doubt, the decline in drunkenness, and indicates an important advance in civility and peaceful living.

1 The concentration of licences in the metropolitan and central west-end areas (the Exchange and former Blythswood wards) is in part explained by the normal needs of hotels, restaurants and clubs, etc.

2 Northern Glasgow, including the area north of Cowcaddens, has a late-Victorian sordidness of its own quite distinct from that of the older parts.

3 In his 1950 report (p. 68) the Chief Constable records many additional applications for an increase of seating accommodation in public houses and suggests that the improved facilities being provided by many licence-holders in the city are having beneficial effect.

There are other indications that licence-holders are co-operating effectively with the police. Recently, for example, there has been successful joint action by publicans and police to reduce drinking by young people.

4 The annual figure of more serious assaults, classified as crimes of personal violence, is by contrast 20 or less.

It may also be bound up with the growth in economic independence of wives.

A clearer sign of major social change is the general increase in traffic offences, paralleling the general decrease in drunkenness, since the early decades of the century. The pavements or footpaths are now free from drunken brawls: but the streets themselves are more dangerous. Indeed the traffic problem is for the police of to-day what the drunkenness problem was for their predecessors in the period before 1914. The first accidents involving motor cars occurred in Glasgow in 1901—six were fatal accidents. In 1904 two persons were killed by motor cars in the city. A Police Traffic Department was formed in 1924—one senior officer and six assistants. By 1955 it had grown to 184 with one Chief Superintendent, 3 Chief Inspectors, 24 Inspectors and Sergeants and 156 Constables. The burden they carry is illustrated by the 1955 total of 11,972 road accidents, 83 more than in 1954. 109 persons were killed and 3,198 injured.

TABLE CXXXVI

OFFENCES AGAINST ROAD ACTS, ETC.
NUMBER OF CASES MADE KNOWN AND PERSONS PROCEEDED AGAINST
DURING THE YEARS 1913, 1925, 1938 AND 1945-1954

	1913	1925	1938	1945	1947	1950	1951	1952	1953	1954
No. of cases made known	2157	3527	13824	3956	7124	7147	6683	7310	8478	8869
(including " Drunk in charge ")	(—)	(—)	(282)	(107)	(182)	(267)	(297)	(299)	(403)	(445)
No. of persons proceeded against	4454	7429	13718	4940	9034	7841	7285	7156	8251	9020
(Including " Drunk in charge ")	(—)	(—)	(202)	(104)	(175)	(146)	(166)	(166)	(239)	(264)

SOURCE: Chief Constable of Glasgow.

Part of the danger is the old evil in a new form. The recent growth in volume of cases of " Drunk in charge of a motor vehicle " is ominous. But apart from this too leniently treated offence (and reserving for the moment the matter of Breaches of the Peace) the general change in the pattern or composition of offences reinforces the lesson of the declining volume of the annual totals. Glasgow is becoming a better-behaved city in so far as fewer of its citizens are rendering themselves liable to prosecution for the more " offensive " types of offences.

CRIMES

The improvement in Glasgow's manners as measured in particular by the reduction in apprehensions for drunkenness is roughly parallel to the general improvement in Scotland as a whole. The improvement in Glasgow's morals, as measured by the trend of crimes over the last half-century, appears to be markedly greater than in the rest of Scotland. This is in such startling contrast to the journalist's stereotypes, and to the preconceptions of the inhabitants of other Scottish cities, that it calls for detailed examination.

In the first place what the statistical records show is simply that Glasgow's *rate* of improvement appears to be faster than that of its neighbours. The present situation is shown in Table CXXXVII.

TABLE CXXXVII

COMPARISON OF CRIMINAL STATISTICS OF GLASGOW AND THOSE OF OTHER AREAS IN SCOTLAND

	Crimes Made Known to Police (*Rate per* 1,000 *Population*)					*Persons Proceeded Against* (*Rate per* 1,000 *Population*)				
	1950	1951	1952	1953	1954	1950	1951	1952	1953	1954
Cities										
Glasgow	27.1	29.0	28.5	25.0	23.8	6.1	6.8	7.3	6.6	6.4
Edinburgh	18.8	22.2	22.7	23.7	23.1	3.3	3.6	4.0	3.8	3.3
Aberdeen	18.7	22.3	19.3	17.5	17.9	4.6	5.2	5.7	4.7	4.5
Dundee	8.7	10.4	11.1	10.5	11.1	4.2	4.7	4.5	4.0	3.7
Large Burghs										
Airdrie	12.3	9.4	9.5	9.3	12.1	5.2	4.5	5.2	3.4	4.7
Ayr	25.2	27.5	30.2	24.9	25.8	5.4	6.3	4.7	6.0	5.3
Coatbridge	6.8	8.3	9.0	10.5	9.1	5.3	8.2	7.7	7.2	7.0
Greenock	32.2	41.4	34.6	35.9	29.8	6.0	7.2	8.0	8.3	7.2
Hamilton	15.6	15.1	13.7	14.6	16.9	6.6	6.1	5.8	5.5	7.6
Inverness	13.2	16.0	19.7	20.0	17.6	5.7	6.4	6.4	7.0	5.5
Kilmarnock	10.4	8.7	8.5	8.2	8.8	7.1	6.9	6.2	5.8	6.3
Motherwell	10.3	10.5	11.1	7.7	7.8	4.2	4.7	4.3	4.6	3.3
Paisley	15.6	22.1	18.7	18.4	21.3	4.7	6.2	5.3	4.5	4.0
Perth	13.9	14.2	12.7	12.9	12.3	3.1	3.6	3.3	3.1	2.8
Scotland	14.5	16.2	16.1	15.0	14.6	4.6	5.1	5.3	4.7	4.5
Cities	22.5	25.0	24.6	22.6	21.9	5.1	5.7	6.1	5.5	5.2
Large Burghs	13.0	19.2	17.9	17.3	12.1	4.2	6.1	5.8	5.6	4.7
Counties	8.8	9.4	9.6	9.1	9.0	4.3	4.4	4.6	4.0	3.8

SOURCE: *Criminal Statistics, Scotland.*

This shows that the incidence or density of crime, stated in the usual form of rate per thousand population, is still comparatively very high in Glasgow. But it is notable that the Glasgow incidence of " crimes made known to the police " has declined between 1950 and 1954 from 27.1 to 23.8 per thousand of the population, while that of Scotland as a whole is almost unchanged in the same period, being 14.5 and 14.6 per thousand of the population in 1950 and 1954 respectively. The next table makes the same point.

It shows that Glasgow's share in the all-Scotland totals of " crimes made known to the police " has declined from 44 per cent in 1938 to 34 per cent in 1954. In the rest of Scotland, omitting Glasgow, the volume of crimes made known has increased by almost 50 per cent

TABLE CXXXVIII

GLASGOW/SCOTLAND CRIME AND POPULATION RATIO IN 1925, 1938, 1951 AND 1954
ALL CRIMES MADE KNOWN

	1925	1938	1951	1954
Glasgow (Totals)	14,677	25,709	31.625	25.732
Scotland (Totals)	33,070	58,976	83.008	74.974
Glasgow-Scotland Crime Ratio	44%	44%	38%	34%
Glasgow-Scotland Population Ratio	22%	23%	21%	21%

SOURCE: *Criminal Statistics, Scotland.*

(33,267 to 49,242). In Glasgow it has remained practically at the same level (25,709 and 25,732).

It can of course be objected that this particular measure—"crimes made known to the police"—is peculiarly affected by changes in method of recording. But even allowing for this some of the rest-of-Scotland increase is a real increase. The comparative stability of the Glasgow figures in the same period is probably in large part a reflection of an actual improvement in the effectiveness of police preventive methods and in the conduct of the citizens. And this happy reflection will be reinforced when we come to examine the totals of charges proved.[1]

So much for the broad quantitative picture. But it is time we got away from statistical totals. They contrast oddly with the general reputation of Glasgow in these matters. And these crime totals, being composed of up to 95 per cent of crimes against property, might conceal an upward trend[2] of the small but vitally important sector of crimes of personal violence, a sector in which Glasgow has obtained an unenviable notoriety. The following sections discuss two of the main sources of this ill-fame: the classical Glasgow murders of the last century, and the interwar episode of the Glasgow gangs.

The Classical Glasgow Murders

Murders were relatively infrequent in Glasgow in the years before the First World War. In the period 1860-1914 there were fifteen separate years in which no murder was committed, fifteen with one murder each, nineteen with two murders, three with three murders, two with four and one with six.[3] But this same period contains three of the four great murder cases which have made the city a *locus classicus* of the dreadful art.[4] It is true that in quality of sheer horror Glasgow

1 See Fig. 34.
2 In fact the trend is downward: see below.
3 See Statistical Appendix, Table 146.
4 See *Notable Scottish Trials Series*: Trials of Madeleine Smith (1857); Jessie McLachlan (1862); Dr. Pritchard (1865); Oscar Slater (1909).

must yield place to Edinburgh. The deeds of Burke and Hare in the West Port, early in the nineteenth century, cannot be matched in the West: and the Robertson double murder of 1954,[1] in its pure destructive obsession, is worthy to be reported by Thomas De Quincey. But the Glasgow record is richer in speculative and sociological interest. All four of the "classical" murders caused immense public excitement, and two if not three of them were "cleared up" in so dubious a manner as to provoke great disquiet, the remarkable case of Oscar Slater in the first decade of this century leading to a major recasting of the criminal law of Scotland.[2] The cases of Madeleine Smith, of Dr. Pritchard, and of "Auld Fleming" in the Jessie McLachlan trial, reveal the passion and the violence at the heart of the solid Calvinist morality of mid-Victorian Glasgow.

The persons chiefly involved as victims or culprits in these famous cases were members or adherents of the respectable and prosperous middle class. In this they are of course exceptional. The tale of Glasgow murder in the nineteenth century, and even more to-day, is most often the typical sordid story of the usually unpremeditated violence of the poor, the mentally dull or the semi-insane. There is one odd exception, a trade union murder in 1913: a man was charged with shooting another man during a collision in the Broomielaw between two rival sections of the Dockers' Union. But for the rest, murder in Glasgow, or serious violence which might have ended in murder, is no different from murder anywhere else. Except for one development. The second and dominant element in the legend of Glasgow violence is the outbreak of gang violence and gang murder which disturbed the city so profoundly within living memory.

Gang Violence[3]

The Glasgow gangs were almost entirely a phenomenon of the interwar years. There is very little left to-day of the organised violence which sprang into life quite suddenly in the nineteen-twenties and which contributed a lurid footnote to the city's social history throughout the hopeless years of unemployment in the 1930's.

The gangs flourished in most of the crowded areas of the near-centre of the city and particularly in Gorbals, Calton, and Bridgeton.

1 v. *Scotsman*, 3 June 1954.

2 The case of Oscar Slater in 1909 let loose an eruption of indignation far beyond the boundaries of Scotland. The extraordinary conduct of the trial, the ineffective inquiry in camera (duplicating the McLachlan case), the breaking and subsequent hounding of Det. Trench of the Glasgow police—the only official person who queried the official case against Slater—and the persistent campaign of William Park and Sir Arthur Conan Doyle culminating in the quashing of the conviction and the release of Slater, is effectively described by William Roughead in "The Slater Case—a Retrospect," to be found in *Classic Crimes* (1951), pp. 369-412.

3 For much of the information in this section I am indebted to the articles published in the *Evening Citizen* for January 7-13 and 17-19 and February 7-11, 1955, the work of Mr. Harold Ballantyne.

Their numbers varied with the occasion, but some of them could muster quite quickly up to three or four hundred. They had a rudimentary organisation. There was usually one leader, a combination of planner and fighting man, an inner ring of " strong-arm " men, and an attachment of girls or " queens " who stimulated the fighting spirit of the gang, acted as a travelling armoury, and occasionally took part themselves in the heat and fury of the battle. The gangs took their names either from the locality or street-corner which was their stamping-ground—the Norman Conks (Conquerors) from Norman Street, the Beehive Gang, the South Side Stickers, the Calton Entry, the Briggate Boys, the Bedford or Parlour Boys—or from other associations. The Billy Boys favoured Prince William of Orange and concluded the evening's proceedings with " God Save the King." The Redskins, and the Black Hand gang, the first to come to the attention of the police in 1919 and 1920, derived their titles significantly from schoolboy reading and make-believe. It may well be that the gangs began as an extension into later adolescence of the collective stone-throwing exploits of schoolboys. Even when they developed later their typical shape of bands of young men and women in the age range of 18 to 30 most of them had junior sections. This aspect of make-believe, of regression to primitive rituals of violence, is characteristic of much of their behaviour in the 1920's. Generally speaking, then and later, and taking the whole range of newly-emerging as well as established gangs, their conduct was riotous rather than criminal.

But they could and did become fully criminal and dangerous. Their private fights spread until they terrified the neighbourhood. Shopkeepers and publicans endured organised banditry, enforced by terror, for months and years at a time. The activity of some gangs masked systematic house—and shop—breaking on a big scale. Sir Percy Sillitoe in his excellent first-hand account of the Glasgow gangs[1] points out that they certainly were never in any sense organised teams of experienced criminals grouped round a " master mind." But by 1924, he goes on, the gangs had become well organised and were undoubtedly ruled by hardened criminals. Thus by the time the Beehive Corner Boys had become the Beehive Gang the inner circle was composed of housebreakers. Around them moved a much larger group of men who could be called upon to take part in fights, intimidation, and occasionally mob attacks and robberies. The leader of this gang was one Peter Williamson, but the real brain of the outfit was a man named Howie, a skilled burglar who kept out of the fights. Instead he planned and executed numerous clever burglaries along with the inner circle of the gang, teaming up with a specially imported English safe-breaker for several months.

This high degree of organisation and specialisation was however exceptional. A much more typical gang development, typical in its confusion and in its meaningless and murderous violence, is provided by the battle on the Albert Bridge in early 1928 between the South

[1] Sir Percy Sillitoe: *Cloak without Dagger* (1955), Chapter 14.

Side Stickers and the Calton Entry, as revealed in the report of the trial,[1] on 28 and 29 June of that year, of James McCluskey, Abraham Zemmil, Alexander McCaughey, Archibald Gaughan, James Walker and George Stokes[2] in connection with the death by stabbing of James Tait. The ages of all concerned ranged from 15 to 17. An older youth, Hugh Martin (19) admitted he was a member of the older Calton Entry gang; but it was the younger gang who were fighting that night.

The Calton Entry belonged to the north side of the bridge; the Stickers to the south side. These units did not exhaust the gang potential of the neighbourhood: according to one witness there were seven gangs in the vicinity of Jail Square alone. The two gangs had been friendly until an incident occurred in a picture-house, when a girl was struck. After that the gangs met and scrapped. The evidence is confusing and evasive, as usual in these cases, but it appeared that the battle of the bridge had been planned originally as a tournament, like the fight of the clans in Scott's *Fair Maid of Perth.* Frank Kerney (16), leader of the Calton Entry, had been told by three girls that Zemmil wanted to fight him. He ultimately agreed and arrangements were made for a fight at the end of the bridge, each principal to bring four supporters. Tait was one of the four who came to support him in the fight. Each side was equipped with a variety of weapons. Andrew McCarthey (17) had given McCaughey (of the Stickers) a dagger in exchange for a bag of cakes. Next day he gave him a sword. Kerney, it appeared, also had a sword. The fight between the two teams of five quickly became general, both sides throwing stones and bottles. But the battle raged fiercest between the picked fighting men. McCluskey (of the Stickers) hit Tait (of the Entry) first with his fist. With that, said Kerney, he himself went to hit McCluskey with his sword, and in a minute all the party were round McCluskey attacking him. McCluskey had to save himself, added Kerney chivalrously. He apparently did so by stabbing Tait to death. Lord Hunter was dissatisfied with this account of the fight. Why, he asked, was Tait struck in the back? Kerney did not know.

The combined tension and hopelessness of the depression years of the early 'thirties gave the gangs an even stronger impetus, so they came to invoke more ancient loyalties. This was the era of the Billy Boys and the Norman Conks. The leader of the Billy Boys, William Fullerton, was a fighting man and a strategist of some quality. In 1955 Fullerton, now for many years a steady worker and a good citizen, described the origin of the Billy Boys. In 1924 a tough football team, the Kent Star from Calton, had the misfortune to lose to a scratch Bridgeton team in a game on the Glasgow Green. Fullerton, then aged 18, scored the winning goal. For this he was marked down by some Kent Star supporters, who later made a mass attack on him. He was literally "given the hammer"! Deciding on reprisals, he organised a

1 *Glasgow Herald,* 29 and 30 June 1928.

2 Stokes' younger brother William, then aged nine, won the Victoria Cross in the Second World War.

small gang of his own, and hit on the name "Billy Boys." A significant feature was the general enthusiasm throughout Bridgeton for the new gang among many who were not at all gangster-minded but who had Orange sympathies. The Billy Boys quickly flourished until they numbered 800 at their peak, attracting recruits from as far out as Airdrie, Coatbridge and Cambuslang. Three other odd developments are worth noting. In 1926 some of the Billy Boys took the side of "law and order" in the General Strike and display their certificates of civic merit to this day. Later Fullerton joined the Fascist Party for a time, and became a section captain in charge of 200 men and women. "I couldn't give you a definition of Fascism to this day," Fullerton says. "It just seemed like a good thing to belong to at the time." Fascists apart, it is reported that some politicians, party unnamed, were not above employing the Billy Boys to break up the meetings of their opponents.

Fullerton's energies were devoted to waging war on the Roman Catholic Norman Conks. Both sides, says Sir Percy Sillitoe,[1] habitually used hatchets, swords and sharpened bicycle chains, which were brought to the field of battle by their "queens." In 1932 Bull Bowman, leader of the Norman Conks, marched his men into the Billy Boys' territory (Abercrombie Street) under cover of a parade of unemployed, his 300-odd gangsters each armed with a pickshaft. The Billy Boys, though taken by surprise, mustered 200 men in a few minutes.

After the fight, in which a number of policemen were wounded, there were several arrests and some fines. The fines were paid by levies on the local shopkeepers. "The usual technique employed upon shopkeepers who did not choose to contribute was to mix all the shop's goods in a smashed heap on the floor, with the proprietor on top of the pile like a bruised Guy Fawkes. Then as they departed, the gangsters would break his window glass. They could accomplish all this damage in less than ten minutes of entering the shop."[2]

The End of the Gangs

In the course of the 1930's order was restored to the streets of the affected areas by a combination of counter-measures. Of these the most direct and immediate was the sharp corrective action of a reorganised and reinvigorated police force. Two episodes in this counter-action, the dispersing of the Billy Boys by a police ambush near Celtic Park, and the offensive-defensive tactics of "Big Tommy from the Toll" (Police-Sergeant Morrison) may well become part of Glasgow's folklore.[3] The gangs, no matter what their ultimate explanation may be,

[1] Sillitoe, *op. cit.* p. 128.

[2] *ibid*, p. 129.

[3] Sergeant Morrison and two young officers arrested Fullerton, fighting drunk, and took him 500 yards to the police station through the thick of the gang—a kind of Chaplin's "Easy Street" in reverse. Fullerton was charged with assaulting Sergeant Morrison. "As each witness of the gang gave his evidence came the constantly

lived for and by violence, and undoubtedly the strongest single factor in their putting-down was this demonstration that the law could not be flouted with impunity.

Reinforcing this direct counter-action from quite a different direction was the effective attempt by a number of socially concerned people to find a more wholesome outlet for the destructive energies of the gangs. Most of this kind of service goes unchronicled and unsung, but one characteristic piece of work has been reported. In 1928 a young minister, the Rev. J. Cameron Peddie, came from the quiet town of Barrhead to assume the charge of Hutchesontown Parish Church. He found that the people of the Gorbals were mostly quiet decent folk, anxious to be rid of the menace in their midst. He found also that the gang rivalries had no deep roots. The South Side Stickers and their chief local enemies, the Liberty Boys, each contained Protestants and Roman Catholics. He sought out the gang leaders, at first with no result, but later he had the good fortune and the courage to intercept a large party of the Stickers on their way to attack the Liberty Boys. To his surprise they agreed to follow him into his vestry, one lad showing with pride a sword concealed down his trouser leg. As the result of that talk a club was formed. The gang drew up a constitution and programme—the keynote, surprisingly enough, was Brotherhood and Good Citizenship. One enthusiast moved that the Liberty Boys should be invited to join them there and then. In the upshot about 30 clubs were formed in the neighbourhood with 4,000 members, and although it continued to be the case that club members got into trouble, the clubs kept them on the roll and there was less trouble as the years went on.

Mr. Peddie and his fellow social workers had seen and proved the social and moral energies which, however perverted, gave the gangs their horrid vitality. Mr. George Blake, in a passage which deserves close study, has summed up the lesson of this insight.

" Much has been made of gang warfare in Glasgow," he says, " and of those bands of pugnacious youths who, under fancy names, banded to fight each other on such pretexts as the old Billy and Danny rivalry, Protestants and Catholics. The pretexts are meaningless. The emergence of a Scoto-Irish breed, mainly huddled in the most degraded areas, did indeed complicate the pattern, but its basis was the essentially Scottish one of the clan system. Strong and violent youth unconsciously organised itself in groups in order, one had almost said, to fight its way out of sombre monotony. Theirs was only a special and unpleasant expression of the motive that bids millions rather more fortunately

recurring phrase . . . ' and then Big Tommy from the Toll hit me, and that is the last I remember.' At last the stipendiary magistrate could contain his curiosity no longer. ' Who is this Big Tommy from the Toll?' he asked. ' If he is in court, will he please stand up?'

" In complete silence Police-Sergeant Morrison got to his feet, bowed and then sat down again. The stipendiary magistrate looked at the huge officer, nodded and said, ' I think I begin to understand. Thank you, Sergeant Morrison.' "
Sillitoe, *op. cit.*, p. 133.

placed to sublimate their sense of frustration in blind loyalty to this or that football team. It is of touching interest that a sympathetic police official of one of the eastern divisions of Glasgow could by 1942 show from his careful records that most of his notoriously bad boys were by then serving, if they had not already fallen, in North Africa or in the various Commando raids on the European coasts. So badly did they need a way of escape from the home environment and from the doldrums of unemployment that so terribly afflicted the industrial regions of Scotland during most years of the third decade of the twentieth century."[1]

And that may be accepted—if we do not press the clan analogy too hard, and if we spare a thought for the police force which bore the brunt of the fight against monotony—as a fair summing up of the episode of the Glasgow gangs.

The Change in the Face of Violence

The ordinary reader of the newspapers might be forgiven for thinking that gang life and gangsters flourished again in Glasgow after the Second World War in the same way as before. Certainly the profound unsettlement of the time led to much and serious violence. There were two cases of gang murder in 1945 and in 1951 a dance-hall stabbing in a northern housing area. There was also a slight recrudescence of terrorism in the late nineteen-forties, when bands of youths were to be found from time to time in the older districts surging along the width of the street brandishing various "weapons." But they never took shape as organised gangs. The conditions which had helped to produce the gangs were in fact disappearing. Mass unemployment was a thing of the past. The slow process of dispersing the crowded populations of the central districts into the newer housing areas was accelerating. What had been perhaps the most spectacular feature of some of the gangs, their ability to muster at short notice an army of fighters from a few blocks of crowded tenements, was no longer so easy. They carried many of their problems and habits to the newer areas, but the wide-spaced houses and avenues in new Glasgow made the old concentrations impossible. Moreover the old spirit had gone. A subtle change had come over the face of violence in this as in other cities. Students of social pathology might regard it as a change for the worse, an indication of a greater degree of social disintegration than had existed even in the 1930's. The semi-organised gangs of that period had to some degree, as Mr. Blake has indicated, banded themselves not simply to challenge the law and order of the wider society but also and more profoundly to resist the social sickness of demoralisation and purposelessness. But the violence of the immediate postwar years was largely the work of individuals or small groups at war with themselves as well as with society. The more outstanding attacks, symbolic of the time,

[1] George Blake (ed.): *The Trials of Patrick Carraher* (1951), pp. 23-4.

were made by rootless individuals, some being deserters on the run, others verging on insanity, the victims in more than one case being complete strangers to them. A typical case is that of Patrick Carraher, who was executed for murder in 1945.[1]

Downward Trend of Violence

It will be a long time before Glasgow outlives the legend embodied in the classical murders and in the folk-lore of the gangs. But such objective indications as are available record improvement. It may be we are already seeing the effects of the expanding civic effort to improve on the past, to create new and better communities and to arrest the decay of the old. The annual totals of crimes of personal violence have been going down since the war.

TABLE CXXXIX

CRIMES OF PERSONAL VIOLENCE 1947-1954 (MURDER, ASSAULTS, ETC., SEXUAL CRIMES INVOLVING VIOLENCE, AND ROBBERY)

	1947	1948	1949	1950	1951	1952	1953	1954
Made Known to Police	869	670	600	604	690	622	574	559
Persons Proceeded Against	292	271	241	163	226	245	227	216

SOURCE: Chief Constable of Glasgow.

The increase between 1950 and 1951, from 604 to 690 " crimes made known to the police," and from 163 to 226 " persons proceeded against," is the result of a recording change. A substantial number of minor assaults which had formerly been classified as " breaches of the peace " (offences not crimes) were up-graded in 1951 to the category of " criminal assaults," warranting severer penalties. But this should not be dismissed as a mere technical reclassification: it reflects one reaction of the authorities and the public to what they considered to be a growth in the degree of violence used in minor and major assaults alike. A second and much better-known public reaction was manifested in the infliction by the High Court of heavier sentences for certain major assaults, from 1952 onwards. The effects were immediately seen in the figures of assaults in which razors were used, which fell from 34 in 1952 to 14 in 1953,[2] and the decline has continued ever since in the more general category of criminal assaults, as Table CXL shows.

The two remaining sub-groups of crimes of personal violence reveal the same recent downward movement. Crimes of sexual violence (rape, assault with intent to ravish, and indecent assault) declined from 290 in 1946 to 103 in 1949 and 56 in 1953. The annual totals between

[1] v. George Blake, *op. cit.*

[2] Report of the Chief Constable for 1953, p. 21. In the same period " assaults in which knives were used " dropped from 60 to 38.

TABLE CXL

ASSAULTS 1951-5, GLASGOW

Year	1951	1952	1953	1954	1955
Cases Made Known	412	333	287	297	254

SOURCE: Chief Constable's Reports 1951 to 1955.

1925 and 1939 were mostly over 200. Likewise with robberies and assaults with intent to rob.[1]

TABLE CXLI

ROBBERIES, 1946-54

	1946	1947	1948	1949	1950	1951	1952	1953	1954
Glasgow	293	313	253	241	261	199	203	206	177
Scotland	381	386	353	325	346	305	303	301	266

SOURCE: Chief Constable of Glasgow and *Criminal Statistics, Scotland.*

But the crime of robbery remains a major problem to police and public alike. Although its volume and incidence are comparatively minute (now one in every two days, affecting one in every 5,000 of the population per annum) the percentage cleared up, in Glasgow as elsewhere, is low, between 19 and 20 per cent: and the table indicates that in spite of the comparatively greater decline in Glasgow it is still the case that at least two out of every three robberies in all Scotland occur within the bounds of the city.

Housebreaking and Theft

We now turn to crimes against property, which make up the great bulk of all crimes. Crimes against property with violence, and crimes against property without violence, have increased greatly since the beginning of the century.[2] The former category, mainly housebreakings, ran in the region of 2,500 cases per annum made known to the police in the period before 1914, 5,000 in the 1920's, 10,000 in the 1930's, 15,000 in the 1940's and early 1950's. Since 1952 there has been a steady decline—11,183 in 1953, 10,876 in 1954, and 10,369 in 1955. The second category, mainly theft, shows less variation, running at an annual average of under 10,000 cases made known to the police in the years before 1914, and fluctuating between 13,000 and 15,000 per annum since the 1920's. Here again the movement in the last few years is a downward one.

1 Robbery etc. is technically a "crime against property with violence." But it is substantially a crime of personal violence.

2 For the figures in detail since 1901 see Appendix Table 148.

It is those figures of crimes against property which are most influenced by changes in recording methods. One main reason for the increase throughout the century is the greater care now being taken to record all crimes made known, even the most minute. Thus, for example, out of 10,167 cases of housebreaking[1] in 1955 no property was stolen in 2,042 cases. Serious housebreakings and thefts in which over £100 was stolen numbered just under 750: of these 30 were cases in which more than £1,000 was stolen. Perhaps the most notable case in recent years however falls into the category of robbery. In July 1955 a bank messenger was clubbed and tied up and a van stolen containing £44,000 in cash. In the next few months six men were arrested. After an eight-day trial three were found guilty, one being sentenced to eight years' imprisonment and each of the two others to six years' imprisonment. The leader of the gang, called the Major, who had lived in comfort with his confederates in an Aberfoyle hotel while planning the coup, was already serving a sentence of imprisonment in England.

This gang is the successor of a number who have given the police much trouble in the past. We have already noted the exploits of the Beehive Gang in the 1930's. In 1908 Chief Constable Stevenson reported that there had been at large in the city a greater number of expert criminals than there had ever been at one time in the past quarter of a century. A large number of serious housebreakings were committed. The thieves worked in small gangs, and as a gang usually went to the country districts after a successful operation in Glasgow, detection was the more difficult and for a time they successfully evaded apprehension. By continuous and persistent efforts these dangerous gangs were broken up, the leaders were convicted, and received sentences of penal servitude varying from three years to fourteen years.[2] Daniel Cooney, leader of the Cooney gang, got ten years' penal servitude. Thomas Rice Reid, leader of the two gangs called by his name, got fourteen years on his second appearance in court, having previously forfeited £700 bail.

Coming back to the present day one main problem is the enormous number of small house- and shop-breakings and thefts, testifying to two things. The first is an increase in petty dishonesty revealed in the figures of cases made known. The second is the much greater opportunity for crime afforded by the modern city. In the last fifty years the city has expanded enormously. A population 30 per cent bigger is dispersed over a much wider area, while the police burden in the near-central areas has not been lightened. Other social developments—the rise of the big department store, the growing tendency for shopkeepers and owners of public houses to live away from their business premises,[3]

1 Housebreaking comprises (a) Theft by housebreaking, (b) Theft by opening lockfast places, (c) Housebreaking with intent to enter and steal, (d) Attempted housebreaking with intent to enter and steal.

2 City of Glasgow Police: Criminal Returns for 1908, p. 4.

3 In Glasgow (1954) there are 1,086 public houses and in no instance does the licensee or any of his staff live in. In Birmingham, in all licensed premises some-

the increase in working-class prosperity and in thievable articles in the vulnerable tenement house—all make things progressively more difficult for the police. Add to this the increasing skill of the professional criminal, and the multiple nature of the contemporary police problem emerges. But the police in Glasgow are not merely holding their own against the growth in the spread of minor criminality and the growth of major criminal skill: they are by all objective indications playing a major part in the general improvement of the city in these matters. The history of the growth of Glasgow's Police Force has already been outlined in a previous chapter.[1] The police organisation has grown in size and complexity with the growth of the city and with the increase in the skill and mobility of the criminal. The advent of the motor car has added a new dimension to crime and to police work. Mobility of criminals has increased; boundaries have lost their previous significance; new problems of crime detection and traffic control now engross the attention of the police.

The Silent Police Revolution

G. A. N. Lowndes gives his account of British educational development since 1870 the striking title of the Silent Social Revolution. The quite as remarkable story of the Silent Police Revolution remains to be written, for it has come about only in the last generation and it is still going on. The Glasgow Police Force has the distinction of pioneering that revolution along with the Metropolitan Force of Greater London. In 1931-2, at the same time as Lord Trenchard was carrying through a similar action in the Metropolitan District, Chief Constable Sillitoe began the reorganisation of the Glasgow Police.

The morale and the efficiency of the Force had been affected by a combination of adverse circumstances. Economic depression had set in earlier and more severely in the West of Scotland than in any other part of Scotland. The gangs were only one manifestation of the human problems which resulted. Another symptom of the social malaise of the time was the existence of petty corruption among some councillors and magistrates, including, as it turned out, the convener of the Police Committee itself. The aftermath of the Oscar Slater case had shaken the police in a very special way. The successful campaign to release Slater in the 1920's had exposed certain deficiencies in the Scottish system of criminal justice, as we have seen; it had also revealed, among other things, major weaknesses in the methods of detection employed by the police. Finally a series of head-on conflicts between police and unemployed, and between police and strikers in the General Strike of

1 Chapter 13.

one lives in. In Glasgow nearly all shops are locked-up premises. In many of the English cities the shopkeeper lives above the shop, thus giving added security to his premises.

1926, had considerably impaired the relations between the police and various important sections of public opinion.

The reforms initiated by Chief Constable Sillitoe and carried on by his successors are most comprehensive. The mere technical record of the early 'thirties is impressive in itself. The Force was made more mobile. The fleet of patrol vans and cars was increased, and a Mechanical Transport department was created to man and maintain the cars. The number of police divisions in the city was reduced from eleven to seven. Thirteen Police Offices were closed down, and each division was given fast motor transport. The system of Police Boxes (inaugurated in the 1870's) was extended and modernised. A police radio transmitter was installed at Pinkston, maintaining constant wireless communication with the patrol cars. Communications with forces throughout Scotland were strengthened. A teleprinter service was established between Glasgow and Edinburgh in 1934: in the same year a daily police newspaper, the Scottish Police Gazette, was inaugurated for issue throughout Scotland. The Criminal Investigation Department was increased, and the appointment established of an Assistant Chief Constable in charge of the department. More important, the training and equipment of the C.I.D., as of the force in general, was improved.

Scientific Aids to Detection

A notable development was the inauguration of the Finger Print Bureau. Glasgow had been the first police force in Scotland to adopt the finger print system of identification.[1] Ten identifications of criminals by finger prints were made in 1899. In 1932, the first year of the Bureau, 11,230 finger print records were available for reference and some 400 criminals were identified by this means. At the end of 1954 the reference collection numbered 118,894, 5,772 forms having been added during the year. 15,445 finger print forms were submitted for search, 5,493 from Glasgow and 9,952 from other towns: and 9,420 were identified as belonging to persons having a previous criminal history.

The most outstanding instance of the effectiveness of the new methods occurred in 1935 in the course of what might be called a combined operation with the Forensic Medicine departments of Glasgow[2]

1 Finger prints were at first used in conjunction with the *Bertillon* anthropometric system of identification, but the latter was discarded in 1903. For details see "Scientific Aids in the City of Glasgow Police" in the *Report of the Chief Constable of the City of Glasgow* (1949), pp. 9-12.

2 The association between medicine and criminal investigation in Glasgow has been officially established since the days of King James VI. This fact is emphasised in the following extract from the Gift and Charter of Erection granted by King James in favour of the Faculty of Physicians and Surgeons of the City of Glasgow in 1599:

"That the said visitors (Mr. Peter Lowe, the King's Surgeon, and Robert Hamilton, Professor of Medicine, and their successors) shall visit every hurt, murdered, poisoned, or any other person taken away extraordinary, and to report to the magistrates the fact as it is."

and Edinburgh Universities. This was the famous Ruxton case. The remarkable feat of identification of the human remains by the medical experts[1] was followed by an equally striking demonstration of the evidence of finger prints. "Among the remains was a hand with the epidermal skin on the fingers still intact though badly distorted. The Glasgow experts examined all parts of Ruxton's house and were finally able to state that many finger print traces found there were identical with the finger prints which had been taken from the above-mentioned hand."[2]

The use of scientific aids by the Glasgow C.I.D. was greatly extended in 1945, when a Scientific Branch was formed, including the now celebrated Identification Bureau, and serving all Scottish police forces. On various occasions the officers of the Scientific Branch have given specialist evidence on ballistics, botany, chemistry, instrument marks, spectographic analysis, typewriting identification and ultraviolet examination. But the most remarkable recent case falls broadly within the finger print category: it is the conviction in 1952 of a criminal on the evidence of a toe print left on a safe. This form of identification, frequent in eastern countries, had never before been used in a British court.[3]

Measures of Improvement

We have already noted one effect of the reorganisations just described—the decline in Glasgow's share in the all-Scotland totals of crimes made known to the police.[4] A second effect can be seen in the increase in the percentage of detections from 1932.[5]

As Table CXLII shows, the percentage of crimes cleared moved up from 19 per cent in 1932 to an annual average of 31 per cent in the four years 1936 to 1939. With the weakening of the police in the war years the percentage cleared went down till in 1946 it stood again at 19 per cent. Since that year it has climbed steadily, and stands now at the high level of 34 per cent.

The clearest evidence of the improvement in police efficiency over the past generation is however to be seen in the quite remarkable

[1] This broke new ground in forensic medicine: see Glaister and Brash: *Medico-Legal Aspects of the Ruxton Case* (1937).

[2] "Scientific Aids in the City of Glasgow Police" in *Report of the Chief Constable of the City of Glasgow* for 1949, p. 12. See also Blundell & Wilson (ed.): *Trial of Buck Ruxton* (1937), pp. 196-201.

[3] *Report of the Chief Constable for the City of Glasgow* (1952), pp. 47-9.

[4] See pp. 649-50 above.

[5] The figures are strictly comparable from 1932 onwards. In that year a recording change was made—one of the minor reorganisations of the period—which had the effect of adding to the total about 9,000 very minor crimes against property formerly omitted from official records as either unimportant or unsubstantiated. A similar change, with even more striking results, was carried out in the Metropolitan Police District in the same year. (See Chapter on "Crime," by J. Mack, in *The Scottish Economy*, ed. Cairncross (1954), p. 230).

TABLE CXLII

CRIMES, GLASGOW, 1931-1954

Year	*Made Known*	*Cleared Number*	*Cleared Percentage*
1931	18,633	4,493	24
1932	27,525	5,172	19
1933	27,492	6,478	24
1934	26,735	6,731	25
1935	28,716	7,265	25
1936	26,639	8,211	31
1937	26,040	8,445	32
1938	25,709	7,768	31
1939	26,534	8,117	31
1940	28,067	7,713	27
1941	30,203	7,301	24
1942	30,150	7,685	25
1943	31,279	7,176	23
1944	31,939	6,953	22
1945	41,243	8,513	21
1946	33,823	6,536	19
1947	32,248	6,515	20
1948	34,531	7,696	22
1949	28,376	6,954	24
1950	29,504	7,816	26
1951	31,625	8,777	28
1952	30,943	8,790	28
1953	27,116	8,794	32
1954	25,732	8,663	34

SOURCE: Chief Constable of Glasgow.

decline in crimes committed by adults. The following graphs[1] trace the trend of criminal charges proved in Glasgow and in the United Kingdom for the years from 1938 to the present, separating the totals for each year into charges proved against adults (17 years and over) and charges proved against juveniles (8 to 16 inclusive).

This shows that in recent years the burden of adult crime in Glasgow has been very much lighter than it was in 1938. In 1949 it actually fell to 70 per cent of the prewar figure, and in 1954 it stood at 84 per cent of that figure. This contrasts sharply with the trend in England and Wales and in Scotland where the level of adult crime is still above the prewar figure. It is a surprising and gratifying result. It means that though the burden of crime in Glasgow is still very heavy, it is made up to an increasing extent of juvenile misbehaviour. And juvenile delinquency—if we disregard for the moment its wider social implications—is a less serious matter than adult crime. The important thing is to ensure that the juvenile delinquent of to-day is prevented from becoming the adult criminal of to-morrow. The graph shows that the enormous wartime increase in juvenile crime in Glasgow has had no apparent effect on the adult crime statistics of ten years later. This

[1] For the data on which the graphs are based see Appendix Table 149.

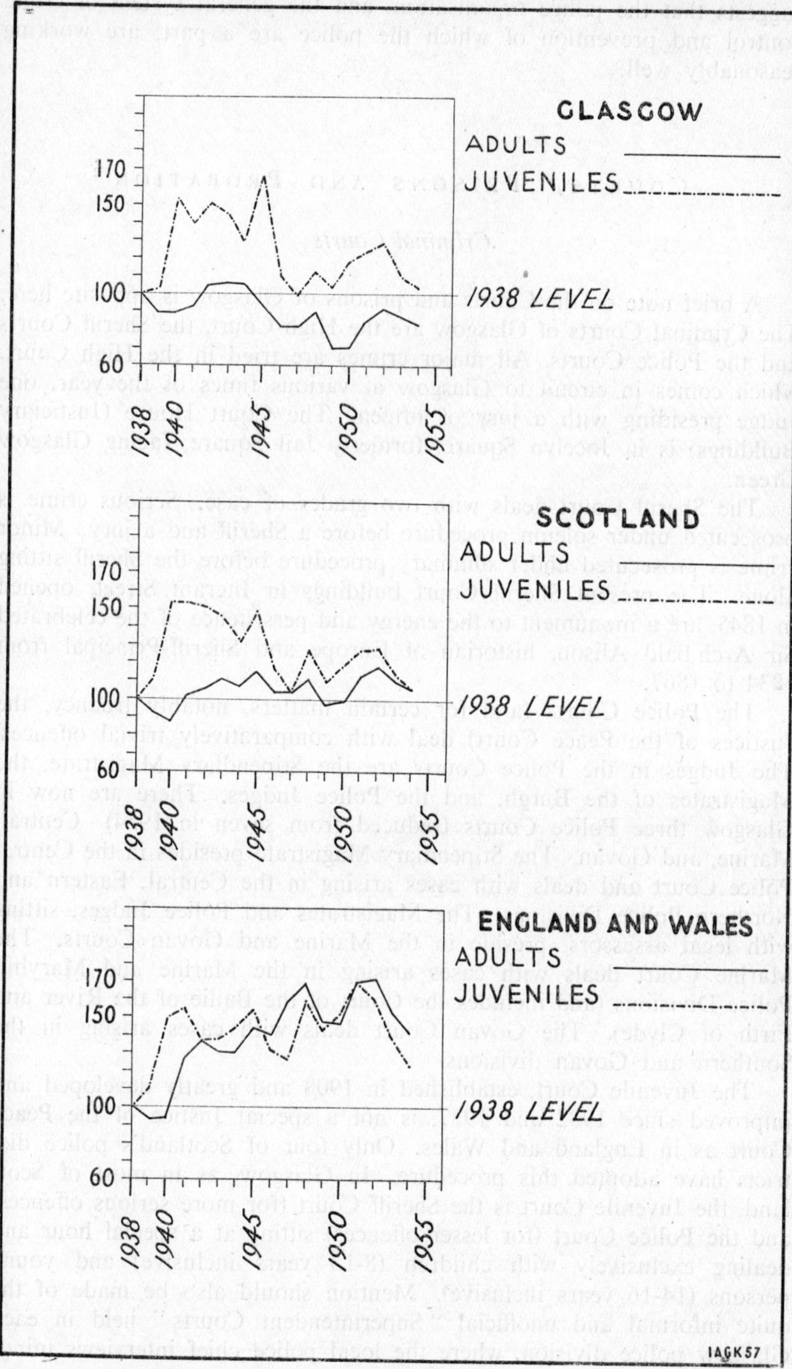

FIG. 34. Criminal Charges Proved Against Juveniles and Adults, 1938-54.

suggests that the police organisation, and the general system of crime control and prevention of which the police are a part, are working reasonably well.

COURTS,[1] PRISONS AND PROBATION

Criminal Courts

A brief note on the Courts and prisons of Glasgow is apposite here. The Criminal Courts of Glasgow are the High Court, the Sheriff Courts and the Police Courts. All major crimes are tried in the High Court, which comes in circuit to Glasgow at various times of the year, one Judge presiding with a jury of fifteen. The Court House (Justiciary Buildings) is in Jocelyn Square, formerly Jail Square, facing Glasgow Green.

The Sheriff Court deals with two grades of case. Serious crime is prosecuted under solemn procedure before a Sheriff and a jury. Minor crime is prosecuted under summary procedure before the Sheriff sitting alone. The present Sheriff Court buildings in Ingram Street, opened in 1845, are a monument to the energy and persistence of the celebrated Sir Archibald Alison, historian of Europe and Sheriff-Principal from 1834 to 1867.

The Police Courts (and for certain matters, notably truancy, the Justices of the Peace Court) deal with comparatively trivial offences. The Judges in the Police Courts are the Stipendiary Magistrate, the Magistrates of the Burgh, and the Police Judges. There are now in Glasgow three Police Courts (reduced from seven in 1954)—Central, Marine, and Govan. The Stipendiary Magistrate presides in the Central Police Court and deals with cases arising in the Central, Eastern and Northern Police Divisions. The Magistrates and Police Judges, sitting with legal assessors, preside in the Marine and Govan Courts. The Marine Court deals with cases arising in the Marine and Maryhill Police Divisions (and includes the Court of the Bailie of the River and Firth of Clyde). The Govan Court deals with cases arising in the Southern and Govan divisions.

The Juvenile Court, established in 1908 and greatly developed and improved since 1932 and 1937, is not a special Justice of the Peace Court as in England and Wales. Only four of Scotland's police districts have adopted this procedure. In Glasgow, as in most of Scotland, the Juvenile Court is the Sheriff Court (for more serious offences) and the Police Court (for lesser offences) sitting at a special hour and dealing exclusively with children (8-13 years inclusive) and young persons (14-16 years inclusive). Mention should also be made of the quite informal and unofficial "Superintendent Courts" held in each Glasgow police division, where the local police chief interviews minor

[1] For a further account of the Courts, see Chapter 13.

first offenders with one or both parents, thus dispensing with the need for a formal court appearance.

Prisons

The only prison remaining within the bounds of the city is Barlinnie. Opened in 1882 it was one of the first products of the revolution in prison management initiated by R. A. Cross as Home Secretary in 1877, whereby the prisons of the country were placed entirely under the control of the Imperial Government.[1] The biggest prison in Scotland, it has a daily population of 800-900 male prisoners of all classes and all ages.[2] Duke Street prison, which was closed in 1955 and whose inmates were transferred to the more modern buildings of Greenock Prison, had functioned as a women's prison for many years. In its last year it had a daily average of 65 women prisoners. There is little more to be said here on this subject. The main features of prison development belong to the history of the Scottish prison system rather than to that of the city. The most obvious change in the last fifty years has undoubtedly been, along with the progress of prison reform, the reduction of the number of persons annually committed to prison from over 50,000 at the turn of the century to under 10,000 in recent years.[3]

Probation

This reduction has been expedited by the development of the practice of probationary supervision, in which Glasgow is a pioneer in Scotland. At about the same time as the Birmingham justices were carrying through similar reforms, Bailie John Bruce Murray was arguing that short sentences were not only neither deterrent nor reformative but positively detrimental. Reporting to the Corporation in December 1905 he pointed out that in 1904 43,000 persons sentenced to pay fines were received into prison because they did not possess the required sum, making 80 per cent of the total prison population: and that in Scotland one person in 75 of the population was sent to prison against one person in 145 in England and Wales. At that meeting the Corporation approved the proposal to strengthen the system of probation of offenders, inaugurated by the Act of 1887, by appointing full-time Probation Officers to supervise persons put on probation. These officers were drawn from the ranks of the police. Six officers were appointed (operating in plain clothes) and later three women for super-

1 Bell and Paton: *Glasgow, Its Municipal Organization and Administration* (1896) p. 97. The land of Blackhill had been acquired in 1875 by the Corporation as the site of a new prison, but the Government, superseding the Corporation as the prison authority, planted the new buildings at Barlinnie, and what had been intended for a prison was turned later into a golf course. Blackhill is now a housing estate.

2 It now also accommodates a few women prisoners awaiting trial.

3 Scottish totals.

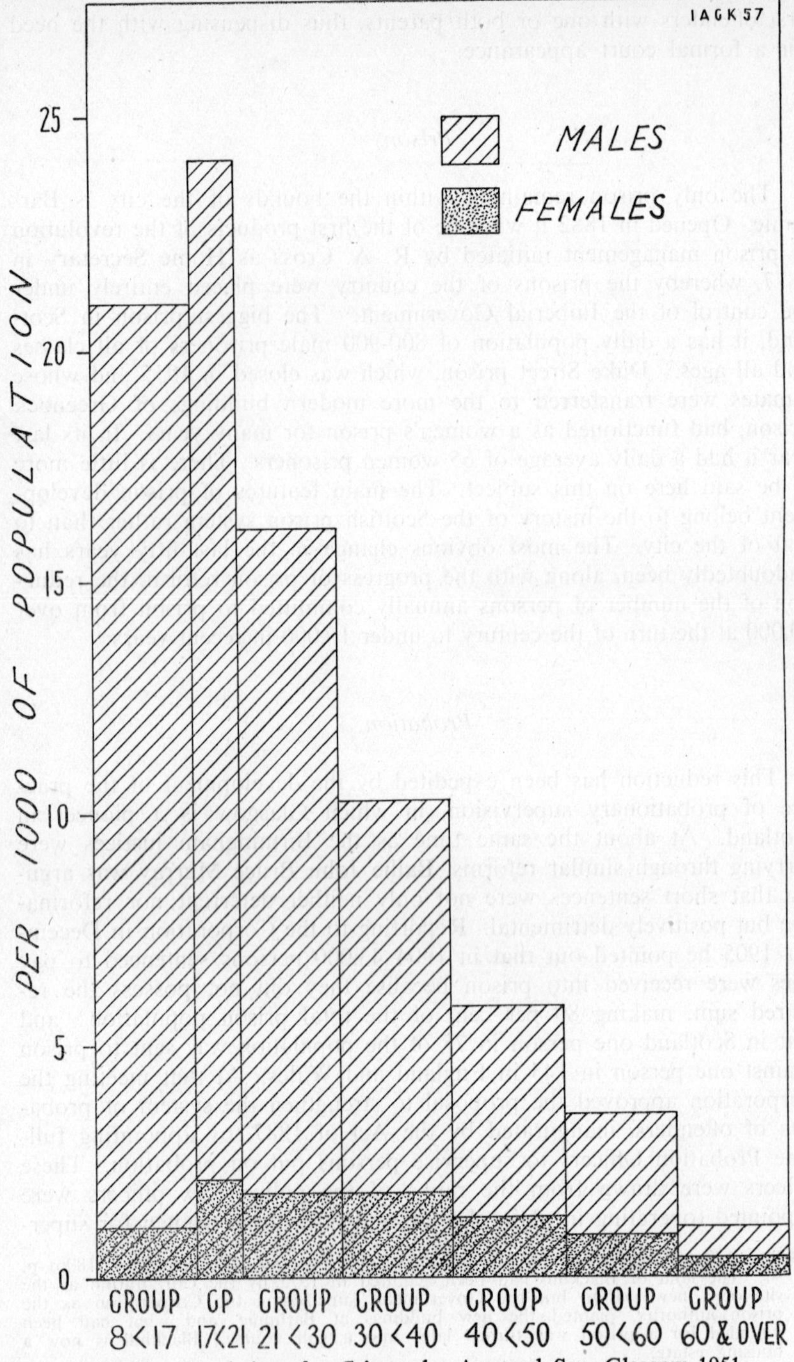

FIG. 35. Convictions for Crimes, by Age and Sex, Glasgow 1951.

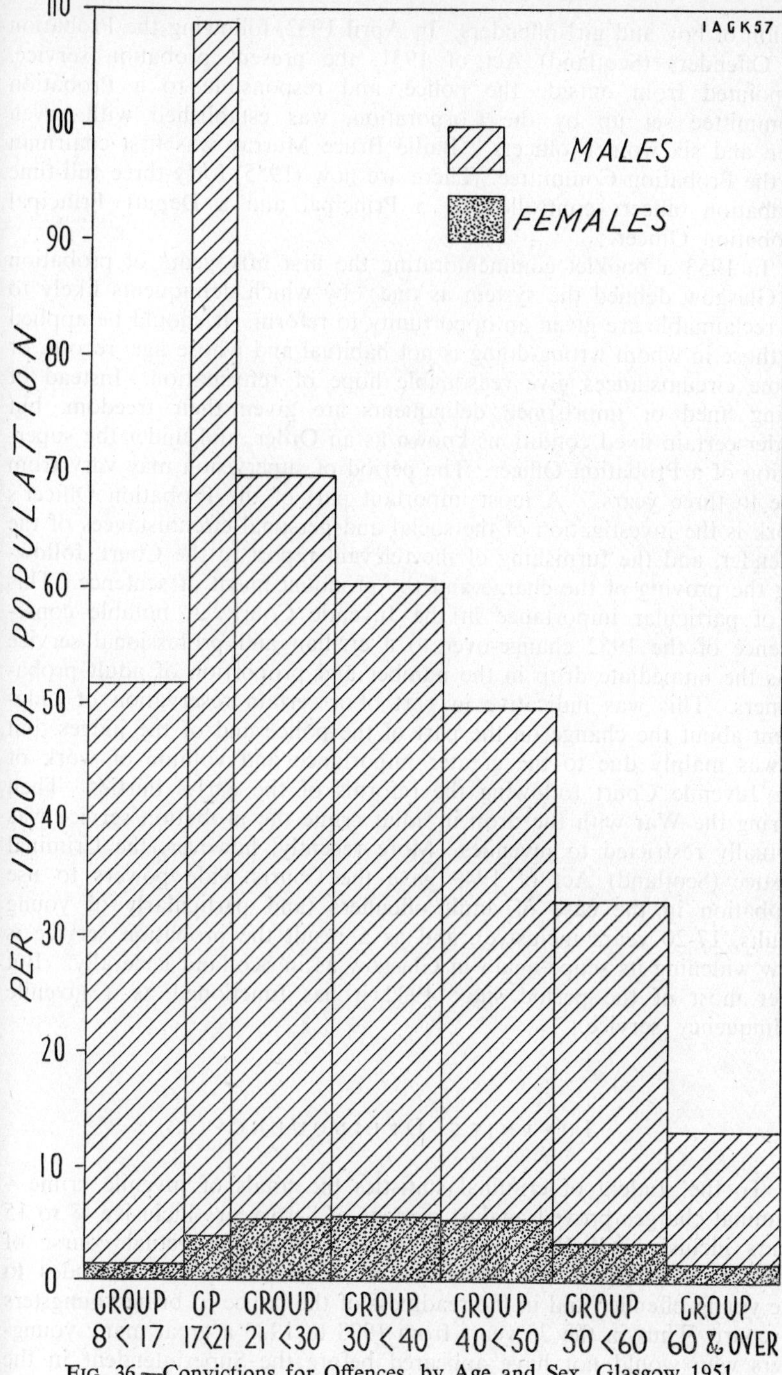

FIG. 36.—Convictions for Offences, by Age and Sex, Glasgow 1951.

vision of boy and girl offenders. In April 1932, following the Probation of Offenders (Scotland) Act of 1931, the present probation service, appointed from outside the police, and responsible to a Probation Committee set up by the Corporation, was established with seven men and six women officers.[1] Bailie Bruce Murray was first chairman of the Probation Committee. There are now (1955) forty-three full-time probation officers controlled by a Principal and a Deputy Principal Probation Officer.

In 1953 a booklet commemorating the first fifty years of probation in Glasgow defined the system as one " by which delinquents likely to be reclaimable are given an opportunity to reform. It should be applied to those in whom wrong-doing is not habitual and whose age, record, or home circumstances give reasonable hope of reformation. Instead of being fined or imprisoned delinquents are given their freedom, but under certain fixed conditions known as an Order, and under the supervision of a Probation Officer. The period of supervision may vary from one to three years." A most important part of the Probation Officer's work is the investigation of the social and personal circumstances of the offender, and the furnishing of the relevant report to the Court, following the proving of the charge and the pronouncement of sentence. This is of particular importance in the Juvenile Court. A notable consequence of the 1932 change-over to a civilian and professional service was the immediate drop in the number and proportion of adult probationers. This was indicative in part of a certain reservation of judgment about the change on the part of the police and of the judges, but it was mainly due to the greater importance and volume of work of the Juvenile Court following the reforms of the early 'thirties. Then during the War with the drop in adult crime the probation service was virtually restricted to juveniles. More recently, however, the Criminal Justice (Scotland) Act of 1949 gave the Courts wide powers to use probation in the case of adult offenders (and particularly of young adults, 17-20 years inclusive), and as a result the probation service is now widening its scope again in Glasgow as in Scotland generally. But over most of the period since 1932 it has functioned as a juvenile delinquency service.

Juvenile Delinquency

To the student of criminal statistics the totals of juvenile crime—criminal charges proved against persons of 8-16 years inclusive (8 to 15 years inclusive till 1934)—record not so much the actual course of juvenile offending as the variation in police and public attitudes to the young offender and in the readiness of the police to bring youngsters to court. Thus in the 25 years from 1908 to 1933 a great many youngsters who would not have appeared before the Superintendent in the

[1] The first Chief Probation Officer was Mr. Buchanan and his successor the present Principal Probation Officer is Mr. Robert Thomson.

Juvenile Court were given rough justice on the spot by police or parent. Since 1933 the Juvenile Court has been more generally used. But the recorded Court totals have to be read along with those of "Warnings administered by Superintendents." And these, given to child and parents in cases of very petty first offences, have varied in number with the readiness of the police to use this unofficial "warnings" method. During the war, for example, the police had less time for this practice, and in more recent years the number of unofficial warnings has again gone down. Thus if we add together the totals of Court charges proved and "Warnings administered by Superintendents" we get the general impression that the volume of juvenile crime, more serious and more petty lumped together, has decreased rather than increased!

TABLE CXLIII

JUVENILES: CHARGES PROVED AND WARNINGS ADMINISTERED BY SUPERINTENDENTS 1938-55

Year	*Juvenile Court Criminal Charges Proved against Juveniles*[1]	*Warnings Administered by Superintendents to Juveniles*	*Total*
1938	2188	3160	5348
1945	3609	1566	5175
1946	2406	1209	3615
1947	2159	1431	3590
1948	2483	2573	5056
1949	2275	2450	4725
1950	2599	2602	5201
1951	2747	1975	4722
1952	2813	1280	4093
1953	2416	1397	3813
1954	2287	1146	3433
1955	2480	1171	3651

SOURCE: Chief Constable of Glasgow.

But if we are to consider, as we must, that the significant totals are those recording the crimes considered by the police to be serious enough to warrant an appearance in Court, then the significant movement of juvenile delinquency in Glasgow is recorded in Fig. 34, which shows an enormous wartime increase, repeating on a greater scale the increase in the First World War, and a continuing level in recent years above that of 1938.

It should not be inferred from Glasgow's general reputation for juvenile delinquency that the city as a whole has an exceptionally heavy burden in comparison with the rest of Scotland. Mr. Bernard Queenan[2] has analysed the incidence of juvenile delinquency in the thirty-five police areas in Scotland for the five years 1946-50 inclusive, and finds

[1] These are the figures on which Fig. 34 is based.
Note that these totals do not coincide with the totals given in the annual Police reports, which exclude Malicious Mischief, classing the latter under Offences.

[2] Queenan: *A Statistical Survey of the Policy of Scottish Courts on the Disposal of Cases of Juvenile Delinquency* (1946-50): A Thesis submitted in part fulfilment of of the Regulations for the Degree of Bachelor of Education in the University of Glasgow: 1952.

that Glasgow ranks twelfth in the list.[1] The heaviest incidences are found in the large burghs. Kilmarnock with an incidence of 2.75 per cent (2.75 per cent of the population at risk, i.e. boys and girls of 8-16 years, in the period), comes first, followed by Greenock (2.70 per cent), Coatbridge (2.51 per cent), Ayr Burgh (2.18 per cent) and Hamilton (1.99 per cent).[2] The city of Dundee is ninth (1.74 per cent), Aberdeen is sixteenth (1.40 per cent) and Edinburgh twenty-fifth (0.82 per cent).

Mr. Queenan has also analysed the " methods of disposal " employed by the Juvenile Courts in each area. The key to the rather complicated table (CXLIV) is as follows:

Method of Disposal (Our classification)	*Method of Disposal (Official Classification)*
A—Release	Absolute Discharge, etc. Admonished or otherwise disposed of.
B—Conditional Discharge	Bond only with or without sureties. Caution with or without sureties.
C—Probation	Probation Order with Supervision. Probation.
D—Fining	Fine imposed on Offenders. Fine imposed on parent or guardian of Offenders.
E—Detention	Remand Home. Approved School. Borstal Institution. Prison.

To the general student of these matters the main interest of Table CXLIV is the demonstration that in the high delinquency areas, those in which the courts are presumably overworked, the tendency is to prefer fining to probation and in some cases absolute discharge to both.[3] As far as Glasgow is concerned the table shows an average use of probation, a comparatively low use of absolute discharge, and a comparatively high rate of detention.

But these comparisons do not answer the question—how effective are these methods of disposal? The usual way of testing a method of disposal, e.g. probation, is to give the percentage of probationers—usually about 70-80 per cent—who do not appear in the courts again during the period of the probation order. But over a longer period this percentage would probably go down somewhat. A special follow-up study was made in 1954 by Chief Superintendent Gilbert McIlwrick of Glasgow C.I.D. He traced the subsequent record of all those juven-

1 See Table CXLIV.

2 The high incidences in the burghs as compared with Glasgow are to be explained (a) by the closer supervision exercised by the burgh police in their more manageable areas; (b) by the absence of the vast areas of middle-class suburbia which keep the Glasgow average down; and (c) (possibly) by the absence or non-use of the unofficial method of " Warnings administered by Superintendents." For an indication of the incidence in Glasgow's more central areas see below p. 670.

3 Compare Dr. Max Grünhut's study of the English and Welsh Courts—*Juvenile Offenders Before the Courts* (1956). Dr. Grünhut suggests that an excessive use of absolute discharge—which means that the Courts wash their hands of the case —is probably due to the bringing before the court of many petty cases which might be dealt with by an unofficial " warnings " system, improved and made uniform throughout all courts.

TABLE CXLIV

ANALYSIS OF METHODS OF DISPOSAL OF PERSONS AGAINST WHOM CHARGES WERE PROVED IN JUVENILE COURTS IN SCOTLAND, 1946-1950

National ranking by Incidence of juv. del.	*Area*	*Incidence of j.d. as % of pop. 8-16*	*Percentage of I-VI charges disposed of by different methods* A	B	C	D	E
	Cities						
9	Dundee	1.74	30.7	2.4	34.6	23.9	8.3
12	Glasgow	1.59	28.4	1.4	31.7	24.7	13.7
16	Aberdeen	1.40	49.6	4.2	30.7	9.7	5.7
25	Edinburgh	0.82	33.4	6.1	29.2	14.6	16.7
	Large Burghs						
1	Kilmarnock	2.75	34.8	0.3	16.2	45.5	3.2
2	Greenock	2.70	27.7	0.5	22.7	39.9	9.2
3	Coatbridge	2.51	55.6	0.1	17.5	23.7	3.1
4	Ayr (Burgh)	2.18	48.4	0.3	26.1	21.9	3.3
5	Hamilton	1.99	58.5	1.5	19.8	14.2	5.9
7	Airdrie	1.78	31.7	0.4	34.0	34.0	3.6
8	Inverness (Burgh)	1.77	47.7	1.5	26.5	12.9	11.4
10	Paisley	1.71	38.5	0.3	31.2	15.5	14.5
17	Motherwell & Wishaw	1.37	44.2	1.7	17.1	30.4	6.5
21	Perth (Burgh)	0.98	39.2	0.9	50.2	2.2	7.5
22	Kirkcaldy	0.94	39.0	1.0	33.1	12.1	12.8
27	Dunfermline	0.74	43.5	1.2	46.8	4.0	4.4
	Counties						
6	Lanarkshire	1.83	35.2	1.2	11.8	47.6	4.1
11	Renfrew/Bute	1.65	38.1	1.0	20.4	33.1	7.4
13	Dunbartonshire	1.58	44.8	1.2	33.9	12.2	7.8
14	Ayrshire	1.55	42.7	1.1	20.0	32.2	3.9
15	Stirling & Clackmannan	1.50	46.7	0.5	25.1	23.9	4.8
18	Perth & Kinross	1.33	43.4	3.5	38.6	10.7	3.7
19	Caithness	1.21	34.8	0.0	1.1	56.8	7.3
20	Fife (excl. Kirkcaldy & Dunfermline)	1.01	45.3	0.6	32.5	15.8	5.7
23	Argyllshire	0.89	51.8	1.8	30.6	11.1	5.1
24	Lothians & Peebles	0.88	51.5	1.9	24.6	18.7	3.2
26	Dumfries & Galloway	0.78	42.0	4.9	40.4	5.8	6.8
28	Berwick, Roxb'gh & Selkirk	0.73	35.1	0.2	33.2	26.2	5.2
29	Sutherland	0.69	(50)	(0.0)	(40)	(10.0)	0.0
30	Ross & Cromarty	0.62	40.8	0.0	18.0	39.0	2.1
31	Inverness-shire	0.61	34.7	3.9	29.7	22.1	9.5
32	Angus	0.52	51.4	4.8	21.8	13.9	8.1
33	Orkney	0.50	(55.1)	(1.5)	(20.5)	(20.5)	(1.3)
34	Shetland	0.16	(30)	(0.0)	(55)	(10.0)	(5)
?	North-East Counties	n.a.	55.1	0.0	25.7	15.6	3.6

Figures in brackets show that the percentage indicated was calculated on a total of less than 100.

SOURCE: Queenan, *op. cit.*

iles, 1,275 in number, who appeared in court in 1946 on criminal charges for the *first time* and were dealt with in various ways. As Table CXLV shows 49 per cent in all reappeared in court on one or more occasions between 1946 and 1953.

TABLE CXLV

JUVENILES—FIRST COURT APPEARANCE—1946

Order of Court	*Number*	*No. reappeared in Court;* 1946-1953 *inclusive*	*Percentage*
Probation	490	254	51.8
Admonished	179	80	44.7
Sentence Deferred	144	60	41.7
Fined	341	166	48.6
Detention	35	16	45.7
Approved School	33	13	39.4
Borstal	2	1	50.0
Cautioned	42	30	71.4
Birched	9	3	33.3
Totals	1,275	623	48.8

This would appear to suggest that the Glasgow Juvenile Courts are making rather heavy weather. But this kind of estimate is highly defective. Much more important is the long-term outcome of the entire correctional process, legal and extra-legal, remedial and preventive. By this test, as we have seen, the general system in Glasgow is working well. In spite of the high level of juvenile delinquency ten years ago, the present level of adult crime is well below that of pre-war years. The probation service as the main instrument at the court's disposal for the majority of not too serious offenders, must share the credit for these developments with the police and the " Superintendent's courts."

It remains to mention some other services. The Remand Home and the Approved Schools are the Court's resort in the more serious and troublesome cases. Quite as important but more long-range in its effects is the work of the education authority in the schools and in co-operation with numerous voluntary groups in the provision of club and community activities in all parts of the city. But possibly the main factors in the civic improvement of Glasgow (as measured by the crime barometer) fall outside the remedial and preventive measures now being undertaken.

Residential Provision for Young Delinquents

The Glasgow Remand Home, unsuitably housed (until recently) in a Georgian terrace in St. Vincent Street—just opposite Greek Thomson's famous church—moved in 1955 to its present specially built accommodation at Larchgrove in Springboig. The Remand Home, which is the responsibility of the Children's Committee of Glasgow Corporation, houses young offenders before they appear in court: it also serves as a short-term detention centre—maximum period twenty-eight days. The daily average complement of residents in 1955 was 35-40 boys and 1-2 girls.

Mossbank Approved School in Millerston is the only Scottish approved school whose governing body is the local authority: that is, in this case, Glasgow Corporation acting through its Education Committee. The present building was erected about 1870, as a result of a public subscription launched by the Glasgow Industrial School Society.[1] Mossbank Industrial School provided for potential not actual delinquents, children whose surroundings and circumstances were such as to make delinquency seem inevitable. Actual delinquents were sent to Reformatories. In 1933 the distinction between Industrial Schools and Reformatories was abolished, and the term Approved School was adopted. This changed the whole character of Mossbank as Table CXLVI shows:

TABLE CXLVI

ADMISSIONS TO MOSSBANK SCHOOL, 1920 AND 1937

Reasons for admission	*Number of admissions* 1920	1937
Criminal offence (theft, housebreaking, etc.)	20	51
Beyond control of parents	4	0
Persistent truancy	1	10
Care and protection (wandering and neglect)	54	1
Total admissions	79	62

SOURCE: See footnote below.

Mossbank Industrial School trained boys for work. Half of the day was spent in class-rooms and half in the work department—tailoring, shoe-making, paper bag-making, farming, gardening and the like. When the boys left some were placed out on farms, some entered the services, some emigrated, and some returned to their parents. Many of them had successful careers. There come to mind (writes the headmaster) a Deputy Speaker of the House of Commons, the Mayor of a Canadian city, and a holder of the Victoria Cross.

Mossbank Approved School to-day has a roll of around 80 pupils. Three quarters of them have committed criminal offences, and in many cases have had three or more Court appearances. The remaining quarter is made up of truants, and of children beyond control of their parents. The age-range is 8-15 years. All pupils spend their time in ordinary school work. Nearly all the boys return to the care of their parents, often before the age of 15. The school welfare officer supervises each boy after he returns home until his eighteenth birthday. For pupils who have no homes or whose homes are unsuitable a place is provided in the Mossbank Auxiliary Boys' Home in Dennistoun. This is of particular value to lads who could not meet the cost of lodgings.

[1] This account is based on information kindly provided by Mr. J. T. Wilson, the present headmaster of the school. The Glasgow Industrial School Society came into being in 1874 and organised day schools in North Frederick Street in 1847-51 and in new premises in Rottenrow in 1851-68. In 1855 the school became residential. In the following decade legislation greatly extended the classes of children eligible for admission to Industrial Schools, until in 1866 the Directors decided to build the present school.

Looking to the future it is obvious that the barrack-like buildings intended to house 400 boys are quite unsuited for the rehabilitation of 80 young and immature delinquents. Recent studies advocate the use of a number of cottages or villas, each housing about 15 boys, where the children can learn the meaning of living together as a family, instead of becoming units in an istitution. The Corporation of Glasgow was thinking in terms of a new Mossbank before the war, and the question is still receiving consideration. "Whether a new school is provided or not," concludes the headmaster, "there is one problem which must be faced by all Approved Schools and the general public —the education, training, and supervision of the parents who provide our population of young delinquents. Divorce, desertion, cohabitation, illegitimacy, police records, on the part of the parents, still show in our records with the same alarming frequency as in the Industrial School records of a hundred years ago. There will be no real progress until as much time and energy is devoted to changing the parents as to changing the boy."

The Schools and the Parents

The rapid increase in juvenile delinquency in the Second World War caused local authorities throughout Scotland much concern. A notable report on the subject, prepared in consultation with various authorities, and incorporating suggestions from Head Teachers and their staffs in every Glasgow school, was approved by the Education Committee and subsequently by the Corporation in 1944. Two main developments in the prevention of juvenile delinquency may be traced to these discussions. The first, which has its counterpart in every area, is the more intensive development of the Glasgow Corporation Child Guidance Service, first established in 1937. While this is primarily an educational service, closely connected with the work of the schools, it is of great value in detecting and treating those indications of emotional disturbance and maladjustment which may if unchecked develop into serious delinquency; and it has sought, particularly in recent years, to help not only the child but also wherever possible the parents and the family situation behind the child. There are now four main and seven subsidiary clinics, together with a residential school and clinic at Nerston, East Kilbride. Table CXLVII shows the progress of the work in recent years.

TABLE CXLVII

GLASGOW CORPORATION CHILD GUIDANCE CLINICS

Year	1947	1948	1949	1950	1951	1952	1953
No. of cases	2,932	3,045	3,309	3,232	3,409	3.427	3,680

SOURCE: Director of Education.

NOTE—These figures may indicate a growing willingness on the part of parents and teachers to use the clinics and not an actual increase in the number of children (and parents) in difficulty.

There is also the Notre Dame Child Guidance Clinic in Dowanhill, made famous by the work of the late Sister Marie Hilda, and strongly supported by the Corporation.

The second development coming out of the 1944 Report has no counterpart in other areas. It is the establishment of welfare officers, trained teachers seconded for welfare work in schools with a high incidence or potential of truancy and delinquency. "Essentially," says a recent report, "the welfare officer serves as a link between home and school, providing the school with information about the domestic circumstances of the pupil which enable the school to provide more effectively for his education and inviting the parents to co-operate in the steps taken by the school to help the pupil. The welfare officer is able to bring to bear on families in trouble the resources of the appropriate social agencies: from time to time she has to attempt the rehabilitation of the family if the individual child is to be helped." The activities initiated are most varied. For example in the Abbotsford School in Gorbals, where in the mid-1940's a great change was effected, the Welfare Officer in co-operation with the staff introduced

(1) Swimming Clubs for boys and girls;
(2) A Junior Club;
(3) A School Football Club affiliated to the Schools League;
(4) A School Holiday Camp;
(5) Visits to places of interest around Glasgow; and
(6) A Parents' Day.

In the other schools similar innovations have been made, and close associations developed with the local boys' and girls' clubs. But the heart of the matter is in the home visits. "Parents usually welcome a visit from the Welfare Officer and very often ask that such visits may be repeated. It is in many instances a source of encouragement to parents to feel that someone knows and understands their particular problems and many confidences have been disclosed during these visits which have relieved parents of anxiety and feelings of despondency and reflected favourably on the children."

In the years immediately following 1944 the scheme was tried out in three schools: Abbotsford; St. John's Boys; and St. Patrick's Boys; all junior secondary schools. The record of the first three years shows a decided improvement in all three cases in both school attendances and delinquency.

In more recent years the scheme has been extended to four other schools: Lambhill Street Junior Secondary School, St. Columba's Junior Secondary School, St. Joseph's Boys' Junior Secondary School, and St. Roch's Junior Secondary School: while Abbotsford has dropped out. It may be tentatively concluded that this most interesting experiment is proving itself, and may well be extended to other schools as time goes on.

TABLE CXLVIII

ATTENDANCE PERCENTAGE

	1944-5	1945-6	1946-7
Abbotsford	80.5%	83.8%	86.9%
St. John's Boys	81.0%	86.0%	87.6%
St. Patrick's Boys	82.3%	86.9%	87.4%
All-Glasgow average	85.4%	87.3%	88.3%

DELINQUENCY TOTALS (CRIMES ONLY)

	1944-5	1945-6	1946-7
Abbotsford	37	33	11
St. John's Boys	65	52	24
St. Patrick's Boys	46	45	30
	(1944)	(1945)	(1946)
All-Glasgow Totals (all ages 8-16)	2,266	2,540	2,406

SOURCE: Director of Education.

THE OCCASIONAL CRIMINAL

It was suggested at the beginning of this chapter that the burden of crime in Glasgow is largely a carry-over from its hundred years and more of too rapid expansion between 1800 and 1920. This is borne out by the continuing pattern of crime in the city. That pattern is set by the distribution of the mass of petty crimes against property. Glasgow, like any other great city, has three types of criminal—the professional criminal, now highly mobile, the young or adult criminal whose behaviour is the product of psychological disturbance, and the non-professional, psychologically normal, occasional criminal whose behaviour is mostly determined by the standards of his neighbourhood and of his companions. The vast majority of crimes, the petty crimes, are traceable to this third category. In Glasgow this mass of petty criminality is still largely concentrated in the comparatively under-privileged groups, living in the overcrowded and decaying districts surrounding the centre of the city. As we have seen, a growing proportion of it is juvenile crime. It is probable that these districts have the heaviest juvenile delinquency incidence of any in Scotland, much heavier than that of Kilmarnock, Greenock, and the other burghs mentioned earlier. This is supported by various records and studies. Annual analyses of delinquency in Glasgow schools were prepared for the Education Committee up till two or three years ago. The 1950 report shows that all the schools[1] with more than 5 per cent of delinquents on their total roll were located in the wards of Gorbals, Govan, Calton, Anderston, and Hutchesontown. Professor Thomas Ferguson's study of delinquency in Glasgow[2]

[1] Excluding special schools. The high-delinquency schools are all boys' schools or boys' sections of mixed schools.

[2] Thomas Ferguson: *The Young Delinquent in His Social Setting* (1952).

supports this generally. He analysed the delinquent performance of that cross-section of Glasgow boys who left school at 14 in a certain month of 1947—a true cross-section of children of Glasgow's poorer or less provident families. Of the 1,349 boys studied, 165 or 12.2 per cent had appeared in court on criminal charges on one or more occasions between the ages of 8 and 18. The corresponding figure for all Glasgow boys, taking in those who stay at school after 14, would be nearer 3 per cent.

Professor Ferguson studied a cross-section of Glasgow boys and not any particular area. But he confirms that delinquency was found to increase as the type of district in which the boy lived deteriorated. He found also that in those new housing areas reserved for slum clearance the delinquency rate was as high as in the slums themselves.

TABLE CXLIX

INCIDENCE OF DELINQUENCY (AS PERCENTAGE OF BOYS "AT RISK") IN RELATION TO TYPE OF HOUSING DISTRICT

Type of district	*No. of boys "at risk"*	*Boys convicted During school years* %	*Boys convicted After leaving school* %	*Boys convicted at least once between ages of 8 and 18*[1] %	*Boys with more than one conviction* %
Residential, and good working-class	188	4.8	2.6	6.9	2.6
Fair working-class	381	5.8	4.7	9.1	4.9
Bad working-class	252	5.2	9.5	14.2	6.3
Slum	139	7.9	15.8	22.3	8.6
Local Authority housing	389	4.6	8.7	12.3	3.3
"Rehousing" (slum clearance)	142	10.6	13.3	21.8	7.7
Other L.A. housing	247	1.3	6.0	6.8	0.8
All boys in study	1,349	5.4	7.6	12.2	4.8

SOURCE: Ferguson, *op. cit.*

Among boys from these rehoused slum families, even families that have been rehoused for upwards of ten years, delinquency (he concludes) "is still as prevalent as among boys continuing to live in slums: it is much easier to alter a causal environment than to change a way of living . . . much easier to improve physical attributes than those that are less material."[2]

More generally speaking, however, the effect of new building and of the transfer of families with children from the older crowded districts into the newer housing areas is to reduce crime and delinquency in the long run. J. H. Bagot shows in his study of Liverpool in the interwar years[3] that while the crime-experienced members of families

[1] In this table the figures shown in this column may be rather less than the total of the two preceding columns because of the inclusion in each of these of a few boys convicted both during and after school years.

[2] *op. cit.*, p. 145.

[3] J. H. Bagot: *Juvenile Delinquency* (1936).

moving into new and better houses continued in their anti-social behaviour, the younger children showed a progressively lessening degree of delinquency. This seems to be broadly true of the Glasgow experience. As the people sort themselves out and get to know each other there is a steady improvement in the morale and the general security of the district. This has certainly happened in a striking manner in Househillwood. On the whole therefore it is arguable that when the rehousing of Glasgow's population is carried through and the central areas are redeveloped, much of the crime and social disorganisation of the old and familiar kind described in this chapter may eventually disappear.

One consideration, peculiar to Glasgow and Liverpool among the greater British cities, is the degree of change to be expected in the behaviour of the poorer sections of the large Roman Catholic Irish community. For it is still the case—a matter generally glossed over in discussions of crime in Glasgow—that the poorer members of that community contribute to the crime totals, and notably to the juvenile-crime totals, more than proportionately to their numbers in the total population. Roman Catholic children have more criminal charges proved against them, in proportion to their numbers, than are proved against Protestant children. Of the 2,282 young delinquents attending school in 1953, 1,286 attended Protestant schools and 996 attended Roman Catholic schools. The schools population of Glasgow in that year was:

Attending Protestant schools	126,663
Attending Roman Catholic schools	56,672

That is to say, 1.01 per hundred of the pupils attending Protestant schools were reported for crime while of those attending Roman Catholic schools the figure is 1.75 per hundred. In other words the proportion of Roman Catholic children reported for crime was 75 per cent higher than that of Protestant children. A similar conclusion emerges from the study of Approved School admissions in 1951. The proportion of Roman Catholic children in the general school population of Glasgow was 31 per cent; the proportion of Glasgow Roman Catholic children in Approved Schools was 45 per cent.

It would be highly unscientific as well as unmannerly to deduce any causal connection here. It is primarily a matter of social and economic conditions. In other countries, or other parts of this country, where Roman Catholics are not predominantly drawn from the lower income groups, they are correspondingly non-delinquent. These figures indicate simply that a high proportion of children and adults, living in Glasgow in those conditions of comparative poverty and squalor which conduce to a high delinquency rate, happen to be Roman Catholic. But this is not all. There is also the element of culture-conflict. Besides being comparatively poor, they are mostly Irish by blood and sentiment, and this national difference, with its strong overtones of historical antagonism to England and to Protestant Scotland, has undoubtedly contributed among many of the more recently settled groups to a certain sympathy or at least tolerance for whoever is against authority. Even the settled community—as recorded elsewhere in this book the Irish in Glasgow are now largely third and fourth generation and have contributed notably to civic welfare—is still to some extent on its guard.

These points are worth stressing in any attempt to estimate the trend of social development in the city using crime as an indicator. Properly considered they tend to reinforce the general impression built up in the earlier part of this chapter on the somewhat uncertain foundation of comparative statistics: the impression namely that the diminution in Glasgow's share in the Scottish totals of crime—whether measured by crimes made known or by criminal charges proved—indicates a real change for the better in Glasgow's behaviour relative to other comparable areas. For if crime in the city is largely a product of such centres of social decay as continue to fester in Glasgow's central districts, if it is fostered by what remains of social and national antagonism, then it will diminish as these diminish. The rebuilding of Glasgow, and the redevelopment of the central districts, is now well under way. Likewise there is plainly visible the progressive weakening of the old social and religious enmities described elsewhere in this book. Thus we may infer that the picture of progress revealed by Glasgow's crime figures is no mere statistical conjuring-trick, but is the outward result of profound social changes. One of these changes is manifest in the physical renewal of Glasgow. The other, no less important, is seen in the gradual reception of a formerly alien community into the multi-group life of the great city.

As this book approaches publication a case described by *The Glasgow Herald* as " surely destined to become the most famous in the record of famous Scottish trials " has just closed with the execution of Peter Manuel. This thirty-two-year-old man was found guilty of seven murders, committed just outside the Glasgow boundary, between September 1956 and January 1958; and was probably responsible for two more. He elected halfway through his trial to defend himself, and did so with such fluency, assurance, and sharp intelligence as to demolish any case for a plea of diminished responsibility which might have been founded on the apparent lack of motive for the murderous crimes he had committed. The public interest evoked by the trial is probably unequalled in Scottish judicial history, surpassing in intensity of impact even the Slater and Madeleine Smith cases recorded above. The people of the West of Scotland were appalled to have revealed to them what appeared to be a flourishing criminal underworld in which house-breaking, gun-peddling, and vicious violence were all in the day's work. Equally alarming was the fact that Manuel's murderous career was not intercepted earlier.

Chapter 21

POVERTY, DISTRESS AND SOCIAL AGENCIES

AGNES R. CLEVELAND

Introduction

It has been said that during the last hundred years our technological advances have far outpaced developments in social organisation, yet if one compares the social services of Glasgow as they exist to-day with those described in the *New Statistical Account* one finds changes which are almost comparable with those which have taken place in technology. At the same time much that is traditional remains and particularly the tradition of taking voluntary action to mitigate the hardships, lack of opportunities, and crises experienced by fellow citizens.

The difference between the social services of to-day and a hundred years ago is that we now take collective action either through the local authority or the central government departments to deal with matters which previously were left either to the individual, or to a self-constituted voluntary association. Yet even in 1850 the change had been foreshadowed, for already compulsory assessment for the maintenance of the poor had been in existence for five years and Dr. Chalmers's far-sighted experiment in St. John's Parish had failed.

Thus the main change which has taken place since the *New Statistical Account* was written is that the Glasgow Corporation is now the very senior partner in the social service firm. The Corporation as a matter of policy has long been prepared to use its powers, both obligatory and permissive, to the full for the purpose of initiating social services: on occasions (as in the case of supplementary allowances to the unemployed) it has even been prepared to exceed its powers when circumstanccs seemed to justify such action. The history of the Glasgow local authority departments can produce many examples of progressive action which forestalled legislation: for example the provision, before the passing of the Children's Act, of higher education facilities for boarded-out children, and the building of the Crookston Homes for old people.

The legislation which was implemented in 1948 gave to local authorities the opportunity of developing services which had previously been left to voluntary action or of permitting voluntary organisations to continue to undertake certain of these services. In Glasgow the tendency has been for the Corporation gradually to extend its own direct responsibilities. Youth Clubs and play centres have been opened for young people, an after-care department for the mentally handicapped has been set up, a start has been made with a welfare service for the handicapped, and at the time of writing (1955) the Health and Welfare Department has just taken over the welfare work for the blind in the city, while as a result of powers given by the Employment and Training Act the Corporation has taken over the Youth Employment Service from the Ministry of Labour and National Service.

Nevertheless in extending its direct responsibility for the provision of social services, the Corporation has not ignored the work which has long been carried on by voluntary organisations. By grants in aid, equipment, accommodation, and the advice and co-operation of departmental officials, voluntary social work has been stimulated and encouraged and both long-established organisations such as the University Settlement and new ones like the Glasgow and West of Scotland Branch of the Scottish Epilepsy Association have received support from official sources.

We now accept the need for statutory social services, but as a Christian community we also recognise the need for individual charity. Indeed it has been a characteristic of recent social legislation for clauses to be inserted defining the part which voluntary organisations may play in improving social conditions. And so it is that in spite of the financial difficulties with which voluntary services are certainly struggling at the present time, their number continues to increase.

Voluntary organisations are essentially local organisations, though they may be affiliated to national bodies. Their nature in a given locality tends to be governed by local needs and very great diversity exists. Further while the framework of the welfare system is applicable to all parts of the country local authorities retain considerable discretion in relation to the extent to which they may co-operate with existing voluntary organisations; so that in the structure of the statutory local authority services there is also diversity. Thus a description of the social services, statutory and voluntary, of any given locality is essentially a local document. It is then the local authority services and the voluntary organisations operating in Glasgow which will be described in this account.

At the time when the account of Glasgow was being compiled (1835) for the *New Statistical Account of Scotland,* the problem of poverty was much in the minds of the people of Glasgow. Though statistics were few and imperfect there can be no doubt that considerable numbers were living in great poverty and distress. Even under the unreformed Poor Law the number of poor on the Parish in 1830, according to the Glasgow Account, amounted to 5,066 or 2.5 per cent of the population; and in 1847, two years after the passing of the Poor Law Amendment Act in 1845, the parishes of Barony, Glasgow, Gorbals and Govan with a total population of 282,343 had 14,460 (5.1 per cent of the population) on their regular Poor Roll and in addition 30,746 casual poor, 700 orphans or deserted children and 229 lunatics. Moreover, the condition of the Glasgow poor was far below anything conceivable even in the worst slums of to-day. Poverty then too often meant actual lack of food, an appalling degree of overcrowding, an almost complete lack of sanitation, and in consequence filth and dirt and disease.

Up to 1845 the means existing to relieve poverty consisted of a number of charitable and benevolent societies and funds, and a Poor Law, whose revenue was made up of certain assessments levied on the inhabitants, supplemented by Church collections and certain donations. The *New Statistical Account* names 33 "Benevolent and Charitable Institutions of Glasgow, exclusive of Widows' Funds, Benefit Societies, Charity Schools and Maintenance of Paupers." This list of institutions, mainly religious, began with the Glasgow Missionary Society, founded in 1796; together they had annual subscriptions in 1834 amounting to over £30,000. It adds a list of about 30 charities (besides the 14 incorporations) with an annual income of over £15,000; the oldest of which was St. Nicholas Hospital, founded about 1460.

On the alternative methods of dealing with the problem of poverty —by the Poor Law or by voluntary charity—there was already controversy, in which a prominent figure was that of Dr. Chalmers, whose ideas were to have a remarkable influence on the future of social work.

Development of Voluntary Agencies

Dr. Chalmers

Before he came to be known for his practical experiments, Dr. Chalmers (1780-1847) had already written extensively[1] on the problem of poverty. He had criticised strongly the principles and practice of the Poor Law on the ground of its failure to distinguish (except by the mechanical work-house test) between those who could not and those who would not maintain themselves. While he was so far in accord with the *laissez-faire* philosophy of his time as to condemn the placing of the burden of relief on the tax-payer, and to insist on the responsibility of relatives and friends to maintain those in need, he was far in advance of his contemporaries in his conception of poverty as not merely lack of means, but as a condition arising from a combination of defects—individual and social—bad habits, bad legislation, bad administration, and unthinking charity. Hence in place of the harsh device of the work-house test he demanded the careful investigation of each individual case.

In 1822 he put his theories into practice in Glasgow in the Parish of St. John of which he was minister. He obtained the consent of the Poor Law Authorities to suspend the operation of the Poor Law within the parish (except as regards those already on Parish Relief who were to be continued) and made himself as minister of the Parish responsible for its poor, raising the necessary funds from voluntary contributions

[1] E.g. *Christian and Civic Economy of Large Towns*: Three Vols. 1820-1826.

from Church members and not by parish assessments. He divided the parish into districts with a deacon in each who was to get to know intimately the families in his district and to "combat all the evil habits prevalent among the people and to encourage all that is good"; and to be responsible for the investigation and subsequent treatment of each case as need arose.

In the end the experiment was abandoned, partly because the poverty of the parish was too great for voluntary charity to combat and partly because of the difficulty of getting suitable visitors for the increasing number of the poor. But although the practice of Dr. Chalmers's principles fell into abeyance the principles themselves were not forgotten.

During the nineteenth century Glasgow grew rapidly and congestion and poverty increased. As always the Glasgow public was generous to those in distress, new charities were founded and private benevolence was practised extensively. As the sources of help multiplied the unscrupulous exploited them, and social reformers recognised that indiscriminate charity could do harm as well as good. Thoughts turned once again to the work which Dr. Chalmers had done in the Parish of St. John and particularly so after the foundation in London in 1869 of the Charity Organisation Society which had been set up to combat the same abuse.

The Charity Organisation Society

In 1874 Glasgow instituted its own Charity Organisation Society. Its founder, James Cleland Burns, spoke at an early meeting on the theme of the principles of Dr. Chalmers. The Society was founded "to investigate thoroughly the cases of all poor persons in the City brought under the notice of the Committee with a view to forwarding them to the proper quarter for relief, to bring existing charities into co-operation with one another and with the Poor Law Authorities, to repress mendicity and by these agencies to improve the condition of the deserving poor."

Although the "detection of roguery" received much emphasis in its early years, the Society was not merely negative in its attitude. Nor was it just another relief-giving organisation though its work as such grew rapidly. Its distinctive contribution was to co-ordinate the charitable efforts of the city. In that capacity it compiled and kept up to date a register of the parish and charitable aid, and undertook investigation of cases on behalf of other organisations. Moreover, it stressed the need for adequacy in the treatment of cases assisted and was quick to note deficiencies and gaps in voluntary effort: in the second year of its existence, for example, it reported that no organisation existed to meet the needs of deserted wives. Some of these deficiencies the Society itself made good: it provided sewing work for women, and a labour yard for men; and opened a register of employment vacancies.

Glasgow felt the full impact of the trade depression of the 1880's and at that time the Society undertook investigations for the "Unemployed Relief Fund" opened by the Magistrates and Town Council. As the severity of the depression declined so did the appeals for help, and the Society had time to isolate new problems, among them the problem of the "intractable case" now familiar as the "problem family." To deal with this phenomenon the society introduced "friendly visitors" (as distinct from investigators), whose function it was to try by example and persuasion to rehabilitate these families. The process of individualisation was taken a step further when the society's "casework" was decentralised to District Committees whose workers knew the local people and co-operated with other voluntary organisations with intimate knowledge of the district.

The early years of the twentieth century saw the beginnings of great changes in the role of voluntary organisations, changes which came with increasing rapidity as the state accepted responsibility which had previously been borne by voluntary effort. The First World War, it is true, made extensive calls on voluntary social service and to these the Glasgow C.O.S. was quick to reply; but once the war was over the country demanded an expansion of the services introduced before the war, and these demands were fortified by the postwar economic situation.

In 1925 therefore the Society set up a committee to review the needs which the new conditions were creating. As one result of the Committee's recommendations, the name of the Society was changed to the City of Glasgow Society of Social Service—a change which recognised the fact that the Society was now mainly concerned with the improvement of social conditions and the re-establishment of individuals and families, rather than with the more negative investigation of "fraud and roguery." The casework function of the Society was thus officially recognised. Secondly the representative element in the Society's governing body was strengthened so as to bring into closer association the voluntary organisations and the statutory departments which new legislation was creating.

The severe industrial depression of the 1930's, and after it the disruptions of the Second World War, tested these administrative changes and found them adequate. During both of these prolonged crises there was a need for the voluntary and statutory social services to work harmoniously together and because it was in a position to secure this co-operation the Society was able to promote such projects as the occupational centres for the unemployed and later still an Old People's Welfare Committee. At the same time it was able to develop its casework through its district committees and so to deal with the individual difficulties which social pressures were producing in individual families.

Since the Society was founded in 1874 what amounts to a revolution in social conditions and social outlook has taken place and this has naturally been reflected in the activities of the Society. The old labour yard and the register of employment of the late nineteenth century and the occupational centres of the interwar period have all been closed down. On the other hand new work has been undertaken, notably the Citizens' Advice Bureaux, which were brought into being as a national service under the stress of the Second World War. But its basic work, the need for which is no less than it was, has persisted. The Society is still the co-ordinating agency for the social services of Glasgow. It has its Mutual Registration of Assistance, the heir of the register of Parish and Charitable Aid started in the early years of the Society. It is the central collecting agency for the convenience of the citizens of Glasgow who wish to support several of Glasgow's multifarious voluntary organisations. It provides a training ground for students of the University School of Social Study, and for the Health Visitor students. On its Council are the Lord Provost, the Medical Officer of Health and the Director of Education, *ex officio*; and the magistrates and town council, the Churches, the Royal Faculty of Physicians and Surgeons, the University, the Trades of Glasgow, and the Education Committee are represented, while on the District Committees which are responsible for local casework many practising social workers serve. Sixty-one local charities and institutions are affiliated to the Society, which is itself represented on 19 societies and associations.

Finally at the basis of the Society's activity is casework. To be effective casework has to co-ordinate the services available so that the individual may be able to use these resources in accordance with his own requirements. It is therefore appropriate that the Society which was founded to bring method into the distribution of relief should now use its knowledge and experience for the benefit of the individuals and families who are experiencing social breakdown or difficulty, and that the erstwhile Charity Organisation Society should now be the Family Casework Society in the city.

Settlements

Among the voluntary organisations for social service there has always been room for the organisation which serves a particular district instead of providing a specific service. A Settlement is such an organisation, and of Settlements there have been two in Glasgow, only one of which, however, now survives.

The first was the University Students' (residential) Settlement, opened in 1889 at the "Roon' Toll," Garscube Cross, by a group of Divinity students, inspired by Professor Henry Drummond. At first strongly evangelical, it came to lay more emphasis on social and educational work. Although it survived the First World War it suffered severely from the stresses of that time, and it closed its doors in 1925.

The other Settlement, which is still active in Anderston, arose out of the "Glasgow University Settlement Association," which opened a building in Townhead, where, on the model of Toynbee Hall in

London, members of the Association, mainly women connected with Queen Margaret College, carried on educational and social work. In 1897 the work was transferred to Anderston. The Settlement became residential when the present premises in Port Street were acquired in 1903.

The Settlement was founded at the time when the Glasgow Charity Organisation Society was decentralising its work by setting up district committees, and from the beginning it was able to co-operate by providing staff for the local office and volunteer collectors for the local savings bank which the C.O.S. was pioneering as a means of encouraging thrift. But the Settlement workers found other problems which were equally urgent, among them the needs of children and young people.

Because of the unhealthy nature of this congested district child ill-health was endemic, and in the first year of its existence the Settlement became active in the care, convalescence, and after-care of sick children. This work is still going on under the name of Invalid Children's Aid and children are sent away regularly for convalescent treatment and convalescent holidays. In 1902 the Settlement opened a school for invalid and defective children which was the forerunner of the Local Education Authority special schools. This was followed, in 1905, by a milk depot which was opened in conjunction with a mothers' clinic and infant health visitation scheme, carried on by the Corporation. For healthy children the Settlement undertook the organisation of playground games. In 1899 the Settlement opened a club for girls and in 1914 the first nursery school in Glasgow. This nursery school is still carried on in the Settlement premises though it has now been taken over by the Glasgow Education Authority.

Like other settlement workers before them the members of Queen Margaret College Settlement Association soon saw the need for formal knowledge of social science subjects; so in 1904 a Lecture Committee was formed to organise courses for helpers. These lecture courses were the forerunners of the course in Social Study, now a University course. The connection between the University School of Social Study and the Settlement has remained a close one: students of the former still attend at the Settlement for part of their practical training, and some of them, as well as students from other University Departments, reside in the Settlement.

After the First World War further expansion of the work took place. In co-operation with the Law Society of Glasgow the Free Legal Dispensary was opened under the title of Poor Man's Lawyer. Clubs for men and boys were started. As the postwar slump grew worse more positive measures were needed to counteract its effects in the district and in 1932 occupational centres were opened for both men and women; these were run in co-operation with the Society of Social Service.

The work of the Settlement in Anderston had been at first carried on by women and had concentrated on the needs of women and children. Because of the needs of the district the work had been extended to include men and boys and in 1935 the constitution of the Settlement was altered so that men could be admitted to membership of the Association.

During the Second World War the Settlement Association, recognising the need for hostel accommodation for members of the services, acquired additional premises in Port Street and started a hostel which remained open until 1946.

When the war ended the Settlement Association was faced with the need to replan its work in the light of the social changes which the war had wrought. In Anderston, as elsewhere, the accent was on youth work. In addition the Settlement for the first time initiated work outside Anderston by sponsoring mothers' clubs in the Maternity and Child Welfare Clinics. These clubs were run in the true tradition of settlement work as they were organised and staffed entirely by voluntary helpers, many of whom have close ties with the University.

While these changes were being made the nursery school was taken over by the Glasgow Corporation just as the health clinic, special school and milk depot had been taken over previously, though the nursery school remained on Settlement premises.

As Glasgow housing plans have matured many families with young children have been moved out of the district, but the old people have remained and one of the growing postwar needs has been for social and other facilities for old people. In 1949 an old ladies' group was formed and in 1950 dinners for old people were provided twice a week in the café, which had originally been opened for the use of the youth club. This luncheon club has brought many old men to the Settlement and within the last year it has been decided to enlarge the old ladies' group into an Old People's Centre. The Settlement is now a centre for the young and old alike. Its links with the University remain and the work now brings it into ever closer touch with various departments of the Corporation.

The Society of Social Service and the Settlements have been described at length as the two organisations engaged in general social work. In the city there are now many voluntary agencies, some old, some new, which deal with every kind of social problem, as well as many funds from which monetary assistance is forthcoming for those in need. Some of the former will be mentioned in the section dealing with the various types of need.[1] But certain organisations whose social work has sprung from a religious or moral concern are characteristic and demand a brief description.

[1] For a full list of such organisations and brief descriptions of their work, see the *Directory of Social Services in the City of Glasgow* (compiled by the Glasgow University Settlement—1951) and the annual *Appeal* of the Society of Social Service.

Evangelism and Social Work

During the nineteenth century evangelism and social work frequently went hand in hand. Adverse social conditions, gross overcrowding, poverty, sickness, and intermittent wage earning, were all factors contributing to the apparent godlessness of the people, and those who sought converts were brought face to face with the misery which was bred in the slums.

Of national organisations of this kind working in Glasgow the outstanding example is the Salvation Army, which carries on many-sided activities such as the provision of homes for the aged and for unmarried mothers and their babies, work among the homeless in the lodging houses, and cultural and recreational work among young people.

The specifically local missions often serve a comparatively small area and depend to a very great extent on the support of voluntary helpers.

The Grove Street Institute serves the congested district of Cowcaddens as a mission and social work centre. In 1895 it started as a ragged school with a class of two boys and two girls in a disused room which the founder, J. Wakefield MacGill, had to heat with a lump of borrowed coal. Now the Institute has classes and services for people of all ages and in addition provides recreational facilities for boys and girls in its B.B. company and choirs. For men and women there are meetings, choirs and a silver band. All the work of the Institute is interdenominational and the members of the recreational groups contribute towards the evangelistic work.

The Canal Boatmen's Institute and Port Dundas Mission is another evangelistic organisation working locally. Founded in 1871 for the social, moral, and religious welfare of canal boatmen, it now includes in its activities the relief of the poor and distressed in the Port Dundas District.

In Oxford Street, Gorbals, the *Glasgow Medical Mission,* which was instituted in 1867, still carries on social, religious and medical work among the people of the district.

Two evangelistic organisations whose work is now city-wide are the Glasgow United Evangelistic Association and the Glasgow City Mission.

The Glasgow United Evangelistic Association started as a noon-day prayer meeting in 1874. Free breakfasts for adults each Sunday and poor children's sabbath day dinners were introduced during the same year and in 1875 a children's refuge was opened and help was provided in finding work for boys and girls. In 1899 the Association began its work for physically infirm children when it founded the Cripple Children's League, whose convalescent homes for cripples and the craft training centre and social club for cripples remain complementary to the National Health Service.

The Glasgow City Mission, founded in 1826, is one of the oldest of the undenominational missions in the city. The Mission carries on home visitation of the aged and sick, and work with Glasgow taxi-drivers (formerly cab-drivers); and provides a distinctive social service in the police courts of Glasgow where a missionary attends daily at each court.

As one would expect, the various denominations undertake social work in the city.[1] This work undertaken by the Churches is now more extensive than it has ever been and it may tend to overshadow the contribution made by the undenominational missions which did so much for the people without church connections during the late nineteenth and early twentieth centuries.

Temperance

Police statistics show a remarkable reduction in the number of cases of drunkenness[2] in Glasgow during the present century, but at the time of the Fair, at Hogmanay and at the week-ends, Glasgow could not yet be described as an entirely sober city. The drinking habits of the people do however appear to be changing. Drinking is becoming more a social pastime than a serious business, the pubs are improving and are being used by women as well as men with the result that they are less often places in which quick oblivion is sought. Nevertheless there remains in the city plenty of scope for the temperance movement—even on the new municipal housing estates, to which a long-standing council order is still (1955) applied prohibiting the erection of public houses or other places in which intoxicating liquors are sold.

The temperance movement has strong links with the Churches and with the Missions, nearly all of which have their own temperance groups for both educative and preventive work and support the Scottish Band of Hope Union which through its Glasgow office is getting into touch with young people in schools and social groups. The Band of Hope is using to an increasing extent the technique of the film, both sound and technicolour, to put over its message in a way which is acceptable to the younger generation. Special propaganda has been prepared for use among lads conscripted for national service.

The Glasgow Abstainers Union, founded in 1854, uses the more traditional methods of the temperance movement. Meetings are organised and sewing classes for women, while the Union maintains a woman missionary who undertakes house to house visitation in the Garscube Road area.

The Scottish Temperance Alliance combines educational work for promoting abstinence from intoxicants among all age groups with the work of protecting areas from undesirable licences and supporting measures in Parliament for the promotion of national sobriety.

Since the war, branches of Alcoholics Anonymous have been

[1] See under "Those in Need," pp. 694-711.

[2] See Appendix Table 143, and Chapter 20 (Crime).

started in Glasgow, centred on Community House. The purpose of this organisation is to give to confirmed alcoholics mutual support in their endeavour to overcome their disability. Anonymity is maintained and at the same time each member has the responsibility of helping another member to overcome the habit by overcoming it himself.

Thrift

The *Friendly Society* Movement in Glasgow predates the Savings Bank of Glasgow by nearly a hundred years, for the Bell's Wynd Society, probably the first society open to non-members of the Incorporations, was started in 1746. In the eighteenth century the movement developed rapidly: the first *Statistical Account* lists 92 Societies, including the Incorporations, and Cleland in his *Annals of Glasgow* (1816) gives the names of 129. The life of the early societies, however, tended to be short, for most of the Societies lacked the backing of men of business experience. Nevertheless some of the early societies did survive—an example is the Glasgow Water of Endrick Friendly Society which was instituted in 1771 and registered as a Friendly Society in 1843 and which survived until 1953.

As standards of management improved in the nineteenth century, failures were less frequent, though the life of a society still tended to be fairly short. During the present century however the number of Friendly Societies has diminished and the report of the Registrar of Friendly Societies for 1952 showed that there had been a further decline in membership since the introduction of the National Insurance Scheme in 1948.

The Joint Stock Banks provided far greater security than the Friendly Societies but even in Scotland they did not cater for the very small depositor. There was therefore room for some new means of both inculcating thrift and providing security for the savings of the thrifty, and the Savings Bank was evolved to meet this need.

The present *Savings Bank* of Glasgow was founded in 1836. On 30 July it opened the doors of its first office, two rooms in Hutchesons' Hospital, and collected on that day £497 14s. 6d. from 92 depositors. From this small but confident beginning, the bank was to become the greatest trustee savings bank in Britain and through two of its actuaries, William Meikle and Thomas Henderson—in their time "elder statesmen" of the Trustee Savings Bank movement—was to exert an influence reaching far beyond the bounds of the city.

The Savings Bank of Glasgow was sound and well managed from the start, but it did not at first entirely meet the needs of the small investor, the minimum deposit being 1s. and the very formal procedure of depositing money being somewhat alarming even to those workers who could in fact attend the office of the bank during working hours. Consequently in 1838 centres were opened at which quite small sums could be deposited for transmission to the office when a minimum deposit had accumulated. These centres were conducted on informal lines and were similar to the "penny banks" which were being started about this time in such industrial concerns as the Glasgow Gas Works. Mr. William Meikle was an advocate of these penny banks and it was largely as a result of his enthusiasm that some 200 were opened by Churches and Missions of the city and, after the introduction of compulsory education in 1872, in the schools; the majority being run in close association with the Savings Bank of Glasgow. A Special Investment Department of the Savings Bank was opened in 1870, again through the initiative of William Meikle.

A Savings Bank which holds (in 1955) funds due to depositors amounting to £100,633,119 must have many different departments. The Glasgow Savings Bank does offer a variety of facilities to its clients. It has a Government Stock Department holding Stocks and Bonds to the amount of £8,582,491; and a Government Annuity Department. There are also in operation 237 Penny Savings Banks and there is a Direct Transfer Scheme which enables workers to have a weekly stoppage from their wages transferred directly to the bank.

The Savings Bank provides facilities for those who know they want to save, but many need direct encouragement to save. This is met in Glasgow as elsewhere by the National Savings Movement and by the local thrift clubs whose history is older than the National Savings Movement.

Three voluntary organisations have shared the development of the Thrift Clubs—the Society of Social Service, the Guild of Aid and the Settlement. The clubs were started by each organisation as a means of teaching and encouraging thrift. All three organisations are still collecting regularly week by week from their members and in 1955 the Guild of Aid had 500 subscribers who saved a total sum of £15,675 for such purposes as rent, clothing and special emergencies.

Moral Welfare

In spite of the changing pattern of many of our social services Moral Welfare work still remains the monopoly of the Churches and Voluntary Organisations. The early attitude of the Church in Glasgow is illustrated by an enactment of the Kirk Session in November 1725 that "the elders and deacons should go through their proportions and take notice of all young women who keep chambers alone, especially those suspected of lightness and warn them that they will be taken notice of and advise them to get honest men or take themselves to service." During the 250 years which have intervened since this enactment our ways of life have changed and the Corporation now include flats for single women as a normal part of essential housing. Methods of prevention have also changed, but the essential problem remains as Glasgow grows in opulence, importance and size and will remain so long as the notorious communal toilet on the common stair continues to be, as it is at present (1955), a too prevalent feature of the city's housing and a source of anxiety to responsible parents.

The prevention of immorality and the understanding care of the unmarried mother and her child are now carried on side by side. The Church of Scotland, the Roman Catholic Church and the Salvation Army all provide mother and baby homes. This concern of the Churches with the problems of moral welfare is nation-wide. It is in the development of lay voluntary organisations for moral welfare that Glasgow's own attitude to this service can best be seen.

In 1805 the Lock Hospital was founded. Ten years later the Magdalene Society was formed for the repression of prostitution and the reformation of "penitent females." The Magdalene Asylum was opened shortly after and co-operation was soon established with the Lock Hospital, and the interchange of cases became the accepted practice. In 1859 the Glasgow Magdalene Institution was founded and the original Magdalene Asylum was merged in it in 1867. This institution aimed at the suppression of "the resorts of profligacy" and at the same time sought to provide "a temporary home for females who have strayed from the paths of virtue and are willing to return to them: also a similar refuge or other protection to females who are in imminent danger of being led astray." At the present time the Magdalene Institution has a home at Lochburn which can accommodate about 116 girls who are in need of training and discipline. Training for up to two years is provided in cooking, housework, sewing or laundry work. Discipline is attained through the sympathetic supervision which is the basis of Christian home life.

The Glasgow Home for Deserted Mothers was founded in 1873 with the object of affording temporary shelter and maintenance to destitute and houseless mothers and their children. It has always been and still remains the policy of this organisation that only unmarried mothers with a first baby should be accepted.

The National Vigilance Association of Scotland is one of two organisations for Moral Welfare which made their appearance during the first 25 years of the twentieth century. It exists for the care and protection of women and children. The work includes advisory and protective work for an average of over 600 cases per annum and close co-operation has been established with the women police, children's departments, probation department, public health department, marriage guidance clinic, clergy, doctors, nurses and the women's services. In Renfrew Street there is a hostel for women and girls and a domestic training home. The Society is a registered adoption society. The outdoor work of the society includes the meeting of long-distance trains at the Central Station and contact with the Irish boats as these arrive.

The other organisation, the Women's Help Committee, was inaugurated to deal with the social problems which were the aftermath of the 1914-18 war. One of its main interests is the welfare of the unmarried mother and her child. In addition to the social casework which such work involves the Committee maintains a mother and baby home at Atholl House where mothers may stay after confinement and eventually return to work knowing that their babies are being cared for while they are away. On the preventive side the Committee has a hostel in Burnbank Gardens for twelve working girls where judicious supervision and freedom are combined to prepare the girls to live responsibly on their own.

Since the war a Marriage Guidance Council has been started in Glasgow and is already making an important contribution to the moral welfare of the city by the educative and the remedial work which the counsellors are undertaking. Great care is taken in the selection of counsellors who have to complete successfully a course in marriage guidance before they can take a full part in the work.

•

Charitable and Benevolent Funds

Glasgow is as well endowed as any city in the country with funds to provide financial aid for residents who are experiencing material difficulties which cannot be fully alleviated from statutory sources. Many of these funds date from the time when statutory help for the poor was kept to the minimum and originated either in the incorporations of the city or in the mortifications of individuals.

(1) For the *aged* there are:
- Buchanan's Aged Persons' Mortification (1725).
- Hamilton Annuity Fund for residents in the Barony of Gorbals (1806).
- Glasgow Aged Women's Society (1811).
- The Glasgow North Parish Washing Green Society for residents living around Glasgow Cathedral.
- St. Nicholas Hospital (1456).
- William Hamilton Trust.

(2) *Infirm and handicapped* persons are also provided for through:
- The dorcas and samaritan societies of the hospitals.
- The Colquhoun Bequest Fund for Incurables (1873).
- The Association for the Relief of Incurables in Glasgow and the West of Scotland (1875).
- The Mission to the Outdoor Blind for Glasgow and the West of Scotland (1859).
- The Mission to the Adult Deaf and Dumb for Glasgow and the West of Scotland.

(3) There are funds for *Indigent Ladies*:
- The Balmanno Bequest for natives of Glasgow over 40 (1856).
- E. McLaren Fund for Indigent Ladies.
- The Isobel Robertson Trust.
- The Ladies' Work Society of the West of Scotland.
- The Stevenson Bequest.
- The Ure Elder Fund for Indigent Widow Ladies.

(4) The *trades and incorporations* of Glasgow make very considerable provision for members and their immediate dependants who are reduced to necessitous circumstances, through the following funds:
- Glasgow Eastern Merchants' and Tradesmen's Society.
- Glasgow Southern Merchants' and Tradesmen's Society.
- Glasgow Fishmongers Company (Incorporated by Royal Charter).
- Glasgow Fruit Trade Benevolent Society.
- Grocer Company of Glasgow.
- Glasgow Master Wrights' and Builders' Association.

Slate Trade Benevolent Association.
The Company of Stationers of Glasgow.
Wholesale and Retail Drapers' Benevolent Fund.
Govan Weavers' Society.
The Weavers' Society of Anderston.
The Society of Deacons and Free Preses of Glasgow.
Both the Merchants' House and the Trades' House of Glasgow have funds at their disposal.

There are a number of other funds which are available to people of specified occupations:

Glasgow Society of Sons of Ministers of the Church of Scotland (1790).
Miss Mary Barclay's Trust for the use of ministers or the sons of ministers studying for the ministry.
Glasgow Society of Musicians' Benevolent Fund.
W. F. Frame Benevolent Fund for theatrical and variety artists.
Mrs. Susannah Dinwiddie's Mortification for daughters or grand-daughters of burgesses.
Mitchell's Mortification for old burgesses, their widows or unmarried daughters.
The Paterson Nursing Fund for Bridgeton Girls working in cotton mills.
Tennant Mortification for widows of Ministers, Merchants or Tradesmen.

(5) Glasgow has several *family funds*:

The Buchanan Society.
The Graham Charitable Society.
Maxwell and Hutchison Charitable Fund.
Maclean Trust.
The Coulter Mortification.

(6) The extent of Glasgow's links with *other parts of Scotland, both highlands and lowlands,* is evidenced in the number of charitable funds which exist for the benefit of those who have associations with parts outside the city:

The Glasgow Aberdeen Society.
The Arran Society of Glasgow.
Glasgow Border Counties Association.
The Glasgow Bute Benevolent Society.
Fife, Kinross, Clackmannan Charitable Society.
Galloway Association of Glasgow.
Glasgow Highland Society.
The Glasgow Kilmarnock Society.
The Kintyre Club.
Lewis and Harris Association and the Lewis Society of Glasgow.
Glasgow Moray and Banffshire Friendly Society.
The Mull and Iona Association.
Glasgow Northern Highland Benevolent Society.
Glasgow Perthshire Charitable Society.
Glasgow Renfrewshire Society.
Glasgow Skye Association.
The Incorporated Glasgow Stirlingshire and Sons of the Rock Society.
Tweedside Society.
Uist and Barra Association.

(7) Some funds are available only to *residents in certain parts of the city* and these date from the time that provision for the poor was made through the parish:

The Barony of Gorbals Benevolent Society (1806).
The Couper Bequest for the deserving poor in the villages of Old and New Cathcart.
The Old Maryhill Neighbourly Society.

Other funds are less local in their application:

The Glasgow Benevolent Society (1832).
Macalpine's Mortification.
Robert Hart Trust, limited to men over 50.
The Widows' Friend Society (1856).

The Society of St. Vincent de Paul (1848).
The Glasgow Jewish Board of Guardians (1877).
Thomas Wharrie Morrison Bequest Fund for the benefit of disabled ex-service men of the 1914-18 war.

The Lord Provost of Glasgow has his own fund which he administers for the benefit of citizens.

In this list no mention has been made of the national funds which are supported by Glasgow people and may be applied to the use of Glasgow citizens. The Services and some trades and professions all have such funds. Many individual churches provide financial help for members who are facing difficulty or crisis.

In spite of the very considerable number of funds which are available in the city there are still individuals and families whose particular circumstances do not come within the terms of reference of any particular society. So that these cases shall not fall through the net of voluntary benevolence when their need arises the Society of Social Service maintains a general fund from which help can be forthcoming, though now as at the time of its institution the society is not primarily a relief-giving organisation.

Many people are concerned in many different ways in raising money for the voluntary organisations in the city. Methods of raising money are as individual as the societies are but many of the latter benefit from two well established institutions, the Central Collecting Agency operated by the Society of Social Service and Students' Charities Day Organisation.

The Central Collecting Agency enables subscribers to more than one organisation to send a composite cheque to the Society of Social Service where the money will be allocated in accordance with the subscriber's wishes.

Students' Charities Day is organised by the students of the institutions for higher education in the city. It takes place on the third Saturday in January and is preceded by a week of intense activity in the suburbs and surrounding towns and of " stunts " in the city itself. On Charities Day the city is invaded by students in fancy dress, and fancy undress (for primitive man in a scanty leopard's skin and blue and pink with cold can extort silver in mid-winter from great-coated citizens). At the end of the day the money is counted and it is then for the Committee to decide what charities are to benefit from the efforts of the students. Some organisations receive large sums, others a few pounds, and some may get nothing at all. The money allocated as a result of Charities Day is a great help to the organisations which benefit from it. But since the allocation changes from year to year no organisation can budget ahead on the assumption that financial help will in fact be forthcoming from this particular source and one of the essentials for sound planning is an assured income.

Growth of Statutory Welfare Services

The Poor Law

The Poor Law Amendment Act of 1845 provided the legal basis for municipal social services, and the numerous services which are now provided by the Health and Welfare and the Children's Department have developed slowly out of the powers which in 1845 were vested in the parishes to make assessments for the support of the sick, the aged, and the young who had no visible means of support.

In Glasgow as elsewhere the Poor Law was unpopular, but that it was administered with a sense of humanity would seem to be demonstrated from the city records. For example Glasgow children were regularly boarded out on the farms and crofts of Scotland. In 1850 the Barony Parish Account Book shows among other items a sum of £561 spent on education for pauper children and this sum included contributions to the Deaf and Dumb Institution, to the Asylum for the Blind and to the Glasgow Industrial School. As early as 1853 the Parochial Board of the City Parish set up a special Children's Committee. From the records it is evident that indoor relief was not widely used in Glasgow even in the nineteenth century. An example, picked at random, illustrates this point. In the three parishes of City, Barony and Govan in 1881 there was a total of 11,262 people on out-relief, a figure which included Irish, English, foreign and non-resident poor, while only 3,340 were in the poorhouse of the parishes concerned. Side by side with the policy of boarding out pauper children and granting out-relief went the policy of boarding out pauper lunatics, either in the country or with their own relatives, and at least some supervision was provided. But although the administration of the Poor Law was less harsh and unimaginative in Glasgow than in some other comparable cities it was still the Poor Law.

Public Assistance

Throughout the nineteenth century the Poor Law authority remained the only authority responsible for the prevention of destitution; and such changes as the substitution of the Parish Councils for the Parochial Boards in 1894 hardly affected the spirit of the Poor Law or the adequacy of its provision. But the twentieth century brought a revolution in social outlook, first expressed in the reports published in 1909, of the Poor Law Commission, the Majority Report advocating the drastic reform and the Minority Report the break-up and abolition of the Poor Law. The revolutionary changes that have since taken place are in the main the working out of the implications of these reports.

Under the Local Government (Scotland) Act, 1929, poor relief became "public assistance," the basis of its administration was widened from the parish to the city, and the Town Council set up a Public Assistance Committee. The duties of that Committee were partly the traditional poor law duties—the relief of the impotent and weak, the sick, the aged, and widows with young children. But new duties were added. Under the Act of 1930 it was given the administration of the scheme for Blind Persons, and under the Economies Act of 1931 was made responsible for the investigation of needs in connection with the granting of transitional payments to the able-bodied unemployed. Thus during the early 1930's the Public Assistance Department had the invidious duty of administering three different schemes involving three different rates of payment. For Public Assistance the rates were:

For a single person, 12s. 6d.
For a married couple, 22s. 6d.
For a married couple with one child, 27s. 0d., plus 4s. for a second child, and 3s. for each additional child.

For Transitional Payments the rates were:

For a single man, 15s. 3d.
For a married couple, 23s. 3d.
For a married couple with one child, 25s. 3d., plus 2s. for each additional child.

For a blind person the Public Assistance scale could be increased by 5s. 0d. at the discretion of the committee. In addition to these sums payments could be made in respect of rent. The Committee also laid down rules as to the income which could be ignored when assessment was made in each case.

The anomaly of the three different scales of relief did not continue long. In 1935 the administration of the Blind Persons' Act was transferred to a special committee for Necessitous Blind Persons, though the executive functions remained with the Director of Public Assistance and the administrative change had little effect on the recipients. The second change was more far-reaching. In 1936 the transfer of responsibility for the able-bodied unemployed from the Public Assistance Committee to the newly established Unemployment Assistance Board, removed the large majority of the able-bodied from public assistance, but it left the difficult cases with the Public Assistance Department. These cases were comparatively few in number but they did prove intractable and right up until the outbreak of war in 1939 the Committee was considering ways and means of dealing with the "long-term unemployed, the dissipated, the discouraged, and the physically sub-normal" who, the Director suggested, needed "a short term of regular hours, nourishing food and work to rehabilitate them."

The years during which the three scales had been administered were years of widespread unemployment and its attendant hardship in Glasgow. It was the considered view of the Public Assistance Committee that the transitional grants approved by the government for the relief of the able-bodied unemployed were inadequate. The Committee therefore took responsibility for supplementing these grants, a decision with which the Director of Public Assistance disagreed as there was no statutory sanction for such action. For some years all these grants were signed individually by a member of the Public Assistance Committee, the Director of Public Assistance signifying his disagreement.

The Public Assistance Committee was also responsible for the administration of the Children's Acts and had a staff of ten officers dealing with child life protection and the boarding out of children who were without homes or suitable guardians. At the other end of the age scale the Committee had to provide for the aged. Finally it had responsibilities resulting from the Lunacy Acts and it had to maintain an institution for the provision of indoor relief.

From its inception in 1929 the Public Assistance Committee was a welfare committee and its liberal policy is demonstrated not only by the supplementation of government grants and its concern over the rehabilitation of the unemployed but also by the action which it took in relation to children and to the aged.

In his report for the year ending May 1938 the Director of Public Assistance states that "when a child proves outstanding in school the Committee sanction higher education followed by university or other advanced courses to give their ward every opportunity to make good." He then goes on to say that four girls and two boys were training for the teaching profession, that one girl had graduated M.A., that a boy was going through the medical school, that two were training for the ministry, that two boys and three girls were studying for the civil service and that four girls were probationer nurses. In addition 30 to 40 boarded-out children were in the higher grade schools.

In the same report mention is made of the adaptation of a home in Kirn as a short-stay home for healthy children and later reports show that the experiment was so successful that another home was to be opened. Though one may regret, in the light of modern knowledge, that the children at this home had their own teacher and did not attend the local school and that when additional accommodation was needed it was a bigger house which was sought and not another small and homely one, yet there is no doubt that Glasgow was progressive in its care of homeless children.

For old people the Committee showed itself equally enlightened in its provision of the Crookston Homes.[1]

In Glasgow as in the rest of Britain the responsibilities of the Public Assistance Committee for the administration of relief declined during the years 1939-48. The first large group to be removed from public assistance during the war was the Old Age Pensioners, who were transferred to the Unemployment Assistance Board as supple-

[1] See pp. 696ff.

mentary pensioners. Soon the Widows joined the supplementary old age pensioners and the title of the U.A.B. changed to Assistance Board. Next to go were those who were undergoing treatment for T.B. This group was transferred to the Local Health Authority.

Social Welfare

Between 1939 and 1948 the work of the Committee (renamed the Social Welfare Department) was being gradually reshaped. With less responsibility for financial assistance there was more opportunity for the promotion of welfare and Glasgow was already welfare conscious. Thus when under the National Assistance Act of 1948 the social welfare committee was finally relieved of its obligations to provide financial relief it was ready to take up new duties in association with the Health Department for the promotion of the welfare of the aged and the mentally and physically handicapped, and moreover the committee could call upon the services of staff who had been trained in its tradition.

1948 is a significant date in the history of local government because of the extensive reorganisation of the social services which then took place throughout the country. In Glasgow the Corporation Health and Welfare Committee was created and made responsible for both public health and welfare services. It works through the Health and Welfare Department, which was given the duties previously carried out by the social welfare department and not transferred by the new legislation, and in addition it was made responsible for the new services permitted under the National Assistance Act for the benefit of the aged and the handicapped.

Its duties are many and diverse. It provides temporary accommodation for those in need through unforeseen circumstances such as flood, fire, the collapse of buildings or eviction. This last-mentioned duty brings the department into touch with some of the most difficult families in the city and the lack of suitable alternative accommodation makes the rehabilitation of some of these families a particularly difficult task. The department has the duty of investigating applications for relief of rates, of registering and inspecting homes for the aged and disabled and of administering the Clydeside Air Raid Distress Fund.

In addition it is the department responsible for the welfare of the aged and handicapped and it is this aspect of its work which brings the department into close touch with voluntary organisations in the city.

THOSE IN NEED

Numbers

In a Welfare State enjoying something near full employment it may be surprising that there should be a place for such numbers of benevolent funds and public boards to provide assistance for people who cannot maintain themselves and it would be of interest to know who and how many they are who need such assistance. But definite information on these points is hard to come by.

Table 157 in the Appendix shows that in the Glasgow area, during the year 1954, over 161,000 applications for assistance were made to the National Assistance Board, and that about 48,000 were from people in fairly continuous need. But applications are not applicants, for in the course of the year one applicant may make many applications.

Appendix Table 158 is more helpful. It shows that on a particular day in 1954 (21 December) there was a live load of 57,446 individuals on the books of the National Assistance Board, all receiving allowances of longer or shorter duration. Together these made up over 40 per 1,000 of the population of the area.[1]

This figure is a minimum estimate. It is a minimum because it covers only those who made their needs known to the National Assistance Board. There are still those who will not ask for such assistance; and there are also those who receive assistance from voluntary societies and charitable funds and not from the State. The number of the latter it is impossible to estimate.[2] Few voluntary societies state the number they aid; and there is little doubt that, in spite of the registration work of the Society of Social Service, there is still overlapping and many people receive assistance from more than one source.

But Table 158 tells something about the 57,446 in receipt of National Assistance. They fall into three categories. The first consists of those whose allowances from the National Assistance Board were in supplementation of non-contributory Old Age Pensions. These numbered 2,743. The second consists of those whose assistance allowances were in supplementation of Insurance Benefits of one kind or another. These numbered 35,247, the allowances of 23,578 being in supplementation of Retirement Pensions, 5,348 of Sickness and Industrial Injury Benefits, 3,875 of Widows' Benefits and 2,446 of Unemployment Benefits. In the third category were those who were not in receipt of either pensions or benefits. These numbered 19,456 of whom 4,943

[1] This figure may be compared with the 32.8 per 1,000 who were in receipt of ordinary Outdoor Relief under the Public Assistance Committee in the last year of its operation, 1948.

[2] The Society of Social Service dealt with 1,845 cases during the year 1955/6, but not all of these cases required financial help.

were persons registered for employment and 14,513 were miscellaneous cases such as persons over pensionable age but without pensions; married women under 60 with or without children, who were separated from their husbands; other women with dependent children; persons incapable of work because of sickness or disability but not in receipt of sickness benefit; blind persons and tuberculous cases on a special scale; persons in residential accommodation, and persons receiving pocket money only who were in hospital and without resources. These figures show that among those who, at a date in December 1954, were considered by the National Assistance Board to be in need of assistance, two out of every three were already in receipt of State pensions or benefits. Assuming that these State payments are adequate for the normal person under normal circumstances (admittedly a big assumption particularly in the case of the Old Age Pensioners) there must be special circumstances affecting at least the first two categories to account for their need of supplementary assistance. This is as far as the official data carry us. To measure more accurately the extent and depth of need persisting in a city with all the resources of the Welfare State at its command, and with the will to use them; and to understand more fully the many causes which in varying degrees contribute to it, from fecklessness or ill-luck to pride and independence, would demand an enquiry at the personal level not yet attempted on the necessary scale. We proceed therefore to an account of the ways in which recognised types of need are met.

Old People

Since the Second World War there has been an increased interest in the older section of the population. Because of this, and the expansion of the services for the aged which has accompanied it, it is easy to overlook the work that has been done in Glasgow in the past by long-established voluntary organisations and by the Poor Law Authorities. As early as 1460 St. Nicholas Hospital was making provision, among other things, for the maintenance of "twelve old men and a priest." Hutchesons' Hospital, founded in 1639, performed a similar service. The Merchants' House and the Trades House (established by Letter of Guildry in 1605) from the first included the care of the aged among their duties. The Town's Hospital or Poorhouse, opened in 1733, provided an "asylum for the old." Special Funds, like the Buchanan Aged Persons' Mortification (1725), were available to help old people to maintain their independence. As Glasgow grew in population and in wealth the need increased and the means were forthcoming. Early in the nineteenth century, the Aged Women's Society (1811) and the Old Men's Friendly Society (1814) were formed (later amalgamated in the Incorporated Glasgow Old Men's Friend Society and Old Women's Home). Most of these early provisions and others added in the nineteenth century still exist and function alongside of the statutory provision which has been the main feature of the twentieth century.

The long-established social services for the aged had two main ends in view: the provision of an income for those who had been unable themselves to provide for old age, and the provision of a home for those who had no one to care for them. In the nineteenth century when wages were low and often irregular and families nearly always large, the first of these ends tended to be the more important; the second was generally accepted as the duty of a daughter or daughter-in-law as long as the aged relative survived. But as the size of family decreased and greater statutory financial provision was made for the elderly the emphasis changed and the new local social services have concentrated on the provision of homes, companionship and occupation, and of the personal services which enable old people to continue to live independently.

Before the Second World War Glasgow Corporation had shown an enlightened appreciation of the material needs of the aged. In September 1938 the Crookston (Cottage) Homes were opened. The opening of these homes did much to break down the reluctance which the aged had always had to accepting institutional help, and there was soon a waiting list of candidates when a vacancy occurred.

The Crookston Homes were for old people "of a higher standard" than the general poorhouse level. Individual houses were provided consisting of a living-room, bedroom, kitchen and bathroom. The houses were available for single persons and married couples and each house was fitted with a wireless loud-speaker. With the exception of dinner, residents could make their own meals and rations were provided for the purpose. There were day-rooms and a dining-room in which the lonely could find communal life and where newspapers were available. The qualification for residence was receipt of public assistance and each resident was allowed 2s. 0d. pocket money. When Crookston Homes were opened they set the standard for the whole of Britain and not least in the insight and understanding which was shown in allowing the residents to have their own furniture and personal possessions and encouraging them to have such companions as birds in their homes.

Crookston Homes were built around Crookston House in which there was additional provision for the aged in small dormitory wards. These beds were reserved for those old people who could no longer look after themselves and were available also for residents of the homes who might be taken ill. In 1938 Crookston became a colony for old people, a little remote perhaps from the community, but remote also from the institution at Barnhill which so many old people feared. The planners of Crookston had seen, more than ten years before it was officially recognised in the National Assistance Act, that special accommodation should be provided to suit the varying needs of the aged.

But the Crookston Homes could not house all the aged persons in the city who needed accommodation. Some were still living in the poorhouse, renamed Foresthall, but still almost a prison in the eyes of many. Many more were living in the Local Authority Hospitals, where as bedridden patients they were accommodated in the wards for the chronic sick. Others lived on sufferance with unwilling relatives or managed somehow on their own. By the end of the war in 1945 part of Glasgow's housing problem was the provision of homes for old people, and the National Assistance Act of 1948 gave the local authorities final responsibility for such provision.

In Glasgow the problem was a formidable one. First there were the able-bodied elderly who could look after themselves if they had somewhere to live. Next there were the frail whom new medical techniques had enabled the hospitals to discharge provided some care could be provided for them, and finally there were the bedridden who might or might not respond to treatment.

The contribution of the Local Authority to the provision of accommodation for the able-bodied elderly has taken several forms. In the first place, as part of the housing programme the Housing Department has built houses for special allocation to old people, not in isolated groups, but as part of the new communities which are being created. Secondly, the Health and Welfare Department has acquired large houses and had them converted into hostels for the elderly. Third, the Corporation has given grants to voluntary organisations engaged in similar work.

These voluntary organisations are many of them long-established, and the kind of provision they make varies from one organisation to another. The Guild of Aid has opened service rooms with cooking facilities where old people can take their own furniture and live in complete independence yet confident that in time of illness the Guild workers will be at hand to help. The Incorporated Glasgow Old Men's Friend Society and Old Women's Home has room for 90 men and 60 women at 81 Rottenrow and 32 cottages for old married couples at Milncroft. The Whiteinch Homes for Old Men and Women have 40 houses, some single apartment and some two apartment. There is a residence for Ladies of Limited Means in Victoria Crescent. In addition the Church of Scotland has eventide homes in the city, and the Salvation Army, the Catholic Church and the Jewish Community all maintain homes for old people. One of the newest developments is the formation of a Housing Association, Glasgow Old People's Homes Ltd., for the purchase and conversion of houses into accommodation for old people.[1]

The problem of providing homes for the able-bodied aged is thus being attacked with initiative and imagination.

The care of the frail and the bedridden presents a problem less easy of solution since the cost in terms of wages and salaries for essential domestic and nursing staff is heavy and recurring. For this reason the provision of this kind of accommodation, which is still insufficient, would appear to be a form of social service which must fall to the

[1] Even more recently (in 1957) the Soroptimists have opened a house for gentlewomen of over 60 whose means are limited.

Health and Welfare Department rather than to the voluntary organisations. Nevertheless the Little Sisters of the Poor take the aged sick of both sexes and all denominations into their home at Royston Hill. The local authority makes provision in several ways. Some of the chronic sick are accommodated at Foresthall, the erstwhile poorhouse. The Department has also opened a hostel in Burnbank Gardens for "frail ambulant" old people. And those inhabitants of Crookston Homes who can no longer look after themselves receive nursing care in the Annexe.

To provide means of social intercourse, clubs for the old have been started since the war in all areas of the city and in the promotion of these the Glasgow Old People's Welfare Committee has been particularly active. This Committee was formed in 1948 on the initiative of the Glasgow Society of Social Service. Primarily it is a co-ordinating body but through its district committees it is able to make an effective contribution to the organisation of local services for old people, particularly by the promotion of clubs and home visitation of the housebound. How pressing was the need to relieve the loneliness of old people can be judged by the fact that within four years of its formation the Committee had started fifty clubs which had a total membership of 6,500. Workers are convinced that there are many who have not yet been reached.[1]

Among the newer postwar services for the aged there are the "meals on wheels" organised by the Women's Voluntary Services, the luncheon clubs organised locally and the Chiropody Service inaugurated by the City of Glasgow Branch, British Red Cross Society. To provide a continuing interest for old people and to enable them to supplement their income, the Guild of Aid has a work centre for women in Coburg Street which produces knitted and woven garments.

Most of the organisations which are sponsoring services for old people arrange annual outings, bus runs, trips down the Clyde, and visits to the circus and to the theatre. Some of the Youth Clubs in the city are encouraging their members to give displays and concerts for old people, who get great enjoyment from these contacts with young folk.

The special needs of old people are brought before the notice of the citizens each year by means of an Old Folks Week which is planned not only to raise money, but also to remind people of the loneliness and even hardship which still exist for many during the last years of life and of the ways in which younger people can contribute towards their mitigation. Old Folks Week is now a national institution but it owes its existence to the imagination of the Glasgow Old People's Welfare Committee to which 50 voluntary organisations are affiliated.

The services for old people in Glasgow show that a high degree of

[1] In October 1957, at the instigation of the Lord Provost, a conference was held in the City Chambers at which it was decided to set up a council to study the two questions of preparation for retirement and the provision of occupational activities for the retired in relation to the economic situation in the city and the social needs of its older inhabitants.

co-operation does exist between local authority and voluntary organisations.

The Handicapped

Prior to 1948 when the local authorities were given new and far wider powers for preparing schemes for the welfare of the handicapped much though by no means all of the responsibility for the welfare of the handicapped had been carried by voluntary organisations such as the Mission to the Outdoor Blind for Glasgow and the West of Scotland (1859), the Mission to the Adult Deaf and Dumb for Glasgow and the west of Scotland (1822), and the Glasgow Cripple Children's League (1899). As specialist organisations these had amassed a great deal of experience of the particular problems of the special group served. There were however groups of handicapped people for whom no special voluntary organisation existed—epileptics for example—and it was apparent that an extension of such services was urgently needed.

This extension could be carried out in two ways. A general service for all handicapped persons could be provided; this is the direction in which the Glasgow Corporation has been developing. It works through the Health and Welfare Department which has already a wealth of general experience of disablement gained during the days of public assistance. Alternatively new specialist organisations could promote the welfare of special groups; and this is the main trend among voluntary organisations. Both methods are being adopted in Glasgow at the present time and close co-operation has been established between the Health and Welfare Department and the new voluntary organisations so engaged.

The Corporation's work in this field has been developed by stages and priority has been given to the after-care service for the pupils of the special schools. Contact is made with every child who leaves the special schools and supervision is provided for as long as necessary. Special care is taken over the placing in employment of these young people, and there is close co-operation with the Youth Employment Service. Handcraft training centres have been opened for boys and girls and arrangements are made for the sale of completed goods. For the home-bound a start has been made in providing employment in the home. Through the Health and Welfare Committee the Corporation is responsible for the Mental Health Services in the city and by a special arrangement with the Regional Hospital Boards the Department's officers undertake the supervision of certified mental patients boarded out under guardianship. Ever since the Blind Persons Act came into force the Local Authority has co-operated with the Outdoor Mission to the Blind and with the Royal Glasgow Asylum for the Blind. At the time of writing the Health and Welfare Committee has just taken over from the former the responsibility for the welfare of the blind within the city.

The new voluntary organisations, such as the Glasgow and West of Scotland Branch of the Scottish Epilepsy Association, are encouraging the handicapped to join so that they can participate directly in the promotion of schemes for their own welfare. The clubs which have been started enable the handicapped to meet regularly with others suffering from similar disabilities for educative, recreational, and occupational activities.

The Glasgow Branch of the British Red Cross Society has also extended its work since the war. Now in addition to the casework service which it has provided for so long for the benefit of disabled ex-service men and women the local branch has started a club for disabled old folk; a therapeutic treatment centre for psycho-neurotic and orthopædic cases and diversional work in hospitals for long-time cases. The Society also has a guide and escort service for those who have to take long journeys by land, sea or air to undergo hospital treatment, and maintains a loan depot of medical equipment.

Children Deprived of a Normal Home

From the time that Hutchesons' Hospital was founded in 1639 it has been recognised in Glasgow that children who have been deprived of a normal home and parental guidance need special care and provision. The early records of the Town Hospital or Poorhouse show considerable expenditure on child welfare during the eighteenth century, including items for boarding out of pauper children. Traditionally the Glasgow public has expressed its sense of responsibility for local children by the provision of municipal services and by voluntary action.

The Poor Law Amendment Act in 1845 placed the responsibility for pauper children on the Parochial Boards, and the problem of their care became one of increasing dimensions as the population of the parishes increased. The creation in 1853 of a Children's Committee by the Parochial Board of the City Parish did not result in any sudden change of policy towards pauper children as it was already customary to board them out. The Committee did however evolve a policy in relation to boarding out, the two main features of which were first that the number of children sent to any one home or community should be limited so that the children could be more easily assimilated and pauperisation minimised: and second that the children should be boarded out in rural areas, as it was believed that "country air would benefit their health, and the thrifty habits of the cottars would help to reform their morals." The records for the year 1875 show that considerable progress had been made in implementing this policy. By that year the majority of the children were boarded out, at the rate of not more than two in any one home. The rural policy was also consistently carried out, so much so, indeed, that their supervision in the remote parts of Scotland became a time-consuming business. By 1875 there was a special inspector for boarded-out children who was instructed to visit each child four times a year and Committee members were expected to undertake an annual inspection of every home.

In spite of the declared policy of the Children's Committee to prevent the concentration of pauper children in any area, such concentration did in fact take place as the rapid growth of Glasgow and the social and economic difficulties of the twentieth century increased the number of children in care. In 1939 the Director of Public Assistance had to report that in one northern parish 50 per cent of the 67 children in the local school were Glasgow children.

By the end of the Second World War when Glasgow, in common with other local authorities, had to set up an independent Children's Department, the city already had a long tradition of child care and the reputation of fitting its children to take their rightful place in society. Nevertheless there have been changes since the new department was established.

Since 1948 there has been a gradual but steady reduction in the number of children boarded out in the remoter parts of Scotland as it is now the policy of the Children's Committee to board out children in areas in which employment can be expected to be available and in which educational and other facilities are adequate. This inevitably is a slow process since homes given up in distant places have to be replaced by others in more suitable areas and good foster homes are not easy to find. The importance now attached to boarding out all members of a large family together adds to the difficulty of the problem.

When the boarded-out children reach working age many of them return to Glasgow and fresh accommodation has to be found for them in the city. Comparatively few are ready to live independently in lodgings even under the supervision of the Children's Officer. Some are placed in hostels run by voluntary organisations and the Children's Committee has its own hostel for boys.

For children who are not suitable for boarding out the Committee has opened several homes since its inception. On the whole these homes accommodate smaller groups of children than did the older homes, though some still have over 40 children. Most of the new homes take children of either sex and two take children of all ages so that the large family coming into care need not be broken up. As the number of vacancies in local authority homes is increased less use is made than formerly of the homes run by voluntary organisations, and the small but regular reduction in the number of children placed in the care of voluntary organisations each year suggests that this is a matter of considered policy.

In the annual reports of the Children's Department it is recorded that the number of children coming into care is no longer increasing as it tended to do immediately after 1948.[1] More time is now being given to preventive work as it is realised that the child who can stay in his own home where the standard of child care has been improved has a

1 The number of cases in care and under supervision has fallen steadily from 3,202 in 1950 to 2,545 in 1955. See Appendix, Table 159.

better chance of full development than has the child who has had to be separated from his parents because of their incompetence. This policy of prevention does inevitably require generous staffing since very close supervision may have to be maintained over a long period, but it must be remembered that the annual salary of an additional qualified officer who can give home supervision to more than four children per annum is less than the cost of taking four children into care for a year.

Apart from the special work of the Children's Department, the Health and Welfare Department through its maternity and child welfare visitors is in touch with every home in which there are young children. Much of the health visitor's time is devoted to the less efficient mothers. The Education Department through its school welfare officers and school attendance officers is in touch with many of the emotionally and spiritually poorer homes in which breakdown is liable to take place.

The Church of Scotland Social Service Department, The Salvation Army, and the Roman Catholic Church all provide residential care for orphans, deserted children and the children of unmarried mothers who are unable to maintain their offspring. The Lochburn Home, the National Vigilance Home in Renfrew Street and the Women's Help Committee Hostel all take older girls who are unready or unfit by reason of age or personality to live in lodgings on their own. Eastpark Home for Infirm Children makes a very important provision for children who because they are suffering from long-term or chronic disability cannot stay at home.

In Glasgow, as in other cities in Scotland, the Royal Scottish Society for the Prevention of Cruelty to Children is untiring in its efforts to improve the standard of the less satisfactory homes and to protect children from ill-treatment and neglect. At the time of writing (1955) this Society has just appointed women officers in Glasgow whose work will be with the less competent mothers, whose failure is so frequently due not to the absence of strong affection for their children but to frustration, tiredness or lack of common sense.

When a child is deprived of a normal home he is subjected to emotional tensions with which he may be unable to deal alone and he may require psychological or psychiatric treatment. The Glasgow Education Authority has its own child guidance clinics, which are available for the treatment of children from normal homes as well as of those whose family life has broken down. In addition there is the voluntary child guidance clinic established by the late Sister Marie Hilda of the Order of Notre Dame. The Notre Dame Child Guidance Clinic, in which play therapy was pioneered, is open to children of all denominations and is staffed by psychiatrists, psychologists, psychiatric social workers, a family case worker, speech and play therapists and a remedial teacher. In this clinic the treatment is based on the assumption that the child is not only "an individual but also a member of a family group and of wider communities at school or in leisure." This approach is of very special value to the deprived child who has to build up a substitute for the family group which has disintegrated around him.

All this effort, statutory and voluntary, requires co-ordination. In Glasgow, the Children's Officer has been appointed Co-ordinating Officer and in addition to personal contact between the different workers he arranges periodic meetings for representatives of all the departments and voluntary organisations concerned with child care. At these meetings matters of general importance and of policy are discussed. In the final count however co-ordination depends on the casework co-operation of the workers who are in actual touch with the children and their families. It is a personal matter for the officers concerned rather than one of administrative machinery. It demands considerable freedom of action for the caseworkers rather than departmental directives so that by confidential discussion of individual cases a common policy can be agreed in every case which is on the books of more than one department.

Young People

Youth Work in Glasgow has a long tradition and many of the older organisations have strong links with the Churches or with the Missions. For example the Glasgow Foundry Boys Religions Society was founded in 1865 "to promote the religious, educational and social welfare of lads and girls employed in all descriptions of labour throughout the city." The purpose of this youth work was constructive and the early youth workers, like their successors of the present day, strove by means of the recreational activities which they provided to educate for responsible citizenship and a realisation of spiritual values.

An organisation which exemplifies this attitude towards youth work is the Boys' Brigade, whose founder, William A. Smith, came to live in Glasgow in 1869 and started his Young Men's Society as a sunday school attached to the North Woodside Road Mission.[1] William Smith was the son of a soldier. He joined the Lanarkshire Rifle Volunteers soon after his arrival in Glasgow and he had a profound admiration for considerate discipline.

The Boys of the North Woodside Road area were "tough" and Smith discovered that "much of the time which should have been given to teaching was wasted in efforts to secure order and attention." Smith understood his boys and recognised that they were full of energy for which the Woodside Road district provided insufficient outlets. He therefore set himself to solve the problem of directing this energy "into the right channels" so that "the boys will enjoy themselves far more than when running wild; and instead of becoming hooligans and loafers they will gain manliness; and more than that, they may be led to the service of their Master."

[1] This was a Mission of the Free College Church, whose minister was then the Rev. George Reith, father of Sir John Reith, the first Director-General of the B.B.C.

To this end boys of 12 and over were to be formed into a " Brigade " and taught elementary drill and physical exercises. Obedience, punctuality and cleanliness were to be insisted upon. The mission authorities were dubious about this new approach to sunday school teaching but Smith was allowed to go ahead and the original company of the Boys' Brigade was formed. The Boys' Brigade is no longer a local organisation. In Scotland, England and Wales and Ireland there are 2,815 companies with an individual membership of over 80,000; in addition there is an overseas strength of 18,000 in 30 different countries. The junior section, the Life Boys, is almost equally numerous. Glasgow is still the strongest B.B. centre in Scotland with over 250 companies and a membership of 9,000 boys, a membership which is only exceeded in Greater London. The objects of the B.B. remain unchanged and are still summarised as " The advancement of Christ's Kingdom among boys and the promotion of habits of Obedience, Reverence, Discipline, Self-Respect, and all that tends towards true Christian Manliness."

At the present time much youth work has still a direct association with the churches. In two different parishes the Church of Scotland has sponsored youth centres. At the Pearce Institute, Govan Old Church has a centre where club activities are provided for adults and old people as well as for adolescents. St. Francis-in-the-East has founded Church House Community Centre in Bridgeton.

The encouragement of clubs among the youth of their own congregations has been a marked feature of the churches in Glasgow in recent years, not only in the older districts, but significantly in the new housing estates. In the Church of Scotland at the present time some 15,500 of its boys and 14,600 of its girls[1] are members of uniformed groups (like the Boys' Brigade and Girl Guides) and some 1.570 boys and 1,590 girls of non-uniformed groups. In the Congregational Union a total of over 1,200 boys and girls are in uniformed and 2,170 in non-uniformed clubs. In the Methodist Churches there are some 2,400 members of young men's and young women's societies; in the United Free Churches over 2,000; and there are smaller numbers in several of the smaller denominations. The Roman Catholic Church has two full-time clubs, the Sacred Heart Youth Club in Bridgeton and St. Aloysius Youth Club in Rose Street; and St. Peter's Youth House in Myrtle Street is under the auspices of the Episcopal Church in Scotland. The Jewish Community supports the Jewish Lads' Brigade and Club in Butterbiggins Road. Others with a definitely religious background are the six centres and the hostel for students and apprentices run by the Y.M.C.A. The Y.M.C.A. has also its own fully equipped theatre, the Lyric (formerly the Royalty) in Sauchiehall Street, first used mainly for concerts but now, with the growth of amateur dramatic companies, more as an ordinary theatre.

Much of the motive force of the Church of Scotland Clubs has come from Community House, which was founded by the Iona Youth Trust after the War. Working in Community House there is a specialist

[1] See Chapter 22 (The Churches).

Glasgow Corporation Baths Department

Plate 20. OLD VIEW OF GLASGOW GREEN

Showing first public wash-house dating from 1742

Scottish Tourist Board

Plate 21. AN INTERNATIONAL FOOTBALL MATCH AT HAMPDEN PARK

The Glasgow Herc

Plate 22. HIKERS HOMEWARD BOUND FROM LOCH LOMOND

staff who organise courses of study on subjects relating to work among young people. Community House provides a meeting place for leaders and older members of youth organisations and there is a chapel, a library, and a cafeteria.

At the present time not all the voluntary youth work has a direct association with the churches or other religious bodies but though the individual clubs may be non-sectarian, in the voluntary youth movement there is emphasis on the importance of spiritual and moral values.

In Glasgow many of the voluntary clubs are affiliated according to sex, either to the Glasgow and West of Scotland Association of Girls' Clubs, or to the Glasgow Union of Boys' Clubs. The work of these two organisations is advisory and co-ordinating. Both have a holiday centre for the use of members. Many of the clubs affiliated to these two organisations are run entirely by voluntary leaders and helpers and are open one or two nights a week; others are open nightly and provide a wide range of activities catering for many different age groups.

The Hew McCowan Club in Shakespeare Street is sponsored by the Hew McCowan Trust. This club works towards the strengthening of the family and there are therefore groups for very young children and for young mothers as well as the usual youth groups. The active co-operation of members' fathers is sought though it has proved very difficult to keep a fathers' group in being. Also in Maryhill there is the Maryhill Youth Club, which has made a reputation for itself by the high standard which it has achieved with its entertainments and by the holidays abroad which it has organised. In Anderston the University Settlement has clubs for young people of both sexes and a feature of its accommodation is a well-equipped café decorated by murals executed by students of the Art School.

With the great and growing activity on the part of voluntary associations it is perhaps not realised that from the point of view of numbers the Local Education Authority is now undertaking directly the larger share of the youth work in the city and is almost entirely responsible for the development of the work in the new communities which have grown so rapidly since the war. Much of the work in the new communities is based on the schools, some of which are already opened most nights during the week for the benefit of youth or adult organisations.

In some areas however churches or church halls have now been built and in them the youth work of the churches is being started and the voluntary movement is beginning to penetrate into the new communities. In all districts, both old and new, there is a shortage of voluntary helpers and trained club leaders and this shortage is undoubtedly handicapping the development of the voluntary movement and leaving to the Education Committee the main responsibility for extending the youth service.

The Corporation's policy on the Service of Youth as set out in the Progress Report of the Education Department for the years 1950-2 is twofold:

(1) To assist voluntary organisations to extend their provision for youth and
(2) To set up, where necessary, clubs and centres for young people who are not attached to voluntary organisations.

In order to implement the first part of this policy the Education Committee has made grants to individual clubs and it has helped others by providing specialist instructors or giving the use of Corporation premises. As to the second, the Education Authority has set up and staffed its own youth centres and play centres. In order to train the staff of these centres the Authority organises an annual training course which is attended by youth workers from voluntary as well as local authority clubs.

The Education Committee does not confine its work in connection with informal education to youth groups only. Five Community Centres have been opened catering for all age groups, and in the new housing estates parents' clubs have been started. These clubs are based on the schools and they serve as recreational groups for the adult population and provide a link between the school and the parents in the new areas where community life for the resettled families is being established slowly and sometimes painfully.

The Sick

The care of the sick whether in hospitals or at home has been a State Service since 1948. The number of hospitals supported by voluntary effort has been radically reduced, but voluntary effort has not been entirely disassociated from the hospital movement. Within the hospitals the Glasgow Hospitals Auxiliary Association is doing much to provide comforts and amenities for patients and staff beyond the minimum supplied by the Regional Hospital Boards. In carrying out this work the Assocation is in touch with such organisations as the W.V.S. and the British Red Cross Society, both of which are interested in the provision of such amenities as ward trolley shops and libraries, while the Glasgow Branch of the British Red Cross Society provides diversional and occupational activities for long-term ex-service cases in hospital.

The Social Service Departments in the hospitals provide another outlet for voluntary action within the hospitals since the almoners in these departments require funds to help cases which are not entirely covered by statutory or other sources. These medical social caseworkers are dealing with the difficulties of individual patients, and the general rules of eligibility, which are bound to govern the administration of the National Insurance and National Assistance schemes, do not always make adequate provision for the very individual problems which are brought to the Almoner's Office.

Thus voluntary organisations are finding needs both new and old for their initiative and goodwill within the National Health Scheme. Much of the work undertaken by the voluntary organisations may seem unspectacular to the outsider but to the patient in the wards the trolley which comes round with the things he needs to buy, and the regular supply of books, can provide an interest which is as much a part of his treatment as skilled nursing care, while the money which the almoner may be able to provide to meet a pressing debt may give the peace of mind which the Health Service alone could not provide.

For the after-care of these patients, the hospitals make considerable use of the voluntary Convalescent Homes, of which there are many, both old and new, within the city and within easy reach of it. Three of the homes which are closely associated with Glasgow are now nearing their centenary. The Glasgow and District Coast Homes, instituted in 1866, have a Convalescent Home in Saltcoats open for adults and children, with 114 beds. The Glasgow Kilmun Convalescent Home was opened in 1867 and is managed by the Directors of Glasgow Abstainers' Union. The Home provides accommodation for 210 patients and there is an annexe for mothers and children. The Glasgow and West of Scotland Convalescent Seaside Homes were founded in 1869; both adults and children are admitted to the home at Dunoon, which claims to be the largest of its kind in Scotland, having accommodation for 206 adults and 30 children. The Co-operative Convalescent Homes Ltd. has four homes open to subscribers. The Guild of Aid, as one of its many activities, runs a home at Callander for women in need of rest after illness. Moore Convalescent Home for Nurses provides convalescent care for nurses associated professionally with Glasgow institutions.

For children the Glasgow Poor Children's Fresh Air Fund and Cripple Children's League has two homes, one in Maybole and one in Dunoon. St. Vincent de Paul Society has a country home for children at Langbank.

The maintenance of a convalescent home at the present time by a voluntary organisation is a difficult financial undertaking because of the annually recurring charge for domestic and nursing staff. One of the tasks undertaken by the Glasgow and West of Scotland Hospital Sunday Fund, which is supported by 20 denominations and religious bodies, is to help towards the upkeep of convalescent homes, though the homes depend as well on the support of their own subscribers.

Seamen

As a great port and shipbuilding centre Glasgow's association with the sea is close. Many Glasgow men go to sea and even more seamen come to Glasgow. One expects to find therefore that most of the national organisations for the welfare of seamen have offices in the city and this is in fact the case. In addition there are a number of local voluntary organisations for seamen, all of them long-established.

The oldest is the Glasgow Seamen's Friend Society, which was founded in 1822 for the religious, moral and social welfare of all sailors who visit the Port of Glasgow. The Society still maintains an Institute in the Broomielaw and a Bethel in Eaglesham Street. Out of the Glasgow Seamen's Friend Society there has grown up a Ladies' Auxiliary which undertakes the work of visiting all widows and dependents of merchant seamen whose homes are in Glasgow and helps with "grants of money, practical advice and sympathy."

In 1857 the first Glasgow Sailors' Home was opened; now there are three hostels, including one for Asiatic seamen. Married quarters are provided at Atlantic House in York Street.

The Glasgow Aged Seamen's Relief Fund is now over fifty years old and still gives relief to old, infirm and disabled seamen.

The Forces

During the Second World War Glasgow had the reputation of being the most hospitable large town in Britain. Many of the voluntary organisations which were not essentially service or ex-service organisations responded quickly to the new needs of troops on the move and troops away from home and opened canteens and hostels to supplement the private hospitality of the citizens. During the ten years since the end of the war the needs have changed and although sailors' hostels and the Soldiers' Home are part of the permanent voluntary social provision of the city the continuing need has been primarily for casework for the families of service, ex-service, and disabled ex-service men, backed by adequate financial resources to meet applications for material relief.

The Sailors', Soldiers' and Airmen's Families Association maintains a full-time office in the city for the benefit of the families of men and women of Glasgow serving in the forces at home and overseas. The City of Glasgow Branch of the Red Cross Society provides a full-time casework service for ex-service men and women who are suffering from ill-health. The Forces Help Society, which works in close co-operation with the Society of Social Service, is responsible for the welfare of service and ex-service men and their families, while the Ex-Services Mental Welfare Society specialises in work with those suffering from war psychoses and neuroses.

Many of the Scottish Regiments have local associations or branches, including of course the H.L.I., and there are also branches of the Airborne Forces Security fund, the Royal Artillery Association and the Royal Engineers Old Comrades Association.

As the family casework organisation in the city the Society of Social Service comes into contact with many families of ex-service men and the Mutual Registration of Assistance provides administrative machinery for securing adequate aid to individual families without the overlapping which could easily take place in a city which supports so many service and ex-service organisations.

The Homeless

Once Glasgow was caught up in the Industrial Revolution the population grew rapidly. Newcomers in search of work crowded into the city and found a space to sleep in the small and already overcrowded dwellings in the back courts and narrow lanes.

There was no control whatever of the letting of lodgings. Lodging houses (" flea barracks ") were kept by those in search of " easy money," who for 2d. to 4d. a night packed the sick and well, the drunk and the sober, men and women, adults and children, into small, squalid, airless rooms. Disease was rife, especially typhus because of the dirt and vermin, cholera from polluted water, and fever which was passed from one resident to another, as ventilation was non-existent and blankets were never disinfected.

The Glasgow Police Act of 1843 provided powers to license lodging houses, of which 489 were officially listed in 1846, although 600-700 actually existed;[1] but the regulations proved abortive. The first effective step to improve the standard of lodgings was taken by a group of responsible citizens who, with Lord Provost Hastie, started the Model Lodging Association. The Association rented a house in Mitchell Street in 1847 and followed this up by buying property in Greendyke Street, McAlpine Street, and Carrick Street, with the object of providing tolerable conditions and setting a standard which would be a challenge to private owners.

Under the City Improvements Act of 1866, which was passed for the purpose of clearing the most congested districts of the city, in which many of the lodging houses were situated, there was set up the City Improvements Trust which accepted the responsibility of providing lodging houses. The Trust opened the first municipal lodging houses in 1871, one in the Drygate for men and one in East Russell Street for women, and took over the Model Lodging Association's houses in the cleared areas. The Houses opened by the Trust were run in accordance with the regulations made for the control of lodging houses by the Glasgow Police Act of 1866, and a better standard was gradually enforced throughout the city after the appointment of the first Sanitary Inspector in 1870. By 1896 there were 18 of these " Model " Lodging Houses, including one family house for widows or widowers with children.

Glasgow was still however an overcrowded city and lodgings were at a premium, a factor which continued to depress the standard of many lodgings which were run for profit. In 1897 new bye-laws were drawn up which, with small amendments, remain in force to-day. The most important of these are that a lodging house keeper must produce

[1] Laidlaw: *Glasgow Common Lodging Houses and the people living in them.* (1956).

a certificate of good character, all lodging houses must be registered annually and none can open without registration, adequate cooking and washing facilities and toilet accommodation must be provided, drains must be kept in good repair, good discipline must be maintained and the sexes segregated, and illness must be notified and bedding fumigated. In 1912 an additional bye-law was made prohibiting the admission of lads under 18 and this regulation was extended to girls in 1922.

The strict enforcement of these bye-laws weeded out the worst of the remaining lodging houses and the general improvement of standard was encouraged by the opening of Workmen's Hotels during the early years of the present century. These hotels were slightly more expensive and rather more comfortable and competition with them put the lodging house keepers on their toes.

In 1913 lodging house accommodation reached its peak (14,000 beds) in Glasgow. Thereafter there was a gradual decline in demand, and the keener competition for custom brought improved standards. More comfortable beds, enclosed single cubicles, a chair, a wardrobe, were offered one by one as attractions, and thick netting was put over the cubicles to enable sleepers to remove their boots and outer garments at night without the fear that these articles would be missing by the morning. A recreation room was an added attraction. Some model lodging houses provided hot water and central heating and many had shops at which the residents, usually known as "modellers," could purchase food in small quantities. All these improvements added to costs. At the same time progressive welfare legislation, and the gradual reduction of overcrowding in the city as a whole, were reducing the number of their clientele. Lodging house keeping thus became less profitable.

At the present time there are 19 lodging houses in the city, 15 for men and 4 for women. Six of these are owned by the Corporation, three by the Salvation Army and ten are privately owned. In most of them the residents cook their own food, the Salvation Army houses providing the exception. Charges range from 1s. 6d. to 2s. 0d. a night for men and 1s. 0d. to 1s. 6d. for women.

The demand for accommodation in lodging houses is still declining, but the need for them has not disappeared. The "modellers" are mainly people without family ties, many of them drift from one lodging house to another, and three quarters of them are sick, retired or unemployed. Most of them are over forty. Prison sentences are not unknown among them but are ignored, since the one rule observed by all is to "mind one's own business." This does not promote friendliness, and modellers tend to be more than usually self-contained and to include in their ranks many social misfits who could not live elsewhere. Drunkenness is prevalent but is not excessive as chronic alcoholics, trouble makers and methylated spirit drinkers tend to prefer the brick kilns where no charge is made and no resident superintendent interferes with their liberty of action, though a visit from the police is a recurring hazard.

In a hundred years the physical standard of the lodging houses has been improved. The flea barracks have been replaced by the reasonably hygienic barracks of the present, in which the occupants are moved round according to the time of day to ensure that all rooms are adequately cleaned. But except for the work of the Lodging House Mission, started by the Presbytery early in the century, little is yet done for the social and spiritual welfare of the residents, who tend to be very largely people apart from the community as a whole, friendless and too often hopeless.

Conclusion

The changes of the last one hundred years have created new problems for those who administer the social services.

The number and scope of the services have increased and there is now a need for improved co-ordination. Glasgow is aware of this problem. In 1954 the University and the Corporation jointly sponsored a conference, which was held at Kilmacolm, so that the matter could be fully and frankly discussed. This conference has been followed by further meetings and by Extra-Mural courses and the latter have provided a meeting place for the field-workers of many organisations and departments and has resulted in an interchange of opinions and ideas. In addition there is in Glasgow an Association of Social Workers which is open to all who are engaged in full-time social work and which holds monthly meetings throughout the winter. The Children's Officer has been designated Co-ordinating Officer for all the services which make provision for children deprived of a normal home, and he arranges meetings at which all the organisations engaged in this work are represented. In spite of these provisions the problem of co-ordination has not been fully solved: nevertheless there is an awareness of it and of its importance, for without good co-ordination the citizen is unable to benefit to the full from the services which the city provides.

Because our social services are now highly developed both the local authority services and the voluntary organisations are able to concentrate more and more on the individual. This has caused a demand for more professional caseworkers for both preventive and remedial casework.

This demand for more caseworkers has itself created a grave problem for the voluntary organisations since it increases administrative expenses at a time when it is difficult to maintain even the existing income. Effective casework must always take more time than the general relief work which was characteristic of the last century and the caseload which any one professional worker can carry is limited. Thus the agencies which are doing casework may not be able to show either a large number of cases dealt with nor large amounts of money spent on relief. Their work is the prevention of social breakdown and the re-establishment of those families which have collapsed under the stress of modern life. Thus the citizen of Glasgow is gradually becoming used to requests from voluntary organisations for financial support so that more professional workers can be employed for the individual and personal work which is now so essential.

Chapter 22

THE CHURCHES

JOHN HIGHET

INTRODUCTION

PRACTICALLY everyone knows of Glasgow's reputation for bad weather, slums, razor gangs, and the friendliness of its people. The first is not wholly deserved, the second and third may be somewhat exaggerated; and wave after wave of visiting servicemen of other nationalities testified during the Second World War to the fourth. But has the city, like the country whose commercial capital it is, a reputation for "churchmindedness"? It is not the commonest of the attributes conventionally ascribed to Clydeside's metropolis.

Whether this is an injustice to Glasgow is a matter that can in the end be settled only subjectively. But subjective judgment is not one whit absolved from the obligation to base itself on such relevant facts as can be assembled. To present at least some of the facts concerning the religious life of Glasgow is the purpose of this chapter.

Whatever may be said, at the end of the day, by way of verdict on Glasgow's Christian denominations, it is unlikely that anyone will complain of lack of variety: indeed, the fact that so many of the components of the Church Ecumenical have a foothold within the city may well be thought to be the chief feature of its ecclesiastical life. Its religious groups, numbering over 30, range numerically from large to small; in doctrine from Fundamentalism to a moderate Modernism; in type of government from loosely knit gatherings enjoying complete local autonomy, through democratic communities linked by a national system of graduated representative courts, to component units of extranational associations varying from the lightly to the tightly organised.

This number and diversity makes any attempt to describe the city's churches severally and in detail an impossible task in the space available. Here our interest is chiefly in aspects of the city's churches *qua* social institutions. Even so, the problem of covering that ground in the space of a chapter is still formidable, and our account is unavoidably incomplete and selective. No significance should be attached to the allocation of space to the different bodies or to the number of words devoted to this or that topic: neither is to be taken as indicating the writer's idea of their relative importance.

In the following section we shall review the city's Christian denominations, and in the next two discuss, respectively, membership and attendance. Subsequent sections give an account of recent evangelistic activities and briefly review the non-Christian religious groups in the city. In the final section a little is said about some of the matters a statistical emphasis is apt to ignore. For it is freely admitted that the sort of approach attempted in this chapter leaves many, and almost certainly the most important, aspects of a community's religious life out of account. A word is said on this issue in our concluding section; meantime the point may reasonably be made that quantitative aspects have been astonishingly neglected by observers not merely in recent years but over recent decades, and even as only part of the picture they carry their own interest.

The Christian Denominations

Information on a number of points has been gathered for 23 of the city's Christian denominations—the 23 listed in the Table of Membership (Table CL). It has been thought best (in order to economise in space) to present this information in the form of a Synopsis. In this, Synopsis A, the order of treatment corresponds to that in which the denominations are set out in the Table of Membership (Table CL): starting with the non-Roman Catholic denominations,[1] it deals first with the Presbyterian Churches, next with the Episcopal Church, then with the Methodist Church and the larger Independent "Federations," and next again with a group varied in doctrine and organisation and brought together (in Table CL) under the comprehensive head "Others." This classification is not put forward as other than broad and general and no implications should be read into it. The group "Others" includes, for example, some small denominations which, like the Churches of Christ, the Unitarian Church, and the Assemblies of God, can no doubt be regarded as "independent churches," but it is convenient for our present purpose, and in particular from the point of view of tabular lay-out, to place them with the newer denominations, the Pentecostal churches and the other bodies grouped under "Others."[2] Finally—and again as a matter of tabular convenience—comes the Roman Catholic Church.

At the time of the gathering of the data for this chapter six Presbyterian denominations were represented in the city; but in May, 1956, the three Glasgow congregations of one of these bodies, the United Original Secession Church, joined with the majority of U.O.S. congregations in Scotland in acceding to the Church of Scotland. This event has reawakened interest in the very fact—as puzzling to many church folk as it is to those non-churchgoers who are aware of it—that there is a group of small Presbyterian bodies holding themselves apart from

[1] This term, which for convenience will frequently be shortened in the pages that follow to "non-Roman," is preferred by many churchmen to the more lay term "Protestant."

[2] In this chapter no attempt has been made at a definitive or technical use of such terms as "denomination," "group" or "sect."

the Established Church (the Church of Scotland). How this comes about is a story much too complicated to recount here.[1] But it may serve some purpose simply to mention the dates of the various secessions from the Church of Scotland. The Reformed Presbyterian Church claims continuity with those " Dissenting Covenanters " who refused, in 1689-90, to enter the Church of Scotland of the Revolution Settlement. The United Original Secession Church, dating in that form from 1852, claimed to be the direct ecclesiastical descendants of Ebenezer Erskine and the other " Seceding Fathers " of 1733. The Free Presbyterian Church came into existence in 1893, formed by a group that severed connection with the then Free Church (of 1843 origin). In 1900 the Free Church joined the United Presbyterian Church (whose origins went back to 1847 and the re-uniting by devious routes of a number of secession groups) to form the (original) United Free Church.[2] But a minority stood apart from this 1900 union and retained the name " Free Church " (familiarly, the " Wee Frees "). To-day's Free Church is this body in continuance. A majority of the United Free Church as constituted in 1900 returned to the main Presbyterian stream by uniting with the Church of Scotland in 1929; but a minority holding by the Voluntary principle stood apart and constituted themselves the United Free Church (Continuing). In 1934 the terminal word was dropped from the title; nonetheless the U.F. Church of to-day is the 1929 " dissenting " minority in continuance.

Thus the six Scottish Presbyterian churches of 23 May 1956 became five as from 24 May, when the General Assembly of the Church of Scotland received back the Original Secession Church. Whether this will lead the way to further accessions to the main stream is for the future to tell, but it must be borne in mind that the Original Secession Church, regarding itself as " part of the Established Church " (which it referred to as the " Mother Church ") *" in a state of secession,"* was always the most likely of the five small bodies to go back.

The great majority of the churches reported on in the Synopsis have one interesting sociological feature in common: within their membership women out-number men. This applies to the Church of Scotland, the U.F., F.P., R.P., and Methodist Churches, to the Congregationalists and the Baptists, the Churches of Christ, the Latter-Day Saints, the Seventh-Day Adventists, the New Church, the Assemblies of God, the Elim Church, and the Unitarian Church; and it may well apply to some of the others who did not submit information on this head. The extent of female predominance varies from a slight majority in, for example, the cases of the Latter-Day Saints and the New Church

1 A historical sketch and an account of the principles distinguishing the Presbyterian bodies one from another is to be found—along with an account of the doctrinal and organisational features of most of the denominations mentioned in this chapter—in the author's *The Churches in Scotland To-day* (1950), pp. 4-30.

2 The year before the union of 1900, there were 100 congregations of the Established Church in the city, 95 of the Free Church and 96 of the United Presbyterian Church.

to a 3-to-1 ratio in the case of the Reformed Presbyterian Church. The only recorded case of an estimated balance of the sexes is that of the Assemblies of Christian Brethren. But however it may be in terms of numbers, in almost all the denominations under review men are more active than women in the administration of the affairs of the local fellowship. Only in a few cases, indeed, is any alternative constitutionally a possibility. The United Free Church, for example, admits women to all offices within the church, not excluding the ministry; in the case of the Latter-Day Saints, women can hold practically every office except those demanding priesthood; a few churches in the Congregational Union have women ministers while another few have women office-bearers; and there are women office-bearers in some churches in the Baptist Union. In the majority of cases, however, tradition continues to restrict the use of female talents and resources in the higher conduct of the affairs of the church; and there is evidence of growing dissatisfaction—and not wholly among women members—with this situation. In the majority of cases where women predominate in the membership they are not thought to be, proportionately to their numbers, any more regular than male members in attendance at public worship; but exceptions may be the Baptists, the Spiritualist churches and the Elim Church.

Although the question of the social class composition of the churches' following requires fuller investigation, available information suggests this broad classification: predominantly middle-class and lower-middle-class—the Church of Scotland, the Episcopal Church, the Reformed Presbyterian, the Churches of Christ, the Latter-Day Saints, the Society of Friends, and the Unitarians; predominantly upper-working-class, but with a professional sprinkling—the Methodists, the Congregationalists, and the Christian Brethren; mainly working-class —the Roman Catholic Church, the Free Presbyterian, the Baptists, the Church of the Nazarene, the Assemblies of God and the Elim Church; "mixed" in social background—the United Free Church, the U.O.S. Church, the Seventh-Day Adventists, the New Church, and the Christadelphians.

Synopsis A

CHRISTIAN CHURCHES IN GLASGOW

SUMMARY OF DATA

NOTE: This Synopsis summarises data about the 23 Christian denominations in the city listed in the Table of Membership (Table CL). Other information about some of them is given, more generally, in other parts of this chapter.

Other religious bodies, Christian and non-Christian, exist in the city, but for reasons mentioned in the text little information concerning them has been forthcoming.

Key to Symbols

(a) No. of churches in city.
(b) No. of members in city.
(c) Sunday Schools: No./Enrolment/No. of teachers.
(d) Bible Classes: No./Enrolment/No. of teachers.
(e) Other Youth statistics.
(f) No. of vacant charges.
(g) Minimum stipend/No. of charges on M.S.
(h) Congregational Givings/Givings per member (approx.).
(j) Baptisms.
(k) Historical date—e.g. date of first church in city.
(l) Other data.

Where no year is given, the information relates mostly to 1955.

A dash (—) following a symbol indicates that no information is available or that the item is not applicable.

Church of Scotland

(a) 217. (b) 171,213. (c) 215/46,520/1,280 men and 6,890 women (1953). (d) 196/11,120/— (1953). (e) 15,560 boys and 14,600 girls in uniformed organisations; 1,570 boys and 1,590 girls in organisations without uniforms (14-18 years); 1,600 in Societies of Young Men and just over 2,000 in Societies of Young Women; about 550 male and about 60 female leaders of the various organisations (1953). (f) 20 (June 1956). (g) £600 with manse or £675 without manse/53. (h) £530,914 ("Christian Liberality")/£3 2s. (j) 8,131 (including 1,017 adult baptisms). (k) See text. (l) An account of the considerable evangelistic activity in which the church has been engaged in Glasgow is given on pp. 734ff. Social welfare activity is engaged in to varying extent by a number of congregations, but the bulk of the Church's substantial contribution to this aspect of the city's life is made through central agencies and departments such as the Social Service Committee, and to these (as to other Church purposes) the Glasgow congregations devote a proportion of their financial givings. For a description of the Church of Scotland's Social Service (which has been described as "the largest and most varied of any single organisation in Scotland") both in general and as applying to Glasgow, see the author's *The Churches in Scotland To-day*, pp. 112-119.

United Free Church

(a) 17. (b) 4,895. (c) 17/2,243/360. (d) 15/272/—. (e) 338 in 20 "organisations for young men and young women"; 1,744 in 52 other groups officially described as "young people's organisations" (such as the Boys' Brigade). (f) One, with 2 other charges being attended to by lay missioners in training. (g) £500 + manse (1956)/10. (h) £20,925/£4 6s. (j) 293 (including 57 adult baptisms). (k) See text. (l) Takes part in local and wider evangelistic campaigns so far as resources allow; took part in the All-Scotland—Billy Graham Crusade (see below).

Free Church

(a) 8. (b) 2,502 (including adherents). (c) and (d) in 1952, 8 Sunday Schools and 6 Bible Classes had 478 pupils and 50 teachers. (e) 70 members of youth organisations. (f) 2 (1956). (g) —/—. (h) £12,216 (1952)/£4 14s. (j) 46 (1952). (k) See text. (l) Evangelistic activities to the extent resources allow tend to take the form more of inter-congregational united campaigns than of association with other denominations. The Free Church did, however, associate itself with the All-Scotland—Billy Graham Crusade. Individual congregations maintain benevolent funds for relief of hardship and support and co-operate with a number of organisations engaged in promoting social and spiritual welfare.

Free Presbyterian Church

(a) 1. (b) 686 (including adherents). (c) 1/40/2. (d) Nil. (e) No youth organisations. (f) —. (g) —/—. (h) —/—. (j) Annual average 25. (k) See text. (l) 4 services (one in Gaelic) are held each Sunday, and on first Sunday of month a service is held in Pollok (a new housing estate). Average attendances at Sunday Services: Gaelic (morning) 120 (20 aged under 20); English (morning) 45 (10); English (afternoon) 70 (10); English (evening) 450 (60). Allowing for those attending more than one of these services, about 580 are estimated to attend at least one service each Sunday. Within its limited resources the congregation makes its contribution to the relief of want, distributing to the poor of the city about £170 annually.

United Original Secession Church

(a) 3 in 1955: on 24 May 1956 these (with other Secession congregations in Scotland) re-united with the Church of Scotland. (b) 353. (c) and (d) 2 congregations have 13 teachers instructing 54 Sunday School and 14 Bible Class pupils. (e) One congregation has a youth club of 19 members, a Children's Club of 40, and 41 in two other youth organisations. (f) to (j) —. (k) See text. (l) On average 225 attend at least one service.

Reformed Presbyterian Church

(a) 1. (b) 130. (c) to (j) —. (k) See text. (l) About 70 attend regularly.

Episcopal Church in Scotland

(a) 25. (b) 6,641. (c) 26/1,776/130 (1953). (d) 21/487/— (1953). (e) —. (f) 4 Assistant Curates and one Curate-in-charge required (at end of 1953). (g) To be £504 + a house or house allowance for 1957; in 1953 only six clergy stipends were above the then minimum of £425 etc. (h) £28,145 (1953)/£4 4s. (j) 334 (including adults) (1953). (k) There has been a congregation in Glasgow since at least 1750, the date of the building of the chapel St. Andrew-by-the-Green. By the end of the nineteenth century there were 23 churches in the city. In 1947 there were 33. (l) At the end of 1953 there were, in addition to the Bishop, 12 Rectors, 3 Priests-in-charge, 7 Curates-in-charge, 8 Assistant Curates, 2 Supernumeraries (and Hospital Chaplains), and 1 Chaplain to Missions to Seamen. While the Church does not appear to do much evangelistic activity on its own, it has in recent years been associated in varying degree with inter-denominational campaigns. Through the Glasgow Diocesan Social Service Board, the Church engages in a fair amount of social work in Glasgow: for example, 2 chaplains and a woman worker carry out prison visitation; the Mission to Seamen (mainly dependent on the Episcopal Church although supported by workers from other denominations) caters for the spiritual and material welfare of seamen of all denominations and creeds in the Clyde area. In addition, there are hospital and student chaplains, and chaplains to the Actors' Church Union and to St. John's Guild for the Blind.

Methodist Church

(a) 17. (b) 4,167. (c) 17/2,634/478 (1953). (d) 15/471/— (1953). (e) 2,428 in youth organisations. (f) 2 (1953). (g) £430 (1955-56) at top of scale (i.e., for over 20 years' service) with an additional £20 for Superintendent Ministers (i.e., those in charge of a group of churches working together in a given area)/—. (h) £19,720 (1953)/£4 16s. (j) 199 (including 4 adult) (1953). (k) First Methodist Society in Glasgow, 1765. (l) Evangelistic and welfare activities include house-to-house visitation by ministers and members, work in local factories and tram depots, young wives' and young mothers' clubs, dining clubs for old people, and concerts in hospitals and old people's Homes; co-operated in the All-Scotland—Billy Graham Crusade.

Congregational Union

(a) 23 in May, 22 in autumn, of 1955. (b) 8,370. (c) 21/3,192/—. (d) —. (e) 1,212 members of youth groups; 2,170 members of uniformed organisations. (f) 1. (g) £400 plus manse (to be raised to £520 plus manse from 1 July 1956)/4. (h) —. (j) —. (k) Of the Glasgow churches in the Union at present, the oldest is Hillhead (1800), followed three years later by Elgin Place. In 1899 there were 25. Montrose Street congregation closed in autumn, 1955, leaving 22 at end of 1955. (l) Active in evangelism so far as resources allow, and readily co-operates in interdenominational missions; actively supported the All-Scotland—Billy Graham Crusade.

Baptist Union

(a) 22. (b) 4,247. (c) 25 (including missions associated with congregations)/ 2,739/510. (d) 10/220/—. (e) —. (f) 2. (g) £380 plus manse and rates, and children's allowances/—. (h) —. (j) 265 (Believers' Baptism by Immersion). (k) 1769. At end of nineteenth century there were 12 Baptist churches in the city. (l) Engages in evangelistic work (e.g. at holiday resorts during summer months) so far as resources allow; actively supported the All-Scotland—Billy Graham Crusade. Willingly co-operates in interdenominational campaigns.

Assemblies of Christian Brethren

(a) 31. (b) 3,138. (c) 30/attendance 3,131/—. (d) 27/attendance 822/—. (e) to (h) —. (j) 26 Assemblies administered 196 baptisms. (k) 1877. Most recently established was in 1942. (l) Of the membership, 2,013 or 64 per cent on average attend the Sunday morning meeting for Breaking of Bread. Most of the Assemblies hold week-night meetings. The following figures show the average attendances, with in brackets the number of Assemblies holding the type of meeting mentioned: Prayer meeting 939 (31); Bible Reading 602 (19); Youth Fellowship 509 (15); Women's Meetings 1,035 (23); and "Children's or Other Work" 1,067 (15). On occasion assemblies co-operate with other denominations in evangelistic campaigns, and most of them undertake evangelism either on their own account or in association with fellow-assemblies. Some Brethren in the city took an active part in the All-Scotland—Billy Graham Crusade. The assemblies are locally autonomous, there being no central administrative or other body controlling, answering for, and representative of, the local groups. In each assembly there are Elders or Overseers who take responsibility for the maintenance of spiritual order. Conference meetings are held in Glasgow on the Spring and Autumn holiday week-ends for Bible teaching and Missionary reports. There is no ordained ministry, but there are "teaching Brothers" or "ministering Brothers" and "Evangelist preachers" or "Evangelist Brethren." It should be noted that the foregoing figures and statements refer to what are known as "Open Brethren"; there are other assemblies, generally referred to as "Exclusives," not covered by this summary.

Churches of the Spiritualists' National Union

(a) 7. (b) 763. (c) 2/120/—. (d) to (j) —. (k) The largest of the seven, the Glasgow Association, is also the oldest. Dating from January 1866, it is described as "the Mother Church of Scotland." Until 1941, there were 9 churches within the city, but in that year 2 linked up with the Glasgow Association. (l) All seven churches practise Spiritual Healing, one having a Healing Sanctuary and a second, a Healing Clinic; and healing services are open to the public. Since many visitors attend services, particularly in the evening, attendance exceeds the reported membership.

Churches of Christ

(a) 4. (b) 737. (c) 4/509/96 (1954). (d) —. (e) 370 in Youth Organisations (1954). (f) —. (g) —. (h) £3,523 (this sum, however, does not include contributions from individuals to national committees)/£4 16s. (j) —. (k) 1839. There were 4 Churches of Christ in the city at end of nineteenth century. (l) 250 on average attend morning service (always communion). From time to time congregations have engaged in united evangelistic efforts, the preachers on occasion coming from Australia or America.

Church of The Nazarene

(a) 3. (b) 260. (c) to (j) —. (k) Glasgow is the birthplace of the Nazarene Church in the British Isles, the first church, Sharpe Memorial, having been established at Parkhead (Glasgow) in 1906. (l) In Barlanark, a new housing area, an extension of the Parkhead church has recently been developed but it has not yet been organised as a separate congregation. Average attendance for Sharpe Memorial, Govan, and Parkhead (including Barlanark extension) together is about 270.

Church of Jesus Christ of Latter-Day Saints (Mormons)

(a) 1. (b) 189. (c) and (d) What is termed the Sunday School is divided into junior and senior sections with classes to cover all ages. Enrolment 105. (e) to (j) —. (k) A branch of the Church has existed in the city since 1840, but it was not until February 1951 that its followers became established in a building of their own—in Claremont Terrace (dedicated by the head of the Church, David O. McKay, in June 1952). (l) Generally known as "Mormons" because of their acceptance of "The Book of Mormon" as a companion sacred volume to the Bible. Followers of this Church number one-and-a-half million throughout the world. No paid ministry.

Seventh-Day Adventists

(a) 1. (b) 180. (c) and (d) 1/30/6. (e) to (g) —. (h) About £2,000 annually/ £11. (j) —. (k) The Glasgow congregation has been in existence for a little over 50 years. (l) Average attendance at morning worship, approximately 130. A few years ago an evangelistic campaign, consisting of a series of lectures in a city cinema and in the McLellan Galleries, brought in between 60 and 70 new members.

New Church, or Church of the New Jerusalem

(a) 1. (b) 170. (c) to (j) —. (k) Date of first church not known; until a few years ago there were 2 congregations in the city. (l) Average attendance, approximately 55.

Ecclesias of Christadelphians

(a) 2. (b) 160. (c) Sunday School enrolment of about 40. (d) to (j) —. (k) 1851. Following a visit to the city that year of Dr. John Thomas, founder of the movement, a group detached themselves from the sects of their allegiance and formed themselves into a separate body. (l) About 100 are regular attenders. The members are active in evangelism, including occasional week-night suburban meetings and open-air meetings at Queen's Park Gates during the summer.

Assemblies of God (Glasgow Pentecostal Church)

(a) 2. (b) 125 (in addition, adherents estimated at 50). (c) 2/180/—. (d) 2/50/—. (e) 2 Youth Fellowships with 50 members. (f) to (j) —. (k) 1929. The other Assembly dates, as such, from 1952. That year the East Campbell Street Mission of the Elim Church was closed and some of its members formed the nucleus of the second Assembly. (l) Notably active in holding public meetings and in other forms of evangelism: in 1955 a month's Revival and Divine Healing Crusade was conducted by Pastor Howell Harris, with attendances averaging 200 each evening. A special "Youth Campaign and Crusade" was also held in 1955. Members of the two Assemblies acted as counsellors and stewards for the All-Scotland Crusade (1955). Generally referred to as the "Pentecostalists."

Society of Friends ("Quakers")

(a) One "Meeting." (b) 123 members and 48 in category termed "Regular Attenders" (corresponding broadly to "adherents" in other cases). (c) 30 children, classified as "Temporary Members," are associated with the Meeting. There is a Children's Class on Sundays at 11 a.m. (d) to (j) —. (k) 1716. (l) For its size, the group is notably active in social and welfare work, both of its own initiative and as the local implementation of projects planned centrally by the London Yearly Meeting. An Adult School is held on Sundays at 6 p.m. Study Groups are held from time to time. Average adult attendance at the Meeting for Worship is 53. Commonly if unofficially known as "Quakers."

Elim Church (Elim Foursquare Gospel Alliance)

(a) 1. (b) 100. (c) 1/50/7. (d) —. (e) The youth organisation, the Elim Crusaders, had 20 members in 1955. (f) and (g) —. About £600 annually/£6. (j) —. (k) Date of first church in Glasgow not known. Up to 1952 there were two congregations in the city, but in 1952 the East Campbell Street Mission ceased to function as an Elim branch and became the second of the two Assemblies of God. (l) Average attendance: at morning service, 80; at evening service 120 (some of the latter number being adherents). Active in evangelistic drives, usually with aid of visiting preachers. In one such campaign over 4 weeks in September 1953, about 1,000 professed conversion and attendances on occasion reached 3,000.

Unitarian Church

(a) 1. (b) 80. (c) 1/20/3. (d) to (j) —. (k) 1791. A second Unitarian church was started in 1871, but closed in 1948, when the congregation united with the founder church. (l) Average attendance at Sunday morning service, 35.

Roman Catholic Church

(a) 58 (mid-1954). (b) 194,550: estimated adult population in city at mid-1954 (including an estimate for St. Mungo's, Garthamlock, which although outside the Archdiocese of Glasgow is inside the city boundaries). (c) to (h) —. (j) 8,636 in 1954 in the wider area of the Archdiocese of Glasgow. (k) Date of first R.C. church not known. In 1778 there were 30 "known" Roman Catholics in Glasgow. In 1898, twenty years after the Roman Catholic hierarchy was re-established in Scotland, there were 27 churches and 97 clergymen. (l) In mid-1955, in the Archdiocese of Glasgow (taking in Dunbartonshire and parts of the environs of the city) there were 80 parishes, 330 priests, 14 Religious Houses for men and 24 for women. The officially estimated R.C. population (including infants and children) in the Archdiocese was 330,450 (compared with 330,415 the year before). In this wider area there were, in 1954, 92 Catholic schools with 66,434 pupils; 3,231 marriages were recorded. Through a variety of associations and institutions extensive social work is carried out in the city. Evangelistic activities of the type familiar to observers of the larger non-Roman denominations are little in evidence and such mass campaigns as the All-Scotland Crusade are officially shunned by the hierarchy.

These 23 denominations, varied though they may be, do not complete the picture of the religious groups at work and worship in the city. But they do exhaust the list of denominations for whom membership figures and other data have been ascertained. It remains to make bare mention of such other bodies as are known to the writer to exist but have been omitted from the foregoing synopsis and the Membership Table in the next section because they are not strictly denominations or units of denominations, or because they do not divulge their membership or, again, because for other reasons this and other information concerning them has not, despite extensive enquiries and repeated requests, been forthcoming. Foremost among these in social work and evangelistic activities, and almost certainly also in numerical strength, is the Salvation Army, of which there are about 30 centres in the Glasgow area.[1] There are three branches in Glasgow of the Church of Christ, Scientist; a number of companies of Jehovah's Witnesses (none thought to be very large); several meetings of Associated Bible Students; one congregation of the Catholic Apostolic Church; possibly one congregation of the Liberal Catholic Church and possibly one also of the Apostolic Church.[2] There is a place of worship known as the City Temple, and the city also houses a congregation—St. Silas'—of the English Episcopal Church. There is a handful of churches of the Greater World Christian Spiritualists' Association, and there are almost certainly a number of independent Spiritualist centres. Further, there are, as we have seen, groups known as Exclusive Brethren—they themselves, it is understood, repudiate the name; and it is likely that Glasgow contains one assembly of each of the two groups (the "Needed Truth" group and the "Green Pastures" group) into which the Churches of God movement has divided. Again, there is the non-denominational Tent Hall, opened in 1877 and operating under the control of the Glasgow United Evangelistic Association (founded by D. L. Moody). There is no official membership, but 1,800 on average attend the Evangelistic Rally on Saturdays, about 1,200 the Sunday evening service, about 350 the Sunday afternoon service, and about 300 the Thursday mid-week service. In addition there are a number of self-contained, unitary Missions, Gospel Halls and Meeting Houses; and there are numerous groups which, while (like the Carters' Mission, the Seamen's Chapel and the Seamen's Mission) administering to the spiritual as well

1 An account of the Salvation Army's organisation and work in Scotland and Glasgow is given in *The Churches in Scotland To-day*; and as there explained, the Army authorities courteously but firmly refuse to divulge membership data.

2 There is some doubt as to whether the latter two still exist; it is indeed by no means clear whether the separate identity of the three last-mentioned was ever rooted in fact and not simply an apparent distinction arising from verbal confusion. What is certain is that the city holds one congregation of the Catholic Apostolic Church—a congregation that has been in existence for about 120 years:

as temporal needs of specific segments of the community, are not perhaps properly to be regarded as full religious agencies.[1] But it is a labyrinthine maze one wanders in here, and he would be a bold investigator who would swear to having unravelled to its last knot the tangled skein of Glasgow's "religious fringe."

Membership of Christian Churches

The membership figures of the 23 Christian denominations surveyed in Synopsis A above are brought together and shown as percentages, first of the adult population of the city, and secondly of the known church membership as a whole, in Table CL.

By "membership" is here meant, with two exceptions, communicant, full or official membership according to the relevant qualifications of the various denominations, and the figures given in Table CL are in most cases those reported by denominations, in some cases are compiled from the returns submitted in connection with the 1955 Attendance Census,[2] and in a few others are official estimates where for one reason or another the denominations could not give an exact figure.

The first exception is the case of the Roman Catholic Church. No intelligible meaning can be given to the concept of "membership" as applied to the Roman Catholic Church. That Church itself speaks in terms of "Roman Catholic population," and by this is generally meant all of whatever age who have been baptized into the Roman Church. Figures reported in Roman Catholic official publications therefore include infants, children and teenagers as well as adults, and they cannot therefore be used as they stand for the purpose of comparison with the membership figures of other denominations. Accordingly, it is necessary to seek a figure that would represent the number of adult Roman Catholics in the city. No such figure is possessed by the hierarchy in Glasgow, and the one given in Table CL has been arrived at by a method sanctioned by the Roman Catholic authorities when used by the writer in previous studies of this kind.[3]

The second exception is provided by the Free Church and the Free Presbyterian Church. In their cases it is necessary, in order to obtain a figure comparable with other non-Roman denominations, to add to their communicant membership the reported number of their "adher-

[1] Here it may be in place to mention the Glasgow City Mission, a non-denominational "Christian lay agency" of evangelism and philanthropy. An account of its activities is given in the author's earlier work on the Churches, already cited, pp. 93-5.

[2] See next section.

[3] The method is to apply to the total figure of the Roman Catholic population the over-20-years and under-20-years proportions of the relevant population as a whole —in this case of the city of Glasgow. Since the Roman Catholic birth-rate is higher than that of the non-Roman section of the community the estimate arrived at in this way slightly overestimates the Roman Catholic adult members. Alternative methods, however, are equally open to objection, and the estimate here offered will serve our present purpose.

ents."[1] In Table CL, then, the figures given for these two Churches combine adherents and communicant members.

The data in Table CL relate (as do other figures in this chapter unless otherwise indicated) to the area within the municipal boundaries of the city.[2] From this it follows that some figures given here may not correspond to the "Glasgow" figures given for the relevant item in a denomination's Year-book (or other official publication) if the latter include, as frequently happens, one or several churches outside the city limits but inside the denomination's Glasgow unit of administration. The greatest discrepancy of this kind occurs in the case of the Church of Scotland, whose nearest official figures to the ones required for the present purpose relate to churches within the Presbytery of Glasgow. This unit, however, includes several churches in Clydeside districts adjoining the city's boundaries, while on the other hand it excludes ten city churches that are administratively part of neighbouring Presbyteries—four in the Presbytery of Paisley and six in the Presbytery of Dunbarton.

Most of the figures in Table CL are of membership as at a date in 1955, the others referring to a date in 1954. It is in this sense, and not as relating to the sessional period 1954/5, that the symbol "1955/54" is to be understood.[3]

With these points of explanation before us, we may turn to commenting briefly on aspects of the data Table CL presents. The first thing to be said is that the total it shows is a minimum index of the size of Glasgow's church-connected community. This is so for two reasons. First, the majority of the figures relate to full membership and exclude adherents. How many of these potential members the city may hold is, quite literally, anybody's guess. The number might well be somewhere in the region of 50,000. Secondly, there are, as we have seen, several religious denominations in the city whose numerical strength is not known. Here again we can only guess at this number, but it is unlikely to be much more than 15,000 and may well be much

[1] The term "adherents" has no precise connotation but the concept is a familiar one at least among Presbyterians. By "adherent" is generally meant one who accepts the Christian faith and subscribes to the doctrine of his denomination, attends public worship, takes part in the congregational life, and has his Church's welfare at heart, but who, for one reason or another, has not taken full communion. In the Free and Free Presbyterian Churches the number of such followers—in their case, persons who feel themselves not yet ready or "good enough" for the serious step of taking communion—is relatively greater than in other denominations, and many of these adherents are often more regular attenders at public worship, and more active in the affairs of their congregation, than are many full members of other denominations.

[2] This admittedly gives rise to difficulties: for example, some churches located within that area draw their following from districts bordering on the city's boundaries. Other worshippers travel the other way—crossing the line from homes inside to churches sited just outside. There is no possibility of adjusting figures to take account of this complication; in any case the two-way movement of these ecclesiastical commuters, if they might be so called, may go some way to cancelling itself out.

[3] This is also the explanation, *mutatis mutandis,* of the symbol 1956/55 in Table CLI and elsewhere.

less.[1] If we accept 15,000 as a reasonable guess, our total of church membership in the city would then become about 420,000, and this, which we may well have to regard as the outside limit, would bring the city's churchfolk up to 57 per cent of the adult population. If, pursuing this speculation, we were to accept the figure of 50,000 as a tolerable guess at the number of city adherents, we get a total of 470,000 members-plus-adherents, or 64 per cent of the adult population. Perhaps, then, we might risk saying that something of the order of two thirds of the city's adults have a connection of some degree of directness with the city's churches.[2]

All this, however, is conjecture. What we can say with reasonable confidence is that at least 404,000, or 55 per cent of the city's adult population, are church members.[3] And even if some of the constituent items in this total have undergone a modicum of official inflation, this is likely to be more than counter-balanced by the "margin of unknowns."

Of the city's adult population very nearly one half (49.9 per cent) are Church of Scotland members (23.4 per cent) and Roman Catholics (26.5 per cent), while 5.2 per cent are distributed over the remaining 21 denominations of Table CL.[4] These two ecclesiastical giants together account for 90.6 per cent of the city's church membership—the Church of Scotland for 42.4 and the Roman Catholic Church for 48.2. This numerical lead of the Roman Catholic Church on the Church of Scotland is perhaps the most striking fact that emerges from an examination of Table CL. Nor is the gap markedly narrowed if one sets against the Roman Catholic figures those for the Presbyterian group as a whole—adding, that is, to the Church of Scotland the 8,566 "wee Presbyterians" who might in different historical circumstances have been in the fellowship of the Established Church—for the Presbyterians claim 24.5 per cent of the city's adults as against the Roman Church's 26.5 per cent. Indeed, if the interest lies in the relative attachment of Glasgow citizens to one or other of the major competing ecclesiastical forms—Presbyterianism and Episcopacy—as distinct from the Reformed issue, the Scottish Episcopal Church brings the lead of devotees of Episcopacy up to almost 3 percentage points—27.4 per cent as against 24.5 per cent. It is not until the basis of comparison is between

1 These "unmeasured" groups will also have their adherents in the sense here understood.

2 We are here excluding those who, while not churchgoers, would if asked for their "religious affiliation" cite one or other denomination, even if simply on the ground that they were brought up in it or, again, would declare that in any fundamental philosophical conflict they would be found "on the side of the angels." These coupled with our two thirds would reduce the proportion of out-and-out atheists and agnostics to probably between 10 and 15 per cent of the city's adults.

3 For the sake of brevity we will agree to understand by this term the equivalent concept in the case of Roman Catholics.

4 Tables showing Christian Church membership in Scotland in 1951, 1901 and 1871, and in England and Wales in 1951, are to be found in the author's Chapter, "The Churches," in *The Scottish Economy* (ed. by A. K. Cairncross, 1954).

TABLE CL

KNOWN MEMBERSHIP OF CHRISTIAN CHURCHES IN GLASGOW, 1955/54

No. of Churches in City	*Denomination*	*Membership*	*Percent. of Adult Population (733,000 est.)*	*Percent. of Known City Church Membership*
	Protestant or non-Roman Catholic			
	Presbyterian			
217	Church of Scotland	171,213	23.4	42.4
17	United Free Church	4,895	0.67	1.21
8	Free Church	2,502	0.34	0.62
1	Free Presbyterian Church	686	0.09	0.17
3	United Original Secession Church	353	0.05	0.09
1	Reformed Presbyterian Church	130	0.02	0.03
247	Presbyterian	179,779	24.53	44.52
	Anglican Communion			
25	Episcopal Church in Scotland	6,641	0.91	1.64
	Methodist			
17	Methodist Church	4,167	0.57	1.03
	The Larger Independent "Federations"			
23	Congregational Union	8,370	1.14	2.07
22	Baptist Union	4,247	0.58	1.05
31	Assemblies of Christian Brethren	3,138	0.43	0.78
365		206,342	28.15	51.10
	Others			
7	Churches of the Spiritualists' National Union	763	—	—
4	Churches of Christ	737	—	—
3	Church of the Nazarene	260	—	—
1	Church of Jesus Christ of Latter-Day Saints	189	—	—
1	Seventh-Day Adventists	180	—	—
1	New Church, or Church of the New Jerusalem	170	—	—
2	Ecclesias of Christadelphians	160	—	—
2	Assemblies of God (Glasgow Pentecostal Church)	125	—	—
1	Society of Friends	123	—	—
1	Elim Church (Elim Foursquare Gospel Alliance)	100	—	—
1	Unitarian Church	80	—	—
			0.39	0.72
389	Protestant or non-R.C.	209,229	28.54	51.82
58	Roman Catholics (adults)	194,550	26.54	48.18
447	Total	403,779	55.09	100.00

NOTES: Where summations do not add up to totals this is due to "rounding-off."

In the cases of the Free and Free Presbyterian Churches the figures given include adherents.

The Roman Catholic figure is an estimate of the Roman Catholic adult population (see text).

the Roman Catholic Church and all the others that the former loses its numerical ascendancy, and even then the position is turned only marginally, the non-Roman churches claiming 28.5 per cent of the city's adults compared with 26.5 per cent who are Roman Catholics. This margin of 2 percentage points is equivalent to a difference in numerical strengths of 15,000 persons—relatively an aggregate of no great magnitude.[1] In 1947, the Church of Scotland Glasgow membership was 170,525 and the estimated number of adult Roman Catholics in the city was 185,565.[2] Thus in a period of between 7 and 8 years the Church of Scotland has increased by 688 members while the Roman Catholic population has gone up just short of 9,000.

These findings lend support to the forebodings often indulged in by non-Roman Catholics. On the other hand, since Table CL was compiled, membership figures for seven non-Roman Catholic churches (those who took part in the Attendance Censuses described in the next section) relating partly to dates in 1955 and partly to the spring of 1956 have been obtained. These show the membership total for this group to have increased by 5,197, compared with their total twelve months previously. Further, the Roman Catholic adult population in 1955, estimated by the writer at 193,000, is 1,500 less than the estimated number for 1954. This decrease is likely to be temporary; and it is improbable that the marked increase in the membership of the seven-church Protestant group will prove a regular annual achievement, since almost certainly part of it at least was a result of the All-Scotland—Billy Graham Crusade and another part a consequence of follow-up activities deriving some of their dynamic from that campaign. Nevertheless, these figures show that for the time being at least a halt has been called to the trend shown by the earlier postwar years.

It is right also to point out the increasing feeling on the part of some non-Roman (and even, indeed, some Roman Catholic) observers that the actual situation may not be as the figures indicate. It is argued that the published official estimates of the Roman Catholic population fail to take account of the loss of persons (in general baptised as infants) through death, emigration, apostasy or conversion to a non-Roman faith; and, while there are as yet no published statements citing documentary evidence, indications pointing towards a substantiation of this contention are known to not a few non-Roman clergymen from their own pastoral experience.[3]

[1] It must be remembered that we are here speaking of the city of Glasgow as such: if our study took into account such neighbouring residential areas as, e.g., Giffnock and Bearsden (which are to all intents and purposes part of Glasgow as a community for all that they are outwith the municipal boundaries) the Protestant churches and in particular the Church of Scotland would come out of a numerical comparison with the Roman Catholic population more favourably.

[2] cf. *The Churches in Scotland To-day,* p. 74. Not sufficient was known to the writer about the 1947 Glasgow membership of some of the small bodies listed in the present membership table to allow, here, of a firm comparison between Roman Catholic advance and that of the non-Roman Churches.

[3] It is, for example, widely held that all mixed marriages " go Catholic." This is certainly not the experience a number of non-Roman clergymen in developing areas have reported to the writer.

It is noteworthy that in his pastoral letter for Advent the Roman Catholic Archbishop of Westminster, Cardinal Griffin, speaks of real ground for concern over evidence that a number of young Catholics "abandon their religion within a short period of their leaving school," and adds that most of the lapsed boys and girls "come from homes where the parents have themselves lapsed" and that the "leakage" is particularly prominent in industrial areas.[1] May it not be that for some areas, Glasgow among them, the official figures are not corrected to take account of this loss?

Indirect evidence that official Catholic figures may be over-estimated seems to be provided by the 1954 Attendance Census finding that on average only 47 per cent of adult Catholics in Glasgow attended morning masses over the census period. For Catholics are under obligation to attend Mass, and it is charitable to assume that the half who did not were in the main—illness and other variable factors would account for the absence of some—no longer practising Catholics rather than believing Catholics falling short in a major duty implied by their faith. At any rate the issue is clear: either a substantial number of Catholics have renounced their faith, or the official estimates of Catholic population are inflated. The actual, operative gap between the non-Roman and the Roman Catholic strengths may in fact be wider than our analysis of the available figures suggests.[2]

CHRISTIAN CHURCH ATTENDANCE

Church membership is one thing: attendance quite another. How many of Glasgow's churchfolk turn out to public worship?

Apart from subjective guesswork or, at best, a minister's private

1 cf. *Glasgow Herald,* 28/11/55.

2 In an instructive article on "The Catholic Population of Scotland in the Twentieth Century" in *Scottish Survey, 1878-1955* (an informative series of essays published by the *Glasgow Observer* and the *Scottish Catholic Herald* in 1956 to mark the 70th anniversary of their founding), James Darragh draws the following among a number of conclusions:

"The rate at which the Catholic population of Scotland has been increasing has tended to fall over the last 50 years and is now only half of what it was at the beginning of the century."

"The absolute increase in Catholic population conceals an effective real loss which was most serious in the years between 1931 and 1950—and probably most serious between 1931 and 1940."

"Examination of the statistics between 1945 and 1954 suggests that there has been some halt—perhaps only temporarily—to this loss of Catholic population. *This does not mean that it is not continuing* but merely that it is being concealed and outbalanced by unexpected gains of population from immigration."

More generally, the Archbishops of St. Andrews and Edinburgh and of Glasgow state, in their Foreword to the Survey:

"It is an encouraging story that it (the Survey) has to tell of numerical expansion of clergy and people, of the growth of chapel and school, of convent and monastery, charitable institution and welfare society, shrine and pilgrimage, religious art and culture, but while we rejoice in this manifestation of the progress of the Church in Scotland we must beware of succumbing to complacency, for there has been loss as well as gain, and the difficulties and the dangers that encompass our community to-day are more grave than at any time in the past seventy years."

assessment of the record in this respect of his own people, no information existed on which to base an answer to this question. It was decided, therefore, in connection with the present study, to replace guesswork by a special enquiry—to hold a Church Attendance Census within the city. After negotiations with eight Christian denominations (seven non-Roman Catholic and the Roman Catholic Church), teams of local lay enumerators, working in collaboration with the author, counted and recorded the number attending the main service of public worship on Sundays 25 April, 2 May and 9 May 1954.

Normally one would allow an interval of up to 10 years to elapse before carrying out a follow-up enquiry. Within twelve months, however, a major factor had rendered the situation far from normal: the All-Scotland—Billy Graham Crusade centred on the city from 21 March to 30 April 1955. Accordingly, it was decided to undertake a follow-up three-week investigation, starting on Sunday 1 May, in order to record the immediate impact of the Crusade and its attendant activities on church-going. This second enquiry showed an increased level of attendance; and the question at once arose, would it last—even twelve months? To find out, a third census was carried out on Sundays 29 April, 6 May and 13 May 1956.[1]

The results of the three-year investigation are presented in Tables CLI and CLII of this chapter and in Tables 162, 163 and 164 in the Appendix: the first pair giving average (adult) attendances over the census period of each year and summarising comparisons, and the latter three providing Sunday-by-Sunday figures and bringing out the differences shown by the corresponding Sundays in the three periods. Before the reader examines these data, however, one or two further points of explanation are in order: (1) the findings here presented relate to the number of adults attending the main religious service—in all but a fraction of cases, the morning service—held in the city churches of the participating denominations:[2] (2) for this reason, and also because not all the city's religious denominations were included,[3] the recorded figures for 1954 (and, as we shall see, those for 1955 and 1956 even more so) are a minimum index and do not represent the total city turn-out at public worship over the periods covered; (3) even so, the 1954 census covers about 98 per cent of the known city church membership and probably about 95 per cent of total membership, and there are indications that the number of adults attending a subsidiary

1 The dates of the 1955 census, deliberately fixed so that the first enumeration followed a matter of hours after the closing of the Crusade at the Hampden Park Rally on the evening of 30 April (Saturday), were one week later than the Sundays of the 1954 census. The 1956 dates were of Sundays equivalent to those covered by the 1955 enquiry. This difference does little to affect the comparison of the 1954 findings with those of the two later censuses.

2 The attendances at all morning masses in Roman Catholic and in Episcopal churches were taken.

3 The reason why only eight denominations were invited to take part was a practical one solely: some of the others could not be approached centrally, others (as has been made clear earlier) are so withdrawn as to be virtually inaccessible, while the remainder, who might have agreed to take part if asked, were numerically so insignificant as to make little difference to the relative results.

service who were not also at the main service is small: so that the complete picture of adult turn-out can differ only very slightly from that presented by the 1954 enquiry;[1] (4) the Roman Catholic Church was invited, along with the other Churches, to take part in the 1955 and 1956 censuses, but each time the Archbishop of Glasgow replied that for reasons of his own he was unable to associate himself and his Church with these resumed enquiries. Thus, while the 1954 Roman Catholic figures are recorded, the comparisons set out in the tables relate to the 7 non-Roman Catholic denominations only; (5) the 1955 and 1956 enquiries had no link, official or unofficial, with the Crusade organisation.[2] (6) neither the 1955 nor the 1956 census is to be regarded as specifically an investigation into the effects or success of the Crusade; in registering the level of adult attendance immediately following and a year after the campaign they give only a partial answer to that question and, obviously, have nothing to say about the possible qualitative effects; (7) weather conditions were fairly uniform and the distribution of Communion and other special services was more or less even over the three census periods, and the differences shown by the results are not to be accounted for by factors of this kind.[3]

A comparison of the figures for the seven non-Roman denominations shows that the three-Sunday average rose from 56,503 in 1954 to 67,078 in 1955, and fell in 1056 to 62,224—respectively 27.8, 33.2 and 30 per cent of the city membership of these seven bodies, and 7.6, 9.2 and 8.5 per cent of the estimated adult population of Glasgow. The peak attendance recorded was 72,079 on Sunday 1 May 1955. By the end of the 1955 census period attendance had fallen to 61,620—a level below that shown by two of the 1956 census Sundays (6 May and 13 May). All three 1956 census Sundays had higher attendances than the Sundays of the 1954 census.

The 1956 average, at 4,854 below that for 1955 and 5,721 above that for 1954, represents a position a little above the midway point between the 1954 and 1955 levels.

It is not possible on the basis of the census figures to say what accounts for the fall of nearly 5,000 from the immediate post-Crusade level. It may be that the Crusade stirred some existing but dormant members into attendance for a week or two, and that after this first flush of revived enthusiasm they relapsed into "paper" membership

[1] Each year an enumeration of children and young people attending public worship was taken, and in 1955 and 1956 a count of adults and those under 20 years of age was taken at subsidiary (usually evening) services; but a number of considerations have led to the exclusion of the resultant data from this report.

[2] The censuses were, in the highest sense, a combined operation in which clerical and lay representatives of city congregations joined forces with an academic observer in an enquiry of both ecclesiastical and sociological import; and the author gratefully pays tribute to these collaborators for their enthusiastic support and practical help.

[3] Further information concerning the census enquiries—e.g., on the practical arrangements made, on the reason for the choice of the 1954 dates, and on other points —is set out in two articles the author published in the *British Weekly* of 10 and 17 November 1955. See also articles in the *Glasgow Herald*, 11 October 1954 and 23 September 1955.

TABLE CLI

AVERAGE ADULT CHURCH ATTENDANCE, GLASGOW, OVER CENSUS PERIODS 1954, 1955 AND 1956, BY DENOMINATIONS, WITH PERCENTAGES OF MEMBERSHIP AND ADULT POPULATION

	1954			1955			1956		
		Average Adult Attendance as Percent. of—			*Average Adult Attendance as Percent. of—*			*Average Adult Attendance as Percent. of—*	
Denomination	*Average Adult Attendance over Census Period*	*City Membership (1953)*	*City Adult Popn. (estd.)*	*Average Adult Attendance over Census Period*	*City Membership (1955/54)*	*City Adult Popn. (estd.)*	*Average Adult Attendance over Census Period*	*City Membership (1956/55)*	*City Adult Popn. (estd.)*
Church of Scotland	45,294	26.2	6.1	53,151	31.0	7.3	49,959	28.4	6.8
Baptist Union	2,022	47.8	0.3	2,671	62.9	0.4	2,240	49.6	0.3
Congregational Union	2,848	34.9	0.4	3,658	43.7	0.5	3,201	39.3	0.4
Episcopal Church	1,975	29.4	0.3	2,299	34.6	0.3	2,198	31.8	0.3
Free Church	1,407	54.0	0.2	1,575	62.9	0.2	1,562	64.4	0.2
Methodist Church	1,599	38.6	0.2	1,932	46.4	0.3	1,607	38.2	0.2
United Free Church	1,357	27.9	0.2	1,792	36.6	0.2	1,456	28.7	0.2
7 Non-Roman Catholic Denominations[1]	56,503	27.8	7.6	67,078	33.2	9.2	62,224	30.0	8.5
Roman Catholic	92,300	46.9	12.5						
8 Denominations	148,803	37.2	20.1						

[1] Where summations do not add up to totals this is due to "rounding-off."

TABLE CLII

Attendance and Membership Comparisons, by Denominations, 1954, 1955 and 1956

Comparison	Church of Scotland	Baptist Union	Congregational Union	Episcopal Church	Free Church	Methodist Church	United Free Church	7 Non-Roman Catholic Denominations
1955 with 1954								
Average Adult Attendance, increase, +	+7,857	+649	+810	+324	+168	+333	+435	+10,575
Per Cent increase, +	*+17.3*	*+32.1*	*+28.4*	*+16.4*	*+11.9*	*+20.8*	*+32.1*	*+18.7*
Membership,[1] increase, + decrease, −	−1,516	+15	+211	−66	−104	+27	+38	−1,395
Per Cent increase, + decrease, −	*−0.9*	*+0.4*	*+2.6*	*−1.0*	*−4.0*	*+0.7*	*+0.8*	*−0.7*
1956 with 1955								
Average Adult Attendance, decrease, −	−3,192	−431	−457	−101	−13	−325	−336	−4,854
Per Cent decrease, −	*−6.0*	*−16.1*	*−12.5*	*−4.4*	*−0.8*	*−16.8*	*−18.8*	*−7.2*
Membership,[2] increase, + decrease, −	+4,712	+271	−234	+267	−75	+36	+220	+5,197
Per Cent increase, + decrease, −	*+2.8*	*+6.4*	*−2.8*	*+4.0*	*−3.0*	*+0.9*	*+4.5*	*+2.6*
1956 with 1954								
Average Adult Attendance, increase, +	+4,665	+218	+353	+223	+155	+8	+99	+5,721
Per Cent increase, +	*+10.3*	*+10.8*	*+12.4*	*+11.3*	*+11.0*	*+0.5*	*+7.3*	*+10.1*
Membership,[3] increase + decrease, −	+3,196	+286	−23	+201	−179	+63	+258	+3,802
Per Cent increase, + decrease, −	*+1.9*	*+6.8*	*−0.3*	*+3.0*	*−0.7*	*+1.5*	*+5.3*	*+1.9*

[1] Membership as returned for 1955 census (202,035) compared with 1953 membership (203,430).

[2] Comparison between returns for 1956 (207,232) and 1955 censuses.

[3] Membership as returned for 1956 census compared with 1953 membership.

only, while some new, post-Crusade attenders fell away during the months that followed, some before becoming members of a church and some after joining. As against this, nearly 6,000 of the 10,575 increase shown by the 1955 average over 1954 were still in the pews in 1956; and the city membership of the seven denominations (as returned for the 1956 census and relating to 1956/55) showed, at 207,232, an increase of 5,197 on the total made up by the 1955 returns (relating to 1955/54).

The three-year enquiry does not allow of conclusions as to the respective impact, on attendance and membership, of the Crusade on the one hand and, on the other, of the local mission campaigns which preceded and followed Mr. Graham's visit to the city and the work currently going on in the new housing areas; but it is highly probable that the 1956 attendance and membership figures would have been lower but for the follow-up work carried out in connection with the Tell Scotland Movement.[1] What is certain is that the sceptical predictions put forward by some commentators in the spring of 1955 that, whatever immediate effect the Crusade and its supporting activities might have on attendance and membership, there would be little evidence of it twelve months later, have not been borne out.

Over the 1954 census period, the average attendance was 148,803, or 37.2 per cent of the city membership of the eight participating bodies and one fifth of the estimated adult population of the city. It is tempting to speculate on what the findings would have been if the Roman Catholic churches had taken part in the follow-up enquiries. A moderate Roman Catholic increase can probably be assumed, although it is not likely to have been of the relative magnitude of the non-Roman increase. If in 1955 and 1956 the Roman Catholic turn-out rose to somewhere around 95,000, this would give an 8-denomination attendance of approximately 162,000 and 157,000 respectively. These estimates would result in the following proportions of city membership (8 denominations) and adult population respectively: 1955, 40.8 per cent and 22.1 per cent; 1956: 39.2 per cent and 21.4 per cent.[2]

Even allowing for the denominations not included in the censuses, it is patently clear that something like three quarters of Glasgow's adults, and about three fifths of those at least formally attached to the city's denominations, either stay aloof from or are relative strangers to public worship.

It may be readily granted that one cannot expect a turn-out that will be 100 per cent of the membership roll: on any given Sunday there will always be some churchfolk absent from public worship for reasons that have nothing to do with the force of their religious convictions. The author's own estimate would put the "realistic maximum expectation" at about 65 per cent to 70 per cent for normal services and perhaps 75 per cent to 80 per cent for communion and special services. Even so, an attendance level of one third of the membership still leaves much to be desired.

The task that faces the Glasgow Churches would therefore seem to be not merely to make impact on the thousands in the city who are without even formal attachment to any religious body, but also, and perhaps even more, to stir into closer association with, and more active participation in, congregational life at least half of their non-attending members. Perhaps the two sides of the problem may best be tackled at the one time and in the one way; it may be that the way to stir the more dormant members is to bring home to them the magnitude of the

1 See following section.

2 The estimated number of adult Roman Catholics for 1954 is 194,550 and for 1955 193,000, giving membership figures for the eight denominations of 396,600 and 400,232. The estimated adult population of the city at the end of 1954 is 733,000 and at the end of 1955, 733,900.

missionary task and win them over to discharging the obligation resting on the laity to supplement the efforts of the clergy. What has recently been attempted and done in this way in the city forms the subject of the next section.

THE "OUT-REACH" OF THE CHURCH

The ten years following the Second World War have seen evangelistic activities on a scale which in extent and variety must surely be unprecedented in the history of the Scottish Churches. Overshadowing all else in the brilliance of its organisation, in the blaze of publicity it won in press and on radio, and in the immediate impact of its skilfully presented message, was the All-Scotland—Billy Graham Crusade of March-April 1955. But if pre-eminent in these and other respects, the Crusade was no sudden, disparate, out-of-the-blue affair: it had its smaller-scale and (at any rate up-to-now) largely unsung precursors; and, one can say even from this near-point in time, it has had its smaller-scale successors. The part these local enterprises make of the general picture badly needs heightening.

In order to fulfil that aim even partially, it has been necessary to resort once again to the device of a synopsis. At this writing no comprehensive account of recent evangelistic activities in Glasgow exists, at all events in publicly-accessible form; and it has accordingly been thought of service to set down some record, based on memoranda submitted for the purpose by participating ministers, of what has been done.[1]

Even so, the projects summarised in Synopsis B (all non-Catholic, some otherwise inter-denominational, and some by individual congregations) are only a selection. This is unavoidable, and not only because of space restrictions. Not all the ministers who have carried out this work have found time to do more than jot down scattered notes of what they and their "co-missioners" were about: and these notes are not always usable source-material for the investigator. Again, since few of these enterprises are planned and co-ordinated by a central agency, the enquirer's learning that a particular work was undertaken in a particular district all too often rests on a chance remark or a fortuitous hint. Nevertheless, this section may provide at least a sketch, so far as Glasgow is concerned, of a situation which, if a fuller picture were possible, might well warrant description as a veritable ferment of activity.

There is another reason why the synopsis accounts may seem unsatisfactory: based as they are on memoranda which speak falteringly on this matter, they are admittedly somewhat vague in their assessment of results. This, to be sure, cannot be otherwise. For the fruits of the seeds these "missioners" seek to sow do not all burgeon at the one

[1] Thanks are expressed to these ministers—named, if not in the appropriate synopsis-entry, then in the List of Acknowledgments at the end of this volume.

moment of time; so that assessment, if possible at all, is a continuing process. Further, much of the fruition is a blossoming of faith, a ripening of commitment; and if there is any index of the richness of such a crop it is not a quantitative one.

To say this is not to run counter to the preceding section on the results of the Attendance Censuses. As is there conceded, the attendance figures give only a partial answer to questions about the effects of the Crusade—or, for that matter, of the supporting local campaigns. The difficulty is to find the other parts of the answer. In the end one has to make do with generalisations. This is well illustrated by the All-Scotland Crusade itself, and although a brief summary of the campaign is given (for all that it concerned a wider area than Glasgow) in the synopsis,[1] it is in place to offer here the following summary of assessments elicited by extensive enquiries about the Crusade's impact.

For months before and for weeks after the Kelvin Hall meetings, and for all the six weeks they were in process, religion was assuredly, as Tom Allan has put it, "a talking-point in a way that is without parallel in our generation."[2] But whether this, and what people heard from Mr. Graham, discernibly brought a new quality to the life of Glasgow and of Scotland, few would care to judge. Changes in some few individual lives there undoubtedly were—the evidence is on record; and it is probably good realism to say that this is effect enough. On the other hand, it is right to record that a good many people are of opinion that the gains are much less than might have been expected from a campaign of such a magnitude. Nor is this solely an extra-Church speculation: not a few ministers have told the writer that as far as churchfolk and churchless in their areas are concerned, the Crusade had negligible impact or none at all. As against this, however, it may well be that with the All-Scotland Crusade as with other activities of the kind the best results have been where a local cadre (lay and ministerial) had prepared the way and were ready to consolidate and expand the position. Certainly, and however that may be, other ministers reported a "spiritual quickening" in the life of their congregations.

The synopsis review starts with an account of a project undertaken in the late 1940's,[3] but the real genesis of the story goes back at least to the "hungry 'thirties" of this century and the concern aroused in

[1] The synopsis summary should be supplemented by consulting *Crusade in Scotland . . . Billy Graham,* edited by Rev. Tom Allan (1955). This book, published within three months of the end of the campaign, is the only report on the Crusade so far made public.

[2] *op. cit.*, p. 112.

[3] A fuller account of activities in Glasgow and elsewhere in the late 1940's is given in the writer's *The Churches in Scotland To-day* (1950), while some of the gaps this section leaves in the story of Glasgow and Scottish activities in the early 1950's are closed in a report by a panel convened by the Rev. T. R. Morton and published in 1954 under the title *Evangelism in Scotland* by the Iona Community, Glasgow, on behalf of the Secretariat for Evangelism of the World Council of Churches, Geneva. This brochure, the text of which was written by Mr. Morton, also contains stimulating passages that discuss changes in attitudes to the Church and other aspects of the background against which contemporary evangelism in Scotland moves.

the minds of many of the young men coming through the Divinity Colleges in that period by the awareness of the gap between the Church and a disturbingly large section of the population and of its industrial workers in particular. They could not easily shake from their thoughts the evidence that to many of the bruised souls that had been through the years of depression what the Church was saying seemed despairingly meaningless or tragically irrelevant. Some found in the work the Rev. G. F. MacLeod had been doing in Govan, and was continuing through the agency of the Iona Community, a promising pointer to, if not blue-print for, a line of attack on this problem.[1] Then came the war; and in their experiences then many of these younger ministers found reinforcement for the growing conviction that some at least of the troubled, anxious minds that looked everywhere but to the Church for solace and guidance were its for the taking if orthodox ways could be supplemented by newer lines of approach. If the full story of recent evangelistic campaigns could be told, it would be in essence a story of the testing of hypotheses that arose out of developments and refinements of this conviction.

It would be wrong to give the impression that these younger men have been alone in this work: they have been joined by many of their older colleagues—some of the men who have been active in the campaigns to be described are their seniors by a generation or thereby—and few among them would not acknowledge as guide and trainer that *doyen* of Scottish evangelists, the Rev. D. P. Thomson. But indisputably they are the shock-troops of the new assault. It requires to be said also that these experimenters have not all been doing the same things, are not all in agreement about the most effective methods to pursue. There is no dogmatic conviction on the part of any one of them that his ways are the only ways possible. Activity has not put all thought to flight. To be persuaded of this one has only to read the Rev. Tom Allan's concluding chapter in *Crusade in Scotland . . . Billy Graham*. There Scotland's most active evangelist of the younger school, a man who has addressed himself most competently and tirelessly to experimenting with new approaches, in particular perhaps with " indirect " or mission evangelism, asks himself whether the older way of " direct " or mass-meeting evangelism might not, after all, be a good deal less outmoded than he had at one time considered it to be.

He was certainly of that conviction nine years or so ago when he set out on one of his first ventures, the North Kelvinside Mission. It is with this mission that our synopsis review of postwar activities starts.

[1] For a short account of the Iona Community see *The Churches in Scotland To-day*, pp. 129-137.

Glasgow Corporation Health & Welfare Department

Plate 23. A GLASGOW COMMON LODGING-HOUSE

The Scotsman

Plate 24. INTERIOR OF GLASGOW CATHEDRAL FROM THE CLERESTORY

Synopsis B

SUMMARY OF EVANGELISTIC CAMPAIGNS AND PARISH MISSIONS

NOTE: This Synopsis summarises information, in most cases submitted by a participating minister, of recent campaigns and missions in Glasgow—all non-Catholic, some otherwise inter-denominational, some by individual congregations.

As the neighbouring text explains, the following is but a selection illustrative of recent and current evangelistic activity, the genesis of which goes back to the period between the two World Wars.

KEY TO SYMBOLS

(a) Background notes.
(b) Type and method.
(c) Participants.
(d) Results and/or assessment or other comments (in each case those of the relevant informants).
(e) Sources of further information.

A dash (—) following a symbol indicates that no information is available.

NORTH KELVINSIDE MISSION, 1947

(a) In 1946, membership of North Kelvinside Church of Scotland stood at just over 400 out of a parish population of 10,000. Out of about 2,000 homes nearly 700 had no church connection of any kind. (b) A fortnight's mission of visitation of homes in the area (north-central). (c) Rev. Tom Allan, minister of North Kelvinside, and a team of missioners under the leadership of Rev. D. P. Thomson. (d) Three months after the mission almost 100 new members were added to the Communion Roll; two years after the mission the congregation had doubled itself; 5½ years after, 800 new members had joined. But the mission was not without its less happy features. Only a small number of the "original" members took part, while among the rest was a substantial section who opposed the mission. Not all new members were fully assimilated into the congregational life, and some in consequence drifted away as the months passed. On this Mr. Allan has written: "Far from being the minister of a growing congregation I was in fact in danger of becoming the minister of two congregations, worshipping in the same building and called by the same name, but separate in every other sense." But, on the credit side, he could also say, "Gradually . . . the gulf between the parish and its church is being bridged." (e) *cf.* Mr. Allan's *Face of My Parish* (1954). The quotations are from p. 33 and p. 82.

RADIO MISSIONS, 1950 AND 1951-2

(a) Starting-point was the discovery that 50 per cent of listeners to religious broadcasts are non-churchgoers. (b) Concentrated series of broadcasts (church services, talks, family services, a few dramatic presentations) over several weeks (e.g. 90-odd broadcasts in a six-week period of 1952). (c) Team of preachers drawn from six non-Catholic denominations, under the general leadership of Rev. R. H. W. Falconer, Organiser of Religious Broadcasts in Scotland, whose idea it was. (d) Of the Missions' three aims the first, "to challenge the careless," was achieved to some extent; the second, "to reclaim the lapsed," was the most adequately fulfilled of the three; and the third, "to strengthen the faithful," was largely fulfilled. But, on the debit side, there was little support from the laity. Those lay members, however, who did "go out" found "that in the process their beliefs took on a new meaning for them; congregations too did some self-examination." (e) *cf.* Mr. Falconer's *Success and Failure of a Radio Mission* (1951) and his article in *The Student Movement* (December, 1952). The quotation at end of item (d) is from the latter, *cf.* pp. 12-13.

The Glasgow Churches' Campaign, 1950

(a) The 1950 Radio Mission was timed intentionally to coincide with this Campaign (sometimes also called the Glasgow "Commandos' Campaign"). (b) A programme of long-term preparation and training—district surveys, witness weeks, campaign "socials," training schools, prayer meetings, open-air meetings and house-to-house visitation culminated in the inter-denominational "Commandos' assault" of 3-13 October. This took the form of lunch-hour factory addresses, night-shift meetings, meetings at works gates and in shipyards, visits to Transport Department depots, schools, the teachers' training college, other colleges and the University, cinemas, dance halls, football matches, hospitals, R.N.V.R. and Army depots, "model lodging houses" and a city prison—the whole amounting to about 1,500 assignments. Street plays and films shown in a mobile cinema and converted vans were also used as methods of "getting the message across." (c) Under a sponsoring committee the Rev. R. Leonard Small (who was joint chairman of the Edinburgh "Commandos' Campaign" of 1947) led the campaign, with the Rev. J. B. Donald in the early months, and latterly the Rev. J. T. Wotherspoon, acting as organiser. The "Commando" team composed of some local (and a number of visiting) ministers was under the convenership of the Rev. Johnston R. McKay, and the Congregational Mission under that of the Rev. Tom Allan. (d) No attempt made at statistical assessment, but there was very little opposition to meetings anywhere, many serious and sympathetic questions were asked and discussions held, and a number of conversions were made. Several churches had increased attendances for a time and cases were reported from all districts of "individuals challenged and completely changed by the campaign." A longer-term effect was an impetus to industrial chaplaincy in the city (31 factories asked for a regular chaplain, and a chaplaincy service for transport depots was developed). (e) —.

Partick Mission, 1949 and 1950

(a) —. (b) (i) Parish visitations before and after the 1950 Churches' Campaign, and (ii) series of meetings and services in which the Partick churches united. (c) Over 50 members of Partick Anderson Church of Scotland (west-central district) took part in (i) above, in association with their minister, the Rev. K. J. Turnbull; some members of other Partick churches joined in (i) later; the Rev. Tom Allan was special or visiting preacher for (ii). (d) The visitation showed that of the 10,537 households visited 32 per cent claimed connection with the Church of Scotland, 12 per cent with the Roman Catholic Church, and a further proportion (not stated) with other churches, while 11 per cent of households contained persons who expressed a desire to join a church. Two things, wrote Mr. Turnbull, "driven home to us again and again" were the need for the Church to do regular open-air work and the "urgent and vital need" for each church member to become an active missionary in his own particular circle of families, friends and workmates. (e) —.

The Gorbals Mission, 1952-3 and 1954-5

(a) This Mission followed a smaller-scale visitation over part of the area (south-central) in 1952-53 by the Rev. John Lang and colleagues. (b) Inter-denominational house-to-house visitation, special meetings and services. (c) Ministers of the area and some lay members, with the Rev. Tom Allan as special preacher and leader of a six-weeks' training school. (d) No "official" assessment; but one participating minister, the Rev. James Wood of Augustine-Buchanan Church of Scotland, stated in a memorandum that the work of follow-up proved difficult, partly because the great majority of members live outside the area where the churches are situated, and partly because few of the area churches (for other reasons besides the foregoing) made any effort to cope with the task. As a result of a follow-up by himself and his office-bearers, 65 new members had been added to the Augustine-Buchanan roll by the date of his communication, with others preparing to join. The survey part of the project showed that in one section of the mission area 45 per cent claimed Protestant and 43 per cent Roman Catholic affiliation of some degree, 12 per cent being Jews, Hindus or Pakistanis. In the other section there were very few of the three latter, 45 per cent professing Protestant and 55 Catholic connection. "Very few householders declared themselves to be Communists or unbelievers." Full details are not available, but it would appear that only about 10 per cent of the self-declared adult Protestants in the combined area attended church regularly. (e) —.

MISSION IN CARNTYNE, 1952-53

(a) Out of a membership of about 800 only about 170 reside within the parish. (b) House-to-house visitation, special meetings and services. (c) The minister of Carntyne Old Church of Scotland (eastern district), the Rev. G. K. Mortimer, and members of the congregation. (d) Some addition was made to the roll, but the most marked effect of the missionary activity was on the congregation itself—increased attendance and participation in the life of the church, and heightened interest in Bible study. (e) —.

NORTH GLASGOW MISSION, 1953 AND 1954

(a) —. (b) After a "Teaching Mission" for the preparation of church members as missioners, a fortnight's series of public meetings was followed by visitation in the northern districts of the city each weeknight for three weeks—over the period, a total of 15,000 visits paid. (c) District ministers and lay members of 12 congregations of several denominations, and 120 students from the Scottish Universities—the combined team under the leadership of the Rev. Tom Allan, then Field Organiser of the "Tell Scotland" Movement. (d) No statistical assessment, but in a report the Rev. William Burnside, of Springburn North Church of Scotland, a participating minister, wrote that the meetings drew large crowds, the overall activities made religion a talking-point and were "a means of conversion, heart-searching and quickening in the Church." A follow-up (1955-6) by his own congregation at the time of his submission of a memorandum to the author held promise "of bringing many people into the membership of the Church." (e) —.

AN EXAMPLE OF CHURCH EXTENSION AT WORK:

ST. JAMES (POLLOK)

(a) Church extension in the new housing areas of the city is going ahead as rapidly as finance and materials allow—in some places, indeed, well in advance even of the erection of temporary halls. (In the new and expanding estate of Castlemilk, for example, the Rev. David Reid, Castlemilk East, and the Rev. D. A. MacLeod, Castlemilk West, were on the spot and at work almost as soon as the first houses were occupied, ready to welcome subsequent arrivals and holding services of worship where they could—in Mr. MacLeod's case in a neighbouring school, in Mr. Reid's in a workmen's canteen hut for a year before he too obtained the use of the school in his parish.) An account of the newest parishes, however, with the population itself still in process of settling in, would at this stage be premature: the time for their story will come. Here we take St. James Church of Scotland, Pollok, set up in August 1948 on the southern outskirts of the city, as an example both of extension work and of out-going mission: in both senses it well illustrates the "outreach" of the Church. The current membership of St. James is about 2,150, half of whom are entirely new to the Church of Scotland. In Pollok, as in many other postwar housing areas, people have virtually "stormed" the place (temporary or permanent) of public worship. But for all that the ministers and their lay helpers have not simply held out their arms in welcome to this inflow: they have gone out and about in their parishes and brought into the fellowship those who might not have come on their own initiative. So, taking up our symbols once again, we pass on to: (b) Regular and sustained missionary work over the parish area. (c) The joint ministers—Revs. J. Clarence Finlayson and James Currie—the assistant minister, some office-bearers and some members. (d) Whereas in 1950-1, out of 4,183 houses 33 per cent had a Church of Scotland connection, 28 per cent Roman Catholic, 9 per cent a connection with other denominations, and 30 per cent no religious affiliation at all, by 1955 these percentages had changed to 48.3, 27.2, 6.0 and 18.5 respectively. The figure of 48.3 per cent of houses is made up of 24.5 per cent (of all houses) with membership at St. James, 14.1 per cent with children at St. James Sunday School, and 9.7 per cent with other Church of Scotland connection. Youth Fellowships and uniformed organisations are also steadily increasing in numbers. The present situation at St. James is described by Mr. Finlayson as "interim only"; future developments may see a determined attempt "to get at the working man at his own level." (e) Article, "Some Further Facts from a Scots Church Extension Parish" in the *British Weekly,* 3 November 1955.

THE ALL-SCOTLAND—BILLY GRAHAM CRUSADE, 1955

(a) It is this Crusade which, naturally and on the whole justifiably, most people think of when they hear mention of "Tell Scotland" (see neighbouring text, *infra*) and recent evangelistic activities. The "Tell Scotland" Movement invited Mr. Graham to Scotland, and played a very considerable part in the preparations for, and quite brilliant organisation of, the Crusade. This contribution is recorded (in the Rev. William Fitch's chapter) in *Crusade in Scotland . . . Billy Graham.* (b) A six-weeks series of meetings in Kelvin Hall, Glasgow, for hymn-singing and prayer and, after a sermon by Mr. Graham each evening, for people to "come forward" and "take decisions for Christ"; ancillary meetings in other Scottish towns, including Edinburgh; television and radio links with congregational groups meeting all over Scotland and places in England; television and radio broadcasts; mass rallies at Glasgow's great football stadiums —at Ibrox Park on the second-last, and at Hampden Park on the last, evening of the campaign; careful training of stewards and counsellors and husbanding of decision-takers until received by the minister of the church of their choice. All this and much else is described in the book mentioned above (to date the only publication of book length on the Crusade). (c) Mr. Graham's own team and many ministers from Scotland, England and America, men and women from many parts of Scotland serving as members of various committees, stewards and counsellors and members of the massed choir—the whole, it might be said, led as to day-to-day operational arrangements by the Rev. Tom Allan in his role as chairman of the All-Scotland Executive Committee. (d) For comments on the effect of the Crusade see neighbouring text, *supra.* Here we shall record data that in some measure indicate the Crusade's immediate impact. In Chapter I of *Crusade in Scotland . . . Billy Graham,* Mr. Allan writes (p. 8): "Between the 21st of March and the 30th of April, 1955 . . . a total of 1,185,360 people in Scotland attended meetings of one kind or another directly connected with the Crusade. Of these, 830,670 were at the nightly meetings in Kelvin Hall and at the closing rallies in Ibrox Stadium and Hampden Park; 217,700 were at services of the Relay Mission in various parts of the country; and 136,990 were at other meetings addressed by Mr. Graham and Team members during the Crusade. And the total number of enquirers in Scotland during these weeks was 26,547." Of these enquirers—the general term used to describe converts, those who publicly re-affirmed their faith, and those "simply seeking guidance or comfort or encouragement"—19,835 came forward at Kelvin Hall, Ibrox or Hampden; and of these 29 per cent were men and 71 per cent were women, while 79 per cent indicated that they were making "a first-time decision for Christ." The six-weeks campaign provided a surplus of £26,722 from a total income of £71,618. Collections at the Kelvin Hall meetings amounted to £51,980 and at the Ibrox and Hampden Parks rallies £1,690 and £3,574 respectively. The expenses of Mr. Graham and his team were met by the Billy Graham Organisation, and the All-Scotland Executive Committee have made a donation of £12,000 out of the surplus to that body. Whatever may be the eventual assessment of the longer-term effects, few will dismiss as partisan Tom Allan's judgment—a judgment which in any case is shared by many others of authority—that the Crusade was "the greatest evangelistic campaign in the history of Scotland." (e) —.

The Work Goes on: Youth Rallies and the "House-Church"

The work of mission by inter-church teams and congregational groups goes on—in Govanhill, in Maryhill, in Newlands, in Pollokshields, in Shawlands, and in other districts of the city. New things are being tried. This synopsis concludes by mentioning two out of several. By coming back, through this particular choice, to the evangelist and the parish of our first account, we underline the fact that methods have not been allowed to set in a rigid pattern.

Youth Rallies.—The Rev. Tom Allan, recently inducted to a "down-town" charge, St. George's Tron, is seeking to make of it a "city centre of evangelism." Among several new ventures already put in train is a series of monthly Saturday youth rallies. These speedily became so successful—regularly attracting attendances of well over 1,000—that the venue was changed, in the late spring of 1956, to Kelvin Hall. So that, a little more than a year after its precincts had held the huge congregations who came to hear Mr. Graham, its doors opened to hundreds of young men and women come from the city and beyond to be challenged by Mr. Allan to "make their decisions for Christ." On one Saturday evening in May, over 4,500 young people attended the rally, of whom 88—one third of them in the 17-20 age group—made decisions of commitment.

The "House-Church."—As Mr. Allan does all this the work he started in North Kelvinside is being carried on by his successor in that parish, the Rev. Hamish Kennedy, through the medium of what is called the "house church." (This relatively new medium of mission is not confined to North Kelvinside: much activity of this kind is going on in Burntisland, Port Glasgow, Greenock and elsewhere.) In practice this is house-based fellowship of members with members for Bible study, discussion and acts of worship, and of members with families as yet outside the church. The congregational groups active in these house-fellowships have two objectives—to integrate the membership of the congregation and to go out into the streets of the parish in friendship and mission.

These ventures have not won total support from the people inside the churches. Especially in the earlier projects a major disappointment to the leaders and organisers was the failure of too many lay churchfolk to provide the support expected—to supplement in their own way an endeavour whose purpose is theirs as well as their ministers'. Later experience has shown what was in any case obvious, that without the backing of a trained and enthusiastic laity the full fruits of even the most zealous ministerial efforts cannot be reaped. In some cases those who hold back do so from personal motives the sincerity of which their ministers and others respect; in other cases the reasons are alleged lack of time, lack of interest, uncertainty of their own convictions and unwillingness to be put to the test of defending them against challenge and of witnessing to them more positively.

However, it is possible, towards the end of 1956, to see signs that inroads are being made into the conservatism of the bulk of churchgoers. This is partly an effect of the All-Scotland Crusade; it is equally, if not more, to the credit of "Tell Scotland," itself the motivating force behind the Graham campaign. In "Tell Scotland" the more recent and current campaigns have behind them, as earlier ventures had not, a sustaining force, a behind-the-scenes impetus, a framework of ideas loosely patterning local thought and action. In it, too, the Scottish Churches have in their evangelistic endeavours a focus and a potential agency of consolidation.

The roots of this Movement—for that is the one word that sums up its character—go back at least twenty years: possibly, as many have suggested, to the situation and reactions described in the opening paragraphs of this section. Doubtless, too, these roots were nurtured in the soil richly tilled by the Church of Scotland pamphlet of 1946, *Into All The World*. It took form as something more than vague aspirations and inarticulate intentions in 1953, when ministers of six denominations—joined later by representatives of other two—formed themselves into a "Tell Scotland" Committee. Before long, the Rev. Tom Allan was appointed field organiser and evangelist,[1] and plans for a programme conceived in three phases began to form. The first, running from September 1953 to June 1954, was a period of general discussion on the theme of mission among ministers and office-bearers. During the second (September 1954 to June 1955), "the emphasis passed to the preparation of the congregation and the recruitment and training of the lay forces of the Church for the task of witness." Phase III, begun in September 1955, saw lay groups "moving out in witness—in the community, at work, in the place of leisure."[2]

Future missions, then, are likely to move within the broad framework of "Tell Scotland." Development has not proceeded evenly in all areas, either of the country as a whole or of Glasgow; but the hope cherished by the "Tell Scotland" leaders that the Hampden Park closing of the Crusade on 30 April 1955 would be thought of not as an end but as a fresh beginning has been demonstrably fulfilled. The "out-reach" of the Church goes on.

Non-Christian Religious Groups

In addition to the Christian denominations with which we have been concerned in the foregoing sections, the city houses followers of non-Christian faiths.[3] Only about some of these, however, is information of any sort obtainable without embarking on a specific and exhaustive survey.[4] It is known, for example, that the city has its devotees of Buddhism, but just how many it is impossible without a census-type enquiry to tell.

Similarly, the total number of Muslims and Hindus in the city is

1 Mr. Allan's successor in this post is the Rev. Ian MacTaggart.

2 The quoted phrases are taken from the report of the Home Board to the General Assembly of the Church of Scotland (see *Reports to the General Assembly*, 1955, p. 177).

3 A brief discussion of the social inter-relations between Christians and non-Christians in Glasgow—and among the devotees of the different Christian denominations—is to be found in Chapter 23.

4 Among the reasons for this are: (1) the decennial Population Census has nothing to say on this matter; (2) not all religious minorities are numerically large enough to maintain a place of worship or other focus of their common interests; and (3) a religious minority may be made up of persons of several nationalities, not all of whom may have official representatives in a position, through their supervisory and welfare duties, to furnish data about their immigrant countrymen.

not known, but it is estimated that there are about 1,000 Pakistani Muslims and about 500 Indian Hindus resident in the city.[1] Each estimate excludes the "floating" population of Pakistani and Indian seamen (numbering, on an average day, about 500 and 200 respectively) and the student groups.

The majority of both Pakistanis and Indians live in the South Side of the city, in the central near-river areas, but some are to be found in central northern districts (for example, around St. George's Cross and North Woodside Road) and an increasing number (Pakistanis rather more than Indians) are finding it financially possible to move out to middle-class areas and are settling in such districts as Pollokshields and Kelvinside. Most of the Pakistanis and Indians are travelling salesmen on their own account, with a few (Pakistanis again rather more than Indians) owning small grocery or women's clothing shops. Of the total of approximately 1,500, somewhere between 300-400 are employed in factories, on the railways, and in the Corporation transport service.

Nearly all the Pakistanis are thought to be devout Muslims, regularly attending the Holy Day (Juma or Friday) prayer-meetings held in the Mosque (situated in the Gorbals area), and observing the regulations of their religion governing fasting days and diet. They do not eat pork or bacon, and have their own butchers providing them with Kosher-type food. Despite the lack of a Hindu temple as such in Glasgow, the majority of the city's Indians are practising Hindus, for example abstaining from beef-eating and observing such practices as cremation in accordance with Hindu rites. A small Sikh temple, established in 1911, serves the few Glasgow Indians who are members of this sect.

In addition to these relatively "settled" communities, there are about 800 overseas coloured students attending courses at the University and the Royal College of Science and Technology. Of these, about 200 are Hindus, about 100 Muslims and about 50 Buddhists. About 350 are at least nominally Christian or with a Christian background, the remaining 50-100 being attached to other religions or of atheist or "rationalistic" persuasion. In each case about one quarter of the students included under the heads of these four religious groups attend services of worship regularly or are in other respects religiously active. Very few non-Christian students, whether active or not in the observance of their own faith, attend Christian church services, although Hindus have been known willingly to attend such services if invited to do so by Glasgow Christians with whom they may be spending a week-end. Practically all Muslim students and about half of the Hindu students

[1] By, respectively, Mr. Mustapha Ellam, Pakistan High Commissioner's representative in Scotland and Mr. G. C. Dass, formerly Indian Welfare Officer and presently Secretary of the Indian Association (Glasgow). These gentlemen, whose assistance is gratefully acknowledged, are the authorities for statements made in this Section and in Chapter 23 concerning the Pakistani and Indian communities in Glasgow. Mr. N. Bose who, with 40 years of residence in Glasgow behind him, is very probably the city's oldest Indian inhabitant, was kind enough to read an early draft of both these Sections and to make comments.

are thought to observe the prescriptions of their religion governing diet.[1]

Of the non-Christian religious groups in the city the Jewish community is the most considerable—numerically and by any other reckoning. The first Jewish citizen of whom there is record was Isaac Cohen, a hatter, who was admitted a Freeman of the city in 1812. From that time on the evidence is of growth—slow for the better part of a century but increasing in pace in recent decades—in numbers, in activities, and in assurance of acceptance as fellow-citizens by the non-Jewish population.[2] At the beginning of this century the city's Jewish community probably numbered somewhere between 2,000 and 3,000. Now, in 1956, its numerical strength is in the region of 15,000.[3] From three 50 years ago the total of synagogues has risen to thirteen. The location of recently established synagogues or meeting-places—serving Giffnock and Newlands; Langside; Netherlee and Clarkston; Pollokshields; and Queen's Park—is an interesting indication of another development in the life of Glasgow Jewry: the move from the older, near-river south-side area in which for decades the great majority were concentrated to newer, middle-class, residential (but still mainly south-side) districts.

The concepts of "membership" and "regularity of attendance" cannot meaningfully be applied to the Jewish community. The number of synagogue seat-holders is not known to the central council of the community; and, since many devout Jews worship in family groups—a congregation may properly be constituted if a minimum of ten males are present—and may attend synagogue only occasionally (perhaps only once a year, on the Day of Atonement), there is no possibility of arriving at a statistical measure of degree of attachment that could even broadly be set alongside the figures for Christian denominations in the foregoing sections. Jewish authorities hesitate even to concede

[1] The author is indebted to the Rev. A. Scott Hutchison, Church of Scotland Chaplain to Overseas Students, for these notes and estimates.

[2] Leaning heavily on Mr. A. Levy's *The Origins of Glasgow Jewry, 1812-1895* (1949), the following is a summary of the growth of Glasgow Jewry in the nineteenth century: The first Jewish place of worship in the city was opened in 1823; until the late 1890's there was only one congregation in Glasgow, worshipping in a succession of buildings until the consecration and opening of Garnethill Synagogue in 1879 gave it a more permanent home. In 1831 the number of Jews in Glasgow was still under 50; about a century ago the number of Jewish families was thought to be about 26. In 1879 there were "upwards of 700" Jewish inhabitants; as a result mainly of the influx soon after of refugees from Russian persecution, there was a sufficient increase in numbers to create a demand for an additional place of worship. A second synagogue, this time on the south side of the river, where increasingly the Jewish incomers were making their homes, was consecrated in 1899 and a third, in the same district, in 1901.

[3] It can be stated quite literally that no one knows the exact figure. The estimate here quoted is that put forward by a well-known (perhaps the best-known) Rabbi in Scotland, the Rev. I. K. Cosgrove, minister, Garnethill Synagogue. There are a small number of Jews residing temporarily in the city whose social relationships are confined to their own circle or extend to non-Jewish groups, and who have little or no connection, religious or otherwise, with the Jewish community or its component associations. They are not included in the above estimate. Glasgow's Jewish community is fourth in size in the United Kingdom, London having about 250,000 Jewish inhabitants and Manchester and Leeds between 25,000 and 30,000 each.

the possibility that among the estimated 15,000 there may be some Jews of the younger age-groups who have only mild religious convictions or none at all; one gathers that even an agnostic or atheist may, for reasons of family loyalty, attend gatherings for worship and so be one of the Jewish community.[1]

General Assessment and Conclusion

As was stated in the opening paragraphs of this chapter, it is readily admitted that the factual, mainly quantitative approach attempted in this review leaves unanswered such questions as—and these are probably the ones that matter most of all about a community's religious life—what does it mean for the city of Glasgow that there are these 404,000 Christians (and some thousands of followers of other religions) in its midst? What difference does it make to these individuals and the life they lead that they are professing members of a religious denomination?

If justification is required for eschewing these high matters,[2] it is sufficient simply to state that their investigation would have called for a long-term and large-scale enquiry reaching far beyond the resources available to this study. But there is more to it than that. It is debatable whether the most perfect methods of opinion-sounding, attitude-testing and behaviour assessment likely to be available to social scientists for some time would provide answers to our questions that would not lose through qualifications and caveats a great deal of what they seemed to gain.[3]

One difficulty is that in this as in other Western societies people live their lives in a cultural milieu that is very considerably coloured by Christian beliefs themselves, and the more palpable contrasts between mid-twentieth Christian and non-Christian lives are hard to come by.

[1] While this is not a sociological account of Glasgow Jewry, the following observations may be of interest as filling in part of the background to the above sketch. Undoubtedly there is a widespread impression among non-Jews that the great majority of Glasgow Jewish citizens are in business, however small-scale, on their own account. Since no statistics of Jewish occupational distribution are available for Glasgow it is not possible to confirm or correct this guess; but according to Jewish spokesmen with a working knowledge of the community, hundreds of the city's Jews are employed in tailoring factories and as large-store salesmen, while many others are in cabinet-making and other types of manufacture; a sizeable proportion are in various professions, and another considerable segment of the community work as agents on a commission basis for Jewish stores and businesses. Clearly the Jewish community, like the city as a whole, has its well-to-do and its poor and a range of strata in between; but how the proportions in each stratum compare with their non-Jewish equivalents, and whether the former is marked by greater or lesser social status consciousness, are questions on which no one can speak with authority.

[2] A partial and tentative discussion of a few of the issues raised by these questions is to be found in Chapter 23.

[3] One could, of course, enquire into a number of things: for example, the extent to which regular churchgoers are leaders of the voluntary organisations of their community. But what to do about the problem of assessing the difference this makes to these associations' lives—their constitutions, their primary group relations, the pursuing of their purposes?

Ethically these lives will in very many cases reveal a close similarity—both in the success and lack of success in living up to self-imposed standards. Moreover, the Christian faith is, for the believing Christian, more than a source of standards of conduct: it concerns much that is private to the individual's solitary "cool-hour" reflection but will not necessarily issue in an observably different pattern of conduct from that of the non-Christian. To say that it ought to and that if it does not the man is not really a Christian is, if not to beg the question, certainly to confuse it. The problem is not: what difference would it make to the life of Glasgow (or any other community) if x per cent of its citizens were a communion of saints?

Further, there is a wide variation in the willingness of men to excuse or charitably to suspend judgment upon an individual Christian's short-comings; there is also an elasticity about the number and character of short-comings regarded by men as necessary before an individual forfeits all claim to the name of Christian. For this among other reasons a considerable element of subjectivity would be virtually ineradicable from any "scientific" investigation of the matters here raised.

But this having been said, and these deep issues set aside, there follow a few observations—resting on hints and pointers picked up in the course of this study but in the final analysis no more than subjective comments—on some "qualitative," background aspects to the matters discussed in the foregoing sections, and (by way of summary) a general assessment of the contemporary Church situation.[1]

Every minister and office-bearer knows that a congregation carries with it a fringe of "paper" or nominal members—members who are strangers, to greater or lesser degree, to its communal life and its service of public worship. But there is also, in most if not all congregations, a fringe of another sort—a body of quite regular attenders whose church-going is motivated by such peripheral objectives as the acquiring of social status or the winning of acceptance into a social circle for whom churchgoing is a potent norm. There can be no doubt that there is still a lingering element of prestige-seeking and prestige-conferring about the churchgoing of a number among the following. The harsh economic and social sanctions of an earlier time are no longer brought to bear on non-members and poor attenders; but here and there in the middle-class strata of the city pockets of a powerful social status pressure towards membership and attendance still exist. For some, churchgoing is still the thing you do—and for extra-religious reasons.

It is, however, right to record that in a good many congregations such people are finding that another sort of pressure is bearing in upon them as upon their more earnest brethren in the pews: the relentless attack by many of the younger ministers on extra-religious motives and the implied if not always explicit challenge from the pulpit Sunday after Sunday to throw off the "Sunday-church-going-clothes" mentality

[1] It should be noted that the discussion to follow relates exclusively to the non-Roman Churches and mainly but not only to the Church of Scotland.

and live every day of the week a life dedicated to Christ.[1] It is no secret that many younger ministers would rather reduce their congregations by half than carry with them a load of paper members and conventional attenders.

Within the membership of the Church there has been a change of attitude to the minister—such a change, indeed, as would have shocked our churchgoing grandmothers: the minister's judgment is no longer accepted in silent reverence as the final word, even his *obiter dicta* as the pronouncements of infallible authority; there is not the same frantic, last-minute scatter to tidy up when the knock on the door is suspected to be his. Indeed, frequently in their pastoral visitations even to their own members ministers have to compete with a radio or television programme. And if the menfolk, to whose fathers disputation with the minister was always an attractive diversion, are less inclined now to engage him in philosophical arguments, this is due more to the complexity of contemporary problems and the change in accepted thought-forms—and possibly also to the general decline in the art of conversation—than to any latter-day obsequiousness in the ministerial presence. In lesser matters, indeed, there is in minister-member social relationships a tendency to forthrightness of comment and even to light-hearted banter without disrespect that is refreshingly in keeping with the current " down to earthness " of much pulpit address. We may say, in sum, that diminishing though the gap may be between ministerial stipends and the monetary rewards of a wide range of non-professional occupations, the social status of the minister is, if lower than it was, still relatively high.

Our fathers would see change also in the contemporary outlook on Sunday Observance. The rigid Sabbatarianism of an earlier day, with even the family's church-going shoes brushed and polished by Saturday evening, is with us no longer, at least in the towns and cities. Though it breaks out from time to time, one cannot say that Sunday Observance is currently a very burning issue. The Church unsuccessfully fought the decision of the magistrates in 1954 to allow the Sunday commercial opening of (on average) 12 out of 73 central and suburban cinemas on rota; and the same year it failed to prevent the Sunday opening of Corporation bowling greens. Such attempts by the Church to restrict Sunday diversions create a certain amount of resentment among the churchless, but this soon passes as they cheerfully pursue on Sundays the secular delights which Church and Local Authority alike are powerless to forbid. Even among churchfolk the feeling is forming that a Sunday bus- or car-ride to the coast after Church, a bathe or a game of cricket on the beach on a holiday Sunday, maybe even a quiet non-

[1] An interesting development in this connection is Scottish Christian Industrial Order (" SCIO " for short). SCIO's concern—as the Chairman, Mr. George Taylor, points out in a communication to the author—is not with industrial relations: its aim is " to further the application of the principles of the Christian Faith throughout industrial life and society . . . to assist its members in making their working life a more real and effective part of their Christian life." The Order has two types of branches. There are 10 Church Branches in the Glasgow area, and efforts are now being made to form branches of the second type, Work Branches,

holiday hour on the tennis courts between services—that these and similar diversions are not the last word in pagan indulgence. As against this, it should be added not only that belief and practice vary but that this tendency, described by some churchfolk as a growing capitulation to the "Continental Sunday," has aroused not a little disquiet. By and large, however, there is a growing tendency towards what by contrast with its predecessor can be called a liberal outlook on these matters.

If the foregoing pages have established anything, it must surely be that an outstanding characteristic of the church situation in Glasgow (as elsewhere in Scotland) to-day is the realisation that—as many church leaders have expressed it—"only if it is a missionary 'outgoing' force will the Church in our time be effective." We have noted some examples of recent attempts by ministers and a number of lay members to win back or introduce to the fellowship of the Church the lapsed, the wavering, and the undiscovered well-disposed. Only as the work proceeds is the magnitude of this task being fully appreciated and the realisation being driven home that it is a continuing endeavour to be given up only on peril of losing hard-won gains. But the prospects are not everywhere discouraging. Even if little headway is likely to be made in the older areas of the city where church-avoidance by the (now) older age-groups set into a fixed pattern of beliefs and behaviour during the interwar period—and it is by no means certain that such areas are irretrievably lost to the Church—the situation in both the between-the-wars suburbs (such as King's Park and Croftfoot) and the postwar housing districts on the city's outskirts is of an entirely different character. Pollok forms an excellent example of the latter, and if the Rev. J. Clarence Finlayson is right, it is only the limitation of man-power and other practical resources that prevent the Church there from claiming about four fifths of the population. Two features of the situation in Pollok are especially notable. One is the fact that many of the people coming into the Church are working-class or upper-working class people who previously reflected in their life and beliefs "the non-Church-mindedness" of the older areas from which they have moved. The other is that the great majority of the reclaimed or newly-won are coming to the Church not—as the writer along with other observers thought likely to be the case—primarily as a means of cultivating new social relationships but primarily for what the Church *qua* spiritual agency has to offer them. Many who have joined the Church refuse to have anything to do with such related associations as the Woman's Guild or the Men's Association: the felt need is for the Church's specific message.[1] This attitude is, to churchmen, the true ground of encouragement: the essential condition is satisfied, and integration into the full community life of the congregation can if

1 These points were made by Mr. Finlayson in conversation with the author. In this connection an interesting suggestion made by Mr. Finlayson was that with more money in their purses these men and women are not now deterred, as some were in the past and might in less comfortable circumstances still be, by the "fashion parade" aspect that unhappily characterised and still characterises too much of the city's attendance at public worship.

ultimately sought follow without difficulty. In such areas the situation is, for the Church, one of heartening promise.

As for the intellectuals, it can at least be said that they do not constitute a solid *bloc* of atheists and that a number outside the Church have in recent years shown towards it an open-mindedness increasingly touched with goodwill. This has been won partly at least by the evidence of a revitalised zeal, a willingness to face up to the challenge of the day, on the part of the Church itself. The Church would, however, be unwise not to realise that the fundamentalism of Mr. Billy Graham was a hard pill for these men and women to swallow, and may well have lost to the Church bridgeheads it was beginning to consolidate.

There remains the hard core of the "just not interested." As stated earlier, there may be no bright prospect of much advance among the working-class population still residing in the older areas with a non-church "culture" going back at least to the 1920's. The physical move to a new house in a new neighbourhood seems for some to touch off a mental re-rooting, a kind of intellectual re-decorating and re-furnishing; and when this occasion is lacking the Church may find it difficult to break through. Even so, inroads are beginning to be made, through the agency of industrial chaplaincies and in other ways, into this sector of working-class indifference. The fact that it is now correct to use the word "indifference" rather than the terms, such as "hostility" and "resentment," that could not have been avoided in the 'twenties and 'thirties, is in itself one sign of change. It behoves the Church, nevertheless, to recognise that (justly or unjustly) it is given little or no credit by these people for the transformation in living conditions which, a little paradoxically, has been a major factor working towards that change of attitude. In this very fact there lurks the warning that this indifference may prove no easy nut for the Church to crack.

It falls to be said also, however, that evidence from house-to-house missions suggests that the "just not interested" form a minority among the unconnected, and that many in this category still send their children to Sunday School—a practice which is not in every case motivated solely by a desire to get them out of the way and leave the reading of Sunday newspapers undisturbed. Indeed, not merely does this category display little hostility to the Church: more positively it appreciates that the Church has a part to play in the lives of others if not in theirs and should be left to get on with it. It also contains, it should be added, its quota of "four-wheel Christians";[1] and the nub of their attitude is: "We are not much interested in the Church but it is a good thing to have around when you need it." So, too, the minister is a useful fellow to have about the place; and, in magnanimous mood, it is conceded that the job he has to do is no easy, one-day-a-week assignment. The respect the churchless extend to the ministers of the city is, indeed, not

[1] This delightfully succinct phrase has gained useful currency recently as a summary description of those whose only connection with the Church is on the occasions when they are wheeled there for baptism in a perambulator, arrive in a taxi for the solemnisation of their marriage, wheel their children to church for their baptism and, finally, are driven in the company of a minister to their grave.

unconnected with the attempts many of the latter have been making to reduce the number to whom the adjective " churchless " applies.

What success may attend these efforts is for a later observer to establish; what we can record here, in concluding this study, is that in the postwar decade the Church has lived through a period of activity, of experiment, of clarification of aims, of rededication to its missionary obligation, on a scale and to an extent unprecedented in its recent history. In foregoing sections we have noted some of the fruits of this industry; to these may be added the following among the gains of the " Tell Scotland " movement listed by the Rev. Tom Allan at a press conference on 13 October 1956: the various branches of the Church in Scotland are working more harmoniously together than at any time in the past; the contributions to the work of the Church are on the increase; and more students are coming into the ministry than at any time since the war.

Altogether, then, there is much in the postwar story the Church has already written from which it may justifiably take heart. " It is easier," said Mr. Allan on the occasion referred to above, " it is easier to preach the Gospel in Scotland to-day than at any time since the First World War—that, at least, is my experience and the experience of older ministers." His point here was that there are signs of " a greater willingness to receive the Gospel," not that the Church is watering down its message to make it more acceptable to churchless and church-folk. That is not the mood of the contemporary Church: the people in many of the city's pews, the audience at many public meetings, are not being allowed to remain in any doubt that the Church in Glasgow to-day is a challenging and a demanding Church.

Chapter 23

SOCIAL RELATIONS

RELIGIOUS AND RACIAL RELATIONS

JOHN HIGHET

As the previous Chapter shows, there are in Glasgow Christians, Jews, Muslims, Hindus, Buddhists, and followers of one or two other religious faiths. Some Christians are Roman Catholics, some are not. Some of the non-Romans are Presbyterians, while the others are distributed over a wide range of ecclesiastical groupings. How does this variety of religious and denominational attachment affect social relationships?

Few non-coloured Glaswegians are moved on purely religious grounds to any sort of hostility towards Muslims, Hindus, Buddhists and other non-white religious minorities within the city; and this is so even if the main reason for it is simply that these groups *are* minorities. As long as we restrict our questions to the context of religious loyalties this short and plain statement is in fact all that need be said. Inevitably, however, this matter becomes entangled with the more general issue of race relations. The testimony of both Mr. Ellam and Mr. Dass, speaking on behalf of the Pakistani and Indian communities, is that social and economic discrimination on grounds of colour is almost entirely non-existent. This is not necessarily a tribute to Glasgow's enlightenment; doubtless things might be otherwise in a more competitive economic situation and if the city's coloured inhabitants were more numerous. For example, the Rev. A. Scott Hutchison tells of the reluctance of Glasgow landladies to take in overseas coloured students as boarders —out of 1,350 landladies on the University list only 60 have stated their willingness to accept overseas students—and if the majority of Glasgow citizens were similarly placed in a situation in which their social relationships with coloured people were of this regularly direct and personal kind, no one can be confident that something like the beginning of widespread colour prejudice might not show itself. On the other hand, this reluctance on the part of landladies is partly connected with the complication of providing acceptable food; and it is not symptomatic of the attitude of others who are in fairly regular contact with coloured students. More generally, over the past year Mr. Hutchison has had more than 100 requests from churches and church groups for overseas students to address meetings, and invitations to them to attend " socials," or to visit the homes of church people; and as we have seen, coloured students are frequently invited by their hosts to attend

Christian religious services, even if not all feel free for reasons of faith to accept. In summing up, in a private communication, his own experience of their reactions to their sojourn in the city, Mr. Hutchison writes that overseas students, on the whole, feel genuinely " at home " in Glasgow.

Essentially the same opinion was expressed independently by Mr. Ellam and Mr. Dass in respect of the non-student coloured groups whose welfare is their concern; the gist of their comments can be summed up in the statement, " Our countrymen have no grievances, no complaints; they like the Glasgow people and the Glasgow people seem to like them." The coloured men who have recently been brought into the city's transport service have been well received—and often helped—by the travelling public; and in this and in other spheres of employment their relations with their white workmates are in the main cordial. There is some inter-marrying and a fair amount of visiting of " white " homes by coloured people. It is a story of generally harmonious acceptance and contented " settling in "—a happy condition to which the great majority of coloured people have themselves contributed by their quiet, law-abiding living as they get on with their jobs.

In the attitude of the Jew and (white) non-Jew to one another the lines of demarcation between religious and non-religious ingredients are blurred even more. The lay Christian is conscious of differences in mode of living—in the dates of communal holidays, in diet, in greater (or at anyrate apparently greater) family solidarity—but there is little evidence that he is greatly exercised over the reflection that a source of these is ultimately the cleavage in religious beliefs: he takes them simply as here-and-now ways that are not his. Less happily, he is aware also of another order of difference—difference this time in physical appearance. He is conscious, too, that, for whatever reason, other nations and other cities have traditionally treated their Jewish inhabitants as an " out-group." He is therefore communally predisposed to the unreflecting reception of signs marking the Jew off from himself and his fellows; and, similarly historically conditioned, the Jewish community, if it does not positively flaunt these differences, of set purpose maintains them.

The lay Christian's attitude to the Jew is, in short, a product of varied sociological and psychological forces rooted deep in folk-experience; so that the assignment of such grating as there may be in the wheels of their social intercourse expressly to the grit of religious dispute is a hazardous enterprise. It is equally a risk to assert categorically that awareness of the fundamental rift in matters of faith may never be present in the mind of this or that Christian. But it would seem safe to say that such awareness seldom leads by itself to anything more hostile than " social distance."[1]

[1] And, of course, not always to that. Through the efforts of a Church of Scotland Committee and office-bearers of the Jewish Representative Council, meetings have been held in recent years in Glasgow at which two Christian and two Jewish speakers have addressed mixed audiences of Jews and Christians, with, it is

This term, "social distance," if not taken too technically, best sums up the prevailing state of Jewish—non-Jewish relations: in the normal course their paths seldom cross in formal and informal leisure activities. The Jewish community's associational life is rich and varied, with its cultural societies—prominent among which is their amateur dramatic group, the Jewish Institute Players—athletic and youth clubs and organisations, women's guilds, and so on; and it gets along by itself for the most part happily,[1] while opening its doors to any non-Jews who might wish to participate. Where they do come together, either in working hours or in off-duty informal groupings, they rub along, on the whole, pretty well. In the general run of the city's life what the careful observer would note is a somewhat cool reciprocal aloofness punctuated from time to time by the exchange of social courtesies as circumstances demand, and warmed now and again by more intimate association on a basis of mutual respect. His ears would pick up an undertone of enmity here and there, but he would normally look long before he saw signs of its expression in action.

There is, indeed, little in the attitude of Glasgow's non-Jews to Jews that merits the name of anti-Semitism, as the term has unhappily come in recent history to be understood. Dr. Cosgrove, invited as a leading figure in the religious and social life of Glasgow Jewry to comment freely on this issue and submit what relevant evidence the Jewish Representative Council might have before it, dismissed economic discrimination as extremely infrequent and seldom seriously handicapping, and social ostracisation as limited to a few non-Jewish institutions and establishments operating a bar against Jews as a set policy.[2] In neither practice, however, did Dr. Cosgrove see any ground for accusing non-Jewish Glaswegians of anti-Semitism as normally understood. This judgment is borne out by Mr. Maurice J. Roston, of the Board of Deputies of British Jews, who stated in a letter to the writer: "As far as can be ascertained there is no overt anti-Semitism in Glasgow, and good relations exist—as they have always done—between Jew and non-Jew. No organised outdoor or indoor activities are

[1] This is not to suggest that Jews make no contribution to the city's life and public affairs. Bailie Myer Galpern is at present Convener of the Corporation's Education Committee; Bailie Dr. Maurice Miller is Convener of the Planning Committee; Lord Greenhill was formerly City Treasurer and is Chairman of the West of Scotland District of the W.E.A.; and Benno Scholtz is a well-known sculptor. A lengthy list of Jews prominent in a wide variety of fields is to be found in an article published by the Rev. Dr. I. K. Cosgrove in the *Weekly Scotsman* of 19 September 1956. *Later*: Mr. Galpern was elected Lord Provost of Glasgow in May, 1958.

[2] Some Glasgow golf clubs and swimming clubs, and a city bridge club, debar Jews from membership. A Jewish golf club, formed recently partly as a result of this, has now acquired ground as a course. Membership of this club, it must be added, is open to non-Jews. For these and other facts and for many useful observations on the question of Jewish—non-Jewish relations in the city, I am indebted to my colleague, Miss Miriam J. H. Boston.

---

claimed, a resultant breaking down of prejudices and removal of misunderstandings on both sides. (cf. e.g. *Reports to the General Assembly of the Church of Scotland*, 1955, p. 189)

carried out by anti-Jewish organisations in Glasgow, or indeed—as far as we know—in the 'hinterland of Scotland.' The proverbial Scottish commonsense and an inherent dislike of intolerance, coupled with the historic independence of outlook, would make it more than difficult for any organised anti-Jewish prejudice to take root." Dr. Cosgrove, indeed, went further: Glasgow, he said, was sociologically speaking a much pleasanter place for Jews to live in than most others in Europe.[1]

The members of the "newer," non-traditional Christian Churches tend to restrict their relationships to within their own circle, but there is little evidence that this is as a result of deliberate social ostracisation by members of other denominations. A Seventh-Day Adventist working in an office where his workmates either have no church connections or are members of the Established Church may possibly be thought a little "queer" in his ideas, and the non-churchgoers may subject him from time to time to banter that is predominantly good-natured; but he is unlikely to be the victim of any discrimination other than this. He is not, for example, likely to be refused employment because of his particular religious beliefs.

Church of Scotland members may think it a pity that some Christians are "Wee Frees" and Baptists and Congregationalists and Episcopalians and so on, but between them and these others, and among these others themselves, relations are predominantly harmonious. No cases are known to the writer of social alienation or economic discrimination by members of one of the more traditional non-Roman denominations against members of others. This is not to say that doctrinal differences are no longer matters of real personal and group concern, or that the goal of denominational unity is about to be achieved: we are speaking here of everyday social relationships. Nevertheless, there can be little doubt that this widespread spirit of toleration owes a good deal to the easier relationships that have happily come to prevail recently at official levels and to the practical inter-denominational co-operation in evangelism that is one of the outstanding features of the postwar church situation.

An issue more widely regarded as of the essence of Glasgow's religious and social life is that of the relationships between the two great divisions of the city's Christian followers, the Roman Catholics and other Christians. (In what follows we shall use the popular terms "Catholics" and "Protestants" for these two categories.) Unfortunately, little recent research has been done on this question, and the remarks that follow must be regarded as the merest tentative reconnoitring of the ground. In preparing these observations I have been greatly aided by discussions with and memoranda from Mr. Frank MacMillan, a Catholic school-teacher and writer who has devoted con-

1 If the area of comparison is limited to the United Kingdom, it may be stated that precisely the same sentiment, *mutatis mutandis*, was expressed independently by Mr. Ellam and Mr. Dass as spokesmen for the Pakistani and Indian communities respectively.

siderable time to the study of Catholic social problems in the Clydeside area.[1]

Those whose information about Glasgow is based on what they glean from articles in Sunday newspapers and illustrated weekly magazines probably imagine that the Catholic-Protestant issue is Glaswegians' over-riding concern, and that the city is full of warring groups of Catholics and Protestants breaking bottles over each other's heads. This fantasy has obviously been engendered chiefly by the prominence given to the clashes that break out from time to time (usually just before, during or after a game) between segments of the followers of two of the city's football clubs, Rangers (objectified by the protagonists as representing Protestant Glasgow) and the predominantly Catholic club, Celtic. On this several things can be said that are likely to stand full-scale systematic investigation. First, these outbursts of violence (speedily, it should be added, controlled by the police) and foul-mouthed vocal demonstrations are the work of the merest minorities on each side: the vast majority of the supporters of both teams not merely disclaim any association with these factions but abhor their behaviour.[2] Secondly, the great bulk of these minorities are men with no religious faith whatsoever or with at best an extremely formal attachment, in the Protestant cases far short of church membership and in the case of the Catholics constituted by infant baptism and up-bringing in a Catholic family and background: their conduct is an embarrassment as much to the Churches whose cause they seem to imagine they espouse as to the honest-to-goodness spectator whose enjoyment of the game they effectively spoil. Thirdly, while on occasions in recent years this hooliganism has had a disquieting revivification, it is on the whole less regular and on a smaller scale now than at times between the wars.

Mr. William Maley, until 1937 secretary and manager of Celtic Football Club, put forward the theory that this trouble, unknown in the city up until the First World War, arose through the importation of workmen from Northern Ireland to meet the labour demands of Clydeside industry, many of these men bringing with them their strong, almost native, anti-Catholic prejudices, which were fanned afresh by the mere presence in the city of considerable numbers of Southern

1 Even so (and Mr. MacMillan agrees that this should be said), what follows is at best an amalgamation of the mainly subjective assessments by two observers representing—most amicably, it should be added, and far from dogmatically—each side.

2 Relations between the two football clubs are, at an official level, harmonious and even cordial. This applies no less to the respective Supporters' clubs, who have jointly backed up the efforts of magistrates and police to eliminate hooliganism and who have taken what steps are in their power to expel the worst offenders from attendance at Rangers-Celtic matches. At their annual rallies recently each Supporters' Club has invited one or two outstanding personalities from among the other's players to attend to receive presentations. Other facts relevant to an appreciation of this whole issue are these: the Rangers team is staffed exclusively by Protestant players, whereas the Celtic Board, although composed predominantly of Catholics, is not averse to "signing-on" non-Catholics: there are five or six Protestants among top-line Celtic players at this writing. There is little evidence of hostility on the part of Celtic supporters to these non-Catholic players, and none of strained relationships, on this ground, among the playing staff themselves.

Irishmen; and that the mutual antagonism of the two groups came to be linked with Rangers-Celtic rivalry in football. The rowdyism of to-day, however, would seem to be to only a limited extent an objectification in the context of football of divergent religious loyalties and antagonisms. It is just as likely that the football rivalry is a rationalisation of feelings arising from real or imagined social deprivation past or present, and doubtless in some cases of more deep-seated psychological disorders, with the element of religious enmity and intolerance entering as a further order of rationalisation playing back upon the other. Whatever the true account of this phenomenon should turn out to be, we mislead ourselves if we regard it as a manifestation of purely religious animosity even on the part of the small minority of Glasgow citizens directly involved.

Not only is this minority behaviour deprecated by the city as a whole: beyond the socio-economic stratum and the confined localities to which the protagonists belong, it has had practically no adverse effect on Catholic-Protestant relations generally. These are, on the whole, good. There is a certain amount of mutual dislike and suspicion among the under-educated on both sides, and similar attitudes may be shown to some extent in business, again on both sides. Further, there is a certain amount of middle-class Protestant disquiet over what it regards as Catholic infiltration into the city's local government and the administration of the city's affairs: allegations are not infrequently made of disproportionate Catholic influences on Corporation Committees and in the staffs of administrative departments, leading to decisions and policies favouring the Catholic community generally if not also discriminating against Protestant interests. Whether and how far these allegations are justified it is impossible on the basis of the information at present available to say; and this applies also to Catholic complaints of discrimination against them by Protestant industrial and business firms.[1]

That there should be this undercurrent of veiled animosity, and that a dossier of real or imagined instances of economic and social discrimination could doubtless be compiled, is probably only to be expected.[2] What calls to be said is that there is little organised expression of hostility and no physical manifestation of it outside of delinquent groups who would find excuse for resort to violence in any case.[3] In

1 Mr. Frank MacMillan advances the hypothesis that complaints of discrimination may be partly at least rationalisations, on both sides, of individual failure "to make the grade." At all events, to balance cases of missed promotion, other things being equal, because of Catholic affiliation there are instances of promotion being gained on this ground.

2 The issue is, of course, complicated by the existence of nationalistic feelings and by such sociological factors as working-class Protestant feelings of superiority at maintaining a higher level of home and child-care than they judge many working-class Catholics to achieve and, associated with this, Protestant condemnation of large Catholic families. Attitudes of this kind are common, for example, among Govan Protestants, and it is a social (even moralistic) judgment that has nothing to do with fears about population trends.

3 I add—without self-commitment—that some would hold that one "organised expression of hostility" towards Catholics is the annual Orange Walk on 12 July. For the purpose of this demonstration Glasgow Orangemen—in any case no more typical of Glasgow Protestantism than its self-appointed votaries among Rangers' football "fans"—are said to enlist the aid of "contingents" and speakers from Northern Ireland.

Glaswegian Protestants and Catholics suspicion, resentment and dislike are for the most part tacit, or if expressed in mumbling invectives of criticism and condemnation in the "in-group" associations, seldom break out in vindictive action. On the occasions when the Education Department has been forced by overcrowding in a Catholic school to transfer some Catholic classes to a conveniently placed and under-populated non-Catholic school, Protestant parents have usually been quick to protest: but their reaction seldom goes beyond threatened or temporary withholding of their children from school.

Coolness of personal relations, a maintaining of "social distance" beyond polite formalities, there may be when Protestants and Catholics find themselves together in their daily concerns; but even this is not uniform throughout the city's life—many individuals maintain cordial social relationships on a basis of mutual respect with devotees of the other religious persuasion[1]—and it is in any case of a quite different order from organised antagonism and soul-devouring bigotry.

A city tennis club recently banned an 11-year-old girl from membership because she was a Catholic.[2] But the prominence given to this case in the city's press was a measure of the infrequency of this type of action, and leader-writers' comments and readers' reactions showed that public opinion is much more unfavourable now than it has often been in the past to social discrimination on religious grounds.

No doubt one factor in the generally easier situation of to-day is the fact that so many non-Catholics are only nominally Protestants. Mr. MacMillan suggests others: "My own personal view is that the quite startling change of the general climate of opinion in this matter is due to these facts:

(a) the Catholic contribution to both world wars, and especially the second. This operated in two ways:
   (i) the non-Catholics could scarcely call in question the loyalty of their Catholic fellow-citizens, and such theories as that of a prior loyalty to the 'Vatican' or, again, of irredentist Irish-ism, began to wear thin;
   (ii) where such an anti-Catholic attitude persists, Catholics feel more disposed to smile at it, confident in their war record, whereas before the 1914-18 War there was no such possible appeal to the tribute of blood.

(b) the disappearance of the Irish question as a major issue in British politics, such as it was up till the Treaty of 1922. The generation of Catholics in this country to whom that meant a great deal, from atavistic tradition reinforced by surrounding hostility, gradually died out—as did the ancestral voices from beyond the

1 Mr. MacMillan gives an example from his own profession: "Where there have been non-Catholic teachers on the staff of any Catholic school I have known, relations have always been of the most cordial . . . this applies also to the professional teachers' associations."

2 Soon afterwards the girl was admitted to a neighbouring Protestant Tennis Club.

Irish Sea calling for aid, loyalty and aspirations to nationhood. Nowadays the great majority of Scots Catholics are Scots-born to the third or even fourth generation."

Certainly when one reflects that Protestants might have been moved by alarm over the recent growth in Catholic numbers to vindictive attitudes and actions, the degree of tolerance that at present marks the city's life in this respect is the more gratifying.

THE CHANGING CITY

J. A. MACK

A New Glasgow in the Making

THE main effect of the social changes of the last half-century on Glasgow families is plainly visible. The average family is smaller, the individual children are bigger, and there is more room for them to move about in. There are some reservations to make, for Glasgow may take all of the next half-century to overcome the ravages of its past. Although families on the whole are smaller, having an average of two children to the turn-of-the-century average of four or five, there survives in Scotland an excessive proportion of very large families. As the table shows, Scotland's proportion of households with 5 or more children under 16, small as it is, is twice that of England and Wales. We may safely infer that the great majority of these comparatively large families are poorly off, and that they are concentrated in Glasgow and the West.

TABLE CLIII

HOUSEHOLDS WITH 5 OR MORE CHILDREN AS PROPORTION OF TOTAL HOUSEHOLDS: ENGLAND AND WALES, AND SCOTLAND, 1951

1 *Area*	2 *Total Households*	3 *Households with 5 or more children under* 16	4 *Column* 3 *as Percentage of* 2
England and Wales	13,043,500	134,400	1.03%
Scotland	1,438,000	31,300	2.2%

SOURCE: *Census 1951, Great Britain, One per cent Sample Tables,* Part II.

The older built-up areas of the city, too, are still greatly overcrowded in places. Play-grounds for the children and recreation grounds for the older boys and girls are all too few: and Glasgow easily maintains its unwanted lead over all other western cities of comparable size in the proportion of its people living in houses of one or two rooms.[1] But the interwar and postwar rehousing drives are steadily increasing the amount of living space. In 1928 the million people in the city lived in just over a quarter of a million houses fairly closely crowded together except in the better-class suburbs and in new housing schemes such as Knightswood and Mosspark. In 1953 a slightly diminished population occupied 310,000 houses, reaching into nearly every corner of the city's expanded boundaries. But the pressure of the population on houses built and building is much more intense now than in the early part of the century. In the Glasgow of 1911 more than one house in ten stood empty. Now with a steadily expanding supply of houses and a stationary population, there is a very long waiting-list for Corporation houses. Some of this may be fictitious, but there is a big nucleus of genuine demand. It bears witness not only to improving standards of living, but also to a greater determination on the part of young couples to set up house for themselves. There is still a lot of sharing of houses, of married sons or daughters staying on in the parental home, but not nearly so much, we may guess, as in the unrecorded past. The horizon has widened. The growing demand is for a house of one's own and more room for the children. In discussions with mothers and fathers of growing families who have moved from two-apartment houses in the city to four and five apartment houses in the newer areas, the writer has been told again and again of the great blessing it is to be able to give the boys and girls a room or rooms of their own.

So much, and a great deal more, we may infer from the figures of housing and from economic and other surveys of households in Glasgow and kindred cities. But it does not take us very far. If we are to get anything like an adequate picture of family and social relations in all their variety, if we are to grasp the inner and deeper aspects of social change, we must go beyond the kind of information derived from surveys to the incidental writings in which Glasgow abounds—reminiscences, sketches, belles-lettres and novels. This material may not be scientifically organised, but it is authentic—fine rich confused feeding, like the sheep's head on which Glasgow business men were wont to lunch on a Wednesday well into this century.

It shows for example that it was at some point in the last fifty years that Glasgow suffered its sea-change, lost its narrow but comforting small-town atmosphere, abandoned its sheep's head on a Wednesday, and fell apart into the metropolitan agglomeration it is to-day. Glasgow in 1901 was a populous place, with over three quarters of a million people living within its bounds, but it still held together a recognisable community of citizens. The little book entitled *Glasgow in 1901*,[2] written by "James Hamilton Muir," describes a compact and

[1] See p. 454ff.
[2] Published in 1901.

self-sufficient society, living on top of its work. its business and professional classes still as much part of it as in the days of Adam Smith and Provost Cochrane. This compactness can be illustrated from the family background of two of the three young men who composed "James Hamilton Muir."[1] James and Muirhead Bone (their equally eminent brother David was already on the high seas) came of Ayrshire and Glasgow stock.[2] Their father's grandfather, a Chartist and occasional journalist (his broadsheet was entitled the *Mustard Plaster*) was a school-fellow of Robert Burns in the farm school taught by John Murdoch. Their mother's father supplied uniforms for the City of Glasgow Police. The children of the modern city have often only the haziest idea of what their father and other grown-ups do for a living. There was no doubt in the minds of the young Bones that Glasgow and the Clyde lived by building ships. Their father, a journalist on the staff of the *North British Daily Mail,* wrote authoritatively on Clydeside shipping and ship-building. They moved from house to house in Partick and Glasgow, but Sir David Bone's most vivid memory is of Glenavon Terrace, a tenement building almost on the summit of Partickhill, from which the windings of the Clyde could be followed from downstream at Clydebank to the shipyards at Meadowside and Govan. "It was in keeping with that inspiring maritime prospect that most of our nearby friends and neighbours were in some way occupied with the building of the ships or the construction of the engines for them." A launching at the Govan shipyards could best be seen from the pasture-fields on the heights of Partickhill and it was there the children of the district assembled to watch the spectacle. "But even on Clydeside not all ship launchings go smoothly and according to plan. I remember returning from school on a summer afternoon in early July of 1883 and seeing my mother's serving-maid rushing frantically down the Crow Road towards the river, shrieking wild cries and from time to time throwing her apron over her head to veil her grief, in the way Highland people do. I learned later that the newly-built *Daphne,* on which her father was employed, on being launched at Linthouse, had overturned in the river and that many workmen—our Mirren's father among them—were believed drowned."[3] Experiences like these prepared the way for the great shipyard etchings of Muirhead Bone and for the voyages, and the books, of the future Commodore of the Anchor Line.

Glasgow in 1901 is best on middle-class Glasgow, its business men and merchants and shopkeepers. Some of its types are recognisable to-day, notably the small business man, independent, cautious, shrewd, "decent," clearly of the people. But whereas in those days he mostly lived in the suburbs, West-end or more probably South Side, now he is as likely to be found beyond the city's bounds. So too the old cross-

[1] James Bone, later London Editor of the *Manchester Guardian* and doyen of London journalists; Archibald Hamilton Charteris; and Muirhead Bone, painter and etcher.

[2] Like the Arthur Moorhouses in Guy McCrone's Glasgow family saga *Wax Fruit* (1947).

[3] Sir David Bone: *Landfall at Sunset* (1956), pp. 15-16.

river rivalries are gone. Glasgow in 1901 was not so compact as not to draw the line, sharply, between South Side and Kelvinside. "Demn' snob" said young South Side and young Kelvinside retorted with "poisonous bounder." Their athletic interests differed. Kelvinside was all for Rugby: South Side was divided between Rugby and Association. They differed too in their ways of amusing themselves. "South Side is the friend of bars and pantomimes and lighted streets: Kelvinside stays at home, or in each other's homes, dancing or billiard-playing and performing, in fact (as it will tell you), the ordinary social duties of civilised man."[1] And so on. The 1920's saw the last of this mutually cherished duality. It was the finest hour of the Glasgow Accies,[2] and, across the river, the Queen's Park Football Club[3] were still going strong. But then and since the process of dispersal has gone on fast. As new housing schemes leap-frogged over the older Western and South-side suburbs into Knightswood and Mosspark and King's Park and Pollok, the middle-class Glaswegian leaped over these again (or, as in King's Park, moved into them) leaving only a small occupying force to uphold the old traditions in a spreading desert of nursing homes, business premises, offices of public boards, and houses broken up into apartments.

The foregoing picture is of course a gross simplification: there is still a recognisable Dennistoun, and a Queen's Park district, and a Hyndland, and a Crosshill, as Mr. House makes clear later in this chapter. Likewise there is still a recognisable framework of old Glasgow residents and families, their representatives now rather elderly, sustaining the surprisingly complex system of benevolent and charitable societies which have retained their identity even in the Welfare State. Some future researchers into the minute books of the voluntary organisations of the city will doubtless note how often the same names recur in generation after generation. There is a great deal of ruin in a city, as Adam Smith might have said—meaning that it takes a vast amount and extent of social change to transform the basic character and structure of a civic entity so vigorous as Glasgow has shown herself to be over the last three centuries. And it may be that the tide is on the turn. The first steps are being taken to clear the slums not merely street by street but district by district; and it may be that by the end of the century the older crowded areas will have been entirely developed. There are some signs too that business and professional men, tired of the petrol fumes in the Great Western or Kilmarnock roads, are beginning to think of coming to live nearer to their work again. But there can be no return to the former social balance. A new Glasgow is in the making. The condition of the working people who form the majority of the citizens

1 J. H. Muir, *Glasgow in 1901*, pp. 162-3 For more about these Kelvinside and Hillhead parties see James Bridie: *One Way of Living* (1939) and J. J. Bell: *I Remember* (1932).

2 The Rugby fifteen of the old boys of Glasgow Academy.

3 Queen's Park, the most famous of all Scottish amateurs in the Association game, have now in the later 'fifties played themselves back into the First Division (one hopes) after a period of partial eclipse in the Second Division of the Scottish League.

has been and is being steadily improved. The old social divisions are less well marked. The middling well-off and small business men and industrialists and merchants and professional men who set the tone of the city up till the 'twenties and early 'thirties now (many of them) live outside its bounds and no longer feel they belong. But until the changes now in process work themselves out more fully it will be difficult to grasp the emerging pattern of the city or to determine whether and how the social groups now rising in the civic scale will come to assume the functions of social integration and leadership discharged up till the 1930's by the former middle class.

Family Life and Social Mobility

Meantime underneath the flux of social and civic change the essential business of family life goes on. It might indeed be said that the foregoing discussion about middle class and working class is all rather conventional and superficial. Fundamentally speaking there is only one broad division between social classes in Glasgow and Scotland, and it cuts across all differences in income, education or accent. On the one side there is the great majority of families who agree with the incomparable Robert Burns's

> " To mak' a happy fireside clime
> For weans an' wife
> That's the true pathos and sublime
> O' human life."

This great majority of families consists of man and wife devoting themselves to the task of bringing up their children to be reasonably honest and kindly and well-behaved men and women. On the other side there is the minority of families in which the children, for a variety of reasons, are the victims of physical or moral or emotional neglect or of all three combined. Let us look first at the minority. It is of course a very varied group. Those households in which the children have least chance of a decent upbringing are the few which conform most nearly to the older pre-industrial pattern of family with several generations and aunts and uncles living under the same roof or in adjacent houses or streets. But it is the older pattern debased. In some parts of Govan, writes Mr. Brennan,[1] the organisation of many households is very loose indeed. The " official " inhabitants of a house are not clearly known from day to day. Temporary changes as a result of quarrels, reorientation of affections or simply convenience of sleeping arrangements are very common. In such households where there are children there is, strictly speaking, no parental control. The parents may change partners and one or other move out temporarily. Even without this type of instability, the large and varying number of adults of different genera-

[1] T. Brennan: *Pilot Survey of* 100 *Households* (Unpublished Paper).

tions, with different standards of behaviour, all taking turn, so to speak, in disciplining or indulging the children, makes it impossible for the children to be brought up to any pattern of behaviour consistent with the ethic of the wider society. These children may be fundamentally normal as individuals. They may even welcome any chance of undergoing the firm and consistent discipline of the wider ethic. But home conditions soon restore the original morality. The story of the approved school youth whose conduct in school had improved so vastly that his house master gave him a special holiday of a week at home, on which his equally gratified parents (or extended family elders) rewarded him further by putting him to bed with his young prostitute aunt, is not a Glasgow story: but it vividly illustrates the clash of cultures. These debased survivals of the older "extended family" are comparatively rare.[1] But it is to be suspected that they provide a high proportion of those persistent young criminals whose criminality has nothing psychologically abnormal about it.[2]

A more numerous group of socially incompetent families are those of the more ordinary pattern where the parents, and the children as they grow up, live from day to day, or rather from drinking-session to drinking-session. As living and housing standards improve, and particularly as families move out into the new housing areas, the proportion of families who waste their substance in drinking is going down. But such families, and the environments which provoke and half-justify them are still too numerous to be ignored. One such environment was the Townhead area in the late 1940's, described by George Blake in *The Trials of Patrick Carraher*.[3] The family, whose eldest son, a quiet reserved soldier, was stabbed to death by Carraher, was apparently conducting itself as usually on a Saturday when the father and grown-up sons went the round of pub after pub from four in the afternoon till nine at night, without solid food, consuming a series of whiskies followed by beer, varied by occasional draughts of cheap wine. Another such environment was the Gorbals of the early part of the century, and of the interwar years, which the Glasgow novelist Edward Gaitens has captured so well in his *Dance of the Apprentices*.[4] This story is much more true to the life of the mean broad streets of this famous quarter than are the more well-known play and novel of the same period.[5] Its young men can see the stars even in the Gorbals sky. They talk politics and books against a background of seductive triviality.[6] They grow

[1] Mr. Brennan in a sample of 100 Govan households finds six out of forty-five families with children to be of the "extended" type. He is not to be taken as agreeing with the inference made above.

[2] v. J. A. Mack: *Delinquency and the Changing Social Pattern,* the fifth Charles Russell Memorial Lecture (1956).

[3] Published in Notable British Trials Series, 1951.

[4] First published 1948 by William Maclellan, Glasgow.

[5] *The Gorbals Story,* by Robert McLeish (first published 1946) and *No Mean City,* by A. McArthur and A. K. Long (published 1935: reissued 1956).

[6] v. pp. 107-9. The young men standing in the close, out of the rain, have just listened to an essay on Individualism by Neil Mudge, constitutional and democratic socialist:

". . . they began an argument with Neil vigorously attacking, heartened by

up hopefully, in much the same way as young men do the world over, against the dispiriting background of the Gorbals streets, and, in the hero's case, in spite of his drunken parents.

"'Never any peace!' Every member of his family had cried so at one time or another but none had made an intelligent move to establish peace. He recalled how his mother had become really ill later that night. The doctor was summoned and discovered that her nose was broken. His father had shown up after a month, slouching in unkempt, unshaven, out of work, weeping in shoddy condition, swearing he would make it up to his wife for all the pain he had done her."[1]

The Macdonnels are that distinctive but now fast diminishing Glasgow problem, the more boisterous type of poor Irish Catholic family, alternately staging fights and throwing parties. The most memorable Macdonnel party (these were always informal affairs; guests just got to know and drifted in) began unpromisingly. Jimmy, the sailor son, came home sober from one voyage. He had become engaged to a good-living girl, and had promised her to give up the drink. Mr. Macdonnel had glared wildly at his son. He was dumbfounded. Every time Jimmy had come home from sea there had been a party and a few more after it until his pay was burned right up. And once again it happened just as before. Three hours later the hapless Eddy, who had been entranced by Jimmy's miraculous conversion, looked out at a sudden clamour in the street to see Jimmy stumbling happily along with his Aunt Kate's hat on his head and his arm round his father's neck. ". . . large bottles of whisky waggled from the pockets of the two men. Behind them, laughing like witches, came Mrs. Macdonnel and Aunt Kate with the sailor's cap on, followed by six of Jimmy's pals who were carrying between them three large crates of bottled beer." There follows a wild evening, lachrymose and violent by turns, erupting into transvestism, and seducing even the Glasgow police, who came to stop but remained to join the party. Eddy, student of psychology, was staggered. "Human behaviour" had passed his understanding . . . "He was thinking of Jeannie Lindsay and wishing he might find her standing at her close in South Wellington Street. But it was very late.

[1] E. Gaitens: *Dance of the Apprentices,* p. 25.

his literary success. Eddy Macdonnel lit a Woodbine and listened with a broad amiable smile, drinking in their erudition: Paddy Maguire and Bobby Logan strayed to the middle of the close singing "Alexander's Ragtime Band," Paddy contributing a tuneless bass, Bobby's Punchlike features moving up and down crazily as he moaned a nasal tenor . . . (Bobby) was secretly convinced that his voice was exactly similar in volume and style to that of a famous American ragtime singer and always wondered why he was never asked to sing at parties. "You made me love you," he crooned, "I didn't want to do it, I didn't want to do it."

Eddy Macdonnel was suddenly overcome by a great weariness with learning and Neil's genteel voice. A deep longing for love and rag-time troubled his heart, but in the ghastly light shed by the broken (gas) mantle he glanced impatiently to the end of the close that held the drum of relentless rain and the echoes of song and debate. He wanted to be standing there with Bobby, humming "Itchy Koo" and "Casey Jones" and shuffling his feet to syncopation. But Neil, taking his arm . . ."

He hurried round the corner in a queer, emotional tangle of sexual shame and desire, his romantic thoughts of Jeannie mingled with the shameful memory of his mother and the women dressing up in men's clothes and Bridget Delaney pulling up her skirts to the hips to show her bare legs to the men."[1]

* * * * * *

The alchemy of civic transformation has doubtless brought the present generation of Macdonnels up in the world. But let us turn now to a third of the many categories of families in which the children are let down—the families of those otherwise well-conducted and averagely competent individuals who cannot get on together as man and wife, and who break up their marriage or who live together at the cost of such strain as to impose a great emotional burden on themselves and their children.[2] Early in the century the number of divorces and marital separations in Scotland was very small. In 1939, following the Act of the previous year adding to the ground for divorce, the total of Scottish divorce cases was under 1,000. It rose to 3,000 in 1946 and is now settling at a level of about 2,000 cases per annum, plus about 300 marital separations and an unknown number of unofficial separations. Many of these divorces are no doubt unavoidable and justified. Given the greater economic and social freedom of women and the general toleration of divorce by society, it is perhaps surprising that the totals are so low.[3] But most divorces and separations carry with them a great deal of pain and wretchedness not only for both of the parties but also for the unoffending children. (There are children involved in two out of three divorces.) And for every broken marriage there are probably several near breaking-point.

It was to meet this problem that the voluntary marriage guidance movement came into existence. It is often thought that voluntary associations have had their day, and are due to be superseded by the statutory and professionalised social services. This is partly true of some of the older pre-1939 type of associations: but the voluntary principle is justifying itself in new fields, and notably in the field of marriage guidance. The Glasgow Marriage Guidance Council was not the first in Scotland—that distinction belongs to Edinburgh—but it has since its conception in 1948 made steady progress and is now the largest of the Scottish councils. Its counsellors are volunteers, carefully selected and trained for the work: its clients likewise come voluntarily for help and advice in preparation for marriage or in marriage relationship

1 *Ibid*. p. 45.

2 Two notable novels about interwar Glasgow, George Blake's *The Shipbuilders* (1935) and James Barke's *Major Operation* (1936), describe the shattering effect on middle-class husbands of the breakdown of their marriage.

3 The English peak year of 1947 showed a five-fold increase over 1939 (10,000 to 50,000). The number is now settling at 30,000 per annum, three times higher than in 1939.

difficulties. The total numbers of cases in the last three years have been as follows:

TABLE CLIV

MARRIAGE GUIDANCE CASES

	1953	1954	1955
Preparation for Marriage	40	62	60
Circumstances outside the Marriage Relationship	70	67	57
Marriage Relationship Difficulties	290	340	298
	400	469	415

It is interesting to note, says the latest annual report, that those seeking help are not confined to any particular age or social or religious group, but comprise a complete cross-section of the community.

Certainly the increase in marital friction is evidence of the growing isolation of families and their greater independence of local opinion: just as the response of the voluntary marriage guidance movement shows the healing and recuperative powers of the civic and national organism.

* * * * * *

Problem families and other kinds of defective family relationship are dealt with in the chapter on social services. Here it remains to indicate the main fact about social and family relationships in Glasgow in the mid-century, which is that they continue to exhibit a remarkable strength and adaptability in the face of the great strains imposed by the tempo of social change in war and peace. The bulk of families continue through all the crises and emergencies to give their children a safe and happy childhood and to bring them up in the way they should go. It should be added that the majority of the parents concerned also strive to ensure that their children shall have the opportunity of a higher standard of living than they themselves have had. This is of course the driving force behind the collective provision of the social services: but it also operates in every group in the traditional way. This element of unselfish ambition is to be detected in the two outstanding expressions in this century of Glasgow family folklore: J. J. Bell's *Wee MacGregor*—published in the 1900's—and the episodes from the life of the " McFlannel " family broadcast in the 1950's. It is of course clearly to be distinguished from the social pride and stuck-up-ness of " those and such as those " who think themselves superior to their more easy-going neighbours. The affected Aunt Purdie in the MacGreegor stories, and Mrs. McCotton in the McFlannel series, are usually figures of fun and derision, very occasionally figures of pathos. But the " ideal type " of Glasgow family, to judge from these very popular fictional exemplars, is one which finds its central purpose and daily task in lifting the children up a little higher in the social scale. This is particularly obvious in the McFlannel family, which is nearly grown up. Willie the father is promoted from craftsman to foreman in the shipyard and the family moves into a bigger tenement house. Later the family tries out a big house in its own grounds in the country: but this is strictly temporary and therefore not evidence of sinful pride. The son is a draughtsman, a white-collar and highly skilled job: the daughter is a teacher, and marries a minister. In *Wee MacGregor*, an altogether more profound and cautious study, the promptings of unselfish ambition are barely hinted at. Here too the father is made a " foresman." But there is no change of residence. Wee MacGregor is sadly humiliated by a hat, Alpine style, which causes the neighbours, old and young, to call after him the dread epithets

" Gentry pup
Wi' yer tail tied up."

He has no white-collar ambition and will be a house-painter when he grows up. But when he does grow up (as he does in a later book) and falls in love, his young lady, Christina, makes no bones about bullying him into taking steps to better himself. But *Christina* is a much cruder work, and made no such impact on the popular mind as did its famous predecessor.

It may be that the transition from *Wee MacGregor*, with its lack of emphasis on moving up, to the consciously mobile McFlannels, marks a greater readiness to admit ambition, a more pronounced status-consciousness, now than in the days before 1914. In this J. J. Bell may have been describing a more easy-going and satisfied society which is now no more. But in most other respects *Wee MacGregor* is perennially fresh. It is sentimental and even mawkish in parts. But it is strikingly true to present-day family life in its main outlines. The family is small for its time, the average size of ours (Wee MacGregor has one sister, wee Jeannie the baby). The guidance of the parents is supplemented from time to time by that of the grandparents, Grandpa and Grandma Purdie, but they live elsewhere, not with the MacGregor Robinsons. The supreme importance—rediscovered by contemporary psychologists—of warm mutual affection, in those relationships so chillingly named " parent-child " and " husband-wife," was no secret to John Joy Bell. Wee MacGregor is heart-broken when he gets paint on his good knickerbockers, not because his mother is angry with him, but because she is angry with his father for trying to help him conceal the crime. But all comes out well in each instalment of the chronicle. And it is as clear about the importance of moral guidance and discipline as it is about the child's need for love. When Wee MacGregor takes the putty—the " daud o' potty "—from the bigger but spindle-shanked Wullie Thomson, he is made to take it back, and with it, neatly done up in a parcel, his own Saturday supply of coconut ice, or " taiblet." It is true that the two boys eventually share both putty and coconut ice, all ill-feeling forgotten. But right and wrong have been clearly distinguished. This difference between the " decent " families, who check their children from doing or repeating such a thing as stealing and bullying, and those others who tolerate or encourage it in *their* children, is one of the burning questions in the neighbourhood life of many Glasgow housing schemes to this day. It is also, along with accompanying differences in the use and non-use of bad language, and in parental attitudes to their children's schooling, likely to be the chief determinant of the non-economic class differences and social discriminations of the immediate future in this country.[1]

* * * * * *

There is a striking parallel between the structure of family authority in the very comfortably off middle-class world of late Victorian and Edwardian Glasgow and the more backward and less mobile sectors of the lower-income groups of to-day. Probation officers report that among the poorer families, poorer as to both income and intelligence, it is still widely held by the women of the house that "the man's the maister." (Mr. Brennan suggests[2] tentatively that in the more poorly off Catholic families the women in the home, daughters and mothers, have more responsibility with lower status than elsewhere: and that this is a matter of culture rather than of individual mental backwardness). The wife does not know the size of the weekly pay-packet. She takes what she is given. A broadcast feature programme produced by A. P. Lee and J. S. Campbell in 1953[3] illustrated this most aptly. A foundryman said: "When I was serving my time and when my time was out my mother always impressed upon me that I should keep one thing to myself after I was married, and that was my wages—the amount of my wages. She told me never to stint your wife but at the same time never let her know just exactly how much you earn, because if you do she'll look for more and more and more until a time comes when you'll be completely unable to satisfy her, and then there'll be trouble. So I have never at any time disclosed to my wife my gross earnings. Now I think this is a general practice among Clydeside workers. On a Friday night in the Govan Road you will see carried along by the wind thousands and thousands of torn pay-packets, strewing and littering the streets, which I think is sufficient proof that every

1 Cf. also J. A. Mack: *op. cit.* "I suggest that we might worry less about the group of people who send their children to fee-paying schools. At least it can't be said of them that they don't believe in education. The real source of educational inequality is that much larger group of people who set their face against any schooling at all for their children after 14, and who frustrate the work of the school by throwing their influence against the teacher, or by displaying no interest at all in the education of their children.. And this is only one aspect of the forces in the family structure of some parts of our society which are working against the chances of the children to win to a better kind of life. These studies show the strength of the anti-egalitarian resistance movement among the under-privileged groups themselves. It is hard to see what political action, or legislation, or administration can do here. The teacher or the school welfare officer, the social worker or the youth club organiser, represent the kind of things these families don't want. They have their own opposed values." Cf. Dr. Highet's views on pp. 529ff.

2 *Op. cit.*

3 *Me and the Pay-Packet,* 29 September 1953.

man tears up his pay-packet, and segregates his earnings—something for himself and something for his wife."

This is no doubt a prime source of secondary poverty. The husband may be making more money than before, with or without overtime, but the wife still gets his £4 or whatever it is for housekeeping in spite of rising prices. One particularly dull woman, applying for a charitable grant to go on a holiday, was advised to spend her own money instead since her husband was making £14 a week. But of this, she said, she got only £4 as always. The extra money, as she pointed out, was "his" money, not hers.

This picture is probably true of a relatively narrow section only. A more prominent development in both older and newer Glasgow is the pattern of both parents working, and arranging the sharing of the household costs in a variety of ways. This is the source of perhaps the most vigorously debated single family issue of our time, the effects of mothers' working on the conduct and happiness of their children. A surprising sidelight on this issue is given in an enquiry made by Professor Ferguson of Glasgow University. He finds in a statistical survey of a true cross-section of boy school-leavers that those whose mothers went out to work had a lower rate of delinquency than those whose mothers stayed at home.[1] And the more capable and intelligent of the non-working wives in all economic groups have established a working economic partnership with their husbands: either the wife manages the entire household expenditure, or they plan their expenditure together. But the principle that "the man's the maister" is still widely held. And it corresponds closely with what we know of the older middle-class pattern. Take for example the insights yielded incidentally by James Bridie the dramatist and Guy McCrone the novelist. Both would repudiate the title of social historian. But both are acute social observers. Consider, for example, Bridie's family comedy, *The Black Eye*. (In this play, by the way, a nice lesson in family discipline is provided by the two boys who go out into the garden to settle their differences. This it is said was the practice in a family James Bridie knew very well.) The point of the play for our present purpose is the absolute ignorance of the mother and daughters of the sources of the family income and their consequent general ineffectiveness. This is well brought out also by Guy McCrone in his trilogy *Wax Fruit*, almost against his intention. He would perhaps have liked to have made Bel Moorhouse, wife of the successful Arthur, into a matriarch. But she fails, or blunders, both with her half-sister Phœbe and her son Arthur. And it is not only a matter of her personal failings, her conventionality, her maternal selfishness obscuring her grasp of reality. The social stars in their courses are fighting against her. Arthur is the master: she not only enjoys having him lay down the law: she accepts it from him. She is of course the more active agent in the upward social movement of the Moorhouses. Thus she rounds on her husband for his cautious slowness in deciding to leave the house in Montrose Street for a big solid house in the West

[1] T. Ferguson: *The Young Delinquent in his Social Setting* (1952).

End. But he gives way only because he has simultaneously been given the same advice by a respected senior in the business world. An even more striking example of the invisible limits set by Victorian and Edwardian Glasgow on its stirring young women is that of Phœbe Moorhouse. Clearly intended as a sketch of the New Woman, determined to live her own life, Phœbe too is enveloped by the family ethos, as powerful in its unassuming way as that of any London Forsytes. Her failure to strike out for herself makes a less exciting story, but it is all the truer to the facts of Glasgow middle-class life. And so tough and pervasive are these traditions and attitudes that there is to this day a certain old-fashionedness in these matters to be detected in the demeanour of the Glasgow middle-class matron, at least in its ritual aspects. She may have more than 50 per cent control of the domestic economy, but she likes to have it appear that her husband decides.

The structure of authority in the family is a static affair. But family life is essentially dynamic, a constellation of forces making for change while striving to maintain social equilibrium. And the dynamic element is undoubtedly the wife and mother. The continual subtle drive upwards in the social scale, the continual watch on the children to see that they learn their lessons, scholastic and social, the continual pressure on the husband to keep him also on the right path, is admirably observed both by the vignettist J. J. Bell and the novelist Guy McCrone. It is the woman who can tell at once what is fitting in matters of furnishing, deportment, nuances of meaning of word or manner. It is the woman who sets the standards and decides the priorities. This is as true of Lizzie Robinson, wife of the respectable craftsman, as it is of Bel Moorhouse, wife of the successful merchant. Each has her sense of due limit, of what is fit and proper. Lizzie is as clear about the folly of aping the fake small-shop-keeping "gentry" as Bel is about her inability to capture the manner and the confidence of the members of the county families.

From the point of view of Glasgow's future Lizzie's is the more relevant case-study. The new social constellation now taking shape in middle- and working-class Glasgow, among the solid majority of all those families in all economic groups who are out to do their best by the children, will be determined by Lizzie and her like.

And here a postscript may be added to reassure those who may be somewhat alarmed by this recurring insistence on the continuing upward-moving social tropism which is the implicit dynamic of the broad stream of Glasgow family life. It is also true that this broad multiple-centred movement is probably less caste-ridden, less influenced by considerations of birth or colour or accent or schooling, than in any comparable urban centre. There is a comparative absence of colour prejudice in these parts. The city's nearest approach to a Public School, the Glasgow Academy, is cheerfuly derisive of the Public-School ritual.[1] The Glasgow accent is not confined to the manual workers. The almost

[1] See James Bridie: *One Way of Living,* Ch. III. See also Dr. John Highet above for a statement about the status of the Glasgow Academy.

gyroscopic tendency of Lizzie Robinson and women like her to keep her family in order and on the move is accompanied by a genuine friendliness or at least fellow-feeling for her fellow-creatures and neighbours.

DISTRICT LOYALTIES

JACK HOUSE

GLASGOW may not, as Mr. John Mack suggests, be the closely-knit city it was in 1901, but there is still a decided difference between the North and South sides of Glasgow—though it may not be as easy to distinguish a Northerner from a Southerner as it was fifty or more years ago.

Outwardly the inhabitants of both sides of the River Clyde look the same. But most of them say flatly that they would not want to live on the other side of the river. There are numerous cases of South Side families who, for various reasons, have to " flit " to the North Side, but are soon complaining about their new surroundings and often are arranging to go back to the other side of the Clyde. This applies to all classes of Glaswegians. South Siders, in particular, attach some sort of magic to living south of the Clyde. Several South Siders, interviewed when they had returned to the south after a short sojourn in the north, complained about the " different air " on the north of the Clyde. A middle-class housewife confessed that she felt " unwell " all the time she was living in North Kelvinside. When she returned to Pollokshields, her health improved immediately. A Glasgow journalist, accustomed to living in Ibrox, said that he was " unsettled " when he had to reside in Hillhead.

The North Siders do not seem to worry so much about the change of air. Few North Siders have had to make the change to the South Side. The North Siders' attitude, however, is well exemplified in the case of the Citizens' Theatre. Most of the entertainment of Glasgow is situated north of the river. The only theatre on the other side is the Citizens'. Many North Siders say they will not go to the Citizens' Theatre because " it's so far away." In actual fact, it is just across the Clyde and it is well served by bus routes from the north and the west. From the centre of the city—Central Station, for example—the Citizens' Theatre takes less than a minute longer to reach than the King's Theatre, near Charing Cross. And you can get to the Citizens' Theatre from the centre more quickly than you can reach the Empress Theatre at St. George's Cross. This has been pointed out many times to North Siders, particularly by the management of the Citizens' Theatre, but they still talk about the " distance " to the theatre, and the " difficulty " of getting there. South Siders, in the main, *must* cross the river to get their entertainment, and they do not appear to object to this. North Siders make exceptions, by the way, of the Plaza Palais de Danse and Crossmyloof Ice Rink. They never refer to "difficulties" in connection with getting to these two places.

In Glasgow there is the customary feeling between East Enders and West Enders, but it is by no means as strong as the "differences" felt by South Siders and North Siders. This is partly because Glasgow originally spread to the East. The move to the West did not take place until nearly half way through the nineteenth century. By that time there were many well-established district communities in the East. The result is that, though, very broadly speaking, the West End is "well off" and the East End is "working class," the East Enders do not envy or look up to the Glaswegians of the West. It is in the East End particularly that vestigial remains of "village" life are still to be found. Most of the districts of Glasgow that existed up to the First World War retain an independent ambience. In the East End, for example, inhabitants of adjacent districts like Shettleston and Tollcross are annoyed if outsiders mix them up. Two sisters, well-known Motor Rally drivers in Britain and on the Continent, expressed their exasperation at being referred to in newspaper reports as "Andy and Chris Neil of Shettleston." They pointed out in the strongest terms that they did not come from Shettleston. They came from Tollcross.

An examination of several districts of Glasgow will illustrate the depth of local feeling and local pride, and the strong sense of individuality which marks one cluster of buildings from another along the same tram lines. In some cases these feelings are kept alive by clubs formed partly of those who still live in the district and partly by those who were brought up in the district and have moved elsewhere. Very often this local pride is really nostalgia, and a number of district clubs are really the equivalent of school Old Boys' associations. The members of this sort of club are usually middle-aged or older, and it is difficult to estimate how long some of these clubs will last.

As has been indicated, the natural place to start a survey of individuality in districts is the East End of Glasgow. Bridgeton is a good example. It was originally a village on its own, and rather troubled by "roughs" who came into it from Glasgow. In the 1830's Bridgeton boys dug along the banks of the River Clyde for "cockadoos." These were mussels, and the attraction was that some of the shells contained tiny pearls. Bridgeton colliers still held Penny Weddings, and the Bridgeton Band was turned out on ceremonious occasions. It was known as the Gentlemen's Band because of its uniform of black coats and trousers, white vests, and tall hats. Bridgeton is now largely tenements and factories, and there are few if any signs of the former village. Nevertheless, the Bridgeton Business Club and the Bridgeton Burns Club (which claims to be the largest Burns Club in the world) have members who can recall vestiges of village life, and who are proud of the fact that they were born and brought up in Bridgeton. This pride is an interesting corollary to the popular idea of Bridgeton as a centre of gang warfare.

Young people in Bridgeton have also a strong local pride—partly due to the existence of John Street Secondary School, where local pride has been nurtured. An investigator who was searching for the single tree which is all that remains of a Tea Garden and Menagerie which existed in Bridgeton in the 1830's found the tree in a grimy backyard behind the tenement close at 182 Main Street. A young married couple watched him taking notes and then came forward and volunteered information about the Tea Garden which had been handed down to them by their Bridgeton-born parents. The same investigator, touring Bridgeton with the comedian Tommy Morgan (born in Bridgeton), found that Morgan was greeted everywhere as a Bridgetonian who had done well for himself, of whom they were proud, and for whom they had a special regard because he had not forgotten (on the contrary, proudly proclaimed) that he came from Bridgeton.

Another East End district, Shettleston, has an intense local pride even to-day. It was a village, The Sheddens, mentioned in a Papal Bull of 1170. There are practically no signs of village life in Shettleston to-day. Nevertheless, middle-aged men in Shettleston public houses will talk for hours about the weavers' cottages, the farms and the independent nature of the place. They would not live anywhere else, even though the village atmosphere has been replaced by the odours of a number of "offensive" industries. They ask visitors to name any other place the size of Shettleston which has given three Members of Parliament to the House of Commons. (The late John Wheatley, the late Lord Kirkwood, and John McGovern, M.P., were all born and raised in Shettleston.)

Tollcross, which lies south of Shettleston, was another "original" village. There has been a good-natured feud between Tollcross and Shettleston for many years. In *Old Shettleston,* by the Rev. J. F. Miller, Tollcross was described as "the aristocratic and exclusive part of Shettleston"—a description which caused some offence in Tollcross, because the natives refused to be considered as living in "part of Shettleston." In Shettleston there is a saying that such and such a man is "an explorer—he went all the way to Tollcross to find a wife."

There are many more signs of the original village in Tollcross than there are in Shettleston. The farm of Egypt still stands on the hill overlooking Shettleston, though the farmlands are now covered by houses, with the exception of a single field. There are small, tiled cottages with outside stairs. Behind Tollcross Central Church, which was opened in 1806, are the remnants of the village of Auchenshuggle (from the Gaelic—"the field of rye"), with a farmhouse which is said to be 300 years old. With such evidence before them, Tollcross natives are inclined to be more of the "villager" type than natives of Shettleston. But neither district has organisations like the Bridgeton Business Club or the Bridgeton Burns Club.

Perhaps the most remarkable East End district is Dennistoun, which was never a village, and yet to-day is probably the most " individual " district in the whole of Glasgow. Until about 1860 it consisted of a number of small estates. Then it was developed as a garden suburb of Glasgow, but fell in the social scale from detached villas to terrace houses, and from terraces to tenements. It is difficult to say why Dennistoun should be regarded by its natives as a place apart from any other in Glasgow, although (as in the case of John Street School and Bridgeton) considerable local pride was fostered in Whitehill School. But it is a strange fact that, even to this day, the natives of this district, when asked where they come from, do not say " Glasgow." They reply, as if it were the only answer, " Dennistoun."

A club called the Old Dennistounians' Association holds an annual dinner, at which the past glories of the district are sung. It is generally agreed by the members that Dennistoun is not what it was, and few of the members live in the district now. Almost all of them, however, mention Dennistoun in the course of any convenient conversation. This is the kind of club whose future, owing to the average age of its members, would seem uncertain. At the moment, however, the number of members continues to grow, particularly among those who no longer live in Dennistoun.

Across the Clyde local pride, albeit of a somewhat defiant character, will be found in the Gorbals. It exists also in districts like Crosshill and Polmadie, where the old Glasgow expression—" Oot o' the warld and into Polmadie "—is still known among the older inhabitants. For an intensity of local pride comparable with that of the East End, however, one must go farther south, to Pollokshaws. This is another case of an independent village. As far as local pride is concerned, what can be better than the opening sentence of *The History of Pollokshaws* by Andrew McCallum? It reads: " Few small communities are so famous as Pollokshaws."

The inhabitants of this district are known generally in Glasgow as " the queer folk o' the 'Shaws." Various theories have been put forward to explain this nickname. Its general use comes from a song by James Fisher, " The Queer Folk o' the 'Shaws," written in Glasgow about 1850. It tells the experience of a Glesca keelie at the 'Shaws races, and one verse goes—

" Look smart and keep your eyes about,
Their tricks will make you grin;
The Barrhead train will take you out,
Thae folk will take you in."

The village history starts about 1600. Local industries were so well developed that the population a hundred years ago was around 5,000. Pollokshaws retained much of its village look until the 1920's. There were many eighteenth-century houses still standing in 1925. Most of these have been knocked down, and the 'Shaws is now a strange mixture of ancient and modern. But, though the buildings of the past have vanished or are disappearing, the spirit of the Queer Folk is maintained, and a large number of the inhabitants regard themselves as 'Shaws folk first and Glaswegians a bad second. An investigator going round some of the old "lands" in Pollokshaws asked an elderly lady what age the buildings were. She replied, "They're gey auld-fashioned, like the people living in them." The people of Pollokshaws are most anxious not to be confused with the people of Pollokshields. This feeling is reciprocated, because Pollokshields is to the South Side of Glasgow what Kelvinside is to the West End. Mr. Mack has already drawn comparisons between these groups.

Local pride exists to a limited extent in Southern districts such as Bellahouston, Dumbreck and Ibrox. Again there is the influence of a local school, Bellahouston Academy. It was originally a boarding school and was founded to keep South Siders on the south side, so that they need not cross the river to schools like Glasgow Academy. But for real pride, one must go up towards the Clyde, to Govan. Before being absorbed by Glasgow in 1912, Govan was the fifth largest burgh in Scotland. It fought desperately against being absorbed, and most old Govanites still think that the absorption was the greatest mistake ever made—especially as the old boundaries of Govan no longer exist and Govan Town Hall is, officially, outside Govan.

Govan was not only a village which grew into a town, but it was also a recognised holiday place for Glasgow people. This was in 1800, when Govanites could still drink water from the Clyde, and porpoises came as far up the river as Govan Ferry. Govanites are also proud of their Parish Church, which contains an amazing collection of sculptured pre-Christian stones, including the mysterious hog-back stones and a sun stone from the Druids' Circle which stood where the kirkyard is now. There are 41 of these stones in Govan Parish Church, compared with 21 at St. Andrews, 13 at Iona, and 12 at Whithorn. Elderly Govanites will boast about the Druidical remains in the same breath as they tell you that the oldest co-operative society in Britain was founded in Govan—the Govan Old Victualling Society, which was started in 1777.

But the especial prides of Govan, which link the present group of districts with the town of the past, are Govan Old Fair and the Govan Weavers' Society. The origin of Govan Old Fair is wrapt in mystery, but the Fair is held by tradition on the first Friday of June. It consists nowadays of a children's fancy dress parade, with lorries decorated by local firms and organisations, and headed by Govan Burgh Band. Whatever the weather, the whole population of Govan turns out for this parade, which is the only one of its kind in Glasgow. On the same evening the Govan Weavers have their annual meeting. Shortly before the Govan Old Fair march, the Weavers, wearing their sashes, aprons and chains of office, march along the main street. They carry with them the Sheep's Head (the stuffed head of a large ram) which is part of their insignia. They also possess an old spear, which is called King Robert the Bruce's Spear (without any justification), and the Sheriffmuir

Flag which was carried by Govan men at the Battle of Sheriffmuir in 1715, when Govan was on the side of the Government and against the Jacobites.

The Govan Weavers were founded on 30 August 1756. To-day there is not a single weaver member. But the original Weavers welcomed outsiders, and in 1758, out of 614 members, less than half (303) were weavers. The rest included 15 distillers, 13 tailors, 9 shoemakers, and 3 fiddlers. A fair proportion of the Govan Weavers to-day are connected with shipbuilding, for Govan's northern boundary consists almost entirely of shipbuilding yards. At their annual meeting, held in a restaurant at Govan Cross, they have a traditional meal of boiled eggs, washed down with "white wine." The "white wine" is an ancient euphemism for whisky. Until the Second World War started, salmon was included in this meal. Traditionalists among the Govan Weavers eat the already peeled eggs and drink the whisky. But for weaker vessels there are sandwiches and tea.

The independence of Govan is also fostered by the Old Govan Club, and by the local weekly newspaper, *The Govan Press*. This organ of Govan opinion was founded in 1878, and the outside of the newspaper office in Govan Road shows six busts—two of the founders of printing, Gutenberg and Caxton; two literary lions, Robert Burns and Sir Walter Scott; and the founders of *The Govan Press*, Mr. and Mrs. John Cossar.

Across the river, on the north side of the Clyde, is another Glasgow district which preserves its independence in spirit if not in fact. It is Partick, which was known as a village far to the west of Glasgow in the twelfth century. Many Partickonians to-day talk of the great past of Partick, when it had its own Town Council and Police Force (which won the tug-o'-war championship of the world). On 4 November 1912, when Partick ceased to be a burgh and became merely part of Glasgow, the Partick Town Council met for the last time in Partick Burgh Hall. An organist played "Lochaber No More" as Provost Thomas Stark Brown took off his Provost's chain and robe. "There they lie," he said, "the abandoned habits of the Provost of Partick, taken from him by Act of Parliament."

Partick Business Club meet in the Burgh Hall, and use some of the old chairs with the arms of Partick still emblazoned on them. Another centre of local feeling is Partick Bowling Club, founded in 1844. Here tales are told of the two sides of Partick—north and south of Dumbarton Road. Some elderly members can recall when local coalmen sold coal on the south side cheaply, and then changed their price boards as they crossed to the north. To this day, old Partickonians refer to the "hauf-croon" side, and the "five bob" side of Partick.

Local pride exists in small pockets throughout the districts to the north of Glasgow, but to nothing like the same extent as that found in Partick, Govan, Tollcross and Bridgeton. Probably the two most independent districts are Maryhill and Springburn, both of which are former villages. In both districts there are also vestiges of village houses. If

Govan can boast the first co-operative society, Maryhill can claim the first temperance society in Britain. The first pledge was signed at Gairbraid on 1 October 1829 by Lilias Graham, daughter of the Mary Hill who gave her name to the district. In England the first temperance society is claimed to be the one formed at Preston, but that was not until 1832.

Springburn retains an aura entirely of its own. Within its boundaries are enormous railway works and a huge locomotive factory. A representative of British Railways estimated that the number of men, women and children who were " connected " with the railways was not less than 20,000. Railway workers have always been known as men with a pride in craft and a determination to " better " themselves. To an outsider that feeling is still to be observed in Springburn.

It could hardly be expected that the spirit of independence and local pride would show much in the new suburbs of Glasgow, where, naturally, there is no village history, and where a district did not grow up gradually, but was countryside one day and a proliferation of living boxes the next. Nevertheless, one can see the beginnings of a local pride in some of the suburbs which were built in the early 1920's. This has been observed particularly in Knightswood, Riddrie and Mosspark. Conversation with the inhabitants, however, makes it clear that a principal reason for the formation of this local pride is that newer housing schemes have been built near the original ones, and even newer are being erected farther out. So some people in Knightswood, Riddrie and Mosspark feel that they are now old inhabitants, and even that they have higher standards than the newcomers.

STATISTICAL APPENDIX

STATISTICAL APPENDIX

CONTENTS

(*A detailed Index to the Statistical Tables will be found on pp.* 959ff)

STATISTICAL APPENDIX

THE purpose of this appendix is to bring together the most significant statistics relating to the City of Glasgow, in greater detail and completeness than was possible in the text if the flow of the narrative was not to be unduly interrupted. Some of the tables relate to the present, some to developments from the past. Together they cover the most important measurable aspects of the growth of the city and its contemporary life and activities. The order of the tables roughly follows the order of treatment of subjects in the text.

Some of the tables, in the form in which they are here presented, have been prepared for us by officials of Government Departments, Central and Local, and of other authoritative bodies, some are reproduced from Government reports and other official sources, and some have been compiled from original data. The sources are in all cases indicated at the foot of the tables. Acknowledgment is hereby made to all who have provided special statistical information, in tabular form or otherwise, or permitted the reproduction of material already published.

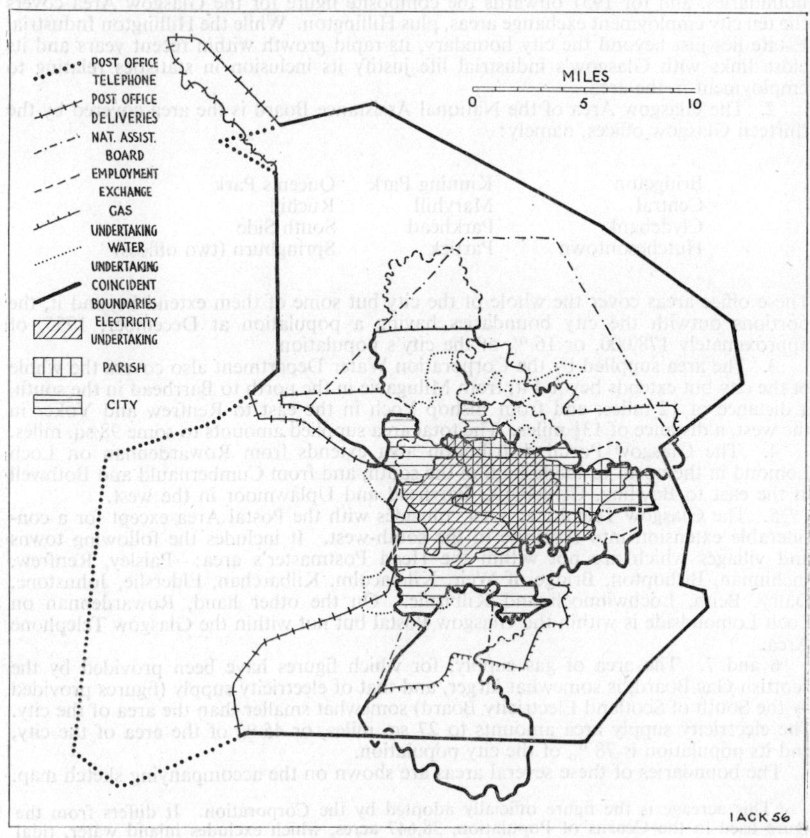

Fig. 37. The Several Areas of "Glasgow," 1956

NOTE ON THE SEVERAL AREAS OF 'GLASGOW' IN 1956

The City of Glasgow, whose boundaries were last extended in 1938, now covers an area of 39,725 acres, or some 62 square miles.[1] That is the area of reference for the majority of the statistics given in the tables.

In certain cases, however, the only available statistics have reference to administrative areas which differ, to a greater or less extent, from that of the city.

1. The area taken to be 'Glasgow' by the Ministry of Labour and National Service has undergone a number of changes in recent years. Up till 1948 it was the area covered by the ten city employment exchanges, namely:

Bridgeton	Maryhill
Central	Parkhead
Finnieston	Partick
Govan	South Side
Kinning Park	Springburn

The figures of insured persons up to 1948 were for that area, which extended beyond the city boundaries at many points. In 1949 and 1950, after the introduction of National Insurance in 1948, the figures of insured employees were based on National Insurance Local Office areas, and for 'Glasgow' they were in the form of a composite figure covering ten National Insurance Office areas, equivalent to the ten city exchange areas, plus Hillington and Rutherglen. In 1951 there was a revision of Ministry of Labour boundaries, and for 1951 onwards the composite figure for the Glasgow Area covers the ten city employment exchange areas, plus Hillington. While the Hillington Industrial Estate lies just beyond the city boundary, its rapid growth within recent years and its close links with Glasgow's industrial life justify its inclusion in statistics relating to employment in the area.

2. The Glasgow Area of the National Assistance Board is the area covered by the thirteen Glasgow offices, namely:

Bridgeton	Kinning Park	Queen's Park
Central	Maryhill	Ruchill
Clydebank	Parkhead	South Side
Hutchesontown	Partick	Springburn (two offices)

These office areas cover the whole of the city but some of them extend beyond it, the portions outwith the city boundaries having a population at December, 1955, of approximately 178,000, or 16 % of the city's population.

3. The area supplied by the Corporation Water Department also covers the whole of the city but extends beyond it, from Milngavie in the north to Barrhead in the south, a distance of 12 miles, and from Bishop Loch in the east to Renfrew and Yoker in the west, a distance of 13½ miles. The total area supplied amounts to some 98 sq. miles.

4. The Glasgow Postal distribution area extends from Rowardennan on Loch Lomond in the north to Eaglesham in the south, and from Cumbernauld and Bothwell in the east to Bowling, Clydebank, Barrhead and Uplawmoor in the west.

5. The Glasgow Telephone Area coincides with the Postal Area except for a considerable extension into Ayrshire in the south-west. It includes the following towns and villages which are not within the Head Postmaster's area:—Paisley, Renfrew, Inchinnan, Bishopton, Bridge of Weir, Kilmacolm, Kilbarchan, Elderslie, Johnstone, Dalry, Beith, Lochwinnoch and Kilbirnie. On the other hand, Rowardennan on Loch Lomondside is within the Glasgow Postal but not within the Glasgow Telephone Area.

6 and 7. The area of gas supply, for which figures have been provided by the Scottish Gas Board, is somewhat larger, and that of electricity supply (figures provided by the South of Scotland Electricity Board) somewhat smaller than the area of the city. The electricity supply area amounts to 27 sq. miles, or 45 % of the area of the city, and its population is 78 % of the city population.

The boundaries of these several areas are shown on the accompanying sketch map.

[1] This acreage is the figure officially adopted by the Corporation. It differs from the figure used in the Census of Population, 38,647 acres, which excludes inland water, tidal water, and foreshore.

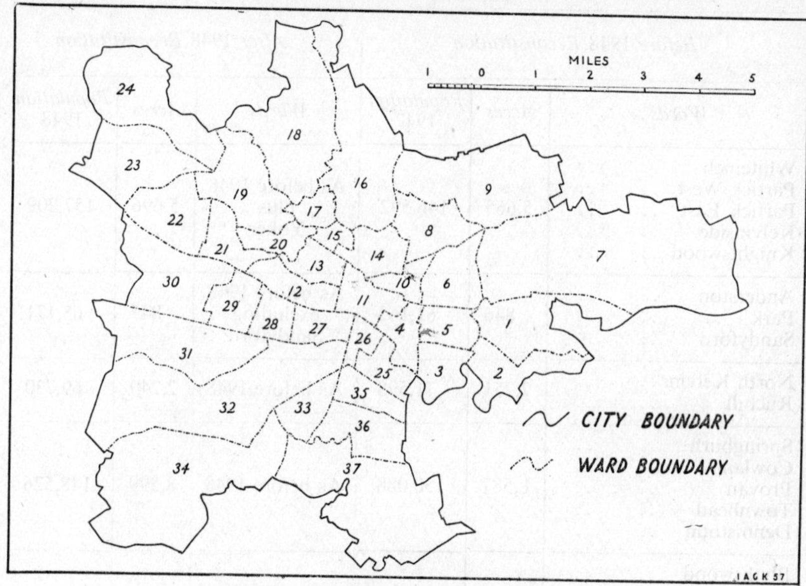

Fig. 38. The Present Wards of the City

The City Wards

Internally the City of Glasgow is divided into Wards, now numbering 37. Before 1948 there were 38. Since 1926 these had, with very slight exceptions, remained unaltered in their boundaries. But owing largely to the development of housing schemes the peripheral wards had acquired large populations, while many wards in the centre of the city had been steadily losing their population. It was largely to rectify the consequent disparities in numbers that it was decided, in 1948, to adjust the boundaries of the wards, and authority to do so was obtained in the Local Government (Scotland) Glasgow Wards and Councillors Order, 1948.

The result of the adjustment was to reduce the number of wards from 38 to 37, and to add to some wards at the expense of others. Three wards disappeared, namely Whitevale, Blythswood and Sandyford; two new wards were created, Yoker and Craigton. Only six wards remained unchanged after the adjustment, namely Cowcaddens, Woodside, Maryhill, on the north side; and Hutchesontown, Gorbals and Govanhill on the south. Except in these six wards, therefore, it is not possible to make direct comparisons between pre-1948 and post-1948. But certain contiguous wards taken together form groups whose areas are almost identical before and after 1948. These are shown overleaf.

Before 1948 *Reconstitution*			*After* 1948 *Reconstitution*		
Wards	*Acres*	*Population* 1947	*Wards*	*Acres*	*Population* 1948
Whiteinch Partick West Partick East Kelvinside Knightswood	5,665	146,592	As before 1948 plus Yoker	5,696	157,209
Anderston Park Sandyford	846	61,162	As before 1948 excluding Sandyford	847	65,171
North Kelvin Ruchill	2,251	71,598	As before 1948	2,240	69,730
Springburn Cowlairs Provan Townhead Dennistoun	8,587	150,088	As before 1948	8,599	148,526
Blythswood Exchange Calton Mile-end Dalmarnock Parkhead Shettleston Tollcross Whitevale	3,875	204,133	As before 1948, excluding Blythswood and Whitevale	3,827	194,423
Kingston Kinning Park Govan Fairfield	2,596	125,756	As before 1948	2,597	118,727
Pollokshields	4,837	55,857	Pollokshields Craigton	4,805	68,731
Camphill Pollokshaws	3,690	46,383	As before 1948	3,704	53,052
Langside Cathcart	3,506	48,526	As before 1948	3,538	53,443
Total of above groups	35,853	910,095		35,853	929,012
Unchanged Wards					
Maryhill	2,210	27,524		2,210	25,202
Woodside	170	29,681		170	28,689
Cowcaddens	488	29,527		488	27,688
Hutchesontown	387	34,536		387	31,240
Gorbals	252	38,823		252	38,849
Govanhill	365	29,814		365	29,320
All Wards	39,725	1,100,000		39,725	1,110,000

PART I: THE BACKGROUND

NOTE ON STATISTICS OF AREA AND POPULATION

THE growth of the area of the city as a unit of local government from before 1800 to the present time, is traced in Table 1. The dates of the successive extensions are shown, and at each date the number of acres added and the total resulting acreage.

It is unfortunately not possible, for the earlier part of the period, to relate the known facts of population to these known acreages. This is due to the lack of continuity in the meaning attached to 'Glasgow' by the Census authorities and consequently in the area whose population they enumerated.

In the first six Census Reports, 1801 to 1851, the area whose population was counted was one called at first 'The City and Town of Glasgow,' later 'Glasgow City and Burgh,' and later again 'Glasgow City and Suburbs.' The population of Glasgow, in this sense, was not again enumerated after 1851. There is doubt about the acreages of those areas, but they certainly did not correspond to the acreages of the growing municipal area shown in Table 1.

The Report of the Census of 1841 published the result of an enumeration of the population of another 'Glasgow.' This was the Parliamentary Burgh created for electoral purposes under the Reform Act of 1832, and the population of Glasgow in this sense has been enumerated at every Census since then. The acreage of this area in 1841 was 5,063 acres, and it remained unchanged until it was extended (to 6,111 acres) under the Redistribution of Seats Act, 1885. The Census Report of 1851 provided a link between the past and the future. Reviewing the progress of the past half century, it made a special retrospective calculation of the population of an area 'nearly the same' as that of the Parliamentary Burgh, as at each Census back to 1801. The population, acreage and density of this constant area are therefore known from 1801 to 1881.

Forwards, it provides a link with the Municipal Burgh. By an Act of 1846 the boundaries of the municipal area had been made to coincide with those of the Parliamentary Burgh, and these areas remained unchanged and equal until the former was extended in 1872; so that in enumerating the population of the Parliamentary Burgh in 1851, 1861 and 1871, the Census was at the same time enumerating the population of the municipal area. In 1881 (i.e. at the first Census date after the extension of the municipal area in 1872) the Census began to enumerate separately the population of the Municipal Burgh, and it has continued to do so at each Census date up to 1951. For the period 1851 to 1951, therefore, we know the population, acreage and density within the municipal limits (an expanding area after 1871).

To enable Glasgow to be seen in its setting, Tables are included giving the statistics of population of two wider areas within which it is situated. These are:-

(1) *The Central Clydeside Conurbation*

Conurbations as defined by the Registrar-General for Scotland are 'continuously urbanised areas surrounding large population centres, which are, to a greater or less extent, focal points of economic and social activity.' They are 'defined in terms of complete local authority areas,' which 'ensures the maximum degree of comparability with other statistical series.' The Central Clydeside Conurbation consists of the administrative areas shown in Table 13.

(2) *The West Central Regional Division*

Recent Census Reports divide Scotland into four regional Divisions, West Central, East Central, Northern and Southern. The West Central Division consists of Glasgow City and the Counties of Lanark, Renfrew, Dunbarton and Ayr.

PART I - SECTION 1

Area & Climate

TABLE 1

THE EXTENSION OF THE CITY'S BOUNDARIES SINCE 1800

Date	Districts Incorporated		Area Added (Acres)	City's Total Area (Acres)
Before 1800	—		—	1,768
1800	Part of the Green and part of the present centre of the city between Ramshorn Church and St. Enoch's Burn		96	1,864
1830	The Necropolis and the lands of Blythswood, and adjacent lands		317	2,181
1843	The portion of the city between Castle Street and Garscube Road, south of the Canal ..		192	2,373
1846	Areas, including the Burghs of Anderston and Calton, the major portion of the Barony of Gorbals, and parts of the counties adjoining	3,418		
	Less northern portion of ancient royalty cut off by new municipal boundary, now made to coincide with the boundary of the Parliamentary Burgh created in 1832	728		
		2,690	2,690	5,063
1872	Areas, including Glasgow University and part of Alexandra Park, etc. ..	242		
	Plus northern portion of ancient royalty formerly excluded ..	728		
		970	970	6,033
1878	Coplawhill and the remainder of the Barony of Gorbals		78	6,111
1891	Burghs of Govanhill, Crosshill, Pollokshields East, Pollokshields, Hillhead and Maryhill; the districts of Mount Florida, Langside, Shawlands, Kelvinside, Possilpark, Springburn, and extensions of Belvidere, etc.		5,750	11,861
1896	Bellahouston Park, Craigton, etc.		450	12,311
1899	Blackhill and Shawfield areas		377	12,688
1905	Burgh of Kinning Park		108	12,796
1909	Moss Park		179	12,975

Date	*Districts Incorporated*	*Area Added (Acres)*	*City's Total Area (Acres)*
1912	Burghs of Govan, Partick and Pollokshaws; Lanarkshire—Shettleston and Tollcross, and portion west of Govan; Renfrewshire—Cathcart and Newlands, and portion west of Partick; Dunbartonshire—Dawsholm, Temple, and Knightswood (North)	6,208	19,183
1926	Lanarkshire—Lambhill, Robroyston, Millerston, Carntyne and Aikenhead; Renfrewshire—Mansewood, Kennishead, Nitshill, Hurlet, Crookston, Cardonald, Scotstoun and Yoker; Dunbartonshire—Knightswood	10,326	29,509
1931	Hogganfield, Carntyne (East)	535	30,044
1938	Lanarkshire—Balmuildy, Auchinairn, Cardowan, Gartloch, Easterhouse and Queenslie; Renfrewshire—Linn Park, Jenny Lind, Darnley and Penilee; Dunbartonshire—Drumry, Drumchapel, and Summerston	9,681	39,725

SOURCE: *Glasgow Corporation. Boundary Commission Reports.*

TABLE 2

Land Use in the City of Glasgow as at 1944/45[1]

Description	*Acres*		*Per Cent*
RESIDENTIAL:			
Private	3,677		
Corporation	2,630		
Private (with Shops)	399	6,706	16.9
COMMERCIAL	959	959	2.4
INDUSTRIAL	2,522	2,522	6.3
RAILWAYS	1,774	1,774	4.5
PUBLIC BUILDINGS:			
Municipal and Government	172		
Schools	555		
Churches	179		
Institutions	1,003		
Entertainment	49		
Baths, Halls, Libraries	89		
Ancient and Historic Buildings	25	2,072	5.2
OPEN SPACE:			
Public	2,749		
Private	1,084		
Cemeteries	510	4,343	10.9
UNURBANISED LAND			
Agricultural, arable	9,458		
Agricultural, pasture	2,016		
Woodlands	723		
Allotments and Nurseries	584		
Policies	590		
Unused Land	2,645	16,016	40.3
ROADS AND STREETS	4,206	4,206	10.6
RIVERS AND WATER	1,127	1,127	2.9
TOTAL	39,725	39,725	100.0

SOURCE: *Glasgow Corporation Planning Department.*

[1] No more recent survey of this nature had been carried out by the Corporation's Planning Department at the time of going to press.

TABLE 3

LAND USE WITHIN THE CITY OF GLASGOW, BY WARDS AS AT 1944/45
(Acres)

Ward	Residential	Commercial	Industrial	Railways	Public Buildings	Open Space	Un-urbanised	Unused Land	Roads Streets	Rivers Water	Total
1. Shettleston and Tollcross ..	418	15	97	36	81	212	369	71	172	2	1,473
2. Parkhead ..	147	9	185	38	69	144	91	63	89	48	883
3. Dalmarnock ..	53	2	119	27	12	1	—	8	54	12	288
4. Calton	48	8	39	1	19	135	—	7	55	21	333
5. Mile-End ..	43	1	70	7	13	5	—	8	43	1	191
6. Whitevale ..	35	20	39	31	7	2	—	11	34	1	180
7. Dennistoun ..	105	8	20	13	21	16	—	33	64	—	280
8. Provan	299	8	189	129	166	165	1,426	256	228	69	2,935
9. Cowlairs ..	66	2	88	98	41	53	28	31	49	—	456
10. Springburn ..	305	12	39	125	331	416	2,644	518	193	158	4,741
11. Townhead ..	43	10	14	2	23	36	—	7	40	—	175
12. Exchange ..	21	73	7	65	28	5	—	3	73	10	285
13. Blythswood ..	20	100	—	11	17	2	—	2	82	8	242
14. Anderston ..	42	94	58	37	32	13	—	7	70	89	442
15. Sandyford ..	37	29	—	1	16	2	—	4	43	—	132
16. Park	80	16	1	5	20	72	—	1	66	5	266
17. Cowcaddens ..	53	20	142	79	11	5	—	98	80	22	510
18. Woodside ..	58	12	24	—	15	3	—	4	48	6	170
19. Ruchill	253	12	119	116	74	122	849	308	148	88	2,089
20. North Kelvin ..	68	2	1	—	8	16	—	5	39	7	146
21. Maryhill ..	133	3	67	73	98	193	1,143	319	110	71	2,210
22. Kelvinside ..	305	16	83	74	94	193	74	62	180	39	1,120
23. Partick East ..	89	7	5	9	55	36	—	7	54	6	268
24. Partick West ..	101	47	29	43	10	13	37	18	76	28	402
25. Whiteinch ..	319	33	156	51	103	202	60	65	198	41	1,228
26. Hutchesontown..	55	2	109	13	12	72	5	42	58	19	387

(Continued overleaf)

TABLE 3 (*Continued*)

LAND USE WITHIN THE CITY OF GLASGOW, BY WARDS AS AT 1944/45
(*Acres*)

Ward	*Residential*	*Commercial*	*Industrial*	*Railways*	*Public Buildings*	*Open Space*	*Unurbanised*	*Unused Land*	*Roads Streets*	*Rivers Water*	*Total*
27. Gorbals	69	11	24	38	16	3	—	5	72	14	252
28. Kingston ..	40	53	28	59	9	2	—	6	64	24	285
29. Kinning Park ..	64	85	37	26	15	17	2	12	62	59	379
30. Govan	116	20	146	43	22	40	8	19	90	25	529
31. Fairfield	134	117	195	50	87	136	446	30	113	95	1,403
32. Pollokshields ..	1,264	31	81	204	277	909	1,372	95	559	48	4,837
33. Camphill ..	139	14	3	9	20	97	—	17	66	1	366
34. Pollokshaws ..	340	13	104	56	91	216	2,139	136	213	16	3,324
35. Govanhill ..	93	14	39	19	17	6	17	93	67	—	365
36. Langside.. ..	143	10	1	12	27	99	99	98	65	3	557
37. Cathcart.. ..	526	15	28	68	68	470	1,468	67	219	20	2,949
38. Yoker & Knightswood	582	15	136	106	47	214	1,094	109	270	74	2,647
	6,706	959	2,522	1,774	2,072	4,343	13,371	2,645	4,206	1,127	39,725

SOURCE: *Glasgow Corporation Planning Department.*

TABLE 4

ABSTRACT OF METEOROLOGICAL OBSERVATIONS TAKEN AT SPRINGBURN PUBLIC PARK, GLASGOW, 1925-1955

YEAR	SHADE TEMPERATURE			RAINFALL		SUNSHINE
	Highest	*Lowest*	*Mean*	*Days*	*Inches*	*Hours*
1925	83	18	46.7	222	38.24	1,224
1926	86	22	47.7	242	45.91	1,174
1927	77	20	46.8	245	49.12	1,162
1928	79	20	46.8	255	49.35	1,121
1929	80	14	46.3	226	43.01	1,223
1930	79	20	47.7	234	42.94	1,022
1931	73	19	46.5	251	43.06	1,078
1932	83	25	47.3	223	42.98	1,126
1933	87	20	48.4	203	29.17	1,255
1934	86	24	48.5	248	39.98	1,186
1935	80	15	47.2	230	43.44	1,211
1936	80	17	47.2	230	40.85	1,076
1937	80	15	47.0	212	31.66	1,183
1938	76	20	48.1	242	49.76	1,174
1939	88	18	47.6	212	38.41	1,177
1940	85	6	46.5	210	39.52	1,111
1941	80	12	46.3	204	33.34	1,035
1942	80	18	46.3	220	40.64	1,067
1943	86	23	48.0	252	45.43	1,094
1944	80	21	47.3	231	44.44	953
1945	81	11	48.6	233	43.62	1,199
1946	77	19	47.3	222	39.93	1,220
1947	86	8	46.7	209	38.63	1,086
1948	85	25	48.1	233	53.33	1,157
1949	84	19	49.3	222	43.20	1,310
1950	88	18	46.7	226	45.37	1,181
1951	81	21	46.8	221	41.46	1,182
1952	79	15	46.3	195	35.32	1,280
1953	80	20	48.6	206	36.51	1,078
1954	73	19	46.2	247	56.31	1,030
1955	85	12	47.2	199	31.67	1,563
1955						
January ..	52	15	34.5	25	3.10	35.6
February ..	45	12	32.5	18	2.05	91.6
March ..	55	22	37.3	11	1.55	119.8
April ..	69	30	48.4	14	1.69	159.9
May ..	77	31	48.9	19	3.48	238.3
June ..	74	36	54.8	16	2.55	162.7
July ..	83	43	63.1	5	1.23	292.1
August ..	85	41	62.2	9	1.15	177.1
September	79	41	55.7	23	3.72	124.1
October ..	64	26	46.3	20	2.88	78.7
November ..	57	28	44.0	16	2.02	48.5
December ..	53	21	38.3	23	6.25	34.8

SOURCE: *Glasgow Corporation Parks Department.*

PART I - SECTION 2

Vital Statistics

TABLE 5

LIVE BIRTHS IN GLASGOW, 1861-1955

Year	LIVE BIRTHS Legitimate	Illegitimate	Total	Birth Rate per 1000 Population	Illegitimate Births as % of all Live Births
1861	15,084	1,453	16,537	41.6	8.8
1871	17,112	1,755	18,867	38.4	9.3
1881	17,617	1,526	19,143	37.4	7.9
1891	18,308	1,549	19,857	35.0	7.8
1901	22,725	1,481	24,206	31.8	6.1
1902	23,211	1,511	24,722	32.4	6.1
1903	23,636	1,499	25,135	32.9	6.0
1904	23,194	1,560	24,754	32.4	6.3
1905	22,722	1,544	24,316	31.8	6.4
1906	22,944	1,616	24,560	31.5	6.6
1907	22,488	1,518	24,006	30.7	6.3
1908	22,400	1,515	23,915	30.6	6.3
1909	21,566	1,574	23,140	29.6	6.8
1910	20,728	1,494	22,222	28.4	6.7
1911	20,286	1,469	21,755	27.7	6.8
1912	20,572	1,472	22,044	28.1	6.7
1913	26,843	1,845	28,688	28.1	6.4
1914	27,571	1,891	29,462	28.6	6.8
1915	26,300	1,643	27,943	27.0	5.9
1916	25,438	1,656	27,094	26.0	6.1
1917	22,259	1,771	24,030	22.9	7.4
1918	21,612	1,912	23,524	22.3	8.1
1919	23,905	1,930	25,835	24.3	7.5
1920	30,420	2,206	32,626	31.5	6.8
1921	27,794	1,918	29,712	27.6	6.5
1922	26,570	1,728	28,298	26.3	6.1
1923	25,218	1,492	26,710	24.9	5.6
1924	23,846	1,484	25,330	23.6	5.9
1925	23,935	1,481	25,416	23.7	5.8
1926	23,081	1,460	24,541	22.7	5.9
1927	22,132	1,446	23,578	21.6	6.1
1928	22,078	1,571	23,649	21.7	6.6
1929	21,249	1,550	22,799	20.9	6.8
1930	21,799	1,523	23,322	21.4	6.5
1931	21,504	1,422	22,926	21.1	6.2
1932	21,402	1,330	22,732	20.9	5.9
1933	20,069	1,292	21,361	19.6	6.0
1934	20,501	1,321	21,822	20.1	6.1
1935	20,789	1,313	22,102	20.3	5.9
1936	20,952	1,321	22,273	20.5	5.1
1937	20,905	1,271	22,176	20.4	5.7
1938	20,722	1,257	21,979	20.1	5.7
1939	20,435	1,247	21,682	19.8	5.8
1940	19,760	1,205	20,965	19.2	5.4

Year	LIVE BIRTHS			Birth Rate per 1000 Population	Illegitimate Births as % of all Live Births
	Legitimate	*Illegitimate*	*Total*		
1941	19,024	1,341	20,365	18.6	6.6
1942	19,196	1,419	20,615	18.9	6.9
1943	20,732	1,631	22,363	20.5	7.2
1944	20,443	1,760	22,203	20.3	7.9
1945	18,610	1,684	20,294	18.6	8.3
1946	22,111	1,449	23,560	21.6	6.1
1947	24,465	1,364	25,829	23.7	5.2
1948	21,027	1,265	22,292	20.4	5.7
1949	19,758	1,165	20,923	19.2	5.6
1950	18,934	1,097	20,031	18.4	5.5
1951	19,030	1,061	20,091	18.4	5.3
1952	19,378	959	20,337	18.7	4.7
1953	19,213	1,019	20,232	18.6	5.0
1954	19,954	1,023	20,977	19.3	4.9
1955	20,037	987	21,024	19.4	4.7

SOURCE: *Glasgow Corporation Health and Welfare Department.*

TABLE 6

MARRIAGES IN GLASGOW

Rate per 1000 *of Population*, 1861-1955

Ten-year Averages, 1861-1950
Annually, 1951-1955

Period	*Rate*	*Period*	*Rate*
1861-1870	9.2	1931-1940	9.7
1871-1880	9.1	1941-1950	10.2
1881-1890	9.3	1951	9.6
1891-1900	9.4	1952	9.5
1901-1910	8.8	1953	9.7
1911-1920	9.7	1954	9.6
1921-1930	8.9	1955	9.8

SOURCE: *Calculated from number of marriages shown in Annual Estimates of Registrar-General for Scotland and the population of the City as estimated by the Medical Officer of Health, Glasgow*

TABLE 7

BIRTH RATES PER 1000 POPULATION IN SANITARY DISTRICTS, 1881-1890 AND 1891-1900

Sanitary District	1881-1890	1891-1900	*Sanitary District*	1881-1890	1891-1900
Blythswood	22.6	20.1	Anderston	39.8	38.1
Exchange	30.0	29.6	Kingston	32.2	29.5
Port Dundas	39.6	38.1	Lauriston	37.3	37.5
High Street and Closes, West	31.9	33.7	Hutcheson Square ..	43.5	39.3
St. Rollox	39.4	36.2	Gorbals	36.8	38.5
Bellgrove and Dennistoun	38.1	35.8	Springburn and Rockvilla	43.0	39.1
High Street and Closes, East	36.4	38.3	Govanhill	—	33.2
Greenhead and London Road	40.9	40.4	Crosshill	—	15.6
Barrowfield	38.6	39.0	Langside and Mount Florida	—	22.4
Montieth Row ..	25.7	24.4	Pollokshields East and Strathbungo	—	17.1
St. Andrew's Square ..	30.8	31.8	Pollokshields West and Bellahouston ..	—	12.0
Calton	38.6	38.4	Hillhead	—	13.1
St. Enoch Square ..	29.2	28.8	Kelvinside	—	13.4
Brownfield	37.1	40.6	Maryhill	—	38.8
Bridgegate and Wynds	35.8	37.4	Possilpark and Barnhill	—	40.2
Woodside	36.9	33.0			
Cowcaddens	42.8	43.9			
Kelvinhaugh and Sandyford	29.0	25.1	City of Glasgow[1] ..	36.5	33.4

SOURCE: *Glasgow Corporation Health and Welfare Department.*

[1] Including Institutions and Harbour.

TABLE 8

BIRTH RATES PER 1000 POPULATION, BY WARDS, 1910-1955

Ward	1910	1920	1930	1940	1945	1950	1955
Blackfriars	30.8	32.2	—	—	—	—	—
Broomielaw	28.9	37.6	—	—	—	—	—
Blythswood	9.1	17.6	20.8	20.5	14.5	—	—
Sandyford	21.9	28.7	21.6	19.0	20.2	—	—
Whitevale	31.3	35.5	23.7	23.1	20.0	—	—
Govan Central	—	34.8	—	—	—	—	—
Ibrox	—	34.0	—	—	—	—	—
Jordanhill	—	21.5	—	—	—	—	—
Partick Central	—	28.8	—	—	—	—	—
Plantation	—	32.0	—	—	—	—	—
Shettleston and Tollcross	—	31.3	22.1	19.0	18.5	10.4	19.5
Parkhead	—	—	25.1	21.1	18.6	18.5	16.0
Dalmarnock	35.9	37.6	28.2	26.2	22.3	20.5	23.3
Calton	31.3	36.9	28.6	25.9	20.7	20.5	23.3
Mile-End	38.1	36.4	28.9	25.3	22.5	21.8	26.0
Dennistoun	23.8	22.1	17.1	14.8	16.1	15.8	17.1
Provan	—	—	26.0	20.9	19.8	16.8	17.2
Cowlairs	32.4	32.7	23.4	20.8	19.6	18.3	23.3
Springburn	36.2	35.8	22.7	18.6	16.1	18.1	15.8
Townhead	29.5	30.0	21.2	25.4	20.0	21.1	28.6
Exchange	20.1	18.6	26.9	26.4	19.9	16.5	27.6
Anderston	30.2	34.4	25.1	24.0	20.6	18.2	21.8
Park	8.7	17.0	9.5	13.7	17.9	15.7	19.2
Cowcaddens	29.6	35.3	27.9	26.9	23.5	20.6	25.2
Woodside	26.3	29.3	25.5	23.2	22.2	19.6	27.4
Ruchill	—	—	25.8	17.8	19.4	19.5	17.8
North Kelvin	—	—	19.3	18.6	19.9	18.0	24.2
Maryhill	31.6	29.9	23.2	18.9	17.5	18.3	22.6
Kelvinside	10.4	12.9	8.2	8.3	13.0	11.7	14.4
Partick East	—	24.5	19.0	19.4	17.7	14.8	17.1
Partick West	—	26.0	20.9	23.5	19.7	18.0	21.3
Whiteinch	—	—	18.1	15.7	18.6	16.0	19.6
Yoker	—	—	—	14.1	18.2	{12.6	11.9
Knightswood	—	—	—			14.3	20.4
Hutchesontown	38.4	36.3	27.1	25.2	20.8	23.0	28.5
Gorbals	26.0	28.7	26.7	27.9	27.6	24.0	26.0
Kingston	27.9	31.3	27.1	26.4	21.4	21.8	25.8
Kinning Park	34.2	37.4	25.6	25.0	23.5	20.7	22.6
Govan	—	—	27.9	24.9	24.2	22.0	24.9
Fairfield	—	26.6	20.9	16.2	17.4	18.4	17.2
Craigton	—	—	—	—	—	14.0	10.9
Pollokshields	9.6	10.4	10.5	11.9	17.9	15.0	11.5
Camphill	—	—	10.2	12.1	14.6	11.6	12.4
Pollokshaws	—	27.5	15.9	14.4	18.3	20.6	13.7
Govanhill	31.0	29.5	18.2	15.7	17.3	15.6	19.1
Langside	17.7	18.8	9.4	11.2	12.2	11.9	11.1
Cathcart	—	17.8	11.1	10.5	13.6	11.1	16.6
City of Glasgow	27.6	29.4	21.4	19.1	19.3	18.2	19.4

SOURCE: *Glasgow Corporation Health and Welfare Department.*

[1] The city wards were reconstituted in 1912, 1920 and 1948. At these reconstitutions some names were dropped and some added; and even where names remained unaltered, the areas of some wards were changed. In consequence, direct comparisons can be made only between 1930, 1940 and 1945, and between 1950 and 1955.

TABLE 9

Deaths by Age Groups, and Death Rates per 1000 Population

Every tenth year, 1861 *to* 1931. *Annually thereafter*

Year	Deaths from All Causes					*Total Deaths*	*Death Rate per 1000*
	Under 1 year	1-4 *years*	5-19 *years*	20-59 *years*	60 *years and over*		
1861	2,544	2,906	1,109	2,988	1,385	10,932	27.5
1871	3,608	4,064	1,753	4,463	1,897	15,785	32.1
1881	2,765	2,601	1,452	4,154	1,942	12,914	25.2
1891	2,946	2,484	1,270	4,892	2,732	14,324	25.3
1901	3,602	2,788	1,154	5,150	3,022	15,716	20.6

Year	Deaths from All Causes								*Total Deaths*	*Death Rate per* 1000
	Under 1 year	1 *and under* 2 *years*	2-4 *years*	5-14 *years*	15-24 *years*	25-44 *years*	45-64 *years*	65 *years and over*		
1911	2,944	1,078	784	650	584	1,774	2,684	2,400	12,898	16.4
1921	3,135	992	502	601	722	2,020	3,790	3,863	15,625	14.5
1931	2,397	793	548	532	710	1,696	3,816	5,013	15,505	14.2
1932	2,542	631	417	515	738	1,911	4,049	5,268	16,071	14.7
1933	2,061	408	316	469	664	1,675	3,901	5,253	14,747	13.4
1934	2,140	655	471	501	613	1,675	3,916	5,263	15,234	13.7
1935	2,169	382	289	419	636	1,760	4,086	5,795	15,537	13.8
1936	2,429	541	327	391	684	1,732	4,295	6,007	16,406	14.5
1937	2,313	393	293	391	658	1,761	4,362	6,208	16,379	14.6
1938	1,919	440	313	412	666	1,587	4,002	5,677	15,016	13.3
1939	1,737	232	264	374	607	1,631	3,999	6,166	15,010	13.3
1940	1,983	307	376	390	737	1,861	4,712	7,237	17,603	16.8
1941	2,267	288	347	374	651	1,703	4,154	6,517	16,301	15.6
1942	1,863	179	241	345	707	1,570	3,841	5,933	14,679	14.0
1943	1,825	179	215	359	638	1,462	3,893	6,253	14,824	14.2
1944	2,108	178	190	338	590	1,370	3,708	6,121	14,603	13.9
1945	1,379	133	198	297	557	1,338	3,719	6,320	13,941	13.3
1946	1,588	123	153	236	480	1,488	3,819	6,615	14,502	13.5
1947	1,989	120	134	272	536	1,345	3,992	6,879	15,267	13.9
1948	1,241	110	109	215	493	1,331	3,578	6,543	13,620	12.3
1949	1,033	105	98	193	466	1,268	3,803	7,237	14,203	12.8
1950	879	77	114	123	352	1,138	3,937	7,470	14,090	12.8
1951	922	80	91	128	235	998	3,967	7,891	14,312	13.1
1952	831	63	77	96	226	875	3,828	7,845	13,841	12.7
1953	723	54	64	120	170	847	3,549	7,300	12,827	11.8
1954	736	37	55	94	152	755	3,672	7,249	12,750	11.7
1955	765	43	56	99	134	726	3,702	7,750	13,275	12.3

Source: *Glasgow Corporation Health and Welfare Department.*

PART I - SECTION 3

Population

TABLE 10

POPULATION OF GLASGOW—CENSUS ENUMERATIONS

Census	*Area Enumerated*	*Population*		
		Males	*Females*	*Total*
1801	City (including suburbs) ..	35,007	42,378	77,385
1811	City (including suburbs) ..	45,275	55,474	100,749
1821	City (including suburbs) ..	68,119	78,924	147,043
1831	City (including suburbs) ..	93,724	108,702	202,426
1841	City (including suburbs) ..	130,478	143,846	274,324
	Parliamentary Burgh ..	120,044	135,606	255,650
1851	City (including suburbs) ..	162,933	182,053	344,986
	Parliamentary Burgh (=Municipal area as extended in 1846)	154,930	174,167	329,097
1861	Parliamentary Burgh (=Municipal area as extended in 1846)	185,556	209,947	395,503
1871	Parliamentary Burgh (=Municipal area as extended in 1846)	230,995	246,737	477,732
1881	Parliamentary Burgh ..	236,593	251,995	488,588
	Municipal Burgh	248,366	263,049	511,415
1891	Municipal Burgh (=Parliamentary Burgh as extended under the Redistribution of Seats Act, 1885)..	277,798	288,041	565,839[a]
1901	Municipal Burgh	373,540	388,169	761,709
	Parliamentary Burgh ..	308,958	313,414	622,372
1911	Municipal Burgh	381,304	403,192	784,496
	Parliamentary Burgh ..	296,493	303,121	599,614
1921	Municipal Burgh (= Parliamentary Burgh as extended under the Representation of the People Act, 1918) ..	504,568	529,606	1,034,174
1931	Municipal Burgh	524,475	563,986	1,088,461
	Parliamentary Burgh ..	495,199	532,220	1,027,419
1951	Municipal Burgh[1] ..	518,871	570,896	1,089,767

SOURCE: *Census of Scotland*, 1801-1951.

(*a*) The population of the Municipal Burgh, plus suburbs which were brought within the Municipal Burgh later in the same year, was 658,073.

[1] Under the Representation of the People Act, 1948, the City of Glasgow was divided for parliamentary purposes into fifteen " Burgh Constituencies."

TABLE 11

GLASGOW. DENSITY OF POPULATION[1]

Year	Area	Population	Acres	Persons to Acre
1801	An area approximately equal to that of the Parliamentary Burgh created in 1832 ..	77,058	c.5,063	15
1811	Do.	103,224	c.5,063	20
1821	Do.	140,432	c.5,063	28
1831	Do.	193,030	c.5,063	38
1841	Parliamentary Burgh ..	255,650	5,063	50
1851	Parliamentary Burgh (=Municipal area)	329,097	5,063	65
1861	Do.	395,503	5,063	78
1871	Do.	477,732	5,063	94
1881	Parliamentary Burgh ..	488,588	5,063	97
	Municipal Burgh	511,415	6,111	84
1891	Municipal Burgh	565,839	6,111	93
1901	Do.	761,709	12,688	60
1911	Do.	784,496	12,975	60
1921	Do.	1,034,174	19,183	54
1931	Do.	1,088,461	29,509	36
1951	Do.	1,089,767	39,725	27

SOURCE: *Population figures from Census of Scotland,* 1801-1951.

[1] See Note on Area and Population, p. 787.

TABLE 12

MUNICIPAL BURGH OF GLASGOW

Estimates of Population, 1932-1955

Year	*Population*	*Yearly Change %*	*% of Census Population 1931*
1931	Census Population, 1,088,461		100.00
	Registrar-General's Estimates[1]		
1932	1,104,689 Total	—	101.49
1933	1,109,371 „	+ 0.42	101.92
1934	1,113,330 „	+ 0.36	102.28
1935	1,119,414 „	+ 0.55	102.84
1936	1,115,834 „	− 0.32	102.51
1937	1,119,863 „	+ 0.37	102.88
1938	1,127,825 „	+ 0.71	103.52
1939	1,128,473 „	+ 0.06	103.68
1940	1,045,333 Civilian	− 7.37	96.04
1941	1,008,435 „	− 3.53	92.65
1942	1,000,060 „	− 0.83	91.89
1943	993,249 „	− 0.68	91.25
1944	992,434 „	− 0.08	91.18
1945	1,001,523 „	+ 0.92	92.01
1946	1,054,928 „	+ 5.33	96.92
1947	1,108,549 Total	+ 5.08	101.85
1948	1,106,072 „	− 0.22	101.62
1949	1,099,691 „	− 0.58	101.03
1950	1,089,303 „	− 0.94	100.08
1951	1,090,364 „ (Census: 1,089,767) ..	+ 0.10	100.17
1952	1,086,791 „	− 0.33	99.85
1953	1,084,253 „	− 0.23	99.61
1954	1,083,417 „	− 0.08	99.54
1955	1,082,467 „	− 0.09	99.45

SOURCE: *Census of Scotland,* 1931 *and* 1951; *and Annual Estimates of Registrar-General for Scotland,* 1932-1955.

1. Estimates of Population

Estimates of the population are published in the ' Annual Estimates of the Registrar-General for Scotland.' Up to and including 1939 the estimates were of total population at 30th June in each year. From 1940 to 1946 inclusive, the estimates were of the civilian population only and were based on the National Register amended for changes (including enlistment) known to have taken place. For these years, each annual estimate was the mean of four quarterly estimates.

Since 1947 the estimates (now taken, as before the war, as at 30th June) have again been estimates of the total population. In 1947, 1948 and 1949 the figures in the National Register continued to be used as the basis but were modified by estimates of persons leaving and entering H.M. Forces since the beginning of the war. In 1950 the total population estimated was the civilian population (including members of the Mercantile Marine at home and abroad), plus H.M. Forces stationed at home; but in 1951 and since, members of the Mercantile Marine for the time being outwith Scotland have been excluded.

TABLE 13

The Central Clydeside Conurbation[1]

Population of the Conurbation, 1951, and of the same area 1921 and 1931[2]

Administrative Area	*Acres*[3] 1951	*Population* 1921	*Population* 1931	*Population* 1951
Glasgow City	38,647	1,056,436	1,093,337	1,089,767
Airdrie Burgh	2,071	26,215	26,734	30,313
Coatbridge Burgh	3,513	44,466	43,513	47,541
Hamilton Burgh	2,877	39,746	38,112	40,174
Motherwell and Wishaw Burgh	4,640	69,956	65,611	68,154
Rutherglen Burgh	1,039	24,777	25,182	24,213
Clydebank "	2,831	46,674	47,033	44,638
Kirkintilloch "	1,041	11,775	11,952	14,826
Milngavie "	1,600	4,515	5,178	7,885
Barrhead "	1,154	11,714	12,373	12,971
Johnstone "	1,232	12,781	13,182	15,660
Paisley "	6,217	86,584	88,384	93,711
Renfrew "	2,214	14,206	15,012	17,091
Lanark 5th District	27,565	22,900	22,275	24,255
" 6th "	13,251	59,401	59,002	60,232
" 8th "	8,122	31,035	36,908	38,319
" 9th "	37,718	47,619	53,842	64,255
Renfrew 1st "	28,565	12,700	17,238	38,201
" 2nd "	17,365	9,715	9,972	13,740
New Kilpatrick District ..	7,281	4,319	5,325	12,508
Total	208,943	1,637,534	1,690,165	1,758,454

Source: *Compiled from Census of Scotland*, 1951.

[1] See Note on the Conurbation, p. 787.
[2] Boundaries as in 1951 in all cases.
[3] Exclusive of inland water, tidal water and foreshore.

TABLE 14

Population of Scotland and West Central Division. Census, 1951

	Males	*Females*	*Total*
Scotland	2,434,358	2,662,057	5,096,415
West Central Division[1]			
Glasgow City	518,871	570,896	1,089,767
Lanarkshire	254,632	269,964	524,596
Renfrewshire	153,760	170,900	324,660
Dunbartonshire	79,441	84,828	164,269
Ayrshire	153,114	168,123	321,237
Total, W. Central Div.	1,159,818	1,264,711	2,424,529
W. Cent. Div. % of Scot.	47.6%	47.5%	47.6%

Source: *Census of Scotland*, 1951.

[1] See Note on the Regional Divisions of Scotland, p. 787.

TABLE 15

POPULATION OF WEST CENTRAL DIVISION OF SCOTLAND AT EACH CENSUS, 1801-1951

Census Year	*Population of West Central Division of Scotland*	*% of Total Population of Scotland*	*Intercensal Change %*
1801	331,110	20.6	—
1811	412,491	22.8	+ 24.6
1821	511,178	24.4	+ 23.9
1831	628,528	26.6	+ 23.0
1841	790,696	30.2	+ 25.8
1851	926,221	32.1	+ 17.1
1861	1,060,132	34.6	+ 14.5
1871	1,241,952	37.0	+ 17.2
1881	1,460,638	39.1	+ 17.6
1891	1,657,616	41.2	+ 13.5
1901	1,976,640	44.2	+ 19.2
1911	2,169,754	45.6	+ 9.8
1921	2,288,480	46.9	+ 5.5
1931	2,307,594	47.6	+ 0.8
1951	2,424,529	47.6	+ 5.1

SOURCE: *Census of Scotland*, 1951.

TABLE 16

GLASGOW. SUMMARY OF COMPARATIVE AGE DISTRIBUTION 1851, 1901, 1931, 1951.

AGE GROUP	MALES *Per Cent of all Males*				FEMALES *Per Cent of all Females*				BOTH SEXES *Per Cent of Total Population*			
	1851	1901	1931	1951	1851	1901	1931	1951	1851	1901	1931	1951
0-14	34.9	32.8	28.5	26.4	30.8	31.6	26.2	23.3	32.8	32.3	27.3	24.8
15-64	63.1	64.7	66.4	65.8	66.4	64.8	67.7	67.3	64.8	64.8	67.1	66.6
65 & over	2.0	2.4	5.0	7.8	2.8	3.6	6.0	9.3	2.4	3.0	5.6	8.6

SOURCE: *Calculated from Census of Scotland*, 1851, 1901, 1931, 1951.

TABLE 17

POPULATION OF THE CITY OF GLASGOW BY AGE AND SEX. PERCENTAGE DISTRIBUTION. 1851-1951

Age Group	1851 *M*	1851 *F*	1901 *M*	1901 *F*	1911 *M*	1911 *F*	1921 *M*	1921 *F*	1931 *M*	1931 *F*	1951 *M*	1951 *F*
All Ages	154,930	174,167	373,540	388,169	381,304	403,192	504,568	529,606	524,475	563,986	518,871	570,896
	%	%	%	%	%	%	%	%	%	%	%	%
Under 1	13.2	11.7	2.8	2.6	2.4	2.3	2.5	2.3	2.0	1.8	1.9	1.6
1-4			9.4	9.1	9.2	8.6	7.6	7.2	7.5	6.9	7.9	6.9
5-9	11.0	9.7	10.7	10.2	10.7	10.1	9.9	9.5	10.0	9.2	8.4	7.4
10-14	10.7	9.5	9.9	9.7	9.9	9.5	10.1	9.6	9.0	8.4	8.2	7.5
15-19	11.2	11.5	10.1	10.0	9.6	9.6	9.9	9.7	9.2	9.2	7.1	7.6
20-24	11.5	12.6	11.0	10.9	9.3	9.9	8.8	9.7	8.9	9.2	7.3	7.6
25-29	9.5	10.1	9.8	9.8	8.9	9.3	7.9	8.7	8.3	8.5	8.0	7.5
30-34	7.9	8.2	7.9	7.6	8.3	8.1	7.2	7.7	7.3	7.9	6.9	6.9
35-39	6.2	6.2	6.7	6.7	7.4	7.1	6.9	7.1	6.6	7.1	7.4	7.3
40-44	5.7	5.7	5.8	5.6	6.2	5.8	6.7	6.6	6.1	6.4	7.4	7.2
45-49	3.9	3.9	4.7	4.6	5.2	5.1	6.5	5.9	5.8	6.0	7.0	6.8
50-54	3.4	3.8	3.9	3.9	4.3	4.3	5.3	4.7	5.6	5.4	5.9	6.4
55-59	2.0	2.2	2.8	3.0	3.3	3.3	4.0	3.7	5.0	4.5	4.8	5.4
60-64	1.7	2.2	2.1	2.6	2.4	2.5	3.0	2.9	3.7	3.5	4.0	4.6
65-69	0.9	1.2	1.2	1.6	1.6	1.9	2.0	2.0	2.5	2.6	3.2	3.7
70-74	0.6	0.8	0.7	1.1	0.9	1.5	1.0	1.4	1.5	1.9	2.5	2.8
75-79	0.3	0.4	0.4	0.6	0.3	0.6	0.5	0.8	0.7	1.0	1.4	1.7
80-84	0.1	0.2	0.1	0.3	0.1	0.3	0.2	0.4	0.2	0.4	0.5	0.8
85& over	0.0	0.1	0.0	0.1	0.0	0.1	0.0	0.1	0.1	0.1	0.1	0.4

SOURCE: *Census of Scotland*, 1851 to 1951.

TABLE 18

THE CENTRAL CLYDESIDE CONURBATION[1] POPULATION BY AGE AND SEX: 1951

Age Group	POPULATION *Males*	*Females*	*Total*	*Age Group*	POPULATION *Males*	*Females*	*Total*
All Ages	838,697	919,757	1,758,454	45-54	106,975	119,608	226,583
0- 4	83,856	80,363	164,219	55-64	72,832	90,603	163,435
5-14	141,840	138,981	280,821	65-74	47,560	58,953	106,513
15-24	119,229	138,004	257,233	75 and over	18,649	25,892	44,541
25-34	123,723	133,711	257,434	Not stated	101	147	248
35-44	123,932	133,495	257,427				

SOURCE: *Census of Scotland*, 1951.

[1] See Note on the Conurbation, p. 787. The Central Clydeside Conurbation consists of the administrative areas shown in Table 13.

TABLE 19

GLASGOW

Number of Females per 1,000 *Males*, 1851, 1901, 1951, *by Age Groups*

Age Group	1851	1901	1951	*Age Group*	1851	1901	1951
0- 4	993	1,002	954	50-54	1,260	1,039	1,197
5- 9	990	986	967	55-59	1,267	1,110	1,239
10-14	999	1,014	997	60-64	1,459	1,258	1,268
15-19	1,141	1,038	1,176	65-69	1,432	1,401	1,288
20-24	1,226	1,032	1,140	70-74	1,547	1,537	1,241
25-29	1,200	1,038	1,034	75-79	1,651	1,633	1,326
30-34	1,158	1,012	1,106	80-84	1,599	2,164	1,539
35-39	1,129	1,036	1,089	85-89	1,707	2,628	2,173
40-44	1,115	1,016	1,067	90 & over	4,063	2,846	3,703
45-49	1,141	1,008	1,067	All Ages	1,124	1,039	1,100

SOURCE: *Calculated from Census of Scotland*, 1851 *and* 1901. *For* 1951 *the figures are as given in the Census of that year.*

TABLE 20

Population of the City of Glasgow by Age, Sex and Marital State, 1951

Age Group	Males: Total	Males: Single	Males: Married	Males: Widowed or Divorced	Males: Not Stated	Females: Total	Females: Single	Females: Married	Females: Widowed or Divorced	Females: Not Stated
All Ages	518,871	261,444	234,056	22,747	624	570,896	271,796	240,333	58,188	579
0-4	50,833	50,833	—	—	—	48,515	48,515	—	—	—
5-9	43,598	43,598	—	—	—	42,164	42,164	—	—	—
10-14	42,673	42,673	—	—	—	42,564	42,564	—	—	—
15-19	36,946	36,774	172	—	—	43,451	41,998	1,449	4	—
20-24	38,117	30,117	7,872	45	83	43,435	26,798	16,487	96	54
25-29	41,462	17,335	23,752	280	95	42,885	13,034	29,257	543	51
30-34	35,559	8,718	26,311	467	63	39,343	7,601	30,609	1,100	33
35-39	38,445	6,523	31,030	838	54	41,866	7,158	32,929	1,746	33
40-44	38,478	5,383	32,051	1,012	32	41,064	7,522	31,144	2,360	38
45-49	36,395	4,862	30,143	1,357	33	38,826	7,724	27,503	3,572	27
50-54	30,388	3,718	24,921	1,703	46	36,373	6,762	24,078	5,477	56
55-59	24,809	2,826	19,810	2,143	30	30,746	5,525	18,153	7,028	40
60-64	20,777	2,601	15,504	2,632	40	26,354	4,777	13,053	8,467	57
65-69	16,514	2,332	10,871	3,277	34	21,277	3,920	8,319	8,971	67
70-74	12,757	1,805	7,097	3,811	44	15,830	2,865	4,787	8,129	49
75-79	7,428	950	3,368	3,067	43	9,848	1,776	1,956	6,081	35
80-84	2,818	318	963	1,524	13	4,338	760	489	3,069	20
85-89	709	56	149	501	3	1,541	263	75	1,193	10
90-94	101	7	19	75	—	373	56	11	302	4
95-99	9	1	—	8	—	37	7	3	26	1
100 & over	1	—	—	1	—	1	—	—	1	—
Not stated	54	14	23	6	11	65	7	31	23	4

Source: *Census of Scotland*, 1951.

TABLE 21

GLASGOW

Population by Age and Marital State, 1881, 1901, 1931 *and* 1951

AGE GROUP	1881				1901			
	Total	*Single*	*Married*	*Widowed or Divorced*	*Total*	*Single*	*Married*	*Widowed or Divorced*
0-14	176,831	176,831	—	—	245,136	245,136	—	—
15-19	52,549	51,677	863	9	76,627	75,604	1,020	3
20-24	54,004	40,431	13,339	234	83,643	66,595	16,889	159
25-29	46,543	19,455	26,174	914	74,352	36,865	36,664	823
30-34	37,291	9,333	26,391	1,567	59,043	18,200	39,283	1,560
35-39	31,952	5,586	24,247	2,119	50,775	11,276	36,913	2,586
40-44	29,167	4,136	21,695	3,336	43,415	7,656	32,349	3,410
45-49	22,728	2,652	16,469	3,607	35,561	4,945	26,312	4,304
50-54	19,738	2,099	13,206	4,433	29,783	3,655	20,597	5,531
55-59	13,559	1,324	8,236	3,999	22,113	2,388	14,131	5,594
60-64	12,330	1,242	6,261	4,827	17,915	1,953	9,425	6,537
65-69	6,811	712	2,885	3,214	10,937	1,140	4,808	4,989
70-74	4,474	472	1,414	2,588	6,910	744	2,232	3,934
75-79	2,126	257	500	1,369	3,457	384	841	2,232
80-84	947	103	146	698	1,503	158	208	1,137
85 & over	365	37	48	280	539	65	44	430
All Ages	511,415	316,347	161,874	33,194	761,709	476,764	241,716	43,229

AGE GROUP	1931				1951			
	Total	*Single*	*Married*	*Widowed or Divorced*	*Total*	*Single*	*Married*	*Widowed or Divorced*
0-14	297,596	297,596	—	—	270,347	270,347	—	—
15-19	100,006	98,415	1,580	9	80,397	78,772	1,621	4
20-24	98,667	79,948	18,538	161	81,552	56,715	24,359	141
25-29	91,470	47,038	43,747	669	84,347	30,369	53,009	823
30-34	82,525	24,637	56,354	1,513	74,902	16,319	56,920	1,567
35-39	74,698	16,115	55,847	2,718	80,311	13,681	63,959	2,584
40-44	68,340	12,800	51,575	3,959	79,542	12,905	63,195	3,372
45-49	64,179	11,497	47,301	5,374	75,221	12,586	57,646	4,929
50-54	59,717	10,300	42,475	6,932	66,761	10,480	48,999	7,180
55-59	51,514	8,394	34,488	8,624	55,555	8,351	37,963	9,171
60-64	39,159	6,082	23,352	9,716	47,131	7,378	28,557	11,099
65-69	27,999	4,229	13,797	9,967	37,791	6,252	19,190	12,248
70-74	18,348	2,614	7,051	8,674	28,587	4,670	11,884	11,940
75-79	9,368	1,149	2,573	5,641	17,276	2,726	5,324	9,148
80-84	3,529	443	602	2,483	7,156	1,078	1,452	4,593
85& over	1,336	162	135	1,038	2,772	390	275	2,107
All Ages	1,088,461[a]	621,423	399,420	67,478	1,089,767[a]	533,240	474,389	80,935

SOURCE: *Census of Scotland*, 1851-1951.

(*a*) In the Census of 1931 totals include 140 persons who failed to state their marital condition, and 10 persons their age. In 1951 the corresponding figures were 1,203 and 119 r espectively.

TABLE 22

Birthplaces of Inhabitants of Glasgow

Where Born	1851	1861	1871	1881	1891	1901	1911	1921	1931	1951
Glasgow	145,022	201,555 [a]	226,115	262,146	312,265	652,933	482,455	656,580	749,653	809,508
Scotland (excluding Glasgow)	114,145	118,822 [b]	164,733	161,452	169,161		205,402	252,837	230,864	191,382
England	8,057	10,266	14,286	15,677	18,495	27,537	29,059	40,515	39,060	37,032
Wales	111	149	214	349	399	567	665	1,086	1,045	1,584
Isle of Man and Channel Islands ..	115	125	134	185	170	237	235	333	264	299
Ireland: N. Ireland									28,962	16,665
Ireland: Eire ..	59,801	62,084	68,330	67,109	59,822	67,612	52,828	65,688	23,260	17,661
Ireland: Not stated									157	149
British Colonies and Dependencies ..	923	1,134	1,436	1,761	1,966	3,138	3,183	4,923	5,093	5,478
Foreign Countries ..	854	1,275	1,788	2,637	3,486	9,600	10,530	10,940	9,798	9,960
(*British Subjects*)	(*242*)	(*772*)	(*794*)	(*1,084*)	(*1,276*)	(*2,822*)	(*2,206*)	(*3,139*)	(*3,420*)	(*4,885*)
(*Foreign Subjects*)	(*612*)	(*503*)	(*994*)	(*1,553*)	(*2,208*)	(*6,778*)	(*8,324*)	(*7,801*)	(*6,378*)	(*5,043*)
(*Citizens of Irish Republic*) ..	—	—	—	—	—	—	—	—	—	(*32*)
At Sea	69	93	120	99	75	85	139	142	104	44
Not Stated	—	—	—	—	—	—	—	1,130	201	5
Total Population of Glasgow	329,097	395,503	477,156 [c]	511,415	565,839	761,709	784,496	1,034,174	1,088,461	1,089,767

Source: *Census of Scotland*, 1851-1951.

(*a*) Born in Lanarkshire.
(*b*) Born in Scottish Counties other than Lanarkshire.
(*c*) Shipping Population excluded (576).

TABLE 23

BIRTHPLACES OF SCOTTISH-BORN INHABITANTS OF GLASGOW BY REGIONAL DIVISIONS, 1951, AND EQUIVALENT AREAS, 1901 AND 1851

Division	*County of Birth*	1951	1901	1851
West Central	Ayr	17,537	24,976	13,866
	Dunbarton	12,761	9,941	5,641
	Lanark (excluding Glasgow) ..	41,738	468,542 (Lanark and Glasgow City)	15,565
	Glasgow City	809,508		145,022
	Renfrew	22,546	29,959	20,658
Total	Number	904,090	533,418	200,750
	Per cent of Glasgow Scottish-born	90.7%	81.7%	77.5%
East Central (Excluding Dundee)	Clackmannan	1,411	1,927	743
	Fife	5,921	7,073	3,083
	East Lothian	711	1,123	852
	Midlothian (excluding Edinburgh)	1,684	15,890 (Midlothian and Edinburgh City)	8,477
	Edinburgh City	10,267		
	West Lothian	2,734	2,876	1,456
	Stirling	13,927	12,594	9,138
Total	Number	36,655	41,483	23,749
	Per cent of Glasgow Scottish-born	4.1%	6.4%	9.2%
Northern (Including Dundee)	Aberdeen (County)	4,092	8,136 (Aberdeen County and City)	1,527
	Aberdeen (City)	3,713		
	Angus (including Dundee) ..	7,016	8,479	1,646
	Argyll	7,625	11,587	11,858
	Banff	1,872	2,432	225
	Bute	1,887	2,127	1,630
	Caithness	1,245	2,133	638
	Elgin	1,668	2,366	513
	Inverness	6,596	7,122	2,434
	Kincardine	856	1,252	271
	Kinross	133	575	268
	Nairn	257	424	100
	Perth	4,861	8,967	6,183
	Orkney	420	1,257 (Orkney and Shetland)	342
	Shetland	308		
	Ross and Cromarty	3,731	4,187	815
	Sutherland	656	1,049	447
Total	Number	46,936	62,093	28,897
	Per cent of Glasgow Scottish-born	4.3%	9.5%	11.1%
Southern	Berwick	447	999	524
	Dumfries	3,427	5,541	1,930
	Kirkcudbright	1,220	2,177	580
	Peebles	574	555	181
	Roxburgh	783	1,366	446
	Selkirk	484	508	85
	Wigtown	2,204	4,064	2,025
Total	Number	9,139	15,210	5,771
	Per cent of Glasgow Scottish-born	0.9%	2.4%	2.2%
Not stated	.. ..	4,070	729	—
Total born in Scotland		1,000,890	652,933	259,167

SOURCE: *Calculated from Census of Scotland,* 1851, 1901 *and* 1951.

TABLE 24

Inhabitants of Glasgow Born in the Crofting Counties, 1851-1951

Where Born	1851	1861	1871	1881	1891	1901	1911	1921	1931	1951
Orkney	342	281	439	468	703	420	788	817	712	420
Shetland		130	227	245	324	308	339	426	388	308
Argyll	11,858	12,380	12,685	10,651	12,161	11,587	10,177	12,191	10,794	7,625
Inverness	2,434	2,687	3,893	4,097	5,766	7,122	6,985	8,777	8,189	6,596
Ross and Cromarty	815	1,074	1,828	2,143	3,210	4,187	3,663	4,910	4,596	3,731
Sutherland	447	362	639	619	939	1,049	893	1,064	894	656
Caithness	638	760	1,138	1,258	1,646	2,133	1,869	2,119	1,828	1,245
Crofting Counties (*a*) ..	16,534	16,682	21,849	19,481	24,749	26,806	24,714	30,304	27,401	20,581
Scotland (*b*)	259,167	320,377	390,848	423,598	481,426	652,933	687,857	909,417	980,517	1,000,890
(*a*) as % of (*b*)	6.4%	5.2%	5.6%	4.6%	5.1%	4.1%	3.6%	3.3%	2.8%	2.1%

Source: *Census of Scotland*, 1851 *to* 1951.

TABLE 25

WARD POPULATION, ACREAGE AND DENSITY, 1951

Ward	Male	Female	Total	Acreage	Density Persons to the acre
NORTH SIDE.					
1 Shettleston & Tollcross	20,624	21,985	42,609	1,167	37
2 Parkhead	10,160	11,418	21,578	819	26
3 Dalmarnock	19,523	21,098	40,621	487	83
4 Calton	13,214	13,059	26,273	404	65
5 Mile-End	19,563	20,608	40,171	443	90
6 Dennistoun	12,469	14,475	26,944	689	39
7 Provan	11,936	12,299	24,235	4,846	5
8 Cowlairs	13,564	14,434	27,998	645	43
9 Springburn	17,005	18,644	35,649	2,118	17
10 Townhead	16,819	18,186	35,005	301	116
11 Exchange	10,045	10,044	20,089	507	40
12 Anderston	15,728	16,174	31,902	530	60
13 Park	10,795	12,963	23,758	317	75
14 Cowcaddens	13,444	13,785	27,229	488	56
15 Woodside	12,796	14,150	26,946	170	158
16 Ruchill	22,295	23,634	45,929	1,962	23
17 North Kelvin	11,956	13,861	25,817	278	93
18 Maryhill	12,347	13,168	25,515	2,210	12
19 Kelvinside	8,406	12,626	21,032	1,160	18
20 Partick East	10,212	13,164	23,376	351	67
21 Partick West	12,518	14,296	26,814	464	58
22 Whiteinch	11,008	12,233	23,241	894	26
23 Yoker	14,611	15,587	30,198	1,213	25
24 Knightswood	8,394	9,136	17,530	1,614	11
North Side	329,432	361,027	690,459	24,077	29
SOUTH SIDE					
25 Hutchesontown ..	15,032	15,933	30,965	387	80
26 Gorbals	18,074	18,574	36,648	252	145
27 Kingston	13,191	13,704	26,895	355	76
28 Kinning Park	13,810	14,314	28,124	402	70
29 Govan	17,242	17,910	35,152	489	72
30 Fairfield	12,082	13,050	25,132	1,351	19
31 Craigton	19,080	21,368	40,448	1,566	26
32 Pollokshields	18,623	21,333	39,956	3,239	12
33 Camphill	9,778	12,751	22,529	481	47
34 Pollokshaws	19,473	20,244	39,717	3,223	12
35 Govanhill	12,160	14,217	26,377	365	72
36 Langside	11,243	14,335	25,578	801	32
37 Cathcart	9,651	12,136	21,787	2,737	8
South Side	189,439	209,869	399,308	15,648	25
GLASGOW	518,871	570,896	1,089,767	39,725	27

SOURCE: *For population, Census of Scotland*, 1951.
For acreage, Report of Medical Officer of Health for Glasgow, 1951.

TABLE 26

Density of Population in each Municipal Ward, 1949, 1951, 1953, 1955

Ward	Persons per Acre			
	1949	1951	1953	1955
1 Shettleston and Tollcross	36	37	36	41
2 Parkhead	26	26	25	24
3 Dalmarnock	94	83	81	77
4 Calton	72	65	62	59
5 Mile-End	97	90	89	85
6 Dennistoun	41	39	38	36
7 Provan	4	5	6	8
8 Cowlairs	49	43	42	41
9 Springburn	13	17	18	19
10 Townhead	126	116	112	107
11 Exchange	49	40	37	35
12 Anderston	66	60	58	55
13 Park	80	75	70	65
14 Cowcaddens	62	56	53	51
15 Woodside	180	158	148	140
16 Ruchill	22	23	26	26
17 North Kelvin	100	93	90	86
18 Maryhill	12	12	11	12
19 Kelvinside	19	18	17	17
20 Partick East	72	67	64	60
21 Partick West	63	58	59	57
22 Whiteinch	27	26	25	25
23 Yoker	24	25	24	24
24 Knightswood	10	11	11	17
25 Hutchesontown	89	80	78	75
26 Gorbals	162	145	136	128
27 Kingston	85	76	73	70
28 Kinning Park	77	70	68	66
29 Govan	77	72	70	67
30 Fairfield	18	19	18	17
31 Craigton	25	26	25	25
32 Pollokshields	8	12	13	13
33 Camphill	51	47	45	44
34 Pollokshaws	8	12	15	15
35 Govanhill	77	72	69	67
36 Langside	33	32	32	32
37 Cathcart	8	8	8	9
City ..	28	27	27	27

Source: *Reports of Medical Officer of Health for Glasgow.*

TABLE 27

Distribution of the Child Population (under 15 years) by Wards, 1951

Ward	*Number of Children*	*Children % of total population of Wards*
1 Shettleston & Tollcross	10,881	25.5
2 Parkhead	5,181	24.0
3 Dalmarnock	11,440	28.2
4 Calton	6,734	25.6
5 Mile End	11,695	29.1
6 Dennistoun	5,653	21.0
7 Provan	5,285	21.8
8 Cowlairs	7,086	25.3
9 Springburn	9,296	26.1
10 Townhead	9.282	26.5
11 Exchange	4,421	22.0
12 Anderston	8,623	27.0
13 Park	3,987	16.8
14 Cowcaddens	8,185	30.1
15 Woodside	7,254	26.9
16 Ruchill	11,878	25.9
17 North Kelvin	6,381	24.7
18 Maryhill	6,506	25.5
19 Kelvinside	3,205	15.3
20 Partick East	4,184	17.9
21 Partick West	6,834	25.5
22 Whiteinch	5,224	22.5
23 Yoker	6,564	21.8
24 Knightswood	3,889	22.2
25 Hutchesontown	8,883	28.7
26 Gorbals	10,790	29.4
27 Kingston	7,871	29.3
28 Kinning Park	7,412	26.4
29 Govan	10,280	29.3
30 Fairfield	5,773	23.0
31 Craigton	8,977	22.2
32 Pollokshields	10,183	25.5
33 Camphill	3,674	16.3
34 Pollokshaws	12,488	31.5
35 Govanhill	5,743	21.8
36 Langside	4,440	17.4
37 Cathcart	4,165	19.1
Total	270,347	24.8

Source: *Census of Scotland*, 1951.

TABLE 28

Ward Population by Sex and Age, 1951

Ward	Males			Females		
	Under 15	15-64	65 and over	Under 15	15-64	65 and over
1 Shettleston and Tollcross ..	5,531	13,765	1,328	5,350	15,098	1,537
2 Parkhead ..	2,626	6,765	769	2,555	7,920	943
3 Dalmarnock ..	5,815	12,465	1,243	5,625	13,845	1,628
4 Calton ..	3,370	8,524	1,320	3,364	8,456	1,239
5 Mile-End ..	5,977	12,368	1,218	5,718	13,326	1,564
6 Dennistoun ..	2,903	8,483	1,083	2,750	10,032	1,693
7 Provan ..	2,627	8,429	880	2,658	8,588	1,053
8 Cowlairs ..	3,503	8,659	1,402	3,583	9,442	1,409
9 Springburn ..	4,704	11,358	943	4,592	12,958	1,094
10 Townhead ..	4,679	10,607	1,533	4,603	11,971	1,612
11 Exchange ..	2,233	6,728	1,084	2,188	6,854	1,002
12 Anderston ..	4,325	10,070	1,333	4,298	10,504	1,372
13 Park	1,992	7,709	1,094	1,995	9,162	1,806
14 Cowcaddens ..	4,101	8,330	1,013	4,084	8,727	974
15 Woodside ..	3,646	8,187	963	3,608	9,224	1,318
16 Ruchill ..	6,099	14,847	1,349	5,779	16,393	1,462
17 North Kelvin ..	3,244	7,809	903	3,137	9,280	1,444
18 Maryhill ..	3,302	8,117	928	3,204	8,832	1,132
19 Kelvinside ..	1,668	5,740	998	1,537	8,804	2,285
20 Partick East ..	2,143	7,002	1,067	2,041	9,094	2,029
21 Partick West ..	3,379	8,168	971	3,455	9,268	1,573
22 Whiteinch ..	2,657	7,236	1,115	2,567	8,341	1,325
23 Yoker	3,330	10,225	1,056	3,234	11,158	1,195
24 Knightswood	1,971	5,867	556	1,918	6,539	679
25 Hutchesontown	4,568	9,536	928	4,315	10,414	1,204
26 Gorbals ..	5,551	11,346	1,177	5,239	12,040	1,295
27 Kingston ..	4,018	8,267	906	3,853	8,865	986
28 Kinning Park ..	3,801	9,003	1,006	3,611	9,371	1,332
29 Govan	5,265	10,875	1,102	5,015	11,575	1,320
30 Fairfield ..	2,914	8,174	994	2,859	8,974	1,217
31 Craigton ..	4,553	13,182	1,345	4,424	15,178	1,766
32 Pollokshields ..	5,070	12,281	1,272	5,113	14,219	2,001
33 Camphill ..	1,910	6,689	1,179	1,764	8,779	2,208
34 Pollokshaws ..	6,396	12,235	842	6,092	13,043	1,109
35 Govanhill ..	2,928	8,130	1,102	2,815	9,806	1,596
36 Langside ..	2,224	7,744	1,275	2,216	10,030	2,089
37 Cathcart ..	2,081	6,510	1,060	2,084	8,298	1,754

SOURCE: *Calculated from the Census of Scotland*, 1951.

TABLE 29

POPULATION OF CIVIL PARISHES IN 1951, AND OF THEIR PORTIONS LYING WITHIN GLASGOW CITY (1951 AREA) IN 1951 AND 1931

Civil Parishes	*Population of portion within City (1951 area)*			*Population of portion outwith City*		*Population of entire Parish*
	1931 (*a*)	1951 (*b*)	% *change* (*c*)	1951 (*d*)		1951 (*b*) + (*d*)
Glasgow . .	590,893	539,942	−8.6	9,889	(Lanarkshire)	549,831
Govan . .	364,786	311,984	−14.5	9	(Burgh of Renfrew)	311,993
Cadder . .	2,116	7,855	+271.2	19,727	(Lanarkshire)	27,862
Carmunnock . .	120	271	+125.8	2,731	,,	3,002
Old Monkland . .	949	395	−58.4	71,045	,,	71,440
Rutherglen	73	1,385	+1,797.3	32,940	,,	34,325
Cathcart . .	58,684	58,666	0.0	11,630	(Renfrewshire)	70,296
Eastwood	20,198	40,551	+100.8	15,143	,,	55,694
Neilston . .	35	42	+20.0	13,748	,,	13,790
Paisley . .	11,588	65,614	+466.2	122,343	,,	187,957
Renfrew	25,548	34,405	+34.7	17,439	,,	51,844
New Kilpatrick	18,347	28,657	+56.2	26,281	(Dunbartonshire)	54,938
Totals . .	1,093,337	1,089,767	−0.3	343,205		1,432,972

SOURCE: *Census of Scotland*, 1951.

TABLE 30

GAELIC-SPEAKING PERSONS IN GLASGOW: 1901, 1931, 1951

	Total Population	*All Gaelic-speaking Persons*	*Gaelic only*		*Gaelic and English*	
			Males	*Females*	*Males*	*Females*
1951	1,089,767	12,556	1	2	5,507	7,046
1931	1,088,461	16,276	3	14	6,788	9,471
1901	761,709	12,621	59		12,562	

SOURCE: *Census of Scotland*, 1901 *and* 1951.

TABLE 31

Registered Aliens in Glasgow by Nationality

	1931			1954		
	Male	*Female*	*Total*	*Male*	*Female*	*Total*
Afghan				2		2
American (U.S.A.)	239	229	468	147	64	211
American (Central)	3	2	5	2		2
„ (South) ..	12	9	21	5	2	7
Armenian	1		1		1	1
Austrian	58	56	114	15	33	48
Belgian	27	30	57	13	12	25
Bulgarian	1	1	2	1		1
Burmese				14		14
Chinese	5	1	6	13		13
Cuban				1		1
Czechoslovakian ..	5	4	9	8	4	12
Danish	36	34	70	20	7	27
Dutch	18	11	29	55	16	71
Egyptian	18	5	23	17	1	18
Esthonian	1	3	4	4	5	9
Ethiopian				2		2
Finnish	4	4	8	2	1	3
French	46	72	118	52	48	100
German	88	127	215	114	159	273
Greek	18	15	33	26	7	33
Hungarian	5	2	7	5	4	9
Icelandic	1		1	5		55
Iranian				3		3
Iraquian				17	1	18
Israeli				5		5
Italian	1,008	921	1,929	567	458	1,025
Japanese	1	2	3	3	1	4
Korean				2		2
Latvian	1	4	5	5	4	9
Lebanese				1		1
Lithuanian	103	100	203	67	45	112
Norwegian	29	33	62	121	17	138
Palestinian	4	1	5	3	2	5
Persian	1		1			
Polish	48	65	113	852	123	975
Portuguese		2	2	5	3	8
Roumanian ..	16	14	30	4	2	6
Russian	1,485	1,696	3,181	385	412	797
Sengalese				1		1
Siamese				7	1	8
Spanish	17	25	42	23	10	33
Swedish	30	27	57	9	6	15
Swiss	51	47	98	39	31	70
Syrian		1	1			
Transjordanian ..				2		2
Turkish	5	6	11	3		3
Yugoslavian ..	21	8	29	17	1	18
Uncertain	103		103	74	19	93
Total	3,509	3,557	7,066	2,738	1,500	4,238

Source: *Chief Constable, City of Glasgow.*

PART II: THE CITY'S ECONOMY

Note on Statistics of Insured Employees

The figures of insured employees and their distribution by industries have been supplied by the Ministry of Labour and National Service. The area to which they refer has been explained in the note on Areas, p. 784. It does not coincide with that of the City of Glasgow, but extends beyond it at many points, and it is not possible, with the available information, to make precise allowance for the difference in areas. Moreover, the Ministry's Glasgow area has been changed several times in recent years, as explained in the note referred to. The selection of years for which figures of insured persons are given in the following tables has been determined by these considerations. Comparative figures are given for 1938 and 1947, when the area consisted of the ten city employment exchange areas; and again for 1951-55, when it included those ten city exchanges plus Hillington. No comparisons are attempted between the pre-1948 and the post-1948 position. Apart from the changes in the area, there was a change, in 1948, in the official classification of industries which in itself would have made such comparison impracticable. The pre-1948 classification is used in Table 32 and the post-1948 Standard Industrial Classification in Table 33.

PART II - SECTION 1

Industry & Commerce

TABLE 32

ESTIMATED NUMBER OF INSURED PERSONS, BY SEX AND INDUSTRY, IN THE GLASGOW AREA (10 EMPLOYMENT EXCHANGES) AT MID-1938 AND MID-1947

Industry	*Mid*-1938			*Mid*-1947		
	Males 14-64	*Females* 14-64	*Total*	*Males* 14-64	*Females* 14-59	*Total*
Building	23,539	1,116	24,655	26,115	1,173	27,288
Public Works Contracting	8,397	113	8,510	4,662	139	4,801
Electrical Wiring and Contracting	1,585	222	1,807	2,103	313	2,416
Shipbuilding and Ship Repairing	17,830	421	18,251	19,458	1,361	20,819
General Engineering, Engineers' Iron and Steel Founding	27,637	1,875	29,512	33,365	4,790	38,155
Stove, Grate, Pipe, etc., and General Ironfounding	5,070	124	5,194	2,512	208	2,720
Electrical Engineering ..	1,063	216	1,279	1,286	317	1,603
Marine Engineering, etc.	9,740	204	9,944	8,712	717	9,429
Constructional Engineering	4,538	197	4,735	4,395	348	4,743
Motor Vehicles, Cycles and Aircraft	4,671	571	5,242	6,242	1,317	7,559
Carriages, Carts, etc. ..	252	49	301	576	74	650
Railway Carriages and Wagons, etc.	1,804	42	1,846	1,476	47	1,523
Sawmilling and Machined Woodwork	2,463	197	2,660	1,765	255	2,020
Furniture Making, Upholstering, etc.	3,757	1,668	5,425	3,253	1,360	4,613
Wood Boxes and Packing Cases	599	144	743	392	88	480
Other Woodworking ..	874	365	1,239	757	517	1,274
Explosives	8	5	13	204	138	342
Chemicals	2,003	1,145	3,148	2,625	1,932	4,557
Oil, Glue, Soap, Ink, Matches, etc.	865	294	1,159	869	464	1,333
Coke Ovens and By-product Works	7	—	7	485	1	486
Paint, Varnish, Red Lead, etc.	792	309	1,101	975	480	1,455
Pig Iron (Blast Furnaces)	1,302	7	1,309	764	37	801
Steel Melting and Iron Puddling, I. and S. Rolling, etc.	6,191	152	6,343	4,670	308	4,978

Industry	Mid-1938			Mid-1947		
	Males 14-64	Females 14-64	Total	Males 14-64	Females 14-59	Total
Brass, Copper, Zinc, Tin, Lead, etc.	741	171	912	1,128	298	1,426
Tin Plates	4	1	5	3	—	3
Electric Apparatus, Cable, Lamps, etc.	497	184	681	651	788	1,439
Files	438	34	472	228	48	276
Iron and Steel Tubes ..	2,226	173	2,399	1,428	318	1,746
Wire, Wire Netting, Wire Ropes, etc.	517	482	999	582	688	1,270
Bolts, Nuts, Screws, Rivets, Nails, etc.	556	391	947	498	597	1,095
Heating and Ventilating Apparatus	1,307	72	1,379	2,226	220	2,446
Brass and Allied Metal Wares	195	92	287	56	11	67
Metal Industries not separately specified	3,637	693	4,330	3,885	823	4,708
Watches, Clocks, Plate, Jewellery, etc.	258	86	344	375	179	554
Musical Instruments ..	125	57	182	78	67	145
Scientific and Photographic Instruments and Apparatus	2,123	1,328	3,451	1,722	956	2,678
Toys, Games and Sports Requisites	244	63	307	141	29	170
Rubber	1,226	1,464	2,690	1,170	829	1,999
Tanning, Currying and Dressing, etc.	920	650	1,570	1,072	891	1,963
Leather Goods	414	375	789	491	585	1,076
Brick, Tile, Pipe, etc., making	1,049	80	1,129	537	72	609
Pottery, Earthenware, etc.	262	223	485	128	153	281
Cement, Limekilns and Whiting	92	50	142	175	29	204
Cast Stone and Cast Concrete Products, Patent Fuel, Stone Grinding, etc.	311	16	327	723	32	755
Glass Manufacture (excluding Bottles, Lenses and Prisms)	444	179	623	559	552	1,111
Glass Bottles, Jars, etc. ..	506	5	511	420	68	488
Hotel, Boarding House, Restaurant, Club Catering Service	4,719	8,059	12,778	4,544	8,024	12,568
Laundry Service	742	2,320	3,062	535	1,932	2,467
Job Dyeing, Dry Cleaning, etc.	228	832	1,060	119	614	733
Commerce, Banking, Insurance and Finance ..	3,086	1,810	4,896	2,132	2,343	4,475
Railway Service	6,004	541	6,545	12,929	1,764	14,693
Tramway and Omnibus Service	10,239	522	10,761	9,418	2,147	11,565

Industry	*Mid*-1938			*Mid*-1947		
	Males 14-64	*Females* 14-64	*Total*	*Males* 14-64	*Females* 14-59	*Total*
Other Road Passenger Transport	1,469	158	1,627	1,074	145	1,215
Goods Transport by Road	6,499	264	6,763	6,383	484	6,869
Fishing	24	—	24	4	1	7
Shipping Service	7,172	708	7,880	3,648	511	4,159
Harbour, River, Canal Service	2,188	24	2,212	2,117	50	2,167
Port Transport (Dock Wharves, etc.) Registered Workers	3,547	10	3,557	3,848	76	3,924
Port Transport (Dock Wharves, etc.) Others	631	6	637	46	2	48
Other Transport, Communication etc.	844	782	1,626	791	643	1,434
Coal Mining	2,519	44	2,563	2,055	62	2,117
Iron Ore and Ironstone Mining, etc.	4	—	4	1	—	1
Lead, Tin and Copper Mining	2	—	2	—	—	—
Stone Quarrying and Mining	433	10	443	498	52	550
Slate Quarrying and Mining	1	—	1	—	—	—
Other Mining and Quarrying	12	3	15	2	—	2
Clay, Sand, Gravel and Chalk Pits	126	5	131	30	11	41
Paper and Paper Board ..	662	390	1,052	671	302	973
Cardboard Boxes, Paper Bags and Stationery ..	365	1,631	1,996	491	1,477	1,968
Printing, Publishing and Bookbinding	7,917	7,526	15,443	6,719	5,892	12,611
Wallpaper Making ..	99	87	186	59	67	126
Stationery and Typewriting Requisites (not paper)	54	21	75	87	138	225
Cotton Preparing, Spinning, etc.	94	302	396	436	646	1,082
Cotton Manufacturing (Weaving, etc.)	676	2,591	3,267	328	1,090	1,418
Woollen and Worsted ..	111	246	357	163	466	629
Rayon, Nylon, etc., Yarn Manufacture	3	3	6	1	4	5
Silk Spinning and Manufacture of Rayon, Nylon, etc. Weaving etc.	8	105	113	1	3	4
Linen	95	105	200	94	62	156
Jute	71	43	114	8	16	24
Hemp, Rope, Cord, Twine, etc.	77	132	209	237	442	679
Hosiery	164	2,815	2,979	133	1,794	1,927
Lace	80	88	168	39	27	66
Carpets	1,061	3,441	4,502	847	2,020	2,867
Other Textiles	469	882	1,351	263	1,113	1,376
Textile Bleaching, Printing, Dyeing, etc. ..	629	558	1,187	358	296	654

Industry	*Mid*-1938			*Mid*-1947		
	Males 14-64	*Females* 14-64	*Total*	*Males* 14-64	*Females* 14-59	*Total*
Tailoring	2,410	9,371	11,781	1,724	8,891	10,615
Dressmaking and Millinery	320	1,986	2,306	515	3,065	3,580
Hats and Caps (including Straw Plait)	159	985	1,144	87	653	740
Shirts, Collars, Underclothing, etc.	288	3,862	4,150	224	3,585	3,809
Other Dress Industries ..	86	252	338	10	6	16
Boots, Shoes, Slippers and Clogs	1,497	814	2,311	1,307	653	1,960
Bread, Biscuits, Cakes, etc.	8,013	7,833	15,846	6,205	5,311	11,516
Tobacco, Cigars, Cigarettes and Snuff	245	1,073	1,318	460	1,654	2,114
Grain Milling	854	69	923	833	190	1,023
Cocoa, Chocolate and Sugar Confectionery ..	673	3,115	3,788	313	1,362	1,675
Other Food Industries ..	1,202	1,981	3,183	1,367	2,632	3,999
Drink Industries	2,684	1,961	4,645	2,811	2,202	5,013
Gas, Water and Electricity Supply	7,531	252	7,783	7,370	409	7,779
Oilcloth, Linoleum, etc. ..	18	19	37	3	7	10
Brushes and Brooms ..	102	90	192	168	115	283
Distributive Trades ..	50,962	51,303	102,265	34,333	45,932	80,265
National Government Service	3,745	924	4,669	7,362	5,557	12,919
Local Government Service	12,854	3,420	16,274	9,743	5,751	15,494
Professional Services ..	3,978	5,330	9,308	4,902	7,678	12,580
Entertainments & Sports	3,946	2,080	6,026	2,182	2,357	4,539
Other Industries and Services (Manufacturing)	3,603	1,866	5,469	672	423	1,095
Services (Non-manufacturing)				3,921	1,410	5,331
Chauffeurs, Lorry Drivers, etc., in Private Domestic Service	164	25	189	31	6	37
Farming, Forestry, etc. ..	85	5	90	24	7	31
Market Gardening, Horticulture, etc.	66	9	75	14	6	20
Total—General Scheme	311,688	151,994	463,682	293,627	159,195	452,822
Farming, Forestry, etc. ..	765	126	891	623	245	868
Market Gardening, Horticulture, etc.	352	64	416	241	79	320
Other Employments ..	1,460	52	1,512	1,180	42	1,222
Private Gardening ..	179	3	182	100	—	100
Total—Agricultural Scheme	2,756	245	3,001	2,144	366	2,510
Ex-Service Personnel not allocated to any industry	—	—	—	2,850	282	3,132
GRAND TOTAL.. ..	314,444	152,239	466,683	298,621	159,843	458,464

SOURCE: *Ministry of Labour and National Service.*

TABLE 33

ESTIMATED NUMBER OF INSURED EMPLOYEES, 15 YEARS AND OVER, BY SEX AND INDUSTRY, IN GLASGOW AREA (10 CITY EMPLOYMENT EXCHANGES AND HILLINGTON EXCHANGE) AS AT MID-1951 AND MID-1955

Standard Industrial Classification (introduced 1948)	*Mid*-1951			*Mid*-1955		
	Males	*Females*	*Total*	*Males*	*Females*	*Total*
Agriculture & Horticulture	968	269	1,237	640	256	896
Forestry	67	7	74	21	3	24
Fishing	13	—	13	1	—	1
AGRICULTURE, FORESTRY, FISHING TOTAL	1,048	276	1,324	662	259	921
PER CENT ..	0.29	0.13	0.23	0.20	0.13	0.17
Coal Mining	2,581	345	2,926	2,042	278	2,320
Stone Quarrying & Mining	696	60	756	151	46	197
Slate Quarrying & Mining	76	4	80	25	2	27
Clay, Sand, Gravel and Chalk Pits	31	7	38	—	—	—
Other Mining & Quarrying	58	5	63	12	9	21
MINING AND QUARRYING TOTAL ..	3,442	421	3,863	2,230	335	2,565
PER CENT ..	0.94	0.20	0.67	0.66	0.16	0.47
Bricks and Fireclay Goods	669	87	756	619	70	689
China and Earthenware (including Glazed Tiles)	281	245	526	234	139	373
Glass (not containers)	533	307	840	741	461	1,202
Glass Containers	411	42	453	570	59	629
Cement	23	11	34	26	18	44
Other Non-Metalliferous Mining Manufactures ..	1,932	204	2,136	1,474	141	1,615
TREATMENT OF NON-METALLIFEROUS MINING PRODUCTS OTHER THAN COAL TOTAL ..	3,849	896	4,745	3,664	888	4,552
PER CENT ..	1.05	0.43	0.83	1.09	0.43	0.84
Coke Ovens and By-Product Works	412	—	412	520	2	522
Chemicals and Dyes ..	2,550	822	3,372	2,256	811	3,067
Pharmaceutical Preparations, Toilet Preparations, Perfumery ..	191	683	874	194	495	689
Explosives and Fireworks	1,453	645	2,098	609	287	896
Paint and Varnish ..	1,185	512	1,697	1,087	543	1,630
Soap, Candles, Glycerine, Polishes, Ink, Matches	335	272	607	309	288	597
Mineral Oil Refining ..	227	60	287	109	47	156
Other Oils, Greases, Glue, etc.	835	243	1,078	448	125	573
CHEMICAL AND ALLIED TRADES TOTAL ..	7,188	3,237	10,425	5,532	2,598	8,130
PER CENT ..	1.97	1.56	1.82	1.64	1.26	1.50

Standard Industrial Classification (introduced 1948)	*Mid*-1951			*Mid*-1955		
	Males	*Females*	*Total*	*Males*	*Females*	*Total*
Blast Furnaces	1,139	34	1,173	1,346	54	1,400
Iron and Steel Melting, Rolling, etc.	5,672	401	6,073	4,885	538	5,423
Iron Foundries	4,007	255	4,262	4,099	347	4,446
Tinplate (including Melting and Rolling) ..	9	—	9	—	—	—
Other Sheets (including Melting and Rolling) ..	501	5	506	786	4	790
Iron and Steel Tubes (including Melting & Rolling in Integrated Works)	1,948	355	2,303	1,742	456	2,198
Non-Ferrous Metals Smelting, Rolling, etc.	2,540	526	3,066	2,294	498	2,792
METAL MANUFACTURE TOTAL ..	15,816	1,576	17,392	15,152	1,897	17,049
PER CENT ..	4.33	0.76	3.04	4.50	0.92	3.14
Ship Building and Ship Repairing	19,616	1,237	20,853	17,018	1,297	18,315
Marine Engineering ..	9,012	612	9,624	9,616	633	10,249
Agricultural Machinery (except Tractors) ..	312	39	351	172	23	195
Boilers and Boilerhouse Plant	1,795	221	2,016	1,987	324	2,311
Machine Tools, and Engineers' Small Tools ..	919	163	1,082	1,155	206	1,361
Stationary Engines ..	17	6	23	1,334	124	1,458
Textile Machinery and Accessories	676	166	842	538	196	734
Ordnance and Small Arms	53	8	61	150	25	175
Constructional Engineering	4,768	412	5,180	3,975	306	4,281
Other Non-Electrical Engineering	22,748	4,574	27,322	21,889	4,868	26,757
Electrical Machinery ..	1,240	253	1,493	1,410	280	1,690
Electrical Wires & Cables	215	192	407	197	206	403
Telegraph and Telephone Apparatus	52	5	57	90	6	96
Wireless Apparatus (except Valves) and Gramophones	61	39	100	328	160	488
Wireless Valves and Electric Lamps	66	105	171	203	136	339
Batteries and Accumulators	55	20	75	76	31	107
Other Electrical Goods ..	555	509	1,064	1,100	876	1,976
ENGINEERING, SHIPBUILDING AND ELECTRICAL GOODS TOTAL ..	62,160	8,561	70,721	61,238	9,697	70,935
PER CENT ..	17.03	4.11	12.35	18.20	4.69	13.06
Manufacture of Motor Vehicles and Cycles ..	3,964	613	4,577	3,389	519	3,908
Motor Repairers and Garages	4,185	686	4,871	4,611	904	5,515

Standard Industrial Classification (introduced 1948)	*Mid-1951*			*Mid-1955*		
	Males	*Females*	*Total*	*Males*	*Females*	*Total*
Manufacture and Repair of Aircraft	4,124	847	4,971	5,868	1,459	7,327
Manufacture of Parts and Accessories for Motor Vehicles and Aircraft ..	156	56	212	230	105	335
Railway Locomotive Shops	6,765	376	7,141	—	—	—
Other Locomotive Manufacture	5,029	238	5,267	9,700	578	10,278
Manufacture and Repair of Railway Carriages and Wagons and Trams	3,681	162	3,843	2,843	111	1,954
Carts, Perambulators, etc.	131	60	191	61	28	89
VEHICLES TOTAL ..	28,035	3,038	31,073	26,702	3,704	30,406
PER CENT ..	7.68	1.46	5.43	7.94	1.79	5.60
Tools and Cutlery ..	488	228	716	207	147	354
Bolts, Nuts, Screws, Rivets Nails, etc.	955	703	1,658	854	697	1,551
Iron and Steel Forgings, not elsewhere specified	420	72	492	405	76	481
Wire and Wire Manufactures	895	813	1,708	669	513	1,182
Hollow-ware	108	80	188	182	129	311
Brass Manufactures ..	757	91	848	900	126	1,026
Metal Industries not elsewhere specified.. ..	3,588	686	4,274	2,517	735	3,252
METAL GOODS NOT ELSEWHERE SPECIFIED TOTAL ..	7,211	2,673	9,884	5,734	2,423	8,157
PER CENT ..	1.98	1.29	1.73	1.70	1.17	1.50
Scientific, Surgical and Photographic Instruments, etc.	2,423	1,114	3,537	2,268	987	3,255
Manufacture and Repair of Watches and Clocks	124	72	196	204	91	295
Jewellery, Plate and Refining of Precious Metals	99	16	115	104	18	122
Musical Instruments ..	89	64	153	148	20	168
PRECISION INSTRUMENTS JEWELLERY, ETC. TOTAL ..	2,735	1,266	4,001	2,724	1,116	3,840
PER CENT	0.74	0.61	0.70	0.81	0.54	0.71
Cotton Spinning, Doubling, etc.	1,766	2,208	3,974	915	1,170	2,085
Cotton Weaving, etc. ..	397	1,107	1,504	334	946	1,280
Woollen and Worsted ..	220	586	806	199	643	842
Rayon, Nylon, etc., Production	—	—	—	10	14	24
Rayon, Nylon, etc., Weaving and Silk	59	134	193	7	26	33
Linen and Soft Hemp ..	33	52	85	6	14	20
Jute	15	15	30	11	9	20
Rope, Twine and Net ..	257	491	748	185	402	587

Standard Industrial Classification (introduced 1948)	*Mid-1951*			*Mid-1955*		
	Males	*Females*	*Total*	*Males*	*Females*	*Total*
Hosiery and other Knitted Goods	298	2,278	2,576	207	1,969	2,176
Lace	68	60	128	—	3	3
Carpets	1,512	2,783	4,295	1,378	2,408	3,786
Narrow Fabrics	20	10	30	48	80	128
Made-up Textiles.. ..	229	562	791	188	474	662
Textile Finishing, etc. ..	698	698	1,396	375	407	782
Other Textile Industries ..	357	503	860	450	439	889
TEXTILES TOTAL ..	5,929	11,487	17,416	4,313	9,004	13,317
PER CENT ..	1.62	5.53	3.04	1.28	4.35	2.45
Leather (Tanning and Dressing) and Fellmongery	947	414	1,361	841	320	1,161
Leather Goods	223	455	678	247	552	799
Fur..	246	479	725	246	429	675
LEATHER, LEATHER GOODS AND FUR TOTAL ..	1,416	1,348	2,764	1,334	1,301	2,635
PER CENT ..	0.39	0.65	0.48	0.40	0.63	0.49
Tailoring	3,391	13,548	16,939	2,801	13,438	16,239
Dressmaking	104	1,188	1,292	81	979	1,060
Overalls, Shirts, Underwear, etc.	244	3,357	3,601	289	3,031	3,320
Hats, Caps and Millinery	96	633	729	70	614	684
Dress Industries not elsewhere specified.. ..	90	278	368	137	627	764
Manufacture of Boots, Shoes, Slippers and Clogs (excluding Rubber)	685	709	1,394	501	531	1,032
Repair of Boots and Shoes	576	158	734	590	177	767
CLOTHING TOTAL ..	5,186	19,871	25,057	4,469	19,397	23,866
PER CENT ..	1.43	9.56	4.38	1.33	9.38	4.39
Grain Milling	879	159	1,038	941	180	1,121
Bread and Flour Confectionery	7,358	5,135	12,493	6,442	4,870	11,312
Biscuits	1,171	2,810	3,981	1,599	4,307	5,906
Meat and Meat Products	1,345	934	2,279	1,066	861	1,927
Milk Products	551	330	881	879	403	1,282
Sugar and Glucose ..	50	94	144	81	146	227
Cocoa, Chocolate and Sugar Confectionery ..	453	1,967	2,420	641	1,869	2,510
Preserving of Fruit and Vegetables	378	754	1,132	392	662	1,054
Food Industries not elsewhere specified.. ..	902	1,026	1,928	897	776	1,673
Brewing and Malting ..	1,320	705	2,025	1,426	600	2,026
Wholesale Bottling ..	1,356	1,595	2,951	1,786	1,952	3,738
Other Drink Industries ..	1,191	898	2,089	1,191	884	2,075
Tobacco	562	1,374	1,936	767	1,205	1,972
FOOD, DRINK & TOBACCO TOTAL ..	17,516	17,781	35,297	18,108	18,715	36,823
PER CENT ..	4.80	8.55	6.16	5.38	9.05	6.78

Standard Industrial Classification (introduced 1948)	*Mid-1951*			*Mid-1955*		
	Males	*Females*	*Total*	*Males*	*Females*	*Total*
Timber	2,041	249	2,290	1,356	204	1,560
Furniture and Upholstery	3,846	1,733	5,579	3,398	1,407	4,805
Shop and Office Fitting ..	421	125	546	505	106	611
Wooden Containers and Baskets	1,171	430	1,601	1,332	349	1,681
Miscellaneous Wood and Cork Manufactures ..	593	359	952	378	275	653
MANUFACTURES OF WOOD AND CORK TOTAL ..	8,072	2,896	10,968	6,969	2,341	9,310
PER CENT ..	2.21	1.39	1.91	2.07	1.13	1.71
Paper and Board	530	211	741	717	261	978
Wallpaper	157	89	246	1	1	2
Cardboard Boxes, Cartons and Fibre Packing Cases	512	1,398	1,910	679	1,441	2,120
Manufactures of Paper and Board not elsewhere specified	388	592	980	380	561	941
Printing and Publishing of Newspapers and Periodicals	3,672	528	4,200	4,570	597	5,167
Other Printing and Publishing, Bookbinding, Engraving	4,057	5,528	9,585	4,271	5,253	9,524
PAPER AND PRINTING TOTAL ..	9,316	8,346	17,662	10,618	8,114	18,732
PER CENT ..	2.55	4.02	3.08	3.16	3.92	3.49
Rubber	1,142	519	1,661	1,045	509	1,554
Linoleum, Leather Cloth, etc.	16	4	20	7	1	8
Brushes and Brooms ..	205	96	301	179	71	250
Toys, Games and Sports Requisites	297	174	471	317	197	514
Miscellaneous Stationers' Goods	96	179	275	134	179	313
Production and Printing of Cinematograph Films ..	8	5	13	—	1	1
Miscellaneous Manufacturing Industries	354	191	545	467	209	676
OTHER MANUFACTURING INDUSTRIES TOTAL ..	2,118	1,168	3,286	2,149	1,167	3,316
PER CENT ..	0.58	0.56	0.57	0.64	0.56	0.61
Building	29,476	1,614	31,090	26,769	1,379	28,148
Electric Wiring and Contracting	2,156	263	2,419	1,870	282	2,152
Civil Engineering Contracting	4,416	163	4,579	4,147	237	4,384
BUILDING AND CONTRACTING TOTAL ..	36,048	2,040	38,088	32,786	1,898	34,684
PER CENT ..	9.88	0.98	6.65	9.75	0.92	6.39

Standard Industrial Classification (introduced 1948)	Mid-1951 Males	Mid-1951 Females	Mid-1951 Total	Mid-1955 Males	Mid-1955 Females	Mid-1955 Total
Gas	4,490	140	4,630	2,901	168	3,069
Electricity	4,133	526	4,659	2,224	541	2,765
Water	813	28	841	768	26	794
GAS ELECTRICITY AND WATER TOTAL ..	9,436	694	10,130	5,893	735	6,628
PER CENT ..	2.58	0.33	1.77	1.75	0.36	1.22
Railways	21,053	1,639	22,692	15,884	1,861	17,745
Tramways and Omnibus Service	8,127	3,483	11,610	7,364	4,286	11,650
Other Road Passenger Transport	827	156	983	733	125	858
Goods Transport by Road	5,886	781	6,667	5,987	659	6,646
Sea Transport	4,683	639	5,322	3,968	628	4,596
Port, River and Canal Transport	4,029	112	4,141	4,032	134	4,166
Harbour, Dock, Canal, Conservancy, etc., Service	2,398	214	2,612	1,837	102	1,939
Air Transport	14	1	15	6	4	10
Postal, Telegraph and Wireless Communication	1,561	1,149	2,710	472	612	1,084
Other Transport and Communication	274	154	428	436	393	829
Storage	883	527	1,410	855	599	1,454
TRANSPORT AND COMMUNICATION TOTAL ..	49,735	8,855	58,590	41,574	9,403	50,977
PER CENT ..	13.63	4.26	10.23	12.36	4.55	9.38
Dealing in Coal, Builders' Materials, Grain and Agricultural Supplies (Wholesale and Retail)	2,578	892	3,470	2,569	847	3,416
Dealing in Other Industrial Materials and Machinery	2,432	1,534	3,966	2,377	1,770	4,147
Wholesale Distribution of Food and Drink ..	5,199	3,252	8,451	4,377	2,445	6,822
Retail Distribution, Food, Drink (excluding Catering)	8,239	11,419	19,658	7,123	12,153	19,276
Wholesale Distribution of Non-Food Goods ..	11,971	10,459	22,430	9,472	9,062	18,534
Retail Distribution of Non-Food Goods	8,777	19,762	28,539	9,471	19,769	29,240
Retail Distribution, Confectionery, Tobacco, Newspapers	363	2,072	2,435	325	1,706	2,031
DISTRIBUTIVE TRADES TOTAL ..	39,559	49,390	88,949	35,714	47,752	83,466
PER CENT ..	10.84	23.76	15.53	10.62	23.09	15.37
INSURANCE, BANKING AND FINANCE TOTAL ..	6,532	4,387	10,919	6,859	4,908	11,767
PER CENT ..	1.79	2.19	1.91	2.09	2.37	2.17

Standard Industrial Classification (introduced 1948)	*Mid-1951*			*Mid-1955*		
	Males	*Females*	*Total*	*Males*	*Females*	*Total*
National Government Service	3,557	1,821	5,378	1,277	917	2,194
Local Government Service	11,226	4,554	15,780	13,652	4,709	18,361
PUBLIC ADMINISTRATION AND DEFENCE TOTAL ..	14,783	6,375	21,158	14,929	5,626	20,555
PER CENT ..	4.05	3.07	3.69	4,44	2.72	3.78
Accountancy	1,883	1,426	3,309	1,869	1,567	3,436
Education	5,332	11,889	17,221	6,245	13,725	19,970
Law	866	1,732	2,598	791	1,922	2,713
Medical and Dental Service	4,490	12,846	17,336	4,555	13,624	18,179
Religion	286	322	608	206	224	430
Other Professional and Business Services ..	3,450	1,362	4,812	2,833	1,452	4,285
PROFESSIONAL SERVICES TOTAL ..	16,307	29,577	45,884	16,499	32,514	49,013
PER CENT ..	4.47	14.22	8.01	4.90	15.72	9.02
Theatres, Cinemas, Music Halls, Concerts, etc. ..	1,804	2,446	4,250	1,616	2,376	3,992
Sport	470	191	661	356	164	520
Other Recreations ..	331	288	619	253	286	539
Betting	434	1,109	1,543	649	1,621	2,270
Catering, Hotels, etc. ..	5,011	9,321	14,332	4,568	8,973	13,541
Laundries	507	1,880	2,387	558	1,608	2,166
Dry Cleaning, Job Dyeing, Carpet Beating, etc. ..	216	744	960	202	790	992
Hairdressing and Manicure	577	762	1,339	584	941	1,525
Private Domestic Service (Resident)	153	2,213	2,366	60	1,565	1,625
Private Domestic Service (Non-Resident) ..	57	1,574	1,631	47	1,298	1,345
Other Services	1,669	1,165	2,834	1,337	1,371	2,708
MISCELLANEOUS SERVICES TOTAL ..	11,229	21,693	32,922	10,230	20,993	31,223
PER CENT ..	3.08	10.44	5.75	3.01	10.15	5.75
EX-SERVICE PERSONNEL NOT YET ALLOCATED TO ANY INDUSTRY TOTAL ..	313	16	329	313	1	314
PER CENT ..	0.09	0.01	0.06	0.09	0.00	0.06
GRAND TOTAL ..	364,979	207,868	572,847	336,395	206,786	543,181

SOURCE: *Ministry of Labour and National Service.*

TABLE 34

PERSONS TRAVELLING INTO GLASGOW TO WORK, AT 1951 CENSUS DATE

Place of Enumeration	Population (1951)	No. Travelling into Glasgow to Work			Approx. Distance to City Centre (miles)
		Males	Females	Total	
LANARK COUNTY (excluding Glasgow)	524,596	23,754	16,096	39,850	—
Large Burghs:					
Airdrie	30,313	753	483	1,236	12
Coatbridge	47,541	1,533	1,841	3,374	10
Hamilton	40,174	1,083	548	1,631	11
Motherwell and Wishaw ..	68,154	988	716	1,704	12
Rutherglen	24,213	3,554	1,957	5,511	3
Small Burghs:					
Biggar	1,437	2	8	10	38
Lanark	6,219	55	32	87	25
Villages (over 1,000 pop.) ..	251,976	13,629	9,296	22,925	—
Rural Areas	54,569	2,157	1,215	3,372	—
RENFREW COUNTY	324,660	15,226	4,890	20,116	—
Large Burghs:					
Greenock	76,292	664	100	764	23
Paisley	93,711	2,863	703	3,566	7
Port Glasgow	21,618	225	45	270	19
Small Burghs:					
Barrhead	12,971	655	256	911	9
Gourock	9,107	143	50	193	26
Johnstone	15,660	361	89	450	11
Renfrew	17,091	887	342	1,229	6
Villages (over 1,000 pop.) ..	62,577	8,583	3,044	11,627	—
Rural Areas	15,633	845	261	1,106	—
DUNBARTON COUNTY	164,269	9,608	4,115	13,723	—
Large Burghs:					
Clydebank	44,638	2,861	1,217	4,078	7
Dumbarton	33,702	497	167	664	14
Small Burghs:					
Cove and Kilcreggan ..	890	37	3	40	38
Helensburgh	8,760	370	127	497	22
Kirkintilloch	14,826	953	528	1,481	8
Milngavie	7,885	1,183	470	1,653	7
Villages (over 1,000 pop.) ..	48,051	3,322	1,413	4,735	—
Rural Areas	15,517	385	190	575	—
Counties of Lanark, Renfrew and Dunbarton	1,013,525	48,588	25,101	73,689	
Elsewhere in Scotland	—	7,039	2,407	9,446[a]	
Total Travelling into Glasgow to Work		55,627	27,508	83,135	

SOURCE: *Census of Scotland*, 1951.
(*a*) Of this number, 2,839 came from Stirling County.

TABLE 35

ESTATES ADMINISTERED BY SCOTTISH INDUSTRIAL ESTATES, LTD., IN THE GLASGOW EMPLOYMENT AREA, 1955

Estate	*Year Opened*	*Distance from City Centre*	*Factory and Administrative Space Built (sq. ft.)*	*Space available for Development (sq. ft.)*	*Approx. Employment*	*Number of Firms*
Hillington ..	1937	4 miles	4,220,968 [a]	39,897	20,000	144
North Cardonald (ext. to Hillington)	1949	4 miles	336,054	163,964	700	13
Queenslie ..	1946	4 miles	702,508	581,224	3,000	23
Thornliebank	1947	5 miles	222,207	35,059	700	15
Carntyne ..	1946	3 miles	190,306	nil	750	7
Craigton ..	1947	3 miles	370,367 [a]	150,000	600	12
All estates in Glasgow[1] Employment Area ..			6,042,080	970,144	25,750	214
All estates in Scotland ..			15,599,015	2,585,000	67,000 [b]	—

SOURCE: *Scottish Industrial Estates, Ltd.*

[1] In addition to the estates named, there are 13 firms on individual sites in the Glasgow Employment Area employing approximately 6,000 people.

(*a*) At Hillington, 1,801,237 sq. ft. of space is ex-Government. At Craigton all space was formerly Government premises.

(*b*) This number includes approximately 2,000 people who are employed by firms on industrial estates but not employed on the estates themselves.

TABLE 36

Manufacturing Establishments in Glasgow (including Hillington) with more than 10 Employees

Classified by Number of Employees, November, 1954, and November, 1955

No. of Employees	Establishments[1] Nov. 1954	Establishments[1] Nov. 1955	No. of Employees	Establishments[1] Nov. 1954	Establishments[1] Nov. 1955
5,000 or more	1	1	300-399	38	32
4,000-4,999	—	—	200-299	59	57
3,000-3,999	4	3	100-199	166	178
2,000-2,999	4	3	75-99	112	101
1,000-1,999	24	24	50-74	216	204
750-999	16	20	25-49	384	417
500-749	36	32	11-24	403	383
400-499	14	23			

Source: *Ministry of Labour and National Service.*

[1] Where a firm has more than one establishment (with more than 10 employees) in Glasgow, each establishment is entered as one.

TABLE 37

INDUSTRIAL FIRMS

ANALYSIS (BY SIZE AND BY INDUSTRIAL GROUPS) OF FIRMS IN THE GLASGOW AREA (INCLUDING HILLINGTON) EMPLOYING 50 OR MORE WORKERS 1956

Industrial Group	*Firms Employing*				
	50 to 100	101 to 250	251 to 500	501 to 1,000	1,000+
Building and Road Construction materials	5	4	—	—	—
Coal Mining	1	1	—	2	1
Glass and other non-metalliferous Mineral Manufactures	4	6	3	2	—
Chemicals, Paints, Oils, Rubber, etc.	18	15	5	2	—
Foundries, Smelting and Rolling	6	11	9	8	2
Shipbuilding and Repairs ..	3	9	5	3	12
Electrical Engineering.. ..	10	3	2	—	—
Transport—Repairs and manufacture	17	12	2	3	7
Other Engineering	38	39	18	16	6
Textiles and Allied Industries	18	14	5	2	2
Leather and Leather Goods ..	9	2	1	2	—
Dress Industries	52	42	11	2	—
Food, Drink and Tobacco ..	35	39	11	8	7
Timber and Wooden Manufactures	17	17	5	—	—
Paper, Printing & Stationery..	35	15	8	1	4
Miscellaneous Manufactures ..	3	5	—	—	—
Building	37	29	4	5	1
Electrical and Civil Engineering Contracting	15	18	2	1	—
Public Utilities (other than Transport)	—	3	2	1	4
Transport & Communications	18	18	6	1	8
Wholesale and Retail Distribution	126	73	26	7	3
Public, Professional and Business Services	61	33	13	4	8
Entertainment and Recreation (including Betting)	7	4	1	2	—
Catering and Hotels	28	13	3	1	1
Laundries and Dry Cleaning..	7	4	1	—	—
Miscellaneous Services ..	10	1	—	1	—
	580	430	143	74	66

SOURCE: *Ministry of Labour and National Service.*

TABLE 38

INDUSTRIAL BUILDING: GLASGOW CITY
LININGS GRANTED BY THE DEAN OF GUILD COURT, 1872-1955

Year	*Warehouses, Stores and Workshops*		Year	*Warehouses, Stores and Workshops*	
	No. of Linings	*Valuation £000*		*No. of Linings*	*Valuation £000*
1872-73	240	399	1914-15	155	345
73-74	202	242	15-16	138	352
74-75	201	176	16-17	158	547
75-76	205	445	17-18	121	472
76-77	172	320	18-19	186	750
77-78	149	241	19-20	293	1,779
78-79	65	105	1920-21	183	725
79-80	86	103	21-22	174	293
1880-81	79	106	22-23	161	209
81-82	93	155	23-24	122	392
82-83	89	292	24-25	128	416
83-84	99	233	25-26	139	273
84-85	59	86	26-27	174	393
85-86	66	69	27-28	172	627
86-87	77	73	28-29	217	557
87-88	60	86	29-30	162	250
88-89	103	263	1930-31	151	339
89-90	162	183	31-32	131	122
1890-91	119	179	32-33	150	875
91-92	121	225	33-34	137	244
92-93	106	462	34-35	155	390
93-94	105	176	35-36	144	297
94-95	107	166	36-37	162	734
95-96	86	194	37-38	160	594
96-97	146	486	38-39	142	770
97-98	136	489	39-40	60	307
98-99	113	516	1940-41	49	142
99-1900	115	758	41-42	44	173
1900-01	113	396	42-43	46	243
01-02	166	349	43-44	33	46
02-03	134	269	44-45	25	296
03-04	131	829	45-46	101	490
04-05	124	280	46-47	158	944
05-06	99	394	47-48	168	978
06-07	133	218	48-49	110	529
07-08	100	280	49-50	152	427
08-09	106	212	1950-51	210	1,151
09-10	82	194	51-52	147	1,023
1910-11	95	225	52-53	165	806
11-12	77	197	53-54	196	1,677
12-13	115	474	54-55	194	2,617
13-14	152	547	55-56	345	3,716

SOURCE: *Glasgow Corporation Office of Public Works.*

TABLE 39

Industrial Building

In Central Clydeside Conurbation, and Completions in Whole of Great Britain, 1945-1956[1]

Year	Central Clydeside Conurbation						Great Britain	
	Approved in Period		Started in Period		Completed in Period		Completed in Period	
	No.	*Area ('000 sq. ft.)*	*No.*	*Area ('000 sq. ft.)*	*No.*	*Area ('000 sq. ft.)*	*No.*	*Area ('000 sq. ft.)*
1945	64	1,818	10	542	—	—	5	82
1946	138	3,694	148	2,747	14	262	176	3,201
1947	67	1,647	86	3,206	65	1,280	613	11,425
1948	47	1,075	21	555	74	1,468	970	23,329
1949	64	1,221	49	920	80	2,481	1,015	21,800
1950	45	1,128	35	865	61	1,410	1,198	24,564
1951	50	2,048	48	2,018	49	982	1,423	33,873
1952	36	916	26	468	39	1,292	1,446	29,181
1953	64	1,298	55	1,264	43	1,808	1,444	31,391
1954	71	2,794	69	2,099	67	1,354	1,727	38,761
1955	97	2,527	72	2,173	67	1,549	2,091	40,538
Jan.-June, 1956	36	1,233	47	1,006	29	742	992	20,521
Total	779	21,399	666	17,863	588	14,628	13,100	278,666

Source: *Board of Trade Office for Scotland.*
[1] Based on information available up to the end of September 1956.

TABLE 40

Industrial Building

In City of Glasgow (plus Hillington Industrial Estate) and Completions in Scotland, 1945-1956[1]

Year	City of Glasgow (plus Hillington)						Scotland	
	Approved in Period		Started in Period		Completed in Period		Completed in Period	
	No.	Area ('000 sq. ft.)	No.	Area ('000 sq. ft.)	No.	Area ('000 sq. ft.)	No.	Area ('000 sq. ft.)
1945	38	1,020	3	103	—	—	1	5
1946	75	1,678	80	1,182	9	108	24	564
1947	33	499	50	1,580	26	390	117	2,391
1948	26	681	7	181	44	696	138	2,825
1949	30	556	25	365	47	926	148	3,777
1950	18	336	19	558	27	456	127	2,065
1951	26	592	20	476	26	401	114	2,830
1952	24	499	12	276	18	601	99	3,483
1953	42	638	35	475	21	874	111	3,268
1954	44	1,266	43	710	42	653	153	3,132
1955	60	1,491	46	1,069	41	754	134	3,119
Jan.-June, 1956	19	366	30	756	19	457	87	1,817
Total	435	9,622	370	7,731	320	6,316	1,253	29,276

Source: *Board of Trade Office for Scotland.*

[1] Based on information available up to the end of September 1956.

TABLE 41

City of Glasgow (including Hillington Industrial Estate) Factory Buildings Approved, Started and Completed

By Industries. 1945-June, 1956

Industry	*Approved*		*Started*		*Completed*	
	No.	*Area '000 sq. ft.*	*No.*	*Area '000 sq. ft.*	*No.*	*Area '000 sq. ft.*
Treatment of Non-Metalliferous Mining Products other than Coal:						
Glass (other than containers)	4	158	4	158	3	109
Others	10	246	7	114	7	114
Chemicals and Allied Trades:						
Chemicals and Dyes	11	184	9	141	7	110
Coke Ovens and By-Products Works	1	120	1	120	1	120
Others	9	132	7	110	7	110
Metal Manufacture:						
Iron and Steel	28	619	23	564	22	504
Non-ferrous Metals Smelting, Rolling, etc.	5	47	3	30	3	30
Engineering, Shipbuilding and Electrical Goods:						
Shipbuilding and Marine Engineering	37	873	33	730	26	578
General Mechanical Engineering ..	92	1,631	83	1,478	71	1,260
Electrical Engineering	17	325	14	287	12	146
Vehicles:						
Motors and Aircraft (including engines, repairs, etc.)	41	553	34	459	29	417
Locomotives and Rolling Stock.. ..	5	68	3	36	3	36
Metal Goods not elsewhere specified:						
Brass Manufactures	12	100	12	100	10	88
Miscellaneous Metal Goods	20	407	17	367	15	211
Scientific, Surgical and Photographic Instruments:	4	49	3	29	2	23
Textiles:						
Textile Finishing	2	141	2	141	2	141
Others	21	209	16	141	15	134
Leather (Tanning and Dressing) and Fellmongery	3	33	3	32	2	20
Clothing:						
Tailoring	8	132	8	132	8	132
Others	1	5	1	5	1	5
Food, Drink and Tobacco:						
Bread and Flour Confectionery ..	8	132	4	38	3	24
Biscuits	11	308	10	230	6	115
Others	23	528	21	303	20	286
Drink Industry	6	190	6	190	6	190
Tobacco	2	509	2	509	1	482

Industry	Approved No.	Approved Area '000 sq. ft.	Started No.	Started Area '000 sq. ft.	Completed No.	Completed Area '000 sq. ft.
Manufactures of Wood and Cork:						
Timber	9	361	8	345	7	332
Furniture and Upholstery	9	190	5	157	5	157
Others	7	93	7	93	6	87
Paper and Printing:						
Paper and Board	3	478	1	12	—	—
Printing and Publishing of Newspapers and Periodicals	4	174	3	78	2	14
Others	15	260	14	255	14	255
Other Manufacturing Industries:						
Rubber	6	311	5	291	3	30
Others	4	56	4	56	4	56
TOTAL ..	438	9,622	373	7,731	323	6,316

SOURCE: *Board of Trade Office for Scotland.*

TABLE 42

NAVAL SHIPBUILDING ON THE CLYDE, SEPTEMBER, 1939, TO AUGUST, 1945

VESSELS COMPLETED

Year	Battleships and Carriers[1]		Cruisers and Destroyers[2]		Minor and Ancillary Vessels[3]		Total	
	No.	Displacement Tons	No.	Displacement Tons	No.	Displacement Tons	No.	Displacement Tons
3-9-1939 to 31-12-1939	—	—	4	6,840	4	3,500	8	10,340
1940	—	—	14	38,420	73	35,156	87	73,576
1941	1	35,000	20	31,535	117	100,894	138	167,429
1942	1	35,000	33	57,235	110	41,553	144	133,788
1943	1	13,825	14	38,610	193	94,462	208	146,897
1944	2	46,000	14	23,980	180	44,176	196	114,156
1-1-1945 to 31-8-1945	1	14,000	3	5,735	54	34,746	58	54,481
Total 3-9-1939 to 31-8-1945	6	143,825	102	202,355	731	354,487	839	700,667

SOURCE: *Admiralty*.

[1] Battleships, Fleet Carriers, Light Fleet Cruisers, Escort Carriers.

[2] Cruisers, Flotilla Leaders and Destroyers, Escort Destroyers.

[3] Monitors, Aircraft Transports, Submarines, Sloops, Frigates, Corvettes, Fast Minelayers, Minesweepers, Trawlers, Boom Defence Vessels, Tugs, River Gunboats, Steam Gunboats, Destroyer Depot Ships, Submarine Depot Ships, Salvage Vessels, L.S.T.s, Small Craft (all types).

TABLE 43 (*a*)

Ships Launched on the Clyde, 1864-1900

Year	TONS			Sail Tonnage as Percentage of Total
	Sail	*Steam*	*Total*	
1864	47,527	130,978	178,505	26.6
1865	31,457	122,475	153,932	20.5
1866	31,164	93,349	124,513	25.0
1867	43,926	63,418	107,344	40.9
1868	76,103	92,983	169,086	45.1
1869	76,482	115,828	192,310	39.8
1870	31,569	148,832	180,401	17.5
1871	9,233	186,996	196,229	4.7
1872	11,263	219,093	230,356	4.9
1873	12,674	220,252	232,926	5.4
1874	66,019	196,411	262,430	25.2
1875	92,134	119,348	211,482	43.6
1876	73,447	101,377	174,824	42.1
1877	75,542	93,941	169,483	44.6
1878	61,035	150,862	211,897	28.8
1879	9,036	148,569	157,605	5.7
1880	21,765	226,891	248,656	8.8
1881	34,838	292,175	327,013	10.7
1882	67,932	314,737	382,669	17.8
1883	56,949	347,434	404,383	14.1
1884	33,116	228,906	262,022	12.6
1885	99,452	92,940	192,392	51.7
1886	59,527	113,238	172,765	34.5
1887	34,954	149,840	184,794	18.9
1888	52,120	221,511	273,631	19.1
1889	77,559	258,506	336,065	23.1
1890	81,825	270,299	352,124	23,3
1891	104,377	222,098	326,475	32.0
1892	159,002	163,176	322,178	49.0
1893	91,829	169,707	261,536	35.0
1894	71,900	261,524	333,424	22.0
1895	36,081	304,146	340,227	10.6
1896	35,361	352,737	388,098	9.1
1897	20,557	282,284	302,841	6.8
1898	1,965	429,440	431,405	0.5
1899	473	462,600	463,073	0.1
1900	6,279	451,232	457,511	1.4

Source: *Lloyd's Register of Shipping, Reports of Glasgow City Chamberlains, and* Glasgow Herald,

TABLE 43 (*b*)

Ships Launched on the Clyde, 1901-1919

Total

Year	*Vessels*	*Tonnage*	*I.H.P.*	*Year*	*Vessels*	*Tonnage*	*I.H.P.*
1901	297	511,990	440,125	1911	413	630,583	786,889
1902	312	518,270	480,870	1912	389	640,529	878,326
1903	277	446,869	455,221	1913	370	756,976	1,111,440
1904	329	417,870	432,815	1914	339	653,332	1,149,407
1905	319	539,850	518,547	1915	293	306,415	1,284,130
1906	372	598,841	606,600	1916	393	506,382	1,862,410
1907	526	619,919	668,527	1917	432	459,959	1,588,370
1908	569	355,586	474,400	1918	440	555,803	1,900,595
1909	354	403,187	610,983	1919	422	646,154	1,479,771
1910	358	392,392	593,840				

Source: Glasgow Herald *Shipbuilding, Engineering and Commerce Supplements. Annual.*

TABLE 43 (*c*)

Ships Launched on the Clyde, 1920-1955

	MERCHANT			NAVAL			TOTAL		
Year	*Vessels*	*Tonnage*	*I.H.P.*	*Vessels*	*Tonnage*	*I.H.P.*	*Vessels*	*Tonnage*	*I.H.P.*
1920	330	672,438	620,615				330	672,438	620,615
1921	249	511,185	478,760				249	511,185	478,760
1922	143	388,481	345,729		*NONE*		143	388,481	345,729
1923	122	175,528	166,956				122	175,528	166,956
1924	251	538,021	456,258				251	538,021	456,258
1925	280	523,322	433,243				280	523,322	433,243
1926	171	275,140	433,465	2	11,210	—	173	286,350	433,465
1927	268	441,383	400,584	6	21,182	247,240	274	462,565	647,874
1928	238	583,071	509,507	3	21,540	164,400	241	604,611	673,907
1929	229	558,058	609,837	5	7,740	140,400	234	565,798	750,237
1930	243	526,564	532,734	5	3,280	68,000	248	529,844	600,734
1931	97	152,101	181,390	2	562	2,250	99	152,663	183,640
1932	29	63,757	54,805	1	2,880	112,400	30	66,637	167,205
1933	29	55,058	172,204	2	1,310	2,470	31	56,368	174,674
1934	61	238,300	204,753	6	29,821	508,770	67	275,894	713,523
1935	67	162,037	231,771	7	9,893	180,600	74	171,930	412,371
1936	100	296,366	449,156	5	30,491	371,000	105	326,857	820,156
1937	103	344,204	302,508	9	36,900	678,800	112	381,104	981,308
1938	104	415,093	595,189	13	28,522	319,450	117	443,615	914,639
1939	70	239,417							794,522
1940	52	261,842			Comparable figures				1,304,529
1941	65	350,591			not available				1,355,935
1942	62½	335,984							1,653,360
1943	46	284,869							1,271,422
1944	50	248,519			Comparable figures				1,431,700
1945	60	248,638			not available				1,158,820
1946	98	341,778							589,255
1947	98	374,293	487,339	1	450	2,150	99	374,743	489,489
1948	119	358,483	449,981	1	1,700	—	120	360,183	449,981
1949	88	439,794	449,534	1	2,610	—	89	442,404	449,534
1950	84	442,633	518,109	3	7,830	160,000	87	450,463	678,109
1951	79	426,969	434,424	1	380	1,400	80	427,349	435,824
1952	74	451,345	404,346	3	3,200	53,000	77	454,545	457,346
1953	70	398,617	435,687	4	7,400	30,000	74	406,017	465,687
1954	86	477,805	508,606	6	2,500	17,500	92	480,305	526,106
1955	85	485,438	498,505	10	9,000	—	95	494,438	498,505

Source: Glasgow Herald *Shipbuilding, Engineering and Commerce Supplements* (1920-1930), *and Trade Reviews*, 1931 *onwards*.

TABLE 44

NUMBERS OF TRADESMEN AND APPRENTICES EMPLOYED IN THE CLYDE SHIPBUILDING AND SHIP REPAIRING INDUSTRY AS AT 1930, 1939 AND 1955

Class	*April,* 1930		*April,* 1939		*May,* 1955	
	T'men	*Apps.*	*T'men*	*Apps.*	*T'men*	*Apps.*
Platers	1,340	533	1,358	465	1,881	357
Riveters	1,578	207	850	150	383	26
Holders-on	1,034	0	590	0	302	4
Caulkers	982	319	869	291	695	81
Burners	[a]	[a]	[a]	[a]	364	69
Welders (Electric)	73	[a]	452	381	1,806	480
Shipwrights (including Loftsmen)	2,083	708	1,599	697	1,855	572
Riggers (not Labourers)	158	[a]	[a]	[a]	113	4
Joiners and other Woodworkers ..	2,268	631	1,611	513	2,038	562
Drillers	532	358	540	327	414	52
Shipsmiths or Blacksmiths ..	281	67	247	57	192	33
Coppersmiths	40	[a]	[a]	[a]	4	0
Plumbers	642	294	679	323	791	263
Sheet Iron Workers and Sheet Metal Workers	339	10[b]	549	281	466	166
Electricians	675	213	664	343	953	308
Painters	555	[a]	367	106	485	115
Mechanics:						
Fitters	491	131	712	237	710	224
Turners	59	[a]	99	33	113	29
Other Tradesmen	1,168	52	360	42	282	19
Women (all skilled trades) ..	198	[a]	78	118	211	37
	14,496	3,523	11,624	4,364	14,058	3,401
Labourers and General Workers (including semi-skilled classes):						
Men over 21 .. .. }	11,267	0	6,190	0	9,169	0
Boys and Youths .. }			1,916	0	587	0
Women and Girls ..	24	0	16	0	120	0
	25,787	3,523	19,746	4,364	23,934	3,401
Total	29,310		24,110		27,335	

SOURCE: *Clyde Shipbuilders' Association.*

(*a*) Not known.
(*b*) Sheet *metal* workers' apprentices only.

TABLE 45

RETAIL TRADES OF GLASGOW, 1950

Kind of Business[a]	*Estab-lish-ments*	*Sales*	*Persons Engaged*		*Wages and Salaries*	*Estab-lish-ments per 10,000 Inhabi-tants*	*Average Sales per Estab-lish-ment*	*Average Sales per Full-time Worker*
			Full-time	*Part-time*				
	No.	£000s	*No.*	*No.*	£000s	*No.*	£000s	£000s
Grocery ..	2,094	25,392	9,200	1,150	1,763	19.2	12.1	2.8
Other Food Retailers ..	2,934	19,943	9,427	1,633	1,914	26.9	6.8	2.1
Dairymen ..	448	4,227	1,590	467	320	4.1	9.4	2.7
Butchers ..	697	5,971	2,764	170	663	6.4	8.6	2.2
Fishmongers, Poulterers ..	341	2,114	1,130	203	233	3.1	6.2	1.9
Greengrocers (including with fish) ..	769	3,223	1,681	(459)	281	8.1	4.2	1.9
Bread & Flour Confectioners	487	2,849	1,790	210	333	4.5	5.9	1.6
Confectioners, Tobacconists, Newsagents	2,145	14,990	3,945	1,862	522	19.7	7.0	3.8
Confectioner-Tobacconist-Newsagents[b]	1,093	5,015	1,833	752	209	10.0	4.6	2.7
Tobacconist-Newsagents[c]	1,028	9,926	2,082	1,092	311	9.4	9.7	4.8
Clothing ..	1,734	26,933	10,141	1,707	2,510	15.9	15.5	2.7
Boots and Shoes ..	262	4,291	1,431	189	366	2.4	16.4	3.0
Men's Wear	288	6,056	1,997	258	586	2.6	21.0	3.0
Women's Wear[d] ..	551	10,388	3,911	—	—	5.1	18.9	2.7
Men's and Women's Wear	330	5,157	2,173	289	562	3.0	16.4	2.4
Hardware ..	538	3,282	1,580	295	315	4.9	6.1	2.1
Domestic Hardware ..	346	1,528	783	181	125	3.2	4.4	2.0
Radio and Electrical (with repairs)	124	1,129	572	68	141	1.1	9.1	2.0
Booksellers, Stationers	172	2,126	851	171	206	1.6	12.6	2.5
Chemists' goods, Photographic Goods ..	371	3,419	1,638	246	442	3.4	9.2	2.1
Furniture ..	285	7,598	2,440	230	725	2.6	26.7	2.7
Domestic Furniture ..	105	5,211	1,435	105	455	1.0	49.6	3.6
Jewellery, Leather, Sports Goods ..	232	2,265	959	137	246	2.1	9.8	2.4

(*Continued overleaf*)

TABLE 45 (*Continued*)

Kind of Business	*Estab-lish-ments*	*Sales*	*Persons Engaged*		*Wages and Salaries*	*Estab-lish-ments per 10,000 Inhabi-tants*	*Average Sales per Estab-lish-ment*	*Average Sales per Full-time Worker*
			Full-time	*Part-time*				
General ..								
Department	34	18.486	7,322	978	2,047	0.3	543.7	2.5
Stores ..	18	12,738	4,950	749	1,321	0.2	707.7	2.6
Variety Stores, Other General	16	5,748	2,372	229	727	0.1	359,3	2.4
Coal, Builders' Materials, Corn	366	3,984	1,671	131	413	3.4	10.9	2.4
Coal ..	234	3,131	1,074	82	224	2.1	13.4	2.9
Other Non-food	308	1,493	940	129	203	2.8	4.9	1.6
Total retail	11,213	129,912	50,114	8,669	11,305	103.0	11.6	2.6

SOURCE: *Census of Distribution and Other Services*, 1950.

(*a*) Main groups with selected sub-groups inset.
(*b*) Includes only those tobacconists and newsagents who also sell sweet confectionery.
(*c*) Tobacconists and tobacconist-newsagents.
(*d*) All specialist sellers of women's garments. Totals of part-time workers and wages and salaries are not given owing to non-disclosure of some figures.

TABLE 46

SERVICE TRADES OF GLASGOW, 1950

Kind of Business	*Estab-lish-ments*	*Sales*	*Persons Engaged*		*Wages and Salaries*	*Estab-lish-ments per 10,000 Inhabi-tants*	*Average Sales per Estab-lish-ment*	*Average Sales per Full-time Worker*
			Full-time	*Part-time*				
	No.	£000s	*No.*	*No.*	£000s	*No.*	£000s	£000s
Catering	1,150	7,447	7,789	1,884	1,464	10.6	6.5	1.0
Hairdressers ..	493	672	1,487	197	256	4.5	1.4	0.5
Funeral Furnishers	67	530	232	31	64	0.6	7.9	2.3
Portrait Photographers ..	48	112	181	19	31	0.4	2.3	0.6
Repairers	444	533	982	119	136	4.1	1.2	0.5
Motor Vehicles, Cycles, Accessories	127	5,629	1,045	74	334	1.2	44.3	5.4
Motor Vehicle Repairers, Garages	170	5,206	2,334	85	677	1.6	30.6	2.2
Total Service	2,299	20,129	14,050	2,409	2,962	22.9	8.1	1.4

SOURCE: *Census of Distribution and Other Services*, 1950.

TABLE 47

Wholesale Trades of Glasgow, 1950

Kind of Business[a]	Establishments	Sales	Persons Engaged[b]		Wages and Salaries
			Full-time	Part-time	
	No.	£000s	No.	No.	£000s
Agricultural Products, Supplies..	53	15,358	541	29	226
Builders, Materials, Hardware ..	168	13,344	2,211	71	777
Coal	93	20,324	552	37	204
Metals, Metal Products	119	17,827	1,350	57	508
Iron, Steel	80	12,885	1,040	43	387
Timber	41	3,388	362	21	145
Scrap and Waste Materials ..	86	3,414	653	24	179
Other Industrial Materials ..	100	49,807	1,974	133	909
Yarns	38	38,892	1,352	97	—[c]
Machinery (except Electrical), Vehicles	144	12,845	2,322	69	840
Electrical Goods	73	4,942	1,032	72	341
Groceries, Confectionery, Drinks	363	107,029	5,523	234	1,893
Groceries, Provisions	200	79,809	2,846	86	923
Alcoholic Drinks	101	20,702	1,583	101	585
Other Food	180	52,822	3,872	118	1,171
Fresh Milk, Cream	10	17,950	562	11	163
Meat, Poultry	21	16,909	814	36	261
Fresh Fruit, Vegetables, Nuts	102	15,268	2,162	56	647
Clothing, Footwear, Textiles:					
Women's Wear	208	11,362	1,026	88	305
Men's and Women's Wear ..	142	20,456	2,515	122	890
General	46	17,548	2,731	127	872
Chemicals, Oils, Drugs	99	11,460	1,208	63	411
Furniture, Musical Instruments	27	4,212	832	11	260
Glass, China, Earthenware ..	36	884	246	9	80
Paper, Stationery, Books ..	134	8,457	1,713	71	541
Petroleum Products	41	5,138	1,193	—[c]	555
Tobacco	53	5,427	299	37	81
Other Manufactured Goods ..	99	3,241	818	38	274
General	148	11,765	1,510	112	537

Source: *Census of Distribution and Other Services*, 1950.

(a) Main groups, with selected sub-groups inset.
(b) Includes working proprietors.
(c) Total not given owing to non-disclosure of figures.

TABLE 48

The Foreign Trade of Glasgow, 1938, 1948 and 1951, by Value

Exports

	£000[1]			Percentage of Total Exports		
	1938	1948	1951	1938	1948	1951
Class I—Food, Drink and Tobacco						
Spirits	5,819	11,606	20,290	17.9	13.0	13.2
Other	913	3,068	5,617	2.8	3.4	3.7
Total ..	6,732	14,674	25,907	20.7	16.4	16.9
Class II—Raw Materials						
Coal	355	736	207	1.1	0.8	0.1
Other	685	675	2,342	2.1	0.8	1.6
Total ..	1,040	1,411	2,549	3.2	1.6	1.7
Class III—Manufactures						
Machinery	7,155	17,703	29,139	22.0	19.8	19.0
Iron and Steel and manufactures thereof	4,899	9,234	17,099	15.1	10.4	11.1
Cotton Goods	2,798	7,403	12,977	8.6	8.3	8.5
Vehicles (excluding ships) ..	1,410	6,475	11,966	4.3	7.3	7.8
Woollen Goods	584	4,015	9,234	1.8	4.5	6.0
New Ships for Foreign Owners..	2,065	5,946	9,202	6.3	6.7	6.0
Jute, Linen and Hemp Goods ..	1,173	3,144	7,505	3.6	3.5	4.9
Chemicals	554	2,030	3,580	1.7	2.3	2.3
Linoleum	390	2,847	3,040	1.2	3.2	2.0
Other	3,402	13,266	19,630	10.5	14.9	12.8
Total ..	24,431	72,061	123,372	75.1	80.8	80.4
Classes IV and V						
Animals (not for food) and Parcel Post	325	1,064	1,692	1.0	1.2	1.0
Total Exports ..	32,528	89,211	153,521	100.0	100.0	100.0

Source: *Board of Trade, Annual Statements of Trade of the United Kingdom.*

TABLE 49

The Foreign Trade of Glasgow, 1938, 1948 and 1951, by Value

Imports

	£000			Percentage of Total Imports		
	1938	1948	1951	1938	1948	1951
Class I—Food, Drink and Tobacco						
Grain and Flour	4,272	14,883	16,463	15.4	20.4	14.9
Fruit and Vegetables	1,866	3,087	7,756	6.7	4.2	7.0
Dairy Produce	3,013	4,706	4,441	10.8	6.4	4.0
Tobacco	159	2,011	2,890	0.5	2.8	2.6
Meat	2,524	4,252	1,391	9.1	5.8	1.3
Other	3,656	9,551	7,179	13.1	13.1	6.5
Total ..	15,491	38,490	40,119	55.7	52.8	36.3
Class II—Raw Materials						
Crude Petroleum	Not separately shown		11,072	Not separately shown		10.0
Wood and Timber	1,139	2,900	7,861	4.1	4.0	7.1
Rubber	283	1,609	5,953	1.0	2.2	5.4
Iron Ore and Scrap	1,314	2,626	3,975	4.7	3.6	3.6
Hemp and Flax	217	1,024	4,496	0.8	1.4	3.9
Wool	146	994	2,561	0.5	1.4	2.1
Other	2,425	7,280	13,236	8.7	10.0	12.4
Total ..	5,523	16,432	49,154	19.8	22.5	44.5
Class III—Manufactures						
Manufactured Oils	1,065	6,543	5,612	3.8	9.0	5.1
Non-ferrous Metals and Manufactures	447	2,749	3,031	1.6	3.8	2.7
Machinery	893	2,542	2,687	3.2	3.5	2.4
Paper and Cardboard	505	862	2,544	1.8	1.2	2.3
Iron and Steel Products	1,255	631	578	4.5	0.9	0.5
Other	2,352	3,651	6,142	8.5	5.0	5.6
Total ..	6,517	16,978	20,594	23.4	23.4	18.7
Classes IV and V						
Animals (not for food) and Parcel Post ..	293	1,066	543	1.1	1.5	0.4
Total Imports ..	27,823	72,906	110,409	100.0	100.0	100.0

Source: *Board of Trade Annual Statements of Trade of the United Kingdom.*

TABLE 50

Foreign Trade of Glasgow by Value, 1954

Imports	£000	% of Total
Class A—Food, Drink and Tobacco:		
Grain and Flour	12,976	12.3
Fruit & Vegetables	8,228	7.8
Meat	5,177	4.9
Tobacco	4,250	4.0
Live Animals for Food	3,497	3.3
Dairy Produce ..	1,446	1.4
Other	7,684	7.3
Total ..	43,258	41.1
Class B—Basic Materials:		
Iron Ore and Scrap ..	6,408	6.1
Wood and Timber ..	3,084	2.9
Oil Seeds	3,014	2.9
Rubber	2,740	2.6
Wool	2,306	2.2
Hemp and Flax ..	1,763	1.7
Other	6,962	6.6
Total	26,277	25.0
Class C—Mineral Fuels and Lubricants:		
Crude Petroleum ..	17,555	16.7
Refined Oils ..	2,061	2.0
Coal	1,061	1.0
Other	425	0.4
Total	21,100	20.1
Class D—Manufactured Goods:		
Machinery	3,313	3.1
Paper & Cardboard	1,885	1.8
Non-ferrous Metals	1,472	1.4
Chemicals	1,174	1.1
Other	6,197	5.9
Total	14,041	13.3
Class E—Miscellaneous:	535	0.5
Total Imports ..	105,213	100.0

Exports	£000	% of Total
Class A—Food, Drink and Tobacco:		
Whisky	26,650	17.0
Other	6,868	4.4
Total	33,518	21.4
Class B—Basic Materials:		
Total	2,463	1.6
Class C—Mineral Fuels and Lubricants:		
Total (including Coal and Coke—238)	738	0.5
Class D—Manufactured Goods:		
Machinery—Non-electric	34,135	21.8
Iron and Steel ..	13,854	8.8
Vehicles—Road, Rail and Air ..	11,675	7.4
New Ships for Foreign Owners	10,194	6.5
Cotton Yarns, Threads & Fabrics	6,835	4.4
Metal Manufactures	6,189	3.9
Floor Coverings ..	5,266	3.4
Jute, Linen, Hemp & Miscellaneous Goods	4,892	3.1
Chemicals	4,201	2.7
Electrical Machinery and Appliances	3,592	2.3
Paper & Cardboard	3,183	2.0
Woollen Yarns and Fabrics	2,991	1.9
Other	11,386	7.3
Total	118,393	75.5
Class E—Miscellaneous	1,725	1.1
Total Exports ..	156,838	100.0
Re-exports	921	—

Source: *Annual Statement of Trade of the United Kingdom.*

TABLE 51

Annual Tonnages of Goods Imported and Exported[1] at the Harbour of Glasgow, 1861-1955

Year Ended June 30	Thousand Tons		
	Imp'ts	*Exp'ts*	*Total*
1861	613	754	1,366
1862	626	754	1,380
1863	661	777	1,437
1864	647	835	1,483
1865	615	836	1,451
1866	648	839	1,487
1867	668	928	1,596
1868	771	948	1,719
1869	746	965	1,710
1870	860	1,062	1,921
1871	896	1,090	1,986
1872	943	1,157	2,101
1873	1,069	1,168	2,237
1874	1,095	1,124	2,219
1875	1,089	1,257	2,347
1876	1,121	1,213	2,333
1877	1,251	1,222	2,473
1878	1,245	1,316	2,561
1879	1,176	1,290	2,466
1880	1,252	1,401	2,653
1881	1,553	1,500	3,053
1882	1,563	1,803	3,367
1883	1,772	1,952	3,725
1884	1,780	1,929	3,709
1885	1,856	1,876	3,732
1886	1,821	1,915	3,736
1887	1,809	1,914	3,723
1888	1,836	2,248	4,084
1889	2,246	2,495	4,383
1890	2,118	2,678	4,795
1891	1,870	2,607	4,478
1892	2,303	2,594	4,897
1893	2,329	2,550	4,879
1894	2,300	2,771	5,070
1895	2,441	2,064	4,505
1896	2,647	2,661	5,308
1897	2,792	2,881	5,673
1898	3,054	4,048	7,102
1899	3,048	3,912	6,960
1900	3,106	4,110	7,215
1901	3,131	4,142	7,274
1902	3,192	4,280	7,472
1903	3,430	5,138	8,567
1904	3,881	5,257	9,138
1905	3,761	5,265	9,026
1906	3,913	5,344	9,256
1907	4,009	5,786	9,795
1908	3,776	5,755	9,531
1909	3,656	5,903	9,619
1910	3,992	6,105	10,097
1911	3,986	6,373	10,359
1912	3,572	5,952	9,525
1913	4,041	6,377	10,418
1914	3,761	6,306	10,068
1915	3,691	5,889	9,580
1916	4,003	5,708	9,711
1917	3,750	4,683	8,433
1918	3,470	4,503	7,974
1919	3,606	3,336	6,942
1920	3,601	3,427	7,028
1921	3,059	2,763	5,822
1922	2,307	3,715	6,021
1923	2,953	5,089	8,042
1924	2,970	4,697	7,667
1925	2,987	4,460	7,447
1926	2,551	4,195	6,746
1927	3,496	3,269	6,765
1928	3,028	4,350	7,378
1929	2,808	4,153	6,962
1930	2,988	4,459	7,447
1931	2,523	3,739	6,263
1932	2,271	3,399	5,670
1933	2,137	3,180	5,317
1934	2,660	3,456	6,116
1935	2,814	3,667	6,481
1936	3,169	3,268	6,437
1937	3,408	3,334	6,743
1938	4,072	3,192	7,265
1939	3,253	2,936	6,189
1940	4,220	3,755	7,975
1941	5,345	3,399	8,744
1942	4,860	3,129	7,989
1943	5,084	3,714	8,798
1944	5,628	3,591	9,220
1945	5,372	3,578	8,949
1946	3,740	2,487	6,227
1947	3,371	1,889	5,259
1948	3,697	1,899	5,596
1949	3,821	1,933	5,754
1950	3,604	1,935	5,539
1951	3,412	2,244	5,655
1952	3,952	2,058	6,010
1953	3,764	1,869	5,634
1954	4,013	1,906	5,920
1955	4,724	1,995	6,719

Source: *Clyde Navigation Trust Annual Reports, and additional information supplied by the Trust.*

[1] The figures are for the whole of the Trust's area, from Albert Bridge, Glasgow, to Newark Castle, Port Glasgow, a distance of 18 miles.

PART II - SECTION 2

Transport and Communication

TABLE 52

MEAN DAILY FLOWS OF TRAFFIC AT MINISTRY OF TRANSPORT CENSUS POINTS IN GLASGOW, 1935, 1938 AND 1954

(*Census taken from* 6 *a.m. to* 10 *p.m. one week in August*)

Census Point	*Mean Daily Flows—All Vehicles*[1]			*Mean Daily Flows as Percentages of* 1938 *Mean Daily Flows*		
	1935	1938	1954	1935	1938	1954
Alexandra Parade (Glenfield St.)	10,256	11,273	13,688	91	100	121
Paisley Road (Carnoustie Street)	12,756	15,477	13,668 [a]	83	100	88
Great Western Road (Southpark Avenue)	11,737	13,409	13,143	88	100	98
Pollokshaws Road (Springhill Gardens)	10,960	11,536	11,868	95	100	103
Gallowgate (Graham Square) ..	not available	8,408	8,596	not available	100	102
Argyle Street (Pitt St.)	7,759	7,219	7,947	107	100	110
Maryhill Road (Maryhill Barracks)	6,488	6,948	7,717	93	100	111
Springburn Road (Sighthill Cemetery)	6,049	6,244	7,610	97	100	122
Duke Street (Prison)	not available	6,791	7,537	not available	100	111
Great Western Road (Garscadden Road)	not available	4,729	7,447	not available	100	157
Renfield Street (West George Street)	7,877	8,288	6,944 [a]	95	100	84
Dalmarnock Road (Poplin Street)	5,329	5,405	6,481	98	100	120
London Road (Belvidere Hospital)	4,380	5,093	6,066	86	100	119
Dumbarton Road (Yoker Ferry Road)	5,130	5,969	5,995	86	100	101
Cumbernauld Road (Monkland Canal Bridge)	4,650	5,540	5,957	84	100	108

SOURCE: *Glasgow Corporation Office of Works, National Traffic Census within Glasgow,* 16*th*-22*nd August*, 1954.

[1] Both directions.

Notes: (*a*) The reasons for the substantial decrease of traffic in the case of Paisley Road and Renfield Street appear to be as follows: *Paisley Road*—The resurfacing of West Street and Scotland Street, which has led to diversion of traffic by this alternative route. *Renfield Street*—The withdrawing of the several bus routes which used to operate in this street.

TABLE 53

MECHANICALLY PROPELLED VEHICLES REGISTERED AT GLASGOW IN QUARTER ENDING SEPTEMBER 30, 1927-1955

	Private Cars	Motor Cycles	Goods Vehicles	Hackney Carriages other than Tramcars	Tramcars	Exempt Vechiles and Miscellaneous	Total
1927	9,300	3,891	4,988	714		1,198	20,091
1928	10,132	4,030	5,388	713		1,202	21,465
1929	10,958	4,154	5,767	754		1,266	22,899
1930	11,744	4,349	6,204	793		1,275	24,365
1931	11,990	3,869	6,264	813		1,280	24,216
1932	12,150	3,472	6,245	708[a]	1,079	200	23,854
1933	13,003	3,396	6,584	705	1,080	201	24,969
1934	13,670	3,390	6,842	721	1,084	188	25,895
1935	14,862	2,968	7,138	746	1,084	192	26,990
1936	16,733	2,971	7,611	777	1,084	216	29,392
1937	17,891	2,979	7,946	776	1,086	223	30,901
1938	19,158	2,928	8,386	945[a]	1,147	242	32,806
1946	15,459	2,321	9,373	1,353	1,206	390	30,102
1947	17,002	2,705	11,376	1,457	1,207	391	34,138
1948	16,921	2,702	13,869	1,676	1,207	472	36,847
1949	17,965	3,271	15,292	1,935	1,201	597	40,261
1950	19,088	3,916	16,521	2,110	1,229	684	43,548
1951	19,712	4,452	17,536	2,136	1,175	546	45,557
1952	20,640	5,013	17,908	2,078	1,155	558	47,352
1953	22,550	5,635	18,263	1,632[a]	1,109	524	49,713
1954	25,497	6,232	18,997	1,591	1,081	441	53,739
1955	29,071	6,979	20,253	1,562	1,031	439	59,335

SOURCE: *Ministry of Transport Returns of Mechanically Propelled Road Vehicles, and Local Taxation Office, Glasgow.*

(*a*) The abrupt changes in the numbers of hackney carriages registered are due largely to changes in registration conditions, resulting in certain types of vehicles being transferred from the hackney class to the private car class, and *vice versa.*

TABLE 54

DRIVING LICENCES CURRENT IN GLASGOW, 1928-1955
(*Excluding provisional licences*)

Year Ending December 31

1928	30,520	1934	38,753	1940	37,276	1946	41,290	1952	63,338
1929	32,009	1935	41,074	1941	31,627	1947	50,036	1953	68,201
1930	33,329	1936	47,383	1942	23,963	1948	52,020	1954	72,421
1931	33,451	1937[1]	47,095	1943	20,102	1949	55,169	1955	78,138
1932	34,459	1938	45,649	1944	20,789	1950	58,335		
1933	35,690	1939	48,423	1945	31,916	1951	61,399		

SOURCE: *Local Taxation Office, Glasgow.*

[1] Driving test introduced in 1937.

TABLE 55

Glasgow Corporation Transport

Annual Vehicle-mileages Run and Passengers Carried, 1895-1955

Year Ending 31st May	VEHICLE-MILES RUN (000s)				PASSENGERS CARRIED (000s)			
	Trams	*Motor Buses*	*Trolley Buses*	*Under-ground*	*Trams*	*Motor Buses*	*Trolley Buses*	*Under-ground*
1895	5,192 [a]				57,105 [a]			
1900	9,657				127,628			
1905	17,944				195,768			
1910	20,974				222,731			
1915	24,214				336,201			
1920	26,459				509,340			
1925	30,937	227 [b]		1,227 [c]	439,341	1,340 [b]		20,008 [c]
1930	35,868	5,566		1,173	470,021	48,067		19,969
1935	35,678	13,056		1,061	449,062	78,962		14,413
1940	36,892	15,819		1,328	459,181	110,231		26,748
1941	37,036	16,253		857 [d]	478,222	129,185		17,074 [d]
1942	37,539	15,710		1,339	526,781	130,899		28,511
1943	36,365	15,464		1,346	556,204	137,168		31,271
1944	36,224	14,905		1,478	563,941	137,914		33,705
1945	36,042	14,939		1,486	571,653	136,263		34,210
1946	36,925	15,353		1,484	584,287	140,627		35,003
1947	38,361	17,128		1,485	587,334	142,729		36,582
1948	38,865	18,172		1,489	595,673	152,845		37,187
1949	38,489	20,396	75 [e]	1,486	583,748	178,133	1,675 [e]	37,344
1950	36,607	23,174	1,104	1,548	537,727	209,485	20,105	37,290
1951	35,909	25,230	1,416	1,504	504,646	214,568	25,430	36,669
1952	35,111	25,586	1,295	1,504	478,561	218,067	24,100	37,113
1953	32,581	25,108	1,589	1,476	442,270	216,470	26,313	35,971
1954	30,397	25,596	2,775	1,453	396,913	211,209	42,660	33,621
1955	29,640	25,761	2,947	1,470	383,861	211,728	45,083	34,371

SOURCE: *Glasgow Corporation Transport Department.*

(*a*) 11 months.
(*b*) 6 months.
(*c*) Underground opened, 1924.
(*d*) Bomb damage.
(*e*) 2 months.

TABLE 56

Numbers Killed and Injured in Traffic Accidents in Glasgow, 1928-1955

	Killed	Injured		Killed	Injured		Killed	Injured		Killed	Injured
1928	126	4,543	1935	123	5,413	1942	241	3,648	1949	111	2,730
1929	148	4,825	1936	123	4,647	1943	193	3,041	1950	109	2,807
1930	180	5,552	1937	120	4,165	1944	180	2,854	1951	97	2,645
1931	135	5,401	1938	115	4,444	1945	139	2,766	1952	92	2,371
1932	116	5,023	1939	215	4,452	1946	119	2,781	1953	108	2,969
1933	114	5,309	1940	260	4,394	1947	125	2,934	1954	115	3,059
1934	125	5,710	1941	258	4,150	1948	97	2,608	1955	109	3,198

Source: *Annual Reports of Chief Constable.*

TABLE 57

Road Casualties by Class of Persons

Class of Persons	Killed				Injured			
	1938	1953	1954	1955	1938	1953	1954	1955
Pedestrians	88	83	95	79	2,584	1,381	1,543	1,483
Pedal Cyclists	9	5	6	7	541	266	248	276
Motor Cyclists	2	0	2	6	80	143	133	195
Motor Drivers	1	6	2	3	158	175	216	233
Passengers	15	13	8	13	985	976	891	975
Drivers and Passengers[1] of Horse-drawn Vehicles	0	—	—	—	75	—	—	—
Pillion Passengers ..	0	1	2	1	21	28	28	36
Total	115	108	105	109	4,444	2,969	3,059	3,198

Source: *Annual Reports of Chief Constable for Glasgow.*

[1] *This class omitted from Police returns after 1949.*

TABLE 58

ROAD CASUALTIES BY AGE OF PERSONS

Age Group	*Killed*				*Injured*			
	1938	1953	1954	1955	1938	1953	1954	1955
Under 5 ..	14	12	14	17	325	247	202	206
5 to 9 ..	14	25	14	12	718	453	465	475
10 ,, 14 ..	13	5	4	6	465	277	247	256
15 ,, 19 ..	6	4	5	5	501	246	288	311
20 ,, 29 ..	6	3	5	6	578	434	427	485
30 ,, 39 ..	9	6	5	8	610	295	319	342
40 ,, 49 ..	9	10	8	10	430	336	356	391
50 ,, 54 ..	12	4	5	5	179	155	177	171
55 ,, 59 ..	4	7	6	7	145	116	125	154
60 ,, 64 ..	5	3	9	6	199	127	132	119
65 ,, 69 ..	5	7	9	5	143	98	100	102
70 ,, 74 ..	9	9	10	12	95	97	110	84
75 ,, 79 ..	6	11	11	6	40	57	67	58
80 and over ..	3	2	10	4	16	31	44	44
Totals ..	115	108	115	109	4,444	2,969	3,059	3,198

SOURCE: *Annual Reports of Chief Constable for Glasgow.*

TABLE 59 (a)

Glasgow Harbour—Development of Quays and Docks from 1792 to 1852

Date	*Locality*	*Length of Quays in Yards*	*Area of Harbour in Acres*
Unknown	Glasgow Bridge to Robertson Street ..	262	2½
1792	Glasgow Bridge to York Street	382	4
1814	Glasgow Bridge to Royalty Burn ..	697	7
1823	Glasgow Bridge to Clyde Street	865	9
1827	Glasgow Bridge to Hyde Park Recess ..	1,114	11
1828	Temporary Wharf, South Side, added to West Street ..	1,543 (N[1] 1,114) (S[2] 429)	14
1837	New Quay on South Side in place of temporary one there, and near Glasgow Bridge to Hyde Park Recess	(N. 1,107) 1,512 (S. 405)	17
1838	Windmill Croft Quay added	1,847 (N. 1,107) (S. 740)	21
1840	Hyde Park Quay added	1,973 (N. 1,233) (S. 740)	23
1844	Lancefield Quay added, also Upper Harbour Quay and Stairs, and part of Springfield Bank removed	2,322 (N. 1,582) (S. 740)	33
1848	Finnieston Quay added, also temporary Wharf at Springfield	2,819 (N. 1,879) (S. 940)	39
1849	Part of Springfield Quay added	3,019 (N. 1,879) (S. 1,140)	42
1850	Remainder of Springfield Quay added, and the temporary Wharf removed ..	3,391 (N. 1,879) (S. 1,512)	49
1851	Mavisbank temporary Wharf added ..	3,591 (N. 1,879) (S. 1,712)	51
1852	The Upper Harbour Quay, 100 feet added this year	3,624 (N. 1,912) (S. 1,712)	52

Source: *John F. Ure: Report on the Extension of the Harbour of Glasgow* (1854).

[1] N=North side of river.
[2] S=South side of river.

TABLE 59 (b)

Extension of Quays & Docks, 1860-1955

Date	*Length in yards*		*Date*	*Length in yards*	
1860	4,376		1910	18,620	
1870	5,604		1920	19,284	
1880	7,464		1930	19.106	
1890	10,956		1931	21,180	*King George V Dock opened.*
1900	15,109		1940	21,102	
1907	16,072	*Rothesay Dock Opened*	1950	21,546	
1908	17,404	*Yorkhill Quays & Basins opened.*	1955	21,546	

Source: *Clyde Navigation Trust.*

TABLE 60

Number and Net Tonnage of Ships Registered at Glasgow, 1810-1954

Year	*No. of Ships*	*Net Tonnage*	*Year*	*No. of Ships*	*Net Tonnage*	*Year*	*No. of Ships*	*Net Tonnage*
1810	24	1,956	1870	892	428,262	1930	1,164	1,617,568
1820	77	6,131	1880	1,207	776,780	1938	1,060	1,371,433
1830	217	39,432	1890	1,571	1,274,021	1953	710	874,485
1840	403	185,707	1900	1,605	1,582,229	1954	703	840,896
1850	507	137,909	1910	1,729	2,026,954			
1860	660	212,028	1920	1,169	1,461,990			

Source: *Annual Returns relating to the Navigation and Shipping of the United Kingdom, and information supplied by H.M. Customs, Glasgow.*

TABLE 61

Number and Tonnage of Ships arriving at the Harbour of Glasgow, 1831-1955

Year Ending June 30

Year	*Sailing Ships*		*Steam Vessels*		*Total*	
	No.	*Tons*	*No.*	*Tons*	*No.*	*Tons*
1831	4,005	186,576	7,537	545,751	11,542	732,327
1841	5,785	314,262	9,421	828,111	15,206	1,142,373
1851	6,212	424,785	11,062	1,021,821	17,274	1,446,606
1861	4,804	474,740	11,281	1,029,480	16,085	1,504,220
1871	3,087	461,009	12,713	1,588,699	15,800	2,049,708
1881	1,948	369,563	15,815	2,687,970	17,763	3,057,533
1891	1,280	239,334	14,855	3,135,775	16,135	3,375,109
1901	585	108,641	14,696	4,276,782	15,281	4,385,423
1911	393	71,780	16,316	6,097,166	16,709	6,168,946
1921	45	9,145	9,668	4,573,093	9,713	4,582,238
1931	295	7,110	12,558	6,637,926	12,853	6,645,036
1941[1]	11	1,510	10,453	6,458,581	10,464	6,460,091
1946					8,109	4,774,765
1951					8,119	6,127,140
1952					8,076	6,194,140
1953					7,707	6,397,761
1954					7,882	6,606,394
1955					8,996	7,408,000

Source: *Figures up to 1901 from Marwick,* The River Clyde (1909), *Appendix Table III, pp. 239-40, 1911 onwards—Clyde Navigation Trust.*

[1] 1941 was the last year in which sailing ships were separately enumerated.

TABLE 62

AIR TRANSPORT. PASSENGER, FREIGHT AND MAIL STATISTICS

Renfrew Airport

(Dashes indicate not available)

	Pas-sengers	Freight (Short tons)	Mail (Short tons)		Pas-sengers	Freight (Short tons)	Mail (Short tons)
1947	77,000	—	—	March ..	16,318	81.2	46.0
1948	107,000	—	—	April ..	22,868	108.0	46.0
1949	133,000	349	—	May ..	23,209	138.2	46.7
1950	138,000	410	—	June ..	32,459	445.3[1]	254.5[1]
1951	139,500	496	—	July ..	47,555	88.9	27.4
1952	160,000	493	340	August ..	40,857	92.6	32.6
1953	210,000	770	354	September	33,080	112.2	30.7
1954	258,000	969	456	October ..	24,676	120.5	38.9
1955 (Total)	306,000	1569	685	November	18,918	109.2	36.1
January ..	13,279	60.6	45.6	December	19,474	124.1	44.7
February	12,881	81.9	46.0				

SOURCE: *Ministry of Transport and Civil Aviation.*

[1] The high figures of freight and mail traffic for June, 1955, are due to diversions of traffic to special air services during the railway strike.

TABLE 63

GLASGOW POST OFFICES, STAFF AND SERVICES

Selected Dates, 1906-1955

Numbers of	1906	1913	1920	1938	1954	1955
Post Offices	142	151	153	199	247	254
Total Staff (including Telephonists)	3,214	4,020	4,214	4,975	6,791	6,957
Telephonists	—	—	—	1,893	2,083	1,795
	1905/6	1912/13	1919/20	1937/38	1953/54	1954/55
Letters posted (000s) ..	143,748	181,776	164,004	226,756	262,247	263,735
Letters delivered (000s) ..	130,802	148,749	160,862	233,005	291,803	275,557
Letters in transit (000s) ..	50,076	55,948	70,309	84,550	83,642	89,112
Parcels posted (000s) ..	3,307	4,013	4,469	4,754	6,241	6,549
Parcels delivered (000s) ..	2,138	3,055	3,063	3,389	4,926	6,508
Parcels in transit (000s) ..	1,873	2,595	2,501	3,445	6,915	7,571
Telegrams handed in ..	—	—	—	—	1,210,790	940,997
Telegrams delivered ..	—	—	—	—	1,239,140	981,364
Telephones (Exchange connections)				59,450	107,946	187,280
Calls (000s)	—			80,000	164,400	170,276

SOURCE: *Head Postmaster, Glasgow.*

TABLE 64

BROADCAST RECEIVING LICENCES ISSUED IN RESPECT OF GLASGOW POSTAL AREA. 1946—1955[1]

Dec.	*Radio only*	*Radio & Tele-vision*	*Car Radio*	*Total*
1946	292,386	—	29	292,415
1947	292,981	—	57	293,038
1948	298,761	—	109	298,870
1949	301,609	—	134	301,743
1950	303,115	—	2,490	305,605
1951	301,035	34	2,803	303,872
1952	312,356	14,195	4,181	330,732
1953	309,740	40,839	4,235	354,814
1954	263,855	68,911	4,930	337,696
1955	252,348	100,764	4,710	357,822

SOURCE: *Head Postmaster, Glasgow.*

[1] Local records relating to the period before 1946 have not been preserved.

PART III: PUBLIC ADMINISTRATION & SERVICES

SECTION 1

Parliamentary and Municipal Government

TABLE 65

OCCUPATIONS OF GLASGOW TOWN COUNCILLORS, 1900, 1914, 1920, 1955

	1900	1914	1920	1955
Large Manufacturers and Owners				
Shipbuilders	2	1	—	—
Ironfounders	2	1	—	—
Shipowners	3	4	2	—
Coach-builders	2	—	—	—
Coal-master	1	—	—	—
Others and unspecified	10	12	13	2
Merchants				
Provisions	3	4	2	—
Grain and Flour	4	1	—	—
Wine and Spirit	1	—	1	2
Coal	1	2	—	—
Others and unspecified	11	15	7	7
Professions				
Doctors	4	4	3	2
Accountants	3	3	4	4
Solicitors	1	8	12	5
Others	1	3	5	3
Miscellaneous				
Secretaries and Organisers	1	7	12	15
Insurance Agents, etc.	1	5	7	12
Small Shop-keepers and Shop Assistants	10	21	15	8
Industrial Employees	9	15	16	11
Housewives	—	—	—	6
Others	3	5	12	36

SOURCE: *Town Council Diaries.*

The occupational descriptions are those given by the councillors themselves and are sometimes vague. Doubtful cases are grouped under " others."

TABLE 66

Municipal Election Returns, 1920-1938, and 1945, 1947, 1955

Numbers of Wards with Various Percentage Polls

Year	*Unop-posed*	*Under* 20%	20+ to 30%	30+ to 40%	40+ to 50%	50+ to 60%	60+ to 70%	70+ to 80%	80+ %
1920	4/37				1	3	13	16	
1921	7/37					9	19	2	
1922	13/37			1		1	12	10	
1923	10/37				1	15	11		
1924	5/37				2	11	18	1	
1925	8/37				1	17	9	2	
1926	11/37				3	12	11		
1927	8/37				5	12	12		
1928	6/37				7	17	6	1	
1929	10/37	1 [a]		5	16	4			1
1930	3/37			1	6	22	4		
1931	7/37			2	7	14	7		
1932	8/38			2	6	18	3		
1933	4/38				4	15	15		
1934	2/38				1	18	17		
1935	6/38			1	6	20	5		
1936	8/38			1	11	15	3		
1937	5/38			2	5	24	2		
1938	3/38		1	5	22	7			
1945	7/38		3	11	14	3			
1947	2/38		1	2	11	18	4		
1955	2/38	2	9	11	13	1			

Source: *The Glasgow Herald*

(*a*) Abortive Communist attempt to challenge Labour in Gorbals. The Communist candidate polled only 201 votes.

TABLE 67

Glasgow Parliamentary Elections, 1950, 1951, 1955

Electors and Votes Cast—by Constituencies

Constituency	1950			1951			1955		
	No. of Electors	*No. of Votes Cast*	%	*No. of Electors*	*No. of Votes Cast*	%	*No. of Electors*	*No. of Votes Cast*	%
Bridgeton ..	44,382	34,125	76.9	43,570	33,485	76.9	53,733	35,470	66.0
Cathcart ..	44,859	37,594	83.8	44,881	37,037	82.5	45.969	34,779	75.7
Central ..	36,739	27,203	74.0	36,379	27,043	74.3	42,068	26,981	64.1
Gorbals ..	53,859	41,609	77.3	53,795	40,910	76.1	56,627	36,897	65.2
Govan	49,189	41,336	84.0	49,025	41,631	84.9	55,743	40,034	71.8
Hillhead ..	46,455	38,173	82.2	46,238	38,013	82.2	40,802	29,754	68.0
Kelvingrove ..	38,899	30,640	78.8	38,472	30,243	78.6	39,672	26,820	67.6
Maryhill ..	44,903	35,924	80.0	45,032	36,344	80.7	48,197	33,710	69.9
Pollok ..	54,688	44,463	81.3	62,961	51,923	82.5	51,800	32,105	75.5
Scotstoun ..	49,010	41,460	84.6	49,814	42,369	85.3	46,370	36,880	79.5
Shettleston ..	51,801	41,402	79.9	52,267	42,430	81.2	53,533	37,109	69.3
Springburn ..	55,756	42,886	76.9	57,019	44,497	78.0	40,537	28,021	69.1
Woodside ..	43,728	35,046	80.1	42,950	34,763	80.9	48,632	35,389	72.8
Camlachie[1] ..	50,515	40,779	80.7	49,732	40,963	82.4			
Tradeston[1] ..	53,711	42,302	78.8	53,404	42,737	80.0			
Craigton[1] ..							48,071	38,030	79.1
Provan[1] ..							41,326	30,886	74.7

Source: *Sheriff Clerk, Lanarkshire.*

[1] Under the Representation of the People Act, 1948, Glasgow was divided, for parliamentary electoral purposes, into the 15 Burgh Constituencies which come first in the table. In 1955 adjustments were made in some boundaries, Camlachie and Tradeston ceased to be constituencies, and Craigton and Provan took their place.

PART III - SECTION 2

Housing Conditions

SINCE the first Census, taken in 1801, changes have taken place in the meaning of terms employed and in the manner of presentation of data, which must be noted for the proper understanding of the tables.

Houses.—Up to the Census of 1841, the meaning of a " house " was left largely to the discretion of the enumerator. For the purposes of the Censuses of 1851, 1861 and 1871 a house was to be understood as " all the space within the external and party walls of a building." This (English) definition was found to be unsuitable to Scottish conditions, and in the Scottish Census of 1881 every building (*a*) with a distinct outside entrance from a street, court, lane, road, etc., or (*b*) with a door opening directly into a common stair, was deemed a separate house. This definition has remained substantially unaltered to 1951. These changes mean that the numbers of occupied houses for 1851, 1861 and 1871, shown in Table 68, are not comparable with those for earlier and for later years.

Private House.—Since the Census of 1911 a distinction has been drawn for some Census purposes between " private houses " and others. Private houses are those with fewer than twenty-five rooms and accommodating households with fewer than twenty persons.

Rooms.—In reckoning the number of rooms in a house, kitchens are counted as rooms, but not kitchenettes, sculleries, closets, bathrooms, landings or rooms occupied as offices, shops, or for other business purposes. The standards have been consistently applied in previous censuses back to 1881.

TABLE 68

Glasgow

NUMBER OF HOUSES OCCUPIED, UNOCCUPIED AND BUILDING, WITH NUMBER OF FAMILIES OR OCCUPIERS, AND THE POPULATION, 1801-1951

Year	*'Families' or 'Occupiers'*	NUMBER OF HOUSES[1] *Occupied*	*Unoccupied*	*Building*	*Population*	*Area*
1801	20,967	20,276	1,184	—	77,385	City and Suburbs
1811	23,567	17,543	706	72	100,749	City and Suburbs
1821	31,956	31,644	1,917	244	147,043	City and Suburbs
1831	41,965	41,598	1,759	156	202,426	City and Suburbs
1841	35,309	52,441	2,337	529	274,324	City and Suburbs
1851	64,611	11,965[a]	221	140	329,097	Parliamentary Burgh
1861	83,454	13,866[a]	144	176	394,864[b]	Parliamentary Burgh
1871	106,722	14,652[a]	166	205	477,156[b]	Parliamentary Burgh
1881	114,910	106,238	12,264	377	511,415	Municipal Burgh
1891	126,296	117,424	5,170	768	564,981[b]	Municipal Burgh
1901	163,258	155,414	7,279	1,535	761,709	Municipal Burgh
1911	167,896	163,057	20,903	487	784,496	Municipal Burgh
1921	233,808	225,059	11,539	1,409	1,034,174	Municipal Burgh
1931	265,784	256,399	6,465	Not given	1,088,461	Municipal Burgh
1951	307,833[c]	295,472	6,036	Not given	1,089,767	Municipal Burgh

SOURCE: *Census of Scotland*, 1801-1951.

[1] In this table the houses include all residential establishments irrespective of size.

(a) See notes on houses in introduction to this section;

(b) Exclusive of population on board ships in the harbour.

(c) "Separate occupiers"—Defined in 1951 Census.

TABLE 69

Distribution of Families in Houses of Different Size at each Census, 1861 to 1951

Year		*Percentage of Families in Houses with Number of Rooms as under:* 1	2	3	4	5	6 and over	*Total[1] Families*
1861[1]	%	(34.1	39.3)	(12.6	6.4	2.4)		82,842[a]
	%	73.4			21.4		4.8	
1871[1]	%	(41.3	37.2)	(11.2	4.8	1.7)		106,717[a]
	%	78.5			17.7		3.7	
1881[1]	%	(35.6	41.0)	(13.5	5.1	1.6)		114,759[a]
	%	76.6			20.2		3.2	
1891[1]	%	(33.4	42.8)	(14.6	4.8	1.5)		126,262[a]
	%	76.2			20.9		2.9	
1901	%	(26.1	43.6)	(16.6	6.1	2.5)		163,258[a]
	%	69.7			25.2		5.1	
1911	%	(20.0	46.3)	(18.9	6.6	2.8)		162,788[b]
	%	66.3			28.3		5.4	
1921	%	(18.1	48.4)	(19.4	6.1	3.1)		224,826[b]
	%	66.5			28.6		4.9	
1931	%	(14.5	43.6)	(24.0	9.0	4.2)		256,171[b]
	%	58.1			37.2		4.7	
1951	%	(14.7	35.9)	(27.0	15.2	4.3)		306,725[b]
	%	50.6			46.5		2.9	

Source: *Computed from Census of Scotland*, 1911-1951.

(*a*) From 1861 to 1901 all houses are included.

(*b*) From 1911 to 1951 only private houses are included, large establishments, i.e. houses with 25 or more rooms and containing 20 or more persons, being excluded.

[1] In 1861, 1871, 1881 and 1891 there were in addition respectively 241, 3, 1 and 1 families living in houses of one room with no windows. Over 100 of these families were of 3, 4 or 5 persons, and 17 of them were of more—two being of 9 and 10 persons respectively.

TABLE 70

Housing—Rooms and Persons, 1911, 1921, 1931, 1951

Year		*Percentage of persons living in Houses[1] with Number of Rooms as under*						*Total Persons[1]*
		1	2	3	4	5	6 and over	*Number*
1911	%	(13.8	48.7)	(21.2	7.2	2.9)		754,534
	%	62.5			31.3		6.2	
1921	%	(13.2	51.5)	(20.8	6.3	3.0)		998,419
	%	64.7			30.1		5.2	
1931	%	(11.0	44.4)	(25.4	9.6	4.1)		1,053,258
	%	55.4			39.1		5.5	
1951	%	(8.2	33.3)	(28.8	20.1	5.5)		1,054,097
	%	41.5			54.4		4.1	

Source: *Computed from Census of Scotland*, 1861-1951.

[1] Private houses only and persons living in them.

TABLE 71

Persons per 100 Rooms, 1861-1951

	1861	1871	1881	1891	1901	1911	1921	1931	1951
Glasgow City	204	210	194	189	187	185	176.1	153.6	126.8

City Wards, 1951

Shettleston & Tollcross ..	147.5	Park	89.3	Gorbals ..	165.8
Parkhead ..	136.7	Cowcaddens..	171.6	Kingston ..	156.4
Dalmarnock	179.5	Woodside ..	150.6	Kinning Park	140.6
Calton ..	158.4	Ruchill ..	145.8	Govan ..	161.7
Mile-End ..	172.9	North Kelvin	125.7	Fairfield ..	137.7
Dennistoun ..	116.0	Maryhill ..	141.9	Craigton ..	98.5
Provan ..	122.4	Kelvinside ..	68.3	Pollokshields	98.4
Cowlairs ..	159.1	Partick East..	85.4	Camphill ..	83.7
Springburn ..	140.0	Partick West	129.5	Pollokshaws..	130.3
Townhead ..	151.4	Whiteinch ..	108.5	Govanhill ..	122.4
Exchange ..	135.1	Yoker ..	115.1	Langside ..	80.0
Anderston ..	150.5	Knightswood	115.8	Cathcart ..	77.8
		Hutchesontown	181.6		

Source: *Census of Scotland*, 1951.

TABLE 72

Private Houses: Density of Occupation

Percentage of City Population living at the following Densities per Room —at various Years

Year	*Not more than 2*	2-3	3-4	*More than 4*
1951	75.6	16.3	5.1	3.0
1931	57.7	23.4	11.4	7.5
1921	45.9	26.3	16.3	11.5
1911	44.3	27.8	13.7	14.2

Ward Details for 1951

	Not more than 2	2-3	3-4	*More than 4*
Shettleston & Tollcross	72.7	19.5	5.5	2.3
Parkhead	75.1	17.3	5.3	2.3
Dalmarnock	56.8	25.1	10.4	7.7
Calton	62.8	23.6	9.1	4.5
Mile-End	59.2	25.3	9.2	6.3
Dennistoun	83.8	12.3	2.6	1.3
Provan	82.7	13.9	2.9	0.5
Cowlairs	67.8	21.7	7.0	3.5
Springburn	81.4	14.1	3.3	1.2
Townhead	67.6	21.5	7.1	3.7
Exchange	70.6	18.4	7.1	3.9
Anderston	66.8	20.5	7.8	4.9
Park	91.4	6.5	1.3	0.8
Cowcaddens	58.4	25.4	9.9	6.3
Woodside	63.6	21.5	8.3	6.6
Ruchill	75.8	18.6	4.2	1.4
North Kelvin	73.2	17.8	5.7	3.3
Maryhill	72.0	19.8	5.9	2.3
Kelvinside	98.0	1.6	0.4	0.0
Partick East	91.6	6.5	1.4	0.5

	Not more than 2	2-6	3-4	*More than 4*
Partick West	70.4	17.1	6.9	5.6
Whiteinch	81.7	13.3	3.6	1.4
Yoker	89.9	9.0	1.1	0.0
Knightswood	89.6	9.4	0.6	0.4
Hutcheson-town	55.8	25.3	11.2	7.7
Gorbals	58.1	25.2	9.9	6.8
Kingston	64.9	22.1	7.9	5.1
Kinning Park	69.5	19.2	7.1	4.2
Govan	61.4	25.2	8.5	4.9
Fairfield	77.7	16.9	3.9	1.5
Craigton	94.8	4.9	0.3	0.0
Pollokshields	94.3	5.4	0.3	0.0
Camphill	96.5	2.8	0.4	0.3
Pollokshaws	81.5	14.9	2.6	1.0
Govanhill	84.4	12.5	2.3	0.8
Langside	98.6	1.3	0.1	0.0
Cathcart	96.2	3.1	0.5	0.2

Source: *Census of Scotland*, 1951.

TABLE 73

NUMBERS OF PERSONS, AND PROPORTIONS OF TOTAL PERSONS RESIDING IN VARIOUS SIZES OF HOUSE AND AT THE FOLLOWING DENSITIES OF OCCUPATION IN 1861, 1911, 1931 AND 1951

Year	*Persons per Room*				*Total Persons*
	Not more than 2	2-3	3-4	*More than 4*	
In Houses of 1 Room	%	%	%	%	
1861	13.5	17.4	20.1	49.0	105,752
1911	21.0	22.0	22.2	34.8	103,815
1931	21.8	22.1	20.5	35.6	115,490
1951	29.7	24.6	21.7	24.4	86,592
In Houses of 2 Rooms					
1861	28.5	36.0	25.0	10.5	160,363
1911	29.6	33.6	25.0	11.8	367,341
1931	42.8	31.7	17.7	7.8	467,725
1951	65.0	25.0	7.5	2.5	350,739
In Houses of 3 Rooms					
1861	59.0	36.9	3.3	0.8	52,372
1911	56.2	33.2	9.7	0.9	160,083
1931	72.0	22.6	4.9	0.5	267,814
1951	85.2	12.3	2.2	0.3	303,332
In Houses of 4 Rooms					
1861	78.9	19.0	1.8	0.3	29,137
1911	82.4	16.2	1.4	—	54,238
1931	89.1	10.1	0.8	—	101,191
1951	89.7	9.4	0.9	—	212,016
In Houses of 5 Rooms					
1861	90.9	8.2	0.9	—	11,431
1911	95.0	5.0	—	—	21,961
1931	97.2	2.8	—	—	43,584
1951	91.0	9.0	—	—	57,855

SOURCE: *Calculated from information in Census of Scotland,* 1861, 1911, 1931 *and* 1951.

TABLE 74

Private Houses

Proportions of Houses of Different Size and of Persons Living in Them

By Wards: 1951

		Houses with Rooms as under:				*Total Number*
		1	2	3-5	6 *and over*	
		%	%	%	%	
Glasgow City	Houses	11.0	36.3	49.8	3.4	294,467
	Persons	8.2	33.3	54.4	4.1	1,054,097
Ward						
Shettleston and Tollcross ..	Houses	10.5	35.3	53.5	0.7	10,940
	Persons	7.2	31.0	61.1	0.7	42,442
Parkhead	Houses	9.6	38.3	51.0	1.1	5,755
	Persons	6.6	33.9	58.1	1.4	20,957
Dalmarnock	Houses	29.8	52.9	17.2	0.1	11,893
	Persons	24.6	52.4	22.9	0.1	40,592
Calton	Houses	19.6	48.6	30.6	1.2	6,971
	Persons	13.2	48.1	36.4	2.3	24,696
Mile-End	Houses	22.9	55.0	22.1	0.0	11,199
	Persons	18.5	53.1	28.3	0.1	39,745
Dennistoun	Houses	6.1	32.3	59.2	2.4	8,070
	Persons	4.7	27.3	64.7	3.3	26,825
Provan	Houses	2.5	7.1	88.9	1.5	5,618
	Persons	1.1	5.2	92.0	1.7	22,806
Cowlairs	Houses	17.7	57.3	24.8	0.2	7,964
	Persons	13.8	54.0	32.2	0.0	26,769
Springburn	Houses	7.7	28.1	63.1	1.1	7,819
	Persons	4.8	21.5	72.7	1.0	32,903
Townhead	Houses	14.9	53.0	31.6	0.5	9,561
	Persons	11.0	50.2	37.9	0.9	32,956
Exchange	Houses	13.1	38.0	46.4	2.5	4,600
	Persons	8.4	36.0	51.6	4.0	16,607
Anderston	Houses	12.2	49.6	36.7	1.5	8,285
	Persons	9.2	47.2	41.1	2.5	30,108
Park	Houses	4.5	14.7	66.4	14.4	6,128
	Persons	2.4	12.0	64.8	20.8	21,572
Cowcaddens	Houses	19.0	59.0	21.8	0.2	7,483
	Persons	14.8	58.6	26.1	0.5	26,734
Woodside	Houses	19.2	55.6	22.7	2.5	7,736
	Persons	15.8	55.3	23.4	5.5	26,226

Ward		Houses with Rooms as under:				Total Number
		1	2	3-5	6 and over	
		%	%	%	%	
Ruchill	Houses Persons	5.0 3.1	25.2 20.0	69.5 76.6	0.3 0.3	10,684 45,093
North Kelvin	Houses Persons	14.6 12.0	49.8 49.6	31.0 32.0	4.6 6.4	8,069 25,598
Maryhill	Houses Persons	8.6 6.3	48.3 43.4	41.6 48.6	1.5 1.7	6,846 24,466
Kelvinside	Houses Persons	7.6 3.5	12.3 10.2	62.5 61.6	17.6 24.7	6,525 18,573
Partick East	Houses Persons	6.6 3.4	16.6 15.2	61.9 61.1	14.9 20.3	6,875 21,977
Partick West	Houses Persons	14.0 13.7	53.7 54.4	28.4 27.2	3.9 4.7	8,392 26,646
Whiteinch	Houses Persons	5.2 4.1	38.6 36.6	50.1 52.7	6.1 6.6	6,765 22,944
Yoker	Houses Persons	0.1 0.0	11.9 8.9	86.9 90.1	1.1 1.0	7,772 29,858
Knightswood	Houses Persons	6.2 0.1	3.5 2.5	95.2 96.3	1.1 1.1	4,331 17,313
Hutchesontown	Houses Persons	31.1 26.3	57.7 59.6	11.2 14.1	0.0 0.0	9,407 30,917
Gorbals	Houses Persons	17.1 12.6	45.7 43.2	36.2 41.8	1.0 2.4	9,291 36,289
Kingston	Houses Persons	16.0 12.2	45.4 43.3	38.1 43.5	0.5 1.0	7,262 26,609
Kinning Park	Houses Persons	11.9 9.8	53.1 52.3	32.7 34.7	2.3 3.2	8,007 27,413
Govan	Houses Persons	13.6 10.2	51.7 48.4	34.0 40.2	0.7 1.2	9,044 34,716
Fairfield	Houses Persons	9.4 6.5	45.7 41.6	44.7 51.6	0.2 0.3	6,613 23,177
Craigton	Houses Persons	0.3 0.2	1.7 1.1	93.7 94.6	4.3 4.1	10,499 40.098
Pollokshields	Houses Persons	0.6 0.3	3.0 1.9	83.0 85.6	13.4 12.2	8,667 37,591
Camphill	Houses Persons	3.0 1.8	20.2 17.7	69.5 70.4	7.3 10.1	7,668 22,055
Pollokshaws	Houses Persons	5.3 3.1	15.4 10.9	76.0 83.3	3.3 2.7	8,691 38,797

(Continued overleaf)

TABLE 74 (*Continued*)

Ward		Houses with Rooms as under:				Total Number
		1	2	3-6	6 and over	
Govanhill	Houses	2.8	50.4	46.5	0.3	8,272
	Persons	2.3	46.5	50.6	0.6	25,954
Langside	Houses	0.9	8.9	82.2	8.0	7,830
	Persons	0.5	6.8	81.9	10.8	24,462
Cathcart	Houses	1.1	18.8	65.4	14.7	6,935
	Persons	0.8	16.6	65.5	17.1	21,613

SOURCE: *Census of Scotland*, 1951.

TABLE 75

1935 Overcrowding[1] Survey

Overcrowded Fit Houses in Municipal Wards

Municipal Ward	*Actual Number of Fit Houses found Overcrowded*	*Number of Overcrowded Fit Houses as Percentage of Total Fit Houses in Ward*
1. Shettleston & Tollcross	3,560	32.0
2. Parkhead	3,980	43.7
3. Dalmarnock	4,085	54.6
4. Calton	2,193	39.6
5. Mile-End	2,357	52.9
6. Whitevale	2,039	40.0
7. Dennistoun	1,264	19.4
8. Provan	2,746	29.6
9. Cowlairs	2,044	36.5
10. Springburn	1,814	35.2
11. Townhead	1,955	34.5
12. Exchange	1,076	36.9
13. Blythswood	506	23.5
14. Anderston	1,871	36.9
15. Sandyford	901	27.5
16. Park	436	11.5
17. Cowcaddens	3,174	43.3
18. Woodside	2,574	36.2
19. Ruchill	3,435	31.0
20. North Kelvin	1,445	28.2
21. Maryhill	2,134	32.3
22. Kelvinside	121	3.5
23. Partick (East)	1,837	30.4
24. Partick (West)	1,664	28.0
25. Whiteinch	1,687	23.1
26. Hutchesontown ..	4,544	48.1
27. Gorbals	3,075	37.7
28. Kingston	2,526	39.7
29. Kinning Park	3,155	38.5
30. Govan	3,158	38.6
31. Fairfield	2,521	31.0
32. Pollokshields	351	4.5
33. Camphill	339	6.8
34. Pollokshaws	1,069	19.2
35. Govanhill	1,925	23.1
36. Langside	248	5.6
37. Cathcart	465	6.1
38. Yoker and Knightswood	678	9.0
	74,952	30.3 (Average)

Source: *Corporation Housing Department. "Review of Operations, 1919-1947," p.* 82.

[1] For 1935 overcrowding standard, see Chap. 14 (Housing), p. 464.

TABLE 76

GLASGOW, 1935, OVERCROWDING SURVEY (UNDER HOUSING (SCOTLAND) ACT, 1935)

(*Italicised figures represent overcrowded families*)

Number of "Adults" in Family	*Number of Families Occupying Number of Apartments as under:*							*Totals*
	Half	1	2	3	4	5	6 & over	
1	*16*	8,182	6,134	1,845	735	229	36	17,177
1½	—	329	245	42	12	3	—	631
2	*12*	13,173	25,674	12,431	5,354	1,317	168	58,129
2½	*5*	*6,617*	10,012	4,090	1,629	261	17	22,631
3	*9*	*6,694*	23,111	13,512	5,331	1,594	273	50,524
3½	*2*	*2,523*	*7,125*	3,798	1,000	286	29	14,763
4	*1*	*2,027*	*14,214*	11,755	4,623	1,466	247	34,333
4½	—	*868*	*4,673*	3,164	811	213	30	9,759
5	—	*791*	*7,991*	7,788	3,283	935	173	20,961
5½	*1*	*367*	*3,140*	*2,218*	639	129	17	6,511
6		*286*	*4,099*	*4,268*	2,067	495	133	11,348
6½		*129*	*1,737*	*1,396*	529	85	21	3,897
7		*92*	*1,824*	*1,951*	1,210	238	87	5,402
7½		*35*	*805*	*665*	353	50	17	1,925
8		*17*	*673*	*808*	*607*	155	58	2,318
8½		*13*	*269*	*305*	*215*	22	8	832
9		*10*	*215*	*314*	*274*	64	31	908
9½		*1*	*81*	*101*	*89*	23	10	305
10		*1*	*57*	*101*	*85*	29	15	288
10+		*1*	*26*	*72*	*98*	*32*	25	254
Total Families ..	46	42,156	112,105	70,624	28,944	7,626	1,395	262,896
Families overcrowded owing to number of occupants	*46*	*20,472*	*46,929*	*12,199*	*1,368*	*32*	*1*	*81,047*
Families overcrowded owing to factor of sex-separation ..	—	*1,062*	—	—	—	—	—	*1,062*
Overcrowded Families Totals ..	*46*	*21,534*	*46,929*	*12,199*	*1,368*	*32*	*1*	*82,109*
Percentage Total Families	*100*	*51.6*	*42.8*	*18.2*	*5.3*	*0.9*	*1.7*	*31.3*

SOURCE: *Corporation Housing Department.*

Note: Survey limited to houses not exceeding £45 rental per annum, i.e. 259,769 out of a total of 276,130 in the City at 1935 or 94.1 % of total.

TABLE 77

OVERCROWDING IN GLASGOW, 1951 (1944 STANDARD OF OCCUPANCY)[1]

(Italicised figures represent overcrowded houses)

Number of Persons in each House	Private Houses with Number of Rooms as under: 1	2	3	4	5	6	7	8	9	10 & over	Total Private Houses
1	*8,575*	11,920	5,221	1,960	800	241	101	41	19	29	28,907
2	*8,450*	26,824	18,092	7,428	3,229	1,012	497	229	106	118	65,985
3	*7,086*	*25,965*	20,350	8,711	3,132	998	564	263	146	166	67,381
4	*4,687*	*21,081*	18,050	9,365	2,461	850	514	272	148	161	57,589
5	*2,049*	*11,144*	*10,310*	7,905	1,420	549	369	164	126	144	34,180
6	*958*	*5,371*	*5,384*	5,242	890	281	197	138	101	121	18,683
7	*418*	*2,471*	*2,817*	*3,387*	614	178	98	82	71	66	10,202
8	*147*	*1,097*	*1,397*	*1,940*	476	88	57	33	30	59	5,324
9	*70*	*526*	*710*	*1,047*	*339*	68	33	28	26	45	2,892
10	*25*	*246*	*366*	*564*	*247*	35	25	14	14	27	1,563
11	*9*	*87*	*175*	*282*	*149*	*23*	18	9	9	26	787
12	*2*	*40*	*92*	*117*	*103*	*10*	11	6	5	25	411
13	*1*	*16*	*32*	*63*	*76*	*8*	*3*	5	6	10	220
14	–	*3*	*22*	*34*	*39*	*3*	*12*	5	3	8	129
15 & over	–	*3*	*8*	*34*	*53*	*34*	*11*	*17*	17	37	214
Total occupied private houses	32,477	106,794	83,026	48,079	14,028	4,378	2,510	1,306	827	1,042	294,467
No. of houses overcrowded	*32,477*	*68,050*	*21,313*	*7,468*	*1,006*	*78*	*26*	*17*	–	–	*130,435*
Percentage overcrowded	*100*	*63.7*	*25.6*	*15.5*	*7.1*	*1.7*	*1.0*	*1.3*	–	–	*44.2*

SOURCE: *Calculated from 1951 Census figures by the application of the 1944 Standard of Occupancy.*

[1] For definition of 1944 Standard see Chap. 14 (Housing) pp. 467-8

TABLE 78

Household Amenities, 1951

Use	Piped Water Supply Within House		Water Closet		Fixed Bath	
	Number and Percentage of Households having					
	Number	%	Number	%	Number	%
Exclusive ..	282,404	92.0	191,506	62.4	135,277	44.1
Shared	24,243	7.9	114,960	37.5	17,786	5.8
None	178	0.1	359	0.1	153,762	50.1
Total Households	306,825	100.0	306,825	100.0	306,825	100.0

Source: *Census of Scotland*, 1951.

PART III - SECTION 3

Municipal Housing

HOUSES built by the Corporation fall into three groups on the basis of rentals charged. These are:—

1. *Rehousing*

The houses in this group have very low rentals made possible by the high subsidies given under certain Acts. They are provided (*a*) for persons to be rehoused from slum clearance schemes or (*b*) for those who require houses and whose incomes are below a fixed minimum. They are built under the provisions of the various Housing Acts dealing with Slum Clearance.

2. *Ordinary*

These are let at much higher rents, being built to meet the general housing needs of the community, namely:—

(*a*) In homeless families.
(*b*) In overcrowded families.
(*c*) In the case of occupants who are not eligible for houses in Rehousing Schemes but are nevertheless in unfit houses.
(*d*) Where change of house is justified on medical grounds, as certified by the M.O., or where changed conditions call for special consideration.
(*e*) In a percentage of newly married couples.

3. *Intermediate*

These are houses with intermediate rentals, made necessary because of the existence of applicants not eligible for re-housing but yet unable to pay ordinary rents. They are normally let only to over crowded families of four or more persons subject to an agreed limit on family income.

TABLE 79

HOUSES BUILT IN GLASGOW, 1919-1955

	Permanent	Temporary
1. By Corporation	86,056	2,550
2. By private enterprise		
(*a*) With financial assistance from Corporation	10,235	—
Transferred to City from Lanarkshire, Renfrewshire and Dunbartonshire	184	—
(*b*) Without financial assistance from Corporation	10,404	—
3. By Scottish Special Housing Association	2,012	—
Scottish Veterans' Garden City Association Inc.	40	
British Legion Haig Homes	10	
Total ..	108,941	2,550

SOURCE: *City Architect.*

TABLE 80

Glasgow Corporation

Houses Completed each Year, Permanent and Temporary, 1920-1954

	1 *Apt.*	2 *Apts*	3 *Apts.*	4 *Apts.*	5 *Apts.*	*Houses Completed*	*Total Apartments*
1920	—	—	250	18	—	268	822
1921	—	—	305	51	48	404	1,359
1922	—	—	799	531	240	1,570	5,721
1923	—	162	1,122	833	244	2,361	8,242
1924	—	400	232	137	8	777	2,084
1925	—	324	315	198	86	923	2,815
1926	—	344	1,048	477	79	1,948	6,135
1927	—	428	2,329	859	93	3,709	11,744
1928	—	370	2,372	816	54	3,612	11,390
1929	—	278	4,659	1,379	51	6,367	20,304
1930	—	474	2,098	595	61	3,228	9,927
1931	—	472	1,823	387	3	2,685	7,976
1932	—	190	1,874	350	2	2,416	7,412
1933	33	288	2,079	433	10	2,843	8,628
1934	33	318	3,310	775	3	4,439	13,714
1935	—	762	2,386	774	4	3,926	11,798
1936	33	84	1,384	478	6	1,985	6,295
1937	—	12	1,066	667	96	1,841	6,370
1938	—	—	1,154	1,394	240	2,788	10,238
1939	—	—	771	1,215	201	2,187	8,178
1940	—	—	376	481	123	980	3,667
1941	—	—	271	466	54	791	2,947
1942	—	—	459	539	126	1,124	4,163
1943	—	—	373	446	112	931	3,463
1944	—	—	168	238	78	484	1,846
1945	36	—	176	254	106	572	2,110
1946	—	—	859	760	112	1,731	6,177
1947	—	—	1,548	1,172	124	2,844	9,952
1948	—	—	607	1,989	198	2,794	10,767
1949	—	—	667	2,634	332	3,633	14,197
1950	56	—	708	3,263	108	4,135	15,772
1951	72	—	1,259	2,280	128	3,739	13,609
1952	439	—	1,506	1,328	142	3,415	9,473
1953	124	—	3,073	1,779	166	5,142	17,289
1954	321	—	3,336	2,349	206	6,212	20,755
Totals	1,147	4,906	46,762	32,345	3,644	88,804	297,339
Houses taken over from Counties ..		42	232	98	8	380	1,212
Grand Totals	1,147	4,948	46,994	32,443	3,652	89,184	298,551

Source: *City Architect.*

Includes 2,012 houses built by the Scottish Special Housing Association; 198 war-damaged houses, in the year in which they were originally built and again in the year in which they were rebuilt; 2,550 temporary houses; 12 houses at Edmiston Drive subsided and rebuilt; 2 houses at Knightswood subsided and demolished.

TABLE 81

Glasgow Corporation

Summary of Permanent Houses Erected, 1919 to 1954, under various Acts

Act	*House[1] Purchase*	*Ordinary*	*Inter-mediate*	*Rehousing*	*Total*
1919 Act	—	4,690	—	—	4,690
1923 Act	428	2,052	—	6,546	9,026
1924 Act	—	13,435	8,151	—	21,586
1930-35 Acts	—	868	2,961	8,001	11,830
1938 Act	—	1,754	2,573	212	4,539
1946/50/52 Acts ..	—	32,190	1,114	—	33,304
Unassisted	248	664	169	—	1,081
Totals ..	676	55,653	14,968	14,759	86,056
Scottish Special Housing Association	—	2,012	—	—	2,012
Grand Totals ..	676	57,665	14,968	14,759	88,068

Source: *City Architect.*

[1] Houses taken over by the Corporation.

TABLE 82

Glasgow Corporation

Cost per House, 1919 to 1955. 3- and 4-Apartment Flatted Type (*4 in a Block*)

Year	*3 Apt.*	*4 Apt.*	*Year*	*3 Apt.*	*4 Apt.*	*Year*	*3 Apt.*	*4 Apt.*
1919	£721	£—	1930	£330	£366	1940	£503	£575
1920	823	913	1931	325	360	1941	518	600
1921	847	953	1932	320	358	1943	700	810
1922	507	578	1934	298	327	1944	744	870
1923	392	540	1935	283	318	1945	840	925
1924	425	488	1936	320	365	1946	1,020	1,140
1927	410	461	1937	366	417	1947	1,062	1,249
1928	365	411	1938	400	456	1948	1,230	1,350
1929	345	380	1939	400	456	1949	1,310	1,450

Source: *City Architect.*

Since 1949 changes in types of houses and variations in site conditions make strict comparison of costs impossible. The latest (1955) costs of a typical 3- and a typical 4-apartment house in a 4-storey tenement are approximately £1,400 and £1,550 respectively.

TABLE 83

ASSESSMENTS IMPOSED FOR HOUSING PURPOSES, 1920-1955

Year	*Rateable Value*	*Assessments Imposed for Housing Purposes*	*Representing Assessment per £ of*
1920-21	£8,932,681	£35,584	.98d.
1921-22	9,743,958	41,359	1.04d.
1922-23	9,926,163	37,253	.94d.
1923-24	10,151,003	57,453	1.39d.
1924-25	10,424,040	133,064	3.15d.
1925-26	10,579,818	118,360	2.74d.
1926-27	11,032,431	139,221	3.11d.
1927-28	11,046,963	171,395	3.78d.
1928-29	11,197,954	182,981	3.99d.
1929-30	10,918,908	223,491	4.74d.
1930-31	10,876,988	191,390	4.37d.
1931-32	11,055,202	182,560	4.14d.
1932-33	11,061,528	180,345	4.08d.
1933-34	10,964,530	272,838	6.21d.
1934-35	10,961,962	86,282	1.97d.
1935-36	10,921,212	75,370	1.72d.
1936-37	10,984,365	78,060	1.73d.
1937-38	10,989,189	95,974	2.12d.
1938-39	11,138,431	97,902	2.14d.
1939-40	11,135,298	170,208	3.74d.
1940-41	11,114,386	214,574	4.73d.
1941-42	11,052,492	306,574	6.78d.
1942-43	11,074,722	196,067	4.30d.
1943-44	11,187,533	270,323	5.85d.
1944-45	11,216,832	329,580	7.12d.
1945-46	11,269,814	331,986	7.13d.
1946-47	11,428,681	344,811	7.30d.
1947-48	11,550,941	460,116	9.64d.
1948-49	11,875,152	455,671	9.30d.
1949-50	12,197,855	503,427	10.00d.
1950-51	12,361,475	532,748	10.46d.
1951-52	12,597,612	782,547	1/3.07d.
1952-53	12,934,132	1,196,934	1/10.48d.
1953-54	13,447,764	1,449,872	2/2.21d.
1954-55	14,132,105	1,673,082	2/4.76d.

SOURCE: *City Chamberlain.*

TABLE 84

APPLICATIONS FOR MUNICIPAL HOUSES FROM JANUARY 1, 1945, TO DECEMBER 31, 1955, AND APPLICANTS ACCOMMODATED EACH YEAR[1]

Year	NUMBER OF APPLICATIONS LODGED					No. of Applicants Accommodated
	Houseless	Tenants of Houses		Single Persons about to be Married	Total	
		Over-crowded	Not Over-crowded			
1945	9,073	2,322	1,327	1,654	14,376	1,097
1946	8,377	2,013	1,321	2,393	14,104	2,397
1947	6,834	1,834	953	2,587	12,208	3,670
1948	6,060	1,963	1,058	2,603	11,684	3,685
1949	5,438	2,481	1,347	2,085	11,351	4,991
1950	5,162	1,873	1,496	1,988	10,519	4,532
1951	5,085	1,475	1,949	2,227	10,736	4,734
1952	4,991	1,202	1,916	2,059	10,168	4,913
1953	4,562	1,506	2,173	2,148	10,389	7,210
1954	4,153	1,617	2,914	2,046	10,730	7,431
1955	4,203	1,361	3,466	2,222	11,252	7,219
Total 1945/55	63,938	19,647	19,920	24,012	127,517	51,879
Percentage	50.14	15.41	15.62	18.83	100.00	—

SOURCE: *City Factor.*

[1] The number of applicants accommodated has no relation to the number of applications lodged each year. In 1945 there were 86,000 applicants on the waiting list. By 1949 this figure had risen to approximately 127,000; but in that year a revision of the list and cancellation of applications which were no longer effective reduced the number to 89,100 live applications. Since the revision of 1949 no further revision has been made and the list has continued to grow.

TABLE 85

Glasgow Corporation

(Including Scottish Special Housing Association)

Housing Schemes

(Only the Schemes with 500 houses or more when completed are shown separately. The total number of smaller schemes and of the houses in them are shown at the end of the Table.)

Scheme	*Distance from Glasgow Cross (miles)*	*Period of Construction*	*Total No. of Houses in Scheme when Completed*	*No. of Shops in Scheme when Completed*
North				
Balmore	2½	1927-1930	734	—
Balmore Road	2¼	1931-1934	768	—
East Keppoch	1¾	1932-1934	1,105	—
Hamiltonhill	1¾	1922-1927	728	—
Milton	2¾	1947-1954	2,934	28
North-East				
Balornock	2¼	1925-1938	1,416	9
Balornock & Robroyston[1]	2½-3½	1939-1956	1,570	18
Barmulloch	2½	1949-1954	1,656	7
Blackhill	2½	1933-1938	1,324	5
Germiston	1¾	1927-1932	690	5
Riddrie	2¼	1920-1933	1,074	9
East				
Barlanark	4	1951-1954	2,322	16
Barrowfield	1¼	1939-1947	590	—
Carntyne and Carntyne South	2½	1927-1950	3,877	19
Cranhill	3	1949-1954	2,289	18
Cuthelton Street	2¼	1932-1934	534	—
Easterhouse	4-6	1955-1959	7,200	71[a]
Garthamlock	4	1953-1957	1,519	8
Greenfield	3	1946-1949	500	6
Haghill	1½	1928-1937	1,176	—
Newbank	2	1923-1927	606	13
Ruchazie	3¼	1952-1955	1,578	14
Shettleston	3½	1926-1929	616	—
Springfield Road ..	1½	1934-1936	628	—
Tollcross	3½	1922-1933	604	5
South				
Castlemilk	3-4	1954-1958	8,596	66[a]
Eastwood	3¾	1949-1955	571	4
Govanhill & Hollybrook Street	1½	1926-1937	979	3
Mansewood	3¾	1949-1956	734	4
Merrylee Road	3	1951-1955	664	4
Toryglen[1]	2	1947-1955	1,963	6

TABLE 85 (*Continued*)

Scheme	*Distance from Glasgow Cross (miles)*	*Period of Constructi on*	*Total No. of Houses in Scheme when Completed*	*No. of Shops in Scheme when Completed*
South-West				
Arden[1]	5	1953-1957	1,356	6
Berryknowes	4	1936-1943	796	6
Broomloan Road ..	2½	1933-1935	516	
Carnwadric and Boydstone Road	4½	1930-1943	1,048	10
Mosspark	3½	1921-1935	1,533	16
Old Nitshill ..	5¾	1957-1959?	1,000?	?
Penilee	5	1940-1948	1,912	7
Pollok Area	4-5	1937-1953	5,052	39
Priesthill Area	5	1932-1952	4,123	25
West Drumoyne	3½	1931-1935	838	7
West				
Blairdardie	5½	1950-1954	589	4[b]
Drumchapel	6	1952-1957	7,480	55[a]
Knightswood Area ..	4½-6	1923-1947	8.989	72
Scotstoun, Scotstoun W. & Queen Victoria Drive	4¾	1924-1937	1,472	—
North-West				
Cadder Road[1]	3	1946-1956	1,058	4
Possil	1¾	1925-1930	584	
Ruchill	2¾	1927-1930	920	10
Schemes with 500 houses or over, as above .. (48)			90,811	
Smaller Schemes (not detailed) .. .. (84)			19,377	
All Schemes .. (132)			110,188	

Of the total of 110,188 houses, 90,961 had been built by December 31, 1955

SOURCE: *City Architect.*

[1] Part of scheme built by Scottish Special Housing Association.
(*a*) Shops partly in suites and partly in centre of scheme.
(*b*) Shops privately built.

PART III - SECTION 4

Health

TABLE 86

STILLBIRTHS REGISTERED[1] 1939 TO 1955

Year	*No.*	*After Correction for Transfers*	*Percentage of all Births (live and still)*	*Year*	*No.*	*After Correction for Transfers*	*Percentage of all Births (live and still)*
1939	1,144	1,009	4.4	1948	809	735	3.2
1940	1,084	963	4.4	1949	716	639	3.0
1941	1,004	945	4.1	1950	682	596	2.9
1942	1,035	942	4.4	1951	646	580	2.8
1943	979	847	3.6	1952	635	572	2.7
1944	901	832	3.6	1953	599	551	2.7
1945	800	730	3.5	1954	675	636	2.9
1946	995	886	3.6	1955	612	578	2.7
1947	973	868	3.2				

SOURCE: *Health and Welfare Department.*

[1] Registration of Stillbirths (Scotland) Act, 1938, came into operation on 1st January, 1939.

TABLE 87

INFANT MORTALITY

NUMBER OF DEATHS UNDER ONE YEAR, BY AGE AT DEATH, AND SEX

FIVE-YEARLY AVERAGES, 1904 TO 1953; AND 1954, 1955

5-Year Period	*Under 4 Weeks*		*4 Weeks and under 3 Months*		*3 Months and under 6 Months*		*6 Months and under 12 Months*		*All Deaths under 1 Year*		*Total*
	M	*F*	*M*	*F*	*M*	*F*	*M*	*F*	*M*	*F*	
1904-8	559	418	332	279	326	267	602	503	1,820	1,466	3,286
1909-13	555	424	307	214	297	226	531	456	1,690	1,320	3,010
1914-18	622	473	not available						1,827	1,469	3,296
1919-23	636	474	291[1]	217[1]	285[1]	222[1]	532[1]	408[1]	1,731	1,309	3,040
1924-28	535	366	232	164	285	197	469	379	1,521	1,105	2,626
1929-33	463	349	225	154	264	186	402	316	1,353	1,005	2,358
1934-38	484	374	226	147	253	173	293	245	1,255	939	2,194
1939-43	495	368	207	151	220	158	181	155	1,103	832	1,935
1944-48	454	339	193	126	177	123	142	106	966	695	1,661
1949-53	283	213	93	67	71	58	49	42	496	381	877
Year											
1954	271	179	68	50	57	44	44	23	440	296	736
1955	287	192	65	59	49	51	28	34	429	336	765

SOURCE: *Health and Welfare Department.*

[1] Average of 4 years, 1920-1923.

TABLE 88

Neo-natal Mortality Rates and Infant Mortality Rates (Per 1,000 Live Births), 1903-1955

Year	Neo-natal Mortality Rates			Infant Mortality Rates				
	Male	*Female*	*All*	*Male*	*Female*	*Legitimate*	*Illegitimate*	*All*
1903	47.7	36.8	42.3	158	128	132	298	146
1913	48.4	37.0	42.8	143	113	121	227	129
1914	51.1	38.5	44.8	145	117	127	211	133
1915	48.7	38.3	43.6	154	130	140	206	143
1916	40.3	35.7	38.1	116	103	105	194	111
1917	45.7	36.2	41.1	143	112	125	169	129
1918	45.3	32.8	39.2	125	95	108	168	113
1919	47.4	34.6	41.1	126	97	110	164	114
1920	44.5	34.0	39.3	115	92	101	181	106
1921	45.8	34.1	40.0	117	92	102	163	105
1922	41.4	34.1	37.8	134	105	116	181	120
1923	38.4	32.1	35.3	99	79	85	163	89
1924	43.2	32.6	38.1	130	104	115	182	119
1925	41.8	27.4	34.8	118	83	99	157	102
1926	44.2	28.6	36.6	118	88	101	157	104
1927	39.1	32.2	35.7	119	95	105	147	107
1928	44.3	32.6	38.6	120	93	102	176	107
1929	42.1	32.3	37.4	118	95	103	165	107
1930	36.7	30.8	33.8	112	89	91	146	101
1931	38.3	33.2	35.8	120	88	99	173	105
1932	40.3	29.5	35.1	122	100	101	169	112
1933	42.1	32.3	37.3	110	82	95	127	96
1934	36.9	29.3	33.2	112	83	97	112	98
1935	48.8	36.0	42.6	111	85	96	112	98
1936	44.9	35.3	40.2	121	97	101	129	109
1937	44.4	40.6	42.6	114	94	97	135	104
1938	39.9	31.5	35.8	99	75	84	139	87
1939	41.6	31.8	36.8	88	72	78	95	80
1940	44.6	34.5	39.6	106	83	92	117	95
1941	54.3	41.6	48.1	125	96	100	148	111
1942	47.8	37.5	42.8	100	79	86	142	90
1943	40.0	33.4	36.8	90	73	78	121	82
1944	49.0	36.1	42.7	107	82	92	127	95
1945	33.3	28.2	30.8	77	59	66	92	68
1946	38.9	30.6	34.8	76	58	65	96	67
1947	38.4	32.4	35.5	87	67	75	103	77
1948	33.0	25.4	29.3	63	47	54	81	56
1949	28.0	22.4	25.3	55	44	48	66	49
1950	27.5	21.5	24.6	48	39	44	44	44
1951	28.6	23.1	25.9	49	43	45	58	46
1952	24.5	23.7	24.1	44	38	40	53	41
1953	26.2	17.9	22.2	40	31	35	55	36
1954	25.0	17.7	21.5	41	29	35	35	35
1955	26.4	19.0	22.8	39	32	36	36	36

Source: *Health and Welfare Department.*

[1] Neo-natal and Infant Mortality Rates = No. of deaths per 1,000 live births in each category.

TABLE 89

INFANT MORTALITY AND 'TODDLER' MORTALITY, SELECTED YEARS, 1900-1955

Year	*Infant Mortality Rate per 1,000 Births*	DEATHS 1-5 YEARS	
		Actual Number	*Rate per 1,000 Population at Ages 1-5 Years*
1900	153	2,754	39.2
1911	139	1,862	26.7
1921	106	1,494	19.2
1931	105	1,341	17.2
1938	87	753	9.8
1943	82	394	5.3
1946	67	276	3.6
1947	77	296	3.7
1948	56	219	2.7
1949	49	203	2.4
1950	44	191	2.2
1951	46	171	2.1
1952	41	140	1.8
1953	36	118	1.5
1954	35	92	1.2
1955	36	99	1.3

SOURCE: *Health and Welfare Department.*

TABLE 90

Infant Mortality Rates: by each of the Eight Major Groups of Causes of Death, 1947-1955

Deaths under one year: per 1,000 births of each sex

Groups of Causes	1947		1948		1949		1950		1951		1952		1953		1954		1955	
	M	*F*	*M*	*F*	*M*	*F*	*M*	*F*	*M*	*F*	*M*	*F*	*M*	*F*	*M*	*F*	*M*	*F*
Immaturity	35	30	33	26	28	22	29	24	31	26	27	25	27	19	27	19	28	22
Diseases of the Respiratory System ..	14	9	8	6	9	7	7	6	6	5	5	4	5	3	4	4	5	5
Diseases of the Digestive System	28	18	14	9	10	6	5	4	4	3	4	2	2	3	3	1	2	2
Diseases of the Nervous System ..	3	2	3	1	2	3	1	0	1	1	1	1	0	0	1	1	–	–
Tuberculous Diseases	1	1	1	1	1	1	1	1	0	1	1	1	0	0	0	0	–	–
Infectious Diseases ..	2	3	–	1	1	1	1	1	1	1	1	1	1	1	1	1	–	–
Suffocation	1	1	1	1														
All Other Causes ..	3	3	3	2	4	4	4	3	6	6	5	4	5	5	5	3	4	3
All Causes ..	87	67	63	47	55	44	48	39	49	43	44	38	40	31	41	29	39	32

Source: *Health and Welfare Department.*

TABLE 91

INFANT MORTALITY BY WARDS; 1930, 1935, 1940 AND 1945, AND ANNUALLY, 1950-1955

Wards before 1948 Reconstitution	*Infant Deaths per 1,000 Births* 1930	'35	'40	'45	*Wards after 1948 Reconstitution*	*Infant Deaths per 1,000 Births* 1950	'51	'52	'53	'54	'55
Whiteinch ..	72	88	76	55	—Whiteinch ..	29	32	37	45	27	28
Partick West	78	84	81	37	—Partick West	41	39	42	27	37	21
Partick East	104	94	99	81	—Partick East	30	24	29	43	16	35
Kelvinside ..	11	80	62	43	—Kelvinside	20	34	19	13	12	33
Knightswood		51	62	47	—Knightswood	43	48	25	30	25	35
					—Yoker ..	41	42	30	30	41	18
Anderston ..	105	123	117	79	—Anderston ..	42	45	44	48	49	42
Park ..	54	108	58	40	—Park ..	46	41	50	36	29	31
Sandyford ..	100	114	89	66							
North Kelvin	81	103	82	44	—North Kelvin	53	28	28	19	32	49
Ruchill ..	96	88	81	63	—Ruchill ..	35	40	34	26	27	49
Springburn	98	85	71	59	—Springburn ..	48	51	21	46	35	37
Cowlairs ..	73	79	74	72	—Cowlairs ..	52	78	37	40	33	31
Provan ..	101	90	90	64	—Provan ..	37	43	48	48	21	45
Townhead ..	87	119	109	93	—Townhead ..	51	42	55	38	41	49
Dennistoun	70	92	91	49	—Dennistoun	50	56	37	36	24	33
Blythswood	124	122	88	89							
Exchange ..	153	171	151	121	—Exchange ..	63	67	43	31	36	59
Calton ..	131	133	118	79	—Calton ..	42	52	20	39	56	42
Mile-End ..	128	101	107	75	—Mile-End ..	58	50	48	51	32	38
Dalmarnock	96	112	124	72	—Dalmarnock	41	48	51	32	47	28
Parkhead ..	104	92	108	78	—Parkhead ..	43	37	29	44	36	48
Shettleston & Tollcross	87	99	82	54	—Shettleston & Tollcross ..	56	51	42	28	31	34
Whitevale ..	126	98	94	99							
Kingston ..	118	110	94	82	—Kingston ..	51	59	51	41	40	36
Kinning Park	89	96	96	67	—Kinning Park	32	41	53	30	41	39
Govan ..	122	95	106	89	—Govan ..	45	42	45	50	26	41
Fairfield ..	84	83	57	46	—Fairfield ..	34	38	49	24	31	29
Pollokshields	66	60	64	41	—Pollokshields	47	42	41	34	26	37
					—Craigton ..	33	38	30	28	28	38
Camphill ..	69	62	41	35	—Camphill ..	25	27	25	31	23	15
Pollokshaws	49	72	66	68	—Pollokshaws	48	57	31	37	42	39
Langside ..	49	45	62	24	—Langside ..	23	33	40	19	28	11
Cathcart ..	50	61	55	23	—Cathcart ..	37	13	15	17	21	25
Maryhill ..	102	64	87	53	Maryhill ..	49	54	47	26	29	31
Woodside ..	103	84	98	94	Woodside ..	46	51	56	39	47	31
Cowcaddens	120	106	121	100	Cowcaddens	34	46	35	41	42	36
Hutchesonto'n	124	106	97	72	Hutchesonto'n	35	46	39	44	37	38
Gorbals ..	128	131	132	113	Gorbals ..	63	54	54	36	55	50
Govanhill ..	83	75	93	51	Govanhill ..	30	32	41	23	24	17
City of Glasgow	101	98	95	68	City of Glasgow	44	46	41	36	35	36

SOURCE: *Health and Welfare Department.*

[1] See Note on reconstitution of Wards, 1948, on p. 785.

TABLE 92 (a)

Male Neo-natal Mortality Rates—per 1,000 Births—by Causes, 1945-1955

Causes	MALES										
	'45	'46	'47	'48	'49	'50	'51	'52	'53	'54	'55
I. Congenital Malformations	2.2	3.3	4.1	2.8	2.9	3.0	3.2	3.5	3.8	4.1	2.8
II. Diseases of Early Infancy:											
(a) Injury at Birth	3.3	3.9	2.3	2.8	3.7	6.0	5.1	4.0	4.8	4.9	4.3
(b) Atelectasis ..	1.7	3.4	2.9	2.6	3.1	5.7	5.4	5.3	5.7	6.1	7.4
(c) Pneumonia of Newborn ..	—	—	—	—	—	—	3.0	1.3	1.4	1.5	1.7
(d) Diarrhoea of Newborn ..	—	—	—	—	—	—	0.6	0.5	0.4	—	0.1
(e) Haemolytic Disease of Newborn (Erythroblastosis)	—	—	—	—	—	—	1.2	1.1	0.8	0.6	0.7
(f) Congenital Debility, Sclerema and Ill-defined Causes ..	3.4	2.2	2.3	0.8	1.3	0.9	0.7	1.1	0.9	0.8	0.3
(g) Premature Birth	16.1	18.9	16.4	18.7	11.8	6.7	7.2	5.9	5.6	4.5	6.9
(h) Others ..	0.9	1.7	1.7	1.4	1.1	4.1	0.9	0.9	1.2	1.4	1.2
III. Diseases of Respiratory System	2.3	3.6	3.8	1.5	2.0	0.1	0.4	—	0.3	—	0.2
IV. Diseases of Digestive System:											
(a) Diarrhoeal ..	1.6	0.9	3.4	1.4	0.7	} 0.3	0.3	0.1	0.2	0.1	0.3
(b) Others	0.2	0.1	—	—	0.1						
V. Diseases of Nervous System	0.7	0.5	0.2	0.5	0.4	0.1	—	0.2	0.1	0.2	—
VI. Tuberculous Diseases	—	—	—	—	—	—	—	—	—	—	—
VII. Infectious Diseases ..	0.2	—	—	—	—	—	—	—	—	—	—
VIII. Syphilis	0.1	—	—	—	—	0.1	0.1	—	—	—	—
IX. Overlaying	—	—	0.4	0.3	0.1	0.1	—	—	—	—	—
X. Other Violence ..	0.1	0.1	0.2	0.1	0.5	—	0.1	0.3	0.8	0.3	0.1
XI. All Other Causes ..	0.5	0.2	0.7	0.3	0.3	0.5	0.5	0.3	0.3	0.5	0.4
All Causes ..	33.3	38.9	38.4	33.0	28.0	27.5	28.6	24.5	26.2	25.0	26.4

Source: *Health and Welfare Department.*

TABLE 92 (*b*)

FEMALE NEO-NATAL MORTALITY RATES—PER 1,000 BIRTHS—BY CAUSES, 1945-1955

	FEMALES										
Causes	'45	'46	'47	'48	'49	'50	'51	'52	'53	'54	'55
I. Congenital Malformations	2.8	3.2	3.4	3.4	2.6	3.2	3.0	4.0	3.5	4.0	3.6
II. Diseases of Early Infancy:											
(*a*) Injury at Birth	1.8	2.3	2.2	1.6	1.9	4.1	4.0	4.1	2.7	1.8	2.5
(*b*) Atelectasis ..	1.1	2.0	2.6	2.0	3.3	3.4	4.3	4.8	4.3	3.9	4.4
(*c*) Pneumonia of Newborn ..	—	—	—	—	—	—	2.4	1.3	0.5	0.4	0.8
(*d*) Diarrhoea of Newborn ..	—	—	—	—	—	—	0.3	0.5	0.1	0.1	—
(*e*) Haemolytic Disease of Newborn (Erythroblastosis)	—	—	—	—	—	—	0.6	0.5	1.0	0.7	0.5
(*f*) Congenital Debility, Sclerema and Ill-defined Causes ..	2.3	1.0	1.7	1.1	0.9	0.9	0.6	0.7	0.2	0.3	0.2
(*g*) Premature Birth	16.1	16.0	14.9	13.0	9.2	5.2	6.0	5.7	4.0	5.0	5.7
(*h*) Others	0.8	0.9	0.9	1.3	0.9	3.9	0.8	0.9	0.6	0.5	0.4
III. Diseases of Respiratory System ..	1.1	3.0	2.7	0.8	1.3	—	0.2	0.1	0.1	0.1	0.1
IV. Diseases of Digestive System:											
(*a*) Diarrhoeal ..	1.1	1.0	2.4	1.2	0.8	} 0.1	—	0.1	0.2	—	0.2
(*b*) Others		0.1	0.2	0.1	0.1						
V. Diseases of Nervous System	0.4	0.1	0.4	0.3	0.4	—	0.1	0.1	—	—	0.1
VI. Tuberculous Diseases	—	—	0.1	—	—	—	—	—	—	—	—
VII. Infectious Diseases ..	0.3	0.1	0.1	—	0.1	—	0.1	—	—	—	—
VIII. Syphilis	—	—	—	—	—	—	—	—	—	—	—
IX. Overlaying	—	0.3	0.2	0.2	—	0.1	—	—	—	—	—
X. Other Violence ..	0.1	0.3	0.2	0.1	0.6	0.2	0.1	0.4	0.2	0.5	0.2
XI. All Other Causes ..	0.2	0.3	0.4	0.3	0.5	0.3	0.6	0.5	0.5	0.4	0.3
All Causes ..	28.1	30. 6	32.4	25.4	22.4	21.5	23.1	23.7	17.9	17.7	19.0

SOURCE: *Health and Welfare Department.*

TABLE 93

Maternal Mortality

Death Rates per 1,000 *Live Births*, 1921-1955

Year	Death Rate	Year	Death Rate	Year	Death Rate
1921	6.39	1933	5.90	1945	3.47
1922	7.60	1934	6.05	1946	2.82
1923	7.08	1935	7.01	1947	2.32
1924	5.84	1936	5.87	1948	1.56
1925	7.63	1937	4.96	1949	1.58
1926	6.68	1938	5.68	1950	1.02
1927	7.21	1939	4.61	1951	0.97
1928	8.79	1940[a]	4.93	1952	1.29
1929	8.33	1941	5.67	1953	1.06
1930	8.57	1942	5.10	1954	0.74
1931	6.37	1943	5.19	1955	0.33
1932	7.87	1944	3.99		

Source: *Health and Welfare Department.*

(*a*) Before 1940, death rates were calculated on live births; since then on all births (live and still).

TABLE 94

Maternal Mortality. Classification by Causes, 1950-1955

Causes	Rates per 1,000 Births (Live and Still)					
	1950	1951	1952	1953	1954	1955
Accidents of Pregnancy	0.24	0.15	0.19	0.29	0.28	0.05
Puerperal Haemorrhage	0.05	0.34	0.48	0.19	0.09	0.09
Puerperal Septicemia, including Post-Abortive Sepsis	0.19	0.24	0.24	0.24	0.14	0.05
Toxaemia of Pregnancy, Albuminaria, Convulsions	0.24	0.05	0.29	0.24	0.18	0.09
Other Puerperal Diseases	0.29	0.19	0.09	0.10	0.05	0.05
Total	1.02	0.97	1.29	1.06	0.74	0.33

Source: *Health and Welfare Department.*

TABLE 95 *(a)*

Infectious Disease. Case Rates per Million, 1935-1941

	1935	1936	1937	1938	1939	1940	1941
A. Notifiable							
Enteric Fever and Paratyphoid ..	169	200	65	52	54	320	73
Puerperal Fever and Pyrexia	775	663	795	747	674	617	285
Scarlet Fever	3,711	3,960	5,153	3,703	2,711	1,715	1,752
Diphtheria and Membranous Croup ..	2,272	899 68	2,143	2,596	2,877	4,751	3,698
Erysipelas	932		955	886	763	600	615
Cerebro-spinal Fever	76	1,801	97	81	74	418	374
Ophthalmia Neonatorum	691	649	732	711	653	565	497
Acute Poliomyelitis ..	2	24	1	38	4	30	43
Acute Polio-Encephalitis	—	—	1	1	—	1	1
Acute Encephalitis Lethargica	13	12	27	7	5	3	6
Acute Primary Pneumonia ..	5,302	5,359	5,391	4,882	3,221	5,049	5,664
Acute Influenzal Pneumonia ..	372	191	517	105	209	282	144
Whooping Cough[1] ..	1,148	3,903	8,018	3,776	5,776	801	10,059
Dysentery	124	220	251	240	149	333	292
Pulmonary Tuberculosis	1,616	1,515	1,522	1,599	1,440	1,747	1,892
Other forms of Tuberculosis ..	620	654	591	640	513	612	605
Other notifiable[2] ..	33	29	35	31	25	53	36
B. Not Notifiable							
Measles	821	18,576	2,090	14,492	1,338	10,095	1,477
German Measles ..	387	1,502	190	447	3,470	598	214
Chickenpox	5,310	6,300	5,727	5,805	3,533	1,874	3,748
Other not Notifiable	63	70	45	42	25	301	119
Totals	30,437	46,595	34,346	40,881	27,514	30,765	31,893

[1] Whooping Cough became notifiable as from 1st January, 1950.

[2] Including Smallpox—26 cases in 1942, 2 in 1945, aud 16 in 1950.

TABLE 95 (*b*)

Infectious Disease. Case Rates per Million, 1942-1948

	1942	1943	1944	1945	1946	1947	1948
A. Notifiable							
Enteric Fever and Paratyphoid ..	63	40	28	35	40	33	14
Puerperal Fever and Pyrexia	559	635	498	451	456	415	341
Scarlet Fever	2,837	2,853	3,130	3,131	3,145	3,270	3,584
Diphtheria and Membranous Croup ..	3,045	2,674	2,178	1,805	1,336	460	262
Erysipelas	668	650	517	481	441	434	440
Cerebro-spinal Fever	181	113	118	119	208	121	89
Ophthalmia Neonatorum	614	570	487	300	312	280	241
Acute Poliomyelitis ..	5	2	22	6	2	272	5
Acute Polio-Encephalitis	2	1	1	—	2	17	1
Acute Encephalitis Lethargica	4	8	3	4	5	4	5
Acute Primary Pneumonia	4,826	6,163	5,204	4,468	5,638	4,947	4,331
Acute Influenzal Pneumonia ..	83	173	82	71	201	81	32
Whooping Cough[1] ..	1,076	5,119	3,381	2,543	2,499	5,002	1,562
Dysentery	250	401	1,153	1,351	524	254	1,080
Pulmonary Tuberculosis	2,128	2,544	2,527	2,420	2,575	2,535	2,545
Other forms of Tuberculosis	654	673	615	509	466	469	342
Other Notifiable[2] ..	66	24	30	37	74	40	39
B. Not Notifiable							
Measles	7,604	7,184	5,831	5,509	8,887	3,878	7,457
German Measles ..	385	3,618	658	542	1,001	1,032	201
Chickenpox	7,549	5,124	6,885	4,831	4,473	5,091	6,305
Other not Notifiable	109	57	146	68	62	111	55
Totals	32,708	38,626	33,492	28,681	32,347	28,746	28,931

[1] Whooping Cough became notifiable as from 1st January, 1950.

[2] Including Smallpox—26 cases in 1942, 2 in 1945, and 16 in 1950.

TABLE 96 (c)

INFECTIOUS DISEASE. CASE RATES PER MILLION, 1949-1955

	1949	1950	1951	1952	1953	1954	1955
A. Notifiable							
Enteric Fever and Paratyphoid ..	9	16	48	20	17	27	45
Puerperal Fever and Pyrexia	281	243	308	288	302	298	205
Scarlet Fever.. ..	2,138	1,742	2,102	2,495	1,762	1,245	1,107
Diphtheria and Membranous Croup ..	141	79	123	79	46	11	2
Erysipelas	281	259	207	218	203	195	182
Cerebro-spinal Fever	93	105	116	93	113	83	88
Ophthalmia Neonatorum	121	160	171	131	92	70	47
Acute Poliomyelitis	26	260	50	32	46	36	226
Acute Polio-Encephalitis..	2	5	1	—	1	—	3
Acute Encephalitis Lethargica	4	1	2	4	2	2	2
Acute Primary Pneumonia	4,126	3,244	3,403	4,845	3,609	3,040	4,201
Acute Influenzal Pneumonia	70	38	115	114	138	30	66
Whooping Cough[1] ..	3,620	4,938	6,673	1,296	6,083	3,050	1,255
Dysentery	1,285	2,176	1,422	2,110	2,509	5,755	5,823
Pulmonary Tuberculosis	2,595	2,244	2,025	2,083	2,182	2,029	2,010
Other forms of Tuberculosis	358	339	326	277	272	222	256
Other Notifiable[2] ..	28	41	24	36	38	21	16
B. Not Notifiable							
Measles	3,698	6,272	3,934	6,323	4,496	5,298	3,516
German Measles ..	249	3,027	588	242	1,599	296	354
Chickenpox	3,394	6,426	7,390	5,474	6,771	6,847	4,149
Other not Notifiable	44	41	83	57	135	89	85
Totals	22,562	31,656	29,111	26,217	30,416	28,644	23,638

SOURCE: *Medical Officer of Health Report, 1955.*

[1] Whooping Cough became notifiable as from 1st January, 1950.

[2] Including Smallpox—26 cases in 1942, 2 in 1945, and 16 in 1950.

TABLE 96

TUBERCULOSIS

Number of New Cases Registered, and Rates per 1,000 of the Population, 1930-1955

Year	TUBERCULOSIS					
	Pulmonary		*Non-Pulmonary*		*All Forms*	
	Number	*Rate per 1,000 of Population*	*Number*	*Rate per 1,000 of Population*	*Number*	*Rate per 1,000 of Population*
1930	1,687	1.55	1,047	0.96	2,734	2.51
1931	1,702	1.56	976	0.90	2,678	2.46
1932	1,722	1.58	957	0.88	2,679	2.46
1933	1,616	1.48	794	0.73	2,410	2.21
1934	1,646	1.51	677	0.62	2,323	2.13
1935	1,757	1.62	674	0.62	2,431	2.24
1936	1,647	1.51	711	0.65	2,358	2.16
1937	1,654	1.52	642	0.59	2,296	2.11
1938	1,748	1.60	700	0.64	2,448	2.24
1939	1,574	1.44	561	0.51	2,135	1.95
1940	1,908	1.75	669	0.61	2,577	2.36
1941	2,066	1.89	661	0.60	2,727	2.49
1942	2,324	2.13	714	0.65	3,038	2.78
1943	2,778	2.54	735	0.67	3,513	3.21
1944	2,758	2.53	671	0.61	3,429	3.14
1945	2,641	2.42	555	0.51	3,196	2.93
1946	2,809	2.58	508	0.47	3,317	3.05
1947	2,765	2.53	512	0.47	3,277	3.00
1948	2,775	2.54	373	0.34	3,148	2.88
1949	2,829	2.59	390	0.36	3,219	2.95
1950	2,446	2.24	369	0.34	2,815	2.58
1951	2,207	2.02	355	0.33	2,562	2.35
1952	2,264	2.08	301	0.28	2,565	2.36
1953	2,368	2.18	295	0.27	2,663	2.45
1954	2,201	2.03	241	0.22	2,442	2.25
1955	2,181	2.01	278	0.25	2,459	2.26

SOURCE: *Health and Welfare Department.*

TABLE 97

Deaths from Tuberculosis, per 1,000 of the Population, 1855-1955

Year	Pulmonary T.B. (Phthisis)	Non-Pulmonary T.B. (Other Tuberculous Diseases)	All Forms of T.B. (All Tuberculous Diseases)
1855	3.98	1.79	5.77
1860	4.33	1.67	6.00
1865	4.13	1.77	5.90
1870	4.31	1.91	6.22
1875	3.95	1.66	5.61
1880	3.15	1.60	4.76
1885	2.97	1.19	4.16
1890	2.50	0.97	3.47
1895	2.28	0.90	3.18
1900	1.98	0.84	2.82
1905	1.52	0.81	2.33
1910	1.21	0.72	1.93
1915	1.39	0.55	1.94
1920	1.06	0.40	1.46
1925	0.92	0.36	1.28
1930	0.80	0.34	1.14
1935	0.87	0.21	1.08
1936	0.86	0.26	1.12
1937	0.85	0.21	1.06
1938	0.85	0.24	1.09
1939	0.86	0.23	1.09
1940	1.13	0.32	1.45
1941	1.11	0.32	1.43
1942	1.05	0.30	1.36
1943	1.01	0.32	1.33
1944	1.08	0.28	1.36
1945	1.03	0.25	1.28
1946	1.10	0.23	1.33
1947	1.07	0.22	1.29
1948	1.14	0.14	1.28
1949	1.01	0.13	1.14
1950	0.87	0.12	0.98
1951	0.64	0.09	0.73
1952	0.52	0.07	0.59
1953	0.43	0.04	0.47
1954	0.39	0.03	0.42
1955	0.34	0.03	0.37

Source: *Health and Welfare Department.*

TABLE 98

MORTALITY OF THE COMMONER INFECTIOUS DISEASES EXPRESSED AS A RATE PER MILLION OF CHILDREN UNDER TEN YEARS, 1860-1955

Average of Period	*Scarlet Fever*	*Diphtheria and Croup*	*Whooping Cough*	*Measles*
1860-64	4.724	3,165	6,480	3,663
1865-69	5,860	2,106	5,954	3,687
1870-74	5,732	2,627	5,202	3,376
1875-79	2,631	2,252	5,454	2,351
1880-84	2,942	2,308	5,379	2,942
1885-89	1,777	1,969	4,755	2,536
1890-94	1,478	1,707	4,108	3,956
1895-99	1,019	874	3,830	3,404
1900-04	710	722	3,798	2,247
1905-09	441	957	3,823	3,036
1910-14	721	993	2,535	2,558
1915-19	514	763	2,865	2,583
1920-24	323	683	1,939	2,737
1925-29	218	579	1,720	1,291
1930-34	284	536	1,195	1,353
1935-39	108	715	959	630
1940-44	27	575	484	227
1945-49	14	87	163	98
1950-54	1	13	60	40
1955	0	0	0	25

SOURCE: 1860-1929, *from Evidence on the Medical Services, submitted to the Committee on Scottish Health Services* (1936), *Table I, p.* 15. 1930-1955, *Medical Officer of Health's Reports.*

TABLE 99

DIPHTHERIA IMMUNISATION, 1946-1955

Year	NO. OF CHILDREN IMMUNISED				NO. OF REINFORCING DOSES			
	Under 5 Years	*5 Years & over*	*Age not stated*	*Total*	*Under 5 Years*	*5 Years & over*	*Age not stated*	*Total*
1946	8,745	3,734	—	12,479	61	1,723	—	1,784
1947	10,560	10,143	—	20,703	32	4,809	—	4,841
1948	12,701	9,819	16	22,536	691	6,959	7	7,657
1949	11,403	6,106	—	17,509	24,283	65	—	24,348
1950	7,624	5,771	28	13,423	84	19,758	3	19,845
1951	11,864	7,832	1	19,697	130	23,851	—	23,981
1952	9,859	7,375	1	17,235	76	17,794	—	17,870
1953	11,053	8,074	—	19,127	95	21,657	—	21,752
1954	11,380	9,515	—	20,895	99	23,839	—	23,938
1955	9,569	8,598	9	18,176	38	21,607	1	21,646

SOURCE: *Medical Officer of Health Report*, 1955.

PART III - SECTION 5

Education

TABLE 100

SCHOOLS UNDER THE MANAGEMENT OF GLASGOW EDUCATION AUTHORITY

ANALYSIS OF SCHOOL ROLL, 1954 AND 1955

	On October 15, 1954			*On October* 14, 1955		
	Prot.	*R.C.*	*Total*	*Prot.*	*R.C.*	*Total*
Primary						
I and II (Infants)	25,986	12,385	38,371	24,313	12,128	36,441
III-VII	59,418	26,407	85,825	60,291	27,384	87,675
Total Primary Pupils ..	85,404	38,792	124,196	84,604	39,512	124,116
Secondary						
1st Year	10,950	5,850	16,800	11,590	5,161	16,751
2nd Year	10,669	5,072	15,741	10,680	5,634	16,314
3rd Year	8,153	3,350	11,503	7,962	3,121	11,083
4th Year	1,914	577	2,491	1,889	605	2,494
5th Year	1,115	293	1,408	1,055	325	1,380
6th Year	423	167	590	436	170	606
Total Secondary Pupils	33,224	15,309	48,533	33,612	15,016	48,628
Handicapped Pupils						
Mentally	2,229	1,257	3,486	2,184	1,226	3,410
Physically	693	468	1,161	652	419	1,071
Blind	26	28	54	31	28	59
Deaf and Semi-Deaf ..	218	148	366	211	142	353
Myopic	48	32	80	44	28	72
Total Handicapped Pupils	3,214	1,933	5,147	3,122	1,843	4,965
Totals—Primary, Secondary, and Handicapped	121,842	56,034	177,876	121,338	56,371	177,709
Total Roll for all Schools		177,876			177,709	

SOURCE: *Education Department of Glasgow Corporation.*

TABLE 101

Pupils on Register of All Glasgow Schools

Analysis by Age-group of Pupils and Type of School and Class at January 15, 1954

	Numbers on Registers			Born in			
	Total	*Boys*	*Girls*	1949 *or Later*	*Period* 1942-1948	*Period* 1939-1941	1938 *or Earlier*
Total receiving Education[1] ..	182,697	92,937	89,760	1,801	123,712	49,993	7,191
In Public and other Grant-aided Schools: Total	177,333	90,274	87,059	1,472	120,505	48,934	6,422
Nursery Schools and Classes ..	1,506	738	768	1,379	127	—	—
Primary Departments: Total	124 864	63,524	61,340	28	117,592	7,244	—
P I	20,097	10,391	9,706	28	20,069	—	—
P II	21,030	10,580	10,450	—	21,030	—	—
P III	17,897	9,056	8,841	—	17,896	1	—
P IV	16,488	8,451	8,037	—	16,485	3	—
P V	16,777	8,548	8,229	—	16,760	17	—
P VI	16,455	8,386	8,069	—	15,922	533	—
P VII	16,120	8,112	8,008	—	9,430	6,690	—
Secondary Departments: Total	46,248	23,406	22,842	—	302	39,998	5,948
S I	17,000	8,558	8,442	—	301	16,692	7
S II	16,118	7,992	8,126	—	1	15,994	123
S III	8,585	4,260	4,325	—	—	7,145	1,440
S IV	2,378	1,358	1,020	—	—	166	2,212
S V	1,514	837	677	—	—	1	1,513
S VI	653	401	252	—	—	—	653
Special Schools and Classes ..	4,715	2,606	2,109	65	2,484	1,692	474
Receiving Authority education elsewhere than at School ..	473	272	201	4	329	105	35
In Independent Schools	4,580	2,105	2,475	325	2,845	812	598
In Approved Schools	311	286	25	—	33	142	136

Source: *Scottish Education Department.*

[1] Of the total of 182,697 children receiving education in Glasgow, a number equivalent to less than 1% are resident outwith Glasgow.

TABLE 102

Pupils Finally Leaving Public and other Grant-aided Schools

Analysis by Type of Course, Stage of Progress and Age on Leaving. Year Ended June 7, 1954

	Grand Total	From Three-Year Courses							From Five-Year Courses										
		Total	*On attaining school leaving age*		*Before 16*		*16 or over*		Total	*On attaining school leaving age*		*Before 16*		*Before 17*		*Before 18*		*18 or over*	
			Boys	*Girls*	*Boys*	*Girls*	*Boys*	*Girls*		*Boys*	*Girls*	*Boys*	*Girls*	*Boys*	*Girls*	*Boys*	*Girls*	*Boys*	*Girls*
Pupils leaving School[1]	16,442	10,233	4,968	4,978	163	112	7	5	6,209	1,391	1,787	560	565	384	329	381	302	326	184
Without completing S I	42	9	5	4	–	–	–	–	33	14	13	6	–	–	–	–	–	–	–
After completing:																			
S I but not S II	993	492	231	249	9	3	–	–	501	249	219	20	10	2	–	–	1	–	–
S II but not S III	7,254	5,480	2,712	2,721	23	23	–	1	1,774	649	849	143	96	24	12	–	1	–	–
S III but not S IV	6,293	4,246	2,017	2,003	130	86	6	4	2,047	467	690	330	352	98	80	18	7	2	3
S IV but not S V	548	6	3	1	1	–	1	–	542	12	16	60	106	144	117	43	36	6	2
S V but not S VI	799	–	–	–	–	–	–	–	799	–	–	1	1	112	118	238	179	101	49
S VI or beyond	513	–	–	–	–	–	–	–	513	–	–	–	–	4	2	82	78	217	130

Total secondary school pupils leaving on attaining school leaving age, 13,124; before 16, 1,400; before 17, 725; before 18, 683; age 18 and over, 510.

Source: *Scottish Education Department.*

[1] In addition 584 pupils finally left school from special schools and classes.

TABLE 103

Teachers Employed for the Whole Day in Schools under the Management of Glasgow Education Authority

Analysis by Type of Certificate held, Employment and Sex, at October 1, 1954

	Teachers			PRIMARY AND SECONDARY EDUCATION											
				Employed wholly or mainly in one School								*In more than one School*			
				Nursery		*Primary*[1]		*Secondary*[1]		*Special*[2]		*Supervisors, etc.*		*Supply and Relief*	
	Total	*Men*	*Women*	*Men*	*Women*	*Men*	*Women*	*Men*	*Women*	*Men*	*Women*	*Men*	*Women*	*Men*	*Women*
A. *Certificated Teachers*															
General															
Non-graduate	2,409	202	2,207	–	32	188	1,985	10	28	4	134	–	8	–	20
Graduate	2,288	964	1,324	–	3	432	145	482	461	48	90	2	16	–	9
General and Special ..	449	338	111	–	–	6	4	316	96	1	2	14	7	1	2
General and Technical															
Non-graduate	32	16	16	–	–	4	3	3	10	1	–	8	3	–	–
Graduate	34	24	10	–	–	7	–	10	9	1	–	6	1	–	–
Special	231	134	97	–	–	5	3	127	89	–	–	2	3	–	2
Special and Technical ..	2	2	–	–	–	–	–	2	–	–	–	–	–	–	–
Technical															
Non-graduate	1,166	589	577	–	–	–	–	481	452	13	12	95	113	–	–
Graduate	8	5	3	–	–	–	–	5	3	–	–	–	–	–	–
Teachers of the Deaf[3] ..	1	–	1	–	–	–	–	–	–	–	1	–	–	–	–
Total Graduates	3,012	1,467	1,545	–	3	450	752	942	658	50	92	24	27	1	13
Total Non-graduate ..	3,608	807	2,801	–	32	192	1,988	494	490	18	147	103	124	–	20
Total Certificated Teachers	6,620	2,274	4,346	–	35	642	2,740	1,436	1,148	68	239	127	151	1	33
B. *Retired Teachers*	173	39	134		–	20	104	16	9	1	12	–	2	2	7
C. *Uncertificated Teachers* ..	32	6	26	–	–	–	17	6	6	–	1	–	1	–	1
D. *Grand Total*	6,825	2,319	4,506	–	35	662	2,861	1,458	1,163	69	252	127	154	3	41

SOURCE: *Based on Tables prepared by the Scottish Education Department and the Education Department of Glasgow Corporation.*
[1] Excluding Nursery and special classes. [2] Including child guidance clinics and occupational centres. [3] Qualified under footnote (*e*) to Article 32 (*b*) of the Regulations for the Training of Teachers.

TABLE 104

UNIVERSITY OF GLASGOW—MATRICULATED STUDENTS (INCLUDING STUDENTS OF THE ROYAL COLLEGE OF SCIENCE AND TECHNOLOGY) SELECTED YEARS 1913-14 TO 1955-56

Year		Arts	Divinity	Law	Medicine[1]	Science	Engineering[2]	Single Class Enrolments	Totals
1913-14	M	776	69	178	712	509		10	2,254
	F	499			109	39		15	662
	T	1,275	69	178	821	548		25	2,916
1918-19	M	390	47	43	1,290	343			2,113
	F	389		4	475	71		16	955
	T	779	47	47	1,765	414		16	3,068
1919-20	M	628	57	183	1,388	919		1	3,176
	F	453		6	468	100			1,027
	T	1,081	57	189	1,856	1,019		1	4,203
1928-29	M	1,604	81	512	784	436	380	6	3,803
	F	1,425	2	28	96	134		8	1,693
	T	3,029	83	540	880	570	380	14	5,496
1938-39	M	1,022	176	495	1,032	489	362	92	3,668
	F	739	2	17	217	119	1	8	1,103
	T	1,761	178	512	1,249	608	363	100	4,771
1946-47	M	1,130	114	509	848	833	712	116	4,262
	F	944		41	227	208	1	5	1,426
	T	2,074	114	550	1,075	1,041	713	121	5,688
1947-48	M	1,410	159	592	1,417	1,071	831	156	5,636
	F	897		46	321	220		6	1,490
	T	2,307	159	638	1,738	1,291	831	162	7,126
1948-49	M	1,465	160	564	1,349	1,224	1,058	251	6,071
	F	853	2	42	329	239		4	1,469
	T	2,318	162	606	1,678	1,463	1,058	255	7.540
1949-50	M	1,360	127	635	1,583	1,147	1,129	67	6,048
	F	840	1	44	343	231	2	9	1,470
	T	2,200	128	679	1,926	1,378	1,131	76	7,518
1950-51	M	1,115	110	648	1,534	1,115	1,032	102	5,656
	F	816	2	46	297	235	2	13	1,411
	T	1,931	112	694	1,831	1,350	1,034	115	7,067
1951-52	M	981	101	587	1,397	1,039	1,021	99	5,225
	F	766	1	46	291	230	1	17	1,352
	T	1,747	102	633	1,688	1,269	1,022	116	6,577

(*Continued overleaf*)

TABLE 104 (*Continued*)

Year		*Arts*	*Divinity*	*Law*	*Medicine*[1]	*Science*	*Engineer-ing*[2]	*Single Class Enrol-ments*	*Totals*
1952-53	M	967	85	559	1,301	1,015	858	87	4,872
	F	765	1	50	269	220	2	13	1,320
	T	1,732	86	609	1,570	1,235	860	100	6,192
1953-54	M	970	64	533	1,213	1,018	871	101	4,770
	F	694	1	39	278	238	1	26	1,277
	T	1,664	65	572	1,491	1,256	872	127	6,047
1954-55	M	948	88	585	1,217	1,023	889	25	4,775
	F	719	3	37	297	259		23	1,338
	T	1,667	91	622	1,514	1,282	889	48	6,113
1955-56	M	870	88	448	1,196	1,014	827	*a*	4,443
	F	703	4	31	303	267	2	*a*	1,310
(*at Nov.* 1955)	T	1,573	92	479	1,499	1,281	829	*a*	5,753

SOURCE: *Registrar's Office, University of Glasgow.*

[1] The figures for Medicine include Dental Surgery and Veterinary Medicine and Surgery.
[2] Engineering was created a separate Faculty in 1923.
(*a*) Included under Faculties.

TABLE 105

UNIVERSITY OF GLASGOW

MATRICULATED STUDENTS, 1954-55, BY SEX AND COURSE

	New Enrolments			Total Enrolments		
	Males	*Females*	*Total*	*Males*	*Females*	*Total*
Arts:						
M.A.	193	190	383	724	575	1,299
Ed. B.	1		1	75	31	106
B.Mus.	1		1	5	3	8
B.Litt.	2	1	3	9	2	11
Dip. in Pub. Admin.	5		5	28	5	33
Social Study	5	15	20	10	36	46
Social Welfare	7	1	8	39	13	52
Biblical Studies		5	5	2	14	16
Private	13	18	31	28	26	54
Research	1	1	2	14	6	20
Dramatic Studies				14	8	22
Divinity:						
B.D.	1		1	31	2	33
Church Qualification	18		18	30		30
Special	8		8	12		12
Private	4	1	5	4	1	5
Research	1		1	11		11
Law:						
B.L.	25	2	27	125	18	143
LL.B.	2		2	87	7	94
C.A.	52	1	53	368	12	380
Law Agent	1		1	2		2
Private	1		1	1		1
Research			2			2
Medicine:						
M.B., Ch.B.	128	44	172	856	238	1,094
D.P.H.	3		3	9	1	10
Research	1		1	20	3	23
B.D.S.	15	10	25	147	31	178
L.D.S.	2		2	6		6
B.V.M.S.	34	5	39	168	23	191
M.R.C.V.S.				7	1	8
Dental Research				1		1
Veterinary Research				3		3
Science:						
Pure	159	52	211	523	162	685
Private		1	1		1	1
Research	3		3	106	17	123
Agriculture	19	3	22	72	8	80
Agric. Research		1	1	10	1	11
Applied Chemistry	51	2	53	77	2	79
Architecture				1		1
Engineering:						
B.Sc.	147		147	543		543
Research				17		17
Totals	903	353	1,256	4,187	1,247	5,434

SOURCE: *Registrar's Office, University of Glasgow.*

TABLE 106

University of Glasgow
Degrees Awarded in Various Faculties, Selected years, 1913-1954

	1913-14	1923-24	1933-34	1953-54
Arts	282	352	586	351
Divinity[1] ..	14	10	24	15
Law[1] ..	19	32	69	89
Medicine ..	139	423	187	205[a]
Science ..	112	278	135	277
Engineering ..	—	—	71	145
Totals ..	566	1,095	1,072	1,082

Source: *Registrar's Office, University of Glasgow.*

[1] Honorary Degrees awarded are included under the Faculties of Divinity and Law.

(*a*) The figure given for Medicine for 1953-1954 includes Dentistry and Veterinary Medicine.

TABLE 107

University of Glasgow

Homes of Students [1] 1934-1955

	1934-35	1949-50	1954-55
Students whose homes are in the United Kingdom and under 30 miles from Glasgow ..	3,121	4,563	3,660
Students whose homes are in the United Kingdom and over 30 miles from Glasgow ..	1,105	1,197	789
Students, other than the above, whose homes are in the British Commonwealth	79	102	167
Students whose homes are in foreign countries	85	92	132
Totals	4,390	5,954	4,748

Source: *Registrar's Office, University of Glasgow.*

[1] This analysis is of University students only (i.e. students of the Royal College of Science and Technology not included).

PART III - SECTION 6

Other Public Services

TABLE 108

Scottish Gas Board—Glasgow Division

(Glasgow District[1])

Year	*Gas Sold (millions of cubic feet)*	*Number of Meters in Use*	*Year*	*Gas sold (millions of cubic feet)*	*Number of Meters in Use*
1921	8,455	296,662	1950	13,364	346,170
1931	8,776	319,671	1951	13,927	349,180
1938	9,332	336,513	1952	13,592	351,451
		Number of Consumers	1953	13,405	353,377
1946	12,325	342,059	1954	13,670	358,991
1949[2]	12,743	342,954	1955	13,668	360,226

Source: *Divisional Controller, Scottish Gas Board (Glasgow District).*

[1] The area supplied extends beyond the City of Glasgow. See note on areas, p. 784.

[2] The Gas Department passed out of the control of the Corporation of Glasgow on 1st May, 1949, when it was vested in the Scottish Gas Board.

TABLE 109

South of Scotland Electricity Board—Glasgow Sub-Area

Consumption of Electricity, 1949-1955

	At March 31							*At Dec.*31
	1949	1950	1951	1952	1953	1954	1955	1955
Consumers								
Domestic ..	216,550	221,686	225,665	228,511	228,913	231,022	231,785	231,544
Commercial, etc. ..	33,796	33,903	34,043	34,103	30,616 [a]	30,566	30,574	30,600
Industrial ..	281	280	300	340	4,708 [a]	4,804	4,757	4,675
Total ..	250,627	255,869	260,008	262,954	264,237	266,392	267,116	266,819
Units Sold (Millions)								
Domestic ..	257	225	245	238	234	227	239	244
Commercial etc. ..	235	247	273	226	237	225	247	255
Industrial ..	292	290	306	384	393	427	459	488
Total ..	784	762	824	848	864	879	945	987
Maximum Demand .. *(Megawatts)*	249	231	238	272	284	286	295	321

Source: *South of Scotland Electricity Board.*

[a] 4,000 consumers were transferred from " Commercial " to " Industrial."

TABLE 110

Glasgow Corporation Water Supply

Population Supplied and Consumption, Selected Dates, 1852-1956

Year	*Population Supplied (Estimated)*	*Average Daily Consumption (gallons)*	*Consumption per Head per Day (gallons)*	
			Unmetered	*Metered*
1852	360,000	14,000,000	34	4
1861	436,901	18,020,000	35	6
1871	595,224	28,847,451	38	10
1881	724,702	38,678,025	38	15
1891	845,564	41,956,791	32	17
1901	1,021,158	56,344,681	36	20
1911	1,080,030	67,565,658	39	22
1921	1,261,894	77,066,834	39	22
1931	1,191,263	73,198,102	41	20
1941	1,303,000	76,976,219	35	24
1951	1,217,000	84,744,991	41	29
1954	1,218,791	87,444,500	42	30
1955	1,219,163	90,245,411	44	30
1956	1,221,614	91,801,784	44	31

Source: *Glasgow Corporation Water Department.*

TABLE 111

WATER SUPPLY

RAINFALL ON GATHERING GROUND AND RESERVOIRS. INCHES

Year	Loch Katrine Area Average	Loch Arklet Area Average	Loch Vennachar Area Average	Duchray Valley and District Average	Near Reservoirs Average	Gorbals District
1920	99.81	107.00	75.50	101.79	56.65	53.70
1930	86.17	87.40	71.11	90.88	50.70	50.35
1940	69.77	65.64	60.97	72.93	45.00	43.45
1941	58.72	57.73	50.95	63.35	39.85	34.85
1942	86.81	86.17	73.89	87.63	51.80	46.56
1943	97.55	99.02	82.88	99.64	58.20	56.86
1944	81.64	91.54	68.98	80.73	53.45	53.76
1945	81.95	87.63	70.45	88.11	54.40	52.37
1946	80.22	83.49	71.54	86.14	51.69	49.40
1947	80.43	82.24	71.47	86.55	49.27	48.41
1948	107.34	118.81	95.24	122.56	74.18	64.53
1949	91.07	98.00	79.31	98.99	60.85	57.86
1950	89.64	97.25	77.19	99.23	61.90	55.61
1951	79.87	80.42	68.27	86.90	55.28	51.25
1952	63.79	72.92	53.19	72.81	45.22	41.45
1953	81.61	93.51	66.68	86.39	49.65	44.71
1954	102.51	117.29	90.51	107.02	69.42	64.51
1955						
Jan.	5.28	5.91	4.80	5.50	3.49	3.39
Feb.	4.04	4.31	3.36	4.60	2.40	3.59
Mar.	2.31	2.04	2.84	2.17	1.65	1.89
April	5.21	6.22	4.29	5.27	3.29	2.53
May	4.99	5.25	4.55	5.11	4.43	4.49
June	4.12	5.06	3.90	4.47	3.45	2.61
July	1.38	1.06	0.97	1.24	1.67	1.51
Aug.	1.59	1.66	1.38	1.57	1.03	1.40
Sept.	7.03	8.51	5.76	6.93	5.46	5.11
Oct.	7.16	7.76	5.97	6.57	4.14	3.42
Novr.	4.79	5.13	3.89	4.96	2.33	1.83
Dec.	14.33	16.98	12.81	15.11	8.80	8.11
Total 1955	62.23	69.89	54.52	63.50	42.14	39.88
St'nd'd Aver'ge 1916-50	84.48	87.39	72.15	89.81	53.05	49.45

SOURCE: *Glasgow Corporation Water Department.*

TABLE 112

Glasgow Corporation Water Supply Analysis

Results expressed in parts per million, except for pH value and colour test.

	Loch Katrine Water	*Gorbals Water*
Free and Saline Nitrogen	0.007	0.128
Albuminoid Nitrogen	0.046	0.105
Oxygen absorbed from Permanganate in 15 mins. at 27 deg. C.	0.62	1.02
Oxygen absorbed from Permanganate in 4 hours at 27 deg. C.	1.28	1.86
Chlorides (as Chlorine)	8	11
Nitrates (N)	0.11	0.60
Nitrites (N)	nil	nil
Total Solids	32	98
Mineral Solids	14	62
Organic	18	36
Total hardness (as Calcium Carbonate) ..	10	47
pH value	6.3	7.0
Colour (Hazen units)	14	20
Free Chlorine	nil	nil
Chloramine	nil	0.16

ANALYSIS OF MINERAL CONSTITUENTS

Results expressed in parts per Million

	Loch Katrine Water	*Gorbals Water*
Hardness (E.D.T.A. Method)		
Calcium Hardness ($Ca\ CO_2$)	6.4	35.5
Magnesium Hardness ($Ca\ CO_3$) ..	2.5	9.5
Total Hardness ($Ca\ CO_3$)	8.9	45.0
Calcium (Ca)	2.40	14.90
Magnesium (Mg)	0.79	2.63
Iron (Fe)	0.03	0.08
Sodium (Na)	4.24	7.98
Manganese (Mn)	0.007	0.002
Aluminium (Al)	0.03	0.02
Silica ($Si\ O_2$)	0.30	3.20
Sulphate (SO_4)	4.70	14.87
Phosphate (PO_4)	0.007	0.06
Chloride (Cl)	7.00	11.50
Fluoride (F)	0.01	0.05

Source: *City Analyst.*

TABLE 113

Baths Department

Attendances per 1,000 of Population, 1886 to 1955

Year ended May 31

Year	No. of Establishments	Attendances per 1,000 of Population		Year	No. of Establishments	Attendances per 1,000 of Population	
		Baths and Ponds	Wash-houses			Baths and Ponds	Wash-houses
1886	5	709	—	1943	28	2,068	1,347
1890	5	818	234	1944	28	2,483	1,637
1895	5	761	284	1945	28	2,592	1,636
1900	8	998	387	1946	28	3,183	1,685
1905	10	911	630	1947	28	3,120	1,757
1910	13	925	879	1948	28	2,815	1,743
1915	20	1,229	899	1949	28	3,241	1,700
1920	22	1,776	907	1950	27	3,252	1,814
1925	23	1,800	1,034	1951	27	2,989	1,959
1930	27	1,986	1,160	1952	27	3,222	1,914
1935	28	2,415	1,199	1953	27	3,215	1,836
1940	29	1,542	1,327	1954	28	3,106	1,764
1941	28	1,671	1,437	1955	28	3,277	1,685
1942	28	1,938	1,287				

SOURCE: *Corporation Baths Department.*

TABLE 114

Baths Department. Analysis of Attendances, 1949-1955

Year ended May 31

Year	Attendances per 1,000 of Population					Total
	Slipper Baths	Turkish Baths	Sun-ray	Swimming-ponds	Free Admissions (not classified)	
1949	1,367	50	36	1,755	33	3,241
1950	1,304	51	31	1,822	44	3,252
1951	1,295	52	32	1,562	48	2,989
1952	1,369	58	35	1,712	48	3,222
1953	1,385	58	34	1,689	49	3,215
1954	1,342	63	36	1,621	44	3,106
1955	1,398	75	41	1,713	50	3,277

SOURCE: *Corporation Baths Department.*

TABLE 115

Cleansing Department. Material Handled In Tons, 1939-1955

Year	Method of Disposal				
	Separation and Incineration (4 *works*) A	*Incineration for Generation of Electric Current* (1 *works*) B	*Controlled Tipping at Coups —Direct* C	*Controlled Tipping of Residue from Works* (A+B) D	*Total* A+B+C
1939-40	163,920	197,615	48,363	175,969	409,898
1940-41	165,242	190,871	37,216	193,471	393,329
1941-42	169,875	176,133	26,496	190,686	372,504
1942-43	173,855	168,209	32,687	205,044	374,751
1943-44	197,615	167,027	21,654	218,369	386,296
1944-45	218,747	163,027	19,170	222,263	400,944
1945-46	239,051	160,150	17,489	250,287	416,690
1946-47	239,102	164,221	40,861	245,634	444,184
1947-48	254,440	180,109	21,642	239,850	456,191
1948-49	251,642	180,078	13,756	239,824	445,476
1949-50	249,841	186,146	12,748	244,191	448,735
1950-51	241,832	195,602	11,191	244,165	448,625
1951-52	220,346	191,320	10,703	235,475	422,369
1952-53	224,260	192,259	7,090	260,940	423,609
1953-54	225,443	199,281	5,380	253,932	430,104
1954-55	236,333	211,512	2,936	245,950	450,781

Source: *Corporation Cleansing Department.*

TABLE 116

SALVAGE MATERIAL RECOVERED BY CLEANSING DEPARTMENT, AND ELECTRIC CURRENT GENERATED AT REFUSE POWER WORKS, 1939-1955

Year	*Waste Paper*	*Scrap Metal*	*Waste Food*	*Textiles*	*Bones*	*Total*	*Electric Current Generated*
	Tons	*Tons*	*Tons*	*Tons*	*Tons*	*Tons*	*Thousand Units*
1939-40	3,258	2,492		140		5,890	32,586.0
1940-41	8,757	4,146	1,508	204	236	14,851	22,817.5
1941-42	9,568	3,702	9,139	196	97	22,702	12,281.0
1942-43	8,850	6,463	12,701	393	234	28,641	7,918.0
1943-44	7,948	9,323	13,985	359	219	31,834	8.428.0
1944-45	7,477	5,160	12,949	350	141	26,077	8,798.5
1945-46	7,169	5,332	10,746	313	64	23,624	8,195.5
1946-47	7,031	5,126	8,758	237	40	21,192	6,139.5
1947-48	8,480	5,744	9,075	286	31	23,616	7,980.5
1948-49	9,036	5,702	8,952	319	23	24,032	9,040.5
1949-50	5,058	6,435	8,135	252	25	19,905	10,420.0
1950-51	6,842	7,397	6,831	232	15	21,317	14,325.0
1951-52	8,370	6,964	6,812	222	8	22,376	13,589.5
1952-53	8,701	6,859	6,330	166	6	22,062	13,890.5
1953-54	9,349	7,389	5,532	275	7	22,552	13,631.0
1954-55	10,769	7,538	3,984	228	4	22,523	14,339.0

SOURCE: *Corporation Cleansing Department.*

TABLE 117

FIRE SERVICE.[1] CALLS RECEIVED. YEAR TO MAY 31

Nature of Call	1949 (*7 mos.*)	1950	1951	1952	1953	1954	1955
Fires	1,089	1,940	1,894	2,013	1,839	1,858	2,914
Chimney Fires	756	2,222	2,088	2,286	2,270	2,099	2,452
Total Fires ..	1,845	4,162	3,982	4,299	4,109	3,957	5,366
Special Services:							
Opening doors for locked-out tenants	15	21	33	48	44	49	59
Pumping out flood water	4	3	7	9	20	14	10
Rescue of animals ..	—	—	14	31	26	26	27
Rescue of persons ..	—	—		11	17	16	30
Precautionary stand-by ..	—	—	—	6	6	11	14
Tracing suspected burglar	—	—	—	6	6	2	1
Miscellaneous	13	24	5	3	8	11	7
Total Special Services ..	32	48	59	114	127	129	148
False Alarms:							
Good Intent	372	739	823	952	1,112	1,025	1,297
Malicious	229	446	518	615	514	476	549
Automatic and Accidental	55	107	120	123	193	187	187
Uncertain	103	226	205	265	257	283	296
Total False Alarms ..	759	1,518	1,666	1,955	2,076	1,971	2,329
Total Calls ..	2,636	5,728	5,707	6,368	6,312	6,057	7,843

SOURCE: *Firemaster's Annual Reports.*

[1] Authorised operational strength at 31st Dec., 1955, 643; actual operational strength at 31st Dec., 1955, 610.

TABLE 118

FIRE SERVICE. TYPE OF PREMISES IN WHICH FIRES[1] OCCURRED, 1949-1955

Premises	1949 (*7 mos.*)	1950	1951	1952	1953	1954	1955
Buildings:							
Factories	24	46	61	55	56	68	56
Workshops	71	143	149	199	165	133	140
Offices	16	34	32	49	38	41	49
Warehouses	27	45	53	46	48	39	62
Shops	83	155	151	187	138	145	140
Farm Steadings	4	—	3	7	6	3	13
Railway Premises	65	61	63	51	33	33	48
Ships	5	12	9	18	12	8	33
Hospitals, Schools, etc. ..	9	20	23	23	29	25	30
Churches, Halls, Clubrooms	17	23	30	18	13	34	30
Hotels and Public Houses ..	24	23	39	47	28	56	59
Theatres, Music-halls, etc. ..	5	17	2	10	9	12	10
Private Dwellings	415	763	727	764	683	668	903
Unoccupied Buildings ..	37	66	61	48	48	58	81
Miscellaneous	19	52	91	71	92	91	179
Other than Buildings:							
Streets and Yards	41	53	73	58	105	112	107
Vehicles	60	102	98	92	101	123	150
Grassland	—	—	—	—	—	—	242
Miscellaneous	167	325	229	270	235	209	582
Total ..	1,089	1,940	1,894	2,013	1,839	1,858	2,914

SOURCE: *Calculated from data in Firemaster's Annual Reports.*

[1] Exclusive of chimney fires.

TABLE 119

FIRE SERVICE. SUPPOSED CAUSES OF FIRES,[1] 1949-1955

Causes	1949 (7 mos.)	1950	1951	1952	1953	1954	1955
Back-fire of motors, etc. ..	4	6	6	9	4	4	9
Boiling over of fat, tar, etc.	33	51	50	57	72	61	77
Children playing with lights ..	176	281	318	327	306	268	607
Cinematographic or celluloid film igniting	—	1	—	—	—	1	—
Defective fireplaces, hearths and vents	175	433	381	337	259	286	328
Dropped lights	162	250	263	321	301	317	420
Electric circuit defects ..	98	186	218	208	240	237	238
Friction of machinery ..	33	11	15	18	13	17	17
Gas escapes and explosions ..	9	15	12	15	17	25	20
Goods in contact with lights ..	63	95	97	92	73	89	178
Heat from stoves, flues, etc.	27	28	45	19	9	21	11
Lightning: sun's rays ..	2	3	—	2	4	2	9
Hot ashes, hot metal	79	196	143	164	181	175	373
Incendiarism	8	19	18	7	8	10	8
Oxy-acetylene burners ..	5	17	21	33	26	18	32
Radiated heat	37	66	74	93	71	63	87
Sparks from chimneys, fires and locomotives	138	197	173	225	198	197	427
Spontaneous combustion: chemical action	3	6	3	7	2	3	9
Television	—	—	—	—	—	1	—
Vapour or chemicals in contact with lights	24	60	44	63	45	53	57
Unknown	13	19	13	16	10	10	7
Total ..	1,089	1,940	1,894	2,013	1,839	1,858	2,914

SOURCE: *Firemaster's Annual Reports.*

[1] Exclusive of chimney fires.

TABLE 120

MUNICIPAL CEMETERIES. ACREAGE AND INTERMENTS, 1939-1955

Cemeteries	Acreage	1939	1951	1952	1953	1954	1955
Eastwood ..	26	604	1,374	1,327	1,318	1,309	990 Jan.-Aug.
Sighthill[1]	55	597	215	197	160	176	103 " "
Southern Necropolis[2]	12	79	43	45	33	27	13 " "
Total ..	93	1,280	1,632	1,569	1,511	1,512	1,106

SOURCE: *Corporation Parks Department.*

[1] Taken over by Corporation, September, 1953.

[2] Taken over by Corporation, April, 1954.

Note: There are eleven City Burial-grounds no longer in use, with a total area of 24 acres.

TABLE 121 (*a*)

Local Taxation (Scotland) Returns, 1880-1881

Burgh Returns—Receipts

Sources[3]	Glasgow Police Commissioners	Glasgow City and Burgh	Govan	Govanhill	Hillhead	Maryhill	Partick
	£	£	£	£	£	£	£
Property Investments and Common Good Assessments under General or Special Police Acts ..	5,616	88,703	108	213	312	—	346
Police Assessment ..	—	—	8,373	919	3,080	3,368	6,734
General Sewerage ..	—	—	153	—	—	—	238
Special Sewerage ..	—	—	—	—	807	618	278
Water Assessment ..	—	—	—	—	—	—	—
General Improvement	—	—	—	132	281	242	473
Private, Special or Other Improvement	—	—	392	—	1,194	—	35
Assessments under Public Health Acts:							
General and Special	23,802	—	675	131	1,120	1,030	1,788
Authors of Nuisances, etc.	—	—	5	—	—	—	7
Assessments under Other General Acts:							
Registration of Births, etc.	—	4,318	—	—	—	—	—
Registration of Voters and Election of Councillors	—	2,159	—	—	—	—	—
Valuation of Lands and Heritages	—	1,439	—	—	—	—	—
Contagious Diseases (Animals) Act ..	—	720	—	—	—	—	—
Cess and Land Tax Act	—	2,342	—	—	—	—	—
Other Assessments under Special Acts:							
Roads Act	39,476	—	—	—	—	—	—
Water Rates[1]	—	—	—	—	—	—	—
Other Acts[2]	167,490	61,358	—	—	—	—	—
Her Majesty's Treasury:							
On a/c. of cost of pay and clothing of Police..	36,405	—	2,125	—	—	749	1,480
Penalties, fees, etc. ..	11,711	—	1,033	42	13	126	506
Sale of Property ..	14,799	—	71	—	—	—	—
Borrowed during the year	118,970	325,683	1,550	275	1,206	4,175	
Any other receipts ..	35,611	6,292	160	221	202	70	52
Totals ..	453,880	493,014	14,650	1,933	8,215	10,378	11,937

Source: *Local Taxation Returns (Scotland)*, 1880-1881.

[1] In respect of Glasgow Corporation Water Works, Water Rates amounted to £147,301.

[2] Including Statute Labour under Glasgow Police Act, Police Lighting of Common Stairs, cleansing of private streets and courts.

[3] Other sources against which no receipts are recorded for this year included, e.g., Burial Grounds Act, 1855, Public Libraries Acts, 1867-77, Artisans' Dwellings Acts.

TABLE 121 (*b*)

Local Taxation (Scotland) Returns, 1880-1881

Burgh Returns—Expenditure

Item[2]	*Glasgow Police Commis-sioners*	*Glasgow City and Burgh*	*Govan*	*Govan-hill*	*Hill-head*	*Mary-hill*	*Par-tick*
	£	£	£	£	£	£	£
Public Works—Maintenance and Repair ..	39,801	—	—	—	1,558	817	—
Pay and Clothing of Police	75,572	—	4,173	—	—	1,602	2,833
Lighting, Cleansing, Paving, etc.	116,033	—	3,687	579	1,918	1,039	1,411
Drainage	1,029	—	104	—	546	376	302
Water Supply[1] ..	—	—	—	—	—	—	—
Removal of Nuisances	—	—	—	66	136	—	1,212
Hospitals	13,875	—	269	4	867	1,165	2,111
Registration of Births, etc.	—	3,872	—	—	—	—	—
Registration of Voters and Election of Councillors	—	2,948	145	53	83	138	106
Valuation of Lands ..	—	4,615	—	—	27	—	—
Contagious Diseases (Animals) Act ..	—	3,260	—	—	—	—	—
Sheriff Court Houses	—	—	52	—	—	—	35
Cess and Land Tax ..	—	2,298	—	—	—	—	—
Prisons Act, 1877 ..	834	—	44	—	—	—	—
Salaries, Fees, etc. ..	24,358	—	1,516	236	332	359	899
Contributions to School Board	—	570	—	—	—	—	—
Loans repaid with interest, etc.	99,112	285,730	1,301	474	879	5,323	69
Turnpike Roads ..	920	—	—	—	—	—	—
Any other Expenditure	82,314	136,502	1,865	518	1,869	215	1,793
Total ..	453,848	439,795	13,156	1,930	8,215	11,034	10,770
Gross Rental	(3,426,730)	3,432,112	188,585	40,401	78,908	62,271	148,859
Loans on Security of Rates:							
Outstanding at beginning of the year[1] ..	628,478	2,420,540	10,400	4,252	9,669	9,500	21,600
Borrowed during year	118,970	325,683	1,550	275	1,206	5,675	—
Outstanding at close of the year[1] ..	672,464	2,460,493	11,100	4,327	10,875	15,131	20,310
Sinking Funds:							
At close of the year..	111,467	94,695	—	—	3,850	—	1,016

Source: *Local Taxation Returns* (*Scotland*), 1880-1881.

[1] In respect of Glasgow Corporation Water Works, there were also the following items:-
Water Supply, Expenditure, £121, 902
Loans on Security of Rates:
(*a*) Outstanding at the beginning of the year, £1,404,922
(*b*) Outstanding at the close of the year, £1,387,758
Sinking Fund at the close of the year, £212,405

[2] Other items, against which no expenditure is recorded for this year, included e.g., Burial Grounds, Public Libraries, Artisans' Dwellings and Public Parks.

TABLE 122

RETURN OF THE REVENUE AND EXPENDITURE FOR YEAR TO MAY 31, 1913; AND OF THE LOAN DEBT AS AT SAME DATE

Department	*Revenue*	*Expenditure*[1]	*Loan Debt*
I. Non-rating Departments	£	£	£
Common Good, including Tramways ..	1,196,347	1,216,009	825,882
Ardgoil Estate, including Pole Farm ..	2,301	2,988	—
Fire Insurance Fund	3,740	1,325	—
Gas Measures Acts	970	842	—
Markets:			
(*a*) Cattle, Fish, etc.	34,069	39,644	284,078
(*b*) Bazaar, etc.	13,065	13,871	207,891
Water	259,719	276,233	2,830,816
Gas	1,022,918	1,022,918	1,627,975
Electricity	345,750	345,750	1,911,964
Town-Clerk's Fee Fund	17,607	13,383	
	2,896,485	2,932,963	7,688,606
II. Rating Departments			
Police, viz.:			
(*a*) Police, Lighting, Cleansing, Baths, etc.	684,656	711,159	3,749,231
(*b*) Statute Labour	242,389	241,906	
(*c*) Sewage Purification	178,418	181,575	
(*d*) Sanitary	202,204	204,917	
Improvements Acts:			
(*a*) 1866-1912	72,237	80,157	1,220,894
(*b*) 1897-1909	37,954	37,236	487,216
Parks, etc.	108,302	108,364	696,503
Libraries	37,726	31,386	67,018
Municipal Buildings	48,147	46,415	557,284
Registration of Births, etc., Acts	9,307	10,130	—
City Assessor's Department:			
(*a*) Valuation of Lands Acts	8,350	9,016	—
(*b*) Registration of Voters Acts ..	10,765	13,854	
(*c*) Assessments, etc.	7,821	7,821	
Prison Payment Act	805	805	5,818
Diseases of Animals Acts	57,388	21,167	61,884
Clyde Embankments	7,466	6,427	94,334
Boundaries Acts, 1891-1912	23,689	27,374	185,060
	1,737,624	1,739,707	7,125,243
Combined Total	4,634,109	4,672,670	14,813,849
Year to May 31, 1912 ..	4,074,734	4,082,852	14,773,570

SOURCE: *Municipal Glasgow*, 1911-1914.

[1]Including interest, year's fund, and depreciation and reserve funds.

TABLE 123

Burgh Fund, 1954-1955

Departmental Accounts	*Expenditure*	*Revenue*[1]	*Burgh Rate*
			Expenditure
	£	£	£
POLICE ACCOUNT:			
Police	2,210,276	1,185,938	1,024,338
Lighting	1,076,896	73,832	1,003,064
Fire	459,581	127,065	332,516
Cleansing	1,622,695	268,204	1,354,491
Baths and Wash-houses	590,782	156,537	434,245
Halls, etc.	22,996	13,953	9,043
	5,983,226	1,825,529	4,157,697
LIBRARIES	307,950	10,010	297,940
MISCELLANEOUS:			
Registration of Voters	24,742	11,049	13,693
Valuation of Lands	61,288	1,825	59,463
Registration of Births, etc.	60,861	10,179	50,682
Diseases of Animals	3,471	127	3,344
Municipal Buildings	140,335	71,890	68,445
Rating (Scotland) Act, 1926	186,673	28,315	158,358
Clyde Embankments	8,364	1	8,363
Extension of Boundaries	21,606	—	21,606
Probation of Offenders	33,430	17,331	16,099
Weights and Measures, etc.	28,822	13,459	15,363
Sundry Accounts	51,294	6,890	44,404
PARKS AND MUSEUMS, ETC.			
Parks	709,388	103,412	605,976
Burial Grounds	36,844	6,636	30,208
Museums and Art Galleries	91,207	10,456	80,751
STREETS AND SEWERS:			
Streets, Bridges and Planning	1,318,791	158,962	1,159,829
Sewers	120,371	2,400	117,971
Sewage Purification	600,953	58,176	542,777
EDUCATION	11,528,787	7,833,305	3,695,482
CHILDREN ACT, 1948	388,259	206,953	181,306
HEALTH AND WELFARE	2,005,059	1,090,342	914,717
CIVIL DEFENCE	46,727	37,323	9,404
HOUSING	5,566,857	3,893,775	1,673,082
CITY IMPROVEMENTS ACT, 1866	167,955	141,571	26,384
CITY IMPROVEMENTS ACT, 1897	42,003	44,886	2,883cr.
PUBLIC WATER	130,488		130,488
	29,665,751	15,584,802	14,080,949
General Account			
RATES RESERVE ACCOUNT	100,000	—	100,000
	29,765,751	15,584,802	14,180,949
			Revenue
CONTRIBUTION IN LIEU OF RATES	—	357,922	357,922
BURGH RATE	—	13,496,449	13,496,449
	29,765,751	29,439,173	13,854,371
SURPLUS BROUGHT FORWARD	—	554,041	554,041
BALANCE BEING SURPLUS CARRIED FORWARD	227,463	—	—
	29,993,214	29,993,214	14,408,412
		Surplus	227,463

SOURCE: *Facts and Figures*, 1955.

[1] Including Government Grants.

PART IV: COMMUNITY LIFE - SECTION 1

Occupation and Unemployment

TABLE 124

CENTRAL CLYDESIDE CONURBATION—OCCUPATIONS IN 1951

Occupation	*Males*	*Females*	*Total*	*% of all Gainfully Occupied*
1. Fishermen	28	—	28	—
2. Agricultural, horticultural & forestry occupations	5,685	695	6,380	0.79
3. Mining and quarrying occupations	11,162	24	11,186	1.38
4. Workers in treatment of non-metalliferous mining products	2,155	581	2,736	0.34
5. Coal gas and coke makers, workers in chemical and allied trades ..	2,203	220	2,423	0.30
6. Workers in metal manufacture, engineering and allied trades ..	121,822	5,462	127,284	15.67
7. Textile workers	4,695	14,208	18,903	2.33
8. Tanners, etc., leather goods makers, fur dressers	3,439	1,313	4,752	0.59
9. Makers of textile goods and articles of dress	5,505	22,661	28,166	3.47
10. Makers of foods, drinks & tobacco	7,513	6,680	14,193	1.75
11. Workers in wood, cane and cork ..	20,237	817	21,054	2.59
12. Makers of and workers in paper and paper board, bookbinders, printers	6,295	5,249	11,544	1.42
13. Makers of products not elsewhere specified	3,412	988	4,400	0.54
14. Workers in building and contracting	34,066	87	34,153	4.21
15. Painters and decorators	10,040	1,406	11,446	1.41
16. Administrators, directors and managers	11,342	1,003	12,345	1.52
17. Persons employed in transport and communication	59,563	7,906	67,469	8.31
18. Commercial, finance and insurance occupations	48,283	38,243	86,526	10.66
19. Professional and technical occupations	27,996	21,198	49,194	6.06
20. Persons employed in defence service	13,593	328	13,921	1.71
21. Persons professionally engaged in entertainment and sport	3,138	588	3,726	0.46
22. Persons engaged in personal service	14,788	45,015	59,803	7.37
23. Clerks, typists, etc.	31,083	58,501	89,584	11.03
24. Warehousemen, store-keepers, packers, bottlers	13,894	9,256	23,150	2.85
25. Stationary engine drivers, crane drivers, tractor drivers, etc., stokers, etc.	12,814	139	12,953	1.60
26. Workers in unskilled occupations ..	68,775	17,091	85,866	10.57
27. Other and undefined workers ..	6,596	2,074	8,670	1.07
Total gainfully occupied	550,122	261,733	811,855	100.00
Total population 15 years and over	613,001	700,413	1,313,414	

SOURCE: *Census of Scotland*, 1951.

TABLE 125

GLASGOW—OCCUPATIONS IN 1951

Occupation	*Males*	*Females*	*Total*	*% of all Gainfully Occupied*
1. Fishermen	22	—	22	—
2. Agricultural, horticultural & forestry occupations	1,802	157	1,959	0.38
3. Mining and quarrying occupations	1,183	2	1,185	0.23
4. Workers in the treatment of non-metalliferous mining products (other than coal)	1,052	399	1,451	0.28
5. Coal gas and coke makers, workers in chemical and allied trades ..	1,357	168	1,525	0.30
6. Workers in metal manufacture, engineering and allied trades ..	76,451	2,935	79,386	15.47
7. Textile workers	1,581	6,220	7,801	1.52
8. Tanners, etc., leather goods makers, fur dressers	2,514	1,147	3,661	0.71
9. Makers of textile goods and articles of dress (not boots and shoes) ..	4,313	17,609	21,922	4.27
10. Makers of foods, drinks & tobacco	5,222	4,758	9,980	1.94
11. Workers in wood, cane and cork	13,372	567	13,939	2.72
12. Makers of and workers in paper and paper board; bookbinders, printers	4,551	4,282	8,833	1.72
13. Makers of products not elsewhere specified	2,383	781	3,164	0.62
14. Workers in building and contracting	20,805	56	20,861	4.06
15. Painters and decorators	6,941	1,034	7,975	1.55
16. Administrators, directors, managers	5,745	634	6,379	1.24
17. Persons employed in transport and communication	43,210	5,547	48,757	9.50
18. Commercial, finance and insurance occupations (excluding clerks) ..	30,047	25,201	55,248	10.76
19. Professional and technical occupations (excluding clerks)	15,665	13,029	28,694	5.59
20. Persons employed in defence services	9,058	241	9,299	1.81
21. Persons professionally engaged in entertainments and sport	2,181	419	2,600	0.51
22. Persons engaged in personal service (including institutions, clubs, hotels, etc.)	10,225	30,240	40,465	7.88
23. Clerks, typists, etc.	19,525	38,058	57,583	11.23
24. Warehousemen, store-keepers, packers, bottlers	10,161	6,524	16,685	3.25
25. Stationary engine drivers, crane drivers, tractor drivers, etc., stokers, etc.	7,417	62	7,479	1.46
26. Workers in unskilled occupations ..	41,965	8,776	50,741	9.88
27. Other and undefined workers ..	4,437	1,306	5,743	1.12
Total gainfully occupied	343,185	170,152	513,337	100.00
Not gainfully occupied (including retired persons)	38,582	267,501	306,083	
Total age 15 and over	381,767	437,653	819,420	
Total population under 15 years ..	137,104	133,243	270,347	
Total estimated population.. ..	518,871	570,896	1,089,767	

SOURCE: *Census of Scotland*, 1951.

TABLE 126

Industrial Status of Gainfully Occupied Persons in Glasgow, 15 Years and over, in 1951

Status	*Males*	*Females*	*Total*
Employers	5,593	1,072	6,665
Employees[1] ..			
Managers	8,251	1,674	9,925
Mainly salaried persons	24,283	18,201	42,484
Mainly wage-earners	278,748	141,678	420,426
Working on own account	7,905	2,491	10,396
Out of Work	18,404	5,035	23,439
Total	343,184	170,151	513,335

Source: *Census of Scotland*, 1951.

[1] Included among employees are:
Apprentices and articled employees, 20,639 males; 2,147 females.
Part-time workers, 466 males; 10,141 females.
Unpaid family workers, 82 males; 242 females.

TABLE 127

Glasgow[1]

Insured Persons Wholly Unemployed,[2] Numbers and Percentages, by Sex, 1938, 1947 and 1951-1955

Year[3]	MALES			FEMALES			TOTAL		
	Number Insured	*Number Insured Unem-ployed*	*% Unem-ployed*	*Number Insured*	*Number Insured Unem-ployed*	*% Unem-ployed*	*Number Insured*	*Number Insured Unem-ployed*	*% Unem-ployed*
1938	314,444	55,409	17.6	152,239	11,985	7.9	466,683	67,394	14.4
1947	298,621	14,276	4.8	159,843	5,253	3.3	458,464	19,529	4.3
1951	364,979	9,846	2.7	207,868	2,743	1.3	572,847	12,589	2.2
1952	334,712	11,625	3.5	203,880	6,053	3.0	538,592	17,678	3.3
1953	334,202	11,519	3.4	203,162	4,806	2.4	537,364	16,325	3.0
1954	333,695	10,558	3.2	206,644	4,147	2.0	540,339	14,705	2.7
1955	336,395	9,594	2.9	206,786	3,313	1.6	543,181	12,907	2.4

Source: *Ministry of Labour and National Service.*

[1] For 1938 and 1947, the area is that of the 10 Glasgow City Employment Exchanges. For 1951 onwards it includes also the Hillington Exchange area.

[2] Excluding temporarily stopped and casuals.

[3] All figures for mid-year, except those of the unemployed in 1938, which are for December.

TABLE 128

GLASGOW[1] REGISTERED UNEMPLOYED[2] AT JUNE AND DECEMBER, 1927 TO 1955

	Men	*Women*	*Juveniles*	*Total*
1927 June	34,743	5,713	2,833	43,289
December ..	35,204	6,254	2,795	44,253
1928 June	36,993	6,319	2,374	45,686
December ..	44,985	9,859	3,157	58,001
1929 June	39,898	7,471	3,216	50,585
December ..	47,574	10,520	2,966	61,060
1930 June	58,040	15,019	4,188	77,247
December ..	85,510	20,422	5,145	111,077
1931 June	91,934	20,762	6,440	119,136
December ..	96,793	17,531	6,124	120,448
1932 June	98,930	15,979	6,951	121,860
December ..	105,569	17,192	7,129	129,890
1933 June	97,757	15,094	6,018	118,869
December ..	101,550	15,712	6,358	123,620
1934 June	83,697	13,909	5,607	103,213
December ..	87,294	15,021	6,810	109,125
1935 June	81,044	13,115	5,399	99,558
December ..	79,233	13,947	6,821	100,001
1936 June	69,865	12,560	5,239	87,664
December ..	67,181	13,335	4,818	85,334
1937 June	58,917	12,257	3,608	74,782
December ..	61,551	13,909	3,743	79,203
1938 June	56,481	13,332	3,467	73,640
December ..	63,308	15,174	4,437	82,919
1939 June	52,451	13,064	2,901	68,416
December ..	37,105	19,314	3,132	59,551
1940 June	22,138	14,327	1,723	38,188
1945 December ..	9,026	6,726	910	16,662
1946 June	17,533	7,800	898	26,231
December ..	18,974	6,596	840	26,410
1947 June	14,642	5,459	527	20,628
December ..	13,683	4,686	429	18,798
1948 June	14,163	4,232	289	18,684
December ..	17,089	4,241	457	21,787
1949 June	15,333	3,640	346	19,319
December ..	17,082	4,064	477	21,623
1950 June	15,302	4,204	455	19,961
December ..	14,141	3,712	376	18,229
1951 June	10,303	2,832	247	13,382
December ..	11,837	5,152	581	17,570
1952 June	11,995	6,524	746	19,265
December ..	14,643	6,288	377	21,308
1953 June	11,967	4,947	399	17,313
December ..	12,100	4,852	344	17,296
1954 June	10,852	4,378	470	15,700
December ..	11,761	3,882	454	16,097
1955 June	9,925	3,843	453	14,221
December ..	10,066	2,878	394	13,338

SOURCE: *Ministry of Labour Gazette.*

[1] The figures are for the 10 City Exchanges, plus Rutherglen.

[2] Exclusive of people on systematic short time but including those "suspended" or "stood off."

TABLE 129

NUMBER OF WHOLLY UNEMPLOYED PERSONS IN THE GLASGOW AREA (TEN EMPLOYMENT EXCHANGES) IN 1938 AND 1947, BY AGE, SEX, AND DURATION OF UNEMPLOYMENT

Duration of Unemployment	*Men* 21-64	*Young Men* 18-20	*Boys* 16-17	*Boys* 14-15	*Women*[1] 21-59/64	*Young Women* 18-20	*Girls* 16-17	*Girls* 14-15	*Total Males*	*Total Females*	*Grand Total*
December 12, 1938											
Under 4 weeks ..	6,424	766	509	Not available	1,401	415	336	Not available	7,699	2,152	9,851
4-8 weeks ..	4,917	547	337		1,605	385	197		5,801	2,187	7,988
8-26 weeks ..	11,172	1,093	546		2,811	693	287		12,811	3,791	16,602
26-52 weeks ..	6,467	456	128		1,137	233	75		7,051	1,445	8,496
1-2 years ..	6,399	290	62		1,055	139	43		6,751	1,237	7,988
Over 2 years ..	15,152	144	—		1,106	66	1		15,296	1,173	16,469
Total ..	50,531	3,296	1,582		9,115	1,931	939		55,409	11,985	67,394
December 8, 1947											
Under 4 weeks ..	2,108	151	151	48	658	105	83	35	2,458	881	3,339
2-4 weeks ..	1,321	73	41	1	372	34	1	—	1,436	407	1,843
4-8 weeks ..	1,719	100	40	—	588	31	—	—	1,859	619	2,478
8-26 weeks ..	3,145	120	15	1	1,546	28	—	—	3,281	1,574	4,855
26-52 weeks ..	1,567	40	1	—	652	2	—	—	1,608	654	2,262
1-2 years ..	1,937	17	—	—	390	1	—	—	1,954	391	2,345
Over 2 years ..	832	4	—	—	49	—	—	—	836	49	885
Total ..	12,629	505	248	50	4,255	201	84	35	13,432	4,575	18,007

SOURCE: *Ministry of Labour and National Service.*

[1] In the case of women the upper age limit was 64 in 1938 and 59 in 1947.

TABLE 130

NUMBER OF PERSONS REGISTERED AS UNEMPLOYED (EXCLUDING TEMPORARILY STOPPED AND CASUALS) ACCORDING TO SEX AND AGE GROUPING AND DURATION OF UNEMPLOYMENT IN THE GLASGOW AREA (TEN EMPLOYMENT EXCHANGES) AND HILLINGTON, AS AT DECEMBER, 1951, 1952, 1953, 1954, AND JUNE AND DECEMBER, 1955

Duration of Unemployment	MALES								FEMALES							
December, 1951	65 & *over*	55-64	50-54	40-49	20-39	18-19	*Under* 18	*Total*	60 & *over*	55-59	50-54	40-49	20-39	18-19	*Under* 18	*Total*
Not more than 2 weeks	30	151	144	381	1,057	105	179	2,047	8	39	54	196	714	115	106	1,232
,, ,, ,, 8 weeks	50	348	279	646	1,472	150	99	3,044	16	82	138	318	853	110	54	1,571
,, ,, ,, 26 weeks	35	424	290	593	1,115	88	13	2,558	10	112	184	310	615	42	4	1,277
,, ,, ,, 1 year	26	267	196	342	335	9	1	1,176	3	47	45	96	92	8	—	291
1-2 years	9	266	169	261	274	8	—	987	2	38	47	39	37	1	—	164
Over 2 years	18	612	317	465	300	4	—	1,716	—	45	19	17	2	—	—	83
Total ..	168	2,068	1,395	2,688	4,553	364	292	11,528	39	363	487	976	2,313	276	164	4,618
December, 1952																
Not more than 2 weeks	20	213	211	385	1,352	139	148	2,468	12	29	54	174	579	96	101	1,045
,, ,, ,, 8 weeks	62	362	276	668	1,979	183	71	3,601	10	82	149	340	989	128	27	1,725
,, ,, ,, 26 weeks	41	451	345	741	1,700	146	15	3,439	16	119	190	411	1,159	104	1	2,000
,, ,, ,, 1 year	27	393	260	484	724	40	3	1,931	2	66	125	234	442	35	—	904
1-2 years	18	316	175	307	344	10	—	1,170	1	68	61	105	98	4	—	337
Over 2 years	31	485	300	414	304	3	—	1,537	2	47	36	26	7	—	—	118
Total ..	199	2,220	1,567	2,999	6,403	521	237	14,146	43	411	615	1,290	3,274	367	129	6,129
December, 1953																
Not more than 2 weeks	29	167	141	320	1,236	100	157	2,150	5	34	66	213	608	86	92	1,104
,, ,, ,, 8 weeks	45	281	219	542	1,483	130	60	2,760	16	86	101	256	678	70	14	1,221
,, ,, ,, 26 weeks	55	410	286	586	1,146	83	25	2,591	9	110	142	291	721	34	4	1,311
,, ,, ,, 1 year	18	299	205	396	512	19	4	1,453	3	56	67	118	257	8	1	510
1-2 years	16	290	161	400	396	9	—	1,272	4	51	73	91	133	8	—	360
Over 2 years	37	512	292	419	304	2	—	1,566	2	58	41	31	20	—	—	152
Total ..	200	1,959	1,304	2,663	5,077	343	246	11,792	39	395	490	1,000	2,417	206	111	4,658

(*Continued overleaf*)

TABLE 130 (Contd.)

Duration of Unemployment	MALES								FEMALES							
	65 & over	55-64	50-54	40-49	20-39	18-19	Under 19	Total	60 & over	55-59	50-54	40-49	20-39	18-19	Under 18	Total
December, 1954																
Not more than 2 weeks	38	177	175	332	1,202	110	176	2,210	12	29	60	162	598	87	132	1,080
,, ,, ,, 8 weeks	50	296	237	492	1,449	141	102	2,767	13	80	109	211	557	56	21	1,047
,, ,, ,, 26 weeks	49	425	301	572	1,212	87	31	2,677	8	109	125	205	511	25	2	985
,, ,, ,, 1 year	26	256	203	367	488	17	4	1,361	1	51	51	101	181	4	1	390
1-2 years	13	262	170	249	272	8	—	974	—	41	27	53	64	2	—	187
Over 2 years	33	552	289	425	311	2	—	1,612	3	45	43	25	24	—	—	140
Total ..	209	1,968	1,375	2,437	4,934	365	313	11,601	37	355	415	757	1,935	174	156	3,829
June, 1955																
Not more than 2 weeks	20	129	119	326	945	109	160	1,808	6	40	53	133	480	105	97	914
,, ,, ,, 8 weeks	27	250	170	439	854	136	90	1,966	8	72	99	175	470	45	12	881
,, ,, ,, 26 weeks	28	323	259	451	835	73	56	2,025	7	85	112	190	378	19	6	797
,, ,, ,, 1 year	20	266	229	332	451	28	4	1,330	3	57	65	118	170	4	—	417
1-2 years	10	262	161	254	269	7	—	963	—	29	29	47	73	1	—	179
Over 2 years	34	541	282	388	257	—	—	1,502	3	43	34	30	15	—	—	125
Total ..	139	1,771	1,220	2,190	3,611	353	310	9,594	27	326	392	693	1,586	174	115	3,313
December, 1955																
Not more than 2 weeks	14	116	127	315	1,040	79	167	1,858	12	30	67	137	474	70	94	884
,, ,, ,, 8 weeks	40	285	228	451	1,244	117	75	2,440	12	69	102	178	426	48	16	851
,, ,, ,, 26 weeks	41	362	264	500	984	89	23	2,263	3	71	98	186	304	24	1	687
,, ,, ,, 1 year	18	235	188	272	315	14	13	1,055	3	40	37	67	72	2	—	221
1-2 years	10	253	187	235	229	7	—	921	1	40	25	28	21	—	—	115
Over 2 years	22	519	258	341	184	—	—	1,324	1	27	23	19	10	—	—	80
Total ..	145	1,770	1,252	2,114	3,996	306	278	9,861	32	277	352	615	1,307	144	111	2,838

SOURCE: *Ministry of Labour and National Service.*

TABLE 131

Number of Registered Disabled Persons as at January and July, 1951, 1952, 1953, 1954 and 1955

Glasgow (Ten E.E.s) and Hillington

	Males	*Females*	*Total*		*Males*	*Females*	*Total*
1951				1953			
January ..	20,552	2,931	23,483	July ..	19,196	3,110	22,306
July ..	20,045	2,854	22,899	1954			
1952				January ..	19,003	3,017	22,020
January ..	20,305	2,921	23,226	July ..	18,478	3,062	21,540
July ..	19,734	3,098	22,832	1955			
1953				January ..	18,573	3,066	21,639
January ..	19,307	3,030	22,337	July ..	18,503	3,189	21,692

Source: *Ministry of Labour and National Service.*

TABLE 132

Number of Unemployed Registered Disabled Persons in Sections I and II[1] of the Disabled Persons Register as at June and December, 1951, 1952, 1953, 1954 and 1955

Glasgow (Ten E.E.s) and Hillington

		Section I			Section II		
		Males	*Females*	*Total*	*Males*	*Females*	*Total*
1951	June	1,596	151	1,747	133	12	145
	December ..	1,751	208	1,959	145	14	159
1952	June	1,831	262	2,093	139	14	153
	December ..	1,924	269	2,193	130	15	145
1953	June	1,671	208	1,879	122	16	138
	December ..	1,593	199	1,792	116	16	132
1954	June	1,469	205	1,674	93	23	116
	December ..	1,434	186	1,620	89	16	105
1955	June	1,376	213	1,589	87	18	105
	December ..	1,322	201	1,523	68	20	88

Source: *Ministry of Labour and National Service.*

[1] Section I = Disabled Persons capable of employment under ordinary conditions; Section II = Severely Disabled Persons capable of employment under sheltered conditions.

PART IV - SECTION 2

Leisure

TABLE 133

Museums and Art Galleries

Annual Attendances, 1901-1955

	Opened	1901	1911	1921	1931	1941	1951	1955
Kelvingrove ..	1902	—	543,571	618,864	551,124	242,953[1]	435,395	357,226
Camphill, Queen's Park ..	1896	85,862	70,617	82,283	101,763	58,535	24,604	34,619
People's Palace, Glasgow Green	1898	474,865	342,777	262,488	242,413	135,179	67,700	52,080
Tollcross, Tollcross Park..	1905	—	105,795	93,947	81,171	79,231	101,489	61,578
Mosesfield, Springburn Park	1905	—	43,894	40,794	61,833	33,065	14,039[3]	—
Aikenhead, King's Park ..	1936	—	—	—	—	—[2]	—	—

Source: *Director, Museums and Art Galleries.*

[1] Kelvingrove closed for three months in 1941 because of war damage.
[2] Aikenhead taken over by military authorities and has not been open to public since
[3] Mosesfield—closed as a museum in October, 1951.

TABLE 134

Glasgow Parks Department: Garden Allotments, 1916-1955

Number of Plots			*Approximate Acreage*	*Number of Plots*			*Approximate Acreage*
April	1916	273	15.00	Nov.	1935	1,537	76.85
	1917	3,975	198.75		1939	1,056	52.80
	1918	5,778	288.90		1940	2,010	100.50
Nov.	1920	5,720	286,00		1942	4,613	230.65
	1923	2,454	122.70		1945	4,281	214.05
	1925	1,674	83.70		1950	2,698	134.90
	1930	1,165	58.25		1955	1,793	89.65

Source: *Corporation Parks Department.*

Note: There were no Allotments under the administration of this Department prior to 1916.

TABLE 135

GLASGOW CORPORATION PUBLIC LIBRARIES. GENERAL STATISTICS, 1931-1955

	1955	1954	1953	1952	1951	1941	1931
Number of Reference Libraries	4	4	4	4	4	4	4
Number of Home Reading Libraries (Senior) ..	31	30	29	29	28	25	22
Number of Home Reading Libraries (Junior) ..	30	29	28	28	27	24	21
Total number of volumes in stock in:							
(1) Reference Libraries	670,893	659,236	649,582	638,557	627,581	498,698	407,650
(2) Home Reading Libraries (Senior) ..	583,517	587,219	552,982	537,003	521,072	423,830	307,901
(3) Home Reading Libraries (Junior) ..	102,363	94,883	87,562	83,807	76,244	78,996	74,316
Total number of volumes issued by:							
(1) Reference Libraries	890,489	946,475	956,189	986,679	1,038,005	956,745	1,637,919
(2) Home Reading Libraries (Senior) ..	3,570,340	3,369,677	3,297,860	3,047,294	2,865,244	2,291,039	2,319,456
(3) Home Reading Libraries (Junior) ..	736,097	720,181	688,959	628,724	647,193	642,974	775,130
Total number of registered readers	182,242	172,344	168,579	161,832	159,293	138,643	133,484
Total tickets in use:							
(1) Senior (General)	129,704	123,374	120,474	114,636	110,588	87,425	87,369
(2) Senior (Non-fiction)	142,398	135,229	131,454	125,083	119,386	91,366	79,267
(3) Junior (General)	52,538	48,970	48,105	47,196	48,705	51,218	46,115

SOURCE: *City Librarian.*

TABLE 136

GLASGOW CORPORATION PUBLIC LIBRARIES. SUMMARY OF BOOKS ISSUED BY EACH LIBRARY, 1954-55

Home Reading Libraries	*Date of Opening*[1]	*General Literature*	*Theology and Philosophy*	*History, Biography & Travel*	*Sociology*	*Arts, Sciences, Nat. Hist.*	*Poetry and the Drama*	*Language*	*Prose Fiction*	*Juvenile*	*Books for the Blind*	*Total*
Anderston ..	1904	4,020	1,574	11,853	1,481	8,015	569	606	51,232	18,687		98,037
Bridgeton ..	1906	4,194	1,724	13,705	2,721	10,292	610	634	61,066	18,165		113,111
Campbell ..	1882 (1915)	2,599	912	11,403	1,301	5,547	304	407	56,802	15,464		94,739
Cardonald ..	1953	3,310	1,789	16,095	2,778	13,689	736	591	81,236	28,196		148,420
Carnwadric ..	1947	429	342	3,842	526	1,885	144	92	30,324	18,376		55,960
Couper ..	1887 (1912)	7,661	1,636	15,952	2,658	11,897	635	701	68,659	23,625		133,424
Dennistoun ..	1905	6,107	1,732	15,464	2,501	12,039	715	674	62,738	18,350		120,320
Elder Park ..	1925	6,728	1,634	18,439	3,204	13,433	755	518	83,297	28,812	464	157,284
Gorbals ..	1901	3,047	1,196	9,125	2,185	6,557	356	4,762	41,255	20,304		88,787
Govanhill ..	1906	6,915	2,708	16,515	2,481	12,403	721	757	76,433	26,820		145,763
Hillington ..	1939	1,674	685	9,651	2,189	6,933	182	222	43,524	21,013		86,073
Househillwood	1949	4,127	1,337	16,155	2,035	10,221	554	592	71,821	36,164		143,006
Hutcheson-town ..	1906	2,560	895	10,335	2,097	5,217	277	253	46,255	19,255		87,144
King's Park	1952	7,538	2,832	24,595	3,941	18,352	894	906	140,947	39,549		239,554
Kingston ..	1904	4,594	1,354	9,977	1,881	8,465	571	420	47,761	14,513		89,536
Kinning Park	1904 (1905)	4,497	789	9,235	2,196	6,313	254	303	41,783	24,757		90,127
Knightswood	1934	3,879	1,086	14,061	1,905	10,302	494	571	63,004	22,712		118,014
Langside ..	1915	9,503	3,223	24,202	4,266	15,789	922	1,105	96,292	26,507		181,809
Maryhill ..	1905	4,485	1,368	14,227	2,205	9,632	592	706	57,658	22,878		113,751
Milton ..	1954	1,298	986	9,016	1,745	7,611	349	273	56,431	49,689		127,398
Mosspark ..	1949	1,652	732	12,000	1,565	5,799	237	222	52,245	17,416		91,868
Parkhead ..	1906	3,838	1,506	11,753	2,022	7,340	396	447	61,843	20,049		109,194
Partick ..	1925	9,232	2,566	21,693	4,397	17,338	1,314	1,070	87,944	29,708		175,262
Pollokshields	1907	5,243	1,577	16,327	2,395	9,726	632	560	59,139	14,069		109,668
Possilpark ..	1913	4,914	1,534	12,054	2,490	9,260	379	529	69,820	30,903		131,883
Riddrie ..	1938	5,531	1,251	13,130	2,221	10,304	655	491	59,134	27,858		120,575
Shettleston ..	1925	6,893	1,357	12,134	2,272	10,399	611	656	63,567	25,707		123,596
Springburn ..	1906	3,834	1,797	14,181	2,770	11,588	485	628	68,567	19,512		123,362

Home Reading Libraries	*Date of Opening*[1]	*General Literature*	*Theology and Philosophy*	*History, Biography & Travel*	*Socio-logy*	*Arts, Sciences, Nat. Hist.*	*Poetry and the Drama*	*Language*	*Prose Fiction*	*Juvenile*	*Books for the Blind*	*Total*
Stirling's ..	1792 (1912)	20,111	8,922	43,070	12,033	58,522	3,907	3,485	221,889			371,939
Townhead ..	1907	5,271	1,562	13,785	2,858	9,083	487	485	65,176	18,635	1,371	118,713
Whiteinch ..	1926	8,534	2,389	19,527	3,227	16,081	953	913	74,354	19,340		144,018
Woodside ..	1905	8,674	5,431	26,697	6,450	20,577	1,976	1,761	93,997	19,064		184,627
Hospital Service ..									50,400			50,400
Prisons ..				1,770					6,000			7,770
Gartcraig School ..		32							11,273			11,305
Totals ..		172,924	60,426	491,968	90,996	380,619	22,666	26,340	2,322,566	736,097	1,835	4,306,437
REFERENCE LIBRARIES: The Mitchell Library, Commercial Library, etc.												890,489
Grand Total ..												5,196,926

SOURCE: *City Librarian.*

[1]Date of incorporation within the City system given in brackets.

TABLE 137

Public Parks Administered by the City of Glasgow, showing Recreational Facilities, 1955

	Park Acreage	*Situation*	*Golf Courses*	*Bowling Greens*	*Putting Greens*	*Pitch and Putt*	*Tennis Courts*	*Running Track*	*Cricket Pitches*	*Hockey Pitches*	*Football Pitches*	*Rugby/Shinty*	*Boating Loch*
Alexandra Park	101	N.E.	1	5		1	12				3		
Auldhouse Park	19	S.W.		2	1		6						
Bellahouston ..	175	S.W.		6		1	6				7		
Botanic Gardens	42	N.W.											
Castlemilk Estate	74	S.E.											
Cowlairs Park ..	33	N.		4	1		5				9		
Dawsholm Park	94	N.W.		2		1					10		
Elder	91	S.W.		4	2		5				16		
Glasgow Green	159	E.		8	2		14				22		
Glenconner Park	18	N.E.		4			4				4		
Govanhill Park	4	S.											
Hogganfield ..	242	N.E.	1			1					8		1
Househill ..	128	S.W.									3		
Kelvingrove ..	97	N.W.		6	2		6				2		
King George's Field	35	S.W.		2			4				5		
King's Park ..	98	S.E.	1										
Knightswood ..	142	N.W.	1	6	1	1	6	1	1	1	3		
Loch Lomond Park (Balloch)	200				2								
Maryhill Park ..	23	N.W.		2	1		5			2			
Maxwell Park ..	21	S.W.			2		4						
Newlands Park..	14	S.W.					4						
Plantation Park	15	S.W.		3			5				3		
Pollok Grounds	121	S.W.											
Queen's Park ..	152	S.W.		9		1	17				7		
Richmond Park	49	S.W.		6					1				
Ross Hall ..	42	S.W.											
Rouken Glen ..	227	S.W.	1			1		1	1				1
Ruchill Park ..	92	N.	1	4							2		
Springburn Park	171	N.	1	3	2		6		1	2	4		
Linn	212	S.W.	1		3								
Tollcross ..	150	E.		3		1	8		1	1	7		
Victoria Park ..	77	W.		6	2		12	1	1	1	3	1	
Westthorn ..	19	E.		2						2			
Total ..	3,137		8	87	21	8	129	3	6	9	118	1	2

Source: *Corporation Parks Department.*

TABLE 138

PERSONNEL IN THE REGULAR POLICE FORCE[1]

Rank	Authorised Establishment 1955	Actual Strength at December 31								
		1955	1954	1953	1952	1951	1950	1949	1948	1947
MEN										
Chief Constable	1	1	1	1	1	1	1	1	1	1
Assistant Chief Constable	2	2	2	2	2	2	2	2	2	2
Chief Superintendent ..	10	10	10	4	3	3	3	3	2	2
Superintendent	4	4	3	9	10	8	9	9	10	11
Chief Inspector	28	27	28	28	28	27	27	28	28	27
Inspector	118+2	108+2	108	109	110	99	98	94	92	92
Sergeant	274+10	252+10	249	250	250	222	224	221	223	223
Constable	2,101+4	1,765+4	1,773	1,813	1,813	1,813	1,845	1,833	1,909	1,821
Total	2,538+16[2]	2,169+16[2]	2,174	2,216	2,217	2,175	2,209	2,191	2,267	2,179
WOMEN										
Chief Inspector	1	1	1	1	—	—	—	—	—	—
Inspector	1	1	1	1	1	1	1	1	1	1
Sergeant	4	3	3	—	1	1	1	1	1	1
Constable	43	44	39	26	26	26	26	26	25	26
Total	49	49	44	28	28	28	28	28	27	28

SOURCE: *Reports of the Chief Constable of Glasgow*, 1947-1955.

[1] Excluding officers seconded for special duties.
[2] The plus figures refer to Secondments, mainly to the Scottish Police College.

TABLE 139

Strength of the Special Constabulary[1]

Rank	MEN						WOMEN					
	1955	1954	1953	1952	1951	1950	1955	1954	1953	1952	1951	1950
Commandant	1	1	1	1	1	1	—	—	—	—	—	—
Assistant Commandant	1	1	—	1	—	1	—	—	—	—	—	—
Divisional Commandant	8	8	8	8	7	7	—	—	—	—	—	—
Deputy Divisional Commandant	7	5	8	8	3	5	—	—	—	—	—	—
Inspector	30	35	36	32	37	40	—	—	—	—	—	—
Sergeant	73	75	75	87	99	99	—	—	—	—	—	—
Constable	577	627	641	681	808	746	38	37	32	18	12	—
Total ..	697	752	769	818	955	899	38	37	32	18	12	—

SOURCE: *Reports of the Chief Constable of Glasgow, 1950-1955.*
[1]Authorised strength, 2,000.

TABLE 140

PERSONS PROCEEDED AGAINST FOR CRIMES (CLASSES I-VI) AND OFFENCES (CLASS VII) DURING THE PERIOD 1897-1955. NUMBER AND PROPORTION PER 1,000 OF POPULATION

	CRIMES		OFFENCES			CRIMES		OFFENCES	
Year	*Number*	*Per 1,000 of Population*	*Number*	*Per 1,000 of Population*	*Year*	*Number*	*Per 1,000 of Population*	*Number*	*Per 1,000 of Population*
1897	4,731	6.6	50,111	70.1	1927	5,369	4.8	35,173	31.4
1898	6,277	8.6	50,439	68.9	1928	5,053	4.4	35,685	31.1
1899	6,611	8.9	54,162	73.2	1929	5,430	4.7	34,962	30.1
1900	7,208	9.7	52,331	70.4	1930	5,733	4.9	31,031	26.7
1901	7,666	10.1	56,300	74.1	1931	5,947	5.5	29,498	27.1
1902	7,278	9.4	52,825	68.1	1932	6,629	6.1	25,625	23.5
1903	7,452	9.5	43,367	55.5	1933	6,739	6.1	25,064	22.7
1904	7,624	9.8	43,710	56.1	1934	7,305	6.5	30,303	27.2
1905	7,910	10.1	45,795	58.4	1935	7,423	6.6	36,095	32.0
1906	7,498	9.4	53,810	67.4	1936	7,106	6.3	40,041	35.5
1907	7,171	8.9	55,774	69.1	1937	7,047	6.3	42,199	37.7
1908	7,113	8.9	53,566	66.9	1938	7,248	6.4	41,469	36.8
1909	5,949	7.4	46,140	57.6	1939	6,914	6.1	37,782	33.5
1910	6,348	8.3	39,164	50.9	1940	7,665	6.8	40,086	35.5
1911	6,123	7.9	40,914	52.2	1941	7,858	7.0	38,234	32.3
1912	7,328	7.2	43,676	43.2	1942	8,615	7.6	34,705	30.8
1913	8,356	8.1	53,115	51.5	1943	8,378	7.4	30,517	27.0
1914	7,797	7.4	48,963	46.4	1944	8,064	7.1	27,928	24.7
1915	6,738	6.3	43,277	40.3	1945	9,081	8.0	22,492	19.9
1916	6,077	5.5	37,225	34.0	1946	6,842	6.5	26,618	25.3
1917	6,608	6.0	30,238	27.3	1947	6,725	6.5	30,345	29.1
1918	5,873	5.3	22,299	20.0	1948	7,372	6.7	28,392	25.8
1919	6,412	5.8	28,629	25.7	1949	6,172	5.6	27,695	25.0
1920	7,646	6.8	43,711	39.0	1950	6,672	6.0	28,666	25.8
1921	6,780	6.1	30,777	27.6	1951	7,415	6.7	28,771	25.9
1922	6,167	6.0	30,052	29.1	1952	7,904	7.3	28,373	26.1
1923	6,626	6.1	28,801	26.4	1953	7,203	6.6	32,472	29.9
1924	6,277	5.7	30,124	27.5	1954	6,947	6.4	33,211	30.6
1925	5,705	5.2	32,388	29.5	1955	7,122	6.6	36,612	33.8
1926	6,541	5.8	33,568	29.9					

SOURCE: *Calculated from information supplied by Chief Constable of Glasgow.*

TABLE 141

SEX AND AGE GROUPS OF ALL PERSONS CONVICTED OF CRIMES, 1947-1955

Year	*Under 14*		*14 and under 17*		*−21*		*−30*		*−40*		*−50*		*−60*		*60 and over*		*Totals*	
	M	*F*	*M*	*F*	*M*	*F*	*M*	*F*	*M*	*F*	*M*	*F*	*M*	*F*	*M*	*F*	*M*	*F*
1947	816	32	506	46	636	78	1,097	142	766	141	494	95	174	49	51	17	4,540	600
1948	855	24	592	57	711	71	1,303	138	785	142	436	124	177	65	53	26	4,912	647
1949	936	14	545	35	603	57	1,013	116	623	114	358	81	138	46	59	17	4,275	480
1950	1,034	10	524	37	572	65	1,005	130	630	116	352	97	150	49	48	18	4,315	522
1951	964	27	646	50	652	75	1,170	142	762	149	432	107	193	62	65	28	4,884	640
1952	925	32	732	60	757	91	1,279	159	812	162	517	108	197	68	83	22	5,302	702
1953	775	39	648	54	681	67	1,257	155	816	185	406	110	184	65	62	24	4,829	699
1954	646	27	541	50	581	109	1,106	160	753	162	456	141	153	76	58	29	4,294	754
1955	643	48	612	53	635	89	1,159	157	771	159	422	120	168	74	53	24	4,463	724

SOURCE: *Annual Reports of Chief Constable of Glasgow*, 1951 *and* 1955.

TABLE 142

SEX AND AGE GROUPS OF ALL PERSONS CONVICTED OF OFFENCES, 1947-1955

Year	Under 14		14 and under 17		−21		−30		−40		−50		−60		60 and over		Totals	
	M	F	M	F	M	F	M	F	M	F	M	F	M	F	M	F	M	F
1947	1,727	16	3,330	123	2,351	153	4,857	532	5,255	716	3,795	619	1,554	307	696	176	23,565	2,642
1948	1,516	16	3,475	151	2,959	161	4,803	418	4,402	544	3,173	420	1,316	226	578	136	22,222	2,072
1949	1,435	16	3,065	90	3,103	95	4,858	336	4,137	497	3,234	405	1,420	222	617	165	21,869	1,826
1950	1,315	31	3,096	93	3,406	123	5,013	377	4,403	505	3,458	408	1,591	258	717	129	22,999	1,924
1951	1,173	20	2,800	91	2,912	141	5,078	410	4,451	464	3,731	414	1,824	218	792	121	22,761	1,879
1952	937	11	2,410	128	2,520	127	4,803	457	4,584	564	3,914	440	2,031	250	855	131	22,054	2,108
1953	1,033	30	2,846	170	3,093	162	5,718	454	5,350	568	4,518	566	2,254	277	875	138	25,687	2,365
1954	830	20	2,801	173	3,211	142	6,109	490	5,564	678	4,652	488	2,482	296	900	142	26,549	2,429
1955	856	25	2,583	116	3,554	156	6,881	591	6,600	1,036	5,226	595	2,625	312	1,046	129	29,371	2,960

SOURCE: *Annual Reports of Chief Constable of Glasgow*, 1951 *and* 1955.

TABLE 143

Drunkenness and Licensed Premises in Glasgow, 1899-1955

Year	*No. of Persons proceeded against for Drunkenness*	*Per 1,000 of population*	*No. of Licensed Premises*	*Population per Licensed House*	*Year*	*No. of Persons proceeded against for Drunkenness*	*Per 1,000 of population*	*No. of Licensed Premises*	*Population per Licensed House*
1899	19,874	26.8	1,742	424	1927	7,964	97.1	1,521	737
1900	18,689	25.1	1,739	427	1928	8,373	7.2	1,519	755
1901	19,571	25.7	1,730	439	1929	8,130	7.0	1,511	768
1902	17,565	22.6	1,692	458	1930	6,725	5.7	1,499	774
1903	14,176	18.0	1,650	473	1931	6,445	5.9	1,484	733
1904	13,617	17.4	1,644	475	1932	6,075	5.5	1,480	735
1905	14,309	18.3	1,636	479	1933	5,674	5.1	1,454	759
1906	19,334	24.2	1,651	483	1934	6,230	5.5	1,437	776
1907	21,055	26.1	1,631	495	1935	6,466	5.7	1,424	792
1908	18,615	23.2	1,627	492	1936	7,057	6.3	1,404	804
1909	14,167	17.7	1,626	492	1937	8,121	7.3	1,411	794
1910	12,029	15.6	1,609	494	1938	7,658	6.8	1,390	811
1911	13,147	16.7	1,565	501	1939	7,641	6.8	1,391	810
1912	14,072	17.1	1,786	565	1940	8,293	7.3	1,384	815
1913	17,402	16.8	1,772	582	1941	7,124	6.3	1,365	827
1914	15,929	15.1	1,755	601	1942	4,596	4.1	1,358	830
1915	17,078	15.8	1,727	622	1943	3,885	3.4	1,360	829
1916	11,735	10.7	1,696	645	1944	2,469	2.2	1,356	832
1917	7,244	6.5	1,644	673	1945	1,813	1.6	1,351	835
1918	4,108	3.6	1,621	686	1946	2,340	2.2	1,353	776
1919	9,143	8.2	1,614	690	1947	2,773	2.7	1,350	771
1920	18,709	16.6	1,602	700	1948	2,574	2.3	1,348	815
1921	10,465	9.3	1,534	727	1949	2,897	2.6	1,353	820
1922	8,001	7.7	1,531	675	1950	2,933	2.6	1,355	819
1923	7,496	6.7	1,521	716	1951	3,444	3.1	1,353	813
1924	7,710	7.0	1,519	721	1952	3,473	3.1	1,354	812
1925	7,835	7.1	1,517	723	1953	3,653	3.3	1,355	803
1926	7,618	7.0	1,528	733	1954	3,717	3.4	1,353	805
					1955	4,055	3.7	1,347	805

Source: *Chief Constable of Glasgow.*

TABLE 144

Distribution by Wards of Premises Licensed for the Sale of Intoxicating Liquors, 1954

(Arranged in ascending order of population per licence)

Ward	Number of Licensed Premises				*Population per Licence*
	Hotels	*Public Houses*	*Grocers*	*Total*	
Exchange ..	12	160	49	221	81
Calton	1	82	8	91	269
Kingston	—	80	12	92	276
Gorbals	—	108	4	112	295
Anderston ..	1	74	12	87	346
Cowcaddens ..	—	63	7	70	360
Woodside ..	—	44	13	57	430
Park	6	29	14	48	442
Townhead ..	—	59	7	66	496
Mile-End ..	—	62	10	72	531
Dalmarnock ..	—	53	2	55	695
Kinning Park ..	1	27	10	38	712
Hutchesontown ..	—	35	6	41	715
Govan	—	29	13	42	797
Partick West ..	—	25	8	33	820
Camphill ..	—	14	10	24	896
Partick East ..	—	9	12	21	1,042
Cowlairs	—	20	4	24	1,115
Maryhill	—	14	3	17	1,543
Fairfield	—	10	5	15	1,604
Parkhead ..	—	8	3	11	1,831
Govanhill ..	—	5	8	13	1,901
Sh'eston & T'lcross	—	18	6	24	1,949
North Kelvin ..	—	10	2	12	2,048
Pollokshaws ..	—	15	4	19	2,555
Springburn ..	—	8	4	12	3,301
Ruchill	—	9	3	12	4,316
Kelvinside ..	—	—	4	4	4,983
Langside	—	2	3	5	5,191
Dennistoun ..	—	3	1	4	6,370
Yoker	—	4	—	4	7,271
Pollokshields ..	1	—	—	3 [a]	14,337
Provan	—	2	—	2	16,362
Craigton	—	2	—	2	19,652
Cathcart	—	—	—	—	—
Knightswood ..	—	—	—	—	—
Whiteinch ..	—	—	—	—	—
Total ..	22	1,083	247	1,345 [a]	801

Source: *Licensing Court.*

(*a*) Includes 2 wholesale dealers in Spirits, Beer, etc.

TABLE 145

All Crimes (Classes I-VI), 1897-1955

Year	No. of Cases made known	No. of Cases Cleared	Percentage Cleared	Year	No. of Cases made known	No. of Cases Cleared	Percentage Cleared
1897	8,916	4,281	48	1926	13,605	4,071	30
1898	10,477	5,757	55	1927	11,993	3,261	27
1899	10,697	5,934	48	1928	13,478	3,429	25
1900	11,038	5,972	54	1929	16,272	4,086	25
1901	12,247	6,910	56	1930	17,040	4,531	27
1902	11,920	6,557	55	1931	18,633	4,493	24
1903	12,829	6,442	50	1932	27,525	5,172	19
1904	15,670	6,340	40	1933	27,492	6,478	24
1905	16,428	5,612	34	1934	26,735	6,731	25.2
1906	17,428	5,901	34	1935	28,716	7,265	25.3
1907	17,397	5,659	33	1936	26,639	8,211	30.8
1908	16,555	5,729	35	1937	26,040	8,445	32.4
1909	15,124	4,146	27	1938	25,709	7,768	30.8
1910	15,021	5,300	35	1939	26,534	8,117	30.6
1911	15,309	5,041	33	1940	28,067	7,713	27.5
1912	16,358	5,850	36	1941	30,203	7,301	24.3
1913	18,244	6,642	36	1942	30,150	7,685	25.5
1914	18,432	6,274	34	1943	31,279	7,176	22.9
1915	15,719	5,273	34	1944	31,939	6,953	21.8
1916	16,248	4,275	26	1945	41,243	8,513	20.6
1917	15,028	4,271	28	1946	33,823	6,536	19.3
1918	14,087	4,025	29	1947	32,248	6,515	20.2
1919	16,436	4,391	27	1948	34,531	7,696	22.3
1920	20,146	5,991	25	1949	28,376	6,954	24.5
1921	18,770	5,077	27	1950	29,504	7,816	26.5
1922	17,940	4,953	28	1951	31,625	8,777	27.7
1923	18,188	5,174	28	1952	30,943	8,790	28.4
1924	14,840	4,964	33	1953	27,116	8,794	32.4
1925	14 677	3,993	27	1954	25,732	8,663	33.7
				1955	26,357	8,155	30.9

Source: *Chief Constable of Glasgow.*

TABLE 146

MURDERS—ATTEMPTS TO MURDER—CULPABLE HOMICIDE

NUMBER OF CASES MADE KNOWN AND CLEARED,[1] 1860-1955

Year	*Murder*	*Attempt to Murder and Culpable Homicide*	*Year*	*Murder*	*Attempt to Murder and Culpable Homicide*	*Year*	*Murder*	*Attempt to Murder and Culpable Homicide*
1860	2	3	1892	2	2	1924	5	7
1861	2	1	1893	—	—	1925	4	16
1862	1	—	1894	—	7	1926	2	12
1863	1	2	1895	2	5	1927	3	13
1864	1	6	1896	—	3	1928	8 (7)	16
1865	2	1	1897	2	6	1929	2	15
1866	1	1	1898	2	7	1930	1	21
1867	1	1	1899	1	11	1931	1	11
1868	—	1	1900	—	18 (17)	1932	2	7
1869	2	5	1901	—	8	1933	5 (4)	7
1870	—		1902	4	14	1934	5 (3)	10
1871	—	3	1903	2	18	1935	8 (3)	12
1872	—	5	1904	6	12	1936	5 (1)	11
1873	—	5	1905	2	12	1937	6 (4)	2
1874	3	4	1906	2	12	1938	7	8
1875	1	1	1907	4	13	1939	1	4
1876	1	4	1908	1	13	1940	2	7
1877	—	7	1909	2	6	1941	1	6
1878	2	6	1910	2	12	1942	5 (4)	8
1879	3	6	1911	1	19	1943	1	7
1880	1	10	1912	3 (2)	19	1944	4 (3)	4
1881	1	5	1913	2	11	1945	10 (8)[a]	10 (9)
1882	—	9	1914	2	11	1946	3 (4)	5
1883	2	6	1915	3	21	1947	3	7
1884	1	5	1916	3	15	1948	3 (2)	6
1885	1 (0)	5	1917	3 (2)	8	1949	5 (3)	5
1886	—	5	1918	1 (0)	9	1950	5 (4)	3
1887	—	7	1919	3 (2)	20	1951	1	9
1888	2 (1)	1	1920	7 (5)	20	1952	4 (3)	9 (8)
1889	1	7	1921	7 (6)	17 (16)	1953	8 (7)	5
1890	2	4	1922	4 (3)	15	1954	6 (5)	7
1891	—	—	1923	3 (2)	11	1955	5 (4)	10

SOURCE: *Chief Constable of Glasgow.*

[1] Where there is less than 100% clearance, the number of solved cases is shown in brackets.

(*a*) At the end of 1945 two cases of murder remained unsolved. In the following year, however, one of these was cleared up and this accounts for the extra solved case shown in 1946.

TABLE 147

CLASSIFIED CRIMES—SELECTED YEARS, 1897-1954

Class of Crime	1897	1913	1925	1938	1951	1954
I Crimes against the Person						
(*a*)	209	2,160	1,353	1,628	1,156	1,132
(*b*)	209	2,109	1,111	1,415	823	951
(*c*)	100	98	82	87	71	84
II Crimes against Property with violence (house-breaking and robbery)						
(*a*)	1,872	2,685	4,078	8,353	13,305	10,876
(*b*)	352	405	438	1,559	2,256	2,245
(*c*)	19	15	11	19	17	21
III Crimes against Property without violence (mainly theft)						
(*a*)	6,251	12,187	8,448	13,426	15,162	11,800
(*b*)	3,136	3,011	1,857	4,218	5,034	4,815
(*c*)	50	25	22	31	33	41
IV Malicious injuries to Property (mainly malicious mischief)						
(*a*)	548	511	244	2,095	1,595	1,402
(*b*)	548	446	197	669	519	452
(*c*)	100	87	81	31	33	32
V Forgery and Crimes against Currency						
(*a*)	10	19	46	37	62	108
(*b*)	10	9	15	17	50	106
(*c*)	100	53	33	46	81	98
VI Other Crimes not included above						
(*a*)	26	682	508	315	345	414
(*b*)	26	662	375	85	95	94
(*c*)	100	97	74	27	28	23
All Crimes (I-VI)						
(*a*)	8,916	18,244	14,677	25,854	31,625	25,732
(*b*)	4,287	6,642	3,993	7,963	8,777	8,663
(*c*)	48	36	27	31	28	34
VII Miscellaneous Offences ..						
(*a*)	39,156	45,955	23,554	40,685	25,490	29,612
(*b*)	37,897	45,637	23,432	36,152	23,637	27,731
(*c*)	97	99	99	89	93	94

SOURCE: *Chief Constable of Glasgow.*

(*a*) Numbers known to the Police.
(*b*) Numbers in which one or more persons were apprehended.
(*c*) Percentage of crimes cleared.

TABLE 148

CRIMES AGAINST PROPERTY, 1901-1955

Five Years Average	With Violence		Without Violence		Malicious Damage	
	Cases made Known	*Cases Cleared*	*Cases made Known*	*Cases Cleared*	*Cases made Known*	*Cases Cleared*
1901-1905	2,577	428	8,807	3,661	655	544
1906-1910	2,586	472	11,624	2,911	489	394
1911-1915	2,572	398	11,396	2,745	492	417
1916-1920	3,448	552	10,990	2,351	430	342
1921-1925	4,003	678	10,683	2,345	325	215
1926-1930	5,524	528	6,791	1,785	316	241
1931-1935	10,678	1,264	12,883	3,088	361	326
1936-1940	8,477	1,642	13,779	4,057	2,460	876
1941-1945	12,662	1,696	16,573	4,148	2,384	723
Year						
1946	15,118	1,711	15,211	3,717	2,182	483
1947	14,515	1,552	14,306	3,791	2,099	409
1948	16,516	1,992	14,846	4,399	1,842	495
1949	13,102	1,776	12,749	3,889	1,287	468
1950	13,292	2,134	13,358	4,393	1,496	485
1951	13,305	2,256	15,162	5,034	1,555	519
1952	13,035	2,363	14,883	4,996	1,509	435
1953	11,183	2,226	12,817	4,933	1,556	521
1954	10,876	2,245	11,800	4,815	1,402	502
1955	10,369	1,873	12,771	4,669	1,678	549

SOURCE: *Calculated from information supplied by Chief Constable of Glasgow.*

TABLE 149

PERSONS AGAINST WHOM CRIMES WERE PROVED, 1938-1955

With index 1938 = 100

Year	*Juveniles*	*Index*	*Adults*	*Index*
1938	2,188	100	4,777	100
1939	2,288	102	4,275	89
1940	3,381	154	4,248	89
1941	3,053	139	4,568	93
1942	3,283	150	5,037	105
1943	3,137	143	5,051	106
1944	2,803	128	5,025	105
1945	3,609	165	4,625	94
1946	2,406	110	3,794	80
1947	2,159	99	3,876	81
1948	2,483	113	4,207	88
1949	2,275	104	3,348	70
1950	2,599	119	3,452	72
1951	2,747	125	3,990	84
1952	2,813	129	4,411	92
1953	2,416	110	4,189	88
1954	2,287	105	3,998	84
1955	2,480	113		

SOURCE: *Chief Constable of Glasgow.*

TABLE 150

NUMBER OF JUVENILES UNDER SEVENTEEN YEARS OF AGE PROCEEDED AGAINST FOR CRIMES DURING THE YEARS 1938-1945 AND 1954-1955

Year	DISPOSAL													
	Charge withdrawn or acquitted	Charge proved Dismissed	Put on Probation	Sent to Prison	Sent to Borstal	Sent to Approved School	Sent to Remand Home	Fined (inc. Parent fined: ordered to find Caution)	Committed to care of fit person	Whipped	Admonished	No order made	Detention of Mental Defectives	Total
1938	109	149	931	—	13	189	20	333	—	5	548	—	—	2,297
1939	151	188	883	1	17	182	49	241	2	14	593	—	1	2,322
1940	141	226	1,127	—	17	273	60	724	—	111	857	—	1	3,537
1941	117	113	954	—	37	241	76	911	2	110	569	—	—	3,130
1942	112	124	890	—	51	226	124	1,286	—	100	521	—	—	3,434
1943	139	94	824	4	58	323	106	1,101	7	103	571	—	—	3,330
1944	165	75	826	4	47	217	102	1,064	4	21	518	—	—	3,043
1945	255	70	887	8	67	226	127	1,424	—	29	544	227	—	3,864
1954	188	55	968	—	22	151	227	422	—	—	380	43	19	2,475
1955	180	57	1,070	—	27	151	234	403	—	—	443	81	14	2,660

In addition Warnings were administered by Superintendents
in 1,146 cases in 1954
„ 1,171 „ „ 1955

SOURCE: *Chief Constable of Glasgow.*

TABLE 151

NUMBER OF JUVENILES AGAINST WHOM CHARGES PROVED DURING THE YEARS 1938, 1953, 1954 AND 1955, AND ANALYSIS BY TYPE OF CRIME OR OFFENCE

Crimes and Offences	*Number of Juveniles against Whom Charge(s) Proved*			
	1938	1953	1954	1955
All Crimes and Offences	6,197	6,562	6,179	6,137
Crimes	2,188	2,416	2,287	2,480
Offences	4,009	4,146	3,892	3,657
Class I—Crimes against the Person				
Murder	—	2	—	—
Assaults and Threats	—	4	—	10
Sexual Crimes	3	29	18	25
Other Crimes against Person	—	15	18	20
Class II—Crimes against Property with violence				
Housebreaking and robbery and assault with intent, etc.	635	844	891	790
Class III—Crimes against Property without violence				
Theft	1,077	1,142	1,070	1,295
Others	51	69	84	66
Class IV—Malicious injuries to Property				
Fire-raising	—	—	4	4
Malicious mischief	415	298	196	265
Class V—Forgery and Crimes against Currency ..	—	—	—	—
Class VI—Other Crimes	7	13	6	5
Class VII—Miscellaneous Offences				
Betting, Gaming, etc.	454	403	289	268
Breach of the Peace, etc.	1,303	1,885	1,638	1,488
Cruelty to Animals	—	—	—	1
Offences connected with Explosives	13	1	—	—
Offences against Intoxicating Liquor Laws ..	—	19	12	7
Offences against Police Acts, By-laws and Regulations	1,419	388	263	281
Offences connected with Railways	—	—	—	—
Offences connected with bicycles	123	93	95	112
Offences connected with motor vehicles	192	88	109	92
Obstructions and Nuisances	1,422	1,218	1,419	1,304
Offences against Vagrancy and Trespass Laws ..	10	—	1	3
Other Offences	73	51	66	101

SOURCE: *Chief Constable of Glasgow.*

TABLE 152

Poor Law

Number of Poor Relieved in each of the undernoted Parishes during the Year Ending May 14, 1847

Parishes		*Population*	*Number of Poor on the Roll or Registered*			*Number of Casual Poor*			*Number of Lunatics*			*Number of Orphans or Deserted Children*		
			M	*F*	*T*	*M*	*F*	*T*	*M*	*F*	*T*	*M*	*F*	*T*
Barony		106,075	789	1,984	2,773	6,423	10,155	16,578	42	57	99	118	107	225
Glasgow		120,183	2,719	7,577	10,296	2,903	3,274	6,177	36	41	77	175	196	371
Gorbals		10,200	44	212	256	390	616	1,006	3	4	7	18	11	29
Govan:														
Gorbals District	38,075 }	45,885	{ 251	707	958	1,086	5,695	6,781	16	17	33	26	39	65 }
Govan Proper District	7,810 }		{ 45	132	177	67	97	164	6	7	13	13	6	19 }
		282,343	3,848	10,612	14,460	10,869	19,837	30,706	103	126	229	350	359	709

Source: *Health and Welfare Department.*

TABLE 153

Poor Law

Expenditure for the Relief and Management of the Poor in the undernoted Parishes, for the Year ending May 14, 1847

Parishes	Expenditure				
	Relief of Poor on the Roll or Registered	*Relief of Casual Poor*	*Medical Relief*	*Management and Litigation*	*Total Amount of Money Expended*
Barony ..	£9,716 16 0	£4,980 10 0	£574 3 0	£1,229 10 9	£16,501 0 3
Glasgow	27,285 8 5	662 10 1	1,896 11 4	11,247 10 0	41,091 19 10
Gorbals ..	543 18 0	404 19 9	55 0 6	655 9 7	1,659 7 10
Govan:					
Gorbals District	2,852 5 0	1,283 4 10½	88 16 8	493 18 6½	4,718 5 1
Govan Proper District	748 13 7	238 13 6	38 3 3	104 7 11	1,129 18 3
Totals ..	£41,147 1 0	£7,569 18 2½	£2,652 14 9	£13,730 16 9½	£65,100 11 3

Source: *Health and Welfare Department.*

TABLE 154

POOR LAW

STATISTICS OF PAUPERISM IN GLASGOW AND GOVAN PARISHES AS AT NOVEMBER 15, 1901

	Glasgow	*Govan*	*Total*
I—*Out-door Poor*			
Poor resident in Glasgow	3,037	2,044	5,081
Poor resident in other Parishes	193	174	367
Interim Poor	114	78	192
Irish, English and Foreign Poor	64	68	132
Dependants of above	4,246	3,311	7,557
Boarded-out Children	1,507	482	1,989
Industrial Schools and Orphanages	51	56	107
Asylum for the Blind	8	5	13
Deaf and Dumb Institution	1	1	2
Lock Hospital	—	—	—
Total of Out-door Poor	9,221	6,219	15,440
II—*In-door Poor*			
Ordinary Inmates	2,870	917	3,787
III—*Lunatic Poor*			
In Asylums	1,405	739	2,144
In Larbert and other Institutions for Imbeciles ..	86	33	119
Boarded-out with strangers	325	98	423
Boarded-out with relatives	25	39	64
Total of Lunatic Poor	1,841	909	2,750
Grand Total	13,932	8,045	21,977
Other Parish Poor resident in Glasgow (Out-door and In-door)	391	245	636
Dependants of above	626	362	988
Total	1,017	607	1,624
Parish Populations, 1901	571,569	341,450	913,019

SOURCE: *Health and Welfare Department.*

TABLE 155

POOR LAW

PARISH OF GLASGOW EXPENDITURE, 1901

	£
I—MAINTENANCE	
Out-door Poor	30,012
Non-resident Poor	3,006
Children Boarded	15,511
Casual Poor	294
	48,823
In-door Poor	28,287
Lunatic Poor—Certificates, Warrants, Removals and Board in other Asylums	2,298
Lunatics Boarded in Private Dwellings	7,061
Board in Glasgow District Asylums	34,573
	43,932
II—MANAGEMENT	
Inspector's Department	8,806
Collector's Department	953
Poorhouse Department	9,130
	18,889
III—MEDICAL RELIEF	
Out-door	4,176
In-door—Poorhouses	4,299
General Laboratory Salaries	397
	8,872
IV—LAW CHARGES	454
V—COST OF OTHER PARISH POOR	7,107
VI—INTEREST	668
VII—ENLARGEMENTS: REPAIRS, ETC., OF BUILDINGS NOT DEFRAYED OUT OF LOANS	
Poorhouses	2,851
VIII—VACCINATIONS	101
IX—COLLECTION OF SCHOOL AND SPECIAL RATES ..	1,084
X—ELECTION OF PARISH COUNCIL	—
	160,968

SOURCE: *Health and Welfare Department.*

TABLE 156

Poor Law and Public Assistance. Ordinary Poor and Able-bodied Unemployed in Receipt of Outdoor Relief, 1921 to 1948[1]

Year Ending	*Total Ordinary Relief*	*Total A.B. Relief*	*Grand Total of Ordinary & A.B. Relief*	*Total Rate per 1,000 of Population*	*Rate per 1,000 of Population in Receipt of Ordinary Relief*	*Rate per 1,000 of Population in Receipt of A.B. Relief*	*Necessitous[2] Blind Persons*
15/11/21	22,440	61,921	84,361	81.5	21.7	59.8	
15/11/22	25,298	90,615	115,913	112.0	24.4	87.6	
15/11/23	28,226	70,514	98,740	95.4	27.3	68.1	
15/11/24	28,310	40,313	68,623	66.3	27.4	38.9	
15/11/25	30,194	48,657	78,851	76.2	29.1	47.1	
15/11/26	28,025	56,713	84,738	81.9	27.1	54.8	
15/11/27	28,405	48,934	77,339	74.7	27.4	47.3	
15/11/28	29,482	39,116	68,598	66.3	28.5	37.8	
15/11/29	32,366	34,096	66,462	64.2	31.3	32.9	
15/ 5/30	33,871	20,355	54,226	52.4	32.7	19.7	
15/ 5/31	43,501	23,872	67,373	65.1	42.0	23.1	
31/ 5/32	51,480	37,134	88,614	81.4	47.3	34.1	
31/ 5/33	62,011	54,252	116,263	106.8	56.9	49.9	
31/ 5/34	69,011	69,099	138,110	126.8	63.4	63.4	
31/ 5/35	78,860	70,168	149,028	136.9	72.4	64.5	
31/ 5/36	87,689	63,292	150,981	138.7	80.5	58.2	
31/ 5/37	86,853	8,238	95,091	87.4	79.8	7.6	
31/ 5/38	79,324	6,268	85,592	78.5	72.8	5.7	1,175
31/ 5/39	79,616	6,521	86,137	79.0	73.1	5.9	1,324
31/ 5/40	69,675	4,075	73,750	67.6	64.0	3.6	1,320
31/ 5/41[3]	36,432	1,177	37,609	34.4	33.4	1.0	1,254
31/ 5/42	35,097	438	35,535	32.6	32.2	0.4	1,265
31/ 5/43	35,002	120	35,122	32.2	32.1	0.1	1,293
31/ 5/44	33,871	100	33,971	31.2	31.1	0.1	1,301
31/ 5/45	35,119	140	35,259	32.3	32.2	0.1	1,272
31 /5/46	36,411	325	36,736	33.7	33.4	0.3	1,256
31/ 5/47	36,514	404	36,918	33.9	33.5	0.4	1,199
31/ 5/48	35,745	443	36,188	33.2	32.8	0.4	1,199

Source: *Health and Welfare Department.*

[1] The figures for 1921 to 1937 include Other Authority Poor resident in Glasgow and exclude Glasgow Poor resident in Other Authority areas. The figures for 1938 to 1948 are those of Glasgow Poor wherever resident. To be strictly comparable the latter should be increased by an average of 1.5 %.

[2] From 1921 to 1937 Blind Persons and their necessitous dependants are included in the Ordinary Relief figures. From 1938 to 1948 the dependants of Blind Persons are included in the Ordinary Relief figures but Blind Persons are shown separately.

[3] The big fall in 1941 was the result of the operation of the Old Age and Widows' Pensions Act, 1940, under which the old age pension was granted to women at sixty and their supplementation transferred from the Local Authority to the Assistance Board. Under the Pensions and Determination of Needs Act, 1943, the supplementation of widows who had a pension and dependent children was transferred to the Assistance Board.

TABLE 157

NATIONAL ASSISTANCE, APPLICATIONS—GLASGOW OFFICES, 1954 (53 WEEKS)

Office	*Applications Un-cleared Dec., '53*	*Applications*	*R.O.s*[1]	*I.P.s*[2]	*Not Granted Withdrawn, etc.*	*Applications Un-cleared Dec., '54*	*R.F.L.*[3]
Parkhead ..	28	17,052	4,689	15,794	2,893	13	4,587
Glasgow Central	5	27,691	7,252	31,437	2,632	2	7,061
Partick ..	35	7,752	2,458	5,822	1,843	27	2,398
Springburn I ..	11	12,424	4,145	15,273	1,439	8	3,950
Springburn II	17	6,501	2,337	6,205	896	13	2,399
Bridgeton ..	18	20,313	5,029	20,092	1,438	5	4,856
Kinning Park ..	5	17,674	6,470	15,393	2,588	14	6,346
Maryhill ..	14	5,480	1,864	5,774	456	5	1,779
Glasgow S. Side	57	13,394	3,540	14,775	1,173	9	3,203
Ruchill ..	8	13,124	3,819	14,026	921	16	3,578
Queen's Park ..	13	6,737	1,737	6,201	606	2	1,674
Hutchesontown	13	7,697	2,507	8,511	1,263	17	2,417
Clydebank ..	17	5,313	1,941	4,281	595	21	1,921
	241	161,152	47,788	163,584[4]	18,743	152	46,169

SOURCE: *National Assistance Board, Central Office in Scotland.*

[1] R.O. = Running orders resulting in continuing weekly grants.
[2] I.P. = Immediate payments resulting from applications.
[3] R.F.L. = Removed from live load.
[4] Of these, 97,506 were single payments.

TABLE 158

Persons in Receipt of National Assistance

Live Load in the Glasgow Area at December 21, 1954

Numbers receiving National Assistance in supplementation of the following insurance benefits:	
(*a*) Retirement Pensions	23,578
(*b*) Sickness and industrial injury benefits	5,348
(*c*) Widows' benefits	3,875
(*d*) Unemployment benefits	2,446
	35,247
Numbers receiving National Assistance in supplementation of Non-contributory Old Age Pensions	2,743
Numbers receiving National Assistance who are not in receipt of such pensions or benefits:	
(*a*) Persons registered for employment	4,943
(*b*) Persons not registered for employment	14,513
Total	57,446
Included in the above figures are the following numbers of persons assisted in the Special Scale for Blind Persons	1,412
for Tuberculous Persons ..	2,240

Source: *National Assistance Board, Central Office in Scotland.*

TABLE 159

GLASGOW CHILDREN'S DEPARTMENT

CHILDREN IN CARE AND UNDER SUPERVISION, 1949-1955

	1949	1950	1951	1952	1953	1954	1955
Boarded out with foster parents and relations	2,153	2,072	1,975	1,868	1,701	1,576	1,652
In Corporation Residential Homes	385	377	415	397	449	443	439
In Voluntary Homes	278	312	278	250	235	230	163
In private lodgings or residential employment	—	—	—	—	—	—	166
In Corporation Boys' Hostel—"Lochaber"	—	—	—	—	8	11	18
In Working Boys' Hostels ..	91	119	99	62	64	46	93
Temporarily in Hospitals ..	45	42	23	15	19	8	—
On After Care Register[1]	207	280	335	251	200	236	14
	3,159	3,202	3,125	2,843	2,676	2,550	2,545

SOURCE: *Children's Department, Glasgow Corporation.*

[1] From 1949 to 1954 children over school age; in 1955, those over 18 years.

TABLE 160

REASONS FOR CHILDREN BEING IN CARE OF GLASGOW CHILDREN'S COMMITTEE, AS AT MAY 31, 1955

	Legitimate	*Illegitimate*
Orphans	106	113
Deserted or Abandoned	308	355
Neglected	466	63
Parent/s immoral, in prison, etc.	95	102
Parent/s Homeless	26	183
Widowers unable to care for children	97	—
Parent/s unable to provide for various reasons ..	15	159
Truancy of child	53	2
Care and Protection Cases	27	—
Foundlings	—	16
Illness of Parent/s: T.B.	65	9
Mental	55	104
Other	59	67
Total ..	1,372	1,173

SOURCE: *Children's Department, Glasgow Corporation.*

Included in the above are the following cases committed by Court to the care of the Corporation:

289 Boys
274 Girls

563

Of this number, children committed as offenders (Truancy) number 38.

TABLE 161

CHILDREN IN CARE OF GLASGOW CHILDREN'S COMMITTEE AT MAY 31, 1955

	Under Two Years			*Two Years to Compulsory School Age*			*Compulsory School Age*			*Over Compulsory School Age*			*Total*		
	Boys	*Girls*	*Total*	*B*	*G*	*T*	*B*	*G*	*T*	*B*	*G*	*T*	*B*	*G*	*T*
Boarded Out															
(*a*) In Glasgow City Area	2	4	6	14	33	47	146	123	269	62	45	107	224	205	429
(*b*) Outwith Glasgow	7	11	18	54	45	99	453	410	863	118	125	243	632	591	1,223
Total ..	9	15	24	68	78	146	599	533	1,132	180	170	350	856	796	1,652
In Children's Homes provided under Children's Act, 1948															
(*a*) Reception Homes[1] (*b*) Residential Homes } .. .. —	37	29	66	42	26	68	180	125	305	—	—	—	259	180	439
Total ..	37	29	66	42	26	68	180	125	305	—	—	—	259	180	439
In Voluntary Homes															
(*a*) Within the City	—	—	—	—	—	—	1	3	4	—	—	—	1	3	4
(*b*) Outside the City	1	—	1	7	6	13	79	58	137	—	8	8	87	72	159
Total ..	1	—	1	7	6	13	80	61	141	—	8	8	88	75	163
In Corporation Boys' Hostel, "Lochaber" ..										18	—	18	18	—	18
In Working Boys' Hostels										93	—	93	93	—	93
On After Care Roll										7	7	14	7	7	14
Total ..										118	7	125	118	7	125

SOURCE: *Children's Department. Glasgow Corporation.*

[1] There are no complete and separate Reception Homes but there are Reception Sections in Residential Homes.

PART IV - SECTION 5

The Churches

TABLE 162

CHURCH ATTENDANCE, GLASGOW, ON THREE SUNDAYS,

SPRING, 1954

Denomination	*Number of Churches*	*Adult Attendance, 1954*		
		April 25	*May 2*	*May 9*
Church of Scotland	215	44,330	44,572	46,981
Baptist Union	22	1,957	1,990	2,120
Congregational Union	23	2,730	2,851	2,962
Free Church	8	1,508	1,090	1,624
Methodist Church	17	1,468	1,571	1,759
United Free Church	17	1,235	1,435	1,402
	302	53,228	53,509	56,848
Episcopal Church	26	1,886	2,010	2,029
Non-Roman Catholic	328	55,114	55,519	58,877
Roman Catholic	57	91,137	92,031	93,732
Total (Eight Denominations) ..	385	146,251	147,550	152,609

SOURCE: *Dr. Highet's Census of Church Attendance.*

TABLE 163

CHURCH ATTENDANCE, GLASGOW, ON THREE SUNDAYS, SPRING, 1955, WITH INCREASE OVER CORRESPONDING SUNDAYS, 1954

Denomination	*Adult Attendance, 1955*		
	May 1	*May 8*	*May 15*
Church of Scotland	57,443	53,404	48,605
Baptist Union	2,752	2,763	2,497
Congregational Union	3,988	3,420	3,566
Episcopal Church	2,445	2,298	2,154
Free Church	1,468	1,860	1,398
Methodist Church	1,936	2,072	1,788
United Free Church	2,047	1,717	1,612
Total (Seven Denominations)	72,079	67,534	61,620
Increase over corresponding Sunday, 1954 ..	16,965	12,015	2,743
Per Cent Increase	30.8	21.6	4.7

SOURCE: *Dr. Highet's Census of Church Attendance.*

TABLE 164

CHURCH ATTENDANCE, GLASGOW, ON THREE SUNDAYS, SPRING, 1956 AND COMPARISONS WITH 1955 AND 1954

Denomination	*Adult Attendance*, 1956		
	April 29	*May* 6	*May* 13
Church of Scotland	48,054	50,893	50,931
Baptist Union	2,275	2,182	2,264
Congregational Union	2,992	3,289	3,322
Free Church	1,463	1,575	1,649
Methodist Church	1,564	1,646	1,611
United Free Church	1,401	1,516	1,452
	57,749	61,101	61,229
Episcopal Church	2,172	2,204	2,217
Total (Seven Denominations)	59,921	63,305	63,446
Comparison with 1955: Increase(+) or Decrease (−)	−12,158	−4,229	+1,826
Percentage Increase or Decrease	−16.9	−6.3	+3.0
Comparison with 1954: Increase (+) or Decrease (−)	+4,807	+7,786	+4,569
Percentage Increase or Decrease	+8.7	+14.0	+7.8

SOURCE: *Dr. Highet's Census of Church Attendance.*

INDEX TO STATISTICAL APPENDIX

LIST OF CONTRIBUTORS

Robert Baird, *Department of Social & Economic Research, Glasgow University.*

Roy H. Campbell, *Department of Economic History, Glasgow University.*

Agnes R. Cleveland, *School of Social Study, Glasgow University.*

G. D. Costain, *Department of Industrial Administration, Royal College of Science & Technology, Glasgow.*

Rev. Wm. C. Galbraith, *Minister of St. George's-in-the-Fields, Glasgow.*

Maxwell Gaskin, *Department of Political Economy, Glasgow University.*

W. Allan Gay, *Department of Industrial Administration, Royal College of Science & Technology, Glasgow.*

J. B. S. Gilfillan, *Department of Scottish History & Literature, Glasgow University.*

Zygmunt Grosicki, *Department of Textile Technology, Royal College of Science & Technology, Glasgow.*

Paul Hanika, *Department of Industrial Administration, Royal College of Science & Technology, Glasgow.*

John Highet, *Senior Lecturer in Sociology, Glasgow University.*

Wm. A Horne, *Medical Officer of Health, Glasgow.*

Jack House, *Feature Writer,* Evening Times.

C. E. V. Leser, *Formerly Lecturer in Economic Statistics, Glasgow University.*

John Loudon, *Department of Industrial Administration, Royal College of Science & Technology, Glasgow.*

John A. Mack, *Stevenson Lecturer in Citizenship, Glasgow University.*

Douglas MacKenzie, *Department of Industrial Administration, Royal College of Science & Technology, Glasgow.*

Alfred W. Marvin, *Department of Textile Technology, Royal College of Science & Technology, Glasgow.*

James Orr, *Department of Mechanical Engineering, Glasgow University.*

Sarah C. Orr, *Department of Political Economy, Glasgow University.*

Andrew M. Robb, *Professor Emeritus, John Elder Chair of Naval Architecture, Glasgow University.*

Donald J. Robertson, *Department of Political Economy, Glasgow University.*

J. F. Sleeman, *Department of Political Economy, Glasgow University.*

Donald G. Southgate, *Lecturer in Political and Constitutional History, Queen's College, Dundee, University of St. Andrews.*

SOURCES OF INFORMATION

Because of limitations of space an exhaustive bibliography relating to the City of Glasgow cannot be attempted here; nor is it possible to acknowledge adequately the valuable assistance rendered by numerous individuals in the preparation of this Account. A short list of books and of helpers is given below under the relevant chapter headings, preceded by a note of some general statistical works, official reports and other sources of information drawn upon by contributors.

GENERAL

Census of Scotland, Reports, 1801-1951.
Sir John Sinclair—*The Statistical Account of Scotland* (1791-99).
Sir John Sinclair—*General Report* (1814).
Sir John Sinclair—*Analysis of the Statistical Account of Scotland* (1825).
The New Statistical Account of Scotland (1834-45).
John Strang—*Report on the Vital and Economic Statistics of Glasgow for 1856* (1857).
John Strang—*Report on the Vital and Economic Statistics of Glasgow for 1858-1861* (1862).
Wm. West Watson—*Report upon the Vital, Social and Economic Statistics of Glasgow for 1863 and 1864* (1865).
Wm. West Watson—*Report upon the Vital, Social and Economic Statistics of Glasgow for 1876* (1877).
Wm. West Watson—*Report upon the Vital, Social and Economic Statistics of Glasgow for 1878* (1879).
Wm. West Watson—*Report upon the Vital, Social and Economic Statistics of Glasgow for 1880* (1881).
James Nicol—*Vital, Social and Economic Statistics of the City of Glasgow, 1881-85* (1885).
James Nicol—*Vital, Social and Economic Statistics of the City of Glasgow, 1885-91* (1891).
Corporation of Glasgow—*Facts and Figures* (Annual).

Corporation of Glasgow—DEPARTMENTAL REPORTS:

Baths—Commenced 1900; no breaks; Annual.
Children's—Commenced year 1949/50; no breaks; Annual.
Cleansing—Commenced 1869; no publications 1941-45; Annual.
Education—Commenced 1872; published triennially till 1907; from 1908 published annually; period 1939-48 issued in one volume; after 1948-49 reverted to triennial publications.
Education Health Service—Commenced 1907/8 (Govan Parish School Board); commenced 1909/10 (School Board of Glasgow); combined in 1919 (Education Authority for City); from 1930 report issued under auspices of Health Committee; no breaks; Annual.
Fire—Commenced year to May 1900; breaks 1940/41 to 1947/48; now published in calendar years; Annual.
Housing—All material in the one volume, 1919-47 (the only publication).
Libraries—Commenced 1874; break from 1895 to 1947; recommenced 1948/49; Annual.
Medical Officer of Health—Commenced 1863; break 1914-19; Annual.
Sanitary Inspector—Commenced 1871; break 1914-19; merged with M.O.H. Report from 1920 (this also covered the 1914-19 period); Annual.

Museums and Art Galleries—Commenced 1876 (as City Industrial Museum Report); in 1902 changed title to Art Gallery Report; no publications from 1918 to 1941; publications resumed 1942; Annual.

Office of Public Works—Commenced 1895/96; break 1916/17—1924/25; recommenced 1925/26 to 1937/38; 1938-48 produced in one volume; latest publication June 1949-May 1955.

Police—Commenced 1859; no breaks; Annual.

Probation—Commenced 1934; no breaks; Annual.

Transport—Commenced 1947; no breaks; Annual.

Water—Centenary volumes 1836/1936 and 1855/1955. Annual.

Welfare—Earliest records commence in 1858; from 1895, annual statistics of pauperism in respect of the Barony, Govan and City Parishes; from 1929/30 to 1947/48, the Welfare Department published an Annual Report, and from 1948 the Medical Officer of Health has dealt with Welfare in his report.

CHAPTER 1—THE SITE AND ITS DEVELOPMENT

Bibliography

Reports of the Boundary Commissioners

City of Glasgow—*Municipal Extension Acts.*

Glasgow Corporation—*First and Second Planning Reports to the Highways and Planning Committee* (1945 & 1946).

Glasgow Corporation—*Report on Activities of the Office of Public Works, 1938-48* (1949).

L. Becker—*The Climatology of Glasgow* (1918).

Dugald Bell—*Among the Rocks around Glasgow* (1881).

British Association—*Handbook on the Fauna, Flora and Geology of the Clyde Area* (1901).

James Cleland—*Annals of Glasgow* (1816).

F. Groome (Ed.)—*The Ordnance Gazetteer of Scotland* (1885).

Stuart I. A. Laidlaw—*The Menace of Polluted Air* (1952).

W. J. McCallien—*Geology of Glasgow and District* (1938).

Hugh MacIntosh—*The Origin and History of Glasgow Streets* (1902).

David Murray—*The Streets of Glasgow and their History* (1925).

Blaeu's *Atlas* (1654).

Joseph Swan's *Select Views of Glasgow and its Environs* (1828).

Acknowledgments

Cyril A. Halstead, Lecturer in Geography, Glasgow University.

Dr. W. M. Smart, Professor of Astronomy, Glasgow University.

City Architect and Planning Officer, Glasgow Corporation, and members of his Department.

Director, Parks Department, Glasgow Corporation, and members of his Department.

Master of Works and City Engineer, Glasgow Corporation, and members of his Department.

Medical Officer of Health for Glasgow, and members of his Department.

Chemist and City Analyst, Glasgow Corporation.

The Meteorological Office, Edinburgh.

Members of the Meteorological Office, Renfrew Airport.

CHAPTER 2—POPULATION—PAST AND PRESENT

Bibliography

Census of Scotland, Reports, 1801-1951.
Annual Estimates of the Registrar General for Scotland.
Annual Reports of the Medical Officer of Health for Glasgow.
Annual Reports of the Chief Constable, Glasgow.
A. K. Cairncross (Ed.)—*The Scottish Economy* (1954).
Enid Charles—"*Differential Fertility in Scotland,* 1911-1931," in *Transactions of the Royal Society of Edinburgh,* Vol. 59, 1936-9.
C. E. V. Leser—"*Variations in Mortality and Life Expectation*" in *Population Studies,* Vol. IX, July 1955.
D. F. Macdonald—*Scotland's Shifting Population* (1937).

Acknowledgments

The Registrar General for Scotland.
The Department of Health for Scotland.
Aliens Registration Department, City of Glasgow Police.
City Architect and Planning Officer, Glasgow Corporation.

CHAPTER 3—THE HISTORICAL SETTING

Bibliography

Sheriff Barclay—*Reminiscences of Glasgow* (1880).
J. J. Bell—*I Remember* (1932).
British Association—*Handbook on Archæology, Education, Medical and Charitable Institutions* (1901).
Colm Brogan—*The Glasgow Story* (1952).
T. C. F. Brotchie—*History of Govan* (1905).
Andrew Brown—*History of Glasgow* (1795).
J. D. Burn—*Commercial Enterprise and Social Progress* (1858).
R. G. Cant & I. G. Lindsay—*Old Glasgow* (1947).
Alexander Carlyle—*Autobiography* (1860).
P. MacGregor Chalmers—*The Cathedral Church of Glasgow* (1914).
James Cleland—*Annals of Glasgow* (1816).
James Cleland—*The Rise and Progress of the City of Glasgow* (1820).
James Cleland—*The Former and Present State of Glasgow* (1840).
Henry Cockburn—*Journal, 1831-54* (1874).
James Coutts—*A History of the University of Glasgow* (1909).
James Cowan—*From Glasgow's Treasure Chest* (1951).
James Denholm—*History of the City of Glasgow* (3rd edn. 1804).
W. J. Duncan (Ed.)—*Notes and Documents illustrative of the Literary History of Glasgow* (1886).
George Eyre-Todd and Robert Renwick—*History of Glasgow* (3 vols. 1921-34).
Thomas Ferguson—*The Dawn of Scottish Social Welfare* (1948).
R. Gillespie—*Glasgow and the Clyde* (1876).
Glasgow Academy: the First Hundred Years (1946).
J. F. S. Gordon (Ed.)—*Glasghu Facies* (1872).
James Grant—*History of the Burgh Schools of Scotland* (1876).
John Gunn (Ed.)—*The City of Glasgow: its Origin, Growth and Development* (1921).
R. Harvey—*Early Days of Engineering in Glasgow* (1919).
James Hedderwick—*Backward Glances* (1891).

Thomas Howarth—*Charles Rennie Mackintosh and the Modern Movement* (1953).
J. Knight—*Glasgow and Strathclyde* (1931).
Theo Lang (Ed.)—*Glasgow, Kyle and Galloway* (1953).
H. Lumsden—*Records of the Trades House of Glasgow* (1910 & 1934).
W. F. MacArthur—*History of Port Glasgow* (1932).
A. McCallum—*History of Pollokshaws* (1925).
Hugh Macdonald—*Rambles Round Glasgow* (1854).
J. K. McDowall—*The People's History of Glasgow* (1899).
Andrew MacGeorge—*Old Glasgow* (1880).
George MacGregor—*The History of Glasgow* (1881).
Peter Mackenzie—*Old Reminiscences of Glasgow and the West of Scotland* (1865-6).
J. D. Mackie—*The University of Glasgow, 1451-1951* (1954).
John Macky—*A Journey through Scotland* (1723).
John McUre—*History of Glasgow* (1736).
James Maidment's *Topographical Collection* (*Lanarkshire*).
D. M. Malloch—*The Book of Glasgow Anecdote* (1912).
David Martin—*The Glasgow School of Painting* (1897).
J. D. Marwick—*The Water Supply of the City of Glasgow* (1901).
J. D. Marwick—*The River Clyde and the Clyde Burghs* (1909).
J. D. Marwick—*Early Glasgow* (1911).
W. H. Marwick—*Adult Education in Glasgow 80 Years Ago* (1931).
Herbert Maxwell (Ed.)—*The Lowland Scots Regiments* (1918).
J. O. Mitchell—*Old Glasgow Essays* (1905).
James Muir—*Glasgow Streets and Places: notes and memoranda* (1899).
"James Hamilton Muir"—*Glasgow in 1901* (1901).
David Murray—*Early Burgh Organization in Scotland, as illustrated in the history of Glasgow and of some neighbouring burghs* (2 vols., 1924-32).
David Murray—*Memories of the Old College of Glasgow: some chapters in the history of the University* (1927).
James Nicol—*Vital, Social and Economic Statistics of the City of Glasgow 1881-1885* (1885).
James Nicol—*Vital, Social and Economic Statistics of the City of Glasgow 1885-1891* (1891).
C. A. Oakley—*The Second City* (1946).
J. Ord—*Barony of Gorbals* (1919).
Archd. Orr-Ewing—*View of the Merchants' House of Glasgow* (1866).
James Pagan—*Sketch of the History of Glasgow* (1847).
D. Pollock (Ed.)—*Dictionary of the Clyde* (1891).
James Primrose—*Medieval Glasgow* (1913).
J. M. Reid—*Glasgow* (1956).
Robert Reid ("Senex")—*Glasgow, Past and Present* (1851).
Robert Reid ("Senex")—*Old Glasgow and its Environs* (1864).
Report on the Burgh and Middle Class Schools of Scotland (1868).
John Guthrie Smith & others—*The Old Country Houses of the Old Glasgow Gentry* (1870).
Rev. John Smith—*Andrew Melville: an Oration delivered in the University of Glasgow on Commemoration Day* (1910).
Rev. John Smith—*Broken Links in Scottish Education* (1913).
G. Stewart—*Curiosities of Glasgow Citizenship* (1881).
John Strang—*Glasgow and its Clubs* (1856).
John Strang—*Social and Economic Statistics of Glasgow* (1862).
Tait's *Glasgow Directory* (1783).
Rev. W. M. Wade—*The History of Glasgow, Ancient and Modern* (1821).
Andrew Wallace—*Popular Traditions of Glasgow: Historical, Legendary and Biographical* (1889).

Acknowledgments

Members of the staff of Glasgow Corporation Libraries, Museums and Art Galleries.
J. L. Leckie, of the Glasgow "Ours" Club.

CHAPTER 4—INDUSTRIES—PRELIMINARY SURVEY

Bibliography

Ministry of Labour Gazette.
Digest of Scottish Statistics (annual).
City of Birmingham—*Abstract of Statistics, No. 2* (1952).
C. E. V. Leser—*Some Aspects of the Industrial Structure of Scotland* (1951).
C. A. Oakley—*Scottish Industry To-day* (1938).
C. A. Oakley—*Scottish Industry* (1953).
Scottish Industrial Estates (Brochure) (1954).

Acknowledgments

Ministry of Labour and National Service.
Board of Trade, Office for Scotland (Research Section)
The Scottish Council (Development and Industry).
Federation of British Industries.
Scottish Industrial Estates Ltd.
South of Scotland Electricity Board.
Traffic Superintendent, Scotland, British European Airways.
Commercial Manager, British Railways.
Secretary, Clyde Navigation Trust.
J. D. M. Bell, formerly of the Social and Economic Research Department, Glasgow University.

CHAPTER 5—IRON AND STEEL

Bibliography

General

Balfour Committee on Industry and Trade—*Survey of Metal Industries* (1928).
Board of Trade—*Industrial Survey of the South West of Scotland,* by the staff of the Political Economy Department, Glasgow University (1932).
Import Duties Advisory Committee—*Report on the Present Position and Future Development of the Iron and Steel Industry, 1936-7,* Vol. 12.
Clydesdale & North of Scotland Bank—*Annual Survey of Economic Conditions in Scotland.*
D. L. Burn—*The Economic History of Steel-making, 1867-1939* (1940).
J. V. Day—*The Iron and Steel Industries of Scotland* (British Association Handbook, 1876).

Histories of Firms

Shaw & McInnes Ltd.—*One Hundred Years of Family Business* (1946).
Stewarts & Lloyds Ltd. 1903-1953 (Commemorative volume published by the Company).

Acknowledgments

J. Gray Buchanan, Chairman, William Jacks & Co. Ltd.
Dr. P. T. Carter, Lecturer in Metallurgy, Royal College of Science and Technology.
M. W. Flinn, master, Isleworth Grammar School.
Dr. R. Hay, Professor of Metallurgy, Royal College of Science and Technology.
R. Liston, Metallurgist.

Sir Robert Shone, Iron & Steel Board, London.
P. W. Thomas, Secretary, West of Scotland Iron & Steel Institute.
Dr. G. Thomson, Lecturer in Chemistry, Glasgow University.

The following firms replied to questionnaires:

Colvilles
Dixon's Ironworks.
William Beardmore & Co.
The Steel Company of Scotland.
Govan Shafting & Engineering Co.
Smith & McLean.
Stewarts & Lloyds.
John Inshaw.
McCallum & Hope.
Kerr & Co. (Maryhill).
Ferromac Foundries.
J. & A. Law.
Colston Iron Works.
Shaw & McInnes.
The Carron Co.
Mirrlees Watson Co.
Wilson Pipe Fittings.
William Cook & Sons (Glasgow).
Ever-Ready Razor Products.
William Reid & Sons (Wireworkers).
Begg, Cousland & Co.
Guest, Keen & Nettlefolds (Midlands).
William Motherwell & Co.
George Boyd & Co..
Watson & McLean.
Associated Metal Works.
James G. Carrick & Co.

CHAPTER 6—SHIPBUILDING AND MARINE ENGINEERING

Bibliography

General

The Glasgow Herald Annual Trade Reviews.
Lloyd's *Register of Shipping.*
British Association—*Handbook on the Local Industries of Glasgow and the West of Scotland* (1901).
James Cleland—*Annals of Glasgow* (1816).
W. S. Cormack—*An Economic History of Shipbuilding and Marine Engineering* (unpublished thesis, 1931, in Glasgow University Library).
John Shields—*Clyde Built* (1949).

Histories of Firms

Barclay, Curle & Co. Ltd.—*Development of Shipbuilding on the Upper Reaches of the Clyde* (1911).
Sir Allan Grant—*Steel and Ships* (1950) (A history of John Brown's).
Denny, Dumbarton, 1844-1932 (1932).
Two Centuries of Shipbuilding by the Scotts at Greenock (1920).
J. L. Carvel—*Stephen of Linthouse. A Record of Two Hundred Years of Shipbuilding, 1750-1950.*

Acknowledgments

Department of the Chief of Naval Information, The Admiralty.
The Clyde Shipbuilders' Association.
The Shipbuilding Conference.

The following firms replied to questionnaires:

Barclay, Curle & Co.
British Polar Engines.
Harland & Wolff.
D. & W. Henderson.
A. & J. Inglis.
Miller Insulation & Engineering.
David Rowan & Co.
Scottish Lion Shipbuilding & Engineering Co.
Alexander Stephen & Sons.
Simpson-Lawrence.
The Bergius Co.
The Fairfield Shipbuilding & Engineering Co.
Yarrow & Co.

CHAPTER 7—OTHER ENGINEERING

Bibliography

General

Reports of Census of Scotland.
British Association—*Handbook on the Local Industries of Glasgow and the West of Scotland* (1901).
British Association Handbook—W. R. Scott, *The Industry and Commerce of the Clyde Valley* (1928).
H. Hamilton—*The Industrial Revolution in Scotland* (1932).
C. A. Oakley—*Scottish Industry* (1953).

Histories of Firms

Sir William Arrol & Co. Ltd.—*Bridges, Structural Steel Work and Mechanical Engineering Production* (1909).
H. Cunningham—*Sir William Arrol & Company Ltd., 1909-1950.*
Messrs. Barr & Stroud Ltd. (Souvenir Handbook, 1919).
James Howden & Co. Ltd.—*A Hundred Years of Howden Engineering, 1854-1954.*
Mavor & Coulson Ltd.—*Fifty Years of Pioneering, 1881-1931.*
North British Locomotive Company Ltd.—*A History of the Company* (1953).
Sir Samuel Beale—*L. Sterne & Company, Ltd., 1874-1949.*

Acknowledgments

J. Martin Baxter, of P. & W. MacLellan Ltd.
G. H. Cutbush, Editor, *Motor World.*
A. Donaldson, late of Albion Motor Works.
Hugh W. Fulton, Albion Motor Works.

The following firms replied to questionnaires:

Innes Walker (Engineering) Co.
Penman & Co.
Muir & Findlay
James Howden & Co.
M. Macdonald & Son.
The North British Locomotive Co.
Anderson, Whan & Co.
Wickman.
Hugh Smith & Co. (Possil).
Nicol & Andrew.
James Bissell & Co.
Mercer & Garside.
Vertimax.
Scottish Machine Tool Corporation.
William Wilkie & Son.
Stewart & McKenzie.
J. & T. Boyd.
John Dalglish & Sons.
British Olivetti.
Remington Rand.
The Glacier Metal Co.
Mavor & Coulson.
Mine Safety Appliances Co.
James Combe & Son.
Winsor Engineering Co.
Charles McNeil.
Myreside Engineering Co.
James Ferguson & Munro.
Laurence, Scott & Electromotors.
The Macfarlane Engineering Co.
P. & R. Fleming & Co.
P. & W. MacLellan.
R. Smith & Co. (Dennistoun).
Sir William Arrol & Co.
Acme Welding & Constructional Engineering Co.
Fleming Bros. (Structural Engineers).
The Pennycook Patent Glazing & Engineering Co.
Frederick Braby & Co.
Lambhill Ironworks.
Rolls-Royce.
Albion Motors.
Argyle Cycles.
King Aircraft Corporation.
H. Churchill & Sons.
Cockburn Bros. (Govan).
Lancefield Foundry Co.
Fry's Metal Foundries.
William Stevenson & Co. (Lead).

Jamieson & Co. (Ventilating Engineers).
Kilday & Co.
Mechans.
Thermotank.
Parkinson & Cowan Gas Meters.
George Orme & Co.
A. & P. Steven.
Butters Bros. & Co.
Glasgow Engineers.
Paterson Hughes Engineering Co.
Parker Mitchell Engineering Co.
J. H. Carruthers & Co.
Matthew Wylie & Co.
L. Sterne & Co.
David Scott & Co.
Glass & Steel Products.
Alley & Maclellan (Polmadie).
Duncan Stewart & Co.
Drysdale & Co.
G. & J. Weir.
Blairs.
Andrew Young & Son.
John McNeil & Co.
West of Scotland Wringer Co.
Acme Wringers.
Robertson Bakery Engineering Co.
Ultra Rapid Machines (Scotland).
Cockburns.
Watson, Laidlaw & Co.
A. Cockburn & Co. (Engineers).
Scottish Precision Engineering Co.
G. B. Montgomery Manufacturing Co. (Glasgow).
Burdon Furnaces
E. Chalmers & Co.
D.C.M. Metals (Glasgow).
Robert Currie & Sons.
Dewrance & Co.
Chloride Batteries.
Claude-General Neon Lights.
Scottish Telecommunications.
Atkins, Robertson & Whiteford.
Craigpark Electric Cable Co.
Heatovent Electric.
Duncan Low.
James Grindlay & Co.
Thomas Bishop.
William Rome (Files).
Andrew Fraser (Safes).
Electro-Platers.
Docherty & Co.
Glasgow Expanded Metal Co.
L.M.S. Products.
Chromium Platers.
William McPhail & Sons.
Bull's Metal & Marine.
C. & A. Stewart.
The Horne Engineering Co.
Kingston Brass Co.
William Ross & Sons.
Scottish Precision Castings.
John Glover & Sons (Bridgeton).
Steven & Struthers.
Barr & Stroud.
Kelvin & Hughes.
John Jamieson (Glasgow).
Robert MacLaren & Co.
Dobbie, McInnes.

CHAPTER 8—TEXTILES AND CLOTHING

Bibliography

General

Factories Enquiry Commission, 1832—*First and Second Reports* (1833).
Factory Commission, 1832—*Analysis of Evidence.*
E. Baines—*History of the Cotton Manufacture in Great Britain* (1836).
D. Bremner—*Industries of Scotland* (1869).
J. Ingram—*Notes on Early Textiles in Scotland.*
A. W. Marvin—*The Rise of the Scottish Knitwear Industry* (Articles in *The Times Weekly Review,* July 25 and Oct. 17, 1951, and Jan. 2, 1952).
C. A. Oakley—*The Second City* (1946).

Histories of Firms

D. & J. Anderson Ltd.—*Famous Fabrics, 1822-1952* (1952).
The Gourock Ropework Co. Ltd.—*The Gourock* (1954).
J. E. Lyle—*The Carpet House of Lyle* (1953).
F. H. Young—*A Century of Carpet-making, 1839-1939* (A history of James Templeton & Company) (1944).

Acknowledgments

Ministry of Labour and National Service.
National Union of Hosiery Workers (Scottish Section).

The following firms replied to questionnaires:

Dunlop Cotton Mills.
George Melville.
The Scottish Towel Co.
John Lean & Sons.
William Strang & Son.
Wilson Bros. & D. G. Howat & Co.
William Wiseman & Sons.
J. Macarthur & Co.
D. & J. Anderson.
William Hollins & Co.
F. Friedlander (Great Britain).
The Gourock Ropework Co.
Kid-Knit Manufacturing Co.
Twomax Knitwear (McClure & McIntosh).
J. Clark & Co. (Knitwear).
Moray Textiles (Glasgow).
James Sharpe (Knitwear).
The Kidmar Hosiery Co.
Strathclyde Hosiery Co.
James Templeton & Co.
John Lyle & Co.
James Park & Co.
Wallace & Co. (Netherplace).
J. & H. M. Dickson.
Robert Douglas & Brittain.
William Burns (Glasgow).
John McFarlane & McAlister.
J. K. Mills & Co.
Andrew D. MacNair & Co.
West Flock Co.
Corrance & Yuill.
John Allan & Sons.
James Walker (Insulators).
John W. Hannay & Co.
The Scottish Wool Flock Co.
M. & H. Harris.
B. Aiken.
M. Barr & Co.
Charles Konchater.
Albert Granet.
Edward MacBean & Co.
Norman N. Taylor & Co.
Canda Manufacturing Co.
A. Simmons.
G. J. Mason & Co.
Fraser Ross (Glasgow).
Glassford Tailoring Co.
D. & H. Silver.
Joyce Tailored Wear.
Gymoza Products.
Mastercraft (Tailoring).
Harris & Samuel.
Balfrae Clothing Manufacturers.
Cowen & Bryer.
William Hall (Junior).
Glen-Har.
Delcoats.
Barnett Taylor & Sons.
A. Taylor & Co. of Bridgeton.
D. & H. Cohen.
Charles A. Orr.
Ralph Burns.
James Brodie & Co.
A. Field.
J. H. Lindsay & Co. (Lindsay Maid).
Brook Manufacturing Co. (Northampton).
A. & J. Gelfer.
Connal & Bannatyne.
James Ritchie & Co.
Gardner & Johnston.
Salton Brown & Co.
J. & E. Shinwell.
Alexander S. Clark.
A. W. Cook & Co.
David Neilson & Co.
Neil Meiklejohn & Co.
Pollock & Green.
Muir Young & Martin.
James Young Sons & Co.
Southbank Leather Co.
Haven Products.

CHAPTER 9—OTHER MANUFACTURING INDUSTRIES

Bibliography

General

British Association—*Handbook on the Local Industries of Glasgow and the West of Scotland* (1901).
Corporation of Glasgow—*Glasgow Industrial Guide* (1955).
David Murray—*Robert and Andrew Foulis and the Glasgow Press* (1913).
C. A. Oakley (Ed.)—*Buyers' Guide to Scottish Industries* (Annual).
C. A. Oakley—*Industrial Map of Scotland* (compiled for the Scottish Development Council, 1939).
C. A. Oakley—*Scottish Industry* (1953).
Stratten & Stratten—*Glasgow and its Environs: a Literary, Commercial and Social Review Past & Present; with a Description of its Leading Mercantile Houses and Commercial Enterprises* (1891).

Histories of Firms

Blackie & Son Ltd.—*Sketch of the Origin and Progress of the Firm, 1809-74* (1897).
W. W. Blackie—*John Blackie, Senior* (*1782-1874*) (1933).
W. W. Blackie—*Walter Graham Blackie* (*1816-1905*) (1936).
David Keir—*The House of Collins* (1952).
R. & J. Dick Ltd.—*100 Years of Guttapercha* (1946).
Farquharson Bros. Ltd.—*Milestones: a Brief Review of 50 Years' Progress* (1950).
J. Maclehose—*The Glasgow University Press, 1638-1931* (1931).
R. D. MacLeod—*The Scottish Publishing Houses* (1953).
J. & J. Murdoch Ltd.—*The First Hundred Years* (1944).
S. Straker & Sons Ltd.—*Fifty Years Together* (1943).
William Thomlinson Ltd.—*The Story of a Famous House* (n.d.).
W. D. & H. O. Wills—*Tobacco: its Culture and Manufacture* (1949).

Acknowledgments

E. Dawson, Secretary, Glasgow and West of Scotland Aerated Water Manufacturers' and Beer Bottlers' Defence Association.
L. I. Macbeth and staff of Research Section, Board of Trade, Office for Scotland.
C. A. Oakley, former Controller (Scotland), Board of Trade.
The Secretary, The Imperial Tobacco Co. (of Great Britain and Ireland) Ltd.

The following firms replied to questionnaires:

Brownlee & Co.
Robinson, Dunn & Co.
James Adams & Co.
James Kennedy & Co.
A. & T. Begg.
The Timber Fireproofing Co.
H. Morris & Co.
John McGregor & Sons.
Wylie & Lochhead.
L. Levin & Sons.
Sragowitz & Gillman.
D. MacDonald & Bros.
Thomas W. Wilson.
Clydesdale Cabinet Works.
Archibald Stewart & Co. (Furnishers).
James D. Bennet.
Andrew Thomson & Sons (Furniture Manufacturers).
The Steadfast Furniture Manufacturing Co.
L. Strang & Son.
Walker & Clark (Ryse-Rite).
J. Dykes.
Dollar-Rae Shopfitters.
Colin Hunter.
British Basket & Besto Co.
Clyde Cooperage Co.
Robert Burley & Sons.
Daniel Montgomery & Son.
Wm. Rankin & Sons.
Wm. Rankin (Crown Corks).
James Anderson & Co. (Colours).
British Dyewood Co.
R. & J. Garroway.
Askit.
Ault & Wiborg (Scotland).
Sandeman Bros.
W. B. Dick & Co.
Ferguson Shaw & Sons.
Percy & Halden.
Archibald H. Hamilton & Co.
Montgomerie, Stobo & Co.
Simpson, Thomson & Shannon.
Federated Paints.
Sandeman's Varnish.
MacArthur & Jackson.
Thomas Hinshelwood & Co.
Craig & Rose.
Lewis Berger (Scotland).
Imperial Chemical Industries.
Thomas Taylor.
Donaldson Golf Club Manufacturing Co.
William Thomlinson.
Gymnastic Equipment Engineering Co.
John Letters & Co.
Ioco.
"Colonel" Rubber Manufacturing Co.
R. & J. Dick.
The Regent Tyre & Rubber Co.
The City India Rubber Co.
George MacLellan & Co.
Andrew Muirhead & Son.
W. & J. Martin.
Millars.
The Ronson Fur Service.
H. M. & W. Sochart.
Edmund Taylor & Son.
John Fraser & Sons.
Universal Covers.
Robert Alford & Sons.
M. Segal (Travelware).
John Paterson & Son.
Garrowhill Brickworks.

Aerox.
D. McDougall & Co.
Wilson's Terrazzo Manufacturing Co.
Marinite.
Unit Concrete Co.
Bath & Portland Stone Firms.
Oswald Toffolo & Co.
Scott & Rae.
Val de Travers Asphalte.
Limmer & Trinidad Lake Asphalte Co.
Marley Tile Co.
Toffolo Jackson & Co.
Chance Bros.
Fibreglass.
John Baird.
Edward Collins & Sons.
George Stark & Sons.
The Dalsholm Paper Co.
John Laird & Son.
New Safety Containers.
Charles Sprenger & Sons.
William Clark Stephen.
William Vass Graham & Parata.
Charles G. Donald & Co.
James Munro & Co.
Donaldson & Filer.
William Collins Sons & Co.
Blackie & Son.
Robert MacLehose & Co.
McCorquodale & Co.
D. Mills Duncan & Co.
John McCormick & Co.
Glasgow Numerical Printing Co.
Wilson Guthrie & Co.
Alexander Woodrow & Son.
Millar & Lang.
J. & J. Murdoch.
Livingstone Bros.
John Watson & Co.
Duncan Campbell & Son.
Gilmour & Dean.
John Thomlinson.
Farquharson Bros.
Gray Dunn & Co.
Bilsland Bros.
Beatties Bakeries.
Welma Bakeries.
Walter Hubbard.
A. F. Reid & Sons.
R. A. Peacock & Son.
Thomas Lennie & Son.
Galbraith's Stores.
John Dalziel & Co.
T. & W. Weir.
J. & R. Caldwell.
Montgomerie & Co.
J. & R. Snodgrass.
Edward Mackenzie.
Reeves.
MacMillan & Monro.
John Buchanan & Bros.
Drysdale & Gibb.
Clyde Confections.
T. D. Finlayson (Confectioners).
R. S. McColl.
Sister Laura's Food.
East Kilbride Dairy Farmers.
Sloan's Dairies.
Norie.
Mellis (Glasgow).
Fletcher & Sons.
Ingram Bros. (Glasgow).
Creamola Food Products.
James Marshall (Glasgow).
Jean MacGregor.
R. Paterson & Sons.
Malga Products.
Stoddart & Bansford.
W. A. Parker & Co. (Grain).
Cardowan Creameries.
William Brock & Son.
Andrew Motherwell.
Glasgow Curers.
J. & R. Tennent.
Scottish Grain Distilling Co.
A. G. Barr & Co.
G. & P. Barrie.
Citrus Products Co.
Robertson Fruit Products.
The Imperial Tobacco Co. (of Great Britain & Ireland).

CHAPTER 10—TRANSPORT AND COMMUNICATIONS

Bibliography

Aer Lingus—Official Time-tables.
British European Airways—Official Time-tables.
Board of Trade—Annual Statement of Trade of the United Kingdom, Vol. IV Supplement.
Board of Trade—Annual Statement of the Navigation and Shipping of the United Kingdom.
British Transport Commission—*Report on Passenger Transport in Glasgow and District* (*Inglis Report*) (1951).
Ministry of Transport and Civil Aviation—*Census of Mechanically Propelled Vehicles licensed in Quarter ending Sept. 30* (Annual).
Chief Constable of Glasgow—Annual Reports.

Clyde Navigation—*Report by Mr. John F. Ure on the Extension of the Harbour of Glasgow* (1854).
Clyde Navigation Trust—Annual Statistics.
Clyde Navigation Trust—*The Port of Glasgow* (1947).
Glasgow Corporation—*Development Plan, 1951.*
Glasgow Corporation Office of Public Works: National Traffic Census—*Return of Traffic Census within Glasgow, 16 & 22 August,* 1954.
Glasgow Corporation Transport Department—Annual Reports and Accounts.
Glasgow Corporation Transport Department—*50 Years of Municipal Transport* (1944).
J. D. Marwick—*The Water Supply of the City of Glasgow from the earliest times, with notes on various developments of the city till the close of 1900.* (1901).
J. D. Marwick—*The River Clyde and the Clyde Burghs* (1909).

Acknowledgments

British European Airways, Traffic Superintendent, Scotland.
British Railways—District Goods Superintendent.
British Railways—District Passenger Superintendent.
British Road Services, Scottish Division.
Clyde Navigation Trust.
David MacBrayne Ltd.
Department of Scientific and Industrial Research, Road Research Laboratory, Scottish Branch, Thorntonhall.
General Post Office, Head Postmaster, Glasgow.
Glasgow Corporation: Chief Constable.
Glasgow Corporation: Master of Works and City Engineer.
Glasgow Corporation: Motor Taxation Officer.
Glasgow Corporation: Town Clerk.
Glasgow Corporation: Transport Manager.
H.M. Customs and Excise, Glasgow.
Hunting-Clan Air Transport Ltd.
Ministry of Transport and Civil Aviation—Scottish Civil Aviation Divisional Office.
Ministry of Transport and Civil Aviation—Aerodrome Commandant, Renfrew.
Road Haulage Association Ltd., Scottish Area.
H. A. Moisley, Lecturer in Geography, Glasgow University.

CHAPTER 11—COMMERCE

Bibliography

General

J. Flanagen—*Wholesale Co-operation in Scotland, 1868-1918* (1920).
J. B. Jeffreys—*Retail Trading in Great Britain, 1850-1950* (1953).
J. B. Jeffreys (with M. MacColl and G. L. Levett)—*The Distribution of Consumer Goods* (1950).
Charles Madge—" War and the Small Retail Shop " in *Bulletin of the Institute of Statistics, Oxford,* Vol. 4, April 1942, Supplement No. 2.
W. Maxwell—*History of Co-operation in Scotland* (1910).

Histories of Firms

J. F. Barclay—*The Story of Arthur & Co. Ltd.* (1953).
Asa Briggs—*Friends of the People: the Centenary History of Lewis's* (1956).
Sir Thomas Lipton—*Leaves from the Lipton Logs* (1932).
Arthur Wilson—*Walter Wilson, Merchant, 1849-1917* (1920).
Royal Polytechnic Warehouse, Glasgow (Jubilee Celebrations Volume) (1887).

Acknowledgments

N. Carrick Anderson, Secretary, Wholesale Textile Association.
Arthur and Co.
G. S. Beattie, Secretary, Scottish Retail Drapers' Association.
G. T. Bookless, of Bookless Brothers (Glasgow).
Caledonian Clothing and Supply Co.
The Chairman, Glasgow Wholesale Fruit and Vegetable Traders' Association.
The City Factor.
Andrew Cochrane Ltd.
Copland and Lye.
John Cowie, of Cowie Brothers and Co.
Mary E. Dunn, of Ideal Dairies.
Elliott and Hetherington.
J. H. Gardner, of Cooper and Co.'s Stores.
The General Managers of the following Co-operative Societies: Clydebank, Cowlairs, Glasgow Eastern, Glasgow South, London Road, Rutherglen, St. George, St. Rollox, United Co-operative Bakeries.
The General Manager of Markets, Glasgow Corporation.
The House of Fraser.
R. Hunter, of Roxburgh, Colin Scott and Co.
Macdonald, Fraser and Co.
T. H. McHugh, of Campbells and Stewart and McDonald.
John H. McKenzie, of A. R. Brown, Macfarlane & Co.
W. H. Marr, of James Finlay and Co.
The President, Scottish Provision Trades Association.
The President, Wholesale Grocers' Association of Scotland.
The Registrar, Glasgow City Police.
A. F. Reid and Sons.
The Secretary, Chamber of Commerce and Manufactures of Glasgow.
The Secretary, Scottish Co-operative Wholesale Society.
The Secretary, Scottish Credit Traders' Federal Board.
James T. Skarrott, of Scottish Retail Investments.
J. H. Smith, Secretary, Treasurer and Statistical Secretary of the Glasgow and District Co-operative Association.
Tréron Ltd.

CHAPTER 12—FINANCE

Bibliography

G. Clayton—*The Provincial Stock Exchanges* (Paper delivered to Section F of the British Association, 3 Sept. 1953).
D. M. C. Donald—"Scottish Investment Trusts" in *The Scottish Bankers Magazine,* February 1956.
J. C. Gilbert—*The History of Investment Trusts in Dundee* (1939).
G. Glasgow—*The Scottish Investment Trust Companies* (1932).
T. Henderson—*The Savings Bank of Glasgow: One Hundred Years of Thrift* (1936).
R. F. Henderson—*The New Issues Market and the Finance of Industry* (1951).
G. G. C. Kennedy—"The Union Bank of Scotland: Its Contribution to Scottish Banking" in *The Scottish Bankers Magazine,* May 1955.
Sir John Mann—"Glimpses of Early Accountancy in Glasgow" in *The Accountants' Magazine,* June 1954.
D. Morrah—*A History of Industrial Assurance* (1955).
R. S. Rait—*A History of The Union Bank of Scotland* (1930).
J. M. Reid—*The History of The Clydesdale Bank, 1838-1938* (1938).
A. C. Stalker—"Scottish Insurance Companies" in *The Scottish Bankers Magazine,* May 1956.
Investment Trust Companies (Annual Statistics published by Messrs. Laing & Cruickshank, London).
Records of the Glasgow Stock Exchange Association, 1844-1926 (1927).

Acknowledgments

A. K. Brown, Manager, Glasgow Chief Office, Bank of Scotland.
City Chamberlain of Glasgow.
The Chairman, The Association of Underwriters and Insurance Brokers in Glasgow.
The Chairman and Secretary, The Glasgow Stock Exchange Association.
S. M. Duff, Assistant Manager, Glasgow Office, The British Linen Bank.
John Dunlop, of Moores, Carson & Watson, Chartered Accountants.
The General Manager, The Savings Bank of Glasgow.
J. F. A. Gibson, Secretary, Glasgow Industrial Finance.
W. T. Henderson, of S. M. Penney and MacGeorge, Stockbrokers.
The Manager, Bank of England Exchange Control Office, Glasgow.
D. F. McCurrach, of the Alliance Trust Co.
Olds Discount Co.
Regional Manager, Export Credits Guarantee Department, Glasgow.
Scottish Legal Life Assurance Society.
The Secretary, Associated Scottish Life Offices.
The Secretary, The Clydesdale and North of Scotland Bank.
The Secretary and Investment Secretary, Scottish Amicable Life Assurance Society.
United Dominions Trust.

CHAPTER 13—GOVERNMENT

Bibliography

Reports of the Boundary Commissioners.
Report of the Royal Commission on Municipal Corporations in Scotland (1833).
Report of the Commissioners on the Courts of Law in Scotland (1869).
Glasgow Corporation—*Second Planning Report to the Highways and Planning Committee* (1946).
Abercrombie & Matthew—*The Clyde Valley Regional Plan, 1946* (1949).
Glasgow Corporation Diaries (various dates).
Glasgow Citizens' Union—Annual publications, 1900-20.
Robert Alison—*Anecdotage of Glasgow* (1892).
George Baillie—*Reminiscences.*
D. H. E. Butler—*The Electoral System in Britain, 1918-1951* (1953).
S. B. Chrimes (Ed.)—*The General Election in Glasgow, February 1950.* Essay by members of the staff of Glasgow University (1950).
Thomas Johnston—*A History of the Working Classes in Scotland* (1920).
David Kirkwood—*My Life of Revolt* (1935).
John Tweed—*The Lord Provosts of Glasgow, 1833-83* (1883).
G. B. Young—*Reminiscences of the Glasgow Sheriff Court* (1907).
Oliver & Boyd—*The Edinburgh Almanac.*
The Glasgow Herald (Election analyses, various dates).
The Times—House of Commons.
Constitutional Year-books (various dates).
Dod—*Parliamentary Companion.*

Acknowledgments

Office of the Sheriff Clerk of Lanarkshire.
Town Clerk, Glasgow.

CHAPTER 14—HOUSING

Bibliography

Census of Scotland. Reports 1801 to 1951.
Report of Committee on Rentals of Small Dwelling Houses in Industrial Districts in Scotland (1916).
Report of Royal Commission on Housing in Scotland (1918).
Return of Rents of Houses owned by Local Authorities in Scotland (1953).
Report of Glasgow Municipal Commission on the Housing of the Poor (1904).
Glasgow Corporation Housing Department—*Review of Operations,* 1919-1947.
Glasgow City Architect & Planning Officer—*Report on Glasgow's Housing Needs* (1952).
Robert Baird—*Council Houses and Local Rates* (1949).

Acknowledgments

City Architect & Planning Officer, Glasgow, and members of his Department.
The City Assessor, Glasgow, and members of his Department.
The City Chamberlain, Glasgow, and members of his Department.
The City Factor, Glasgow, and members of his Department.
Manager, Housing & Works Department, Glasgow Corporation, and members of his Department.
Master of Works & City Engineer, Glasgow, and members of his Department.
Scottish National Building Trades Federation.

CHAPTER 15—HEALTH

Bibliography

Census of Scotland. Reports, 1801 to 1951.
Poor Law Commissioners—*Reports on the Sanitary Condition of the Labouring Population of Scotland* (1842).
Poor Law Commissioners—*Report on the Health of Towns* (1844).
Sir John Boyd Orr—*Report of the Committee on Infant Mortality in Scotland* (a sub-committee of the Scientific Advisory Committee) (1943).
Reports by the Medical Officer of Health for Glasgow (Annual).
Corporation of Glasgow—*Education Health Service* (Annual).
Corporation ofGlasgow—*Education Health Service* (Annual).
A. K. Chalmers, M.O.H. Glasgow—*Report on Certain Cases of Plague occurring in Glasgow in 1900* (1901).
James Burn Russell, M.O.H. Glasgow—*Evolution of Public Health Administration* (1895).
James Burn Russell, M.O.H. Glasgow—*Vital Statistics of the City of Glasgow, 1871 to 1885* (1886).
John Strang—*Report on the Vital and Economic Statistics of Glasgow for 1856* (1857). *Do. 1858-61* (1862).
Thomas Ferguson—*The Dawn of Scottish Social Welfare* (1948).

Acknowledgments

This chapter, prepared by the Medical Officer of Health for Glasgow, includes material supplied by members of the Health & Welfare Department, and by Dr. A. K. Bowman, Senior Administrative Medical Officer, Western Regional Hospital Board, and H. Cumming, Statistical and Records Officer, Western Regional Hospital Board.

CHAPTER 16—EDUCATION

Bibliography

Scottish Education Department—*Education in Scotland* (annual).
Corporation of Glasgow, Education Committee—*Progress Reports* (triennial).
The Book of the Fifth Centenary (of Glasgow University), *A complete record of the Celebrations* (1952).
Fortuna Domus: a series of lectures delivered in the University of Glasgow in connection with the Fifth Centenary of its Foundation. (1952).
H. M. Knox—*Two Hundred and Fifty Years of Scottish Education, 1696-1946* (1953).
J. D. Mackie—*The University of Glasgow, 1451-1951: A short History* (1954).
J. B. Neilson (ed.)—*The University of Glasgow through Five Centuries: a pictorial history* (1951).

Acknowledgments

Schools

The Scottish Education Department.
H.M. Chief Inspector of Schools for the Western Division.
H.M. Inspectors.
The Director of Education, Glasgow.
Administrative Assistant to the Director of Education.
Assistant Director of Education (Further Education).

Central Institutions

Dr. David S. Anderson, Director, Royal College of Science and Technology.
George H. Thomson, Secretary-Treasurer, Royal College of Science and Technology.
W. H. Masson, Secretary and Treasurer, Scottish College of Commerce.
David C. Black, Secretary & Treasurer, Glasgow School of Art.
John B. Morrison, Secretary, Royal Scottish Academy of Music.
Miss I. S. Gibson, Principal, Glasgow & West of Scotland College of Domestic Science.
Nigel B. Bain, Secretary & Treasurer, West of Scotland Agricultural College.

The University

Dr. Robert T. Hutcheson, Secretary of the University Court and Registrar. (Supplied a statement on the University.)
George P. Richardson, Assistant Secretary of the Court and Assistant Registrar. (Prepared statistical data on enrolment, courses and degrees.)
Miss Hilda R. Kahn, Assistant in Applied Economics (permission to quote from her unpublished paper *University of Glasgow: Sundry Information about degrees and graduates*).

CHAPTER 17—OTHER PUBLIC SERVICES

Bibliography

Local Taxation (Scotland) Returns

GLASGOW CORPORATION DEPARTMENTAL REPORTS:
Office of Public Works (Lighting, Sewers, Halls) (Latest Report 1949-55).
Annual: Baths & Wash-houses. Fire Service (report for 1954 contains a short history of the Fire Service). Chief Constable. Cleansing. Libraries. Museums & Art Galleries. Transport.

Glasgow Corporation—*Municipal Glasgow* (1914).
Glasgow Corporation—*Glasgow Advancing: A Civic Exhibition* (1944).
Glasgow Corporation—*Fifty Years of Municipal Transport* (1944).
The Water Supply of Glasgow: A Century of Public Ownership 1855-1955.
J. D. Marwick—*Glasgow: The Water Supply and Various Developments of the City till the close of 1900* (1901).
Colin MacFarlane—*The Public Cleansing of the City of Glasgow* (1933).
J. L. MacKenzie—*Glasgow: A Short Account of Municipal Undertakings* (1938).

Acknowledgments

Glasgow Corporation, Parks Department.
Scottish Gas Board, Glasgow District.
South of Scotland Electricity Board.

CHAPTER 18—WORKING CONDITIONS

Bibliography

Census of Scotland, 1951, Vol. IV.
Ministry of Labour Gazette.
J. D. M. Bell—*Strength of Trade Unionism in Scotland* (1950).
J. D. M. Bell—Chapter on Trade Unionism in *The Scottish Economy* (ed. Cairncross) (1954).
Phyllis Deane—"Regional variations in U.K. incomes from employment, 1948" in *Journal of Royal Statistical Society*, Vol. 116 (1953).
T. Ferguson & J. Cunnison—*The Young Wage-Earner* (1951).
Sarah C. Gillespie—*A Hundred Years of Progress* (A Record of the Scottish Typographical Association, 1853-1952).
H. S. Kirkaldy—"Industrial Relations in Great Britain" in *International Labour Review*, Dec. 1956.
C. E. V. Leser—"Earnings in British Regions in 1948" in *Scottish Journal of Political Economy*, Vol. I. (1954).
A. N. MacPhail & T. Ferguson—"Long-continued Unemployment in Glasgow" (in the *Glasgow Medical Journal*, Oct. 1955).
W. H. Marwick—*Labour in Scotland* (1948).
D. J. Robertson—"Wages" in *The Scottish Economy* (ed. Cairncross) (1954).

Acknowledgments

The Ministry of Labour & National Service.
Scottish Trades Union Congress.
Glasgow Trades Council.
Trade Unions with offices in the Glasgow Area.
Glasgow Offices of the Workers' Educational Association.
J. D. M. Bell, formerly of the Social & Economic Research Department, Glasgow University.

CHAPTER 19—LEISURE INTERESTS

Bibliography

Glasgow Corporation—Departmental Reports on: Baths, Libraries, Museums and Art Galleries.
Walter Boynham—*The Glasgow Stage* (1892).
James Cowan—*From Glasgow's Treasure Chest* (1951).
John K. McDowall—*The People's History of Glasgow* (1899).
Duncan McLellan—*Glasgow Public Parks* (1894).
C. A. Oakley—*The Second City* (1946).

CHAPTER 20—CRIME

Bibliography

Scottish Home Department—*Criminal Statistics, Scotland* (Annual).
Annual Reports of Chief Constable, Glasgow.
Glasgow Corporation—*Annual Reports of Probation Department.*
City of Glasgow Police—*Criminal Returns for 1908.*
J. H. Bagot—*Juvenile Delinquency* (1936).
Harold Ballantyne—Articles on Gang Violence in *Glasgow Evening Citizen* (Jan. 7-13 and 17-19, and Feb. 7-11, 1955).
Bell & Paton—*Glasgow, Its Municipal Organisation and Administration* (1896).
George Blake—*The Trials of Patrick Carraher* (1951).
Thomas Ferguson—*The Young Delinquent in his Social Setting* (1952).
Glaister & Brash—*Medico-Legal Aspects of the Ruxton Case* (1937).
John A. Mack—" Crime " in *The Scottish Economy* (ed. Cairncross) (1954).
Duncan MacLaren—*The Rise and Progress of Whisky Drinking in Scotland*, quoted by " Shadow ": *Midnight Scenes and Social Photographs, Glasgow* (1858).
Notable Scottish Trials Series: Trials of Madeleine Smith (1857); Jessie McLachlan (1862); Dr. Pritchard (1865); Oscar Slater (1909).
Bernard Queenan—*A Statistical Survey of the Policy of Scottish Courts in the Disposal of Cases of Juvenile Delinquency* (Unpublished thesis in Glasgow University Library) (1952).
William Roughead—" The Slater Case—A Retrospect " in *Classic Crimes* (1951).
" Shadow "—*Midnight Scenes and Social Photographs, Glasgow* (1858).
Sir Percy Sillitoe—*Cloak Without Dagger* (1955).

Acknowledgments

The Procurator Fiscal.
The Chief Constable.
Assistant Chief Constable Robertson, Ex-Chief Superintendent McIlwrick and Inspector Watt, City of Glasgow Police.
The Director of Education.
The Principal Probation Officer.
The City Librarian and members of his staff.
James Adair, formerly Procurator Fiscal in Glasgow.
Harold Ballantyne, of the *Evening Citizen.*
George Blake (permission to quote from *The Trials of Patrick Carraher*).
Professor Thomas Ferguson (permission to quote from *The Young Delinquent in his Social Setting*).
Rev. J. Cameron Peddie, Hutchesontown Church of Scotland.
D. J. Wilson-Reid, Archivist, Glasgow University.
J. T. Wilson, Headmaster, Mossbank Approved School.

CHAPTER 21—POVERTY, DISTRESS AND SOCIAL AGENCIES

Bibliography

Corporation of Glasgow—*Annual Reports of the Children's Committee.*
Corporation of Glasgow—*Annual Reports of the Public Assistance Committee* (to 1948).
Corporation of Glasgow—*Annual Reports of the Health and Welfare Committee.*
Grove Street Institute—*Annual Reports.*
The Boys' Brigade—*Annual Reports.*
Glasgow Society of Social Service—*Annual Reports.*
Glasgow Charity Organisation Society—*Handbook of Glasgow Charities and Beneficent Institutions* (1907).
The Glasgow Herald Year Book (1914).
Glasgow University Settlement—*Directory of the Social Services in the City of Glasgow* (1951).
Thomas Chalmers—*Christian and Civic Economy of Large Towns,* Three vols. (1820-1826).
James Cleland—*Annals of Glasgow* (1816).
J. Cunnison—"Casual Recollections of the Students' Settlement" in *The College Courant,* Martinmas 1955.
Thomas Ferguson—*The Dawn of Scottish Social Welfare* (1948).
F. P. Gibbon—*William A. Smith of the Boys' Brigade* (1946).
Thomas Henderson—*The Savings Bank of Glasgow. One Hundred Years of Thrift* (1936).
Report of the One Hundred and Twentieth Annual Meeting of the Savings Bank of Glasgow (1955).
Stuart I. A. Laidlaw—*Glasgow Common Lodging Houses and the People Living in them* (1956).
Stuart I. A. Laidlaw—*The Domiciliary Care of the Aged* (Paper read at the 76th Annual Meeting of the Royal Sanitary Association of Scotland, 1951).
Week-end Conference at Kilmacolm on Social Agencies and the Family in Glasgow. *Handbook of Facts and Figures* (1954).
T. Brennan—*The Work of a Glasgow Relief Agency* (Unpublished paper 1956).

Acknowledgments

Children's Officer, Glasgow.
Chief Administrative Officer, Health and Welfare Department.

James Campbell, Deputy Controller for Scotland, National Assistance Board, Glasgow.
James D. Campbell, Assistant Actuary, Glasgow Savings Bank.
William Glen, formerly Secretary of the Glasgow Society of Social Service.
William Muir, Secretary, Glasgow Society of Social Service.
George Hood, Secretary, Grove Street Institute.

CHAPTER 22—THE CHURCHES

Bibliography

Tom Allan—*Face of My Parish* (1954).
Tom Allan (ed.)—*Crusade in Scotland . . . Billy Graham* (1955).
R. H. W. Falconer—*Success and Failure of a Radio Mission* (1951).
R. H. W. Falconer—Article in *The Student Movement* (December 1952).
John Highet—"The Churches," Chapter 20 in *The Scottish Economy* (ed. A. K. Cairncross, 1954).
John Highet—*The Churches in Scotland To-day* (1950).
A. Levy—*The Origins of Glasgow Jewry, 1812-1895* (1949).
G. F. MacLeod—*Only One Way Left* (1955).

Acknowledgments

Denominational Data

Mrs. William Bell, General Secretary, United Free Church.
William L. Bond, Secretary, and Rev. Robert Kay, Minister, Glasgow Pentecostal Church.
Rev. Canon J. Bullough, Synod Clerk, Scottish Episcopal Church.
Rev. James M. Calder, Secretary, Congregational Union of Scotland.
John Carberry, Hon. Secretary, Glasgow Unitarian Church.
John Elliott, Secretary, Churches of Christ, Glasgow District.
Rev. R. L. Findlater, Clerk of the (then) United Original Secession Synod.
Rev. J. Clarence Finlayson, St. James (Pollok) Church of Scotland.
W. E. Foote, Priesthood Supervisor in Scotland, Church of Jesus Christ of Latter-Day Saints.
Rev. A. R. Fraser, Clerk, Free Presbytery of Glasgow.
Rev. G. M. Hardie, Secretary, Baptist Union of Scotland.
H. U. Hall, Secretary, Scottish Association of the New Church.
Murdoch M. Henry, Superintendent and Secretary, Glasgow City Mission.
Hugh Hood, Recording Brother, Glasgow Ecclesias of Christadelphians.
Rev. W. W. Kelly, Elim Church.
Bernard Kinman, President, Scottish Mission of Seventh-Day Adventists.
K. S. Laurie, Society of Friends.
James McNee, Secretary, Scottish District Council of the Spiritualists' National Union.
Rev. Sydney Martin, Church of the Nazarene (Parkhead).
Rev. D. J. Matheson, St. Jude's Free Presbyterian Church.
John M. Moore, Superintendent, Glasgow United Evangelistic Association.
Rev. Edward Page, Methodist Church.
Rev. Charles Presho, Reformed Presbyterian Church (Nicholson Street).
Rev. J. D. B. Robertson, Glasgow District Association Representative, Baptist Union of Scotland.
Rev. Dr. Mortimer Rowe, Secretary, British and Foreign Unitarian Association.
Rev. Dr. John Sinclair, Clerk, Presbytery of Glasgow (Church of Scotland).
Rev. R. R. Sinclair, Clerk, Free Presbyterian Synod.
Martin Smith, Baltic Hall.
Andrew Stewart, Glasgow Seamen's Friendly Society.

Rev. Leonard Sykes, Convener, Glasgow District Council, Congregational Union of Scotland.
Rev. William Young, (then) Synod Clerk, Reformed Presbyterian Church of Scotland, and certain members of the Christian Brethren in Glasgow who wish to remain anonymous.

Attendance Census

The Revs. Bullough, Page, Robertson, Sinclair, Sykes, as above.
Also Rev. F. Coyle, Secretary, Archdiocese of Glasgow.
A. J. A. Fergusson, Secretary, Glasgow Elders' and Office-Bearers' Association.
Rev. Alex. Macdonald, Free Church.
His Grace the Most Rev. Donald A. Campbell, Archbishop of Glasgow.
Rev. Robertson Taylor, Clerk, United Free Presbytery of Glasgow.
Miss Jean G. Macfarlane, Secretary to the Clerk of the Presbytery of Glasgow (Church of Scotland),
And congregational office-bearers and their colleagues too numerous for individual mention.

Evangelism

In addition to those mentioned in Synopsis B, Rev. Duncan Campbell (" Churchman " of the *Evening Citizen*); Rev. Thomas Crombie (St. Andrew's Parish); Rev. G. N. Duff (Albert Drive Church of Scotland); Rev. James Munn (Newlands South Church of Scotland).

Non-Christian Religious Groups

The persons named in footnote 1 to p. 743, and the Rev. A. Scott Hutchison. Church of Scotland Chaplain to Overseas Students.

General

Rev. Tom Allan. St. George's Tron Parish Church.
Rev. R. H. W. Falconer, Organiser of Religious Broadcasting, Scotland, B.B.C.
Rev. J. Clarence Finlayson, St. James (Pollok) Church of Scotland.
Rev. J. G. M. Watt, Pollokshields East Church of Scotland.
Rev. James Wood, Augustine-Buchanan Church of Scotland.

CHAPTER 23—SOCIAL RELATIONS

Bibliography

James Barke—*Major Operation* (1936).
James Barke—*The Land of the Leal* (1939).
J. J. Bell—*Wee MacGreegor* (1900).
J. J. Bell—*The Braw Bailie* (1925).
J. J. Bell—*I Remember* (1932).
J. J. Bell—*Do You Remember?* (1934).
George Blake—*The Shipbuilders* (1935).
George Blake—*The Trials of Patrick Carraher* (1951).
David Bone—*Landfall at Sunset* (1956).
" James Bridie " (O. H. Mavor)—*One Way of Living* (1939).
Anna Buchan—*The Setons* (1917).
John Cockburn—*Tenement, A Novel of Glasgow* (1925).
T. Ferguson—*The Young Delinquent in his Social Setting* (1952).
Edward Gaitens—*Dance of the Apprentices* (1948).

Glasgow Observer and Scottish Catholic Herald, Supplement, 24 Feb. 1956.
James E. Handley—*The Irish in Modern Scotland* (1947).
A. Levy—*The Origins of Glasgow Jewry, 1812-1895* (1949).
J. A. Mack—*Delinquency and the Changing Social Pattern.* (The fifth Charles Russell Memorial Lecture, 1956).
A. McArthur & H. K. Long—*No Mean City* (1935).
Andrew McCallum—*History of Pollokshaws* (1925).
Guy McCrone—*Wax Fruit* (1947).
Robert McLeish—*The Gorbals Story* (1946).
J. F. Miller—*Old Shettleston* (1919).
"James Hamilton Muir" (James Bone, Archibald Charteris and Muirhead Bone)—*Glasgow in 1901* (1901).
Neil Munro—*The Looker On* (1933).
Neil Munro—*Erchie, my Droll Friend* (1904).
Neil Munro—*The Vital Spark* (1906).
Neil Munro—*In Highland Harbours with Para Handy* (1911).
Neil Munro—*Jimmy Swan, the Joy Traveller* (1917).
Neil Munro—*The Brave Days* (1931).
Frederick Niven—*The Justice of the Peace* (1914).
Frederick Niven—*The Staff at Simson's* (1937).
Old Glasgow Club—*Transactions* (various dates).
T. Brennan—*Pilot Survey of* 100 *Households in Govan* (unpublished paper).

Acknowledgments

The City Librarian and members of the staffs of the Mitchell Library and the Glasgow District Libraries.
T. Craig Annan, present proprietor of T. & R. Annan & Sons, Glasgow.
N. Bose, an old Indian inhabitant of Glasgow.
Miss Miriam J. H. Boston, of the Department of Social & Economic Research, Glasgow University.
Rev. Dr. I. K. Cosgrove, Garnethill Synagogue.
G. C. Dass, Secretary of the Indian Association (Glasgow).
Miss K. E. Doak, and the Glasgow Marriage Guidance Association.
The late John Dunlop of Baillie's Institution.
Mustapha Ellam, Pakistan High Commissioner's representative in Scotland.
A. P. Lee and J. S. Campbell, British Broadcasting Corporation, Glasgow.
Frank MacMillan, schoolmaster and free-lance journalist.
Maurice J. Roston, of the Board of Deputies of British Jews.

The secretarial and typing work involved in the production of this volume was carried out, at successive stages, by Miss E. Hatrick and Miss M. A. Scott, whose valuable assistance is hereby gratefully acknowledged.

COPYRIGHTS

GENERAL INDEX

F

G

H

I

N

Q

R